GOD IN EXILE
Modern Atheism

GOD IN EXILE

A Study of the Internal Dynamic of Modern Atheism,

by

TRANSLATED AND EDITED BY

Modern Atheism

from Its Roots in the Cartesian Cogito *to the Present Day*

CORNELIO FABRO

ARTHUR GIBSON

University of St. Michael's College
Toronto, Canada

Westminster, Md. Glen Rock, N. J.
New York, N. Y. Amsterdam Toronto

A Newman Press edition, originally published under the title *Introduzione all' Ateismo Moderno,* © 1964, Editrice Studium.

Library of Congress
Catalog Card Number: 68-20846

Published by Newman Press
Editorial Office: 304 W. 58th St., N.Y., N.Y. 10019
Business Office: Westminster, Maryland 21157

Printed and bound in the
United States of America

Contents

PART II

DEISM AND ATHEISM IN ENGLISH EMPIRICISM

PART III

ENLIGHTENMENT ATHEISM

PART IV

DISINTEGRATION OF IDEALISM INTO ATHEISM

PART V

Explicit and Constructive Post-Hegelian Atheism

PART VI

The Religious Atheism of Anglo-American Empiricism

PART VII

Freedom as an Active Denial of God in Existentialism

PART VIII

Theology of Atheism
Dialectical Theology and Death-of-God Theology

PART IX

The Inner Nucleus of Modern Atheism

Foreword

Atheism has become a widespread phenomenon of the contemporary world. Everywhere its challenge is being felt, and even those who still believe in God are sometimes bewildered and confused by the rising tide of unbelief, and may wonder whether their destiny is to be that of a mere remnant, while the great mass of mankind swing forward into a new era that will be devoid of faith in God.

In some countries, atheism has become the official dogma of the State. In these lands, Christianity and other faiths are sometimes violently persecuted, usually subjected to disabilities, and always exposed to the incessant stream of atheistic propaganda that is designed to weaken the faith of those who still believe and to prevent the awakening of faith in the younger generation.

But even in the free world, in countries where the Christian faith has been long established and where there is no hindrance to its profession and practice, atheism has made remarkable advances. Men have become so much masters of their own destinies and have achieved so much control over their environment that to many, God seems quite irrelevant. Even among Christians in recent years there has been talk of the "death of God" and attempts to understand Christianity itself as a humanistic ethic compatible with an atheistic view of the world.

There are also the younger countries of the world, the new nations that have suddenly acquired independence and have now to make their way and develop their resources. As they are thrown into the technological era, their ancient cultural and social patterns and their ancient beliefs are everywhere crumbling. Are we going to see in these lands renewed and more mature forms of faith such as will be able to sustain men in the strange new world into which they are being thrust, or are we going to witness the take-over of these lands also by atheism, in one or other of its forms? For atheism is not only widespread; it is also multiform. If in some countries it appears as the jaded cynical conviction that the world is absurd and all human effort self-frustrating, in others it appears in optimistic guise and exhilarates men as it calls on them to take over responsibility for their future and to rely no more on the caprice of the gods.

Atheism is a fact of life in the contemporary world. It will continue to be a fact—perhaps an even more insistent fact—in the foreseeable future. We may not like this fact. We may think (and certainly this is my own conviction) that atheism is fundamentally mistaken and that in the long run it must lead to a serious impoverishment and disfigurement of human life. But the fact of atheism is there, and it does little good just to bewail it or to look the other way.

What is required is that we should try to understand this pervasive and multiform phenomenon. There is no doubt either that as we try to understand it, we shall find that mixed with its errors, there are elements of truth. If Christians have sometimes permitted their belief in God to become an anodyne, or if they have held that belief in immature and superstitious ways, then the criticisms of the atheist have had a partial justification. They should be understood as a kind of judgment on the innumerable ways in which men prevent the understanding of God and try to domesticate him for their own purposes. The error of the atheist is that he takes these distortions to be the substance of the belief in God, and so he rejects this belief entirely. He may be contrasted with the Old Testament prophets who, in their detestation of idolatry and their awareness of the crippling effects of perverted belief, were just as much iconoclasts as the atheist, but who had the wisdom to see further, and to understand that their ultimate aim must be to recall men to a truer knowledge of God.

One obvious way in which to gain an understanding of this complex phenomenon of modern atheism is to study its history—the roots which gave rise to it, the positions against which it has been reacting, the factors which have called forth the many diverse forms of atheism. This book, which it is my privilege to commend to the reader, performs this great service of providing a detailed historical investigation into modern atheism. Beginning with Descartes, the father of modern philosophy, Father Fabro leads us through the twisting paths of European thinking in the past few centuries, keeping our gaze directed all the time at the emerging phenomenon of atheism. Although one may not always agree with Father Fabro's judgments, one can only admire his erudition and the clarity with which he sets forth his great store of material. This book makes the most notable and sustained contribution toward the understanding of that phenomenon of atheism with which we all have to live nowadays, and inevitably it makes its contribution also to the more affirmative task toward which the fact of atheism directs the theologian

—the task of setting forth in clearer, more adequate and more convincing concepts a renewed understanding of God.

Equally commendable is the work of the translator, Father Gibson. With great patience and skill, he has made Father Fabro's monumental study available to the English-speaking world, and he has succeeded in doing this in English that is unusually elegant for a translation.

JOHN MACQUARRIE
Union Theological Seminary
New York, N.Y.

January 5, 1968

Translator's Introduction

Atheism is almost as old as religious belief, almost but not quite. By its very nature atheism is a phenomenon of negation and thus can never be ascribed to a thinker of any positive stature as the constitutive element of his system of thought. The negativity that is his atheism nestles in the positive assertions that constitute the real body of his philosophical thought. Atheism may be a preliminary methodological assumption or moral option; it may be a terminal conclusion from the philosophical analysis of reality undertaken by the human thinker. But it can never itself constitute the essence of any system of human thought.

Atheism is never an exclusively theoretical phenomenon. It always has practical effects in the dimension of human conduct. Often, indeed, a practical atheism is combined with a theoretical stance that is professedly theistic. Still more often, until very recent times, a theoretical approach entailing atheistic overtones and consequences has been combined with a practical conduct and indeed volitional profession that is devoutly theistic.

A creeping atheism now burgeoning into its full somber flower has been characteristic of human thought since the inception of modern philosophy. Atheism as such did not, of course, begin with Descartes; but a new, radical and volatile *form of atheism* did. The present volume traces the internal dynamic of that new atheism, *modern atheism.*

BACKGROUND AND LIMITS

Two preliminary observations are therefore of capital importance to a proper positioning of the present work: in no sense does its author intend to suggest that the phenomenon of atheism sprang suddenly into being for the first time with the Cartesian system; nor does the author wish his work to be received as an overall *history,* even of modern atheism.

A proper realization of the existence and a concomitant understanding of the dynamic of pre-Cartesian atheism is an essential preliminary to the author's very drastic contention that the Cartesian *cogito* represents a qualitatively novel germ already containing in embryo the numerous subsequent stages of the evolution of modern atheism. A proper understanding of the author's explicitly restricted intention is indispensable to a right appreciation and evaluation of his effort to chart the dynamic of a specific *principle of thought*.

Fabro himself points up, in his Introduction, two crucial distinctions between modern atheism as derived from the *cogito* and all antecedent atheistic phenomena: modern atheism is militantly universal in its appeal and constitutes a professed dimension of the philosophical stance of organized schools of thought and even of political power structures, whereas pre-Cartesian atheism was always a phenomenon of limited appeal and a way of thinking restricted to single individual philosophical lone wolves; modern atheism loudly proclaims the denial of God as an indispensable preliminary to the construction of a happy life for man, whereas pre-Cartesian atheism was usually almost apologetic about its undermining of the bulwarks of belief in God.

Fabro has virtually no explicit and certainly no systematic reference to pre-Cartesian atheism: it simply transcends the scope of his own present work. There are, however, a number of references, especially to the later decadent Scholastics and the whole phenomenon of nominalism, which evince a keen appreciation of the fact that the modern aberrations he pillories are not without roots in the pre-Cartesian past of Western thought. As he proceeded with this translation, the present translator became more and more convinced of the imperative need for a systematic treatment of pre-Cartesian atheism in Western thought. He has been generously encouraged by Professor Fabro in this resolution to attempt such a charting of pre-Cartesian atheism. This work will require at least five years for its completion; meanwhile the present volume represents a definitive and permanent charting of Western atheism from Descartes to our own day.

It will be useful here to adduce a few of the chief strands that will be treated in detail in the forthcoming work on pre-Cartesian atheism, a work that will be modelled on Fabro's meticulous scholarship, even though it can never hope to match his exhaustive and impressive erudition.

The atheism of the ancient Greek and Roman world has often been described as a protest by philosophical sophisticates against the rank anthropomorphic jungle of the popular gods of Olympus. It was much more than this if it was atheism at all. The real atheism of classical Greco-Roman thought entailed a radical depersonalization of ultimate reality and, at least in the atomists, a drastic pluralization of that reality, as against the pre-Socratics' persistent search for an underlying principle of (even impersonal) unity.

The atheism of early Christian times, epitomized in the dramatic sunburst that was Emperor Julian, was likewise far more than a misguided effort to restore ancient pagan monotheism. It entailed the first unsystematic practical (as opposed to the Cartesian theoretical and the Sartrian systematic ethical) protest against a deity conceived as degrading man's status and hampering the freedom of his operation. Julian sought to replace that too personal God by a benignant cosmic force whose supreme manifestation was to be the Emperor.

The considerable and often underestimated Platonic influence on evolving Christian philosophy impelled the jelling Christian philosophical tradition in the direction of a pernicious essentialism. Fabro bears repeated and eloquent witness to Thomas Aquinas' heroic resistance to this trend. Aquinas' key notion of Being (*esse*) as transcendent internally dynamic act, far beyond the mischievous tension of essence (*essentia*) and existence (*existentia*), could have saved the evolving theistic tradition from its tendency lethally to granulate God, opening thereby the floodgates to the vigorous protests of subsequent thinkers against a God rendered static and less than genuinely omnipotent.

The atheism of numerous Renaissance scientists might be (and has been) considered a merely methodological precaution intended to guarantee their own strictly delimited fields of scientific investigation against the intolerable restrictions of an oppressive theology. Yet these scientists, by their very selection of an area of interest, were indicative of a swerving of man's focus of concentration from the whole sphere of theological and even ontological enquiry to the disjunctive fields of specialized research in the natural sciences. The tools utilized with preference by these scientists (experimentation; tentative hypothesis; verification by man's senses or by their mechanical extensions in scientific instruments; induction and the partially justified but already exaggerated revolt of empiricism against all manner of rationalism) all tended to reorient not only man's interest and manner of thinking but even his criterion of certitude. They represent a faltering of what Etienne Gilson in a recent lecture felicitously termed "the will to metaphysicize".

Descartes, says Fabro, simply effected still another swerve, the next logical one, from the external world to the interior of man's mind. There Descartes located the fountainhead of meaningfulness and the criterion of certitude. The former was the *cogito,* the act of thinking pivoted on and manifested as the individual thinker who in turn no longer recognizes any distinction between this act and his very being: the new atheist identifies himself by a first person singular indicative verb form, *cogito,* even as the God of Western theistic tradition identified himself by the first person singular indicative verb form, *sum*. The latter are the *clear and distinct ideas,* those new surrogates of created objects; but these clear and distinct ideas, which for Descartes are the focal points of meaningful reality, have been produced not by the creative act of God but by the *creative act of the human mind.*

It is the developing saga of the human mind in quest of ultimate meaning within the vanishing point-instant of its own epistemologico-criteriological act which Fabro undertakes to trace. His treatment is therefore expressly restricted to the *philosophical parameter* of modern atheism. Repeatedly he warns, especially in his treatment of Nietzsche and the Marxists, that this is but one parameter, that modern atheism, as a drastically complex phenomenon, cannot safely be reduced to or confined exclusively along this parameter alone. The reasons for the current widespread phenomenon of modern atheism go far beyond the mere philosophical method of modern man. They involve moral indignation at the lapses of theists, the new spirit of devotion to this world, the powerful thrust by man toward a complete mastery of nature, the disturbing revelations of modern depth psychology concerning the dubious motivation of much of man's volitional and confessional activity, the distrust of any transcendental commitment that could trigger a holy war or lethal crusade in a context big with the menace of total destruction.

Yet, if Fabro insists on the importance of these other motivations and the impermissibility of neglecting them, he insists equally on the cardinal significance of the philosophical parameter of modern atheism which he has set himself to trace.

PREFACE AND PURPOSE

In a brief Preface and lengthy Introduction, Fabro pinpoints the guiding purpose of his investigation and delimits that purpose, both positively and negatively. The immediate purpose of the volume, as evidenced by a fleeting perusal of its pages, might seem to be simply a staggeringly exhaustive examination of all the major and many of the minor philosophers of modern times, from the point of view of the atheism inherent in their systems. The Preface, however, clearly reveals an intensely practical motivation for the research here undertaken. Just as Fabro commends Nietzsche for calling modern thought to the bar for an accounting and forcing it to face up to its own implications, so he obviously feels that the time has come for a casting of a balance sheet of modern thought, more extensive and meticulously systematic than Nietzsche attempted, a balance sheet encompassing likewise those systems of modern thought subsequent to that Nietzsche, in whose shadow, Heidegger maintains, every 20th century philosopher lives and thinks. The motivation of this systematic research is no mere scholarly yen for an orderly and comprehensive coverage of a sprawling and complicated phenomenon. The motivation is an intensely practical concern with the fate of modern man: Fabro is persuaded that the eruption of an active nothingness in the very center and fulcrum of the human mind, in our day, threatens the foundations of Western civilization and leaves man mortally exposed to the lowering weapons of total destruction that mind has excogitated.

The investigation is undertaken frankly and explicitly from a theistic point of view. Theistic criteria of judgment and evaluation which Fabro contends to be amply substantiated in non-theological dimensions are employed throughout in the critique of the developing phenomenon of modern atheism. But the critique invariably follows a meticulous and scrupulously fair exposition of the thought-pattern of the philosophers in question, and the book is commendably free of all polemical or catechetical intent.

A number of preliminary critical observations concerning modern atheism are presented in the Introduction and amply substantiated and documented throughout the lengthy work itself. Chief among these are: the unjustified tendency to select one area of reality, empirical reality whether conceived in function of the rational human mind or of the sense-manifold, and to pronounce it the only reality existent or admissible; the erroneous thrust toward a total freedom for the human existent, a freedom whose very guarantee of autonomous hegemony is held to lie in its self-derived nature and autogenesis, but which reveals itself terminally as elusive and mortally vanishing into the nothingness that lies at the root of the immanentized human mind, or more exactly the human thinking act when that act is deprived of all transcendent substantiation and foundation; and the curious phenomenon of that monism which Fabro characterizes as the ontological structural principle of all atheism, a monism which does violence to the drastic, radical and irreducible duality between transcendent creator and immanent creation by abolishing the creator, blurs the irreducible and drastic duality between cognizing man and the brute material complex that is nature, either by reducing mind to an epiphenomenon of that nature (a reductive tendency that reaches its acme in the speculations of Toland and the thinkers of the French Enlightenment on "thinking matter") or by a pernicious and impertinent reduction of the whole complex of material reality to a mere epiphenomenon of mind (a tendency initiated by Berkeley and forced to its logical conclusion by Hegel); and operates in an entirely illicit (and diametrically opposed) fashion with the logical principle of identity, extrapolating that principle, entirely licit within the dimension of human logic, into a staticizing and restrictive grid, a Procrustean bed, on which the rich diversity of ontological reality is stretched and wracked into a mere logical construct, or else, in excessive reaction against this staticization, denying any even analogical reality to this principle and opting for a total, brute, radical and irreducible heterogeneity as the irrational, pluralistic pattern of ultimate reality.

One especially ticklish question which receives thorough and meticulous treatment in the Introduction and to which the author recurs repeatedly throughout the work is the problem of a working definition of atheism and atheist. Surely all modern thinkers, even the most redoubtable atheists, will be willing to admit the phenomenological historical fact that Western thought, until a century ago at the earliest, has developed against a background of theistic persuasion, in a context permeated by theistic assumptions. It is this theistic sediment in the very river-bed of modern thought which renders so difficult in our day a fair and acceptable definition of atheism. One might say that the tonality and implications of the term atheist depend on the pronunciation. If this nounal adjective is pronounced in the usual way, with the first syllable lengthened and stressed, it inevitably becomes a term of opprobrium and reproach, with overtones of moral turpitude. If, however, the first syllable be shortened and the stress shifted to the second syllable, the term becomes rather a descriptive designation of a system of thought substantially diverging from the mainstream of theistic philosophizing. It is this second meaning which Fabro elects to utilize and to which he adheres throughout. And this is of crucial importance for an evaluation of his judgments on several philosophers.

No reader, surely, will object to the designation atheist being applied to such philosophers as Marx, Nietzsche or Sartre; reservations could be entertained here solely on the adequacy or fairness of the presentation of the content of their systems of thought. There will probably be widespread agreement with the author's application of the designation of atheist to such philosophers as Spinoza, the French Enlightenment thinkers and Hegel. The most strenuous objections are likely to arise in connection with the application of this designation to such thinkers as Descartes, Berkeley, Alexander, and particularly Whitehead. It should here be stated in frankness and fairness that the author himself derives from and approaches his task in the light of the historical religious tradition of Roman Catholicism and the philosophical tradition of Thomism (*not* Scholasticism!). The legitimacy of such a conditioned approach is indisputable: no thinker can approach the mass of historical material in total abstraction from a personal viewpoint. The adequacy of his treatment of the material will depend on the extent to which he manages to refrain, in his expository and critical operations, from any illegitimate transgressions of the boundaries of philosophy into an appeal to that aphilosophical substantiation of principles provided by the dimension of faith. In an age of uneasy and even finicky ecumenism, it is refreshing to encounter a thinker and commentator who patiently and persistently insists that the act of faith, the historical religious traditions, the teaching authority of a religious body, are at least phenomenological events demanding to be taken seriously by any thinker aspiring to genuine phenomenological fairness. Fabro will not allow any of these realities to be called in question *a priori*. As for his own fairness to the thinkers whose systems he expounds, it need only be remarked that no work of comparable scope and size contains more exhaustive textual citations from the thinkers in question.

It should be noted that the present volume does not represent simply an English version of the first Italian edition of 1964. Numerous new appendices have been added; the text itself has been considerably modified by expansions and deletions effected by the author; one entire new chapter (on the Death-of-God theologians) has been specially written for this volume. The bibliography has been updated to November 1, 1967.

The work of translation of this sort of document, in which the author's personal stylistic idiosyncrasies in his mother tongue play a key interpretative role, presents difficulties of a particularly delicate kind. The translator wishes to express his sincere gratitude to the author for his generous concession of entire freedom of maneuver in the rendering. Translator and author were in complete agreement that it was the sense behind the words and not the exact phrases of the original that had to be made available to the English reader. The original Italian edition was drastically polyglot; in this English version the entire text has been rendered into English with the exception of book titles. References to the original works will enable the specialist to check non-English citations.

SCOPE AND SEQUENCE

It will be useful, in the face of the mass of detail that constitutes the body of the work itself, for the reader to bear in mind two considerations that have animated the author throughout: the first is his contention that the *cogito* principle itself contains in germ and imposes as a necessary internal dynamic of development every further stage in the development of modern atheism; the second is the author's persuasion of the complexity, zigzag course, frequent instances of cross-pollination, substantial modification of a thought content in function of its contact or merging with another thought-stream, even in function of its geographical migration. In the light of these guiding principles, the body of the text may be usefully divided into: a preamble (Parts I and II) and a three-stage treatment of the progressive anti-God polemic: his indictment by Enlightenment atheists as the author of or conniver with moral evil (Part III); his imprisonment within the bounds of ungodding immanentism (in transcendental idealism [Part IV], Feuerbachian and Marxist anthropologism-naturalism [Part V] and empirical theological evolutionism [Part VI]); and his definitive exile by the existentialists in the philosophical realm (Part VII) and by the Death-of-God theologians in the theological realm (Part VIII). A concluding section explicitates the intimate and persistent nexus between immanentism and atheism.

Parts I and II: Preamble on Principles

The preamble is devoted to a meticulous explicitation and development of the latent consequences of the *cogito* principle which is traditionally associated with Descartes but which Fabro contends can be extended, in its most basic sense, to include Spinoza as well. It will be useful to the reader to realize in advance at least the outline of a complex of contentions which Fabro quite legitimately develops very gradually throughout this immense work. For him the *cogito* principle involves, in the first instance, a swerving of the fundamental ontological axis to the creative constitutive act of the human mind. Henceforth the quintessence of meaningfulness is sought in the *mental dimension:* the criterion of certitude for the human thinker is his own primordial product, clear and distinct ideas, indivisible from the thinking act that constitutes them, even as this act itself is indivisible from the very being of the thinker. Thus we have here a strict analogue to the traditional Western theistic conception of God as that Being whose act is indivisible from his nature and whose products (creation) issue from the unaided operation of that act, operating to communicate a participation in his act of Being.

Fabro considers one of the basic mystery-truths of the Western theist tradition to be precisely the insistence that God can communicate his Being less than completely. This is the indispensable fulcrum of the real distinction between creatures and creator. The *cogito* approach, on the other hand, is structurally and constitutively atheistic, however it be articulated, however developed. The principle itself is polyvalent and hence contains in germ and explains in fact the zigzag tergiversations of subsequent modern thought, founded upon it.

The absolutely fundamental characteristic of the *cogito* principle and the *cogito* approach consists in a subjection of being to thought. In its extrapolation to God on the part of the professedly theistic Descartes, it imposes on the Creator the radically restrictive parameters of human logical operation. It seeks primarily, however, in the Cartesian tradition, to arrive at an anterior terminal of human operation, theoretical and practical, which shall be located within a region directly accessible to every human being by his unaided efforts. In this sense of its total abstraction from the phenomenon of faith, the Cartesian *cogito* already heralds subsequent systematic immanentism.

The Cartesian *cogito* amounts to a radical monism, no less drastic than Spinozism for being epistemological rather than (at least initially) ontological. For the Cartesian *cogito* attempts to derive all meaningfulness from a single point-instant act. The Cartesian *cogito* is much more polyvalent than the Spinozan *cogito* approach: initially it contains an unresolved ambivalence and tension which can give rise either to rationalism or to empirical materialism. For its criterion of certitude (clear and distinct ideas) can be restrictively articulated and explicitated either in function of abstract science (mathematics, logic, etc.) or in function of the specialized sciences of nature (physics, chemistry, biology, etc.). Moreover, the Cartesian *cogito* can swerve into a theoretical or into a practical bias in either of these subsequent resolutions: the abstract theoretical bias gives rise to and nurtures strict rationalism; the abstract practical bias gives rise to and nurtures the vaguer effort at elucubration of a rational morality (Bayle, Toland); the concrete theoretical bias gives rise to dogmatic materialism; the concrete practical bias engenders all manner of immanentistic moral systems, by no means always rationally grounded (from the curious systems of the French Enlightenment through the professed anti-rationalism of Nietzsche down to the cult of the absurd in 20th-century existentialist atheism). *It all depends on how the clear and distinct ideas are further articulated and developed,* whether into the fundamentals of logic, the universal moral truths of incipient humanistic ethics, the ontological persuasion of the adequacy and perspicacity of matter-in-motion as absolute, or, quite simply and most drastically, the brute facticity of man-and-world-in-situation.

The Spinozan approach has traditionally been described as a radical ontological dualism, articulating Thought and Extension as the two co-eternal and eternally distinct Attributes of a God already effectively depersonalized (or, at least, transpersonalized). But Fabro sees that Spinoza's towering monotheism, or more accurately, his yen for monism, cannot be safely neglected: in effect his dualism is unstable and contains an internal dynamic inevitably tilting the system in the direction of a radical preponderance of one of the Attributes over the other.

Therefore, there is observable, on the one hand, a confluence of Cartesian and Spinozan influences in the genesis of full-blown rationalism (when Thought takes hegemony over Extension); and since Spinozism is more ontologically pretentious than Cartesianism there is a further bias of Spinozism toward that transcendental idealism that culminates in Hegel. On the other hand, there is an equal disjunctive anterior bias in Spinozism toward rank materialism, (when Extension takes hegemony over Thought); in this event, Thought is reduced, in the essentially depersonalized cosmos of the would-be stabilizer, Spinoza, to an unstable sport of a comforting continuum of mechanistically governed eternal material substance. This substance, in turn, with the progress of science, reveals its radical and terrifying instability and indeterminacy and the comforted seeker after monistic certitude is finally left bemused before the phenomenon of mindless flux.

The third chapter of Part I points up Fabro's own determination, within the predetermined bounds of his chosen dimension of investigation, to canvass the full multidimensionality of the phenomenon of atheization. For this Chapter is devoted to Pierre Bayle, a thinker intent far more on arriving at a humanistic substantiation of human ethical conduct than on explicitating any definitive theoretical description of the totality of reality. Fabro ascribes capital importance in the overall dynamic of atheization of Bayle's plaidoyer for a religionless morality and his contention that a society of atheists can indeed live a morally unobjectionable and even heroically ethical life, relying solely on natural inhibitions against predatory conduct and ultimately on enlightened self-interest.

The latter part of the preamble (Part II) deals with the dynamic of the materialistic fork of Cartesianism in the specific cultural context of 17th and 18th century England. The pendulum-swings (both in attitude and area of interest) through Cherbury, Hobbes, Shaftesbury, Locke, Toland, Berkeley and Hume should not obscure the fatal simultaneous bias toward the *cogito*-type natural morality that seeks to ground human ethical conduct on a basis other than the direct creaturely personal relationship of the individual human being to his Creator-God, and toward a hopelessly inimical dichotomy between the two dimensions of man and nature, mind and matter (ultimately derivable from and reducible to Spinoza's two co-eternal and unstably tensional Attributes of Extension and Thought). This inimical dichotomy is nowhere more forcibly and ominously articulated than in the brief and pregnant passage cited by Fabro from the Anglican Bishop Berkeley:

"Nay, so great a difficulty has it been thought to conceive Matter produced out of nothing, that the most celebrated among the ancient philosophers, even of those who maintained the being of a God, have thought Matter to be uncreated and co-eternal with him. How great a friend *material substance* has been to atheists in all ages were needless to relate. All their monstrous systems have so visible and necessary a dependence on it, that when this cornerstone is once removed, the whole fabric cannot choose but fall to the ground; insomuch that it is no longer worth while to bestow a particular consideration on the absurdities of every wretched sect of atheists." (Cf. Part II, Chapter 4, Note 44, p. 291).

Already in cruder form is here adumbrated the audacious Hegelian monstrosity of a total consignment of material "Nature" to the realm of unreality, an impertinence which certainly conspired to produce the all-out systematic Marxist revolt into dogmatic atheistic dialectical materialism. Already a devout and well-intentioned theist is affixing the name of God to a reality no longer worthy of it, or conversely is restricting God into an ungodly mold. *And all because of an absolutely fundamental abandonment of the radical primacy of being over thought.* Depersonalization of ultimate reality signifies a procedure quite other than the laudable thrust toward removal of anthropomorphic restrictions from the concept of God. It signifies a sudden, often unperceived, letting-go of the intuition of the *Living God,* who so transcends all created reality and so thoroughly and substantially permeates it, as to render superfluous any concern with real dichotomies and resolve those superficial dichotomies within creation in the potent simplicity of his creative and Loving Being. Once man lets go of this intuition and initiates a search for a univocal all-embracing ontological foundation within creation, he must inevitably do violence to one or other of the complex realities, mind and matter, which Spinoza so rightly intuited as coexistent and so fatally erroneously ascribed not to creation but to creator.

The stage is therefore set by the end of Part II for the whole of the ensuing drama. It is indicative of the cogency of Fabro's basic guiding principle that no Chapter in this work can be hermetically sealed off from those that precede it or those that follow it. Throughout rages the see-saw conflict between equally unstable ultimates, the emergent human thinking act and the cosmic material flux.

Part III: Indictment and Defense of God

With the French Enlightenment thinkers, La Mettrie, Helvétius, Diderot, d'Holbach and Meslier, Fabro pursues the saga of the search for ultimate meaning in function of human science. But he also introduces and highlights another dimension, the protest against God in function of the scandal of physical and moral evil. In this Part, as in the preceding (on English atheistic empiricism), the Appendices assume a capital importance. For they furnish textual reports of the spirited and often well-informed and impressively articulated critical reaction from theist circles against the mounting waves of atheism. In the Appendices to Part II, Fabro assigns a place of special honor to the Anglican divines who delivered the Boyle's Lectures for sounding the alarm against progressive and ever more audacious atheization of English philosophy on the part of English sense-impressionists and radical empiricists. In the Appendices to Part III, on the French Enlightenment, he furnishes very lengthy textual excerpts from important documents issued by the Archbishop of Paris, the French Episcopate and the High Court of France, against the writings of the Enlightenment thinkers, who were paving the way for the French Revolution. Obviously opinions will vary on the cogency of these documents and on the desirability of the censorship and punitive action they intimate. But even professed Marxist atheists should advert to the fact, amply documented in these excerpts, that the establishment reaction could argue incisively as well as simply censor or imprison.

In their curious ambivalence (theoretical perceptivity and bemusing obtuseness to the urgent need for socio-political change), these documents highlight the tragedy of those critical decades immediately preceding 1789: the smug failure of theists to grapple with the real socio-political problems or indeed *to take creation seriously;* and the enraged excesses of the atheists driving for this needed change but *indicting God as bitterly as government* and thus preparing the exile of him in whose absence their own ambitious revolutionary states would degenerate into inhuman tyrannies, unbridled by any transcendental future to tame the Moloch of the temporal future which devours so many children of each today, in the unremitting struggle to implement justice and human concord in abstraction from their Author.

Parts IV-VI: Threefold Imprisonment of God

The French Revolution explodes into a holocaust of freedom betrayed into licence by humanist fanaticism. It sends shock waves far beyond the country of its origin and begins the age of the New Man, to whom nothing is sacred and all risks permissible and exhilarating. Fabro now turns to another climate and cultural context, the Teutonic preserve, to trace the dynamic of the first imprisonment of God within the jail of radical idealistic immanentism (Part IV). From this saga, he shifts to the Slavic scene via the bridge of Feuerbach and the Hegelian Left to trace the second imprisonment of God within the dungeon of dialectical materialism (Part V). Thereafter, he veers to the Anglo-American scene of the 19th and 20th centuries to report on the third imprisonment of God within the amorphous quagmire of cosmic evolutionism.

It is in this portion of the work that the gravest problems of interpretation arise. The transcendental idealists rarely admitted even to agnosticism, though they were often enough accused of downright atheism: Hegel indeed considered himself the supreme defender of God. Conversely, the Marxist materialist atheists could object violently to any allegation that they retain even an ungodded God within their system. Finally, all the Anglo-Americans treated (with the exception of Dewey and possibly James) lay claim to being theists; and A. N. Whitehead has exercised a profound and impressive influence on Protestant religious thought in our own day.

Another Fabro principle must here be invoked in the interests of clarification for theists. The translator himself will answer the Marxist possible objection: he has had many pleasant and spirited contacts with them and wants them to know that his remarks on Fabro's treatment of their system represent his own gloss though he is persuaded that that gloss can be substantiated by reference to Fabro's text.

The Fabro principle here of importance and significance to theists is this: Fabro contends that atheism can represent and be constituted by either a downright denial of the existence of a transcendent personal creator or by the denial or distortion of any one of the *essential attributes* of that creator, if such a denial or distortion amounts to an ungodding of God. In such circumstances, Fabro is quite outspoken in contending that the mere use of the Name does not save the reality. On the other hand, throughout the entire book, as we have already indicated, and most especially in this Part, he is scrupulously fair to the thinkers involved: he does not question their goodwill nor their sincerity, merely their consistency and perceptivity. Indeed, he considers this whole phenomenon of vagueness and inconsistent assertions about the Living God to be one of the most serious internal dysfunctions of the theist philosophical and theological world.

As for the Marxists, they certainly do deny the existence of God. But we do not believe that it is a mere trick of mental gymnastic to apply in inverted fashion the Fabro principle just stated above: the denial of a reality under one name does not suffice to banish that reality entirely from a system if it be readmitted equivalently under another name. And Fabro himself quite clearly shows that the Marxist system defies matter-in-motion, ascribing to it not only equivalently divine creative powers but above all things an anterior independent consistency over against man, so that man is at the terminal issue of the Marxist system faced with an at least relatively transcendent reality over against himself; and the principle of the *cogito* has been utterly betrayed, or say rather has revealed its own logical inconsistency and incapacity to support a systematic and systematized universe.

Though the indictment of God is followed by a manifold and multidimensional phenomenon of imprisonment, this imprisonment is of quite different sorts; and the form of imprisonment chosen imparts its stamp to the whole fabric of the system in question. Thus, transcendental idealism as epitomized in Hegel radically denies God's transcendent immutability and incarcerates him in a jail, in the strictest sense: the boundary line between creator and creatures has been hopelessly blurred and the creator is subjected to the same temporal dynamic of evolutionary march to perfection which is the quite genuine lot of all creatures and of creation as a whole. Marxist dialectical materialism has been well identified recently by Leslie Dewart in his *The Future of Belief* as not an atheism at all but rather an anti-theism. We would simply recommend taking this approach one step further: for the Marxist dialectical materialist is in effect denying the Living God while elevating to a divine status the mindless will-less flux of matter-in-motion, a stupefying somersault which can be adequately articulated only by saying that the Living God has been thrown into an underground dungeon, his essential attributes of eternity and ultimate immutability having been torn loose from their substrate of Living Being and subterraneanly incarcerated in the mindless dungeon of moving matter.

The Anglo-American streams of philosophical and theological thought treated by Fabro in Part VI run the entire gamut from the Platonic staticism of Bradley to the radical evolutionism of Whitehead. Bradley in fact appears here as the thinker who, in Fabro's estimation, has succeeded in extirpating from Hegelianism its single redeeming feature, namely, the notion of change and possible progress; though Fabro does indeed insist that this kind of Hegelian mutability is totally inapplicable to the Living God as transcendent reality, he yet agrees that, in the context of immanentism, the ascription of change and possible progress to the imprisoned God is less appalling than the leering ontological standpattism of Bradley's super-Platonism. The other thinkers, from the professedly theistic theologian, Alfred North Whitehead, to the radically dubiously theistic agnostic philosopher, John Dewey, are all concerned with the thrust to progress and change. It is precisely this thrust and emphasis, in the context of a too drastically Platomism-dominated theological tradition, which makes Whitehead's contributions so valuable if the proper corrective modifications be applied to them. But the effort to force theists to take creation seriously, in its temporally-channelled thrust to ever greater perfection, assumes in these thinkers the erroneous form of an attempt to introduce temporal and even material mutability into the transcendent God, who should indeed never be conceived in terms of Platonic staticism but whose explosive internal dynamism must not, on pain of distortion, be reduced to progress along a temporal parameter from lesser to greater perfection. Such drastic cosmic evolutionism may indeed spur man to very noble efforts; but it deprives him (and he well knows it) of the sustenance and support of the eternal God who, in such systems, is reduced to a becoming entity, himself in quest of his own perfection. The imprisonment here is in a quagmire, a treacherous shifting flux, out of which the imprisoned God strives perpetually to emerge.

1. *Dynamic of Hegel Syndrome*

Part IV is devoted to a meticulous investigation of the complex dynamic of philosophical thought and controversy in Germany which culminated in the Hegelian phenomenon. Fabro reports on the famous Lessing-Jacobi controversy, the Forberg-Fichte case with its drastic overtones of State interference resulting in Fichte's dismissal from the University of Jena on charges of atheism, the Jacobi-Schelling controversy and the final emergence of full-blown Hegelian idealist pseudo-theology. Copious appendices position and comment on the significance of Schlegel, Goethe, Herder and report von Baader's critique of "Hegelian Spinozism".

It is significant that the whole phenomenon of Spinozism is the fundamental subject of the first controversy here reported. Jacobi's chief charges against Spinoza are that his excessive rationalism inevitably leads to atheism and fatalism. In his controversy with Lessing, Jacobi is at special pains to point out that pure philosophizing inevitably comes down to a simple reflection on the sense-manifold and is compelled to proceed solely in terms of an application of the principle of identity within the sphere of the finite. This, according to Jacobi, entails an inevitable imprisonment of the purely philosophical thinker within the confines of the finite. If he persists in insisting that there is no other way of knowing open to man, he will inevitably first imprison God within this restrictive sense-manifold and finally end by denying God altogether, to be left with nothing more than mindless will-less moving matter mechanically governed by intrinsic brute laws, and so will be pushed to pessimistic and even despairing fatalism. Jacobi therefore comes out very strongly in favor of the admission of a new and generically different method of knowing, namely, knowing by faith, which responds to the initiative of God's own revelation of himself and the whole of that transcendent reality which exists beyond the bounds of the sense-manifold. While giving Jacobi throughout full credit for his vigorous protest against the illicit restrictiveness, first of Fichte and then of Schelling, Fabro cautions against the dubious character of Jacobi's concept of faith: it is too drastically antithetical to reason and Jacobi's championing of faith implies and involves an undue depreciation of the powers of reason.

With the emergence of full-blown Fichtean *Wissenschaftslehre,* we are already in the antechamber of Hegelian idealism. For now the Ego, the Self, is being touted as the structural producer of the real via its positing of the Not-Self. The Self here (*das Ich*) is certainly intended by Fichte to designate God; but this is a God already operating in his creative act in the fashion of a human logical manipulator. Creation by logical operation has replaced creation by overflowing Loving.

The ungodding of God proceeds another gigantic step with Schelling's famous formula: without the world, there is no God. The boundary lines are blurring: the infinite creator has first been conceived as limiting himself by a logical operation; then this act of limitation has been conceived as somehow internally necessary. For the supreme and sovereign freedom of the transcendent God has been substituted the dubious and teacherous freedom of an essentially immanent Self, i.e., a self which does not really transcend the limits and restrictions of that total reality which man cognizes by direct knowledge. The Cartesian thinking act, which in the first flush of the new dawn of naturalism seemed possessed of unlimited freedom precisely because not anteriorly grounded, begins to reveal itself as dominated by implacable fatalistic laws, the laws of logic, which spur and goad it into a creative act that is simply not free.

With the emergence of full-blown Hegelianism, the transcendent God is entirely corrupted: the real distinction between God and creatures is hopelessly blurred and even the internal dynamic of God's "private life" has been reduced to a mere objectivization of the logical process of the subjective concept: Father, Son and Holy Spirit amount simply to concept, judgment and conclusion. The Real and the True become the Whole. It is but a step from this quintessence of Hegelianism to the explicit anthropologization of religion effected by Feuerbach.

The phenomenon of Hegel dominates the whole of the rest of Fabro's exposition; and he returns insistently to this epitome of modern thought, this acme of the *cogito* principle extrapolated to an ontological ultimate, in his extensive concluding Part. He gives full credit to the subtlety and manysidedness of Hegel. Indeed this very scrupulous fairness in the critique may initially bewilder the reader in his effort to pinpoint the quintessence of the Hegelian atheistic syndrome and to trace the guiding thread from Descartes-Spinoza to Hegel. The following observations may here be of some assistance:

Hegel is obviously a drastic and supreme *mentalist.* Notoriously unhappy himself with the apparent chaos and unclassifiability of material nature, he ascribed hegemony to mind over matter: it was indeed this very mentalism against which the Marxist materialist revolt was preeminently directed. In this sense, then, of locating the creative fulcrum of reality within the mental dimension, Hegel is faithful to the Cartesian *cogito* principle.

But Hegel is also an *unstable dualist.* Spinoza's trenchant if also inherently unstable dualism of the co-eternal Attributes of Extension and Thought has been in Hegel refined to the still more unstable pseudo-dualism of the logical operation. Creation in fact amounts to nothing more than the *total* (*never* partial or participational) extrinsicization or alienation of the Absolute from itself in order the better to know itself.

A recent conversation with the present leader of the Sufi movement furnished us with a dramatic illustration of the irreducible tension between Hegelian theologizing and the genuine mainstream of Western theistic theology, an illustration the more poignant for coming from an entirely different tradition, the climate and context of Oriental religious thought.

This Sufi leader, Pir Zade Inayat Viliyat Khan, described a conversation between a Sufi holy man and another Asian religious leader. They were discussing the optimal fashion in which to describe creation to the believer. The other religious leader said: "Tell the believer that God so wished to know himself that he was willing to pass over into the state of an object and create you that he might the better know himself; be worthy therefore of the status and dignity of being an object of the divine knowledge." The Sufi holy man gently but firmly objected: "Say rather to the believer, God so loved you that he was willing to pass over into the state of an object and create you so that you might share in his loving; be worthy therefore of so great a love." The mainstream of Western theistic tradition has likewise ascribed to God's creative act the mysterious motivation of overflowing Loving; Hegelian theologizing ascribes to that creative act the internal necessity of a logical operation and the theological motivation of the realization and conquest of a perfection not anteriorly present in the creator.

Finally, Hegel is a *radical ontological monist.* This monism has many consequences but the most significant to our present purpose is its blurring of the distinction between creator and creature: it is the treacherous slippery slide into atheism, which we must shortly trace through Feuerbach and the Marxists on the one hand, and through Nietzsche and the existentialists later on. In effect, Hegel's monism represents a congealing or subversive merging of two drastically distinct realities, creator and creatures. It is not that the creator is denied outright, though Hegel was often accused in his own day of equivalently doing just that. It is not that creation is promoted to the status and dignity of the divine, though Hegel's defenders retorted that the previous charge was precisely a misinterpretation of just such an audacious, though still entirely orthodox, exaltation of creation. Fundamentally, Hegelian monism meshes with Hegelian mentalism into a cameo of the *cogito*-approach: it attempts to explain reality comprehensively in terms of logic and the dimension of logic alone; it therefore subverts the transcendent dynamism of God into the necessary tension of a logical operation; and so finally it causes creator and creature to coalesce into an inherently temporally dynamic, i.e., mutable, totality evolving according to the laws of logic.

2. *From God through Man to Nature*

Faced with this inherently unstable merger, thinkers of stature were not long in pinpointing and attacking its crucial points of instability. In his Part VI, after a brief excursus on Bruno Bauer, D. F. Strauss and the Hegelian Left in general, Fabro launches into a detailed treatment of the degenerative process triggered by Ludwig Feuerbach and pushed to its conclusion by the Marxists, which latter manifest an internal dynamic of their own.

In Hegel's subtle and extraordinarily comprehensive outline of reality, there was a real place for the attitude that spatio-temporal creatures were less than entirely real, were real only as parts (*never* participants) of the supremely real, the Absolute. Thus, the way was open to those interpretations which perhaps culminate in Heidegger (though the philosophical and even linguistic subtlety impose a certain caution on any unidimensional interpretation of his thought) and which speak of a process of the falling away of the veils of the relative unreality of the created in order to reveal the genuine and brilliant reality of the Truly Real, of the diaphany of Being in the wake of the vanishing or deliberate removal of the veils of the being of beings. Such interpretations would apparently likewise proceed to describe creation in terms that would be barely acceptable to the mainstream of theistic tradition: namely, as a voluntary self-veiling of Being so that beings might be allowed to be. Even such interpretations are perilously close to a logicization or at least a negativization of the creative act.

But it is patently obvious that the Hegelian merger in its fundamental instability left the way open to a diametrically opposed approach:

namely, the contention that all talk of the transcendent Absol[illegible] was nothing more than an objectification of those internal [illegible]es which the human thinker had discovered in [illegible] was this path that Ludwig Feuerbach [illegible] found God to be the mirror-image of man. [illegible] animal demonstrably capable of setting his individual imperfections over against a generic concept of the perfection of humanity, mistakenly objectifies that still unattained perfection and calls it God. For Feuerbach, applying once again the Hegelian dialectic in the context of the history of human thought, this objectification is not necessarily lethal or even meaningfully erroneous at a certain stage of human development. There is such a thing, there has been such a phenomenon as the legitimately religious age. But in order to attain genuine adulthood, man must issue from this troubled adolescence into genuine maturity, relocating within himself the mistakenly objectified concept of humanity and realizing that his own productive effort alone is the power that can achieve this perfection. And so, no longer do we have even an evolving God; what we have is evolving humanity, powered by the internal thrust of its own distinctive power. For Feuerbach, still basically faithful to the *cogito* principle, this power was the power of rationality.

For Engels and the subsequent Marxists, however, in a crescendo of "naturalization", this motive power was successively displaced from the purely rational operations of the human individual to the social labor of the human species; then to the conflict-producing and progress-generating class-struggle; finally to the embattled and dramatic effort by man to win mastery over and subject entirely to his own interests the very implacable external material nature from which, without remainder, he has sprung.

And so, at the extremity of the Marxist dynamic, man is again faced with a reality possessing some of the essential attributes of God. But the relationship is no longer the paralyzed reverence of a Hegelian part to the Whole, for man represents in some mysterious fashion an eruption out of the entire level of the anterior ultimate; the relationhip is not a personal relationship even of tragic love, either, for the anterior ultimate has been deprived of all personality. It is the most somber and taxing of all conceivable relationships of man to the ultimate, a relationship of implacable strife and enmity on the part of a provisionally weaker emergent to a stronger but incomparably more stupid matrix.

3. *The Vanishing God*

The progressive vanishing of God into the quicksands of cosmic evolution can be almost palpably traced from Mill, who exiles him entirely from all direct miraculous intervention in the implacable natural laws of the cosmos, through Royce who characterizes him almost as a bemused and benignant onlooker upon the unstable and unpredictable evolution of a phenomenon-complex he did not create but strives to bring into harmony, Alexander who represents God and man alike as caught in the powering surge of an ultimate creative upthrust into novelty which is deeper-lying than either, Whitehead who institutes a subtle but (on Fabro's reading, at least) dangerously ambiguous investigation into the substantive nexus between God and the world, to Dewey for whom God is but a useful term to signify the active relation between ideal and actual.

From the outset, the thrust is toward a highlighting and underscoring (and hortatory intensification) of man's own real responsibility for the future of the cosmos. This thrust toward real human executive function and commitment has an internal dynamic of its own which tends ever more energetically to depress the role of any anterior creator until he has been first reduced to a substantially evolutionary or emergent status, and finally evaporated into a useful self-invented catalyst of the human mind's own creative grappling with the Herculean task of orphaned administration, rectification and perfection of an eternal world, neutral at best and hostile at worst, and of a human reality instinct with destructive and centrifugal powers that must be tamed and channelled by man's individual and collective effort unaided by any transcendent Power.

Parts VII-VIII: Banishment of God

It is only with the phenomenon of atheistic existentialism in philosophy and "Christian atheism" or the Death-of-God school in theology, that Fabro espies the total, consistent banishment of God. To Schopenhauer and especially Nietzsche he ascribes the crucial transformation of the *cogito* into the *volo* and the definitive *moral option* against God.

Here, as throughout, Fabro readily admits, nay insists upon, the multidimensionality of the ecology of this Nietzschean revolt: among its causes are not only a voluntaristic fabric of philosophizing, but also a passionate devotion to the present world, a violent enmity against the warping and shrivelling effects of excessive Christian asceticism and otherworldliness, a noble determination to assume full responsibility for the destiny of the cosmos, and above all a trenchant commitment to the irrational or a-rational forces in man, too long suppressed, vilified and neglected, and actually indispensable to the flowering of man's full potential (Part VII).

The bemusing phenomenon of "Christian atheism" or Death-of-God theology as purveyed by men who insist they are Christians and are writing meaningful (indeed the only or the first really meaningful) theology, is for Fabro equally complex in its origins. Some readers may be astounded to see this Part (VIII) of the investigation commenced with a thorough examination of Karl Barth, followed by equally meticulous treatments of Tillich and Bultmann (though I should imagine that the number of the astounded would decrease in direct proportion to the Chapter progression!). But throughout this whole portion of Part VIII, as throughout the less unexpected subsequent treatment of the specifically Death-of-God theologians, two already articulated principles are rigorously and consistently applied:

The first has been adumbrated in the treatment of Jacobi and is here explicitated with more specific reference to the Luther phenomenon of *sola fides*. It might be globally positioned thus: *atheism can eventually stem just as much from a heresy of the Right as from a heresy of the Left*. An undue skittishness in regard to human reason, an excessive transcendentalization of God as the Wholly Other, a too drastic rupture between the dimensions or levels of reason and faith, of the natural and the supernatural, of the transcendent and the immanent, will by its own internal dynamic, even in defiance of the explicit intention of the thinkers embracing such an approach and attitude, impel in the direction of psychological fideism and ontological deism, both antechambers of atheism.

And the second principle is the converse of the first and is explicitated in this Part VIII in its most subtle and trenchant form: any effort to tamper with the supreme mystery dimension of God's actual ingress into the space-time continuum in hypostatic union with our humanity will more seductively, subtly and definitively ungod the redeemer than any, even extreme, Hegelianism can ungod the creator. Indeed, the supreme tragi-comedy of the Death-of-God school is that every substantive theological remark they make is strictly true though not the whole truth; and by their empiricist bias against any mystery element in theological articulations, they are impelled to push the partial truth articulated in their daring statements to the distorted extreme of a downright heresy. There is no mystery about a God who becomes man so thoroughly as to cease effectively being God; there is only a logical (and ontological!) inconsistency. There is mystery in the Incarnation of God. There is no mystery in a death which is human and definitive; there is supreme mystery in a death which is indeed human but hypostatically transfigured into a trailblazing of immortality for all mortal flesh. God did indeed assume to himself in personal union a human nature capable of death; in a certain sense, though theologians tend to be most skittish about this sort of statement, it might be said, at least poetically, that God died on Calvary. But he did not stay dead—to pursue the poetic articulation; he rose again and therein lies the whole meaning of his death. What is far more orthodox and therefore consistent is to assert, in the somewhat more crabbed terms of strict theological articulation, that Christ died in his humanity and gloriously raised that human body he had taken, conjoining it again to its human soul, by the power of his undying divinity. Not in the grandiose gesture of total self-immolation which the Death-of-God theologians claim furnishes the pledge of man's total freedom and the earnest of his responsible executive position is the majesty of Christ's sacrifice to be sought; rather it lies in the glorious miracle of resurrection whereby in the power of his divinity he transfigured definitively the lowliness of his humanity so that henceforth death should have no dominion over him or those who believe in him and are conjoined to him.

1. *The Ungodding of Philosophy*

Fabro's survey of the existentialist dimension of the phenomenon of modern atheism (or the atheistic dimension of modern existentialism, a philosophical stance by no means essentially irreconcilable with theism) begins with Schopenhauer, proceeds through Nietzsche and Jaspers, includes a lengthy and extremely nuanced treatment of Martin Heidegger (easily the most enigmatic thinker, in Fabro's opinion, among all those treated in this volume), and concludes with an investigation of French atheist existentialism, ranging over Sartre, Merleau-Ponty and Camus.

Examining in some detail the enigmatic Nietzschean slogan, *God is dead,* so often discussed and interpreted today with such dubious penetration, Fabro adverts to the strong element of moral option in the articulation. The transformation of the *cogito* into the *volo,* the dissolution of being into sheer willing, the trenchant identification of self-awareness with ultimate life, constitutes, in Fabro's judgment, the death-knell of all true metaphysics, the final exasperated revenge of the *cogito* on its adherents, the nemesis of the ungrounded or self-grounded finite desirous of conquering the world and winning total hegemony for itself over being and terminally revealed and revealing itself in all the barrenness and even nihilism of its own insubstantial evanescence.

The doughty Will-to-Power becomes imperceptibly the Will-to-Death in a clear-eyed acceptance of the terminal mortality of the ungrounded finite; the Will-to-Death itself merges into the nadir of nihilism, the Will-to-Nothingness. What the *cogito* as initially articulated by Descartes actually was, though in him it was not even potentially recognized to be such, that *cogito* has finally become, not only in professed and admitted theoretical stance but also in practical action. An act requiring for its true substantiation a *being,* whose being is neither exhausted in, nor entirely actualized by, that act, has been itself elevated to the status and [illegible] egregious blunder but a remediable one) but rather to the absolutely primordial creative fountainhead of all meaning and ultimately of all reality. The more it is appealed to as God, the more it reveals the dizzying evanescence of its own nothingness *when torn loose from its only true grounding in being*. Now the actual finite creature shows his true face, as that face is inevitably distorted when it seeks to become not only the world but God as well: the creature, determined to cast off the yoke of the creator, entrusts himself to the enormous power of the negative and thus of evil as a motive power of history; the voluntarist philosopher determines to overcome the antithesis of true and false by the assertion, as an act of will, of the equivalence of truth and error.

This radical Nietzschean revolt against any transcendence coupled with Nietzsche's equally trenchant insistence on the finite creature accepting fully the consequences issuing from the absolutization of this finitude, constitutes for Fabro the only fruitful line of approach to, and interpretation of, the entire phenomenon of modern existential atheism or atheistic existentialism.

Heidegger is highly praised for his directing of philosophical attention to forgotten *Being* and for his revolt against the essentialist formalization of philosophy; but Fabro is extremely dubious as to whether Heidegger himself has not unwarrantedly and anti-theistically temporalized this very Being which always comes to presence as the being of beings. Still more dubious is Heidegger's (admittedly extremely subtle) introduction of nothingness into the philosophical and preeminently into the ontological picture.

Sartre will develop this crucial function of nothingness to drastic extremes, speaking in eloquent terms of man's own contradistinction of himself from the amorphous mass of the *en-soi* precisely by his tunneling of a little refuge of nothingness in the very heart of being so that the *pour-soi* may come to birth and continue its embattled fight against the slimy *en-soi* that would swallow it up again and disintegrate it. And Sartre seems entirely unaware that he is most poignantly articulating the very fate of modern man who, having rejected the creative fountain of living water, must indeed try desperately to bring into play the only power left, his own nothingness in abstraction from the exiled Living God. It is not simply that man as creature is powerless in divorce from his creator; it is rather that man as free creature still retains a power, even in divorce from his creator, the power to multiply nothingness or to smother and dissipate being, to disintegrate being ultimately into the desperate finite will beating madly against the barriers of its own finitude.

2. *The Ungodding of Theology*

It would seem at first glance the height of absurdity to speak of a theology of atheism. In fact, all self-styled Christian atheism reduces either to simple dogmatic atheism under a deceptive adjectival cloak or else to the inconsistency of a Christian theological heresy. The attribute of God denied by the Death-of-God school globally might perhaps most usefully be characterized as his *presence-in-power within the created space-time continuum.*

When such theologians speak, like Bonhoeffer, of a God who, in such very presence demands of us that we live as if he were absent, they are either writing rhetorical hortatory poetry or hybris-engendered theological absurdity. The nobility of their own witness cannot be allowed to obscure the inconsistency of their theological stance. The much greater and more fruitful and more taxing mystery is *the technique* whereby this God, radiantly and powerfully present, compelling even our rebellious wills, manages to effect all this without violating our human freedom. But that is precisely a mystery and as such (proclaimed explicitly as such by the mainstream of Western theological thought) not susceptible of exhaustively satisfactory human explanation. But the refusal to accept that mystery entails a gradual and accelerating elimination of God from the spatio-temporal universe.

The cultural-psychological observations interpolated by Fabro into this Part VIII are of capital importance: the penetration of a creeping atheism into even Christian theology is indicative of the peril to which the message of Christ is always exposed in any age or cultural pattern. No human activity, not even theologizing, can occur in a vacuum and the baneful influences of an age living under the sign of the *cogito,* of radical empiricism and even more baneful radical epistemologization of being, are bound to infiltrate the realm of Christian articulation. Fabro does not call for any ghetto-mentality; but he does remind Christian philosophers that their duty demands that they not only avoid contamination by the spirit of the age, not only articulate Christian truth in unflawed fashion in some secluded cloister, but precisely and preeminently that they issue forth into drastic and intimate congress with this world, in order to transform it, in order to strive manfully to cure the *cogito*-sick civilization in which we live in the West today by the power of him who personalized epistemology by his solemn declaration: *I am the Truth.*

PART IX AND CONCLUSION: COGITO AUT SUM

Apart from an interesting terminal excursus on the relevance and witness of modern science in the ontologico-theological dimension, Fabro's concluding Part IX is devoted to a closely-reasoned, all-sided explicitation of the finitization, negativization, epistemologization and ultimate atheization of *being itself* in the wake of the *cogito*.

Descartes ratiocination *Cogito ergo sum,* contends Fabro, ultimately reveals itself as making being dependent on thinking and finite thinking at that. If I choose to proceed in the Cartesian fashion, if I choose to make my thinking act the anterior terminal and fountainhead of meaningfulness and ultimately of reality itself, then I shall indeed conclude eventually, driven to this extreme by the very internal dynamic of the principle I have chosen, to a sort of *sum,* to the *I-am-in-the-world* of brute facticity, to the *Sein-zum-Tode* of radical terminal mortality, to the spine-chilling fact of total aloneness in a universe depersonalized at its core.

The choice therefore is between the *cogito* of atheistic nihilism and the *Sum* that is the Name of God. This massive volume explicitly proclaimed at its outset the absence of all polemical or catechetical intent. Meticulous analysis and patient efforts at correct understanding and interpretation of all the thinkers studied can, we believe, be said to have characterized it throughout. It contains many a sharp rebuke to theists for defalcations both in the theoretical, the homiletical and the practical spheres. But the book is most certainly written with a totally committed *persuasive* intent. Its author sees modern atheism neither as a passing aberration nor yet as the new wisdom of the human future. He sees it as a desperate sickness, a dreadful affliction issuing from a fundamentally distorted view of reality, an initial distortion-act big with the most lethal consequences.

The English title is calculated to express the precise thrust of the entire volume: *God in Exile* articulates a capsule-declaration of the dynamic of the exposition and the evaluation contained in this volume. In the heyday of theism in the West, God throned in splendor and heretics who dared to question his smallest right were themselves sent into the exile imposed on traitors to the People of Israel or, later, to the Christian Empire. Then came a day when man decided to ground his being upon himself, upon his own most distinctive act, thinking. Gradually it became possible even to indict God. Albert Camus, the most limpid of all modern atheists, has pointed out in *The Rebel* that this sort of initial indictment represents not all-out rebellion nor yet any fundamental questioning of the autocrat, merely a determination to stand and talk with him on an equal footing. But, again gradually, the transition occurred from indictment to imprisonment, as the finite human mind sought to reduce God to its own limits. Eventually came the definitive sentence of banishment passed, in stormy assembly, on the basis of a plethora of shreds all bearing that one Name, the name of him who was accused of aspirations to tyranny, illicit circumscription of man's rights, connivance at or imbecility in consent to evil, inaccessibility to man's reason or defiance of that reason, logical inconsistency and mythical monstrosity.

The supremely free, radically loving creator has obviously accepted this sentence of exile, abstaining from any interference in the free functioning of his free creatures. It would be grotesque to suppose he could be restored by force, he who disdains himself to use his unbounded power to thwart that adventurous freedom he has created. It would be childish to imagine that a merely blatant and slavish repetition of the articulations of a vanished age will serve to hasten his restoration. It would be pointless to insist with a modern atheist that this restoration is a duty owed to the God that atheist proclaims to be non-existent in the first place! But one can inquire if that atheist does not begin to see how vital restoration is for man, for that very humanity to which the modern atheist is almost always sincerely devoted, more consequentially committed than many a renegade theist.

The translator wishes to thank Rev. James Sheridan for his invaluable assistance in coping with the bastard Latin of Renaissance Holland, France and England and with the elliptical Greek of classical antiquity; Mr. Peter Ahr for his tireless proofreading of a virtually infinite manuscript and for his compilation of the cumulative bibliography and the Index of Names; Mrs. Margaret McGrath, librarian at St. Michael's College, for her consistent dispatch in providing arcane volumes needed in this enterprise; Rev. Kevin Lynch, C.S.P. and Mr. Urban Intondi of Newman Press for their unflagging kindness, patience and expert editorial advice in preparing this volume for publication.

ARTHUR GIBSON

December 25, 1967 Toronto, Canada

Author's Preface

In the evolution of modern thought, the wheel has come full circle: the adventure of freedom has already been pushed through all its contrasting phases, and the indifferent neglect of being, heralded by the Cartesian *cogito,* has led, as was inevitable, to the loss of the Absolute. It has left man to wander, an aimless nomad, within the confines of a world that lowers around him as a deadly menace. In our day, science has succeeded for the first time in fathoming the forces hidden in the heart of the atom and has even now harnessed these forces for a noisy invasion of the immemorial quiet of deep space. Yet, never has man been so painfully aware of the imminent threat that his civilization may vanish utterly, that the human race itself may be destroyed; indeed, the very impetus given modern man by his mastery of the forces of the universe has pushed him to the verge of the void; chaos may erupt at any moment from a will that is no longer anchored in objective truth nor bridled by it. And contemporary thought, by making nothingness the ground of being, has wrenched from man's mind all objective tether.

The eruption of this active void in the very core of man's mind has sent shock waves far beyond the area of a philosophy drained of the living God: literature, art, politics and the whole complex of the social and psychological disciplines have banished the true God from their field of vision. In ages past, God was the mainstay of the founders of civilization and the champions of freedom. They saw him as the Father of mankind and the one sure refuge in times of doubt and grief.

The chief aim of this volume is to chart the main thrust of the void gouged by the Cartesian *cogito* insofar as it has driven man to that blank despair that wells up from the inevitable issue already latent in the initial principle, an issue in trenchant contrast with the aim of a freedom rendered richer at each succeeding stage. For the outcome has been a plain demonstration of man's incapacity to save himself and of the consequent admissibility of his praying for salvation. Therefore, here we shall not present a history of thought—the gaps are far too numerous and the perspective too foreshortened to warrant such a designation—but rather a sectional analysis of the latest effort of freedom, starting from the innermost recesses of the supreme aspiration to liberation from the tyranny of the finite, a tyranny to which modern thought has been condemned by its own theoretical consistency. With copious direct textual citation and unremitting attention to the crucial point, we have thus elected to stress that theoretical kernel whose adventurous history has been marked at the speculative level by a series of restructurings and restatements in the course of its manifold articulations.

It will be our aim to catch and interpret, in the light of its motive force, the gripping saga of modern thought, a saga unparalleled in the history of the human spirit. Our immediate interest will be directed not only to the problem of God, nor to the problem of man or the world, nor again to the problem of the epistemological and the ontological dimensions, nor to that of the One and the many; rather, it will focus on the flash point, the critical point of all these tensions. This is the point of origin of the vacuum and the aspiration, the suspense element or the judgment made by thought upon itself in order to endorse a reality so intimately present as to preclude the very possibility of delusion. Our age has exhausted all the vain and illusory shadows of the temporal dimension. Therefore, it must be closer than any other to the substantial hope and more capable of redirecting philosophy to its primal mission of serving as a guide to wisdom and a reinforcement in the struggle to put freedom on a firm foundation.

Consequently, we have avoided slavishly chronological exposition, unconsidered polemics and discredited apologetics. We prefer to direct our search and confrontation solely to principles, from which alone man's posture in the world and the ultimate meaning of his destiny can be derived. This is our prime and overriding interest, so that we may come to know whence he comes through the gates of birth and whither he goes through the gates of death.

INTRODUCTION

Toward a Delimitation of the Notion of Atheism

1

Present-Day Atheism as a Universal Positive Phenomenon

It is no easy matter to articulate a verdict on the age in which one lives. In the riverbed of history, the present is inescapably the narrows that each and every one of us is navigating. We cannot pull out of these narrows. Yet, such an act of abstraction is mandatory for anyone preparing to make a judgment, especially that definitive judgment on which depends the fate and, indeed, the very meaning of man. Yet, no one can get through life without making that judgment, without taking a bearing on the meaning that existence has acquired for him in that temporal environment, which is at once the fulcrum and the scaffolding of his being. Indeed, in a certain sense, a contemporary must be admitted to be the only qualified judge of his own era, for he alone is actually living through the very process represented by that era; above all, he alone is compelled to face the risk inherent in each succeeding hour, in every passing moment of his own age. The judgment that succeeding generations claim to pass on former ages—when the banquet hall is deserted or the curtain has rung down on the tragedy, and which they call the "verdict of history"—can only have a probability value at most. This is of interest to science but not pertinent to the ontological truth that must necessarily engage the freedom of anyone judging in a special temporal environment: judging not indiscriminately but rather in function of his self-identity and of his recognition of himself in that spiritual mold, which is the only one that really fits him.

And so we have a prior right over posterity to speak about our own era, about its spiritual countenance, about what it is and must be for each one of us. Our first assertion must be this: our age is more intensely interested in truth than any other age has ever been—or at least let us say (in order to avoid transgressing the principle we have already laid down concerning historical judgments) that our age, in its truth-seeking, has a passion for clarity second to none, but it can be described as typical and definitive, at least in some respects, precisely because of the lack of all those objective guarantees which were, to a greater or lesser degree, available to the other ages.

We must note at once that the absence of objective criteria is raised to the level of a principle in the present age by "radical humanism", which defines it as spiritual reality in act. In our day, this radical humanism is expressed in the total exclusion and rejection of transcendence in both of its constitutive elements: the existence of God as First Principle and creator of the world (metaphysical transcendence) and the personal immortality of the human individual (temporal transcendence of the human person).

A human being can admit God and speak of God only insofar as he is a free and spiritual person who aspires to attain, athwart death, participation in divine life; this is the prospect, only vaguely hinted at by the philosophy of antiquity, which was proclaimed by the Christian religion but has always been undermined by philosophy and definitively rejected by modern thought. To avoid any ambiguity, let us make it quite clear: the assertion that the present-day world is under the aegis of atheism does not, by any means, signify that the whole world has become atheistic or that religion, especially Christianity, has ceased to exist.[1] It may even be that a strictly personal census of interior convictions taken today would uncover more convinced theists than in any other age; it may well be that the Christian religion, especially in our own day, is more than ever before on the verge of bearing that witness to the presence of God in Christ and to its own commitment to the universal salvation of man; it may well be that this will bring clearly to light the irrefutable truth of Christianity, after man has shown by the atrocity of two world wars that he cannot save mankind, that he can do nothing better than leave humanity prey to the terror of an impending nuclear conflict.

But we must still take account of still another state of affairs, unburdened with fatuous optimism or vain regrets: both atheist and believer, in the wake of the evolution of modern thought, have today been forced back to confront one another openly at the level of their respective

[1] From a more spiritual point of view, it may even be true that atheism represents a protest against the inadequate notions of God and of religion; this would make atheism into a plea for a more solid grounding of the problem of God and a more effective witness to his presence in the world of free beings. In this inverse sense we can agree with E. Frank's remarks concerning "the paradoxical statement that the real proof of God is the agonized attempt to deny God. It has often been remarked that atheism is but a kind of negative theology. The atheist may feel the inadequacy of all human concepts of God compared with what God would really be, the author of all things, even of the atheist." See E. Frank, *Philosophical Understanding and Religious Truth* (Oxford University Press, 1945), pp. 43f.

principles. For we are not going through any mere "weekend crisis". No, ours is an age of decision, of radical import for whole peoples as much as for individuals. Indeed, it can be said without fear of exaggeration that, in our day as never before, unlimited masses of men are under the professedly atheist and areligious rule of governments and parties. This represents a reversal of the situation: whereas in the past atheism was restricted to an elite, and thus a strictly individual phenomenon of limited scope, it has admittedly become more and more a mass phenomenon in our time. This would be a distressing and hopeless diagnosis, provided it could be unquestionably ascertained that the masses are solidary with the ideologies of their leaders, or that they must resign themselves to their state because of the practical impossibility of any egress from the state of political violence (and, often, of physical and social violence) in which they are confined, even to the point of being restricted in, or indeed completely deprived of, the right of proclaiming their own convictions.

Present-day atheism[2] stems from various cultural roots and may appear in various forms having a greater affinity of methods than of ideology.

There is the *atheism stemming from materialism,* its best-known form, in which the exclusion of God is motivated by the alleged incapacity of man to transcend the horizon of sensory experience. This is a rather vague attitude that manifests itself simply as agnosticism if it stops at the affirmation of this incapacity, it becomes atheism as soon as it affirms that man can have no other vital environment than that of the sensible world. It is the atheism of the man who is "God-less", the man who cannot manage to establish any contact with God because there is no God.

There is the *atheism stemming from illuminism, i.e., rationalism,* which affirms that we must appeal to human reason alone to discover the "why" of things and of our knowledge of them. This is the position of those who call themselves freethinkers and of the most drastic variety of laicism as applied to the life of society and of the individual. The mounting achievements of science, which have upset all the old pictures of the universe and, perhaps, are close to threatening the very foundations of that picture, have provided an imposing pretext for modern atheism as a whole, which has still not lost its fascination for those who are most intolerant of the metaphysical outlook.

Finally, there is the latest brand of *atheism, stemming from immanentism*—phenomenology, Marxism, existentialism and the like. This brand of atheism starts from the principle of consciousness and stops at the reality of human nature in its immediate social or individual actuality. This brand subsumes the forms of atheism most prevalent to-

[2] *L'Athéisme contemporain* (Geneva: Edition Labor et Fides, 1956).

day, such as neopositivism, Marxism in all modalities, and negative existentialism.

Contemporary atheism has certain features differentiating it from preceding forms which have coexisted with belief in God throughout human history. These distinguishing features can be subsumed under the two attributes of *universality* and *positive militancy*.

(a) *Universality*. Whereas in the past, prior to the appearance of Marxism, atheism had been a sectarian stance among philosophers, "free livers" and initiates of secret societies, today it is laying siege to the masses brought into the foreground by the principle of democracy: the masses of workers in the West and the masses of the ex-colonial and underdeveloped nations of Asia and Africa, who are in process of attaining independence, and into whose minds Soviet propaganda is insinuating the contention that religion and Christianity have been and still remain the chief allies of capitalists and colonial overlords.

(b) *Positive Militancy*. Whereas the old kinds of atheism were predominantly theoretical in nature and operated in clandestine fashion, atheism today is coming right out into the open in its operations and organization, with the professed aim of eliminating Christianity as the chief bulwark of resistance. Present-day atheism affirms that man will take possession of his own being to the extent that he expunges from himself and society all awareness of God. Thus, the designations *humanistic atheism* and *atheistic humanism* are used to denote the restoration of human nature from the thrall of capitalist and religious alienation. Neither paganism nor idolatry, neither the wars of Islam nor the Reformation itself, neither Illuminism nor the French Revolution were in any sense as radical and dangerous as this "constructive atheism" which claims, with good reason, to be the ultimate and most consistent issue of modern thought.[3]

In this state of affairs, our chief fear must be an ever wider outburst of practical atheism (or social and political atheism, if you will), an outburst of which numerous symptoms can already be seen among the great peoples of Asia and Africa who have hitherto been culturally isolated from the West. Among these peoples the expansionist drive of Marxist Communism finds the raw material which is at once the most artless and the most greedy, inflamed with demands for freedom and material progress. To these peoples, atheistic Communism is incessantly presenting religion in general and Christianity in particular as the historical allies of capitalist oppression and, therefore, as co-responsible for that oppression. Ample proof of this propaganda line may be found in Marxist writings.

[3] I have it on first-hand evidence that in Japan and China the translations of the main works of Hegel, Feuerbach, Marx, Engels, Stalin, etc. now outnumber the French, English and Italian translations!

We can thus speak of a *positive atheism.* We shall directly see the most salient features of those forms of atheism that could be called *constructive atheism,* as opposed to the destructive atheism of the materialism of antiquity and of the illuministic currents. Whereas this older materialism was entirely directed to demolishing the Absolute by unhinging the metaphysical presuppositions on which it was based, present-day atheism in contrast claims to be dedicated to the edification of man

as starting point, that man must be edified and saved via man. In other words, it implies the negation of God, not as an end in itself, but as a means to an end and, as it were, as a repercussion. Modern atheism is fighting for man and asserts that God must be eliminated in order to save man, that eternity must be set aside in the best interests of a full life in the temporal dimension. This is the most radical atheism; it sees in the denial of God the fundamental condition of the salvation of man (Marxist, existentialist, sociological, historical and kindred brands of atheism).

Dialectic of the Concept of Atheism

It is no easy matter to dissipate the confusion and inaccuracies encumbering the concept of atheism in our present-day culture. Let us work through the problem by stages. The first assertion must be that of the existence of atheism. Today atheism does in fact exist and flourish in broad daylight on every continent and under the most varied forms of civic life, and it is not just that practical atheism to which theists of the first order (Christians included!) often succumb; it is, rather, theoretical atheism. The point is that today we can find in all social classes, albeit in varying proportions, men who are convinced that there is no God and who *say* that they have valid reasons for denying God and his providence.

Apart from the traditional denial by Catholic theology of the possibility of speculative atheism or theoretical atheism as such, there have been some recent philosophers who have summarily denied this possibility. Such philosophers (e.g., J. Lagneau) advance as a prime counterargument the consensus of all peoples in past ages in favor of the existence of God. Such an argument is nugatory at best because the problem relates to the modern and present-day world which has laid down a new principle (the Copernican revolution of thought) as the foundation of being. Then, too, there is the fact that in most cases the religions of antiquity (polytheistic, hedonistic, etc.) were nothing but more or less disguised forms of pantheism or materialism and consequently denied God. Lagneau's strongest argument, however, is a different one; he admits that there does exist among men such an attitude as the denial of God, but maintains that such rejection is aimed only at the false or inadequate notions of God current in some circles and thus reduces atheism to a verdict of dissatisfaction with the current idea of God.

Aside from these theoretical atheists who, in Lagneau's argument, are not atheists at all but rather witnesses to the demand for the true God, Lagneau contends that there are only practical atheists, i.e., those who do not take account of God in their own actions. "Practical atheism is moral evil, which does not imply a denial of the absolute value of the moral law but simply a rebellion against that law. Aside from this practical atheism, there is no true atheism at all." [4]

Lagneau's sincere and profound discussion of this matter follows substantially the pattern of the Cartesian concept of the perfect Being. Every discussion on the existence of God, notes Lagneau, presupposes the assertion of an absolute truth, to which particular truths must be related, and this assertion implies the affirmation of the existence of God in more or less confused fashion. Furthermore, continues Lagneau, the affirmation of the perfect Being implies the negation of all formulations not expressing this Being completely. In this sense, concludes Lagneau, what is ordinarily called atheism is necessary not only to progress but to the very existence of the true and genuine belief in God. The point is that our reason for asserting the existence of God always comes down, in the final analysis, to the impossibility of finding in reality the entire object of our thought. And so God can be posited only as transcendence and thus on the basis of negation, at least a certain kind of negation.

Lagneau elaborates this variant of "negative theology" in stages. Thus, the demonstration of the impossibility of God's existence, in the sense of his being directly accessible to our senses or even a necessary object of our reason, is the necessary condition for our being able to know that God is, because the reality of God would be illusory unless it consisted in a surpassing (or transcendence!) of reflection on things. Thus, God is not the impossible but rather the reason of the impossible, i.e., of the transcendence both of the immediate and of the mediate (object of human reason). God, therefore, is the Absolute, and this means that God cannot exist either as do the objects of our senses (contingently) or as do the objects of the intellect (necessarily). The end of the matter is a complete reversal of the situation as ordinarily pictured and the conversion of atheism into the indispensable condition of the affirmation of God. In fact, when criticism has demonstrated the impossibility of explaining the absolute method of operation of thought

[4] J. Lagneau, *Célèbres leçons et fragments* (Paris: Alexandre, 1950), p. 229.

either by sense experience or by the presence in that thought of a law which would determine it to affirm being necessarily, the resultant impossibility of accounting for this affirmation constitutes the proof of the objective reality of God.

Summing up Lagneau's argumentation in his own words: "It can be understood why atheism is not only the salt that prevents belief in God from being corrupted, as it otherwise might well be, into an unreason- [illegible] that atheism which can only consist in showing that God is not given, either as a sensible reality or as an essence, for then God would be nothing but necessity, i.e., he would not be. Genuine atheism would consist in denying, not the existence, but the reality of the Absolute." [5] But this atheism is, in Lagneau's view, impossible because the Absolute is always being affirmed at the aim and end toward which nature tends and as the object of the intellect and the will.

Unquestionably, there is great cogency in this "positive critique" of atheism, but it is a cogency that remains on the Augustinian-Cartesian level of essence and does not arrive at a judgment on existence. Therefore, it does not break out of the circle of immanence. For why cannot the Absolute, of which Lagneau speaks, be in fact reason itself in its own increasing self-transcendence as thinking activity? This thinking activity as Absolute has been entirely eroded, as we shall see, by the Hegelian left wing, by Schopenhauer and Nietzsche, and by present-day philosophy; for all these schools of philosophy, atheism coincides with the very essence of the modern philosophy of immanence, and no other philosophy is any longer possible.

Atheism is thus surveyed and judged from the interior of the act of thinking. In this sense, J. Maritain has distinguished a dual atheism, *negative* and *positive:* whereas the first limits itself, in Maritain's opinion, to rejecting the idea of God and then leaving blank (vide) the place formerly occupied in man's mind by this idea, the second actively combats the idea of God and concurrently makes every effort to substitute the world of man and of human values in place of this idea—thus Nietzsche, Marxism, existentialism. But the distinction seems to us somewhat forced and fictitious for two reasons: the 18th-century philosophers also combated the idea of God only in order to establish the kingdom and hegemony of man; present-day atheists (e.g., the Marxists) are, for their part, also furnishing at every turn tangible proofs of their fury against God and religion, organizing museums and literary exhibitions on atheism, etc. And so we contend that modern atheism as a whole is *absolute* and *positive,* but it is not so much—or, at least, no primarily and preeminently—the result of a free act of moral choice, as

[5] *Ibid.,* p. 231.

Maritain thinks, and consequently strictly an explicit rejection of God; it is rather a way of thinking which from the outset, i.e., from the first step of reflective awareness, involves the impossibility of encountering and acknowledging the problem of God.

Maritain himself realized this when he asserted absolute atheism to be founded upon "an insistent claim on the part of man to become the sole master of his own fate, entirely freed from all alienation and all outside domination, drastically and entirely independent of any last end and any eternal law imposed upon him by any transcendent God".

Today atheism is no longer a marginal episode; rather, it takes us to the heart of the modern principle of immanence: "What, then, is the actual culmination in our own day of the philosophy of absolute immanence which is inseparably identical with absolute atheism? Everything that was once considered to be superior to time and to possess some sort of transcendent quality—an ideal value or a spiritual reality—is henceforth absorbed into the dynamic of temporal existence, submerged in the omnipotent ocean of becoming and of history. Truth, justice, good, evil, faithfulness, all the norms of conscience, are henceforth thoroughly relativized and no longer amount to anything more than the changing molds of the process of history, even as for Descartes they were nothing but the contingent creation of the divine freedom." [6] Yet, Maritain is the thinker who has provided a masterly analysis of the Cartesian *cogito* as potentially atheist, inasmuch as the *cogito* constitutes a highlighting of existence in a way that is destructive of (negating of) essence. Descartes then, while abandoning St. Thomas and following the line of Scotist voluntarism, is the ancestor of the modern libertarians and the forerunner of Jean-Paul Sartre: "It is this same form of existentialism—in which the primacy of existence is asserted, but paid for by the abolition of intelligible nature or essence—that we find again in the atheistic existentialism of today; wherefore the author of *Being and Nothingness* has more reasons than he realizes to hark back to the philosopher of the *cogito*." [7] The author of *Being and Nothingness* is known,

[6] J. Maritain, *La signification de l'athéisme contemporain* (Paris, 1949), pp. 16f. But whereas Maritain concludes that "a total rejection of transcendence logically involves a total adherence to immanence" (p. 18), we think (and this is the central object and guiding principle of our investigations) that exactly the reverse process is what actually occurs: it is the principle of immanence that leads, in roundabout fashion perhaps but nonetheless irretrievably, to atheism in the form of radical humanism.

[7] J. Maritain, *Court traité de l'existence et de l'existant* (Paris, 1947), p. 15f. Eng. tr.: Vintage Books (Alfred A. Knopf and Random House Inc., 1966), p. 5. In this sense of the *cogito* being an essential cause and motif of modern thought in its evolution from Descartes to existentialism, whether right-wing or left-wing, we can likewise agree with Gabriel Marcel when he remarks that "the application of the category of causality to the problem of God" has been "the chief fountainhead of atheism" (J. Lacroix, "Sens et valeur de l'athéisme con-

as we shall see in due course, to accept unreservedly this rapprochement.

Therefore we cannot accept the idea of continuity in the development of modern thought: in its "drive for consistency" atheism is essential to that modern thought, as constituting the negative formula calculated to guarantee the positive formula of the "freedom of being" of man which is the new essence of the *cogito,* i.e., of the new concept of freedom. This also enables us to understand why Marx, and quite a few others (non-Marxists) in his wake, should have asserted that atheism itself had been superseded, i.e, that the very discussion of God must be relegated to the oblivion of a dark ages of mankind. The Marxist stand is of exceptional importance for an understanding and clarification of the modern principle. It will be worthwhile to take note of it at once:

"*Atheism* as negation of this inessentiality no longer has any meaning, for it is a negation of God and posits the *existence* of man by means of this negation. But socialism as such no longer has any need of this intervening link: it starts from the *sensible, theoretical and practical knowledge* of man and of nature, as the essence. It is the *positive self-awareness* of man no longer because of the suppression of religion, just as *effective* life is no longer a function of the suppression of private property, i.e., of *Communism.* Communism is a negation of the negation and thus the *real* element necessary for the imminent historical development of the emancipation and restoration of man." [8]

Now this is the crux of the question: whether modern and contemporary atheism is nothing more than a practical attitude, a "matter of opinion" as it is often said to be.[9] We hold modern atheism to have its roots primarily and preeminently in the philosophical sphere; it goes back to the assumption of the *cogito* rather than to the later negation of the supernatural, which many religious-minded philosophers continued to maintain after having posited and accepted the virtually atheistic *cogito* and which these philosophers still continue to maintain today. The atheism of which we are speaking (and our remark is valid generically for any form of atheism) is the direct consequence of initiating

---

temporain," in *Monde moderne et sens de Dieu* [Paris, 1954], p. 45). This remark recurs in Marcel's *Le sens de l'athéisme moderne* (Paris-Tournai, 1958, p. 20, i.e., of that denial of God that stems from the principle of immanence (granted by Marcel himself) which subverts transcendence and the causal relation between God and creature (cf. in this regard P. Henry's appeals to the doctrine of Vatican Council I in *Monde moderne et sens de Dieu,* pp. 69ff., 75).

[8] K. Marx, *Zur Kritik der Nationalökonomie, Oekonomisch-philosophische Manuskripte aus dem Jahre 1844:* M.E.G.A. Abt. I, Vol. 3, p. 126. The assertion of an anti-Marxist like M. Merleau-Ponty, more than a century later, about this "supersession" differs little from that of Marx; cf. *Éloge de la philosophie* (Paris, 1953), especially pp. 58ff.

[9] Cf. the basic essay of A. del Noce, "Riflessioni sull'opzione ateistica, in *Il problema dell'ateismo* (Brescia, 1962), pp. 171ff.

philosophical thinking in a way and at a point necessarily involving the forcible exclusion of God. Now this kind of beginning would have been possible even in the hypothesis that man was created in the purely and exclusively natural order. The question of the loss of grace simply does not enter here in the matter of the theoretical initial moment as understood for instance, by St. Thomas.

Atheism appears in various modalities and according to various methodologies.

An initial atheism can derive, for example, from the *phenomenological* insistence on the fact that man's mind is initially in a state of pure potency, inasmuch as it is devoid of all content at the moment of its first actuation and consequently devoid of the notion of God.

Again, a *psychological* atheism can be admitted inasmuch as, for every finite intellect, God is incommensurable as object of intuition or as presence in the proper sense of that word. Even though God be immanent in every being and, in a very special way, in the consciousness and awareness that is spirit and therefore *capax infiniti et capax Dei,* nonetheless God remains beyond the reach of any finite intellect unless that intellect be aided by grace and elevated to the state of supernature. This is just what is expressed by the principle of the absolute "transcendence" of God, a basic element of the concept of genuine "theism".

Or, again, there may be such a phenomenon as *pedagogical* (or didactic, if this term be acceptable) atheism, stemming from the fact that neither man's sensible nor his intellectual knowledge encounters God in himself as long as they operate in their own sphere and as long as they are actuated *directly* and immediately. For then their proper objects are the finite objects making up the world of knowledge directly facing man and entering into the fabric of his everyday life. Neither the Church nor traditional theology have ever favored the mythological imaginings of antiquity nor the older or more recent fantasies of ontologism or pantheism; both the Church and traditional theology have preferred to tangle with the difficulty of mounting to the infinite from the springboard of finite things.

Finally, at times there has been a tendency to speak of *methodological* atheism within the limits of the sciences; this has been taken simply in a privative rather than an outright negative sense. But caution must always be exercised here, when it is a question of science in the sense that term has assumed in modern times, especially in the sphere of the specifically mathematical, physical and natural sciences. For they actually deal with objects that are by definition limited to the sphere of the sensible, the imaginative and the conceptual faculties of a finite reason, and God would no longer be God, i.e., the transcendent Absolute, were he the object of such methods of investigation. To avoid misunderstanding, let us state quite clearly that if science as such does not find God in the object proper to its own research and investigation, this does not preclude—indeed, it makes it mandatory—that the *scientist himself as a man* shall pose to himself the problem of God, i.e., the problem of the meaning and ultimate ground of the natural laws and phenomena,[10] as we shall mention in due course.

Adopting Dilthey's terminology,[11] we can say that the restrictive observation is valid only for the natural sciences and not for the psychological and social sciences such as law, ethics, politics, philosophy of history and the like, and preeminently not for philosophy. Indeed, the mind cannot articulate a single absolute statement without first having determined the First Principle and decided on its own relation to the last end.

The problem of God, then, concerns the whole man as "a person" and not any particular element of his cognitive actuation. The above observations are therefore not intended to restrict the eidetic sphere of the problem of God, but rather to specify it in its real comprehension. Indeed, it is historically certain that men have spoken of God in the most diverse and (at least apparently) contradictory fashions. But surely it must be equally evident that if God is God (as he must be), he can be spoken of properly in one way only, the way that is at once appropriate to the creator of the world and Father of men and suitable for man as a rational being, seeking the cause and ground of beings outside the circle of finite things.

[10] In this context, the problem of God in the sciences emerges rather as a *problem of the man* who is dealing with science than as a problem internal to science itself. I mean that the demand for God does not make itself felt so much in the effort to penetrate to the core of the *object* of a science in its physical structure as such as rather in the effort to comprehend the "groundwork" of being itself. It is a demand of the subject, of the scientist, who, after science has had its say, proceeds to address himself to the "problem of being" and of his own fate; cf. C. Fabro, *Dio, Introduzione al problema teologico* (Rome, 1953), pp. 86ff.

[11] W. Dilthey, *Einleitung in die Geisteswissenschaften,* Collected Works, Vol. I (Leipzig, 1933). Dilthey holds to an intimate interconnection between religion and metaphysics and conceives of religion as bound up preeminently with interior experience, which latter, in turn, he specifies as being the birthplace and the fountainhead of the *Geisteswissenschaften* (psychological and social sciences). Metaphysics is the basis of the psychological and social sciences, while religion is the basis of metaphysics (p. 137); the new notion of religious experience is a heritage of Schleiermacher with his critique of the intellectualist practice of basing religion on the unconscious (pp. 139ff.).

2
Theoretical Features in the Problematic of Atheism

In view of the foregoing, it must be borne in mind that the disintegration of the modern principle of immanence into atheism has rendered the terms "theism", "atheism" and "pantheism" radically dialectical, from whatever point of view they be considered. It may very well be—and the history of Western spirituality at least bears this out—that the mystic, at the very moment of reaching the summit of union with God, sees in a "darkness" (Pseudo-Dionysius, St. John of the Cross, *et al.*) and feels himself "empty of God", desperately far removed from God and poised, as it were, in frightening balance over the abyss of nothingness; whereas the immanentist, like the metaphysical idealist, may claim, in virtue of his interpretation of the *Ich denke überhaupt* (the sheer "I think") as absolute Act, to be plunged in the divine life, because he identifies the divine and God himself with cosmic life via the nexus of the cognitive act. This sort of nexus first effaces, as Kierkegaard has noted, the infinite difference separating the finite from the Infinite, and then makes impossible the recognition and admission of sin as an existential difference of man from God in the historical flux of human liberty.[1] For these reasons and others which may emerge and whose consideration we shall postpone until we reach the various stages

[1] "Between God and a human being (let us leave to the speculative thinkers the notion of *humanity* for them to conjure with), there is an absolute difference. The neat relation of the human being to God can thus express the absolute difference and the divine resemblance perverted into impudence, insult and arrogance" (Kierkegaard, *Afslutt. uvid. Efterskrift,* P. II. Sec. II, cap. 4). In the existential realm, the relation of the human being to God, expressive likewise of the absolute difference between them, is articulated in the act of "worship": "Worship is the *maximum* expression of the relation of the human being to God and simultaneously of his resemblance to God, since the qualities are absolutely different. For worship signifies precisely that God is absolutely everything for the human being and that the worshiper in his turn is the one who makes the absolute distinction" (*ibid.,* Vol. II, p. 219).

of the development of atheism at which they do emerge, we are persuaded that the greatest caution must be used in navigating the whole of this arduous passage.

Historically, the misunderstanding perpetrated by atheism may spring from many and mixed motives. The prime motive is the assertion of the impossibility of transcending the finite world of experience; it gives rise to skeptical and phenomenalistic atheism. Then there is the difficulty of [illegible] and of pinpointing the distinction between them; this gives rise to materialist and idealist atheism respectively. The simple admission of matter or spirit does not of itself involve the exclusion of God; that comes from the profession of materialist or spiritualist *monism*. The "distinction", at the ontological level, between spirit and matter is the first step in theism, and this for two reasons: God can be conceived only as spirit, and man can seek God only insofar as man feels himself as "spirit, i.e., only as man is open to the Absolute. In antiquity, we find this nexus between materialist monism and atheism in Democritus and his school.[2]

In modern thought, materialist monism stems preeminently from the mechanism of Descartes, the empiricism of Locke and the humanism of Feuerbach. More difficult to detect but deeper and more crucial is the nexus of atheism with the spiritualist monism that is proper to modern idealism, as we shall point out in due course. The atheism of that skepticism prevalent in antiquity comes down to materialist atheism; an example is Carneades, who held that the gods needed sense objects to sustain their life even as did man, and so were themselves mortal.[3] The implicit or explicit atheism of modern skepticism (Hume), on the other hand, comes down to the principle of immanence.

Then there is the alleged impossibility of "combining" the life of the spirit, i.e., the "freedom" of man with the freedom of God: this gives rise to humanistic atheism.

A natural consequence of this last problem is the urgent need to "reconcile" the problem of evil with the existence of God—and then we have pessimistic atheism (Schopenhauer). Each of these features (which seem to us to be all the main ones) has its own cultural "atmosphere" and environment, which later ages sometimes succeed in clear-

[2] Even Plato in his day made a critique of materialist atheism (*Laws*, X, 891c-892b); in modern thought, the outstanding critiques come from Berkeley. (*A Treatise concerning the Principles of Human Knowledge*, P. I, 92, Berkeley's Works, ed. A. C. Fraser, Vol. I [Oxford, 1901]; *Alciphron*, I, 9 *C.W.*, Vol. II) and Leibniz (*Confessio naturae contra Atheistas, C.W.*, ed. Gerhardt, Vol. IV [Hildesheim, 1961]).

[3] Sextus Emp. *Adv. Mathem.*, 139-140.

ing away. Thus, many stands taken by philosophers, especially in antiquity, which were considered in their own day to be atheistic positions, amount rather to a positive critique of as many inadequate notions of God. Among the philosophers actually taking such a positive line, although accused of atheism, may be listed Parmenides, Heraclitus, Anaxagoras, Socrates, Plato, Aristotle *et al.* However, the same cannot be said for the modern philosophers whose point of departure is the principle of immanence.

Theoretically, the meaning of the error committed by atheism emerges in the gratuitous selection of a particular realm of the real, which in principle, is exclusive of all oppostion and diversity. "Monism" constitutes in point of fact the ontological structure proper to atheism, and the assertion of a single homogeneous reality necessarily entails the effacement of the manifold and of all distinctions within the real. Monism thus yields the speculative formula of atheism. For the materialist and vitalist monism of antiquity and of the Renaissance, the exclusion of God is overt and avowed. But modern Spinozan and idealist monism, though brimming with God, *becomes* atheism in practice, inasmuch as it is pantheism or panentheism, effacing the metaphysical distinction (i.e., the distinction at the level of being) between God and the created universe, including man. For Spinoza, being is one and integral, i.e., Substance (Nature, in the widest sense); within it, the two worlds of thought and extension are distinguished only as necessary "attributes" and the individual existents only as "modes"; for metaphysical idealism, likewise, being is one, the Ego or the Absolute Idea, and the individuals are nothing but its epiphanies or manifestations.

In this sense, we feel it is inaccurate to characterize as "pantheism" the idealism of Fichte-Schelling-Hegel, inasmuch as this idealism is founded precisely upon the distinction between appearance (the many) and reality (the one). Thus, we position the atheism of metaphysical idealism at the opposite pole from Spinozan atheism: whereas Spinozan atheism disintegrates the foundation of nature, the atheism of metaphysical idealism disintegrates the foundation of spirit. The negation of God amounts to the same thing in either case, but its meaning is not identical in both cases. Both can be bracketed adequately only under monism and panentheism, its equivalent.

Existentially, the error of every type of atheism lies in the inhibition or inversion of *freedom,* which is essentially reduced to necessity, i.e., to nothing. Materialist monism reduces it to a psychological gravitation or to the result of the convergence of instincts and feelings. Idealist monism does not go much farther; indeed, it complicates matters by conceiving freedom as transcending the realm of contingency and operating in accord with the strict necessity of the Idea, the impersonal or social Ego or the like. The distinction between materialism and idealism loses all pith when viewed from the bedrock of freedom as a primordial act of the human being. Atheist existentialism itself falls into the same trap, and even more drastically than materialism or idealism, because its desire is to accomplish, even as its antagonist Marxism is determined to [illegible]

existence is for existentialism a choice, but it is a choice of being simply what one is, i.e., of not choosing, because if the human being were to have to choose something beyond himself, and if his choice were to be conditioned by anything different from himself, it would no longer be a choice. Therefore, if God were to exist, man would not be free. Nor can Marxist atheism escape from the pinch of this quandary by its express rejection of the nihilistic individualism of existentialism. For in Marxism, even as in monism, the subject of being and value is *a unitary entity* just as in materialism and idealism: mankind, the working class, the Party, i.e., in each case a universal. Thus, both existentialism and Marxism represent a blend of materialism and idealism, in varying proportions but in both cases fluctuating between the two extremes, patently precluded from any stabilization in either. What is clear, however, is that the actual human being, the individual who is the primary subject of being, does not choose, and therefore is not free, *is* not, radically speaking.

Phenomenologically, the error of atheism lies in its befuddlement of the very notion of "experience" to which it claims to confine itself: atheism dismisses any conception of the *intentionality* of cognition as a relation of compresence. Atheism either asserts that being is matter and spirit is an epiphenomenon, or, conversely, it maintains, as do materialism and idealism, that one or the other reduces to zero and consequently the distinction between them evaporates. Every opposite, it contends, has meaning in virtue and function of its contrary; and so, matter can have meaning as set over against spirit and vice versa. But, in fact, to say that everything is matter or that everything is spirit is to say nothing at all, because with the evaporation of all distinction there vanishes likewise all possibility of any meaningful contraposition, and the very notion of a "compresence", which has given rise to the problem as such, is deprived of all meaning. These atheist sets of mind wreak a brutal but inevitable vengeance upon themselves: materialism, with its exclusive self-restriction to the perceptually immediate, and idealism, with its exclusive self-restriction to the reflectively immediate, have abrogated the distinction between immediate and mediate, have extirpated intentionality root and branch, and with it the very basis of cognition.

Logically, the error of atheism can be pinpointed and therefore confuted in the primacy it assigns to the "principle of identity", a primacy so drastic as to dethrone entirely the principle of (non-) contradiction. The principle of identity cannot be primary for several cogent reasons: (1) precisely, the created universe is not all that exists; (2) man[4] is distinct from the world around him; (3) man initiates his own cognitive process not simply on his own but rather via the presence of the many and proceeds to judgment on the basis of the distinction between himself and the world around him.

Therefore, since the world cannot be identical with man, neither can man be identical with the world, and the difference between them is the very basis of compresence in cognition and of the possibility of a relationship. Hence, the world cannot be explained in terms of man or man in terms of the world; rather, each must be explained in terms proper to itself. Yet, even such an explanation cannot suffice, for it, too, would involve a regress to the bastard primacy of the principle of identity. There is need for a deeper probing via the principle of contradiction.

There is no need of philosophy in order to assert the sheer presence and distinction of the world and man; experience itself suffices for such an assertion. But experience, together with reality, also affirms the multiplicity, the diversity, the finitude, both of the world and of man: man has a "jump" on the world because he knows it and transforms it; but the world, for its part, has a "jump" on man because it conditions him, and because it stands over against him as a kind of helpful partner and a recalcitrant menace. Hence, the principle of identity is meaningful only if it is founded on the principle of contradiction; the genuine principle of identity reveals itself to be a principle of verification of the real, not a principle capable of serving as a universal basis for the primary nexus between being and knowing. The "jump" that the world and man have on each other is a sign of the "lag" both have with respect to sheer being as such. Thus, the inescapable compulsion to accept the principle of contradiction implicitly poses the problem of God, i.e., it levies the demand for transcendence and the transcendent. Admittedly, the theist must tangle with quite demanding problems in his defense of the need for God and, preeminently, of the attributes of God; but the atheist, in

[4] Man here signifies, obviously, the actualization of the human individual in his originality as *mind, awareness, consciousness,* not that human individual in his physical reality, in function of which he is part of the physical world and in constant precise physical relations with the world.

denying the existence of God, is abandoning, at the level of logic, all vestige of a solid basis and all hope of a synthesis, because at the outset he has, with his monistic approach, voided of all significance that exclusion of contradiction which is the very vital principle of thought.

Historians of philosophy traditionally seem to have limited the problem of atheism to the stand taken by the odd individual philosopher, a kind of marginal episode in the history of thought. Actually this problem is the expression of the crucial constitutive drama of thought in search of its own ultimate basis. Any assertion of the identity of thought (awareness, cognition) and being, such as is made by modern monism, whether materialist or idealist, is a denial of reality to the relationship between them, to that association of the one to the other which excludes identity precisely because it is defined *as* a relationship of *association.* Now, it is precisely this essential association of thought to being (and, in its own way, of being to thought, as we shall see later) that constitutes the primary nucleus of the problem of God; for the human being, such association really signifies distinction and dependence of cognition upon being, as we have said.

The relation of thought to being cannot be reduced to a univocal judgment of presence ("being there", *Dasein:* Heidegger) such as that involved in the simple acceptance of the given, whether matter or spirit; rather, this relationship must be actualized in a "mutual" process of substantiation, which necessarily requires a transcending of the relationship itself, i.e., the positing of a supreme Principle which in turn posits the terms of that relationship without being subject to the relationship itself. Materialist monism leaves *spirit* (awareness, mind) without any foundation; idealist monism leaves *the world* without any foundation. And the reason is that both ignore or forget, as Heidegger says, the fact that being belongs to (is associated with) thought and thought to (with) being. Consequently they both render themselves incapable of explaining why thought is based on being and being is illuminated in thought. At this point, strictly speaking, the distinction between materialism and idealism, e.g., between Hegel, on the one hand, and Marx and Sartre on the other, is irrelevant. The evolution of present-day thought will be devoted to showing that consistence favors Marx and Sartre, rather than idealism and the theologizing spiritualism of the lesser heirs of idealism.

Semantics is of little use to us in the theism-atheism tension; metaphysics must speak the decisive word. After the artificial theological tumescence of rationalism, the evolution of modern thought has seen atheism step by step win for the principle of immanence the rights accruing to a consistent principle, and that principle of immanence is now deploying unopposed throughout the thinking of our own day. In classical antiquity the neat concept of God was diluted into the indeterminate ocean of "the divine"; that concept of God as First Principle that emerges in Platonism and idealism is more indicative of a radical separation of God from the world than it is of God as the creating cause of the world. Nor can the celebrated distinction, attributed to Averroes,[5] here suffice; for this distinction between *natura naturans* and *natura naturata* cannot of itself, as Schopenhauer notes, ensures an ultimately theistic stand, even though it is not pantheism either and in fact remains extraneous to the theism-atheism tension. As for the notion of pantheism itself, far from serving to mediate between atheism and theism, it is simply intrinsically contradictory (*ein sich selbst aufhebender Begriff*), inasmuch as the notion of a God presupposes the notion of a world distinct from him as an essential correlative. And if the world takes over the function of God, it becomes an absolutized world, without God. Pantheism is thus but a "euphemism for atheism".[6]

The essential features of the notion of God are inextricably interwelded. The omission or abandonment of any one of them inevitably involves the penalty of losing God, of being without God. Atheism is therefore involved not only in the exclusion of God and the assertion that there exists nothing but the world and man; atheism is also implicit in any assertion that God alone exists, with the consequent denial of the reality of the world and man by way of a degradation of both to the status of mere elements or phenomena of the Absolute. The striking solidity of the world is an obvious fact, but theism contends that this very solidity is calculated to demand and to manifest as its foundation spirit differing entirely from the solid material world. Man's spiritual faculty is an obvious fact and constitutes the sustaining principle of his freedom which sets him off from nature, but theism contends that the human soul is infinite only in the realm of potency or capacity (and herein lies its distinguishing mark, as opposed to nature), while remaining finite in its actualization and being always conditioned and limited by nature and its fellow human beings. Thus, not only is the human soul not God; it feels the need of seeking God and of turning to God to overcome such limitations and to fix itself on the Infinite, adhering to the Infinite as to its proper ultimate, τέλος. From this point of view the notion of theism is losing ground and the notion of atheism is gaining.

[5] Averroes attributes the term "*natura naturata*" to the visible universe: "Et hoc ita fuit quoniam natura naturata ita fecit, ut nos sequimur suum opus" (*In l. I de Coelo et Mundo,* tc. 2; ed. ven. minor, [Venice, 1560], fol. 7r.)

[6] Schopenhauer contends that this expression contains a "gratuitous insinuation" (*Erschleichung*), a usurpation, because the burden of proof rests with the theist; whereas it would be more exact to call atheism and atheist "non-Judaism" and "non-Judaic" (*Ueber die vierfache Wurzel des Satzes vom zureichenden Grunde, C.W.*, ed. Frauenstädt, Vol. I [Leipzig, 1916^2], ch. 5, p. 129; cf. *Parerga und Paralipomena, C.W.*, Vol. V, p. 125).

Confirmation of this can be seen in the spread of the blemish of atheism in recent years over the whole face of the globe. But even in the philosophy of the last half of the 19th century and the first half of the 20th century, that blemish of atheism had ravaged almost the whole of man's spiritual countenance.

We must conclude that there is but *one* genuine notion of God and, consequently, but one valid form of theism, namely, that which admits God as the supreme ontological Principle who is the supreme Being, distinct from the world created by him, and who is simultaneously the supreme spiritual Principle, i.e., a knowing and a willing and hence a personal Being, therefore the all-embracing and free cause of the world.[7] A God conceived as act of the world and immersed in the world or "emerging" from the flux of the world's becoming, as the inexhaustible and always immanent aim of universal evolution, is simply an "event" of the world and in no case the God man seeks and begs to save him.

[7] "This latter [theism] demands not only a Cause of the world distinct from the world, but also an intelligent, i.e., knowing and willing and therefore personal, nay more, individual Cause: such a One and only such a One is the One designated by the Word of God. An impersonal God is no God at all, is nothing but a misused word, a pseudo-concept, a *contradictio in adiecto,* a shibboleth for philosophy professors, who are at pains to slip through with a verbal subterfuge in the wake of their intellectual discomfiture" (Schopenhauer, *Parerga und Paralipomena,* ch. 5, p. 123).

3
Critique of the Notion of Atheism

The nominal "notion" of atheism is quite clear, but it is a difficult business to define the essence of atheism, to pinpoint its content and structure.[1] The theist sees atheism simply as an error, the acme of all errors; for him it comes down to a simple process of intellectual or emotional aberration. But the atheist sees things in a diametrically opposite fashion: for him the believer is a victim of a psychological tendency to unwarranted extrapolation or of a simple mental delusion, whereas the atheist has arrived at the truth. This attitude is evident in modern atheist writings which we shall cite in some detail later.

I

The first thing that can be said of theoretical atheism is that it issues either from some *particular difficulty* encountered by the human mind in considering the notion of God, or that it derives from some *erroneous principle* taken for granted as an initial postulate of philosophizing. Thus, it would seem logical that atheism of the first kind would be overcome once the difficulty in question has been resolved, and that atheism of the second kind would be precluded when the inconsistency of the initial principle which leads to atheism has been demonstrated. The particular difficulties arise in almost every case from the limitation of the human mind: e.g., the incapacity of man to conceive of pure Spirit, pure Being and such definite attributes proper to God; the inability to reconcile divine providence with the existence of evil (as noted above) and, above all, with the misfortunes of the innocent and the prosperity of the wicked; similarly,

[1] On the complexity and difficulty presented by the concept of atheism, cf., e.g., the remarks of a modern historian of atheism, F. Mauthner, *Wörterbuch der Philosophie,* Vol. II (Leipzig, 1927[2]), pp. 16ff. (under *Gott*).

the inability to harmonize the infinite divine goodness with the inexorable divine justice; further, the inability to make the infinite divine omniscience and omnipotence square with human freedom, and other analogous apparently insoluble problems presented by the notion of God.

These difficulties can readily be admitted to constitute real and grave problems for the theist, but this admission by no means involves any concession that they constitute, simply for that reason, "positive" argument for the atheist. When the theist has demonstrably solid arguments for asserting the existence of God, such difficulties stimulate rather than paralyze his search for a knowledge [illegible] ever more intimate "appropriation" (*Aneignung*) of his own relation to the Absolute. Such difficulties are not really arguments in favor of the atheist position, because they arise out of the human situation or stem from our own human limitations which restrict us to projecting the radial nexus that binds us to God from our own human center. This is peripheral in the ontological circle, since God himself, the absolute Principle and Good, is the real center from which not only the radial nexus actually connecting God to the world and to man is projected, but also that nexus binding the world and, above all, man to God. No wonder the theist cannot entirely dispel the shadows of these difficulties; if he could, man would no longer be the finite being he is; he would be God himself. The real reason for man's inability, as a finite being, to "resolve" these difficulties is quite simply the fact that their solution lies precisely in that "infinitude" of the divine attributes that unknots the cramp of finitude.

II

The notion of "positive" or constructive atheism is peculiar to the modern era; more exactly, it is the quintessential distillation of the principle of immanence. In order to grasp the significance of this capital event in the modern world, we must consider certain difficulties connected with what might be called the "ontological structure" of atheism, or better, of the mind of the atheist.

First, there is a point of elementary semantics to be clarified. Atheism is a professedly negative term, expressing the denial of a supreme Principle of the real, of a Being whose essence is existence. How then can the adjective "positive" [2] be legitimately used to modify the noun "atheism" which is *a priori* a purely and radically negative term? We feel the

[2] Cf. C. Fabricius, *Der Atheismus der Gegenwart, Seine Ursachen und seine Überwindung* (Göttingen, 1922), pp. 2ff.

answer must be that we have here a new semantics that modern atheists wish to set up on the basis of the new principle of the "subjectivity of being". Down to the period of the Renaissance, all atheist schools of thought (and the cognate schools of monism, pantheism, naturalism, and the like) were the outcome of a "reduction" or degradation of man to the ontological common denominator of matter; man's being was traced back to some form or other of an element or principle of nature. Modern thought, and the atheism that has issued from it, operates on a quite different constitutive principle—man's claim to originality over against nature. This claim finds its expression in the "new" principle of immanence, i.e., the elevation of man's being to the level of the *cogito* (the act of thinking) or, alternately, the reduction of the actualization of being to the actualization of the *cogito,* the limitation of the structure of being to the structure of the *cogito*—to cite but a few of the ways in which this crucial claim may be expressed. Consequently, truth is not simply, as it was for classical naturalistic atheism, a simple turning of man to nature; rather, it stems from the activation and actualization of man's potency, his capacity, considered as freedom of being. This positive character of the new atheism (whether Marxist, existentalist, neo-positivist or pragmatist, or any other variety) finds expression in the ambitious title of "humanism" claimed as the adequate substantive, descriptive of their stand by atheists of the modern era, especially after Feuerbach.

Therefore, here we are dealing with a claim that is specious rather than seriously founded. Indicative in this regard is the stand of Spinoza, who was quite early accused of atheism and can indeed be considered, despite the impassioned defense advanced on his behalf by Hegel,[3] to be one of the founders of modern atheism. Yet Spinoza, far from claiming to be an atheist or favoring atheism in any way, merged and dissolved everything into God and referred everything back to God: he gave the impression of taking a semantic and ontological tack diametrically opposed to what began to come into vogue with the materialist Illuminism of the 18th century and was to gain the upper hand after the death of Hegel.

III

In light of the justified contention that man has a natural inclination to turn to God, to seek God, and, consequently, to come to know God, just as man has a natural inclination to live in society, to seek happiness,

[3] Cf. especially *Enzyklopädie der philosophischen Wissenschaften,* §573, ed. Hoffmeister (Leipzig, 1949), p. 484. Text and context will be examined later.

etc.,[4] atheism seems an impossibility. It appears to be a psychological syndrome or a pathological state of disarray, rather than a genuine theoretical attitude; thus it seems that the very possibility that there can be such phenomena as theoretical atheists must be denied. Theoretical atheism seems to be a contradiction in terms, for at least two cogent reasons: (1) because it is a denial of the fact that man is naturally inclined or destined to seek God as his First Principle, the mandatory goal and consummation of man's rational nature; (2) because it claims —and this is expressly asserted by modern atheism—that an ultimate basis of the real can be arrived at via the exclusion of the Absolute and the simultaneous admission that neither nature nor man can rise to the level of the Absolute in order to occupy the place left vacant by the denial of God. Consequently, theoretical atheism, as *a rational objective posture or attitude,* is as inconceivable and unfeasible as a square circle. This may afford a partial explanation of the lack of interest shown by theologians of this last century in theoretical atheism and the common tendency to resolve it into practical atheism.

But the situation is much less straightforward when viewed from the inside of modern thought. The point is this: atheism has never been nor can it ever be, a starting point, but it does constitute the terminal point of a certain way of seeing the world and man or of a modified "attenuation" of the being either of man or of the world. This atheism may in turn become a starting point for other elaborations and conclusions relative to the being of man and of the world. The starting point of modern atheism is the new notion of being and of freedom stemming from the *cogito* in any of its modalities. Thus, there can exist such phenomena as a theoretical (positive) atheism, theoretical atheists, even convinced theoretical atheists: all those who have opted to effect an exhaustive comprehension and elaboration of the modern principle of immanence. As a cultural phenomenon and a state of mind, atheism can therefore be *real,* in the sense of being "subjective conviction", which is all that is presently in question. The yen for God and for the knowledge of God can be called inherent to man, in the sense that man is impelled to find a rational explanation of the world and of his own experience and is therefore compelled to effect a regression to some "foundation" of being. This yen is innate, this impulsion to look for the fountainhead, this curiosity to find the principle; but actually the ultimate object of man's (re)search is neither innate nor anteriorly determined. The innate

[4] "Inest homini inclinatio secundum naturam rationis, quae est sibi propria, sicut homo habet naturalem inclinationem ad hoc quod veritatem cognoscat de Deo et ad hoc quod in societate vivat" (Man has an innate inclination in accord with the nature of the very pith of his being: thus man has a natural inclination to know the truth about God and to live within society) (St. Thomas, *S.T.,* I-II, q.94, a.2.).

element of knowledge as such is intrinsically indeterminate as "potency", as the germ of an idea which man must proceed to elaborate and clarify. Therefore, the "conviction" of awareness of God, the assertion of his existence and the definition of his nature represent the conclusions or outcome of a process that has to be effected by man. The issue of this process naturally depends to some extent on the process itself, but it is transcendentally determined preeminently by the *beginning*, i.e., by the initial attitude assumed by the mind with regard to being.

Thus, anyone adopting the Parmenidean stand that being is the foundation of thought [5] is thereby positively setting out on a road that will eventually lead to the Absolute, provided he does not get bogged down underway or take a wrong turn as a result of some methodological blunder. Conversely, anyone starting from the notion of thought as the foundation of being is thereby ruling out in advance any genuine penetration to a notion of transcendence, no matter what determination the mind later elects to impose upon being, whether empiricist, rationalist, idealist, phenomist, materialist, intuitionist or other. So it is a reflexive principle, this acceptance of the *cogito* in all its implications, which blocks at the outset the movement of the natural inclination to the Absolute, by swerving the mind in a diametrically opposite direction, so that the thinker is bound to arrive at the terminal conviction that there is no such being as God in the sense of a transcendent Principle, that the problem of the Absolute is therefore meaningless, even that God must be denied in order to guarantee man's freedom, etc.[6] Thus, such phenomena as theoretical atheism and theoretical atheists do, or at least can, exist in the sense that atheism represents, or at least can represent, the conclusion from a principle or point of departure which renders that conclusion logical and inevitable.

In antiquity and, indeed, right down to the point at which modern thought emerges, atheism represented a sporadic phemonenon occurring within the confines of a cultural elite, but as soon as the *cogito* comes on

[5] Cf. the chief Parmenidean text, 28 B 8, Diels I, 238, 34ff. In this connection, cf. C. Fabro, *Partecipazione e causalità secondo S. Tommaso d'Aquino* (Turin, 1961), pp. 69ff.; French translation: *Participation et causalité* (Paris-Louvain, 1960), pp. 87ff.

[6] In this sense we feel that the critique of those who identify modern atheism with a denial of all values is not penetrating to the theoretical kernel of this atheism: e.g., such remarks as: "Truly irreligious atheism is to be found only where there is complete skepticism about any value of life. He who believes that there is nothing worthwhile is the thoroughgoing atheist. For him there is no value distinction" (E. S. Brightman, *A Philosophy of Religion* [New York, 1946] pp. 202f.). Beginning with Bayle, as we shall point out, the protagonists of the divorce of morality from religion and later the explicit atheists like d'Holbach, Feuerbach, the Marxists, the existentialists and the like insist on atheism precisely as mandatory in order to guarantee freedom and therewith the very foundation of value.

the scene, atheism assumes an all-embracing structure simultaneously invading public life and individual behavior. Therefore, we must bypass all pointless polemic pro and con and zero in on this principle of the *cogito* in order to make an exhaustive study of its significance, its theoretical implications and the subsequent intellectual processes it can trigger.

IV

Consequently, those theologians [illegible] the possibility of theoretical atheism and deny the very existence of theoretical atheists—and it seems that hitherto the majority of theologians have done just that—are considering the problem in *se* and *per se,* in its abstract and objective dimension; and they may well be right in so doing, for the alternative here would be the admission that the non-existence of God could be objectively demonstrated and the consequent avowal that God has given man reason in order that that very human reason may drift away from God, exclude God, itself take over the place of God.

It may easily happen that the ordinary believer disagrees with theologians on this point, for we have here an observation going to the very roots of ontology, an observation that we shall indeed bear in mind in the whole of our discussion of atheism. But we must also bear in mind that even though, obviously, God's stand (so far as God is concerned) with respect to man has not changed and cannot change, man's stand with respect to God, on the other hand, has changed radically in modern thought as compared to preceding eras and even as compared with the natural tendency of man as such. In past ages the sporadic assertions of atheism stemmed from more or less evident (and therefore rectifiable) warpings of the principle of realism, warpings that could be refuted by thought as compared to preceding eras and even as compared with the an appeal to the basic principle of realism, inasmuch as this basic principle maintained intact the demand for transcendence; but the principle of immanence strikes at the very root of transcendence. So the situation is now reversed: the existence of a large number of theists in modern thought proves nothing, unless it be the lack of consistency, even—nay, especially—in such men as Descartes, Malebranche, Leibniz, Kant, the later Schelling, Hegel and those others who really do posit and admit God as a "principle" of being and knowing. We have here one of those staggering illusions, of which as always only a great genius is capable.

At this point a new problem arises at the level of religious phenomenology and of theology. Once the real possibility of a speculative atheism and the existence of theoretical atheists has been admitted, it would seem that it must also be admitted that such men are what they are, i.e., *atheists in good faith,* inasmuch as they be admitted to have arrived at the denial of God by way of a process endowed with an intrinsic consistency of its own. But this would amount to admitting that a man can become an atheist and remain one, *even for his whole life,* without incurring any guilt, and that, in the final analysis, man can discharge the offices of his life as man without reference to God and, indeed, dispensing with God entirely. We are grazing the famous contentions of Bayle, whose thought will come in for detailed consideration later, concerning the nexus between atheism and morality. As far as I can establish, theologians have given direct consideration only to the less radical problem, i.e., whether a person can lose his faith through no fault of his own, and there have certainly been theologians who have admitted that this might happen in individual cases. But as far as I know, no theology has ever discussed the question of the possibility we have here broached for atheism; still less has any theologian given an affirmative reply to this question. The reason is that theologians are treating these problems from the point of view of divine truth rather than from the point of view of the modern error, i.e., the modern principle of immanence.

From the point of view of philosophy, the problem is whether it is possible for a thinker in good faith to accept the principle of immanence, and then elaborate and develop it from a chain of thought concluding with atheism. And it is the state of man rather than the state of God that creates difficulties militating against an affirmative reply. Certainly, if God were an evident object, a perceptible entity, i.e., an object proper to direct and immediate sense-experience, or even an "analytic conclusion" like the formal conclusions of mathematics or the demonstrations of natural science that remain within the dimensions of the finite, then there would be no room for any radical mental deviation such as the one involved in the denial of God via the principle of immanence.

As things actually stand, however, it can happen that the environment in which a man lives and the education, training and conditioning he receives may impel him to absorb the principle of immanence until it becomes intellectual blood and bone to him; then he may indeed elaborate and work on this principle to the point where he distills from it its inevitable atheist marrow, on which he then may gnaw for nourishment "for some time". *But not for always!* For he is living in a world with an historical past and "ought to" ask himself, first of all, why philosophy was never atheistic prior to the appearance of the *cogito* on the scene; then, why some philosophers, even after the *cogito* had appeared on the scene, still continued to impugn the principle of immanence as intrinsically meaningless and contradictory; and further, why some philosophers have returned and are returning to the metaphysical principle precisely in order to escape the ontological void of the principle of immanence, well aware that this contradicts the logic of the principle of immanence but bowing, nonetheless, to the "demand and need for a foundation, a basis".

Therefore, "atheist" good faith, even though it may have existed or can have existed at the outset as an effect of environment and training, cannot and may not persist for long and certainly not for a whole lifetime. And this, not only because it is inadmissable that God should not have furnished man with enough principles so that he may find and have a valid certainty of God's existence, but [illegible] sible that man should be incapable of finding the basis of truth.

V

There remains the problem of "implicit atheism", i.e., the problem of the stand of those philosophers who found that their own philosophizing on initial principles or positions, which must logically culminate in atheism, has in fact led to atheism in the course of its subsequent historical development by other thinkers, whereas the original philosophers often kick against the pricks of the logic of their own principles and assert the existence of God or of the gods. It may be that the theism professed by the Epicureans and the Stoics (and perhaps even by some of the neo-Platonists) can be judged to be a simple articulation in esoteric language of contemporary popular belief, with the philosophers in question professing for their own part a naturalistic pantheism equivalent to atheism. But the same certainly cannot be said of such subtle and erudite philosophers as Descartes, Malebranche, Leibniz, Locke, Berkeley, Kant, Hegel and others, who come out quite strongly as theists, even declaring that their whole philosophy aims at a defense of this assertion.

Whatever may be said about the theoretical problem as such, we have here a problem of *the very thinking pattern of the philosopher* in question, the pattern according to, and within which, he was convinced that he was excogitating a better defense than anyone else for the existence of God. The crucial point here seems to us to be the fact that a "new" principle has been insinuated into the proofs advanced by these philosophers (e.g., Descartes, Leibniz, *et al.*), a principle that inhibits the "atheist conversion" of the principle of immanence. Such an inhibitory principle would be the "Idea" of the most perfect Being, the Idea of the Infinite, and the like, which ideas cannot be explained within the limits of the dimension of purely human intellection and thus entail the mandatory admission of a supreme Being, etc. In this way, such a principle might give the impression of having cogent conclusive force.

This crucial drama of modern thought brings into play and manifests something that can almost be termed a "constitutional ambiguity". The starting point is the obvious principle of the association of truth to man, but this is conceived immediately as a principle of the subjectivity of truth. Thus, for several centuries and in many ways we can discern in many philosophers an absence of any awareness of an opposition or strict incompatibility between the "subjectivity of truth" and a convinced theism; the opposition, articulated as atheism, manifests itself only in isolated cases. The main and most widespread consequence of the "subjectivity of truth" notion is not atheism but deism and Illuminism, not the rejection of God but the critique of positive religions and, in particular, of Christianity as an historical religion. And here we encounter a whole gamut of positions.

There may be a peaceful coexistence of the principle of immanence and theism and Christianity, as in Descartes, Malebranche, Leibniz, Bacon, Locke, Bayle, Hegel, *et al.*

There may be a coexistence of immanentism and theism or natural religion or something similar, but a critical attitude toward Christianity: then we have the *deism* of Cherbury, Shaftesbury, Mandeville, Hobbes, Tyndal, Toland, Voltaire, Rousseau, the early Diderot, *et al.* This is a sort of momentary halt on the bridge toward atheism.

There may be an accord between immanentism and atheism: just as the ambiguity of rationalist theism made possible deism and the championing of a religion of pure reason, so the ambiguity of deism may cause it to drift into atheism.[7]

The intensifying drama involved here lies in the fact that neither essence nor existence can stand alone in the theoretical process. And so the theism that is not specified and actualized as an historical religion (Christianity) ceases to be theism, i.e., a conviction that there is a personal and providentially causal God, and becomes deism, i.e., the assertion of God often reduced to the status of universal cosmic Reason or Mind. Such deism, in its turn, fluctuates between the universal impersonal Reason and the human reason, lapses eventually into a deification of the latter and so breaks down into atheism to which it impels its protagonists. In this sense, the drama of the 17th- and 18th-century European thought, which runs the entire gamut of theism-deism-atheism, is the background drama that provides the key to an understanding of 19th-century atheism.

This is true *a fortiori* of the pietist and deist, Kant, who first rules out

[7] E.g., Shaftesbury's influence shows itself as decisive both for the trenchant deism of Voltaire and Rousseau and for the no less trenchant atheism of Diderot and d'Holbach (Cf. D. B. Schegel, *Shaftesbury and the French Deists* [Chapel Hill: Univ of North Carolina Studies, 1956], especially pp. 77ff.).

the metaphysical proofs of the existence of God in *The Critique of Pure Reason* and then appeals to *Practical Reason.* This Kantian "switch-over" has a certain depth of vision all its own, inasmuch as it recurs in a certain sense to the radical yen for happiness and the supreme Good, that yen lies in man's innermost depths and which, rightly understood, is the first and last ground of all his other longing, aiming and endeavor. It recalls that *appetitus naturalis* of St. Thomas that we have already noted in passing. There is no doubt, then, about Kant's subjective conviction of the existence of God, just as there is no less doubt about his "objective atheism."

But the most typical instance, from this point of view, is *pantheism* (and panentheism), especially as it begins to take form in modern thought beginning with Spinoza. There is in Spinoza's own system neither let nor hindrance to atheism, as we shall point out in due course. Philosophical criticism has been almost unanimous on this point.

At first glance, Spinozism might be called theism or at least deism,[8] but in reality it is atheism. Hegel was a convinced and outstanding defender of Spinoza's "theism" (!). Hegel admits that the "absolute Substance" is not yet "Absolute Spirit" (as Hegel conceives it!) but contends that Spinoza should not be said to have "confounded God with nature, with the finite world, or to have made the world into God", since for Spinoza the world is a "mere phenomenon" (*ein Phänomen*). Therefore, far from denying God, Spinoza, on the contrary, denies the world and asserts "that God and only God is": this is not atheism; it is acosmism,[9] if any negative term be applicable to it. At the end of the "system", Hegel returns to a more extensive discussion of the accusation of atheism (and of pantheism) and it will be worthwhile briefly to follow this discussion with careful attention.

Hegel again recalls that the accusation of atheism is the one leveled by theologians against (modern) philosophy, whereas the accusation leveled by certain intellectualist philosophers is rather one of pantheism, the reproach that there is too much God in the philosophy in question (Spinoza's and Hegel's own). Hegel notes that it has been preeminently the philosophy of the recent past that has preferred to level the reproach of pantheism instead of that of atheism, an accusation that seems at first glance more severe and invidious. The accusation of atheism, then, collapses of itself: philosophy is recognized by the very accusation of pantheism as being able to recognize God everywhere; further, philoso-

[8] Voltaire classes Spinoza as a deist (cf. *Questions sur les miracles*).

[9] *Enzyklopädie der philosophischen Wissenschaften,* §50; Hoffmeister, pp. 76f. This §50 contains the theoretical pith of Hegelianism, even as §573 contains the most spirited summary of it (Hegel himself in §573 refers the reader expressly to §50: ed. Hoffmeister, p. 484).

phy for Hegel is superior to religion and, as such, in a position to comprehend the truth of the religious sphere, i.e., "to recognize its own forms in the categories of the religious mode of representation", whereas religion is not capable of the converse. The reason for this is that the religious sphere is dualistic and conceives truth in rigid intellectualist separation, whereas philosophy moves in a sphere superior to reason (*Vernunft*). Thus, philosophy is impervious alike to the accusation of atheism and to that of pantheism; both accusations merely betray the limitations of the accusers' points of view. The transition from the accusation of atheism to that of pantheism, concludes Hegel, has its foundation only in the superficiality of representation which makes the finite an external entity, and the Infinite likewise an external entity. Now, contends Hegel, these critics then proceed to declare that the position contrary to their own must assert that everything is God, that everything is dissolved into, somehow bathed in, God. But, objects Hegel, these critics ought to sharpen their perception of what constitutes the "substantiality" of which philosophy is speaking; that is, they ought not to transform formal universality into real universality and assert indiscriminately that all things, the most trivial just as the most noble, possess substantiality and that this being of terrestrial objects is God for Hegel; such being is sheer exteriority (*Dasein*) and mere appearance (*Schein*).

And here we have the heart of the matter. The "All" of which pure philosophy speaks (the Invisible, the Eternal of Krishna, the One of the Eleatics,[10] the Substance of Spinoza and, we would add, the Absolute Idea of Hegel himself) is the only entity that is divine, who is God; all the rest of the world is accidental. The progress held to have been achieved in the modern (and especially the Hegelian!) way of thinking consists in the transition to a conception of the Absolute not only as substance but also as spirit. Hegel is persuaded (and Schleiermacher as well) that this accords with and gives satisfaction not only to the theism of natural religion but also preeminently to Christianity. Hegel holds that in philosophy, considered as the ultimate and adequate expression of the truth that is the unity of contraries, the true definition of God's relation to the world is derived from the determination (*Bestimmung*) of the nature of God. Initially, God is separated from the world as essence from phenomenon, the Infinite from the finite, but this very

[10] It is typical that Hegel, while hastening to defend Spinoza against the accusation of atheism, tends to class the whole of Greek thought, on the other hand, as atheist because, in Hegel's opinion, it was unaware of God as a person: "The definition of *the subjectivity of the Supreme Idea,* of the personality of God, is a much richer, more intense and therefore much later concept" (*Vorlesungen über die Geschichte der Philosophie, Introduction:* ed. Hoffmeister [Leipzig, 1944], p. 67. In the margin, Hegel noted: "All the *ancients thus atheists,* not *Christian philosophers*").

separation is calculated to entail (and *involve*) a conviction of the relation (*Beziehung*) of the appearance to the essence, of the finite to the Infinite. In the profoundest sense, this is what constitutes the *dialectic* in Hegelian speculation.

Hegel has achieved two important results at this ultimate and conclusive point of his system; first, he has shown that his own philosophical system is not entirely God-centered but also calculated to overcome the inadequacies of the ways in which past thinkers conceived of God, by starting, in contrast to these thinkers, within the interior of pure thought and within the interior of God himself, secondly, [illegible] Hegel has clarified the essential relation of God to the world and thereby likewise clarified the essential relation of the world to God. Since this relation is one of dialectical unity, it is the only one conceived in the order of essence that contains at once the *necessity* of the relation and the distinction of the components, of appearance and essence, of the finite and the Infinite, within the confines of their unity.

The critics who accuse philosophy of atheism or of pantheism, concludes Hegel, are proceeding from their own abstract way of conceiving this unity and identity, and, therefore, they attribute to philosophy the notion that God is "composite" (*Zusammengesetzt*), being made up of God and the world; they then go on, "in utter heedlessness of justice and truth", to accuse philosophy of affirming such a unity and identity. Hegel's polemic is directed primarily against the conservative theologians [11] who were alarmed at the Spinozism and consequent pantheism of the new philosophy, and it is significant as an indication of Hegel's own personal conviction that only a transferrence of reality to the Absolute-One and a reduction of the finite to the status of phenomenon could provide truth for man and thus a genuine identification and proper recognition of the divinity. But if Being is one, it embraces within itself all truth and reality; and if truth and reality lie in the historical actualization of historical reason, then man can at one and the same time boast of being everything, inasmuch as he is the actual subject of this reason, and of being nothing inasmuch as he passes with time, being the empirical subject he is, a transient element and fleeting moment in the universal becoming.

It is significant in this connection (and for a deeper awareness of the nexus between the Protestant principle and modern philosophy) that the prince of modern theology, Schleiermacher, is no less knee-deep in Spinozism than Hegel, his most tenacious and relentless opponent. In

[11] In §573, Hegel recalls the famous theologian Tholuck (Hoffmeister, p. 484) as an adversary, but the strongest and final attack on Tholuck comes in the Preface to the second edition of the *Enzyklopädie* (Hoffmeister, pp. 10f., 15ff.), dating from 1827.

the 1799 *Reden über die Religion,* published in the heat and frenzy of the *Atheismusstreit,* God is designated by such expressions as *Weltgeist* (World-Soul), *Geist des Universums* (Spirit of the Universe), *Ganze* (All), which are all expressly Spinozan in origin and were soon to be taken up into Hegel's own system. And yet, it was precisely by recourse to the "higher realism" of Spinoza that Schleiermacher counted on barring the way to metaphysical idealism which tends to make of the world and God a simple reflection of the human mind; it even goes so far as to identify with the totality of the Universal Spirit. Let us then sacrifice a lock of our hair, says Schleiermacher, to the hands of this excommunicated saint, Spinoza, who enables us to rein in the frenzy for annihilation of the universe that pervades the whole of speculative idealism: "The sublime World-Soul (*Weltgeist*) penetrated him entirely; the Infinite was his Alpha and Omega, the universe was his one abiding love; in holy innocence and profound humility he gazed upon himself in the mirror of the eternal world and he saw himself there in his turn as the most attractive mirror of that eternal world; he was full of religion and of the Holy Spirit and therefore he towers unique and unattainable, master of his own art but exalted above mundane controversy and without rights of citizenship." Within the ambit of the One-All of Spinoza, Schleiermacher presents his own central idea, that of the "intuition of the universe" (*Anschauung des Universums*), which he also calls the "supreme and most general formula of religion and the pivot (*Angel*) of its message".[12]

Schleiermacher, like Hegel, hopes to use Spinoza's all-out exaltation as a buffer against the shoals of speculative atheism. Surely Spinoza's cosmic monism is superior to the polytheism of a pious Roman, just as the view of a Lucretius is superior to that of a fetishist (*Götzendiener*)! At this point, there are two possible conceptions of God: that of metaphysics, which conceives God as the Absolute and the Infinite, and consequently the ineffable All; or else the point of view of religion, according to which God is rather the "divine" (*das Göttliche*) who reveals himself either in an "actual vital experience" or in an intuition of the Universe as the ineffable All. Whereas metaphysics starts from the finite, which it then cannot transcend, religion, according to Schleiermacher, has its beginning in the intuition of the All, with the accompanying "sense of dependence", as we shall note in due course. What is important to note here is that, for Schleiermacher, the idea of God is thereafter not as important for the genuinely religious man as is generally believed, that there are not, among truly religious men, such phenomena as zealots, enthusiasts or fanatical proponents of the existence of God; such truly religious men have reacted quite calmly to what

[12] Schleiermacher, *Ueber die Religion, II Rede:* Selected Works Vol. IV (Leipzig, 1911), p. 243.

in their environment is called atheism and have always felt that there was something still more irreligious than this.[13]

For Schleiermacher, therefore, intuitionist pantheism may be an expression of the sublimest form of theism and of piety (*Frömmigkeit*), for to Schleiermacher the question of whether God be within or beyond the world is meaningless, just as materialist pantheism is the most serious aberration.[14] If in fact religion is a feeling, then the aim and purpose of all religious emotions and feelings is the shedding of a clearer light upon the immediate being of God in us, by the instrumentality of [illegible] therefore it is God who becomes conscious in us, who appears immediately to our self-awareness as in his native seat. So we have dialectical Spinozism in Hegel with his notion of a meditation, and "immediatistic" Spinozism in Schleiermacher with his notion of direct experience; but both are convinced that the being of God and that of the world cannot be distinct, that they form a single whole within the ambit of consciousness, of the mind.

This formal unification of self-awareness Schleiermacher calls precisely the "sheer sense of dependence" (*das schlechthinnige Abhängigkeitsgefühl*) which thus constitutes the essence of universal finite self-awareness and is identical in everyone; it is actualized as soon as sensory self-awareness is stimulated from the outside.

This sense of dependence is not something accidental; in it our own self-awareness acts as the universalized finitude of being, making it a universal element of life which replaces all the so-called proofs of the existence of God.[15] Schleiermacher thus categorically judges atheism to be simply and solely the result of a defective and stunted mental development. In its most drastic manifestation, it can be only delirium and illusion (*Wahn und Schein*). Schleiermacher distinguishes and describes three forms of atheism or "lack of God" ("godlessness", *Gottlosigkeit*). The first is typical and proper to *infancy,* whether individual or phylo-

[13] *Ibid.*, p. 288. This text approaches the Buddhist notion; cf. F. Heiler, *Die Religionen der Menschheit,* (Stuttgart, 1959), p. 284.

[14] In a lengthy note in the 1831 edition of *Zur Theologie* (Collected Works, Vol. I; 7th ed. of M. Redeker [Berlin, 1960], pp. 279f., Note 19) on the text cited in our Note 13 immediately above, Schleiermacher defends himself against the accusation of atheism by appealing to *Der christliche Glaube*, §8, Appendix 2, to which we shall return in due course. Schleiermacher has no scruples about defending Spinoza against the accusation of pantheism and eulogizing his piety (cf. Note 3 on p. 267, in which Schleiermacher expresses his disagreement with the critique of Jacobi and his surprise that Novalis should have gone over to Catholicism after having been an adherent of Spinoza). These lengthy notes, written after Schleiermacher's theological *magnum opus,* are of great importance for a proper grasp of Schleiermacher's final notion of religion. As we shall see, Schleiermacher remained substantially faithful to the stand he had taken in the famous *Reden* of 1799, as he himself asserts (in Note 5 on p. 269).

[15] Schleiermacher, *Der christliche Glaube,* §§8, 12 and 33; Redeker edition, Vol. I, pp. 52ff. and 174f.).

genetic. It amounts to a total lack of any awareness of God, due to the underdeveloped state of the mind. It is also found among primitive peoples, contends Schleiermacher, even though difficult to demonstrate from the historical point of view. The second form of atheism Schleiermacher calls *sense-hampered:* it involves the adulteration of a really present sheer sense of dependence with some extraneous element that eventually destroys its efficacy, as when God is objectivized in the forces of nature and the phenomena of the world of the senses (polytheism, fetishism). The third form of atheism (*Atheismus*), properly speaking and full blown, has a dual modality. One aspect is a malignant fear in the face of the sternness of the demands involved in the knowledge of God; this fear is a product of unbridled license and is thus a sickness of the soul (*Krankheit der Seele*); such an atheism must actually be denied all genuine ontological status because it is totally lacking in interior genuineness. The other aspect is simply an opposition to vulgar religious practice and is directed against the more or less inadequate current explanations of religious knowledge or against the diseased anthropomorphic conceptions (*anthropopatische Vorstellungen*) of religion favored by ecclesiastical tyranny. Such was, in Schleiermacher's view, the atheism of the 18th century; and if this sort of atheism later slipped into a misunderstanding of even the interior facts of self-awareness, this was due to a debility (*Kränklichkeit*) of the intelligence.

This "knowledge and awareness of God" is thus the basic fact and act for the human subject in this synthesis of the Substance of Spinoza and the "sense of the sublime" of Kant. Once this "knowledge and awareness of God" is developed, both the proofs of the existence of God and the attacks of atheism collapse simultaneously.[16] Whereas during the first half of the 19th century, the main current in theology was the Hegelian mediation teaching, the theology of "immediatism" (echoed in the phenomenon of Modernism) later recovered its vigor and still maintains it today in the Protestant world.

VI

At this point a new problem is cropping up here and there in religious criticism, intimately connected with the problem of atheism: it is the much-discussed question as to the relationship between *religious piety, theism* and *atheism.* Can an atheist still feel that he is "religious" and be

[16] Schleiermacher, *Der christliche Glaube,* §33 and appendices 2 and 3; Redeker edition, Vol. I, pp. 174f., 176ff. The Spinozan origin of Schleiermacher's intuitionist pantheism had been spotted by Kierkegaard as early as the first texts of the Diary; cf. *Papirer* (Copenhagen, 1915), 1836, I A 273; cf., in this connection C. Fabro, *Dall'essere all'esistente* (Brescia, 1957), pp. 329ff.

admitted to be so?[16a] The question seems a contradictory one, inasmuch as the proper scientific object of religion is God and consequently there can be no talk of religion without God; from this formal point of view, God and religion are inseparable. But the problem does seem to us to persist from the subjective point of view, in the phenomenological sense of the development of the mind. We have ourselves admitted, with St. Thomas, the existence of a natural inclination of man to seek God, and this is what constitutes the primary kernel of *religious piety*. Such religious piety is purely potential in its initial impulse and thus, as such, [illegible]
and attained by the exercise of specifically critical and cognitive faculties.

Suppose, now, that the mind's activity misses its ultimate mark which is God and swerves into a denial of God's very existence; will this serve of itself to eradicate entirely all religious devotion? This is the problem and there is no easy answer. Any property pertaining to a nature belongs immutably to that nature. Therefore, religious feeling, piety, remains in "germ", even in the atheist, preeminently as a "capacity", and even if it has hitherto been suffocated or warped, it still remains in the depths of the mind like a principle always susceptible of germination. Furthermore, it is not even certain that this religious piety will remain entirely inoperative in the atheist. This religious feeling, in virtue of its goal and its dynamic, has a tendency toward the transcending of the egotistical striving of the individual. As a result, many atheists devote themselves to humanitarian initiatives, to the defense of moral and social values; and if this course of action is lacking in "logical consistency", it has, nonetheless, a deeper "existential consistency". Religious piety further shakes man loose from the thrall of immediate impressions; it instills into him the suspicion that reality is in fact extremely complex, and it makes clear to him what a noble task it is to study the laws of that complex reality in order to put them into the service of life and to enable all to benefit from their planned and conscious manipulation. Thus, atheist philosophers and scientists have applied themselves in the past and continue to apply themselves in our day with boundless dedication to researches in science and technology. In every human action and scientific investigation, a tendency toward transcendence is inherent, a desire to get above and beyond the empirical and the immediately individual and singular; it is such a tendency toward transcendence which, by an existential paradox not yet investigated in depth, leads to atheism itself, inasmuch as the atheist, too, is seeking the foundation of being, even though he be in error both in the matter of method and in the matter of his conclusions. This is the explanation of the passionate

[16a] Schopenhauer contends he can; cf. *Parerga und Paralipomena,* § 13, p. 138; cf. also M. Joel, *Religionsphilosophische Zeitfragen* (Breslau, 1876), pp. 17ff.

devotion of many atheists to the arts, to science and to politics, a devotion so intense as to take on the complexion of patent fanaticism.

There are well-known examples of such attitudes. One obvious example is the *Religion de l'Humanité* (Religion of Humanity), proclaimed by the leftist wing of the Deists and, in their wake, by the Illuminists, by the leaders of the French Revolution and, in general, by movements calling themselves laicist. And the anthropology which Feuerbach desired to set over against theology is pregnant with religious feeling and piety; it conceives of mankind as an integral whole possessed of an absolute value; it exalts the *Gattung* (species) to which individuals must subordinate their egotistical instincts, and its dialectic of the "I and Thou", which is regarded as the structural basis of any fully human act, bears limpid witness to the *dynamic survival* of religious feeling and piety.

The same can be said, and perhaps with still greater emphasis, of Marxist atheism itself, whose course of action has been and continues to be quite simply the deflection of the subliminal energy of religious feeling and piety into the "class struggle" conceived precisely as a deliverance from evil. In our own view it must be admitted that the dynamic impulse of religious feeling and piety is operative wherever there is a yen and a drive impelling the human being as a whole to transcend the bounds of the here and now, on singular individual reality. The vague notion of the real to which man attains in all these chains of thought ought to be tethered to the here and now; the proponents of atheism ought to be sheer nihilists and end up as suicides. Such is the theory propounded by Dostoevski in *The Possessed,* and such is the logical substance of Sartre's atheism, even though Sartre gives evidence of being quite satisfied to remain on this nauseating earth of ours.

The point, then, is not that there can be such a thing as religion without God, as some have claimed,[17] with an appeal to the phenomenon of Buddhism which is intrinsically atheist both in its deposit of doctrine and in its practice; it is simply that, in the transition from the objective plane to the existential-subjective level, the individual human being can effect a *transference,* channeling that innate thrust toward transcendence, which is religious feeling and piety, to the pursuit of finite reality, attributing to the content of the latter and to the vital thrust itself a teleological status and the capacity to provide a consummation of being. He exalts the finite to the status of the infinite and exchanges the baneful infinity for the beneficent infinity, to use Hegelian terminology.

[17] Schopenhauer cites Brahmanism and Buddhism as examples of such a claim (cf. *Ueber die vierfache Wurzel des Satzes vom zureichenden Grunde,* ch. 5, pp. 125f.).

This "reduction" of transcendence to the limits of immanence can take various forms. In theological romanticism and in the religious phenomenology of which it is the inspiration, the practice is to speak not of God as subsistent Being and perfect Spirit but rather of "the divine" (*das Göttliche*), a term indicative of everything and nothing, inasmuch as every adjective always presupposes a substantive to which it is referred, and there seems no good reason why philosophers should be exempt from this rule of language! In this way of looking at things, God is reduced to a mere "property" (albeit the most sublime one) of the real, or more accurately to a category of the mind, a category [illegible] accorded other designations, such as "the sacral" (*das Heilige*), "the "Awe-Inspiring" and the like. In any case, such a God cannot be the God of religion.

But atheists often turn the tables by loudly accusing the champions of theism not only of ulterior motives and exploitation of the ignorance of others, but also and indeed primarily of a weird mixture of naiveté and overweening fanaticism, of mistakenly seeing God as a reality immediately present to themselves, of daring to deal with God as with any mere mortal, of claiming experimental knowledge of God and the ability to enter into communion with him at their own whim. They insinuate that it has been precisely in order to prevent such shameful anthropomorphism that philosophy has effected a gradual clarification of the situation in its successive transitions via pantheism, panentheism and monism to eventual atheism. This would make theism the cause of atheism! This is substantially the accusation later to be leveled by Feuerbach and Marx, using the famous Hegelian term "alienation" (*Entfremdung*).[18] This accusation does indeed seize upon one undoubted aspect of human cognition in its historical development, especially those forms of intuitionist metaphysics which claim to rest on a direct apprehension of God (neo-Platonism, ontologism, and the like), asserting that God is the point of origin and departure of their ratiocination or that they can and do effect a direct leap from immediate experience to the experience of God; or again, those forms of rationalist metaphysics that make a "direct transition" from abstract principles and the *cogito* to the reality of God as actuality and actualization of an "idea" or a concept (the most perfect Being, the Infinite: thus Descartes, Malebranche, Spinoza, Leibniz, Clarke, *et al*).

Hegel, too, in the final analysis makes a "direct transition" from the finite to the Infinite, because for Hegel the finite is mere appearance (*Erscheinung*) and fortuitiousness (*Das Zufällige*) and only the Absolute is the All and the True. But this accusation does not stand up in the

[18] Cf. K. Marx, "Kritik der Hegelschen Dialektik und Philosophie überhaupt," in *Oekonomisch-philosophische Manuskripte: M.E.G.A.*, Abt. I, Vol. 3, pp. 150ff.

case of Thomistic metaphysics which prescribes finite being as the proportionate object of the human intellect and posits the Infinite as shrouded in mystery, accessible only by way of analogy, i.e., in a fashion more negative than positive and via the reason which effects the outward thrust to its own limits or the reduction to the fundamental. Thus, for St. Thomas, man manages to get to know not so much what God is as what God is not.[19] This Thomistic conception, therefore, is the exact opposite of the alienation of which religion is accused; for the Thomistic conception asserts precisely the priority and epistemological worth and solidity of the finite against all forms of intuitionism and idealism. The Thomistic conception is also the exact opposite of the anthropomorphism charged against religion because Thomism, instead of making a God of man and conceiving of God after the fashion and in the image of man, isolates God entirely in the loneliness of supreme transcendence and conceives the real ontological and spiritual attributes of God precisely in terms of the negation of all the modalities and limits accessible to human experience. However nuanced and complex this Thomistic stand may be (and undoubtedly it is both), it is the exact opposite of the "alienation" leveled as a blanket charge against religion.

It must be concluded from all we have said that the notion of atheism, like that of theism, appears in an extremely dialectical form, which fact should put us on our guard against any attempt at glib oversimplification.

[19] "Quia de Deo scire non possumus quid sit, sed quid non sit; non possumus considerare de Deo quomodo sit, sed potius quomodo non sit" (For we cannot know concerning God what he is, but what he is not; we cannot consider how he is but rather how he is not) (St. Thomas, *S.T.*, I, q. 3, Prologue).

4
Atheism and Dialectic of the Notion of God

The problem of God, then, becomes the keystone or crux of the elucidation of human existence. Contemporary man scorns the Absolute and prefers to identify himself in terms of his attitude to history and the finite goods of this earth, the arts, science and politics. But these are simply diversionary tactics to mask the inner void and the lack of a criterion of truth and value capable of steadily buttressing man, especially in this world of ours, against the despair that must otherwise invade him at the knowledge of his own capacity to resist the forces operative within the temporal dimension. If God really does not exist, then there are no essences; there are only existents that time relentlessly propels and pillages. Therefore, there is nothing at once more pressing and more demanding than the problem of God, nothing at once more immediate and more far-reaching, more concrete and at the same time more universal, nothing more urgent for the substantiation of any value and at the same time more nuanced and difficult to define univocally even in its problematic.

This paradoxical nature of the problem of God can be described as simultaneously *universal* or *inescapable* and yet optional.

In saying that the problem of God is universal, we mean primarily that it is accessible to every normal mind and does not require, radically and ineluctably, any special technical training, as has been pointed out already. This means that it is not the proper and exclusive object of any one particular type of reflection or a privilege of special cultural patterns; rather, it is anterior to, and concurrent with, them all.

In saying further that the problem of God is *inescapable,* we wish to point up the fact that the ultimate problems relative to being and truth, the ultimate notions relative to good and evil, the radical feeling for justice and a truly human life—all involve an inescapable regress to the problem of the final and ultimate grounding of all in God who is the sheer Beginning, Source and Principle of all being, truth and justice.

Finally, in saying that the problem of God is somewhat *optional,* it is not exactly our intention to assert that it is a matter of indifference whether or not man shows interest in God. Such interest is not optional like the choice of a profession or of a particular field of study or action easily interchangeable with another; for in these latter cases, the objects of the possible choices are objectively on the same plane of finite interests. The problem of the knowledge of God is optional in the sense that man must seek it over and beyond the evidence provided by the visible world and must retain it despite the hobbles of the finite reason and the difficulties that may arise from the practical sphere of existence. In this sense God can be called the *existential* problem *par excellence,* and this for two reasons: first, because God is the foundation of every existence; second, and preeminently, because the admission of God on the part of man decides and alters the inmost bent of freedom itself by grounding it in transcendence: by the very fact of being the First Principle, God is the Final God.

We can thus sum up these reflections on the subjective aspect of the problem of God by asserting that God is the *crucial problem of man as such:* the crucial problem, in the sense of being the problem of the ontological foundation of all else, imparting meaning for man and, indeed, a special meaning to everything; this problem of God is the problem of "man as such" or "Everyman" (the *almindelige Mennesket* of Kierkegaard), in the Kierkegaardian sense of the human mind in its basic orientation to the truth and the good that is accessible to every man.

Finally, in a more radical sense, we can speak of the *universality* and *transcendentality* of the problem of God, understanding *universality* and *transcendentality* here in the existential methodological sense rather than the formal systematic sense.

Here, the *universality* of the problem of God means that this problem is posed and its solution is accessible to each and every kind of human knowledge and cognitive activity, whether it be the "immediate cognition" of the child, the primitive man and the common man, or the "reflective cognition" of the scientist, the moralist, the politician, the philosopher or the like. This means: (a) that this problem is accessible in some degree to each of such kinds of cognitive activity, to each of these types of mind, and at the same time (b) that no one of these types exhausts the problem as such or is able to appropriate it entirely. Man is always pursued and confronted by the problem of God and its demand, whether that man be child, teenager, adult or oldster; whether he be primitive or highly civilized, a professional man or a scientific researcher; whether he be an artist, a man of culture or one endowed with a rigorous philosophical mentality. No matter what the social class or status of the individual, no matter what his cultural level, he is inevitably faced with the problem of God, and the urgency of this problem is unaffected by the changing face of events or by the succeeding ages. Although it is the most complex and demanding of all problems, the problem of God is present to all minds, to all human knowers, even the rudest and most primitive. And, what is stranger still, this problem of God does not present itself in a rigorous ascending succession of degrees of conceptual clarity, with philosophy as the supreme zenith of its lucidity and perspicuity, and immediate cognition as a mere flickering gleam [illegible] insignificance on the appearance of reflective thought. Religious feeling is rather a "primordial property" of man similar to society's inclination to life; man is moved by a natural impulse toward the "not-self" to seek a vital and ontological communication with his fellow human beings in the visible world and with God, his creator and Father, in the invisible world.

By the *transcendence* of the religious problem we intend to signify the fact that the religious element cannot be exhaustively articulated in any of the forms of cognition or knowledge, not even the most sublime and universal, like philosophy or even theology and mysticism; there is always *a something more,* always an unarticulated remainder. This does not mean that the realms of cognition and the degrees of knowledge are all on the same level or that they remain isolated and indifferent to one another; this would imply that knowledge was sheer symbolism and would lead to agnosticism of the skeptical and relativist schools of philosophy, culminating in Jaspers' empty cryptography (*Chiffreschrift,* cipher). Rather, the problem of God, inasmuch as it cannot be the exclusive object of any special particular science or knowledge, engages the whole gamut of knowledge and the mind at all levels; by transcending each one of those levels, it predisposes each in some way to a dynamic and importunate clamor for the others.[1]

Atheism is thus the dissenting stance assumed by man in the theoretico-existential area when faced with the problem of the admission of the existence of the First Principle. The term was in vogue during the Renaissance to indicate the position of anyone refusing to admit the existence of the divinity, but the term is almost as ancient as philosophy itself: it suffices to recall the accusations of *αθεοτής, ἀσεβεῖα, αθεία, δυσσεβεία* and the like, leveled against the ancient philosophers.

These distinctions are derived from the subjective sphere. But it seems to us no less important to consider the object as such, i.e., God, in terms of the metaphysical demand of his essence. Obviously God is only in one way, and thus the concept of God should have quite precise

[1] C. Fabro, "The Problem of God," in *Problemi e orientamenti de Teologia dommatica,* Vol. II (Milan, 1957), pp. 5f.

content. Hence, in the case of man, the admission of God ought to have a univocal bent and be manifested in one way only, i.e., with a content excluding all ambiguity. This demand will result in a vast dilation of the scope of atheism, for it will not only brand as atheists those who assert outright that God does not exist, that the concept of God is contradictory, but it will also clarify as atheism all those conceptions of God that are demonstrably erroneous and inadequate, i.e., those that deny or erode any of his fundamental attributes. Whereas the explicit denials of God constitute an atheism "by defect", these other conceptions constitute an atheism "by excess", inasmuch as they corrupt the very notion of God and attribute to him a way of being in contradiction to his nature.

The mandatory conditions of an adequate concept of God are:

(a) that *God* be recognized and admitted as the *Supreme Being,* an object of truth that must be affirmed in order to afford an effective foundation to any truth. Thus, any *agnosticism* which declares the existence of God to be inaccessible to the human intellect is already slipping downgrade toward, and will ultimately reveal itself as, atheism, because it does not get through to God, does not recognize and admit God and so leaves man "God-less"; [2]

(b) that *God* be *One and Supreme;* thus, pagan *polytheism* throughout the ages, with its admission of several gods, is equivalent to the denial of God;

(c) that *God* be *Spirit,* i.e., that his being actualize in the supreme degree the highest form of being that is intelligent and volitional life; thus, all forms of *naturalism, panpsychism,* and *vitalism* are so many forms of atheism.

(d) that *God* be *transcendent* in himself and not merely the sum or totality of the world or immersed in it as a force, life or universal Mind; thus, any form of monism (and therefore *pantheism*) is atheism: [3] we shall see in the sequel the many forms of monism in the thought of antiquity and in modern philosophy;

(e) that *God* be *a supremely free, personal being* in his relations with the world and with man and that, consequently, the creation of the world and of man proceed from the sheer liberality and generosity of

[2] Obviously a distinction can be made between the agnostic (who says: "I have no proofs to demonstrate that God exists") and the atheist (who declares: "I have proofs to demonstrate that God does not exist"). Therefore many have thought in the past that "positive" atheism was rare or downright impossible, but this has been fully disproved by the evolution of contemporary thought. The strict nexus between agnosticism and atheism is recognized and admitted by such a benevolent and balanced critic as Flint (*Agnosticism* [Edinburgh and London, 1903], pp. 50f.).

[3] "Pantheism slipped more and more from the noble form to its vulgar form, from *acosmism* to *atheism*" (M. Scheler, *Vom Ewigen im Menschen;* Collected *Works,* Vol. I [Berne: Francke Verlag, 1954[4]], p. 109).

God and not from any intrinsic necessity of his nature; thus, all *rationalist schools of philosophy* (*idealist and immanentist*), identifying intellect and will in man and in God, are atheist.

We can then speak of an *explicit* or *professed atheism* (overt and explicit denial of God). With it must also be classed the *absolute* or *metaphysical materialism* of antiquity and the modern brand derived from illuminism and Kant (Forberg) or from Hegel-Feuerbach (existentialism and Marxism being its two main distinctive currents), or from scientific positivism (evolutionism, neopositivism, and the like).

But we must also speak of a *presumptive* or *inferential atheism* (implicit denial of God) that is a property of those philosophies which, while affirming God, deprive him of one or other of the attributes [4] that the human mind must posit as inseparable from God's essence.

Such philosophies may deny:

1. the knowableness of the existence and nature of God as such (and then we have *skepticism* or agnosticism);

2. God's *oneness* and *perfection* (and then we have *polytheism* or *fetichism);*

3. God's *transcendence* (and then we have *acosmism, pantheism, panentheism* or *monism*)*;*

4. God's *spirituality* (and then we have *naturalism, panpsychism* or *vitalism);*

5. God's *personality* (and then we have *rationalism, idealism* or *theory of values.*

This classification seems to us substantially in agreement with the Diderot *Encyclopedia* which proposes a threefold division: "Atheists are designated as those who deny the existence of a God as author of the world. They can be divided into three classes: the first deny that there is a God; the second affect incredulity of skepticism on this point; the third class, who differ little from the first, deny the principle attributes of the

[4] In this sense Feuerbach was right in his analysis of atheism. That analysis may have been radical and paradoxical but it was entirely consistent. He writes: "Empiricism does not deny existence to God; rather, it denies to him the positive determinations, for their content is finite, empirical, whereas the Infinite cannot be an object of man. The more numerous the attributes I refuse to a being, the more do I render that being extraneous to me, the more do I make myself free of him. The more numerous the qualities that I possess, the greater likewise is the sphere of my action and of my influence. And the more [God] is One, the more likewise is known about him. Every negation of an attribute of God is thus a partial atheism, an area of godlessness (*Jede Negation einer Eigenschaft Gottes ist daher ein partialer Atheismus, eine Sphäre der Gottlosigkeit*). In proportion as I remove from God a property, I remove from him his very being. If, for example, compassion and mercy are not attributes of God, then I am alone in my suffering—God is not anymore my comforter" (*Grundsätze der Philosophie der Zukunft,* § 16; Collected Works, ed. Bolin-Jodl, Vol. II [Stuttgart, 1904], pp. 266f.; edition of M. G. Lange [Leipzig, 1950], p. 111).

divine nature and hold God to be a being devoid of intelligence who acts purely from necessity, i.e., a being who does not act at all, properly speaking, but rather is perpetually passive. The error of the atheists derives necessarily from one of these three approaches. It comes from ignorance and stupidity. . . ." [5]

On the philosophical level, i.e., in the sphere of speculation properly so-called, these and similar forms of atheism are the reflection on the principle, source and foundation of things.

After Hegel's death, the crisis with the assertion of atheism by the left-wing Hegelians was in turn the reply and counterpart to the crisis rampant among the right-wing Hegelians concerning the attributes of God and particularly God's "personality" and the concomitant immortality of man. These were no mere verbal disputes; they showed that the "new principle" of philosophy had finally broken the provisional dam that had thus far contained it, at least in appearance, as theism and orthodoxy. Above all else, the problem of the "personality" of God (and, hence, of man) is crucial to a proper grasp of the essence of modern philosophy and, indeed, of philosophy in general,[6] because for man this problematic constitutes the decisive point insofar as the substantive worth of the spirit is concerned; this problematic is also of capital importance for the very meaning of truth.

[5] "Athée", in the *Encyclopédie ou Dictionnaire raisonné des sciences, des arts et de metiers,* edited by D. Diderot and d'Alembert, Vol. I; 1st ed. (Paris, 1751), p. 798b; 2nd ed. (Lucca, 1758), pp. 692aff., where the atheist is held to be punishable according to the natural laws because he is destroying the basis of morality and society.

[6] "The old controversies as to whether or not the Absolute is divine, as to whether or not God is a personal being, are no mere academic excuses for mental gymnastics; they are the fundamental questions of all speculative endeavor: upon the answers given to them depend all other organic constituents of a system of philosophy, and therefore they must be coped with and clearly resolved before any other speculative problem can be adequately resolved. Nay, more! In those apparently so academic-sounding questions lies the focus of the entire intellectual and cultural life of our day; they contain the banners and the slogans under which the great struggle between the old and the modern outlook and philosophy is going to have to be fought out. There is so much talk these days about a 'new outlook and philosophy', but only a handful see clearly that it is here a question of the struggle between atheism, theism and pantheism. There is abroad today the almost unanimous feeling that especially the present state of our religion stands in urgent need of improvement, and there is a most passionate longing for this revolution to be effected. Yet our age is presently curiously oblivious to the realization that this revolution depends solely on whether it is the personal or the impersonal notion of God that emerges as victor from this struggle; modern man therefore generally adopts a downright indifferent attitude to the above-mentioned problematic" (A. Drews, *Die Spekulation seit Kant mit besonderer Rücksicht auf das Wesen des Absoluten und die Persönlichkeit Gottes,* Vol. I [Berlin, 1893], pp. VIf.).

5
Structural Features of Modern Atheism

The problem of the atheism of antiquity presents no more serious difficulties than those involved in the definition of materialism and skepticism as encountered in classical philosophy. By contrast the atheism that has more and more been gaining the upper hand in modern thought has been following the checkered fate of the new principle of immanence, and any study in depth of this positive and constructive atheism is fated undoubtedly to renew the clashes and polemics, inside and outside the ambit of idealism, in which the civilization of our day is still locked. By aiming the thrust of our definition of the essence of modern atheism squarely and head-on at the constitutive element, which is precisely this principle of immanence, we unequivocally opt for a solution of the problems of atheism at their bedrock level. It is the mind's first step, the "start", that is decisive; it is an initial act of postulation already pregnant with the final solution, and it imparts an internal specification to reflection because it already implies and expresses the "method".

Realism and immanentism (in all its forms) are such from the very outset; a definitive stand has already been taken with the first step. As we shall point out in due course, being is for realism the foundation and the criterion of the activity of the mind, whereas in immanentism mind must provide the sources and the criterion of being: the *esse* is a function of the *cogito;* however the *cogito* may subsequently be conceived in the various systems.

So the first question a realist has to pose to the idealist cannot be topical and systematic; it must be drastic and preliminary: What is being for the mind? This is preeminently a request for a statement on the primordial being-mind nexus.

Thus, Leibniz's question, repeated by Schelling and Heidegger and again by Gilson in his debate with Brunschvicg—"Why is there rather being and not nothing?"—is for us secondary and can have no meaning until it has been established "what" is being and *be-ing* (*esse* = the act of existence). For us the primary obvious fact is that being is there: it is there from the first awakening of the mind, of consciousness, beyond which there is (and will be for a long time, i.e., until the "foundation" has been resolved into its component elements) nothing but the darkness of the spirit.

In the immediacy of its *givenness,* being lights up on its own; thus the givenness of *"be-ing"* (the act of existence) to the mind, as articulated in the statement "being is", is a *synthetic* act for the mind and cannot be otherwise, whatever may be said of the grammatical formulation. Therefore, all knowledge of the real, whether immediate or mediate, will be synthetic; analytic cognition is reserved to the formal sphere of the merely possible. The theologian who knows that creation depends sheerly on the free act of God, and that it has not been coexistent with God, cannot but confirm and highlight the significance of this synthetic character which is self-evident and included in the very notion of being. If formalistic philosophies, realist and immanentist, have reduced being to essence, so much the worse for them! Over against all these philosophies we set the genuine one of St. Thomas who was the first, after Parmenides, to begin directly and absolutely with *ens* (being).

Once there has been affected a firm orientation of the mind upon *being* (*ens*), there has also been achieved a clarification of the dual relation, the existence-mind nexus and the mind-existence nexus; there has been attained likewise a virtual clarification of the fundamental meaning of nature and spirit. Thereupon, the traditional arguments advanced against the existence of God from the (undeniable) existence of physical or moral evil lose the cogency they were thought to possess. For if being is synthetic and the spirit is the *capacitas entis in veritate sua,* then no physical evil, not even death itself, can decide the be-ing of man as such, a be-ing (a mode of existence) that perfects itself solely as freedom; even moral evil is never terminal or definitive so long as there is life, for freedom can always overcome it or forswear it and cleave to the good.

So, too, throughout the ages, the frequent and bitter invectives of atheism against the *divine attributes* collapse: for example, the contention that an infinitely good and just God should not have permitted evil, death, disease, treachery of friends, sufferings of the innocent and all the other miseries of existence.

Atheists, ancient and modern, conceive of God as a metaphysical monolith and deny any sort of freedom and transcendence to God just as much as to man; this leaves them a wide-open field to distort existence into a charge sheet against God. Thus, though the problem of the divine attributes is not so easily solved and has always tantalized the mind of man, the atheists' denial is too cheap a trick entirely and can readily be unmasked in its assumptions.

Consequently, we ourselves do not wish to deny that the problem of the existence of God presents constant and grave difficulties to philosophical reflection for the theist as well, or at least for those theists who follow St. Thomas in refusing to admit any direct and proportionate knowledge of God, allowing only a mediate knowledge via demonstration and analogy. The central metaphysical difficulty, which in its own way likewise contains the principle of the single valid solution, is that of the coexistence and [illegible] and identity in God of the purely ontological attributes and the spiritual attributes that precisely seem irreconcilable among ourselves. The purely ontological attributes are God as the Being who is Absolute, as the One, the True, the Immutable, the Necessary—these are the attributes that separate him from the world. The spiritual attributes are God as the Pure Spirit who is intelligent, volitional, loving, prescient and provident—these are the attributes that bind him *somehow* to the world or at least show him as involved in a real relation to the world. Here, too, theology goes considerably further, in showing that God in Christ has assumed human nature, taking part in man's earthly Odyssey itself in order to redeem man from error and sin. But this difficulty serves only to shed further light—in its own way and as a kind of confirmation that is of supreme speculative value —on that *synthetic nature of being* wherein is expressed, in the final analysis, the very presence of the real, both for man and for God, even though the basis of that synthetic nature is exactly opposite in man and in God. In man the finitude of his mind separates him from being and constrains his mind to recognize and admit the presence of the real; in God, it is the infinity of Being that distinguishes him from every being, even as he ingresses with creation into the most intimate depths of the finite (*per essentiam, per potentiam et per praesentiam*)[1] and penetrates with the incarnation to a direct and more intense participation than that of any human being in adversity and suffering, pushed to the most shameful death of the cross. Hence, also, light is shed on the precarious and shaky position of Illuminist deism which, after refuting revealed historical religion, has shown itself in fact powerless, even prior to the appearance of idealism, to defend natural religion.

Clearly, then, there does indeed exist a "possibility of atheism" other than the simple argument from the fact to the possibility. The root lies in man and not, obviously, in God who cannot deny himself, as St. Paul declares.[2] Man can really deny God because he is a creature of sense-

[1] Cf. St. Thomas, *S.T.* Ia, q. VIII, a. 1-4; also C. Fabro, *Partecipazione e causalità,* pp. 470ff.; French translation, pp. 472ff.

[2] 2 Tim. 2, 13.

perception and tethered to time and space; therefore, man is enticed primarily by those things that seem good to his senses and by the events in the temporal dimension. Man never feels, sees or encounters God in his everyday sense-experience; and so impatience, discouragement and pride put man in constant danger of falling out of the orbit of God into all manner of sub-orbital divagations, of becoming an outsider to religion and even an opponent of it.

Nor is it any cause for wonder that man can deny God who is Pure and Absolute Spirit, when man can and frequently does in fact deny the spiritual nature and the freedom of his own soul, i.e., that finite spirit which he bears within himself and of whose existence and activity he has constant personal experiential evidence. Thus, the materialist denial of the freedom and spirituality of the soul is, in this structural analysis, parallel to, and coincident with, the immanentist denial of the personality of the One who is sacrificed to the monistic All of the Spinozan brand of atheism or simply to the spontaneous act of the actualist or phenomenological variety.

Thus, there is a dual dialectic of atheism, one extrinsic, in the historical dynamic of culture, and one intrinsic, in the theological investigation of the demand of God on the part of the human mind. To the former element belong the polemics and accusations of atheism launched against philosophers from ancient times right down to the modern age. These accusations bear witness to the way in which philosophy and certain individual schools of philosophy find themselves clashing with the common thinking and the dominant trend of their own society. To the second element, which in a certain sense develops within the ambit of the first and constitutes its cause and catalyst, there belongs what could be called the "dynamic of the idea of God" in progressive articulation via an exhaustive and absolutely valid concept. To any theoretical historian of atheism dealing with the gradual emergence and solidification of this denial, this element presents itself as the gradual loss of the "attributes of God", from the initial one of Absolute and Spirit up to and including that of a Person which is the keystone attribute. In this passage, the sea of philosophy becomes more and more stormy, and finally, in the ever stronger tempest of modern thought, the ship of religious knowledge sinks to the bottom. Here precisely is the object of our investigation: a synthesis of the two elements that will examine the most significant "crises" in the history of modern thought in order to shed light in each case on a new stage of the "loss of God" and the excogitation of a new notion of "human freedom" based on the persistent drive of man to find the basis of his own existence in himself alone.

The extrinsic genesis of atheism certainly seems at least to trace the entire arc of the development of Western philosophy from the dawn of Greek thought to the twilight of modern philosophy. It should be noted that this development is characterized by an obvious inversion of the theoretical axis. This inversion consists in the transition from transcendence to immanence; this transition is likewise clear enough, at least from the stage of the Cartesian *cogito* which is the primary theoretical nucleus of positive atheism. The true significance of this inversion is exposed when immanence solidifies as "finitude" and tethers the fate of the touted "freedom" of the mind to the "situational" dialectic of the world. The rebound produces by interior dialectic an inversion or transmutation of all concepts and all values. An immanence linked to an idea of the worth or the freedom of the spirit of man can maintain itself as such only to the extent that, and as long as, the being and freedom of man are posited against a background of transcendence and relate themselves to this transcendence with a resolution that defines and consolidates the immanence itself in this relation as an assumption of man's own being and man's own responsibility. And so, an immanence is no longer dialectical once the transcendence is taken away.

The immanence of the *cogito,* set over against transcendence and gradually absorbing that transcendence from Descartes to Hegel, ended up by disappearing as immanence. Modern philosophy wanted to stake a claim for the freedom of man over against the interfering ingress of God; by submerging itself in its own principle, it has placed man either at the mercy of the "collective", which is the impersonal All, or at the mercy of the "world" in the shape of a blind irruption of amorphous and extraneous forces, often opposed to the spirit. In his unwillingness to exist for the true God man has not succeeded, with the new principle of mind or consciousness, in substituting himself for God; rather, he has lost man together with God, the much-touted immanence having perished concurrently with the decline of transcendence. From the mid-19th century right down to our own days, man has indeed been defined simply as a "potency of finitude", i.e., as a "being-for" science, politics and technology; in other words, man is a "being-in-the-world" and is casually defined in terms of the spatio-temporal that contains him. The abyss of human freedom is certainly a forward step on the road of the mind, but unless it is grounded in God, it sinks into the groundless, bottomless void. It seems that man, as a finite spirit, can of himself give meaning to a finite world, and this is precisely the effort of Prometheus, whose perfect formula lies in the principle of immanence and whose realization is to be found in technological civilization. Yet, man is experiencing, in the midst of such conquests, a mounting uneasiness, rising like a sinister tide from all the margins of his mind. And so, in fleeing

God, man is fated to lose himself because he "falls into the world", with no remaining feature save exteriority and finitude. Thereupon, the dialectic evaporates and freedom is lost.

The problem of atheism, of the loss of God, provides the key to the burning problem in our day: the loss of man, the radical desperation, the profound despair that is presently throttling all the peoples of the world at the very moment when man is so justly proud of his drastic advances in the mastery of the most hidden forces of nature. The difficulty does indeed lie at a deeper level than would appear from a purely structural analysis of the opposing teachings: the riddle of man is not simply phenomenological; it is strictly metaphysical. The uneasiness gnawing at modern man is not to be eliminated by a simple formal recourse to the Absolute. Indeed, this improperly assimilated Absolute solves nothing and even represents a new danger, only increasing the uneasiness and confusion of mind. This sort of damage has been done by all the stunted forms of religious practice in every environment of human history, both outside and (unfortunately!) sometimes inside of Christianity, as often as they twist or bend religion to personal whims. Only a natural religion lived in its fullness or a total commitment to Christianity can cope with the task of an effective cleansing of existence and provide the real foundation of freedom.

The dialectic of atheism as a lapse into the finite is simply the concave aspect of a single phenomenon whose convex aspect is the upward thrust of theism toward the Infinite. The finite into which man lapses even as he protests his own freedom over against the Absolute dissipates and dissolves this freedom into the greedy caprice of the τέλος, of the individual and his fellows. The Infinite, to which man elects to submit even as he confesses his own creaturely finitude, musters and exalts his freedom, which finds its best foundation in total submission to the Absolute. This is the ultimate alternative in the confrontation between theism and atheism, an alternative becoming ever more ominously meaningful for the fate of mankind-to-be. Kierkegaard has pithy comments in this regard:

"The greatest thing that can be done for a being, much greater than anything that a man can do with or for it, is to make it free. Nothing less than omnipotence is needed in order to be capable of such an operation. This seems strange, for omnipotence is thought of as causing dependence. But a genuine notion of omnipotence will clearly show the concept to connote precisely the resolve so to restrain the manifestation of omnipotence as to allow what is created to be independent, thanks to the omnipotence. For this reason, no one man can ever make another man entirely free; the power-holder will always be bound by the very power he holds and therefore be in a false position in relation to the one whom he wants to make free. Furthermore, there is always a finite self-love in every finite power (natural gifts, etc.). Only omnipotence can restrain itself even as it gives itself, and it is this relationship precisely that constitutes the independence of the one who receives. God's omnipotence is therefore identical with his goodness, for goodness consists in giving without stint but with such omnipotent-style self-restraint as to render independent the one who receives. Every finite power makes dependents; only omnipotence can make independents, can produce out of nothingness what has self-consistency because of the very restraint of the omnipotence. Omnipotence is not bound by its relation to the other because there *is* no other to which it relates; thus it can give, without losing the least fraction of its power, i.e., can make dependents. Herein lies the mystery whereby omnipotence is able to produce not only the most imposing thing of all (the sum total of the visible world), but also the most fragile thing of all (i.e., a nature independent in relation to the omnipotence). Thus, the same omnipotence that can, by its powerful hand, deal so hard with the world can at the same time make its touch so light that what is created enjoys independence. It is but a wretched and vulgar notion of the dialectic of power to think that it increases in proportion to the ability to cramp and make dependent. Socrates had a better understanding of the matter when he insisted that the art of power consists in making men free. But in the relations between man and man, this is not possible (much as it must always be stressed to be the highest and noblest thing to aim at); it is a prerogative of omnipotence. Thus, were man to enjoy the least autonomous consistency over against God (like that of prime matter), God would not be able to make him free. Creation out of nothing involves the ability of omnipotence to make free. The One to whom I owe everything absolutely, but who at the same time absolutely preserves everything in being, has precisely made me independent. Had God lost any of his power in creating men, he would no longer have been able to make men independent." [3]

The fight for and against God is not merely an epistemological struggle but also a freedom fight; it is no mere conquest of results; rather is it primarily a search for the source.

[3] Kierkegaard, *Journals* 1846 VII A 181.

6
Atheism and the Principle of Contradiction

Is atheism contradictory in itself? The question seems superfluous, both for theists and for atheists, since both have resolved the problem, albeit in diametrically opposed fashions. Although accused of atheism by the theologian Budde, Wolff stands firmly on the side of theism and formulates his proposition in the most categorical form: *Atheismus contradictionem involvi,*[1] The core of Wolff's argument is taken from the fact that the world is obviously contingent, whether considered in its immediate reality or viewed in its constitutive principles, whereas the atheists' suppositions would make it necessary (*a se*): "For in the atheist's hypothesis the world is self-originating (*ens a se*). Now manifestly the visible world is not self-originating, nor yet the elements of material things out of whose aggregation come into being the bodies constituting the world; if indeed it be granted that the world originates from material atoms or a homogeneous, uniform, undivided matter, neither these atoms nor that matter can be said to be self-originating. Hence, in the atheist hypothesis there is asserted what ought to be denied. Wherefore, the implications of the atheist hypothesis contradict a true proposition, since there is a contradiction contained in two propositions, one of which denies the same thing which the other asserts. Now, there is a contradiction involved in any assertion whose implications contradict some true proposition. And so it is evident that atheism involves a contradiction."

Wolff appends a brief explanation repeating that the world cannot in any sense be considered as self-originating being (*ens a se*), and that the denial of God would immediately involve the admission of an uncreated world. Thus, "the principles we have presented both in the first part of our Natural Theology and in this second part patently demonstrate the

[1] C. Wolff, *Theologia Naturalis,* P. II §485 (Frankfurt and Leipzig, 1741), pp. 460f.

absurdity of atheism" (*loc. cit.*). Thus, Wolff contends, all discussion with the atheist is entirely useless.

For Rosmini, too, atheism involves an evident contradiction, but he considers it to reside more in the subjective sphere, in an error of method. This error begins with the atheists' claim to "comprehend" God, whereas God is not susceptible to this sort of comprehension and thus the atheist denies and rejects him, passing from the incomprehension of the essence to the denial of the existence of this elusive Being. This is what Rosmini calls the "sophism of the uncomprehended Infinite": "Every so often a philosopher is pricked by the desire to engage in ratiocination concerning the Infinite and Absolute Being, not limiting himself to that negative knowledge he can have of this Being but presuming to comprehend this Being, i.e., to attain a positive and total knowledge of the said Infinite and Absolute Being; inevitably he simply pleats sophisms because he is obliged to attribute to God what belongs to the finite being, since this finite sort of being is the only one of which he has positive knowledge. Such a philosopher is thus basing his whole claim of reasoning on an erroneous cognition of God himself." [2]

This was the defect of the Anthropomorphites and the Epicureans, and a like sophism has been the basis of all kinds of idolatry. A sophism of the same kind, continues Rosmini, is the basis of atheism that the philosopher exposes in the realm of ethics and to which he seems to attribute a Ciceronian inspiration: "If the gods exist, they must have virtues; but they cannot have human virtues; therefore, they do not exist! This fallacy is based on the following attitude of mind: We are unwilling to admit ignorance of the nature of the virtue proper to the divinity; seeing, therefore, that this divinity cannot have human virtue, which is the only one we know, we deny the existence of the divinity." [3] Rosmini is not here treating directly of atheism; rather, his intention is the clarification of the nature of the "sophism of the atheist". Here, it seems to us, is a case of an "existential" difficulty, rather than of a logical contradiction: man is denying what he does not succeed in comprehending, and is denying it for the simple reason *that* he does not understand it; man who comprehends only the finite is claiming to comprehend the infinite: there lies the contradiction.

We feel that St. Thomas would have been more queasy about such a line of argument, for man can, by way of analogy, have a certain kind of knowledge or awareness even of the nature of God, whether he takes the world or his own spiritual operations as a point of departure. The tension between the Rosminian and the Thomistic approach becomes

[2] Rosmini, *Logica,* n. 714 (Intra, 1867[2]), pp. 283f.; cf. for this text C. Riva, *Pensiero e coerenza cristiana,* (Brescia, 1963), pp. 13f.

[3] Rosmini refers to Cicero, *De natura deorum,* Bk. III, cc. 8ff.

clearer if we consider the overall Rosminian teaching on Being as a notion present to all in its most general and virtual sense, and revealing to the scanner of its inner depths a fullness that is the *Ipsum esse subsistens,* i.e., God in his fullest reality.[4] For St. Thomas, on the other hand, this *ens communissimum* as the first object of the mind articulates only *id quod habet esse* (that which has being) and is objectified directly in the field of the objects of external and internal experience. This *ratio entis* (sum total or basic notion of being) extends in its comprehension *as such* only to finite being.[5]

The ascent to God requires rigorous demonstration via the principle of causality; it thus necessarily involves a "passage" and an act of transcending. The direct and proportionate aim and goal of man's understanding is not God but the finite; the operative principle *whereby* man understands is likewise not God but man's own intellect; even though this intellect is caused by God, nevertheless God does not in any sense fall either within the constitutive fabric of the object or within the constitutive fabric of the subject. The only ones, therefore, who can assert that atheism *as such* is contradictory are those who assert the notion of God to be analytical, as do Rosmini and the Ontologists in general.

A recent protagonist of the alleged "self-contradiction of philosophical atheism" seems to us to be operating in just such an environment of onto-theological immediatism. His contention is: "Any doubting of the existence of an independent (of the world), unitary, thinking creator-God and *a fortiori* the outright denial of God is a self-contradiction." [6] For those not familiar with the analogy of being, this may appear exaggerated. It is certainly possible to pass from *doubt* of God to the *"demonstration* of God" but only because the existence of God can be the object of a doubt that is more poignant, trenchant, radical and certainly more skeptical and deeper-going than the first vulgar superficial doubt. But doubting as such is in no sense the highest form of living, nor is it genuinely autonomous; rather does genuine and more conscious doubt lead precisely to God. What, indeed, would the demonstration of God amount to, were it not cogent, could it be swept aside, did its adversaries not contradict themselves, were their very counterarguments not a tissue

[4] Cf. Riva's clear statement in *op cit.,* pp. 14f.

[5] "We call 'a being' that which participates in a finite degree in being, and this is proportionate to our intellect whose object is that which is something; wherefore our intellect is capable of grasping only that which has an essence participating in being; but the essence of God is being itself, and therefore is beyond the intellect" (*In librum de Causis,* lect VI; ed. Saffrey, p. 47; ed. Pera, n. 175, p. 47).

[6] "The burden of the present work is the contention that any doubting of the existence of an independent, unitary, thinking creator-God and *a fortiori* the outright denial of God *is a self-contradiction*" (E. von Fürstenberg, *Der Selbstwiderspruch des philosophischen Atheismus* [Regensburg, 1960], p. 7).

of contradictions? Whoever does not include God—being as being—in his living and thinking is living in a state of contradiction, and all his talk is at cross-purposes.

Being, then, can fall short of the Absolute. In other words, there is a dual manner of being: one manner is the manner of the relative, the conditioned, the contingent; the other is that of Absolute Being, being as being, *ens ut ens*. For example, any doubt of the existence of God necessarily entails an idea of what this God, whose existence is being doubted, should be and can be. But if God is being as being (*das Sein als Sein*), can there be any more legitimate doubt relative to God? Is he not, in a sense, Being, detected and identified? Is not such a doubt on the part of the knower rather a kind of rejection, a makeshift, rough-draft, gimcrack notion of that God? Does not this rejection itself involve a liberation from the vapid vicissitudes of being in flux and thus reveal already the features of the divine autonomy of being?

To put it in a catchy phrase: It may be that God is, but it may also be that God is not! That seems fair enough, but there is still one more aspect to be considered. If God is simple, if he is possibility as possibility, then the human mind would affirm it: "It may be that God is" rather than "It may be that possibility is possible". Actually, the opinion that it may also be that God is not would mean in this case: "It may be that there is no such thing as possibility as such!"

What we understand by a "demonstration" of the existence of God is inherent in things and in thinking. It partakes of the inevitability of breathing, rather than of the forensic cogency of a chain of criminal court evidence or of the force of conviction of a reckoning that could simply be disregarded.

There is a kind of doubt that is genuine and a kind of skepticism that is honest; there is also a spurious skepticism that mires itself in simple-minded superstition. The first kind involves a kind of faith; the latter kind involves a species of dogmatism (von Fürstenberg, *op. cit.*, p. 9). Thus, the demonstration of the existence of God is not the final sum total of a balance sheet; rather, it is the premise, in a sense, of the first entry of the balance sheet. It is the premise of every thought, of every being and demonstration. Furthermore, this "demonstration" is nothing other than the proof that God is not simply a self-subsistent entity of this world, whether nation or golden calf; that God is no mere idol, but rather, as the Tree of Porphyry proclaims, him to be: *extra omne genus*. Any doubting of God or denial of God would thus be and is in fact nothing else than the divinization or deification of some mundane entity (*ibid.*, p. 11). This is precisely the contradiction in which the atheist is involved.

This line of argument claims to be perfectly loyal to the thinking of St. Thomas, inasmuch as those who deny God are obliged to deify the creature (an argumentation somewhat reminiscent of Rosmini). In actual fact, the crux of this whole stand also smacks of ontologism. For we read (*idem,* p. 18): "The first principles (contradiction, causality, etc.) hold both for thought and for being, inasmuch as they can, in accord with their structure, be valid only for thought dependent on being, only for a being dependent on thought; their validity in the ontological sphere entails their validity in the noetic sphere and *vice versa.* Every necessary nexus refers immediately to being as being. The 'demonstration of the existence of God' is the Alpha and Omega of the whole of philosophy. Being as being consists in the structure of being; or, to put it more exactly, it sustains every being".

There are many sciences and disciplines that can be called philosophy. Within philosophy in the stricter sense there are modifications, gaps and leeway. But there is also something that is not subject to variations and mutations and that persists everywhere. The demonstration of the existence of God also belongs to this something, the structure of being and knowing.

Here is the definitive formulation: "Any doubting of an independent, thinking creator-God is a self-contradiction. It is impossible to evade the 'demonstration' of the existence of God, the elaboration of *being as being,* without running into an internal contradiction. Any teaching attempting such an evasion would be making a mundane entity into God. This holds obviously for everything that is. Everything that is not referred to God is, in the final analysis, nonsense. This contention may well be at odds with the majority of the philosophers of the last three centuries, but that is because their philosophies have never really confronted Thomism, having been rather predetermined in almost every case by the bias of atheism banishing God *a priori* as an object of 'faith' " (*ibid.,* p. 19).

Now this trap can, in our opinion, be a dangerous one. *In se,* there is indeed nothing more necessary than the existence of God who is *ipsum esse.* But *quoad nos,* God is not *per se notum* but only via the meditation of the finite: and von Fürstenberg also seems to us to be confusing expressly *ens per se notum,* indicating the first and fundamental step of the mind, with God. Now, as we shall see, the Jesuit Hardouin is going to accuse Descartes and the Cartesians of atheism precisely on account of this confusion between the initial *ens* and the terminal *Esse,* God.

Von Fürstenberg appeals specifically to the Thomistic argument that God is "total cause" (*Totalursache*), whereas any created being is "partial cause" (*Teilursache*) and thus no created being can act without the direct and continuous cooperation of God (pp. 12, 42, and esp. 90 and 111). Be it noted, however, that all of this has universal and permanent validity only *in ordine essendi et operandi* (in the order of being and operating), *not,* however, *in ordine cognoscendi* (in the order of knowing), in which God is the most toilsome and remotest object of knowledge. Moreover, this whole notion seems to us to be reviving a kind of radical "contingentism" entirely foreign to Thomistic metaphysics in which the creature is not, properly speaking, simply a "partial" cause, with the other "part" being supplied by God,[7] but rather the creature is total cause in its own order (of secondary causality) just as God is total cause in his own order (Primary Causality) and thus pervades the innermost depths of the being and the acting of all beings, from the lowliest element to the most exalted intelligence.

Summing up, then, we admit that any denial of the existence of God, *in a realist metaphysics* which starts from being, is indeed most certainly contradictory; but its contradiction is a "secondary contradiction", if this term be permissible, for the primary contradiction lies in the denial of the objects that are primarily evident, i.e., immediate, whether in experience or in reflection. For modern philosophy, on the other hand, with its foundation and designation of being in terms of thought or upon the fulcrum of the act of knowing, the denial of God is actually in no sense contradictory; rather, it constitutes the essential and inevitable end result of the very principle of immanence pushed back to its ultimate basis. The fundamental reason for modern atheism, that point at which the very judgment on the feasibility of atheism must begin, lies not in formal logic but in the downright constitutive sphere and is to be found further back, in the first step of the thinking process.[8] Once the *cogito* has been taken as the starting point, once the sheer act of thinking, voided of all content of being, has been posited as the anterior terminus, philosophy has thereby already denied that it is founded on being; it has made being dependent on a function of thought, mediated by the act of thinking, no matter how the act of such mediation may thereupon be conceived by the various systems of modern philosophy. This inversion of the foundations of the truth of being likewise involves the very meaning and significance of the first principles that are conformed to their new foundation (*Grund*), which is here the act of knowing. For the realist, the denial of God's existence turns out to be or at least shows itself to be contradictory upon mature reflection; this denial does not in fact constitute a contradiction for the immanentist but is simply a consistent stand, as we shall explain later. And the fact that some of the major modern philosophers (Descartes, Spinoza, Leibniz, Locke, Kant,

[7] The classic distinction made by St. Thomas is between the created and finite causes of *becoming* and the cause of *being,* which latter cause is precisely God. He also makes a distinction between *causa universalis* and *causa particularis,* but this distinction likewise is understood in function of the notion of participation (cf. C. Fabro, *Partecipazione e causalità,* pp. 448ff.).

[8] Yet we can agree with Fürstenberg in his fundamental critique of Kant, Hume, Hartmann, Hegel, Heidegger, Hessen *et al.* (*op. cit.,* pp. 10, 47ff., 144ff., 158ff. and *passim*).

Hegel, *et al.*) continued for several centuries to admit the existence of God merely shows how complex are the factors operative during an age of history in the molding of men's notions of the world.

Kant's critique of the ontological argument,[9] seems to us formally valid in this whole discussion which is grappling with the speculative root of the problem. The ontologists hold the denial of God to imply an instant and immediate contradiction. But the ontological argument is not a clinching one either for Kant or, indeed, for St. Thomas, even though these two great thinkers adduce divergent arguments against its cogency and are indeed at opposite poles in their epistemology. However, it is not our purpose to treat this point in depth.

Kant distinguishes a dual negation, depending on whether the negation is aimed at the predicate or the subject. If in a judgment I deny the predicate while maintaining the subject, then there does arise a contradiction; therefore, I say that this predicate necessarily pertains to this subject. But if I deny the subject together with the predicate, then in such an event there arises no contradiction at all; *there is in fact nothing left that could be contradicted.* To posit a triangle and then deny the three angles of that same triangle is to fall into a contradiction, but there is no contradiction whatever involved in denying the triangle together with its three angles. And exactly the same thing holds for the notion of an aboslutely necessary being. For if you deny the existence (*Dasein*) of an entity and thereupon deny the entity itself with all its particulars, whence can any contradiction arise? Externally there is nothing that could be contradicted because the entity is not supposed as being externally necessary; nor is there any ground for internal contradiction, for by your negation of the thing itself, you have denied simultaneously everything that is internal to it. The omnipotence of God is a case in point. The judgment "God is omnipotent" (*allmächtig*) is a necessary judgment. The omnipotence cannot be denied if you posit a divinity, i.e., an infinite essence (*Wesen*) whose notion is identical with omnipotence. But when you say: "God is not," then there is no longer either omnipotence or any other of his predicates, for all have been eliminated together with the subject, and there is no contradiction in evidence in such a thought.

In this very case, the situation is still more radical. Immanentist philosophy does not limit itself to a formal contradiction; rather, it inverts the primary meaning of the knowing-being nexus. Immanentism does not confine itself to a denial of the subject of the proposition; it deprives the thinking subject (the human mind) of any possibility of adverting to, or posing in any fashion whatever, the problem of God.

[9] Cf. *Kritik der reinen Vernunft,* Elementarlehre, II Theil, II Abt., 3 Abschn.; A 594, B 622.

7
Atheism as Logical Conclusion in Present-Day Rationalism

When the theologian sees that the attitude assumed by modern thought on the problematic of theology is steadily becoming more patently negative, he hastens at once, in his proper office as defender of the faith, to a critique and condemnation, accusing atheism of involving damaging and absurd consequences and entailing a total inversion of the very structure of existence. A philosophical analysis, on the other hand, must grapple with the element anterior to the "fall into atheism", for philosophy has the assignment of clarifying principles and illuminating the speculative horizon with the light of a logical circuit welded step by step; philosophy cannot allow itself to be ruffled by consequences but must concern itself primarily with principles and, above all, with the "first principle" involved in the mind's first and crucial contact with being. A consideration, therefore, of present-day rationalism's peremptory claim to be able to dispose entirely of the problem of God provides some surprises but also sheds a great deal of light on the whole matter, calculated to aid in the formation of a valid speculative and theological judgment on modern thought. Theism is disposed of by the simple stratagem of stigmatizing what is usually called common sense as a species of dogmatism amounting to simple-minded, unreflective and irrationally fanciful thinking. This rationalism alleges that there are two sources of the God-problem: the specious argument from order to artificer, and animism.[1]

The ordinary man, confronted with the continuous flux of becoming in nature, has in fact learned how to forge his own practical instruments to mold matter to his needs; but in the process he is carried away by his own imagination to conceive of a primordial origin of the world and of

[1] Cf. L. Brunschvicg, "La querelle de l'athéisme," in *De la vraie et de la fausse conversion* (Paris, 1950), pp. 207ff. The discussion which this article records took place at the Société française de philosophie, on March 24, 1928 (cf. *Bulletin de la Soc. fr. de Philosophie,* Vol. 28, n. 3).

matter—to wit, a first creation of things by a Supreme Being, conceived of as having precision-welded nature and events to the perfection of an ideal machine; thus, the whole world becomes a precision watch and God the master watchmaker.[2]

The other bulwark of theistic metaphysics is alleged to be animism. This animism conceives not only of man, animals and plants but even of the sun and the stars as living beings; the rationalist critique proceeds to dismiss theism's assertion of transcendence as a simple supposition that the hierarchy of beings (which vitalistic dynamism holds to extend from the sublunar to the supralunar world) continues on even beyond the heaven of astronomy to attain a region populated by invisible and supernatural entities. The supernatural beings of these celestial regions, alleges rationalism, are held by theism to have originated by the same process of generation (paternity and filiation) as can be observed here below. Thus common-sense realism and whimsically imaginative extrapolation are held to have been the crucial elements operative in the genesis of religion and belief in God, and these elements, it is alleged, have been swept away by the new rational method, by science and by modern thought.

Modern science does not in fact recognize any such entity as a single homogeneous matter; rather, matter resolves itself into a manifold of elements, each one of which precludes, in virtue of the exteriority essential to it, the very existence of any other element. Since the 18th century, mathematical physics has forced the previously dominant religious and metaphysical outlook to give way to rational and scientific explanation. The activity of reason has come to constitute the genuine sphere of the spiritual and has entirely eliminated the extravagant fancies of an otherworldly sphere of supernature. Thus a transcendent supernatural reality is intrinsically contradictory for rationalism: God cannot be beyond human reality, those truths and those values that man is in process of constructing and recognizing with his own reason. Therefore, in the recognition of human reason as the fountainhead and abode of truth, modern man finds that ultimate basis of all things which simple-minded and mythologically-bent thinking had transferred into the realm of

[2] In Voltaire's famous verse: "All round me ticks the universe; and in my wildest dream I cannot see how, if there be no watchmaker, this great precision watch could come to be" (in L. Brunschvicg, *Héritage de mots, héritage d'idées* [Paris, 1945], p. 51). Brunschvicg cites Voltaire's phrase, in his *Lettre au marquis de Villevielle,* which Brunschvicg finds too Thomistic in inspiration (!), to the effect that "the atheists have never replied to this difficulty that a watch proves the existence of a watchmaker" (*La raison et la religion* [Paris, 1939], p. 56). The analogy of the watchmaker is frequently encountered in 18th-century English philosophy with which Voltaire was quite familiar (cf. Leslie Stephen, *History of English Thought in the Eighteenth Century* Vol. I. [London, 1881], p. 409 and note 1).

transcendence. Rationalism insists that it is only in this fashion that God can exist in spirit and in truth in his Logos, and rationalism charges that the accusation of atheism can be leveled against rationalist thought only by those who persist stubbornly in confusing imagination with thought.

The patent caricature represented by this sort of presentation of theism seems to facilitate a head-on pertinent critique: [3] theism in its metaphysical form, as elaborated by a St. Thomas, for example, posits the requirement of a first principle of being, without in any sense distending images beyond their proper scope or basing its elaborations on imaginative and whimsical notions. The problem is whether nature can be reduced to science (rationalism) and science to the life of the spirit, without remainder, as a man like Brunschvicg asserts in his consistent and consequential immanentism. The famous text of Pascal, setting the God of Abraham, Isaac and Jacob over against the God of the philosophers, merely points up that circumvention of the real theist stand which turns back on the theists themselves the accusation of atheism!

Brunschvicg must be praised for his deliberate effort to tether his rationalism to the ultimate source of radical immanentism; for this reason the Catholic theologian can read him with very great profit and derive much clarification from such a perusal. Any critique that does not attain to the root principle of thinking in its primary latent power can never interest but only irritate the philosopher who has the right to a first hearing.[4] Indeed, in his own reply, Brunschvicg has an easy time of it, simply observing that the essential problem has to do with the principle and not the conclusions; the confrontation between metaphysical theism and modern thought must be effected in the area of beginnings, of principle. In an excess of generosity, Brunschvicg designates modern thought as "spiritualism". And here is the way in which he presents idealism as spiritualism, i.e., as a doctrine that identifies the cognition of the real with the activity of the human spirit. This human spirit realizes itself to have been liberated from the order of matter and of life from the very moment of its first appearance on the scene, from its first flash of awareness that it actuates in the scientific thought of its first creative power. It would be betraying itself were it to descend below itself. Hence, the deep-cutting inversion effected by modern thought via the principle of immanence: it amounts, in fact, to the substitution of the reality of a human creation, in the context in which this creation is

[3] This critique can be found in E. Gilson's reply to Brunschvicg's "La querelle de l'athéisme," in *De la vraie et de la fausse conversion,* pp. 214ff.

[4] As an attempt to circumvent this radical demand, Gilson's recourse to the Leibnizian principle of sufficient reason (*ibid.,* pp. 216f.), which Brunschvicg easily refutes (pp. 222f.), does not seem to us to be very much to the point, either for the debate or for the metaphysical grounding of the God-problem. Gilson returns to this later (p. 229) and Brunschvicg consolidates his own critique (p. 233).

really experienced and verified, for the ideal of an absolute creation posited by the theological imagination (!) in the notion of God. This is radical idealism, founded on the evidence of science and sharply distinguished by Brunschvicg from the *a priori* German idealism, which is still metaphysical and therefore nothing but an imitation of realism, still tethered to an imaginative notion of the Absolute. This radical idealism is therefore synonomous with loyalty to the modern principle of progress.[5] For it, mathematics was nothing at all until man by his own labor throughout the whole of his history had formulated its principles and pursued its elaborations, applications and conclusions. This scientific idealism can be summed up in one single contention: *"It is within history that the spirit naturally and necessarily conquests the awareness of its own eternal actuality"* (*loc. cit*, p. 225; italics Brunschvicg's).

Idealism of any stripe simply disregards the criticisms leveled against it by realism and theism for the very simple reason that idealism does not accept the principle on which such criticisms are founded, namely, realist dogmatism, i.e., the conceptual world struck down by Descartes with his methodical doubt. Prior to Descartes, mutters idealism, the idea was modeled on its object which was presupposed by heaven knows what sort of magic or, better, begging the question. But since Descartes, the object is modeled after the Idea in such a way that "the principles of human knowledge exercise hegemony over the principles of philosophy". Brunschvicg insists that this does not in any sense mean that idealism should take on the assignment of deducing things from thought, for it was precisely the *Discourse on Method* that robbed the syllogistic process of all prestige and based the new culture on the substitution of scientific knowledge for purely conceptual knowledge, i.e., on the replacement of the abstract Aristotelian method of descent from the general to the particular by the modern method of an attempted ascent from the simple to an attainment and explanation of the complex.

Cartesianism demands supreme clarity in the inception of thought in general. At the outset there exists no distinction between time and eternity and thus no opposition between finite and infinite either. Brunschvicg cites as an example in parallelism the following: Just as there do not exist any imaginary spaces in which the creator could be supposed to be located prior to creation and from which his transitive action could be supposed to have been exercised to draw up out of the void the heaven and the earth, just so was there no moment in which there did not already exist eternity, and similarly is there no moment in which the time of immortality will succeed brusquely to the time of life and death.

[5] "I am an idealist because idealism is *the only doctrine which encounters no difficulty,* which involves no reservation, in the definition of being by progress" (*ibid.,* p. 225).

And Brunschvicg is gratified to conclude that this is the crucial significance of the set imparted by Descartes to modern thought, a set which has resulted in science restoring thought to the interior of the human mind and recovering the genuine sense of reason and of truth so as to displace the axis of the entire life of religion, with the end effect, we would add, of severing the taproot of the validity of religious knowledge.

But Brunschvicg firmly asserts, this time in accord with illuminism and idealism of the transcendental variety, that he does not in fact wish to deny natural religion or even the revealed Judeo-Christian religion, but rather to purify it by restoring it to its pristine simplicity and also to expand and complete it by transforming (!) the transcendence of revelation into the immanence of reason. This is the central nucleus of philosophy from Descartes onward: "There is in history a line of division, not simply between two eras but between two types of mental makeup, and this line of division is firmly traced by the decisive criticism by Cartesianism of the dogmatism that had gone before, a criticism that can never henceforth be effaced. And this is what I was pleased to recall when I said that science, by carrying thought back from the outside to the inside, by restoring the genuine sense of reason and of truth, had displaced the axis of the life of religion." [6]

The crux of the controversy is touched on by Brunschvicg himself in his final reply to Gilson, in which Brunschvicg alleges that the problem of the existence of the world is not in fact a problem at all; it is only when the imagination makes the leap at its own whim to some moment of time which we fancy to be anterior to this universe that this problem can be posed in the first place. But, says Brunschvicg, the progress of scientific idealism over dogmatism consists precisely in that scientific idealism had eliminated that imaginative notion, and herein lies the true power of the principle of immanentism. For his own part, Brunschvicg asserts that "consciousness and mind are the condition, not of being, but of the knowledge of being".[7] This was what had to be highlighted: the nexus between mind and being; for it is here that realism and idealism diverge, even before they part company on the point of the notion of creation.

[6] Brunschvicg concludes: "Must we conclude that this felicitous effort to sift out the pure gold of religion involves a break with the past, that it specifically shatters the religious fervor and upsurge which is manifested athwart the vicissitudes of the Judaeo-Christian world? I am going to say rather that it perfects that religious upthrust to the extent that the immanence of reflection gains precedence over the transcendence of revelation" (*ibid.,* p. 226).

[7] *Ibid.,* p. 235.

8

Conclusion: Curtain Up on the Tragedy of Modern Man!

Exaggerated as the above title may sound, it is meant to indicate the basic thrust of present-day culture which has already been outlined in its constitutive elements. The point is that modern thought is essentially atheistic because it is founded on the principle of immanence; thus, it must be granted that it is legitimate for the atheism of present-day philosophers to claim in its favor the logic of the *cogito*. And so the professions of theism, made more or less explicitly by a goodly portion of modern philosophers up to the 19th century, belong solely to the realm of good intentions and reveal merely the subjective attitude of individual philosophers; such professions are inexorably subverted by the logic of the *cogito* principle. In his dedicatory epistle for the *Meditationes de prima Philosophia* to the Dean and Doctors of the Theology Faculty of the Sorbonne, Descartes declared: "I have always held the two questions, concerning God and concerning the soul, to be the chief among those that are to be treated by philosophy rather than by theology." [1] Kant himself composed his *Critique of Pure Reason* for the

[1] *Meditationes de prima Philosophia, Oeuvres,* ed. Adam-Tannery, Vol. VII (Paris, 1909), p. 1. It is worthwhile to cite the intervention of H. More, who in May 1655 wrote from Cambridge a complacent eulogy *contra murmurantes* of the apologetic effectiveness of the Cartesian philosophy: "Nor is this Cartesian philosophy merely pleasant reading; above all it is useful, the mutterings and pratings of some to the contrary notwithstanding, for that supreme end of all philosophy, to wit, religion. For the Peripatetics hold that there are certain substantial forms that arise out of the potency of matter and so merge with matter that they cannot subsist in default of matter and therefore necessarily return in the end into the potency of matter (among which forms they rank the souls of almost all living beings, even those to which they attribute sense-perception and reflection); the Epicureans for their part reject those substantial forms and assert the power of sensing and reflecting to be innate to matter itself; Descartes is the only one I know among the Physiologists who has provided a philosophical grounding for those substantial forms and souls that arise out of matter and has totally denied to matter itself any faculty for sensing and reflecting. Wherefore

purpose of routing atheism and unbelief: "Therefore through such [a critique] alone can there be utterly eradicated materialism, fatalism, atheism, the unbelief of the free-thinkers, and that fanaticism and superstition which can prove so universally noxious, and, finally, the idealism and skepticism which represent a greater danger for the schools and will have a hard time taking firm root among the general public." [2]

Better known is the declaration of Bacon: "Shallow sips of philosophy may move toward atheism but ample draughts bring back to religion." [3] The words are taken from Leibniz's *Confessio Naturae contra Atheistas.*[4] For Hegel, too, we know the main aim of philosophy and of the whole of human life to have been the "knowledge" of God via reason.[5] Such instances could be multiplied. But as early a thinker as Jacobi had already recorded a "prophecy" of the paradoxical Lichtenberg: "Our world is en route to a state of affairs in which it will be as ridiculous to believe in a God as it is today to believe in ghosts." [6] It seems to me that it is not too pessimistic to say we have already arrived at this state of affairs!

For the theological problem of modern thought seems to have reached, in present-day philosophies, the "moment of truth". Its issue does not represent any "value" whose development is left to the free option of subsequent thinkers; rather, that issue flows inexorably from the "structural analysis" of the *cogito.* The contention that atheism is implied in the very principle of immanentism is by no means new or revolutionary; but what is more important to grasp is the deep-rooted affinity between the most diametrically opposed systems of modern thought, an affinity that is also the reason for their mutual clashes. Rationalism and empiricism, deism, sense-perceptionism, critical realism, idealism, phenomenalism, positivism and the like, together with the minor systems that might be mentioned, constitute the stages in the authentication of the *cogito.* It is true that, in the atheist degeneration

---

an adherence to Cartesian principles would provide a most certain method and way of demonstrating both that God exists and that the soul of man cannot be mortal, which two are the most solid foundations and fulcra of all true religion. I note this but briefly though I could also add much that is relative thereto. But let me say in summing up that there exists no philosophy, save perhaps the Platonic one, which so firmly bars the way for the atheists to those perverse cavils and subterfuges to which they are prone to have recourse, as does this Cartesian philosophy if it be thoroughly understood" (In Descartes, *Correspondance,* ed. Adam-Tannery, Vol. V, pp. 259f.).

[2] *Kritik der reinen Vernunft,* Foreword to 2nd ed., p. xxiv.

[3] *De augm. scient.* I; *The Works of Francis Bacon,* ed. J. Spedding, R. L. Ellis and D. D. Heath, Vol. I (London, 1879), p. 436.

[4] *Opera philosophica,* ed. Dutens, Vol. I, (Geneva, 1768), pp. 5ff.

[5] *Philosophie der Welgeschichte; C.W.,* ed Lasson, Vol. I, (Leipzig, 1925) pp. 17ff.

[6] Jacobi, *Werke* III, 199, *Vermischten Schriften,* Vol. I (Göttingen, 1800), p. 166.

of the *cogito,* materialism seems to express a jarring note and a patent absurdity; therefore, the rationalist and idealist wing always indignantly used to repel any attribution of atheism. But since the works of Feuerbach, Nietzsche and Sartre, such indignation has become steadily rarer and can be said today to have disappeared entirely among philosophers. This must be admitted to constitute a notable contribution to honesty and clarity in the speculative field.

Undoubtedly, modern philosophy has constituted the most daring attempt of the human spirit to attain total and radical autonomy and to mold thought within the confines of its own self. Neither ancient philosophy, with its Olympian calm and serenity, nor even Christian thought, bulwarked by revelation, can sustain comparison with the restlessness, vitality and inexhaustibility of the modern systems, insofar as speculative boldness and variety of fields of investigation in the whole sphere of the spirit are concerned. And so, whatever our judgment on the modern philosophy of immanence which has not reached its zero point, we must admit that it has molded the modern world in which we, too, find ourselves. If this world has gone adrift and needs to get a new bearing on the Absolute which is a true lodestar and fills the void of the Absolutes of rationalism and idealism, this is also a service that has been rendered by the principle of immanence. In its degeneration and dissolution into the void, it has shown that the questioner and the answerer can be none other than Being and that it is up to man to make every effort to assume a listening posture and to repeat the truth he has heard and harvested in the presence of Being.

The road of our own researches will be lit up for us by the very progress of the interior dynamic of the *cogito* in its three basic stages of the *Via Crucis* or speculative Good Friday of God (Hegel): (1) the rationalist stage in which the Absolute is posited as a Principle; (2) the critical idealist stage in which the Absolute is interpreted as a resultant Principle; (3) the post-Hegelian stage in which the Absolute in our own day has been liquidated entirely as nothing more than the result of an illusion.

These same stages could be indicated in the progress of thinking with respect to the new "notion" of man (mind) as absolute: in rationalism the mind of man claims for itself the status of initial act; in transcendental idealism, it affirms this initial act as the principle of the content itself; in present-day thought it reveals the sheer identity of act and content. The importance of this route of research is that it should begin from the zero point of doubt (*cogito*), patenting itself as assertion of action (*volo*), i.e., as the zero point of thought, and terminating in the finitude of being as the zero point of being and of thought alike and with the reduction of man to a futile anguish.

The methodological principle that must be "laid hold of" with greatest "seriousness of application" [7] must be the principle seen in, and as the development and end result of, this ultimate "tragedy of man". This "human tragedy" is replete with the depth and anguish of classical tragedy and plays out the very plot of that tragedy on the stage of a culture and civilization where fate is represented by the impersonal menace of nuclear weapons and the setting is a world deprived of man himself who has been overpowered and overwhelmed by the machine. And just as the Christian message of salvation could appear more radiant to the man of classical tragedy, it may without presumption be hoped that the free highway of a better-founded hope may open up to present-day man out of the holocaust-mottled dead-end in which he sees the *cogito* consuming itself.

The present interpretative analysis, therefore, strives for a rigorously unitary character, whose efficacy the reader must judge. Inasmuch as we hold the question of the *cogito* to be crucial, we proceed to a treatment of the individual immanentist positions from the interior structure of the *cogito* in order to analyze away, as foreign bodies or extrinsic residues, the ever feebler and more equivocal interpolations of the Absolute. This interpretation therefore distrusts as a radical contamination and incomprehension every effort at systematic or structural compromise between the classical philosophy of transcendence and the modern one of immanence; but our interpretation takes over at the same time the element of radicalism from the fascinating adventure of modern thought. It is directed, however, not to the imposition of thought as act of being (an imposition which can be demonstrated to be impossible by even the most elementary analysis of the structure of thought and which has been demonstrated irrefutably to be impossible by the whole evolution of modern philosophy), but rather to the presentation of being as act and foundation of thought.

The perusal of modern thought is as decisive for the actuation of the metaphysical ideal as was that of Greek thought for the molding of Christian philosophy; indeed, it is more crucial because of the formalistic deviation. And when the new contribution to the demand for the transcendental is recognized, as it must be, as coming from Being itself, it ought to preclude the aridities and deviations that have rendered the transcendental ambiguous and inoperative for so many centuries and clarify truth in its authentic language, which is the mind in act.

[7] This method of ours (the method itself, not the problematic which imposes itself with a most trenchant insistency) is therefore diametrically opposed to recent concordist formulas according to which "the gap between the way of thinking which is being proposed by [atheist] existentialism and that of barely thirty or forty years ago is more drastic than the gap between modern philosophy and medieval or between medieval philosophy and classical"; cf. L. Stefanini, *Esistenzialismo ateo ed Esistenzialismo cristiano* (Padua, 1952), p. 4.

Appendices

I. Difficulties Surrounding Any Definition of Atheism

Anyone having an entirely clear notion of God would not have any difficulty in defining atheism; but the concept of the Supreme Being has introduced an element of strain into the philosophical investigation of every age and there has thus been a continuous fluctuation in the definition of this concept.

For our present purpose we can distinguish primarily *three stages or levels* of the concept of God: (1) the popular-mythical; (2) the philosophico-speculative; (3) the revealed-personal. At each of these levels the denial can be effected, and hence we shall have various types of judgments concerning the atheism involved. The content and validity of such judgments is bound up with the semantics proper to the respective intentional area. Socrates and the others who refused to accept mythological religion were judged atheists; so, on the other hand, were the theologians and "philosophers" of antiquity and the moderns who stopped at the concept of the Absolute without conceiving that Absolute as a free and foreseeing Person; so, too, the Christians themselves were called atheists by the pagan philosophers like Julian.

A further consequence of this state of affairs is the necessity of distinguishing, in any judgment concerning theism and, above all, concerning atheism, between the *objective* aspect of the judgment itself (i.e., the "content" of the neat notion of God, as that notion is expressed by the philosopher, measured against the crucial point of the problem itself, i.e., what should be posited as an adequate concept of God) and the *subjective* "intention" or conviction of the philosopher. In this way there may be many *pantheists, monists* and *panentheists* who believe themselves to be theists and notoriously reject any designation of themselves as atheists (e.g., Spinoza, Toland, Fichte, Hegel, *et al.*). Thus, two classes of atheists could be indicated: (a) *explicit* or avowed atheists,[1] and (b) *implicit* or inferential atheists.

Finally, even the traditional division between practical and theoretical atheism, which seems obvious at first glance, is not in fact so obvious in the case of either of the two terms involved. It does not really seem

[1] N. Abbagnano calls it "professed atheism" (*Dizionario di filosofia* [Turin, 1961], pp. 79f.). In this lucid article, Sartre's atheism is attributed to materialism rather than to the doctrine of freedom in virtue of the principle of immanence.

possible that anyone should admit the existence of God and then live *entirely and in all respects* (N.B. in *all* respects) as though God did not exist, for the very notion of God expresses a reality too compelling for anyone calling himself a "theist" not to feel in some fashion the resulting influence and responsibility. On the other hand, the theoretical atheists themselves can scarcely escape the influence of the category of the "sacred" even if they refer it to nature or to man; and this category of the "sacred" is notoriously the subjective nucleus of the origin of the idea of God.

An examination of the definitions of atheism given in the history of philosophy would lead us very far afield and yield no appreciable advantage for our present research which is mainly confined to the theoretical order. Let us cite, for example, among the most famous treatments of the subject, that of the adversary and accuser of Wolff, namely, J. F. Buddaeus, in his *Theses de Atheismo et Superstitione* (Jena, 1714).[2] Buddaeus distinguishes, for example, two main classes of atheists in the following order:

1. "Those who perpetrate a brazen and forthright denial of the existence of God, or who, being in bad faith, cannot deny or plead unawareness of the fact that atheism necessarily follows their principles:" among such Buddaeus lists the Epicureans, Spinoza (God-Nature) (V: I,§26: pp. 78ff.).

2. "Those who set up principles from which conclusions can be legitimately drawn that are either prejudicial or injurious to the providence and the freedom of God [= Aristotle, the Stoics = God tethered to the world—but they did not see these consequences], who make God and nature into a single Being and confound them one with the other, which is the same thing as denying the existence of God, although the authors of this system disavow these consequences and refuse to admit the nexus of such consequences with their own principles." [3]

But Buddaeus declares forthwith that such a benign criterion cannot be used in the case of Spinoza: "We cannot give the same benefit of the doubt to Spinoza who understood quite well the monstrous consequences of his wicked system and whose artful adjustment and arrangement of that system (an artifice which is nevertheless so transparent as

[2] In 1717 this same Buddaeus (Budde) published in Jena a German edition (*Sätzen von Atheisterey und Aberglaube;* cf. J. Trinius, *Freydenker Lexikon* [Leipzig & Bernburg, 1759; abridged edition, Turin, 1960], p. 61). A French translation was made, edited by L. Philon (Amsterdam, P. Mortier, 1740), from which we have taken the quotations.

[3] Among the dogmas bound up with atheism, Buddaeus lists the denial of providence (hence Bayle was accused of atheism), of the immortality of the soul, of the existence of pure spirits (materialism), of the prophecies and the miracles, and, in particular, of the divine origin of Christianity (accusation against Spinoza, pp. 143ff.) and of sacred Scripture (pp. 116ff.). The notion of *inferential atheism* can be found as early as Moreri: "The name of atheist can be merited not only by teaching in so many words that there is no God, but also by propounding ideas necessarily entailing the non-existence of a Supreme Being" (*Le Grand Dictionnaire Historique,* Vol. I [Basle, 1733[2]], fol. 611a).

such) can leave no doubt that he saw quite clearly that the inevitable consequence would be that there was no God, according to that Spinozan system, aside from Nature. Thus, we shall be doing him no injustice whatever in assigning him one of the first places among top-flight atheists" (French translation, fol. 3).

In Section I, Buddaeus offers a quite comprehensive lift of dogmatic atheists: in addition to such classical philosophers as the Eleatics, the Stoics, Epicurus and Aristotle himself, Buddaeus includes from among the moderns such men as Campanella, Cardanus, Machiavelli, Cesalpinus, Berigardus Cremonini, G. Bruno, Pomponazzi, Vanini, Politianus, Ermolaus Barbarus, G. Della Casa, *et al.* And among the Scholastics the Scotists are accused of having paved the way for Spinoza (pp. 52f.).

At the beginning of Section 2, atheism is called "a malign and perverse disposition of mind" (p. 98), and among the main causes are indicated human corruption, evil education, conversation with the impious, reading of atheist books, disordered studies, etc. (p. 149).

No less exhaustive and punctilious is the exposition and critique of atheism effected by Wolff whom Buddaeus accused of falling into the same error as will be pointed out in due course.[4] Wolff ranges Spinoza among the atheists (*Theol. Nat.,* p. 11, §717, p. 730). Another classic of the history of atheism is the work of Theophilus Spitzel [5] who asserts that the pagans accused the Christians of atheism (Clem. Alex. *Strom.* VII and Julian in Sozom. *Hist.* lib. V, c. 15) and that the Catholics leveled the same accusations against the Protestants: "Just as the papal writers [6] in no way hesitated to brand our Churches with the most shameful stigma of *atheism:* thus, Possevinus (*Bibl.* lib. VIII), Claudius de Sionctes (*Tract. pecul.*), Chiconius (*Contra Cavillum*), Campanella ". . . in *Atheismus Triumphatus,* intemperately and overtly throughout", Mersenne (*Comm. in Genesim, passim*), the Jesuit Cornelius à Lapide (*In II Tim.* III, 9) did not hesitate to assert Lutheranism and Calvinism as having strayed into atheism and their adherents to have become libertines, etc. And in his *Comm. in II Petr.* III, p. 374 he states: "Rightly, therefore, does Cardinal Hosius call atheism the perfection of the Lutheran and Zwinglian perfidy. . . . With what degree of reliability, however, and with what truth (comments Spitzel) will mayhap appear more clearly elsewhere" (p. 6; on p. 7 Buddaeus turns the tables by accusing the Jesuits of atheism; on p. 8 he declares that there is *real equivocation* involved in calling atheists "all who deny or oppose the true religion" and in accusing the Mohammedans and modern Judaism of atheism!).

Writing about the concept of atheism, Spitzel distinguishes in Section

[4] *Theol. Nat.,* Pars II, c. 1. "De Atheismo," §§411-527, pp. 369ff.

[5] *Scrutinium Atheismi historico-aetiologicum* (Augsburg, 1663).

[6] "With a like viciousness, each kind of our Lutheran religion has been accused by papal writers of atheism, as can be seen in Gisbert Voetius and Spitzel" (M. J. F. Herttenstein, *Quo jure antiqui quidam Philosophi Athei vocentur* [Ulm, 1709], p. 8).

3 a *direct* and an *indirect* concept: "To the former species are said to belong such as attempt, as much as in them lies, to snuff out in their heart all knowledge and sense of the Spirit and all faith in the Spirit, to such an extent that they strive so mightily to *απιστία* (disbelief) as to will sometimes to have arrived at that state and to have persuaded themselves and others thereof, or such men as deny God out of a fixed persuasion of their mind and without any prick of a rebelling conscience or impugn the essence of the said God unto their last breath. Debate has begun among the experts as to whether there are such atheists, whereas all the words and examples of the Holy Book seem to touch upon an *INDIRECT atheism,* involving an elimination or subversion of all knowledge of God at least as a necessary consequence. . . . The existence of such atheists is attested by scripture which mentions them throughout and is confirmed by sad experience which patently manifests monsters of this sort within the ranks of sounder and faithful men.

Now this *INDIRECT* atheism in turn is conveniently divided into *theoretical* or speculative and *practical;* the strongest reason for this division lies in the fact that the one is distinguished from the other by the ultimate act of specification on account of the respectively predominant element, despite the fact that they revolve around mutually common principles: for *practical atheism* is effected more by the will, while yet requiring of the intellect a certain *γνῶσις* (knowledge), whereas *theoretical atheism* recognizes the will as cause and at least tends to some sort of usefulness (imaginary, to be sure, and not real). And although the intellect does indeed give its anterior knowing in support of the will, nevertheless the will does not always depend upon the intellect, preeminently if the actions take their origin from a vicious habit" (pp. 11f.).

There follows the distinction of atheism into *theoretical* or speculative and *practical.* Theoretical atheism depends on the intellect "which out of a fixed persuasion of the mind attempts by some firm sequence of reasoning to deny God or eliminate the deity" (p. 13), whereas practical atheism depends on the will, as instanced by those "who not so much by intellectual attitude and profession, as rather by their life, practical operation and habitual morals, attempt to deny God and all religion: for example, someone who neglects all offices and exercises of piety as useless, while yet professing some religion". And Spitzel laments: "For speculatively such persons can advance to such a stage of impiety that they not only deny God indirectly but even dare to impugn anything that is either known or believed concerning GOD." And he concludes: "In this group of atheists can be conveniently classed those vilest men of all religions, together with Machiavelli's adherents and disciples, to wit, the crooked politicians, those most shameful slaves of popularity and every ambition; to whom we may add the swine from among the herd of Epicurus and all lovers and followers of all manner of wickedness and impurity" (pp. 14f.).

Either type of atheism may be *inchoate* or *consummate* and each such subdivision is in turn divided into *crass* or *subtle* (covert) (p. 16). There follows an ample list of atheists arranged by countries (Italy—Aretino is called the author of *De Tribus Impostoribus*—France, Spain: p. 17ff.). England is called "today the scum of all religions and pestiferous dogmas. . . . From the foundation of the world there have not been so many monstrous opinions as presently in England" (p. 32).

Among the causes of atheism, Spitzel indicates "human corruption and aversion from God, foolishness, μωρός [stupid], ἀσύνετος [brainless], ἀπαιδεύτος [ignorant] pride, disordered study, abominable books" (of which there follows an ample list: *De Tribus Impostoribus;* Cardanus, *De subtilitate;* Godof. a Valle, *De arte nihil credendi; Simonis religio* published in Poland; Sim. a Valle, *Cur receptum sit Evangelium;* Bonav. de Perez *Cymbalum Mundi;* Vanini *Amphitheatrum,* etc. Says Spitzel: "Concerning the writings of Campanella, Portelli, Cardanus, Gaffarelli, Taurelli and their like, let others judge" (p. 60). He also includes "debates and colloquia, free exegesis of the Bible, the impious religion of the Machiavellians or pseudo-politicians, the *Ratio Status*" (condemned, incidentally by St. Pius V), alteration of religion, bragging about fake miracles, touting of natural wisdom" (pp. 64ff.).

The article on the atheists appearing in the *Encyclopedia* and attributed to a certain Abbé Yvon [7] hews approximately to this same line. The notion of atheism is presented in descriptive terms: "Name applied to those who deny the existence of a God, author of the world. They can be divided into three classes: the first class denies that there is a God; the second attempts to pass for agnostics or skeptics on this point; finally, the third class, differing little from the first, denies the chief attributes of the divine nature and supposes God to be a being who, properly speaking, does not act at all but rather is always passive." Among the causes of atheism are indicated "ignorance and stupidity, debauchery and corruption of manners and morals" inasmuch as "the atheism of the heart often leads to the atheism of the mind" (fol. 678b; I ed. 798a). Atheism is defined as, "the opinion of those who deny the existence of a God-author of the world" and not, therefore, simple doubt or ignorance.

This article distinguishes *four types* of theoretical atheists (*"atheists in virtue of speculation and reasoning"*) as follows:

(a) Those who brazenly (*effrontement*) deny the existence of God: "Critias of Athens, Diagoras of Miletus, Theodores, Prodicus, Eumeros, Bion of Boristene and Stilpon; moderns: Giordano Bruno, Vanini, Mahomet Essendi, John Toland, etc."

(b) Those who set up principles from which atheism necessarily derives—skeptics: Arcesilaos, Carneadas, Clitomachos, Anasarxos,

[7] *Encyclopédie,* 1st ed., coll. 798b-815a; 2nd ed., cols. 677b-694a. On the origin of the article in question, we read at the bottom of the page the following interesting statement: "This article is taken from the papers of M. Formey, Secretary of the Royal Academy of Prussia," 2nd ed., 693b).

Pyrrho, Protagoras and Cotta of Cicero; moderns: Cl. Berigardus, Come Ruggerius, Gotofredus a Valle, Thomas Browne; the protagonists of the principle that the One is the All: Xenophon, Parmenides, Zeno, Melissos; moderns: Vanini and Spinoza admit the name of God but deny the reality.

(c) Those who, although they speak of God and ascribe to him attributes worthy of him, nevertheless have principles and a system from which derive consequences destructive of the existence of God. Thus, the pantheists, i.e., all the pagan philosophers (with their *Anima mundi,* and the like): Strato, Pliny the Elder, Alfonso of Castille; among later philosophers: Averroes, Amalricus, David of Dinant, Achillini, Zimara, Vicomercatus, Pomponazzi, Campanella, Cremonini, Hobbes, Collins, Bayle.

(d) Hedonists who have embraced theoretical atheism: the Cyrenaics; moderns: Pietro Aretino, Fr. Poggio, Marcello Palingenio, Jonathan Swift, M. de Saint-Evremond, the Abbé de Challien" (fol. 679ab).

Of note in particular is the sharp refutation of Bayle's famous contention (to be treated in due course) that atheism is not a greater evil than idolatry and that atheism is not destructive of society (fol. 681a—683b).

Perhaps the most important aspect of the article is to be found in the conclusion where atheism is judged punishable according to the natural laws inasmuch as it subverts the foundations of morality and politics, even though it may leave room for the notions of what is honest and what dishonest, for such virtue remains sterile: "Thence we conclude that atheism publicly professed is punishable according to natural law. Certainly many of the barbarous measures and inhuman executions occasioned by the mere suspicion of atheism, or indeed the pretext of atheism, can only merit the strongest disapproval. On the other hand, the most tolerant man will surely not disagree that the magistrate has the right to repress those who dare to profess *atheism* and even to put them to death if there be no other means open to him to save society from them.

"No one calls in question the fact that the magistrate has full authority to punish what is evil and vicious and to reward what is good and virtuous. If he can punish those who do wrong to a single individual, he undoubtedly has as much right to punish those who do wrong to an entire society by denying that there is any God; he likewise has the right to intervene in the conduct of the human race to recompense those who work for the common good and to chastise those who attack it. Such a man can be regarded as the enemy of all his fellowmen, since he subverts all the foundations on which are chiefly established their conservation and their happiness. Such a man could be punished by anyone within the law of nature. Consequently the magistrate must have the right to punish not only those who deny the existence of a divinity but also those who render vain this existence by denying God's providence, or by preaching against worshiping him, or such as are guilty of formal blasphemies, profanations, perjuries, or vain oaths. Religion is so necessary for the support of human society that it is impossible, as the pagans have recognized as well as the Christians, for society to subsist in default of the admission of an invisible power governing the affairs of the human race" (fol. 693b; I ed. 816b—817a).

The article is thus adhering to the canons of orthodoxy and was probably inserted to ward off any condemnation by the royal censor, an aim which we know it has failed to achieve!

II. The Atheist's Faith

Under this surprising title (*Der Glaube des Atheisten*) an eminent historian of classical thought defends the contention that there have never really been any theoretical atheists in earnest, despite accusations (K. Joel; "Antibarbarus," in *Vorträge und Aufsätze* [Jena, 1914], pp. 14ff.). Joel here shares the opinion of Hume who is supposed to have said, while dining in Paris with d'Holbach, that he did not believe that there were any atheists because he had never seen one. But it must be remembered that the host replied: "We are eighteen here at table; fifteen are atheists and the other three do not know what to think" (cf. P. Hazard, *La pensée européenne au* XVIIIe *siècle. De Montesquieu á Lessing,* Vol. I [Paris, 1946]. The attempt to acquit the "confessed and professed" atheists of antiquity (Hippo, Eumeros, Diagoras and Theodoros the Atheist) does not seem to square with an objective reading of the sources. This is true, e.g., in the case of Diagoras (5th century B.C.) in his book Ἀποπυργίζοντες Λόγοι, according to the most recent studies: "That the main thesis of Diagoras' book consisted in the assertion that gods did not exist at all: 'There are no gods'; not 'There are no man-made gods' or any similar statement, but a repudiation pure and simple of the whole concept, an atheism radical, extreme and uncompromising. That is an opinion rarer in antiquity than it is in modern times. But it is the opinion ascribed directly to Diagoras by all our witnesses down from Aristoxenos and Epikuros, and obviously by Aristophanes too. There simply is no contradictory evidence. Philodemos (III, 5), rather anachronistically, merely gives him the benefit of the doubt that, perhaps, the whole thing was meant as a huge joke, a prank. It was this radical denial which earned him the surname *the atheist,* shared only (and rarely) by Theodoros of Kyrene, and on account of which he was regarded as the ἄθεος κατ' ἐξοκήν. In his limited sphere, and as far as a comparison is admissible at all, the opinion of Diagoras stands side by side with the complete nihilism of Gorgias in his first main thesis ὅτι οὐδὲν ἔστιν (that nothing is). I regard this evidence as a sufficiently strong basis for a conclusion *e silentio:* the book of Diagoras was of a purely negative (or perhaps it would be better to say polemic) character, confining itself to attacking the belief in the existence of god(s) and not developing a theory of his own belief" (F. Jacoby, "Diagoras, Ὁ Ἄθεος [The Atheist]," in *Abhandl. d. deutschen akademie d. Wiss., Klasse f. Sprachen, Literatur u. Kunst* [Jahrgang, 1959], Nr. 3 [Berlin, 1959], p. 26).

Joel, on the contrary, finds the whole business quite simple: the mechanistic attitude of modern rationalism is not really radically atheist but rather extremely theistic; even the brutal *Homme machine* of Lamettrie is not atheistic as such, and it is well known to what extent Hobbes and Spinoza assert the reality of God! So no account should be taken of the accusations of atheism; even d'Holbach, asserts Joel, has no desire to be atheistic, because he identifies God with the primordial energy of Nature (p. 80).

The theists dominate 19th-century science, claims Joel, citing the famous apologetic book *Dieu et la Science* by Elie de Cyon. Joel really feels that anyone admitting the *Urkraft* (primordial energy) or the *Weltseele* (world-soul) is not to be classed as an atheist. Now it is clear that such a principle, either identical with or totally immersed in matter, is admitted even by the most radical atheists and materialists, not only by men like d'Holbach but even by men like Czolbe and Haeckel.

In the case of Feuerbach, insists Joel, "the rejection of God is basically nothing more than a rejection of Hegel. He protests only against God as a projection of the thinking process, against the abstract, objective, alien God out there and up there; but against the subjectively experienced God, against the God felt within man, he has no objection" (p. 180). Thus, even Moleschott and D. F. Strauss (who preaches God as "the Being in all being and the Life in all life") would not be atheists. And so there is no such thing as atheism; Joel claims that this is F. A. Lange's contention in his famous *Geschichte des Materialismus* (Leipzig, 1905). The accusation of atheism, renewed century after century, is the result of religious fanaticism and intolerance. The theists have not understood the problem of God: what is branded as atheism is nothing other than "negative theology" which is called to purge "positive" or affirmative theology, because, according to the teaching of Nicholas or Cusa, the true *mystical theology* can rise above every yes and every no (pp. 190ff.).

It can be said to have been the merit of present-day philosophy to have made a clean sweep of these oversimplifications which do violence to philosophy and religion at once. An old English theologian was therefore not wrong in declaring: "But we must begin at the beginning so as to demonstrate by arguments from reason and by the authority of the learned that there can really be such men who persuade themselves that there is no supreme Spirit or (to put it in the terms used here by theology) that there can be speculative atheists, as against the commonly accepted opinion asserting that there can be no atheist properly speaking, because the proposition *God is* is so inscribed in the hearts of men that it can never be effaced, albeit it may be buried, as in the case of the practical atheists. Therefore, if in fact the theologians would attend to the fact that the doctrine of innate ideas is borne out neither by sound reason nor by experience nor yet by revelation, they would not be so diffident about conceding that there can on occasion be speculative atheists." [8]

III. Religion, Superstition and Atheism

In contradistinction to Plutarch, the theologians and apologists consider atheism as the worst aberration of the human mind and therefore judge any religion, even the most superstition-riddled, to be preferable to atheism. Plutarch's contention is taken up again by Bayle: "That atheism is not a greater evil than idolatry" (*Pensées diverses sur le comète,* Vol. I [Rotterdam, 1704], §§214-225, pp. 225ff. and *Addition* . . . Vol. IV, pp. 561f.). Bayle's sharp reproof of this Plutarchian thesis does not prevent Bayle from admitting that "idolatry renders men more difficult to convert than does atheism" (*op. cit.,* Vol. I, p. 232; cf. *Addition,* Vol. IV, pp. 592ff.). The crux of Bayle's position seems to be that a distinction must be made between the area of abstract judgment and the practical area. In the case of the former: "Any inspection of the atheists' judgment concerning the divinity reveals a horrible excess of blindness, a prodigious ignorance of the nature of things, a frame of mind subversive of all the laws of common sense and productive of a disordered and false fashion of reasoning that defies description" (*op. cit.,* §223; Vol. I, p. 237).

In the practical area, however: "Are you going to say that these atheists have effaced from their heart the image of God with which they were born, whereas the other Athenians 'have retained it?' You would be quite wrong to say that because it is certain that the idolaters have not at all preserved the idea of God that nature might have given them.

[8] J. T. Philipps, *De Atheismo or a History of Atheism in Which Many Writers, Ancient and More Modern, Falsely Accused of Impiety, Are Freed from the Shameful Stigma of Atheism, While Others Who Seem To Have Thought Less Correctly of the Supreme Spirit Are Rightly Refuted* (London, 1735), p. 2. On p. 3 is recorded Locke's polemic against the Cartesian innate ideas, but the author defends Descartes against the accusation of atheism (pp. 12f.), and in Article III ("Quid vox atheus") he protests against the exaggerated attribution of atheism effected by Voetius: "In Voetius there are so many divisions, subdivisions, degrees and species of atheism that all mortals, so many as to be innumerable, will fall into one or other class, and in this visible world there are left no worshippers of GOD" (p. 26). A moderate approach is typical likewise of M. J. F. Herttenstein, in his *Quo jure antiqui quidam Philosophi Athei vocentur:* after §1, entitled "A Consideration of the Heinous Nature of the Crime of Atheism," he warns in §2: "One should be cautious in branding with the stigma of atheism" (p. 6). The same position is taken by the Protestant, J. F. Reinmann, *Atheismi et Atheorum falso suspectorum apud judaeos, ethnicos, christianos, mahumedanos* (Hildesheim, 1725).

They know only false gods, abominable gods, and it would be an impiety to say that they were born with the image of God stamped upon their heart; for this would be to maintain that the true God had engraved in their heart this monstrous idea of the divinity. If our souls are united to our bodies with the imprint of the image of God, this image must necessarily be that of the true God, and consequently the idolatrous Athenians were as guilty as the atheists of the crime of having effaced from their hearts the idea of God which nature had given them" (*Pensées* . . . , c. 104, Vol. III, pp. 483f.).

Bayle's position is therefore intentionally highly nuanced: the idolaters are held to have been already true atheists in a certain sense (§217; Vol. I, p. 228) and idolatry precisely was the source of atheism. In support of his contention, Bayle cites ample witnesses of Fathers like Lactantius, Tertullian, Cyprian, Augustine and Gregory Nazianzen, and even pagan authors (§216, pp. 227f.; *Addition* . . . , Vol. IV, pp. 622 and 625). Thomas Aquinas is also cited: "The Angelic Doctor is taking the same line when he writes. . . ." and Bayle cites *S.T.* IIa-IIae, q. 94, a. 3 (whether idolatry be the most serious sin), which does in fact consider idolatry as the most serious sin from the objective point of view: "It must be said that the gravity of any sin can be considered from two points of view: first, from the standpoint of the sin itself, and from this point of view the sin of idolatry is the most serious. For even as it seems to be the most serious offense in an earthly state for someone to give and ascribe the kingly honor to another than the true king, because such an action as such upsets the order of the whole of the state; even so in the sins which are committed against God, which sins are certainly the greatest, the most serious seems to be for divine honor to be given and ascribed to a creature, because such an action as such makes another God in the world, diminishing the divine sovereignty."

To this statement of the question correspond several sections in Bayle, e.g.: "Atheism does not lead to corruption of morals" (*Pensées* . . . Vol. I, §233, p. 261); "Would not a society of atheists make good and honorable laws?" (Vol. II, §172, p. 349; *Addition,* Vol. II, p. 576). His reply is squarely in the affirmative here as also in the matter of the mortality of the soul: "The mortality of the soul does not interfere with the immortalizing of its name" (*Pensées* . . . , Vol. II, §173, p. 352).

Voltaire, as we shall point out, vigorously opposes Bayle's contention. The controversy occupied a prominent place likewise among the 18th-century theologians and apologists, e.g., a man like Valsecchi who sides with Voltaire, contending: "Superstition is not worse nor yet more pernicious to society than is atheism" (*Dei fondamenti della religione e dei fonti dell'empietà,* Bk. III, p. I, c. 14 [Padua, 1805[7]], pp. 119ff.). Valsecchi, indeed, makes a strong point precisely of an assertion of Bayle himself: "All the religions of the world, the true and the false alike, pivot on this great point that there is an invisible Judge who punishes and recompenses after this life the actions of man, both exterior and interior. Thence is supposed to flow the chief usefulness of religion" (Bayle, *Dictionn. hist. et crit.,* Vol. IV [Basle, 1738[5]], fol. 256b). In his own demonstration, Valsecchi makes a great display of classical authors, such as Euripides, Sophocles, Homer, Hesiod, Virgil, Terence, Plutarch, Plautus *et al.* As for the disorders provoked by religious fanaticism and adduced by Bayle and Toland in defense of the superiority of atheism over pagan and idolatrous religions, Valsecchi deplores such excesses but observes that they are not due to religion but to the vices of man, and he cites on his side Voltaire (*op. cit.,* Bk. III, p. II, c. 15, Vol. III, pp. 130ff.).

In this connection it is to the point to cite also a passage from Kierkegaard in which he considers with great precision both unbelief and superstition, i.e., atheism and idolatry as being on the same level: "They are in perfect correspondence: both lack inwardness; it is just that unbelief is passive athwart an activity and superstition is active athwart a passivity; the one can be said to be the masculine mold, the other the feminine, and the content of both molds is auto-reflection. In their essence they are perfectly identical. Both unbelief and superstition are the anguish of faith, but unbelief commences in the activity of unfreedom, whereas superstition commences in the passivity of unfreedom. Usually attention is paid only to the passivity of superstition; therefore superstition seems less imposing and more excusable according as it is judged under the categories of aesthetics or ethics. There is a deceptive weakness in superstition, but there must always be in it an activity sufficient to enable superstition to maintain its passivity. Superstition is unbelieving toward itself; unbelief is superstitious toward itself. The content of both is auto-reflection. Superstition is moved by its apathy, cowardice and faintheartedness to deem it better to stay superstitious than to abandon superstition; unbelief is moved by its stubbornness, haughtiness and pride to deem it more daring to persist in unbelief than to abandon it. The subtlest form of such auto-reflection is always that which makes the self interesting to itself with the desire of emerging from this state while complacently remaining in it" (S. Kierkegaard, *Il concetto dell'angoscia,* Italian translation by C. Fabro [Florence 1953], pp. 179f.).

IV. Negative Atheism (Bouterwek)

Only after the death of Hegel and especially with Feuerbach, as we shall point out in due course, does immanence begin to reveal its atheistic taproot and, more precisely, headway begin to be made in imparting its distinctively positive character to modern atheism on the basis of the principle of knowledge and consciousness. In passing, it is worthwhile to note here an effort made by F. Bouterwek (1765-1828), a contemporary of Fichte-Schelling-Hegel, in his work *Die Religion der Vernunft* (Göttingen, 1824), Ch. III, pp. 155ff., to bring out positive atheism in clearer relief.

Bouterwek distinguished four basic attitudes in the face of the problem of religion: *atheism, pantheism, hylozoism* and genuine *theism.* For hylozoism, God is the principle of the world, the world-soul (*Weltseele*), the life of all life, etc., and this is the way of thinking most frequently encountered in antiquity (Aristotle, the Stoics, *et al.*); some forms of modern idealist pantheism (not, however, Spinoza!) slip into hylozoism so that it is legitimate to speak of a "natural transition" (*natürlicher Uebergang*) from pantheism into hylozoism (cf. pp. 218, 221ff). Whereas the origin of atheism is to be found, according to Bouterwek, in "an intellect submerged in the sensible" (*aus einem in der Sinnlichkeit versunkenen Verstand*), pantheism, on the contrary, is expressive of the rising of the thinking mind above the sensible by way of the pure metaphysical consideration of the Absolute; pantheism is evidence of a predominant desire to know the Absolute by means of pure thought, as something which is exalted (*erhaben*) over all manner of sense-perception.

Bouterwek thinks or appears to think that Jacobi's critique of Spinozan pantheism is calculated to convince only someone operating on the religious level. All of Jacobi's criticisms, claims Bouterwek, are relevant for religion but not for philosophy: the criticisms that pantheism gives to the term "religion" a meaning foreign to the other schools; that it renders void the moral elements of religion and tends to submerge the individual ego in a mystical All-One-God (*All-Eins-Gott*); that this All-One is mindless and cannot really be prayed to; that the eternal guidance and action exercised by such an All-One would be totally subject to blind necessity, like the eternal nature of which the atheists speak; that pantheism, therefore, precludes all rational faith in a divine providence, even as does atheism. Pantheism aims at deducing the finite from the Infinite, time from eternity, either in dialectical or in mystical fashion, but its mystical theology relapses in turn into a dialectic: the incomplete pantheism of Xenophon and Parmenides (cf. pp. 188ff., 246ff.), as also that of Heraclitus, is purely dialectical; genuine Spinozism and Hegelianism are recent derivatives, under the heading of subjective Logic, of a mystical doctrine of intuition. All these systems proceed from a "fragmentation" (*Zergliederung*) of certain general ideas, especially the notions of Being and Becoming, to demonstrate that the Absolute is something absolutely unique and that in this One is unified the whole of the possible and the real. It is called God, whether it be an eternal Reason (*ewige Vernunft*) or the self-cognizant Reason in human nature (p. 185). Giordano Bruno's pantheism occupies a position midway between dialectical and mystical pantheism.

Bouterwek thus has not the faintest suspicion of the radical difference between the pantheism with a cosmological (or, as he calls it, hylozoistic) background and the pantheism of idealist Spinozism; he expressly admits the transition from the idealist pantheism to the hylozoistic, without noticing the profound inversion produced in modern thought by the *cogito* and the act of freedom erected by it. A similar narrowness of perspective is evident in Bouterwek's definition of the notion of *atheism* (pp. 156ff.). Here, too, he distinguishes two sorts of atheism: *skeptical* and *dogmatic*. The first is negative inasmuch as it asserts that it does not have sufficient reasons to admit God; the second is positive or genuine inasmuch as it advances reasons for denying the existence of God. The principle of dogmatic atheism is, according to Bouterwek, the dogmatic concept and notion of *nature;* hence modern French atheism is dubbed by Bouterwek a "system of nature" (an evident allusion to d'Holbach's *Système de la nature,* to which Bouterwek devotes a lengthy and significant note, which begins suggestively enough with the words: "The well-known *Système de la nature* by its very title exercises a power of attraction on the human understanding which sets a high store upon the natural in all things and equates the unnatural with the unreasonable and the fantastic"—note a, p. 241).

Influenced by his fixed idea that atheism is exclusively the result of sense-perception naturalism, according to which matter is eternal and everything proceeds from the forces of matter (*als eine Wirkung von Kräften der Materie*), Bouterwek concludes that atheism with all these premises, is primarily bound up with "sensism" (*Sensualismus*), both in antiquity and in the 18th-century French illuminism when it becomes the "fashionable philosophy". But the central idea of dogmatic atheism is that there is proper to matter a "primordial force" (*Urkraft*), for the idea of such a primordial force is inseparable from the Idea of an Absolute: "The notion of a primordial force, in turn, is inseparable from the idea of the Absolute of which experience teaches us nothing. Thus the atheistic concept of nature is at variance with itself. Though claiming to be founded to the hilt on sense-perception, it yet assimilates features that are wholly alien to sense-perception. It interpolates into nature an entity Absolute and Eternal, an entity of which experience knows nothing; and its reason for this interpolation is to arrive at an explanation of nature within its own confines as this Absolute and Eternal. . . . What impinges upon the senses is not a dynamic totality of things; it is only an infinitely regressing chain of phenomena" (p.170).

In the final analysis, therefore, positive dogmatic atheism is as cogent as the notion of matter on which atheism stands and falls (*mit dem . . . steht und fällt*)—hence, its intrinsically contradictory structure. Bouterwek does not think of God as Absolute, with no concern for his relation as principle to the world and to man; it is therefore not surprising that he can acquit even Spinoza himself of the accusation of atheism (p. 249). Bouterwek seems to feel that the assertion of a free and personal God (pp. 328ff.) can find its best footing in the moral realm.

A vehement and trenchant critique of Bouterwek's stand was made by Krause from the idealist point of view in *Die absolute Religionsphilosophie,* Vol. I, *Prüfung und Würdigung von Fr. Bouterwek's Schrift "Die Religion der Vernunft,"* ed. Leonhardi [Dresden and Leipzig, 1834], especially "Kritik der dritten Abhandlung 'Der Atheismus, der Pantheismus und der Hylozoismus,' " pp. 343ff.). Krause reproaches Bouterwek with having restricted the term "God" to a too limited meaning and of having inflated that of "atheism" by extending it to cover even those who do not admit the one or the other of the properties which Bouterwek himself judges should be attributed to God: "For he admits as being theism, pure and unalloyed, only that doctrine of God that imparts in anthropomorphic and anthropopathic fashion a content to the vacuous idea of the Absolute and, in particular, maintains in consequence of these assumptions that God is an extramundane being and the world an entity separate from God; further, that God is personal in knowing, perceiving and willing, as the living God, as the infinite Providence. The author brands as at least mediately an atheist (initially as a pantheist and therefore a crypto-atheist, since pantheism coincides with atheism in most of its end results) anyone who does not arrive at a recognition of these properties of God in his theologizing or even to a *scientific* contemplation of them; or who defines these properties in a different way, even though such a one be motivated by the intention of preserving himself intact from illegitimate anthropomorphism and anthropopathism; or who maintains that the finite mind is not capable of effecting any definition in respect of these properties of God; and, further, anyone who maintains that there is nothing whatever outside of God and that the world therefore is in God, under God and through God, even though such a one admits God as being a personal being. Therefore, even though a student of philosophy admits God to be the One Infinite Absolute Being, the cause of everything finite, including the spirit and man; even though he accepts and admits all other fundamental attributes of God; even, indeed, though he ascribes to God infinite cognition, should he but ascribe it among other attributes divergent from those approved of by Bouterwek, then the doctrine of such a man is branded by Bouterwek as *atheism* and its author as an *atheist,* an 'a-theologist', a God-denier!" (pp. 346f.).

But this is to behave anti-scientifically and unjustly: it is sheer anarchical arbitrariness so to restrict the notion of theism and to broaden to such an extent the notion of atheism. Krause goes on specifically to contest the legitimacy of a reduction of atheism to sensism-materialism; this will not hold water even in the case of d'Holbach or Helvétius, in both of whom can be found assertions having evident suprasensible content (p. 357, note 2). Krause contends that the crucial point in the God-problem and therefore likewise in the problem of atheism is a different one:

"For the real question which must be answered in order to determine if theism or atheism be well grounded is rather the question as to whether the human mind is empowered or entitled to affirm the existence of a Being, wholly and in every sense infinite, unlimited and absolute, exalted above the awareness of the finite mind and above the finite mind and spirit as such, indeed, above everything finite whatsoever, both the temporally and the eternally finite; or whether, on the contrary, the human mind is empowered or entitled to deny the existence of such a Being; or, finally, whether the human mind must leave this question entirely undecided. The concept of an *extrinsic, external* nature as such and, above all, the assumption as to whether this nature be material or immaterial or both, have no decisive influence on this main question; indeed, this whole notion can and must be entirely ignored in the process of deciding on the main point" (p. 351).

Over against Bouterwek's formula for the solution of the problem of atheism, Krause sets a formula stemming from a drastically ontologistic idealism. Bouterwek had written on this point: "From this critical analysis of the atheist concept of nature it follows (*a priori*) that man cannot find God in nature unless reason has previously found him in the awareness of its own self" (Bouterwek, *Die Religion der Vernunft,* p. 179). Krause retorts: "Say rather: unless it [reason] has found God in himself, in the untrammeled, immediate ontological vision or vision of the Absolute. For *in* and *of* itself, reason would, even if given all eternity, find only itself in its narrow finitude, were it not able, through God who reveals himself to it, to think and cognize God by the subordinate collaborating efficacy of its own finite power of understanding. The knowledge and cognition of God transcends the finite self-knowledge and self-cognition of the finite rational being just as much as it transcends the finite knowledge and cognition which that same finite rational being has of nature which is partially external and extrinsic to the finite rational being itself. Whoever does not know and cognize God in himself is not going to find so much as a trace of God either in himself or in nature" (p. 360f. (On the controversy concerning the knowledge and cognition of the Absolute, cf. pp. 224ff.).

Consequently, claims Krause, Bouterwek's definition of the notions of pantheism and theism emerge as not much more convincing; Bouterwek's accusations are mere windy polemic and have no scientific foundation (p. 367n). Thus it is a case of one contention against another with no way out of the impasse.

The stand taken by W. Vatke can be mentioned as a position calculated to stabilize a position midway between the two extremes (*Religionsphilosophie oder allgemeine philosophische Theologie,* ed. Hermann G. S. Preiss, [Bonn, 1888], Part II, pp. 205 ff.). He makes the distinction between a practical atheism and a theoretical atheism, which latter in turn, Vatke (like Bouterwek) indicates, can be skeptical or dogmatic. The full-blown form of theoretical atheism is to be found in the materialism of Lamettrie and d'Holbach who declare total war on the very idea of God. But atheism can also derive from an idealist system, and Descartes, Spinoza and Leibniz were accused of atheism; Kant denies that God is a personal being, and there are many others in the same line. This is the *Atheismus der Idealität,* to which Goethe also alludes in *Faust.* Vatke goes on to caution that there is a great difference between denying a given formulation of the Absolute and denying the very idea of this Absolute; it is the latter sort of denial which produces the atheist, but such an atheist is but a practical atheist—theoretical atheism as such is not possible: "For it is not possible by thinking to eliminate the Unconditioned, the Absolute; and where this attempt is made notwithstanding, thinking is feeble and does not grasp or understand itself" (p. 207). Not even the slightest notice is taken of the origin of atheism from the principle of immanence!

V. From Skepticism to Atheism (G. Rensi)

The confessed Italian atheist, G. Rensi (1871-1941), provided a notable contribution to a clarification of the semantics of atheism. His work was wholly directed to a denunciation of a wily maneuver of deception and hypocrisy within the then dominant idealist immanentism which under the verbal cloak of a certain spiritualism, was hiding nothing other than a purely materialist and equally atheist conception of the positivism it was combating (cf. his *Realismo* [Milan, 1952], especially pp. 139ff.: "L'autocapovolgimento dell'idealismo," where Rensi shows how Kant and Locke are fundamentally in accord and cites Windelband on his own side; cf. also pp. 225ff.: "La rivendicazione del materialismo dedotta dall'idealismo," a direct attack on the Italian neo-Hegelians, Croce and Gentile).

For his own part, Rensi starts from the *cogito* as well and interprets this *cogito* within the finite limits of "possible experience" (space, time and the categories); he then goes on to identify being with sensible reality: "Being signifies what can be seen, touched, perceived" (*Apologia dell'ateismo* [Rome, 1925], p. 15); God, therefore, is logically indicated to be non-being pp. 37ff.). We, for our part, hold the immanentism of the *cogito* always to be fundamently atheism, and the various labels of materialistic sense-perceptionism, idealist spiritualism, etc., to be a matter of complete indifference. The immanentism of the *cogito* is already atheism at bottom because it gives a human grounding to truth and therefore an anthropological background to the principle of being, i.e., confines that principle within the limits of possible human experience, nature and history.

Rensi's position is exemplary for the consistency with which he manages his own stand of radical atheism. Theism, metaphysics and intolerance are for him synonomous because a metaphysical philosophy posits truth as existent and knowable and immutable in itself. This belief in absolute truth is in reality but a remnant of the primitive mentality proper to savages and children; Rensi cites with approval Guyau's remark: "Intolerance, initially theoretical and later practical, derives from the faith in the absolute under its various forms" (M. Guyau, *L'irréligion de l'avenir* [Paris, 1896], p. 111). Rensi therefore contends that the free man must make it his business "to combat this notion of absolute truth exalted to the status of an ism, to oppose the idea held by barbarians, illiterates and infants concerning the absolute nature of truth, the existence of an absolute truth (which is always *my* truth) which allegedly gives the right to bend others forcibly to think this truth. . . . It is supremely useful to be stubborn in combating the savage idea that absolute truth exists, or, in more rigorous terms (since absolute truth is but a more drastic designation for truth as such), that *the* truth exists" (G. Rensi, Preface to the Italian translation of F. Le Dantec, *L'ateismo* [Milan, 1925], p. 8). Rensi therefore levels the charge of intolerance not only against Catholicism but against Protestantism and Bolshevism itself as well, that Bolshevism "which imposes on all minds a State-dictated opinion" (p. 14); indeed, Rensi finds that Protestantism and Bolshevism are even more drastically in conflict with the modern principle of liberty for claiming to profess it.

Toward the end of his life, Rensi summed up the chief motive of his own atheism as being the shock of seeing that on this earth the just are oppressed and the wicked enjoy happiness and good fortune and that everywhere virtue is despised and vice exalted: Christ himself was abandoned on the cross by the Father. Man must react from the depths of his own mind against this hegemony of evil, must find in himself the divine element (the θεῖον), so as to rescue within himself that which differs in nature from the atoms and the void. Therefore, Rensi poses to himself the question:

"When men like Jesus and Brutus are compelled to submit to such supremely bitter ultimate experiences; when Plato must sadly note the good fortune of wicked and unjust men both in private and public life, the fact that wicked men have grown old and have lived a full life, leaving their children's children in positions of the highest honor, the fact that other men have climbed by just such impiety and godlessness and wickedness from humble beginnings to imperial domination and the highest rungs of the ladder—such facts are calculated to impel to unbelief; when Euripides is forced to the embittered conclusion that any hope in a divine intelligence ruling the world is annihilated by the sight of what happens in the world, and more especially in the world of man; when Cicero must put into the mouth of a character in one of his dialogues the reminder that 'a certain Diogenes the Cynic used to say that Harpalus, who in those days was a lucky and successful robber, was bearing witness against the gods by the very fact of living so long in such good fortune' (*De Nat. Deor.* III, 34); when Seneca is compelled to admit that 'such a successful Sulla was a crime of the gods' (*Ad Marc.*, XII, 6); when men who are deep thinkers and rich in experience of life are obliged to make such statements and admissions; when, in a word, in real life, if not in that represented by Greek tragedy, wicked actions are seen to be honored and paid obsequious homage and their authors to continue to enjoy the durable and thriving prosperity of solid and steady success—what, in such circumstances, is the response that seems to be enjoined upon the Sophoclean, if not this: 'What thing, then, is there going to be to make me pour forth songs of joy?' And so, shattering within me the tenuous gossamer of the rationalist dream, there breaks forth from the innermost roots of my being this statement of my PHILOSOPHICAL TESTAMENTS: *Atoms and Void. . . .*

"But when, on the other hand, I perceive within myself the insurmountable impossibility of acquiescing in this Evil that holds triumphal hegemony in the world, that is prince of the world, even God in that world; when I see that I cannot knuckle under to that Evil despite my clear vision of the advantages I lose by my refusal to do so and the detriments I am going to encounter in this transitory life which yet is all there is; when, despite the loss of the former, alluring as they are, and the impending threat of the latter, harsh and painful as they are, I feel persisting and blazing up within me invincibly this stubborn determination, which from the human and rational point of view can only be described as *folly,* to stand up against this Evil, in total defiance of all my own interests, to stand squarely on the side of the Good; when I surprise within myself this absurdity—this miracle, this divine phenomenon—of the insuperable impossibility of placing myself in the retinue and service of Evil and of repudiating and abjuring the Good; when I find myself forced to act thus without any pragmatic reason whatever, indeed in defiance of every such pragmatic reason at least so far as I can determine; when I thus sense as present within me, in a guise considerably more intimate and vivifying and inspiring than in many, the God in whom they believe and whom they revere or whom they venerate with mere outward show and perfunctory homage, this upward thrust and impulse (*élan vital*) of the eternal Will to the True and the Good . . . then it is apparent to me that, in addition to the atoms and the void outside, in addition to the Platonic *materia* of the *Timaeus,* there is within a certain something uncorrelated with them and differing from them in nature and origin; then I feel rising within me a belief, if not in θεός [God] then at least in the θεῖον [divine], and consequently I expand and complete thus the title of my PHILOSOPHICAL TESTAMENT: *Atoms and Void and the Divine in Me.*" (Cf. the *Testamento filosofico,* related by E. Buonaiuti, *Giuseppe Rensi, Lo scettico credente* [Rome, 1944], pp. 221–234).

PART I

CONTROVERSIES SURROUNDING THE ATHEISM OF RATIONALISM

1

Ontological Apriorism and Atheism of the Cartesian *Cogito*

The philosophical thought of Descartes is the real starting point of the adventure of modern thought which owes its origin to this Cartesian thinking rather than to the systems of Telesio or Bruno or Campanella. Before Descartes, there were only hints, only the ferment of elements and free radicals. This seething mass was waiting for the interpreter who could penetrate to its nucleus, grasp its radical novelty and consistently structure all man's problems starting from man himself, seizing the yawning gulf of man's freedom and filling it with satisfying meaning for man.

Modern thought is in essence simply the progress of the claim to that radical freedom pinpointed by Descartes as that open-ended ability of man to make and unmake the first step of the pilgrimage of truth. As it forces the immanentist principle to its logical conclusion which is its disintegration, this radical libertarian tendency will gradually reveal itself as responsible for that positive and constructive atheism which is typical of modern philosophy. This modern philosophy can appropriately be called "the philosophy of freedom, considering freedom an ultimate and therefore a viable first principle". Such a philosophy, therefore, has neither need nor use for God as principle or foundation; hence, it is atheist. Nor is it any accident that Descartes proposes his own philosophical system, founded on the *cogito* principle, precisely as a counterweight to those very atheists (Averroists, Pomponazzians, Macchiavellians, free-livers and their like) [1] who had been infiltrating everywhere.

[1] Exhaustive studies of these great upheavals in modern thought have been made by R. Pintard in his *Le Libertinage érudit dans la première moitié du XVIIe siècle* (Paris, 1943) and especially by H. Busson in his *Le Rationalisme dans la littérature française de la Renaissance* (Paris, 1957 [2]), cf. especially Book VII, c. 17: "Athées et Déistes," pp. 516ff. Busson's work gives a striking picture of the cultural and spiritual substrate of 16th-century culture (from 1533 to 1601), a meeting point of the restless Reformation spirit, all manner of critiques of religion and Christianity, the humanist inclination to the skepticism and atheism of antiq-

To the fashionable atheism then rampant in high society and among the intelligentsia, Descartes opposes his radical doubt as a voluntary option; the sovereign intellect is dethroned and the monarchy of the will is established as the quintessence of subjectivism, hewing the royal road of ontological truth out of the very fabric of the human subject and confining it entirely to the realm of the self. Cartesian immanentism concentrated itself in man's most intimate and all-embracing act, that of willing; it was therefore bound to close to man all avenues of escape from the long straight road leading down to d'Holbach, Feuerbach, Nietzsche and Sartre. Atheism was going to be nothing more than thoroughgoing immanentism, consequential immanentism, which is a theory of the will radically aware of its own inescapable internal logic.

The paradox of modern thought in its ascendant phase and in the period of its greatest splendor, stretching from Descartes to Hegel, is the evermore insistent accusations of atheism leveled against its major representatives, despite the explicit intent of these representatives to make the Absolute the principle and center of philosophizing in the demonstration of the existence of God and of his attributes. Their adversaries recognize and admit the explicit "theological intent" of such philosophies, but they do not agree that the God at whom these philosophies arrive emerges as sufficiently well founded, i.e., as a God to whom is guaranteed all his fundamental attributes, not only the attribute of Absolute, but also those of personality and freedom. The objections usually come from the theologians, for whom the concept of God obviously cannot be left in suspension or limited to functions of a gnoseological foundation, but must rather be posited as creator of the world and Father of men. Does the new concept of God that begins with Cartesian speculation satisfy these conditions?

The sweeping contention that it does not is advanced in an attack on the entire trend of French neo-Augustinianism by an eminent historian of the councils, G. Hardouin, who sees in the manifold Augustinian attempts at *a priori* proofs of the existence of God nothing but a trick to mask their own atheism. In fact Hardouin's extensive work bears the title *Athei detecti* [1a] (Atheists Unmasked), a title quite suggestive in

---

uity, and the persistent, pervasive and versatile Averroism that had spread from Padua to France where it found the most motley group of allies in all social circles. Suffice it to recall, among the most outstanding, such skeptics as Rabelais, Montaigne, Bodin and their like. So it is no accident that the first protagonist of the controversy surrounding modern atheism should be the out-and-out Cartesian Bayle or that the first philosopher of modern times to be specifically labeled an atheist should be Spinoza, the most famous of all the Cartesians.

[1a] Included in *Opera varia.* Folio edition bears the inscription: Amstelodami, Apud Henricum du Sauzet, et Hagae Comitum, apud Petrum de Hondt, M. DCC. XXXIII. The volume of the *Opera varia* was put on the Index, because it was

itself. The argument of indictment is presented forthwith in the brief Preface: What these men are touting as God is not the God of believers but simply Being, the Being of every being, the Essence of every essence, universal Truth, universal Goodness, the intelligible Form of every truth, goodness, unity and the like.[2] Some of those writers (Hardouin is alluding specially to Descartes) have thought to collect these diverse attributes under a single term, the Infinite or the infinitely perfect Being (*Ens infinite perfectum*).[3] If, in fact, urges Hardouin, God were reducible merely to this sort of Infinite, then there would be no possibility of atheism; everyone, modern and ancient alike, would have admitted God, there would never have been any atheists, and it would have been entirely pointless and out of place to write against atheism.[4]

The crowded ranks of the accused can be divided, we feel, into two groups: (1) Augustinians in the strict sense, including C. Jansen, Ambrosius Victor, P. Quesnel, L. Thomassin and P. Nicolle (the first named is the famous author of the *Augustinus*); (2) Descartes and the

---

"published arbitrarily and without those corrections which the author had made to it" (cf. *Enc. Catt.* VI, 1362). The "Atheists Unmasked" include Cornelius Jansen, Ambrosius Victor (André Martin), Louis Thomassin, François Malebranche, P. Quesnel, P. Nicolle, Blaise Pascal, René Descartes, Antoine Le Grand and S. Regis.

2 "For what, when all is said and done, are they touting as God? Simply Being, the Being of all being, that Being which excludes no genus of being, and thus infinite or indefinite and indeterminate Being; Essence in general, the Essence of all essences; universal Truth or Truth in general; universal Goodness or the Good in general, indefinite indeterminate, the Good of every good; Beauty in general, or the Beauty of everything beautiful, whether bodily or spiritual; the intelligible Form of unity and reality, wherein agree all things that are; the intelligible Form of the true, the good, the beautiful, the upright and virtuous, according to which both all things are formally true and good and beautiful and upright and virtuous and we judge and pronounce concerning the truth, goodness, beauty, uprightness and virtue of singular essences and natures; and therefore the universal Reason is called by them by other names as well. For when they discourse concerning God, they consider the object of such discourse sometimes as Reality, sometimes as sheer and simple Being, sometimes as the True, as the Good, as the Beautiful, as the Virtuous in general, as the Essence of all essences and truths, as that which is fitting, or that which must be" (Hardouin, *op. cit.* Praefatio, fol. 2a).

3 "And so those men teach that not one name only but many names are proper to God. Although when the discussion revolves around the existence of God, inasmuch as it is desirable to establish first what is that entity concerning which the question is being asked as to whether it exists, so that there is the necessity of assigning one subject of the question, here some of them have esteemed that one name ought to be used which would embrace all these notions, *viz.*, the *Infinite* or the *Infinitely Perfect Being*" (*ibid.*).

4 "But if this is to be taken as being God, what African or American native is there at this present time, who was there ever in the past or who will there be ever in the future, who would not know the true God and often love him? To what purpose would we take up the pen against the atheists, since there are none such nor can there be, if this is God or if there is no God but this?" (*ibid.*).

Cartesians A. Le Grand and S. Regis. Malebranche is founder and in a certain sense intermediary between the two groups.

The charge against the representatives of the first group is almost always leveled in the same terms that we have already heard: they have reduced God to universal Truth, impersonal and immanent in finite minds.[5] Against the Augustinians, Hardouin takes vigorous exception to the notion that God can be reduced to purely abstract perfection, and he concludes adamantly: "But Catholics deny altogether that beauty or the intelligible form of beauty is God; to profess the contrary, they say, is to be of the atheist party. Then deny that God is loved in this life because he is beautiful; they say this God ought to be loved, not as the good in general, but only because he is good." [6] The weak point, in this conception, which reduces God to the fullness of those universal perfections, lies in the fact that such a God cannot be conceived as a living "person" except metaphorically: "And the Catholics are certainly not afraid of anyone objecting to them that they do not see the God whose existence they prove in their writings to be a living entity according to his substance. The only ones to fear this are those for whom the entity they designate as God is one to which properly pertains nothing more than a metaphorical life, a metaphorical nature or substance and a metaphorical subsistence. Among this class of atheists belong those to whom God is but the truth of things, by which whatever is true and beautiful is formally so." [7]

[5] On Jansen, Hardouin writes: "He holds God to be nothing other than Truth, the Truth which he sees shining forth in every mind; which he consults and hears replying to him when he considers within himself what is to be said about anything; which everyone follows when judging truly and rightly about anything; according to which each one is compelled to pronounce a judgment concerning everything, which acts as a rule of judging if someone asks a decision, verdict, judgment or opinion of him. . . . Universal Reason, the intelligible order, wisdom universal and eternal: not otherwise, I say, does the Bishop of Ypres hold God to be" (*ibid.*, fol. 1). There follows an exhaustive exposition of texts of the *Augustinus,* and Hardouin concludes: "From the writings of Jansen we have now cited sufficiently: whoever does not see atheism in these texts, we do not scruple to assert that such a one is blind and dull of mind" (fol. 6). The Oratorian Ambrosius Victor is accused of atheism in virtually the same terms (fol. 6-10).

[6] *Ibid.,* fol. 7 (Hardouin is treating of A. Victor who wrote a *Philosophia Christiana* in 56 chapters, each one of which is briefly summed up).

[7] *Ibid.,* fol. 8b. This is the line of argument which recurs constantly and which Hardouin protests he has gathered from the works of these famous authors: "On occasion, when I am expounding to my friends this impious opinion and saying that, in the opinion of Jansen, Thomassin and their like, God is nothing other than the Truth which shines before the mind so that a sound judgment can be made concerning anything, these friends object that such a Truth is not a living and subsisting entity and thus cannot be God. But, mark it well, Jansen himself, Thomassin and other like-minded men go contrary to this as-

The error becomes more evident still in the extensive theological output of the famous Oratorian L. Thomassin, whose whole work is based, according to Hardouin, on the pernicious doctrine "which removes from the world the true God and substitutes in his place the unity and truth of things, the One, Being, the Good as such, the indeterminate and the absolute". From this substitution likewise derives the basic error on grace: "Whence that teaching of Chapters XIIIff., to the effect that men sin only because they have been forsaken by God: a contention which follows necessarily from the fact that God is simply τὸ ὄν (Being). For wherever there is anything in the way of a good, there likewise must be a certain something coming from Being; and this something, they say, is simply this, that man is aided by supremely invincible, omnipotent and irresistible grace. For whatever is, cannot not be, so long as it is. Whence it follows in turn that this something must necessarily be lacking when the good is lacking to man; this means that in such a situation man is forsaken by Being and the Good and the True, and thus by God (as they would have it), so that a man so forsaken cannot but fail and sin. This is the origin and root of the five propositions of Jansen." [8]

It can be seen how the controversy is broadening out and invading the whole field of theology: the polemical thrust is bursting all bounds and overflowing almost obsessively, without the faintest suspicion that the reviled opponents were aiming at just the same end result, that of erecting a dam against the profligate free-thinker philosophers. Nor is any consideration being given to the fact that these writers are expressing a type of spirituality active under the eyes of all and with the approval of authority, which latter indeed is virtually accused of direct connivance: "Is this Truth, this ontological and epistemological Necessity existing in things themselves, is this, I say, God? This is what the French, this is what the Calvinists, are writing openly with no one gainsaying them?" [9]

Hardouin alleges, for instance, that it is certain that Thomassin

---

sertion, for they are of the opinion that it can be opposed by Catholics. And so I tell my friends that this very thing is what Jansen, Thomassin, Ambrosius Victor, Malebranche and others teach, and that I have not been making any false accusation against them" (fol. 11a). The common source is considered to be M. Ficino in his *Theologia Platonica* (cited are lib. II, c. 3; lib. VII, c. 7); Ficino is called αθεος (atheist) outright and ranged with Vanini (fol. 11b-12ab).

[8] *Ibid.*, fol. 14a. Thomassin is considered one of the founders of positive theology with his basic capital work on the *Dogmata theologica* (Paris, 1680ff).

[9] Hardouin, *op. cit.*, fol. 20b. Later on (fol. 26) we read an explicit charge of Arianism, based on the fact that the Father is called *Unitas* and the Son *Veritas* (*Patris*). Hardouin examines here the other work of Thomassin: *La Méthode d'étudier et d'enseigner Chrétiennement et solidement la Philosophie* . . . (Paris, 1685).

"teaches, at length and in detail, that the existence of God is the first principle of all reasoning, inborn in children from the outset . . . without which no reasoning whatsoever can be effected nor any certain cognition can be had. . . . For God himself is the law of reasoning and vice versa".[10] But Hardouin does not penetrate to the cardinal principle involved here nor does he even pose the problem of that principle, contenting himself with a perpetual repetition of the charge.

The indictment against Malebranche is the most detailed and deep-cutting, as also the broadest and most biting: "He indeed advanced the impious hypothesis most openly of all and most boldly did proclaim it in public, defending it and polishing it with the elegance of his French language." There follows the indictment that also sums up in the various phases the method of operation of the preceding authors, a method that is alleged to have attained a more explicitly radical stage in Malebranche himself: "For him there is, in place of God, Being or the True as such, Being or the True without any end or limit, from which and through which is truly whatever is in the nature of things, and which is in that Being the indeterminate Good (the good, the fulcrum, the right), the rightness of beings, the order of things, the order of immutable wisdom, the wisdom whereby each single thing is what it ought to be, the laws of which wisdom he likewise calls immutable and supremely simple. Such are the laws of motion and of the mechanical arts, the Eternal Law, the necessity of existing thus and not otherwise, and simultaneously the Truth because it is the universal form of all that is true and right in all entities that are or could be; therefore, the Reason of men and Angels, as many as are endowed with minds, compels them to make a right judgment concerning anything whatsoever—this should be thus, that should not. Whence it is also called and is the Light of souls, according to which we judge concerning things physical, geometrical, ethical and others. Therefore, for the same reason the Word of God is also rightly called both universal Reason and our Master. And so he boasts of himself seeing all things in the Word of God and in God, even though he knows that this furnished the occasion for the bandying about of this doggerel against him and its singing by the common people themselves:

[10] Hardouin, *op cit.*, fol. 20f. F. Bouiller brought out in detail the especially favorable reception accorded Descartes in the Oratory of France by Bérulle himself (F. Bouiller, *Historie de la philosophie cartésienne,* Vol. I [Paris-Lyon, 1854], pp. 412ff.). It is curious that the most famous apologist of the 18th century, the responsible Dominican Valsecchi, should have come out in defense of the philosophers charged with atheism by the capricious Jesuit; Valsecchi expresses his regret that the gifted accuser "in the famous Treatise *Athei detecti*" should have "displayed as atheists excellent writers certainly deserving of no incrimination less than that of atheism" (A. Valsecchi, O.P., *De fundamentis religionis et fontibus impietatis* [Venice, 1770 [2]], p. 144b.).

'He who sees all things in God
Does not see himself's a clod.' "[11]

Beginning with the main work, the *Recherche de la vérité,* Hardouin reviews all Malebranche's works with a stubborn punctiliousness not at all difficult to achieve with a line of thought so exposed to criticism as the Malebranchian ontologism, in order to gather his own contentions and the material for his own charges against Malebranche.[12] Malebranche's position is not basically far removed from that of Thomassin, which consists in conceiving God as the universal, indeterminate Good —the usual Trojan horse whereby to smuggle in atheism: "The indeterminate Good is merely the God of the atheists; and while they preach him so loudly and strongly, they are bearing in atheism and putting it forth artfully and covertly."[13]

The indictment continues with a demonstration of how such an indeterminate Being and Good must therefore be the first object of the intelligence and the will. The first and apodictic proof of the existence of God is that based on the idea of the Infinite, because for Malebranche and for this whole Cartesian-Augustinian school the *Ens indeterminatum* (indeterminate Being) coincides with God: "For indisputably what the mind knows, as they keep saying throughout, is certainly being which is that unlimited and infinite Good and True that is contained in Being, and the mind does not make being true and good, for the universal True and Good combines within itself whatsoever is true and good or can be. Therefore it is infinite. Therefore likewise it is uncreated. For what is unlimited and infinite cannot be created. Therefore the being which every created mind necessarily knows and cognizes, to which it is conjoined from the outset, the idea of which is innate within every created mind, from which no mind can disjoin itself, is God himself. Nor can there be any finer demonstration of the existence of God than this which is taken from the idea of unlimited and indeterminate and therefore infinite and infinitely perfect Being . . . this demonstration in which nothing is presented as being God, save only τὸ ὄν (being), i.e., the formal being or the formal truth of all beings, whereby the thinking and knowing mind itself is molded so that it will rightly be and rightly think. Moreover, what atheist would not embrace this God of his own accord?"[14]

[11] Hardouin, *op. cit.,* fol. 43a. Since he had located the "principle of atheism" (of the new Augustinian spiritualism) in the notion of God as *"Ens, Verum, Bonum . . . absolutum, indeterminatum"* and in the preference for the ontological argument for the existence of God, Hardouin felt justified in presenting his exposition of Malebranche before that of Descartes.

[12] Cf. *ibid.,* fol. 45a, 45b, 50a, 54a, 55a, 57a, 60b, 67a, 71b, 72b, 79a, 90b, and *passim.*

[13] *Ibid.,* fol. 43b-44a. There is here a hint, although a vague one, of what Malebranche may have owed to Descartes.

[14] *Ibid.,* fol. 44a. A little later on Malebranche is called "Atheologus" (fol. 45b).

To this argument, proposed in various forms by Anselm, Descartes, Leibniz, Hegel, *et al.* down to and including K. Barth, Hardouin opposes a tortuous and virtually *a posteriori* argument: "Necessary existence is contained in the idea of an infinitely perfect Being. This proposition is to be distinguished thus: in the idea of an infinitely perfect Being really distinct from the universe and extrinsic cause of that universe (an idea, incidentally, which is far from clear but is nonetheless certainly true, as is evident from elsewhere), *concedo;* in the idea of a perfect Being not really distinct from the universe and cause of it not properly in the order of efficient causality but rather merely as a kind of exemplar of things, even possible things, in the mind, and their true and necessary mode, while being outside the mind the formal being of all beings, *subdistinguo:* in such an idea is contained absolutely necessary existence, *nego;* in such an idea is contained existence necessary on the hypothesis of a world already created by God, again *subdistinguo:* and that idea is not the idea of the true Spirit but only of the true or of Truth (*du Vrai*) *concedo;* and that idea is the idea of the true God, *nego.* But it is merely Being of this first kind of idea of which Malebranche contends to be innate to us; he is joined in this contention by others whose words we present in this study." [15]

The crux of Malebranche's whole method is the doctrine of *divine illumination,* understood as a "seeing" in God, in the divine wisdom which is the Word of God, which "would shine directly upon my mind" as we have seen already in Thomassin.[16] It is from this erroneous confusion at the outset between *Ens* (Being), *Bonum* (the Good), *Verum* (the True) *indeterminatum* (in the indeterminate sense) and God that there derive the other grave theological errors on sin, grace and redemption.[17] All of this is borne out and confirmed, contends Hardouin, in a work of Malebranche himself, wherein a Christian philosopher and a Chinese philosopher are represented as conversing together about the problem of God.[18] This work, claims Hardouin, shows clearly that Malebranche is really in accord with the atheism admitted

[15] *Ibid.,* fol. 47a. Here the difference between Descartes and Malebranche is taken to be simply verbal (*verbo tenus*) (fol. 48b). On the idea of the perfect Being, cf. also fol. 74a.

[16] *Ibid.,* fol. 49a. On the derivation of this doctrine from St. Augustine, cf. fol. 50b.

[17] This is expounded in the examination of the other works of Malebranche, especially *De la nature et de la grâce,* fol. 56bff., *Méditations Chrétiennes,* fol. 64bff. Other excerpts from the *Traité de la Nature et de la Grâce* are given and commented upon earlier: fol. 87a-104b, where Hardouin is dealing directly with the controversies on grace.

[18] Published in 1704 ("hoc anno!" ["this very year!"]) under the title *Entretien d'un Philosophe Chrétien et d'un Philosophe Chinois sur l'Existence et la Nature de Dieu,* by the author of the *Recherche de la Vérité.*

by the scholars of China, despite a few slight shades of difference: the *Li* of the Chinese scholars, which is simultaneously reason and nature, matter and spirit, from which all things derive, is the very *ens indeterminatum* of Malebranche. But while they can be pardoned, Malebranche cannot, "for if they be atheists, is he not surely a Christian?" [19]

Hardouin's charge and indictment thus seems to be based on the following principles or criteria:

1. God, in order to be God, must be distinct from the world and thus is going to be conceived as extrinsic efficient cause and not as the perfect Infinite in the sense of a mere formal cause.
2. God, in order to be God, must be free in his creative activity and not compelled to it by any necessity.
3. God, in order to be God, must be able to move individual creatures and in particular to move individual human beings by his grace; he must not unfold his own causality in a universal, generic or undifferentiated fashion.

Even abstracting from the polemical thrust here in evidence,[20] we cannot but point up the vigor of this effort to save the transcendence of God and the status (dignity and responsibility) of the individual which begin to fracture and disintegrate at the very first stage of modern thought and which, after the all-out effort of Leibniz to erect the monad as a bastion against pantheism, will corrode at a very deep level the whole development of the principle of immanence.

The second constellation of atheists, after the Jansenist one to which belong the authors mentioned above, is the Cartesian school. Hardouin actually considers *Descartes'* thought solely from the metaphysical point of view, i.e., the point of view of his notion and way of conceiving God, and he surreptitiously passes over the problem of the method, the principle of the *cogito,* which inaugurates modern thought. On the problem of God, Hardouin tells us, Descartes' position coincides entirely with the position of the preceding authors: "The principle of the Cartesian philosophy is none other than this: he assigns to the place of God the same thing that we have seen assigned by those whom we have already sum-

[19] Hardouin, *op. cit.,* fol. 79a. At fol. 84bff. begins the exposition of a work by a certain Lelevel (*De la vraie et fausse métaphysique*), intended to defend Malebranche against the attacks of the Cartesian Regis. Both the exposition of P. Quesnel (fol. 104a-159b) and that of P. Nicolle (fol. 162a-200b) are concerned with predominantly theological problems and errors that Hardouin sees as being intimately bound up with the basic philosophical error.

[20] This was also stressed, as might be expected, by Voltaire: "The Jesuit Hardouin, more learned than Garasse and no less rash, accuses the Descartes, the Arnaulds, the Pascals, the Nicoles, the Malebranches, of atheism in his book entitled *Athei detecti;* fortunately they did not meet with the fate of Vanini" (*Dictionnaire philosophique,* ed. J. Benda and R. Naves [Paris: Garnier, 1954], p. 40).

moned before our tribunal: Being as such, τὸ ὄν, unlimited Being, Being, Thing, Entity, Perfection in general—and therefore infinite Being with no definite name proper to it, whence also it is called by some the Unnameable, almost what the French call *Chose.* Thus this philosophy is rightly designated by the more expert among Catholics as the philosophy of the atheists." [21] Hardouin considers first the arguments used in the demonstration of the existence of God (§ 1) and then the considerations of the essence and the attributes of God (§ 2), following the *Meditationes Metaphysicae* of 1641.

In the opening paragraph, Hardouin touches in passing on the problem of doubt, but without giving this point any prominence; he does not consider this "doubt" the real starting point of Descartes, nor does he pay any real attention to what has been called, in the wake of Gassendi's objections, the "Cartesian vicious circle". Gassendi's point was: "It is a circular argument to prove that God exists and is truthful because the notion of him is clear and distinct, and that the notion of God is clear and distinct because God exists and is truthful. The method which was to satisfy all desires still leaves much to be desired!" [22] Hardouin, on the contrary, concentrates the Cartesian criterion of truth solely on the "ontological way": "[Descartes] himself professes that all his ideas, however clear and distinct, would be doubtful and recondite, were they not illuminated by his proof of the existence of God." And Hardouin explains: "This is the capital dogma of Descartes: When the mind has a clear idea of anything, it sees this idea . . . and thus it can affirm or deny. For whoever sees anything this way is seeing in God, than which vision none can be more certain." [23]

The first Cartesian proof of the existence of God is the one taken from the *idea of the infinite,* which Hardouin summarizes in special detail: "This is the summary of the third meditation in which he proves God's existence. Nothing can be in an effect that was not formerly in an efficient and total cause. But the idea or perception of the Infinite, i.e.,

[21] Hardouin, *op. cit.,* C. IX, fol. 200a. No one has ever raised any doubts about the personal sentiments of Descartes as a practicing Catholic. Baillet, his biographer, asserts that Descartes convinced many atheists and became most enthusiastic when speaking of God (cf. J. Orcibal, "Descartes et sa philosophie jugés à l'Hôtel Liancourt," in *Descartes et le Cartésianisme hollandais* [Paris, 1950], p. 101). We have mentioned above that Descartes undertook his work on the *cogito* precisely for the purpose of overcoming unbelief and atheism. On the floodtide spread of skepticism and atheism, as a result of humanism, and on its diffusion in France and especially in Paris (where Mersenne reckoned there to be a good 50,000 atheists!), cf. Bouiller, *op. cit.,* Vol. I, pp. 27ff.

[22] Descartes, *Meditationes de Prima Philosophia,* ed. Adam-Tannery, Vol. VII, In Med. V, Dub. IV, Instantia 2 (Paris, 1909), p. 405. Cf. O. Hamelin, *Le Système de Descartes,* (Paris, 1921 [2]), pp. 139ff. Hardouin is familiar with the objections and cites earlier Descartes' replies, but I have not seen him citing those of Gassendi.

[23] *Athei detecti,* c. IX, fol. 200b-201a.

of perfect Being as such, or of sheer Perfection considered as such rather than as it is this or that perfection, considered as it is Perfection and Being in general, is the idea or perception of an infinite reality; it is actual. Therefore the object of that idea or perception, since that object is the efficient cause of this idea, is an infinite and actual reality. Therefore God exists in act. For that which is infinite and exists in act is God."

Descartes is convinced he can legitimately conclude to the existence of God from the idea of God, because the idea that I have of God is not an idea like other ideas; it is not a contingent idea of contingent things, but rather a necessary Idea of the necessary Being and must therefore be admitted to be able to be produced only by necessary Being, for it certainly cannot come from nothingness which is not, nor yet from us who are contingent. But Hardouin retorts that the God of Descartes as such is not God but rather a pure formality: *Perfection* is general and a *mere metaphysical entity,* whereas God is conceived as *He Who Is* and such a *He Who Is exceedingly and uniquely* can then be designated as a cause: *"This is that altogether perfect entity and this made that which is, of what kind soever."* And the idea of God as Infinite Being, that idea which Descartes so exalts, says nothing more than the idea of *Being in general, the True in general,* etc. And it is the idea of the non-finite rather than the idea of the positively Infinite which is the product of reflection (*idea factitia* = idea-making), and it is stupid and impious to call God the object of such an idea: "For the God concerning whom the serious question is being asked as to whether he exists is a singular intellect-possessing Spirit, and incommunicable; of such a God there is no trace or but a tenuous one in the Cartesian demonstration." [24] And the other arguments adduced by Descartes here prove just as little.

Let us now point up the most important observations. Descartes also introduces the argument from the impossibility of an "infinite regress": if we wish to find a basis for the truth of ideas, we cannot go on *ad infinitum* passing from one idea to another; rather we must reach a First Idea which contains them all: "Although one idea may perhaps be born out of another, there is no such thing here as an infinite regress; rather, in the end, we must arrive at SOME FIRST IDEA, whose cause is like an archetype, in which all the reality is contained formally which is in the idea only objectively." [25] Hardouin replies that the infinite regress can be avoided by arriving simply at the idea of *Being in general, Reality in the universal sense,* which is the first idea in the formal ambit.

[24] *Ibid.*, fol. 201ab. There follows an extensive documentation of texts from the original Latin of the *Meditationes* III, IV and V.

[25] Descartes, *Meditat. de prima philos.*, Medit. III, p. 42 (cf. *Athei detecti*, fol. 201b).

When Descartes goes on to claim that the idea of God is included in the nature of structure of the other ideas, he is making a meaningless assertion: "As far as the ideas manifesting other men or animals or angels are concerned, I easily understand that the ideas of both corporeal things and of God can be compounded out of the ideas that I have of myself, even though there were no men except myself and no animals or angels in the world." [26]

This is a supremely false assertion, observes Hardouin: only the man who is reducing the idea of God to that of indeterminate *Being* can make such an assertion, inasmuch as it is clear that every particular idea points back to the most general idea of *Being*. The whole method of procedure in the third Meditation is wrong, with its assumption that the existence of God can be demonstrated from the objective being of the *idea,* from its mere presence in the mind and from the perfections that are signified in it; for all of this, and any like method of procedure, can be explained away via the idea of *Being* "which the mind abstracts from the idea or the sensation of its own being and of that of other beings like to itself, whether these exist or not". [27] Hardouin's critique is therefore categorical: all the attributes that Descartes ascribes to the objective being of the idea come down to aspects of the idea of *Being* rather than of the idea of God; and so from the objective being of the idea, the existence of God as transcendent and personal principle is not in fact proven.

No more apt is the argument of the fourth Meditation in which Descartes starts from the awareness of his own imperfection as doubter and goes on to the clear and distinct idea of the most perfect Being: "When I watch myself doubting, i.e., being an incomplete and dependent thing or entity, then does there occur to me the clear and distinct idea of an independent and complete Being, i.e., God. And from the mere fact that such an idea is in me, or that I having that idea exist, thus palpably do I conclude that *God* too *exists* and that my existence depends on him in each several moment, so that I am confident that nothing can be known by human wit more evidently or more certainly." [28]

True enough, that last part, saying that I am aware of my own imperfection, signifies that I perceive, at least confusedly, that some perfection is lacking to me that I desire to have. But from this it does not follow that such a perfection is God, unless God is *Being* as formal principle of my being: "But this God is the God of the atheists." [29]

Nor is Meditation V in any better prospect with its development of

[26] *Ibid.*, p. 43.
[27] Hardouin, *op. cit.*, fol. 202b.
[28] Descartes, *Meditat. de prima philos.*, Med. IV, p. 53.
[29] Hardouin, *op. cit.*, fol. 203a.

the argument from the truths of geometry and mathematics: "And although they are thought by me in some sense arbitrarily, yet they are not entirely fabricated by me; rather, they have their own true and immutable natures, as, for example, when I imagine a triangle; even though such a figure perhaps does not exist anywhere in the whole wide world outside of my knowing, nor ever will exist, yet it is an entity having a really determined nature or essence or an immutable and eternal form, which has not been produced by me and does not depend on my mind." [30]

This is likewise a sophism, claims Hardouin, and quite similar to the preceding ones: there is always this shift from the idea of the perfection of the idea to the proclamation of the actual existence of a principle located in another order, i.e., in the existential order: "The more expert theologians say, and metaphysical reasoning itself teaches, that existence is in no way contained in the idea [of God] but only the understanding that, if the object of the idea does exist, it is but fitting that it exist from iself (*a se*). These two points are mightily different. For existing from oneself is clearly a divine perfection." [31] The order of the truths of mathematics abstracts, as such, from existence; their properties are purely formal.

But the argument to which Descartes seems to have attributed the greatest cogency is the one presented last, and actually it is simply one more variation of the ontological-formal argument—the argument from the transition from the necessity of the idea (as possibility) to the

[30] Descartes, *Meditat. de prima philos.*, Medit. V, p. 64. In the *Secundae responsiones,* Descartes specifies: "That the atheist can clearly know the three angles of a triangle to be equal to two right angles, however, I do not deny; it is just that I assert that this cognition and knowledge of his is not true scientific knowledge; for no knowledge which can be rendered doubtful seems fit to be called scientific" (p. 141). In fact, Descartes has recourse rather to the veracity of God than to the *cogito* in order to dispel the doubt.

[31] Hardouin, *op. cit.*, fol. 204a. As far as the concept of *existentia* (existence) is concerned, Hardouin writes: *"Existence,* however, as the metaphysicians teach, *is not a perfection, but rather the mode of the individual perfections" (ibid.).* This is the formalistic notion of "existence" as the simple extrinsic "fact", as the *"positio rei extra causas"* (positing of a thing outside of its causes) and can therefore be called, as Hardouin calls it, a "mode" of the essence to which is then opposed the "state" in the mode or order of potency. This way of looking at things derives in the Latin world from Arabic Scholasticism and more precisely from Avicenna and is bound up with the controversies on the distinction between the *esse essentiae* and the *esse existentiae* (the being of essence and the being of existence) made by the anti-Thomistic schools (Henry of Ghent, Nominalism, Fonseca, Suarez, Arriaga *et al.*). To the approach which makes existence extrinsic, St. Thomas opposes the approach which holds the *esse* (being) or *actus essendi* (act of being) to be an intrinsic principle of being, a proportionate participation of the pure Act which is God (*Esse ipsum*) and therefore act of every act and perfection of every perfection" (cf. C. Fabro, *La nozione mestafisica di partecipazione secondo S. Tommaso d'Aquino* [Turin,[3] 1963], pp. 191ff.).

reality of fact. In the reply to the first objections, we read: "We cannot think his existence to be possible, without simultaneously recognizing and admitting, in the wake of our attention to his immense power, that he can exist *by his own power,* and CONSEQUENTLY does in fact exist and has existed from all eternity. For it is perfectly well known to the light of natural reason that what can exist by its own power always exists." [32] But the idea of God is not innate; rather it has been formed "either discursively out of a consideration of this universe, just as we at least surmise that any author of any outstanding work will himself be eminent, or by tradition and parental training and education acquired from teachers."

Nor is the idea of God supremely simple; rather it is the end product of a synthesis of the many infinite perfections forming our notion of God. But in the context of the Cartesian method, it is more proper to speak always of the "idea of Being or universal Perfection abstracted by the reasoning mind out of beings of every kind" rather than of the idea or concept of God; this idea of Being or universal Perfection is not "the idea of God . . . but rather the idea of supremely universal Being which cannot exist at all outside of created things themselves, with which the idea itself is identified". And even this "idea of Being" is not actually innate, insists Hardouin; it rather derives from experience.[33]

The fact of the matter is, says Hardouin in concluding his indictment, that Descartes like Vanini is falling upon the atheists only in order to cover up his own atheism, as Voetius has rightly observed.[34] The arguments of the Cartesians Antoine Le Grand and S. Regis are nothing but a rehash of the errors of Descartes.

Examination of the Cartesian teaching on the divine essence and attributes affords Hardouin the opportunity to repeat and strengthen his unfavorable verdicts which we have already heard in his treatment of Descartes' proofs of the existence of God: the whole teaching comes down to an admission of God as "Something, Thing and Being, Essence of essences" rather than as *Someone* i.e., a *substance or person* with an intellect of his own. Further, God is held to be present in things only by

[32] Descartes, *Meditat. de Prima Philos.,* Ad primas Ob. p. 119. Also in the reply to the Second Objections where Descartes is explaining in what sense the idea of God is "innate" in us: "For I myself have expressly said . . . that this idea is innate to me, i.e., that it reaches me not otherwise than from myself. I further concede that this idea could be formed even though we did not know that a Supreme Being existed, but not if in fact such a Being were not to exist. For on the contrary I pointed out that the whole force of the argument lies in the fact that it is impossible that the capacity for forming that idea should be in me, *unless I were created by God*" (*ibid.,* p. 133).

[33] Hardouin, *op. cit.,* fol. 205ab.

[34] *Ibid.,* fol. 207. The same charge was made by P. Petit and is noted by the Cartesian J. Amerpoël.

his power, not by his essence; there is absolute likeness and coexistence of will and intellect in God, according to the statement made to P. Mersenne: *"In God, willing and knowing is the same."* [35] Hence derive the assertions that essences depend on God's will, that the world has been created *ab aeterno* (from all eternity), and all the many other errors that are repeated in the chorus of the Cartesians (Le Grand, Regis, Foucher, *et al.*).[36]

In the third part of the critique, Hardouin goes on to reproach Descartes for admitting the existence of the external world only on divine revelation. In the Cartesian theory the senses have no veridical value whatever; this is a point which was explicitly asserted by Malebranche later on, and the Malebranchian way of putting it is quite revealing and ought to have put Hardouin onto a critical track which would have been less extrinsic and more to the point than the one thus far followed.

Here is the Malebranche statement: "I believe this to be a quite simple demonstration of the fact that there can be no assurance of the existence of the world except by a general or a particular revelation, and that no exact scientific demonstration can be adduced. The world is not a necessary emanation of the divinity. It depends on the divine decrees, radically free in this respect and radically indifferent. The existence of the world is by no means necessarily involved in the idea of the infinitely perfect Being. Now no truth has been demonstrated until it has been made clear that this truth has a necessary nexus with its principle. And so the saints themselves who are contemplating the divine essence in heaven still need God to teach them *by revelation* whether he has created or whether he is conserving the world." [37]

In this context, Hardouin limits himself to the observation that, for such a position, the proof taken from the spectacle of the world has no value and the *Caeli enarrant gloriam Dei* (the heavens proclaim the glory of God—Ps. 18, 1) is rendered meaningless, with the result that the Christian faith, as a faith that comes *ex auditu* (from hearing), evaporates into a mere opinion: a doctrine proper to Quacquers and Tremolanti.[38]

[35] *Ibid.*, fol. 211b.

[36] *Ibid.*, fol. 214-223b. We stress in particular the anticipation of the occasionalism of Malebranche and the negation of the divine cooperation with the secondary causes (fol. 220b-222a).

[37] Malebranche, *Dial. de metaph. et relig.*: cited *ibid.*, fol. 223b-224a.

[38] *Ibid.*, fol. 224a. There follows a violent attack on Descartes' defense of heliocentrism, in accord with Copernicus and Galileo, who are called *"primi huius amentiae assertores"* (the first to purvey this madness) (fol. 224b)! Then stress is laid on the errors of *animal mechanism* (fol. 225b), of Pelagianism in the matter of the essence of original sin (fol. 226a), of Traducianism in the matter

A few remarks on the method and basic content of the indictment presented in the *Athei detecti* by Hardouin are necessary. In the first place, it seems to us that the work merits more attention than it has hitherto received in the study of modern thought. To be sure, its author is no philosopher and evades the purely philosophical problem of the "method" on which everything depends; or let us say rather that Hardouin evinces a bemusing failure to notice this problem. Yet, though Hardouin is motivated chiefly by considerations of theological polemic against Jansenism, his critique of the "content" merits highlighting. Thus, Hardouin is substantially accurate in his judgment that the essence or primary intent of the new Augustinian philosophy and of Cartesianism as well lies in its continuous and direct recourse to God as to the *prius cognitum* (the anteriorly known); therefore, Hardouin is also justified in considering the new rationalism to be the full-blown display of the ontological argument.

This is a crucial observation for the whole process of systematization, to be undertaken unhesitatingly and remorselessly, first by Spinoza, and later on, after the critical interlude of Kant, by Hegel, and destined to provide the stimulus for Schopenhauer and, above all, for Feuerbach, to proclaim the positive or constructive atheism of modern thought, as we shall point out in due course.

Pertinent and cogent likewise is the observation that the God of this Augustinianism has been stranded on the reef of *Ens formale* (formal being), *Veritas* (Truth), *Unitas* (unity), *Bonitas* (goodness) etc. *in universali* (all considered in the universal sense), and is thus incapable of presentation as a free Person: God is an *Aliquid* (Something) and not an *Aliquis* (Someone). This is an apt admonition, frankly existentialist in inspiration, susceptible of much more telling application to the entire problem of the Method in philosophy, and especially in metaphysics, than Hardouin himelf even suspected. However, the main gap in Hardouin's resounding critique is his total silence on the "problem of the Method" as a way of attaining truth; there is barely the vaguest hint of the importance of methodical doubt in Hardouin's whole critique of the Augustinian group and of Descartes in particular. Hardouin has no interest whatever in the problem of error as an initial event which prejudices all the rest; he does not seem to see the necessity of establishing an undisputed point of departure for the entire epistemological Odyssey.

These same arguments are taken up and refuted by the prince of

---

of the origin of the human soul (fol. 227b), the equivocations and misunderstandings on the immortality of the soul (fol. 228b-230a) and on the doctrine of grace (fol. 230a-233a). Hardouin leveled a similar charge of atheism against the Jansenists; cf. A. R. Desautels, *Les Mémoires de Trévoux et le mouvement des idées au XVII e siècle* (Rome, 1956), pp. 129f.

Illuminist atheism, Baron d'Holbach, who continues in his own way the indictment initiated by the fiery Jesuit, although there is no evidence that d'Holbach knew the haughty and high-spirited polemicist. D'Holbach snipes at Descartes as one of those typical busybodies whose pretentious chatter is productive of no significant conclusion. He initiates an examination of the central argument from the innate idea of God: "The conclusion is inescapable," we read in the fifth Meditation, "from the very fact that I exist and that a certain idea of a most perfect being, i.e., of God, is in me, that God also is most evidently demonstrated to exist." [39]

D'Holbach also reports the central text of the Cartesian demonstration. (The original Latin text is reported by d'Holbach in French and its English translation is as follows: "The whole force of the argument lies in the fact that I recognize that it cannot be that I exist as the sort of being that I am, i.e., having an idea of God within me, unless God in fact also exists: God, I say, that same God the idea of whom is in me, i.e., a God having all those perfections that I cannot comprehend but can attain in some way by reflective thinking and entirely free of all defects." [40]) Against this text d'Holbach vigorously levies the following objections:

1. In general it is entirely illegitimate for us to conclude to the existence of a thing simply because we have an idea of that thing; our imagination proffers to us the idea of a sphinx or a hippogriff, but this does not give us any right to conclude that such things exist.

2. Then Descartes must be told that we cannot have any positive and real idea of a God who would be in the existential order the kind of Being the theologians are at pains to demonstrate that he is. It is impossible for any human being, for any material nature, to form for itself a real idea of a spirit, of a substance without extension, of an incorporeal entity capable of acting upon a corporeal and material nature. This is the fundamental principle of materialistic sense-perceptionism.

3. Finally, Descartes must be told that man cannot have any positive and real idea of the perfection, of the infinity, of the immensity and of the other attributes ascribed by the theologians to God. (D'Holbach here refers his reader to his critique of the Clarke demonstration of the existence of God, i.e., to Proposition XII: "The supreme cause must necessarily possess infinite goodness, justice and truthfulness, and thus all the other moral perfections which are proper to the Lord and Supreme Judge of the world." [41]).

[39] *Meditationes de Prima Philosophia,* Med. III, p. 51.

[40] *Medit. III,* pp. 51f.

[41] D'Holbach, *Système de la nature,* Vol. II (London, 1774), P. II, ch. IV, pp. 125ff.

The Cartesian proofs, therefore, conclusively prove exactly nothing! Descartes transforms God into a thought, into an intelligence, but how can an intelligence or a thought be conceived without a subject in whom these properties subsist? Descartes asserts that we can conceive God "only as a form communicating itself a little at a time to the parts of the universe" and further says that "God cannot be understood as extended except in the sense that extension is predicated of the fire in a piece of iron; the fire has no other dimensions than those of the iron itself". But this way of looking at the question can legitimately be reproached with proclaiming quite clearly that there is no other God than nature, and this is pure Spinozism. Spinoza is in fact known to have drawn on Cartesian principles for his own system which necessarily derives from those principles. Consequently, concludes d'Holbach, Descartes has been able to be legitimately accused of atheism because he himself destroys, in quite considerable measure, the feeble proofs he advances for the existence of God. In reality, prior to his creation of some sort of matter, God obviously could not have coexisted with that matter nor could he have been extended; in this case, according to Descartes, there would not be any God, because the modifications must likewise disappear when their subject is removed. If God is nothing other than nature for the Cartesians, then they are confessed Spinozans; if God is the motive force of matter, then this God no longer exists by and through himself; he exists only to the extent that there exists the subject to which he adheres, which is called nature, whose motive force he is. In this case, what would this force be without matter; and so, what would God be without the world? [42]

We shall see later how Hegel will make of the last formula of d'Holbach's critique of Descartes the formula of his own philosophy, asserting in his transcendental Spinozism that "without the world, God is not God." [43]

D'Holbach finds the same contradictions in the position taken by the other Cartesians, beginning with Malebranche, who is just as unable to avoid Spinozism, as shown when he writes: "The universe is an emanation of God; we see everything in God; everything that we see is only God; God alone produces all that happens; he alone is the entire action and the whole of the activity; in short, God is the whole of being and the only being." Is not this, says d'Holbach, an assertion that God is nature?

[42] *Ibid.*, ch. V, pp. 148ff.

[43] Hegel, *Philosophie der Religion; C.W.*, ed. Lasson, Vol. I (Leipzig, 1925), p. 148. A little earlier, d'Holbach observed: "Descartes, Pascal and Dr. Clarke were accused of atheism by the theologians of their time" (P. II, ch. 4; Vol. II, p. 107, note 26).

At the same moment, then, that Malebranche is asserting that we see everything in God, he also says: "It has not yet been demonstrated that there exists a matter or that there exist any bodies; and only faith teaches us such great mysteries, of which we should otherwise have no awareness whatever." In this connection, the question could be posed to Malebranche: How can the existence of a God who has created matter be demonstrated if the existence of this matter itself is called in question? The indictment can be frankly admitted to have a certain consistency all its own and to lay bare the exposed flank of rationalism and highlight its responsibility for modern atheism, as we shall see in due course.

Besides, insists d'Holbach, Malebranche himself acknowledges that a valid proof can be had only of a thing necessarily present, and adds: "A more attentive observation will disclose that it is impossible to know with perfect certainty whether God is really the creator of a material and sensible world or not." These notions make it evident, contends d'Holbach, that for Malebranche men have no other basis for the existence of God except faith: but faith, for its part, presupposes this existence; how, then, can there by any conviction that what God says should be believed when there is no certainty that God exists? [44] The logic of the atheist must again be agreed to sweep the field effortlessly. Finally, and with equal justification, d'Holbach accuses Malebranche of making creatures into nothing more than passive instruments in the hands of God, with his conception of God as the only active Principle. But this entails virtues and vices being attributable to God and precludes men from meriting either reward or punishment. Is not this an annihilation of all religions? [45]

D'Holbach's critique of every demonstration of the existence of God is implacable, no matter where the protagonists of such proofs may turn for their material: whether to experience, science or the moral life, all such efforts of theistic philosophers, theologians and scientists, maintains d'Holbach, are primarily open to the objection that they are founded on the false principle that "matter does not exist of itself, that it cannot move itself in virtue of its nature and consequently is incapable of producing those phenomena that we see in the world"; [46] now this is the Locke-Toland principle concerning active matter. When in the sequel God is claimed to be being conceived as "spirit", intelligence, will, goodness, providence and the like, this amounts to nothing more

[44] D'Holbach, *op. cit.*, P. II, ch. 5, Vol. II, p. 152.
[45] *Ibid.*, ch. 5, p. 153.
[46] *Ibid.*, ch. 6, Vol. II, p. 179. For this doctrine, d'Holbach refers the reader to P. I, ch. II, which we have expounded above.

than illegitimate extrapolations from human experience. As has been seen, such attributes indicate merely qualities of human experience which remain in the sphere of the sensible and do not really indicate a reality independent of matter; furthermore and consequently such attributes lose all meaning when referred to a being independent of man. (Hence the ruthless critique of the theism defended by the great Newton in the *Principia mathematica*: "His immense genius enabled him to penetrate nature and her laws but this genius took a false track to the extent that he lost sight of this nature: slave of the preconceptions of his childhood, he did not dare to raise the torch of his illumination against the foolish notions which have twined round that nature like so many accretions." [47] It is the principle of immanence, developed with the implacable rigor of the Bacon-Hobbes-Locke empirical version, that d'Holbach carries through to a definitive consistency, in antithesis to the irresolutions of deism.

Earlier d'Holbach had radically criticized the theologian Samuel Clarke, Newton's deputy in the field of metaphysics. In his *Treatise on the Existence and Attributes of God,* Clarke had pivoted his proof of the existence of God primarily upon the attributes of eternity and necessity. His point was that all the metaphysical or theological attributes, when applied to God in abstraction from that nature and those things that contain them, transform God into an abstract and inconceivable nature, while the moral attributes of justice, mercy and the like, if applied to God, lower him to the level of human nature.[48]

The God of metaphysics is but the infinitized world; the God of ethics, for his part, is but infinitized man. In any event, the God conceived of by the theologians is an internally contradictory essence. Speculative German idealism will try (as we shall see) to transpose Spinoza into a spiritualistic key in an effort to save that God whom atheist illuminism had destroyed by developing and interpreting Spinoza in an empiricist key. This is the main route we are preparing to take in our tracing of the real itinerary of modern atheism.

[47] *Ibid.*, p. 153.

[48] The critique of Clarke takes up the whole of Ch. 4, Part II, Vol. II, pp. 95ff. As we have pointed out, d'Holbach knows that Clarke (together with Descartes, Pascal *et al.*) has been accused of atheism. At the beginning of his critique, he reproves the famous theologian for his pretension in claiming to be able to demonstrate the existence of God *a priori,* something which other theologians hold to be impossible and consider rightly to be a begging of the question (*petitio principii*). This demonstration, adds d'Holbach, was rejected by the Scholastics (e.g., Albert the Great, St. Thomas Aquinas, John Duns Scotus) and by the majority of the modern philosophers, with the exception of Suarez (*ibid.*, pp. 108ff., note 27). In the last part of the note, d'Holbach recalls and approves the criticism of Clarke by Edmond Law, *An Inquiry into the Ideas of Space, Time, Immensity, etc.* (Cambridge, 1734).

The accusation of atheism leveled against Descartes may have savored of a hoax when directed against the man himself who always professed himself to be a theist and convinced believer, but it also had the import of a historical and prophetic judgment on the outcome of Cartesianism and of the new road taken by philosophy. Descartes died too soon to learn of the charge leveled against him by Hardouin, who, as we have seen, deduced atheism from the ontologism or pantheism he believed to confront him in Cartesian innatism. Descartes would probably not have been very surprised at this charge and would have certainly replied to it with his characteristic elegance, the more so since it had been made by a Jesuit, a member of that Order whose schools Descartes had frequented and in which he counted several of his best friends.

But Descartes was surprised and hurt by the charge of atheism leveled against him by the Calvinist theologian Gisbert Voetius (and by his disciple Martin Schook) of Utrecht who phrased the charge in the following terms: "I have known a man who is a match for Vanini and who, even as he desires to be thought to be opposing the atheists with Achillean arguments, is cunningly, deceitfully and most covertly rubbing off the poison of atheism on those who, because of the weakness of their wit, cannot spot the serpent hiding in the grass in any of his lurking places." [49]

Descartes refers to the confession of Schook himself as grounds for the assertion that the mordant expression "that I rub off on others cunningly, deceitfully and most covertly the poison of atheism", i.e. the charge of bad faith and crypto-atheism, was added by Voetius (p. 254). Descartes tells us that the charge is repeated "throughout the entire second last chapter of his book" (p. 187).

In Descartes' own wordy exposition, from which I am borrowing, there seem to be two main points of the charge: the insufficiency of the Cartesian proofs of the existence of God and the skepticism that Descartes chooses as a starting point. These two points are diametrically opposed but are quite pertinent for the purpose of the accuser. Descartes easily acquits himself of the first charge: "Here you pretend that the reasons which I use to prove the existence of God are valid only for those who already make him to exist, because they depend solely on notions innately implanted within us."

But this is a patent equivocation because "innately" signifies only that the ideas are not derived from the senses but rather produced by reflec-

[49] The charge is found in the *Praefatio* to the work *Admiranda Methodus Novae Philosophiae Renati des Cartes* (Utrecht, 1643), with no author's name mentioned. We cite from p. 13 but take the text of Descartes himself in the "Epistola ad G. Voetium," in *Oeuvres,* ed. Adam-Tannery, Vol. VIII, p. 142.

tion alone. Innate, therefore, corresponds to "implicit" and holds for all the truths of the pure sciences: "But it must be noted that all those things, the cognition and knowledge of which is said to be imparted to us by nature, are not, for that reason, known expressly by us; they are simply such that we can know them without any practical experience of the senses, by the powers of our own natural disposition, wit and intelligence. Of such a kind are all the truths of geometry, not only the most obvious ones but even the rest as well, however abstruse they may appear."

Descartes appeals expressly to the maieutics (intellectual midwifery) of Socrates in the *Meno* and goes over to the counter-offensive, aiming at making his adversary contradict himself. Descartes here takes his cue fromVoetius' assertion that there could not be such phenomena as speculative atheists: "And of this same kind is the knowledge of God: and so, when you drew the inference, whether in the *Thersites* or in the pamphlets on atheism, that no one could be an atheist speculatively, i.e., there could be no one who does not recognize at all that God exists, you were no less far off the mark than you would have been, had you said that, because of the fact that all the truths of geometry are innate to us in the same way, there could therefore be no one in the whole world who did not know the elements of Euclid." [50]

The second source of Descartes' atheism is pinpointed by Voetius in the "skepticism" proper to the Cartesian method, and it is a pity that the charge is given scant emphasis, either by Voetius or by Descartes who reports it. In the *Paralipomena ad Praefationem,* Voetius presents Descartes "as an inscrutable outsider, by external profession a papalist and by intellectual attitude a candidate for skepticism if not atheism". And Voetius' son speaks out still more clearly in his apology for his father entitled *Pietas in parentem:* "Nor would my sire have any cause for shame, had he himself (as in fact he did not) composed a part of the text beforehand—especially that part in which the absurd Cartesian philosophy of dizzying skepticism, and consequently of atheism, is struck down." [51]

This charge of skepticism seems to have been developed (more exhaustively and thoroughly) by Voetius in the *Theses de Atheismo,* his first anti-Cartesian work, although Descartes is there not mentioned by name. In this work, Voetius indisputably evinces a quite lively sense of the peril that existed for the cause of truth and of the faith by the new

[50] Descartes, *Epistola ad G. Voetium,* pp. 166f.

[51] I take the texts from the *Lettre apologétique aux Magistrats d'Utrecht,* ed. Adam-Tannery, Vol. VIII, p. 255 (note) and p. 265 of text. The letter can readily be understood to have been written by Descartes to prevent his being tried for atheism.

trend of thought: "But if someone once warned persists in playing the fool and entangling himself and the truth in sheer beggings of the question or obscure and uncertain chains of reasoning, such as *cogito, ergo sum* (I think, therefore I am) and *cuius idea in me est, illud ipsum* (that of which the idea is in me, is itself), etc., so that skepticism is first introduced and then all natural knowledge, innate and acquired, is erased or sequestered in forfeit by doubt, all the principles and demonstrations hitherto in common use in Christendom are denied and stripped away so that a situation will have developed in which all knowledge of God and of the worship of God, of virtue and vice, of the imperative of doing hurt to no one and of rendering unto each his due, shall once have been cast aside and abandoned and the principles of natural reason and of the rule of natural sequences shall have been degraded—whence shall such a one restore at will to himself or others natural and supernatural theology? Whence shall he find forthcoming the weapons wherewith to defend both against infidels, fanatics, heretics and libertines? These things, inasmuch as they are not limited to the field of geometry or optics or mechanics, merit the serious consideration of theologians and of those who set store by true religion and piety." [52]

Descartes' defense, backed up by his friends, came off well and the philosopher was left in peace; it is to be deplored that the scanty speculative capacity of the theologian Voetius and the personal and at least partially the denominational animosity between the two men prevented an effective confrontation of the ideas of the two opponents.[53] Descartes himself, in his running self-defense, loses himself in copious lamentations and protests, but he takes very good care not to reply to the charge which even today retains its ample justification, whatever may be said of Voetius' comparison of Descartes with Vanini, a comparison which occasioned the philosopher such agitation (even anguish and fear!).

Voetius' charge must have provoked a vast echo in the Protestant world, to judge by the invective of a Lutheran theologian, Theophilus Spitzel (1639-1691), no less inflamed with zeal for orthodoxy. Let us divide the Spitzel text into its main elements:

[52] The text is taken from the Editors' Appendix to the Letter to Mersenne, dated December 7, 1642: *Correspondance,* ed. Adam-Tannery, Vol. III, p. 604.

[53] The more or less direct echoes of Voetius' charge against Descartes in the rich flowering of Cartesianism in the Netherlands have been collected directly from the sources adduced by C. L. Thijssen-Schoute, "Le cartésianisme aux Pays Bas," in *Descartes et le cartésianisme hollandais,* pp. 183ff; *idem, Nederlands Cartesianisme* (Amsterdam, 1954) (*Verhandelingen der Koninklijke Nederlandse Akademie van Wetenschappe,* Afd. *Letterkunde,* Nieuwe Reeks, Deel LX).

1. *The Charge or Suspicion of Crypto-atheism*

"The *Cartesian Method* is justly called a perverse method of natural wisdom and the surest road to atheism, but it is better to speak of the skepticism revived by René Descartes [the Latin pun "renatus ille a Renato des Cartes" is necessarily lost in English translation—Translator's Note], and the free rein demanded for philosophizing, yes even of removing and calling in question all the principles and axioms of natural reason, hitherto accepted by the common consent of Christian and non-Christian philosphers, and of the doltish boasting of unheard of and startling methods, and the mandatory and highhanded deletion, consignment to oblivion and effective evasion of all preconceived dogmas, and the rejection of all knowledge, whether of science or of faith.

"And since Descartes, in his Method, openly levies this demand on anyone aspiring to a sound and genuine learning, hence it happens that many have suspected him of many things; for when, after being educated among the French and having deeply imbibed the Gallic mercurial temper, he disseminated his philosophisms in secret throughout Belgium and *roused* hitherto *concordant brothers to battle,* an uncertainty assailed the minds of some as to whether this *self-knower* was philosophizing frankly or disingenuously, whether he was directing his *discoveries* to the repair of the sciences or to the destruction of theology and its principles! Indeed, there were those who, on examining this new method, dared to compare Descartes with I. C. Vanini, the standard-bearer of the atheists, and reckoned Descartes to have done more to provide bricks and lime for the building up of the walls of atheism than for the bringing down of those walls." Spitzel's debt to Voetius is clear; indeed, Voetius is mentioned by name near the end, as we shall point out.

2. *Nexus of Absolute Doubt, Skepticism and Atheism*

"Whatever may be the truth of Descartes' intention, it is quite clear that that method, i.e., the mandatory effacement and rejection of all notions, will, no matter where I am aiming, lead straight to skepticism and thence to atheism. If everything that has the faintest semblance of doubt attached to it is thus to be eliminated because it may be false and erroneous, will not the elimination, on this colorable pretext, of even the first principles pave the way to the libertinism of deciding and judging about anything? If all notions are to be wrested from the tablets of our minds, will not even that knowledge of the existence of the Spirit be likewise subject to overthrow? And will not the power of nature be interpolated, after the voluntary and deliberate admission of atheism for a certain space of time, as indeed Descartes does not hestitate to admit? Some superenthusiasts for the Cartesian dogmas reply that that doubt has not been admitted idly or without reasonable cause, that it is not a case of merely frivolous wavering and entertaining doubts about things of utmost importance; rather, all their doubting is permeated with reasonableness, is indeed nothing else than a sheer and simple noncommital consideration, involving no assent, of the reasons for doubting or of the causes on account of which we can doubt so long as we are deprived of the undoubted bases, the apodictic foundations of true scientific knowledge. This κρησφυγετον (evasion) can in no way help their bad cause or purge the rashness of their doubting of the existence of God. For whoever deliberately and voluntarily doubts concerning God and rushes to strip from his mind the very image imprinted, such a man is guilty of rash doubting."

3. *Validity of Voetius' Accusation*

"Nor do we wonder that G. Voetius accused Descartes by name of atheism, although this is barely mentioned in the *Manes Cartesii, ab ipsomet defensi, sive Ren. des Cartes Querela Apologetica ad Sen. Utraicet.* [The Spirit of *Descartes,* His Own Defense Counsel; or René Descartes' Apologetic Complaint to the Senate of Utrecht, p. 27.] Some have held Descartes to be that Brutus of literary fame, a gimlet of subtlety, overthrowing the modes of thought of all the ancients and the more modern thinkers, and excelling in mathematics to an extent that seems to surpass the powers of the human mind, dissolving and severing whatever was once considered ἄλυτον (indissoluble), but no longer so in this business of the new method. Yet, in no way did he present to the educated world another Atlas, a kind of Elias; he introduced true skepticism and its inseparable companion, *atheism,* full tilt by his whole way of acting." [54]

Spitzel certainly does assert the veracity of sensation and the necessity of our cognitional activity having its start in the senses, but he does not advert to the significance of the intrinsic nexus of our spiritual experience with the world in which we live; and so here once again the problem of modern thought is not even touched upon. Specifically, no stress is given to the significance of the *cogito ergo sum* [55] nor is there even the

[54] Th. Spitzel, *Scrutinium Atheismi historico-aetiologicum* (Augsburg, 1663), pp. 115ff.

[55] As a curious sidelight, we might note that Hardouin reports one of the results of his diatribe to have been the *Judicium Societatis* [*Jesu*] *de quibusdam propositionibus Cartesii et Malebranchi,* commissioned by the Jesuit General

vaguest suspicion of the principle of immanence inaugurated in that phrase. Therefore, the charge of atheism as formulated by Hardouin takes a line diametrically opposed to that which will be followed in the development and evolution of modern thought.

Thus the revolution of the *cogito* had come full circle: the atheists of 18th-century French materialism were convinced that they were the legitimate heirs of the Cartesian revolution and it is hard to fault them on the basic point. The rupture between the world and the ego revealed the rupture between the body and the soul, between man and God. Marx and the Marxists latched primarily onto the materialist element in the Cartesian physics which reduces the whole of natural reality to matter and motion, reviving radical mechanism.[56] Their analysis may be too hasty but it is indicative. The *cogito* did in fact hide within itself much more deep-cutting demands for the direct and definitive expulsion of any view or prospect of the Absolute, even as the dialectic of modern idealism was to do later in comparable ways.

The most categorical indictment comes from a believer who is among those most occupied with modern thought and who has denounced the deep-going ramifications of the corrosion produced by the *cogito* in all areas of human life: "The personal faith of a Descartes did not prevent Cartesianism from paving the way for the modern split between metaphysical speculation and religious speculation. It is not normal for the philosopher to effect a specialization of his research (which, as distinct

---

Michelangelo Tamburini and discussed at the 15th General Congregation. This consists of 30 propositions. It is significant that, whereas the second proposition, having to do with the knowledge of the existence of God as basis of all knowledge whatsoever, is followed by an extensive commentary; the first proposition which enunciates the point about universal doubt ("The human mind can and should doubt about everything except the fact that it is thinking and therefore exists") is followed only by the quotation reference "Ex Cartesio, parte I Principiorum, num. 2, 5, 7" (*op. cit.*, fol. 237a) without any commentary whatsoever.

On the anti-Cartesianism of the French Jesuits, cf. F. Bouiller, *Histoire de la philosophie cartésienne,* Vol. I, pp. 557ff.; likewise G. Sortais, "Le cartésianisme chez les Jésuites français au XVII e siècle," in *Archives de Philosophie,* Vol. VI, 1929. Notable is the scanty emphasis given by Bouiller to Hardouin's *Athei Detecti,* with only a passing reference to the argument taken from the notion of the infinite (Vol. I, pp. 565f.) and with no reference whatever to the basic argument of pantheistic monism from the *Ipsum Ens, Ipsum Verum, Ipsum Bonum,* etc.

[56] "In his *Physics,* Descartes had attributed self-creating power to matter and had taken *mechanical* movement as its vital act. He had separated his *Physics* entirely from his *Metaphysics. Within* his physics, *matter* is the only *substance,* the only ground of being and knowing" (K. Marx-F. Engels, "Die Heilige Familie," in *K. Marx-F. Engels Werke* Vol. II [Berlin, 1958], p. 133; cf. also the *Geschichte der Philosophie,* Vol. I, by a Soviet author team [Berlin: VEB Deutscher Verlag der Wissenschaften, 1959], p. 355).

from the positive sciences, ought to bear upon the whole of man and the whole of being). He must not hold, even if he is a believer, that it is permissible and compatible to conduct double-entry bookkeeping in the matter of knowledge, and erect airtight compartments where the need for unity, universality and consistency is the supreme law of the whole intellectual life. Inversely, Leibniz's attempt to bind and suture nature with grace is at once the effect and the cause of an error no less grave, for by displaying the supernatural as a simple blossoming forth of the depths of nature, he is preparing in advance the letter and stirring up the spirit of the modernist illusion." [57]

It is a deep-cutting condemnation which hurls the explicit charge of apostasy against the very orientation of modern philosophy: "We have already indicated how Descartes subverted the sense and import of philosophy. It was not merely by reversing the first upthrust of investigative curiosity and forcing it back upon the *cogito,* whereas the *primus motus mentis* (first movement of the mind) goes toward the truth, toward being, toward God. Another inversion, doubtless the covert result of the first, paved the way, if not for the inversion, at least for the perversion and debasement of the ideal of a refinement of human culture. How? Because Descartes had a firm intention of founding a science and a philosophy that would be intimately linked in order to assure their autonomy, their untrammeled and unlimited development, their hegemony, limited, to be sure, to this world and the human order but independent and self-sufficient in this realm: *mundus nobis traditur* (the world is handed over to us). As metaphysician, Descartes' chief aim is to firm up the certitude of our grasp of nature, to purge the restlessness of souls by appeasing it, to offer an entirely secure scope for the happy future of a culture in process of an evolution so indefinite as to prolong almost beyond any assignable limits the duration of our earthly existence. . . . Is the enormous apostasy of such an approach now clear, this approach which, even when using God, uses him, so to speak, against himself, takes him at his word in the matter of leaving us to ourselves, dispenses with him as much as possible and contents itself more and more with organizing the world and mankind for our enjoyment, our domination, our self-worship?" [58]

No less telling and drastic is the denunciation uttered by the atheist

[57] M. Blondel, *L'être et les êtres* (Paris, 1935), p. 522. In an early study, Blondel had spoken of an "agnosticism" in Descartes ("Le Christianisme de Descartes," in *Revue de métaphysique et de morale* [1896], p. 560). The radical atheism of the Cartesian *cogito* is vigorously asserted in our own day by W. Schulz: "Such a structuring of self-awareness is plainly directed against any conceivable transcendence. . . . Descartes again shows up as quite deliberately atheistic." Schulz also speaks of a "methodical will to atheism" (*Der Gott der neuzeitlichen Metaphysik* [Pfullingen, 1957], pp. 35f.).

[58] M. Blondel, *L'action,* Vol. I (Paris, 1936), pp. 341f.

Sartre, even though his analysis is the inverse of the preceding one and of a greater complexity.[59]

Descartes' basic insight is the realization that every act, every slightest step of the thinking process, involves the whole of thought, is an autonomous thought which is posited in each and every one of its acts in its full and absolute independence. But this *autonomy,* expressed and actuated by radical doubt does not involve, in Descartes' system, *productivity* or efficient causality for thought. For there exists in fact, prior to knowledge and the mind, an objective order of relations, the order of essences, with respect to which the subjectivity of the individual knower can in reality be only the simple freedom to cleave to the truth or else a confused thought, a deformed truth, whose development and clarification will cause the subjective character to disappear. In the latter event, man disappears and there remains no difference between thought and truth: the true is the totality, the sum total of the system of thoughts. And so, if we want to save man, we have no option, in view of the fact that he cannot *produce* a single idea but can only contemplate such ideas, but to endow him with a simple negative capacity: that of being able to say "No!" to everything that is not true.

Thus, concludes Sartre, we find in Descartes, under the guise of a unitary and homogeneous doctrine, two very different theories of freedom, depending on whether he is considering this power of understanding and judging which is proper to him, or is simply at pains to rescue man's autonomy over against the rigorous system of the ideas. In this way, Descartes becomes for Sartre the forerunner of the Hegelian negativity and even of Heidegger's notion of the loneliness of man. But Descartes the *man* is "free" only in name because for Descartes the Christian there exists the Good in itself and it is not up to man to invent it, just as there exists the True in itself and it is not up to man to create it. Thus, Descartes the philosopher and Descartes the man proceed in opposite directions, the one to a denial of God [60] and the other

[59] J. P. Sartre, *Descartes,* Coll. Les classiques de la liberté (Paris, 1946), pp. 12ff. (The Introduction, from which we summarize a few elements, is in our opinion a masterpiece of penetration and lucidity). The crux of this interpretation is there already in *L'être et le néant* (Paris, 1943), especially pp. 563f.

[60] A contemporary Protestant theologian writes: "Thereby Descartes becomes the type of the *free thinker.* From the 17th century on, the notion of prejudice acquires a peculiar force. The thinker proves himself to be such by having cast off his *prejudices.*" And after showing that the work of Locke and Hume is in a direct line with that of Descartes, this Protestant theologian concludes vigorously: "The furtherance of the work takes the form of posing to reason the question as to how it attains its own content and how it bases its thinking methods. The fact that agnosticism has today become the strongest philosophical force in thought generally is but the logical consequence of the dominant theme in Descartes" (A. Schlatter, *Die philosophische Arbeit seit Cartesius nach ihrem ethischen und religiösen Ertrag* [Gütersloh, 1932], pp. 16f.). The last

to an affirmation of him. For Sartre, the true Descartes is obviously Descartes the philosopher; so he is for Blondel and for us, and the evolution of modern thought has provided the proof of it. The deepening and broadening of this atheist consistency of the *cogito* now awaits our investigation.

To this dual (idealist and materialist) interpretation of the *cogito* in an atheist strain could be opposed the theistic interpretation (of Augustinian inspiration) defended by the Cartesians of the Catholic schools and provocative of the sharp destructive criticism of Hardouin. We are persuaded that any talk of a common "ontologism" in Augustine and in Descartes involves a radical equivocation, for we are dealing with two approaches deriving from drastically divergent inspirations: [61] in the case of Augustine, from the theological sphere and geared to the total grounding of man in God; in the case of Descartes, from the sphere of modern science and from a new notion of freedom, which in reality releases both the world and man from dependence on God, even though it admits an initial ingress and intervention of God in the creation of the world and in the odyssey of truth.

It will require but a few decades and precisely the critique of this Cartesian contention concerning inert matter, a critique which will come from the ranks of the French and English deists (Locke, Toland, Voltaire, Diderot, *et al.*), opening up yet another irreparable breach in the theist positions and leading to the irruption of the constructive atheism of modern thought swirling round the mind on all sides.[62]

A final estimate, then, of this first and decisive stage of the principle of immanence seems to admit of no doubt: the "law of being" once basically and radically specified cannot but pursue inevitably its chosen path toward an even more vigorous and radical self-validation. Regrets and second thoughts can no longer avail anything.

---

few decades have replaced the agnosticism, here referred to, by atheism, and this shift reveals an even greater consistency.

[61] Thus, for instance, a specialist in Augustinian studies concludes from a comparison of the Augustinian *cogito* and the Cartesian one that there is no parity between them: "Descartes also finds God by traveling a road that starts with thought, but it is quite clear that Descartes' road is quite a different one" (Charles Boyer, "Le 'Cogito' dans S. Augustin," in *Descartes,* Coll. III Centenario del Discorso del metodo [Milan, 1937], p. 82).

[62] It is indicative for our purpose that these contentions, virtually parallel to the more famous principle of immanence, should have reached differing goals en route in our days, as is borne out by the most eminent historian of modern English thought: "At the worst, we should come to some such conclusion as was adumbrated by Locke in the proposition, which seemed so scandalous to his contemporaries, that God might superadd a faculty of thinking to matter. That would be to become materialist, with the explanation that matter was itself a kind of spirit" (L. Stephen, *An Agnostic's Apology and Other Essays* [London, 1904], p. 34b).

2

Atheism and Pantheism in Spinozan Metaphysics

Spinoza (1632-1677) [1] indisputably led modern thought to a second step toward atheism; and this step was much more crucial than the Cartesian one. But the nature of Spinoza's contribution and especially the internal dynamic of his principles in the direction of the elimination of the theological principle from philosophy is considerably more evident and at the same time more complex and controversial than in the case of Descartes. The reason is to be sought not only in the fact that Descartes continued to remain faithful to his religion whereas Spinoza was expelled from his and thenceforth kept aloof from every faith. The chief reason lies in the fact that, in Spinoza's exposition of his own thought, everything aspires to and culminates in the Absolute; but this Absolute in turn remains solely a metaphysical principle—the only metaphysical principle—which cannot be the object of any religion because God is rendered present to man and man to God solely in the theoretical act. We can say that, whereas the Cartesian *cogito* introduced an epistemological immanence and with it a mandatory tendency toward atheism, Spinoza—as scion of the pantheism and panentheism inherent in Greek, medieval (especially Jewish) and Renaissance philosophy—was the progenitor of the notion of the metaphysical immanence of reason, a notion that instantly compresses the discussion into its native mold. While Descartes intends to start with the act of knowing, to commence from the certainty engendered by the act (the *cog-*

[1] This is the precise contention of Feuerbach: "The Christian philosophers and theologians reproached Spinoza with *atheism. And justifiably so:* for the repudiation of the companionability, the benevolence and the justice, the supernaturalness, the untrammeled freedom and the wonder-working power, *in short, the humanity of God, is a repudiation of God himself.* A God who performs no miracles, who produces no effects differing from the effects of nature, and who thus does not show himself to be a being distinct from nature is in fact *simply not* God" (*Geschichte der neueren Philosophie von Bacon von Verulam bis Benedikt Spinoza, C.W.*, ed. W. Bolin-F. Jodl, Vol. III [Stuttgart, 1906], p. 383).

ito) in its intimate and naked presence, Spinoza thrusts deeper still and intends to start with the content, from the principle of "subsumption" (*appartenentia*) (of the parts by the whole, of the finite by the Infinite, of the world by God).

And Spinoza is not only *de facto* but also *de jure* the herald of the most vigorous critique of religious knowledge in general and of Cartesianism in particular; [2] but Spinoza is also the progenitor of the new modern metaphysic, primarily the rationalistic and later and preeminently the idealist metaphysic proper to the philosophy and theology of the German transcendentalists, a metaphysic in which the need for God, while being pushed formally to the point of the spastic, is in reality contextually shrivelled to the elevation of human reason and reality to the status of the Absolute. This metaphysic of the German transcendentalists paves the way by its own fall, which is in turn its definitive validation, for the consolidation and, indeed, the irreversible appearance on the scene of the positive and constitutive atheism of modern and contemporary thought. While Descartes can be said to have discovered the new "principle of freedom", it must be admitted that Spinoza was the man who put that principle into operation to the limit. New elements will enter into the development of modern thought (and atheism) and new principles will appear on the scene, especially that of the "mind as activity" and thus of the "fieri", the "becoming", the "existential flux" of life and of history, in the line of Leibniz-Hume-Kant and idealism; and these new elements and principles will subject the situation to a rude upset; but the primordial sense of reality will remain that which was anticipated in the "principle of subsumption". This is why the epistemological aspect is compelled, after a brief interlude of supremacy, in Hume and Kant to yield pride of place to the metaphysical outlook of idealism, in anticipation of its complete dissolution in the radical humanism of present-day philosophy.

If we are to judge the content of a thought by the consistency of its principles, we must say that Spinoza's thought begins, continues and ends solely and exclusively in God and hence has often been likened to a kind of mystical theology; [3] but this is a grave error, probably caused by the fascination exercised by Spinoza's writings and by their sweeping summons to the ideal. The study of Spinoza can arouse and has in fact aroused the most divergent and even opposing reactions and impressions: of materialism or of spiritualism, of absolute realism or of ideal-

[2] Cf. L. Strauss, *Die Religionskritik Spinozas als Grundlage seiner Bibelwissenschaft* (Berlin, 1930), especially pp. 84ff.

[3] "Like the Bible, the *Ethics* of Spinoza has often been the subject of homiletical interpretations" (H. A. Wolfson, *The Philosophy of Spinoza,* Vol. I, [New York, 1958], p. v.).

ism, of an inflexible geometric system and of an intuition mounting step by step to the complete deployment of the activity of the spirit (the *Amor Dei intellectualis* [intellectual Love of God]); and, finally, in the area of our own investigations here, of a deep-seated piety and of radical atheism. This is the enigma of the Spinozan theory; the theoretical act is here far more crucially rooted in ambiguity than in the case of the so-called "Cartesian vicious circle" which the Spinozan theory might call to mind and from which it derives, at least in part. The point is that for Spinoza the problem of certainty coincides with that of the totality of being, the solution of the destiny and fate of man is referred back to that of the reality of the world and that the infinite stretches of time are all gathered together into the infinite present of eternity; [4] thus God is all in all, and God cannot be other nor be otherwise conceived. It is precisely because God, as Spinoza conceives him, cannot be thought, whereas on the other hand Spinoza has to think him at the summit of the most drastic ambiguity, that his passion for God is that of an unhappy love that can never have the beloved, that indeed compromises irreparably at every step all possibility of understanding him.

Spinoza's Protest against the Charge of Atheism

Spinoza's freedom of expression and profound conviction that philosophy could fulfill its assignment only by applying itself to the problems as last court of appeal for the human spirit did not cause him to forget the rules of prudence, especially when reflecting on the furor aroused by the charge of atheism levelled against Descartes by the Dutch theologian Voetius. The charge of atheism against Spinoza must have come early, in the wake of his first published writings, since he tells Oldenburg that he is preparing to compose a treatise "concerning my attitude to scripture" in order to meet and cope with the prejudices of the theologians, rebut the charge of atheism and vindicate freedom of thought.[5] The liveliness of his reaction proves that Spinoza was well aware that the problem touched on the very essence and ultimate significance of the problem of truth.

[4] H. F. Hallet sees the essence of Spinozism in the "duration-eternity" nexus (*"Aeternitas", A Spinozistic Study* [Oxford, 1930], p. 4).

[5] "And the grounds impelling me thereto are: (1) The prejudices of the theologians; for I know that these prejudices are a signal impediment in the way of men applying their understanding to philosophy; therefore I am at pains to expose them and to prune them away from the minds of the more knowledgeable. (2) The opinion held of me by the public which does not cease to accuse me falsely of atheism; I am constrained to obviate this opinion as far as possible. (3) The freedom to philosophize and to say what one feels; which freedom I am eager to assert in every way and which is here being trammeled every which way by the excessive power and impudence of the demagogues" (Spinoza, Ep. XXX, *Opera,* ed. C. Gebhardt, Vol. IV [Heidelberg, 1924], p. 166). The work in question is certainly the *Tractatus Theologico-Politicus,* published in 1670.

The *Tractatus Theologico-Politicus* provides, instead of the apology intended by Spinoza, ample material for an indictment against the author as subverter of all religion and of Christianity in particular. The charge, which will be examined in the sequel by Spinoza, is contained in a letter from Lambert de Velthuysen to Jakob Ostens,[6] a correspondent of Spinoza, and can be summarized in the following points:

1. Spinoza has indeed been good at combatting the passions and prejudices that divide men and in felling superstition; but he has ended by falling into the opposite excess, in that "he seems to me to have stripped off all religion in order to avoid the guilt of being superstitious." He has ranged himself squarely on the side of the free-thinker philosophers or "deists" who are baying everywhere; but Spinoza has outdone all of them in the violence and the skill of his attack, and what is more he is himself quite aware of this: "But I reckon that scarcely any one of the Deists has spoken out so malignantly, so artfully and cleverly for that most evil of causes as the author of this dissertation. Furthermore, unless my guess deceives me, this man does not limit himself to the scope of the Deists, but rather suffers not even the remnants of religious worship to remain to men" (p. 207).

2. It is true that Spinoza admits God and considers him as creator, but he proceeds to subject both God and the world and man in particular to the law of the most rigid necessity, rendering vain all human activity and destroying the efficacy of prayer itself and generally tearing out root and branch the very bases of morality and religion. And this is equivalent to the negation of God, a negation that takes the form of identifying God with the universe. This charge on the part of Velthuysen has stood up ever since! "For I fear that our author is not entirely foreign to that opinion; at least they are not far apart in stating that all things necessarily emanate from the nature of God, and that the Universe itself is God" [7] (p. 208). Spinoza conceives ethics as being completely autonomous with respect to God as criterion of good and principle of sanctions: "Yet he places man's highest delight in the cultivation of virtue, which he says to be its own reward and an arena fit for kings; and thus he claims that a man with a proper understanding of things ought to practice virtue, not on account of the precepts and the law of God, nor yet out of any hope of reward or fear of punishment, but

[6] *Ep.* XLII, *ibid.*, pp. 207ff. Ostens came to visit Spinoza in February, 1671 (cf. K. O. Meinsma, *Spinoza und sein Kreis* [Berlin, 1909], pp. 412f.).

[7] "You have here, most illustrious sir, in the summary handed over to you, an abridgement of a theologian and political thinker's teaching, which in my opinion does away with all worship and all religion, subverting their very foundations, which introduces atheism on the sly, or imagines such a God as would not impress on men any reverence for the divinity, in that he is himself subject to fate; nor is any room left whatsoever for divine guidance and providence, and all allotment of rewards and punishments is abolished" (*Ep.* XLII, *ibid.*, p. 218).

because he discerns the beauty of virtue and the joy of the mind which man experiences in the practice of virtue" (p. 209).

3. The so-called revealed religion, proclaimed by the prophets, was intended for the common unlettered multitude, but it is the business of reason and philosophy to interpret scripture (p. 210).

4. From Spinoza's cosmic fatalism derives his denial of the possibility of miracle, in virtue of the necessary and inviolable character of the laws of nature: "For he held the natures of things and their order to be no less necessary than the nature of God and the eternal truths; consequently, he teaches that it is just as impossible for anything to deviate from the laws of nature as for the three internal angles of a triangle not to be equal to two right angles; that God could not bring it about that a less heavy weight should attract a heavier one, or that a body moved with two degrees of motion should overtake a body that is being moved with four degrees of motion" (p. 212).

The accuser has well seen the intimate nexus between the two elements of the critique of a revealed religion based on the admission of miracles and the destruction of natural religion itself which cannot accept the idea of a God identified with the necessity of nature. Here the charge is hitting at the basic principle of Spinozism which is absolute rationalism or the assertion of an *equivalence* between the real and the ideal order,[8] between the order of the divine knowing and the order of things, which latter equivalence amounts to the total identification in God of the area of the intellect and that of the will and in man (and things in general) of the sphere of possibility and that of reality.

The formulation of the charge is perfect and does credit to the acumen of the accuser: "For he holds God to have willed this universe and all that successively happens within it just as necessarily as God knows this same universe. But if God necessarily knows this universe and its laws, as also the eternal truths contained in those laws, he concludes that God could no more have created another universe than he could upset the nature of things and make twice three equal seven" (p. 211). And Velthuysen notes the profound difference between this doctrine and that of Descartes: "For he is not willing to go along with Descartes, whose doctrine he nevertheless wishes to appear to have adopted, in saying that, the natures of all things being different from the nature and essence of God, the ideas of these things will therefore be freely in the divine mind" (p. 212). The critique then proceeds to the more particularized arguments of the treatise concerning the structure of revealed religion and of civil society.

[8] "*Ordo et connexio idearum idem est, ac ordo et connexio rerum*" (The order and nexus of ideas is the same as the order and nexus of things) (*Ethica,* P. II, Prop. VII, ed. Gebhardt, Vol. II, p. 89).

Well worth reading is Velthuysen's disconsolate conclusion concerning the havoc Spinoza has wrought on faith in God and all religion and concerning the atheism being surreptitiously launched by his ideas. Velthuysen feels that this makes it a duty of conscience to denounce Spinoza: "I reckon therefore that I shall not have strayed far from the truth, nor yet that any injury will have been done by me to the author, if I denounce him as teaching sheer atheism by covert and counterfeit arguments." The charge does not seem to have been the improvised outburst of a moment and must have reflected a widespread impression. As soon as Spinoza had heard of this charge, he took time out to consider it.

His reply [9] shows resentment but does not evade the charges, preferring to face them squarely: he proceeds point by point to unmask the snares and plots of his opponent.

1. A man's private life is not a negligible criterion for judging that man's doctrine: "First he says, *it is of little interest to know of what stock I come or what way of life I follow;* now, of course, if he did know this, he would not so easily have persuaded himself that I am teaching atheism; for atheists make a practice of seeking honors and riches above measure, whereas I have always held them in contempt as all who are acquainted with me know. Then, to lay the basis for his charge, he claims me to be of no mean wit, so that he may the more easily convict me of having spoken out artfully, craftily and in bad faith on behalf of the most evil cause of the Deists. Which shows clearly enough that he had not understood my line of reasoning" (p. 219f.). This is the argument which Bayle will expand into a whole conception of life and, above all, of the relations between religion and morality.

2. This is the most crucial point for the reply to the charge of atheism and Spinoza develops it step by step; but it is really not so much a reply as a repetition of his own arguments, which incidentally had already been excellently summarized by the accuser. First of all, in the matter of the charge that he has overturned religion itself with his critique of superstition, Spinoza asks his opponent what is the distinction to be made here between the two, whereas it was really up to Spinoza to clarify the distinction in question, in view of the fact that the accuser had defended Christianity as a genuine religion. Spinoza, on the contrary, identifies religion with the knowledge of God and with morality: "I ask whether he has stripped away all religion, who has held God to be

[9] It is addressed to Jakob Ostens (*Ep.* XLIII; *ibid.,* Vol. IV, pp. 219ff.). The sole motive of the attack, says Spinoza, is the envy felt by the journeymen for the masters, as once Voetius for Descartes: "Nor am I really surprised at this. For even as Descartes was once publicly attacked by Voetius, so at all times and in all places are the elite publicly slandered" (p. 220).

admitted to be the supreme good and this same God to be loved, as such, freely? And who has held our supreme happiness and our supreme freedom to consist in this alone? And who has furthermore held that the reward of virtue is virtue itself and the punishment of folly and intemperance is the folly itself, and accordingly that each man ought to love his neighbor and obey the commandments of the supreme power?" (p. 220).

3. As for the charge of atheism on the grounds of having denied the freedom of God by identifying that liberty with necessity, Spinoza protests against such a charge by asserting that he has said nothing different from the other philosophers in saying that in God freedom coincides with necessity: "For I have claimed that everything follows by inevitable necessity from the nature of God, in just the same way that all philosophers claim that it follows from the nature of God that he knows himself: now certainly no one denies that this necessarily follows from the divine nature and yet no one conceives that God is constrained by some sort of fate; rather they hold that he knows himself entirely freely, even though necessarily" (p. 221f.). Descartes too asserted at one and the same time the total causality of God and our freedom.

4. Such necessity, specifies Spinoza, leaves the moral order intact; but his reply can be cogent only for those who admit the identity of necessity and freedom: "For moral teachings, whether they assume the form of a law from God himself or no, are in any case divine and conducive to salvation; and whether we accept the good as flowing from the divine power and love and as coming from God as judge, or as emanating from the necessity of the divine nature, it will not for that reason be more or less desirable, just as, on the contrary, the evil that flows from evil works will not be feared any the less because it follows from them necessarily; and therefore are we guided by hope or fear whether we act necessarily or freely" (p. 222f.).

5. And for his own part, Spinoza is not in fact opposed to identifying this necessity of God with nature: "Nor is it any more a question for me at this point why it is the same thing or not much different, at any rate, to hold that all things emanate necessarily from the nature of God and to hold that the universe is God" (p. 223).

But he is at pains to highlight the fact that in the love of God all fear is done away with; and that it is a matter of little importance whether our love for God is free or necessary: if the accuser has not understood this, so much the worse for him: the *Tractatus* is simply not a book for his kind!

6. Spinoza proceeds to reject indignantly the charge of having made reason into the sole interpreter of holy scripture and of having raised Mohammed to the rank of true prophet, whereas in fact Spinoza claims

to have treated him as an impostor because he did not show the signs associated with the true prophets. However anyone, no matter to what religion he belongs, who observes justice and charity, has the spirit of Christ: "Now as for the Turks themselves, and the other Gentile heathen, if they adore God with the practice of justice and charity to their neighbor, I believe them to have the Spirit of Christ and to be in the way of salvation, whatever convictions they may have from ignorance concerning Mohammed and prophetic declarations" (p. 226). And so the charge of atheism is turned back upon the accuser: "And so you see, friend, that this man has strayed far from the truth; and yet I grant him to be doing no injury to me but rather the supreme injury to himself when he does not blush to proclaim that I am teaching atheism by covert and counterfeit arguments" (p. 226).

Spinoza's reply, for all that, has in no way mitigated but rather confirmed and clinched the all-out pantheism and determinism on which the accuser had based the charge of atheism: [10] the crux of the whole matter lies in the rationalistic identification of intellect and will, and of will and freedom, and of freedom and necessity; the charge was based on the total immanence of the act maintained by Spinoza.

Spinoza's line of argument in this whole discussion, conducted at various intervals with different opponents and critics, always hinges on the same argument that reality cannot be governed by chance but must rather be governed by reason: hence the absolute dichotomy maintained by Spinoza between the *fortuitum* (chance) and the *necessarium* (necessary). Hence also it is evident that this *necessarium* coincides with the *rationale,* indeed with the real as such; and that therefore we are compelled to the admission of the identity of the necessary and the free: we are in a world admitting of no lacuna whatever, no leeway and no respite: "Similarly it is beyond me by what chains of reasoning you are trying to persuade me to believe that the *fortuitous* and the *necessary* are not contrary. As soon as I notice that the three internal angles of a triangle are equal to two right angles, I deny that this is the result of chance. Similarly, as soon as I notice that heat is a necessary effect of fire, I deny likewise that this happens by chance. It seems no less absurd

[10] "This protest is strong and even vehement in its terms, and there is not the least reason to doubt its sincerity. . . . It is evident that he considered religion as something very real in man's life, and the charge of irreligion or atheism as the grossest and the most wicked of calumnies. But this religion, as he understands it, is not the religion of churches and sects. It is independent of dogmatic theology, independent of any particular knowledge or belief as to revelation, independent even of the so-called natural theology which holds to the conception of God as a Person after all other definitions of his nature have been renounced, and to the expectation of another life which shall redress the balance of the present one in some manner of which all specific knowledge is disclaimed" (F. Pollock, *Spinoza, His Life and Philosophy* [London, 1899], p. 66).

and repugnant to reason to suppose that the *necessary* and the *free* are two contraries: for no one can deny that God knows himself and all other things freely; and yet all concede by common consent that God knows himself necessarily" (p. 251).[11]

Thus, for Spinoza the knowledge that God has of other things is on the same level as the knowledge that God has of himself: inevitably, therefore, if the mode of being of God is necessity, the existence of things in God must also be necessary and things are not and cannot be except in God. Freedom in the vulgarly understood sense, i.e., the freedom of indifference, comes down simply to ignorance or doubt and the will cannot be at the mercy of contingency and thus cannot be anything but necessity: "An ever constant will, determined in all things, is a power and a necessary property of intellect; you will see that my words entirely concord with truth" (p. 259). Any inclination to admit two wills in God, one necessary and the other indifferent, is simply absurd, because it means admitting that God can will a thing and at the same time not intend it, "and consequently we shall conceive God's will as diverse from his essence and his intellect and in this way shall fall into one absurdity after another." [12]

This notion of freedom, which welds shut the circle of being and acting, is understood restrictively and therefore is diametrically opposed to the psychological notion of a freedom of choice: "I call that entity free that exists and acts solely from the necessity of its own nature; and I call that entity under compulsion, on the other hand, that is determined by another to exist and act in a certain and determined way. For example, God exists freely albeit necessarily, because he exists solely out of the necessity of his own nature. Thus, too, God freely understands himself and all things whatever, because it follows simply from the necessity of his own nature that he should understand all things. And so you see that I am locating freedom not in free decision but rather in free necessity." [13]

Spinoza may be justified in claiming that this notion of "closed-circuit" freedom goes back to Descartes; but the formulation is Spinoza's own and represents a deepening of the Cartesian notion to this extent, that the interpolation of the freedom-necessity of Stoic meta-

[11] *Ep.* LVI to Hugh Boxel; ed. Gebhardt, Vol. IV, pp. 259ff. Spinoza attributes to Descartes his own notion of freedom, "for Descartes designated as free what is not compelled by any cause", and he rejects the notion of the freedom of indifference, i.e., of "what is not determined to anything by any cause" (*Ep.* LVII, p. 263). The point is that freedom is not actuated upon external things or upon the movement of one's own members, but solely upon the interior act proper to one, which act proceeds solely from reason.

[12] *Ep.* LVI, *ibid.,* p. 259.

[13] *Ep.* LVIII, to G. H. Schuller, *ibid.,* p. 265.

physics into the interior of immanence effects a perfect weld between knowing and acting.

The "free necessity", supreme paradox that it is, is the new formula of the principle of immanence: it is the perfect mode of self-actuation of God and also, as we have seen, of man in God. It is along this line, rather than the Cartesian one, that the dialectic of the principle of immanence will pursue its main development in modern philosophy; and as soon as it has succeeded in expelling as superfluous the theological reference, there will be nothing left but the area of human knowledge, and freedom will coincide with limit-setting of reason itself. On this point Spinoza does not hesitate to specify his own position as opposed to Descartes and to reject any notion of freedom unless it coincides with the interior necessity of reason.[14]

And so the Spinozan speculation was crucial, as we have now demonstrated, in the development of modern thought, inasmuch as it traced back the roots of the Cartesian immanence of the *cogito* to the immanence of being and thus demonstrated the hopelessness of Descartes' effort to conclude to a transcendent God and so to maintain the multiplicity of particular finite subjects, when once Descartes had started from immanence. Of course Spinoza is not yet Hegel: between the two intervenes the elaboration of transcendental activism, preeminently in the Leibniz-Hume-Kant conjunction. Yet Spinoza must be admitted to have effected an enormous and decisive advance from the point of view of content: subsequent philosophizing will still be at pains for a long time to solve the problem of the act, seeking for that entirely reflexive and all-encompassing immediacy demanded by the avowed immediacy of the content and the elimination of the opposition between finite and infinite, matter and spirit, nature and God, and the like.[15] So there does

[14] "But when Descartes says that that person is free who is not compelled by any external cause, if by a man under compulsion he understands one who is acting against his own will, then I concede that we are not under any compulsion whatever in some things and in this sense do have free will; but if by 'under compulsion' he understands someone who, though not acting against his own will, is nevertheless acting necessarily (as I have explained above), then I deny that we are free in anything" (*Ep.* LVIII to G. H. Schuller, *ibid.*, pp. 266f.).

[15] Seen thus, Spinoza's firm refusal becomes intelligible to apply to God any "human attribute", even in the higher sphere, whether intellectual or volitional (cf. as early as *Ep.* XXI, *ibid.*, Vol. II, pp. 127f.); attributing human qualities of any kind to God would be like attributing the qualities of the elephant to man (*Ep.* XXIII, *ibid.*, Vol. IV, p. 148). On this point, Velthuysen's charge had hit the mark (*Ep.* XLII, *ibid.*, p. 208). To Schuller's objection: "Since God's intellect differs from our intellect both in essence and in existence, therefore it will have nothing in common with our intellect, and consequently (on the basis of the argument advanced in Proposition 3 of Book I) God's intellect cannot be the cause of our intellect", Spinoza made the vigorous rejoinder: "The human mind can only attain to that knowledge involved in the idea of a body existing in act

not exist for Spinoza in the strict sense any "problem" of the existence of God; even though, in imitation of Descartes, he does present his proofs, these are really simply explanations of what was implicit in the first step. And this first step can only be taken with God, or at least with the notion of a single and perfect "Substance" which is therefore identified with God and shows God, viewed in this speculative mirror, to present features of absolute necessity, as we have seen.

Pantheism and Panentheism or Metaphysical Immanence

The atheist content of the Spinozan metaphysic is not anthropological in nature, as will be the case in the wake of Kant's *Ich denke überhaupt* (I think in general); rather it has a cosmic background and is expressed in the interchangeable use of *Deus sive natura* (God or nature) in a context that sums up with special intensity the reduction of being to unity, that reduction on which was based the charge of atheism we have expounded. Spinoza deduces quite justifiably from this identity the denial of any sort of final cause and of finality in general and thus all the categories and values fall by the wayside: "We thus see that men have been in the habit of calling natural things perfect or imperfect, more out of prejudice than out of any true knowledge of them. For we show in the Appendix to the First Part that Nature does not act for an end; for that eternal and infinite Being we call God or Nature, necessarily acts by the very fact that it exists. For we have shown (Prop. 16, p. I) that that Being acts by the same necessity of nature whereby it exists. Therefore the reason or cause why God or Nature acts and why that same God or

---

or to knowledge to which one can conclude from this idea itself." And he explained, with the evident if tacit intention of overcoming the Cartesian dualism: "For the power and capacity of anything is defined only by its essence (cf. Prop. 7, p. 3 *Ethica*), and the essence of the mind (cf. Prop. 13, p. 2) consists solely in being the idea of the body existing in act, and consequently the mind's power of understanding extends only to those things which this idea of the body contains within itself or which follow from that idea. But this idea of body involves no other attributes of God, nor does it express any, save only extension and thought" (*Ep.* LXIV, p. 277). And since this *thought* has *extension* for its object, we have established that no properly human attribute belongs to God. The bad influence exerted by the *Tractatus Theologico-Politicus* must have been virtually universal, to judge from, e.g., the statements of Philip van Limborch in a letter to his friend Velthuysen: "I agree entirely with you that the author is skillfully and covertly teaching atheism. He does indeed make very frequent mention of God, and the power, knowledge and will of God; but these are mere words, for if we attend to the scattered references, often marginal to his main theme, we shall discover that he admits no God other than this universe." And after showing the identity of God with nature in Spinoza and the absorption of the modes in the single substance in the fashion of the three Persons in the Christian Trinity, van Limborch concludes: "What he has to say for himself in his Letter is to no point, nor is it worthy of any refutation" (Letter of September 13, 1671. Cf. K. O. Meinsma, *Spinoza und sein Kreis,* pp. 528f.).

Nature exists is one and the same. Just, therefore, as that Being exists without the impulsion of any cause, so does that Being act without the compulsion of any end; but rather has no end or principle of action and operation any more than of existing." [16]

Any tendency here to introduce or recall the distinction in Spinoza's thought between *natura naturans* and *natura naturata,* as some have thought to do, not only fails to improve the situation but indeed merely confirms the position of absolute monism, centered upon "nature" as such: God is *natura naturans,* i.e., reality brought back to its constitutive unity and constituting itself in act, but *in nature and as nature*—that is the whole point! To *natura naturata* are referred the duality of the attributes and the multiplicity of modes which, far from shattering the unity of substance expressed in the *natura naturans,* weld it indissolubly together!

The first step in Spinoza's philosophy, then, the foundation stone of his atheism is his very basic principle: *"Praeter Deum nulla dari, neque concipi potest substantia"* (Apart from God, no substance can be or be conceived).[17] We can immediately substitute *natura* (*naturans*) for God, in the sense of the Whole or the All as activity, rationality and self-sufficiency. From the theoretical point of view, the metaphysical monism of the doctrine of Substance, itself a kind of panentheism, is already a display of atheism; and this atheism will undoubtedly be aggravated whenever the opposition between the two attributes, extension and thought, tends to be resolved in favor of the former. This is bound to

[16] *Ethica,* P. IV, *Praefatio,* pp. 206f. Spinoza steadily insisted from the outset: "I do not separate God from nature in such a way as did all those of whom I know" (*Epist.* VI to Oldenburg, concl., *ibid.,* Vol. IV, p. 36). As early as in the *Brief Treatise,* he wrote: "From all this it follows that there is predicated of nature all in all and that therefore nature consists of infinite attributes, each one of which is perfect in its kind. But this accords with the definition given of God" (*Korte Verhandeling van God . . .* [*Brief Treatise on God . . .*] c. II, § 12, *ibid.,* Vol. I, p. 22).

[17] *Ethica,* P. I, Prop. XIV, *ibid.,* Vol. II, p. 56. In this connection, Mauthner notes that, according to Jean Le Clerc (1657-1736), the name of God was not included in the first edition of the *Ethica* which spoke only of "Nature" presented as eternal, and that it was the Latin translator of the work, the physician Louis Meyer, who had the name of God inserted with Spinoza's consent. And Le Clerc comments: "A reading of his book will easily reveal that the word *God* is but a *mock* word, a *decoy,* so to speak, to put the reader on the wrong scent. He subjects everything to some mysterious necessity, not imposed by anyone but natural to matter and to whatever intelligences are mixed up in that matter, and he advances no reason for this, at least none with any semblance of probability. Although he has arranged in mathematical order everything he says, so as to entrap the reader and take him unawares, everywhere can be detected false chains of reasoning and a perpetual succession of balderdash" (F. Mauthner, *Der Atheismus und seine Geschichte im Abendlande,* Vol. II [Stuttgart & Berlin, 1921], pp. 349f.). Legend or not, the incident is indicative of the impression produced by Spinoza's main work.

lead to a designation of being, in the final analysis, as nature in the sense of materiality, the material world, and to make thought but a "reflection" of that world. As we shall see, such is preeminently the Marxist interpretation, and it is probably the closest to the logic of the system though not (we feel, at least) to its formal structure, which explains the angry resentment of Spinoza's reply to the charge of atheism levelled against him, a reply not motivated solely by the fear of court proceedings and unfavorable verdicts!

Let us now see how Spinoza demonstrates the validity of the proposition we have cited above. In fact he presents less a demonstration in the proper sense than a restatement of the very notion of God which he placed at the beginning of the *Ethica* in Definition VI: "By God I understand an absolute infinite being, i.e., a substance consisting of infinite attributes, each one of which expresses an eternal and infinite essence." [18] To God therefore belongs every attribute that expresses his essence, so that the divine essence consists of all the infinite attributes, and from this it follows that God exists necessarily, according to Proposition XI: *"Deus, sive substantia constans infinitis attributis, quorum unumquodque aeternam et infinitam essentiam exprimit, necessario existit"* (God, or the substance consisting of infinite attributes, each one of which expresses an eternal and infinite essence, necessarily exists) (p. 52). And so, because all the attributes belong exclusively to God, another substance hypothetically posited as existing outside of God would have to be what it is by some attribute of God and there would thus exist two substances of the same attribute, which is absurd and therefore not possible. In its formal aspect, this line of reasoning reminds me of the Thomistic principle: *Perfectio pura sive separata non potest esse nisi una.* (There can be but one pure and independently existing perfection).[19] But such a reminder merely serves to point up the fact that Spinoza uses the principle in exactly the opposite way from Aquinas, who introduces it as the foundation of his metaphysics of participation in order to assert the transcendence of the *Esse per essentiam* (Being by essence) and the multiplicity of the *entia per participationem* (beings by participation). Spinoza, for his part, takes the diametrically opposed tack of stressing the unity of being and the preceding propositions are the steps of the deductive process leading to the proclamation of God as the one and only substance. The fulcrum of

[18] *Ethica,* P. I, *Definitiones,* p. 45. In the first of the two *Dialogues* included in the *Brief Treatise on God. . . .* Spinoza had arrived at a thoroughgoing formulation of this whole doctrine and in a form still better stated than in the *Ethica* (cf. V. Delbos, *Le Spinozisme* [Paris, 1926 [2]], pp. 15ff.).

[19] Cf. C. Fabro, *La nozione metafisica di partecipazione secondo S. Tommaso d'Aquino,* especially pp. 199ff.

this deduction is the demonstration, or rather the assertion of the identity of essence and existence in Substance, i.e., in God: *"Ad naturam substantiae pertinet existere"* (It pertains to the nature of substance to exist).[20] This assertion likewise recalls the Thomistic doctrine that conceives God as pure *Esse subsistens* (subsisting Being) and creatures as composites of essence and *esse;* but always the contrast is there between the Thomistic and the Spinozan conceptions, despite the similarity of the formulae. The Spinozan formula is in fact the expression of the stand taken by decadent and anti-Thomistic Scholasticism; and this affords us a precise and telling point of reference on this point as well.

But even as Spinoza took over from Scholasticism the doctrine of essence and existence, he inverted that doctrine entirely: For the (anti-Thomistic) Scholastics, existence indicates preeminently the empirical *datum* (given) and thus the *fact* of the divine causality which has effected the "transition" of a finite essence from the state of potency to that of reality and so existence, as the *positio rei extra suas causas* (placing of a thing outside of its causes), is what might be called the "centrifugal" movement of the creature from the Creator. On the contrary, for Spinoza existence indicates actuality but only in the sense that in the creature essence and existence are distinguished solely to indicate that the creature is a "mode" of God and thus to characterize its "centripetal" movement of reabsorption from the reality of the finite into the Infinite. Hence, the proof of Proposition VII, cited above, is concentrated in the famous notion of God as *causa sui* (cause of himself), with which the *Ethica* opens and which is explained with precisely the Scholastic jargon that will pass over from Spinoza to Hegel: "That is, its essence necessarily involves existence, or it pertains to its nature to exist."

In the Appendix to the *Cogitata Metaphysica,* Spinoza has explained this doctrine with a wealth of particulars that we must bear in mind in order to grasp the rigid and inflexible progress and method of the *Ethica.*[21] Spinoza has extensive recourse to Scholastic terminology and

[20] *Ethica,* P. I, Prop. VII, p. 49.

[21] However, there is a certain difference, at least in terminology, between this Appendix and the *Ethica,* for whereas in the *Ethica* the terms "substance" and "God" are synonymous, they are at least semantically distinct in this Appendix: "From the definition, or, if you prefer, the description of being already given, it can easily be seen that being must be divided into being which by its nature necessarily exists, or whose essence involves existence, and being whose essence does not involve existence, or at best only possible existence. This latter is divided into substance and modes" (*Cogitata Metaphysica,* Appendix, c. I, ed. Gebhardt, Vol. I, p. 236). And in Ch. II as well, Spinoza speaks of "uncreated substance" and of other things outside of God; such remarks would be meaningless in the *Ethica.*

this recourse is quite deliberate; but he inverts the sense entirely or rather he demonstrates the inevitable "decline and fall" of this terminology, once the primary meaning of *ens* (being) and of its constitutive semantics has been lost.

In the muddle of decadent nominalistically inspired Scholasticism,[22] Spinoza wants to arrive at clarity and break out of all ambiguity: "Moreover, to the end that what we have already said, as also what will follow, shall be better understood, we shall try to explain what is to be understood by *esse essentiae* (the being of essence), *esse existentiae* (the being of existence), *esse ideae* (the being of idea) and finally *esse potentiae* (the being of potency). To which course of action we are moved also by the ignorance of some who admit no distinction between essence and existence or, even though admitting it, yet confuse *esse essentiae* with *esse ideae* or *esse potentiae*" (*loc. cit.*, p. 237). To the explanation of these terms is devoted all of section II of the Appendix; and this section, which in its way constitutes the systematic preparation for the *Ethica,* can be signalled as being the tremendous toll that a tradition, already dessicated into mere verbalism and void of any real speculative marrow, had bitterly to pay to the new philosophy which thus cut short all fideistic hesitation in order to proclaim the uncontested hegemony of reason as pure *a priori* evidence. Here, too, just as in the *Ethica,* the point of departure is the notion of God: all things are in God, but in eminent fashion. The mode of being that things have in God is expressed in a graduated series of technical expressions: "(a) *Esse Essentiae*—the mode in which created things are included in the attributes of God; (b) *Esse Ideae*—according as all things are contained objectively in the idea of God; (c) *Esse Potentiae*—a term relating the possibilities not (yet) actualized to the power of God; (d) *Esse existentiae*—which is the very existence of things considered in themselves and outside of God; attributed to things after they have been created by God" (p. 238).

The crucial element for the distinction of God from the creature is expressed in the *esse existentiae:* Spinoza seems to accept the Thomistic contention on this point and asserts that, whereas in God essence and existence are identical, they are different in creatures; and Spinoza adduces Avicenna's argument ("In other beings, essence differs from existence and can readily be conceived without existence"). While the thesis could be called Thomistic, the doctrine is rather nominalist and Suarezian and in the final analysis pantheistic, inasmuch as essence and existence are conceived of as standing in the direct relationship of possibility

[22] On Spinoza's relations with Scholasticism, cf. J. Freudenthal, *Spinoza, Leben und Lehre,* Vol. I, ed. C. Gebhardt (Heidelberg, 1927), p. 43.

and reality.[23] In point of fact, however, the terminology in Spinoza takes on an entirely new meaning. Actually the other Scholastics distinguish essence and existence in creatures only as two elements or moments and not as two principles (as possible essence and real essence), in contradistinction to St. Thomas' contention that God is *Ipsum esse subsistens* and that creatures are composites of essence and the participated act of existence. Spinoza agreed with the non-Thomistic Scholastic position and borrowed its terminology as the technical expression of the unity of substance. Decadent Scholasticism likewise called existence a "mode" of essence: the mode of reality as opposed to that of possibility. For Spinoza, God (substance) is the only reality, things are his modes. God expresses the element of essence as possessed of all perfections; things are the element of existence and thus of outward appearance. Thus, Spinoza expresses the God-creature nexus solely in terms of subsumption, whereas decadent Scholasticism expressed it in terms of causality alone: Spinoza is unaware of the Thomistic solution that uses the notion of intrinsic participation of *esse* (being) to link subsumption to causality, founding the latter upon the former; [24] rather Spinoza takes up again the Parmenidean solution within the bounds of the Cartesian clear and distinct idea. Spinoza steadily developed this approach in scope and depth and it finds its definitive expression in the doctrine of the metaphysical immanence of the many in the One, of the diverse in the Identical, i.e., in the intrinsic subsumption of the attributes and the modes under the single substance.

From this approach to the essence-existence nexus, Spinoza deduces that since God alone is the sole existent Being it is only in God that essence is identical with existence: "Therefore there is nothing outside of God; rather it is only God who involves necessary existence." [25] In his formal Parmenidism, Spinoza conceives Substance as *"Ens absolute indeterminatum et perfectum* (the absolutely indeterminate and perfect

[23] Spinoza is *au courant* of the Scholastic controversies on this question, but he feels it sufficient to have touched on the crux of the problem: "Finally, if any philosopher still is in doubt whether essence and existence are distinct in created things, he need not expend much labor on definitions of essence and existence in order to remove such doubt: for if he but visit some sculptor or wood-carver, they will show him how they conceive a not yet existent statue in a certain methodical arrangement, and later present and exhibit it existent" (*Cogitata Metaphysica, Appendicis* P. I, c. 2, p. 239). On the importance attributed by Spinoza to the distinction between essence and existence for his whole system, cf. *Ep.* XXXIV to J. Hudde, Vol. IV, pp. 179f. and 181f.).

[24] Cf. C. Fabro, *Partecipazione e causalità secondo S. Tommaso d'Aquino* (Turin, 1961). Whereas St. Thomas refers the divine attributes to the source and fountainhead of the *Ipsum esse* (Being himself), Spinoza, together with Descartes, deduces them from the *Essentia perfectissima* (supremely perfect Essence).

[25] *Ep.* XXXV, ed. Gebhardt, Vol. IV, p. 183.

Being) which Being I call God". And he explains: "And seeing that the nature of God does not consist in a certain genus or kind of being, but rather in Being which is absolutely indeterminate, his nature also demands all that perfectly expresses *to esse* (being as such), since his nature would otherwise be determined and deficient. Since that is the way things stand, it follows there can be but one Being, to wit God, who exists by his own power." [26] This tie-in of Spinozism with the point most heatedly contested between formalistic Scholasticism and Thomism could be treated at great length; suffice it for our investigation to note that the new Spinozan formula for the essence-existence nexus will be taken up again and watered down by the Wolffian metaphysic but, above all, will constitute the central axis of Hegel's *Wissenschaft der Logik.*

Hegel's progress over Spinoza lies preeminently in his attempt to effect, via the principle of the transcendental, a dialectical absorption of the being in existence and therefore to make existence an apparition (*Erscheinung*) of essence, an apparition constituting the transition from *Dasein* [simple presence or "thereness"] into *Existenz* [existence, a "standing out" (side causes)], or in Hegel's characteristic expression, from the primary immediacy to the secondary immediacy which he calls a mediated, reflexive, resultant, essential immediacy.[27] It was within these Hegelian bounds that theological immanence was dispersed and thinned out into the cosmico-anthropological immanence of the modern and present-day philosophies, in which atheism is no longer an outcome but rather an outlook, hailed as the indispensible preliminary of the freedom of being. Spinoza's idea of metaphysical immanence constitutes a "new beginning" or rather it represents the complete articulation of the Cartesian initiative, which it pushes to that metaphysical level of meaning the *cogito* had to attain in order to impart to the *sum* the necessity of a fullness or totality of presence and subsumption.

This transition, which will be of crucial importance for the evolution of the transcendental in the great idealist systems and especially in Hegel, is managed via the Spinozan doctrine of *causa sui* (cause of itself) which Spinoza has far from accidentally placed right at the outset of

[26] *Ep.* XXXVI, *ibid.,* p. 185. And he retorts: "I conclude, therefore, as in my last Epistle, that there is nothing outside of God; rather, God alone subsists by his own sufficiency" (p. 186). The final word comes in *Ep.* LXXIII: "For I conclude several of God's properties from the simple fact that I define God to be the Being to whose essence it pertains to exist: to wit, that he exists necessarily; that he is one, immutable, infinite, etc.; and I could adduce several other examples on a parallel with these, which for the present I omit" (p. 335).

[27] For the expressions *reflektierte* (reflexive), *zweite* (secondary), *vermittelte* (mediated), *wesentliche* (essential), *Unmittelbarkeit* (immediacy), cf. *Wissenschaft der Logik, C.W.,* ed. Lasson, Vol. II (Leipzig, 1934), pp. 9, 106f., 122, 132 and *passim.*

the *Ethica* in his first definition: "By cause of itself I understand that whose essence involves existence, or that whose nature cannot be conceived of except as existing." [28] Spinoza gives no proofs or explanations of this proposition which is the one on which his whole speculative edifice rests: it amounts to a kind of primordial reflective and reflexive intuition, expressing in its own way a still more primordial basis of the *cogito,* i.e., the reason of the reality of the principle which is a presupposition of the *cogitare* (thinking), i.e., of substance. In virtue of this formula Spinoza can deny any stable reality to the *natura naturata,* i.e., the world, in order to reserve it to the *natura naturans,* i.e., Substance, transferring into God that constitutive actuality to which he traces back the existence of God. This synthetic element comes out quite patently in the clever process of Spinoza's deductions, when he writes in Proposition VII of the first part of the *Ethica:* "To the nature of substance it pertains to exist" and adds the demonstration: "Substance cannot be produced by another (according to corollary of preceding proposition); therefore it will be the cause of itself, i.e., (according to Definition I) its very essence necessarily involves existence, or to its nature pertains to exist. Q.E.D." [29]

Spinoza in fact hastens to show how this Proposition provides the key to the entire system, against the false conceptions of the principle of subsumption on the part of those who would like to designate finite things likewise as substance and therefore subsistent in themselves: "Would men but pay attention to the nature of substance, however, they would have no doubts whatever concerning the truth of Proposition 7; indeed, this Proposition would be an axiom for everyone and would be numbered among the common notions. For by substance they would understand that which is in itself and is conceived in terms of itself, i.e., that which can be known without needing to know any other thing." The assertion that the existence of substance is the direct consequence of its essence, the proclamation of the identity of essence and existence and the affirmation of the unicity of substance—all are simply aspects or elements of substance as *causa sui:* "Now since it pertains to the nature of substance (according to what has already been shown in this Scholion) to exist, its definition must necessarily involve existence, and consequently its existence must be concluded from its definition alone. But

[28] *Ethica,* P. I, def. I, p. 45. This doctrine of so-called immanent causality is encountered as early as the first writings of Spinoza (cf. P. Lachièze-Rey, *Les origines cartésiennes du Dieu de Spinoza* [Paris, 1932], pp. 21ff.).

[29] *Ethica,* P. I, prop. VIII Scholion II, pp. 50-51. On the principle that in God "the essence involves existence" are founded the demonstrations and the *scholia* of the demonstrations treating of the nature of God (cf. *Cogitata Metaphysica,* P. I, c. 2, c. 3; P. II, c. 1).

from its definition (as we have already shown in Notes II and III) there cannot follow the existence of several substances; it therefore follows from that definition necessarily that there exists but one single substance of the same nature, as we stated at the outset."

This is the essence of the new formula for the ontological argument for the demonstration of the existence of God proposed by Spinoza and destined to enjoy special favor with Hegel; and the frequently recurring analogy of the triangle leaves no doubt on the theoretical structure of the argument as it is developed in the demonstration of Proposition XI of the *Ethica:* it is impossible to conceive that God does not exist. It seems strange that Spinoza found to be identical the two propositions: (a) it is inconceivable that God does not exist because in him essence and existence are identical, and (b) God really does exist. St. Thomas accurately and punctiliously distinguishes these two propositions one from the other.[30] But Spinoza's behavior in this matter seems less strange when we consider the direct correspondence between thought and reality inherent in the new principle of immanence, used with ruthless consistency by Spinoza as the fulcrum of his whole system.

Therefore, the meaning of the principle that in God *essentia involvit existentiam* (essence involves existence) has nothing any longer in common with the Thomistic contention apparently identical with it. And the reason is that the divine *essence* of which Spinoza is speaking is the essence of God in the ideal transparency of primary and sole *Essence,* the obviousness of whose existence necessarily corresponds to and derives from its being conceived necessarily, i.e., is a direct consequence, as such, of the syllogism of identity or of interior perfection. And so it is by a reduction of the real to the "essence", by a merely formal enhancement and heightening, and thus via the simple rational comprehension of the necessary *de jure* subsumption of existence under essence, the transition is effected to the comprehension of the *de jure* existence, on the grounds that within the ambit of the principle of immanence the *de facto* necessary subsumption coincides with the formal subsumption. There exists only one real order, that of essence; and in it there is but one existent, Substance, into which are resolved man and the universe, the attributes and the modes, which exist not in themselves and through themselves but in virtue of their subsumption under substance.

For St. Thomas, on the other hand, is not the essence that makes the being exist; rather it is the *esse;* and so we have here a liminal transition, a crossing of a threshold, which precludes the procession of creatures from God being any sort of unbroken or necessary process, as it is asserted to be by Spinoza and the immanentist metaphysic: the

[30] Cf. his critique of the argument of St. Anselm: *S.T.* I, q. II, a. 2.

Thomistic *esse* constitutes a liminal transition, a threshold-crossing, which posits an irretrievable break with essence. It is the essence that is the proportionate object of analytical thought [31] which can deduce the properties from the essence; but the *esse* is not a property of the essence; the *esse* is the fundamental act of the essence, differing thus from the formal properties like necessity, simplicity, infinity, unity and the rest, which are derived from the essence and directly referred to the essence. Spinoza was here misled both by the Cartesian *cogito,* in the way we have indicated, and by the notion of *existence* which he took from anti-Thomistic Scholasticism. In the Spinozan context, therefore, the Suarezian Nominalist contention that extended the *essential involvit existentiam* to creatures as well in its own way—this thesis of *essentia involvit existentiam* is reserved to God, but not in order to prove transcendence, rather to serve as basis for immanence.

The distinction between essence and existence which Spinoza asserts in creatures he does not apply to God; in God he admits a mutual absorption of essence and existence. Hence, the identification: God = *Ens* (Being) = substantia (substance), without remainder! The Thomistic contention concerning the distinction between essence and *esse,* on the other hand, is aimed at guaranteeing the plurality and stability precisely of the created beings which are participant with respect to the *Esse per essentiam* (the Being by essence), i.e., the creator. And so a comparison of Spinoza with St. Thomas is highly instructive for a deeper understanding of the metaphysical problem and thus of the fundamental significance of pantheism or panentheism as a metaphysical expression of atheism.

We are now in a better position to understand the Spinozan notion of God as *causa sui* or *causa immanens* absorbing into himself the casuality of all things and natures, even as he has absorbed their reality of being: the two elements in Spinoza correspond to the point of identity. For we read (and this is the second pillar of the Spinozan system): *"Deus est omnium rerum causa immanens, non vero transiens"* (God is the immanent cause of all things, but not the transient cause).[32] Spinoza's demonstration, as usual, is purely formal and is rather an exposition of the conclusion of the principal stages thus far traversed: (1) First of all, the principle of the unity of substance, according to which "all things that exist are in God and must be conceived through God". (2) Hence, the principle of the *causa immanens:* "God is cause of the things that are in him," i.e., of all things. (3) These things, however, are

[31] Spinoza distinguishes between things "as they are in the imagination" and "as they are in the intellect": the former, for Spinoza, is the mode of appearance; the latter, of reality.

[32] *Ethica,* P. I, prop. XVIII, p. 63.

to the extent that they exist in God and they exist solely in God because outside of God there does not exist any substance.[33]

The principle of the cause is identical with the principle of the substance, because the principle of substance is identical in turn with the principle of being: the point of departure is also the principle of development of the system and its terminal point. The methodological immanence of the Cartesian *cogito* is being asserted as a rigorous metaphysical immanence, in a species of closed-circuit Parmenidism which admits neither multiplicity (the manifold) nor movement (motion). Of this dual "reduction" of the real, Spinoza did not and could not give any demonstration other than the superficial appeal to the first definition at the beginning of the *Ethica,* and this is not in fact a definition at all but rather the summary and essence of the whole system.

The Spinozan principle of the unity of opposites (in substance) was later taken over by transcendental idealism; but this transcendental idealism thought it could overcome the deadlock of the denial of motion and the manifold by invoking the principle of the dialectic, i.e., of the negativity of the particular. This principle made the manifold appear over against the one as a phenomenon or outward apparition of substance; it made essence the foundation of existence and existence the extrinsic exteriorization of essence. But the rescue operation was doomed from the start: once being and the being have been made to coincide, there is no room for the manifold or for motion, because the dialectic consists precisely in the reduction of the manifold without remainder to the One and of motion to rest ". . . aeterno modo" (in the eternal mode), which is the criticism offered of the Hegelian dialectic by Trendelenburg and Kierkegaard: [34] inasmuch as it starts with a vacuum of consciousness, a mental void, it can never attain to a "content" nor can it think of *motion* or "transition" from one contrary to the other except by having recourse to the empirical figure of motion itself. The unity of being is solidary with the totality and this in turn with the closed circuit and this, in its turn, with immobility.[35]

[33] For the basis of this assertion, Spinoza therefore refers the reader to Prop. 15: "Whatever is, is in God, and without God nothing can be nor be conceived"; this in turn recalls Prop. 14: "Outside of God, no substance can be nor be conceived" (*ibid.,* p. 56).

[34] Cf. A. Trendelenburg, *Logische Untersuchungen,* P. I, c. 3: "Die dialektische Methode".

[35] The hypothetical possibility might perhaps be advanced of a Spinozism without an Absolute as systematic or non-theological totality, with the Absolute being rather conceived of as the totality of the present "moment"; in this sense G. Gentile believed he could resolve the ambiguity of the Hegelian dialectic with his doctrine of "Pure Act", as well as the *phénomène d'être* (phenomenon of being) of Sartre and the like. But Being is here not *preeminently* absolute and thus the foundation of the many and the diverse; it is not Being but simply a phenomenon which dissolves itself into the positing of its own becoming.

An equally serious question is that of the "quality" or "texture" of being in Spinoza: once the attributes of extension and thought have been unified in Substance, this latter is not, properly speaking, itself either extended or thinking, material or spiritual. In his demonstration of the unity of substance (Proposition V), Spinoza appeals to the diversity of the attributes: now anyone would expect him to follow up his admission of the distinction and opposition between extension and thought with an assertion of the dualism of matter and spirit, rather than with an assertion of the unity of substance. The fact that Spinoza does indeed assert the unity of substance presupposes that he effected a further act of resolution within the two attributes, resolving the one into the other; and this seems to us the interpretation closest to the actual facts. If Spinoza does indeed at times attribute to Substance a spiritual nature, his more native conception of the bedrock of being is a material one.[36] And so the reductive conversion of Spinozism into materialism is an attempt to resolve the basic ambiguity of the dualism of the attributes; there is just as much justification for such a materialist reading of Spinoza as for the spiritualist or idealist interpretation; and it presents no greater drawbacks or disadvantages.

Basic Character of Spinozan Atheism

The influence and power of attraction exerted by Spinozism upon the most divergent philosophical tendencies derives preeminently from Spinoza's thrust toward the unity of being and of truth which would make it possible for the circuit of logic to be closed tight upon itself: it matters little, from this aspect, whether the content be designated as matter or as spirit. This sort of unity, which is expressed by the definitive formula of immanence, overcomes all the uncertainties and hesitations that still plagued Descartes, the believer. And it is—be it carefully noted—always an immanence of mind, even in the event of an attribution of corporeity or materiality to substance as its ultimate substratum, because this corporeity or materiality is molded into the unity of substance via reflection which reduces the many to the One. And this reflec-

[36] Spinoza in fact speaks, against his adversaries, of a single, infinite, indivisible, corporeal substance: "For a corporeal substance can be conceived which is not other than infinite, not other than single, not other than indivisible" (cf. Prop. 8, 5 and 12), and conceives matter as the substratum of being: "Matter is everywhere the same, nor are parts distinct within it, except insofar as matter is conceived by us as being disposed in various ways, and then its parts are distinguished modally only but not really." And Spinoza's example is indicative: "E.g., we conceive water, inasmuch as it is water, to be divided and its parts to be separated one from the other; but inasmuch as it is a corporeal substance we do not conceive of any such division, for so regarded it is neither differentiated nor divided. Moreover, water, insofar as it is water, is generated and corrupted, but insofar as it is substance, it is neither generated nor corrupted" (*Ethica,* P. I, Prop. 15, pp. 58ff.).

tion, as we have stressed already, has its fountainhead in an initial synthetic intuition and moves within the ambit of that intuition, even though it claims to use an analytic and deductive method. Consequently the *Deus sive natura* is not an isolated expression; it is a frank and forthright manifesto: the "nature" of which Spinoza speaks does not exclude the spirit, indeed it presupposes that spirit, not so that that spirit shall be identified with nature nor yet so that nature shall be identified with spirit, but rather inasmuch as the two worlds which correspond to the two opposing attributes correspond likewise with one another in nature considered as a Whole, an All; the two worlds converge in this Whole of nature to constitute precisely that nature in its infinite expansion.

Thus, Spinoza's philosophy has justly been called the authentic interpretation of the Baroque age,[37] inasmuch as its fountainhead lies in an "experience of the Infinite" or of a continual overcoming and surpassing of the finite, as opposed to the Renaissance which is the age of the triumph of form and limitation, in the fullness of their realization, this limitation being accepted as a positive element of shaping and structuring. The Baroque age, on the contrary, saw the dominance of the vital feel for the Infinite, a sentiment which manifested itself in the Catholic countries in a revival of mysticism in art (the visions of El Greco) and in spirituality (the ecstasies of St. Theresa), and in the Protestant world in an intensification of the feel for the divine immanence within the soul. Spinoza would have fitted into this last line of development. Spinozism can actually be held to be the philosophy of the Shapeless, of Infinity; such is the set of the principle which will be the keystone of panentheistic philosophy, the principle *omnis determinatio est negatio*[38] (every determination is a negation) with which the finite as such is reduced to nothingness, the principle which is the ultimate justification, in the opposite direction, of the unity of substance.

[37] This is the interpretation of Spinoza's best qualified editor: C. Gebhardt, *Spinoza,* c. V: "Der Spinozismus als Ausdruck der Barock" (Leipzig: Reclam, 1932), pp. 94ff.

[38] In this precise form, the one that has come to be best known in the history of philosophy, I do not believe it is to be found expressly in Spinoza, but it is to be found in an equivalent form and quite explicitly stated in an entirely precise context: "As to the point that by shape and form in this sense a mere negation is posited rather than anything positive, it is perfectly clear that matter pure and entire, considered indefinitely, cannot have any shape or form; such shape and form can obtain only in finite and determined bodies. For anyone who says he perceives shape and form is simply indicating that he is conceiving a determined thing together with the way in which it is determined. Therefore this determination does not pertain to the thing according to its being but is rather its non-being. Therefore, because shape and form are nothing else than a determination and a determination is a negation, shape and form cannot be anything else than a negation, as we have said" (*Ep.* I to J. Jelles, ed. Gebhardt, Vol. IV, p. 240). This point was admirably clarified by Hegel, *Geschichte der Philosophie,* Part III, ed. Michelet (Berlin, 1844), p. 347.

This principle has not only a formal systematic significance; it has a still more important methodological significance, for it leaves the way open to the intuition of the unity of contraries in Substance considered not in a vague indeterminate way but as an "Assumption" or possibility of elevation of human thought into the divine thought and thus in the sense of the accomplishment of the immanence of being via knowing. For us this is the guiding thread enabling us to grasp the true novelty of modern thought and thus to gather the true essence of its downfall into atheism. The assumption of human thought into the divine Knowledge is in the spirit of the entire system from beginning to end and is the explicit object of the famous Proposition 36 of Part V of the *Ethica:* "The intellectual love of the mind for God is the love itself of God, whereby God loves himself, not inasmuch as he is infinite, but rather inasmuch as he can be displayed by the essence of the human mind, considered under the aspect of eternity, i.e., the intellectual love of the mind for God is a part of the infinite love wherewith God loves himself." The demonstration leaves no doubt about the precise meaning of this reciprocal immanence of God in man and of man in God, according to which the true thought of man is identified with that of God, but also the thought of God actuates itself in human thought alone: "This love of the mind must be referred to the actions of the mind (according to Corollary to Proposition 32 on this page and Prop. 3, p. 3) which consequently is an action whereby the mind contemplates itself, with a concomitant idea of God as cause (according to Proposition 32 on this page and its Corollary), i.e., (according to Corollary of Proposition 25, P. I and Corollary II, p. 2) an action whereby God, to the extent that he can be displayed by the human mind, contemplates himself with a concomitant idea of himself; and to such an extent (according to the preceding Proposition) this love of the mind is a part of the infinite love wherewith God loves himself. Q.E.D." [39]

In this text special attention ought to be paid to the expression *God to the extent that,* which is to be the paradigm of every form of idealism with theological pretensions, and may also become the principle of a transcendental phenomenology of religious knowledge, with echoes and cross references from every age of thought beginning with Stoic piety and going on down to the lucubrations of the cabalists and Boehme and right on to our own days (e.g., Bergson).

Spinoza could almost be said to proceed in this area in a way opposite to and the inverse of the one pursued by Hegel: whereas the Hegelian dialectic aims at overcoming the opposition and the "difference" between finite and Infinite, by sharpening the opposition itself in which the dialectical process consists, in the tranquillity of the Spinozan *Amor*

[39] *Ethica,* P. V, Prop. 36, p. 302.

intellectuals the key to the overcoming of this opposition lies in the attainment of identity via intuition. [40] To this can be reduced, in the final analysis, the meaning and significance of the *causa immanens,* according to a precise indication given by Spinoza himself to Oldenburg who had inquired of him about the real significance and meaning of the first three sections of the *Tractatus Theologico-Politicus:* "But to speak plainly with you concerning those three sections to which you refer, I tell you . . . that I cherish an opinion concerning God and nature far different from that which the Christian moderns make a practice of defending. For I hold God to be the immanent cause of everything, as they say, but not the transient cause. I do indeed assert that all things are in God and move in God; herein I agree with Paul and perhaps also with all the ancient philosophers, even though my mode of expression be different; and I would risk saying that herein I agree even with all the ancient Hebrews, inasmuch as can be conjectured from certain traditions, even though these have come down to us adulterated in many ways." [41]

In any case, it can be agreed that any interpretation of Spinozism desirous of defining it either as materialist or as idealist on the metaphysical level is doing violence in a certain sense to Spinoza's intention; but it must also be admitted that Spinoza himself provides the spur for both interpretations, because the harmony of his system was a sheer postulate rather than the result of the deeper lying idea that animates it and opens it upon the Infinite. It should give us pause that Spinoza's further critique of religion in general and of positive religion in particular in the *Tractatus Theological Politicus*—on which are modelled the modern critiques of the basic doctrines of Christianity on the part both of illuminism and idealism and on the part of the Hegelian left—constantly refers back to this theory of the *Amor intellectualis* as the consummate form of immanence.

[40] "Intellectual intuition, the terminal limit of human knowledge, is really the same in man as in God. Man's thought merges with the thought of God, and to understand intuitively is nothing else than to be the thought of God. It would even be false to say that God thinks and we think his thought. We must rather say that God thinks himself in us and that, in each of our thoughts, we are God insofar as he constitutes the nature of our soul" (R. Lévêque, *Le problème de la vérité dans la philosophie de Spinoza* [Strasbourg: Publ. da la Fac. des Lettres de l'Univ. de Strasbourg, fasc. 17, 1923], pp. 151f.).

[41] *Ep.* LXXIII, Vol. IV, p. 307. There follows an observation directed against those who wanted to reduce his thought to immediate physical materialism: "However, those who think the *Tractatus Theologico-Politicus* has as its basis some notion that God and Nature (by which latter they understand a sort of mass or corporeal matter) are one and the same entirely on the wrong road" (*ibid.*). It must be remembered that for Spinoza there exists no such thing as the world of the "sensible qualities" but only the world of extended quantity or extension which is an intelligible world, a world of pure intelligibles.

The following point should be stressed: In the speculative search for ultimate certainty, Spinoza attributes an absolute priority to the knowledge of God which is the content and the very basis and foundation of the original theoretical act in which is asserted the victory over doubt.[42] From this aspect, Spinoza overcame the ambiguity of the "Cartesian vicious circle" because Spinoza does not make the first certainty dependent upon the empty consciousness, the awareness without content, of the *cogito,* but rather on the primordial knowledge of God, *causa sui,* and cause of all things in himself: "Moreover, since all our cognition, knowledge and certitude capable of really removing all doubt depends upon the cognition of God alone, both because without God nothing can be or be conceived, and also because we can doubt about all things so long as we do not have any clear and distinct idea of God, hence it follows that our supreme good and perfection depends on the knowledge of God alone, etc." (pp. 59f.). And Spinoza in his own way, granted the complete immanence of the world in God, can say—in almost Thomistic terms but with these terms used in a diametrically opposed sense—that the knowledge of creatures leads us to the knowledge of God as their cause: "Hence, since nothing can be or be conceived without God, it is certain that all things that are in nature involve and express the concept of God, in virtue of their own essence and their own perfection; and that we thus acquire a greater and more perfect knowledge of God the more we come to know natural things; or (since a knowledge of the effect via the cause is nothing else than a knowing of some property of the cause) the more we know natural things, the more perfectly do we know the essence of God (who is the cause of all things)" (p. 60).[43]

Hence, Spinoza's harsh attack on the common herd who perceive God solely in miracles and base their faith in God solely upon these suppressions of the order of the natural laws and thus accuse those persons of denying God or at least his Providence who try to explain and under-

[42] I follow the *Tractatus Theologico-Politicus,* c. IV, ed. Gebhardt, Vol. III, pp. 59ff.

[43] Spinoza continues to show that religion is entirely embraced in this knowledge and awareness which is also love of God, and that, compared with it, the historical Hebrew and Christian religion, with its truths, laws and ceremonies, proves to be quite inferior and thus useless and to no purpose. And he proclaims overtly (it is, indeed, the main contention of the *Tractatus*) the impossibility of accepting any truth whatever that claims to transcend the human intellect: "For the natural light [of reason] does not demand anything which the light [of reason] does not itself attain, but only that which it can indicate to us most clearly to be a good or a means to our beatitude. But those things that are good only by commandment or institution or because they are the token symbols of some good—these things cannot perfect our intellect; nor are they anything else but mere shadows, or fit to be numbered among the actions which are, as it were, the offspring or fruit of intellect and a sound mind" (*Tractatus Theol. Pol.,* c. IV, p. 62).

stand in terms of the natural laws these unusual facts called miracles by the ignorant! [44] Such people, observes Spinoza, are convinced that God and nature are two distinct principles and orders of causality, "therefore they imagine two powers, numerically distinct one from the other, to wit, God's power and the power of natural things, which latter power they hold nevertheless to have been determined or (as is held rather by the greater number today) created by God in a certain way. But they really do not know what they mean by either of these last adjectives or what by God or what by nature" (*ibid.*).[45]

The rejection of religion in the *Tractatus* is therefore the inevitable end result of all the chipping away at God that has been perpetrated in the *Brief Treatise,* in the *Cogitata* and in the *Ethica.* The Spinozan teaching on miracles thus provides the clinching verification of the fact that he has totally immersed God in the world and the world in God, beyond all possibility of misunderstanding.[46] The Western religious

[44] "For the common herd think they are seeing the most limpid manifestation of God's power and providence when they see something unusual happen in nature, something that contradicts their accustomed expectation of nature; therefore, they reckon that those who are at pains to explain or understand miracles in terms of natural causes are eliminating God or, at least, the providence of God" (*ibid.,* c. VI, p. 81).

[45] Hence the drastic conclusion to an absolute natural determinism: "Nothing therefore happens in nature that is at variance with the universal laws of nature, nor anything that does not agree with those laws or does not follow from them: for whatever happens, happens by the will and the eternal decree of God—i.e., as we have already shown, whatever happens, happens according to laws and rules involving an eternal necessity and truth. Nature, therefore, always observes the laws and rules that involve an eternal necessity and truth, even though these laws and rules are not all known to us; thus nature always observes a fixed and immutable order. Nor can a single sound reason be adduced for attributing to nature a limited power and efficacy only, or for holding nature's laws to be applicable to certain things only but not to all" (*ibid.,* p. 83). In his letter to Oldenburg, Spinoza refers expressly to this section of the *Tractatus,* leveling a mordantly sarcastic charge of ignorance against those who believe in miracles: "Finally, in regard to miracles, I am on the contrary persuaded that the certitude of divine revelation can be built only upon the wisdom of sound learning and true principles and *not on miracles, i.e., ignorance.* This point I have shown quite exhaustively in c. 6 concerning miracles." The Christians who appeal to miracles instead of following philosophy are reducing religion to superstition and ignorance "which is the fountainhead of all vice and roguery" (*Ep.* LXXIII, Vol. IV, pp. 307f.).

[46] "Therefore, we can come to an understanding neither of God's essence nor of his existence, nor yet of anything whatsoever concerning God or nature, on the basis of miracles, i.e., an event that exceeds our grasp. On the contrary, since we know all things to be determined and rendered sacred and inviolable in God, and the workings of nature to follow from the essence of God, and nature's laws to be eternal decrees and volitional dispositions of God, our unconditional conclusion must be that we are coming to know God and God's will that much the better, the better we know natural things and the more clearly we understand how these natural things depend upon their first cause and how they are effected according to the eternal laws of nature" (*Tract. Theolog.-Pol.,* c. VI, p. 85).

tradition has always sought, more or less adequately, to conceive of God as a personal being and thus to look upon creation as an extrinsic and entirely free activity which is therefore radically potential and so indifferent with respect to the divine essence and life; as opposed to this whole approach, Spinoza holds with a creation which is a necessary eternal emanation wherein is actualized (be it carefully noted!) the very divine life, in such a way that the laws of nature express the very texture and fabric of the reality of the divine life in its cosmic projection. For Spinoza, therefore, miracle would in no sense be an argument for the existence of God; on the contrary, it would lead straight to a radical denial of him: for the existence of miracle would be an infraction of the divine laws of the cosmos and would thus furnish a proof of chance and chaos and consequently lead straight to atheism.[47] And so this doctrine of miracle removes any lingering doubt concerning the Spinozan conception of God, i.e., concerning the identity asserted by Spinoza between God and nature, in the sense we have indicated and which Spinoza himself admits;[48] thus man has no opportunity left to appeal to religion against the verdict of philosophy.

Spinoza therefore considerably anticipated Hegel in conceiving the course of the real in terms of the perfect circle of reason, eliminating contingency and asserting the perfect confidence in God of freedom and necessity and therefore the inherence of God in the world and of the world in God. This point is crucial for a grasp of the ambivalence of the immanentist metaphysics and consequently for an understanding of the theism-atheism tension in transcendental idealism, especially the Hege-

[47] If, therefore, anything should occur in nature which did not follow from the laws of that same nature, this would be at variance with the necessary order that God has established forever in nature by way of the universal laws of nature; and so it would be against nature and its laws, and consequently a belief in such a thing would cause us to doubt about all things and would lead to atheism" (*ibid.*, pp. 86f.). Spinoza considers this doctrine basic to his system and clings to it to the end: "I have equated miracles and ignorance, because those who try to build the existence of God and religion upon miracles are attempting to make known an obscure thing by another thing still more obscure, a thing concerning which their ignorance is greatest; thus they are bringing forward a new type of argumentation, whose end result is not a reduction to the impossible, as they say, but simply a proof of ignorance. For the rest, I think I have given a sufficient explanation of my opinion concerning miracles in the *Tractatus Theologico-Politicus*" (*Ep.* LXXV to Oldenburg, Vol. IV, p. 313).

[48] It is his last word on the whole discussion: "But here, when speaking of miracles, I needed no such [argumentation] because there is patent philosophical clarity on the point concerning which we are enquiring (namely, whether we can admit anything to happen in nature that is at variance with its laws or does not follow from them); nay, I rather proceeded quite deliberately to elucidate this question on the basis of fundamental principles known from natural reason" (*Tract. Theol.-Pol.*, c. VI, p. 95). Spinoza does not boggle at demonstrating his interpretation of miracles to be borne out by both the Old and the New Testaments!

lian brand: theistic on the surface, atheistic in its depths, as we shall see: "Now I reply that, just as the Fortuitous and the Necessary are certainly two contraries, even so it is obvious that he who asserts the world to be a necessary effect of the divine Nature likewise denies entirely that the world was made by chance: whereas that man who asserts that God could have abstained from creating the world is corroborating, even though in other words, the contention that that same world was made by chance; since it would have proceeded, on this hypothesis, from a will which could have been non-existent. This opinion, however, and this judgment being wholly absurd, they generally concede unanimously that the will of God was never indifferent; and therefore they ought necessarily also to concede [N.B.] that the world is the necessary effect of the divine nature."

This is the cosmico-metaphysical reason for the rejection of a personal God, a rejection that is forthwith backed up by an anthropometaphysical rejection, i.e., an explicit refusal to transfer into God the attributes of the human spiritual substance, intellect and will, so as not to fracture the ring of necessity in God: "For if you ask them whether the divine will does not differ from the human, they reply that the former has nothing but the name in common with the latter; moreover, in general they concede God's will, intellect, essence or nature to be one and the same thing; thus I myself for my part simply do not ascribe to God human attributes, namely, will, intellect, attention, hearing, etc., lest I confound the divine nature with the human. I say, therefore, as I said just now, that the world is the necessary effect of the divine nature and that this world was not made by chance." [49] Therefore, it is hard to exaggerate the importance of Spinoza in the molding of modern thought: The Cartesian "rough draft" of immanence here becomes an accomplished full-blown reality within the circle of eternal reason and desire of the finite for the infinite and, strange as it may seem, the Spinozan outline with its immanentist trend cannot be adapted to all patterns or trends of thought.

Nature and Influence of Spinozan Atheism

Spinoza's own contemporaries, as we have already emphasized, did not allow themselves to be taken in by the continuous recurrence of the term "God" in the Spinozan writings and immediately denounced the

[49] *Ep.* LIV to Hugo Boxel, Vol. IV, pp. 251f. On this point, the opposition between a theology that conceives of God as a personal Being and a universe-based philosophy is irreconcilable (cf. *Ep.* XXIII, *ibid.*, pp. 148f.; *Ep.* XLII, *ibid.*, p. 208). From the absolute determinism of God's action and operation follows the absolute determinism of the human attribute (cf. *Cogitata metaphysica,* P. II, c. II, p. 274).

atheistic core and substance of his thought: and the sharp and vigorous self-defense contained in Spinoza's *Letters* was less than convincing because the "system" admitted of no cracks or fissures whatever.[50] While the similarity of Spinoza's line of thought to the ancient, medieval and Renaissance forms of pantheism may appear to be obvious, it must not be forgotten, for all that, that Spinoza was a modern who followed Descartes in initiating his speculation from within the ambit of thought: it is from the self-supporting and constitutive evidence of the conceptual determinations that the properties of God and man, of knowing and of acting, and of final beatitude are derived. Spinoza's theism is already gravely comprised by the equivalence of *Deus sive Natura,* the chief point of attack of his critics down to Hegel. This Spinozan theism becomes untenable as soon as the critic concentrates on the frankly noetic background of that identification and on its real significance. Spinoza really was not aiming at diluting God into the indeterminate sea of nature or yet at absorbing nature into the transparent heaven of the divine essence; his aim was rather to assert that man finds his supreme happiness (*amor intellectualis*) in the knowledge of the necessary nexus regulating the course of nature (*extension*) and of human activity (*thought*).

The uncertainty among his interpreters as to whether Spinoza might have attributed to God a knowing in act and thus have ascribed to one of the attributes a metaphysical priority over the other [51] seems to us of secondary importance and remains so for the case of idealist metaphysic where the identical situation is repeated. Even if Fichte, Schelling and Hegel do designate God as *Ich* (I, *ego*), it is a question of an I which is an "absolute" Concept and Idea and thus an all-subsuming and all-comprehending Whole, incapable of being a subject of knowledge in the sense of "cognizance" or advertence of something in act. For such an advertence either signifies a duality of subject and act and thus remains open to a multiplicity of subjects and acts, or it does not signify anything; but again a multiplicity of subjects and acts presupposes the priority and substantive character of being with respect to knowing. Knowledge is a transitory presence of being inasmuch as it becomes the object of knowledge; and knowledge is therefore based upon being and refers back to being which is the subsistent and the permanent phenomenon while knowledge is a modification or an "act" of a being relative to

[50] The *Principia philosophiae cartesianae* ed. Gebhardt, Vol. I, p. 51, is generally admitted to derive the Spinozan substance in its final form from the Cartesian substance (cf. E. E. Powell, *Ueber Spinozas Gottesbegriff* [Halle a S., 1899], p. 26. The author touches on the relations with Suarez' notion of substance: *Disp. Metaph.* XXX.).

[51] Renner gives a clear account of the difficulty (Renner, *Das Selbstbewusstsein der Gottheit im Systeme Spinozas* [Godberg, 1906]).

being [52] and is thus something transitory, at least for man as subject of thinking and philosophizing.

It is thus with Spinoza that there begins the ambiguity of the modern doctrine on "existence" which will later be elaborated by Hegel in the *Science of Logic* and transmitted by him to present-day thought (phenomenology, Marxism, existentialism, etc.). And Kierkegaard is here speaking in true Thomistic fashion when he denies that Spinoza has made any real progress in thought with the principle that in God *essentia involvit existentiam,* so long as the implication of existence in essence is deduced *a priori* as a pure nexus of concepts (as is the case in Spinoza); the only legitimate and valid object of Spinoza's discourse is the "concept" of existence, ideal existence; and this reduces the expression *essentia involvit existentiam* to a simple tautology.

Let us follow Kierkegaard's analysis for a moment. Spinoza, Kierkegaard observes, wants to deduce being from thought, by plunging himself into the concept of God; but, note well, he wants to deduce it not as a priority but rather as an essential determination. His method of procedure is the following: "The more perfect a thing is by its own nature, the greater and the more perfect existence does it involve; and, conversely, the more necessary existence a thing involves by its own nature, the more perfect it is." [53] Thus, the more perfect a thing is, the more being it has; the more being it has, the more perfect it is. But this is a tautology. Kierkegaard goes on to say that this tautological nature of the statement becomes still more patent in the light of a note (*loc. cit.,* Note II): "Note that we are here not speaking of beauty and the other perfections which men have been wont to call perfections out of their superstition and ignorance. Rather by perfection I understand only reality or being." Spinoza explains *perfection* in terms of *reality, being.* Thus, the more perfect a thing is, the more it is; but its perfection is that it has more *being* in it, and so the first statement means simply that the more a thing is, the more it is. So much for the tautology. But, continues Kierkegaard, there is something else in the Spinozan chain of reasoning.

There is in fact, in this reasoning, a failure to distinguish between *de facto* factual being and ideal being. In other words—and this is what Kierkegaard condemns—Spinoza is always moving in the ideal area of possibility and from it is deducing reality, instead of basing himself on *de facto* actual being. Spinoza can, in this ideal area, speak of more or less

[52] Thus, according to St. Thomas (*S.T.* I, 79, 13) cognition is an "act" in the sense that it is an actuation and exercise of knowledge already acquired and thus presupposes being: it is phenomenological cognition when it is a simple advertence to presence; it is moral cognition when it is a judgment on the goodness or badness of an act (*De veritate,* q. XVII, a. 1).

[53] *Principia philosophiae cartesianae,* P. I, Prop. VII, Lemma I (p. 164).

being, i.e., of differences of degree in being; but when speaking of actual being, it is meaningless to speak of more or less being. A fly, when it exists, has as much being as God, because with regard to *de facto* being, Hamlet's dictum is valid: to be or not to be! Actual being is indifferent with respect to all the differences of the essential determination and definition, and all that exists participates in being without any petty jealousy and participates in it to the same degree. The situation is different in the ideal order, that is quite true. *But*—and this is the central point in Kierkegaard's critique—*as soon as I start to talk about being in the ideal order, I am no longer talking about being but rather about essence.*

This observation provides Kierkegaard with the opportunity to accuse the Spinozan system of being an irremediably static system [54] and thus leaving no room for motion, for the dialectic of existence: the highest ideal being is the necessary and so it *is*. But this being is its essence preventing it from becoming the subject of dialectical development in the determinations of *de facto* being, because it simply is and cannot even be said to have more or less being with respect to or in comparison with something else. The Leibnizian (*a priori*) proof of the existence of God—if God is possible, *eo ipso* he is real [55]—is presented likewise within the confines of this realist-type immanentism. Spinoza's proposition, concludes Kierkegaard, is thus quite exact and the tautology is in place; but it is also clear that he is achieving nothing but a transposition of the difficulty, because the difficulty lies in breaking through to *de facto* being and effecting a dialectical introduction of the ideality of God into *de facto* being.[56] Thus the inversion of being from transcendence into immanence has already been accomplished with Spinoza and being has been bent to the exigencies of thought, reality to the demands of the concept.

Kierkegaard is justified in seeing Hegel's whole ambivalence already

[54] In a group of texts from the *Journals* for 1864, and thus later than the text we are here expounding, Kierkegaard levels a precise charge against this static nature of the Spinozan system whence derives likewise the Spinozan rejection of final causes and the consequent ambiguity of the whole structure of the *Ethica:* "On the one hand (in order to get rid of theology), he [Spinoza] considers everything as being in a state of rest, and then on the other hand (in virtue of the definition *suum esse conservare* [to conserve its own being]), finite reality proves to be in a state of flux and becoming. This means that there is here a lack of the concept of motion" (*Papirer* [Copenhagen, 1915] 1846, VIII C. I, p. 401). Kierkegaard refers the reader likewise to VII A 28, 29, 31, 34, 35; cf. *Diario,* Italian translation of C. Fabro, 2nd Ed.; Vol. I, nn. 916, 917, 920, 921.

[55] Identical reference to Leibniz in *Papirer* 1849-50, X 2 A 328; Italian translation, n. 2097, Vol. I, p. 1009.

[56] Cf. Kierkegaard, *Briciole di filosofia,* Vol. I; Italian translation of C. Fabro (Bologna, 1962), pp. 131f.

present in Spinoza: "What introduces confusion into the whole doctrine of 'essence' in the logic [of Hegel] is the failure to note that the whole operation is being effected upon the 'concept' of existence. But the *concept* of existence is an ideal entity, and the whole point at issue is whether existence does in fact lend itself to an exhaustive resolution into concepts. Were this to be the case, Spinoza might be right with his *essentia involvit existentiam,* i.e., the concept of existence; in other words, ideal existence.

Against Spinoza, and certainly with greater justification, Kant asserts that no determination of content follows from the concept of existence. Kant is clearly thinking realistically [57] of existence as not coincident with the concept, i.e., he is thinking of an empirical existence. The principle that essence is existence is valid preeminently in the area of the ideal; but obviously here it is a question, as we have seen, of an ideal existence, i.e., of a mere possibility. Real existence on the other hand, specifies Kierkegaard, corresponds to singular reality (as Aristotle had taught even in his day); it remains outside of, and in no sense coincides with, the concept. For an individual animal, an individual stone, an individual man, existence (to be or not to be) is something very crucial; an individual man certainly does not have a conceptual existence. And so the way in which modern philosophy speaks of existence shows that it does not believe in this personal immortality, it understands only "concepts" [58] to be eternal. Spinoza had effected a radical abolition of the problem of God with his resolution of existence into essence, because essence in turn resolves into thought, into matters of thought and is dependent on thought, which is human thought, and thus resolves itself ultimately into human thought. But the point is this: to speak of "existence" as existence in thought is to deny or annihilate existence itself. Spinoza was saddled with the Cartesian theory of the clear and distinct idea, i.e., of the determination of the real in terms of the idea and of the features of the idea; and he was also saddled, from further back, with the decadent Scholasticism that had combatted Thomistic metaphysics of participated *being,* by denying and rejecting the real distinction in creatures between essence and *esse* (being) [59] and thus depriving itself of the only theoretical guarantee protecting the creature against being dissolved into a "mode" of the one and only Substance and enabling it

[57] Cf. *Papirer* 1849, X 1 A 666: "Philosophy has become fancifully imaginative, especially since it abandoned Kant's 'real-life' road and the famous [real-life] 100 talers in order to become theocentric. The 100 talers are the famous example cited by Kant to show the difference between thought and reality" (*Diario,* Vol. I, Italian translation, n. 1949, p. 926).

[58] *Papirer* 1849-50, X 2 A 328; Italian translation, Vol. I, n. 2097, pp. 1008f.

[59] On this point cf. C. Fabro, *La nozione metafisica di partecipazione secondo S. Tommaso,* III ed., Torino, 1963.

to enjoy a durable subsistence via its own act of being, participated from its own singular essence.

Charges of atheism against Spinoza flew thick and fast while he was still alive, as his *Correspondence* bears witness. The man who assumed, with greatest prestige, the function of public prosecutor of Spinozan atheism was, as we have noted, P. Bayle, who, while recognizing and admitting the originality of Spinozan atheism, yet is at pains to find its antecedents in Oriental, Jewish and Medieval philosophies.[60] For Bayle as for subsequent historians of philosophy in general, the basis of Spinozan atheism lies in the principle of the unity of Substance (*Deus sive natura*), i.e., in panentheism, especially in the form propounded by the Stoics and Neoplatonists, the *Anima mundi* (World-Soul) concept; but in Spinoza this takes on a still more rigid form, inasmuch as he admits no providence in the proper sense.[61]

In his refutation of Spinozan monism, Bayle challenges primarily the identification of God with extension; and this for two reasons: because God cannot have parts, and because such an identification would lead to the further identification of God with matter and thus make him subject, like matter, to continuous changes; [62] It is just as absurd, claims Bayle, to identify God with thought and such an identification would end in dragging God down into the errors and miseries of men. In his desire to lift man up to the level of God, Spinoza has dragged God down into nature and human indigence, into a status worse still than that of the anthropomorphic polytheism of the Stoics: "For if man is but a modification [of God], then man does nothing on his own: it would be a pointless, facetious, ludicrous, empty phrase to say that joy is glad, that sadness is sad; well, it is just that sort of phrase we utter, in the Spinoza

[60] "He was a systematic atheist and used an entirely new method, even though the substance of his doctrine was common also to several other philosophers, ancient and modern, European and Oriental" (*Dictionn. hist. et critique,* Vol. IV [Basle, 1738 [5]], art. "Spinoza", fol. 253). On p. 265 we read: "He is said to have died fully persuaded of his atheism." The exposition and critique are based preeminently upon the *Tractatus Theologico-Politicus,* but in the last Notes to the article, Bayle refers expressly to the *Ethica.*

[61] *Ibid.,* Note (A), p. 253b.

[62] Cf. the exposition in Note (N), repeated in Note (DD); *ibid.,* fol. 259b and 269b. Bayle cites a vast volume of anti-Spinozan writing in his own support: Note (D-Q), fol. 255bff., among which the most violent seem to be the Socinian Fr. Cuper, *Arcana Atheismi enervata . . . ,* (Rotterdam, 1676), and J. Bredenbourg, *Enervatio Tractatus Theologico-Politici una cum demonstratione, geometrico ordine disposita, NATURAM NON ESSE DEUM, cuius effati contrario praedictus Tractatus unice innititur* (Rotterdam, 1675). The Cuper or Cuperus mentioned by Bayle is the Dutch writer Kuyper, whose *Arcana Atheismi revelata* deals with Spinoza's first writing, the *Brief Treatise* (cf. S. Dunin Borkowski, "Der erste Anhang der Kurzen Abhandlung," in *Chronicon Spinozianum* [1921], p. 75, previously published in *Der junge Spinoza* [Münster i. W., 1910], pp. 360ff., 374ff.). On Kuyper, cf. below, Appendix V.

system, when we assert that man thinks, man grieves, man hangs himself, etc. All of these propositions must be predicated of the substances of which man is but the mode. How could it have been imagined that an independent nature, existing by itself, and in possession of infinite perfections, should be subject to all the evils of the human race? . . . The very cogent reasons that stand against the doctrine that our souls are a part of God have still greater cogency against Spinoza." And the end of this monism is the impossibility of speaking any longer even of truth and error: what could be more ridiculous than such a philosophy.[63] And everyone will see, concludes Bayle, how Christianity loses all meaning in this system.

From the mass of mid-century polemic, suffice it to select Wolff's statement, an admirably accurate summary of the state of the question in the age of Rationalism and which presents in synthetic form the main heads of the charge: *"Spinozism is not far removed from atheism and is equally harmful, indeed, in a certain sense more harmful than atheism.* For, although Spinoza admits God to be the first and only cause of all things (§ 672), yet he denies him to be possessed of knowledge (*not.* § 712) or to act from a freewill (*not.* § 709) or to govern and direct this universe (*not.* § 714); and he holds bodies and souls and other thinking entities, if such there be, to be in that same God as parts in a whole (*not.* § 708); he imagines a God totally different from the true God who is possessed of the highest wisdom (§ 640, *part. I Theol. nat.*) and a supremely freewill (§ 431 *part. I Theol. nat.*) and governs and directs this universe by his wisdom (§ 902 *part. I Theol. nat.*) and in whom souls and bodies and thinking entities, if there be any other such, do not exist as parts in a whole (§ 708). And so it is the same thing as if he denied that the true God exists. It is therefore clear that Spinozism is not far removed from atheism, since that man is an atheist who denies that God exists (§ 411). *Which was our initial statement."*

Spinozism is further subversive of all moral order: "Moreover Spinozism does away with all religion (§ 714) and divine obligation to perform certain actions and to abstain from others (§ 715); exactly as atheism (§ 516, 539). Since, therefore, atheism is harmful inasmuch as by it religion is done away with and all divine obligation to perform certain actions and to abstain from others, there can be no doubt that Spinozism is equally harmful with atheism. *Which was our second statement."*

[63] Bayle, *loc. cit.,* Note (N), fol. 262 col. a. An examination and critique of the main Propositions of the *Ethica* are to be found in Note (P), fol. 263ab, and especially of Prop. XIV: Aside from God no substance can be or be conceived (cf. also Note (D-D), fol. 268b). F. Erhardt has provided a systematic treatment of the anti-Spinozan polemic, in its historical evolution, in *Die Philosophie des Spinoza im Lichte der Kritik* (Leipzig, 1908). On the atheism charge, cf. especially pp. IIff.

Indeed, because of its fatalism, Spinozism is more deleterious to the moral life than explicit atheism itself: "And this is the reason why there has been unanimous consent in holding Spinozists to be atheists and Spinozism to be an impious hypothesis; and while other authors who were bespattered with the stain of atheism did find those who defended them, there has as yet been no one who has dared to wipe that stain away from Spinoza. Nay, rather the Ethics of Spinoza is admitted to be the only system of atheism which has been publicly set forth; and the overturning of its foundation is precisely what we have felt to be our duty."[64] For Wolff, too, Spinozism is thus the negation of all natural and positive religion.

Once Spinozism had been rescued from the doghouse in the latter half of the 19th century, thanks to the Hegelian left wing (Feuerbach) and the invasion of positivist materialism, it is no cause for surprise that Marxism should consider Spinozism to stand side by side with Hegel as one of the pillars of the Marxist conception of the real and would be at pains to eliminate from Spinozism every remnant of theological coloring. The duality of the attributes leaves the "quality" or texture of Spinozan being still hanging in the balance: thus, idealism resolved this duality into cognition as act of the spirit, while the dialectical materialism of Feuerbach-Marx-Engels preferred to conceive of cognition and mind as a "reflection" of the material world. For Feuerbach, Spinoza is the true Moses of the modern freethinkers and materialists: his error is merely the methodological one of having operated in too abstract a mold and having conceived of God as subject and nature as predicate; but for all that, Spinoza is the true founder of modern speculative philosophy.[65]

At the end of the last century, E. Bernstein and K. Schmidt tried to bring Marxism back to Kantianism, but the Soviet brand of Marxism assumed a decisively Spinozan set: its doctrine of "substance" as a synthesis of opposites enabled it for a time to overcome vulgar materialism (Vogt, Moleschott) and to initiate an interpretation of the real in dialectical fashion as *unity* of extension and thought, of objective nature and spiritual nature, rather than as that *identity* of the two proclaimed by idealism. For strict Marxism, therefore, Spinoza is worth more than either Descartes or Kant; he is the first thinker of modern times to have shown with unusual depth of penetration and power of persuasion that

[64] Chr. Wolff, *Theologia Naturalis* (Frankfurt and Leipzig, 1741), § 716 (the clinching section), pp. 729ff. The exposition of Spinozism begins with § 671 (p. 672).

[65] Cf. Feuerbach, *Vorläufige Thesen zur Reform der Philosophie; C.W.*, ed. Bolin-Jodl, Vol. II (Stuttgart, 1906), p. 223. Engels and Marx agree in considering Spinoza the standard-bearer of atheist materialism which developed later, preeminently in French Enlightenment philosophy (cf. *Die heilige Familie*, pp. 131ff.). The identification of God with nature is a charge, based on the *Deus sive natura* formula, to be found in the very first polemical writings (cf., e.g., in Italy: B. Lucchi, *Spinozismi syntagma*, [Padua, 1738], pp. 30ff.).

there do not exist any transcendent powers ruling the world, that there does not exist any higher reason pursuing its own ends and goals in the world, that the world is intelligible in terms of itself and must be so understood, that its nature has not been created by anyone and that everything within it happens according to necessary laws.[66] Thus, for the Marxists, Spinoza is the man who has escaped from all the dark shadows and obscurities of the spiritualism of transcendence, restored nature to the attention and inspection of science and vindicated for man the freedom that belongs to him via the two essential truths proclaimed by the Spinozan philosophy: materialism and atheism.[67] The so-called "pantheism" of Spinoza is but a deceptive appearance or at most a remnant of his cultural background.

And so, not only did Spinoza's protest against the charge of atheism remain entirely ineffective; it simply made matters worse. Spinoza's weighty defense undertaken by Hegel himself came to nothing because Hegel himself was immediately forced, precisely and preeminently by his Spinozism into the position of defendant against the same charge on the part of orthodox theology and of the Hegelian left wing, especially Feuerbach, as we have already pointed out. Spinoza certainly began simply as one of Descartes' commentators and propagandists; but he can be seen in the light of all this to have emerged as a new, more consistent, consequential and trenchant initiator of modern thought, whose direct or indirect influence has penetrated the most divergent materialist and idealist philosophies, impelling them all irresistibly to the henceforth inevitable solution of the unity of being, which is absolute immanentism or the mutual subsumption of man in nature and nature in man.[68] In this sense, the evolution of modern philosophy right down to the present

[66] Cf. A. Deborin, "Spinozismus und Marxismus," in *Chronicon Spinozanum,* Vol. V (The Hague, 1927), pp. 152f. The road had been opened up in this direction in 1910 by G. W. Plechanov, *Die Grundprobleme des Marxismus* (Berlin, 1958), pp. 13f.

[67] Cf. George L. Kline *et. al., Spinoza in Soviet Philosophy* (London, 1952), p. 34 (Introduction). The other collaborators agree: cf. pp. 88f. (L. J. Akselrod), 98 (A. M. Deborin), 129 (V. K. Brushilki), 170ff. (J. K. Luppol). Spinoza's reaction to the charge of atheism, which we have encountered in the Letters, is interpreted by the Marxists as being a defense against the charge of immorality which the term "atheist" signified in his day. According to Feuerbach (*Vorläufige Thesen,* p. 383), Spinoza may not have wanted to be believed to be an atheist, but the neo-Marxists have on their side the internal logic of the Spinozan principles and the all-out fight against all religion (cf. A. M. Deborin, "Spinoza's World-View," in Kline, *loc cit.,* pp. 101f.: Deborin cites the weighty evidence of Maximilian Lucas, friend and pupil of Spinoza and his first biographer).

[68] On the influence of Spinoza on the philosophy of various nations, cf. A. van del Linden, *Spinoza, seine Lehre und deren erste Nachwirkungen in Holland* (Göttingen, 1862); M. Grünwald, *Spinoza in Deutschland* (Berlin, 1897) (analytical exposition from Poiret to Nietzsche); G. Bohrmann, "Spinoza in England," in *Spinozas Stellung zur Religion* (Geissen, 1914), pp. 59-81; P. Vernière, *Spinoza et la pensée française avant la révolution,* 2 vols. (Paris, 1954).

day has been accomplished in the shadow (or, if you prefer, in the light) of the Spinozan principle.

With the appearance of Spinoza's thought there begins to be in evidence a new conception of the world and of man in that world; and Spinozism is a river that has become an ocean in which converge in various guises the tributary streams of trends that apparently are drastically opposed to each other. Or rather Spinozism is the underground river that feeds them all and which, as soon as any one of them is blocked or dries up due to the exhaustion of its resources, causes others to gush forth, more suited to the new cultural climate which may well be different from the preceding one and even diametrically opposed to it. It is no accident, therefore, that Spinozism has become the central pillar of modern thought before and after Kant and has persisted right down to our own day, despite the profound change of direction and methodology in philosophy. Hegel was right in asserting, from his point of view, that "to be a Spinozan is the beginning of all philosophizing".[69] Such was the new beginning made by Spinoza and it remains today in the philosophy of immanence exactly what Spinoza made it; nor can it be anything else than that "unity of being" as *mental being, being of knowledge, being of mind;* however the activity of cognition and mind may subsequently be understood, it is always cognition, mind that is at the root of being and its determinations. Therefore, there was ample justification for the theists,[70] whether Catholic or Protestant, to take up the cudgels against Spinoza, even as later on against Hegelianism: the unity of being was bound to entail the disappearance of one of the members of the diarchy. In Spinoza and in metaphysical idealism, it seemed to be the finite and man within it that was doomed to disappear; but in reality it was God who paid the price of this new form of immanence surging forward on the two fronts of being and knowing. It is indicative that Spinozan monism should be invoked in their own support by the new forms of materialism[71] and idealism alike which were to dispute the field in subsequent centuries: the gaps, the inconsistencies and the deleterious consequences for which it was flayed by the theologians became the secret nourishment of the new philosophical criticism and were to lead modern thought gradually but irresistibly to the vision of a world (and of man within that world) open exclusively to this-worldly prospects.

69 "It is therefore to be noted that thinking must have adopted the standpoint of Spinozism; being a Spinozist is the crucial point in all philosophical thinking" (Hegel, *Geschichte der Philosophie,* p. 337).

70 For a bibliography, see Appendix to this section.

71 D'Holbach finds Spinoza's atheism, a consequence of his notion of the unity of being, to raise no problems (d'Holbach, *Système de la nature,* Vol. I, p. 118 ("this celebrated atheist") and *passim.*

3

Religion, Morality and Atheism in P. Bayle

While in England empirical rationalism was corroding the religious mind and, with Hobbes, bending it toward sense-perceptionism and materialism, voices of skepticism were becoming more vocal in France. Criticism and distrust were mounting against the metaphysics that Descartes had wanted to revive but which he had in fact driven into a state of crisis from which there was no escape, or rather only one such way, namely, to make the point of departure God himself, the idea of God, the intuition of God; but this was repugnant not only to avowed materialists but even to those who still declared themselves to be theists but had no intention of making religion dependent on the fortunes of metaphysics.

In this struggle against Christianity or this process of dissolution and headlong fall of modern thought into atheism, the Marxists give a special place of honor to the work of Pierre Bayle (1647-1706), who can be considered the chief partisan of religious skepticism or of the irremediable opposition between reason and faith in the modern age.[1] He is the man, according to Marx, who totally discredited 17th-century metaphysics and every metaphysic from the theoretical point of view. His weapon was skepticism, a skepticism forged out of the very magic formulae of metaphysics. He began at the outset with the Cartesian metaphysic.[2] He, like Feuerbach, shifted from a struggle against speculative theology to a struggle against speculative philosophy, inasmuch

[1] On Bayle's stormy life, cf. P. Hazard, *La crise de la conscience européenne,* ch. V (Paris, 1935), pp. 102ff.

[2] Bayle often expressly declares that he is a Cartesian. Cf. the main work here under discussion, the *Pensées diverses,* written to a doctor of the Sorbonne on the occasion of the comet which appeared in the month of December, 1680 (Rotterdam, chez Reiner Leers, 1704), Vol. III, pp. 90 and 531. Vols. II-IV contain the *Addition* to the *Pensées,* in which Bayle replies to the criticism of the (Calvinist) pastor Jurieu who had expressly accused Bayle of atheism in the *Courte Revue des Maximes* (1591).

as he, like Feuerbach, recognized speculation as being the last bulwark of theology; because he had had to force the theologians to take refuge from the seeming science of metaphysics in the repugnant vulgar faith, religious doubt subsequently impelled Bayle to doubt the metaphysics on which this faith was based. He therefore subjected metaphysics to criticism over the entire vista of its historical development. He became the historian of metaphysics but only to write the story of its death. Spinoza and Leibniz were his favorite targets.

The significance of Bayle's work, according to Marx, is not limited, however, to his having paved the way with his skeptical dissolution of metaphysics for materialism and (British) common-sense philosophy to be welcomed in France. He further proclaimed the *atheist society* which ought to have begun to exist at once in the wake of the *demonstration* that a society of pure and outright atheists *could* exist, that an atheist *can* be a respectable human being, that a man does not become degraded through atheism but only through superstition and idolatry. In this sense, concludes Marx, Bayle must be recognized to have been "the last of the metaphysicians in the 17th-century sense of the term and the first of the philosophers in the 18th-century sense of the term".[3]

The occasion of the famous debate on atheism and of the theses defended by Bayle, to which Marx refers, was the appearance in 1680 of a comet that put all Europe in an uproar because the masses judged it to be a divine sign presaging ill, a portent of dire events and dismal happenings: an obvious judgment and scourge of God, preeminently against those who were cultivating unbelief and professing atheism. The contention that Bayle developed in his *Pensées diverses* was that all this alarmist superstition was simply silly, that the comet was in no sense an extraordinary sign from God but a perfectly natural event.[3a] And Bayle

[3] K. Marx, "Die heilige Familie," c. VI, § 2, in *K. Marx-F. Engels Werke,* Vol. II (Berlin, 1958), pp. 134f. The text is reported in abridged form in the Soviet *Geschichte der Philosophie,* German translation (Berlin, 1959), Vol. I, p. 477. Moreri had already called Bayle the "counsel for the atheists": "However, it seems that, despite all the apologies that have been written in favor of M. Bayle, one can scarcely render a favorable verdict upon him when one bears in mind that almost throughout he is the counsel for the atheists, mitigating their crime as much as possible, using all the powers of his intelligence to bolster their arguments, furnishing them with new weapons, extolling them as invincible, attenuating the best replies, and finally drastically debasing reason and yielding the field to the Manicheans and the Pyrrhonists" (Moreri, *Le grand Dictionnaire Historique,* Vol. I [Basle, 1773], p. 612).

[3a] On the cultural background of the work, cf. the new work by E. Labrousse, *Pierre Bayle,* Vol. II (La Haye, 1964), pp. 103ff. The main intent of the famous work seems to have been the launching of a concerted attack on Roman Catholic piety and devotional practice as a preliminary to an attack on the dogmatic and political level (cf. W. Rex, *Essays on Pierre Bayle and Religious Controversy* [The Hague, 1965], pp. 30ff.).

goes on to pose the radical problem, that of a knowledge of God on the part of man: Who can ever really truly bring the attributes of God known by philosophy into alignment with those that are found mentioned in scripture?[4] But let us proceed in order, for the charge of atheism pierced Bayle to the quick.

In the Preface to the *Pensées diverses,* Bayle declares: "The true scope of this work was to refute with a theological reason that which is wont to be said about the presages of comets. The necessity of buttressing this reasoning impelled me into the parallel between atheism and paganism, a parallel without which my proof would have been exposed to an objection that would have rendered it less apt to convince men of what I had to demonstrate. I had, then, either to leave an open breach or to refute the reasons of those who say that the idolatry of the pagans is not in fact as great an evil as is atheism." We must not, therefore, distort or misrepresent the scope and proportions of the work: it never intended to effect a confrontation between atheists and the devotees of true religion and Christianity but rather to institute a comparison of atheism on the one hand and idolatry and superstition on the other.[5] And Bayle protests vigorously against his accuser (". . . who has written so much against the Roman Church") that it is not true, as claimed by the Calvinist pastor (and today by Marxist criticism!) that Bayle's book "tends to diminish the aversion felt toward atheism"; on the contrary: "I verily believe myself to have spoken all the ill against

[4] "By some mysterious fatality, the more one reasons about the attributes of God in conformity with the greatest and most sublime notions of metaphysics, the more one finds oneself in conflict with a host of passages in Scripture. Although this conflict has its roots not in the things themselves but in the difference of styles, it is not at all easy to eradicate it in a manner that will satisfy all minds" (*Pensées diverses* . . ., Preface, Vol. I, pp. 4f.). Bayle refers the reader to the article "Gregoire d'Armini" in his *Dictionnaire.*

Concerning these *Pensées diverses,* it will be of interest to point out that, according to the author, "the entire book was written from the fictive point of view of a Roman Catholic" (*Addition,* Vol. II, p. 563). Attention might also be called to an explicit protestation of subjection to the Roman Church (cf. *Addition,* Vol. II, p. 535). This specification is strange indeed and it did not escape Feuerbach; cf. *Pierre Bayle, Ein Beitrag zur Geschichte der Philosophie und Menschheit, C. W.,* ed. Bolin-Jodl, Vol. V (Stuttgart, 1905), p. 166.

[5] Cf. *Eclaircissement* I: "The remark that has been made upon the good morals of certain persons who have no religion can in no way prejudice the true faith and does no damage to it" (§ XII, *Dictionnaire historique et critique,* Vol. IV, fol. 618). In his recent study *Pierre Bayle,* esp. Vol. II, pp. 103ff. E. Labrousse has made a masterly analysis of the problem of atheism and the subtle polemical passages in Bayle, with a comprehensive investigation of his sources, ancient and modern, and especially of the anti-Roman cast of the entire work. Cf. also W. Rex, *Essays on Pierre Bayle* (The Hague, 1965), pp. 35ff. The basic aim of the work seems indeed to have been to throw back into the faces of the Jansenists and P. Adam the atheism charge they had leveled against the Calvinists with whom Bayle had ranged himself (cf. W. Rex, *op. cit.,* pp. 65f.).

atheism that can be spoken about it generally speaking." And this under two aspects: (a) "Any inspection of the judgment of the atheists concerning the divinity reveals a horrible excess of blindness, a prodigious ignorance of the nature of things, a frame of mind subversive of all the laws of common sense and productive of a disordered and false fashion of reasoning which defies description"; (b)"Any inspection of the dispositions of the atheists' heart reveals that, not being restrained by the fear of any divine chastisement nor animated by the hope of any heavenly blessing, that heart must abandon itself to all that tickles its passions . . . They would have liked me to have left the world with the same conviction it has at present, that an atheist is necessarily plunged in all manner of crimes: for this conviction, however little in accord with history, is of great use to religion." Let the rhetoricians do this if they will, exclaims Bayle, it is not his task.[6]

First of all, what is the connection between the problem of the comet and that of atheism? Bayle specifies this connection in a set of 14 propositions or points in which he himself summarizes the teaching of the book on the comet and which he sends to the universities for them to pass upon. In view of the unusual importance of the text and the no less serious carelessness with which the historians of philosophy in general and of atheism in particular have often treated Bayle's position, we here present quite extensive excerpts from the original text of the basic points of this authoritative summary of the whole controversy.[7] Bayle defends his own position as being orthodox from the point of view of Catholic theology itself.[8]

§§I-II—Attributing every extraordinary fact or event of nature to miracle or special intervention of God, seeing in such facts or events divine portents as do some Christians, may be a fomenting of superstition and idolatry, the more so because it is a question at most of the most trivial, obscure and entirely useless happenings. If Christians do

[6] *Addition,* Vol. II, pp. 538ff. The Jurieu charge claimed, according to Bayle: "(1) that I am an enemy of all religion in general; (2) that I make no secret of my atheism; (3) that I do not edify the public by any act of religion; (4) that the name of my chief divinity is Louis XIV; (5) that I and the fellow members of my cabal throughout the whole land have our closest ties with the Deists, the Spinozists, the Indifferentists and persons suspected of the greatest heresies" (*Addition,* Vol. II, p. 532).

[7] *Addition,* ch. VII, pp. 604ff. This synthetic summary of the *Addition* is paralleled by the 15-point analytical defense in the later article "Eclaircissement I," added to the *Dictionnaire.*

[8] Bayle insists that his thesis has an apologetic character and that it favors Christianity over paganism: "They will permit me to tell them that it suffices to work for wholesome religion, for everything done for religion in general would serve paganism as much as Christianity" (*Eclaircissement I,* § 10, fol. 618). On p. 535 of the *Addition,* there is also included a protestation of subjection to the Roman Church.

not want to repeat the errors of the pagans, they would do better to attribute such happenings to natural causes, i.e., to the generic laws of nature established by God, than to appeal to particular acts of will on the part of God calculated to produce miracles. Thus, what Bayle wants to assert here is a criterion of theological sobriety; he does not actually deny either the reality or the possibility of miracles, but he takes the specific case of the appearance of the comet as an opportunity to observe:

(a) that such events can be simply natural happenings;

(b) therefore, they do not in fact possess the character of a divine "portent", i.e., they do not imply any special nexus with divine providence and its relations with man and the government and direction of the world;

(c) indeed, any such tie-in would but foment idolatry and superstition as happened in paganism.

§§III-IV—God has always shown his abomination for idolatry through the prophets. But any interpretation of these extraordinary happenings as miracles would amount to thinking that God, who well knows the consequences of his own acts, had set for himself, as the aim and fruit of miracles, the preservation of that idolatry in the world for fear that atheism might otherwise win out. The miracle-mongering interpretation . . . is therefore not only unfounded but, as we would say today, it even boomerangs by yielding more advantage to idolatry and superstition than damage and refutation of atheism.[9]

§§V-VII—Thus it can be asserted—and now Bayle is entering into the heart of the question—that God, who proclaims himself a king jealous of his own glory, feels more abomination for idolatry and superstition which have set false gods on his own throne than he does for atheism.[10] Atheism is a simple refusal of allegiance; idolatry is called theft by God himself and, worse still, prostitution. It is more serious to err concerning the essence of the very concept of God and adore creatures as God, than to have no notion of God and not give him any

[9] In the *Pensées diverses,* the thesis read: "That atheism is not a greater evil than idolatry" (§§ 214-225, Vol. I, pp. 225ff.; cf. also *Addition,* Vol. II, pp. 561ff.). The demonstration is effected with a great myriad of quotations from classical and Christian authors.

[10] And later: "I have claimed paganism to be at least as bad as atheism" (*Addition,* Vol. III, p. 4; cf. Vol. I, § 114, p. 225, (on his point that atheism is not a greater evil than idolatry). Cf. also his thought that it is better to be an atheist than to be a pagan (Vol. IV, c. 76, p. 389). Bayle also cites St. Thomas (*S.T.,* II-II, 94, 3): "The Angelic Doctor is taking the same line. . . ." (Vol I, § 216, p. 227).

honor. It suffices in fact to make the most cursory review of pagan mythology, as it presents the gods involved in all kinds of filth and baseness, in order to become convinced that the human race was considerably more corrupted by idolatry than it could be simply by being deprived of religion.

§§VII-IX—Although no man can, according to theology, act out of pure love of God without a special grace, a man can behave in an upright fashion and do good actions for purely human motives, out of inclination, for love of praise or fear of blame. And so it can very easily be the case that certain men, although they have no religion whatever, yet observe a kind of propriety and "civic integrity".[11]

§§X-XI—There is also the well-known fact that a man can admit in theory the principles of Christian morality and of the Gospel and then live in conflict with these same principles, as do many Christians. Thus, consent of the mind to certain principles is not enough to ensure conformity of the will to those principles in practice; nor is it enough to believe the Gospel in order to ensure that one will practice it without further ado.

§§XII-XV—The pagans, despite their errors concerning religion, nevertheless had the same ideas of glory and honor as the Christians, independently of belief in God: "He [the pagan] can, for example, realize that a person lacking in gratitude is worthy of blame, that a son is worthy of praise when he has respect for his father, just as he realizes independently of religion that the whole is greater than its part." [12]

[11] However, in the article "Eclaircissement I" (§ VII), Bayle observes that a recognition of this fact does not involve any belittling of true religion, because such imposing and noble actions of the pagans, "their sobriety, their chastity, their probity, their scorn of riches, their zeal for the public weal, their readiness to do kindnesses for their neighbor, did not proceed from the love of God or tend to honor and glorify him. Their own self was the motive force and the goal of such actions: self-love was the basis, the end, the whole sum and substance of those actions. They were but brilliant sins, *splendida vitia* as St. Augustine called all the fine actions of the pagans" (*Dictionnaire, loc. cit.*, Vol. IV, fol. 617). For the phrase ascribed to St. Augustine, cf. *De civitate Dei*, I, 19, c. 25. It is also recorded in a similar context by Kierkegaard in *Philosophiske Smuler*, c. 3, interpolation (*C. W.*, Vol. IV, 2nd ed., p. 246).

[12] *Addition*, Vol. II, p. 208. Note, however, the different argumentation in the *Pensées diverses*, where Bayle first observes, with the Fathers, that idolatry is the most serious sin (§ 216), and then goes on to say: "The idolaters were true atheists in a certain sense" (§ 217); "For an idolater, the knowledge of God serves only to make his crimes more atrocious" (§ 218); "Idolatry renders men more difficult to convert than does atheism" (§§ 229-230); "Those who were exceeding wicked among the pagans were not atheists" (§ 230)—e.g., Tarquin, Catiline, Caligula, Nero.

Thus, atheists like Epicurus and Pliny were able to live upright and well-ordered lives. So it is not true that the atheist must, by the very fact of his atheism, be immoral and steeped in all manner of vice, nor does it suffice to know a thing is forbidden by God in order to abstain from it.

§XVI—Atheism is thus a lesser injury to God than is the negation and denial of his fundamental attributes and primarily his holiness: "As the notions of the hierarchy of values clearly show us that moral good is superior to a physical good and that the more one loves virtue the more one prefers it to life itself, God who is supremely holy must have more (if such terms as 'more' and 'less' can be used in his regard) love for his own holiness than for his authority; and so those who represent him as covered with crimes from head to foot, as the pagans represented Jupiter, are offending him in a more sensitive spot than are those who, like Epicurus, take away from him the government of the universe".[13]

§XVIII—It is less of an error to conceive of God as separate from, and disinterested in, the world than it is to consider him as being dependent on that world as does paganism: "Inasmuch as independence is the most sublime of all the physical perfections of God and the one that the Schools hold as making the difference between God and every other being, it is a less gross error to hold with Epicurus that God, being perfectly happy in himself, does not meddle in the government and direction of the world, than to hold, as did some pagans, that God needs to nourish himself on exhalations".[14] There can therefore be no possible misunderstandings, and the trepidations are as meaningless and groundless as the charges of unbelief or of defense of atheism: the critics are simply mistaken.

The crux of the question that Bayle wanted to raise under pretext of the controversy about the comet, is stated as follows: There is no generic comparison instituted between religion and atheism; nor is the outright assertion made that religion is not indispensible for the safeguard of good morals; there is simply an effort to draw attention to the following points:

1. Pagan religions tolerate and even substantiate by mythology the most disordered customs; therefore they contribute to a corruption of good morals rather than to their diffusion.

2. The comparison is thus not between religion and atheism taken in a generic sense in both cases, but rather between "paganism" as a corrupt religion and the atheism of certain "theoretical atheists" who

[13] *Ibid.*, p. 609.
[14] *Ibid.*, pp. 609f.

may have taken principles of uprightness and natural decency as inspiration for their lives.[15]

3. The result of the comparison is thus that there may be persons who call themselves religious and yet live a shameless life and persons who are (and call themselves) atheists and live an upright life.

Can it then be concluded that religion as such is not indispensible for the living of an upright life or that atheism does not of itself lead to a shameless life? On the basis of Bayle's own exposition it is exactly the opposite that should be concluded. He is speaking primarily of, and instituting his comparison between, the state of pagan religions (rather than that of religion as such) and a few theoretical atheists (rather than atheism as a worldwide phenomenon); his defense is aimed "at those who have been scandalized at my having said that there are atheists and idolaters".[16] It is therefore unintelligible how Marx could have so categorically concluded that Bayle "proclaimed the atheist society . . . via the demonstration that there could exist a society of pure atheists, that an atheist can be a respectable man, that a man does not become degraded through atheism but rather through superstition and idolatry".[17] For Bayle claimed to be distinguishing, in contrast to Marx, between religion and superstition and, above all, between Christianity and idolatry; therefore Marx's inferences would have elicited an immediate protest from Bayle himself, even as did the downright charges of atheism made against him by Protestant and Catholic theologians.[18]

Yet, it is undeniable that the document on the comet tends to remove the impression of horror that atheism can arouse and to inculcate

[15] "It was a question solely of atheists in theory, like Diagoras, for example, or Vanini, Spinoza, etc., men whose atheism is attested either by the historians or by their own writings. The nub of the matter is simply the morals of this class of men: let anyone who can do so point out to me examples of such men having led an evil life" (*Eclaircissement* I, § XIII, *loc cit.*, fol. 619).

[16] *Ibid.*, fol. 617.

[17] K. Marx, *Die Heilige Familie*, pp. 134f.

[18] Trinius, e.g., observes vigorously that the *Letter on the Comet* contains various "scandalous propositions", to wit: "Bayle poses the question as to whether atheism is more scandalous than superstition, and further as to whether a society of true Christians would be capable of preserving itself in the midst of pagans or in the midst of other unbelievers, and his reply is in the negative. He asserts that Christianity was not given by Christ for all men; that the Gospel is to be considered merely as a model of the greatest perfection; that the denial of God does not lead in and of itself to impiety; that religion does not serve to make men more pious but only to preach fine sermons, etc." (J. A. Trinius, *Freydenker Lexikon,* (Turin, 1960) pp. 62f.). Thus the contention that Bayle taught that "a society can conveniently preserve itself without religion" was not hard to arrive at (J. A. Trinius, "Erste Zugabe," in the 1765 edition of the *Lexikon,* p. 11). Trinius indicates, on the authority of van Helberg, that Doctor Hickes, Sir Francis Bacon and "many other excellent gentlemen" (!) were precursors of Bayle's thesis. Certainly Spinoza was of the same opinion.

a certain respect for speculative or theoretical atheists and to spread an explicit charge or at least suspicion of hypocrisy and insufficiency against religion in general. Indeed, Bayle's final statement, highlighting the fact that "the fear and love of the divinity are by no means the only fountainhead of human actions. There are other principles moving man to act . . ." [19] is no longer a comparison of atheism with superstition and idolatry but rather with religion itself as such; and the course of the demonstration makes it clear that this includes Christianity as well. The statement: "The fear and love of the divinity are not always more active principles than all the others. The love of glory, the fear of infamy, death or torture, the hope of a preferment, act with greater force upon certain men than do the desire to please God and the fear of transgressing his commandments," [20] is no longer a comparison between atheism and the licentiousness of mythological religion but rather an assertion of the inefficacy or moral impotence of religion as such, and the sophistry is all too patent. In fact, if those who claim to be religious fall into errors and disorders, they certainly do not do so through the fear and the love they have for God but rather because they are following their own passions and making bad use of their own freedom. It is not that the real fear and love of God (and thus religion in general and as such) are insufficient in themselves to restrain the passions; indeed, they demand of man that he take upon himself death itself in order to avoid sin. But the point is that God leaves man free so that man shall show his love as a son and not as a slave. The fact that man deviates into evil while professing religion entails no prejudice to the status of religion as such; it counts solely against man who is abusing his own freedom and following his own passions.[21] This is an obvious enough distinction but one for which the reader searches in vain in Bayle.

Expressed in modern terms, Bayle's methodological (and perhaps likewise his substantial?!) error was that of having interchanged existence and essence, of having elevated a *de facto* state of affairs to a *de jure* principle and of consequently having indubitably favored the position of atheism, perhaps in excess of his own intentions. The split between morality and religion, which is admissible in the *de facto* order,

[19] *Eclaircissement* I, § I, fol. 617.

[20] *Ibid.,* § II, fol. 617.

[21] In the *Pensées diverses,* on the other hand, Bayle says the question can be resolved only by an investigation into religious ethnology (§ 229, p. 250). A modern critic observes: "Perhaps Bayle's basic principle is the independence of morals from any theological or religious sanction. This Cartesian principle was of course reinforced by this Protestant orientation. He points out how often religious men are bad, and irreligious men good" (J. H. Randall, *The Career of Philosophy: From the Middle Ages to the Enlightenment* [New York: Columbia University Press, 1962], p. 857).

precisely in virtue of the basic freedom enjoyed by man to choose good or evil, is not admissible in the *de jure* order: it would amount in fact to a recognition of the superiority of atheism over religion and of the atheist society over the religious one.[22] In effect, it must be admitted that Bayle had not covered himself enough against the Marxist deduction of the possibility of a society of atheists who would be perfect gentlemen and whose society would therefore be superior to a religiously grounded one. Thus, there cannot and should not be any cause for amazement at the charge of atheism being levelled against Bayle in an atmosphere of such inflamed confessional controversy as that of late 17th-century and early 18th-century Europe.[23]

Nor was this charge entirely unfounded if the statements of Bayle be read with assertive and not purely polemical overtones, especially as these statements were first formulated:

§ 233: Atheism does not lead to a corruption of morals, with the comment: "That what persuades us that atheism is the most abominable state in which a man can find himself is but a false prejudice formed in the matter of the light of conscience which is imagined to be the rule of our actions in default of a careful examination of the real wellsprings of our actions" [24] And above all:

§ 234: That experience militates against the reasoning accomplished in order to prove that the knowledge of a God corrects the vicious inclinations of man. All that is all very fine and good when we are looking at things in their ideal state and making metaphysical abstrac-

[22] Indicative of the significance of this document on the comet in the context of the whole of Bayle's writings is the statement of Mauthner: "Bayle's whole personality comes out in this early book, even though it was not intended as a statement of principle and seemed mainly directed solely against a popular superstition" (F. Mauthner *Der Atheismus . . .*, Vol. II, p. 254). Mauthner also admits: "Again and again, atheism is rhetorically compared only with idolatry; but in the end the rebellious thinking of the author finally filters through to the reader in its full extent: atheism is not so dangerous as exaggerated religiosity. . . . Accordingly a society of atheists could live just as morally as a pagan or Christian society with the exclusive invocation of the threat of punishment or disgrace for crime" (pp. 256, 258).

[23] Bayle tries to parry the blow by observing that Descartes met the same fate: "Descartes was accused of atheism by a professor of philosophy from this country because of his metaphysical Meditations wherein the existence of the true God was throughout the basis, the key and the pith of the whole system. . . .Perhaps one day the public will get to see a catalogue of philosophers accused of atheism and will boggle in amazement at the stubbornness, the temerity or the ignorance of the accusers" (*Avertissement,* prefaced to the *Addition,* Vol. II, pp. 5f). Grotius, Arnauld and other proven theists have also met the same fate, claims Bayle (*ibid.,* p. 539).

[24] *Pensées diverses,* Vol. I, p. 261; cf. *Addition,* Vol. II, pp. 567f. In milder terms: "The atheists and the idolaters are impelled to evil by the same principle" (*Addition,* § 144, p. 285).

tions. But the trouble is that it does not prove to be in conformity with experience."[25]

Whatever be the final judgment on the famous controversy, the problem of atheism can be admitted to have entered with Bayle into the vital stream of modern thought and to have begun its underground work of corrosion in the sphere of religion and of transcendence. What Descartes had accomplished in the speculative area with the separation of truth and certainty, Bayle is now introducing into the practical area with the separation of truth and morality and between ethics and religion: just as for Descartes man can (indeed "must") arrive at truth by starting from radical doubt or negation of all preceding certitude, so also for Bayle man can arrive at good and moral action (likewise) by starting from the radical denial of all religion. In other words, just as the principle of truth (the *cogito*) can be self-engendered in Descartes' system, so can the principle of morality (the *volo*) be self-engendered for Bayle. The inevitable evolution of the modern principle of knowledge here finds a notably important confirmation and passes through a crucial stage.

Whatever may have been Bayle's intention, his influence on atheist Illuminism and atheist materialism has been enormous: in every question in which the values of the spirit are directly involved, Bayle is always there to pose, analyze and often give the conclusion on the point in question. His fight against the religion-mongers, those who proclaimed the indissolubility of morality and religion; his contention that morality and religion were separable one from the other, evolved rapidly and readily into the contention that reason and faith were irreconcilable and therefore that reason was superior to faith. Bayle's disciples soon went on to assert that there seemed no evidence that Christians were more virtuous than unbelievers and that it was entirely possible that a republic of atheists would be more virtuous and at the same time more disinterested than a republic of Catholic or Protestant hue.[26] Bayle's

[25] *Pensées diverses,* Vol. I, p. 263. To the further question as to why there is so much difference between what is believed and what is done, Bayle replies that this is due to the fact that man is determined to action not by the generic laws but by the particular judgments which he makes on a matter (§ 235, Vol. I, p. 264). Cf. also § 236 which states that man does not act according to his principles (*loc cit.,* p. 266). Cf. also the *Addition,* Vol. II, § 176, p. 361, and § 181, p. 372). The *Pensées diverses* go on to assert that there is need of the impulsion of the Holy Spirit to be able to overcome the passions and the corruption of nature: "Let us say then that, for the man who is not truly converted to God and has not his heart sanctified by the grace of the Holy Spirit, the knowledge of a God and of a providence is too feeble a barrier to dam his human passions" (*Pensées diverses,* § 231, Vol. I, p. 254; cf. *Addition,* Vol. II, p. 566 and Vol. IV, p. 501).

[26] Cf. P. Hazard, *La pensée européenne au XVIII siècle, De Montesquieu à Lessing,* Vol. I (Paris, 1946), p. 44. Hazard has a lively description of the enormous influence of the Dictionary and of the ferment excited by the work in all quarters, friendly and hostile alike; and so, as we shall point out, Bayle himself was instrumental in inciting a surmounting of the very stand he himself took.

critique of Spinoza and atheism receded into the background; his protestations of theism and Christianity rang ever more hollow, and his name remained linked to the defense of atheism, with atheists commending him for having put an end to their clandestinity and admitted their obvious right to hold their heads up in public.

The materialist Baron d'Holbach expressly links up with Bayle; the Baron asks, in his classic of Enlightenment atheism, *Système de la nature:* "Is atheism reconcilable with morality?" [27] The Calvinist refugee Abbadie, whom he cites, gives a dryly negative reply, in clear-cut contrast to Bayle: "An atheist cannot be virtuous; virtue is for him but a chimera, uprightness but a vacuous whim, sincerity mere stupidity . . . : the only law he recognizes is his own interest; wherever this approach has taken root, there conscience is but a prejudice, the natural law but an illusion, justice but an error; consequently, the desire for goodness has no foundation any longer, the ties of society are dissolved, all loyalty disappears; friend is ready immediately to betray friend, the citizen to blacken his own country, the son to kill his father to come into possession of his property: all will do these horrid deeds as soon as they find a propitious occasion and as soon as the authority they enjoy or the silence they can enjoin will protect them from the secular arm which is all they have to fear. Inalienable rights and the most sacred laws can be considered but dreams and visions." [28]

These are but sheer calumnies and utterly baseless charges, protests d'Holbach. An atheist is rather a man who is familiar with nature and her laws, and with his own nature and the duties it imposes upon him; an atheist has experience and this experience shows him at every turn that vice can damage him, that his most hidden error, his most secret learnings may come to light and be revealed; this experience shows him that society is indispensible to his own happiness and that it is therefore in his own interest to ally himself with his country which protects him and puts him in a position to enjoy in security the goods of nature; everything conspires to show him that in order to be happy he must make himself liked; that his father is his most trusted friend; that he must put far from him all ingratitude toward benefactors; that justice is necessary for the maintenance of any social group and that no one, no matter how powerful he may be, can be satisfied with himself so long as he knows himself to be the object of public hatred. Anyone who has reflected calmly and unhurriedly upon himself, his nature and his neighbors, his own needs and his means to satisfy those needs, cannot but realize his own duties and discover at one and the same time what he owes to himself and what he owes to others. Consequently such a one will have a

[27] *Système de la nature,* P. II, c. 12, Vol. II, p. 371.

[82] Cf. Abbadie, *De la vérité de la religion chrétienne,* cited in d'Holbach, *op. cit.,* Vol. II, p. 371, note 78.

morality: he has cogent motives for adhering to that morality, he is forced to recognize that these duties are binding and mandatory; and if his reason is not addled by blind passions or vicious habits, he will recognize that virtue is for every man the surest way to attain to happiness. The atheist and the fatalist found all their systems upon necessity. They are at least as certain of their moral speculations based upon the necessity inherent in things as are those who base these speculations on a mere chameleon God, changing in function of the intellectual and emotional vagaries of all the God-builders. The nature of things and their immutable laws are not subject to change; the atheist must always label as vice and folly whatever harms his own person; he must always label as criminal whatever harms others; and he must always consider to be virtuous whatever is profitable for them or contributes to their lasting happiness.

Consequently, insists d'Holbach, the atheist has principles considerably less flimsy than those of the theist who bases his ethics on an imaginary essence. And even if, in the sequel, the atheist succumbs to passions, this does not mean that he has no principles: he is certainly being inconsistent, but he is less to be feared than the man who claims to be religious, who says he believes in God and then gives himself over to the most abominable transgressions. An atheist tyrant, an unbelieving philosopher, would never, d'Holbach assures us, let themselves go to such excesses as would a fanatical tyrant, a partisan of superstition; therefore they would be less formidable. An unbridled and wanton atheist would be less formidable than a man of religion who abandons himself to vice. And d'Holbach adduces still another reason why the atheist tyrant would be more tolerable than a religious tyrant: the atheist tyrant would be acting inconsistently were he to persecute his subjects for their religious notions. Our actions are determined—and here d'Holbach cites directly from Bayle's *Pensées diverses*[29]—not by generic spiritual notions but rather by the passions. Atheism as a school of thought will no more make a cad out of a gentleman than it will make a decent citizen out of a blackguard. Those who joined the school of Epicurus did not become vicious and dissolute as a result of accepting Epirucus' teaching; rather they touted their own misunderstanding of the teachings of Epicurus because they themselves were vicious already.[30] In like manner, a corrupt man may profess atheism in the hope that this system will give entirely free rein to his passions. But such a man will

[29] Cf. *Pensées diverses,* § 177.

[30] D'Holbach quotes Seneca on this point: "Thus it is not under the impulsion of Epicurus that they so carouse and run riot; it is rather that, given over to vice as they are, they hide their lechery under the toga of philosophy" (*De Vita beata, op. cit.,* Vol. II, p. 380).

be deceiving himself, because atheism rightly understood rests upon reason which, unlike religion, will never justify or pardon the crimes of the perverse.

In any case, whether or not God exists, our duties will always remain the same, and if we inquire of our own nature, it will show us that vice is always an evil and that virtue is a real and genuine good.[31] If, therefore, there have been atheists who have denied the distinction between good and evil or have presumed to relegate all ethical principles to oblivion, the simple conclusion must be that such men have, in this respect, been guilty of a grave error of judgment, in failing to recognize either the nature of man or the true source of his duties; in believing ethics to be, like theology, a purely ideal science; and in concluding that, once the gods had been destroyed, there would remain no bond governing human relationships. Yet, a modicum of reflection would have shown them that the whole complex of ethics is founded on immutable relationships existing between sensible, intelligent and social beings; that without virtue no society can endure; that every man must rein in his own instincts in the interests of self-preservation. Men are constrained by their very nature to love virtue and to fear crime, just as they are constrained to seek well-being and to flee pain; and this same nature constrains them to distinguish those objects that agree with them from those that do them harm. Actually the distinction between good and evil is not dependent on human consensus or yet on the ideas men may have of the deity. Neither is this distinction dependent on the rewards and punishments that may await man in a life to come.

Thus, an honest atheist ought rather to be much more interested than any other sort of person in the practice of that virtue on which depends his well-being in this world. Even though his horizon is bounded by this present life, he should for that very reason at least wish to pass his days here in joy and peace: with a calm mind, in the lee of the passions, he will know how to judge aright and to select those means calculated to ensure a life free of nagging disquiet and gnawing remorse. Such a man will feel a sense of obligation to his fellowmen not because of any fear of offending a hypothetical God by doing harm to his fellows, but rather because of his persuasion that in doing wrong to his neighbor he is offending a human being and destroying the laws of justice in whose

[31] D'Holbach admits, with Bayle, that there have existed philosophers and atheists who denied the difference between good and evil and preached moral depravity, as e.g., Aristippos, Theodore the Atheist and Bio of Boristene (on the evidence of Diogenes Laertios) in antiquity, and among the moderns the author of the *Fable of the Bees* (Mandeville) and the author of *Man the Machine* (Lamettrie). But if these authors had allowed their morality to be but inspired by the counsels of nature, they would have found, insists d'Holbach, that "this in no wise leads to vice and immorality but rather to virtue" (*ibid.*, p. 381, note 81).

preservation every member of the human race has a personal stake. D'Holbach is insistent in his contention that there is a radical distinction between the realm of ideas and that of action and that there is no direct transition assured from the former to the latter: a man may very well have righteous principles and yet behave badly, simply for want of the will power needed to extirpate his own vicious tendencies. Men are what they are impelled to be by their own physical make-up, as modified by habit, education, example, external authority, interior ideals and aims, and the stable and ephemeral elements of their environment. Their religious ideas and the systems of their invention must of necessity either vitalize or conform to their temperaments, their inclinations and their personal interests.

D'Holbach echoes Bayle in asserting that even if the system the atheist has worked out for himself does not free him from his previous vices, at least it does not proffer him new ones. Superstition, on the other hand, offers its adherents a myriad of pretexts for doing wrong with complete complacency and an entire absence of any remorse of conscience. Atheism at least leaves men no more corrupted than before. And d'Holbach cites Bacon as a supporting witness in favor of the superiority of atheism over superstition.[32] But the passage he cites from Bacon has, in the original, a sense diametrically opposed to that given it by d'Holbach in a surprising exposure of his own aims and intentions.[33]

[32] The original text reads: "Atheism leaves a man to sense, to philosophy, to natural piety, to laws, to reputation—all which may be guides to an outward moral virtue, though religion were not—but superstition dismounteth all these, and erecteth an absolute monarchy in the minds of men; therefore atheism did never perturb States; for it makes men wary of themselves, as looking further; and we see the times inclined to atheism, as the time of Augustus Caesar, were civil times; but superstition hath been the confusion of many States, and bringeth in a new *primum mobile,* that ravisheth all the spheres of government" (F. Bacon, *Essays,* Essay XVII, "Of Superstition," ed. F. Fiske Heard and R. Whateley [Boston-New York, 1871], p. 169).

[33] D'Holbach should surely not have forgotten the context, the fact that Bacon is speaking of "superstition" and not of religion and that the Essay commences with the declaration, readily understandable in such a context: "It were better to have no opinion of God at all, than such an opinion as is unworthy of him; for the one is unbelief, the other is contumely; and certainly superstition is the reproach of the deity" (*ibid.*). D'Holbach ought likewise to have remembered that Bacon had dedicated the preceding Essay XVI to the refutation of Bollandist atheism and hits at the "great atheists", i.e., the theoretical atheists quite sharply and in no uncertain terms: "But the great atheists indeed are hypocrites, which are ever handling holy things, but without feeling, so as they must needs be cauterized in the end" (*ibid.,* p. 156). And again, near the end, Bacon maintains a point of view which is the exact opposite of the contention d'Holbach is here at pains to support: "They that deny God destroy a man's nobility, for certainly man is of kin to the beasts by his body; and if he be not of kin to God by his spirit, he is a base and ignoble creature. It destroys likewise magnanimity, and the raising human nature." And just as a dog becomes nobler and braver when it is kept by

Indeed, d'Holbach continues unabashed in his eulogy of atheism, renewing his charges against religion as having fomented all manner of vices, disorders, wars, discords, errors and defalcations. Thus, d'Holbach converts Bayle's concessive contention that *"even* atheists may be upright" or that "an *individual* atheist *may* be upright" into the categorical contention that *"only* the atheists are the *genuinely upright"* and that the partisans of religion are a host of hypocrites or pitiable daydreamers, rotting in superstition and in the tyranny of the despots. D'Holbach anticipates Marx in his ensuing protest against any talk of the practical "utility" of religion.

The importance of Bayle's stand for the emergence and dynamic of modern atheism can, therefore, scarcely be overestimated. He had a profound influence on English deism, especially in its most radical manifestations. Toland, for instance, in the opening lines of his famous *Letter IV to Serena,* welcomes and approves her eulogy of Spinoza and then adds: "And you know that M. Bayle in his *Various Thoughts Upon Comets* has manifestly proved that even atheism does not necessarily lead a man to be wicked." [34] He continues immediately to give an obviously sympathetic exposition of the basic principles of Spinozism, tempered, it is true, by a criticism of the mechanistic conception of inert matter, a criticism to which we shall return in due course.

But the man to discuss Bayle's propositions most outspokenly in France was Voltaire. In his early writings, Voltaire had already expressed his entire agreement with Bayle in a manner that was no less explicit for being somewhat indirect: "Neither Montaigne nor Locke nor Spinoza nor Hobbes nor Milord Shaftesbury nor Mr. Collins nor Mr. Toland nor Fludd nor Becker nor the Count of Boulainvilliers nor their like were the ones to raise the torch of strife in their home country; the culprits were, for the most part, theologians whose initial ambition to be sectarian leaders soon gave way to the ambition to be party bosses. Why, all these books of the modern philosophers put together will never

---

a man who for the dog holds the place of God or is better by nature than the dog, even so it is with man in his relation to God: "So man, when he resteth and assureth himself upon divine protection and favour, gathereth a force and faith which human nature in itself could not obtain; therefore, as atheism is in all respects hateful, so is this, that it depriveth human nature of the means to exalt itself above human frailty (p. 157). Earlier (*op. cit.,* Vol. II, p. 432), d'Holbach cites the famous text of Bacon: "Shallow sips of philosophy may move toward atheism but ampler draughts bring back to religion" (*De augm. sc.* I), a thought which recurs in the *Essays* as well: "It is true, that a little philosophy inclineth man's mind to atheism, but depth in philosophy bringeth men's minds about to religion" (Essay XVI, p. 155); but d'Holbach goes on to chip away at the all too obvious meaning of this sentence.

[34] J. Toland, *Letters to Serena* (London, 1704), p. 134.

create as much stir in the world as did once the grey friars' dispute on the style of their sleeves and cowl." [35]

A still more explicit contention appears in the conclusion of the *Traité de métaphysique:* Voltaire's superficial moral skepticism leads him to an unqualified acceptance of the English utilitarian ethic. Says Voltaire: "Truth and vice, moral good and evil is, in each country, merely what is useful or harmful to society . . . Virtue is the habit of doing what pleases men and vice the habit of doing what displeases them." But he warns that from this it does not follow that it suffices to be powerful and well shielded from public sanctions for a man to be able to give free rein to all his instincts: any man who did this would be proclaiming himself the enemy of the entire human race. And for the less powerful, the ordinary man in the street, vice and crime involve exposing himself to the sanctions of the public magistracy, to all manner of fears and forebodings, to the contempt and horror of his fellows, which last is the most formidable and insupportable of all punishments.

Hence, Voltaire agrees with Bayle that for a man to be upright he ought to be restrained from vice not by any supramundane sanction but rather by the need for human and social coexistence, or simply "on a point of honor": "Thus every reasonable man will conclude that it is palpably in his own interest to be an upright man. His knowledge of the human heart and his conviction that there is no such thing as virtue or vice as such will never prevent him from being a good citizen and fulfilling all his human and civic duties. And it is a point worthy of notice that the philosophers (who are branded as unbelievers and libertines) have in all ages been the most upright of men. Abstracting here from any list of the great men of antiquity, such men as La Mothe la Vayer, the tutor of Louis XIII's brother, such men as Bayle, Locke, Spinoza, Lord Shaftesbury, Collins, etc., were men of strictest virtue; fear of the scorn of their fellows was not the only architect of their virtues; in addition, they had a taste for virtue itself. The upright soul is a right-living man for the same reason that anyone whose taste has not been depraved prefers first-rate Nuits wine to de Brie or le Mans partridge to horsemeat. A sound education and training perpetuates these feelings in all men and thence derives this universal persuasion called *honor,* a sentiment of which even the most corrupt cannot rid themselves and which constitutes the pivot of society." [36] Conversely, those who need the aid of religion in order to be upright are in a deplorable state and Voltaire goes so far as to designate as "monsters" of society

[35] Voltaire, *Lettres philosophiques,* Lettre XIII, ed. F. A. Taylor (Oxford, 1961), p. 45.

[36] Voltaire, "Traité de philosophie, ch. IX, De la vertu et du vice," in *Philosophie,* Paris, n.d., pp. 178f.

those who do not find within themselves the sentiments necessary for this society and thus are obliged to take from elsewhere what they should find exclusively in their own nature.

From 1750 on, however, (i.e., from the publication of the article "Atheist—Atheism" [37] in the *Dictionary of Philosophy,* Voltaire begins to abandon the restrictive notion of God as simply "the supreme architect of the universe" and begins to speak of a "God who rewards and punishes". At this period he considers Bayle's contentions a "paradox" and refutes Bayle's defense of Vanini,[38] both on the ground that this Vanini was by no means the unsullied soul Bayle tried to make him out to be, and on the ground that Vanini was not even an atheist in the strict sense. In a closer examination of Bayle's thesis (*Whether a society of atheists could subsist*), Voltaire resolves to hold himself aloof both from the slanderers and from the excessively ardent partisans; but he ends by judging Bayle to have been wrong in his basic contentions. Here Voltaire returns, at least in part, to the traditional notion of God.

Voltaire shows himself to be anything but a submissive follower of Bayle, so far as the substance of Bayle's stand is concerned. In any choice between fanaticism and atheism, Voltaire leaves no doubt that he, too, feels the former to be incomparably more noxious than the latter; but he forces atheism, too, to face up to its responsibilities. Fanaticism impels of its very nature to bloody passions, whereas atheism does not; fanaticism goes so far as to commit crimes, whereas atheism fails to oppose such criminal activity; fanaticism readily runs to all manner of excesses and does not boggle at massacres, whereas the atheist (of those days!) counsels moderation and concord. Hobbes, who was believed to be an atheist, lived a tranquil and innocent life, whereas the fanatics of his day were drenching England, Scotland and Ireland in blood. Spinoza not only was himself an atheist, he taught atheism openly; yet he committed no assassinations like the Dutch religious fanatics of his day. But then Voltaire attacks the atheists of his day: for the most part, they are daring scholars who have gone astray and, as a result of their incapacity to understand creation, the origin of evil and other problems, have recourse to the hypothesis of the eternity of things and of cosmic necessity.[39]

[37] Cf. article "Athée," in *Dictionnaire philosophique,* pp. 36ff.

[38] Cf. *Pensées diverses,* § 173, p. 353, and especially § 182, Vol. II, pp. 37ff. See also *Addition,* p. 577.

[39] "Atheists are for the most part daring scholars who have gone astray, whose reasoning is faulty and who, not being able to understand creation, the origin of evil, and other difficulties, have recourse to the hypothesis of the eternity of things and of necessity" (*Dictionnaire philosophique,* p. 42). For Voltaire's strictures on the excesses of religious fanaticism, cf. Part II of the article (*ibid.,* p. 44); note Voltaire's insistence that these do not afford any warrant for atheism.

In the realm of politics, Voltaire expressly asserts the harmful nature of atheism and mentions, as an example, the Senate of Rome "whose members were almost all theoretical and practical atheists, i.e., men who believed neither in providence nor in the life to come. . . . a company of philosophers, epicures and power-hungry climbers, all of them dangerous in the extreme to the Republic and pushing it to ruin". And here again Voltaire asserts the need for a personal God to give consistency to the private and public life of man: "I would not want to fall afoul of an atheist prince who might be interested in pulverizing me; I have no doubt that he would make a good job of it. Nor would I want, were I the prince myself, to have any dealings with atheist courtiers who might be interested in poisoning me; I would have to take an antidote every day on the off chance. And so the man on the throne and the man in the street alike simply must have graven deeply in their minds the idea of a Supreme Being who is Creator, Ruler, Rewarder and Avenger." [40]

Bayle argued strongly in favor of his contention from the existence of what he called "atheist peoples" like the Kaffirs, the Hottentots, the Tupinambas and other such primitive peoples. But Voltaire contends that these peoples are at too low a stage of civilization to constitute any cogent argument here: they are neither atheists nor believers; they are simply "children" in this whole area. As for those who had maintained that atheism was "the religion of the government of China" (and whose statements Bayle had accepted uncritically [41]), these men had been entirely mistaken: they need only have read the edicts of the emperors of this vast land to have seen that these edicts are nothing less than sermons, full of references to the Supreme Being who is Ruler, Avenger and Rewarder.[42] Voltaire's conclusion is almost diametrically opposed to Bayle's contention: "That atheism is a most pernicious monstrosity in those who govern; that it is no less pernicious in those who are councillors of rulers, no matter how blameless these councillors may be in their private life, because from their council chamber they can get through to those who are the actual rulers; that, although not as baneful as fanati-

[40] *Ibid.*, p. 43.

[41] Cf. *Addition,* Vol. IV, c. 154, p. 785.

[42] *Dictionnaire philosophique,* p. 40. Voltaire adds that Bayle has, at the same time, forgotten the most pertinent instance in support of his contention, namely, the Jewish people who did not admit any future life or, consequently, any eternal sanction, and yet were the most religious people in the world, believing in God as creator and punisher of evil on this earth; this restraint was sufficient to keep them in line in the matter of practical morality. It might be pointed out preeminently that personal immortality was a notion well known to the Jews (cf. *Encyclopedia cattolica,* article "Immortalità", Vol. VI, col. 1682ff. Further, it is hard to understand how this argument can buttress the contention concerning the "possibility of a society of atheists" in the light of Voltaire's own assertion that "the Jews were the most religious people in the world" (*ibid.*).

cism, it is almost always fatal to virtue." [43] In this latest and definitive stage of the evolution of his own thought, Voltaire is obviously arguing against d'Holbach's atheism and alludes to it explicitly.

Voltaire returns to the question in his late work *Questions sur l'Encyclopédie* (1770) and stands by his new idea that the notion of a "rewarding and avenging God" is an indispensable prerequisite for national life and the preservation of the State, insisting that if Bayle had been in charge of but five or six hundred fellow-citizens he would not have failed to proclaim to them a "rewarding and avenging God". And to those who reminded him that "atheists do live in society" (doubtless Voltaire was thinking of the d'Holbach group), "and therefore it is possible to live in society without religion", Voltaire retorts: "That wolves live together this way and they are not so much a society as rather a company of man-eating savages . . . and I shall always come back to this question: When you have lent your money to some member of your society, would you be easy in your mind if neither your debtor nor your attorney nor your notary nor your judge believed in God." [44] Voltaire then devotes himself at length to a specially zealous defense of "final causality", examining the main arguments advanced against it by the atheist and presenting a spirited refutation of each one of them, even appealing to the authority of Spinoza as one who felt the necessity of admitting the presence of a supreme Intelligence in the world. Voltaire mentions the "new objection of a modern atheist" to the effect that the events in the universe could be the result of chance. This clearly evokes d'Holbach, and Voltaire rejects the whole contention as fatuous: "The functional structure of a fly's wing, the bodily organs of a snail are enough to topple you." [45] He gives a more measured reply to the difficulty—surely not exactly an insurmountable one—raised by Maupertuis who could not manage to see any purposiveness in the freak structures sometimes encountered in animals: a closer observation and a more attentive reflection, says Voltaire, shows new and unsuspected marvels everywhere. And he concludes on a firm note: "We are thus absolutely compelled to recognize an ineffable intelligence, as was admitted by Spinoza himself. This ineffable intelligence must be admitted to flash forth in the meanest insect even as in the stars. And what about moral

[43] *Dictionnaire philosophique,* p. 43. Voltaire ends his exposition with an expression of gratification at the decline of atheism and a resurgence of belief in God, especially due to the rehabilitation among the philosophers of the notion of "final causes". Thus, says Voltaire, God has again become accessible to all: "A catechist proclaims God to children and Newton demonstrates him to the learned."

[44] "Athéisme," in *Questions sur l'Encyclopédie,* Sect. I; *Dictionnaire philosophique,* p. 459.

[45] *Ibid.,* Sect. II, p. 462.

and physical evil? What are we to say and do about these? Console ourselves by the enjoyment of physical and moral good, while adoring the eternal Being who has authored the good and permitted the evil. One final word on this article. Atheism is the vice of great minds and superstition the vice of fools; and as for knaves, they are quite simply knaves."[46]

But one must agree that Voltaire was overly optimistic about the issue of his polemic against atheism: his new demand for God may have been sincere but it was, for all that, less than cogent against the atheists who took their inspiration from Bayle. Bayle's importance and influence in the molding of rationalism and of modern atheism can therefore be admitted to have been decisive and in no way inferior to that of Spinoza, Hobbes or Locke. Himself a theist and perhaps a convinced Christian like Descartes and the Cartesians, Bayle nevertheless opened a new breach in the dike of theism, through which poured in the raging flood of denial of revealed religion on the part of deism and Enlightenment philosophy and of natural religion and any kind of religious notion on the part of radical atheism.[47] Bayle's corrosive action was entirely in the line of the "devout" Descartes, whose admirer and follower Bayle proclaimed himself to be: it was precisely the clarity of the "clear and distinct ideas" that led Bayle to call in question, if not religion generically considered or Christianity as such, at least the universal human phenomenon of "the religious sense" which is the primordial upthrust of man's aspiration to the Absolute, to the Supreme Good, to perfect Justice, and forms the basis of all religious aspiration.

There is by no means perfect clarity in this thrust of the soul toward mysterious depths, for this impetus begins to stir in man from earliest infancy when there is a lack of clarity regarding objects much more readily within human grasp, which lack of clarity, however, does not impel anyone to dream of opposing or rejecting these objects. Furthermore, there are a multitude of elements and aspects involved in this aspiration; not all of them are destined to remain permanent enigmas, of course; but equally certainly some of them can never become clear and distinct for anyone, be he the shrewdest philosopher or the best qualified theologian. Among these latter are the problems relative to the intimate and radical nexus between man's freedom in his subjection to God and

[46] *Ibid.*, pp. 461f., 463. For d'Holbach's attack on "final causes", cf. *Système de la nature,* Part II, ch. 3, Vol. II, pp. 67ff.; ch. 5, *ibid.,* pp. 160f. (against Newton). Bayle's contention is repeated in the Diderot letter: "Yes, indeed, I maintain superstition is more injurious to God than atheism" (*Pensées Philosophiques,* ed. P. Vernière [Paris, 1961], § XII, p. 14). It perplexed even the Jesuits of the *Mémoires de Trévoux* (cf. A. R. Desoutels, *Les Mémoires de Trévoux,* pp. 79ff.).

[47] Cf. the sober but substantial balance sheet of these harmful effects of Bayle's work in P. Hazard, *La pensée européenne,* Vol. III, Notes et références, pp. 32f.

God's providence toward man whom he has created and set in the world to seek him and to love him.

Central to this challenging complex of relationships is the problem of evil. Man must not allow this problem to trip him up as it did Bayle; rather he must hold firmly to the basic certitudes as a strong shield in his battle to maintain himself in grateful submission to God. A religion like that of rationalism, deism or the Enlightenment, with their complete neglect of prayer, is not and cannot be called a religion at all, not even a natural religion, because it amounts to nothing more than a judgment on abstract evidence, to a merely formal assertion of the existence of God; this involves no act of the will on the part of the whole man and consequently no encounter with the living God, creator of the world and father of men. And so the atheists were not entirely wrong in pushing the modern principle relentlessly to its most drastic and ultimate conclusion.

Bayle's contentions concerning the distinction between ethics and religion seem clear at first glance; yet they contain a certain ambiguity. This ambiguity, however, was cleared away in the further course of European thought; and it was cleared away in no uncertain terms, first by a critique of revealed religion and a consequent implacable rejection of revelation on the part of deism, and later by the unqualified condemnation of religion as such. Thus, Bayle emerges as one of the founding fathers of modern atheism, a development which would certainly have surprised him; and his *Pensées diverses,* considered to have been of Catholic inspiration,[48] became the slogan against all religion.

Feuerbach devoted a special study to the thoroughgoing analysis of this unusual phenomenon in the history of thought. He insists that it can no longer be considered to the point to declare that religion necessarily renders men holy. But this simply means that the things done in the name of religion are not done by that very fact in the spirit of religion. Religion is not to be charged with human passions, weaknesses and corruption; and if religion has somehow somewhere impelled men to crime or failed to restrain them from it or to make them better, this is because there was operative in such cases a false religion or at least a false religious sense and practice. Bayle's charges do not touch religion as such, religion in its essence; they leave unscathed that religion which is faithful to its own ideal, i.e., *true* religion. But what is the basis of this distinction between false religion and true religion? Feuerbach poses to himself this question and replies: the *content* of religion, its spirit. But, once again, what is this spirit, this content? The *concept* of God.

The important thing is therefore *how* God is thought, how he is object of awareness and knowledge. If this concept is not worthy of God (*un-*

[48] Cf. L. Feuerbach, *Pierre Bayle, Ein Beitrag zur Geschichte der Philosophie und Menschheit,* p. 166, note.

göttlich), if it is wrong or impoverished, then the religious theory and practice founded upon it will likewise be insufficient and worthless. The Greeks *thought* God in a way that made him an object of the senses; consequently their entire religious system remained at the level of the senses. But the concept of God is not only an object of religion; it is an object of philosophy and of ethics as well: God can be thought of as the supreme principle of duty, without thereby being reduced to an object of religious veneration and worship.

Feuerbach goes on to point out that what constitutes the essence of religion and distinguishes religion from ethics and philosophy is not a self-constituting goodness; here again there is a dependence on content: "holiness" or the sacral character, which is the supreme category of religion, is not a self-constituting value. The "sacred" must also be something rational, something good in itself; thus, it is not a primordial concept, for it depends on the concepts of truth, rationality and morality; therefore, it belongs to philosophy. Feuerbach certainly goes beyond Bayle's "intentions" though perhaps not beyond his principles to conclude that it is therefore not religion which is the basis of ethics but rather ethics which is the basis of religion. Feuerbach's conclusion does, however, presuppose his own new Hegel-inspired notion of religion as belonging in the realm of feeling and thus inferior to philosophy, a notion of which there is no trace in Bayle. Feuerbach therefore concludes that Bayle's charges do hit their mark if religion, abstracting from its content, be thus distinguished from ethics.[49] Indeed the positively operative element in religion is not a part of religion at all; rather it is something opposed to all established religions, a self-affirmation, an absence of God (*Gottlosigkeit*), a purely rational religion free of all authority and with no right or law save that of personal persuasion, of the spirit, of nature. So it was with primitive Christianity, so likewise with the Reformation.[50] And Feuerbach claims to be reasoning in the spirit of Bayle when he concludes: "Only the concession of complete

[49] At this point Feuerbach launches a lengthy attack on the Catholic Church for having permitted all manners of crimes and injury against the heretics (*ibid.*, pp. 181ff.) and on revealed or positive historical religion in general (pp. 186ff.).

[50] St. Thomas makes a distinction between unbelievers as such, who never had the faith, and heretics and apostates: whereas the unbelievers, even if they were brought into subjection by Christians, ought not to be bound to anything more than not to put any obstacles in the way of the practice of the Christian faith; the heretics and apostates, in a like case, ought to be constrained to observe what they had promised (*S.T.*, II-II, q. 10, a. 8); cf. ad. 2, the categorical statement in reference to the Jews: "Such Jews as have never accepted the faith are in no way to be compelled to the faith"—though, here too, this would not hold in the event that they had at some time in the past accepted the Christian faith. Furthermore, St. Thomas appeals to the steadfast tradition of the Church to argue that the children of Jews cannot be baptized against the will of their parents when such children have not attained the use of reason (*ibid.*, a. 12; cf. III[a], q. 68, a. 10; *Quodlib.* II q. IV, a. 2 and *Quodlib.* III, q. V, a. 1).

freedom to unbelief is a convincing proof of honesty in the whole matter of belief. Only where unbelief is free is faith likewise free. Only there is a distinction established between a feigned, affected faith and a genuine unaffected faith." [51] Here there is some justification for Feuerbach's claim to be reasoning in the spirit of Bayle; but such a radical proposition is a Feuerbach conclusion going entirely beyond Bayle's contention.

The next thesis, likewise, on the "autonomy of ethics" (*Die Selbstständigkeit der Ethik*) [52] stems from the German Feuerbach rather than from Bayle who, as we have seen, limited himself to the mention and consideration of existential concrete situations while protesting his acceptance of the principles of religion and Christianity. To posit God as principle of justice is for Feuerbach to identify him with justice, with the Good in itself and by itself, i.e., with the principle of ethics. This makes God into a mere name, nothing but a word. The essence of the concept is the *ethical* notion and, after an amusing sideswipe at the teaching of the theological schools concerning faith in miracles, Feuerbach pauses to ridicule the contention of Nominalism, the most daring contention to come out of decadent Scholasticism, to the effect that the precepts of morality are based exclusively upon the will of God. Feuerbach brands this as an arbitrary immoral principle which destroys the very foundations of ethics. In fact the Good has no power except its own; nor can it bind or determine man otherwise than *via itself;* there is no other moral basis for the duty to do good than the concept of the Good *in itself and of itself.* If therefore the will of God is thought to be the basis of ethics because it is the will of the Good, and God is reduced to the concept of the Good, then the *essential* and *crucial* notion is quite obviously the *ethical* concept, theology ceases to be theology as such and we are left with philosophy viewed for our present purposes as an autonomous ethic.

Accordingly, the human race had a sacred duty to penetrate to an awareness of ethics as an autonomous science; this duty was discharged by Kant and Fichte who conceived philosophy, especially ethics, as being independent of theology. This was a salvific service to themselves and to mankind. It is primarily to their credit that the ethical notion was promoted to a frank and uncontaminated existential status. And Feuerbach's triumphant conclusion is that so reviled an atheism represents simply the necessary and therefore salutary stage of the transition from the *empirical* objective God, conceived as an *extrinsic* entity, to the idealist position, i.e., to the notion of Spirit, the concept of the divine *in se* and *per se,* to an autonomous understanding of the essence in nature as the essence of the ethical Idea.

[51] *Op. cit.,* p. 190. Feuerbach is compelled to acknowledge, however, that for Bayle such Christians are not behaving in accord with the teaching of Christianity but rather in contradiction of it.

[52] *Ibid.,* p. 193.

Feuerbach insists that Bayle's contentions in the *Pensées diverses sur la comète* are directly dependent on, and derived from, Kant's categorical imperative and Fichte's idea of an absolute ethical quality or norm. And Feuerbach concludes: "Ethics alone, therefore, is true religion: it is the *spirit* of true religion, of the honest mind, sure of itself, neither deluding itself with deceptive phantoms nor hiding behind obscure symbols and muddled notions; it is the word of simple truth, frank, honest, far removed from all oriental hyperbole. History bears witness to the fact that ethics alone engenders open, free and noble characters, men who are integral, *natural,* sincere, genuinely religious." A theology, on the other hand, which pretends to be above ethics, is baneful for the body politic, both for the everyday life of the citizens and for all the sciences.[53] Nor has Leibniz's rejoinder to Bayle done anything to recoup the situation.

Bayle's importance in the development of rationalism and modern atheism can hardly be exaggerated: via Bayle, the most radical contentions of Spinoza concerning the self-sufficiency of human freedom and his accusation against all religion and the Christian religion in particular, the accusation that they are quite incapable of restraining man from following the dictates of his own passions, enters in the European cultural stream and is greeted as the definitive and irrefutable apology for atheism.[54] Neither the development of deism and the Enlightenment philosophy in England and France nor the rise of German idealism can be properly understood in abstraction from Bayle. It is true that in formulating the contention that morality is not strictly linked to religion, Bayle's intention (or alleged intention) was to signify by religion the superstitious and pagan religions and to exclude the true religion and the "true faith which is always accompanied by the love of God and is a gift of the Holy Spirit". This restriction we have noted already, and on this last point any theologian could agree with Bayle even as St. Augustine would have agreed. It is also true that Bayle's positive contention that there have in fact been certain individual atheists of blameless life,[55] and that some of the most important truths of ethics were known to man

[53] *Das Wesen der Religion, C. W.*, ed. Bolin-Jodl, Vol. V, p. 215. The chapter ends with the motto of Frederick II of Prussia, one of the "heroes" of the modern morality exalted by Feuerbach: "*Mein höchster Gott ist meine Pflicht*" (My duty is my highest God!).

[54] Bayle has been shown to have taken his own theses verbatim from Spinoza, specifically from the Preface to the *Tractatus theologico-politicus* (cf. P. Vernière, *Spinoza et la pensée française avant la revolution,* Vol. I, p. 29).

[55] In addition to the reflections cited from the *Pensées* (§§ 174, 178, 180, 182) and from the *Continuation* (§§ 144, 145), the reader should consult, with Bayle himself as guide, the apology for the martyrs of atheism in the *Dictionnaire historique et critique* (cf. Hermias; Stilpon; Xenocrates, Note F; Lucretius, Note E; Spinoza, Note O).

considerably earlier than the period of revealed religion—that this whole proposition could be interpreted in conformity with St. Augustine and St. Thomas or quite simply with Catholic teaching. But it is an equally indisputable fact that, in the wake of Bayle's impassioned diatribe on the *de facto* and *de jure* possibility of an ethic disengaged from religion (and this diatribe may well have been the main aim of Bayle's entire life, inspiring him to compile the *Dictionnaire*), atheism emerges with head held proudly erect and is in a position to demand the right of coexistence in a rational and well-ordered society, whereas religion is brought into the dock, even though the charges against it are expressed by indirection.

Finally, Bayle's novel forthright enunciation of the contention that there could be such a thing as a "positive and constructive atheism", a contention that went beyond Spinoza's most daring speculation, this enunciation coupled with Bayle's failure to clarify the principles and bases of that natural ethic upon which the atheist founded his own life—this left the door open for an endeavor at just such a clarification on the part of all those who thought that the elimination of all dependence of ethics, in any sense whatsoever, upon religion (not only positive and revealed religion but even natural religion in general) [56] was something that had already been achieved or would be a task easily accomplished. Ideas are indeed like arrows, which, once released, do not always follow the course intended by those who have launched them, but rather describe the arc dictated by their inherent thrust.

[56] An expert in the history of atheism writes in this connection: "The progress thus consists not in the enucleation of any new ideas concerning the sources and basis of morality, but solely in the quiet removal of the theological superstructure which had hitherto preserved for ethics its autonomous status" (F. Jodl, *Geschichte der Ethik in der neueren Philosophie* Vol. I [Stuttgart, 1882], p. 286).

Appendices

I. Descartes and Pascal

Pascal's somewhat muted reproach amounted almost to an accusation of atheism levelled against the Cartesian system: "I cannot forgive Descartes," writes Pascal. "He would have liked to get along without God throughout his whole philosophy but he could not restrain himself from making God give a little push to set the world in motion; thereafter he is at a loss what to do with God" (Pascal, *Pensées,* Sect. II. n. 77; ed. Brunschvicg minor [Paris, 1917], pp. 360f.). And yet the same Pascal seems to admit the cogency of Cartesian mechanism in general: "The statement 'This is accomplished by form and movement' is mandatory because it is true. But to specify more precisely and fashion the machine —that is absurd, for it is but pointless guesswork and troublesome to boot. And if it were true, we do not feel that the whole of philosophy would be worth an hour's effort" (*Pensées,* Sect. II, n. 79, p. 361). I do not know why Brunschvicg, in his penetrating comparison of the two thinkers, passed this point over so lightly: to me, it seems crucial (*Descartes et Pascal Lecteurs de Montaigne* 2 [New York-Paris, 1944[2]], especially pp. 157ff.). Pascal deduces from this that the world is "mute", does not speak to us of God and cannot lead us to God (on the Cartesianism of Pascal, cf. F. Bouiller, *Histoire de la Philosophie cartésienne,* Vol. I, p. 551f., J. Souilhé, *La philosophie chrétienne de Descartes à nos jours,* Vol. I [Paris, 1934], pp. 92f.). In a world in which bodies are reduced to extension and spirit to thought, the basic act of perfection of bodies is local movement: Descartes thus made God into the one who gave the first push resulting in the motion of the *machina mundi.* This was indeed inadequate. The rapidly ensuing development of the Cartesian teaching by Spinoza with his reduction of these two attributes of the real (extension and thought) to the unity of substance, is not a foreign distortion; it issues from the internal logic of the principles themselves, despite Descartes' persuasion to the contrary and despite his efforts to fashion new proofs of the existence of God, proofs drawn from the realm of reflection. These are the arguments that Hardouin had branded as tainted with ontologism and pantheism and therefore with atheism.

II. Spinoza's Religious Sentiments

There have not been many writers who have sprung to Spinoza's defense in the matter of the atheism charge: one of the most convinced is certainly one of his best informed biographers, J. Freudenthal, in his now classic work, *Spinoza, Leben und Lehre,* Part I: *Das Leben Spinozas,* 2nd edition, ed. Carl Gebhardt; Part II, *Die Lehre Spinozas auf Grund des Nachlasses von J. Freundenthal bearbeitet von C. Gebhardt,* Curis Societatis Spinozanae (Heidelberg 1927). Cf. P. I, Ch. 7; Vol I, p. 163ff.

Spinoza's religious feelings and convictions are attested by the motto inscribed on the frontispiece of the *Tractatus Theol.-Pol.,* taken from St. John: "By this we know that we remain in God and God in us, in that of his spirit he has given to us" (I Jn. 4, 13). On the theoretical level, the knowledge of God is the first certainty and the basis of all certitude and knowledge: in no passage of the entire *Tractatus* does Spinoza combat the biblical doctrine of God. For Jesus Christ, says Freudenthal, Spinoza shows the highest esteem: but he admits that Spinoza considered Christ to be simply a man, even though wise and perfect and closest of all men to God, but always and only a man, so that Jesus cannot in any sense be called God. Spinoza also shows respect for the sacred scriptures of the Old and the New Testament, as containing a teaching of great value for man. How then, concludes Freudenthal, can such a man be designated as impious and atheist? And Freudenthal is well disposed toward accepting even the recently stated opinion that "Spinoza had accepted the Christian faith, even though he did not make any public profession of it" (!—p. 165).

Freudenthal maintains that Spinoza held to the same principles not only in the *Tractatus* but in his other writings as well. It is true, he concedes, that in the *Ethica* God is not a personal being nor yet creator of the world; nor is there any mention in this work of providence or of revelation. Substantially Freudenthal even admits that for Spinoza there can be no talk of an historico-positive religion, i.e., a revealed religion in the proper sense (p. 168). And toward the end of his peroration, Freudenthal goes so far as to admit frankly the pantheistic and immanentist nature of Spinoza's religious sentiments: "Spinoza must appear devoid of religion for anyone who declares piety to be identical with adherence to one of the many historical forms of religions life and equates religion with Judaism or Christianity. And Spinoza will also be called an atheist by anyone who exalts God above nature and rejects as untenable the notion of an impersonal divinity indwelling in the world. But if that teaching is a religious one which leads us beyond the finite to the eternal, delivers us from selfishness and instills into us pure and unalloyed love to God and man, then Spinoza's philosophy was not irreligious. And if a Christianity unencumbered with any ecclesiastical dogmas may still rate as such, then Spinoza can be called a Christian, indeed perhaps with Goethe *Christianissimus,* for he speaks with great respect of Jesus Christ and teaches much that agrees with the moral views of Christianity" (pp. 171f.).

This is what has been called "Johannine Christianity" but is in reality "rational Christianity" as the Spinozist Lessing will call it; it will pass over into idealism which will incline to liquidate Christianity both as revelation and as religion as such, because the final word on being and on man is entrusted to philosophy rather than to religion. Among the most convinced advocates of Spinozan theism in the 19th century in Germany figure, aside from Hegel who was mentioned at the outset, Herder, Mendelssohn and above all Schelling and Goethe, as we shall point out.

The opposition between the Spinozan approach and the Christian one, indeed the theistic approach in general, has been thus indicated to lie in the Spinozan inanition of the finite and of man within that finite, and the consequent deletion of the freedom not only of man but even of God himself: "Spinoza's mythology is theocentric: God in All. For the medievals, the world was the arena in which the Divine Comedy of man was played out: its first act had been the fall of the first man and the perdition of mankind; its second act had consisted in the sacrificial death of the Son of God and the redemption of mankind; and its third act was still outstanding and would consist in the end of the world and the Last Judgment. For Spinozism God is Nature and the phenomenon of mankind but a single one of the infinite manifold that must necessarily follow from the nature of God. Spinoza removes the concept of purpose or finality from the divinity, just as he rejects any humanization of God and therefore keeps out of the Godhead any will, desire, or in short anything that could negate infinity by defining and determining it. God is in the world not as determined by goals, ends and purposes, but rather as operating through causality. There is therefore in the world no finalistic why (no where*fore*) but only a causal why (be*cause*). The immanent God acts out of the mechanism of his own nature; and in this necessity of his operation lies his freedom. It is the freedom of immanence".[1] And logically enough: Spinoza did not want to square God with the spiritual nature of man; so he had to base him on the necessity of nature.

[1] C. Gebhardt, *Spinoza,* p. 107. On the nature of Spinoza's major work, we have a very significant witness (hitherto unique) of J. Le Clerc, reported by F. Mauthner (*Der Atheismus und seine Geschichte im Abendlande* I, 349f.). The original reads: "I have been told by a credible witness, who also gave me this himself in writing, that Spinoza composed his so-called *Ethica demonstrata* in Flemish and given it to a physician, Louis Mayer by name, to translate into Latin, and that the Flemish original did not contain the word 'God' at all, but only the word 'Nature' of which Spinoza predicated eternity. The physician warned him that there were bound to be drastic repercussions on this account and that Spinoza would be accused of denying God and substituting *Nature* in his place, which latter word is more properly used to designate the creation than the creator.

III. Anti-Spinozan Polemical Writings

The pros and cons of the Spinozan controversy from the 17th to the 19th centuries constitute a chapter apart in the history of philosophy. The material has not yet been collated nor coordinated with an understanding of the evolution of modern thought. A preliminary balance-sheet of notable interest is that struck by Bayle in the notes of his article (Notes D, E, H, I, M, P, etc.) from which we select the most important titles: Stoupp, *La Religion des Hollandais* (Utrecht, 1673); S. Kortholt, *De Tribus Impostoribus* (Kiel, 1680) (The three impostors are Herbert de Cherbury, Hobbes and Spinoza); cf. I. Presser, *Das Buch "De Tribus Impostoribus"* (Amsterdam, 1926), pp. 102ff. (there are various writings that go by that title); J. Bredenbourg, *Enervatio Tractatus Theologico-Politici* (Rotterdam 1675) (which Bayle holds to be the most complete critique); F. Cuper (Kuyper), *Arcana Atheismi revelata, philosophice et paradoxe* (Rotterdam, 1676; this is certainly the same work spoken of by S. Dunin Borkowski in "Der erste Anhang zu der Kurzen Abhandlung," *Chronicon Spinozanum* I [The Hague, 1921], p. 75n, which gives the original Dutch title and lists 1677 as year of publication; cf. also C. Gebhardt, *Spinoza, Kurze Abhandlung . . .*, Introduction [Leipzig, 1922], pp. Vf. Kuyper was a Mennonite and likewise conceived extension as being an attribute of God, without however borrowing this notion in any sense from Spinoza: cf. S. Dunin Borkowski, *Der junge Spinoza* [Münster i. W. 1910], p. 360 and Note 43 to p. 574); I. O. L. de Velthuysen, *Tractatus de cultu naturali et origine moralitatis* (1680; Velthuysen was in correspondence with Spinoza, *Ep.* XLII); Aubert de Versé *L'Impie convaincu, ou Dissertation contre Spinoza dans laquelle on réfute les fondements de son athéisme* (Amsterdam, 1685; cited by d'Holbach, *op. cit.*, Vol. II, p. 151, note, 186 note); Poiret, "Fundamenta Atheismi eversa sive Specimen absurditatis Atheismi Spinoziani," inserted in 2nd ed. of Poiret's *De Deo, Anima et Malo* (Amsterdam, 1685); Henry More, *Op. philos.*, Vol. I, p. 600, translated by Kuyper above; F. Lami, *Le nouvel Athéisme renversé ou Réfutation du Système de Spinoza . . .* (Paris, 1696); Jacquelot, *Dissertations sur l'existence de Dieu où l'on demontre cette vérité par l'Histoire Universelle . . ., par la Réfutation du système d'Epicure et de Spinoza, etc.* (The Hague, 1697); Jens, *Examen philo-*

Spinoza agreed to this change and the book appeared with Mayer's correction in it. A perusal of the book readily reveals that the word *God,* as used in this book, is a mere stratagem to put the reader on the wrong scent. He subjects everything to some vague necessity, not imposed by anyone but natural to matter and whatever intelligences there are mixed in with matter, and he advances no reason with any semblance of verisimilitude to account for this necessity. Though Spinoza has indeed arranged his statements in a mathematical order, so as to dupe his readers, the whole work is a mass of unsound reasoning and incessant balderdash" (Jean Le Clerc (1657-1736), *Bibliothèque Ancienne et Moderne,* Vol. XXIV [Amsterdam, 1724], pp 135ff.).

sophicum sextae definitionis Partis I Eth. Benedicti de Spinoza sive Prodromus Animadversionum super unico veterum et recentiorum Atheorum Argumento nempe "una substantia" . . . (Dort, 1698). For his own part, Bayle criticizes Spinoza's atheism especially in Notes N (fol. 259b-262a and P (fol. 263b-264a).

J. A. Trinius in his *Freydenker Lexicon* observes: "The atheist system of philosophy, which has taken from Spinoza the name of Spinozism, has him as its author formally but not materially, i.e., not contextually" and he cites a good 129 works of refutation (Leipzig & Bernburg, 1759, pp. 418ff. and Supp. pp. 75ff.; ed. Bottega d'Erasmo [1960], pp. 105ff., pp. 247f.).

A substantial bibliography of the anti-Spinozan writings is also provided by G. Ch. B. Punjer, *Geschichte der christlichen Religionsphilosophie seit der Reformation,* Vol. I (Braunschweig, 1880), pp. 322ff. where he also cites a *Catalogus scriptorum Anti-Spinozianorum* by Janichen. F. Ehrardt has rather chosen to follow the order of the doctrines in his treatment of the critiques of Spinoza in his *Die Philosophie des Spinoza im Lichte der Kritik* (Leipzig 1908).

The most accurate chronological exposition of the reactions (and charges of atheism) excited by the *Tractatus Theol.-Pol.* is that of J. Freudenthal, *op. cit.,* P. I, c. 9; ed. Gebhardt, Vol. I, pp. 217-252, and for the *Ethica,* P. II, c. 9, pp. 212-241, with the documentation of Gebhardt on pp. 255ff. Despite his defense of Spinoza (cf. Preceding Section of this Appendix), Freudenthal admits the complete change of course effected in the *Tractatus Theol.-Pol.,* and records the suspicion of Spinoza (confirmed by the biographer Lucas) to the effect that the uproar had been caused intentionally by the Cartesians in order to saddle Spinoza with the charge of atheism that they had seen headed for their own system (Vol. I, p. 233f.). Freudenthal's final judgment may also clarify the significance of his apology for Spinoza: "Thus he [Spinoza] declares himself for immanence, for an intracosmic status of God, against theism and transcendence. Thus he decides in favor of the monism of being and thinking against materialism and dualism; thus he presses home the mechanical explanation of the world and thereby determinism in anthropology and ethics against teleology in nature and against free will in ethics" (*op. cit.,* P. II, c. I, Vol. II, p. 14).

The most recent critical synthesis by a specialist of the Spinozan bibliography with important creative collations is that of S. Dunin Borkowski, *Spinoza nach Dreihundert Jahren* (Berlin and Bonn 1932), pp. 112-186.

But Spinozan studies are showing a noticeable revival even since World War II, as attested by the voluminous work of Vernière which we have already cited. Spinoza seems to have had little influence on classical English philosophy which had already in Hobbes its own model of cryptomaterialism (Cf. e.g., the criticisms of Spinoza by Toland: F.

Ehrardt, *Die Philosophie des Spinoza im Lichte der Kritik,* p. 488). A more explicit return to Spinoza is to be noted especially in the English-American neo-Hegelian school, as we shall see.

IV. Henry More on Cartesian Mechanism and Atheism

In his youth, the Platonist Henry More was an enthusiast of the Cartesian method; but in his later years he developed from a faithful follower into a trenchant critic of that metaphysic and especially of the empty Cartesian claim to have opened up new ways to prove the existence of God. Far from achieving this aim, says More, echoing the charge of Voetius, the Cartesian method has rather provided a foothold for materialism and atheism. More's critique seems to us to merit a brief consideration because More remains closer to the spirit of the philosophy of Descartes, even in his critique of that philosophy, than does the fiery Hardouin. More himself reports on this whole crisis of transition in his own thought and in his estimate of Descartes' thought in the list of his own works, in the *Prefatio generalissima* (1679), prefaced to the first part of his *Opera omnia* (I). Here More is outspoken and uncompromising in his candid self-criticism: "And in this same year of 1664 a new edition was published separately of the Letter to V. C. I wrote this letter both to protect the good name of Descartes (for in it I try to remove from him all suspicion of atheism) and to promote the integrity and well-being of Student Youth, by removing the poison that lies hidden in that Cartesian principle whereby all phenomena of nature are reduced to mere mechanical causes. That this cannot be done, I showed in that Letter, and I have proven the same thing elsewhere more fully and more openly." (Henry More, *Opera Omnia,* Vol. II [London, 1679; reprinted Hildesheim, 1966], pp. xf.).

The above statements were developed at some length in the preface to the second edition of the *Enchiridion Ethicum,* where More states that he has appended the *Epistola ad V. C.* to this latter work, intending that this Letter stemming from his Cartesian period should serve not only as an introduction to an understanding of the philosophy of Descartes but also as a salutary warning: "But as a right sound forewarning and preclusion against all in it that might do damage to the unwary or wound piety and religion" (p. 4). More's charges are two: the first has to do with the Cartesian notion of the infinity and eternity of matter which ends up being identical with God; the second regards the mechanistic conception Descartes presents of reality. The first charge is more strictly metaphysical: "And one of these is, that that very matter of which the world consists must of necessity exist indefinitely extended in every direction: and moreover, that that limitless extension to whose existence our minds must needs give consent, is necessarily corporeal, according to Descartes" (*loc. cit.*). This point, More notes he has refuted at length in his second letter to Descartes, (cf. Descartes, *Correspondance,* ed. Adam-Tannery, Vol. V, pp. 376ff.) to which letter Descartes seems not to have made any reply. The second charge has to do with Descartes' rigorously mechanistic explanation of motion and life: "All the phenomena of the world, namely, including plants and organic living bodies, are held to be able to arise out of merely mechanical beginnings, to wit, from merely local motion and matter; and the necessary causes and principles of all of them are held to be deducible from these sources. This insensate notion we have not failed to attack in many places over and over again in this same Letter" (p. 6).

To these charges, there can be added a third, the denial of final causality in the physical world: "Which it seemed to me so unfitting for a philosopher to do, that I preferred to attribute Descartes' removal of them from his own philosophy rather to a certain harmless sleight-of-hand than to any ignorance on his part of such a well-established truth" (p. 7). And More adds that he therefore preferred Aristotle on this point (p. 8). What shocked More and compelled him to backtrack is thus clearly shown to be that mechanism present in the Cartesian philosophy, which More himself had so vigorously touted in his youth as a refutation of the mechanistic atheists; More has subsequently become convinced that the Cartesian mechanism cannot lead to God. More seems genuinely persuaded of the error of his previous devotion to Cartesian mechanism, as comes out clearly in the Scholion to the Letter to V.C.: "These things did I write then as a follower of Descartes, on the supposition that the parts of matter would necessarily cohere, were they not in motion. But I later realized that this statement of Descartes had been a gratuitous one and that no parts of matter are brought together or kept together by their own power but rather by some higher principle, even as I explain at some length in the *Enchiridion Metaphysicum* (Handbook of Metaphysics)" (p. 123).

The preface to this *Enchiridion Metaphysicum,* a work dating from 1671, when More had reached full maturity, certainly contains what amounts to a downright attack on the Cartesian attitude to religion. First and foremost, More is at pains to repeat that the method used by Descartes in the *Meditations* for proving the existence of God has never seemed to More to be convincing: ". . . and even at that time when I felt other writings of his to be superb, I could by no means find these so admirable. For although he seems to agree with me in supposing incorporeal things to be the legitimate and adequate object of metaphysics; yet most assuredly I could never approve of his proofs of their existence nor of his explanations of their nature . . ." And More follows this up with the drastic judgment: "But indeed, to speak freely as to how the matter stands, Descartes most assuredly gives too little consideration to the strengthening and integrity of even natural religion in that method he uses in his Metaphysical Meditations, especially if these be compared with the principles of philosophy" (pp. 135f.). Indeed, More does seem to admit the validity of the ontological argument and proof, albeit not in the exact form in which Descartes presented it: "But equally unfortunate was that assertion of his to the effect that matter existed of necessity; for thereby the whole force of the argument drawn from the idea of God as absolutely perfect Being to prove his existence is quite drastically weakened and diluted" (p. 136).

In this preface, it is the charge of radical mechanism which is put in first place, inverting the order of the *Enchiridion Ethicum:* "For, to begin with, no greater gash and wound could be inflicted on the most essential parts of religion, than the presumption that all phenomena can be resolved into purely mechanical causes (not excepting even the bodies of plants and animals). For then this corporeal world can produce itself, provided only that a motion is imparted to matter as great as that motion that is in fact found in it. But this is the Cartesian hypothesis" (*ibid.*). But it is preeminently the notion of absolute matter that forces Descartes into a blind alley and brings him to deny the possibility of proving the existence of God. Here More abandons all reverential timidity and speaks out as clearly as one could wish: "Then, that matter according to the innate idea of it in our mind cannot exist, or, that existence necessarily belongs to matter, from the bare make-up of the idea of it. Now this blow seems to me no less cruel or more tolerable than the former: for both inflict immense ruin on the certitude and evidence of the knowledge of things metaphysical" (*ibid.*).

Substantially, then, Descartes leaves the entire problem of the existence of God wide open. The ontological proof, taken from Scholastic metaphysics ("taken from the Idea of God itself") has been vitiated by Descartes' idea of matter: "by his fabrication of a wrong idea of matter, Descartes finally severs all the sinews of this (proof)" (p. 136f.). The other two proofs are still less cogent; and so, the entire metaphysical front is left uncovered. And from this point we wish to cite the critique, now unremitting and trenchant, directly in More's own words: "And to this first argument he subjoins two others; but so weak are they that he himself puts little stock in their cogency. And yet for the sake of these two weak arguments, he fells, as it were, at one stroke, a multitude of sound and solid arguments, nay, rather every single one of such arguments that are to be sought in the area of the phenomena of the world; and this he does by that foolhardy mechanical hypothesis of his, whereby he contends that everything can be resolved into purely mechanical causes. He has asserted that motion was imprinted on matter by God, but he has not proved it; yet he will go on to assert most boldly and persistently, with the whole Epicurean School, that atoms move themselves. He has denied that matter could be thought of as modified in any way whatsoever; but he goes on to admit and quite openly to profess something that seems equally hard to grasp if not much harder, to wit, that matter when moved can be harmonized into those most cunningly devised structures we know as living bodies; not one solid argument has he adduced to prove matter incapable of sensation nor yet to prove the soul really distinct from the body. For he does not pursue the business into the deep realm of metaphysics, proving only that a thinking thing can be either material or immaterial: as likewise the formal concept of an animal can include both the brute beast and man . . . But thus, partly as a result of Cartesian concessions about the mechanical structure of animals, and partly as a result of the quite uninformed opinions and bias of a great number of people, this whole corporeal world would be forthwith admitted to have been able to produce itself and it would be alleged that there was no God beyond this corporeal world; then it would be confidently and openly concluded that all incorporeal things not only are not in any spatial location, as Descartes modestly suggests, but simply are not at all or in any sense, since there would be no use for them. Such was Descartes' diligence and solicitude for the integrity and advantage of religion in his metaphysical meditations, after his mind had so avidly yearned for worlds mechanically constructed: And with so few, so weak, so ill-trained and unreliable troops, has this unconquered Hero dared to challenge the whole world of Letters to battle concerning the existence of God; nor is there any doubt that he would have won the day before judges sufficiently unbiased and well-informed, had not one part of his battle-array so treacherously attacked the other, and the idea of a matter necessarily existing completely overthrown the force of the idea of an absolutely perfect Being" (p. 137).[2]

More has at last succeeded in expressing the deepest reason for his disagreement with Descartes and anticipating the interpretation that is going to be given to Cartesianism by materialistic atheism right down the line from Helvétius to d'Holbach. It thus comes as no surprise to hear More declare openly that Cartesianism is already on the slippery slope leading to atheism: "For be it noted that, as things now stand, if the Cartesian philosophy, physical and metaphysical, should manage to maintain itself, I for one shudder to say on what a dangerous cliff's edge, on what a precipitous slope into atheism the minds of man would be left tottering, so true is it that there is no sufficiently firm tether in his principles of philosophizing to hold them back from slipping into this raging madness" (p. 137).

The specter of atheism cannot easily be exorcised from Cartesian philosophy and More concludes his masterly Preface with this charge, seeming almost to call in question Descartes' own good faith in having so stubbornly clung to this mechanical notion of the real which put his followers so dismally on the wrong track: "And this did he hug so tightly to his heart, not so concerned with proving the existence of God

[2] More's reservations about Cartesianism remained steady, as can be seen from the *Scholia* to the Preface to the second part of Vol. II, in reference to the passages cited in this Appendix: "For that part that insinuates that the world was made or is sustained by merely mechanical causes, I not only do not admit but I actively disprove, as is to be seen in the *Enchiridion Metaphysicum* and in the Letter to V. C." (Vol. II, 2, p. 16).

as with precluding any suspicion that he himself was an atheist on account of his mechanical causes of worlds to be made; if, I say, he did this and proposed as true and natural notions that were distorted and forced, dragged in by the hair to bolster his own contention, and violently twisted at that, then he did institute an unending calvary for serious but unguarded minds, who, led astray by their admiration for his mental perspicacity, were bound to let themselves be persuaded that whatever he had said, however wildly removed from common sense and even self-contradictory, was nonetheless true and solidly grounded, and to attribute whatever they understood less well rather to their own slowness of perception than to the obscurity or the falsity of the notions themselves" (p.138).

Descartes' work has been harmful, on balance, for religion, "especially in a point so serious and of such importance as the existence of God and the immortality of the human soul. The profession of these dogmas cannot but be exposed to the most shameful sniggering and contempt of atheists and men foreign to religion so long as it is propped up by such slight and silly proofs, either weak in themselves or weakened by their mutual contradictoriness of which we have warned already. Which consideration ought manifestly to excuse in the eyes of all good men this, our παῤῥησίαν (unvarnished speaking) in setting forth our opinion of Descartes' metaphysical speculations as compared with his mechanical philosophy" (p. 138).

Unless I am mistaken, the polemic of this disenchanted Cartesian is more radical and vigorous than even Voetius' attack! And More seems to have written the *Enchiridion Metaphysicum,* considered to be his most typical and representative work, precisely in order to hold the line against Cartesian mechanism: he even exclaims: "O Philosophy of Mechanism, credulous and foolish beyond all Superstition!" and, as if this were not enough, More brackets Descartes and Hobbes in a single condemnation: " 'What then,' you will ask; 'is it all over with all manner of mechanical explanations of phenomena?' Well I certainly think it is all over with those 'Simon pure' ones touted by Descartes, Hobbes and mechanical philosophers of their ilk, which explanations alone I attack and shatter, not only as less than pious but as most monstrously silly and false beyond the power of words to express" (p. 139). More's own work in fact aims at the defense of the metaphysical truths comprising the world of the spirit, the existence of God and of spiritual substances, a defense based on the admission of the fact that spiritual life has an origin all its own and proper to itself: ". . . *since there will never be seen upon earth a spectacle more vile or abject than the man who is an atheist and refuses to believe in things incorporeal*" (p. 139). And More continues throughout the entire work to attack Descartes' contamination of metaphysics by a mechanistic physics.

We thus see a complete reversal in More's evolution! And I think that Kuyper's refutation of Spinoza and the further pinpointing of the Spinozan position it effected (points to which the next Appendix will be devoted) played no small part in this dramatic reversal in More, the drama of whose philosophical evolution was keyed to a much higher pitch than that of Voetius.

V. Kuyper-More Critique of Spinoza's Atheism

The Dutch theologian, Kuyper, seems to have been the first (according to his own statement) to sound the alarm concerning Spinoza's atheism. Kuyper examined Spinoza's *Tractatus Theologico-Politicus* in a work entitled *Arcana Atheismi revelata et paradoxe refutata, examine Tractatus Theologico-Politico* (The Secrets of Atheism Revealed and Refuted by way of Philosophy and Paradox, through an Examination of the *Tractatus Theologico-Politicus*). The Latin title continues to this effect: by Francis Kuyper of Amsterdam, comprising two books: in the former, the *Tractatus* itself is examined and rebutted; in the latter, the key arguments of the atheists, first against sacred scripture, then against religion and the existence of God, are clarified and invalidated, and it is proven by new arguments that there is a God. Rotterdam, apud Isaacum Naeranum, Anno 1676).

The sense of the work is indicated in the Preface (". . . comprising the underlying plan of the whole work . . ."), written in a brisk and highly personal style, almost autobiographical, opening with a confession of conversion generically similar to, though specifically different from, that of More; for in Kuyper's case, it was a conversion from the atheism in which he had been brought up to the discovery of its error which had dragged with it so many victims: "Since, however, it was my lot from the time I was knee-high to a grasshopper, so to speak, to live and be brought up amongst atheists, whom I often heard examining the arguments whereby the teachers of truth try to prove the existence of God and ferreting out the feebleness of these arguments (something they do not dare to do except when they are among those whom they believe to be of the same opinion as themselves), I was driven to ponder the problem of finding a surer and shorter way whereby we could be sure of the existence of God. And this problem gained new urgency for me when I saw, a few years ago, so many men, and capable and intelligent men at that, rushing everywhere headlong into atheism" (first page of Preface, in which pages have not been numbered by the editor). Hence Kuyper's decision to refute, for a start, the *Tractatus Theologico-Politicus* of Spinoza: "And since I knew that this could happen only if they discovered that certain arguments which heretofore had satisfied them were invalid, I girded my loins as the first man, so far as I have heard, to attempt a refutation of the *Tractatus Theologico-Politicus,* and I compassed this refutation" (p. 1). The same point is made even more forthrightly later on: "And since it was not unknown to me as one brought up from infancy among atheists that these same atheists have many devices wherewith they cajole even themselves, I held it to be absolutely necessary to go still further and to weigh by the assay of the natural light sharpened by the divine revelations of sacred scripture the rest of their secret objections and lines of argument which I drew partly from manuscripts sent me from various places, and partly from other sources" (p. X).

Kuyper held the book back for a long time after its completion in order to rework and deepen it before publication. As an introduction to the work, he enunciates eight preliminary procedural propositions entirely fideist in inspiration and motivated by a defensive attitude toward atheism: these propositions warn against any use of reason in the field of religion. Obviously there is running in the wake of the new atheism the bogeyman of the Averroistic split between science and faith: "To which end he urges a separation of theology from philosophy, so that there may be greater freedom to inculcate atheistical dogmas under the name of philosophy, and the people at large, should they set up any clamor to the effect that these dogmas are perverting religion, may be calmed down by saying (as it is already beginning to be claimed by the theologians) that a thing can be true in philosophy which is false in theology and vice versa. For he wishes philosophy to be called the realm of truth and theology the realm of senseless drivel, so that the people may be easily managed by the philosophers under the specious title of piety and kept in their place by the fear of divine punishments" (p. IV).

The work is divided into two books: the first presents a chapter-by-chapter refutation of the *Tractatus Theologico-Politicus* down to chapter 12 (omitting the succeeding chapters dealing with politics); Kuyper seems not to have known who was the author of this *Tractatus:* Spinoza is mentioned by name later on (p. 267), on the authority of Ludwig Meyer in the preface to his Cartesian Metaphysics, as one who asserted the identity of intellect and will. The second book examines, in ten chapters, the arguments of the atheists; the eleventh chapter presents a good thirteen arguments in defense of the existence of God, while the last chapter (the twelfth) expounds the criteria for the interpretation of sacred scripture.

Kuyper's opinion on the idea of God is quite close to that of More and the English Platonists: "With no less risk do those men defend religion who press the point that God is a non-extended Being, not existing in place or in time. For if these three (extension, place and time) be removed from the essence of God, the existence of God is entirely denied. For it cannot be conceived that a Being having no extension can have any essence nor that that which exists neither in place nor in time ever exists anywhere. And thus such an opinion seems to be sheer atheism" (p. XII). Kuyper's work fell into the hands of More and could not but arouse More's interest. More's remarks on the work are summarized in the *Epistula altera ad V. C.,* published likewise in 1679, and thus barely three years after Kuyper's work.

More shows himself to be well-informed concerning the rumors in circulation, attributing the *Tractatus Theologico-Politicus* to Spinoza; More himself seems to agree: ". . . *Spinoza,* if indeed he is the author of this treatise, as almost everyone asserts" (Vol. II, p. 565). More continues to maintain this attribution of the *Tractatus* to Spinoza throughout the entire essay; and it becomes a *de facto* certainty for More when he comes to know Spinoza's posthumous works, as More himself hastens to point out in the *Adnotationes* to this Epistle: "After I had completed this refutation of the *Tractatus Theologico-Politicus* together with its Scholia and transcribed it all, I happened to chance upon B.D.S.'s *Opera Posthuma* while I was on business in London. I bought these works mainly so that the reading of them might make it clearer to myself and others that I had done Spinoza no wrong, either in attributing the aforementioned treatise to him or in interpreting passages of it more harshly than was fair" (p. 611). More sees a clear affinity between the atheist teachings and theories of Descartes and those of Spinoza: ". . . if one adheres to the Cartesian philosophy which Spinoza so much admired, we cannot deduce whether God exists or not, and still less whether he be good and wise" (p. 571). The taproot of Spinoza's atheism is indicated to lie in his naturalistic and even materialistic monism and in his identification of intellect and will in God, points of expressly Cartesian inspiration (cf. par. 16, pp. 571ff.). But More proceeds further than did Kuyper and examines likewise the chapters of the *Tractatus* devoted to political theory, in which he again discovers the principles of Spinozan atheism (cf. pp. 529f.).

Polemic flares again in More's comment on the 20th and last chapter of the *Tractatus* in which Spinoza is discussing freedom of thought and has promulgated the slogan: *"In a free Body Politic, everyone has the right to have what opinions he wishes and to express the opinions he holds."* More comments brusquely: "An utterly mad and senseless opinion, as you will readily see if you come down to particular instances. Everyone thus has the right, if he so wishes, to hold the opinion that God does not exist, that God is a malignant spirit rejoicing above all in the calamities of men and even bringing such calamities upon them, or that God is ignorant of human affairs, or even that he knows nothing for certain nor lays down any abiding precepts, but that he is more changeable than the wind in spring; and even opinions more horrifying or absurd than these everyone is justified and at liberty, if he will, not only to hold but to state and profess publicly. Now who would advance so insane an opinion unless he were himself an atheist or else completely out of his mind? Yet no one should marvel that streams so polluted should have sprung from such a tainted fountain!" (p. 595).

The latter part of the Letter is unsparing in its trenchant criticism of Kuyper himself for having denied to reason a natural knowledge of God and the ability to make any distinction between good and bad actions in the realm of natural morality, a stand that More feels to be equivalent to atheism. More even claims that it would have cast doubt on Kuyper's own good faith, had Kuyper's personal aim and intention not been evident, an aim, however, that was most ineptly executed: "What then, you will inquire, do you think on balance of him who revealed the secrets of atheism? Did he behave with such a want of discretion as to reveal himself quite plainly as an atheist? God forbid that I should judge thus; that is the very thing I have thus far used every diligence to avoid doing. This one thing only do I aver: that inasmuch as he contends that no one can know God to exist from his works in nature which he has created but only from revelation, so no one can know Kuyper not to be an atheist; they simply have to take Kuyper's word for it. For I do not doubt but that he would profess himself not to be an atheist; and ordinary human kindness and decency requires that we accept his protestation" (p. 600—More speaks more sharply against Kuyper the *Scholia* and the *Adnotationes,* [pp. 614ff.] even to the point of defending Spinoza against the exaggerations of Kuyper's critique [cf. pp. 604, 613f.]). More holds Kuyper to belong with the Socinians, the Enthusiasts and the Shakers.

The most concise summary of Spinozan atheism is to be found in the conclusion of the *Adnotationes* to the Letter (sect. 51): "That this was indeed the exact opinion and contention of Spinoza is abundantly clear from the points cited above from his posthumous works; nor would there have been any difficulty in understanding his writings, had he but come out in the open and written 'Matter' everywhere in those places where in fact he wrote 'God', and pinpointed once and for all that he understood matter to be αὐτόζωον or living by itself, and that it is the only substance existing in the universe with no other whatever at its side. For this is his supreme secret which he nurses in private, even as he so often takes the name of God upon his lips as a blind to con the gulls. But this is as crass an error as any mortal has ever fallen into. Nor could any fallen soul be dragged down into a darker or more squalid pit of atheism nor yet into plunged into a grosser cesspool of ignorance" (p. 614).

But More is not satisfied even yet; and once he is certain of the authenticity of the *Tractatus* as a work of Spinoza, he writes a new critique which seems to me his most considered and forceful: (*A brief and cogent refutation of the proof of two propositions, to wit, that to substance insofar as it is substance, existence necessarily pertains; and that there is one substance and one substance only in the world, which two propositions are the chief pillars of atheism in Spinoza* [pp. 615ff.]. This critique maintains the distinction between spirit and matter and between God and the world; it also cites extensively and frequently for the first time from the *Opera Posthuma,* especially the *Ethics* and the *Letters.* There is a noteworthy bracketing of Spinoza and Descartes near the end of the work, in connection with the absolute determinism of the divine will in the *Ethics* (P. I, prop. 44, pars II: "For it pertains to the reason to contemplate things not as contingent but as necessary"); More comments: "That is as occurring according to some kind of mechanical necessity, even as *Descartes* supposes the phenomena of the world to come about. There is Spinoza's intellectual love of God for you! What a whited sepulchre!" (p. 634).

More's conclusion in unequivocal: Spinoza is a materialist: "Τὸ πρῶτον ψεῦδος. [The first lie] however in Spinoza is this: that he supposes that there is but one substance in the universe and that this substance must necessarily be matter. And this is the bilge of that dull mind of his, elsewhere taken for such a sharp one, that he proffers the world to drink!" (p. 635).

More's critique, which sides with Hardouin's and Voetius' in charging Cartesian rationalism with an atheist overtone, is itself not free of philosophical defects, e.g., the spatial conception of the immensity of God characteristic of English Platonism which recurs often in this controversy (especially in the polemic against Kuyper). All the same, this critique does constitute one of the strongest and clearest warnings against the radical denial of God latent in the new philosophy, and amounts to a unmistakable exposé of the deliberate and conscious manner in which the new principle is identifying the Absolute with nature and reducing Being as such to the dimension of the finitude of the world.

VI. John Toland's Hesitation Concerning Bayle's Hypothesis

John Toland speaks out considerably more firmly; he makes no reservations or supersubtle theological distinctions; yet he effects no substantial break with Bayle's position. He treats the whole problem in his *Adeisidaimon,* citing Bayle directly in the letter of dedication to Collins. Toward the end of the letter we read: "Incidentally, it may seem to savor of paradox that, although I deem SUPERSTITION to be more baneful to the body politic than ATHEISM, I am willing that the former should be tolerated sometimes whereas I am never willing that the latter should be tolerated."

The specific problem of the relations between superstition and religion is treater earlier, with the aim of acquiting Livy of the charges levelled by theologians. This treatment is on balance clearly favorable to atheism and so in line with Plutarch and Bayle, but Toland's own conclusion is a defense of a midway position which he holds to be "true religion". We here present the pith of his argument which seems to us unusually important: "The most renowed Johannes Gerardus Vossius (in chapter 10 of his book on the Latin Historians) amazingly enough admits the most notorious accusation against Livy and feels himself to have established a wonderful defense of Livy by alleging that the attitudes of which Livy is accused *surely are rather deserving of praise in a heathen, since any cult of the deity is to be preferred to atheism.* His disjunction may satisfy the Grammarians but it can only acutely distress the philosophers; for he presupposes that there is no middle term between atheism and superstition; and he argues as if that monstrous and baneful superstition which fills the most flourishing States with discord and tumults, decimates the most powerful kingdoms and not infrequently subverts them entirely, splits off children from their parents, turns friend against friend and ruptures the closest ties, were not much more deadly to the body politic and human society than any atheism, however abominable. *Religion could induce so many evil deeds*—here it must be noted that the term religion is used in many classical authors not to denote genuine piety or an interior worship of the deity, but to designate all manner of the most absurd superstition . . . and preeminently to denote the external rites and ceremonies. Assuredly the atheist does not believe God to be the avenger of crimes nor does he shudder before the chastising flames of hell. He is not restrained by the sacral religious character of an oath but only by the civic respect due to promises. But if he be but well disposed by nature or by art, he is not necessarily going to be impelled by any goad or incitement to bring ruin upon others. No one will he persecute with hate of mind or force of arms because of fluctuating dictates of conscience, for he is concerned not with what others believe but with what they do. He freely and readily admits the difference between virtue and vice, between the shameful and the honorable, as flowing from the very nature of things: and he is always aware of an inner praise or blame depending on whether he has done rightly or not, although he holds nothing to be absolutely good or evil of itself, estimating the goodness or badness of any thing rather in terms of the good or evil use made of it, i.e., in function of the joy or sorrow it brings, the delight or distaste it occasions. Moreover, the less he lives in expectation of any future reward or punishment after death, the more he is constrained to take thought for happiness in this present life which he holds to be the only one there is; and this happiness no one can attain without the aid of others and mutual collaboration. For that man who does not do to others the things that he would wish to be done to him should not enjoy the benefits of society nor is he likely to. Thus the atheist is not deterred from evil by the wheels, the rocks, the serpents, the fires or the torrents of Hades . . ."

There follows a eulogy of the *Chinese Sages:* ". . . although they believe this visible world to be eternal and incorruptible and do not admit any deity distinct from its material fabric; and reject every teaching concerning a future state of souls as mere legend or politically motivated invention. The atheist will therefore perhaps oppress his foes with the worst devices whereas true piety would lead a man to pardon such foes; and will indulge, in evasion of the laws of the state, the vile sensual gratifications which it is to be hoped will have no place in the lives of those aiming at higher things or at least professing allegiance to them. The superstitious man, on the other hand, not only reckons anyone disagreeing with him or casting even the slightest aspersions on the chimeras of his own brain or the fraudulent babblings of his masters to be his own personal deadly enemy, but even damns such men as hateful to God and reprobate: he rouses heaven and earth, yes, and hell itself against them . . . In this one respect the atheists and the superstitious are on a par, in that it comes down to exactly the same thing whether, in the matter of the plighted word, the atheist sins in secret (to the extent his own interests seem to demand), or whether a superstitious man absolves a person from the obligation of an oath (as happens more frequently). In another respect, however, they are by no means on a par, inasmuch as there are some superstitions which are, so to speak, tolerable in civil society, so that, if they cannot be entirely extirpated, the good statesman will do his best to bring them into line with public polity, whereas atheists may not hope for any toleration under any circumstances, since they are impervious to any bond of conscience (or fear of punishment or love of reward) which might impel them to a public declaration of their secret schemes or frame of mind. Superstition, though always undesirable, can sometimes be innocuous; but the atheist, bent on his own advantage, will never dissent from the established religion, to which he will want everyone else, at all costs, to conform, lest he himself appear suspect. Atheism, in short, involves the few; superstition, almost everyone. But that which is evil in itself is not made acceptable by the simple fact that there seems to be something worse, as has been clearly proven by Bayle, whose merits have never been appropriately recognized. His overall position I do not scruple here to support, even though I do not approve certain points he adduced in defense of it nor wish to become involved in the quarrels that have arisen in connection with this whole argument, since I harbor feelings of the greatest respect and friendship for some of Bayle's opponents. ATHEISM, therefore, and SUPERSTITION are like to a Scylla and Charybdis of souls. And both these extremes are just as much to be avoided as RELIGION, which stands midway between them, is to be pursued" (*Adeisidaimon sive Titus Livius vindicatus . . .*, auctore J. Toland [The Hague: Apud Thomas Johnson, 1709], 67ff.).

VII. MONTESQUIEU AND THE "PARADOX OF BAYLE"

Montesquieu was certainly among those taking a very firm stand on Bayle's thesis. After distinguishing between various degrees of falsity among the false religions, Montesquieu insists that true religion never comes into conflict with the interests of the body politic, least of all the Christian religion: "The Christian religion, which commands men to love one another, indubitably desires that every people shall have the best political laws and the best civil laws, because these are, for Christianity, the greatest good that men can give and receive". There follows a concise and tightly-reasoned refutation with the significant title *Paradox of Bayle:*

"M. Bayle claims to have proven that it is better to be an atheist than to be an idolater; in other words, that it is less dangerous to have no religion at all than to have a bad one. 'I would prefer,' says he 'that men should say of me that I do not exist than that they should say I was wicked.' This is nothing but a sophism, for there is no value accruing to the human race from believing that a certain man exists, wheras it is of great value to believe that God exists. From the notion that he does not, there follows the idea of our own total autonomy, or in its default the idea of our rebellion. To say that religion is not a restraining motive because it does not always restrain is to deprive civil laws, by the same token, of the status of a restraining motive. It is bad argumentation against religion to collect into a lengthy work a long enumeration of the evils it has produced without presenting a similar list of all the good religion has done. Were I to recount all the evils that have been produced in the world by the civil laws, the monarchy and the republican government, I should have some dreadful things to say. Even though it were pointless for subjects to have any religion, it would by no means be pointless for princes to have one and to whiten with their foam the only bit that can tame those who do not fear the laws of man.

"A prince who loves religion and fears it is a lion surrendering to the hand that strokes it or the voice that quiets it; he who fears religion and hates it is like the wild beasts who bite the chain that is preventing them from hurling themselves upon the passersby; he who has no religion at all is that dreadful beast who feels his own freedom only when he is rending and devouring.

"The point at issue is not whether it would be better for a certain man or a certain people not to have any religion whatever than to misuse the one he has; it is rather which is the lesser evil, that religion be sometimes misused or that there be no religion whatever among men.

"Idolatry is excessively indicted in order to lessen the horror of atheism. It is not true that when the men of the ancient world raised altars to some vice this signified that they loved this vice: on the contrary, it meant that they hated it. When the Spartans erected a shrine to Fear, this did not mean that this war-like nation was asking that deity to seize upon Spartan hearts in battle and make himself master of them. There were deities who used to be besought not to inspire men to crime and others who used to be besought to avert it."

A little further on, after showing that Christianity is opposed to despotic rule and quite favorable to a moderate government, Montesquieu enters a vigorous protest against Bayle's defamation of the Christian religion:

"Another paradox of Bayle

After having insulted all religions, M. Bayle proceeds to castigate the Christian religion: he dares to contend that real Christians could not form and fashion a viable State. Why not? They would be citizens immeasurably enlightened concerning their own duties and filled with a very great zeal to discharge those duties; they would be very sensible to the demands of the negative natural law; the more they believe they owed to religion, the more they would think they owed to their country. The principles of Christianity well and truly engraved on human hearts would be incomparably more potent than this counterfeit honor of monarchies, these purely human virtues of republics, and this servile fear of despotic states.

"It is a cause for amazement that this great man can be charged with failure to understand aright the spirit of his own religion, with inability to distinguish between the prescriptions for the establishment of Christianity and Christianity itself, nor yet between the evangelical precepts and the evangelical counsels. When the lawgiver gives counsels instead of laws, it is because he has seen that his counsels, were they commanded as laws, would be contrary to the spirit of his laws."

(Montesquieu, *De l'Esprit des Loix,* Bk. XXIV, Ch. 1-2; Vol. II [Paris, An IV de la République], pp. 330-332 and 337). For other texts from *De l'Esprit des Loix* favoring Christianity, cf. Abbé Nonnotte, *Supplément au Dictionnaire Anti-Philosophique* (Avignon, 1767), pp. 372ff. Montesquieu is here presented as an apologist for Christianity against the attacks of Spinoza, Hobbes and Bayle. On Montesquieu's edifying behavior on his deathbed, cf. the letter of P. Ruth, S.J. to the Apostolic Nuncio Gualtiero (pp. 386f.).

VIII. Rousseau and the Inconsistency of Bayle's Thesis

In the profession of theistic faith he inserts in *Émile,* Rousseau makes a spirited defense of the intimate nexus between morality and religion. We cite the crucial passage: "Flee those who, under pretext of explaining nature, sow in men's hearts devastating teachings and whose patent skepticism is a hundred times more aggressive and dogmatic than the trenchant tone adopted by their opponents. Under the haughty pretext that they alone have seen the light, that they alone are sincere and in good faith, they subject us imperiously to their peremptory conclusions and foist upon us, as the true principles of things, the unintelligible systems they have built up in their own imagination. Moreover, subverting, destroying and trampling upon everything that men hold in esteem, they filch from the afflicted the last consolation of their misery and remove from the rich and powerful the last brake upon their passions; they tear out of man's inmost heart all remorse for crime, all hope of virtue, priding themselves the while upon being the benefactors of mankind. Never, they say, is truth harmful to men. I believe this just as they do and this is, in my opinion, a major proof that what they are teaching is not the truth."

At this point Rousseau inserts an extensive note to refute Bayle's contrary contentions which have already been covered quite thoroughly and significantly in the main body of the text:

"The two opposing groups attack one another with so many sophisms that it would be an immense and risky enterprise to undertake to note them all; suffice it to note a few as they come up. One of the most notorious sophistic tricks of the pseudo-philosopher group is to set a supposititious people composed of good philosophers over against a people composed of bad Christians: as if a body of good philosophers were easier to produce than a body of good Christians! I do not know whether the one is easier to discover among individuals than the other. But I am quite sure that as soon as we are dealing with whole peoples we shall have to suppose that there will be those who will misuse philosophy without religion just as people in our society abuse religion without philosophy; and that seems to me to put quite a different face upon the problem. Bayle has done a good job at proving that fanaticism is more pernicious than atheism, and that conclusion is incontestable; but what he entirely omitted to say—and this is no less true—is that fanaticism, though cruel and bloodthirsty, is nonetheless a strong and lofty passion which exalts man's heart, makes him despise death, gives him a prodigious energy, and need only be better channelled so as to yield the sublimest virtues; whereas irreligion and the rationalistic philosophizing spirit in general, binds man to this life, enervates and debases his soul, concentrates all his passions into the mean scope of his own personal interests, the base ambit of the human ego, thus surreptitiously undermining the true foundations of any society; for private personal interests have far too little in common with the interests of the community for any equilibrium to be effected. And if atheism does not occasion the shedding of human blood, this is less from love of peace than from indifference to good; it matters little to the self-styled sage how things go in the outside world, so long as he is left alone in his ivory tower. His principles do not kill men but they do prevent them from being born, by sapping the ethic of fertility, by splitting the individual from the race, by telescoping all affections into a secret egotism, as baneful to human increase as to virtue. The calm of the philosopher type is like tranquillity of the state under despotic rule; it is the quiet of death; it is more destructive than war itself. Thus fanaticism, though more baneful in its immediate effects than what is today called the philosophic spirit, is much less baneful in its long-range consequences. Furthermore, it is easy to parade fine maxims in books; but the crucial point is whether they jibe with the theory involved, whether they flow necessarily from it; and this is what has hitherto been far from clear. It remains to be seen whether philosophy firmly entrenched and enthroned would really master man's vanity, egotism, excessive ambition and mean passions, whether it would practice this gentle humaneness of which it boasts so much to us in writing.

"In principle, philosophy cannot effect any good that religion would not effect still better, and religion effects much that philosophy could not.

"In practice, it is another story; but here again we must take a closer look. No man follows his religion in every particular when he has one; most men have scarcely any religion and do not follow at all such religion as they have; but some men do have a religion and do follow it at least in part; and there is no doubt that their religious motivations often prevent them from doing wrong and prompt them to virtuous and laudable actions that would never have been done in the absence of such motivations.

"A monk has money entrusted to him and later denies he ever received any; what does that prove except that some fool entrusted it to the monk in the first place? If Pascal had lied about such a matter, that would prove that Pascal was a hypocrite and nothing more. But a monk! . . . Are the people who traffic in religion the ones who have religion? All the crimes committed among the clergy, as elsewhere, in no way prove that religion is pointless; they merely prove that very few people have religion. Our national governments today incontestably owe to Christianity the fact that their authority is so firm and revolutions are less frequent; Christianity has even made them less murderous, as can easily be proven by comparing modern states with ancient ones.

"A religion better understood and purged of fanaticism has lent more gentility to Christian behavior. This change is in no sense the work of cultural giants, for in none of the brilliant cultural centers of the world has human dignity been, for that reason, more respected, as is witnessed by the cruelties of the Athenians, the Egyptians, the Roman Emperors, the Chinese. What a multitude of works of mercy are the fruit of the Gospel! How much restitution and how many works of reparation are motivated, among Catholics, by the sacrament of confession! In our own country, how many reconciliations and how much almsgiving we owe to the recurring Easter Duty! How much less rapacious have moneygrubbers been rendered by the Jewish Jubilee Year! How much wretchedness has it obviated! A fraternity grounded in the Law united the whole nation and not a beggar was to be seen anywhere. Nor are they to be seen among the Turks either, where pious foundations are beyond number; this people is motivated by its religious principles to be charitable even to the enemies of their religion" (J. J. Rousseau, *Émile,* Bk. IV; *Oeuvres complètes,* Vol. II [Paris: Hachette, 1856], pp. 104ff.).

On the irrationality of atheism, cf. the statement in the Letter replying to the condemnation of *Émile* on the part of Archbishop de Beaumont of Paris:

"My persuasion is, then, that the soul of man as it emerges from the hands of nature, without progress, without instruction, without culture, is not in a position to mount under its own power to the sublime notions of the Deity; but these notions are presented to us in proportion as our mind is refined; that God manifests himself in his works to the eyes of any man who has engaged in any thought, any reflection; that he reveals himself to the enlightened in the marvels of nature; that eyes once opened must be shut again deliberately to shut him out from the range of vision; that any atheist philosopher is a thinker in bad faith or blinded by his own pride; but equally that a stupid and dull-witted man who is nonetheless ingenuous and sincere may, as a result of involuntary ignorance, fail to rise to the author of his being and thus fail to conceive what God is, without this ignorance rendering him culpable of a fault to which he has never consented in his heart. This sort of man is quite simply not enlightened as a matter of fact; the renegade philosopher is not enlightened as a matter of personal deliberate choice; as this seems to me a very drastic difference" (*ibid.* p. 348).

The crisis of the decent man whose religious faith is shaken by the scandalous life of believers who are false to their religion and the subsequent possible lapse of such a man into atheism or religious skepticism are described in the *Nouvelle Éloise,* Part V, Letter 5; *ibid.,* Vol. III, pp. 528ff. On the significance of Rousseau's opposition to the atheism of the Diderot-d'Holbach-Helvétius clique, cf. P. M. Masson, *Rousseau et la restauration religieuse,* Vol. III (Paris, 1916 [2]), pp. 7ff.

IX. Voltaire and the Absurdity of Bayle's Hypothesis

The Enlightenment philosophers and 18th-century thinkers soon came to realize there was no point in their cherishing the illusion that the greatest writer of the century would come out in their favor: Voltaire remained his whole life long, if not a theist (for he never arrived at a clear notion of providence or on the problem of evil and thus never really penetrated to the notion of a personal God), then certainly a convinced deist. His stay in England had made him unshakeably firm in this position. From the outset we can find a searching critique of Bayle on both scores: the possibility of a society of *atheists* and the contention that idolatry is more baneful than atheism. The passage is one of the classical documents of our researches.

"1. I now pass from considerations of fact to a consideration of the question of ethics raised by Bayle, to wit, *whether a society of atheists would be viable.* Let us note immediately on this point that there is a crying contradiction evident in the position of those opposing Bayle: those who came out with the greatest violence against Bayle's opinion and denied in the most insulting fashion even the possibility of a society of atheists have since maintained with the same boldness that atheism is the religion of the government of China.

"They have certainly been mightily mistaken on the subject of the Chinese government; they had only to read the edicts of the Emperors of this vast land and they would have seen that these edicts are sermons full of references to the Supreme Being who is Ruler, Avenger and Rewarder.

"And they have been no less mistaken concerning the impossibility of a society of atheists; and I do not see how M. Bayle could have forgotten a striking example which might have won the day for him.

"What makes a society of atheists seem an impossibility? The persuasion that men who have no inhibitory mechanism could never live together; that the laws can do nothing against covert crimes; that there must be an avenging God who punishes in this world or the next the wicked who elude human justice.

"The laws of Moses certainly did not teach a life to come, contained no threats of punishments after death, did not teach the ancient Jews to believe in the immortality of the soul; but the Jews, far from being atheists, far from believing they could escape the divine vengeance, were the most religious of all men. Not only did they believe in the existence of an eternal God, they believed him always present among them; they trembled at the prospect of being punished in their own persons, in their wives, their children, their posterity to the fourth generation. The inhibition was a most powerful one.

"But among the Gentiles, several sects had no such inhibition: the skeptics doubted everything; the men of the Academy suspended their judgment on everything; the Epicureans were persuaded that the deity could not meddle in the affairs of men and, at rock bottom, they did not admit any deity at all. They were convinced that the soul is not a substance, but rather a faculty which is born and perishes with the body; consequently they had no restraining yoke save that of morality and of honor. The senators and noblemen of Rome were out-and-out atheists for they held that the gods did not exist for men who neither feared nor hoped for anything from them. The Senate of Rome was thus in reality a company of atheists from the time of Caesar and Cicero.

"The great orator in his plaidoyer for Cluentius tells the assembled senate: 'What harm does death do him? We reject all the silly fables about hell. What, therefore, has death robbed him of? Only of his vulnerability to grief.'

"When Caesar, who was a friend of Cataline, wished to save the life of his friend whom this same Cicero was trying to get condemned to death, does Caesar not object that it is no punishment for a criminal to put him to death, that *death is nothing,* that it is merely the end of our ills, that it is a moment more felicitous than fatal? And do not Cicero and the whole Senate yield to these arguments? The conquerors and lawgivers of the known world thus palpably formed a society of men who feared nothing from the gods, who were out-and-out atheists.

"2. Bayle proceeds to examine whether idolatry is more dangerous than atheism, whether it is a greater crime to fail to believe in the deity at all than to have unworthy opinions of him. He agrees with Plutarch on this point: he believes it is better to have no opinion than to have a bad one; but, with due deference to Plutarch, it is evident that it was incomparably better for the Greeks to fear Demeter, Neptune and Jupiter than for them not to fear anything at all. Clearly oaths must be sacred and one ought to have more confidence in those who think that a false oath will be punished than in such as believe they can swear a false oath with impunity. It is undeniable that in a civilized town it is incomparably more advantageous to have a religion, even a bad one, than to have none at all.

"It thus appears that Bayle should rather have inquired which is the more dangerous, fanaticism or atheism. Fanaticism is certainly a thousand times more baneful; for atheism does not impel to bloody passions whereas fanaticism does; atheism may fail to oppose criminal activity but fanaticism impels to such activity. Let us suppose, with the author of the *Commentarium rerum Gallicarum,* that the chancellor of the hospital was an atheist; he made only wise laws, counselled only moderation and concord; the fanatics committed the St. Bartholomew's Day massacres. Hobbes was taken for an atheist; he led a quiet and blameless life while the fanatics of his day were drowning England, Scotland and Ireland in blood. Spinoza was not only himself an atheist, he taught atheism openly; yet he was certainly not the one who took part in the juridical assassination of Barneveldt; nor was he the one who tore the de Witt brothers in pieces and ate them roasted on the gridiron.

"The atheists are for the most part daring scholars who have gone astray, whose reasoning is faulty and who, not being able to understand creation, the origin of evil and other difficulties, have recourse to the hypothesis of the eternity of things and of necessity.

"The power-seekers and the pleasure-seekers have scarcely any time for reasoning or for formal adherence to a bad system; they have other things to do than compare Lucretius with Socrates. Such is the state of affairs among us today.

"It was not the case with the Senate of Rome whose members were almost all theoretical and practical atheists, i.e., men who believed neither in providence nor in the life to come; this senate was a company of philosophers, epicures and power-hungry climbers, all of them dangerous in the extreme to the Republic and pushing it to ruin. The pleasure-seeking continued under the Emperors: in the days of Sulla and Caesar the atheists had been sedition-mongers; under Augustus and Tiberius they were slave-atheists.

"I would not want to fall afoul of an atheist prince who might be interested in pulverizing me; I have no doubt that he would make a good job of it. Nor would I want, were I the prince myself, to have any dealings with atheist courtiers who might be interested in poisoning me; I would have to take an antidote every day on the off chance. And so the man on the throne and the man in the street alike must have graven deeply in their minds the idea of a Supreme Being who is Creator, Ruler, Rewarder and Avenger.

"There are atheist peoples, says Bayle in his *Pensées sur les comètes.* The Kaffirs, the Hottentots, the Tupinambas and many other small ethnic groups have no God; they neither deny nor assert the existence of God; they have never heard him spoken of. Tell them there is a God and they will believe quite readily; tell them that everything is the result of the nature of things and they will believe that equally readily. The contention that they are atheists is as asinine as would be the contention that they are anti-Cartesians; they are neither for nor against Descartes. They are simply children; a child is neither an atheist nor a deist, he is nothing.

"What conclusion shall we draw from all this? That atheism is a most pernicious monstrosity in those who govern; that it is no less pernicious in those who are councillors of rulers, no matter how blameless these councillors may be in their private life, because from their council chamber they can get through to those who are the actual rulers; that, although not as baneful as fanaticism, it is almost always fatal to virtue. Let it be added that there are fewer atheists today than ever before, since the philosophers have admitted that there is no plant without a seed, no seed without a design, etc., and that putrefaction is not the origin of grain.

"Some geometricians who are not philosophers have rejected final causality but the true philosophers accept it; and, as a well-known writer has said, a catechist proclaims God to children and Newton demonstrates him to the learned" (*Dictionnaire philosophique,* article "Athées," "Athéisme", pp. 40-43).[3]

XI. Natural Law and Atheism (Pufendorf)

Among protagonists of the natural law, S. Pufendorf (1632-1694) spiritedly enters the lists against atheism as an infraction of the primary "natural obligation" of man. He contends that there are two sorts of atheists, those who formally deny the existence of God and those who do not admit his providence; but the two sorts are on a par when it comes to the moral aspect of religion.

The two standard-bearers of modern atheism, as insidious as they are dangerous, are Hobbes and Spinoza, not because of any overt defense of atheism on their part but because of their drastic distortion of the problem of God. Hobbes' error lay in his willingness to exculpate the atheist as more ignorant than guilty: "According to him [atheism] is not properly speaking a sin but rather a simple error and a kind of madness, not

[3] H. T. Mason has made a study of the fluctuations and uncertainties of Voltaire's thought on the problem of atheism and of his consequent changes of attitude toward Bayle (*Pierre Bayle and Voltaire* [Oxford: Oxford University Press, 1965], especially pp. 78ff.).

deserving of any punishment whatever. Hobbes' reasoning in support of this strange paradox is as follows: An atheist, he says, has never recognized the existence of God and consequently has never submitted his will to the will of this Supreme Being. Now no sovereign rule can be exercised over those who have not recognized that rule by their own consent. Thus the atheist having never been under the rule of God is not held to observe the laws of God. But it is quite false that all dominion depends on the consent of those over whom it is exercised. This is true only of human authority which, being established as it is among creatures who are equal according to their nature, is only legitimate to the extent that it is founded on a covenant or contract whereby those who by that covenant become subjects have deprived themselves of the right and power they have to resist whoever might wish to force them to obey him. But shall we dare to maintain that God has no right to govern his own creature without that creature's voluntary consent to his dominion? All the more grotesque does this contention become if it is true, as Hobbes himself teaches elsewhere, that in the natural kingdom of God his right to rule and to punish comes from his own irresistible power: for no one, I am sure, will imagine that atheists can resist the power of God. Thus, atheists are not, properly speaking, simple enemies of God (if by enemies we understand, as does Hobbes, those who are neither in subjection the one to the other nor yet dependent on a common master); rather they are rebellious subjects, guilty of the crime of high treason against the deity (a title Hobbes assigns to them elsewhere): and this for the simple reason that, again according to Hobbes, the crime of high treason in the human domain consists in persistent overt testimony by word and deed to their unwillingness any longer to obey a person or an assembly vested with supreme authority, i.e., high treason is a radical shaking off of the yoke of civic obedience".

Nor does Hobbes in any way justify himself by his reference to Psalm 14, 1, with its designation of the atheist as a simple "fool" for, maintains Pufendorf, scripture implies by this term a moral judgment of culpable foolishness: "For holy scripture habitually brands as fools not only those who sin by error but those who sin out of malice as well. Besides it is incontestably the greatest of all follies to draw down upon oneself by one's malice a most stringent punishment by allowing oneself to bolt into a fancy that gives little or no pleasure. And it is not as difficult to arrive at a knowledge of God by the lights of reason as to find the ratio of a sphere to a cylinder, which is the example used by Hobbes. I grant that the mentally defective and indeed even the unlettered are scarcely in a position to invent or even to comprehend a formal philosophical demonstration of the existence of God. But it does not follow from this that anyone can with impunity deny or cast doubt upon a truth so clear and so universally admitted."

In an obvious allusion to Bayle's thesis, Pufendorf concludes that atheism is a *crime* that entails punishment. (Bayle is cited in Note 2 by the French translator J. Barbeyrac on p. 392: *Pensées sur les Comètes,* § 177. The same Note likewise cites Mr. Bernard who had distinguished Bayle's *atheists from reflection* into *atheists of the mind* and atheists *of the heart*).

Shorter but no less severe is Pufendorf's critique of the position of Spinoza, a follower of Hobbes (as comes out in *Tractatus Theologico-Politicus,* Ch. XVI) and a thinker who in the final analysis does not admit even natural religion:

"The arguments used by Spinoza to support Hobbes' opinion are equally easily refuted. After setting up the initial principle that, in the state of nature, anyone who has not the use of reason can live according to the laws of his own desires, on the strength of the absolute right accorded him by nature so to do, Spinoza proceeds to pose the objection that such a maxim is entirely at variance with the divine revealed law. His reply is that the state of nature is prior to religion, both in the temporal and the ontological order. This proposition is quite untrue, at least so far as natural religion is concerned. Nor are Spinoza's next words any less wide of the mark: Nature does not teach anyone that he must obey God: reason alone and by itself is incapable of rising so high; there is need of a revelation, authenticated by miracles, to furnish this knowledge to us. This again is untenable as referred to natural religion and thus entirely vitiates Spinoza's conclusion that prior to revelation no one is subject to the laws of God (for this is true only insofar as the positive ordinances are concerned) and that the state of nature must be conceived as being entirely devoid of religion and law and consequently devoid of sin and wrong-doing. He adds that the reason why man in a state of nature is free from the yoke of religion is on the one hand because of his ignorance and on the other hand because of the liberty bestowed on everyone upon their coming into the world. For, he says, if men were naturally subject to the divine laws or if the divine laws were the natural laws, why would God have covenanted with men? What would have been the point in binding them by covenants or oaths? But the covenants between God and man occur only in revealed religion, for man is obliged to discharge the duties of natural religion by the very fact that God has made him a rational animal. This vitiates Spinoza's conclusion that the divine law came into force only when men covenanted with God by entering into an express contractual agreement to obey him in all things, renouncing in a certain sense their natural freedom and transferring their right to God, in the same way as is done in civic societies. This absurd proposition would be tenable only on the supposition that in the state of nature men did not receive their existence from God" (Pufendorf, *Le Droit de la Nature et des Gens,* translated from the Latin by Baron J. Barbeyrac, Vol. I (Basle: Chez E. Thourneisen, 1771), pp. 390-393).

XII. Spedalieri on the Impossibility of a Society of Atheists

The Sicilian Abbot N. Spedalieri (1740-1795), who lived in the midst of the age of the Enlightenment, devoted Book III of his major work to the refutation of irreligion as the number 1 danger of his day and the prime root of all ills in society (*Dei diritti dell'uomo* [On the Rights of Man], a work comprising six books, wherein the Christian religion is shown to be the most reliable safeguard of these rights in society and the conclusion drawn that a revival of that religion is therefore the only worthwhile undertaking in the contemporary situation; Vol. I [Milan: Silvestri, 1848], pp. 232ff.). Spedalieri insists in the Preface that his aim is to operate as a "pure philosopher" following through the internal logic of the problems themselves, without any appeal to authority of any kind or to any rhetorical outbursts. He posits happiness as the end of man, an end to which tend man's "natural rights" (Book I) and indicates the main means for guaranteeing the secure exercise of those rights (Book II); then he pinpoints *atheism* as the chief foe of society (Book III), inasmuch as "irreligion robs society of those very means which, fragile though they are, ought nonetheless to be at society's disposal, and renders them all pointless and meaningless" (Vol. I, p. XI). Spedalieri adopts a crisp juridical style, working via pure concepts and mentioning no names except Bayle; and it is clear that his main objective is to refute Bayle's thesis. First of all, he shows a strict connection between atheism, materialism and fanaticism (ch. II, p. 235: "The *pantheists* belong in the same class with the *atheists*") and draws the conclusion that atheism is destructive of all freedom; for "whoever denies man's *free will* must inevitably deny that man has a soul, which is the same as saying that *fatalism* brings *materialism* inevitably in its wake . . . and materialism brings atheism" a veritable three-headed Cerberus which can only snap and bite with all three mouths (Vol. I, p. 238f.).

Atheism therefore cannot be tolerated: "The toleration of *atheism,* with its divisive consequences, its inflammation of hatred between citizen and citizen, its exacerbation of their passions, its opening up of a broad battlefront for their egotism, would destroy the *essence* of society." There follows an indicative reference to the state of affairs that led to the French Revolution and to its consequences: "And we who still have this horrible fact before us as a mirror in which we can see ourselves, we should not doubt that the mournful catastrophes which France is even now suffering are nothing but the results of the *indolence* with which the government tolerated the establishment of *atheism*" (Vol. I, p. 242).

Atheism is condemned for many reasons and because of many consequences flowing from it, all of which strike at the very basic fabric of society: because it "tends to destroy the equilibrium that must be maintained between the passions of all the citizens" (p. 243). Everywhere the atheist perceives only *matter* and has no scruples about concealing his real intentions in everyday life; he is disposed to mistrust of others and ready to perjure himself without hesitation, because he is convinced that the deity is but a fictive stage prop (p. 245); in the final analysis, therefore, the atheist is lacking and must be lacking in all morality or moral sense.

In Ch. III Spedalieri directly attacks Bayle's contention "that a *society of atheists could subsist, because it would have the ethic deriving from the intrinsic nature of man*" (p. 249). All Bayle's proofs are pure sophisms, charges Spedalieri: where God is lacking, there is nothing else but the law of the *useful* and the so-called "natural morality" which does of course exist but is incapable of convincing the atheist who denies God, i.e., denies the very basis and foundation of such a morality. Then Spedalieri consoles himself, in this matter of Bayle's hypothesis, by observing that atheists represent a minority at all times and that there has never been or ever will be a society of atheists, because there is simply no possibility ". . . that an entire people should conspire against the existence of God; the *majority* must always favor the affirmation of the existence of God simply because of the stunning evidence with which it shines before the human mind" (p. 252). The atheist thus constitutes a danger for society, especially for the young, and society must resolutely defend itself: "Among the natural means excogitated by human prudence to promote the interests of society, there is here applicable only one means, namely, the *civil laws* or rather the *penalty* prescribed by the civil laws. This one means alone will be capable of holding the atheist in check: the *cudgel*. Nevertheless, we must recall how circumscribed is the ambit of the civil laws and how many avenues lie open to the wicked to escape from the punishment they deserve" (p. 257). Similar remarks are made about *materialism* (chapters 5-6) and *fatalism* (chapters 7-8) with special mention of Voltaire "who passes for the Patriarch of the Atheistic Sect" (p. 271) and the materialist la Mettrie (p. 274).

We find Spedalieri's final judgment on Bayle in Book IV which deals with deism (which is pronounced to be ". . . a contrivance full of hidden blemishes and rottenness" (p. 352): he is, to be sure, an extraordinary genius, but his Works ". . . make his intention clear enough, and his skill precisely at tearing down rather than building up. He attacks *revealed religion,* he attacks *deism,* he attacks atheism; then he proceeds with the same skill to defend now *atheism,* now *deism,* and now *revealed religion,* so that the reader shall be left no time to get his bearings" (p. 358). Deism likewise eventually leads to atheism, says Spedalieri (pp. 377ff.) and should not be tolerated in society (pp. 284ff.).

PART II

DEISM AND ATHEISM IN ENGLISH EMPIRICISM

Prefatory Note

In diametric opposition to the charge of atheism based on the ontologism of its metaphysic, Marxism and existentialism consider Cartesian rationalism to be a precursor of positive and constructive atheism: the argument is that the Cartesian metaphysical dualism opens up the road to the new materialism and to atheism.[1]

Descartes did indeed, in his physics, confer on matter a self-creating power and he held *mechanical* motion to be its vital act. *Within* the bounds of his physics, *matter* is the only *substance,* the only foundation of being and of knowing. French mechanistic materialism latched onto Descartes' physics as opposed to his theism and discarded his metaphysics: his disciples were *anti-metaphysically minded* and professedly so; they were *physicists.* The physician Le Roy is the founder of this school, which reaches its apogee in the person of another physician, Cabanis; still another physician La Mettrie was its central figure. Thus the key figures of the school might indeed even be said to have been anti-metaphysicians because they were physicians; and the statement would be more than a facile pun. During Descartes' own lifetime, Le Roy had already extended the notion of mechanical structure from the animal to the human soul, just as La Mettrie was to do in the 18th century, explaining the soul as a motion of the body and *ideas* as *mechanical motions.* Le Roy even alleged that Descartes had concealed his real opinion on this matter; but Descartes protested against this allegation. At the end of the 18th century, Cabanis pushed Cartesian materialism to its ultimate conclusion in his work *Rapport du physique et du moral de l'homme.* Marx avers that Cartesian materialism is still in existence in France, its great follow-through having been *mechanistic natural science.*

[1] I here follow Karl Marx, *Die heilige Familie,* ch. VI: "K Marx-F. Engels Werke" Vol. II (Berlin: Dietz Verlag, 1958), pp. 134ff. The large *Geschichte der Philosophie,* prepared by a strictly orthodox Communist team of Soviet historians of philosophy, further develops the summary remarks of the founders of Marxism ([Berlin: VEB Deutscher Verlag der Wissenschaften, 1959], Vol. I, especially pp. 348ff.). On p. 355 we read: "Descartes' philosophy contains a considerable materialist element—his physical theory which takes the materialist conception of nature as its point of departure. . . . The great historical merit of Cartesian physics lay in its demand for an exhaustive explanation of the world on the basis of matter and motion."

1

Cartesian Bifurcation of Being and the New Materialism

The metaphysics of the 17th century, represented in France by Descartes, was from the outset opposed by materialism. Gassendi, the reviver of "Epicurean" materialism was the personality who stood in direct personal antagonism to Descartes himself: English and French materialism always maintained its close tie with the classical materialism of Democritus and Epicurus. Still another current opposing Cartesian metaphysics was the materialism of Hobbes. And Marx rightly observes that Gassendi and Hobbes triumphed over their adversary a long time after their death, precisely at a point when the Cartesian system was still dominant as the official power in all the French schools. And here Marx interpolates the remark that the financial speculations of Law (1671-1729) had more to do than did philosophy with the indifference evinced by the 18th-century French (as opposed to the 17th-century French) to the Jesuit-Jansenist squabbles. Thus, even the explanation of the collapse of 17th-century metaphysics in view of the 18th-century materialist theory presupposes an explanation of this theoretical movement in view of the practical structuring of the French life of that day, a structuring directed to the immediate present, to wordly enjoyment and worldly interests and to the "terrestrial" world. The anti-theological, anti-metaphysical and materialist practice demanded anti-theological, anti-metaphysical and materialist theories. Marx even explains the transition from metaphysics to materialism in view of the new scientific bent: metaphysics had quite simply been entirely discredited in the practical realm.

The 17th-century metaphysics of men like Descartes, Leibniz and their like still retained a "positive" secular content, making discoveries in mathematics, physics and the other specialized sciences that seemed to fall within its domain. But the early 18th-century brought with it a demolition of this facade.

The positive sciences had broken away from metaphysics and hewed out autonomous realms of their own, leaving metaphysics with a badly depleted treasury, limited to the coin of pure thought and celestial currency, as if the real operations and terrestrial matters had begun to get a corner on the market. Metaphysics had become insipid. The same year that saw the death of the last great 17th-century metaphysicians in France, Malebranche and Arnauld, likewise saw the birth of Helvétius and Condillac, whom we shall consider in due course.

English sense-perceptionism formed the headwaters of another current to which Marx ascribes a crucial importance: the classical work here was Locke's *Essay on Human Understanding,* which was greeted with enthusiasm like an eagerly awaited guest. Though modern materialism can be traced also in some sense to Spinoza, it is a "native son" of Great Britain. Even the British Scholastic, Duns Scotus, notes Marx, was wondering *whether matter might not be able to think.* To make such a miracle feasible he has recourse to the omnipotence of God, i.e., forces theology *itself* to preach *materialism.* He was even a "nominalist". Nominalism was one of the main component elements of English materialism, even as it is generically the *first expression* of materialism.

For Marx, Bacon is the deliberate initiator, the "progenitor" (*Stammvater*) of English materialism and of the whole of *modern experimental* science.[2] In this connection, Marx gives a brief outline of materialism as the primordial bent of human thought. Natural science is for him the true and genuine science and the *physics* of sensible objects, its most important component part. Anaxagoras with his homoiomerides and Democritus with his atoms are his favorite classical authorities. He holds the *senses* to be infallible and the *source* of all knowledge. Science is the *science of experience* and consists in the application of a *rational method* to sense data. Induction, analysis, comparison, experimental observation are the basic preconditions for a rational method. *Motion* is the prime and cardinal inherent property of *matter;* and motion is here conceived not merely as *mechanical* and *mathematical* motion but likewise as drive (*Trieb*), vital spirit (*Lebensgeist*) and tension (*Spannkraft*), even as torment (*Qual:* to use a Jakob Boehme term) of matter. The primitive forms of this motion are the *essential vital forces,* the individualizing principles inherent in matter which produce the specific differences. Marx shows not the faintest sign of appreciating the "leaps" implied in such an interpretation of the real, above all, in using the same term "matter" together with its twin "motion" to describe two opposing realities and properties like the purely mechanical and quantitative phe-

[2] The semi-official Soviet *Geschichte der Philosophie,* mentioned above in footnote 1, again takes up and develops point-by-point and word-for-word Marx's interpretation of English empiricism (Vol. I, pp. 328ff.).

nomena on the one hand and the qualitative ones in living beings, such as instinct, vital spirit, etc.

Hobbes,[3] claims Marx, reduced Baconian materialism to a *system.* Sensibility loses its verdant lustre and becomes merely the abstract sensibility of the *geometrician. Physical* motion is sacrificed to *mechanical* and *mathematical* motion; geometry is proclaimed the basic science. Materialism becomes *hostile to man, one-sided.* To overcome this disembodied status, so hostile to man, materialism in its turn must crucify its flesh and become ascetic. It emerges as an *ens rationis* (*Verstandeswesen*) but it develops even logic with no regard to the intellect.

Inasmuch as the senses proffer all of man's knowledge—Hobbes continues to develop the implications of the Baconian principle—intuition, thought, representation and the like are but images of a corporeal world divested more or less of its sensible forms. Science can do no more than give a name to these images. *One* name can be applied to several images. There can even be names of names. But it would be a contradiction to admit on the one hand that all ideas originate in the sensible world and to assert on the other hand that a word is anything more than a mere word, that there is any universal substance over and above the singular imaged substance.

An *incorporeal substance* is therefore the same kind of contradiction as an *incorporeal body.* "Body", "being", "substance"—all are exactly the same real idea. Thought cannot be separated from a matter that thinks. This matter is the subject of all change. The word "infinite" is meaningless, unless it is taken simply to signify the ability of our mind to effect an endless addition. Since only material reality is perceptible and knowable, man knows nothing of the existence of God. The only thing of which I can be sure is my own existence. Every human passion is an initial or terminal mechanical motion. The objects of instinct constitute the good. Man is subject to the laws of nature as such. Power and freedom are identical. Thus, concludes Marx, Hobbes has effected a systematic development of the Baconian principle but has not further substantiated it.

This substantiation was the work of Locke in his *Essay on Human Understanding.* Even as Bacon asserted the priority of the sense faculty over intellect and Hobbes got rid of the theistic prejudices in Baconian materialism, so did Collins, Dodwell, Coward, Hartley, Priestley and their like get rid of the theological restrictions in the sense-perceptionism of Bacon and Locke. Theism is for the English sense-perceptionists or materialists nothing but an easy and lazy way to get rid of religion. Locke was the founder of common-sense philosophy, with his three

[3] K. Marx, *Die heilige Familie,* p. 136.

basic facts or principles which he set up over against the *Deus ex machina* of the Cartesian "innate ideas" and the apriorism of Spinoza, Malebranche, Leibniz (his immediate adversary) and all manner of rationalism:

1. All knowledge originates in experience and from experience.
2. The soul (or intellect) is, as such, a *tabula rasa* at birth.
3. *Nihil est in intellectu quod prius non fuerit in sensu.*

(Nothing is in the intellect that was not formerly in the senses).

Indeed the very logical principles of contradiction and identity are unknown to children, aborigines and certain types of mentally ill persons. The ideas of good and evil are likewise relative. The notion of the deity is not universally prevalent among men. Locke's assertion that all our ideas come from the senses was one of the severest blows dealt to idealism, even though Locke himself seems occasionally to forget his own basic principle and speaks of a "self-generating power of the mind" and even of a specific "thinking" substance. But Marx contends that Locke's effort to accept the sense images produced from the outside world as point of departure for the entire psychic life must be admitted to have been an extremely fruitful effort; for it constitutes, according to Marx, one of the basic theses of the materialist theory of knowledge. Marx notes, however, that the English materialist sense-perceptionist is preeminently inconsistent in his introduction of the notion of "reflection" which is a relapse into idealism; furthermore, his theory of the mathematical combination of ideas and of the receptive nature of knowledge is expressed in entirely mechanistic fashion. In other words, English empiricism has not yet penetrated to the dialectical notion, i.e., to the synthesis of empiricism and idealism or to the "surmounting" of both, as will Marxist dialectic.

The inconsistency of Locke's materialism comes out most strongly, according to the Marxists, in the famous theory of "primary and secondary qualities": extension, figure, impenetrability, motion, repose are primary; they are the quantitative aspects which are susceptible of mathematical measurement and calculation; and these aspects are admitted by Locke to be "objective" and to correspond to reality. The secondary qualities, on the other hand, like colors, sounds, tastes, smells and the like, have no objective value but are merely subjective sensations formed in our mind on the basis of the various combinations of the primary qualities. All of this, say the Marxists, is an artificial mélange of empiricism and idealism; the empiricists have still not come to any real awareness of the theory which explains the process of knowledge as "reflection" in the Marxist acceptation of that word, namely "mirroring" (*Spiegelungstheorie* or *Widerspiegelungstheorie*). Locke, insist the Marxists, did not realize that the qualitative difference, e.g., between two colors is related to, and bound up with, the objective qualitative difference between the sources of the perception itself, and that the sensation is therefore by no means an arbitrary sign but rather is necessarily linked with the object of perception. Locke's theory that sensations resemble written characters on paper and do not in the least resemble the thoughts expressed in them and therefore come down to nothing more than "symbols" and "hieroglyphs" [4] of the real—this theory, charge the Marxists, is a "remnant of idealism" which prepared the way for agnosticism. Locke's fluctuation between materialism and idealism likewise comes out in his notion of truth: his limitation of his researches to the restricted realm of subjective impressions has led Locke often to a downright forgetfulness of objective reality.

On Locke's definition, knowledge comes down simply to the perception of the agreement or non-agreement of our images, and truth thus consists in the agreement of the images among themselves. The great importance ascribed by Locke to introspection is yet another manifestation of the inconsistency of his materialism. But Locke's philosophy must be admitted, on balance, to be more materialist than idealist.

The Marxists claim to see the same compromising tendency in Locke's thinking on religion. Locke was one of the founding fathers of Deism: his notion of religion was relatively progressive for his age, despite the compromise evident in that notion. Locke the deist actually was attempting, after an initial admission of God, to bring faith into accord with reason and to mold a religion that would to some degree be acceptable for a "man of common sense". He rejected the current professions of faith with their dogmas and their ecclesiastical form, but he recognized and admitted a kind of "rational" natural religion. God is, for Locke, the supreme rational Principle, creator of the world with its immutable laws but thereafter a non-interventionist; he therefore resembles a "constitutional monarch" whose rights are limited and to whom "miracle" and other supernatural manifestations are impossible. Religion is not the business of the State; it is an affair of the individual communities of believers, which communities should enjoy a broad, though not unrestricted, tolerance, so long as they are not atheists or Catholics (synonomous with Jacobites!).

Lenin contends that Locke's sense-perceptionism is not yet full-fledged and consistent materialism.[5] He makes this change in the context of a broader attack on the empiricism of Avenarius ("in the world there is only sensation": 1876) and Mach ("bodies are complexes of sensations": *Die Analyse der Empfindungen*); Lenin's main point here

[4] These terms are used by Lenin in *Materialismus und Empiriokritizismus* (Berlin: Dietz Verlag, 1949), ch. IV, § 6.

[5] *Ibid.*, p. 115.

is a strong protest against such forms of subjectivism which inevitably lead to the denial of objective truth. Both the materialist and the subjective idealist may consider sensations as the source of our knowledge: Diderot and Berkeley both derive from Locke. Lenin's conclusion is that a philosopher can begin with sensations and then follow either the subjectivist line which leads to solipsism ("bodies are complexes or syntheses of sensations") or the objectivist line which leads to materialism (sensations are images of bodies, of the external world). For the philosophers following the former point of view—for agnosticism or, if one wishes to follow through still further, for subjective idealism in general—there can be no objective truth. For the philosopher following the latter point of view, i.e., the materialist, the admission of objective truth is mandatory.

Lenin goes on to make another observation that we consider to be of the greatest importance for the interpretation of the basic significance of the principle of immanence: it was Hegel himself, says Lenin, who declared that materialism is the direct consequence of empiricism. We agree that Lenin on the importance of this Hegelian text, wherein Hegel is not speaking explicitly of materialism but does specify the tendency of empiricism to conceive truth as concreteness, inasmuch as it bases its definitions on the content of experience. Hegel goes on in an Appendix to say that the original aspect of empiricism, its "major principle", is that "empirical cognition has its firm anchor on the *subjective* side in the fact that consciousness has *its own immediate presence and certainty* in perception . . . that what is true must be in reality and must be there for perception".[6]

This does away with the Kantian claims involved in the "ought to be" formulation which posits a transcendence; it highlights rather the new principle of *freedom,* i.e., that "what man ought to hold valid in his own knowing he ought to know to be present (*präsent*) in that knowing". This is a logical development of empiricism inasmuch as it limits itself to the finite as far as content of knowledge is concerned while at the same time denying the suprasensible in general or at least denying the possibility of any human knowing of it and refusing to ascribe to it any functional efficacy, and granting to thought alone the power of abstraction and formal universality. This is precisely the basic illusion of empiricism, its uncritical utilization of the metaphysical category of matter and force, of the one, the many, the universal, even the infinite, without realizing that it is here still metaphysicizing.

The appendix to Section 38 develops the significance of concreteness

[6] *Enzyklopädie der philosophischen Wissenschaften,* Part I, § § 37-38, ed. Hoffmeister (Leipzig, 1949), p. 64. The reference to Hegel was suggested to Marx by Engels (Lenin, *op. cit.,* p. 116).

as empiricism's point of departure, of its starting from the present fact of experience, the "here" (*das Hier*) and the "this" (*das Dieses*), just as did rationalism: "The external is *as such* the true, because the true is real and must exist. Therefore the real specification and specificity that reason seeks is in the world, albeit in a singular sensible form rather than in truth." Empiricism's error or shortcoming lies in conceiving truth in the form of "perception" (*Wahrnehmung*); as such it is something singular and transitory, incapable of constituting a permanent terminal for the knowing act which must rather proceed by analysis to discover the universal and permanent element in the perceived singular and thus effect the transition from simple perception to experience (*Erfahrung*). Analysis is therefore the progress (*Fortgang*) from the immediacy of perception to thought, inasmuch as the specifications that the analyzed object contains united in itself conserve their universality when separated. Thus empiricism's error lies in transforming the concrete into something abstract, of killing what was alive. Empiricism's stand in the business of the "content" (*Inhalt*) of knowing is more positive and consistent. It is the sensible content of nature and the content of the finite spirit: even the notion which this finine spirit can have of the infinite is actualized in the finite mold of the human intellect. Empiricism is mistaken, says Hegel, if it thinks that in analyzing objects it is leaving them just as they were before, because in fact it is by this operation transforming the concrete into something abstract. And so it comes about that the living is killed, for only the concrete, the One, is living.

Yet, empiricism tries, observes Hegel, to free itself from the way of thinking of the old metaphysic for which "it is in thought that the truth of things is located" and for which both form and content of this truth is infinite, is *the* infinite. Empiricism claims that the content is expressed in the sensible content of nature and the content of the finite spirit. The infinite content claimed for thought in the old metaphysic is finitized in function of the form of the intellect. In empiricism, we thus have a finitude of form and of content. And this brings us to the text cited by Lenin: [7] "For empiricism the objective generically is the true and the genuine, and even if a suprasensory reality is admitted, it is alleged that there can be no cognition of it but that knowledge must be confined to what is proper to perception. In its implementation, however, this principle produced what was later designated as materialism. This materialism considers matter as such to be the genuinely objective reality." [8]

[7] *Op. cit.*, p. 116.

[8] Hegel, *Enzyklopädie der philosophischen Wissenschaften*, § 38, Appendix, Vol. I, ed. L. von Henning (Berlin, 1840), p. 83.

Lenin stops quoting at this point, for the passage continues with a critique of this sort of materialism and of all materialism: "But matter in itself is an *Abstract* which cannot be perceived as such. So it can be said that there does not exist any matter because it exists always as something specific and concrete. Similarly, the abstract, matter, must be the foundation of every sensible reality in general, absolute singularity as such . . . Now inasmuch as this sensible is and remains for empiricism something given, empiricism is a theory of non-freedom (*Unfreiheit:* bondage, serfdom), because freedom consists precisely in my not having set over against me anything absolutely other but rather depending on a content constituted ultimately by myself. Furthermore, from this point of view rational and irrational are mere subjective categories, i.e., we are faced with the brute datum as it is and have forfeited the right to ask whether and to what extent it is rational." [9]

Deism is the religious philosophy of the Enlightenment,[10] but its roots are complex and intricate and so are its forms. Under the surface appearance of a simple and straightforward school of thought, it effects a merger of the claims of the Stoic ethic and of that universal natural religion attributed to Stoicism, the plaidoyer of the typical Humanist and Italian Renaissance protagonist, the critique of revealed religion accomplished by Spinoza and Bayle. Deism or (as it was very occasionally called) theism of the latter 17th and the entire 18th century amounts basically to anti-supernaturalism, a recall to, and vindication of, reason and therefore of natural religion as opposed to revealed or supernatural religion, especially institutional Christianity.[11] It is thus intimately

[9] *Ibid.* We shall return later on, in our treatment of English idealist neo-empiricism, to the positive side of Hegel's interpretation.

[10] Cf. E. Troeltsch, "Deismus," in *Realencyklopädie für protestantische Theologie und Kirche,* Vol. IV (Leipzig, 1898), p. 533 (abridged in *Aufsätze zur Geistesgeschichte und Religionssoziologie; C. W.,* Vol. IV [Tübingen, 1925], p. 429). The terms "Deist" and "Deism" had been used for at least a century already in a sense contradistinguished from "atheist" and "atheism" (e.g., by the preacher Pierre Viret in 1563; cf. H. Busson, *Le rationalisme dans la littérature française de la Renaissance* [Paris, 1957 [2]], pp. 517f.).

[11] "Deism begins as a strictly *intellectualistic* system; it aims at removing all mysteries, miracles and enigmas from religion and shifting religion into the clear light of knowledge" (E. Cassirer, *Die Philosophie der Aufklärung* [Tübingen, 1932], p. 228). The term "Deist" apparently occurs for the first time in the *Letter to a Deist* (1677) by the English theologian S. Parker, where a distinction is drawn between the Freethinkers, who are out-and-out atheists, and those who, while critical of positive religions and especially Christianity, nevertheless still hold in various ways with natural religion (cf. J. M. Robertson, *A Short History of Freethought,* Vol. II [London, 1915 [3]], p. 91). The great Clarke, as we shall point out, will vigorously reject this distinction. Söderblom contends that there is a close link between the origin and establishment of Deism and the teaching of Confucius and the Chinese philosophers, introduced into Europe by the Jesuit missionaries and, as we have seen, highly esteemed by Bayle (cf. C. von Brockdorff, *Die englische Aufklärungsphilosophie* [Munich, 1924], p. 101).

aligned, initially with the sounder line of the French Enlightenment (the earlier Diderot, Voltaire, Rousseau) and subsequently with the German Enlightenment (Reimarus, Lessing, Herder, Kant himself); but Deism is distinguished by a more pronouncedly moralistic tendency and a clear-cut aim of bringing about that crowning *pax philosophica* among all peoples, for which Nicholas of Cusa, for instance, had expressed such pious hopes, that concord that would surmount all geographical, religious and cultural distinctions.

As a parallel consequence, the content of religion gradually but inevitably metamorphosed from a complex of objective truth concerning the relations between God and man into a complex of subjective duties of man toward God and toward himself and his kind. This metamorphosis culminated in the elimination of any relationship with God and consequently of any obligation of man toward God, leaving a sheerly human and immanent ethic of coexistence. Although usually considered as being a movement of only secondary importance, Deism is expressive of a crucial formative element of the modern world: it crystallized that "principle of tolerance" calculated to put an end to the wars of religion that had been bleeding Europe white. Thus, in its proclamation of the rather obvious tenet that only "natural religion" fell within the realm of reason, Deism paid no attention to the most serious shortcomings of human nature in the field of ethics nor yet to the profound significance of the generic human longing for immortality and salvation in the dimension of eternity.

Having thus abandoned or denied all direct connection of religion with human history, Deism was in no position to prevent the skid into a merely natural morality, based upon emotion or reason depending on the dominant philosophy but in either case determined to make man the source of human truth and basic human values. In Deism, therefore, one of the basic parameters of the development of the human mind and heart attains a quite unique value in practice: this is the persistent attempt of human reason to break the bonds of its own limitations and make itself the sole foundation, thereby surmounting every opposition offered it by fate, history, revelation or faith.[12] It is no mere accident that the ethical element becomes more basic than the theoretical and that knowledge and the cognitive operation metamorphoses—despite Bacon's insistence on the positive factual method—into a tendency and aspiration accommodated to the unrestricted flowering forth of "feeling" posited as antecedent to any reflective operation. And so there takes shape that radical extirpation of all ideological antagonism calculated to restore man to a primordial truth and innocence; and Bayle's drastic and

[12] On this tension, cf. F. Jodl, *Geschichte der Ethik in der neueren Philosophie,* Vol. I (Stuttgart, 1882), pp. 62f.

indiscriminate charge levelled against all positive religions of having fomented strife among peoples in every age and inculpated themselves in the gravest calamities of mankind now begins to bear fruit in this irreversible drift toward atheism. But even in Deism, this drift is a gradual zig-zag affair, impelled on the one hand by internal tectonic shocks and tremors, under the corrosive and encroaching pressure of the principle of religious subjectivity proclaimed in opposition to Catholicism, and on the other hand by the Cartesian principle of speculative abstract evidence converting man himself into the progenitor of truth. The disengagement of philosophy from religion, destined to be one of the constitutive elements of modern thought, is the work of Deism; or at least this disengagement begins, in Deism, to take on a clear-cut and distinctive outline. For Deism represents a marriage of common-sense English empiricism with the Gallic flair of French rationalism; and the subsequent refinement occurs in an atmosphere of expansive understanding productive of challenges and conflicts of ideas which set the pace for the development of a large part of later thought right down to our own day.[13]

[13] There is a list of the main representatives of English Deism contained in the title of a huge apologetic work ascribed to Philip Skelton, *Deism Revealed,* or the Attack on Christianity Candidly Reviewed in Its Real Merits, as They Stand in the Celebrated Writings of Lord Herbert, Lord Shaftesbury, Hobbes, Toland, Tindal, Collins, Mandeville, Doddwell, Woolston, Morgan, Chubb and Others, 2 Vols. (London, 1751 [2]) (cf. British Museum, *General Catalogue of Printed Books,* Vol. 50 [London, 1953], col. 60).

2
The Shaping of Deism (Herbert of Cherbury, Hobbes)

Deism is generally held to be an English product, nurtured mainly by the Neoplatonic school of Cambridge; at its first appearance it seemed innocuous and acceptable enough. Its position was consolidated in the work of Herbert of Cherbury (1582-1648), whose philosophical activity coincided with the age of the Enlightenment, an age which was thought. Cherbury's influence has been ranked with that of Hobbes and Spinoza,[1] though this may be an exaggeration. The guiding principle of Deism seems to be diametrically opposed to atheism: the very name "Deism" would indicate this and the Deists certainly held this view of their own school of thought. Deism's main point, at the level of controversy, is its clear-cut distinction between natural and revealed religion, coupled with its contention that the former can (and should) stand independently on the sole basis of reason. This line of argument was considered patently anti-Protestant and even aligned, not entirely without a semblance of justification,[2] with the position of St. Thomas Aquinas: it asserts the existence and validity of a "natural religion", i.e., a religion of reason, distinct from revealed supernatural religion. This aggressive and doughty defense of natural religion seems to be typical of the English Enlightenment; although it is not entirely lacking in the European Enlightenment (cf. Voltaire), it is much more muted there and conveys an overall impression of an attitude close to connivance

[1] In the anonymous *De tribus impostoribus* (published by Kortholt in 1598), Hobbes is placed in the same category with Spinoza (cf. the bilingual edition of G. Bartsch [Berlin: Akademie-Verlag, 1960], p. 29. The anonymous author seems to be acquainted with Spinoza's *Tractatus Theologico-Politicus,* but does not profess atheism: cf. pp. 32ff.).

[2] Cf. M. M. Rossi, *Alle fonti del deismo e del materialismo moderno* (Florence, 1942), pp. 15f. Rossi calls "religious rationalism" (*sic!*) the Thomistic distinction of the two orders, the natural and the supernatural. Deism and Deist are also taken as synonomous with "freethinking, freethinker"; hence the difficulty of arriving at a strict and univocal notion (cf. C. von Brockdorff, *Die englische Aufklärungsphilosophie,* pp. 32f.).

with explicit atheism or at least of an incapacity to stem the tide of that atheism, as we shall point out later. There has been a consequent inclination to trace the origins or sources of English Deism back to the Renaissance and even to Stoic philosophy; this has concentrated special attention on the famous *Theologia naturalis* of Raimondo di Sabunde (d. circa 1436), a work that had the distinction of being translated into French by Montaigne.[3]

For Cherbury, there are no "atheist peoples"; all peoples have some religion and religion is therefore a "universal notion"; hence derives the criterion of truth valid for the construction of a "natural theology": the 'notitiae communes" (the κοιναὶ ἔννοιαι of the Stoics), i.e., the universal persuasions and convictions of the human race [4] are true. It is God who has instilled into every human being in every age these universal notions which remain constant through all the flux and conflict of the various schools: this capacity for a *consensus universalis* emerges in man in the form of an *instinctus naturalis* [5] that is innate to the mind. These *notitiae communes* are reduced by Cherbury to five main points: [6]

1. *Esse supremum aliquod numen* (There is a supreme deity).
2. *Istud numen debere coli* (Worship is due to this deity).
3. *Virtutem cum pietate coniunctum praecipuam partem cultus divini*

[3] This is noted by H. Scholz in the Introduction to his collection of Cherbury's two main works: *Die Religionsphilosophie des Herbert von Cherbury* (Auszüge aus *De veritate* und *De religione gentilium*) (Giessen, 1914), pp. 7f. Hume pushes the origin of Deism back to the Cromwellian era and even to the first decades of the 17th century. He attributes to Deism an ethico-political significance rather than the religious significance (such as it was!) that it tends to assume with Cherbury: "The second [party] were the Deists, who had no other object than political liberty, who denied entirely the truth of revelation, and insinuated that all the various sects, so heated against each other, were alike founded in error. Men of such daring genius were not content with the established forms of civil government, but challenged a degree of freedom beyond what they expected, under any monarchy, ever to enjoy. Martin, Challoner, Harrington, Sidney, Wildman, Nevil were esteemed the heads of this small division" (D. Hume, *The History of Great Britain,* Vol. II [London, 1757], pp. 48f.). The names of these first Deists are entirely unknown even to such a well-informed historian of Deism as G. V. Lechler, who sees it beginning with Cherbury, Leland, etc. (*Geschichte des Englischen Deismus* [Stuttgart and Tübingen, 1841], pp. 26ff. Lechler counts F. Bacon as a forerunner of Deism). Toward the end of his *History,* Hume presents a second list of Deists, headed by Shaftesbury, followed by another group of virtual unknowns, such as Halifax, Buckingham, Mulgrave, Sunderland, Essex, Rochester, Sidney and Temple (Vol. II, p. 450).

[4] "Religion is a universal notion, for there is no tribe, race or age without religion. It must therefore be discovered what things are admitted in religion by common and universal consent; let a general comparison be instituted—then those things that are admitted as true in religion are to be considered as being universal notions" (*De veritate,* [Paris, 1633], p. 43; Scholz 34).

[5] *Ibid.,* pp. 38ff.; Scholz 31.

[6] *Ibid.,* pp. 208ff. The "properties" of such *notions* are priority, independence, universality, certainty and necessity (pp. 60f.; Scholz pp. 37f.).

habitam esse et semper fuisse (Virtue conjoined with piety [in the sense of a sincere conforming of the faculties with their object] is to be, and has always been held to be, the chief component element of divine worship).

4. *Horrorem scelerum hominum animis semper insedisse; adeoque illos non latuisse vitia et scelera quaecumque expiari debere ex poenitentia* (A horror of evil deeds has always been native to the souls of men; wherefore they have not been unaware that vices and crimes ought to be expiated by penance).

5. *Esse proemium vel poenam post hanc vitam* (There is such a thing as reward and punishment after this life).

A surprising point about this list is that it devotes to the question of the knowledge of God but a single principle embracing both the assertion of the existence of God and of his status as the One True God. In his explanatory gloss, Cherbury makes a rapid transition from the question of existence to the question of status, without any effort at substantiation or proof: "It is not concerning the gods that there is agreement but concerning God. There is no religion that does not profess and confess that there is a certain supreme being within the class of the gods." [7] The unity of God was recognized even in Graeco-Roman paganism and not merely among the Jews, Mohammedans and Western Indians. There follows a somewhat higgledy-piggledy list of divine attributes on which no disagreement is possible: [8] (1) *Deum esse beatum* (God is blessed); (2) *esse rerum finem* (is the supreme end of created things; (3) *esse rerum causam saltem quatenus bonae sunt* (is the cause of things, at least insofar as they are good). Hence it follows that Cherbury articulates the notion of divine providence in a formulation which is daring or, to say the least, odd; (4) *esse rerum medium* (is the means of things). The subsequent attributes relate to the cardinal act of religion and the cardinal truth of the divine providence in individual events: "(5) *esse aeternum* (he is eternal) for a universal notion teaches that what is first among things is certainly eternal; (6) *esse bonum* (he is good), because a universal notion teaches that the cause of all good is itself supremely good; (7) *esse iustum* (he is just), because a universal notion, and the experience of history likewise, bear witness that things are tempered with supreme equity by his providence," whatever may be said concerning the extremely difficult ques-

[7] *Ibid.*, p. 210; Scholz p. 45. On the natural impulse to know and love God, cf. the fragment of the prayer of Cherbury reported by Rossi (*op. cit.*, p. 22), which speaks vaguely of an immediate intuition of God. There is no actual mention of the word "intuition" in the text, nor was this the Stoic position which served as inspiration to Cherbury. St. Thomas, perhaps under Ciceronian influence, speaks of a "natural bent to investigate concerning God" *S.T.*, Ia-IIae, q. 94, a. 2).

[8] *De veritate*, p. 210; Scholz p. 45.

tions posed by philosophy and theology in this connection. "(8) *Esse sapientem* (he is wise) because visible evidences of his wisdom . . . shine forth most brilliantly in his daily works."

The other attributes of God, such as infinity, omnipotence and freedom are more difficult and are described as "supremely controverted". But Cherbury copes with the problem in a somewhat unexpected and odd fashion, using an elliptical series of syllogisms, a reverse sorites, proving God's freedom from his omnipotence and his omnipotence from his infinity, with his infinity being proven, in an anticipation or rather introduction of the famous Clarke-Leibniz controversy, via the infinity of the space that God fills with his presence: "His *infinity* is proven by the very infinity of place or space; for a universal notion teaches that the supreme being permeates all things. His *omnipotence* is proven by his infinity; for it is beyond dispute that the infinite can have no bounds set to its power. His *freedom* is proven by his omnipotence; for no one of sound mind has ever had the slightest doubt that the one who has no bounds set to his power is supremely free." [9] These same attributes are thereupon deduced or rather enunciated in a more pronouncedly metaphysical and anthropological fashion so as to cope with the more obstinate dissenters. Here recourse is had to the notion of participation: God's infinity is deduced from the fact that he exceeds our intelligence, his omnipotence from his having created the world out of nothing, his freedom from his being himself the cause of freedom in man.[10]

Even at first reading, this natural theology which seems so irenic and innocuous, gives rise to considerable perplexity and uneasiness. There is a complete absence of any effort at demonstration and substantiation of the very existence of God; atheism, skepticism and materialism, which had often extensively jeopardized the awareness of God, are ignored or hushed up (and deliberately, at that!). And the reduction of the practice of religion to the practice of virtue and the horror of vice is too immediately reminiscent of the Spinozan ethic; [11] the elimination of any external worship and of the practice of prayer readily gives rise to the suspicion that the God of Cherbury is but a purely metaphysical principle with no further meaning for the world and for man that that of a cosmic

[9] *Ibid.,* p. 211; Scholz pp. 45f.

[10] "But I hold that another approach should be taken to those who judge differently, and my reason is that it is a universal notion that what exists in us by participation is discovered in God in its fullness. If he so exceeds our grasp as to resist entirely any hemming in by any bounds or term, God will be infinite; if he made all things in the absence of any pre-existing matter, he will be omnipotent; and, finally, if he is the author of our freedom, he will be supremely free himself" (*Ibid.,* pp. 211f.; Scholz p. 46).

[11] There are in fact 17th-century references to Spinozism as Deism (cf. H. Scholz, *Introduction* to *Die Religionsphilosophie des Herbert von Cherbury,* p. 13, n. 1).

cause and physical principle and inaccessible to man save as cause to effect, a relationship that excludes any personal choice. In this sense, Deism is no longer theism, admitting a transcendent and personal God; it is rather a step on the road to atheism. And it reveals itself precisely as such in the further evolution of European thought. It is not the content of the Deist thesis as such but rather the new frame of mind which it introduces that is going to become operative in the evolution of modern thought: Cherbury was a contemporary of Descartes and Hobbes and he urges radical positions in the realm of religion just as they did in the realm of pure philosophy. Cherbury's radicalism in the sphere of religion lies in his referring religious awareness and knowledge to a subjective felling of man as individual and as group. This represented a desertion, bag and baggage, into the ranks of the Freethinkers who absorbed the naturalistic bent and the paganism of certain currents within Humanism and the Renaissance mentality and asserted not only a distinction but an opposition and mutual exclusion as between natural and revealed religion.

Deism may have been inspired at the outset with the positive intention of defending religion against materialist and epicurean atheism. Cherbury gave an explicit expression to this notion when he wrote enthusiastically albeit with an explicit ascription of "catholicity" to pure reason as the only Church worthy of man, at the end of the section dealing with the "five truths": "Now these are undoubtedly universal notions wherein the true Catholic or universal Church doth consist. Nor is that edifice hewn out of stone, fashioned of bricks and mortar or cut from marble, to be called the Church that cannot err. Nay, not even men themselves do constitute the truly Catholic Church in their haphazard and slapdash prating of their oral or written *placets;* still less is that band that fights under some one particular standard or that herded flock that is hemmed in within the narrow confines of one section of the globe or one age of time worthy of being designated as a truly Catholic or universal Church; the sole Catholic, the sole μονοειδής (homogeneous) Church is the teaching of the universal notions that doth fill all space and make up the perfect number."

This is the Church which is the realization of divine providence and outside of which there is no salvation: "For this alone doth disclose the divine providence or the universal wisdom of nature. This alone doth expound the reason wherefore the common father is styled the best and greatest God; outside of this, in sum, there is no salvation." [12] This therefore constitutes the criterion for judging the truth of any other religion: any religion that falls away from this complex of principles would by that very fact be falling into error.

[12] *De veritate,* pp. 221f.; Scholz, p. 53.

Cherbury seems to envelop himself in a prudent but indicative silence concerning the relations between the truth of natural religion and the content of the positive Christian religion: "When these our Catholic truths received in the secret places of the soul have been by undoubting faith therein established, what remains can and should be piously believed on the authority of the Church; provided that all contradictions have been eliminated or dissolved and only those things are instilled into the souls of men which shall promote civic peace and concord and nourish holiness of life. Whether now these means suffice for eternal salvation, this will be seen to by him whose business it is, the best and greatest God. As for us, we are far from probing the secret judgments of God." [13] This is certainly a most graceful but at the same time a most drastic way of liquidating positive (revealed) religion by subordinating it entirely to natural religion, which latter Cherbury calls *"rotunda religio"* (a well-rounded religion). And so we have a Church without rites and without dogmas (for, says Cherbury "there is nothing but wrangling about the dogmas of faith") and we have the implicit assertion that the work of divine providence has been limited to the manifestation of those universal first truth to all men from whose own unaided efforts alone we can expect a *pax communis.*

While his main concern is the vindication of natural religion, Cherbury does also mention revealed religion, or more accurately "revelation" to which he devotes the last part of his work. Actually he here treats not of positive religion and the complex of rites of worship but rather of the *particular* way of knowing God or of the way in which God can manifest himself to the individual man, just as in the case of his treatment of natural religion it was not so much a question of "religion" as rather simply of the universal way of knowing God. The value of such "particular revelations" is derived from the "authority of the one who reveals" (*e revelantis auctoritate,*) which for Cherbury means the objective and subjective qualities of the one who claims and asserts that he has had the revelation in question. As a safeguard against the danger of such revelations being false, Cherbury proposes an initial set of four well-defined conditions that have nothing to do with the theological doctrine of the intelligibility of divine revelation but rather articulate certain guarantees or criteria for recognition of what claims to be an individual religious experience. The conditions are: "(1) *That prayer, taking of vows, faith and all dispositions whatsover that call forth universal or particular providence,* shall precede it. (2) That it *be clear to you yourself;* for what is accepted as revealed from others is not to be considered revelation but rather *tradition* or history; and since the truth of history or tradition depends on the narrator, it is based on a relation

[13] *Ibid.,* p. 223; Scholz, p. 55.

outside of us and therefore so far as we are concerned *is simply probable.* (3) It must be *some outstanding good* that is *being taught* or instilled; for thus are sound revelations distinguished from unsound and unholy temptations." [14]

In the matter of the *content* of revelation, Cherbury seems to admit that something does indeed "exceed the human grasp" but he does not seem to be referring to supernatural mysteries in the strict theological sense. In the matter of the "manner" (*vehiculum*) of such revelations, Cherbury refers only to the psychological dimension and variants ("in sleep or waking state or ecstasy or word or reading, etc."). As for the "medium" or instruments of the revelations, he speaks of the work of corporeal spirits endowed with agility, good and bad spirits alike; but he seems quite unclear on this point ("there can be good reason for differences of opinion on these matters"). Up to this point, Cherbury has been speaking of private revelations. But he goes on to impose the same conditions on revelations made or manifested in any way whatever to priests: the priest (like anyone else) has to prove that he has had them in order for the layman to be able to believe the revelations.

The "prudent layman" must levy (and has a perfect right to levy: *"non inepte requirat"*) the following well-defined conditions:

1. "That it be put beyond all doubt that a revelation has indeed befallen the priest" (Certainty of the fact of the revelation).

2. "That the said revelation have been proclaimed by the most high God, speaking either from his own mouth (as the saying used to go) or via the ministry of a good angel" (Certainly that the revelation comes from God).

3. "That the revelation or oracle or word in question have been faithfully recounted and recited by the priest or, where the occasion demanded, written down or inscribed on tablets and transmitted to succeeding generations in the priest's own handwriting so that anything that might have been added, subtracted or altered in later ages can be corrected, restored or emended on the authority of that autograph" (Certainty that the revelation has been faithfully reported orally or in writing).

4. "That the said revelation be so intimately pertinent to succeeding generations as to pass over necessarily into an article of faith, the more so because almost everything of this sort depends on *the faith of an individual witness. Let the priest prove all this* before the layman accord unrestricted faith to his revelation." [15] (Certainty that it is a question of matter pertaining to the articles of faith).

When these conditions have been fulfilled, the layman will have noth-

[14] *Ibid.*, p. 224; Scholz, p. 56.
[15] *Ibid.*, p. 224; Scholz, p. 57.

ing to say against the dogmas that the authority of the genuinely Catholic Church shall have ratified for mankind. The "Catholic Church" here in question seems throughout to be nothing but the assembly of rational beings in the exercise of their rational functions. Furthermore, these conditions are such as to render their fulfillment impossible for any man operating as an individual, priest or no. In order to prove that the revelation in question which he claims to have had has come from God, that this individual has been favored with that revelation and has been authorized by God to communicate it to others, the individual in question must have signs or extraordinary portents as credentials: the prophets, Jesus Christ and the apostles proved their own mission with miracles and with prophecies fulfilled, but Cherbury makes no mention of this whatever. Furthermore, the legitimate question arises as to how succeeding generations are going to be able to decipher in oral and written tradition the authentic outlines of this divine revelation in the midst of so many errors of mythology and heresy. For this there is need of a visible teaching authority grounded in divine authority and endowed with a supernatural charism enabling it to point through the centuries to the true meaning amid all the various interpretations of these texts. But Cherbury has nothing whatever to say on this point either. Indeed, he even seems to be reducing the reality of revelation to the activity of the "inner sense",[16] anticipating by a good three centuries the principle of immanentism in modernism. We have in Cherbury substantially the "principle of free investigation" tempered by him with the theory of "common consent".

The single and supreme criterion of truth for Cherbury is rationality, evidence of non-contradictoriness; and so faith must dissolve into scientific knowledge "so that here science doth precede faith and firm it up" [17] and the truths of faith are bound to end up being nothing more than the *rationes communes*.

Thus, in the revelation concerning the creation of the world and the redemption of man, Cherbury distinguishes what is doctrinal as such from what is historical fact; the doctrine, which is what counts, can be and is in fact found in every religion and has nothing to do with history: "But I do so distinguish acquiring and possession of certain knowledge from faith by hearing that I give attention to what can be known, what can be believed in any religion." [18] The historical element as such is of

[16] "*Properly speaking, however, revelations will be only those things that the inner sense tells us to have been established over and above the providence of things in general*" (*ibid.*, p. 225; Scholz, p. 57; italics mine). This "inner sense" is further specified as being a "supernatural sense". Cherbury then proceeds to show that the Ten Commandments come down to "universal notions" because they are found in all codes of laws and in all religions (p. 227f.; Scholz, p. 59).

[17] *Ibid.*, p. 229; Scholz, p. 60.

[18] *Ibid.*, p. 230; Scholz, p. 61.

no importance to the truth as such; rather it has to do with the accidental circumstances, the manner, the style and the milieu of the authors; and this is the object of faith which is therefore inferior to reason. Cherbury's position is thus the exact opposite of the traditional Catholic one—as also of Kierkegaard on this point [19]—for which faith is, and is admitted to be, superior to reason both because it proceeds from an illumination coming from God and resting on his authority and because it communicates to us truths that transcend the light of reason. Cherbury, for his part, dissects the "content" of faith, confining what is purely doctrinal within the limits of the *"five notions"*, making it relevant to the knowledge of the necessary which is proper to reason, and assigning what belongs to history as a reality (as a matter of fact) of the past to the category of the "probable" which pertains to faith.[20]

Critics have found Cherbury's position to be vacillating and confused; [21] and it cannot, in all conscience, be said to sparkle with critical and speculative vigor; yet it is both typical and revealing. It shows us that scarcely a century after the Reformation, which had proclaimed the superiority of the Bible over the authoritative Magisterium of the Church in matters of faith, the situation had been turned upside down with reason assuming complete ascendency over faith and philosophy over religion. This was precisely the contention of the "libertarian philosophers" of France who were already touting a combination of scorn for revealed religion and absolute glorification of reason; this amounted to an implicitly atheistic posture. In the wake of an admission that "Herbert *forgets* Christ and passes lightly over the personal nature of God",[22] it should be no cause for wonder that the critics delve to the core of the position and suspect atheism.

Thus, in asserting the validity and universal sufficiency (the "catholicity") of natural religion, Cherbury emerges as the ally of the "libertarians" or Freethinkers who were attacking the bases of Christianity and

[19] Cf. C. Fabro, "Foi et raison dans l'oeuvre de Kierkegaard," *Revue de sciences philosophiques et théologiques* (1948), pp. 169ff.

[20] The section on faith has the indicative title: *De verisimili* (Concerning the Probable) (*op. cit.*, p. 60). The future, which constitutes the object of the prophecies, is classed rather in the category of the "possible" (*De possibili*, p. 63), the understanding of which "is based on pure conjecture" (*in coniectura simplici nituntur*, p. 64). Cherbury does admit likewise the possibility of a prophecy by the "divine spirit" but he hedges it with a plethora of conditions of a kind calculated to render it practically impossible or entirely subject to the dictates of reason.

[21] Cf. A. W. Benn, *The History of English Rationalism in the Nineteenth Century*, Vol. I (New York-London, 1906), p. 90.

[22] M. M. Rossi, *Alle fonti del deismo e del materialismo moderno*, p. 23f. There is an explicit charge of atheism levelled against Cherbury by the polemical writer Kortholt in *De tribus impostoribus* (G. V. Lechler, *Geschichte des englischen Deismus*, p. 53).

revealed religion in general: for, if man is capable of fashioning for himself or even if he finds innate within himself a natural religion and ethic, what need is there of a revealed religion,[23] especially when this religion stands accused of being full of incomprehensible mysteries and dogmatic formularies which divide men among themselves? And if the best way to honor God is to practice morality in everyday life, of what use are the complicated religious observances and the hair-splitting casuistry of positive moral theology, which exasperate consciences to the point of desperation and muddle them to such an extent as to render impossible the practice of virtue and to preclude any moral consensus? And so the Deist principle, which gave the impression of stretching a rainbow of peace over 17th-century Europe lacerated by the wars of religion, proves in fact to have loosed the hurricane that tore up religion by the roots and prepared the way for the atheism of the 18th-century Enlightenment. And "Deist" very soon became synonomous with "atheist" in spite of morphology! Preeminently its radical opposition to Christianity ultimately favored the men who were denying all religion.[24] It is just the same thing that happened to Bayle who, in his desire to glorify

[23] Even in the late 17th century, the Deist C. Blount was attacking headon the authority of Holy Scripture, the doctrine of miracles and the authority of the Church; such attacks were continued throughout the 18th century by men like T. Woolaston, A. Collins, T. Morgan, T. Chubb. Especially J. Toland in his work. *Christianity Not Mysterious,* and M. Tindal in his *Christianity as Old as the Creation: On Gospel, a Republication of the Religion of Nature* deprive Christianity of any supernatural element and conceive of religion as "an inner revelation".

[24] Stephen paints the following picture of the stance of the most typical personalities involved: "But Shaftesbury, though a man of real power, attacked orthodoxy in the most oblique fashion; and Bolinbroke's blunderbuss missed fire, because discharged when the controversy was nearly extinct. Mandeville, perhaps the acutest of the Deists, made, like Shaftesbury, an indirect and covert assault. Collins, a respectable country gentleman, showed considerable acuteness; Toland, a poor denizen of Grub Street, and Tindal, a Fellow of All Souls, made a certain display of learning, and succeeded in planting some effective arguments" (L. Stephen, *History of English Thought in the Eighteenth Century,* Vol. I [London, 1881], p. 87). On the relations between modern (especially English) philosophy and religion, Stephen writes as follows: "Thus we find Descartes elaborately declaring his belief in Catholicism; Malebranche, his disciple, and Gassendi, the opponent of Descartes, were both Catholics [indeed, they were priests!]; Leibniz was a Lutheran. If Spinoza and Hobbes were accused of atheism, each of them sanctioned his speculation by the sacred name of theology. In England, Locke, though attacking the Cartesian philosophy, was a theologian and sincere if a latitudinarian Christian; Berkeley assaulted the older philosophy expressly and most sincerely and passionately in the interests of theology; Hume argued that the premises of Locke and Berkeley led to conclusions irreconcilable with their theology; and Reid—so far agreeing with Hume—attacked their premises in order to support their conclusions. And, finally, Hartley, the materialist founder of a school that altogether repudiated theology, argued in the interests of Christianity. Each philosophical school imputes atheism to its antagonist and declares its own method to afford the only sound basis for theology" (Vol. I, pp. 21f.).

man's freedom and disengage ethics from religion, contributed together with Spinoza and in his wake to provide atheism with its strongest weapons and its most troubling arguments.

Typical for English empiricism is the case of Hobbes (1588-1679): classed by others with the materialists and often with the atheists, he proclaimed himself a vigorous critic of atheism. He considered it to be a sin of supreme imprudence and unwisdom (a most great and ruinous sin: *Maximum damnosissimumque peccatum*) and deserving of punishment both by God and by the civic authority: "For the atheist is punished whether by God immediately or by the kings established under God; not as a subject is punished by his king but rather as an enemy is punished by his foe for refusing to accept the laws; that is, he is punished under the laws of war." [25] The atheist is preeminently the enemy of himself and his own peace of mind: "Those who deny the existence of the providence of the deity do not shake off any yoke; they only banish their own peace of mind." [26]

But the most interesting aspect of Hobbes' thought is his effort to arrive at an objective concept of atheism. His conclusion was that a man should be classed as an atheist not on the basis of his actions but solely on the basis of an oral or written profession involving a direct denial of the existence of God: "Not therefore on the basis of what he has done is the atheist judged to be such. He can therefore inculpate himself only by some sort of statement, whether oral or written, and in no other way saving only by directly denying that God exists." [26a]

And Hobbes is the first thinker to my knowledge to pose the problem of virtual atheism in explicit form. He puts the question: "Will not that man likewise be called an atheist who shall have said or written something from which it necessarily follows that God does not exist?" His reply is more juridical than theoretical, dealing mainly with the question of whether the accused actually himself grasps and is conscious of the atheistic conclusion implicit in his own principles: "So I would say yes in the event that he himself, when he said or wrote it, saw the necessity

[25] Hobbes, *Liber de Cive,* c. 12; *Opera latina,* ed. Molesworth, Vol. II (repr. Aalen, 1961), p. 327. A note apparently of still later date is more explicit: "But I am so much an enemy to atheists that I have both diligently sought for and vehemently desired to find some law whereby I might condemn them of injustice. But when I found none, I inquired next what name God himself did give to men so detested by him. Now God speaks thus of the atheist: *The fool hath said in his heart, there is no God.* Wherefore I placed their sin in the rank that God himself refers to. Next I show them to be enemies of God. But I conceive the name of an enemy to be sometimes somewhat sharper than that of an unjust man" (p. 326). On the necessity of civic sanctions against the atheist, cf. also *Appendix ad Leviathan,* c. 2, *Opera latina,* ed. Molesworth, Vol. III (reprinted Aalen, 1961), p. 549.

[26] Hobbes, *De Homine,* Part II, c. 31, ed. Molesworth, Vol. III, p. 255.

[26a] Hobbes, *Appendix ad Leviathan,* c. II, p. 548.

of such a consequence . . . For the consequences of human utterances are most difficult to pinpoint." In any case, Hobbes has no doubt about the treatment that should be meted out to the explicit atheist: he can be punished by the laws of the State and Hobbes proposes exile as the proper punishment in view of the atheist's total lack of any foundation for civic morality: "Wherefore he who denies that God exists or openly professes to doubt whether he exist or not can be punished, even by banishment, and this in full accord with natural equity and justice."

Hobbes' stand, even though moderated by the "can be" of his formulation, is the diametric opposite of the contention of Bayle and of that "principle of tolerance" which is soon, from Locke onward, to open the road to modern liberalism. Here religion is still, as for Bacon and the Middle Ages, the foundation of society: "For religion and the recognition of the divine power is commanded in every State by law; and it is essential to every State that good faith be observed in contracts, especially if it has been ratified by oath". Hobbes contends that the atheist who does not recognize the authority of God is incapable of swearing an oath and must therefore be sent away as a "public menace": "Seeing therefore that the atheist cannot be bound or put under any obligation by an oath, he ought to be sent away out of the body politic, not as insubordinate, but rather as *a public menace.*" [27]

No less vigorous is Hobbes' condemnation of pantheism which is apparently for him equivalent to atheism: "The philosophers who have said that the world itself or the soul of the world (i.e., a part of that world) is God, have spoken unworthily of God. For they have not attributed anything at all to him but rather have entirely denied that he exists. For that appellation *'God'* signifies *cause of the world;* and in saying that *the world is God,* they are saying that *its cause is non existent,* that there is no cause of it, i.e., that *God does not exist.*"

The same thing holds for those who deny creation by asserting the eternity of the world: "In like manner, those who assert the world to be not created but rather eternal are denying that *there is a cause of the world,* i.e., that *God exists,* since there cannot be any cause of what is eternal." [28] In this passage, Hobbes proceeds to defend the attributes proper to God, taking special care, however, to remove from God any finite or anthropomorphic element, even in the case of the spiritual perfections, and having explicit recourse to analogy: "When therefore

[27] Hobbes, *Appendix ad Leviathan,* c. II, p. 549, italics mine. Yet Hobbes argues against imposing capital punishment on the atheist "since he can sometimes be converted from his impiety. For what is there that man cannot hope for from the divine forbearance before he die?" (*ibid.*). Hobbes even goes so far as to consider as an atheist the blasphemer who "consents with his soul to the words of his mouth" (*ibid.*).

[28] Hobbes, *De Cive,* c. XV, § 14, p. 340, italics in original.

we attribute *will* to God, this is not to be understood as being similar to our own which is called a rational appetite. For if there be *appetite or craving* in God, then God *stands in need* of something, which it were an outrage to say; rather we must suppose in him something analogous which we cannot conceive." [29] The appeal to analogy, which could have an orthodox sense, has here rather a restrictive sense and Hobbes ends up in a stance of overt agnosticism.

Nevertheless there is no doubt that Hobbes did, in his early writings, openly oppose both atheism and pantheism which he equated with atheism; we must therefore conclude that Hobbes belonged on the side of theism.

Actually Hobbes' position is a kind of endorsement or rather anticipation of Deism: [30] there is considerable doubt as to whether he admitted the theological value of miracles; and the acceptance of the Christian religion has in his eyes rather a moral and political value as an act of obedience to the civil law in force which proclaims Christianity as the State religion. Hobbes shows the greatest respect for religion in general and for Christianity in particular; and his condemnation of atheism is so categorical, despite the somewhat summary nature of his analysis, as to put his own good faith apparently beyond doubt. Yet, there have been those who have been inclined to doubt it and have asserted unreservedly that "the guiding norm of Hobbes", i.e., his materialistic sense-perceptionism, "cannot but lead to atheism".[31] Certainly Hobbes had no desire to belong to the group of explicit atheists; together with his absolute allegiance to the civil laws, he evinces the most heartfelt respect for the State religion; he expressly admits "that it can be known by some by the light of reason that *God exists.*"

Yet he seems to restrict such capacity for knowledge of the existence

[29] *Ibid.*, p. 342, italics in original.

[30] Hobbes had indeed been already classed among the Deists by Philip Skelton in his *Deism Revealed.*

[31] S. Holm, "L'attitude de Hobbes à l'égard de la religion," *Archives de la Philosophie* XII, 2 (1936), p. 61. The inevitable nexus in Hobbes' thought between sense-perceptionism and atheism is the main point in the critique by Cudworth, *Systema intellectuale,* Latin trans. by Mosheim (Jena, 1733), Vol II, pp. 750ff. Two recent critics likewise find the charge of atheism justified: George E. G. Catlin, *Thomas Hobbes, as Philosopher, Publicist and Man of Letters* (Oxford, 1922), especially pp. 26ff., 55ff.; George C. Robertson, *Hobbes* (Edinburgh and London, 1910), p. 192 (where there is a reference to the dedication to the King of the *Problemata Physica,* a dedication in which Hobbes expresses the hope that he will be judged orthodox after having subordinated the Church and bishops to the authority of the King: "I hope Your Majesty will think neither atheism nor heresy"). One commentator finds the atheism charge not entirely convincing, inasmuch as it is based preeminently on Hobbes' materialism; this commentator cites the stand of Tertullian in this connection (cf. Samuel I. Mintz, *The Hunting of Leviathan,* Seventeenth Century Reactions to the Materialism and Moral Philosophy of Th. Hobbes [Cambridge University Press, 1962], pp. 41ff.).

of God to a very limited group: "Now that I have said that it might be known by natural reason *that there is a God,* it is so to be understood, not as if I had meant that all men might know this"; rather, the assertion refers to an exceptional case like that of Archimedes' discovery of the theorem on the proportion of the circle to the square. The mass of humanity, in the thrall of the passions, live out their little life in ignorance of God: "Yet men who are continually engaged in pleasures or seeking of riches and honor; also men that are not wont to reason aright, or cannot do it, or care not to do it; lastly, fools, in which number are atheists, cannot know this." [32]

Reference has been made by several critics and commentators to similarities between Hobbes' position and that of Spinoza and a passage from one of Hobbes' later writings, composed during the period of the controversy with Bishop Bramhall, seems to suggest a form of Parmenidism or rather of pantheistic Spinozism: "I mean by the universe the aggregate of all things that have being in themselves; and so do all men else. And because God has a being, it follows that he is either the whole universe or a part of it." [33]

This passage is in embarrassing contrast with the letter of the earlier Latin texts but it may well be in greater harmony with Hobbes' deepest and most genuine and native bent of mind, a sense-perceptionist rationalism, patently closely aligned to Stoic pantheism. Probably Hobbes' stand from the outset on the God-problem was a measured agnosticism, opting for a limitation to the simple assertion of the existence of God and the basic attributes: "For reason dictates only a name signifying the *nature* of God, *He Who Is* or simply *What Is;* and a name signifying a *relation* to us, namely *God,* wherein is contained the notion of both *king* and *lord* and *father.*" [34] This statement, in the Hobbesian context, involves the admission of the impossibility of metaphysics and the unattainability of the life of the spirit in itself, of the dynamic of freedom or of the issue of man's fate.

Yet, few modern thinkers have been more vigorous theists than Hobbes nor proclaimed more unequivocally in their writings the sovereign rights of God; few have given such unhesitating allegiance not only to the principles of reason but to the Bible as well. Hobbes' *De Cive* has

[32] Hobbes, *De Cive,* c. XIV, § 19, p. 326 note.

[33] *English Works,* ed. Molesworth, Vol. IV (Aalen, 1962), p. 349.

[34] Hobbes, *De Cive,* c. XV, § 14, p. 342. The vein of agnosticism comes out more clearly a little later on: "Thus, *there ought to be no disputation concerning the divine nature;* for it is agreed that *in the natural kingdom of God, all things are searched out by reason alone,* that is, from the principles of natural science. But these are so far from being adequate to enable us to know the nature of God that we cannot even attain to a comprehension of the properties of our own bodies or of any creature" (*ibid.,* § 15, p. 343).

a surprisingly fervently religious and almost mystical tone, especially in the section on religion; the title *Of the Kingdom of God by Nature* might sound equivocal but Hobbes' continual recourse to scriptural texts [35] to illustrate his meaning seems to constitute convincing proof of Hobbes' own conviction that he is asserting the kingdom of the true God and not confusing God with nature as Spinoza did. Here is a brief outline of the chapter from which we have already cited the most relevant texts against atheism.

1. The state of nature is asserted (in accord with Vico's notion of it) to be a state of anarchy and savagely clashing (*hostilis*) instincts. Consequently it must be restrained and governed by the *leges naturae* (laws of nature), destined to govern for a time the relations of man to the human collective, the city, and to God. Hobbes calls the life of man as governed by the *Leges naturae,* the *Kingdom of God* (§ 1).

2. The kingdom of God has a moral sense, indicating not merely the dominion of the divine omnipotence but likewise the free recognition and acceptance on the part of man of the laws promulgated by God. It is via this free recognition and acceptance indeed that the kingdom is actualized; hence, the atheists are excluded from it (§ 2).

3. God makes known his laws in three ways: *per tacita recte rationis dictamina* (the voice of reason), *per revelationem immediatam* (the audible voice speaking to the individual human being), *per vocem alicuius hominis* (the prophetic voice); in the last-mentioned case, the prophet presents to the whole Church the divine seal of approval, in the form of miracles, as credentials of his mission (§ § 3-4). God has absolute power over man; yet, although God could have punished and slain man even though man had not sinned, nevertheless, sin was in fact the cause of death and all man's other sufferings (§ § 5-6).

4. Hobbes applies his theory of "contract" or "covenant" in the matter of the way in which man honors God and observes his laws. The individual, having transferred this power to the political authority, it is the business of this latter to establish the meaning and observance of both sacred and civil laws: the only limitation on this State monopoly, even in matters of religion and divine worship, is this, that the State may not make laws that would go directly counter to God (§ § 7-18).

5. Of all the sins man can commit against the kingdom of God, the most serious is atheism: it is a crime of high treason against the deity: ". . . if [the subjects] do not confess before men in word and deed that there is one God, most good, most great, most blessed, supreme king of the whole world and of all the kings of the world. This fourth sin . . .

[35] Hobbes has the following explicit statement on the method he has followed: "In the preceding it has been proved both by reason and by the witness of sacred scripture" (*ibid.,* c. XV, § 1, p. 332). It would be worthwhile making a catalogue or inventory of Hobbes' scriptural citations.

is *the crime of high treason against the divine majesty*. For it is a denial of the divine power, in other words *atheism*" (§ 19).[36] Jesus is here called the Christ but there is no mention of his being God or the Son of God.[37]

It is not easy to make a proper judgment on Hobbes' notion of religion. For always, side by side with his repeated assertions of God, there is his materialistic sense-perceptionism that does not permit of an ontological and therefore transcendent notion of the Spirit. Moreover, side by side with the explicit assertion of human freedom and the ability of man's intelligence to understand and accept the divine "covenant" or contract, there is the conflicting theory of man's *imbecillitas* (weak-mindedness) and his consequent inevitable lapse into idolatry. One assertion may well reveal Hobbes' real and definitive stand, despite the cautious formulation of which he is a master: "Therefore it was quite impossible for men to avoid the twin reefs of *atheism* and *superstition,* without a special assistance of God." [38]

Superstition proceeds from fear without the light of reason, atheism, on the other hand, from an opinion of reason without fear. This creates the impression that belief in God proceeds not from truly philosophical demonstration but rather comes down to an obedience to the laws that assert his existence. Therefore, there is no genuine content of knowledge in the term "God" for Hobbes; rather is this term reduced to the status of a semanteme of socio-historical origin; and this would be in conformity with Hobbes' sense-perceptionist materialism. It is not easy to say what Hobbes the man may have thought in his heart; it may well be that he was more concerned with his own tranquillity than he was avidly desirous of ideological revolutions in a society like this, already all too inflamed with theological controversy.

There is no question but that the assertion of God is an erratic boulder on the surface of Hobbes' philosophy; it has no effective tie-in with his principles and is doomed to be washed away by the flood-tide of subsequent English and European thought.

It becomes evident into what an impasse Hobbes has jockeyed him-

[36] Among the Jews likewise the denial of divine providence and idolatry were considered crimes of high treason against the deity: "For it was to deny that the God of Abraham was their king by a *covenant* entered into with Abraham and themselves" (*ibid.,* c. XVI, § 18, p. 371). The inner core of the religion of Abraham consisted in the recognition of the existence of God and of his providence (c. XVI, § 3, p. 353). Abraham is designated as the first pioneer of monotheism after the flood (§ 1; p. 352).

[37] *Ibid.,* cc. XVI-XVII, pp. 372ff.

[38] *Ibid.,* c. XVI, § 1, p. 352. Historians almost entirely neglect the argumentation and confine themselves to speaking of "agnosticism": "His doctrine of God is, in modern phrase, agnostic. The attributes we ascribe to him only signify our desire to honor him: we understand nothing of what he is, but only that he is" (W. R. Sorley, *A History of English Philosophy* [Cambridge, 1920], p. 67).

self when we read his analysis of the atheist conscience in the context of his political theory concerning the origin of political power and the consent of the citizens. The atheist's sin is not a direct contravention of any law and so he cannot be punished for this sin as such; but he can indeed be punished by the political authority, e.g., by the king, not as a subject is punished by his ruler but rather as one enemy is punished by another enemy, i.e., he can be punished under the laws of war. Therefore, atheism is treated by Hobbes as a sin of imprudence [39] and therefore inexcusable.

But for all his precautions and declarations of theism and orthodoxy, Hobbes did not succeed in escaping the vigilant eye of the theologians. Outstanding among the theologians who initiated a critical examination of the *Leviathan* was Dr. John Bramhall, Bishop of Derry. Hobbes himself sums up Bramhall's objections and comments on the nature of these objections, in the preface to his own voluminous reply: "The late Lord Bishop of Derry published a book called *The Catching of Leviathan*, in which he hath put together divers sentences picked out of my *Leviathan*, which stand there plainly and firmly proved, and set them down without their proofs, and without the order of their dependence

[39] Hobbes has a complicated but significant treatment of this point: "Many find fault that I have referred atheism to imprudence, and not to injustice; yea, by some it is taken so, as if I had not declared myself an enemy bitter enough against atheists. They object further, that since I had elsewhere said that it might be known that *there is a God* by natural reason, I ought to have acknowledged that they sin at least against the law of nature, and therefore are not only guilty of imprudence, but injustice too. But I am so much an enemy to atheists, that I have both diligently sought for, and vehemently desired to find some law whereby I might condemn them of injustice. But when I found none, I inquired next what name God himself did give to men so detested by him. Now God speaks thus of the atheist: *The fool hath said in his heart, there is no God.* Wherefore I placed their sin in that rank which God himself refers to. Next I show them to be enemies of God. But I conceive the name of an enemy to be sometimes somewhat sharper than that of an unjust man. Lastly, I affirm that they may under that notion be justly punished both by God, and supreme magistrates; and therefore by no means excuse or extenuate this sin. Now that I have said, that it might be known by natural reason that *there is a God,* is so to be understood, not as if I had meant that all men might know this; except they think, that because Archimedes by natural reason found out what proportion the circle hath to the square, it follows thence, that every one of the vulgar could have found out as much. I say therefore, that although it may be known to some by the light of reason that there is a God; yet men that are continually engaged in pleasures or seeking of riches and honor; also men that are not wont to reason aright, or cannot do it, or care not to do it; lastly, fools, in which number are atheists, cannot know this" (*Philosophical Rudiments concerning Government and Society,* c. XIV, § 19; *English Works,* Vol. II, p. 198f. Note). In the next chapter (XV *Of the Kingdom of God by Nature*), Hobbes speaks likewise of the natural worship of God and derives it from the obligation incumbent on reason to recognize him; and he adjudges an atheist, as would any orthodox theologian, anyone denying any of the fundamental attributes; cf. the text in the Appendix.

one upon another; and calls them atheism, blasphemy, impiety, subversion of religion, and by other names of that kind." [40]

Hobbes evinces extreme sensitivity in the matter of the charge of atheism and launches into an all-out defense of himself against it. We here sum up the points of the charge as they are presented by Hobbes himself in his dialogue-style reply. Bramhall had charged that in Hobbes' theory of religion, the principal attributes of God are cast in doubt: primarily the *existence* of God and then his "infiniteness, incomprehensibility, unity, ubiquity . . ." (p. 284). Bramhall has further charged that for Hobbes the natural origin of religion is identical with that of superstition: a belief in spirits, ignorance of secondary causes, reverence for him of whom man is afraid, the acceptance of fortuitous events as omens and portents (cf. p. 289). Thus, religion is born exclusively out of the awareness that men have of their own weakness: faced with the amazing spectacle of nature, they believe that there exists an invisible God who has created all things visible.

Bramhall's formulation, as reported by Hobbes ("superstition proceedeth from fear without right reason, and atheism from an opinion of reason without fear"), presents atheism as much more reasonable than superstition.[41] Hence the impossibility of knowing the existence and attributes of God, the uselessness of religion with its practices of prayer, thanksgiving, oblation and sacrifice. It is in this context, charges Bramhall, that Hobbes' contention must be understood when he says in the *De Cive* that atheism is merely a sin of imprudence.

But this is inadmissible, insists Bramhall. It is impossible that what is directly contrary to the light of natural reason should be nothing more than a sin of simple ignorance of imprudence. The laws of nature stand in no need of a new promulgation, having been imprinted naturally by God on the heart of man. Wherefore, seeing that nature has told us that there does exist a God and that this God is owed a debt of worship in a certain fashion, it is not possible that atheism should be a sin of simple ignorance. Besides, a rebellious subject is still a *de jure* subject even though not a *de facto* one; therefore, even the most unbridled atheist ought by rights to be subject to God and ought to be punished not as an enemy but rather as a disloyal traitor. This is indeed admitted, notes Bramhall, even by Hobbes himself when he writes that "this fourth sin is, in the kingdom of God by nature, the crime of high treason against the divine majesty, for it is a denial of the divine power, in other words

[40] *An Answer to a Book published by Dr. Bramhall, to the Reader; English Works,* Vol. IV, p. 281.

[41] "And a little after he telleth us, that *superstition proceedeth from fear without right reason, and atheism from an opinion of reason without fear;* making atheism to be more reasonable than superstition" (*ibid.,* p. 289).

atheism". Hence, the atheist is a traitor to God and to be punished as a disloyal subject and not as a (mere) enemy. Hobbes sums up the conclusion of the charge as an accusation that Hobbes is not a friend of religion and that "I excuse atheism".

Hobbes enters a blanket protest against this charge. Why is there felt to be any monstrous impiety in saying that the savage is led to personify the object of his imaginings and that fear is at the root of his belief in the false gods, even as the fear of the true God is the beginning of wisdom for the Jews and Christians? What is so blasphemous about saying that ignorance of secondary causes impelled man to believe in a First Cause and to give reverence and worship to that First Cause? Had he not also said, protests Hobbes, that superstition is "fear without reason"? Is not atheism perhaps a boldness, based on the false reasoning that "the wicked prospereth; therefore there is no God"? It is therefore not true, concludes Hobbes, that he is presenting atheism as more reasonable than superstition for he has denied all reasonableness to atheism and superstition alike. And because the atheist thinks he is right whereas he is not, Hobbes deems him to be more unreasonable than the superstitious man.[42]

And as to the Bishop's assertion that all men are spontaneously convinced of the existence of God, the same cannot be said, objects Hobbes, in the matter of the other attributes such as infiniteness, incomprehensibility, unity and ubiquity, a knowledge of which is acquired only by a gradual process of reasoning. And as for his assertion that atheism is a sin of ignorance, Hobbes continues, this is no more than a repetition of the words of David: "The fool hath said in his heart, there is no God" (Ps. 13, 1). Hobbes is therefore clearly showing himself to be just as convinced as was David that God does in fact exist; and so the charge that Hobbes excuses and defends atheism simply will not stand up: the Scholastic subtleties of Bramhall are to no avail.

Hobbes now proceeds to defend his stand in the controversy concerning the attributes of God,[43] such as ubiquity, indivisibility, eternity,

[42] Hobbes was thus expressing distrust of Bayle's contention in advance.

[43] Thanks to Hobbes' direct acquaintance with Scholasticism, the importance of the problem of God's attributes both in relation to the problem of the existence of God and especially in relation to the problem of freedom (as we shall point out shortly) is absolutely crucial in Hobbes' thought. His subtle and persistent disquisitions recall the famous controversies of Arabic philosophy on this point.

Thus, for example, he avers that God can be said to be "eternal" but not eternity itself which as such (like every pure abstraction!) has neither reality nor meaning; and he rejects the stand of St. Thomas, shared substantially by his theologian adversaries. Eternity is conceived as an "everlasting succession" and not as an "indivisible point": "To which I answer, that as soon as I can conceive eternity to be an *indivisible point,* or anything but an *everlasting succession,* I will renounce all that I have written on this subject. I know St. Thomas Aquinas

omnipotence, etc. Here Hobbes entrenches himself in a cautious agnosticism and distinguishes between concrete and abstract, between eternity and eternal. Parrying the charge of having conceived of God as being "corporeal" and "infinite", Hobbes appeals to St. Paul (Col. 2, 9): "in him (Christ) the fullness of the Godhead abides corporeally (σωματικῶς)" and the commentary on this passage by St. Athanasius, champion of orthodoxy at Nicea against Arius: "The fullness of the Godhead dwells in him corporeally (θεϊκῶς), i.e., *really*". And in support of his exegesis of Paul and Athanasius, Hobbes appeals to the materialistic theory of Tertullian [44] according to which "all that is not body is nothing"—a doctrine that was not condemned at the Council of Nicea which condemned only the division of the divine substance into God the Father, God the Son and God the Holy Spirit, thus defining that there are not three Gods but one only and one only *individual* Trinity, and adding the statement that "God does not have parts". For the rest, continues Hobbes, whenever scripture speaks of "spirit" (πνεῦμα) it means a corporeal reality, something infinitely subtle (as the obvious meaning of the term indicates), both in the passage speaking of God's breathing into man (*inspiring*) the breath of life and in those passages which say that God "inspires" his prophets. So much for Bramhall's claim that God is to be conceived as an "incorporeal substance".

Proceeding to the question of the nature of the soul and the consequent doctrine on the immortality of the soul, Hobbes specifies his stand to embrace three points:

1. The predestined in Christ will enjoy life eternal and thus will be immortal in virtue of Christ's passion and triumph over death.
2. In that state there will be no soul separated from the body even as there will be no living body separated from the soul.

---

calls *eternity, nunc stans,* an *ever-abiding now;* which is easy enough to say, but though I fain would, yet I could never conceive it; they that can, are more happy than I" (*Of Liberty and Necessity,* A Treatise wherein all Controversy concerning Predestination, Election, Free-Will, Grace, Merits, Reprobation, etc., is fully decided and cleared. An Answer to a Treatise written by the Bishop of Londonderry on the same Subject; *English Works,* Vol. IV, p. 271).

[44] "The soul, then, we define as sprung from the breath of God, immortal, possessing body, having form, simple in its substance, intelligent in its own nature, developing its powers in various ways, free in its determinations, subject to the changes of accident, in its faculties mutable, rational, supreme, endued with an instinct of presentiment, evolved out of one [archetypal soul] (Tertullian, *De Anima,* c. 22; Ante-Nicene Christian Library, Vol. XV, tr. Peter Holmes, [Edinburgh, 1870].—Cf. also: H. Karpp, *Probleme altchristlicher Anthropologie* [Gütersloh, 1950], pp. 46ff.; C. Fabro, *L'anima,* Introduzione al problema dell'uomo [Rome, 1955,] pp. 243ff.). For Tertullian, as for the greater part of the writers of the apostolic age, who draw on Stoic metaphysic or rather physics, matter is synonymous with reality and consequently God himself turns out to be matter, albeit a different sort from that of creatures (cf. M. Spanneut, *Le Stoïcisme des Pères de l'Eglise* [Paris, 1957], pp. 160ff., 288ff.).

3. The damned will come back to life for the judgment and will die a second death in torment and his death will be eternal.

And Hobbes contends that in each and all of these points he is simply basing himself on scripture, which does not know, e.g., the expression "an immortal soul" but rather attributes immortality to God alone (1 Tim. 6, 16), asserting that man can have it only in Christ as a "gift of God" (2 Tim. 1, 10). And scripture should suffice for English Protestants as opposed to Roman Catholics, remarks Hobbes with a waspish irony; and he goes on to say that when he wrote the *Leviathan* there was not yet in England any Church or any bishop; and, finally, he can defend himself against any accusation by an appeal to scripture, as indeed is clearly stated by Article 30 of the Thirty-Nine Articles.[45] It is the Bishop and not Hobbes who is going against scripture; and Hobbes insists the bishop has been speaking not as a bishop but rather as a private individual, as a Scholastic, and so had to be answered.

Hobbes continues with a terse summary of Bramhall's accusation that Hobbes' main intent had been to destroy the existence of God; Bramhall, alleges Hobbes, had wanted to give the world to understand that Hobbes was an atheist. And why? Because Hobbes had said that God was a spirit, but *corporeal.* But Hobbes had the warranty of St. Paul: "There is a physical body and a spiritual body" (1 Cor., 15, 44). The man who asserts that there does exist a God and that this God is something real (for a *body* is indubitably a *real substance*) is very far from being an atheist. But, retorts Hobbes, turning the bishop's own argument against him, the man who says that God is an "incorporeal substance" leaves everyone uncertain as to whether he be an atheist or no; for nobody will ever be able to say whether there exists a substance

[45] We cite the pertinent text of Hobbes: "For the church of England pretendeth not, as doth the church of Rome, to be above the Scripture; nor forbiddeth any man to read the Scripture; nor was I forbidden when I wrote my *Leviathan,* to publish anything which the Scriptures suggested. For when I wrote it, I may safely say there was no lawful church in England, that could have maintained me in, or prohibited me from writing anything. There was no bishop; and though there was preaching, such as it was, yet no common prayer. For extemporary prayer, though made in the pulpit, is not common prayer. There was then no church in England, that any man living was bound to obey. What I write here at this present time I am forced to in my defence, not against the church, but against the accusations and arguments of my adversaries. For the church, though it excommunicates for scandalous life, and for teaching false doctrine, yet it professeth to impose nothing to be held as faith, but what may be warranted by Scripture; and this the church itself saith in the twentieth of the Thirty-nine Articles of religion. And therefore I am permitted to allege Scripture at any time in the defence of my belief" (*An Answer to a Book published by Dr. Bramhall,* pp. 355ff.). Later in this same work, Hobbes declares his intention to submit to the Church of England, if ever that Church should forbid him to treat points of faith except for the statement "that Jesus Christ, the Son of God, died for my sins" (pp. 366f.).

which is not corporeal, nor are any terms such as "immaterial" or "incorporeal" found in scripture. And we have seen already how both St. Paul and Tertullian assert the corporeity of God. Were they by any chance atheists? Indeed they were not! But the bishop takes refuge in the allegation that they were identifying "substance" with "body" and were thus saying that God was a corporeal substance, so that there can be a question of "atheism by consequence". But likewise the man who, like Bramhall, asserts the ubiquity of God and says that God is "wholly here, wholly there, wholly everywhere" is destroying by consequence the infinity and the simplicity of God. So these Scholastics are "atheists by consequence". And the Lord Bishop is likewise an atheist when he releases the will of man from subjection to the necessity of the will and decree of God; he is denying *by consequence* the divine foreknowledge, which thus forces him into *atheism by consequence.*[46] There is need, therefore, for caution in wholesale condemnations and talk of heresy:[47] it is all too easy to treat as a heretic anyone who thinks differently from oneself in matters of religion.

Hobbes and Bramhall were to return to the lists in a debate in Paris on the problem of the relations between the divine causality and human freedom: Bramhall seems here, as in his book already cited, to approach the Catholic position, whereas Hobbes asserts that the term "free will" never occurs in scripture and approves the positions of Luther, Calvin and the other Reformers (in opposition to Arminius and the Arminians).[48] For Hobbes, the infallible foreknowledge of God entails the imposition of necessity on the will of man; thus, although certain events are said to be contingent they " befall" necessarily. The bishop counters that the will is free of compulsion and necessity and that accordingly the judgment of the understanding is not always *practice practicum* (practico-practical), i.e., not of such a nature in itself as to oblige and determine the will *ad unum* (to one thing, end or action): since the will determines itself, external causes can move it only with a moral or

[46] Hobbes says he will pass over in silence the critique of Bramhall (in ch. II of his work) against the political theories of the *Leviathan,* for the mistakes in this critique cannot do him much harm.

[47] Hobbes rounds off this reply with a special disquisition on the notion of "heresy" (cf. *ibid.,* pp. 387ff.).

[48] Hobbes, *The Question concerning Liberty, Necessity and Chance; English Works,* Vol. V, p. 13. Tönnies has this to say on Hobbes' basic attitude: "But Hobbes never denies freedom in the sense of being able to if one wants to; he simply keeps reiterating that the *willing* is *not* free, unless one can want to will; he denies the other meaning of freedom, although his *own* idea of freedom is conditioned by the other earlier one and despite the fact that he himself often mentions the fact that to be free does not mean simply to be able to act if one wants to but rather to be free of constraint and to feel oneself free of constraint" (F. Tönnies, *Thomas Hobbes Leben und Lehre* [Stuttgart, 1925], pp. 173f.).

metaphorical motion, not with any necessary motion. God's foreknowledge therefore does not introduce into the will any necessity whatsoever. A doctrine of necessity, like that of Hobbes, is blasphemous, desperate and destructive. It would be better, according to Bramhall, to be an atheist than to hold it; and the one who maintains it is deserving of being refuted with rods rather than with arguments. Well, concludes Hobbes, we shall leave it to the judgment of posterity to decide which of the two doctrines is more intelligible or more conformable to the word of God.[49] And posterity has, on this point, agreed with the bishop: in a philosophy of radical sense-perceptionism and determinism there cannot be any place either for God or for human freedom, and a transfer of these problems onto the level of an appeal to scripture and of faith cannot but be meaningless unless the world of the spirit and of freedom of individual decision be first firmly grounded on a demand of principle.

Hobbes has been numbered now among the Deists and now among the atheists,[50] even as Spinoza with whom the historians of philosophy have for some time now been showing him to have had many essential traits in common. Like Spinoza, whom he assuredly influenced, Hobbes puts the problem of God in first place, but his God looks like the sumptuous facade of a castle that could not be built for want of a foundation. The basis, the scope and the conclusion of his philosophy is

[49] The exact phrasing of this conclusion is as follows: "That the doctrine of necessity is a blasphemous, desperate, and destructive doctrine. That it were better to be an Atheist, than to hold it; and he that maintaineth it, is fitter to be refuted with rods than with arguments. And now whether this his doctrine or mine be the more intelligible, more rational, or more conformable to God's word, I leave it to the judgement of the reader" (*The Question concerning Liberty, Necessity and Change,* p. 453). In a work written in 1654 against the Bishop of Londonderry, Hobbes had treated the problem of liberty and necessity in a briefer, clearer and more scholarly fashion (*Of Liberty and Necessity,* pp. 229f.).

[50] The charge of "syncretistic atheism" had early been levelled against Hobbes by a certain Adam Rechenberg in 1674 (cf. G. Lyon, *La philosophie de Hobbes* [Paris, 1893], p. 218). Valsecchi reports the critique of Clarke and Cumberland and protests against Bayle who accused Spinoza of atheism and subsequently defended Hobbes (*De Fundamentis religionis et de fontibus impietatis,* [Venice, 1770 [2]], pp. 330ff.). Bayle writes: "He loved his country, was loyal to his King, a good friend, charitable, kindly and obliging; yet he was taken for an Atheist; but those who have written his Life maintain that he held most orthodox opinions on the nature of God"; and in Note (M), Bayle cites the *Vita Hobbesii* (*Dictionnaire historique et critique:* cf. "Hobbes", Vol. II, pp. 776f.). In the title of his major work, Clarke associates Hobbes with Spinoza: *A Demonstration of the Being and Attributes of God more particularly in Answer to Mr. Hobbes, Spinoza and their Followers, Wherein the Notion of Liberty is Stated, and the Possibility and Certainty of it Proved, in Opposition to Necessity and Fate* (London, 1705). The atheism charge is likewise reported by Trinius (*Freydenker Lexikon* [Turin, 1960], pp. 308f.), who tends to exculpate Hobbes from this charge, whereas Kortholt, as we have pointed out, includes Hobbes along with Spinoza and Herbert of Cherbury in his *De tribus impostoribus* which is cited by Bayle himself in the note to the article on Spinoza.

always the same: man; and man's basic activity from which he takes his definition is one and one only: political sociology; and the horizon that bounds the realities of that activity is by definition insuperable: sense activity in a world of institutions actualized in time under the exclusive hegemony of the State. Hobbes' trenchant theism was perhaps more sincere and genuine than that of Spinoza, when due account is taken of the depth of religious feeling native to the English; but actually it was a mask very soon to fall with the appearance, scarcely a century later, of the Enlightenment, of which Hobbes was one of the boldest forerunners and most famous masters.[51] In any event, beneath his surface clarity, Hobbes is a complex and problem-laden thinker, harassed like Descartes by a dying world, the world of authority, and goaded by a new world, the world of freedom: a veritable Janus in the thought-stream of Europe but a man whose work has had an unequivocal and uncontested outcome, despite his own protests.

[51] Diderot has a clear preference for Hobbes over Descartes: "I prefer Hobbes who claims that in order to draw any really meaningful conclusion the line of reasoning had to be: 'I sense, I think, I judge; therefore a piece of matter organized as I am can sense, think and judge.' A second stride, after this first one, puts the reasoner very well along the way indeed." (*Réfutation suivie de l'ouvrage d'Helvétius intitulé l'Homme; Oeuvres philosophiques,* ed. P. Vernière [Paris, 1961], p. 564f.).

Hobbes is one of the admitted sources of d'Holbach and Helvétius. Feuerbach pinpoints the ambiguous position of Hobbes and of the whole of theism in modern thought: "Hobbes is thus no atheist as such; but his theism is in substance and content, like all the theism of the modern world, equivalent to atheism; his God is but a negative being or rather a monstrosity" (*Geschichte der Neueren Philosophie,* c. II; *C. W.,* ed. Bolin-Jodl, Vol. III (Stuttgart, 1906), p. 110). Marx and Engels are more outspoken: "Hobbes annihilated the *theistic* prejudices of Baconian materialism" (*Die heilige Familie,* ch. VI; *Marx-Engels Werke,* Vol. II [Berlin, 1958], p. 136).

3

Theistic Deism and Atheism in Shaftesbury

The most skillful and subtle mediator between the Cartesian rationalism of Bayle and the empiricism of Locke, the mediator who constituted an ideal between the new ferments of English Deism and the French Enlightenment even then in process of preparing the French Revolution was undoubtedly the Earl of Shaftesbury (1671-1713). It is true that Shaftesbury vigorously opposed the utilitarian sense-perceptionism of Hobbes and was averse to the crude and brutal criticism of such pamphleteers as Tindal, Collins, Toland and the like, against positive religion and especially Christianity; indeed, Shaftesbury even openly glorified the positive value of a belief in God and proclaimed the dignity of religious knowledge. Yet his disinterest both in the historical proofs of revealed religion and for the metaphysical bases for belief in the Absolute and his partiality for the realm of feeling served to undermine and sap the bases of an effective assertion of God.

Not only is there no doubt that Shaftesbury abandoned Christianity, going further in this regard, even in the matter of expressions and formulations, than his master Locke; but also that his Deism totters on the brink of atheism and will inevitably precipitate into atheism any follower who resolves to follow through Shaftesbury's principles to their logical conclusion and not merely confine himself to external assertions: [1] it is no mere chance, for instance, that Diderot launches his career as writer by a translation of Shaftesbury's most famous Essay "Concerning Virtue and Merit". There recurs in Shaftesbury, we feel, that same ambiguity that prevailed in the work of Bayle, who, though protesting the while that he was defending true religion from the aberrations of superstition, was in fact opening the road and furnishing the

[1] Shaftesbury has been brought into the foreground by the growing interest on the part of recent historians of philosophy in the Enlightenment and its crucial function in the development of 18th century European thought (cf. F. Meinecke, *Die Entstehung des Historismus* [Munich, 1964 [2]], pp. 16ff.).

weapons to Enlightenment atheism, the first form of positive and constructive atheism in modern thought.

The rapid dissemination of Shaftesbury's writings on the continent, in France and Germany, very soon created that atmosphere of an elevation of the individual conscience to the rank and status of an infallible principle of moral and religious values, an ultimate court of appeal in this area; this exaltation of the individual conscience was in turn to serve as point of departure not only for the "philosophy of feeling" but also for the new trend of European thought as mirrored in Hume and Kant. Shaftesbury follows exclusively the interior rhythm of his own life, unfettered by any precise metaphysical grounding; [2] he succeeds in effecting a singularly skillful description of this interior rhythm, employing a mixture of most novel notions taken both from ancient thought (Stoicism) and the Renaissance and modern rationalism. The result is that there are alternating traces of theism, deism and pantheism in his work; yet there is no possibility of a precise and comprehensive identification of his stand. His thought is clothed in a light and easy style which gives it something of the freshness of the dawn; but it is really heavy with allusions and references to the most important areas of the life of the spirit, from religion to ethics and aesthetics. Shaftesbury clearly stands in the foreground of the molding of the modern world.

The problem with which we are occupying ourselves in these researches stands at the center of Shaftesbury's reflections and is attacked directly in his most famous and best-known work, *An Inquiry Concerning Virtue of Merit,*[3] a work that might almost amount to a new sort of *Discourse on Method,* had the author himself not declared himself to be

[2] Dilthey writes with his usual penetration: "Shaftesbury starts from a certain basic awareness of life . . . This vital consciousness is his starting point: the inner strength and power of the individual to mold himself into a harmonious personality and the subsequent perception of this harmony within himself—such was his milieu. And a man of this sort for whom the proper balance of all powers, their recurrent harmonization as often as necessary within the personality, constitutes the 'peerless bliss of all earth's children', will inevitably perceive this tendency to balance and proportion everywhere in the universe as well. With unwavering persistence he keeps hearing the great symphony sounding throughout the entire cosmos. Each and every area of life has its own rules and its own felicity, and each individual part of the whole is then caught up into the higher harmony of that totality. Thus does he perceive within himself the kinship of his own creative power with that of the universe" (W. Dilthey, *Aus der Zeit der Spinozasstudien Goethes,* Gessamelte Schriften, Vol. II [Leipzig & Berlin, 1940 [4]], pp. 389f.). Dilthey also shows the profound influence of Shaftesbury on Herder and Schiller as well as Goethe.

[3] "It constitutes, then, the very core and basic nucleus of Shaftesbury's entire work and it is also the only work in which Shaftesbury proceeded in a consciously systematic and methodically expository fashion, his other works all being more or less 'miscellaneous' to use his own term (L. Bandini, *Shaftesbury,* Etica e religione, la morale del sentimento [Bari, 1930], p. 33).

opposed to any systematic and abstract line of reasoning. Diderot sums up the pith of the *Inquiry* in masterly fashion as follows: [4]

I. "This essay concerns itself only with moral virtue, that virtue which the Church Fathers themselves admitted could be found in certain pagan philosophers; that virtue which, far from being inseparable from the panoply of institutional ritual and credal definitions which those Fathers professed or pretended to profess, was in fact being utterly destroyed by that institutionalism; that virtue which providence has not left without its reward if it be true, as will be proven in the sequel, that moral integrity constitutes our happiness in this world. But what is integrity?" (p. IIf.).

II. The virtuous man is sufficient unto himself: "A man is upright or virtuous when, without any base or servile motivation, such as the hope of a reward or the fear of a punishment, he constrains all his own passions to conspire to the general good of his species: an heroic effort; yet, one which, for all that, is not at odds with his private interests" (p. 12). Diderot claims to have derived this notion from Cicero (*De Oratore*) but it has much more recent roots, preeminently in Bayle, as Diderot very well knows.

III. And this is the crucial point for Diderot: Shaftesbury is, according to him, at pains to assert theism against atheism ("theism is the only stand of which he is in favor") and thus Shaftesbury feels distrust for deism because of its ambiguity. "A theist" is one who starts with natural religion and remains open to an acceptance of the mysteries of

[4] I am quoting from the Naigeon ed. of Diderot's translation of the *Inquiry: C. W.*, Vol. I (Paris, 1821). I am following and shall be citing in the sequel the Diderot translation not only for its great historical value but also because of its outstanding zeal and meticulous effort to be not simply a word-for-word rendering but a genuinely interpretative translation. On the character of the translation, Diderot writes: "I read and reread the original; I drenched myself in its spirit; and then, so to speak, I closed the book when I took up the pen. Never has any man been freer with another man's goods! I have abridged whatever seemed to me too diffuse, expanded whatever seemed to me too condensed, amended what seemed but bold guesswork; and the reflections that accompany such a text are so frequent that the essay of M . . . S . . . has metamorphosed from its original form as a metaphysical demonstration into a work having a considerable share of ethical elements. The one thing I have scrupuously respected is the order of the original that could not be simplified; and this work still demands a certain restraint" (p. 17). The edition we are following puts the translator's remarks in a note; a comparison with the original has convinced us of the fidelity of this work of Diderot to the original; Diderot's translation remains a classic of its kind. We have consulted the original in the edition: *Characteristics of Men, Manners, Opinions, Times,* with a Collection of Letters by the Right Honorable Antony Earl of Shaftesbury, Vol. II (Basel: Printed for I. I. Tourneisen and I. I. Legrand, 1790) in three volumes; and in Vol. I of the latest complete edition of John M. Robertson (London: Grant Richards, 1900; reprinted Gloucester, Mass.: Peter Smith, 1963), in two volumes.

revealed religion, whereas "a deist" is one who excludes all revelation: "M . . . S . . . who gave meticulous warning of the confusion that could eventuate between the terms *deist* and *theist.* The *deist,* he tells us, is the man who believes in God but denies all revelation; the *theist* on the contrary is the one who is ready to admit revelation and has already admitted the existence of a God. But in English, the word *theist* is used indiscriminately for both *deist* and *theist.* This is an odious confusion, exclaims M. S., who could not abide the prostitution of the name of *theist,* the most majestic of all names, by its application to a band of the ungodly. He was at pains to eradicate the pernicious ideas that had fastened onto the word in his language: he pinpointed with all possible precision the opposition of *theism* to *atheism* and its close ties with *Christianity.* Indeed, while it is true that not every *theist* is already a Christian, it is no less true that anyone must begin by being a *theist* in order to become a *Christian.* The foundation of all religion is *theism*" (p. 13f.). At this point, Diderot notes and approves of two passages in the original English which, to his mind, are crucial for Shaftesbury's orthodoxy and concludes indignantly: "I cannot conceive how, after such solemn protestations of a total submission of heart and soul to the sacred mysteries of his religion, anyone could have been so unjust as to number M. S. together with the Asgils, the Tindals and the Tolands, men whose reputation as Christians is no better in their own Church than is their reputation as writers in the republic of letters: poor Protestants and wretched writers" (p. 15f.).[5]

IV. It is thus no cause for wonder that Diderot could present Shaftesbury's Essay as a solid preliminary to Christianity: "Finally, all that can be said in favor of a knowledge of the God of the nations will apply with a new degree of force in favor of the knowledge of the God of the Christians. This thought permeates every page of this work. And so is the reader led to the door of our churches. The missionary has but to draw him on then to the foot of our altars: that is his task; the philosopher has discharged his" (p. 16). Thus the problem posed in the *Inquiry* seems to be simple enough and the solution accessible to everyone. But even a cursory glance at the body of the work reveals a much more complex state of affairs.

[5] Bandini (*op. cit.,* p. 40) explains Diderot's zeal to acquit Shaftesbury of the charge of *deism* as being a matter of "editorial expediency" in view of the opprobrium attaching to the term "deist". Diderot's spirited defense of Shaftesbury may likewise have been prompted by his own theistic convictions at that period, convictions that were soon to begin to waver, as we shall point out below. A little earlier Shaftesbury had defined as a "theist" the man who admits that everything has been made and ordained and is being governed for the best by a single essentially good intelligence. And Diderot immediately notes: "Be careful not to confuse this word [*theist*] with the other word "deist" (*op. cit.,* p. 25).

The Essay does indeed start off vigorously with a treatment of Bayle's problem which Shaftesbury knew directly because he knew the man even though he is not here mentioned by name: "Religion and virtue appear in many respects so nearly related that they are generally presumed inseparable companions." But this easy assumption is now contrasted with the hard facts of reality: "We have known people who, having the appearance of great zeal in religion, have yet wanted even the common affections of humanity, and shown themselves extremely degenerate and corrupt. Others again, who have paid little regard to religion, and been considered as mere atheists, have yet been observed to practice the rules of morality, and act in many cases with such good meaning and affection toward mankind as might seem to force an acknowledgment of their being virtuous." Indeed, pursues Shaftesbury, "in our dealings with men we are seldom satisfied by the fullest assurance given us of their zeal in religion, till we hear something further of their character . . . But if we hear at first that [a man] has honest moral principles, and is a man of natural justice and good temper, we seldom think of the other question, 'Whether he be religious and devout?' "[6]

The problem is clear in its essentials. Shaftesbury presents it as thorny, ticklish and little studied; and without referring to Bayle, perhaps from motives of prudence, Shaftesbury does refer to the two opposing groups "the religious part of mankind" and "the men of wit and raillery" (Diderot renders: *les beaux esprits et les gens du bel air*), each standing pat in its own exclusivity. Before attacking the problem at hand, Shaftesbury decides to present a brief study in depth of the problem of religion as it presents itself in function of whether the world is admitted to be ordered or whether it is held to be given over to pure chance. The principle of order in the world is, by unanimous consent, called *God* and whoever admits that principle is precisely designated as a *"theist,"* while whoever admits several higher intelligences or minds, all of them essentially good, is a *"polytheist"*, whereas whoever has recourse to capricious intelligences or minds is termed a *"Daemonist"*. A "perfect atheist" on the other hand is whoever does not admit any other cause in nature saving chance only: but these positions fluctuate and intermingle and only atheism excludes all manner of religion.[7]

[6] The concluding sentence is in capitals: "SO GREAT IS THE POWER OF MORAL PRINCIPLES OVER OUR MINDS" (Diderot, p. 20; Basel edition, pp. 1f.).

[7] In a lengthy note, Shaftesbury shows the gamut of such combinations (Diderot, p. 27f.; Robertson, pp. 241f.), among which there figures even that of theism and atheism when chance is admitted together with God. Bayle's problem is presented in the original in these words: "What honesty or virtue is, considered by itself; and in what manner it is influenced by religion: How far religion necessarily implies virtue; and whether it be a true saying, That it is impossible

Shaftesbury devotes a special section to an examination of the tensions and conflicts there may be in men subject to vicious inclinations and passions against which, however, they struggle manfully out of disinterested love for virtue, refraining and holding themselves back from dishonest or cruel acts: this shows, notes Shaftesbury, that there lies hidden in the depths of man a good and virtuous principle that can dominate and master evil impulses. Thus, no nature and no individual man can be totally vicious; each must preserve some traces of virtue. Thus, for instance, a ruffian who out of a certain sense of "fidelity and honor . . . refuses to reveal his associates, and rather than betray them is content to endure torments and death, has certainly some principle of virtue, however he may misapply it." And Shaftesbury concludes that this is applicable to our present problem: even as it seems hard to say of any man that he is absolutely an atheist, so it appears just as hard to say of any man that he is absolutely corrupt or vicious, "there being few, even of the most horrid villains, who have not something of virtue in this imperfect sense".[8]

This parallelism between the moral plane and that of religious convictions must be the guiding thread to the revelation of the substance of Shaftesbury's thought: for Shaftesbury intensifies in the moral realm that claim for positive capacity inherent in the human individual which modern rationalism and especially Deism had first levied as against Protestant pessimism and the pessimism of Hobbes himself. In the human realm, there does not exist any good or evil purely and exclusively such that even good inclinations can degenerate. Thus, for example, religion in its turn, theism included, can go hand in hand with the gravest errors, right down to worshipping the devil or conceiving God as "a being arbitrary, violent, causing ill and ordaining to misery" which is the same thing as identifying him with the devil.

After assigning the proof of the existence of God to the realm of conclusions from finality and beauty in nature, Shaftesbury goes on to clarify the meaning and basis of the notions of justice and injustice and of the extreme variety of such notions in man, independently of the

---

for an atheist to be virtuous, or share any real degree of honesty or merit" (Basel edition, p. 2; Robertson, p. 238). For the background, Robertson refers the reader to: Charles Blount, *Oracles of Reason* (1695); J. Toland, *Christianity not Mysterious* (1696); Rev. Arthur Bury, *The Naked Gospel* (1690); also *The Account of the Growth of Deism in England* (1696); and Leslie, *Short and Easy Method with the Deists* (1697).

[8] *Inquiry. . . .*, I, III, 2; Diderot, pp. 70f. Bayle's thesis is explicit: "As to Atheism, it does not seem that it can directly have effect at all towards the setting up a false species of right or wrong. For, notwithstanding a man may, through custom, or by licentiousness of practice, favored by Atheism, come in time to lose much of his natural sense" (Basel edition, p. 36; Robertson, pp. 261f.).

religion he professes. His conclusion is that a man's religious posture does not as such have any direct effect upon morality: "Since neither deism, theism, atheism, or indeed even demonism, have any immediate and direct operative efficiency relative to the moral distinction of uprightness and injustice; since any belief, religious or irreligious, operates effectively upon this natural and primal idea only via the intervention and revolt of the other affections, we shall not speak of the effect of these hypotheses until the third section where we shall be examining the agreement or disagreement of the affections with the natural feeling by which we distinguish uprightness and injustice" (Diderot translation, p. 63f.).[9]

Meanwhile, in the second section, the entire situation is inverted: it is not religion as such that is able to make men good and to instill into them the sense of the upright and the unjust; rather it is the practice of these virtues that will bring man to conceive of a true and just God and to a religion worthy of God and man. Shaftesbury is quite outspoken here: "As the ill character of a God does injury to the affections of men, and disturbs and impairs the natural sense of right and wrong, so, on the other hand, nothing can more highly contribute to the fixing of right apprehensions and a sound judgment or sense of right and wrong, than to believe a God who is ever and on all accounts represented such as to be actually a true model and example of the most exact and highest goodness and worth. Such a view of divine providence and bounty extended to all and expressed in a constant good affection toward the whole, must of necessity engage us, within our compass and sphere, to act by a like principle and affection. And having once the good of our species or public in view, as our end or aim, 'tis impossible we should be misguided by any means to a false apprehension or sense of right or wrong."[10] And atheism is absolved forthwith; it is religion, rather, which is capable of doing great good or great evil depending on whether its morality is good or bad. Note well and carefully: it seems like a simple statement of obvious fact to say that "religion (according as the

[9] The original is more concise: "Neither *Theism* therefore, nor *Atheism,* nor *Daemonism,* nor any religious or irreligious Belief of any kind, being able to operate immediately or directly in this Case, but indirectly, by the intervention of opposite or of favourable Affections causally excited by any such Belief; we may consider of this Effect in our last Case, where we come to examine the Agreement or Disagreement of other Affections with this natural and moral one which relates to Right and Wrong." (*Inquiry* . . ., I, III, I; Basel edition, p. 35; Robertson, p. 261).

[10] And earlier: "In short: As it seems hard to pronounce of any Man, "That he is *absolutely an Atheist;*" so it appears altogether as hard to pronounce of any Man, "That he is *absolutely corrupt or vitious*", there being few, even of the horridest Villains, who have not something of *Virtue* in this imperfect sense" (*Inquiry* . . ., I, II, IV; Basel edition, p. 30; Robertson, p. 257).

kind may prove) is capable of doing great good or harm", did there not follow an explicit statement of a corresponding incapacity in atheism (which in this context amounts to an overt statement of the superiority of atheism over religion!): "and atheism nothing positive either way. For however it may be indirectly an occasion of men's losing a good and sufficient sense of right and wrong, it will not, merely as atheism, be the occasion of setting up a false species of it, which only false religion or fantastical opinion, derived commonly from superstition and credulity, is able to effect." [11] The entire situation has been stood on its head: of course atheism too can derail and corrupt morality but not *per se,* only *per accidens*; whereas with religion the reverse is true. And, be it noted well, the only value distinction Shaftesbury admits between religions is related to their moral principles.

In the third section, where a solution had been promised, the moral principles of good and evil, of justice and injustice and the like, are presented as something primordial and basic, because simple and immediate and therefore universally admitted, in contrast to the knowledge of God which has always given rise to obscurity and endless contentions and disputes.[12] But coming to the problem as to why men offer worship to God, Shaftesbury claims they do this for two motives: either because they consider God omnipotent and therefore impossible for anything or anyone to resist, or because they consider him to be good, just and merciful. At first glance, Shaftesbury skillfully points out, theism would

[11] Here is the whole text of the original: "But to speak of the Opinions relating to a DEITY; and what effect they may have in this place. As to *Atheism,* it does not seem that it can directly have any effect at all towards the setting up a false Species of Right or Wrong. For notwithstanding a Man may thro' Custom, or by licentiousness of Practice, favour'd by Atheism, come in time to lose much of his natural *moral Sense;* yet it does not seem that Atheism shou'd *of it-self* be the cause of any estimation or valuing of any thing as fair, noble, and deserving, which was the contrary. It can never, for instance, make it be thought that the being able to eat Man's Flesh, or commit Bestiality, *is good and excellent in it-self.* But this is certain, that by means of *corrupt Religion,* or SUPERSTITION, many things the most horridly unnatural and inhuman, come to be receiv'd as excellent, good, and laudable in *themselves.*" The conclusion leaves no doubt as to Shaftesbury's thought: "As to this second Case therefore: RELIGION (according as the kind may prove) is capable of doing great Good, or Harm; and ATHEISM nothing positive in either way. For however it may be indirectly an occasion of Mens losing a good and sufficient Sense of Right and Wrong; it will not, as *Atheism merely,* be the occasion of setting up a false Species of it; which only false Religion, or fantastical Opinion, deriv'd commonly from Superstition and Credulity, is able to effect" (*Inquiry . . .,* I, III, 2, Basel edition, pp. 36 and 40f.; Robertson, pp. 261f., 265.).

[12] At this point, Diderot remarks in a note, citing the Abbé de la Chambre's *Traité de la véritable religion,* that there have existed peoples and societies without God and without worship and indeed even without the name of the Supreme Being, for a long time after they had reached a certain degree of civilization and hence likewise of moral life (*op. cit.,* p. 72 note).

seem to have an obvious advantage: "For where the theistical belief is entire and perfect, there must be a steady opinion of the superintendency of a supreme Being, a witness and spectator of human life, and conscious of whatsoever is felt or acted in the universe; so that in the most perfect recess or deepest solitude there must be One still presumed remaining with us, whose presence singly must be of more moment than that of the most august assembly on earth. In such a presence, 'tis evident that as the shame of guilty actions must be the greatest of any, so must the honor be of well-doing, even under the unjust censure of a world. And in this case, 'tis very apparent how conducing a perfect theism must be to virtue, and how great deficiency there is in atheism." [13] But this seems to be an extreme case, for the discussion comes right back to the two positions already indicated and the solution admits of no doubt: anyone who stops at the idea of a God who is the omnipotent avenger of evil is worshipping him out of simple servile fear of punishment and/or out of a selfish hope of recompense or reward; and this is dishonorable both for God and for man.

The only relationship worthy of God and man is therefore that of virtue and virtuous living, and only that religion is deserving of respect which conceives the enjoyment to be had in a life to come as the enjoyment to be had from the practice of virtue: "In the case of religion, however, it must be considered that if by the hope of reward be understood the love and desire of virtuous enjoyment, or of the very practice and exercise of virtue in another life,[14] the expectation of hope of this

[13] The original text has a limpid summary of the content of the preceding section, which constitutes the central thesis of the *Inquiry:* "That it is possible for a Creature capable of using Reflection, to have a Liking or Dislike, of moral Actions, and consequently a Sense of Right and Wrong, before such time as he may have any settled Notion of a GOD, is what will hardly be question'd: it being a thing not expected, or any-way possible, that a Creature such as *Man,* arising from his Childhood, slowly and gradually, to several degrees of Reason and Reflection, shou'd, at the very first, be taken up with those Speculations, or more refin'd sort of Reflections, about the Subject of GOD'S Existence . . . Before the time, therefore, that a Creature can have any plain or positive Notion one way or other, concerning the Subject of a GOD, he may be suppos'd to have an Apprehension or Sense of *Right* and *Wrong,* and be possess'd of *Virtue* and *Vice* in different degrees; as we know by Experience of those, who having liv'd in such places, and in such a manner as never to have enter'd into any serious Thoughts of Religion, are nevertheless very different among themselves, as to their Characters of Honesty and Worth: some being naturally *modest, kind, friendly,* and consequently Lovers of *kind* and *friendly Actions;* others *proud, harsh, cruel,* and consequently inclin'd to admire rather the Acts of *Violence* and mere *Power*" (*Inquiry* . . ., I, III, 3, Basel edition, pp. 42f.; Robertson, p. 266).

[14] *Inquiry* . . ., P. III. sect. 3; Diderot, pp. 84f. There is here an insert in parenthesis in the Diderot translation "this is the case in Christianity" which is lacking in the original and is an addition of Diderot who had not as yet broken completely with Christianity at this time (1745), as had Shaftesbury.

kind is so far from being derogatory to virtue, that it is evidence of our loving it the more sincerely and for its own sake. Nor can this principle be justly called selfish; for if the love of virtue be not mere self-interest, the love and desire of life for virtue's sake cannot be esteemed so. But if the desire of life be only through the violence of that natural aversion to death, if it be through the love of something else than virtuous affection, or through the unwillingness of parting with something else than what is purely of this kind, then it is no longer any sign or token of real virtue."

And now comes an explicit exculpation of atheism stated in a fashion that represents an advance over both Hobbes and Bayle: "Now as to atheism: though it be plainly deficient and without remedy, in the case of ill judgment on the happiness of virtue, yet it is not, indeed, of necessity the cause of any such ill judgment. For without an absolute assent to any hypothesis of theism, the advantages of virtue may possibly be seen and owned, and a high opinion of it established in the mind. However, it must be confessed that the natural tendency of atheism is very different." [15] But Shaftesbury's reader cannot have failed to notice from the entire tenor of the preceding text that the overwhelming majority of religious cults seem to get man into an even worse pass: note throughout that the distinction, as in the case of Bayle, is based not on something objective (the distinction between true religion and false religions), but rather on something subjective (the practical conduct of individuals). It is exclusively on the basis of a proven superiority in this practical realm that theism can possess and claim a real superiority over atheism. It is indeed more likely that the atheist will lose his equilibrium under the buffeting of the ills and vicissitudes of life than that the theist will lose his balance under similar conditions.

The ensuing passage in Shaftesbury is a model of his "secret code": "There is no creature, according to what has been already proved, who must not of necessity be ill in some degree, by having any affection or aversion in a stronger degree than is suitable to his own private good, or that of the system to which he is joined. For in either case the affection is ill and vicious. Now if a rational creature has that degree of aversion which is requisite to arm him against any particular misfortune, and alarm him against the approach of any calamity, this is regular and well.

[15] *Ibid.,* pp. 87f. A note which Diderot adds to the text here throws an interesting light on his own spiritual state: "Atheism leaves integrity with no support. Worse still, it impels to depravity. Yet Hobbes was a good citizen, a good parent, a good friend, and he did not believe in God at all. Men are not consistent: they offend against a God whose existence they admit; they deny the existence of a God in whose eyes they have been deserving. And if there were any reason for astonishment it would be rather at a Christian living a bad life than at an atheist living a good life" (pp. 87f.). It is difficult to say whether these notes are genuine indications of an inner concern or whether they were inserted simply to evade the censor!

But if after the misfortune is happened, his aversion continues still, and his passion rather grows upon him, whilst he rages at the accident and exclaims against his private fortune or lot, this will be acknowledged both vicious in present and for the future, as it affects the temper, and disturbs that easy course of the affections on which virtue and goodness so much depend. On the other side, the patient enduring of the calamity and the bearing up of the mind under it, must be acknowledged immediately as virtuous and preservative of virtue. Now, according to the hypothesis of those who exclude a general mind, it must be confessed there can nothing happen in the course of things to deserve either our admiration and love or our anger and abhorrence. However, as there can be no satisfaction at the best in thinking upon what atoms and chance produce, so upon disastrous occasions, and under the circumstances of a calamitous and hard fortune, 'tis scarce possible to prevent a natural kind of abhorrence and spleen, which will be entertained and kept alive by the imagination of so perverse an order of things. But in another hypothesis (that of perfect theism) it is understood 'that whatever the order of the world produces, is in the main both just and good'. Therefore in the course of things in this world, whatever hardship of events may seem to force from any rational creature a hard censure of his private condition or lot, he may by reflection nevertheless come to have patience, and to acquiesce in it. Nor is this all. He may go further still in this reconciliation, and from the same principle may make the lot itself an object of his good affection, whilst he strives to maintain this generous fealty, and stands so well disposed towards the laws and government of his higher country." [16]

The Shaftesbury code has yielded its secret: everything depends on the love man evinces for the moral order which is not a matter of speculation but of sentiment, of feeling and of the sense of the harmony of the Universe, of the All: "This too is certain, that the admiration and love of order, harmony, and proportion, in whatever kind, is naturally improving to the temper, advantageous to social affection, and highly assistant to virtue, which is itself no other than the love of order and beauty in society." [17]

The end of the whole matter, then, is simply this: even without God, even were the order of the world to prove to be a chimera, even then the harmony of nature would suffice to impel man to virtue. Yet Shaftesbury

[16] *Inquiry* . . ., I, III, 3; *ibid.*, p. 91. In a long note appended to the text, Diderot insists on the necessary connection between the love of virtue and the expectation of a life to come: "To decry virtue—is it not to give aid and succor to atheism? To inflate the apparent disorders in nature—is it not to shake men's faith in the existence of God without strengthening belief in a life to come?" (p. 90, note).

[17] *Ibid.*, p. 93f.

elects to close this First Book on a positively theistic note: "But if, on the other side, the subject of this passion be really adequate and just (the hypothesis of theism being real, and not imaginary), then is the passion also just, and becomes absolutely due and requisite in every rational creature. Hence, we may determine justly the relation which virtue has to piety, the first being not complete but in the latter, since where the latter is wanting, there can neither be the same benignity, firmness, or constancy, the same good composure of the affections or uniformity of mind. And thus the perfection and height of virtue must be owing to the belief of a God." [18] But text and context remain, for all that, none the less explicit: they constitute an assertion of an anthropocentric view of reality, of the priority of ethics over religion and consequently of the sufficiency of the ethical element independently of the religious one; and finally, of the primordiality and hegemony of feeling, of man's fellow-feeling with his fellowmen and with all of nature, that natural sympathy which is the source and prime reason for every inclination and every action. And this last assertion constitutes the first principle of the whole of Shaftesbury's philosophy.[19]

Consummate artist that he was in the matter of wording, Shaftesbury seems to want to cover his trail at every step as he pursues his steady course to a basic position amounting simply to fidelity to nature, to its inclinations and instincts. The rule of life for man is taken from whatever contributes to the good of his nature and his species: moral laws corrupt him and religion often makes him cruel.

In the relevant passage, almost an aside in praise of the instincts of insect life and of primitive peoples, we find all that polemical violence which English Deism is to hand on to the naturalist school and the atheist Enlightenment thinkers on the continent: "In the other species of creatures around us there is found generally an exact proportionable-

[18] *Ibid.*, p. 95. In his dedication of his translation to his brother (an abbé who appears to have been a very pious man), Diderot speaks much more forthrightly: "Religion and morality are too closely linked for any clash of their basic principles to be feasible. No virtue without religion; no happiness without virtue: these are two truths you will find thoroughly elaborated in these reflections which I have been prompted to write as *useful to us both*" (p. 7). The same turn of phrase is repeated in the *Discours préliminaire* but it can be seriously doubted whether this jibes with the complex dialectical convolutions of the *Inquiry* or, above all, with its specific purpose.

[19] The central thesis recurs in the definitive statement: "Now as to Atheism: Though it be plainly deficient, and without remedy, in the case of ill judgment on the happiness of virtue: yet it is not, indeed, of necessity the cause of any such ill judgment. For without an absolute assent to any hypothesis of Theism, the advantages of virtue may possibly be seen and owned, and an high opinion of it established in the mind. However, it must be confessed, that the natural tendency of Atheism is very different" (*Inquiry* . . ., I, III, 3; Basel edition, p. 55; Robertson, p. 275).

ness, constancy and regularity in all their passions and affections; no failure in their care of the offspring or of the society to which they are united; no prostitution of themselves; no intemperance or excess in any kind. The small creatures, who live as it were in cities (as bees and ants), continue the same train and harmony of life, nor are they ever false to those affections which move them to operate toward their public good. Even those creatures of prey who live the farthest out of society, maintain, we see, such a conduct toward one another as is exactly suitable to the good of their own species. Whilst man, notwithstanding the assistance of religion and the direction of laws, is often found to live in less conformity with Nature, and by means of religion itself is often rendered the more barbarous and inhuman. Marks are set on men; distinctions formed; opinions decreed under the severest penalties; antipathies instilled, and aversions raised in men against the generality of their own species. So that 'tis hard to find in any region a human society which has human laws. No wonder if in such societies 'tis so hard to find a man who lives naturally and as a man." [20]

These principles, expounded with an elegance matching their radicalism, nurture like an underground river the development of modern thought: what Hume was to do for the theory of knowledge, Shaftesbury had done already a half century previously for the area of ethics; and the Humeian revolution would have been impossible without the theory expounded by Shaftesbury in the *Inquiry*. This theory manages with rare skill to maintain a precarious balance between the natural religion of Deism and the denial and rejection of all religion involved in atheism; and its apparent hesitancy has nothing to do with methodological groping or uncertainty in the area of principles. What matters is the provision for man of the possibility of an integral unfolding of his nature, which is the sole and exclusive principle and term of his action and the source of his true happiness. God and religion can also enter into this whole context provided they come down from their throne and adapt themselves to human nature: "We may say of [entire or integral affection as opposed to partial or narrow affection] with justice that it carries with it a consciousness of merited love and approbation from all society, from all intelligent creatures, and from whatever is original to all other intelligence. And if there be in Nature any such original, we may add that the satisfaction that attends entire affection is full and noble in

[20] *Inquiry* . . ., II, I, 2; Diderot, pp. 115f. In a note Diderot recalls the bloody battles among the Arabic theologians occasioned by the disputes on the divine attributes and refers to the battles raging in England: obviously a thrust intended to hit close to home! (Shaftesbury recurs to the business of the wars of religion in *Miscellaneous Reflections,* II, 1 and 2; *Characteristics* . . ., ed. Robertson, Vol. II, pp. 173ff.).

proportion to its final object, which contains all perfection, according to the sense of theism above noted. For this, as has been shown, is the result of virtue. And to have this entire affection or integrity of mind is to live according to Nature, and the dictates and rules of supreme wisdom. This is morality, justice, piety and natural religion."[21]

Thus, far from being shut out, religion is expressly welcomed in, but on condition that it be not "of the dismal or fearful sort" but rather "of the pleasant and cheerful sort", that it make no appeal to anything transcending human nature, that it be quite other than it has become in the hands of its ministers in whose hands the remedy has become worse than the disease; finally, an esthetic religion without any duties or transcendent sanctions.[22] The sanction will be exclusively an immanent one: the distaste that must be provoked by unjust actions or behavior is prompted solely by the fact that such behavior is odious and harmful to oneself and to others—this reference to society, to be made later by Kant in transcendental form, can be designated as taking, in Shaftesbury, the place of the theological basis of morality. But Shaftesbury is still quite cautious and circumspect in his expression: "And thus religious conscience supposes moral or natural conscience. And though the former be understood to carry with it the fear of divine punishment, it has its force however from the apprehended moral deformity and odiousness of any act with respect purely to the divine Presence, and the natural veneration due to such a supposed being. For in such a presence the shame of villainy or vice must have its force, independently on that further apprehension of the magisterial capacity of such a being, and his dispensation of particular rewards or punishments in a future state."[23]

Shaftesbury had never hitherto made mention of this presence of the Supreme Being to man in his internal forum, only of man's presence to his fellowmen. But this supreme Being has all the appearance of being that same universal human Reason to which each and every individual ought to submit himself in his thinking and action, in line with the new course of thought originated by the *cogito*. It is true of course that Shaftesbury does not say this explicitly here; but this presence no less

[21] *Inquiry* . . ., II, III, 1; Diderot p. 132.

[22] "Beauty and harmonious order is the basis of his theism. It is upon beauty, which pleases all men everywhere as becoming, that there is grounded the morally good; that 'enthusiasm' which is the vizualization of the divinely True, Good and Beautiful is the common psychological root of art, religion and ethics, indeed of all that greatness of soul displayed by man in the verve with which he jousts with the chores of everyday living" (G. C. B. Punjer, *Geschichte der Christlichen Religionsphilosophie seit der Reformation,* Vol. I [Braunschweig, 1880]; p. 244).

[23] *Inquiry* . . ., II, II, 1; Diderot, p. 140. For an anticipatory coupling of Shaftesbury with Kant, cf. G. Gizycky, *Die Philosophie Shaftesbury's* (Leipzig and Heidelberg, 1876), pp. 46ff.

truly makes the impression of a frill and an afterthought rather than that of a genuine influence, when Shaftesbury goes so far as to assert the right of a man to renounce life itself. This amounts to a justification of indirect suicide, in cases where life has become insupportable to the individual himself or to others.[24] Thus man's horizon is bounded by his own being, his own life, and the sole rule of life is the feeling for this life and its conformity with the good of his fellowmen: even here, in the matter of the relation of the private to the common or public good, Shaftesbury still walks the tightrope with great skill, for he indicates that the true and genuine private good of the individual ought to coincide with the common or public good and it is precisely the task and assignment of virtue and merit in the good man to effect this coincidence.

Moreover such is the explicit conclusion of the Essay itself, where virtue is conceived in terms of harmony and beauty, inasmuch as it actualizes the conformity of man with the Whole, with society and with the entire universe, in a world in a state of perfect reconciliation with its eternal immanent law: "Thus the wisdom of what rules, and is first and chief in Nature, has made it to be according to the private interest and good of every one to work toward the general good, which if a creature ceases to promote, is actually so far wanting to himself, and ceases to promote his own happiness and welfare. He is on this account directly his own enemy, nor can he any otherwise be good or useful to himself than as he continues good to society, and to that whole of which he is himself a part. So that virtue, which of all excellences and beauties is the chief and most amiable; that which is the prop and ornament of human affairs; which upholds communities, maintains union, friendship, and correspondence amongst men; that by which countries, as well as private families, flourish and are happy, and for want of which everything comely, conspicuous, great, and worthy, must perish and go to ruin; that single

[24] "That life is sometimes a calamity is a fact generally admitted. When a mortal is brought so low by it as to harbor a frank desire for death, it is a great harshness to him to command him to go on living. In such eventualities, although religion and reason restrain the arm and do not permit such a one to make an end of his ills by putting an end to his days, yet if some honorable and plausible occasion of perishing does present itself, it can be embraced without scruple. It is in such circumstances that the relatives and friends rightly rejoice over the death of a person who was dear to them, even though that person may have been pusillanimous enough to eschew the danger and to protract his evil hour as long as in him lay" (*Inquiry* . . ., II, II, 2; Diderot pp. 160f.). This passage is of a disconcerting brutality and Diderot's comment is still more astonishing, for he makes a theological reference which is strange, to say the least, if indeed not openly blasphemous: "Aside from all those exasperating catastrophes that make life insupportable, the love of God produces the same effect, for St. Paul said: *I desire to be dissolved and to be with Christ.* And if Judas the Apostle had contented himself with merely desiring death after his betrayal of his master, he would have been simply pronouncing upon himself the judgment that Jesus Christ had already passed upon him" (*ibid.*, p. 160 note).

quality, thus beneficial to all society, and to mankind in general, is found equally a happiness and good to each creature in particular, and is that by which alone man can be happy, and without which he must be miserable. And thus virtue is the good, and vice the ill of everyone." [25]

This Platonic notion of the identity of the good and the beautiful, which Shaftesbury had in all probability drawn from the Cambridge Platonists, was converted by him into something much more than a mere dry formalistic principle of abstract contemplation. It metamorphosed under his creative touch into the active dynamic notion of the conscience that molds itself via its own ideals. And so it represents the synthesis of the principle of the Platonic "form" and the new principle of conscience and experience pushed to its logical extreme and articulated in its most drastic sense, anticipating by almost two centuries the view of that *Lebensphilosophie* which so exercised such a great number of modern philosophers in the early 20th century.

Shaftesbury's later writings (*The Moralists, A Rhapsody*) represent a development and elaboration of the conclusion of the *Inquiry*. The argument proceeds from the indubitable fact that there exists a natural beauty of figures which even the eye of an infant perceives as soon as it begins to see objects at all [26] and the equally indubitable fact that this beauty is simply the harmony of proportions in the object itself, even the simplest object like a circle, a cube or a painted surface. Shaftesbury goes on to ask if there must not be assumed to be as natural a beauty in *actions?* No sooner has the eye been exposed to figures or the ear to sounds, than the beautiful forthwith imposes itself as an irresistible reality, and grace and harmony are at once recognized and acknowledged as such. No sooner are actions inspected, no sooner are the human affections and passions discerned (and most of them are so contradistinguished as soon as they are felt at all), than an *inner eye* distinguishes and sees the beautiful and the harmonious, the amiable and the admirable, as opposed to what is deformed, odious and despicable. Now, if these distinctions have their foundation in nature, must we not say that the act of distinguishing between them is likewise natural *and nothing more?* [27]

[25] Basel edition, pp. 144ff.; Robertson, p. 338.

[26] Shaftesbury himself refers the reader to the *Inquiry* (I, II, 3) for the substantiation of this principle.

[27] "Is there then, said he, a natural Beauty of *Figures?* and is there not as natural a one of ACTIONS? No sooner the Eye opens upon *Figures*, the Ear to Sounds, than straight *the* Beautiful results, and *Grace* and *Harmony* are known and acknowledg'd. No sooner are ACTIONS view'd, no sooner the human *Affections* and *Passions* discern'd (and they are most of them as soon discern'd as felt) than straight *an inward Eye* distinguishes, and sees *the Fair* and *Shapely*, the *Amiable* and *Admirable*, apart from *the Deform'd, the Foul, the Odious*, or *the Despicable*. How is it possible therefore not to own, 'That as these *Distinctions*

An immediate objection arises: Why is it that men give themselves up to continual disputations about moral matters, with every assertion being contradicted or rejected almost as soon as it is made, if the judgment on the goodness or badness of actions is so immediate and infallible? Shaftesbury's reply is dialectical rather than direct; he points up the transcendental aspect of the problem and distinguishes it from the immediate or empirical aspect. What is important, notes Shaftesbury, is to admit that the basic judgment or discrimination of good and evil, like that of the beautiful and the ugly, is primordial by nature and therefore a constant presupposition of all empirical judgments and events in this area.

Although men behave differently in concrete cases, pursues Shaftesbury, the fact of a primordial judgment is universally admitted. And, as far as that goes, there is not always agreement even in the judgment, in concrete cases, on other sorts of *beauty*. There are disputes and disagreements about which specific building (*"Pile"*) is the most beautiful, which shape or face is the loveliest; but what is beyond dispute (and is admitted without argument) is that there *is* a beauty proper to each group of entities. There is no need for this to be *taught* nor learned by anyone; it is simply *admitted* (*"Confessed"*) by all. *Everyone* is in possession of the *standard,* the *rule,* the *measure.* It is simply in the application of that standard to concrete cases that there arise differences of opinion. Ignorance gets the upper hand, passions and personal interests create disturbances. Nor can it happen otherwise in everyday life, seeing that what interests and engages men as *good* is judged to be different from what they admire and praise as *honest.* But for those who have attained maturity of mind, concludes Shaftesbury, the good and the honest are identical.[28]

---

have their Foundation *in Nature,* the Discernment itself is *natural,* and from NATURE alone?' " (*The Moralists* III, 2; *Characteristics. . .,* Basel edition, Vol. II, pp. 343f.; Robertson II. p. 137). Hence, a radical naturalism and an unhesitating Pelagian optimism, with ethics promoted to a status entirely autonomous and independent of religion: "It was already indicated that Shaftesbury's ethic had been freed, for all practical purposes, from any link with religion. Indeed, no more drastic contrast can be imagined than that between the joyful optimism of Shaftesbury and the gloomy anthropology which forms the basis of the churchly ethical position; for Shaftesbury evinces a boundless trust in the innate goodness of man, the perfection of his structuring and his natural predisposition to moral behavior, whereas the churchly view despairs entirely of man and his powers, sees in human nature nothing but weakness, fecklessness and corruption and has entirely abandoned any hope of making man behave as he ought without supernatural aid and extraordinary means" (F. Jodl, *Geschichte der Ethik in der neueren Philosophie,* Vol. I [Stuttgart, 1882], p. 179).

[28] In view of the importance of this passage, we here cite also the original: "Even by this then, reply'd he, it appears there is Fitness and Decency in Actions; since the *Fit* and *Decent* is in this Controversy ever presuppos'd: And whilst Men

Shaftesbury stops at this point: the discernment of good and evil, like that of the beautiful and the ugly, is simply a question of feeling and taste, a *sui generis* function of a transcendental experience which it is man's task to explicitate and apply to the concrete cases of everyday life. It may well be that this theory of *natural discernment* as a primordial feeling is the first nucleus of the Humeian notion of *feeling* [29] which is to impel Kant in his formulation of his theory of the *a priori*. If English philosophy must be said to have had its beginnings in Bacon, Hobbes and Locke, it must equally be admitted to have attained its specific and unmistakable originality in Shaftesbury, chief of the *Moralists*: he was the first to teach that a man preparing to make a judgment ought not to issue forth out of himself to apply external demands and standards, but rather has only to go into himself and penetrate more deeply into himself, there and there alone to grasp an impulse coexistent with the appearance of the object itself and indeed rendering possible the appearance of beauty or propriety in precisely that form and quality. Shaftesbury was the one to grasp and express the claim (undoubtedly a basically legitimate one) that the esthetic or ethical judgment that man is prompted or inclined to pass on things has its essential nucleus (and therefore the basis and motivating force of its power to cause man to strive toward such things) not so much in the things themselves as in man himself, in the secret dynamism of his own subjective self which burgeons forth and reaches out toward the real, not because of the attractive aspect of the real in itself, but rather in order to actualize the seeker himself, to fill up his inner void and to slake his thirst for justice and beauty.

---

are at odds about the Subjects, the Thing itself is universally agreed. For neither is there agreement in Judgments about other *Beautys*. It is controverted 'Which is the finest *Pile*, the loveliest *Shape of Face*': But without controversy, 'tis allow'd 'There is a BEAUTY of *each* kind'. This no one goes about to *teach:* nor is it *learnt* by any; but *confess'd* by All. All own the *Standard, Rule,* and *Measure:* But in applying it to Things, Disorder arises, Ignorance prevails, Interest and Passion breed Disturbance. Nor can it otherwise happen in the Affairs of Life, whilst that which interests and engages Men as *Good,* is thought different from that which they admire and praise as *Honest*. But with us, PHILOCLES! it is better settled; since for our parts, we have already decreed, 'That *Beauty* and *Good* are still the same'" (*The Moralists . . .,* III, 2; Basel edition, p. 344; Robertson, pp. 137f.).

29 It was Hume himself who numbered Shaftesbury among those philosophers who had begun, in England, in the wake of Bacon, to set man's knowledge on new foundations (cf. *Treatise on Human Nature,* Introduction; ed. Selby-Bigge [Oxford, 1928], p. XXI, note). Mentioned together with Shaftesbury are Locke, Mandeville, Hutcheson, Butler and others. Apart from Locke, who had developed a rationalist ethic, the other authors mentioned agree with Shaftesbury, especially in founding ethics on feeling or spiritual taste (cf. N. K. Smith, *The Philosophy of David Hume* [London, 1941], pp. 18f.).

I do not find evidence of Shaftesbury having ever been expressly charged with atheism:[30] Hobbes might have been ready to classify Shaftesbury among the atheists *by consequence,* if for no other reason than to defend himself from harsh criticisms! We have seen substantially what place Shaftesbury assigns to religion and religious knowledge, i.e., one of total subordination to ethics which becomes the source and standard of every value judgment and discernment. In this sense, Shaftesbury can be said to have "resolved" (or disintegrated) religion into ethics; now this is equivalent to a conversion of transcendence into immanence; and this in turn certainly amounts to atheism pure and simple. For Shaftesbury, all positive religions without distinction are sources of all manner of errors and evils, as we have seen; he took up and continued the Spinozan critique of Sacred Scripture, defending the Deists, his predecessors in this matter. He often readily takes up the defense of the freelivers and freethinkers, the latitudinarians and their kind, against the attacks of the theologians; he praises the breadth of vision of the men under attack and their ample use of intelligence. And Shaftesbury launches an all-out counter-attack on the theologians who are so ready to condemn: "Fain would they [the theologians] confound licentiousness in morals with liberty in thought and action, and make the libertine, who has the least mastery of himself, resemble his direct opposite. For such indeed is the man of resolute purpose and immovable adherence to reason against everything which passion, prepossession, craft or fashion can advance in favor of aught else. But here, it seems, the grievance lies. 'Tis thought dangerous for us to be over-rational or too much masters of ourselves in what we draw by just conclusions from reason only. Seldom therefore do these expositors fail of bringing the thought of liberty into disgrace. Even at the expense of virtue and of that very idea of goodness on which they build the mysteries of their profitable science, they derogate from morals and reverse all true philosophy, they refine on selfishness and explode generosity, promote a slavish obedience in the room of voluntary duty and free service, exalt blind ignorance for devotion, recommend low thought, decry reason, extol voluptuousness, wilfulness, vindicativeness, arbitrariness, vain

[30] If one abstracts from Berkeley's critique about which we shall be speaking shortly. This is likewise the judgment of Stephen, at the conclusion of his analysis of the *Inquiry concerning Virtue* which we have analyzed in the interpretative translation of Diderot: "A belief in God, though hardly in the christian, any more than in the jewish God, is an essential part of his system. The belief in justice must, as he urges, precede a belief in a just God" (*History of English Thought in Eighteenth Century,* Vol. I, p. 25). Shaftesbury's most recent editor insists on the dependence of Shaftesbury's thought "as regards its bases" on Spinoza rather than on Leibniz as some have alleged (John M. Robertson, *Introduction* to his edition of the *Characteristics . . .,* Vol. I, p. XXXIf.).

glory, ane even deify those weak passions which are the disgrace rather than ornament of human nature." [31]

And so we see that Shaftesbury does acquit atheism of the charges levelled by the theolgians; and, whatever his formal declarations of allegiance, he does it with no less zeal than Bayle. And then there is also the matter of the consistently logical conclusion to be drawn from Shaftesbury's stand: if reason must, on principle, justify itself at the tribunal of morality, if morality constitutes the basic and essential element of conscience and religion is therefore true to the extent that it comes down simply to morality, to the exclusion of worship, prayer and sacrifice, this is a clear indication that morality and man as a moral being can subsist and survive without religion at all and that religion is an *αδιάφορον* (a matter of indifference) as Kierkegaard would say.

Dilthey [32] calls Shaftesbury a pantheist because of his ties with Neoplatonism and the naturalistic philosophy of the Renaissance and especially Giordano Bruno; many others have, with more obvious justification, called him a Deist; he has even been acquitted on all counts and presented as a vigorous and convinced theist.[33] It is our opinion that

[31] *Miscellaneous Reflections,* V, 3.—It is also the opinion of L. Bandini in his *Shaftesbury,* pp. 34f. (an excellent study in many respects) that the deepest significance of Shaftesbury's entire inquiry, a significance which makes it most valuable in the modern history of the problem of ethics, lies precisely in this total disengagement of morality from religion. And still earlier Jodl had written: "The ethical has now no longer any need of the religious in order to attain to its perfection or indeed, as had been the case before, even to be able to cross the threshold of existence; rather everything religious now has to be legitimized and justified in function of its agreement with the natural standard of the ethical" (*Geschichte der Ethik,* Vol. I, p. 180).

[32] As also by: O. Lempp, *Das Problem der Theodicee in der Philosophie und Literatur des 18. Jahrhunderts bis auf Kant und Schiller* (Leipzig, 1910), pp. 99f. In Italy: by G. Limentani, *La morale della simpatia* (Genoa, 1914). Cf. also the remarks of I. Osske, in *Ganzheit, Unendlichkeit und Form, Studien zu Shaftesburys Naturbegriff* (Berlin, 1930), pp. 193f.

[33] A strongly-worded passage in the *Letters to a Student at the University* (Letter VI) of 1709 affords full confirmation of our interpretation of Shaftesbury as at bottom a rationalist: "Let it be your chief endeavour to make acquaintance with what is good; that by seeing perfectly, by the help of reason, what good is, and what ill, you may prove whether that which is from revelation, be not perfectly good, and conformable to this standard. For if so, the very end of the gospels proves its truth. And that which to the vulgar is only knowable by miracles, and teachable by positive precepts and commands, to the wise and virtuous, is demonstrable by the nature of the things" (*Characteristics,* Basel edition, Vol. I, p. 339). Thus: 1. it is the court of reason that decides on the truth of Revelation. —2. the highest and thus definitive form of conviction is not that which comes from Revelation or miracles (reserved to "the vulgar"), but solely that which comes from reason. There are other texts, should that one not suffice, to clarify Shaftesbury's attitude and stance which Berkeley, in our opinion, was able to grasp in its true light (cf. J. Wild, *George Berkeley,* A Study of his Life and Philosophy [Cambridge, 1936], pp. 344ff.).

Shaftesbury—at least at the time when he wrote the *Inquiry*—was determined to be taken for an out-and-out theist; but that he no less certainly shifted position over the years, to come closer and closer to the position of the Freethinkers (despite some criticisms of Deism on peripheral points, a critique probably provoked by Shaftesbury's resentment of Toland); and that it is no mere accident that his works have been held to belong among the classics of Masonic writing: It is probable that his disciples of the Scottish school, especially Hutcheson and Butler,[34] inclined to be Deists in this dubious sense of the word. In any case, our main concern in these investigations and interpretations is to seize upon the theories in their nascent state and in the dynamic flux of their crucial components; and from this point of view, Shaftesbury's position is indisputably of prime importance and exceeds in radicalism of outlook and skillful subtlety of exposition that of any other English philosopher with the exception of Hume who precisely closes that whole age of thought to which Shaftesbury, more than anyone else, gave an identifiable character which still remains, despite all the intervening vicissitudes, the foundation of the thought of English-speaking philosophers.

The ambiguity of Shaftesbury's thought and its consequent capacity to function as catalyst of disintegration are attested by the dual and diametrically opposed streams of thought that take their inspiration from it, not only among the English-speaking thinkers but in France and Germany as well: he was certainly bolder and more radical than any Deist who had preceded him, bolder even than Toland or any of his contemporaries. Historians of philosophy in our own day hold that the ambiguity of Shaftesbury's thought derives from the fact that it is a compromise between Platonism and Aristotelianism and see the two elements diverging in 18th-century French thought into the Deism of Voltaire and Rousseau on the one hand and the atheism of Diderot and eventually d'Holbach on the other. [35]

[34] Hutcheson seems most certainly to have been at pains to free himself from the ambiguity in which Shaftesbury's position floundered; but this ambiguity has more theoretical bite and consistency. In any case, it is important to stress the fact that, as opposed to Shaftesbury, Hutcheson sees no clash between goodness and justice in God, esteeming rather, in accord with traditional (especially Thomistic) theology, that God's justice is part of his benevolence: "The Justice of the DEITY is only a Conception of his universal impartial Benevolence, as it shall influence him, if he gives any laws, to attemper them to the universal Good, and inforce them with the most effectual Sanctions of Rewards and Punishments" (Hutcheson, *An Inquiry concerning Moral Good and Evil,* Sect. VII, § 10 [London, 1738]; *British Moralists,* Vol. I, p. 174).

[35] This is the assumption of the brilliant thesis of D. B. Schlegel, *Shaftesbury and the French Deists* (Chapel Hill: Univ. of North Carolina Studies, 1956): "Shaftesbury's deism could, as in the case of Rousseau, lead a disciple to an enthusiastic worship of the Supreme Being. On the other hand, it might lead a

Voltaire says that the best elements of Pope's famous *Essay on Man* are to be found in Shaftesbury: "Pope's *Essay on Man* seems to me to be the finest didactic poem, the most valuable and the most sublime ever written in any language. It is true that the pith of it is to be found *in toto* in Lord Shaftesbury's *Characteristics;* and I do not know why Mr. Pope gives exclusive credit to Mr. de Bolingbroke without saying a word about the famous Shaftesbury, pupil of Locke." [36] We have seen how Shaftesbury served to launch Diderot's writing career and Diderot certainly ended up an atheist; he seems also to have collaborated directly in the editing of some sections of the d'Holbach *Système de la Nature,* and Shaftesbury's writings were the favorite reference work of the d'Holbach set. Schlegel notes that d'Holbach agreed with Shaftesbury that an atheist can in point of fact be more moral than a Christian.[37] Both Voltaire and Rousseau and indeed Hume himself kept away from the "d'Holbach clique". This may have been because they were persuaded that reason could not subsist without a supreme Principle; it may also have been because of a certain diffidence of extremes, a diffidence they shared with Shaftesbury. But their religion, having broken with all concrete historical faiths and with all allegiance to the living

---

follower to no God at all." (*Foreword*). Later in the same work, Schlegel concludes: "Shaftesbury's unorthodoxy therefore offered to the atheists a precedent for their point of view, just as his enthusiasm provided Rousseau with a justification for a reaction in the opposite direction, for the *Characteristics* of Shaftesbury contain germs of thought that were capable of many different types of development. Shaftesbury himself was governed by both reason and enthusiasm; he was both orthodox and liberal, for deism is actually a compromise between atheism and revealed religion; he was both Platonic and Aristotelian" (p. 79). Nor has this ambiguity been resolved by the recent publication of the collection of Shaftesbury's thoughts (*The Life, Unpublished Letters and Philosophical Regimen of Anthony Earl of Shaftesbury,* ed. Benjamin Rand [New York and London, 1900]). The proof of the existence of God is taken from the order and beauty of nature and is basically Stoic in inspiration (redolent of Marcus Aurelius and Epictetus: cf. pp. 13, 22.—On p. 34, Shaftesbury emerges as an Italophile, citing as supreme examples of beauty the Pantheon, St. Peter's, the works of Raphael, Corelli, etc.). On pp. 39ff., Shaftesbury considerably anticipates Jacobi and Kant in using the word "faith" to express this certainty about the deity.

[36] Voltaire, *Lettres philosophiques,* Letter XXII: ed. F. A. Taylor (Oxford, 1961), pp. 82ff.

[37] D. B. Schlegel, *op. cit.,* p. 80. On the preceding page, he writes: "*Although* d'Holbach never actually mentions Shaftesbury by name in the text itself of the *Système de la Nature,* his ethics, polemics, Biblical criticism, and at some points, paradoxically enough, his cosmology, are much like that of the Englishman, . . . Although Shaftesbury's philosophy is skewed and distorted almost to the point of ludicrousness by the change of direction, yet the basic substance of his thought remains strangely intact" (p. 79). The first remark is not entirely accurate, for d'Holbach quotes Shaftesbury expressly at least twice in the *Système de la Nature,* in notes (cf. 2nd ed. [London, 1774], Part II, pp. 251 and 394).

God conceived as being at man's side in times of joy and times of sorrow, evaporated, like Shaftesbury's religion, into a worship of reason's logic and the harmony of the universe,[38] a harmony exposed to constant contradiction by the recurrent woes and the continual mischances of everyday life.

[38] Söderblom considers among the most important factors in the consolidation of Deism in France the reports of the Jesuit missionaries on Confucius and the Chinese sages, all of whom were Deists or radical atheists, and perfect gentlemen (cf. N. Söderblom, *Natürliche Theologie und allgemeine Religionsgeschichte* [Stockholm-Leipzig, 1913], especially pp. 38ff., 58ff.). Even Bayle in his day often buttressed his arguments by appeal to these thinkers.

4

Deism Displayed and Flayed (Locke, Toland, Berkeley)

A Deist still more vigorous and outspoken in discrediting revealed religion was John Toland (1670-1722), who called his major work, significantly enough, *Christianity not Mysterious* (London, 1696).[1] In this work, the subtle tactic of denial of religion proceeds via a complex and skillful process of assertions apparently affirming the need for religion while in fact demolishing all religion. Toland's end product is analogous to Cherbury's but whereas Cherbury had operated in the area of natural religion, Toland initiates a direct examination of Christianity in its doctrinal and general theoretical aspects.

Toland's second-rate philosophical analysis had been preceded, less than a year before, by Locke's *Reasonableness of Christianity* (London, 1695).[2] Locke argues along quite the same lines as Toland; but Locke's work seems to have been inspired by a genuine devotion to Christianity, to judge from the Preface. Locke gives a moderate expression to the hermeneutical principle of Deism, a distrust of the "systems" of theology which Locke claims to undercut by a simple and direct recourse to that Sacred Scripture to which the theologians themselves claim always to be appealing.[3] How, one might ask, can the individual resolve, by

[1] I have consulted the work in German translation, L. von Zscharnack, *John Toland's Christianity not Mysterious* (*Christentum ohne Geheimnis*) *1696*, tr. W. Lunde, Studien zur Geschichte des neueren Protestantismus, 3 (Giessen, 1908).

[2] Cf. *The Works of John Locke, A New Edition Corrected,* (London, 1823; reprinted Aalen 1963), Vol. VII. I also have at hand the French translation of M. Coste, *Le Christianisme raisonnable,* tel qu'il nous est représenté dans l'Ecriture Sainte (Amsterdam: chez Zacharie Chatelain, 1740 [4]). In a prefatory note serving as introduction, the translator states that he is not in agreement with Locke in some of what he says in the book. Locke's works (translated by E. Winckler) form Vol. 4 of the series mentioned above in Footnote 1 to this section. For a recent outline, updating the discussion, cf. C. A. Viano, *John Locke, dal razionalismo all'illuminismo* (Turin, 1960), pp. 311ff.

[3] "The little satisfaction and consistency that is to be found in most of the systems of divinity I have met with, made me betake myself to the sole reading of the Scriptures (to which they all appeal) for understanding the Christian Religion" (*The Reasonableness of Christianity,* p. 3).

personal recourse to Scripture alone, the tremendous problem of truth and salvation, when each and every individual is always limited to his own restricted point of view in thought and in practice? This is bound to result in a divergent interpretation of the Gospel; and hence we see that paradox that is at the same time a real and historically proven and attested fact, namely, the coincidence and intimate nexus between the Protestant principle of "Scripture alone" and the inception of rationalism (biblical and dogmatic) and the advent of Deism. Yet, Locke's Deism can still be called a "Deism of the right": in his *Reasonableness of Christianity,* he accepts and proves from Sacred Scripture that Christ claimed to be the Messiah, that he rose from the dead for man's salvation and that man is saved by faith in Christ and by good works.[4]

Locke prunes his "reasonable Christianity" down to two truths: (1) that there is a God, and (2) that Jesus Christ is the Messiah. The first truth embraces the whole of natural religion, while the second expresses the substance of revealed religion. Man can ascend to God by reason alone and can give worship to God in his own life simply by following the natural law; he can thus obtain God's pardon for his faults. This, claims Locke, is in perfect accord with the Gospel; but this is not enough. Although the works of nature or any part thereof would suffice to show that there does exist a God, nonetheless, notes Locke, men in part likewise to a derailment into superstition. Even those who succeeded in seeing this supreme Being. This failure has been due in part to an excessive attachment to sensible goods, in part to supine indifference, in part likewise to a derailment into superstition. Even those who succeeded by the use of their reason in finding the true God, hid this truth out of fear of reprisals on the part of the priests of the superstitious cults: only in the Jewish religion was there preserved the unalloyed idea of natural religion.

The coming of Jesus Christ dissipated all doubts and shadows and manifested the knowledge of the one true God, creator of all things, showing all men the true life of virtue after which philosophers prior to Christ had striven in vain. Hence, Locke concludes: "He was sent by God; his miracles show it; and the authority of God in his precepts cannot be questioned."[5] Thus Christ's mission, as Messiah sent by the Father, is reduced simply to that of teaching a natural religion and ethic, of restoring both to their primordial purity. This is substantially the

[4] This has given Locke a bad press among the Marxists, who neglect entirely the *Reasonableness of Christianity,* sticking exclusively to the sense-perceptionism of *An Essay concerning Human Understanding* and showing that materialism necessarily follows from this sense-perceptionism, etc. (cf. *Geschichte der Philosophie,* Vol. I, pp. 398ff.).

[5] *The Reasonableness of Christianity,* p. 143.

same notion that will be found later in Kant[6] and in 18th-century Enlightenment theology. The other truths, like the Trinity, the divinity of Jesus Christ, etc., which have been added to these two fundamental articles (existence of God; Christ as Messiah) are, as presented by theology, the work of man and not absolutely necessary to salvation. There may be other truths in Scripture besides these two; but since there is no agreement among the theologians on their interpretation, they are not binding and can thus be left out of account without incurring any guilt of sin.[7] We have here, then, a "Christianity of reason" resting solely on the existence of God and on a life to come.

Locke's position in regard to Christianity was indeed ambiguous: on the one hand, he claimed to be defending the religion and moral personality of Christ against the critique of the libertarians; but on the other hand he admitted only the rational elements in Christianity, rejecting implicitly but nonetheless categorically the specific and typical elements of Christianity as a historical revealed religion. For this reason Locke is considered one of the founders of Deism.[8] It has shown itself, in the dynamic of modern thought, to be one of the great tributaries of the torrent of modern atheism. Locke's theory of knowledge exercised a no less drastic influence in molding the Enlightenment atheism, and this influence was one which was more germane to Locke's entire system of thought: Marx claims that Locke deserves the credit for having substantiated Bacon's materialism. Even as Hobbes had swept away the *theistic* prejudices of Baconian materialism, later English Deists and sense-perceptionists such as Collins, Dodwell, Coward, Hartley, Priestley and the rest, were to sweep away the last *theological* restrictions adhering to Locke's sense-perceptionism.[9]

Starting with Bacon, from the principle that all our knowledge comes from experience, Locke specifies that experience comes from the sensible world, from sensations: refuting Aristotelian abstraction of the intel-

[6] Cf. Kant, *Die Religion innerhalb der Grenzen der reinen Vernunft,* esp. Viertes Stück, I Theil; Reclam., pp. 161ff.

[7] *The Reasonableness of Christianity,* p. 156.

[8] By Soviet historians as well (cf. *Geschichte der Philosophie,* Vol. I, p. 399). The theologian Limborch declares himself in agreement with Locke and sketches a telling picture of the muddle of theology in that age: "It is a crime that he should be considered by the systematic doctors to merit exposure to the infamous abuse of accusations of Socinianism and Atheism: as if anyone refusing to worship according to human tenet is to be considered by that very fact to be forswearing religion altogether" (*Some Familiar Letters between Mr. Locke and Several of his Friends* [London, 1708], p. 381—original in Latin).

[9] Cf. K. Marx, *Die heilige Familie,* p. 136. Cf. also the Marx-Engels treatment of the relations between ideology and economy and of the influence of Locke and English sense-perceptionism on 18th century French materialism, in *Deutsche Ideologie,* III, M.E.G.A., Abt. I, Vol. 3, pp. 394ff.

ligible (for Aristotle, though asserting the senses to be the prime source of knowledge, had nevertheless posited an intellect "separate" from the body as superior to the senses and had alleged this intellect to have as object the universal, in its turn "separate" from the empirical individuality of the contents of experience), Locke reduces intelligence to a mere "reflection on sense data" and accepts the nominalist thesis on universals.[10] For Locke, therefore, universality is not a new and positive step in knowledge; it is simply an accidental aspect of knowing, and consists merely in the fact of the particular ideas from which it originates, being such as to render possible the correspondence of more than one single particular thing to those ideas and the representation of more than one single particular thing by them. This theory of abstraction amounts to a total eradication of any universal structure of being or thought and more precisely the denial of any originality to thought.

For Locke this abstraction simply results in the ideas taken from particular beings becoming representative in general of all the individuals of the same species and their names becoming generic names applicable to anything conformable with such abstract ideas. Anticipating in a sense modern phenomenology, Locke presents abstract ideas as "precise, naked appearances in the mind" with which are usually connected the respective names with which the intellect classifies and arranges the types of real things into the various classes and divisions in such a way that the real existents accord with their models.[11] Locke's abstraction leads only to a generic type of images or representations, a vague type of picture of the reality to which these abstract images refer; and the images themselves hang together really only because of and in the common "name" connected with them. Furthermore, such abstraction does not lead in any sense to the discovery of contents of a new and original order as compared to the data of experience; rather it amounts solely to the "generalization" or de-individualization of such data: it leads not to the knowledge of a real constitutive nucleus of stability but only to the formation of a representative "schema".

In Locke's system, the senses are the sole windows and doors through which the mind communicates with the real, and sensations consequently constitute the primary attestation of reality and existence. Now the realm of sensations is the world of matter and material modifica-

[10] A. Klemmt has made an extensive study of this point in his *John Locke theoretische Philosophie* (Meisenheim-Glan-Wien, 1952), pp. 89ff. The classic Nominalist passage in Locke is *An Essay concerning Human Understanding* (London: George Routledge and Sons, 1854), Book IV, ch. VII, 16 (cf. A. C. Fraser, *Locke* [Edinburgh-London, 1890], pp. 166f.).

[11] J. Locke, *An Essay concerning Human Understanding,* Book II, ch. 11, § 9, p. 104. Universals, like all other ideas, ". . . are . . . particular in their existence" (*Essay,* Book III, ch. 3, § 11; cf. J. Gibson, *Locke's Theory of Knowledge and its Historical Relations* [Cambridge, 1917], p. 322).

tions; this material world is thus the primary and proper object of the human mind, and materialism is the direct consequence of English sense-perceptionism and of Lockeian sense-perceptionism in particular. Locke's assertion that human knowledge is limited exclusively to ideas stemming from the human mode of perception [12] is unequivocal and renders precarious Locke's defense of God and religion; [13] indeed, this defense itself reveals Locke's own aim and attitude and remains quite within the logic of his own principles. It is no cause for astonishment therefore that the Encyclopedists, Voltaire, d'Holbach,[14] and later the dialectical materialists should appeal to Locke and consider him the founder of the new notion of reality. Even as Bayle can be said to have opened the field for the ingress of atheism by shattering the link between morality and religion, Locke can be said to have prepared the ground by showing that the only reality that man can comprehend and of which he can speak is that which presents itself to the senses via sense impressions and perceptions: the material world.

But not only Deism and sense-perceptionism can find good justification for themselves in Locke's philosophy; so can materialism as such and consequent atheism.[15] Descartes (and Malebranche, Spinoza, Leibniz with him) had fixed a great gulf between matter and spirit, confining matter to mathematical extension and reserving to spirit the entire knowing activity. Locke is not persuaded of this absolute separation into two intrinsically opposed and antithetic realms, for he thinks that our ideas do not in fact evince in every case that categorical evidence claimed for them. In the case of the ideas, e.g., of circle, square and equality, we can know with certainty that the circle is not identical with a square. We have likewise the idea of thought and of matter but *probably we shall never be in a position to know if some material being might not be able to think.* That is the famous doubt of Locke, comparable in its consequences to the doubt of Descartes. It is impossible for us, simply by contemplating our ideas (the only form of reflection open to us) to discover without revelation whether the Omnipotent may not have granted to certain systems of properly disposed matter a faculty of

[12] "The whole extent of our knowledge or imagination reaches not beyond our own ideas, limited to our ways of perception" (*Essay,* Book III, ch. 11, § 23, p. 421).

[13] On the proof of the existence of God, cf. *Essay,* Book IV, ch. 10, pp. 527-536.

[14] Cf. the praise of Locke in *Système de la nature,* Part I, ch. 10; Vol. I, p. 178, note 47.

[15] Locke was himself accused by Edwards of promoting atheism; it seems to me, however, that this accusation rested less on philosophical grounds than on the picture of a purely biblical Christianity as presented by Locke in his *Reasonableness of Christianity* (cf. Locke's reply in *A Second Vindication, C. W.,* Vol. VII (London, 1823; Aalen, 1963), pp. 304f.). Peter Browne levelled an explicit charge of atheism against Locke (Cf. L. Stephen, *History of English Thought,* Vol. I, p. 114).

perception and thought or at least have conjoined to matter so disposed an immaterial thinking substance. That radical doubt attributed by Marx to Duns Scotus (as to whether matter might not be able to think) originated in the radical voluntarism of Scotus which was to have its boldest development in the nominalist schools. This doubt is now turning up again in Locke in an explicit and positive form: for Locke is saying we cannot be sure if God, at his good pleasure, can add to matter a faculty of thought or if he can add to matter another substance endowed with the faculty of thought, because we simply do not know wherein the faculty of thought consists, nor yet upon what species of substance the almighty may have deigned to confer this power which cannot be in any created being except by the gratuitous benevolence of the creator. Indeed, Locke concludes this strange substantiation or "theological opening" for the new currents of modern materialism and atheism by saying that he sees no contradiction in God, as first eternal thinking being, giving at his good pleasure to certain systems of created senseless matter, combined as he sees fit, some degree of sense, perception and thought.[16]

The importance of the hypothesis and the danger of this concession would be obvious to everyone: for with the collapse of the barrier between matter and thought there was likewise doomed to fall the distinction between body and soul, with a consequent disappearance of the need of positing in man a spiritual and immortal principle, distinct from the body. Such was in fact the immediate reaction of Edward Stillingfleet, Bishop of Worcester, with whom Locke continued to skirmish till the end, trying to escape by dialectic from the vice of the charge of atheism.[17] Locke recalls to his theologican adversary the proof given in the *Essay* of the existence in us of a thinking substance, deduced from the experience of the act of thought, from which we can ascend to the proof of the existence of God and of his immateriality; and Locke declares that we can argue with great probability that such a thinking substance is immaterial.[18] He grants that he had not succeeded in proving it with absolute certainty; he even grants that it is not possible to

[16] "For I see no contradiction in it, that the first eternal thinking Being should, if he pleased, give to certain systems of created senseless matter, put together as he thinks fit, some degrees of sense, perception, and thought" (*Essay,* Book IV, ch. 3, § 6, p. 441).

[17] The documents relevant to the controversy are included in the Y. A. St. John edition of the *Essay* (*C. W.*, Vol. II [London, 1854], pp. 384ff.). Locke seems to have taken from Newton the direct cue for his contention that the omnipotence of God cannot be limited by the measure of narrow conceptions (cf. *ibid.*, p. 395).

[18] In this connection, Locke makes a brief survey of classical and Christian thought to prove that the immortality of the soul is not in danger because it was admitted likewise by those who claimed the soul to be of a material nature (*ibid.*, pp. 385ff.).

prove it on Locke's own principles which can only prove with a high degree of probability (but not with certainty) that the thinking substance in us is immaterial. Indeed, Locke's entire set of remarks on the subject (an excerpt from which we append as a footnote [19]) show him to have been perfectly aware of the importance of the problem and to have accepted entirely the force of his opponent's objection.

But the opponent insists, observing that "if I admit matter to be capable of thinking, I confound the idea of matter with the idea of spirit". Locke's immediate reply is: "No, no more than I confound the idea of matter with the idea of a horse, when I say that matter in general is a solid extended substance, and that a horse is a material animal, or an extended solid substance with sense and spontaneous motion." And Locke goes on to specify: "The idea of matter is an extended solid substance; wherever there is such a substance, there is matter, and the essence of matter, whatever other qualities not contained in that essence it shall please God to superadd to it." [20] It is clear, therefore, that for Locke the will of God can shatter the confining circumferences of essences and attribute to a material substance operations and properties that are spiritual. Locke sees no valid reason, granted the facility with which it can be admitted that God should have been able to add to extended matter sense, spontaneous motion and the other properties encountered, e.g., in an elephant, why then we should not be able to go further and attribute to matter likewise volitional and intellectual acts, even though he admits that such new properties are not included in the essence of matter. For Locke contends that no possible excellence superadded to matter ever destroys the essence of that matter so long as it leaves it an extended solid substance. Otherwise, asks Locke, what escape is there from the assertion that even life in a plant or sensation in an animal destroy the essence of matter?

But the objection still stands, and Locke cannot conceal it; and it consists precisely in the radical impossibility of attributing to matter the faculty of thinking, of conceiving how matter can think. It is the initial and central objection to which Locke repeats his initial reply now specified so as to signify the agreement of Locke with the most daring deca-

[19] "If by spiritual substance, your lordship means a thinking substance, I must dissent from your lordship, and say, that we can have a certainty, upon my principles, that there is a spiritual substance in us. In short, my lord, upon my principles, i.e., from the idea of thinking, we can have a certainty that there is a thinking substance in us; from hence we have a certainty that there is an eternal thinking substance. This substance, which has been from eternity, I have proved to be immaterial. This eternal, immaterial thinking substance, has put into us a thinking substance, which whether it be a material or immaterial substance, cannot be infallibly demonstrated from our ideas; though from them it may be proved that it is to the highest degree probable that it is immaterial" (*ibid.*, pp. 389f.).

[20] *Ibid.*, p. 390.

dent Scholastic theological extrinsicism. To argue from the radical impossibility of human conception of thinking matter, says Locke, and to conclude that God therefore cannot confer upon matter a capacity for thinking amounts to an assertion that the omnipotence of God is limited to the narrow compass of the human intellect's power to conceive. The Almighty did not take counsel with us when he was creating the world! As we see, Locke is not abandoning his stand one whit, a curious mixture of Augustinianism and Nominalism, of empiricism and rationalism. He is in fact conceiving both material and immaterial substance as not including action in their essence (notion) as such; hence, his conclusion (strange at first sight but not so strange on second thought!), the conclusion from this theological extrinsicism: what power is there that God can confer on one of these substances that he cannot confer likewise on the other, both being intrinsically inactive? In that state of inactivity proper to them as such, neither thinks; since thinking is an action, it cannot be denied that God can put an end to all actions of any created substance without annihilating the substance of which they are the actions. The point is that both of these substances have been created devoid of thought, and neither has of itself the faculty of thinking. Thus God can confer such a capacity upon either of them according to his good pleasure, for he is omnipotent.

There is an exact parallel with the case of self-motion: neither material substance nor spiritual substance can at all easily be conceived as endowed in itself with self-motion: but no one is therefore authorized to deny to the divine Omnipotence the ability to confer the power of self-motion on a material substance, if it please him, just as on an immaterial substance, because neither of these substances can have that power of itself, nor are we able to conceive how such a power can be in either.

For Locke, the situation is identical in the case of thought, as he again insists, reasoning in a way that seems strange to us but appears to Locke himself to be most obvious and evident: "Both these substances may be made and exist without thought; neither of them has or can have the power of thinking from itself; God may give it to either of them, according to the good pleasure of his omnipotency; and in whichever of them it is, it is equally beyond our capacity to conceive how either of these substances thinks. But for that reason to deny that God, who had power enough to give them both a being out of nothing, can by the same omnipotency give them what other powers and perfections he pleases, has no better foundation than to deny his power of creation because we cannot conceive how it is performed." [21]

[21] *Ibid.*, p. 393. This seems to us to sum up the crux of Locke's position.

There can thus be no doubt about where Locke actually stood, even though traditional history of philosophy has tended to pass lightly over this stand of his. This position, Locke specifies, implies no contradiction whatever: there is contradiction only if we say that the divine Omnipotence can cause a substance to be solid and not solid at the same time. But for us (who are of yesterday and know nothing) it is beyond our power to be positive that a solid substance cannot have qualities, perfections and powers which do not have a necessary natural or visible connection with solidity and extension. If God cannot join things together by connections which are inconceivable to us, then we should have to deny likewise the consistency and being of matter itself, since every particle of matter has some bulk and its parts are connected in ways inconceivable to us. Thus, all the difficulties raised against the thinking of matter by our ignorance or our narrow conceptions cannot weigh in the balance against the power of God, if he pleases to ordain it so. Nor can these difficulties in any sense prove that God's omnipotence cannot do anything that does not involve a contradiction. Locke gives exactly the same reply to his opponent's objection that self-consciousness simply cannot be attributed to matter. True, Locke concedes, we cannot comprehend how this is possible but surely the weakness of our intelligence is not a limiting factor in respect of the power of God. The same thing can be said in the matter of the difficulty of attributing to matter the capacity for obtaining ideas by abstraction; here Locke's reply comes down in substance to this: if it be admitted that God's omnipotence can dispose the particles of matter in such a way that they become capable of receiving the faculty of thought, there is then no difficulty in conceiving how God could concede this faculty to various beings in a lesser or greater degree, according to his good pleasure.

Locke concludes by alleging that only Descartes and the Cartesians have maintained an absolute opposition between matter and thought: no Father of the Church has ever denied that matter could receive from the power of the creator the capacity for thought, still less that God "was able" to confer this capacity on matter. To assert such a thing would be in plain and flagrant contradiction of Scripture which asserts that God did give Balaam's ass the power of speaking.[22] Typically, Locke's entire reply is based upon the sole theological foundation of the divine Omnipotence wherewith it is alleged the barrier can be shattered between material substance and spiritual; and to this theological foundation, Locke again typically adds the very criterion of rational evidence. The objection was: I cannot manage to conceive how matter can think and therefore I must deny that God could confer upon matter the faculty of

[22] *Ibid.*, p. 396.

thinking. And Locke's reply has been that this argument is not at all convincing, that in fact it will inevitably lead, if applied in other cases, to a denial of the divine Omnipotence. For example, charges Locke, you cannot conceive how matter can attract matter at any distance, much less at a distance of a million miles; ergo, you argue, God could not make it do so! You cannot conceive how matter can feel, or move itself, or affect an immaterial being, or be moved by it; ergo, you argue, God cannot give it such powers! To deny all this would amount to denying gravity and the revolution of the planets about the sun, to reducing animals to mere machines, without sense or spontaneous motion, to allowing man neither sense nor voluntary motion.[23]

Clearly Locke and his opponent were travelling on different tracks and could never really meet: Locke was starting from the "principle of experience" which reduces the knowledge of nature exclusively to the process of "reflection" on sensations; the "idea" of bodies consequently amounted only to extension and solidity; and the "idea" of spirit to the sense of the human mind, to acts of feeling, thought and will. Since in fact life, sensibility and the rest manifested themselves as present in the greater part of corporeal substances and were yet apparently not necessarily connected with the "idea" of corporeality, Locke went astray: instead of deducing the error in his own theory of knowledge and correcting that error, Locke plunged straight into the much more serious error of making the operations of things dependent solely on God, on divine decree, so that everything could do anything, because there was no genuine and proper necessary nexus between the reality of a nature and the quality of its actions and operations. The result was a philosophy and theology of outright *causal extrinsicism,* if not occasionalism as such,[24] which seems on the one hand to be a relapse into the very Cartesian dualism criticized by Locke himself, and on the other hand to provide a preliminary substantiation for modern mentalistic instrumentalism and actionism. In this connection, we should mention Locke's explicit defense of the originality, novelty and separate character of thought: his opponent had reproached him with the fact that Locke's new principles involved a denial of the immaterial substances Locke had already asserted to exist, in his *Essay.*[25] Locke retorts that it is no more difficult to conceive an immaterial substance than to conceive a material one, and that from the ideas of thought and of a power of moving of matter, which we experience in ourselves (ideas which Locke says do not belong originally to matter as matter), we can conclude to the

[23] *Ibid.,* p. 392.

[24] Which Locke has expressly criticized (cf. "An Examination of P. Malebranche's Opinion of seeing All Things in God," in *Essay, ibid.,* pp. 414ff.).

[25] *Ibid.,* ch. 23.

existence of an immaterial substance in us with no greater difficulty than we can conclude that we have material parts. From these ideas, Locke assures us, we can arrive at the idea of spirit in its strictest sense.[26]

The importance of Locke's influence on the molding of modern materialism and atheism by now are surely quite clear, despite his most outspoken declarations in favor of spiritualism and Christianity which we have mentioned. His position has much in common with that of Bayle. The French polemicist untethered morality from religion, thus removing the aura of reprobation, isolation and revulsion with which atheism had been surrounded; on the other hand, Bayle, for all his verbal distinctions between superstition and true genuine religion and his recognition of the superiority of Christianity over all other religions, in reality opened the gates to the radical critique of religion as such, thus ranging himself with Spinoza. Similarly Locke, for his part, is no less lavish of verbal assertions of the distinction between the material world and the spiritual; yet by the very fact of his having extended to matter the capacity for thought (even though that capacity be conceived as a "divine concession"), Locke was in fact eliminating any such distinction in the theoretical order and drawing the logical conclusion from his basic principle that certainty consists in the perception of the agreement or disagreement of ideas.[27] Henceforth the gates are open to sense-perceptionism and the materialism that will be the destination of that 18th-century French Enlightenment philosophy which is to take its inspiration expressly from Locke, just as the Deists had taken him, together with Herbert of Cherbury, as their instructor in the critique of historical revealed religion.

The young Voltaire, who was one of Locke's most ardent admirers, did not fail to highlight the possibility shown by Locke of matter being able to receive the capacity for thinking: "After having reduced to rubble innate ideas, after having renounced the vanity of believing that we are always thinking, Locke establishes that all our ideas come to us from the senses; he examines our simple ideas and those that are complex; he follows the human mind in all its operations; he shows how imperfect are all human languages and what great abuse of terms we perpetrate at every instant. Finally, Locke comes to consider the extent

[26] *Ibid.*, p. 404. Here Locke makes another survey of the notion of *spiritus* in classical thought, especially in Cicero.

[27] "Certainty consists in the perception of the agreement or disagreement of ideas" (*ibid.*, p. 441). In the *Essay* itself, Locke had written: "The different clearness of our knowledge seems to me to lie in the different way of perception the mind has of the agreement or disagreement of its ideas" (Book IV, Ch. 2, § 1, p. 134). It was on the basis of this analysis that Locke arrived at the admission of the possibility of a matter endowed with the capacity of thought, as we have seen.

(or rather the nothingness!) of human knowledge. In this chapter [28] he presumes to make the modest statement: 'We . . . possibly shall never be able to know whether any mere material being thinks or no' " [29]

And Voltaire forthwith reviews the debate between Locke and Bishop Stillingfleet, claiming that Locke has fully proven his point and totally routed the divine. Voltaire evinces a great fascination with the problem and returns to it often in his writings. He must indeed have grasped most admirably the revolutionary significance of the Lockeian thesis, as can be seen from a letter of Voltaire to the Jesuit Tournemine (historian and critic of atheism!), written in December 1735: "The point is not whether we know if matter can think by itself, a notion rejected by Locke as absurd. The point is not whether we know if our soul is spiritual or not. The point is simple whether we know enough about matter and thought to be bold enough to assert that . . . God cannot communicate thought to the being we call *matter. . . :* to know what a thing is capable or incapable of doing, we must know that thing most thoroughly. Now we know nothing of matter; rather we know ourselves to have certain sensations, certain ideas: in a piece of gold, for instance, we perceive a certain extension, a certain hardness, a certain weight, a yellow color, a certain ductility. But we no more know the substance, the subject, the being in which all this inheres, than we do the make-up of the inhabitants of Saturn. If God has willed certain organized bodies to think, they will not think in virtue of the fact that they are extended and divisible; rather they will have thought independently of all this." [30]

What France was able to give England via the Cartesian *cogito* has now been returned with ample interest—as we see from Voltaire's heartfelt praise of Locke—via the new empiricist principle catapulting Deism forthwith into materialism and atheism; [31] Locke's hypothesis is based

[28] *Essay,* Book IV, ch. 3, § 6, with which we commenced our treatment of the problem.

[29] Voltaire, *Lettres philosophiques,* Lettre XIII, Sur Locke; ed. F. A. Taylor, p. 43. Diderot is doubtless referring to this letter when he writes to Voltaire: "How this reasoning [a form of Spinozan pantheism proposed by Diderot] would be strengthened by the opinion which you share with Locke: that thought might well be a modification of matter" (*A Voltaire,* June 11, 1749).

[30] Voltaire, *Correspondance;* cf. other passages collected by P. Serini in *Voltaire Scritti filosofici* Vol. I (Bari, 1962), pp. 45f., note 12. We note that, in the same year (1734) in which he wrote the *Lettres philosophiques,* Voltaire goes even further than Locke, in a letter to C. M. de la Condamine: "My Letter on Locke comes down simply to this: human reason cannot prove that it is impossible for God to join thought to matter. This proposition is, I believe, as true as the proposition that two triangles with the same base and the same altitude are equal."

[31] This dependence of Deism on Locke in its progressive consolidation is generally admitted: "In a general way Locke and Deism face the same foe, they are associated in time, and they show resemblances that seem to indicate a close relation of some sort" (S. G. Helfbower, *The Relation of John Locke to English*

entirely on the existence of God and his omnipotence, it is true; but his followers, gleeful at the long-awaited breaching of the frontier between matter and spirit, convert the hypothesis into a thesis and assert outright the inherent capacity of matter not only to move itself, but also to feel, to understand and to will. With the sense-perceptionism of Locke, every barrier inhibiting the atheistic element of the principle of immanence collapses: the knowing process is reduced to the perception of "ideas" and therefore dissolves into a mere modification of the subject; the subject in turn is made to belong entirely to the world in which his experience occurs in that arc of time spanning the interval between birth and death, for knowing can easily be an attribute of matter.

John Toland was the thinker who, more than any other, developed Locke's Deism to the point of criticizing all historical religion and accepting atheism to all intents and purposes. Toland likewise developed Locke's sense-perceptionism in the direction of an overtly materialistic outlook. In his outspoken argument against Spinoza [32] contained in his famous *Letters to Serena* (1704), Toland develops a metaphysic of "matter" as the constitutive basis of reality; and his skillful exposition draws its inspiration preeminently from the patently dynamic materialism of the Stoics and Epicureans and from the sense-perceptionism of the great masters Hobbes and Locke. Toland's main line of argument can be summed up in the following four points:

1. There is no matter without action or motion.[33] Motion is immanent to matter; matter is self-caused and of all the sensible properties belonging to matter, motion is the absolute one, rest being a relative property. Action is therefore a necessary property of matter.[34]

2. Therefore matter is inconceivable without motion; for otherwise matter would have to be something without shape or color, neither heavy nor light, neither rough nor smooth, neither sweet nor sour,

---

Deism [Chicago, 1918]. Helfbower cites E. Crous' Dissertation, *Die religionsphilosophischen Lehren Lockes und ihre Stellung zu dem Deismus seiner Zeit,* Abhandl, z. Philos. u. ihre Geschichte, [Leipzig, 1910]).

[32] Cf. especially Letter IV; John Toland, *Letters to Serena* (London, 1704), pp. 133f. However, E. Pracht rightly observes that Toland remains closer to Spinoza (and to G. Bruno!) than he thinks, in his atheistic pantheistic bent (*Einleitung* to his German edition, *John Toland, Briefe an Serena* [Berlin: Akademie Verlag, 1959], p. XXXIX). Toland seems to have translated Bruno's *Spaccio della Bestia trionfante* (though there is no certainty on this point), from which he may have borrowed the notion of panpsychism or universal animism.

[33] *Letter IV,* 8, pp. 139f. Here and in the following pages the heated diatribe against Spinoza flares up again. Later on, we read that the properties of matter are: extension, solidity, motion (*Letter V,* 29, pp. 228f.).

[34] *Letter V,* pp. 165ff. Toland asserts that even the particles of which are composed the hardest and most imposing rocks, are in continuous motion like the particles of fire, air and water.

neither hot nor cold; in short, matter would have be something of no sensible qualities, existing without parts, without proportion, since all of this is immediately dependent upon motion.[35]

3. Matter is eternal and uncreated, impenetrable and indestructible: [36] here, too, Locke is departing drastically from Locke who held that matter is subject to God in its being and in its operation.

4. Consequently Toland rejects the classical notion of the *Anima mundi* (world-soul) and considers life to be immanent to matter, asserting outright that thought is a function of the brain: we cannot have any thought when our cerebral activities cease.[37]

Toland is carrying to its logical conclusion the metaphysical stand or hypothesis of Locke, whom he calls the greatest philosopher since Cicero: the hypothesis of the possibility of "thinking matter". There is, of course, no explicit denial either of the existence of God or of the spiritual nature of the soul to be found in Toland's writings; but it follows from his principles that the former is a useless and superfluous principle and the latter henceforth inconceivable. Toland's cryptoatheism and materialism is therefore already a decisive watershed in the history of the metamorphosis of Deism into atheism: his theory of matter active and capable of thought in itself already heralds that absolute and mechanistic evolutionism that will soon make its appearance with Diderot.

It may be noted that Toland not only excited bitter criticisms on the part of his contemporaries; he has retained an aura of enigma which later critics have not succeeded in dissipating: a difficult character and a man not always easy to fathom, he was distrusted by his contemporaries (also because of his "ex-Catholic" [!] status). Furthermore he made the impression of inconsistency with his own principles, consequently arousing a suspicion of insincerity: [38] the most vexing inconsistency was

[35] *Letter V,* 4, pp. 168f. This Letter V is entitled "Motion Essential to Matter" and is a reply to a friend who had attacked Toland's critique of Spinoza. Toland credits this friend with having grasped the crux of Toland's contention, that "if activity ought to enter into the definition of matter, it ought likewise to express the essence thereof" (pp. 165f.).

[36] *Letter* IV, 16, pp. 159f.

[37] Letter IV, 7, pp. 138f. Toland had expressed himself still more drastically in the *Pantheisticon,* to the effect that thought is a motion proper to the brain which is the special organ of this faculty (Pracht, *op. cit., Einleitung,* p. XXXVIIf.).

[38] "It is difficult to believe in his complete sincerity; but it is true enough that his notions were undigested, and that the argument, though not wanting in vigour, was not carried to a systematic conclusion . . . The proposed excision of mystery from Christianity reduced itself to an excision of mere jargon. The conclusion to which his arguments seem to point would have been contrary to his own belief. For, in truth, there is one way, in which mystery may be expelled from religion, and that is by expelling theology. A religion without mystery is a religion without God" (L. Stephen, *History of English Thought,* Vol. I, p. 110).

that it seemed that for Toland the elimination of all positive and revealed religion (and of that sort alone) left natural religion not only intact but even strengthened and clarified in its basic demands. But this criticism seems to us to apply not merely to Toland but to the entire Deist movement; and it highlights the basic equivocation of this school, that of trying to save and claiming to guarantee the rights of God and to clarify man's duties to God, as demanded by the Christian religion, by identifying that religion with natural religion (as did Cherbury and Locke), throwing overboard the problem of revealed religion, criticizing miracles and prophecies and even the person of Christ himself. Clearly, therefore, the desire was not to oppose to revealed religion any lived religion as such but rather a posture freeing man by the instrumentality of reason from every objective historical bond.

Leibniz's critique of Toland is less polemical in appearance but no less vigorous. In his *Adnotationes subitaneae ad Tolandi "De Christianismo Mysteriis carente"*, dated August 8, 1701,[39] he adverts at once to the inconsistency of the title: though it is true that nothing can be admitted which is contrary to reason, it does not follow from this that religion cannot transcend reason, the more so since everything has in it something infinite: "Everyone does indeed profess that there ought to be nothing in Christian theology which is contradictory of reason, i.e., absurd; but I do not see with what probability it can be said that there is nothing in it which may be beyond reason, i.e., incapable of being comprehended by our reason; since the divine nature itself, as infinite, is necessarily incomprehensible: even as there is something of the infinite in all substances, whence it is that only such incomplete notions can be perfectly understood by us as notions of number, shape and other such standards of measurement abstracted from things by the mind." Thus Toland is unjustified in rejecting at the outset of his work everything that he cannot comprehend.

Nor does Leibniz find any more convincing Toland's notion of truth as the perception of the agreement or disagreement of ideas: "For it seems to me that this holds true for our rational knowledge, viz., that deduced from ideas of definitions, that which we call *a priori;* but it does not hold true for our experimental or *a posteriori* knowledge, in the case of which we often have no distinct ideas at all and consequently do not at all perceive their agreement or disagreement. Thus (to cite an example) we do know from experience that acids distilled from the juices of violets dye red, but we do not perceive any agreement of ideas, for we do not yet have distinct ideas of acid and red and violet. Only God can deduce everything from the ideas of his mind." It is quite strange that a rationalist as determined and vigorous as Leibniz should remind an

[39] Leibniz, *Opera philosophica,* ed. Dutens, Vol. V (Geneva, 1768), pp. 142ff.

empiricist like Toland of the rights and limits of experience: but it might be noted that Toland's notion of an "idea" is not what Leibniz supposes it to be; rather it has the same meaning as for Locke, that of a faithful copy of the sensation, and therefore takes the place of the reality itself as Hume will even more clearly make it do.

Thereupon Leibniz launches an all-out attack on the crucial contention of Toland's entire work, the denial of the possibility of miracles and of divine revelation of truths which are beyond but not contrary to the natural capacity of reason. Miracles, contends Leibniz, represent no difficulty really: "As for the common or universal notions with which the divine truths agree or disagree, prudent theologians have been distinguishing, time out of mind, between those notions that are metaphysically necessary, where the contrary would involve a contradiction and with which no divine truth can possibly disagree; and physical truths which are drawn from experience and, so to speak, from the custom of the world, which nothing prevents God from suspending, since we often see such a thing occurring even in natural events, as the distinguished author himself admits later on. Such a truth is that a piece of iron by its nature sinks in water; now, since this does not happen, as often as the iron is shaped into a hollow cauldron, who doubts that God has many more ways of effecting the same end result, by assisting nature in some fashion hidden from us?"

As for divine revelation, it is based on the very truthfulness of God, on his dignity and not simply on the objective evidence of the concepts: "He [Toland] says that revelation is only a means of information not an argument compelling assent. Now, if this means that revelation has no more authority than does a teacher whom we believe only because he proves something or explains it in clear notions, it cannot stand. For the revealer has not only the status of a teacher or instructor but also of an unimpeachable witness and indeed judge, as soon as we know that the revealer is God himself."

Leibniz's stand is therefore a most drastic and determined one: it amounts to a claim that not only Christianity as a revealed religion but the essence of religion in general is of basic value because not everything can be reduced simply to clear and distinct knowledge or ideas. There are also confused ideas, like those of sensible qualities and generically those ideas encountered in any problem in depth, i.e., as Leibniz penetratingly observes, whenever we encounter the infinite: "I think differently, however, and admit the incomprehensible sublimity of the depths of nature, a sublimity that flows from the influence of the infinite which is the source of ideas which are clear and at the same time confused (such as we have of some sensible qualities), which no creature can ever lay entirely bare and which I deem not to have been sufficiently distinguished from other sorts of ideas in the controversy between the distinguished gentlemen, Stillingfleet and Locke. Now all things conspire to show that there ought to be much less astonishment if such things occur in matters pertaining to the deity, which matters far surpass the powers of reason." Leibniz is courteous and moderate in his tone but his meaning is clear and trenchant: [40] Toland has entirely missed the point.

Leibniz makes a more strictly philosophical attack on Toland's famous thesis, advanced by Locke in the form of an hypothesis, concerning the possibility of attributing to matter the capacity for motion and thought. This Toland thesis is found in the *Letters to Serena:* it has been called "dynamic materialism" and is destined to spread like a floodtide along that channel of modern thought that will culminate in "dialectical materialism". It constitutes a crucial "leap" equal in importance to that of the Cartesian *cogito* and Kant's *Ich denke überhaupt.* It is no mere accident that the French translator of the *Letters to Serena* should have been Baron d'Holbach.

When Toland went to Germany in 1702, he spoke personally with Leibniz and corresponded with him [41] on the crucial point of the possibility of having notions of something completely independent of matter and matter's properties. In his famous letter "On That Which Surpasses Sense and Matter", Leibniz distinguishes between the particular sensible qualities that are perceived (but not comprehended, because sensible qualities are basically occult and hidden qualities) by the individual senses, and the intelligible properties of sensible things, such as number and geometric shapes or figures, which are proper to the common sense and the imagination. Above and beyond all of this, there are objects that cannot really be included at all among the objects of the senses, such as the Ego (*Moy*) as a substance: "Thus it can be said that there is nothing in the understanding that has not come from the senses, except for the understanding itself." To this realm which transcends the contents of the senses belong further being itself and truth, for only the intellect distinguishes the contents of a dream from those of reality and the waking state: only this "natural light" enables man to develop his

[40] In Part I of the "Théodicée" which is the *Dissertatio de conformitate fidei cum ratione* (§ 60), Leibniz associates Toland with Bayle in his critique, as opposed to the distinction between what is beyond reason and what is contrary to it: "The Englishman who authored the ingenious but blameworthy book, entitled *Christianisme (sic!) not Mysterious,* sought to shatter this distinction but, if I am any judge, dealt it no crippling blow at all" (ed. Dutens, Vol. I, p. 100; *Die philosophischen Schriften von G. W. Leibniz,* ed. C. J. Gerhardt, Vol. VI [reprinted Hildesheim, 1961], pp. 83f.).

[41] Cf. *Die philosophischen Schriften von G. W. Leibniz,* ed. C. J. Gerhardt, Vol. VI, pp. 475ff.

own knowledge by reflection and reasoning, whether in the sciences or in ethics. Thus, there exist three realms of objects: "The *merely sensible* ones, which are the objects assigned to each of the individual senses; the *simultaneously sensible and intelligible* ones, which belong to the common sense, and the *merely intelligible* ones, which are proper to the understanding. The first and second are capable of being imagined, but the third is beyond the imagination. The second and the third realms are intelligible and distinct; but the first is confused, even though clear or recognizable."

Toland replies in a letter to a mutual friend, Queen Charlotte of Prussia, observing that even the ideas of the third category demand to be referred back to the senses, even including the notion of the Ego. Leibniz replies in a conciliatory tone that even Toland himself likens the data of the senses to the building materials and the Ego to the Architect; and Leibniz goes on to say that there is a crucial distinction between the two realms (p. 518) and that the interior light of the mind is the radical principle of knowledge. The controversy seems to have been interrupted at this point by Toland's refusal to reply any further to Leibniz' objections, thus provoking from Leibniz the disappointed and bitter judgment: "All of this makes me judge that he is scarcely concerned with the truth and wishes only to acquire the distinction of novelty and singularity. For anyone who really loves truth and has leisure will gladly enter into a meticulous discussion" (p. 520).

As a disintegrating force, the importance of this form of pan-dynamism, equivalent to pan-materialism and different from Leibniz' own pan-activism,[42] cannot be underestimated for the following reasons.

1. Matter and motion are indeed to be found in every sort of materialism from Democritus to Gassendi and Hobbes, but the thesis that "matter is motion and action" is Toland's own. This dynamic materialism stands in the same relation to the mechanistic materialism of Hobbes as does the dynamism and activism of Leibniz to the mechanistic interpretation of man and nature given by Descartes.

2. Therefore, Marxist history of philosophy is right in claiming that Toland's dynamic materialism is the precursor of Marx's dialectical materialism. Toland is not of the same immediate importance for the French Revolution that Marx is for the Russian Revolution; but Toland did start a stream of 18th-century thought that contributed to that eventual explosion.

3. Toland bears the same relation to Leibniz as does Marx to

[42] Cf. F. Heinemann, "Toland und Leibniz," in *Beiträge zur Leibniz-Forschung*, ed. G. Schichkoff (Reutlingen, 1947), pp. 211f.

Hegel: [43] both Toland and Marx translate the idealistic and spiritualistic language of their teachers into materialistic jargon, thereby totally altering its meaning. It is therefore a profound irony of history that the two supreme representatives of theologizing idealism, Leibniz and Hegel, should have served as inspiration for the two pioneers of modern materialism (and atheism), Toland and Marx.

Even as Hardouin held that it was the notion of God as universal Being, Truth, Goodness and the like, that had served to "hurl down" ontologism and rationalism into atheism, so did Berkeley (1685-1753) hold that it was the admission of "matter as a substance" which had ended by excluding God, as Spirit, from reality. Berkeley in fact concludes his critique of matter of corporeal substance by accusing it of having been "the main pillar . . . of skepticism" and alleging that "so likewise upon the same foundation have been raised all the impious schemes of atheism and irreligion". For Berkeley, there is and always has been such an intimate intrinsic nexus between the theory of matter and atheism that the only way to get rid of the latter is to eliminate the former. He expatiates on this point in some detail.[44]

The denial of freedom, intelligence and design in creation and preeminently the denial of any providence, with the attribution of the entire course of nature and history to "blind chance or fatal necessity"—all originate from the same error, that of reducing everything to *"unthink-*

[43] But Leibniz' explicit opposition should be noted to the notion of thinking matter expressed in the *Letters:* "Mr. Toland . . . has published a book in English to prove that matter can think and that it can act on its own. This is simply a case of name-switching; he is calling matter what otherwise is not understood by this name" (*Lettres à La Croze,* ed. Dutens, Vol. V, p. 492). Grua claims that Leibniz does come out expressly in favor of Toland's stand on the possibility of self-motion (and even of thought) on the part of matter, in a letter of which the editor, however, publishes only the prologue (cf. G. W. Leibniz, *Textes inédits,* published by G. Grua, Vol. I [Paris, 1948], pp. 555f.). Leibniz seems to have stood firm on the point that Toland's pantheism is, at bottom, atheistic (cf. K. Hildebrandt, *Leibniz und das Reich der Gnade* [The Hague, 1953], pp. 149f.).

[44] "Nay, so great a difficulty has it been thought to conceive Matter produced out of nothing, that the most celebrated among the ancient philosophers, even of those who maintained the being of a God, have thought Matter to be uncreated and coeternal with Him. How great a friend *material substance* has been to Atheists in all ages were needless to relate. All their monstrous systems have so visible and necessary a dependence on it, that when this corner-stone is once removed, the whole fabric cannot choose but fall to the ground; insomuch that it is no longer worth while to bestow a particular consideration on the absurdities of every wretched sect of Atheists" (Berkeley, *A Treatise concerning the Principles of Human Knowledge,* Part I, § 92; in *Berkeley's Works,* ed. A. C. Fraser, Vol. I [Oxford, 1901], p. 309). In the *Syris,* Berkeley excludes Plato and Aristotle from this condemnation (§ 300; *C. W.,* Vol. III, p. 268). In § 288, Berkeley rejects as erroneous the notion of God as the Whole (τὸ πᾶν) and asserts, against atheism, that it is more respectful and logical to conceive God as completely separated from the world (p. 262).

ing matter", without which, claims Berkeley, "your Epicureans, Hobbists, and the like, have not even the shadow of a pretence, but become the most cheap and easy triumph in the world". Berkeley is both sweeping and drastic: "The existence of matter, or bodies unperceived, has not only been the main support of atheists and fatalists, but on the same principle doth idolatry likewise in all its various forms depend." [45]

In a work of his mature years, *Alciphron* (1732), whose flyleaf presents it as "An Apology for the Christian Religion against those who are called Free-Thinkers", Berkeley traces the inevitable process of logic followed by freethought in his day, beginning with its attack on the mysteries of Christianity and ending with the undermining of all faith in, or persuasion of, the existence of a God. This process has followed the method of reduction, starting from the idea of truth which must be "of a stable, permanent, and uniform nature"; and Berkeley indicates three main stages of the process, as follows: "Having observed several sects and subdivisions of sects espousing very different and contrary opinions, and yet all professing Christianity, I rejected those points wherein they differed, retaining only that which was agreed to by all, and so became a Latitudinarian. Having afterward, upon a more enlarged view of things, perceived that Christians, Jews and Mahometans had each their different systems of faith, agreeing only in the belief of one God, I became a Deist. Lastly, extending my view to all the other various nations which inhabit this globe, and finding they agreed in no one point of faith, but differed one from another, as well as from the forementioned sects, even in the notion of a God, in which there is a great diversity as in the methods of worship, I thereupon became an atheist." [46] Any professing

[45] Berkeley, *Treatise,* Part I, § 94, p. 310. Berkeley continues in the same "Let's get rid of it" vein: "Matter being once expelled out of nature drags with it so many skeptical and impious notions, such an incredible number of disputes and puzzling questions, which have been thorns in the sides of divines as well as philosophers, and made so much fruitless work for mankind" (Part I, § 96, pp. 310f.). Berkeley mentions Vanini, Hobbes and Spinoza as among the "most strenuous" advocates of atheism (*Dialogues between Hylas and Philonous,* Dial. II; *C. W.,* Vol. I, p. 425).

Berkeley likewise refers to Hobbes and Spinoza in stating expressly the religious character of his own philosophy: "My doctrines rightly understood, all that philosophy of Epicurus, Hobbes, Spinoza, etc., which has been a declared enemy of religion, comes to the ground" (*Commonplace Book; C. W.,* Vol. I, p. 52). A little earlier Berkeley has declared that it was "silly of Hobbes" to conceive the will as motion, with which actually it has no similarity (*ibid.*). And a little later, he observes that Hobbes and Spinoza have made God to be extended and Locke seems to have done the same (*ibid.*).

[46] *Alcyphron or the minute Philosopher,* Dial. I, § 8; *C. W.,* Vol. II, p. 45. Berkeley uses names taken from classical Greece to indicate his own contemporaries: thus Diagoras is obviously Collins, Tryphon stands for Mandeville, Cratylus for Shaftesbury, etc. The author's *Advertisement* states that the aim of

freethinker must go the whole way: he neither should nor can stop en route to his atheistic destination.

Highly indicative for our research on the relations between modern thought and atheism is Alciphron's presentation of atheism as "the very top and perfection" of freethinking, touted as the only guarantee of human freedom. Such a claim is certainly true of a factual historical situation in Berkeley's day, a situation that recurs exactly in France as we shall see and has an hereditary nexus with the former situation. In administering the final blow to all religion, atheism is expressing the fact and the claim of the full and genuine freedom of man: that is the sense of the drastic peroration: "Atheism therefore, that bugbear of women and fools, is the very top and perfection of free-thinking. It is the grand *arcanum* to which a true genius naturally riseth, by a certain climax or gradation of thought, and without which he can never possess his soul in absolute liberty and repose."

The notion of God is the merest figment of the imagination: "For your thorough conviction in this main article, do but examine the notion of a God with the same freedom that you would other prejudices. Trace it to the fountain-head, and you shall not find that you had it by any of your senses, the only true means of discovering what is real and substantial in nature. You will find it lying amongst other old lumber in some obscure corner of the imagination, the proper receptacle of visions, fancies, and prejudices of all kinds; and if you are more attached to this than the rest, it is only because it is the oldest."

Atheism is the true destination of freethought and it is this atheism that is to administer the final blow to religion, especially in England, where Alciphron laments there are still too many "who retain a foolish prejudice against the name of atheist". When the root, which is religion, is plucked up, the "scions which shot from it will of course wither and decay. Such are all those whimsical notions of conscience, duty, principle, and the like, which fill a man's head with scruples, awe him with fears, and make him a more thorough slave than the horse he rides. A man had better a thousand times be hunted by bailiffs or messengers than haunted by these spectres, which embarrass and embitter all his pleasures, creating the most real and sore servitude upon earth. But the free-thinker, with a vigorous flight of thought, breaks through those airy springes, and asserts his original independency. Others indeed may talk,

---

the book is "to consider the Free-thinker in the various lights of atheist, libertine, enthusiast, scorner, critic, metaphysician, fatalist, and sceptic"; there follows a reference to ". . . one of the most noted writers against Christianity in our times [Collins] declared he had found out a demonstration against the being of a God" (p. 23).

and write, and fight about liberty, and make an outward pretence to it; but the free-thinker alone is truly free." [47]

Berkeley's contention, therefore, is that atheism is, consciously or unconsciously, the goal and inevitable destination of freethinking. Recent historians of philosophy have shown that, in the whole of this burning controversy with atheism and materialism, Berkeley was aiming at the work of his contemporary and compatriot, John Toland, and the whole of Berkeley's philosophical work amounted to a refutation of Toland's position [48] as leader of the extreme wing of the Freethinkers or "minute Philosophers" as Berkeley calls them. Berkeley returns to the fray in his later work, *The Theory of Visual Language,* whose subtitle shows its polemical intent: "shewing the immediate Presence and Providence of a Deity vindicated and explained". The argument concerning providence was implicit in the first *Theory of Vision,* dating from 1709, but it had been exhaustively treated since then in *Alciphron* (especially in Dialogue IV) and is now presented in the form of "Visual Language" as a "new and irrefutable proof of the existence of the immediate action of God and of the constant care of his Providence" against those who are called "Free-Thinkers". Berkeley develops against the atheists the thesis that the *objects* of vision are *signs* in which is virtually contained a language which is admitted to be of a superior kind, i.e., a "divine language", so that the whole universe of phenomena presented to the senses is in reality a revelation of the Supreme Power as active Mind (§§ 9-18).

The introductory sections (§§ 1-8) [49] are a vehement diatribe against atheism which, Berkeley claims, has made greater headway than some are ready to believe. Atheism is, for Berkeley, the direct offspring of Deism. This claim had already been advanced in Dialogue I of *Alciphron;* but in the meantime the situation has proven to be considerably more serious. In fact, claims Berkeley, anyone who reflects on the fact that the present enemies of Christianity begin their attacks upon it under the specious pretext of a defense of the Christian Church and its

[47] *Alcyphron,* § 9, p. 46. And so we have here ironically stated the rough draft of the atheist and materialist assertions which in a few decades are to be proposed seriously and systematically by d'Holbach and a century later, as refashioned in the light of the Hegelian dialectic, are to constitute the substance of Marxism.

[48] "Toland's philosophy contains the thesis to which Berkeley formulates the antithesis" (F. Heinemann, *loc cit.,* p. 194). This is especially true of Part I of the *Principles,* Dialogue II of the *Dialogues between Hylas and Philonous,* Dialogue I of *Alcyphron* (§ 5, struggle against prejudice; § 6, prejudice at the root of the diversity of religions; § 8, religious development of Toland), and I believe likewise to *The Theory of Vision or Visual Language shewing the immediate Presence and Providence of a Deity vindicated and explained,* written in 1733 (*C. W.,* Vol. II).

[49] *C. W.,* Vol. II, pp. 379ff.

rights,[50] will be inclined to suspect their intentions in taking up the defense of natural religion, and to judge their sincerity in the latter case on the basis of their performance in the former. The symptoms of this Machiavellian tactic are not difficult to spot: the notion of a watchful, active, intelligent, free Spirit with whom we have to do and in whom we live and move and have our being—this sort of notion is not the prevailing one in the writings and conversation of those who are called Deists. Furthermore, no sooner have their plans been implemented in reality than we can easily see that moral virtue and the religion of nature go into a decline; and we can discern, both with our reason and from our experience, that the aim of destroying revealed religion must necessarily culminate in atheism or in idolatry. The protests of the suspects and of a certain writer who is one of their admirers [51] are to no avail when in this very writer himself can be spotted strong traces of atheism and irreligion in every sense of the word,[52] i.e., opposition to both natural and revealed religion; and moreover the introduction of taste as a moral criterion in place of duty, the conversion of man into a necessary agent, the derision heaped upon the very notion of a future judgment, seem to all intents and purposes to be atheistic notions, subversive of any religion whatsoever. Indisputably, observes Berkeley, the best way to disseminate atheism is to repudiate religious principles by insinuations against them and by embellishment of atheism. Of what use is it to the cause of virtue and natural religion to admit the strongest traces of wisdom and power in the structure of the universe, if this wisdom is not held to be observing nor this power to be going to reward or punish our actions, if we do not believe ourselves responsible nor yet believe that God is our Judge? (§ 3).

And Berkeley proceeds in the succeeding section (§ 4): Everything said about a vital principle, order, harmony, proportion, natural decorum and fitness of things, taste and enthusiasm—all this may well be and be admitted without one iota of natural religion, without any notion of law or duty, without any belief in a Lord or Judge or any religious sense of God. For the mental contemplation of the ideas of beauty, virtue, order, fitness and the like are one thing and the sense for religion quite another! So long, insists Berkeley, as we do not admit any other principle of good actions than natural inclination thereto and no reward

[50] Fraser holds this to be an obvious allusion to M. Tindal's *The Rights of the Christian Church* (London, 1709) which is cited here in § 5.

[51] Fraser says this is Shaftesbury against whom is directed Dialogue III of *Alcyphron* and who is here called "a loose and incoherent writer" (p. 381).

[52] Guzzo expresses the same idea thus: "Even though there be no profession of atheism in any of the writings of the free-thinkers, it is covertly present as the foundation of their thought" (*Introd.* p. 36).

or punishment other than the natural consequences; so long as we do not take thought for any judgment, do not cultivate any fear or any hope of a future life, but simply laugh at such things with the author of the *Characteristics* [53] and those he deems the liberal and educated portion of mankind, how can we still be called in any sense religious? Or what is there in all this that an atheist would not find just as much to his taste as a theist? Or could not fate or nature serve just as well as the deity in such a system? And Berkeley's bitter conclusion is that the number of atheists, i.e., those who do not hold any principle of any religion, natural or revealed, is steadily on the increase, even among persons of no mean rank.[54]

Berkeley's charge increases in trenchancy and acrimony: "The principles of atheism have struck deep root," he exclaims, "and have spread much farther than many can bring themselves to imagine: suffice it to note that pantheism, materialism, and fatalism are nothing else than atheism a little disguised." [55]

The notions of Hobbes, Spinoza, Leibniz and Bayle are relished and applauded, laments Berkeley, because they deny the freedom and immortality of the soul, in fact they deny its very existence; thus likewise those who deny that God observes, judges and rewards and punishes human actions are also denying his existence so far as ethics and natural religion are concerned. The fashion of proof affected by the unbelievers leads either to atheism or to unbelief. It is no surprise to find Hobbes and Spinoza listed by Berkeley among these atheists, in view of what he has already said; but it is surprising to find Bayle among them and, above all, Leibniz, apologist of providence (and of Christianity) against Bayle, Toland and the rest, as we have seen. However it is a sign of the

[53] The most explicit and unmistakable reference to Shaftesbury.

[54] A reference to the authors of the *Philosophical Dissertation upon Death* and of the *Rights of the Christian Church,* by the already-cited M. Tindal. The *Dissertation* had been published anonymously in London in 1733 and contained the assertion that the fear of death, like all the other moral feelings and judgments, is based on habit and social convention; the *Dissertation* also called for freedom of morals in function of circumstances and defended the permissibility and even in some cases the expedience and propriety of suicide. The *Disseration* was the work of the Italian exile Alberto Radicati, Count of Passerano, and was translated by John Morgan; Trinius considered it to be ". . . a godless Book" (cf. *Freydenker Lexikon,* p. 401). In the Appendix of 1765, Radicati is characterized as follows: "This Count certainly has an indisputable claim to the title of the boldest and most perverse of thinkers if he be compared with all his predecessors. Only a man who has gone as far as this Right Dishonorable Count, in the denial of humanity and sound reason, can read without a surfeit of horror these accursed and diabolical theories spewing from the inhuman brain of this man" (*Erste Zugabe* to the 1765 edition of the *Lexikon,* p. 73).

[55] The expression "a little disguised" is reminiscent of that used in Hardouin's *Athei detecti.*

gravity of the situation and of Berkeley's deep concern and anguish of mind (§ 6).

He concludes his diatribe with a denunciation of the work of another famous Deist, Anthony Collins (1676-1729), entitled *A Discourse of Freethinking occasioned by the Rise and Growth of a sect called Freethinkers* (London, 1713).[56] Berkeley notes how the author, after having insinuated his own unbelief by describing the various errors and opinions regarding revealed religion, seems to insinuate in the same fashion his own atheism by expounding the divergent notions men have of the nature and attributes of God and especially the opinion that our knowledge of God is according to analogy, as analogy has been understood by some in recent years. Such is the effect of the worst explanations and defenses of our faith and such are the advantages given to their enemies by incautious friends: instead of aiding religion and faith, they end by scandalizing people entirely and preparing the way for the triumph of atheism. It is therefore a duty to disapprove of their works and refute them.

The squall of rationalistic ontologism unleashed on the continent by the Oratorians and Descartes and sweeping away the notion of a personal God was answered in England by the hurricane of Deism, the whirlwind reaped from the wind of sense-perceptionism sown by Bacon and Locke and from Hobbes' materialism. This was just the climate needed to prepare the way directly for the Enlightenment movement as such and to push it forward to all of its principle positions, which were in a few years to invade the whole of Europe and lay the foundations for the radical and definitive transformation of modern life and thought. A

[56] Of this work Trinius writes: "It is one of the most dangerous and worst of Collins' writings, wherein he seeks to prove the necessity and advantages of freethinking, levels charges against the clergy, saddles Christianity itself with the blame for their wrongdoings, reproaches the Church Fathers with a corruption and adulteration of Scripture, calls the Prophets great Freethinkers, accusing them of having stimulated the spirit of prophecy with music and wine, etc." (*op. cit.*, p. 148). On the divergent judgments passed on Collins' work and especially the headlong attack on it by Bentley, cf. J. M. Robertson, *A Short History of Freethought,* Vol. I, pp. 154ff.). Collins expounds a suspect Hobbesian brand of theism but expressly rejects atheism: "Ignorance is the foundation of atheism and freethinking the cure of it" (Collins, *op. cit.,* p. 105). In his first work, *Essay concerning the Use of Reason* (London, 1707), Collins openly attacks revelation, rejecting any distinction between absurdity and mystery, between what is beyond reason and what is contrary to it, and demanding that revelation conform to the ideas of the natural reason concerning God. In 1715, Collins published in letter form the *Inquiry concerning Human Liberty,* in which he embraces determinism. In the essay *Liberty and Necessity,* dating from 1729, the year of his death, he defends this determinism against Clarke's critique. Stephen calls Collins ". . . a favoured disciple of Locke" and founder of "critical deism" (*History of English Thought,* Vol. I, p. 204).

recent critic claims that Berkeley's vigorous and radical stand, as a kind of bulwark between Locke, theist and Deist, and Hume, skeptic slipping toward atheism, served to inhibit temporarily the process of disintegration by a recall to the reality of immediate certitudes: "The abolition of the Cartesian metaphysical doubt concerning the existence of sensible reality restores its traditional purchase to the proof from causality.[57] Materialism, atheism and skepticism, both as regards the reality of external things and as regards God, are refuted simultaneously.[58] By the affirmation and not by the exclusion of the sensible world, everything is eventually reduced to a world of spirits receiving from the divine Spirit the universe of things which is but a universe of ideas." [59] And Hume will be the chief thinker to appeal to Berkeley's critique of abstract ideas and assert the principle of the correspondence between impression and idea, eliminating from the mind all possibility of reference to metaphysical reality.

[57] Cf. Berkeley's *Dialogues between Hylas and Philonous,* Dialogues II and III.

[58] Cf. §§ 92-94, cited above, of *Treatise on Principles of Human Knowledge.*

[59] M. Gueroult, *Berkeley,* Quatre études sur la perception et sur Dieu (Paris, 1956), pp. 119f.

5

Atheistic Elements in the Religious Skepticism of David Hume

In contrast to Berkeley's fervent defense of theism stands Hume's religious skepticism. Hume drives the principle of the new empiricism to its ultimate extreme, the demand for the assertion of being on the basis of the simple and naked presence of sense impressions. Locke had inverted entirely the very meaning of "idea" by reducing it to a mental remnant or residue of sense impressions; but he had advanced no further in the direction of a precise notion in epistemology: his chief merit lay in having denied secondary qualities and effected a radical refutation of the rationalist hypothesis of "innate ideas".[1] Berkeley's merit lay in having taken Locke's principle as starting point and shown that generic ideas are, as such, nothing but particular ideas connected to a certain common term which gives them a wider meaning and serves to recall to the mind other individuals that are similar.[2]

Hume is sharp enough to see a strict connection between Locke's denial of secondary qualities and Berkeley's denial of general ideas or of abstraction. As soon as sensible qualities such as hard and soft, sweet and bitter, white and black, etc., are reduced to mere perceptions of the mind, the same fate is bound to befall the primary qualities of extension and solidity, inasmuch as the idea of extension (and that of solidity as well) is acquired entirely from the sense of sight and the sense of touch, and thus is dependent upon the sensible qualities of these senses, so that if the latter are subjective, extension (and solidity) must likewise and by the same token be subjective. Nor does it make any sense to say they have been obtained by "abstraction" because an extension that is neither

[1] Hume, *Treatise on Human Nature,* ed. Selby-Bigge (Oxford, 1928), p. 35; *An Enquiry concerning Human Understanding,* ed. Selby-Bigge (Oxford, 1936), p. 22, note.

[2] Hume, *Treatise,* p. 17. Berkeley is here not referred to by name but simply as "a great philosopher" and his theory is called ". . . one of the greatest and most valuable discoveries that has been made of late years in the republic of letters".

visible nor tangible cannot even be conceived. It would be just as absurd to try to conceive a triangle in general, neither isosceles nor scalene, having no particular length or proportion of sides. The conclusion which Hume derives from this position of the convinced theist, Bishop Berkeley, fully confirms our criterion of interpretation of the principle of immanence as skeptical and atheistic. Indeed, Hume observes, with subtle irony, that despite the good apologetic intentions of Berkeley, the bishop has in fact favored skepticism and with it the cause of the atheists and free-thinkers he wanted to refute.[3]

For the author of the impassioned refutation of Toland, Collins and the rest, this labelling as a mere skeptic and banner-bearer of skepticism must have sounded like the bitterest of ironies; but that is precisely the irony and the illusion of so many modern thinkers—from Descartes to the would-be Christian idealists of our own day—that they start from immanence and hope to reach God.

Hume's stand on the problem of God derives directly from his skepticism and was expressed quite early in the *Dialogues concerning Natural Religion*, composed between 1751 and 1755.[4] Hume proceeds in the simplest and most consistent fashion imaginable. Since all of our certainty regarding existence comes down to the impression of external or internal experience, psychological habit takes the place of certainty or logical necessity. The principle of causality is the only guarantee we have of the existence of things that are outside the field of immediate experience; but the principle of causality comes down to a *belief*, to a *habit* or *custom,* to a *feeling* of the mind, to something *felt* rather than conceived, something concerning which Hume is at a loss to explain, in his later writings, whether it derives from experience or is a deep-seated impulse of nature.[5] Hence, if our conviction of the causal nexus within the very ambit of sense experience has no philosophical justification, it

[3] "This argument is drawn from Dr. Berkeley; and indeed most of the writings of that very ingenious author form the best lessons of scepticism, which are to be found either among the ancient or modern philosophers, Bayle not excepted. He professes, however, in his title page (and undoubtedly with great truth) to have composed his book against the sceptics as well as against the atheists and free-thinkers. But that all his arguments, though otherwise intended, are, in reality, merely sceptical, appears from this, *that they admit of no answer and produce no conviction.* Their only effect is to cause that momentary amazement and irresolution and confusion, which is the result of scepticism" (*An Enquiry,* p. 155 note).

[4] These *Dialogues* were twice revised, first in 1761, ten years after their composition, and again in 1776, the year of Hume's death (cf. Norman K. Smith, *Hume's Dialogues concerning Natural Religion* [Toronto-New York, 1947 [2]], p. Vf.). The final additions of 1776 seem to have been made under the influence of Hume's visits to Paris in 1763-66, during which he came to make the acquaintance of d'Holbach and his circle.

[5] "Tis *felt,* rather than conceiv'd and approaches the impression from which it is deriv'd, in its force and influence" (*Treatise,* Appendix, p. 627).

loses all meaning whatever when the effort is made to extend it beyond the realm of experience or of the spatio-temporal succession which conditions it. With the collapse of the principle of causality, the principle of substance likewise goes by the board, claims Hume: for this latter principle depends upon the former inasmuch as we conceive substance as the cause of its own qualities and modifications. There disappear likewise the notions of subject, ego, soul, person, which are all based on the notion of substance. For Hume, indeed, the theory of the substantiality of the soul is senseless and leads straight to atheism: those who assert it are simply reiterating Spinoza's stand on the simplicity of the universe and the unity of substance.[6] This is a startling juxtaposition to say the least and it shows at one and the same time Hume's radical phenomenalism and his (apparent or real) horror of atheism.

English Deism, therefore, disintegrates with Hume into skepticism: Christianity, based as it is on the historical reality of the miracles and prophecies and presupposing therefore the validity of the principle of causality, is at once ruled out of court. In his critique of the notion and possibility of miracle, Hume compiles the result of well-nigh a century of attacks by Enlightenment philosophy and Deism on the supernatural character of the Christian religion.[7] There is no sufficient and cogent evidence of miracle either on the part of Moses or of those that came after him; human witness to such a fact as would necessarily change man's entire life is very often wavering and never attains to probability, still less to certainty. But what is at the bottom of this critique is the old principle of absolute determinism in the matter of the laws of physics which, it is alleged, miracles would violate; [8] *therefore,* a miracle is not possible. Hume therefore holds that belief in miracles has its origin in purely subjective psychological factors, such as *surprise and wonder* at the exceptional character of an occurrence, and *giddy credulity* prompting a man to ascribe the occurrence to an extra-mundane principle. Moreover, all religions, even the paganism of antiquity, have appealed to miracles to prove their own truth and their superiority over other

[6] "I assert, that the doctrine of the immateriality, simplicity, and indivisibility of a thinking substance is a true atheism, and will serve to justify all those sentiments for which *Spinoza* is so universally infamous" (*ibid.,* p. 240).

[7] For Hume's critique of the notion of miracle, cf. *An Enquiry concerning Human Understanding,* sec. X, "On Miracles".

[8] "A miracle is a violation of the laws of nature; and as a firm and unalterable experience has established these laws, the proof against a miracle, from the very nature of the fact, is as entire as any argument from experience can possibly be imagined" (*An Enquiry,* p. 114). Belief in the miraculous arises solely from the fact that the event in question is rare and unusual. There follows the definition of miracle as: "*A transgression of a law of nature by a particular volition of the Deity, or by the interposition of some invisible agent*" (p. 115 note; italics Hume's).

religions: hence the proof of miracles does more damage than good to Christianity. Hume is thus shutting himself up in a rigid fideism as the only method proper to the Christian religion, and he warns against the erudite efforts of an apologetic which claims to prove Christianity via the existence of miracles and prophecies. The true and genuine miracle is that produced by faith, moving man's mind to assert to the truth of Christianity and the man so moved is conscious of a continued miracle in his own person, which subverts all the principles of his own intelligence and understanding and makes him inclined to believe what is most contrary to custom and experience.[9] But Hume does not specify whether it is here a case of a "faith" of a higher (i.e., divinely originated) kind or whether it comes down simply to the natural belief in causality and so emerges as an illusion worse confounded, since, unlike the genuine natural belief in causality, this pseudo-supernatural one would be devoid of any objective reference or basis.

After eliminating what he calls the "rational proofs" of the Christian religion, Hume applies his psychological method to the critique of natural religion. The first thing that must be ruled out, says Hume, is any notion that the belief in a supreme Being derives from a natural instinct, for there are peoples who have no concept of religion. Nor can such belief be held to arise out of rational reflection on the causes encountered in nature around us, because the principle of causality is, as he has already pointed up, a purely subjective conviction that loses all meaning when it is extended beyond the field of experience. Nor, finally, can the origin of religion be attributed to a primitive revelation made to mankind. Here we can see an advance by Hume over early 17th-century Deism: whereas the Deists used to attribute the foundations of religions to a trick and fraud perpetrated by the priests, Hume reduces it simply to the psychological behavior of the human individual. Practical de-

[9] "Our most holy religion is founded on *Faith,* not on reason; and it is a sure method of exposing it to put it to such a trial as it is, by no means, fitted to endure . . . We may conclude that the *Christian Religion* not only was at first attended with miracles, but even at this day cannot be believed by any reasonable person without one. Mere reason is insufficient to convince us of its veracity: And whoever is moved by *Faith* to assent to it, is conscious of a continued miracle in his own person, which subverts all the principles of his understanding, and gives him a determination to believe what is most contrary to custom and experience" (*ibid.,* p. 130, 131).

Hegel pinpointed the difference between classical skepticism with its disintegrating bent and that of Hume which makes feeling the basis of truth: "Humeian *skepticism* takes the *truth* of the empirical, of feeling, of sense-perception as basis and attacks generic definitions and laws from that point of view, because they find no justification in sense-perception. The old skepticism was so far from making feeling or perception the principle of truth that it rather set itself first of all against the sensible" (*Enzyklop. d. philos. Wiss.* § 39; ed. Hoffmeister, p. 65).

mands impel man to create religion, primarily the sensations and impressions of fear and hope produced in him by the vicissitudes of life. Let us see the main lines of Hume's argument.

Man's ever unquiet imagination seeks to create for itself a picture of the mysterious powers of nature upon which man feels himself to be completely dependent. Instinct forthwith leads man to picture this power in the guise of a human shape and figure. Thus the multitude of chance events and happenings in life and their attribution to the various forces of nature was bound to lead to the acknowledgment of many deities; and Hume blandly maintains as his central thesis on religion that polytheism is the expression of the primitive religion of man and that monotheism issued out of it by a process of simplification. The mind of man likewise commenced its steep ascent from the imperfect foothills of mythological beliefs and only laboriously and little by little did it rise to the belief in a perfect Being, by way of a subtle process of abstraction.[10] To hold otherwise is to go against the principle of analogy and to ignore the basic principle of the human mind. However the psychological dynamism of analogy comes into play likewise in the transition from polytheism to monotheism. The best-known argument is that taken from providence; but here we have a notion that man immediately confuses with naive and erroneous representations, to such an extent that the most frightening cataclysms of nature and the gravest calamities of human existence, things which as such are diametrically opposed to order and well-being in the world, are rather held to be a means of bringing man closer to the deity.[11] The Humeian original passage here

[10] This is the central thesis of the *Natural History of Religion,* from which we cite a significant passage: "It seems certain, that, according to the natural progress of human thought, the ignorant multitude must first entertain some groveling and familiar notion of superior powers, before they stretch their conception to that perfect Being, who bestowed order on the whole frame of nature. We may as reasonably imagine, that men inhabited palaces before huts and cottages, or studied geometry before agriculture; as assert that the Deity appeared to them a pure spirit, omniscient, omnipotent, and omnipresent, before he was apprehended to be a powerful, though limited being, with human passions and appetites, limbs and organs. The mind rises gradually from inferior to superior: By abstracting from what is imperfect, it forms an idea of perfection: And slowly distinguishing the nobler parts of its own frame from the grosser, it learns to transfer only the former, much elevated and refined, to its divinity" (Hume, *Essays and Treatises on several Subjects,* Vol. II [London, 1788], pp. 364f.). In the five sections devoted to polytheism, Hume refers extensively to ancient Greek and Latin writers.

[11] "Convulsions in nature, disorders, prodigies, miracles, though the most opposite to the plan of a wise superintendent, impress mankind with the strongest sentiments of religion; the causes of events seeming then the most unknown and unaccountable. Madness, fury, rage, and an inflamed imagination, tho' they sink men nearest to the level of beasts, are, for like reason, often supposed to be the only dispositions in which we can have any immediate communication with the Deity" (*ibid.,* p. 387).

is quite significant and seems, in context, to justify a benign interpretation, since it is a subsequent commentary on the famous saying of Bacon to the effect that "a little philosophy makes men atheists; a great deal reconciles them to religion".[12]

This whole theory of the origin of monotheism from polytheism, which latter allegedly represents the primitive stage of religious awareness and knowledge, is a sheer pipe dream of Hume, and of the Enlightenment. It has been debunked not only by modern religious ethnology but likewise by the history of the people of Israel, which, despite its low level of culture, certainly inferior to that of the pagan and polytheistic peoples amid which Israel lived, had the strictest monotheistic religion that history has ever known.[13] Toward the end of his *Natural History of Religion,* Hume highlights with some relish the paradoxical state of religion and unbelief when viewed in the cold and sober light of facts and history: on the one side of the coin, the sublime truths of religion and its lofty moral precepts; on the other, the silly and petty prejudices that have prevailed among the peoples of the world, prejudices that have been based on error to boot, and the painful contrast between the principles professed and the life lived. The greatest and most impassioned

[12] *De augm. scient.* lib. I. The Baconian text recurs in the ensuing *Dialogues concerning Natural Religion* (Part I; ed. Norman K. Smith, p. 139). Here is the context of the famous Bacon passage: "For them that aver that too much knowledge inclineth the mind to atheism and that ignorance concerning secondary causes compelleth to pious belief concerning the primary cause, I would fain arraign with the question of Job: 'Will you speak falsely for God, and speak deceitfully for him? Will you ingratiate yourselves by showing partiality towards him?' (Job 13, 7). For it is patent that God doth not ordinarily operate any thing in nature saving by secondary causes and to be willing to believe anything else would be the merest imposture as it were in favor of God and nothing other than the immolation of an unclean offering of mendacity to the author of truth. Nay rather it is most sure and confirmed by experience that shallow sips of philosophy may move toward atheism but ampler draughts bring back to religion. For at the threshold of philosophy, when the secondary causes obtrude themselves upon the human mind as being nearest to the senses, and the mind doth cleave to them and tarry in them, then may forgetfulness stealthily cover up the primary cause; yet if a man do but proceed further and contemplate the dependency, series and concatenation of causes and the works of Providence, then he will readily believe in accord with the mythology of the poets that the highest link of the natural chain is affixed to the foot of Jove alone" (*The Works of Francis Bacon,* ed. J. Spedding-R. L. Ellis and D. D. Heath, Vol. I [London, 1879], pp. 436f.). The pith of the passage recurs likewise in the *Essays* (Essay XIV, "Of Atheism," ed. F. Fiske Heard and R. Whately [Boston-New York, 1871], p. 155).

[13] "This people [the Jews] is likewise a proof that Hume is in error when he claims that theism is to be found only in higher civilizations. When the Jews came out of Egypt, they were at a cultural nadir and yet the belief in a God remained dominant despite repeated vacillations . . . Despite their low cultural level, the Jews knew their primordial tribal and national God to be the God of heaven and earth" (A. Lüers, *David Humes religionsphilosophische Anschauungen,* Dissertation [Berlin, 1909], p. 9).

zeal is no sure guarantee against hyprocrisy; and the most patent impiety may be accompanied by a secret dread and compunction. The proverb, *Ignorance is the mother of devotion,* says Hume, is borne out by general experience; but he immediately adds that a people entirely destitute of religion is only a few degrees removed from brutes.

The final paragraph pretty clearly recommends a flight from the whirlpool of religion into the calm haven of philosophy: substantially it is the solution offered by the Stoics and by Bayle. "The whole is a riddle, an enigma, an inexplicable mystery. Doubt, uncertainty, suspense of judgment appear the only result of our most accurate scrutiny concerning this subject. But such is the frailty of human reason and such the irresistible contagion of opinion that even this deliberate doubt could scarcely be upheld; did we not enlarge our view, and opposing one species of superstition to another, set them quarrelling; while we ourselves, during their fury and contention, happily make our escape into the calm, though obscure regions of philosophy." [14]

The *Dialogues concerning Natural Religion* return to the same point and especially the problem of founding religion on reason. In the Prologue, belief in the existence of a God is called the most obvious and certain truth that the most ignorant ages have acknowledged and for which the most refined geniuses have ambitiously striven to produce ever new proofs. It constitutes the ground of all our hopes, the surest foundation of morality, the firmest support of society, etc. Thus Pamphilus, who is the first speaker but who immediately adds that no sooner have we begun to apply ourselves to a consideration of the attributes of God, his decrees and his plan of providence, than we find ourselves in a sea of difficulties with no harbor in sight.[15]

It is this skeptical attitude, rather than the original theistic one, that takes the upper hand as well in this work of Hume. On the one hand, Cleanthes does indeed maintain his opinion that the order in the universe proves the existence of a purposive plan; but Demea stresses the incomprehensibility of God and accuses Cleanthes of anthropomorphism. At this point a third speaker, Philo, enters the discussion to throw his support to Demea, asserting that we are completely in the dark on the nature of causes, and that the order that we observe in the world is finite and imperfect, precluding any transition from the finite to the Infinite. None of the traditional proofs of the existence of God, whether *a priori* or *a posteriori,* can withstand the critique wherein Hume combines together the basic points of his speculative skepticism. He grants that the works of nature present a great similarity to works of

[14] *The Natural History of Religion,* p. 425.
[15] *Dialogues concerning Natural Religion,* p. 128.

art and that it is therefore legitimate as such to consider nature to be the work of an Intelligence; and this is the foundation of "Natural Theology". But we are here dealing with a simple analogy which in no way justifies the assertion of a first metaphysical Principle. And Philo, the main speaker, concludes that both the atheists and the extremist theists are in error and that their positions come down actually to the same thing.

We can now pose the question. Was Hume an atheist or a theist? The critics have not found this an easy question to answer; nor do we! During his Paris visit, toward the end of his life, Hume seems to have resolutely refused to ally himself with the circle of atheists headed by d'Holbach who was for a time Hume's host and who is even reported to have stated of Hume that he did not admit the possibility atheism and claimed he had never met an atheist.[16] As far as the issue of the radical skepticism professed by Hume is concerned, there can be no doubt about that: the theists do not have at their disposal a single decisive argument; their arguments are conjectures, faint probabilities and nothing more. But it must be admitted that Hume does not appear to want to burn all his bridges. We have mentioned the explicit statement of theism made by Pamphilus in the Prologue to the *Dialogues*. Demea likewise at the beginning of the second part of these *Dialogues* recalls to Cleanthes his explicit profession of theism: "By the whole tenor of your discourse, one would imagine that you were maintaining the being of a God, against the cavils of atheists and infidels; and were necessitated to become a champion for that fundamental principle of all religion." [17] The

[16] Cf. E. C. Mossner, *The Life of David Hume* (Austin: University of Texas Press, 1954), p. 483 (on p. 603 Mossner reports the episode at Hume's funeral, when one of the crowd exclaimed: "Ah, he was an atheist!" to which another retorted: "For nothing, he was an honest man!"). Cf. also the episode reported by Norman K. Smith, *Dialogues*, Introduction, pp. 37f. Smith admits, however, that the Paris visit had a bad influence on Hume, an influence that can be noted in the last additions and corrections of the *Dialogues*, made at that time. L. Stephens has a good treatment of the ambiguity of Hume's stand on the problem of God (cf. *History of English Thought in Eighteenth Century*, Vol. I, especially pp. 312ff.), and Stephen's conclusions seem to us to be borne out by A. Leroy's painstaking monograph, *La critique de la religion de David Hume* (Paris, 1930). F. Zabceh also inclines to interpret Hume as a downright atheist (cf. *Hume Precursor of Modern Empiricism* [The Hague, 1960], pp. 51ff.). Paulsen maintains that Hume limited himself to a critique of all dogmatism, theist and atheist alike (cf. D. Hume, *Dialoge über natürliche Religion*, German translation [Berlin, 1904], *Introduction*, pp. 8ff.). Hume himself presents his own scepticism as the surest way ". . . to be a true Christian and believer" in the words of his Cleanthes (cf. B. Magnino's monograph, *Il pensiero filosofico di D. Hume* [Naples, 1935], pp. 186f.).

[17] Hume, *Dialogues*, Part II, p. 141. Later on, however (Part VI), Demea raises the whole question again and concludes that no system, neither skepticism nor polytheism nor theism, has any real advantage or edge over the others (p. 175).

fact of the matter is that Hume does not reach any solid steady stand, neither theistic nor atheistic.

If the last page added to the *Dialogues* in 1776 can be taken as indicative, we must designate Hume's terminal position as professed fideistic skepticism. A decisive proof of the existence of God would in any case be beyond the grasp of our human reason: "But believe me," says Philo to Cleanthes, "the most natural sentiment, which a well-disposed mind will feel on this occasion, is a longing desire and expectation, that heaven would be pleased to dissipate, at least alleviate, this profound ignorance, by affording some more particular revelation to mankind, and making discoveries of the nature, attributes, and operations of the divine object of our faith. A person, seasoned with a just sense of the imperfections of natural reason, will fly to revealed truth with the greatest avidity; while the haughty dogmatist, persuaded that he can erect a complete system of theology by the mere help of philosophy, disdains any farther aid and rejects this adventitious instructor. To be a

---

An extensive note inserted into his *The History of Great Britain,* on the harm often done by bigotry and fanaticism in public and private life, shows us a Hume who professes to be critical rather of the abuses of religion than of religion as such: "This sophism, of arguing from the abuse of any thing against the use of it, is one of the grossest, and at the same time, the most common, to which men are subject. The history of all ages, and none more than of the period which is our subject, offer us examples of the abuse of religion; and we have not been sparing, in this volume more than in the former, to remark them: But whoever would thence draw an inference to the disadvantage of religion in general would argue very rashly and erroneously. The proper office of religion is to reform men's lives, to purify their hearts, to inforce all moral duties, and to secure obedience to the laws and civil magistrates. While it pursues these salutary purposes, its operations, tho' infinitely valuable, are secret and silent, and seldom come under the cognizance of history. That adulterate species of it alone, which inflames faction, animates sedition, and prompts rebellion, distinguishes itself on the open theatre of the world, and is the great force of revolutions and public convulsions. The historian, therefore, has scarce occasion to mention any other kind of religion; and he may retain the highest regard for true piety, even while he exposes all the abuses of the false. He may even think, that he cannot better show his attachment to the former than by detecting the latter, and laying open its absurdities and pernicious tendency. It is no proof of irreligion in an Historian, that he remarks some fault or imperfection in each sect of religion, which he has occasion to mention. Every institution, however divine, which is adopted by men must partake of the weakness and infirmities of our nature, and will be apt, unless carefully guarded, to degenerate into one extreme or the other."

And Hume concludes that even the Church of England of that day had not managed to avoid errors and abuses and that one can only anticipate and hope that an age of extravagances and exaggerations will be succeeded by an age that is reasonable and moderate: "For as it is the nature of fanaticism to abolish all slavish submission to priestly power; it follows, that as soon as the first ferment is abated, men are naturally in such sects left to the free use of their reason, and shake off the fetters of custom and authority" (*The History of Great Britain,* Vol. II, pp. 449f.).

philosophical skeptic is, in a man of letters, the first and most essential step toward being a sound, believing Christian; a proposition that I would willingly recommend to the attention of Pamphilus." Hume concludes that Philo's principles are more probable than Demea's; but that those of Cleanthes approach still nearer to the truth.[18] And Cleanthes was precisely the one who, in the course of this same Dialogue, had asserted that religion, even though a corrupt religion, is always better than no religion whatsoever. The doctrine of a life to come is so strong and necessary a guarantee for morality and ethics, that we ought never to abandon or forget it. Indeed, if temporal and finite considerations and punishments exercise so great an effect as we see them do every day, how much greater must we not expect the effect to be when they are infinite and eternal? [19] A great though disconcerting creative writer and a sharp-witted philosopher, Hume was desirous of saving, in terms of man's deep-seated aspiration, what philosophy was in process of destroying; and his chosen method was to describe a way of truth that would go beyond or rather stay this side of both rigid, extrinsic dogmatism and a rationalistic atheism no less arid and dogmatic.

The conclusion of the *Enquiry* seems to us likewise to confirm our interpretation of Hume: "Divinity or theology, as it proves the existence of a deity, and the immortality of souls, is composed partly of reasonings concerning particular, partly concerning general facts. It has a foundation in *reason,* so far as it is supported by experience. But its best and most solid foundation is *faith* and divine revelation." [20] And Hume must be thought to have intended these words to be taken in their obvious and generally accepted meaning. Thus, any accusation of atheism against Hume poses a most subtle problem of doctrinal discrimination.

This explicit charge of atheism was not long in coming; and it came especially from the rationalists of the Leibniz-Wolff school then flourishing in Germany. The main count of the charge-sheet is quite simply Hume's theoretical skepticism, at least in the case of the famous Platner.[21] "Skepticism," writes Platner at the beginning of his analysis, "is a quite special way of thinking, a quicksilver humor of the human

[18] *Dialogues,* p. XII, p. 227f.

[19] *Ibid.,* pp. 219f.

[20] *An Enquiry concerning Human Understanding,* Section XII, P. III, p. 165. In the *Dialogues,* Cleanthes calls Demea "an atheist" because of his anthropomorphic conception of God and so the roles are interchanged. Thus likewise a modern critic has taken up the defense of Hume in these words: "He was no atheist, nor a complete skeptic. He was simply being tossed between a belief and the difficulties he discerned in all beliefs" (Charles W. Hendel, *Studies in the Philosophy of D. Hume* [Princeton: Princeton University Press, 1925], p. 411).

[21] Ernest Platner, *Ueber den Atheismus,* Ein Gespräch; neue Ausgabe, (Leipzig, 1783). The work, in dialogue form, aims at refuting the theory and teaching of the *Dialogues concerning Natural Religion,* which are frequently quoted.

understanding. It does not begin with particular observations or yet with universal principles; rather the observations and the principles it derives take their origin from it. It does not repose upon any nexus of glimpsed truths; rather, if you would pinpoint it, what forms its essence and its spirit at once, is nothing other than a particular earmark of the philosophical mind or rather a working of the spirit. It is atheism, believe me, and nothing else; and the proof is that atheism always and altogether takes its starting point from skepticism." [22] Skepticism has as its effect the "inquietudes of the mind" occurring in periodic cycles and all manner of melancholy.[23] After passing in review Hume's critique of the various proofs of the existence of God, Platner makes Theophilus say that "this book [i.e., Hume's *Inquiry concerning Human Understanding*] contains the most distressing atheism and skepticism conceivable". And Philaletus agrees that skepticism is always the foundation of atheism, saying that the worst enemy of religion has always been the man who has stated that "the human reason is not the measure of truth." [24] Hilarius takes up the conclusion of Hume's *Dialogues* and asserts that it is (divine) revelation in any case that guarantees the truth; and Philaletus retorts that the truth of revealed religion must be firm and certain and therefore proven credible on the basis of facts, witnesses, etc., but that this is not possible in the event of a weak and fragile reason. If man's reason is not the sure standard and measure of truth, how could the historical certainty of religion be proved? [25] Rationalism thus made more evident the demand for an active presence of reason as a preparation for faith. But it was to be rather the Humeian notion of faith that would fertilize the development of modern thought in Hamann, Jacobi, Kant and Lessing, bringing into focus a totally new basis and problematic, the positive generative capacity of the mind which was that *belief* with which Hume hoped to stem the drift to atheism and dogmatism alike.

As opposed to Platner, Jacobi (1743-1819) sees in the suitable rectification and elevation of Humeian *belief* the solid bulwark for a substantiation of our judgment concerning reality: faith (*Glaube*) is not only a

[22] E. Platner, *Ueber den Atheismus,* p. 6. Platner classes Hume's skepticism with that of the Pyrrhonians of classical antiquity (p. 8 and passim).

[23] *Ibid.,* p. 10. A little later we find the expression ". . . the unrest of the mind" (p. 11), which recurs in Hegel where it signifies the constructive restlessness of the dialectic.

[24] *Ibid.,* pp. 144ff.

[25] Jacobi, *Idealismus und Realismus,* Ein Gespräch; *C. W.,* Vol. II (Leipzig, 1816), pp. 127ff. Hume is presented unequivocally as a *Glaubenslehrer* (teacher of faith) and Jacobi adverts to the influence of Hume on Kant. Jacobi quotes from *An Enquiry concerning Human Understanding* repeatedly and in the original; he shows no signs of having been acquainted with the *Dialogues* which Platner, for his part, quotes in the German translation.

theological principle; rather preeminently it constitutes the basis of our conviction of reality and more precisely of our certainty concerning everything not susceptible of rigorous proof, such as the necessary nexus between cause and effect.[26] In this way, Jacobi claims to be effecting a mediation between the "lower idealism" of Berkeley, that idealism that stopped halfway, denying in defiance of common sense the perception of a material world over against us and asserting that we have nothing but sensations, and the higher idealism of Hume, which denies in defiance of the rational sense the truth of the ideas flowing immediately from that sense, at the summit and apex of which stand the indestructible and mutually inseparable concepts or notions of freedom and providence. Humeian *belief* thus assumes the functions of an internal impulse which is elevated, by a convergence of similar needs and demands, first by Jacobi to the status of the receptive subjectivity of the *Glaube,* and later by Kant to the synthetic subjectivity of the *Ich denke überhaupt* as issuing from the *a priori* to bar the way to skepticism and atheism, as we shall be explaining soon.

Jacobi certainly must be admitted, like Hume, to have posed the problem in its most drastic form, reiterating in the atmosphere of modern thought the classical position of the Stoics on the κοιναὶ ἐννοίαι there are primordial cognitions and immediate certainties that do not presuppose any reflection but are themselves the presupposition of all reflection and all knowledge. It is this primordial and unanalyzable knowledge and certainty that Hume and Jacobi call "faith", which in turn is not a blind assent but rather represents the evidence of a theoretical principle; indeed, it reveals the theoretical principle as such, inasmuch as it constitutes the possibility of all knowledge and reflection and is truly that "ultimate basis" to which reflection is brought back by its own analytical activity.

This theory constitutes the positive and constructive aspect of Jacobi's critique of modern pantheism and atheism in his controversy with his friend Mendelssohn, a controversy of which we shall be speaking later, occasioned by the dispute about Lessing's Spinozism. This episode has been accorded little attention in the history of modern thought, but

[26] Jacobi, *Vorrede zugleich Einleitung in des Verfassers sämtliche philosophische Schriften, C. W.,* Vol. II, pp. 76f. This is Jacobi's most mature (1816) work and probably his most forthright: in it he speaks out in no uncertain terms on his speculative odyssey and the precise significance of his basic principles. For this reason I have taken it as a guideline in the following exposition. Jacobi himself asserts he has not only rendered his terminology more precise than it had previously been, but that he has also corrected the error of a failure to distinguish between intellect and reason, an error into which he had fallen in his Dialogue on Hume (cf. *Idealismus und Realismus,* p. 221f., note added to 2nd ed.).

it is so important as to stand out as evidently crucial, both in view of the interest displayed by present-day philosophy for radical phenomenology and ontology and in view of the decisive influence exercised precisely by Hume and Spinoza, for opposite but converging motives, in the molding of modern idealism. There can be no doubt that philosophy today, as a radical and therefore asystematic type of thinking, is closer to Hume and Jacobi than to Kant or Hegel. Jacobi expounds his principle in explicit form preeminently in his famous *Ueber die Lehre des Spinoza in Briefen an den Herrn Moses Mendelssohn* (1785).[27] The Dialogue *Idealismus und Realismus* (1787) takes up the same theme again, with direct reference to Hume.

The central thesis is clearly expressed unequivocally: "All human knowledge proceeds from revelation and faith."[28] This principle touched off a general uproar in the German philosophical world, says Jacobi, because of the unwillingness to admit the existence of a first-hand knowing globally conditioning second-hand knowing (scientific knowledge in the widest sense), a knowing *without proofs* necessarily preceding knowing activity as usually understood, acting as foundation for it, dominating it continuously and completely. The dialogue was intended to constitute a reply to the misunderstandings and apprehensions that had been aroused by Jacobi's principle and to serve as his defense against the charge of being an enemy of reason, a fanatic and a Papist!

Thus Jacobi, a subjectivist like Kant, inverts the Humeian *belief* into the principle of realism and of transcendence. In his last reflections in which he also took a stand on Kant's *Critique of Pure Reason,* Jacobi stresses (in what amounts to an anticipation of Hegel) the distinction between understanding (*Verstand*) and reason (*Vernunft*), something he had not done in *Idealismus und Realismus,* which had appeared in 1788, a year before the publication of *Kant's Critique of Practical Reason.* In *Idealismus und Realismus,* Jacobi had accused Kantianism of leading to nihilism because of its abstraction of being from cognition and its subordination of immediate knowledge to mediate. As soon as philosophy refuses to acknowledge in man a faculty of cognition superior to, and independent of, sense-intuition and attempts to ascend from the sensible realm to the suprasensible, from the finite to the Infinite, solely by way of continual reflection upon the sensible and upon the laws of representation of that sensible to the intellect, the result must

[27] A second edition was published in 1789 and the last edition, which was also Jacobi's last work, in 1819, in which year he died on March 10. This last edition has an extensive Preface (*Vorbericht*).

[28] *Vorrede,* pp. 3f.

inevitably be a pure and simple voiding of knowledge.[29] Kant, says Jacobi, destroyed the rationalistic illusion of nominalism, which had prevailed until Leibniz; that illusion had been to imagine that everything could be solved by the intellect or understanding as a faculty which limited itself to reflecting upon the senses and forming concepts. But Kant's mistake had been to conclude to the impossibility of any knowing of the suprasensible. And this mistake had been caused by his refusal to recognize the second front of knowledge, after the senses, which is reason: Kant at least *implicitly* made the intellect subordinate [30] and that is the way to philosophical perdition. Reason is thus the primary faculty of the spiritual being; it is the very life of that being; therefore, the contention of an absolute and interior irrationalism must be rejected. Thus does Jacobi start from Hume in order to overcome Hume.[31]

Thus Jacobi maintains a qualitative difference between understanding and reason, coming close in this to the Hegelian position, as we have remarked already. He insists that Kant's capital error was that of admitting a single form of intuition only, namely, the sensible one. Since it is a modification of our mind, it cannot attain to the "thing-in-itself". But any talk of phenomena or "appearances" in the absence of something that appears, says Jacobi, is absurd. The understanding, which is only a reflective and judging activity, can do nothing to help here; and no more can the Kantian reason, which is strictly conditioned by the understanding. For Jacobi, on the contrary, reason has the function of positive revelation, of unconditioned decision, or of *natural rational faith:* it is not limited merely to "explaining"; it "reveals" immediately,[32] and so we have a system of absolute objectivity.

[29] Leibniz's position likewise is a dead end: his *"nisi* ipse *intellectus"* (except the intellect itself) does indeed liberate him from materialism and sense-perceptionism but it does not manage to raise him above the sensible world which he had reduced to nothing in order to forge ahead toward the suprasensible, the truly real (*Vorrede,* p. 20).

[30] For a critique of this point of Kantianism, Jacobi refers the reader to his *Von den göttlichen Dingen und ihrer Offenbarung* (1798). For his notion of "reason" which he uses to supplement Humeian *Belief,* Jacobi is indebted specially to Sulzer (1720-1779) and for the identification of reason with the perception of life to Leibniz (cf. *Idealismus und Realismus,* pp. 222ff. note).

[31] "Either the principle of reason must be held to be identical with the principle of life, or the reason must be made into a mere accident of an organized whole. As for me, I do hold the principle of reason to be identical with the principle of life; and I do not believe in any *interior or absolute* unreason" (*Idealismus und Realismus,* p. 222).

[32] "The dynamic of the Jacobi theory, leading as it does with equal cogency to a system of absolute objectivity, is displeasing to the intellect or understanding that grapples solely onto the understandable (after all, this theory speaks precisely of the philosophizing *reason*), and this theory has on its side only the reason that does not explain but reveals directly and immediately, i.e., *natural rational faith.* (*Vorrede,* pp. 36f.).

Kant had initially appealed to sense experience and the existence of the external world in order to refute idealism;[33] but then he proceeded to nullify this experience. Jacobi, on the other hand, observes that it is not enough to assert that "without the *you* there cannot be any *I*"; the very experience of the "I am" is possible only on the presuppósition of external experience. Jacobi seems to us to have effected a penetrating exposure of the pointlessness of Kant's sort of mistaken recourse to experience and rational faith: Kant, says Jacobi, has substituted the *cogito ergo es* for the Cartesian *cogito ergo sum,* but has not been able to get a step further or to substantiate the objective validity of the three transcendental ideas: God, freedom and the substantiality and immortality of the soul. Kant's recourse to "rational faith" (*Vernunftglaube*) is vitiated *ab ovo* by his elimination on principle of all objective knowing: thus, Kantian criticism first inters metaphysics in the dimension of theory out of partiality for scientific knowledge and then gets cold feet at the prospect of subjective nihilism and promptly buries scientific knowledge in the dimension of practice out of a hankering after metaphysics.[34]

Jacobi goes on to show that in the Kantian cosmos, the notion of "freedom" (*Freiheit*) in the moral realm ends up being identical with the notion of "necessity" (*Notwendigkeit*) so that the notions of freedom, rationality and necessity coincide in the single concept of "the unconditioned", "the eternal substance of things" and "the eternal primordial fountainhead of this substance", i.e., of nature. Now this is simply, concludes Jacobi against Spinoza and his transcendental idealist followers, to posit as principle, as primordial beginning, power (*Macht*), a power beyond and above which there is no other power and which can neither be bested nor even managed and directed by knowledge, wisdom or beauty, even granting that they are buried like seeds in its depths, in the innermost reaches of the whole. But such a power is nothing else than blind fate, which is the diametric opposite of God who is pro*vid*ence (Vor*seh*ung); and fatalism and atheism is the inevitable destination of the new philosophy. Fatalism, atheism, Spinozism and idealism therefore come to the same thing.

Jacobi's new "faith" thus stands to scientific knowledge as cause to effect, and scientific knowledge in its turn extirpates that false faith that is superstition. This true faith is the faculty of the suprasensible, even as

[33] Cf. Kant, *Kritik der reinen Vernunft,* Vorrede zur zweiten Ausgabe, Vols. 38-41.

[34] "Kantian criticism first undermines metaphysics theoretically in favor of science; then—because everything is on the point of disappearing into the gaping bottomless abyss of an absolute subjectivity—the same Kantian criticism proceeds to undermine science from the practical point of view, in favor of metaphysics (Jacobi, *Vorrede,* p. 44).

perception is the faculty of the sensible, for even as there is a sensible intuition, an intuition (*Anschauung*) via the senses, so too there is a rational intuition via reason. Both stand over against each other as genuine forms of knowledge and even as the former cannot be deduced from the latter, so the latter cannot be deduced from the former; each is primary and the basis of all certitude in its own order and also the basis of all proof. And Jacobi vigorously asserts the superiority of feeling over every other faculty; it is the faculty that makes man man, the adumbration of the divine knowing and willing in the finite mind of man, and it constitutes the source of the ideas, the upper level of man.[35] Thus, it is not the understanding, which has as its proper object the contents of the external senses and of the material world, but rather it is the faculty of feeling that distinguishes man from the animals. Thus the fundamental significance of Jacobi's positivization of Humeian *belief* lies in the assertion of a dual experience and thus likewise of a dual immediacy: sense perception and the feeling of reason. The original sin of idealism (as also of materialism) is for Jacobi that of having stopped at (or more accurately, started from and based itself upon) the principle of the "unity of experience", which necessarily leads to an imprisonment within the world and nature, with a consequent ruling out of any contact with any suprasensible realities, such as freedom, immortality and God himself. It was the threat of this metaphysical nihilism that impelled Jacobi to oppose himself, as if by prophetic instinct, to Kant and idealism; to transmute the principle of Humeian skepticism into the basis of certitude; and to see in the *cogito* and the *Ich denke* alike the sheer negation of all transcendence and consequently the abyss of fatalism and of atheism, as we shall soon be pointing out.

[35] The original text of this passage we have just paraphrased is of capital importance: "Faith is the adumbration of the divine knowing and willing in the finite mind of man" (*ibid.*, p. 55). And a little later: "The faculty of feeling, we maintain, is the most exalted faculty in man; it is the faculty that specifically distinguishes him from the animals, raising him above them not simply in degree but in kind, i.e., *incomparably*. This faculty is, we maintain, one and the same as reason . . . It is solely and exclusively from the faculty of feeling that there originates what we call reason and exalt over the *mere* intellect or understanding which is geared to nature alone" (p. 61).

6
Conclusion: The Atheistic Implications of Deism

The most thorough overall judgment on the structure and issue of Deism is undoubtedly that of the theologian Samuel Clarke (1675-1729),[1] a contemporary eyewitness of this avalanche of apparently innocuous ideas which Clarke nevertheless judged to be in reality subversive in the long run of all religious values, even those acknowledged and proclaimed by reason alone. The evolution of European thought has amply borne out his most pessimistic anticipations. As an expert observer of the situation, Clarke vigorously maintains that Deism, far from being a stable self-sufficient position, must inevitably end in atheism, to the extent that it does not lead to the acceptance of Christianity: he insists that "a constant and sincere observance of all the Laws of Reason and Obligations of Natural Religion, will unavoidably lead a man to *Christianity;* if he has due opportunities of examining things, and will steadily pursue the Consequences of his own Principles"; and concludes that Deists who do not go this far "can have no fixt and settled Principles at all, upon which they can either argue or act

[1] His major work comprises the two series of Boyle's Lectures given in 1704-1705 in defense of "the being and attributes of God" against the atheists and of the "unchangeable obligations of natural religion" against the Deists, which two series of lectures were collected and published under the overall title *A Discourse concerning the Being and Attributes of God, the Obligation of Natural Religion, and the Truth and Certainty of the Christian Revelation* (London, 1716). On this work, cf. the remarks of W. R. Sorley, *Moral Values and the Idea of God* (Cambridge, 1935 [3]), pp. 450ff. Stephen calls Clarke ". . . the great English representative of the *a priori* method of constructing a system of theology" (*History of English Thought,* Vol. I, p. 119).

The fuller titles of the individual series (both of them representing sermons preached in St. Paul's Cathedral, London) are of interest: 1. *A Demonstration of the Being and Attributes of God:* more particularly in Answer to Mr. Hobbs, Spinoza, and their Followers, Wherein the Notion of Liberty is Stated, and the possibility and Certainty of it Proved, in Opposition to Necessity and Fate. 2. *A Discourse Concerning the Unchangeable Obligations of Natural Religion, and the Truth and Certainty of the Christian Revelation.*

consistently; but must of necessity sink into downright Atheism, (and consequently fall under the force of the former Arguments;)" [which Clarke had used to prove the existence of God].[2] In order to clarify various stages of this lapse of Deism into atheism, Clarke divides the Deists into four classes (without mentioning any names) in function of their way of denying the divine attributes.

1. Some men bear the name of Deists because they pretend to believe in the existence of an eternal, infinite, independent, and intelligent Being, to whom (in order to avoid being dubbed epicurean atheists) they attribute the making of the world. But they are Epicureans in the matter of providence, says Clarke, for they imagine that God does not at all concern himself with the government of the world, paying no attention to what happens in the world nor yet having any concern for intracosmic events.[3] This position is basically nothing else than veiled atheism and close examination proves that it must inevitably terminate in absolute atheism. It is a patent absurdity to assert on the one hand the existence of God and then to proceed to deny his direct intervention in the world, to admit that God has created the world and then to exclude his providence from that world, as though matter and motion alone would suffice, with the course of events in the universe abandoned to the random chaos of infinite possible combinations.[4] If God is an intelligent Being who is likewise omnipotent, omnipresent, possessed of infinite wisdom and untrammelled freedom, then he must direct and govern every event that happens in the world, right down to the minutest cir-

[2] Indicative, in the history of modern atheism, is the fury shown by Enlightenment atheism against the Clarke proof of the existence of God (Cf. d'Holbach, *Système de la Nature,* Part II, ch. II, p. 95 and especially pp. 106ff.).

[3] For the epicurean teaching, Clarke refers the reader to Lucretius (lib. I, v. 57ff.) and cites the following text from Diogenes Laertes' *Life of Epicurus:* "The Blessed and Indestructible hath not private concerns nor yet doth supply them to others, thus having no portion in rages or kindnesses" and Clarke comments: "Nor is the doctrine of those Modern Philosophers, much different; who ascribe every thing to Matter and Motion, exclusive of Final Causes; and speak of God as an *Intelligentia Supramundana:* Which is the very *Cant* of *Epicurus* and *Lucretius*" (*op. cit.,* Part II, p. 15). The position here described certainly agrees with that of Toland in the *Letters to Serena.*

[4] And Clarke adds: "As I shall show presently; after I have made only this One Observation, that as that Opinion is impious in it self, so the late improvements in Mathematicks and natural Philosophy have discovered, that, as things Now are, that Scheme is plainly false and impossible in Fact. For, not to say, that, seeing Matter is utterly uncapable of obeying any Laws, the very original Laws of Motion themselves cannot continue to take place, but by something Superiour to Matter continually exerting in it a certain Force or Power according to such certain and determinate Laws" (*op. cit.,* Part II, p. 16). Clarke goes on to observe that plants and animals cannot be formed out of mere Matter by the laws of motion alone; and that the very law of gravity (then already discovered by Newton) proves the existence of a supreme Being, first cause of the world and preserving and governing Power of that world at the present moment.

cumstance, with due regard, of course, for the nature of subsidiary agents. Hence the conclusion: to take away the government of the world from God is to deny him omnipotence, supreme wisdom and awareness;[5] and this is especially true in any position that would put the government of the physical world ahead of that of the moral, as though the course of the stars were a matter of greater importance to God than the destinies of the human race.

2. A second class of philosophers is listed among the Deists because they make no distinction between moral good and evil: they claim to admit the existence of God and even his providence, but they go on to assert that God is not in fact interested in how men comport themselves in this life. These men are thus admitting the natural attributes of God but denying the moral attributes, justice and goodness, and this again is bound to end in atheism, for the natural and moral attributes in God are inseparable: "It follows unavoidably, that he who denies the Justice or Goodness of God, or, which is all one, denies his exercise of these Attributes in inspecting and regarding the moral Actions of Men; must also deny, either his Wisdom, or his Power, or both; and consequently must needs be driven into *absolute Atheism.*[6] Clarke adds that the conduct of these Deists is entirely in agreement with that of atheists: they condemn all religion, revealed and natural, and every religious practice; they deride all virtue and everything that raises man above the level of the beasts; they seize on the pretext of combatting ignorance and superstition but in reality they are heaping scorn on all that is noblest and most sacred to man, in order to tout the filthy, the dishonorable and the absurd.

With men of this sort, concludes Clarke, the only thing is to explain to them and convince them of the first principles of reason: "And then they must of necessity either retreat into down-right *Atheism,* or be led by undeniable Reasoning to acknowledge and submit to the Obligations of *Morality,* and make open recantation of their profane abuse of God and Religion."[7] For Clarke, who sees the real objectives of the fight even in

[5] "Wherefore the Opinion of this sort of Deists, stands not upon any certain consistent Principles, but leads unavoidably to *down-right Atheism;* And however in *Words* they may confess a God, yet in *reality* and in truth they deny him" (*op. cit.,* Part II, p. 19). Clarke insists that the position of the deists is identical with that of Epicurus, on whom he quotes the famous judgment of Cicero: "Epicurus left God on paper but took him away in fact" (*Epicurum verbis reliquisse Deum, re sustulisse*) (*De natura deorum,* II).

[6] Clarke, *op. cit.,* Part II, p. 22.

[7] *Ibid.,* p. 25. A like ferocity of language recurs often among the theologians, alarmed by the audacity of the Deists: thus, e.g., Oswald, a Scottish common-sense school theologian does not scruple to call every Deist "a madman" (L. Stephen, *History of English Thought,* Vol. I, p. 385).

The clash between the theologians and the Deists was inevitable and the contro-

the midst of the clamor of front-line battle, Deism is raising again the entire problem of man's attitude to truth: the struggle is not limited to the Christian religion alone: what is at stake is the entire life of the spirit.

3. The third class of Deists are entirely orthodox in the matter of God: not only do they admit his existence, they also accept the doctrine concerning his attributes, natural and moral alike, and conceive the doctrine of providence in conformity with these attributes. In regard to man they fall short: prejudiced against the dogma of the immortality of human souls, they imagine that men perish entirely at death. Thus, one generation follows another without anything remaining of the good or evil that men have done; the virtues of God transcend our intelligence, say these Deists in conclusion, and because these virtues of God have nothing in common with what are called human virtues, man ought not to complain about any lack of equity in the distribution of rewards and punishments in this life, and still less ought he to hope for any justice in a life to come. This opinion, says Clarke brusquely, does not stand on any consistent principles: for if justice and goodness are not the same in God as in our ideas, then "we mean nothing when we say that God is necessarily Just and Good",[8] and thus even the existence of God loses all meaning. Those who deny the immortality of the soul, thus, likewise pretend to acknowledge the moral attributes of the deity but in reality they demolish them and thus end up by dropping the natural attributes as well: "And, so upon the whole, this Opinion likewise, if we argue upon it consistently, must finally recur to absolute Atheism." [9]

---

versy flared to high points of extreme bitterness. The Deists were accused not only of destroying Christianity as a supernatural and revealed religion, but even of denying all religion and falling into atheism. Peter Browne, who taught Berkeley in Dublin, considered Toland a madman and hand in glove with the Socinians and the atheists; and he accused Locke, too, of slipping into atheism; Clarke levels the same charge of atheism against Toland; a like charge is brought by Bentley and Bolinbroke against Collins, disciple of Toland; and the controversy reaches its climax of fury in mutual exchanges of the charge of atheism among the theologians themselves (e.g., Clarke and Waterland, Peter Browne and Berkeley) (Cf. L. Stephen, *op. cit.*, Vol. I, pp. 113ff., 121, 178ff., 305, 317, 463 and *passim*).

[8] Clarke cites (Part II, p. 26) a quite pertinent passage of Origen: "For as far as we are concerned, the same virtue belongs to all the blessed, so that the same virtue belongs to man and God".

[9] *Ibid.* Clarke is here obviously aiming at Henry Dodwell, author of a work entitled *The Natural Mortality of the Human Soul clearly demonstrated,* with whom Clarke was at grips precisely on this point (Cf. the final letter in the exchange: *A Letter to Mr. Dodwell,* wherein all the arguments in his Epistolary Discourse are particularly answered [1706]; this letter bears, in the French translation, the plainly Thomistic title: *Sur l'immatérialité de l'âme et son immortalité naturelle;* cf. French translation of A. Jacques, *Oeuvres philosophiques de Samuel Clarke,* nouvelle édition [Paris, 1845], pp. 326ff.).

In this fabric of the spirit everything is interwoven and no rent can be made without unravelling the consistency of the whole notion that man can and must have of the supreme Being.

4. The last class of Deists, the first and best in a descending order of adequacy, embraces all those who admit all the truths of natural religion without distinction, accept providence and profess all the duties to God and men, but reject all divine revelation. These are the only ones who can truly be called Deists and they are the only ones with whom one should enter into discussion; but they are very few and far between, because such men, were they in good faith, would be obliged forthwith to embrace Christianity and acknowledge the supernatural origin of the Christian religion. Deism could subsist, observes Clarke, before Christ, but it cannot now: the philosophers of antiquity were seeking an ever fuller and purer truth and therefore they hoped, in the depths of their heart, for a divinely revealed religion: but "*Deists,* in our Days, who obstinately reject Revelation when offered to them, are not such Men as *Socrates* and *Tully* were; but, under pretense of Deism, 'tis plain they are generally Ridiculers of all that is truly excellent even in natural Religion itself." [10]

Clarke's contention is that a true and genuine Deist cannot remain a Deist in the Christian dispensation but must logically become a Christian: "The Sum is this: There is now no such Thing, as a consistent Scheme of Deism. That which alone was once such, namely the Scheme of the best *Heathen Philosophers,* ceases *now* to be so after the appearance of Revelation; Because (as I have already shown, and shall more largely prove in the sequel of this Discourse,) it directly conducts Men to the belief of *Christianity.* All other Pretenses to *Deism,* may by unavoidable consequence be forc'd to terminate in absolute *Atheism.* He that cannot prevail with himself to obey the *Christian Doctrine,* and embrace Those hopes of *life and immortality,* which our Savior has *brought to light through the* Gospel; cannot Now be imagined to maintain with any firmness, steadiness and certainty, the belief of the *Immortality of the Soul,* and a *future State of Rewards and Punishments after death;* Because all the main difficulties and objections, lie equally against both." [11]

No one step can be taken in this area without incurring the obligation of taking all the other steps; and equally a refusal to take one step necessarily entails the obligation of refusing to take any of the others. Thus, anyone accepting the teaching of reason on the deity cannot refuse to accept revelation: "Wherefore since those Arguments which demonstrate to us the Being and Attributes of God, are so closely con-

[10] Clarke, *op. cit.,* Part II, p. 31.
[11] *Ibid.,* pp. 33f.

nected with those which prove the reasonableness and certainty of the Christian Revelation, that there is Now no consistent Scheme of Deism left; all modern Deists being forced to shift from one Cavil to another, and having no fixed and certain set of Principles to adhere to." [12] Therefore, concludes Clarke, the Deists are to be attacked with the same weapons as are used against the atheists.

The refutation of atheism had been the subject of the work (or "Discourse") devoted by Clarke to the proof of the existence of God, under the significant title "A Demonstration of the Being and Attributes of God: Most Particularly in Answer to Mr. Hobbs, Spinoza, And their Followers". In the first chapter, dealing with the causes of atheism, Clarke divides atheists into three classes: those who do not believe in the existence of God, those who "would be thought to do so"; and those who deny the principal attributes of the divine nature and "suppose God to be an Unintelligent Being, which acts merely by Necessity; that is, which, in any tolerable Propriety of Speech, acts not at all, but is only acted upon: All Men that are *atheists,* I say, in this Sense, must be so upon one or other of these three Accounts.

"Either, *First,* because being extremely ignorant and stupid, they have never duly *considered* anything at all; nor made any just use of their natural Reason, to discover even the plainest and most obvious Truths; but have spent their Time in a manner of Life very little Superior to that of Beasts.

"Or, *Secondly,* because being totally debauched and corrupted in their *Practice,* they have, by a vitious and degenerate Life, corrupted the Principles of their Nature, and defaced the Reason of their own Minds; and, instead of fairly and impartially enquiring into the Rules and Obligations of Nature, and the Reason and Fitness of Things, have accustomed themselves only to mock and scoff at Religion; and, being under the Power of Evil Habits, and the Slavery of Unreasonable and Indulged Lusts, are resolved not to hearken to any Reasoning which would oblige them to forsake their beloved Vices.

[12] *Ibid.,* p. 35. Clarke presents an extensive development of this point, basic to his notion of the relations between natural religion and Christianity, in the first chapter, especially in Proposition X: "That is, Christianity even in this single respect, as containing alone and in one consistent System, all the wise and good Precepts, (and those improved, augmented, and exalted to the highest degree of Perfection,) that ever were taught singly and scatteredly, and many times but very corruptly, by the several Schools of the Philosophers; and this without any mixture of the fond, absurd, and superstitious Practises of any of those Philosophers; ought to be embraced and practised by all rational and considering Deists, who will act consistently, and steddily pursue the consequences of their own Principles; as at least the best Scheme and Sect of Philosophy, that ever was set up in the World; and highly probable, even though it had no external evidence, to be of Divine Origin": p. 11.

"Or, *Thirdly,* because in the way of *Speculative Reasoning,* and upon the Principles of Philosophy, they pretend that the Arguments used against the Being or Attributes of God, seem to them, after the strictest and fullest inquiry, to be more strong and conclusive, than those by which we indeavor to prove these great Truths",[13] and it is to this group alone that Clarke addresses this discourse. The importance of this threefold distinction, an importance acknowledged by Leibniz as well in his famous controversy with Clarke, lay preeminently in the determination to bar the way to the new forms of empiricist and rationalist subjectivism. The shrewd theologian could not be hoodwinked on their long-term consequences. His example was followed by others [14] and in the long run saved Anglican theology from being infiltrated by modern philosophical trends, as was the theology of the continent.

Summing up, then, we may say that Deism has hitherto not been accorded, in the history of modern philosophy, the place it deserves on account of its capital importance in the development of modern thought. This neglect and disregard can be explained in part by the fact that no first-rate philosophers stand out in the Deist tradition; but the main reason why Deism has been overlooked lies in the fact that it is a "philosophy of personalities" rather than of concepts and treats with preference of the concrete existential aspects of personalities and historical events involved in the religion problem. But Deism, like every great current of thought, is a school with varied and complex nuances, extending from the quite vigorous theism of a Cherbury to the atheism threshold of a Toland, Collins or Shaftesbury: it describes the parabola of Diderot's evolution as a thinker, as we shall be pointing out in due course. In his earliest writings, Diderot claims that the Deist is the only one who "can stand up to the atheist", that the Deist actually "renders certain the existence of a God, the immortality of the soul and its consequences;" [15] later he represents the Deist position as not far re-

[13] *Ibid.,* Part I, pp. 1ff.

[14] Joseph Butler, Bishop of Durham, author of the famous apologetic treatise *The Analogy of Religion Natural and Revealed to the Constitution and Course of Nature* (1736), is certainly in the tradition of Clarke, whose work is mentioned in the subtitle of the above work. Like Clarke, Butler divides his work into two parts: "I. Of Natural Religion, II. Of Revealed Religion" and it is interesting to note how he commences the first part with a treatment of immortality (ch. I, Of a Future Life [Glasgow-London,[2] 1827], pp. 185ff.), to which question he had devoted an earlier treatise entitled *Of Personal Identity* (*ibid.,* pp. 517ff.) in which reference is made to the Clarke-Dodwell controversy (p. 521). The polemical overtones, against atheism and Deism, are always muted and veiled in this work (cf., e.g., pp. 171ff., and 337ff.).

[15] "Only the Deist can stand up to the atheist. The superstitious man is simply not up to it: his God is nothing but an imaginary being." "The Deist renders certain the existence of a God, the immortality of the soul and its consequences" (Diderot, *Pensées philosophiques,* §§ XIII and XXIII; *Oeuvres philosophiques,*

moved from Spinozism: "Intelligent being is for him [the Deist] in no sense a mode of corporeal being. To my mind, there is no reason to believe corporeal being to be an effect of intelligent being. It follows, then, from his avowal and my reasoning, that intelligent being and corporeal being are eternal, that these two substances make up the universe and that the universe is God. Our reasons are presently being weighed and if ever a definitive judgment is pronounced, I shall inform you." [16] A closer study of Deism thus brings us up against ambiguities and fluctuations no less serious and striking than those encountered in better known systems of philosophy.

The Deists have in fact been called naturalists, free-thinkers and rationalists by their opponents.[17] Kortholt, as we have seen, judged not only Hobbes and Toland to be atheists, but Collins and Herbert of Cherbury himself as well; later the Deists were called naturalists as being protagonists of natural religion as opposed to supernatural religion, and the term "naturalist" subsequently became synonomous with "rationalist"; [18] the term "free-thinker" goes back to the days of the first Deists and specifically to Collins (*Discourse of Freethinking,* 1763), while Molineux had called Toland "a candid free-thinker" as early as 1697 and the same designation was expressed somewhat more elegantly in France by the term *esprit fort.* Let it be borne in mind, at the same time, however, that the Deists themselves never professed to be denying the deity but solely to be clarifying what the name of God could signify in a rigorously rational conception of the world; nor was it their intention to destroy Christianity but only to criticize a close and dogmatic theology, embroiled in sectarian controversies between the various denominations into which the Reformation had broken Christianity up.[19]

---

ed. P. Vernière, pp. 14, 23). Vernière has a pertinent note to § XXIII: "Voltaire has the marginal note: 'Many Deists do not admit the immortality of the soul at all.' Although himself a Deist, Voltaire had been saying as early as 1734 in his *Traité de métaphysique:* 'I am not claiming to have any proofs against the spirituality and immortality of the soul, but all the probabilities are against both" (p. 23).

[16] Diderot, *Promenade du sceptique. L'allée des Maroniers, ibid.,* pp. CIVf.

[17] This is stated by G. V. Lechler, historian of Deism, in his *Geschichte des Englischen Deismus,* p. 453.

[18] Cf. C. F. Stäudlin, *Geschichte des Rationalismus und Supernaturalismus* (Göttingen, 1826), p. 110. Stäudlin absolves them of the charge of atheism (". . . nor were they atheists or anti-moralists"). The pamphlet *The Necessity of Atheism,* attributed to Shelley (though probably written, in the main, by his friend, Hogg) and responsible for the young poet's expulsion from Oxford University, is considered to be probably in the tradition of English Deism (cf. B. Chiapelli, *Il pensiero religioso di Shelley* [Rome, 1956], especially pp. 40ff.).

[19] But the Deism-atheism nexus seems unavoidable: "The process is a logical one, from the premise that we know only that which is given to us by the activity of the senses, to the conclusion that, if God exists, it must be in a region quite

But the vital dynamic of thought is governed by the logic of its principles and not by the personal intentions or convictions of the philosophers; and by a bitter etymological irony, Deism came to represent one of the most striking stages of the breakdown of theology and the consolidation of atheism in the modern age.

---

beyond the world as we know it through experience. For God cannot be discovered in the sensory sources of knowledge, and therefore, if he exists at all, it must be in a sphere transcending a world which is composed wholly of original elements given in sensation. This is *Deism,* and the way is not far from Deism to atheism, and many there were in that age who found it" (Y. G. Hibben, *The Philosophy of Enlightenment* [New York, 1910], p. 19). The situation was exacerbated especially in the wake of Hume's critique of religion: "The negative assertions of Hume carried more weight, however, than his speculative queries. His argument against natural religion tended to undermine the very foundations of Deism, and to accelerate the tendency of deistical opinion to drift into atheism" (*ibid.,* p. 279). This remark is especially true of France where Hume's writings exercised a considerable influence: "A hatred of the priests, a protest against ecclesiastical authority and a sensationalistic psychology all combined in France to produce a philosophy of atheism" (p. 279).

Appendices

I. Joseph Butler's Refutation of Shaftesbury's Naturalism

The major anti-Shaftesbury work is considered to be Bishop Joseph Butler's *The Analogy of Religion Natural and Revealed to the Constitution and Course of Nature,* published in 1736 (quotations here are all from the 2nd edition, Glasgow, 1827); in an appendix are presented two Dissertations, one *Of Personal Identity* (with reference to the problem of the immortality of the soul) and the other *Of the Nature of Virtue.* Although there are no explicit references to Shaftesbury, either in the main work or in the Dissertations (or, for that matter, in the lengthy introductory Essay of 164 pages by Rev. D. Wilson), a few points will suffice to put it beyond doubt that we are here dealing with a direct refutation of Shaftesbury's ideas:

1. From the *Advertisement* on, there is clear evidence not only of the anti-deistic tone but of the patent anti-Shatesbury bias as well: "It is come, I know not how, to be taken for granted, by many persons, that Christianity is not so much as a subject of inquiry; but that it is now, at length, discovered to be fictitious. And accordingly they treat it, as if, in the present age, this were an agreed point among all people of discernment; and nothing remained, but to set it up as a principal subject of mirth and ridicule, as it were by way of reprisals, for its having so long interrupted the pleasures of the world" (p. 169). The guiding principle of Butler's whole book is the correspondence or "Analogy" between natural religion and revealed religion, both in the negative sense that denials and objections aimed at the one eventually backfire against the other, and in the positive sense that the proofs in favor of the one redound to the advantage of the other (cf. the conclusion of *the Introduction,* p. 182).

2. It is quite probably Shaftesbury who is under attack right from the beginning of Part I, as Butler prepares to launch into his proof of the immortality of the soul: "Strange difficulties have been raised by some concerning personal identity, or the sameness of living agents, implied in the notion of our existing now and hereafter, or in any two successive moments; which whoever thinks it worth while, may find considered in the first Dissertation at the end of this Treatise" (p. 185). The reference is to the Dissertation *Of Personal Identity* (pp. 517ff.).

Chapter II: *"Of the Government of God by Rewards and Punishments, and particularly of the latter"* (p. 208) is certainly aimed against Shaftesbury. Thus, we read concerning the theory of pleasure as the prime motivating force in moral action: "Is the pleasure, then, naturally accompanying every particular gratification of passion, intended to put us upon gratifying ourselves in every such particular instance, and as a reward to us for so doing? No, certainly" (p. 212). Especially patently anti-Shaftesbury is the critique in Ch. III of the theory that only "benevolence" is proper to God and not the justice that punishes in the life to come: "Some men seem to think the only character of the Author of Nature to be that of simple absolute benevolence. This, considered as a principle of action, and infinite in degree, is a disposition to produce the greatest possible happiness, without regard to persons' behaviour, otherwise than as such regard would produce higher degrees of it. And supposing this to be the only character of God, veracity, and justice in him would be nothing but benevolence conducted by wisdom. Now, surely this ought not to be asserted, unless it can be proved; for we should speak with cautious reverence upon a subject . . ." (p. 224; cf. pp. 248ff., 265ff.). Butler insists that such a theory would amount to a removal of all distinction between good and evil.

Similarly, we read in Butler's definition of virtue: "For virtue consists in a regard to what is right and reasonable, as being so; in a regard to veracity, justice, charity, in themselves: and there is surely no such thing as a like natural regard to falsehood, injustice, cruelty" (p. 236—Butler returns to this point in the Dissertation *Of the Nature of Virtue,* pp. 527ff.). There is also a critique of utilitarianism (p. 276ff.) and moral fatalism (pp. 292ff.), as denying freedom and providence.

3. At the beginning of Part II, there is a clear reference to Shaftesbury's deistic critique of revealed religion: "Some persons, upon pretence of the sufficiency of the light of nature, avowedly reject all revelation, as, in its very notion, incredible, and what must be fictitious. And, indeed it is certain, no revelation would have been given, had the light of nature been sufficient in such a sense, as to render one not wanting and useless. But, no man in seriousness and simplicity of mind, can possibly think it so, who considers the state of religion in the heathen world, before revelation, and its present state in those places which have borrowed no light from it; particularly the doubtfulness of some of the greatest men concerning things of the utmost importance, as well as the natural inattention and ignorance of mankind in general" (p. 337; cf. pp. 21ff.). The deistic critique of religion is accused of leading straight to atheism: "The objections against all this, from the perversion of Christianity, and from the supposition of its having had but little good influence, however innocently they may be proposed, yet cannot be insisted upon as conclusive, upon any principles but such as lead to downright atheism; because the manifestation of the law of nature by reason, which, upon all principles of theism, must have been from God,

has been perverted and rendered ineffectual in the same manner . . . Perhaps, too, the things themselves done have been aggravated; and if not, Christianity hath been often only a pretence; and the same evils, in the main, would have been done upon some other pretence. However, great and shocking as the corruptions and abuses of it have really been, they cannot be insisted upon as arguments against it, upon principles of theism" (p. 345).

It is stressed that the critique of miracles (pp. 359ff., 378ff.) or of divine revelation (pp. 368ff.) is unfounded: "But the consequence of the foregoing observation is, that the question upon which the truth of Christianity depends, is scarce at all, what objections there are against its scheme, since there are none against the morality of it; but what objections there are against its evidence: or, what proof there remains of it, after due allowances made for the objections against that proof: because it has been shown, that the objections against Christianity, as distinguished from objections against its evidence, are frivolous. For surely very little weight, if any at all, is to be laid upon a way of arguing and objecting, which, when applied to the general constitution of nature, experience shows not to be conclusive: and such, I think is the whole way of objecting treated of throughout this chapter" (p. 385).

There are two important and explicit references to the Shaftesbury theory of *enthusiasm* as principle of religious fervor in the apostles and martyrs:

(a) "They allege, that numberless enthusiastic people, in different ages and countries, expose themselves to the same difficulties which the primitive Christians did; and are ready to give up their lives for the most idle follies imaginable. But it is not very clear, to what purpose this objection is brought. For everyone, surely, in every case, must distinguish between opinions and facts. And though testimony is no proof of enthusiastic opinions, or of any opinions at all; yet it is allowed, in all other cases, to be a proof of facts. And a person laying down his life in attestation of facts, or of opinions, is the strongest proof of his believing them. And if the apostles and their contemporaries did believe the facts, in attestation of which they exposed themselves to suffering and death, this their belief, or rather knowledge, must be a proof of those facts; for they were such as came under the observation of their senses. And though it is not of equal weight, yet it is of weight, that the martyrs of the next age, notwithstanding they were not eye-witnesses of those facts, as were the apostles and their contemporaries, had, however, full opportunity to inform themselves, whether they were true or not, and give equal proof of their believing them to be true."

(b) "But enthusiasm, it is said, greatly weakens the evidence of testimony, even for facts, in matters relating to religion; some seem to think it totally and absolutely destroys the evidence of testimony upon this subject. And, indeed, the powers of enthusiasm, and of diseases, too, which operate in like manner, are very wonderful, in particular instances. But if great numbers of men, not appearing in any peculiar degree weak, nor under any peculiar suspicion of negligence, affirm that they saw and heard such things plainly with their eyes and their ears, and are admitted to be in earnest; such testimony is evidence of the strongest kind we can have, for any matter of fact" (pp. 454f.).

Butler's conclusion sums up the whole scope of the work, which was to show the close connection between revealed and natural religion and to warn against those who deny it: "Let us then suppose that the evidence of religion in general, and of Christianity, has been seriously enquired into, by all reasonable men among us. Yet we find many professedly to reject both, upon speculative principles of infidelity. And all of them do not content themselves with a bare neglect of religion, and enjoying their imaginary freedom from its restraints. Some go much beyond this. They deride God's moral government over the world: they ridicule and vilify Christianity, and blaspheme the author if it; and take all occasions to manifest a scorn and contempt of revelation. This amounts to an active setting themselves against religion; to what may be considered as a positive principle of irreligion; which they cultivate within themselves, and, whether they intend this effect or not, render habitual, as a good man does the contrary principle. And others, who are not chargeable with all this profligateness, yet are in avowed opposition to religion as if discovered to be groundless. Now admitting, which is the supposition we go upon, that these persons act upon what they think principles of reason, and otherwise they are not to be argued with; it is really inconceivable, that they should imagine they clearly see the whole evidence of it, considered in itself, to be nothing at all; nor do they pretend this. They are far indeed from having a just notion of its evidence; but they would not say its evidence was nothing, if they thought the system of it, with all its circumstances, were credible, like other matters of science or history" (pp. 507f.) [1]

Butler's work certainly constitutes the foundation of the ensuing work of John Brown: the two are alike in structure and character of arguments. Brown, however, makes more extensive references to philosophi-

[1] The best study of Butler's work is still that of L. Stephen (*History of English Thought,* Vol. I, pp. 278ff.). And Stephen insists that, for Butler, God does not constitute a problem at all, being rather a factual *datum* and starting point: "He takes for granted the assumption of the divine existence. We believe, he says substantially, in a God of nature, but the God of nature is such a God as nature reveals, and not the God who is described by your *a priori* speculations. God as known to us by analogy of nature, that is to say, by that kind of imperfect induction which alone is available in these deep problems is no longer different from the God revealed to us in the Bible; on the contrary, he appears, so far as our faculties can be trusted, to be the very same Being" (pp. 281f.).

In his *An Agnostic's Apology* (London, 1904), pp. 17ff., Stephen has made a penetrating study of the vicious circle involved in Butler's analogy and of the backfire potential inherent in such a recourse to the God of revelation with a simultaneous disparagement (inspired by anti-Deist sentiments) of the God of reason.

cal writings and gives us the names of the authors he is citing pro and con.

II. John Brown's Critique of Shaftesbury [2]

I have selected Brown's work because of the courtesy and balance he evinces and the profound esteem he shows for Shaftesbury, whom he quotes on occasion explicitly and by name. The work is divided into three Essays, focussing on the three main points of the Shaftesbury system:

1. *On Ridicule as a Test of Truth.* Brown begins by praising Shaftesbury for his noble aim of defending *Freedom,* but intimates that he cannot accept Shaftesbury's method: "It will ever be our truest Praise therefore, to join the noble Apologist in his Encomiums on *Freedom;* the only permanent basis on which *Religion* or *Virtue* can be established. Nor can we less approve his frequent recommendations of *Politeness, Cheerfulness,* and *Good-humour,* in the Prosecution of our most important Inquiries" (p. 5). Brown's extensive discussion follows exactly Shaftesbury's text, with Copious references to classical sources in the fashion of the day. The conclusion is that it is only reason, not raillery or wit, that is capable of exposing falsehood and proving truth: "and thus Reason alone is the *Detector of Falsehood* and the Test of Truth" (p. 41). Ridicule can never reveal or prove falsehood (p. 47); indeed ridicule not kept in line by reason can itself lead to errors and aberrations of the gravest kind (pp. 64ff.), because only reason can distinguish appearance from reality. The extravagances to which religious fanaticism sometimes abandons itself, as in the cases described by Shaftesbury (cases of French Calvinists in exile in England) are precisely excesses in respect of the judgment of reason and not by the criterion of ridicule: "It implies some further Power, which may be able to distinguish what is *really* ridiculous, from what is only *apparently* so. On the contrary, if by 'that which is ridiculous', he means that which *apparently* ridiculous, it may be affirmed, this may be morally true: Because Imagination and Passion often take up with Fictions instead of Realities, and can never of themselves distinguish them from each other" (p. 89). And Brown concludes: " 'Tis no difficult Matter to

[2] John Brown, *Essays on the Characteristics of the Earl of Shaftesbury* (London: printed for C. Davis, 1751). Brown sets out to play the mediator between the panegyrists and the anathematizers of the *Characteristics* of Shaftesbury, to whom Butler always refers as "the noble Writer".

Stephen has this comment on Brown's critique: "Thus he tries to supplant Shaftesbury's vague declamation and Clarke's nugatory metaphysics by a fixed and intelligible standard. In fact, the criticism strikes at Shaftesbury's fundamental weakness . . . Brown's utilitarianism provides a practical rule, though, of course, it does not attempt to answer the problem of existence of evil" (L. Stephen, *History of English Thought in Eighteenth Century,* Vol. II, pp. 45f.).

point out the Foundation of this Gentleman's Errors concerning Ridicule. They have arisen solely from his mistaking the *Passion of Contempt* for a *judicial Faculty:* Hence all those new-fangled Expressions of—'the Faculty of Ridicule'—'the Sense of Ridicule'—and 'the feeling of the Ridiculous': In the Use of which he seems to have imposed upon himself new phrases for Realities, and Words for Things" (p. 97).

We quote in full the last section (XI) dealing with the religious realm: "To return therefore to the noble Writer. As it is evident, that *Ridicule* cannot in general without Absurdity be applied as a Test of Truth; so can it least of all be admitted in *examining Religious Opinions,* in the Discussion of which his Lordship seems principally to recommend it. Because, 'by inspiring the contending Parties with *mutual Contempt,* it hath a violent Tendency to destroy *mutual Charity,* and therefore to prevent mutual *Conviction'* . . . But if the Way of Ridicule is thus wholly to be rejected in treating every *controverted religious* Subject; it will probably be asked, 'Where then is it to be applied? Whether it is reasonable *to calumniate and blacken it without distinction?* And whether it is not Impiety, thus to vilify the Gifts of our Maker?'

"And 'tis certain, that to do this, were absurd and impious. As on the other hand, there is an equal Absurdity and Impiety in confounding that Order of things which the Creator hath established, and endeavouring to raise a blind Passion into the Throne of Reason. One Party or other in his Debate hath certainly incurred the Censure: The Censure is severe, and let it fall where it is deserved. I know none that endeavour to vilify and blacken Ridicule without Distinction, unless when it presumes to elevate itself into a *Test of Truth:* And then, as a Rebel to the Order and Constitution of Nature, it ought to be resolutely encountered and repelled, till it take Refuge in its own inferior Station.

"The proper Use of Ridicule therefore is, 'to disgrace known Falsehood' and thus, negatively at least, 'to enforce known Truth'. Yet this can only be affirmed of certain Kinds of Falsehood or Incongruity, to which we seem to have appropriated the general Name of *Folly:* And among the several Branches of this, chiefly I think, to AFFECTATION. For as every *Affectation* arises from a false Pretence to *Praise,* so a *Contempt incurred* tends to *convince* the Claimant of his *Error,* and thus becomes the natural Remedy to the Evil.

"MUCH more might be said on this Head. We might run through numerous Divisions and Subdivisions of *Folly:* But as the Task would be both insignificant and endless, I am unwilling to trouble the Reader with such elaborate Trifles.

"It seems an Observation more worthy of our Attention and Regard; that *Contempt* whence Ridicule arises, being a *selfish Passion,* and nearly allied to *Pride,* if not absolutely founded on it; we ought ever to keep a strict Rein, and in general rather curb than forward its Emotions. Is there a more important Maxim in Philosophy than this, that we should gain a Habit of controuling our Imaginations and Passions by the

Use of Reason? Especially those that are rather of the selfish than the benevolent Kind? That we should not suffer our Fears to sink us in Cowardice, our Joys in Weakness, our Anger in Revenge? And sure there is not a Passion that infests human Life, whose Consequences are so generally pernicious as those of *indulged Contempt*. As the common Occurrences of Life are the Objects which afford it Nourishment, so by this means it is kept more constantly in Play, than any other Affection of the Mind: And is indeed the general Instrument by which Individuals, Families, Sects, Provinces, and Nations, are driven from a State of mutual Charity, into that of Bitterness and Dissension. We proceed from Raillery to Railing; from Contempt to Hatred. Thus if the Love of Ridicule be not in itself a Passion of the malevolent Species, it leads at least to those which are so. Add to this, that the most ignorant are generally the most contemptuous; and they the most forward to *deride,* who are most incapable or most unwilling to *understand*. Narrow Conceptions of Things lead to groundless Derision: And this Spirit of Scorn in its Turn, as it cuts us off from all Information, confirms us in our preconceived and groundless Opinions.

"This being the real Nature and Tendency of Ridicule, it cannot be worth while to descant much on its Application, or explore its Subserviency to the Uses of Life. For though under the severe Restrictions of Reason, it may be made a proper Instrument on many Occasions, for disgracing *known Folly;* yet the Turn of Levity it gives the Mind, the Distaste it raises to all candid and rational Information, the Spirit of Animosity it is apt to excite, the Errors in which it confirms us when its Suggestions are false, the Extremes to which it is apt to drive us, even when its Suggestions are true; all these conspire to tell us, it is rather to be wished than hoped, that its Influence upon the whole can be considerable in the Service of *Wisdom* and *Virtue*.

"LORD SHAFTESBURY himself, in many other Parts of his Book, strongly insists on the Necessity of bringing the Imagination and Passions under the Dominion of Reason. 'The only Poison to *Reason,* says he, is *Passion:* for *false Reasoning* is soon redressed, where Passion is removed' And it is difficult to assign any Cause that will not reflect some Dishonour on the noble Writer, why he should thus strangely have attempted to privilege this Passion of *Contempt* from so necessary a Subjection. Let it suffice, in Conclusion, to observe, that Inconsistencies must ever arise and be persisted in, when a roving Fancy, conducted by *Spleen* and *Affectation,* goes in quest of idle Novelties, without subjecting itself to the just Restraints of *Reason*.

"Upon the whole: This new Design of *discovering* Truth by the *Vague* and *unsteady Light* of Ridicule, puts one in mind of the honest *Irishman,* who applied his *Candle* to the *Sun-Dial,* in order to *see how the Night went*" (pp. 99-107).

2. *On Man's Obligation to Virtue and on the Necessity of the Religious Principle*. Brown's second Essay is devoted to the central theme of

Shaftesbury's work, which we expounded in our consecutive analysis of the *Inquiry on Virtue and Merit*. Brown likewise makes such an analysis of this work, reproaching Shaftesbury with wordiness and ambiguity (p. 112). Not only is Shaftesbury's assimilation of virtue to an aesthetic judgment of the elegance, beauty and sublimity of things [3] and the like entirely inadequate; so likewise are Clarke's definitions of virtue as *Fitness, Reason and Relation of Things,* and Wollaston's definition of it as *The Truth of Things:* thoroughly vague notions all of them until it is explained what is meant by beauty, fitness, truth (p. 122). Nor does it suffice to appeal to the common good of mankind: for then Mandeville would be right, as against Shaftesbury, in saying in his *Fable of the Bees* that "Private vices are public Benefits", so that private virtues would be public disasters (pp. 137ff., 146ff., 152ff.). It will never be possible to arrive at a definition of virtue until accord is reached concerning the essence of human nature, the dynamism of its interior faculties whence proceeds that "enthusiasm" that Shaftesbury is all too prone to confuse (like Bayle) with sectarian fanaticism.

At this point, Brown attacks strongly, though with his usual politeness, Shaftesbury's want of understanding of true religion and the hope of a life to come: "to prevent Misinterpretation, it may be proper to observe, that LORD SHAFTESBURY sometimes talks in earnest of the *Nobleness* and *Dignity* of *Religion.* But when he explains himself, it appears, he confines his Idea of it to that Part which consists solely in Gratitude to, and Adoration of, the Supreme Being, without any Prospect of future Happiness or Misery. Now, though indeed this be the noblest Part, yet it is beyond the Reach of all, save only those who are capable of the most *exalted* Degrees of Virtue. His Theory of *Religion* therefore is precisely of a Piece, with his Theory of the *moral Sense;* not calculated for Use, but Admiration; and only existing in the Place where they had their Birth; that is, as the noble Writer well expresseth it, in *a Mind taken up in Vision.*

"He sometimes talks, or seems to talk, in earnest too, on the *Usefulness* of *Religion,* in the common Acceptation of the Word. With regard to which 'tis only necessary to observe, that whatever he hath said on this Subject I readily assent to: But this is no Reason why it may not be necessary to obviate every thing he hath thrown out to the contrary to prejudice common Readers against Religion, though the Vanity of being thought *Original.* To *invent* what is *just* or *useful,* is the Character of *Genius:* 'Tis a far *different* Thing, to broach *Absurdities.*

"FIRST, therefore, he, often asserts, that 'the Hope of future Reward and Fear of future Punishment is utterly unworthy of the free Spirit of a Man, and only fit for those who are destitute of the very first Principles of common Honesty: He calls it *miserable, vile, mercenary:* And com-

[3] Hutcheson, quoted expressly (p. 122 note; cited on p. 162 with the epithet "the most ingenious of his Followers"; p. 166) agrees with Shaftesbury in defining virtue aesthetically ("the BEAUTY of *Virtue*").

pares those who allow it any Weight, to *Monkies* under the Discipline of the Whip.'

"In Answer to these general Cavils (probably aimed chiefly at *Revelation*) which are only difficult to confute, as they are vague and fugitive, let it be observed, first, that whatever can be objected against *religious* Fear, holds good against the Fear of *human* Laws. They *both* threaten the Delinquent with the Infliction of Punishment, nor is the Fear of the one more unworthy, than of the other. Yet the noble Writer himself often speaks with the highest Respect of *Legislators,* of the Founders of *Society* and *Empire,* who, by the establishment of wise and wholesome Laws, drew Mankind from their State of natural Barbarity, to that of cultivated Life and social Happiness: Unless indeed he supposes that ORPHEUS and the rest of them did their Business *literally* by *Taste* and a *Fiddle.* If therefore the just Fear of *human* Power might be inforced without insulting or violating the *Generosity* of our Nature, whence comes it, that a just Fear of the *Creator* should so miserably degrade the Species? The religious Principle holds forth the same Motive to Action, and only differs from the other, as the Evil it threatens is infinitely greater and more lasting.

"FURTHER: If we consider the religious Principle in its true Light, there is nothing in it either *mean, slavish,* or *unworthy.* To be in a *Fright* indeed, to live under the Suggestions of *perpetual Terror* (in which, the noble Writer would persuade us, the religious Principle consists) is far from an amiable Condition. But this belongs only to the *Superstitious* or the *Guilty.* The first of these are *falsely* religious; and to the last I imagine the noble Writer's most zealous Admirers will acknowledge, it *ought* to belong. But to the rest of Mankind, the *religious* Principles or *Fear* of God is of a quite different Nature. It only implies a lively and habitual Belief, that we shall be hereafter miserable, if we disobey his Laws. Thus every wise Man, nay, every Man of common Understanding, hath a *like Fear* of every *possible Evil;* of the destructive Power of natural Agents, of *Fire, Water, Serpents, Poison:* Yet none of these Fears, more than the religious one, imply a State of *perpetual* Misery and Apprehension: None of them are inconsistent with the most generous Temper of Mind, or truest Courage. None of them imply more than a *rational Sense* of these several Kinds of Evil; and from that Sense, *a Determination to avoid them.* Thus the noble Writer himself, when it answers a different Purpose, acknowledges that 'a Man of Courage may be *cautious* without real *Fear*'. Now the Word *Caution,* in its very Nature, implies a Sense of a Possibility of Evil, and from that Sense of a Determination to avoid it: Which is the very Essence of the religious Principle or the *Fear* of God.

"And as to the other Branch of religious Principle, 'the Hope and Prospect of higher Degrees of future Happiness and Perfection': —What is there of *mean, slavish* or *unworthy* in it? Are all Mankind to be blown up into the *Mock-majesty* of the *kingly* STOIC, seated on the

Throne of *Arrogance,* and *lording* it in an empty Region of CHI-MERA'S? Is not the Prospect of Happiness the great universal Hinge of human Action? Do not all the Powers of the Soul centre in this one Point? Doth not the noble Writer elsewhere acknowledge this; and that our Obligations to Virtue itself can only arise from this one Principle, that it gives us real Happiness? Why then should the Hope of a happy Immortality be branded as *base* and *slavish,* while the Consciousness or Prospect of a happy Life on Earth is regarded as a just and honourable Motive?

"The noble Writer indeed confesseth, that 'if by the Hope of Reward, be understood the Love and Desire (he ought to have said, the *Hope*) of *virtuous Enjoyment,* it is not derogatory to Virtue'. But that in every other Sense, the indulged Hope of Reward is not only mean and mercenary, but even *hurtful* to Virtue and common *Humanity:* 'For in this religious Sort of Discipline, the Principle of *Self-Love,* which is *naturally so prevailing* in us (*indeed?*) being no way moderated or restrained, but rather improved and made stronger every Day, by the Exercise of the Passions in a Subject of more extended Self-Interest; there may be Reason to apprehend lest the Temper of this Kind should extend itself in general through all the Parts of Life'.

"This, to say the best of it, is the very *Phrenzy* of Virtue. Religion proposeth true Happiness as the End and Consequence of virtuous Action: this is granted. It proposeth it by such Motives as must influence Self-Love, and consequently hath given the best Means of procuring it. Yet, it seems, Self-Love being not restrained, but made stronger, will make Mankind miss of true Happiness. That is, by leading Self-Love into the Path of *true* Happiness, Religion will inevitably conduct it to a *false;* by commanding us to cherish our public Affections, it will certainly inflame the private ones; by assuring us, that if we would be happy hereafter, we must be virtuous and benevolent, it will beyond Question render us *vile* and *void of Benevolence.* But this Mode of Reasoning is common with the noble Writer.

"However, at other Times his Lordship can descend to the Level of common Sense; and prosecute his Argument by Proofs diametrically opposite to what he here advanceth. For in displaying the Motives to Virtue, after having modelled the inward State of the human Mind according to his own Imagination, he proceeds to consider the *Passions* which regard *ourselves,* and draws another and indeed a stronger Proof from *these.* He there proves the Folly of a vicious Love of Live 'because Life itself may often prove a Misfortune'. So of *Cowardice,* 'because it often robs us of the Means of Safety'. Excessive Resentment, 'because the Gratification is no more than an Alleviation of a racking Pain'.—The Vice of Luxury 'creates a Nauseating, and Distaste, Diseases, and constant Craving'. He urges the same Objections against intemperate Pleasure of the amourous Kind. He observes that Ambition is ever 'suspicious, jealous, captious, and uncapable of bearing the least Disappointment'. He then proceeds thro' a Variety of other Passions, proving them all to be the Sources of some internal or external Misery. Thus he awakens the same Passions of *Hope* and *Fear,* which in a religious View, he so bitterly inveighs against. Thus he exhibits a Picture of future *Rewards* and *Punishments,* even of the most *selfish* Kind: He recommends the Conformity to Virtue, on the Score both of present and future *Advantage:* He deters his Reader from the Commission of Vice, by representing the Misery it will produce; And these too, such *Advantages* and such *Miseries,* as are entirely distinct from the mere Feeling of virtuous Affection or its contrary: From the Considerations of Safety, Alleviation of *bodily* Pain, the Avoidance of *Distaste,* and *Diseases.* Now doth not his own Cavil here recoil upon him? 'That in this Sort of Discipline, and by exhibiting such Motives as these, the Principle of Self-Love must be made stronger, by the Exercise of the Passions in a Subject of more extended Self-Interest: And so there may be Reason to apprehend lest the Temper of this Kind should extend itself in general through all the Parts of Life'. Thus the Objection proves equally against both: In Reality, against neither. For, as we have seen, the *Sense* or *Prospect* of Happiness, is the only possible Motive to Action; and if we are taught to believe that *virtuous Affection* will produce *Happiness,* whether the expected Happiness lies in *this* Life; or *another,* it will *tend,* and *equally* tend, to produce *virtuous* Affection. The noble Writer, therefore, and his Admirers, might as well attempt to remove Mountains, as to prove that the *Hope* and Prospect of a happy Immortality, can justly be accounted more servile, mercenary, or *hurtful,* than the View of those transient and earthly Advantages, which his Lordship hath so rhetorically and honestly display'd, for the Interest and Security of *Virtue.* In Truth, they are precisely of the same Nature, and only differ in Time, Duration, and Degree. They are both established by our Creator for the same great End of Happiness. And what GOD hath thus *connected,* it were absurd, as well as impious, to attempt to *separate.*

"THERE is yet another Circumstance observable in human Nature, which still further proves, that the Hope of a happy Immortality hath no Tendency to produce selfish Affection, but its contrary. For let the *stoical* Tribe draw what Pictures they please of the human Species, this is an undoubted Truth, 'that *Hope* is the most universal Source of human *Happiness:* and that Man is never so sincerely and heartily *benevolent,* as when he is truly *happy* in himself.' Thus the high Consciousness of his being numbered among the Children of GOD, and that his Lot is among the Saints; that he is destined to an endless Progression of Happiness, and to rise from high to higher Degrees of Perfection, must needs inspire him with that Tranquillity and Joy, which will naturally diffuse itself in Acts of sincere Benevolence to all his Fellow-Creatures, whom he looks upon as his Companions in this Race of Glory. Thus will every noble Passion of the Soul be awakened into Action: While the joyless Infidel, possessed with the gloomy Dread of

Annihilation, too naturally contracts his Affections as his Hopes of Happiness decrease; while he considers and despiseth himself, and his Fellow-Creatures, as no more than the Beasts that perish.

"The noble Writer indeed insinuates, that there is 'a certain Narrowness of Spirit, occasioned by this Regard to a future Life, peculiarly observable in the *devout* Persons and *Zealots* of almost every religious Persuasion.' In reply to which, 'tis only necessary to affirm, what may be affirmed with Truth, that with Regard to *devout* Persons the Insinuation is a *Falsehood.* It was prudently done indeed, to join the *Zealots* (or *Bigots*) in the same Sentence; because it is true that *these,* being under the Dominion of *Superstition,* forget the true Nature and End of *Religion;* and are therefore scrupulously exact in the Observation of outward *Ceremonies,* while they neglect the superior and *essential* Matters of the Law, of *Justice, Benevolence,* and *Mercy.*

"And as to the Notion of confining the Hope of future Reward to 'that of virtuous Enjoyment only': This is a *Refinement* parallel to the rest of the noble Writer's System; and like all Refinements, contracts instead of enlarging our Views. 'Tis allowed, indeed, that the Pleasures of Virtue are the highest we know in our present State; and 'tis therefore commonly supposed, they may constitute our chief Felicity in another. But doth it hence follow, that no other Sources of Happiness may be dispensed, which as yet are utterly unknown to us? Can our narrow and partial Imaginations set Bounds to the Omnipotence of God? And may not our Creator vouchsafe us such Springs of yet untasted Bliss, as shall exceed even the known Joys of Virtue, as far as *these* exceed the Gratifications of Sense? Nay, if we consider, what is generally believed, that our Happiness will arise from an Addition of new and higher Faculties; that in the present Life, the Exercise of Virtue itself ariseth only from the *Imperfection* of our State; if we consider these Things, it should seem highly probable, that our future Happiness will consist in something quite beyond our present Comprehension: Will be 'such as Eye hath not seen, nor Ear heard, neither hath it entered into the Heart of Man to conceive' " (Sect. XI, pp. 211-223).

The aberrations and excesses of a false piety are no argument in favor of rejecting and ridiculing the practice of a true piety (p. 235): by reducing the standard of virtue to taste and aesthetic feeling, Shaftesbury is unable to distinguish the true religion and leaves men at the mercy of superstition and despotism.

3. *On Revealed Religion and Christianity.* Shaftesbury's treatment of the very basis of the notion of "virtue" has involved an equivocation; his attitude toward positive religion and Christianity in particular is a veritable tissue of equivocation calculated to make his contract by every cross-ruff and finesse known to man and by surreptitious reneging to boot: "He not only eludes the Force of every Argument the Defenders of Christianity alledge its Support, but even pleads the Privilege of being ranked in the Number of *sincere* Christians. He takes frequent

Occasions of expressing his Abhorrence of *idle Scepticks* and *wicked Unbelievers* in Religion: He declares himself of a more resigned Understanding, a ductile Faith, ready to be moulded into any Shape that his spiritual Superiors shall prescribe. At other Times, and in innumerable Places, he scatters such Insinuations against *Christianity,* and that too with all the Bitterness of *Sarcasm* and *Invective,* as must needs be more effectual in promoting *Irreligion,* than a formal and avowed Accusation. For in the Way of open War, there is fair Warning given to put Reason upon Guard, that no pretending Argument be suffered to pass without Examination. On the contrary, the noble Writer's concealed Method of *Raillery,* steals insensibly on his Reader; fills him with endless Prejudice and Suspicion; and, without passing thro' the *Judgment,* fixeth such Impressions on the Imagination, as *Reason,* with all its Effects, will be hardly able afterwards to efface.

"These inconsistent Circumstances in his Lordship's Conduct, have made it a Question among some, what his real Sentiments were concerning Religion and *Christianity.* If it be necessary to decide this Question, we may observe, that a disguised Unbeliever may have his Reasons for making a formal Declaration of his Assent to the Religion of his Country: But it will be hard to find what should tempt a real *Christian* to load *Christianity* with Scorn and *Infamy.* Indeed, the noble Writer, to do him Justice, never designed to leave us at a Loss on this Subject. For he hath been so good, frequently to remind his Reader, to *look out* for the true Drift of his *Irony,* lest his real Meaning should be mistaken or disregarded.

"Here then lies the Force of his Lordship's Attack on *Christianity;* 'In exciting Contempt by Ridicule'. A Method which, as we have already seen, tho' devoid of all rational Foundation, is yet most powerful and efficacious in working upon vulgar Minds. Thus the Way of *Irony,* and false Encomium, which he so often employs against the blessed Founder of our Religion, serves him for all Weapons; the deeper he strikes the Wound, the better he shields himself.

"We are not therefore to be surprized, if we find the noble Writer frequently affecting a Mixture of *solemn Phrase* and low *Buffoonry;* not only in the same *Tract,* but in the same *Paragraph.* In this Respect, he resembles the facetious Drole I have somewhere heard of, who wore a *transparent Masque:* Which, at a distance, exhibited a Countenance wrapt up in profound Solemnity; but those who came nearer, and could see to the Bottom, found the native Look distorted into all the ridiculous Grimace, which Spleen and Vanity could imprint" (Sect. I, pp. 242-245).

Section II is an all-out attack on the contention in the Shaftesbury *Letter on Enthusiasm* to the effect that it is unworthy of God and man to conceive God as a judge punishing the man of vice: Brown alleges that this exposes the epicurean basis of Shaftesbury's notion of life: "But still the noble Writer proceeds in the Spirit of Derision, to expose the Absurdities and Mischiefs this misguided religious Principle hath occasioned; he often expatiates on the *superstitious Horrors, and furious Zeal* which have had their Source in this Principle; and thence, in the Way of Insinuation, concludes it irrational and groundless" (p. 252). But why should not the divine goodness impel us to have a horror of vice and to fear the just punishment of such vice? [4]

From all of this, it is easy to imagine what treatment Shaftesbury will have in store for revealed religion (Sect. III): a critique of the credibility of biblical history, of the authenticity of the New Testament—which is in fact supported, observes Brown, by a concatenation of testimonies and witnesses such as cannot be boasted of by any book of antiquity (p. 271).

Shaftesbury's subsequent insinuation that Christianity must be false because of the conduct of Christians today must arouse doubts about his sincerity: "Now if his Lordship be indeed in earnest in urging this Insinuation, he must believe, that *one Set* of Men *preached,* and *wrote,* and endured *Bonds* and *Imprisonment, Torments* and *Death;* to the End that *another Set* of Men, some *three* or *four Hundred Years* after, might enjoy the *rich Corporations* and *profitable Monopoly* of *Church Preferments.* How far this may be a Proof of the noble Writer's *Sagacity,* I shall leave others to determine. But if he *believes not* the Insinuation, as indeed he seems to *disbelieve* it, then we cannot surely hesitate a Moment concerning the Measure of his *Sincerity*" (p. 270).

For Shaftesbury miracles are not indeed any proof of the existence of a God: the wisdom, goodness and power of God as seen in nature cannot prove the existence of any such thing as revelation—but why does Shaftesbury insist on the impossibility of God raising man to a degree of happiness superior to the natural one? Only the atheist can doubt here (pp. 287f.).

Shaftesbury commits the further error of designating by the same term, "enthusiasm", the melancholic frenzies of the fanatics and the divine inspiration of Christ and the apostles (pp. 293, 305ff.). Brown is trenchant in his critique: "In examining this Subject, therefore, we shall find, First, that in *some* Respects, *Enthusiasm* must, from its Nature, always resemble *divine Inspiration.* Secondly, that in others it hath generally attempted a further Resemblance, but hath always betrayed itself. Thirdly, that in other Circumstances it is diametrically opposite to divine Inspiration, and void even of all seeming Resemblance" (p. 296). And it is slanderous to attribute to Christianity the origin of all the wars and massacres of history: "So far therefore is Christianity from encouraging Wars and Massacres, on Account of a Difference in Opinion, that its divine Founder hath expressly warned his Followers against the Suggestions of this horrid temper: Nor can these fatal Consequences ever arise among *Christians,* till they have divested themselves of *Christian Charity*, and mistaken the very Principles of their Profession.

[4] Here Brown inserts an extensive quotation from the *Preface* to the Sermons of his contemporary, the noted Dr. Butler (pp. 254f.).

"But the noble Writer proceeds to still more bitter Invectives, if possible, against *Christianity.* For he often insinuates, that the Prospect of Happiness and Misery in another Life, revealed in the Gospel, tends to the Destruction of all *true Virtue.* Indeed we cannot much wonder that his Lordship should treat Christianity in this Manner, when we consider what he hath thrown out against Religion in general, in this Respect" (p. 321).

Nor are Shaftesbury's indiscriminate attacks any better or more solidly founded, when he heaps upon the clergy such titles of opprobrium as *bigots, imposters, formalists, gladiators, incendiary champions of the faith, black tribe* and the rest. This is a patent tactic of "buffooning and disgracing" wholesale, together with the content of Christianity, its institutions, its reality and its historical manifestations in all ages.

III. A Prayer to God by Shaftesbury

"Eternal Parent of Men and all things, the Spirit, Life and Power of the Universe, from whom all order, harmony and beauty is derived, in whom every thing exists, and by whom all things are sustained and ruled, so as to hold *one* order, to concur in *one,* and in their variety of operations to make *one* complete and perfect *whole.* Thou who art the author of all, in and from whom are all things, the order and motion of the heavens and of the infinite spheres: the vigour and flourishing of this earth: the breadth of living creatures, and the intelligence of souls: being himself the universal soul the eternal and infinite mind and wisdom of the whole. Since by thy will, I was made a creature capable thus to know and contemplate thee let it be my thought and study how to follow thee; how to live suitably to Thy appointment and rule, willingly to obey thee, and to seek thy end and purpose in my nature and life: this alone being the end, and, when attained, the good of every rational creature. Let this therefore be my purpose, to learn, how to think Thee, and know Thee more, that I may be more in love with excellence and admire, adore and love, what alone is worthy to be admired, adored and loved. Let it be my labour to purg from my reason those loose and incoherent thoughts which disturb my clearer views of Thee and to purg from amongst my passions, those distempered and unsound ones which are chiefly the occasion of this disturbance of sight, and are withall the occasion of reluctancy to Thy will, of disobedience to Thy law, and of acting contrary to our nature and end. Remembering this, let me be assiduously watchful over my self and intent still on this, how by a right exercise and habit, to have my reason strongly active, true to itself, tenacious of what is clearly learnt, firm in these thoughts of Thee, and invincible in this which is the head of all, the principle and the foundation of all just reasoning, *to know and acknowledge thee, and to consider every thing with respect to the excellence and perfection of Thy*

Government and Rule. Let such be my care of this *principal part:* thus to preserve and to cherish this eye of the mind by which alone (whilst it is unblemished) we are able to keep sight of Thee; and which neglected and grown cloudy, looses us the inestimable view; and leaves us to wander in the horridest of darknesses, *an ignorance of Thee and of ourselves.* But being thus instructed, [317] and armed, let me in the power of reason and of that light which Thou hast infused, make war on all those monstrous thoughts, absurd imaginations, wild and extravagant suggestions of a debauched corrupted mind, or a discomposed entangled or sick reason, which are able at any time to make me think of Thy Being either uncertainly, by falling into those mazes of atheism, or preposterously by superstition. May thy assistant power, which Thou hast placed with me, and Thy character impressed on my mind, set me even far off from such hideous delusions, and make me never but to feel and know not only that a Universe where Thou art wanting, is the greatest of inconsistencies and the absurdest of fancies, but that as Thy Being is certainly demonstrated, so is Thy perfect justice, goodness and wisdom; and that the grounds of superstition, which are imperfections ascribed to Thee, are detestably false, as their effects are miserable.

O thou, who through a cloud of darkness, hast brought me to this free discernment and hast set me in this clear and happy light, let Thy mighty image in my mind and a right sense of Thy goodness, and of the excellence of this high advantage Thou hast bestowed, support me in the work of making myself a worthy spectator of things so goodly to contemplate: and not only a spectator, but an actor, such as Thou wouldst have me to be in this Thy theatre. Let my entire applause accompany whatever is there produced; as knowing *whence* it comes, and to *what perfection* it contributes. Let me adhere to this: incline me only to this: and wish, since nothing is but as it should be, that nothing should be but as it is, and as the Divine Providence has effected it.

For the sake of this, let me extinguish those ardours and inflammations of a mind towards outward things; that I may be ardent and enflamed where *only* I can *rightly* be so, where *alone* the subjects are deserving, and where *alone* I can be earnest and aspire without being frustrated, afflicted, grieved, distressed; without being abject, servile, low, ever poor, ever deficient; without being wicked and corrupt, and without a total disagreement and disorder of life. Let me turn my abhorrence therefore hitherward. That I may no longer abhor or detest what Thy providence makes to be my lot; but what makes Thy providence and my lot to be so ill accepted and makes me unable to receive with calmness and benignity whatever happens, and is.

And since the root of this lies in those wrong ardencies and eager reachings of a feavourish and ulcerated mind towards the enjoyment of such worldly goods as have their high esteem and value from a disproportioned and incoherent fancy, let me bend my whole aversion hitherward, and hate and detest this inward corruption *only* which makes me to know hatred and rancour, and to feel reluctancy and bitterness: that having once unlearnt that violent bent and eagerness of the desire; I may learn how rightly to be moved and affected towards every object in the course of life; and how proportionably to apply my care and concern, my aim and my endeavour, with this reserve and exception still on all occasions that if it otherwise please Thee it shall please me; and that I shall like that as best, when it has happened; since I know it then undoubtedly the best because it happened.

Let this be the measure and temper of all my passions and affections. And let the relation I stand in to every particular one of mankind, and every part of human affairs, guide my disposition, and command that degree of affection and regard which it of right claims [318], and which according to the society of mankind and that order which Thou hast established amongst creatures (and amongst us especially, who are rational ones) becomes due from me to every one respectively; that, as a father, I may be truly a *father;* as a brother, a *brother;* as a son a *son:* and so in every relation. And that nothing ever may turn me from this, and make me to loose my natural and right affections here, or towards mankind *in general:* that thus also as man I may be truly *a man,* a fellow, citizen, a brother amongst men; and never be transported through any abhorrence, enmity or anger, to loose that character of *humanity,* love, kindness, benignity, which whenever I loose, I become savage and unnatural, no longer a fellow creature, nor Thy creature, owning Thee, and living suitably to Thy will.

Let this therefore be ever clearly and fixedly in my mind; that to be deprived of these excellencies, to loose these natural and good affections, this harmony of temper, these orderly and good motions of a soul, is the greatest of punishments, the root of anguish, the ground of horrors, the foundation of bitterness, torment and agony; and that the contrary is peace, tranquillity, assurance, happiness. Be thou ever throughly conscious of this, o my Soul, so as ever to know and have before Thee the Blessedness of Virtue and the inseparable misery of vice, of an aberration from nature, of a revolt from God: that thou mayst never at any time loose thy integrity, thy faith, thy justice, thy modesty, thy simplicity; or think any thing a sufficient price for *these,* or any thing a greater misery than to loose *these* or to suffer *here.* And be Thou o God, by Thy Divine Truth, the author to me of *contemning* that calamitous disastrous foundation of a worldly happiness made from the success of so many various things on which it depends; of contemning the emptiness and poverty of a continual craving and an unsatisfied state; of *contemning* (what every generous nature easily contemns) the sordid bait of a mere sensual gratification, with all those flattering subjects, the most adorned and prosperous of vice; the delicacies of luxury; the glories of ambition, and the flattery of riches and superfluous possessions. That being instructed how to *contemn* that which is even fairest and most promising in vice; whilst I know the foulness and deformity of the rest; the strife, contention and animosity, the envying and repinings, the jealousy and disgusts; the losses and confusions, the shameful condescensions, poorness, and wretched servility inseparable from hence; and on the other side, being fully conscious of the generous state of another order of life; and knowing well the freedom and security, true riches, greatness and exaltedness that attend this other course; I may make *this* my choice and turn all my faculties and powers toward *this,* how to cleanse and purify my soul from all harbourings of sordid and creeping lust, of low and degenerate passions; to preserve chast and inviolable that portion of Thee, and image of Thine within; and to keep that principal part always principal and superior; never *itself* subservient, but chief and presiding over the rest, in a just and absolute dedication to Thee, and as consecrated to Thy service and use.

And since the great foundation of such excellence and that which leads to this, and to all vertue, is temperance, and a command over the sensual appetites; may I still practice this vertue with utmost satisfaction, and know the joy and delight which attends the practice itself: [319] remembering the advantages arising thence both to the body as well as the mind; remembering the wretchedness of that contrary state of impotence and unforbearance; and remembering that sensual pleasure is but a scabb, a sore, the irritation of proud flesh, the appeasing of an itch; and the assuaging of a necessitous and pressing want which gives it being. Let me ever remember that as I make that want *less,* I am myself still *better:* and that as that indigence and want increases, I am naturally more poor, and in a state more calamitous and infirm; that to want nothing is Thy Divine Perfection; and to want nothing but so as easily to dispense with that what is wanting, the next perfection to that Divine one.

Be thou thus o God! the promoter and exalter of my nature; so as to raise me up from a stooping and vile subjection, to Liberty and Manlyness: that hanging now no longer on the events of outward and worldly affairs; being no longer depressed by a low and wretched interest in things contemptible; no longer fawning, trembling on the account of these, having nothing dismally impending, nothing astonishing from any part, nothing gastly or horrid to fear from any side, nothing from death, or in the circumstances of a *natural dissolution,* but willing to restore again that breath and life, which *I have received,* thither *whence I received it,* and to resign my spirit and soul to Thee (Thou *Infinite and Eternal One* of the Universe) I may with perfect resignation, and in firm adherence to Thy rule and order, be able to say to Thee: bring on whatever chance or circumstance to Thy providence seems fitting. All shall be well: every thing agreeable. Such as I shall make right use of, draw advantage from and make to myself subject to piety, of just and generous behavior; and in which I shall still magnify and extoll Thy name. Dispose of me as Thou pleasest, I have a mind *prepared,* a will *instructed;* and I have enough since all contentment, pleasure, joy, success and happiness to me is this, to have my will in conformity to Thine; to accompany that perfect order, that eternal law which is from Thee; who are the Fountain of all good, and the *supreme good* of all" (Shaftesbury Papers, G.D. 24, Vol. XXVI, 7. In F. Heinemann, "The Philosophy of Enthusiasm, with materials hitherto unpublished," *Rev. Intern. de Philos.* VI (1952), pp. 316-319.

IV. Collins and Freethought

The main object of Collins' best-known work, *A Discourse of Freethinking,* seems to be an attack on the clergy and the perpetually squabbling clique of the theologians. Even "As to the Nature of the Eternal Being or God", claims Collins, not only the pagan priests but even the Christian ones have never reached any agreement on the way in which his immateriality or spirituality ought to be understood, so that eventually not a few of them fabricate a notion of God which amounts to atheism: "If any regard is to be had to the malicious Books and Sayings of Priests one against another, several of them make the *material Universe to be the Eternal Being or God,* wherein consists the *Essence of Atheism*" (p. 48). If the theologians are in disagreement on the nature of God, they are still more so on his attributes, on which there is no general agreement either among Protestants or among Catholics: "The whole difference between the *Arminians* and *Calvinists* is founded on different Notions of the Attributes of God; and this dispute is kept up in most Christian Churches on the face of the earth. It is carry'd on in the *Romish* Church under the names of *Jansenists* and *Jesuits, Thomists* and *Molinists,* etc. . . . Indeed the Differences among the Priests in every Church about the *Attributes of God,* are as numerous as the Priests who treat of the *Divine Attributes;* not one agreeing with another in his Notions of them all" (p. 49). In point of fact, it is the clergy themselves who are, by their own confusions and disagreements, more than any other cause provoking the spread of atheism (pp. 91ff.).

Nor is the question of the *Scriptures* in any better state in the various religions, with agreement lacking even in the Christian religion (pp. 55ff.; 86ff.)—and it must be admitted that the discord noted by Collins was at that time particularly disturbing. Collins proceeds to consider in the same fashion the various interpretations of the main dogmas: Trinity, Resurrection, eternity of the pains of Hell, the keeping of feast days, the divine origin of the Episcopate, original sin, etc. (pp. 62ff.). In this diatribe, Collins seems to take a great delight in recounting the most discordant opinions and testimonies, especially among the Anglican clergy, and setting these in mordant contrast with the official decisions of the State. Specifically, he then reproaches the clergy with their constant readiness to burst out into accusations of atheism against anyone disagreeing with them or thinking differently from them: "A fifth Instance of the Priest's Conduct, is, *If any good Christian happens to reason better than ordinary, they presently charge him with Atheism, Deism, or Socinianism:* as if good Sense and Orthodoxy could not subsist together" (p. 84). Among the victims of clerical intolerance, Collins lists by name: Cudworth, Tillotson, Clarke, Carroll and Chillingworth (On Bishop Tillotson, favorably disposed to Freethinkers, cf. also pp. 170ff.).

Freethought is therefore to be welcomed, as an approach that can and should treat of all questions of interest to man: clergy objections to it do not hold water; indeed ". . . *Liberty of Thinking* is the Remedy for all the Disorders which are pretended to arise from Diversity of Opinions" (p. 103). At this point, Collins raises the main objection, namely, the charge that freethinking is the chief culprit in the spread of atheism: "It is objected, *That if Freethinking be allow'd, it is possible some Men may think themselves into Atheism; which is esteem'd the greatest of all Evils in Government*" (p. 104). Collins replies scornfully that it is ignorance alone which is the real cause of atheism, cites Bacon and Hobbes, and appends an anti-Catholic tirade: "And his Observation is confirm'd by Experience. For in ignorant Popish Countries, where *Free-Thinking* passes for a Crime, *Atheism* most abounds; for *Free-Thinking* being banish'd, it remains only for Men to take up their Religion upon trust from the Priest: which being such a Jest upon all things sacred, by making the Truths of God to depend on the various and contradictory Whimsies of interested and fallible Men; half-witted and unthinking People, who can easily see through this, conclude all alike the Priest says. So that Ignorance is the foundation of *Atheism,* and *Free-Thinking* the Cure of it. And thus tho' it should be allow'd, that some Men by *Free-Thinking* may become *Atheists,* yet they will ever be fewer in number if *Free-Thinking* were permitted, than if it were restrain'd" (p. 105).

But Collins goes even further: even though the objection were true, freethought would still be preferable: "But supposing that *Free-Thinking* will produce a great number of *Atheists;* yet it is certain *they* can never be so numerous where *Free-Thinking* is allow'd, as the *Superstitious* and *Enthusiasts*, will be, if *Free-Thinking* were restrain'd. And if these latter are equally or more mischievous to Society than the former, then it is better to allow of *Free-Thinking,* tho' it should increase the number of *Atheists,* than by a *Restraint* of *Free-Thinking* to increase the number of *superstitious People* and *Enthusiasts*. Now that *Enthusiasts* and *superstitious People* are more mischievous to Society, I will prove to you in the judicious Remarks of two Men of great Authority" (pp. 105f.: Bacon and Dr. Hickes).

As to the objection that ". . . Free-Thinkers are the worst subjects in the world", Collins replies that those who use reason and teach others to use it ought to be accounted the most virtuous (p. 120). And he turns against the clergy and their assemblies their own argument, calling them the source of all confusion and claiming that in this they far outdistance any conventicle of atheists: "With respect to the Meetings of Priests in their *Councils, Convocations, General Assemblies, Synods,* and *Presbyteries,* his Enemies record this *Bon Mot* of his, *That he never knew any Good to come from the Meetings of Priests.* But his own words of the *Second General Council* of Nice, more fully show his Judgment of the Authority of such Bodies: *That if a General Council of Atheists had met together with a design to abuse Religion, by talking ridiculously concerning it, they could not have done it more effectually.*" (p. 175).

Collins' work can be considered the modern handbook of Freethought, which he defines at the outset most meticulously in the following terms: "By *Free-Thinking* then I mean, *The Use of the Understanding, in endeavouring to find out the Meaning of any Proposition whatsoever, in considering the nature of the Evidence for or against it, and in judging of it according to the seeming Force or Weakness of the Evidence.*" (p. 5). The proof is quite simple: since we have the "right" to know the truth, we have the right to think *"freely"*. For no proposition can be recognized as true nor set aside as false without the use of reason (p. 6). Every would-be science of Scripture and matters sacred presupposes this freedom and the *Law of Nature* which expresses it: for reason must be allowed its complete freedom so that religion and Christianity may be rid of all the spurious, absurd and abusive notions with which they have been infiltrated (p. 13; cf. on page 14 the reference to the condemnation of Galileo, followed by a critique of the possibility of miracles; cf. on p. 23 the reference to the miracle of the blood of St. Januarius) and it is a source of gratification that freethinking now enjoys in the United Kingdom a most perfect situation, after having shaken off the Papist yoke (p. 28). Truly the only remedy against all oppression and superstition is freethinking; and this was the aim of the Gospel (p. 44), as against all the theological controversies on matters of dogma which have subsequently developed (the standards of Scriptural hermeneutics here presented by Collins—pp. 58ff.—deserve a special treatment, beyond our present scope).

In a further specification of his principle of Free-Thinking, Collins asserts that there is an obligation to make use of this right which is granted to those who are in a position to exercise it and not to the "Bulk of Mankind" for not all are capable of making use of it (p. 100). Nor is it true that Free-Thinking will unleash endless doctrinal splits and all manner of disorders within society: on the contrary, the most divergent schools and opinions have flourished, without causing the slightest difficulties, among the most tolerant civilizations and cultures, such as the Greek and the Moslem, whereas the most furious and bitter controversies are those stirred up by the theologians among themselves. Indeed Freethought even stimulates the practice of virtue, despite the violent reaction it may arouse among the common herd and the despots whose wrath it may provoke, culminating in the Free-Thinkers being branded as atheists (as was Socrates; the early Christians, according to Justin

Martyr!—pp. 124ff.; especially the Stoics, one of whom, Seneca, was held in high regard among the Christians themselves, pp. 135ff.).

And Collins cites Theophrastes who, long before Bayle, held atheism to be a lesser evil than superstition (p. 132). Outstanding representatives of Freethought among the Hebrews were preeminently Solomon, who was slandered as being an atheist (pp. 150f.) and the Prophets themselves (pp. 153ff.). Noted Freethinkers among the Christians were Minucius Felix, Origen and Synesius (pp. 162ff.); among the moderns: "my Lord Bacon" and Hobbes, Bishop Tillotson; and Collins feels there could likewise be included Erasmus, Scaliger, Descartes, Gassendi, Grotius, and all the deists with Locke at their head (p. 177).

Hence, it can be seen that it is a treacherous calumny against the most worthy representative of mankind to accuse the Free-Thinkers of atheism and libertinism (p. 176).

V. Deism and Atheism in Hume

Hume's personal attitude toward religion, at least as it comes out in his Letters, seems to be a mixture of Deism and atheism. For a long while he was, in fact, accused of atheism and the charge was supported (to Hume's own great regret and grief) by his powerful friend Hutcheson: "The accusation of Heresy, Deism, Scepticism, Atheism, etc., etc., etc., was started against me; but never took, being borne down by the contrary authority of all the good Company in Town" (*The Letters of David Hume,* ed. J.Y.T. Greig, Vol. I [Oxford, 1932], Letter 24 [1744], p. 58. In Letter 25 [p. 59] Hume speaks of "a conspiracy of bigots". Some years later, he again recalls: "The violent cry of Deism, atheism, and skepticism, was raised against me" [Letter 77 (1752); Vol. I. p. 165]. Well, says Hume, if atheist he be, "I am an atheist as Bolinbroke" [Letter 105 (1754); Vol. II, p. 214]). In Letter 281, Hume ironically congratulates himself on the fact that the charges of atheism and Deism have not interfered with his business or earning power (p. 501).

But Hume does not fail to turn the charge against his own accusers, as with Mr. W. Leechman, one of whose sermons on prayer Hume had read and judged to be a "very good one"; Hume continues ironically: "Tho' I am sorry to find the Author to be rank Atheist. You know (or ought to know) that Plato says there are three kinds of Atheists. The first who deny a Deity, the second who deny his Providence, the third who assert, that he is influenc'd by Prayers or Sacrifices. I find Mr. Leechman is an Atheist of the last kind" (Letter 21, to William Mure of Caldwell, June 1743; Vol. I, p. 50). From his further comments on the sermon, it becomes apparent that Hume like Bayle reduces religion substantially to the practice of morality.

Hume's friend Boswell provides a most clear-cut witness to Hume's rejection of all positive religion: "He said he never entertained any belief in Religion since he began to read Locke and Clarke. I asked him if he was not religious when he was young. He said he was . . . He then said flatly that the Morality of every Religion was bad, and, I really thought, was not jocular when he said 'that when he heard a man was religious, he concluded he was a rascal, though he had known some instances of very good men being religious' . . . I asked him if it was not possible that there might be a future state. He answered it was possible that a piece of coal put upon the fire would not burn; and he added that it was a most unreasonable fancy that we should exist for ever . . . I asked him if the thought of Annihilation never gave him any uneasiness. He said not the least; no more than the thought that he had not been, as Lucretius observes" (cf. E. Campbell Mossner, *The Forgotten Hume, Le bon David* [New York: Columbia University Press, 1943], p. 181).

Recent investigations have revealed that in 1756 a man by the name of Anderson proposed to the Church Assembly that Hume be excommunicated; the official charge describes Hume as one ". . . who hath arrived at such a degree of boldness as publicly to avow himself the author of books containing the most rude and open attacks upon the glorious Gospel of Christ, and principles evidently subversive even of natural religion, and the foundation of morality, if not establishing direct Atheism" (cf. F. H. Heinemann, *David Hume,* The Man and his Science of Man, containing some unpublished Letters of Hume [Paris, 1940], pp. 19f.).

If we advert to the distinction of a late 18th-century traveller-philosopher between the "sober Deists" who acknowledge the moral law, providence and the life to come, even while denying revelation, and the "atheists" who reject all of this outright, considering religion an illusion and adverting only to earthly existence, then Hume's position seems to us to fall into this second category (cf. R. J. Sullivan, *A View of Nature* in *Letters to a Traveller among the Alps with Reflections on Atheistic Philosophy, now exemplified in France,* 6 vols.; Vol. I [London, 1794], pp. 117f., cf. p. 128.

VI. Theologians' Reaction to Deism (The Boyle's Lectures)

Christian theology may have been less monolithic and orthodoxy less strictly circumscribed in the Churches separated from Rome; but there is no doubt that the authorities, theological and pastoral, of these Churches and in particular the Anglican Church, immediately spotted Deism as a heterodox movement, profoundly anti-Christian and intimately linked with pantheism, the inseparable Siamese twin of atheism. the *Boyle's Lectures,* founded by the scientist-theologian, Robert Boyle (1627-1691), opponent of Hobbes, were certainly intended by their founder to serve as a solid bulwark against the rising tides of unbelief.

In his will, Boyle established a foundation to provide for an annual series of eight lectures or sermons in defense of the Christian religion: "against the notorious infidels, such as the Atheists, the Deists, the Pagans, the Jews and the Mahometans, without descending to those controversies which divide Christians among themselves". The series was initiated in 1692 by Richard Bentley, himself author of two expressly anti-Deist works: *Matter and Motion cannot think; or a Confutation of Atheism from the Faculties of the Soul* (1692) (obviously directed against Locke and Toland); and *Remarks upon a late Discourse of Free-Thinking* (1713) (against Collins), both published under the pseudonym of Phileleutherus Lipsiensis. His *Confutation of Atheism* was stronger and more extensive in its positive theology than in its refutation. After a brief refutation of the atheists' claim that religion demands an "assent to such things as are repugnant to common sense" and a rebuttal of the cryptomaterialism involved in the Locke-Toland deist dogma of matter as capable of thought, there follows a quite ample summary of the *Physicotheologia* (physics-based theology) predominant at that time that saw the dawn of modern science and an upsurge of enthusiasm for that science, especially in the land of Newton.

The Boyle's Lectures series has continued down to our own day. The most notable collection of these lectures was published in English in 1737 as *A Defence of Natural and Revealed Religion: being an Abridgment of the Sermons Preached at the Lecture founded by The Honorable Robert Boyle, Esq., in Four Volumes, With a General Index,* By Gilbert Burnet, Vicar of Coggeshall, Essex. London: printed for Arthur Bettesworth and Charles Hitch, at the Red Lion, in Pater-noster Row. MDCCXXXVII. The following year, there began to appear a French translation of these same Lectures, under the title *Defense de la Religion tant Naturelle que Revélée contre les Infideles et les Incredules:* Extraits des Ecrits publiés pour la Fondation de Mr. Boyle, par les plus habiles Gens d'Anglettere; et traduite de l'Anglois de de Mr. Gilbert Burnet, A la Haye, chez Pierre Paupie, MDCCXXXVIII. This French version comprised six volumes appearing over a period of seven years (1738-1744). The indication "translated from the English of Mr. Gilbert Burnet" in the French title is entirely deceptive. The editor of the French version does indeed note, in his *Foreword*, that this version has rounded out the Burnet text, itself an abridgment of the original Lectures, as its title indicates. There is no mention of the name of the translator; but the editor does indicate that the Burnet text has been rounded out by an inclusion of portions omitted in Burnet and by a more logical arrangement of the material. I originally consulted the French version; a comparison of this French version with the Burnet original revealed drastic discrepancies between the two. In most cases I have been able to verify the authenticity of the French text against the texts of the individual lectures published by their authors. In all cases, I have given a reference to the French edition; in those cases where there is no substantial discrepancy between the French text and Burnet, I have quoted directly from Burnet; in those cases where a drastic discrepancy was evident, I have quoted the relevant passage from the texts of the individual lectures as published by their authors, with the single exception of Bishop Ibbot, whose original text I have not been able to discover. In this last case, I have quoted directly from the French version.

The next speaker after Bentley in the Series to treat of the problem of unbelief and atheism was Bishop Gastrell, whose 1697 lectures were entitled *Of the Certainty and Necessity of Religion in General* (Burnet I, 197-254; Fr. tr. I); especially relevant are sections IV-VII devoted specifically to unbelief, atheism and Deism. Among the consequences of irreligion indicated by Gastrell are: the lack of any real morality (Burnet I, 234ff.; Fr. tr. I, 464ff.: there is no reference to Bayle); disorder in society, a point on which there is nothing to choose between atheism and deism: "What I have said of *Atheism* is applicable to all manner of *Deism,* which is such an Acknowledgment of God, that does not include Religion in it. For if the *Deist* affirms that God *requires nothing* of him, he is at full *Liberty* to *chuse* for himself, and prosecute his own *Happiness* as he thinks fit, which is the Case of the *Atheist.* 'Tis the same Thing, in Effect, with those that make *God a necessary Cause,* and *Men necessary Agents.* For according to this Opinion all Actions are *alike;* and then there can be no general Rules for Men to act by: Which is *Atheism* too." (Burnet I, 240; Fr. tr. I, 473).

A little later, Gastrell sees the basis for atheism in the assertion of the materiality of the soul, conceived as being able to move itself and think by its own power (Burnet I, 245; Fr. tr. I, 484f.). Among the causes of atheism, Gastrell indicates a fear of divine judgment and of Hell, and, as an accessory cause, simple human vanity "of appearing greater and wiser than other Men" (Burnet I, 248; Fr. tr. I, p. 495). There follows, then, the drastic judgment: "Atheists or Deists, whether *real* or *preended,* are generally Persons of no great *Reach;* but Men of strong Lusts, and irregular Imaginations, without a due Ballast of Reason. If some of them have more *natural* Sense, it is *uncultivated:* Or if they have made any Advances in Knowledge by Study, they have either begun *late,* and applied themselves to Books without Direction; or else they have been conversant in *such Studies* as have by no means qualified them to be *Judges of their own Way*" (Burnet I, 250f.; Fr. tr., I, 501f.). The last section (VII) is devoted to clarifying the distinction between the atheist and the Deist: "By an Atheist is commonly meant, one who believes *no God.* And in this Sense of the Word it may be a Question, whether there be an *Atheist* in the World? For 'tis hard to find a Man who has not some Idea in his Mind which he will allow the Name of *God* to, though perhaps it will be found nothing else but a confused Notion of *some vast Power, first Cause, original Mover, or Immortal Being enjoyment eternal Rest and Quiet.* Now according to this Notion of

Atheism, he who believes a God and denies his Providence is called a *Deist.* But where Revelation is owned, he that is called a Deist is one who believes *some Sort of Providence,* but denies *Revelation;* who practises *Justice* for his own *Advantage* and *Interest of Society,* not in Obedience to God, or a *future Prospect,* because he believes no *future Life.* This is the *common Use* of these Words. But by an Atheist, I think, may be meant, not only he that absolutely denies the *Being* of a God, but whoever says, *there is no God that governs the World, or will punish or reward Men hereafter, according to their Actions here.* For *Atheism* is to be considered as a *Vice,* and not a *meer Error in Speculation.* And 'tis all one with Respect to Practice, to say, *there is no God,* as to say, *there is no Obedience due to him,* or *no Punishment for Disobedience,* if there be. For the End of these Opinions is to establish a *Liberty for every Man to live as he pleases;* and what is this, but to say, there is *no God?"* (Burnet I, 252f.; Fr. tr. I. 505f.). The distinction is therefore more formal than real: ". . . by a Deist is to be meant one, who acknowledges *all the Principles of Religion here maintained,* but does *not believe Revelation,* or those *peculiar Doctrines that are discoverable by it.* And, if a Deist be such a one, I don't know whether there be any . . ." (Burnet I, 253; Fr. tr. I, 507). And the impression is created that the good bishop fears the Deists much more than the atheists (which on his own terms are really an impossibility!): "Upon this Account it is that I have several times mentioned the *Deists* as Enemies of natural Religion, and so properly coming within my Subject, and not as meer *Opposers* of *Revelation,* which belongs to another Argument." (Burnet I, 254; Fr. tr. I, 508).

The next lecturer in the Series was Dr. Harris, who spoke in 1698 on the subject *Refutation of the Atheistical Objections against the Being and Attributes of a God* (Burnet I, 257-292; Fr. tr. IIff.). Harris cites moral corruption (Burnet I, 254ff.; Fr. tr. II, 5f.) and pride or vanity (Burnet I, 260f.; Fr. tr. II, 7f.). He admits the existence of "speculative atheists" both in antiquity and in modern times, citing the witness of Bayle, Blount and Vanini who calls Machiavelli *Atheorum facile Princeps* (easily the Chiefest of Atheists) (Burnet I, 261f.; Fr. tr. II, 11). In the matter of the notion of atheism, Harris attains a clarity anticipatory of Feuerbach: "It doth not at all follow, that a Man is not an Atheist, because he doth not openly profess himself so. For if they set up such a God as either cannot, or will not govern the World, and punish or reward Men, according to their Actions, this is in *Reality* to deny there is one; for 'tis a true Belief of *this* only, that can clear a Man from being an Atheist. For if he has not such a Belief of God, as implies a Knowledge of the Perfections of his Nature, he may pretend to the fashionable Name of *Deist,* but he is in Reality an Atheist. And *Blount* in his *Anima Mundi,* and *Vaninus,* in his *Amphitheatrum divinae Provid.* p. 152. say, that to deny a Providence, is the same Thing as to deny a God. This therefore being returned in Answer to the Objection, that there is no such Thing as an Atheist . . ." (Burnet I, 262; Fr. tr. II, 12).

Harris is equally well-informed and terse in his articulation of the arguments advanced by the atheists against the existence of God: these arguments he reduces to two main ones: "1. That we can have no Idea of God. 2. That the Notion of a Deity owes its Original either to the Fears of some Men, or the crafty Designs of others" (Burnet I, 262; Fr. tr. II, 13).

Harris shows himself familiar with the philosophical problematic involved, citing Hobbes (Burnet I, 264; Fr. tr. II, 17) among the opponents and Locke (Burnet I, 266; Fr. tr. II, 21) as a witness favorable to Harris' own contentions; the main opponent seems to be Sextus Empiricus with his sceptical materialism (Burnet I, 269ff.; Fr. tr. II, 27ff.). The chief adversary of that *spirituality* which Harris feels must be the principal attribute of God turns out to be Hobbes whom Harris ranks among the atheists (Burnet I, 271, 277, 280f.; Fr. tr. II, 34ff., 50, 70ff.); Spinoza's deterministic materialism is set side by side with that of Hobbes (Burnet I, 287ff.; Fr. tr. II, 77ff.). It is surprising that Harris should fail to mention the name of Locke in his discussion on the relation between matter and motion.

In 1704 and 1705, Samuel Clarke gave his classics on the being and attributes of God and on natural and revealed religion. Clarke's first treatise begins with a classification of atheists and a vehement attack on these atheists who are the prime target of all Clarke's remarks: "All those, who either are, or pretend to be Atheists, who either disbelieve the Being of God, or, what is all one, suppose him to be an unintelligent Being, who acts by Necessity, which in Truth, is not to act at all, are so upon one or other of these three Accounts. Either, 1. By Reason of their Ignorance and Stupidity, never considering any Thing at all, nor making Use of their Reason. Or 2. Because being debauched in their Practice, they have corrupted the Principles of Nature, and defaced their Reason; and being under the Power of evil Habits, are resolved to hear no Reason, which would oblige them to forsake their Vices. Or 3. From false Philosophy, pretending that the Arguments against the Being and Attributes of God, after the strictest Enquiry, are more conclusive, than those, by which we endeavour to prove them. To the two former Sorts of Atheists I shall not apply myself, the one having not as yet arrived at the Use of his natural Faculties, and the other having renounced them, won't be argued with as a rational Creature. The third Sort, who pretend to defend their Atheism upon Principles of Philosophy, are those to whom I shall direct myself. (Burnet II, 83f.; Fr. tr. III, 1f.).

In his brief diagnosis of the atheistic mind, Clarke stresses the importance of moral considerations: ". . . whether the Being of God can be demonstrated or not, it must be confessed to be a Thing very desirable: And if it be desirable at least that there should be a God, these Men upon their own Principles must be desirous to be convinced of their Errors, and are bound to consider seriously the Weight of the Arguments, by which the Being of God may be proved, and are consequently obliged to exclude all Scoffers at Religion out of their Number, who deride at a venture without hearing Reason" (Burnet II, 84f.; Fr. tr. III, 3).

Thus the existence of God is a thing so much to be desired that it ought to be admitted if it but seem at all possible and still more so if it seem probable. But Clarke obligates himself to prove it with a series of 12 propositions which proceed from the existence of God to the individual attributes. And at the end of his second treatise (on natural and revealed Religion) Clarke quite outspokenly pinpoints the real cause of disbelief of religious truths: " 'Tis not therefore for want of Evidence that Men disbelieve the great Truths of Religion, but for want of Integrity, and of dealing impartially with themselves . . . To conclude; we cannot say, but God may require us to *take Notice* of *some Things* at our Peril; to *inquire into* them, and to *consider* them thoroughly. And Pretence of Want of greater Evidence will not excuse *Carelessness* or *unreasonable Prejudices*" (Burnet II, 183 and 184; Fr. tr. III). Dr. John Hancock's 1706 lectures *On Natural and Revealed Religion* likewise hit straight at the atheists. Before proceeding to the positive proofs of God's existence, Hancock deals with and rejects the objections made by the atheists. Hancock follows the general line set by Bentley, Gastrell, Harris and Clarke, but pays more deliberate attention to the rationalistic origin of modern atheism from Descartes and Spinoza (Burnet II, 194f., 210f.; Fr. tr. III, 246ff., 267ff.). Noteworthy is Hancock's polemic against the materialism of Hobbes who is classed with Spinoza (Burnet II, 221ff; Fr. tr. III, 308ff., 322ff.).

The 1709-10 lectures were given by Josiah Woodward, who advances the somber thesis, anticipatory of Dostoevsky in the *Possessed,* that the only logical conclusion for the atheist is suicide: "The Atheist has also a very *dark* and desolate sort of Life; for, being cut off from the common Succour of Man from GOD, his *Fountain-Good;* he stands alone in all the Shocks of this uncertain Life; and so, in any great Affliction, is crush'd by the Weight of it, and flees to those dismal Refuges, the *Pistol,* the *Knife,* or the *Halter.* These were the Ends of those prime Patrons of irreligion, *Epicurus* and *Lucretius,* as it is affirmed by Two ancient Historians: And the Two Modern Admirers of Lucretius, one of which translated his Book into *English Prose,* and the other into Verse, followed their Author in his sad *Exit,* the one by a *Pistol,* and the other by a *Halter*" (*The Divine Original, and Incomparable Excellency of the Christian Religion, As founded on the Holy Scriptures, Asserted and Vindicated,* By Josiah Woodward, D.D. [London: Printed and sold by Jospeh Downing in Bartholomew-Close near West Smithfield, 1712], pp. 27-28; Fr. tr. IV, 86f.).

The famous physical theology of William Derham was expounded at length in that divine's lectures, given in 1711-12. These lectures bore as title *A Demonstration of the Being and Attributes of God from the Works of Creation* (Burnet II, 409-483; Fr. tr. IV, 141-396) and were translated forthwith into all the major European languages (I have inspected the Italian translation, entitled *Dimostrazione dell'Essenza ed Attributi di Dio dalle opere della sua Creazione,* published in Florence in 1719, "with ample annotations and divers curious observations never hitherto rendered public").

A more direct attack on the anti-theistic polemicists is to be found in Benjamin Ibbot's sixteen talks in the series, given in 1713-14. He takes as text I Thess. V, 21 and the French translator notes that the Treatise seems to be aimed at the *Discourse of Free-Thinking* of A. Collins which had just come out in 1713. Ibbot launches an all-out attack on Deism, aiming his remarks (apparently) against Shaftesbury's essay *Sensus Communis* (1709) and particularly against the Collins essay. Collins is expressly cited (Burnet III, 41; Fr. tr. IV, 465ff.). Ibbot defends Tillotson, Bacon, the Prophets and Solomon against Collin's insinuation that they were all on his side (Burnet III, 42ff.; Fr. tr. IV, 466ff.). In his final judgment, Ibbot closely links atheism and Deism: "It is true, as My lord Bacon has noted, that a slight smattering of knowledge often produces baneful effects, because a man having such has just enough to see and make difficulties. But it is no less true, as the same writer has said, that a broader knowledge brings men back to Religion, because now the light is strong enough effectively to dissipate the clouds. The Atheist reasons so little and so ill that men capable of studying the Atheist System more deeply will inevitably conceive for it the whole measure of scorn that it merits. The snares of Deism are likewise so crass and obvious that they are not really to be feared save for such men as are not in a position to fathom its strategems" (Fr. tr., IV, 514).

Another divine to speak out against the Collins *Discourse* was John Leng, lecturer for 1717-18. His lectures, entitled *Natural Obligations to Believe the Principles of Religion and Divine Revelation* expressly cite Collins (*Natural Obligations to Believe the Principles of Religion and Divine Revelation:* in XVI Sermons, Preached in the Church of St. Mary le Bow, London, in the Years 1717 and 1718, At the Lecture founded by The Honourable Robert Boyle, Esq.; By John Leng, D.D. [London, Printed by W.B. for Robert Knaplock, at the Bishop's Head in St. Paul's Churchyard, MDCCXIX], pp. 33ff.; Fr. tr. V, 15f.); Leng shrewdly imputes to Shaftesbury the chief blame for the Deist attitude (*Natural Obligations,* pp. 51f.; Fr. tr. V, 23f.). Leng cites a multitude of authors, sacred and profane, and ends with a tart reference to both Collins and Shaftesbury: "Though the Morality of the Christian Doctrine has been generally allowed to excel all others in perfection, yet there are not wanting, some who seem to tax it with *deficiency.* An Author, whom I have formerly mention'd in his high admiration of *Epicurean Friendship* (*Discourse* of Free-Thinking, *pag.* 130), tells us, that *we Christians ought to have an higher veneration of* Epicurus *for this virtue of Friendship* than *Cicero* (*By the way, this Author would either impose upon us, or is grossly mistaken himself, in what he there quotes out of Cicero: because it is the* Epicurean *who speakes in that passage, and not* Cicero *himself, who in many places declares, that upon* Epicurean *principles there could be no such things as Friendship. See his* Offices, lib. I, cap. 2. De Amicitia. cap. 13. De Finib. II, 24 &c. III. 21. *and* De Nat. Deor. lib. I. 44. *and elsewhere*), *because even our Holy Religion itself does not any where particularly require of us that virtue.* This hint he took from another Author (*Characteristicks, in the Essay on Freedom of Wit and Humour, pag.* 98.), who has insinuated, that *some of the most Heroick virtues have little notice taken of them in our Holy Religion;* and particularly that *Private Friendship and Zeal for the Publick and our Countrey, are virtues purely voluntary in a Christian. They are no essential parts of his Charity.* And they would both seem to defend this strange kind of Reasoning, from the Concession of an eminent Divine [the French edition identifies this divine as Bishop Taylor], who owns, that the word *Friendship,* in their sense, is not to be found in the New Testament; which though it be true, is nothing to their purpose, but very much the contrary" (*Natural Obligations,* 503ff.; Fr. tr. V, 198f.).

There is a sharp rejoinder to Hobbes: "But if Mr. *Hobbes's* doctrine were true (viz. that [Leviathan, Part 3, ch. 43. p. 271] *at the command of the Magistrate, a man may lawfully deny Christ with his mouth, because then the action is not his that denies him, but his sovereign's* . . . upon the same foot any other Truths may be destroyed, if no man be obliged, either in honour or conscience, to maintain them" (Natural Obligations, 508f.; Fr. tr. V, 200f.).

Dr. John Clarke, brother of the more famous Samuel, lectured on the problem of evil, that problem that has provided atheism with so many pretexts. The starting point of this extensive treatise is Bayle's famous thesis on Manicheanism: Bayle's article "Manichéens" in the *Dictionn. Hist. et Crit.* is directly cited (Burnet III, 223ff.; Fr. tr. V, 209ff.) and discussed point by point throughout the entire Treatise.

Archdeacon Brampton Gurdon, the 1721-22 lecturer, launched a frontal attack on atheism in sixteen sermons on various biblical texts (I Tim. IV, 8; I Thess. V, 21; Act. XVII, 28; Rom. I, 12; Is. V, 28; Io. XV, 24; I Cor. I, 21; II Petr. I, 16). He chose the significant overall title *The Pretended Difficulties in Natural or Reveal'd Religion no Excuse for Infidelity* (under which title these sermons were published by Robert Knaplock in London, 1723—we shall cite from this text). This Gurdon lecture series seems to me to give the most complete and detailed exposition of deist-atheist sources. Spinoza is singled out and referred to as "the only Person, among the modern *Atheists,* that has pretended to give us a regular Scheme of *Atheism*" (Burnet III, 329; Fr. tr. V, 397). Gurdon devotes considerable space to a refutation of Spinoza's arguments and to showing the inconsistency of Spinoza's own system. But it is against Toland's contention concerning motion as a necessary property of matter ("But tho' the Evidence against the Activity of Matter, from its Idea, is so clear, yet Mr. *Toland* has attempted to prove Matter an active Being from its Idea": Burnet III, 344; Fr. tr. V, 409) that Gurdon concentrates his fire. A curious anomaly here is Gurdon's effort to make out Locke's famous hypothesis to be at least reconcilable with theism: "Mr. *Locke,* indeed, supposes a fourth Way of accounting for Intelligence: 'That tho' Matter was a thoughtless and senseless Being, and no Disposition of the Parts of it, how curiously soever they might be put together, would ever naturally rise up into Thought and Understanding, and tho' there was no Principle of Thought in Man distinct from Matter; that yet GOD by his infinite Power might superadd a Thinking Quality to Body or Matter'. But were this possible, it would do the *Atheist* no Service, because it supposes the Being of a GOD as necessary to the producing such an Effect upon Matter as that of Intelligence; or if it could at all favour him, it must then fall in with the second Way of accounting for Thought, *viz.* That such a Quality as thought might *possibly* arise from Matter disposed in such a Manner as are the Bodies of Animals, there being nothing in the Nature of Matter that should make it incapable of receiving Intelligence, and consequently, if the Bodies of Animals could be formed without the Help of a GOD, there would be no Want of Him in accounting for that Thought and Intelligence which belongs to those Bodies. But this, so far as the *Atheist* is concerned in it, is exactly the same with the second Way of accounting for Intelligence; and therefore I shall pass it over without any further Remark" (*Pretended Difficulties,* 208ff.; Fr. tr. V, 426f.). And the entire responsibility is saddled upon the godless Spinoza!

I intend to return to these Boyle's Lectures in my forthcoming investigation of the problem of the person of Jesus Christ in modern thought, an investigation which is intended to supplement and round out the examination of man's horizon and meaning in the face of the void and of death, begun in this present work. These old Anglican theologians and divines must be given credit for having been the first to sound the alarm and hoist the storm signals against the tempest which, blowing in from Averroism and the Italian Renaissance school of thought, and whipped up to a greater frenzy by the French Free-Livers, was to sweep modern thought through the crucial narrows of English Deism into the bottomless gulf of atheistic humanism.

VII. Catholic Critique of Deism (Valsecchi)

The classical study of atheism and Deism produced by 18th-century Catholic theology is indisputably that of the Dominican P. Antonio Valsecchi (1708-1791), *Dei fondamenti della religione e dei fonti dell'empietà.* Books I and II are devoted respectively to the foundations of natural religion (10 chapters) and of revealed religion (18 chapters), Book III dealing mainly with the sources of irreligion under two chief heads (I. *corruptio cordis,* 16 chapters; II *rationis perturbatio,* 8 chapters) and having a third part devoted to the Protestants. It is the work of a theologian well-known and renowned in his day: but what leaps immediately to the eye is the mastery of the material, the restrained style of writing and the wealth of exact information on the authors whom Valsecchi discusses on the basis of their own works, copious quotations from which are found in his text and notes. Faithful to the Thomistic tradition of his order, Valsecchi undertook the grave task of stemming the avalanche triggered by Bayle, Hobbes, Spinoza and 17th century unbelief. The work is directed mainly against the thesis of Bayle in favor of atheism, which we have already mentioned above; Valsecchi quotes from and is thoroughly familiar with Voltaire, Rousseau, Helvétius, Maupertius, Newton, Leibniz *et al.*; he quotes from Diderot's *Pensées philosophiques* (1746) but without the author by name (Part I, c. 2; Latin edition, p. 13 a; 7th Italian edition, Vol. I, p. 17).

Valsecchi has a special section on English Deism. He is familiar with the chief English Deists and their links with the philosophy of Hobbes: the quotations indicate that he knew them only in French translations. Toland is ranked in first place and Valsecchi's refutation deals first with the thesis that motion is essential to matter (Part I, ch. 2; § 5 and cf. Part II, ch. 2, § 9 and ch. 13 § 3 for treatment of the atheist Chinese men of letters), then his critique of the proof of the existence of God (Book I, ch. 3, § 3), his theory of the origin of religion in politics (Book II, ch. 11, § 2) and his arguments for the integrity of free-livers and atheists (Book III, ch. 7, § 5, where the *Adeisdaimon* of Toland is cited, § 23; cf. also c. 11, § 1 on Toland's agreement with the thesis of Bayle).

Valsecchi has specially strong words on the slanted interpretation given to St. Paul's sermon at Athens (Acts 17) by the free-livers and especially by Toland: "I know that some Free-Livers have so far distorted this passage from St. Paul as to claim that it substantiates the pantheism of Spinoza. Toland is the most impudent among all the atheists; desirous of smearing both Moses and the Scriptures with the same grime with which he himself is stained, presumes to write in the *Origines Judaicae* (p. 156): 'Such phrases as: "The supremely perfect Being; the Alpha and Omega, without beginning or end; which was and is and shall be; all in all; wherein we live and move and have our being" are equivocal in the extreme and suit equally well with atheism as with theism; since all are most true when applied to the supposed eternity of the universe'. It is not to my purpose now to prove in detail that it is not true that any one of these expressions can, on any hypothesis, be applied otherwise than to our true God; it suffices for me to note that Toland is operating in the worst of faith when he pretends they are equivocal, when he cannot be ignorant of the fact that in the Scriptures, from which he took them, these expressions always have such riders and are in such a context as renders them inapplicable to any other subject and proves them to be proper only to the good and great God whom we worship. The one in whom Paul says (to speak here but of this passage) 'we live and move and have our being' is the same 'God who made the world and all that is in it, being Lord of both heaven and earth'. Now how can this possibly be made to jibe with the pantheism of Spinoza and Toland, who confuse God altogether with this universal engine, or, to speak more accurately, acknowledge him to be no other than this universal engine, to which they foolishly and impiously give the name of God?

"For St. Paul, God is a being totally different from the world: for Spinoza and Toland he is identical with the world; how then can these men be made to be saying anything even sounding like St. Paul, much less anything identical with the Pauline teaching? The author of the Latin translation of Pope, published in Wittenberg in 1743, dares to claim that this Pauline text and its sequel even provide justification for certain expressions of the poet which had been branded as pantheistic! But despite all the *glossing* and *embossing* he attempts, he will never succeed in making these verses innocuous [The reference here is to Pope's famous *Essay on Man*].

". . . Who is there who does not sense in these verses the Spinozan turn of phrase? The commentator himself cannot deny it: whence, he says: 'The poet speaks with Spinoza but he thinks and feels quite differently. Nay rather he both speaks and thinks and feels in accord with Sacred Scripture.' I do not intend to inquire into *Pope's inner sentiments;* but as for the *actual expressions* of this Poet being in conformity with Scripture (as the Commentator alleges), I defy him to find me any passage of Holy Writ that says that God is a portion of the world, that he changeth hour by hour in changing things, that He is extended together in things, etc." (Book II, ch. 11, § 2; Latin edition, p. 200a-201a; Italian edition, Vol. II, p. 94—the Note goes on to charge that there is pantheism likewise in Pope, Ep. I, v. 170ff. *On Man*).

Valsecchi refutes Collins' sense-perceptionist determinism (Book I, ch. 6, § 4; Collins is cited in the French translation *Recherches sur la liberté*) and praises Bentley's refutation of the *Discourse of Freethinking* (Book III, ch. 6, § 5). Other Deists who come in for criticism are Dodwell, for what he has said about the martyrs' lack of fortitude (Book II, ch. 14, § 4); Woolaston, for his reiteration of the Spinozan denial of the resurrection of Christ (Book II, ch. 16, § 3); Tindal and his master Locke, for alleging that reason is capable of effecting on its own the remission of sins (Book II, ch. 4, § 5): Tindal's *Christianity as Old as the Creation* is cited.

Valsecchi has a special and separate treatment of the ethics of the Deists (and the Naturalists) who claim to be exalting and extolling "uprightness, good faith, virtue and good customs": how, he asks, can this be when they conceive of the Deity as being ". . . blind, inactive, faint-hearted," and when they deprive him "of awareness and governance of the world and especially of watchfulness over human actions in order to reward or punish them?" (Book III, Part I, ch. 10, § 1; Latin edition, p. 336 a; 7th Italian edition, Vol. III, p. 84). It is of interest to note that not a single Deist is cited by name in the entire chapter, but rather anonymous works only, like the *Lettres sur la religion essentielle à l'homme* (§ 2-6) followed by the *Principes de philosophie morale,* for which Valsecchi shows a certain regard (". . . keen insight and methodical exposition are not wanting"). When Valsecchi later treats the "principle of tolerance" (Book III, chapters 14-16), he puts the Deists on the same level as the atheists, holding them to be, like the atheists, partisans of naturalism; and he cites, as agreeing with him in this opinion, Woodward and Gibson (Latin edition, p. 403; 7th Italian edition, Vol. III, pp. 140f). There are extensive quotations from Pascal's *Pensées* included in Valsecchi's exposition of the second cause of atheism, perversion of the mind (Book III, Part II, ch. 1; Latin edition, p. 410a; 7th Italian edition, Vol. III, pp. 151f.).

Another Dominican, a contemporary of Valsecchi, Tommaso Vincenzo Moniglia by name, author of various apologetic works, wrote a lengthy critique of the theory of "thinking matter" (*La mente umana spirito immortale, non materia pensante,* 2 vols. [Padua, 1766]). Moniglia, like Valsecchi, attacks Spinoza (I, 9, 29; II, 84), Hobbes (II, 74f., 131ff., 175), Collins (II, 173), Toland (II, 7, 83ff., 129), Dodwell (I, 66; II, 181). In his refutation of the crypto-materialism of the Deists, partisans of the "thinking matter" concept, Moniglia appeals not to St. Thomas (who is cited but once: II, 71), but rather to contemporary writings, like the anonymous *La Belle Wolfienne* (cited in II, 104ff.), the Platonist Cudworth (cited in II, 120ff.), a dissertation of the English theologian Ditton (cited in II, 125ff.), various treatises of authors of the Wolffian school such as Reinbeck (cited in II, 145ff.), Bulfinger and especially Cantz (cited in II, 152ff.; 158ff.). Moniglia evinces great esteem for Leibniz ("a great Physicist, a great Metaphysician, a great Mathematician": II, 5f.). In Moniglia, too, we find not the faintest suspicion of the speculative cataclysm or inversion effected by the *cogito;* he is quite content to reduce atheism simply to materialism (II, 49ff.). Moniglia seems generally less well-informed than Valsecchi, also more strident and less pithy.

PART III

ENLIGHTENMENT ATHEISM

1

Cartesian and Lockeian Origins of 18th-Century Atheist Materialism

After the death of Descartes, modern thought can be said to have split in two down the middle, with absolute spiritualism on one side and sense-perceptionist materialism on the other. Materialism flourished especially in English philosophy; Hobbes' monumental work can be considered, especially in the field of philosophy of nature and politics, as parallel to, and in some areas still more vigorous than, that of Descartes in its trailblazing of the new line of thought. Hobbes' atheism which was to undermine the development of English philosophy from within was, as we have seen, a logical development patently evident in his principles. But the preponderant and decisive role in the development of the materialist wing of modern atheism seems to have been less the work of English sense-perceptionism than of Descartes himself. The best-informed historians of philosophy [1] claim that Descartes laid down the fundamental principles of the materialism which was to be developed in the French Enlightenment thinkers, the *philosophes;* the claim is that Descartes accomplished this despite and perhaps precisely because of his spiritualistic metaphysic.[2] We might then note that it is no accident that

[1] This is the thesis of A. Vartanian in the basic essay: *Diderot and Descartes,* A Study of Scientific Naturalism in the Enlightenment (Princeton University Press, 1953).

[2] Vartanian's thesis had been formulated in the early 20th century by a Columbia University scholar: "The existence of God and of the soul are made useless from the point of view of his science. Though Descartes asserts that the demonstration of God's existence gains clearness when it is understood that his existence is necessary to assure us of the reality of the occurrences and facts of the material world, he does not show the necessity of God's existence in the development of his scientific ideas concerning the material world. The world being represented as a self-moving mechanism where all phenomena are interconnected by necessary laws and where every effect has its natural causes, there is no place in it for divine grace or providence. All functions of life being described in natural terms, the soul is made superfluous" (L. Kahn, *Metaphysics of the Supernatural as illustrated by Descartes* [New York, 1918], p. 27).

the two main fountainheads of modern atheism, idealism and materialism, can themselves be traced back still further into an ultimate source which is the radical dissociation effected by Descartes between nature and spirit, knowing and being, soul and body.

In the wake of this sort of isolation imposed by the Cartesian Method upon both principles, each one of them, deprived of the contrasting background and the real and intentional substantiation provided by its opposite, was bound to tend to a denial of the grounding of truth in being and in transcendence. On the heels of the denial that being transcends the mind there was bound to follow eventually a "confinement" of being by the mind and a consequent resolution of the immanence of the *cogito* into the finitude (Kant) or the infinitude (Hegel) of the being of the world, culminating in the explicit denial of God in post-Hegelian philosophy. Likewise, on the heels of the rigorously mechanistic conception of nature proposed by Descartes, there followed, less than a century later, the radical expulsion of God from the world, a world conceived as having principles valid and sufficient for its own evolution and government in the mechanism of its necessary laws and its inherent powers.[3] These considerations at least have surprised the professional historians of philosophy;[4] and they merit a brief mention, in the interests of a

[3] Vartanian (*op. cit.*, p. 4) presents three main conclusions: first, that there was a decisive break in theory and in approach in the transition from Descartes to the *philosophes;* second, that there is a basic similarity evident between the thought of Descartes and that of these Enlightenment philosophers; third, that the Enlightenment philosophers, in their section of the Cartesian system to adapt it to their own purposes, were to separate the metaphysics from the physics, but were to carry to full fruition the critical rationalistic method of Descartes. It seems to us that it is not proper to speak of a "decisive break" in principles in the transition from Descartes to the Enlightenment philosophers and hence of a breakdown to the foundation that supports both the idealist and the mechanistic approach, both coexistent in Descartes.

[4] The decisive influence of Cartesian physics upon the Left Wing of French atheist Enlightenment philosophy has been recognized by Brunetière and Lange and more recently by Maritain who maintains Descartes to be a victim of "a natural illusion" which "makes him mistake the quantitative aspects he is considering and the mathematical entities he is manipulating for actually physical causes and principles. A quite privileged victim of that illusion which, with uncompromising obstinacy, he pushes to its final consequences, convinced that physics 'is only geometry', and making of physico-mathematical science natural philosophy itself, Descartes consummates the rupture between the new science and the former wisdom, and he rivets it for several centuries to the most hypocritically tyrannical and most deceiving of metaphysical postulates—to the postulates of a universal mathematism. The scientific truth he brought forth into the light of day, changing into mechanism, becomes in its turn the vehicle of an error" (J. Maritain, *The Dream of Descartes,* English translation by M. L. Andison [New York, 1944], pp. 40f.).

better understanding of the inner torment and staggering complexity of modern thought.

A good case can therefore be made for the fact that it was precisely the Cartesian metaphysical dualism between *res cogitans* and *res extensa* that constituted the first decisive step in the direction both of naturalism as atheistic materialism and of idealism as atheistic anthropologism. The Cartesian world, as Pascal had clearly seen, no longer had any need of God.

Briefly, the situation was this: Descartes had reduced the being of spiritual substance to pure thought (*res cogitans*), and had likewise conceived the material substance as pure extension (*res extensa*); the act proper to spiritual substance was thought, and likewise the *res extensa* had its own proper and essential operation, namely, motion, to which all the activities and properties of bodies had to be reduced.[5] This Cartesian mechanism was thus radically a form of materialism and atheism no less than Spinoza's *Deus sive natura* and perhaps more so. It attributed to matter a primordial power and thus in fact ruled out any intervention of God in the world and conceived nature in terms of the most rigid necessity, entirely excluding any notion of finality. Descartes introduces his "theory of vortices" (*tourbillons*) to explain the entire complex of the development of natural processes from the initial formation of the physical world to the most delicate structures and functions of animals and of man himself. And these *tourbillons* are purely mechanical motions, explanatory of all natural processes without distinction. Matter and motion therefore can be uncreated as they were for the materialism of the Atomists and Epicurus. From this point of view, Pluche's forthright denunciation of the atheism of the Cartesian physics is quite justified:

"Not only is there no profit to be had from this imaginary physics, which pretends to relieve providence of its role in the creation of the universe . . . but there is everything to be lost for man [who] makes an idol of matter once it is set in motion. It is in reality blind, devoid of intelligence and design; nonetheless he attributes everything to it. It is matter in motion that engenders the elements. It is nature which has ordered the spheres, hardened the crust of the planets, and by a residue of lighter dust-like particles has surrounded the planet with an atmosphere. In a word, such a person, preoccupied always with this nature, hardly makes an occasional mention of the Prime Mover. He does not accede to atheism, for that would be the height of folly. But the wisdom

[5] The basic references here made to the "physics" of Descartes come from his later writings, especially *Le Monde ou Traité de la lumière* and *Principes de la Philosophie*.

of the deity, his intentions, foresight, goodness, and the constancy of his favors . . . find themselves absolutely banished from the greater scope of physics, and God is as much forgotten as if he had never existed." [6]

Diderot's remarks in this connection are most significant for he is supposed to have made the transition from Deism to atheism precisely under the impulse of the Cartesian physics: "We cannot but note here how insecure philosophy is in its own principles and how vacillating in its behavior. Motion and matter were once asserted to be the only things needed. If, since then, philosophy has continued to maintain that matter is uncreated, it has nonetheless had recourse to an intelligent being with a view to explaining how matter comes to assume a thousand different forms and how its particles are disposed in an ordered arrangement sufficient to explain the genesis of the world. Today matter is admitted to be created and God is admitted to communicate motion to it; but the assertion is then made that this motion emanating from the hand of God can, if left to itself, express all the phenomena of the visible world. A philosopher who dares to undertake the explanation of the mechanism and even of the original formation of things via the laws of motion alone and who says: *give me matter and motion and I will make a world,* must first prove (which is easy enough to do!) that existence and motion are not in fact essential to matter. Otherwise that philosopher, erroneously believing that there is nothing in the marvelous spectacle of the universe save what could have been produced by motion, risks falling into atheism." [7]

In like manner did the author of the *Summa* of modern materialism, Baron d'Holbach, express his solidarity with the principles of the Cartesian physics: "In supposing . . . the existence of matter, we must suppose it to be possessed of certain qualities from which must necessarily follow its motions or modes of behavior, determined by these very qualities. To make the universe, Descartes called only for matter in motion. A differentiated matter was enough for him; its various motions were the consequence of its existence, of its essence and of its properties. Its various modes of action are the necessary results of its different modes of being. A material substance without properties is nothing but non-being pure and simple. Thus matter must act from the moment it exists . . ." [8]

Descartes with his great sensitivity to criticism would certainly not have failed to express his extreme vexation at this massive pillage and betrayal of his philosophy in favor of that very materialistic atheism he

[6] Abbé Noël-Antoine Pluche, *Histoire du Ciel, considéré selon les idées des poëtes, des philosophes, et de Moïse* (Paris, 1739), II, pp. 225, 256; quoted in A. Vartanian, *op. cit.*, pp. 90f.

[7] Diderot, *Oeuvres philosophiques,* ed. P. Vernière (Paris, 1961), XIV, 9.

[8] D'Holbach, *Système de la Nature,* Part I, c. 2, (London, 1774 [2]), Vol. I, p. 30.

intended to combat and vanquish. For this sacking of Cartesian principles made Hardouin's critique and Voetius' charge seem like mere peccadilloes. Here it was the very notion of the world that was at stake: once its internal structure and its dynamic relations were guaranteed and substantiated in the very simple fashion here being used, i.e., in function of the autonomous distribution of motion and nothing else, with this motion being considered the sole and primordial source of all qualitative distinction and differentiation, then it remained only to assert the self-sufficiency of the physical world in all its manifestations and to make of it a closed circle.[9]

Cartesian physics with its rigid mechanism must, therefore, be admitted to have had a crucial part in the progressive consolidation of immanentism and modern atheism, a part at least equal to, and in any event complementary to, that played by the *cogito* in the realm of the life of the mind and spirit. And the *cogito* itself, as the best-informed historians of philosophy have noted, was only able to offer partially successful and flaccid resistence in the development of modern thought to the irruption of the mechanistic principle which eventually broke the dykes and opened the floodgates to materialism. And it is here not a question merely of the distinctly disturbing ambiguity of the Spinozan *Deus sive natura* which, as we have seen, can be refashioned in Cratesian terms; it is rather a question of an increasing and eventually total liberation attributed by such mechanism to the physical with respect to the metaphysical. Man, grappling with an analysis of motion, becomes the judge and arbiter of the real in its forms and developments as well as in its truth. It is the end of metaphysics as a search for the transcendent and suprasensible.

It is therefore not surprising to find that thinkers like Meslier, Diderot, d'Holbach and La Mettrie himself claim to derive their atheistic materialism directly from Descartes. La Mettrie in particular was able to develop his theory of the Man-Machine from the Cartesian

[9] Cartesian "matter" is actually extension deprived of all form and sensible qualities and consisting solely of dimensions (length, breadth, height), i.e., the purely mathematical body filling space. And the distinction and genesis of the various bodies from matter and Chaos is effected solely by motion and in accord with the laws of motion established by God: "For God hath so marvellously established these Laws that, even were we to suppose that He created nothing more than what I have said, and even that he did not put any order or proportion into it but made it into the most confused and tangled Chaos that the Poets could describe, these Laws suffice to make the parts of this Chaos disentangle themselves of themselves, and to arrange themselves in such good order that they would have the form of a most perfect World, wherein could be seen not only Light but all the other things as well, general and particular, which do appear in this real World" (*Le Monde: Traité de la Lumière; Oeuvres*, ed. Adam-Tannery, Vol. XI, [Paris, 1909], pp. 34f.).

notion of the Animal-Machine.[10] In accord with his rigid dualism between *res cogitans* and *res extensa,* Descartes had had to maintain that all the vital and sensible phenomena in the subhuman realm were reducible to infra-conscious or purely physical processes, resulting from the generic laws of matter in motion; consequently ever apparently conscious and purposive behavior in animals, i.e., any behavior in some sense intelligent in them, could and must be explained, just like the functions of the organism, by purely mechanical causes without any recourse to the existence in these animals of any new principle or "soul" distinct from matter. La Mettrie and the other *philosophes* of the d'Holbach group did to Descartes what Feuerbach and the Hegelian Left did to Hegel: they radicalized the "system" by resolving its ambiguity and the insoluble and, in their eyes, needless tension in which it was floundering. Thus, the materialist Cartesians denied spirit in order better to understand matter, just as the Leftist Hegelians later rejected Hegel's Absolute in order to realize in its concreteness that sensible human reality of which the Absolute was but an empty symbol.

Certainly Descartes and Hegel would both have looked with extremely jaundiced eye on such a treatment and would have attempted a still more vigorous defense of their respective metaphysics; but this would not have prevented the forcing into crisis of the very meaning of the "system" and of its basic principles. La Mettrie makes a significant declaration of principle concerning his debt to Descartes ("this great man"), a declaration that admits of no doubts or uncertainties: La Mettrie is sure he is restoring to Descartes that kudos of which he had been robbed by the Anglophiles, "all these petty philosophers, ludicrous and disgusting apes of Locke, who, instead of impudently thumbing their nose at Descartes, would do better to realize that without him the field of philosophy would perhaps be still lying fallow, even as that of science without Newton."

[10] Descartes is well-known to have thought that the notion of animals as being "pure machines" was calculated to favor faith in the immortality of the human soul. Descartes expresses himself perfectly clearly on the mechanistic notion of the animate: every vegetative and sensitive function is effected by the "animal spirits" conducted by the arteries; these "animal spirits" accomplish all the motions governing the various functions; thus it is an error to believe that it is the soul that gives motion and heat to the body. The difference between a live body and a dead one is thus the difference between a machine in working order and a dismantled one: "Let us say that the body of a living man differs as much from that of a dead man as a timepiece or other automaton (i.e., any machine that doth die of itself) when it is wound up and in working order, having in itself the corporeal principle of the motions for which it is built, doth differ from the same timepiece or other machine, when it is broken and the principle of its motion doth cease to operate" (*Des Passions de l'âme,* c. 6, ed. Adam-Tannery, Vol. XI, pp. 330f.).

And he adds a strange statement: "It is true that this famous philosopher was greatly deceived and mistaken; nobody disagrees on this point. But he *did* know animal nature; he was the first to provide a perfect demonstration of the fact that animals were pure machines. Well, in the face of a discovery of this importance, a discovery that presupposes so much sagacity, how can anyone fail to pardon all his errors unless one wants to be guilty of supreme ingratitude! In my eyes, all these errors are redeemed by this great insight. For, in the final analysis, all his expatiation on the distinction of the two substances is obviously but a sleight of hand, a stylistic ruse to get the theologians to swallow a poison concealed in the shadow of an analogy that is patent to everyone else, and the theologians are the only ones not to see. For it is this potent analogy which compels all scholars and true judges to admit that these proud and vain beings, more distinguished by their pride than by the name of men, however much they desire to give themselves airs, are basically nothing but animals and machines, crawling perpendicularly." [11]

La Mettrie's claim in this matter can easily be verified. Descartes conceives of a living body as a statue or a "farm implement" which, once assembled (by God), continues to accomplish its motions on its own, no differently from a timepiece, a man-made fountain, a mill or other similar machine made by man.[12] This term *machine* recurs with such pervasive and stubborn persistence throughout the entire Cartesian exposition of the vital functions that that encyclopedia of Cartesian science, *Le Monde* can justifiably be considered to be the effective basis for the molding of modern materialism and thus to be a source of prime importance in the constitution of modern atheism. Everything is in fact explained in terms of the motion of the animal spirits impelled in the ". . . concavity of the brain of our machine" by the heart and the arteries and making the entire organism vibrate. This organism proceeds under this impulse to its various functions, both vital and sensitive, in the fashion of an organ—the analogy is Descartes' own in which the air, under the varying action of the organist's fingers, is distributed from the wind-chest into the pipes and produces marvelous harmonies.[13] Indeed the final remarks in the *Traité de l'Homme* provide us with a guidepost for the understanding of the new line that will be taken in subsequent

[11] La Mettrie, *L'Homme machine,* ed. Solovine (Paris: Editions Boissard, 1921), pp. 132f. Also *La Mettrie's L'Homme Machine,* A Study in the Origin of an Idea, Critical Edition with an Introductory Monograph and Notes, by A. Vartanian (Princeton: Princeton University Press, 1960), pp. 191f. The most important chapter of Vartanian's *Diderot and Descartes* is entitled "From Cartesian Mechanistic Biology to the Man-Machine and Evolutionary Materialism" (pp. 203-288).

[12] Descartes, *Le Monde, Traité de l'Homme,* c. 18, p. 120.

[13] *Ibid.,* p. 165.

centuries by the study of man in the most divergent schools: "I would have you consider, in the light of this, that all the functions that I have attributed to this machine, such as the digestion of victuals, the pulsation of the heart and the arteries, the nourishment and growth of the members, respiration, waking states and sleep; the reception of light, sounds, smells, tastes, heat and such other qualities, in the organs of the external senses; the impression of the ideas of them in the organ of common sense and imagination, the retention or imprinting of these ideas in the memory; the interior motions of the appetites and the passions; and finally the outward motions of all the members, which follow so aptly both the actions of the objects presented to the senses and of the passions and the impressions encountered in the memory, as to imitate as perfectly as possible those of a true man:—I would have you, I say, consider that these functions all follow naturally, in this machine, from the simple disposition of its organs, not more nor less than do the movements of a timepiece or other automatic device from the disposition of its counterweights and wheels; so that there is no need, because of these functions, to conceive of their being in this machine any other soul, vegetative or sensitive, nor yet any other principle of motion and of life than its blood and the spirits, excited by the heat of the fire that burns continually in its heart and which is of no other nature than that of all the fires that are in inanimate bodies." [14]

Descartes was therefore the real founder of what Lange has called "psychology without a soul", from which there flowed directly and inevitably in due course the new "philosophy without God." [15] It was precisely the Cartesian conception of the world, veiled indeed in skillful reticences and continual protests of orthodoxy, which took the crucial step, prior to Hobbes and Spinoza and more drastic than they, in radically untethering man from transcendence.

Marx held French Enlightenment atheism, the precursor of the Revolution, to be more than a struggle against the existing political institutions, more even than a struggle against religion and theology. He held it to be also an open fight against the 17th-century metaphysics, especially that of Descartes, Malebranche, Spinoza and Leibniz. Philosophy is set

[14] *Ibid.*, pp. 201f.

[15] Vartanian is categorical on this point and it constitutes the central thesis of his work: "It was the attempt to explain the union of soul and body in terms of Descartes's mechanistic physiology that, in time, transformed the *bête machine* into the *homme machine*" (*Diderot and Descartes*, p. 216). On this basis, Vartanian is impelled to downgrade and even to consider negligible the influence of Locke and English sense-perceptionism in the molding of the materialism of the Enlightenment philosophers in France; this seems to us to be going too far: it suffices simply to read La Mettrie's *Homme-machine* in order to note that Cartesian mechanism and English sensism actually merge.

in opposition over against metaphysics, even as Feuerbach will later do with Hegelian speculation and metaphysics, says Marx, is to succumb before materialism which will represent the definitive starting-point of genuine speculation and will signal the victorious inception of the new Humanism.

Marx sees two trends in French materialism: [16] one stemming from Descartes, the other from Locke; the latter tends mainly to the development of French culture and goes straight to socialism (Helvétius and d'Holbach are the chief representatives); the former, mechanistic materialism, finds its application in the natural sciences properly so-called. The two tendencies intersect in the course of their evolution but Marx is chiefly interested in the trend that stems from Locke and attacks in depth the study of man and the molding of his mind.

Marx follows the authoritative lead of Feuerbach in considering Pierre Bayle to be the precursor of this *destructio metaphysicae*. Bayle corroded with his skepticism the influence of the reigning metaphysics of Spinoza and Leibniz and was no less crucial for the new line of atheism than was the materialism of Bacon and Hobbes. Bayle in fact showed that there could be a society of outright atheists, that an atheist could be an honorable and upright man, that man was not degraded by atheism but by superstition and idolatry.

But the negative element was not enough to create the new revolution in the notion of man: there was need for the positive element as well and this provision of a theoretical basis for the new Humanism was the merit of Locke, with his *Essay on Human Understanding,* which was immediately enthusiastically welcomed in France in the P. Coste translation.[17] The materialist line had already been roughed out in English culture, notes Marx, by Bacon and especially by Hobbes: Bacon had begun by insisting that the senses furnish man with all his knowledge; Hobbes had proceeded to draw the conclusion that thought's intuition, the image and the like, are but phantasms of the material world, more or less divested of their sensible form. The task of science is simply to give a name to these phenomena. The same name can be given to many of these phantasms. And there can even be names for names: hence the

[16] Cf. *Die Heilige Familie,* c. VI, d; Bücherei des Marxismus-Leninismus, Vol. 41 (Berlin: Dietz Verlag, 1953), pp. 25ff.

[17] Generally speaking, they have very little to say about the philosophy of the spirit or mind, for they are quite disposed to believe that Locke has said the last word on this point and they have a deep distrust of metaphysical subtleties: rather than the faculties of the mind, it is nature and society that interest them. In Diderot in particular, and in his materialist friends, d'Holbach and Helvétius and preeminently La Mettrie, there is to be found a progressive predominance of the notion of nature" (E. Bréhier, *Histoire de la Philosophie,* Vol. II [Paris, 1962], p. 444).

assertion of the most radical nominalism as culmination of Hobbes' philosophy. There exist only particular beings, which are designated by individual names; an immaterial substance is no less contradictory than an immaterial body. Body, being, substance are all the very same reality and have the same idea. The idea cannot be separated from the matter that thinks because this matter is subject of all modifications. The term *infinite* is meaningless unless it merely indicates the ability of our mind to keep adding endlessly. Because only what is material is perceptible and knowable, we know nothing about the existence of God. Only my own existence is certain. Every human passion is a terminal or initial mechanical motion. The objects of the drives (*Triebe*) are the good. Man is subject to the laws of nature themselves. Power (*Macht*) and freedom are identical.

Although Hobbes deserves credit for having systematized Bacon's ideas, he did not provide any precise substantiation in the theoretical order for his basic principle that knowledge and ideas originate in the sensible world: this gap was filled by Locke, who appeared to the cultivated 18th-century French public as the philosopher of common sense and of reason founded on common sense. Marx does not enter in detail into the dynamic of Locke's influence in France, limiting himself to crucial elements and vital passages. He notes at once that the *immediate* disciple and interpreter of Locke in France was Condillac, who directed Locke's sense-perceptionism against 17th-century metaphysics, proving that the French had been right in rejecting this metaphysic and the theological prejudices as a mere creation of the imagination. He published a refutation of the systems of Descartes, Spinoza, Leibniz and malebranche. In his *Essai sur l'origine des connaissances humaines,*[18] Condillac developed Locke's principle and showed that not only the soul but the senses themselves, not only the art of fashioning an idea but even the art of material sensations are a matter (*Sache*) of experience and habit. The entire development of human beings depends on education and external circumstances: thus did the Lockeian principle attain, on French soil, consistency and clarity.[19]

[18] Marx writes: *L'essai . . .* (*op. cit.,* p. 259).

[19] "Lange has long since disposed, in his *Histoire du Matérialisme,* of the superficial thesis which made La Mettrie's and d'Holbach's materialism dependent on the sensualist theory of knowledge: we see resolute sensualists like Condillac to be staunch spiritualists; and chronological relations alone make it impossible that the first of the known French materialists, La Mettrie, should have benefited from the works of Condillac. Moreover there had been in existence for a long time an English materialist tradition; we have seen what the "mortalist" faction was in the 17th century; we recall Locke's admission of the impossibility of proving the spirituality of the soul, the books of Toland and the polemic of Collins" (E. Bréhier, *Histoire de la philosophie,* Vol. II, p. 451).

Marx holds that the difference between French materialism and English materialism is to be sought in the difference between the two nationalities as such: the French furnish to English materialism flesh and blood, eloquence, Gallic wit. They endow it with a human warmth and grace hitherto lacking; they civilize it. First on Marx's list comes Helvétius who takes Locke as his starting point and then gives to materialism its typically French character (as we shall be pointing out ourselves in due course). The chief elements contributed by Helvétius are to be found in his book *De l'Homme,* in which the bases of all morality are located in sensible properties and self-love, in enjoyment or pleasure and personal interest properly understood, in the natural equality of human intelligence as between men, in the unity between the progress of reason and the progress of industry, in the natural goodness of man and the all-powerful influence of education. A synthesis of Cartesian materialism and English materialism is to be found, according to Marx, in the writings of La Mettrie: he uses, down to the minutest details, the Cartesian physics and his famous *homme-machine* is but a copy of Descartes' *bête-machine.* In d'Holbach's *Système de la Nature,* the physics is likewise a synthesis of French and English materialism, while the morals depends on the ethics of Helvétius. But the French materialist most closely linked to metaphysics and praised for that reason by Hegel, is Robinet (*De la nature*),[20] who appeals directly to Leibniz.

Marx finds it pointless to go into detail on the other French materialists and atheists (such as Volney, Dupuis, Diderot and the like) or on the physiocrats, once he has demonstrated the dual origin of French materialism from the Cartesian physics and English materialism, and the opposition of French materialism to speculative metaphysics.[21] Even as the first trend of Cartesian materialism ends up in the realm of the natural sciences properly so-called, the other trend leads directly to socialism and communism. Its typical contribution is to have put man at the center of reflection. It does not indeed require any great acuity of insight to discover the necessary connection here with communism and socialism, if consideration be given to the theories of materialism on the original goodness of man, on the equality of human intelligence as between individuals, on the all-powerful influence of education, on the

[20] Cf. Hegel, *Geschichte der Philosophie,* ed. Michelet, (Berlin, 1844), pp. 470ff.

[21] Engels holds that it is with the French Enlightenment that the German philosophy begins which is to give rise to the new dialectic culminating in Hegel: "Meanwhile there had arisen side by side with and in the wake of 18th century French philosophy the more modern philosophy which was to culminate in Hegel. Its great merit lay in having restored the dialectic as the highest form of thinking" (F. Engels, *Herrn Eugen Dührings Umwälzung der Wissenschaft* [Stuttgart, 1904[5]], p. 5).

influence exercised on men by external circumstances, on the great importance of industry, the importance of pleasure, etc. Once man is admitted to be molded from the sensible world and the experience of that sensible world, from sensation, etc., the assignment is quite obviously to organize the empirical world in such a way that man shall experience in it what is truly human, that man shall assimilate this to himself, so as to have an experience of himself as man. If a properly understood self-interest is the principle of all morality, then the private interest of man must coincide with the (generic) human interest. If man is non-free in the materialist sense, i.e., if he is free not in the negative sense of being able to prevent this or that, but rather because of his positive compulsion to assert his own individuality, then there ought to be no punishing of the crimes of individuals but rather a concentration on the destruction of the anti-social evils or motivations from which these crimes spring. Each and every individual ought to be given the social scope for the development of his own proper life. Seeing that man is molded by circumstances, these circumstances must be humanized. Seeing that man is social by nature, he does not develop his true nature except in society, and the measure of the power of that nature ought therefore to be, not the power of the single individual, but rather the power of society.

All Marxist historiography henceforth stresses the decisive influence of atheistic materialism upon the making of Marxism, an influence mediated by 18th-century French Enlightenment thought: Lenin maintains this throughout.[22] He recalls that Engels had recommended to the leaders of the proletariat of his day the translation and dissemination among the masses of the militant writings of the late 18th century atheists; and Lenin complains that this has not yet been done. It is true. Lenin notes, that there are many unscientific and childish points in the works of the 18th-century revolutionary atheists; but these can be left out and the editors can rather highlight the advances made in these works in the scientific critique of religion and noting the works of later thinkers that take their inspiration from these Enlightenment writings.[23]

The most egregious and pernicious error that can be committed by a Marxist, alleges Lenin, is to believe that the popular masses, several millions strong and including masses of peasants and artisans, consigned by the whole of modern society to the darkness of ignorance and preju-

[22] Lenin, "Sur l'importance du matérialisme militant," in *Marx-Engels Marxisme* (Moscow, 1947), pp. 468f.

[23] The Soviet publishers have faithfully executed this program, publishing full-length translations of the French Enlightenment thinkers, whose works constitute one of the basics of Marxist training.

dices, can emerge from this darkness only by the straight road of a purely Marxist training. These masses must be provided with the most diverse documents of atheist propaganda, must be introduced to the greatest possible variety of facts taken from the most divergent fields of life, must be approached from all possible angles to gain their interest and attention, to rouse them from their religious somnolence, to shake them to the core, etc. Now the writings of the old-time atheists of the 18th century, those passionate, lively, clever attacks on the then dominant clericalism are very often a thousand times more suited to shake the masses out of their religious dream-world than are the tedious, dry rehashes of Marxism, second-rate uninspired pedestrian products that dominate the contemporary scene, works almost entirely devoid of skillfully selected illustrative factual material and often guilty of distortions of Marxism. It is simply silly, Lenin continues, to be afraid that a knowledge of the old-time materialism and the old-time atheism could prejudice the advances achieved by Marx and Engels; indeed "a flight from the alliance with the representatives of the bourgeoisie in the 18th century, the very period at which that bourgeoisie was becoming revolutionary, would be tantamount to a betrayal of Marxism and materialism." [24]

Marx had taken his first steps in his critique of religion using the atheist materialism of Democritus' and Epicurus' cosmological atomism: but this was still a static and metaphysical atheism. Enlightenment materialism, on the contrary, was dynamic and probed from the very principle of modern philosophy, the *cogito,* to the taproot of its anthropocentricity; and it combined with this probing a head-on attack on religion in general and Christianity in particular, charging them with corrupting morals and destroying freedom.[25] This sort of polemic was to be an abiding bulwark of Marxist atheism. While claiming to prefer the sensualist materialism deriving from Locke to the metaphysical materialism of those who, like La Mettrie, start from the Cartesian notion of matter, Marxism nevertheless fights just as vigorously as did these

[24] The most thorough and official Marxist exposition at present of 18th century French materialistic atheism, with glossary from the classics of Marxism, is that given in the voluminous *History of Philosophy* edited by the USSR Academy of Sciences, a team of philosophers serving as editorial board. (We refer to the German translation: *Geschichte der Philosophie* [Berlin: VEB Deutscher Verlag der Wissenschaften, 1959], Vol. I, especially pp. 497ff.; cf. also the other work of a team of Russian philosophers, of which we likewise here give the German translation: *Grundlagen der marxistischen Philosophie* [Berlin: Dietz Verlag, 1959], pp. 70ff.).

[25] Cf. M. D. Zebenko's article in *Grundlagen der marxistischen Philosophie,* p. 46.

18th-century French atheists against every form of deism, even against Voltaire himself, who while criticizing Christianity always trenchantly defended the existence of God and immortality.[26]

The Marxist founding fathers acknowledge and openly proclaim the influence of French Enlightenment atheism on Marxist atheism: Marx, Engels and Lenin all accept with special relish the fight against all religion, especially the Catholic faith, and the rude critique of belief in salvation in a life to come. Yet the Marxists have several deep-cutting reservations about these French Enlightenment thinkers. They note that the French materialists were themselves bourgeois and were not aware of the true causes of religious oppression, private ownership of the means of production and oppression of one class by another.

Lenin reiterates two specific criticisms made by Engels.[27] First, that 18th century French materialism was predominantly mechanistic, reducing the animal, as Descartes had done, to a mere machine; whereas the mechanical laws, although they do play a part in chemistry and biology, are pushed into the background by other higher laws. Secondly, that this metaphysical materialism was incapable of conceiving the world and nature as a process or fabric (*Stoff*) subject to a historical fashioning: it knew nature to be subject to a continuous motion but this was a circular motion repeating *ad infinitum* and continually producing the same results. This insufficiency was a mark of the entire culture of the day and

[26] Condillac, Robinet, D'Alembert are likewise taxed with inconsistency for not having gone on to atheism (*Geschichte der Philosophie,* Vol. I, pp. 495, 521 and *passim*).—In the famous *Dictionnaire Philosophique,* in the article *Athée, Athéisme,* Voltaire defends Vanini against the charge of atheism and refutes Bayle's stand on the possibility of an atheist society; then Voltaire proceeds to define what atheists are: ". . . for the most part daring scholars who have gone astray, whose reasoning is faulty and who, not being able to understand creation, the origin of evil and other difficulties, have recourse to the hypothesis of the eternity of things and of necessity." And Voltaire's conclusion is "That atheism is a most pernicious monstrosity in those who govern; that it is no less pernicious in those who are councillors of rulers, no matter how blameless these councillors may be in their private life, because from their council chamber they can get through to those who are the actual rulers: that, although not as baneful as fanaticism, it is almost always fatal to virtue. Let it be added that there are fewer atheists today than ever before, since the philosophers have admitted that there is no plant without a seed, no seed without a design, etc., and that putrefaction is not the origin of grain. Some geometricians who are not philosophers reject final causality but the true philosophers accept it; and, as a well-known writer has said, a catechist proclaims God to children and Newton demonstrates him to the learned" (ed. J. Benda and R. Naves [Paris, 1954], pp. 42f.). Abbé Nonnotte, author of the *Dictionnaire anti-Philosophique* (Avignon, 1767) on the other hand considers natural religion and revealed religion inseparable one from the other (cf. article *Athées,* pp. 31-36) and makes Voltaire responsible for the atheism of Helvétius and his associates.

[27] Cf. F. Engels, *Ludwig Feuerbach und der Ausgang der klassischen deutschen Philosophie,* ed. H. Hajek; *Philos. Bibl.,* Vol. 230 (Leipzig, 1947), p. 18.

the French Enlightenment thinkers cannot be blamed for having been ignorant of the dialectic of nature when even Hegel himself conceived nature as being nothing but an outward phenomenal expression of space itself and reserved to the human reality of consciousness (*Bewusstsein*) the ability to evolve in time. What Lenin does find surprising is that, after Hegel and Marx, materialists like Büchner and Mach (and the Machians in general) should have relapsed into this static materialism.[28]

Finally, the Enlightenment thinkers, in Lenin's opinion, exaggerated the social significance of religion and attempted to label the hegemony of religious ideology as the basic, if not the only, source of every evil in society. This approach is indicative of an atheism still metaphysical in character and neglectful of the importance of the economic element and of the materialistic conception of history. Lenin's high esteem for Enlightenment atheistic materialism does not prevent him from observing that it amounts to a superficial and idealist explanation to see the origin of religion in the ignorance of the masses. Nor is the Enlightenment appeal to "culture" and general education of these ignorant masses the really efficacious way to combat religion: such thinkers did not even suspect that the sole origin of religion, as Lenin will show, is economic and that the only way to overthrow religion is to do away with private ownership of the means of production. Enlightenment thinkers simply did not see through to the class nature of religion; their atheism remained bourgeois: "No Enlightenment tract," says Lenin, "will eliminate religion from the masses held in the thrall of forced labor by the capitalists and dependent on the blind and destructive forces of capitalism until such time as these masses have learned to fight in united and organized fashion, with a prearranged plan against the root of religion, the *rule and hegemony* of capitalism in all its forms . . ." [29] The Marxists thus contend the Enlightenment atheism is not aware of the real state of affairs and remains a prisoner of the bourgeois mentality. But they do credit the Enlightenment thinkers with having prepared the way for the Revolution and the proclamation of the rights of man which will free the masses from capitalist oppression by the instrumentality of a new concept or notion of man.

[28] Lenin, *Materialism and Empiriocriticism* (Moscow: Foreign Languages Publishing House, n.d.), p. 247. Recent Marxist historians of philosophy note and admit certain foreshadowings of the dialectic in the later Diderot; I believe this is because of his references to or hints at a theory of evolution which will be carried further forward by Lamarck and Buffon (cf. G. J. Glesermann, "Der Kampf zwischen Materialismus und Idealismus in der Geschichte, der Philosophie der vormarxistischen Epoche," in *Grundlagen der Marxistischen Philosophie,* p. 75).

[29] Lenin, "Ueber das Verhältnis der Arbeiterpartei zur Religion," in *Ueber die Religion* (Berlin: Dietz Verlag, 1956), pp. 24, 26.

2
La Mettrie's Hedonistic Atheism

D'Holbach's precursor or nearest rival in atheism was the physician Julien Offray de La Mettrie (1709-1751), author of the philosophical works *L'Homme plante* (1748), *Le Système d'Epicure* (1750), and particularly *L'Homme machine* (1748), to which last-named work he owes his fame in the history of thought. One of La Mettrie's recent editors [1] attempts to acquit him of the charge of atheism and present him as a skeptic and agnostic; this editor's argumentation is based on the literal sense of the texts and these can be admitted to have aimed at a coolly ironic tone, avoiding all the violent verbal fireworks in which d'Holbach was later to delight.

The first editor (Luzac) who published *L'Homme machine* anonymously does not rule out the possibility of this work serving in the final analysis as an aid to religion by its very exposition of the arguments against religion, all the more so since nothing is gained by concealing such arguments, and the editor has no doubts about the eventual triumph of religion over unbelief: "Such concealment plays into the hands of the unbelievers; they deride a religion which our ignorance would fain present as incapable of being reconciled with philosophy: they sing hymns of victory in their redoubts which our style of warfare makes them believe to be invincible. If religion is not triumphant, that is the fault of the inept writers defending it. Let the really first-rate ones take up the pen, show themselves to be well-armed champions, and theology will carry the day by force of arms against so weak a rival. I compare the atheists to those giants who wanted to scale the heavens; they will always meet with the same fate." [2]

The same editor makes the penetrating observation that the work is based on a sharply defined notion of the union of body and soul and that the consequences drawn by the author, grave and dangerous though they may be, depend ultimately on this notion which comes down in the final

[1] Cf. M. Solovine, *Introduction* to *L'Homme Machine,* pp. 24f.
[2] *L'Homme machine,* p. 42; Vartanian edition, p. 141.

analysis to a pure hypothesis: this is the hypothesis of the Cartesian dualism of soul and body on which is directly dependent the mechanistic conception of nature and life, up to and including the vital and congitive functions of man. There is no doubt that *L'Homme machine* aggravated the responsibility of Cartesianism for modern atheism; there is equally little doubt that this book was never answered more pertinently and constructively than by the polemical tirades of *Athei detecti,* a work which had as little influence on the subsequent history of thought as did the tart but vague recriminations of Voetius and associates.

La Mettrie begins by dividing (or, more accurately reducing) into two the systems of philosophy treating of the human soul: materialism and spiritualism. Spiritualism is attributed to the metaphysicians and special mention is made of the Leibnizians and the Cartesians: [3] these spiritualists are alleged to make the appeal to the divine revelation of Sacred Scripture their last resort and the basis of their system; but, says La Mettrie, it is experience that must be believed in the event of a conflict between experience and faith, and it is experience that must justify faith. The final word in this controversy on the nature of the soul and the body belongs to the ". . . physicians who have been philosophers" and who have relied upon experience and observation: "These men have explored and shed light upon the labyrinth of man; they alone have revealed to us the mainsprings hidden under outer integuments that reveal to our eyes so many marvels. They alone have calmly contemplated our soul, surprising it a thousand times, both in its misery and in its grandeur; and they have no more despised it in the former state than they have admired it in the latter. Once again, be it said, these are the only physicians who have a right to speak here." [4]

The proper procedure is not the *a priori* one of the philosophers; it is rather the *a posteriori* method ". . . seeking to fathom the soul athwart the organs of the body, that one can, I do not say lay evidently bare the very nature of man, but at least attain to the greatest possible degree of probability on this subject." [5]

La Mettrie devotes special consideration to the "brain" in his study of the nature of the soul: for the brain is the master control of all man's functions, the source of all his passions and actions, the destination of the fibers running from every part of his body. The body is thus sufficient unto itself: "The human body is a machine which is self-winding: it is a living image of perpetual motion. Victuals sustain what fever excites. Without them, the soul languishes, becomes crazed and flickers

[3] *Ibid.,* p. 58; Vartanian, p. 149. Cf. on p. 63 an almost complete list: ". . . The Descartes, the Malebranches, the Leibnizes, the Wollfs . . ."

[4] *Ibid.,* p. 61f.; Vartanian, p. 151.

[5] *Ibid.,* p. 62; Vartanian, p. 152.

out in death. It is a candle whose light revives at the very moment it is going out."[6]

The soul follows the advances of the body, such as those effected by education and training: "The various states of the soul are therefore always correlative to those of the body" and comparative anatomy shows us that man has the most highly developed brain of any animal.[7]

The much-touted "natural law", continues La Mettrie, is a sheer and simple function of the brain, subsequently expressed in a "familiar feeling" that teaches us what we ought not to do because we do not want others to do it to us; thus it is a biological feeling of fear or alarm, a fruit of the imagination, and therefore a sheer product of the brain, like thought, deriving neither from education, training, revelation nor the lawmaker.[8]

The materialist, La Mettrie, adopts a cryptic stance on the God-problem, neither coming out strongly and openly as an atheist nor involving himself in any lengthy discussions of the arguments of theism. He contents himself with hints, insinuations, expressions of doubt. It will be of interest to document from the original text the main stages of this middle road between the Deism of the English philosophers and Voltaire and the atheism of d'Holbach.[9]

1. The existence of God is highly probable but it is a truth which is supremely irrelevant for human life: "It is not that I have called in question the existence of a supreme Being; it seems to me, on the contrary, probable in the highest degree that such a Being does exist; but since this existence does not prove the necessity of one form of worship rather than another, it is a theoretical truth which is hardly useful in practice: so that, as a wealth of experiential data likewise justify one in asserting, religion does not necessarily involve meticulous integrity nor does atheism necessarily exclude it" (p. 104f.; Vartanian p. 175f.).

[6] *Ibid.*, p. 67; Vartanian, p. 154.

[7] *Ibid.*, pp. 73ff.; Vartanian, p. 158. Hence, concludes La Mettrie, the high-sounding words ". . . spirituality, immortality" have no meaning (p. 86).

[8] *Ibid.*, p. 104; Vartanian, p. 175.—The conclusion on the nature of the soul is by now obvious: "The soul is thus but an empty term with no real idea corresponding to it; and a good mind should use it only to designate that part in us that thinks. Supposing the least principle of motion, animate bodies will have all they need in order to move themselves, to feel, to think, to repent and, in a word, to manage themselves in the realm of physics and in that of morality which depends upon it" (p. 113; Vartanian, p. 180).

[9] *Ibid.*, pp. 104ff.; Vartanian, p. 175.—Vartanian has a sober specification of the precise problem involved: "On the propagandist plane, his tendency is frankly atheistic ("l'Univers ne sera jamais heureux, à moins qu'il ne sera athée,' [The world will never be happy until it is atheist], etc.), although what this really expresses is little else besides a general hostility to the established religion. But on the philosophical plane, atheism is presented neither as a premise nor a consequence of the man-machine theory: (*La Mettrie's L'Homme machine,* p. 24.).

The famous thesis of Bayle's *Pensées diverses* will be readily recognized in the last sentence above.

2. The origin of man may be a matter of pure chance: "Who knows, moreover, whether the reason of the existence of man may not lie simply in that existence itself? He may have been thrown by chance upon a point of the earth's surface, with no possibility of knowing how or why; he may only be able to know that he must live and die, like those mushrooms that spring up overnight or the flowers that border the ditches and cover the walls" (p. 105; Vartanian, p, 176). For d'Holbach, on the contrary, as we shall see, there is no such thing as chance; it is a meaningless term with which we conceal our ignorance of causes. Everything must have its own sufficient reason in the world with mathematic precision in terms of the most rigid determinism.[10]

3. We must stop at the observable facts for we are in no position to penetrate to the causes: "Let us not lose ourselves in the infinite, for we are not made to have the least idea of it; it is absolutely impossible for us to penetrate back to the origin of things. It is moreover a matter of indifference for our peace of mind whether matter be eternal or created, whether there be a God or not. What folly so to torment ourselves on account of something it is impossible to know, something that would make us no happier if we were in fact to get to the bottom of it." [11]

On this point too La Mettrie appears in evident contrast with d'Holbach who interprets the structure of the world with a rigidily mechanistic theory and explains all the phenomena of nature and human life as effects of the laws of motion, as we shall be pointing out.

4. The metaphysical proofs of the existence of God (e.g., those advanced by Fénelon, Nieuwentyt, Abbadie, Derham, Rais, etc.) backfire badly: [12] "They are nothing but tiresome repetitions on the part of overzealous writers, each of whom adds only a mass of verbiage to the others, more apt to strengthen than to undermine the foundations of atheism. The proofs drawn from the spectacle of nature gain no additional force from being merely multiplied and heaped up. The structure of a single finger, ear or eye, observes Malpighi, proves everything and undoubtedly proves it much better than Descartes and Malebranche, or else all the rest proves nothing" (p. 106; Vartanian, p. 176).

La Mettrie is less than crystal clear at this point but it is clear that he

[10] D'Holbach, *Le Système de la nature,* Vol. I, p. 56. Cf. pp. 71f.: the order of the world is not an effect of an intelligence; rather it is the result of the various motions. Thus in this sense we do not have mere chance nor any fortuitous caprice; rather everything proceeds according to necessary laws (p. 75).

[11] *Ibid.,* Part I, ch. 2: on motion and its origin; Vol. I, pp. 13ff.

[12] D'Holbach also mentions Abbadie, Derham and Fénelon, among others (*ibid.,* Vol. I, p. 279; Vol. II, pp. 339, 362).

does not consider atheism as yet to have been cogently refused; yet neither does he present any explicit apology for atheism.

5. Indeed, in the sequel La Mettrie puts into the mouth of Deists and Christians as a clinching argument, calculated to reduce the atheists to silence, the observed order and purposiveness governing the phenomena of nature, especially in the animate realm: "The Deists and the Christians themselves ought thus to content themselves with pointing out that in the entire animal kingdom the same designs are executed by an infinity of various means, all of which are, however, of a geometric precision. For what stronger weapons could be used to crush the atheists?" (p. 106; Vartanian, p. 176).

La Mettrie adduces in confirmation an extensive treatment of the marvels of nature and especially of the sense organs, sight and hearing in particular, which he insists cannot be the work of mere chance.

6. But at this point, La Mettrie changes course, abandoning vague generalities and presenting his own stand in explicit terms. He cites at length from Diderot's *Pensées Philosophiques* (". . . a sublime work which will not convince an atheist") and seems to be taking refuge in a form of agnosticism which is certainly not far removed from atheism. His skillfully subtle mode of expression cannot hide his real meaning: "*The weight of the universe* therefore does not even make the atheist stagger, much less crush him; and all these alleged indications of the existence of a creator, indications geared far above the ordinary way of thinking, acquire no greater evidence for their thousandfold repetition, except for the anti-Pyrrhonians or for those who have enough confidence in their own reason to believe themselves capable of making a judgment on the basis of certain appearances, over against which, as you see, the atheists can set others perhaps stronger and absolutely contrary. For if we listen to the naturalists again, they will tell us that the same causes which, in the hands of a chemist and in virtue of the sheer chance of various combinations, made the first mirror, conspired in the hands of Nature to make that clear water that serves as mirror for the humble shepherd; that the motion that conserves the world could have created it; that every body has taken the place assigned it by Nature; that air had to surround the earth for the same reason that iron and the other metals are the work of the bowels of that earth; that the sun is as natural a product as electricity; that that sun was no more made to warm the earth and its inhabitants whom it sometimes burns than was the rain to make the grain crops grow which it often spoils; that neither mirror nor water were made simply so that man could look at himself in them than were any other polished bodies which have the same reflecting capacity; that the eye is in fact a sort of glass in which the soul can contem-

plate the image of objects as they are represented by such glasses; but that it had not been proven that this organ was really made on purpose just for such contemplation nor expressly placed for that reason in its socket; that, in the final analysis, it might very well be that Lucretius, the physician Lamy and all the Epicureans, ancient and modern, were right in their contention that the eye sees only because it is organized and located as it in fact is; that, granting the very laws of motion followed by Nature in the generation and evolution of bodies, it was not possible that this marvelous organ should have been organized or positioned otherwise" (pp. 109f; Vartanian, p. 178).

La Mettrie elects to conclude on an objectively neutral note: "Such is the pro and the con, and an abridgement of the main arguments that have split the philosophers time out of mind. I take no sides". But this neutrality is quite suspect because La Mettrie forthwith proceeds to a defense of atheism as that conception which holds to the simple "natural law" without any superstructure: "Whoever is a strict observer of it is an upright man and deserving of the confidence of the whole human race. Whoever does not scrupulously follow that same law is a knave or a hypocrite and I mistrust him for all his fine external religious pretenses" (pp. 110f.; Vartanian, p. 179).

At this point, La Mettrie proceeds to a consideration of the soul, in regard to which he shows a certitude entirely free of all hesitancy or fluctuations, keeping always straight on course to his goal, which is that of proving the uselessness and therefore the non-existence of the soul. His first step is to reiterate the Locke-Toland hypothesis of matter as principle of motion in the entire gamut of its manifestations which La Mettrie describes with obvious satisfaction, especially in the biological field: each and every part of a living organism has its own proper motions which are products of a power of its own which manifests itself even when some trauma separates or isolates the part from the whole.

La Mettrie is outspoken in his warning against vitalistic rationalism: "Now that it has been clearly proven against the Cartesians, Stahlians and Malebranchians and the theologians unworthy of such illustrious company, that matter moves of itself, not only when it is organized as in a whole heart, but even when this organization is destroyed, man's curiosity would fain know how a body, by the very fact of being initially endowed with the breath of life, finds itself in consequence adorned with the faculty of sensing and even of thinking" (pp. 127f.; Vartanian, pp. 188f.).

At once there appears the same vein of agnosticism as was shown in the consideration of the God-problem: "In the matter of this development, it is folly to waste time seeking for its mechanism. The nature of motion is as unknown to us as is that of matter . . . I am therefore no whit less worried at my ignorance of how matter, from being inert and simple, becomes active and composed of organs, than I am at not being able to look at the sun except through a smoked glass; and I am just as equable about the other incomprehensible marvels of Nature, the genesis of sensation and thought in a being that appears to our bounded eyes to be but a lump of clay" (p. 129; Vartanian, p. 189).[13] At this point, La Mettrie openly professes outright materialism: "Being a machine, feeling, thinking, knowing how to distinguish good from evil, even as blue from yellow, in a word being born with intelligence and a sure instinct of morality, and yet being nothing but an animal—this is no more contradictory than being a monkey or a parrot and yet knowing how to attain pleasure . . . I believe thought to be so little incompatible with organized matter as to seem to be a property of that matter, just like electricity, the motor faculty, impenetrability, extension, etc." (pp. 133f.; Vartanian, p. 192).

The work ends with a eulogy of the "convinced materialist" (convinced, that is, that he is a machine or an animal merely), as the type of man who is upright, wise, just, calmly ready to accept his fate and therefore happy; a lover of life, he will yet await death without fearing it; full of love for mankind, he will love the good human character even of his enemies. This "convinced materialist" will not maltreat his fellows: ". . . too well informed upon the nature of these actions, whose inhumanity is always proportioned to the degree of analogy proven above, and not wishing, in a word, in accord with the natural Law imparted to all animals, to do unto others what he would not have them do unto him" (p. 142). There is no doubt about the meaning of the entire book and La Mettrie is proud of it: "Let us then boldly conclude that man is a machine and that there is in the whole universe but one single substance modified in various ways" (p. 142; Vartanian, p. 197). This moralistic conclusion however constitutes only the obvious facade of an edifice which is all too openly an apology for hedonism.[14] But the crucial point is the undeniable influence exerted by this work upon the

[13] This profession of ignorance in the face of the complexity of the phenomena of life is a recurrent theme (cf., e.g., p. 141: "invincible ignorance" and *passim*).

[14] This was too much even for d'Holbach to swallow and he retorted: "The author who has just recently published *L'homme machine* has argued on morals like a real madman. If these authors had but consulted nature on morality as on religion, they would have found that, far indeed from leading to vice and dissoluteness, it leads to virtue" (*Système de la nature,* Part II, ch. XXII, Vol. II, p. 381 note 80). Granted that *L'Homme machine* was published in 1748, d'Holbach's "just recently" above would lead one to believe that his own *Système* was written about that year, when d'Holbach (born in 1723) was only 25 years old. The dependence therefore does not seem probable.

evolution of those ideas which led to the mental revolution of the modern world. The Cartesian separation of body and soul, of sensation and thought, is here transformed into an unconditional triumph of the former element of each pair and thus all tension and alternative disappears between being and freedom: Bayle's thesis on the independence of morality from religion becomes the overt justification of the atheist as against the believer who is a hypocrite and a bigot. Locke's thesis-hypothesis of self-moving matter is raised to the status of a dithyrambic praise of the senses, an exaltation of the brain as the actual organ of thought, and an apology for pleasure as the supreme goal of existence. In this sense, La Mettrie's position can be considered to be the first consistent and radical form of Enlightenment atheism.

3

Helvétius' Sensualistic Atheism

Present-day atheism differs from classical and Enlightenment materialism not in terms of a denial of the Absolute (for both deny it) but rather in terms of the method of philosophizing employed, more specifically the relationship held to exist between man's being and the world, in the two philosophical streams. Classical and Enlightenment materialism explains man in function of the world and as an element of nature; present-day atheism explains the world from the starting point of man via his mental and conscious activity. Yet both Marx and Marxists of our own day are quick to admit the importance of "dogmatic or metaphysical materialism" in preparing the way for dialectical materialism.[1]

The essence of the atheistic materialism of the Enlightenment can be expressed in the following basic propositions, which are a synthesis of the thought of the two most radical representatives of this stream of thought, d'Holbach and Helvétius.[2]

[1] For a general overall treatment, cf. M. D. Zebenko, *Der Atheismus der französischen Materialisten des 18. Jahrhunderts* (Berlin: Dietz Verlag, 1956). He asserts that the atheistic materialism hinted at or asserted outright by Meslier, d'Alembert, Diderot and La Mettrie becomes explicit and radical with Helvétius and preeminently with the Franco-German d'Holbach. In our own analysis, we have preferred to put Helvétius ahead of d'Holbach, as being less radical than d'Holbach, at least in his formulations.

[2] Cf. *Le vrai sens du Système de la Nature,* posthumously published in London in 1774, pp. 3ff. This little work was attributed to Helvétius as early as its first edition, three years after his death (being designated as "posthumous work of M. Helvétius, at London 1744); but it is no longer considered to have been his work (cf. A. Keim, *Helvétius,* sa vie et ses oeuvres [Paris, 1907], pp. 621ff.). However, it is an admirably clear summary of his ideas and those of the main work of his friend Baron d'Holbach, to which work the title obviously refers (cf., e.g., Ch. XX which discusses the "Proofs of the existence of God" advanced by Clarke and reiterates almost to the letter the treatement given in d'Holbach's *Système de la nature,* Part II, Ch. 4; Vol. II, pp. 95ff., especially pp. 110ff.). *Le vrai sens* was translated into German under the title *Neunundzwanzig Thesen des Materialismus* (Halle a. S., 1873) (There is a copy of the first French edition in the Vatican Library). It is known to have been glossed by Voltaire whose critical notes aim specially to defend the existence of God (cf. S. Ljublinski, *Voltaire-Studien,* Berlin: [Akademie Verlag, 1961], pp. 112ff. Voltaire's marginal notes are given on pp. 125ff.).

I. Man is the work of nature; he is within nature and subject to her laws; from these laws he cannot free himself; thought can never abstract from these laws. Man is not exterior to the great whole of which he is a part. All the other natures supposed to exist above or side by side with nature belong to the realm of fables.

II. The reality of the world is manifested via "motion" and motion constitutes the relation between our organs of perception and the reality that is inside and outside of us. The essence of every body is manifested via motion and everything is in motion in the universe.

III. Matter has always existed and motion is an essential attribute of matter: thus matter received motion from itself. Hence motion is the sole cause of all the metamorphoses, forms and manifestations of matter in every existent being.

IV. By the instrumentality of motion there is accomplished a continuous process of alteration, substitution and circulation of matter; via this process the various beings are differentiated one from another and constitute new relations and new effects.

V. *Man* is a product of nature like any other object, but we do not know how or when he appeared on the scene.[3] He is an organized whole composed of various kinds of matter, each operating according to its own proper qualities.

VI. Man does not enjoy the status of a privileged being within nature but is subject to the same phenomena of energy-exchange as the other beings.

VII. The basic form of knowledge is *sensation* which consists in an impulse or impact administered to our sense organs by bodies via motion; this impulse transmitted to the brain is *perception.* Thought of the realm of "ideas" is nothing but the image or representation of those objects which have first been apprehended by the sensations and perceptions.[4]

VIII. The *soul* is basically constituted by the faculty of sensing; it is distinct from the "spirit" or mind inasmuch as this latter term indicates the complex of "conscious and cognitive" activity, whereas the soul is the sheer and simple principle of life, uniform in all men: thus the soul is properly the "cause" of the spirit or mind, because without sensing there is neither memory nor thought.

[3] The materialist reply to this question will be given a century later in the Darwin theory of evolution.

[4] Helvétius, *De l'Homme,* De ses Facultés intellectuelles et de son education (London, 1776), p. 64. Helvétius' preceding and better known work had already reduced the activity of the mind to the external senses (la sensibilité physique [physical sensibility]) and memory, and its conclusion had been: "I say that physical sensibility and memory, or to speak more exactly, sensibility alone, produces all our ideas" (*De l'Esprit*—written in 1758—I here use the edition published in Paris, Year II of the Republic, Vol. I, pp. 66f.).

IX. Man does not enjoy any *freedom* in his actions, which are in fact the necessary consequence of his temperament and of acquired ideas modified by the examples of others, by education and by experience.

X. Nor does man enjoy any *immortality:* the soul follows step by step the various stages of bodily development and ceases to operate. i.e., to sense (and hence, to exist!), at the death of the body.[5]

XI. The origin of the idea of *God* (and of immortality) is to be sought in man's inclination to fabricate a life of perfect happiness by imagining a Being able to overcome the evil with which man sees himself surrounded.

It would seem that we must look for the key to Helvétius' own thought, as revealed in his major works, especially *De l'homme,* by tracing and identifying the direct line of derivation linking him to Locke's sensism, which trailblazed the second path of immanentism. This will provide us with a crucial insight into the philosophical bias of a great part of 18th century Europe as held in the orbit of French culture. The strictly theoretical part of Helvétius' work opens with the heading: *human mind (or spirit) has been regarded as an effect of the greater or lesser subtlety of organization."* There follows forthwith an enunciation of the theoretical guiding principle crucial to the entire work: "In the wake of the enlightenment provided us by Locke, we know that it is to the sense organs that we owe ideas and consequently our mind or spirit; when, therefore, we note differences both in the sense organs and in the minds of different men, we must agree in concluding therefrom that the inequality of minds is an effect of the unequal subtlety of their senses." [6] And Helvétius sums up his own thinking thus: "It is this principle alone which explains to us how it can be that we owe our ideas to our senses, while at the same time we do not owe the greater or lesser reach of our mind to the mere perfection of those same senses." [7] And on the subject of the *memory:* "The book *De l'Esprit* says that memory in us human beings is but a persisting though weakened sensation. In point of fact, memory is but an effect of the faculty of sensing." [8]

[5] *De l'Esprit,* Vol. I, pp. 63ff.; *De l'Homme,* p. 148.

[6] *De l'Homme,* Sect. II, Ch. 1, p. 61; cf. also Ch. 23, p. 169. An explicit appeal to Locke is also made by d'Holbach who, however, reproaches Locke with inconsistency in having later applied himself to problems of theology (*Système de la nature,* Part I, Ch. 10 pp. 178f.).

[7] *De l'Homme,* p. 64. This amounts to a complete inversion of the Cartesian *cogito* into the act of sensing: "It is properly speaking my sensations and not my thoughts, as Descartes claims, which prove to me the existence of my soul" (p. 69).

[8] *Ibid.,* Sect. II, Ch. 2, p. 71. Later there is presented a synthetic formulation, embracing likewise the practical activity: "The general conclusion of this chapter is that in man everything is sensation; a truth of which I shall give yet another new proof, by showing that sociability is in him merely a consequence of this same sensibility" (*ibid.,* Ch. 7, p. 88).

The immediate conclusion is that, just as the so-called abstract and general ideas are reducible to sensations and perceptions, so, too, judgments consist in a relation or reference to a sensation in the case of present objects and to the memory in the case of absent objects, following which the subject judges, i.e., reproduces exactly the impression he has received. Hence the formula, amounting virtually to a literal version of Hume's famous theory on the basis of judgment: *"Any judgment is thus simply the relation of two sensations, either presently being experienced or preserved in my memory."* [9] Thus, my judgment is constituted by the simple recital or relation of what I am experiencing. With typical Gallic precision, Helvétius pinpoints his definition in the drastic formula: "To judge is *to sense.*" And the sequel is worth noting: the fulcrum of mental life is sensation; all the operations of the mind come down, in the final analysis, to sensations and the faculty of judging is not a function or faculty distinct from sensing; it is simply the ability to compare two sensations, or *"to become attentive to the various impressions excited in us by the objects either actually present to our senses or conserved in our memory."* [10]

Nor is there any exception to this rule in the case of judgments alleged to bear on abstract terms, such as weakness (*faiblesse*), strength (*force*), meanness (*petitesse*), size (*grandeur*) and crime (*crime*), which terms, it is claimed, are not representative of any body; for such terms cannot enter into a judgment until they are applied to some sensible object, i.e., until these terms "become physical" via such application, until the judgment makes "the decision of sensations already experienced" (*le prononce des sensations éprouvées*).[11] Thus the terms "weakness", "strength", etc., notes Helvétius, are indeed indicative of important relationships but they remain extremely vague until they are applied to particular objects and the meaning changes in function of the objects to which they are applied: e.g., the same term "size" will evoke

[9] *Ibid.*, Ch. 4, p. 73; cf. also p. 77. The influence of Hume is here to be felt no less than that of Locke; he is cited expressly later on, in connection with the origin of religion (Sect. II, Ch. 18, pp. 138 and 139), the critique of the notion of causality (Ch. 19, p. 143), the knowledge of universal ideas (Ch. 23, p. 169: where Hume is called "one of the most illustrious writers of England"), and the critique of Catholicism in his *History of England* (Sect. VII, Ch. 3, p. 366 and Ch. 4, p. 370).

[10] *Ibid.*, Sect. II, Ch. 4, p. 74 (italics Helvétius').

[11] *Ibid.*, Ch. 5, p. 75. In the former work: "When I see the size or the color of objects presented to me, the judgment concerning the differing impressions these objects have made upon my senses is evidently nothing more, properly speaking, than a sensation; that I can equally well say 'I judge' or 'I feel' that of the two objects the one that I call 'a fathom' makes a different impression on me than does the one I call 'a foot'; that the color I call 'red' affects my eyes differently than does the one I call 'yellow'; and I conclude that, in this event, judging is never anything other than *feeling, sensing*" (*De l'Esprit*, Vol. I, p. 69).

quite different ideas depending on whether it is applied to a fly or a whale. Exactly the same sort of thing can be said (and here he reveals the real nature of his materialistic sensualism) of what are called "ideas" or "thought": thinking cannot, in fact, be something divorced from matter and extension, something constituting a basis for the immortality of the soul. Thinking is simply "a way of being" of man, certainly different from extension, but not a being apart or a spiritual entity. Thus every idea must ultimately come down to physical facts or sensations. The transition from sensation to judgment is effected by *attention* which confers upon the sensation the "strength" of an impression in order to produce the decision or to achieve the "isolation"—to use a term of the phenomenological school—of a perceptual field or of a particular object of such a field in the confused sea of immediate sensations.[12]

Helvétius' crucial formulation of this notion is: "physical sensibility is the sole cause of our actions, of our thoughts, of our passions and of our social relations" and thus it is "the sole motive force [of life] of man." [13] Sorrow, remorse, friendship, pleasure, power, and even man's social bent itself, depend on the fact that *in* man everything comes down to sensing and thus to pleasure and pain which are the basic powers of mind or spirit.[14] And so even the act of discrimination (or the "method" of judging) not only between true and false, good and evil, etc., but even in the realm of pure science, e.g., geometry, comes down in the final analysis to a sense impression: "The judgments made on the means offered us by chance to arrive at a certain goal are, properly speaking, nothing but sensations and in man, everything is reducible ultimately to sensation." [15]

This free-wheeling phenomenology produces the new definition of "spirit" or mind which is typical of the free-liver Enlightenment tendency. Mind or spirit is formally defined as: *"The natural disposition and capacity to see the resemblances and differences, agreements and disagreements prevailing between various objects."* Mind or spirit is thus a secondary rather than a primary structure, just as it was in Locke's sense-perceptionism: it is a product of man's capacity for physical sensation, his memory, and primarily of the interest he has in combin-

[12] *De l'Homme,* Sect. II, Ch. 6, pp. 78ff. The focussing or isolation here mentioned is caused in the final analysis by the *pleasure* or *pain* that constitute the source and cause of attention (p. 81).

[13] *Ibid.,* Ch. 7, p. 81. And later comes the conclusion: "That in men everything is feeling, all is sensation. That they feel and acquire ideas only by the five senses" (Ch. 15, p. 119).

[14] *Ibid.,* Ch. 8ff. In Ch. 9, Helvétius defends his earlier book *De l'Esprit* against the attacks of the theologians (pp. 93ff.).

[15] *De l'Esprit,* Disc. I, Ch. 1, p. 73, cf. also Ch. 4, p. 107.

ing sensations: "Mind or spirit is thus the result of the comparison of sensations." [16]

The differences between "soul" and "spirit" (in this sense of "mind") are, however, deep-cutting:

1. The mind or spirit is susceptible of development, whereas the soul is not: "The soul exists whole in the child even as in the adolescent. The child is, like the adult, sensible to physical pleasure and pain; but he does not have as many ideas and thus not as much mind (spirit) as the adult. Now if the child has as much soul but not as much mind (spirit) the soul is not the mind (spirit)."

2. The soul has a continuity in its activity that the mind does not have: "The soul does not leave us until death. As long as I live, I have a soul. Can the same be said of the mind? No: sometimes I lose that mind while yet alive, for sometimes I can lose my memory and the mind is almost exclusively the effect of this faculty of memory." Mind (spirit) is defined by Helvétius primarily in function of memory and so, obviously, can be lost when memory goes: "The mind thus differs essentially from the soul, in the sense that the former can be lost while the subject is still alive, whereas the latter cannot be lost except at the moment of death."

3. The essence of the soul is the faculty of sensing, whereas the mind is a result of the complex of ideas: "I have said that the mind of man is composed of the concatenation of his ideas. There is no mind without ideas. Is the same true of the soul? No: neither thought nor mind are necessary for its existence. As long as man is capable of sensing, he has a soul. *It is thus the faculty of sensing* that forms the essence of the soul." [17] The mind is therefore at once something dynamic and acquired which marks the difference between various individual persons. As such, mind is defined as "the result of its own sensations when they are compared." [18] Although men do not all experience the same sensations, all do sense objects in a way which is always proportionately the same and thus all have an identical aptitude, inclination or disposition to

[16] *De l'Homme,* Sect. II, Ch. 15, p. 116.

[17] *Ibid.,* Ch. 2, pp. 66ff. In Sect. III there is a treatment of the "generic causes of the inequality of minds" which are reduced to two: chance (*hasard*) or a different concatenation of events, circumstances and positions in which various men find themselves; and the more or less intense desire or ambition men have to educate themselves" (pp. 172ff.).

[18] *Ibid.,* Sect. II, Ch. 15, p. 116. Helvétius had already written along the same lines: "*The mind . . . consists in comparing both our sensations and our ideas, that is to say, in seeing the resemblances and the differences, the agreements and the disagreements between them.* Now, since judgment is but this perception and realization, or at least the articulation of it, it follows that all the operations of the mind come down to judging" (*De l'Esprit,* Disc. I, Ch. 1, Vol. I, p. 69). Note the (neologistic?) term here used "perception", which may be derived from Leibniz, though here used with a different meaning.

mind. So the course of the human mind, specifies Helvétius, is always the same for all; yet men do manage to get frightfully muddled on the meaning of the basic words of language: e.g., in speaking of "good", "interest", "virtue" and the like, every individual has his own special way of understanding what he is saying and this is what makes meaningful communication virtually impossible. And Helvétius suggests a way out of this uncertainty, vagueness and confusion in the matter of basic semantics: ". . . to compose a dictionary attaching clear-cut ideas and concepts to the various expressions. This is a difficult assignment and can only be executed among a free People." [19] Good Anglophile that he is, Helvétius sees England as being the only nation from which the world at large can expect such a favor.

The impression yielded by these principles in the matter of the problem of religion, of the existence of God and of immortality are ambivalent in the extreme: on the one hand, we find an assertion of respect for religious beliefs and Christianity as such and a polemic against alleged abuses committed by human beings in this whole field; on the other hand, we find the radical demolition of the very principles of all religion and all belief.

Helvétius certainly shows the most drastic distrust of Platonic-Scholastic theology and metaphysics, a distrust perfectly consistent with his principles. He rather favors a *philosophical metaphysics* which might better be called an "experimental metaphysics" based on observation, on Baconian principles: this metaphysics is pervasively present in all the arts and sciences as "the Science of the first principles of any Art or Science. Poetry, music, painting, have their own principles founded upon a constant and generic observation: thus, they have their own metaphysic." [20] The other metaphysics, the transcendental one, amounts simply to man's losing himself in the clouds, to a recitation of philosophical tall tales (*contes philosophiques*). Helvétius anticipates the basic principle of neopositivism in seeing the methodological kernel of this new outlook on philosophical problems in the analysis of language and the consequent reduction of each and every truth to a particular fact

[19] *De l'Homme,* Sect. II, Ch. 19, p. 141. And a little later: "This dictionary translated into all languages would be the comprehensive collection of almost all the ideas of men. To each expression let precise ideas be attached and Scholasticism, which has so often bowled the world over by the magic of words will be but an impotent magician." And in a vein reminiscent of Spinoza: "Moral, political and metaphysical propositions having then become as susceptible of proof as the propositions of geometry, men will have the same ideas of these sciences, because all (as I have shown) necessarily perceive the same relations between the same objects" (p. 143).

[20] *Ibid.,* Ch. 18, p. 140. Helvétius has no doubts about the value of the new Baconian metaphysics: "It is a true and genuine science, when, as distinct from Scholasticism, it is confined to the limits assigned to it by the illustrious Bacon" (Sect. II, Ch. 23, p. 170 note).

grasped by observation: "On the admission of almost all the philosophers, the sublimest truths, once simplified and reduced to their lowest terms, come down to *facts* and thenceforth present to the mind simply such propositions as *white is white, black is black.*" [21] This is the only way to dispel the misunderstandings that occur in an abstract metaphysic that loses itself in word-juggling; and it was Democritus rather than Plato who grasped being in the form of the sign and gave it its primordial significance.[22] This is a pliant and elastic empiricism but at the same time it is much more radical than its English model.

Helvétius is less explicit in his treatment of the religious problem as such but his position seems substantially no less negative than that of d'Holbach. Above all, there is evident in the posthumous work we are following here, from the very first page, a ruthless polemic against all positive religions which are declared to be false, and against Catholic Christianity in particular, which is a veritable pet peeve of Helvétius. The violence of Helvétius' attack exceeds that encountered anywhere else in Enlightenment writings. Helvétius takes his cardinal principle in this critique from none other than Hobbes: *"All religion,* says Hobbes, *which is founded on the fear of an invisible power, is a fabrication which, if avowed by a nation, bears the name of religion, and if disavowed by this same nation bears the name of superstition."* [23] But even in this all-out attack, we encounter the distinction (not a new one, of course, in post-Reformation days) between the Christian religion and Roman Catholicism, which latter Helvétius stigmatizes as "papism": "All religions are false, with the exception of the Christian religion; which latter, however, I do not confound with papism." [24] The utter scum of the earth is constituted by the Catholic nations: Spaniards,

[21] *Ibid.,* p. 165; cf. also p. 169.

[22] "All metaphysics not based upon observation amounts to nothing more than the art of abusing and misusing words. It is this metaphysics which, in the land of fancy, runs ceaselessly in pursuit of soap bubbles, about which it never has said anything but windy nothings. Now relegated to the theological schools, it divides them still, rekindling fanaticism and making human blood to flow anew. I compare these two sorts of metaphysics to the two divergent philosophies of Democritus and Plato. It is from the earth that the former raises himself by degrees to heaven and it is from heaven that the latter lowers himself by degrees to the earth. Plato's system is a cloud castle and the fresh breeze of reason has already begun to dissipate the clouds" (*ibid.,* Ch. 18, p. 140 note).

[23] *Ibid.,* Sect. I, Ch. 12, p. 43; cf. also the tirade on pp. 38ff.

[24] *Ibid.,* p. 43. And for good measure: "*Papism is of human institution.* To a man of any sense, papism is sheer idolatry. The Roman Church certainly saw nothing more in it than a human institution, when it scandalously abused this religion, making it an instrument of its avarice and aggrandizement, using it to further the criminal schemes of the popes and to lend an air of legitimacy to their avidity and their ambition" (*ibid.,* p. 44). Helvétius' attacks on the tyranny and greed of clergy and monks are much more violent in this work than in *De l'Esprit* (cf. *De l'Homme,* Sect. II, Ch. 21, pp. 151ff. and Sect. VII, Ch. 4, pp. 367ff.).

Portuguese, Italians and French are corrupt to the core as a result of Catholic morality.[25] Substantially Catholicism, with its odious superstitions and practices has lapsed back into paganism.

Helvétius proceeds to a deist criticism of all positive religion [26] and proposes a sort of *universal religion* which is a synthesis of Spinozism, Deism and the principles of Bayle. He defines it thus: "A universal religion can only be founded on principles which are eternal, invariable and susceptible, like the principles of geometry, of the most rigorous proofs; these principles must be drawn from the nature of man and of things." The aim or basic law of this religion is to ensure to everyone ". . . right to his goods, his life and his liberty," [27] i.e., the peaceful possession and use of life and of earthly goods, in quiet concord with other men. It is thus *religion reduced to the status of a natural ethic* that forms the proper object of *De l'Homme:* a religion unencumbered with dogmas, mellow and humane, sprightly and joyful in its ceremonies, impelling men to promote the public good. Helvétius is quite explicit: "What is the really tolerant religion? the one which either has no dogmas (like paganism) or which comes down to a sound and exalted ethic (like the religion of the philosophers), which will undoubtedly one day be the religion of the entire world at large." Thus the content of this religion is simply humanity as such: "Humanity is in man the only truly sublime virtue: it is the prime and perhaps the only virtue religions ought to inspire in men; it embraces in itself almost all the other virtues." [28] It is the religion of man, the *Religion des sens* (Religion of the Senses), coinciding with a paganism which has been divested of its fanciful mythology and made to highlight the human and this-worldly values that it was intended to exalt.[29]

[25] Machiavelli himself "attributes the excessive wickedness of the Italians to the falsity and contradictoriness of the moral precepts of the Catholic Religion" (*De l'Homme,* Sect. I. Ch. 10, p. 41). How much better are the Protestants; why, even paganism itself had fewer drawbacks (p. 47 note and pp. 55ff.). Praise for the religious spirit of Northern Europe is one of the recurrent themes of the work.

[26] Helvétius seems to draw his inspiration from the Deism of Voltaire and Hume: he forcefully criticizes the theory of "moral beauty" propounded by Locke and the English philosophers, especially the "idle Shaftesbury" (*De l'Homme,* p. 270); and he is equally energetic in his opposition to the naturalistic optimism of Rousseau (*ibid.,* Sect. V entire, pp. 360ff.).

[27] *Ibid.,* Sect. I, Ch. 13, pp. 47f.

[28] *Ibid.,* Ch. 14, pp. 53f. And a little earlier: "Morality founded on true principles is the only true Religion" (*ibid.,* Ch. 13, p. 50). Hence the vehement attack on religious intolerance which is called the most dangerous of all (Sect. IV, Ch. 18, pp. 234ff.) and contrary to the teaching of Christ itself (*ibid.,* Ch. 19, pp. 238ff.).

[29] Cf. *ibid.,* Sect. I, Ch. 15, pp. 57ff. Cf. also Sect. IV, Ch. 13, pp. 219ff. Section VII has Bayle's thesis as its title: "The Virtues and the Happiness of a People are the Effect not of the Holiness of its Religion but of the Wisdom of its Laws" (p. 354. On p. 356, we find Helvétius' conclusion: "Purity of morals is thus independent of purity of dogmas").

This is religion purged of all normal religious content: it is sheer humanism of the Feuerbachian brand. Is it atheism? Marxist historians of philosophy follow Marx-Engels-Lenin in clamoring that it is [30] and in view of what we have already expounded of Helvétius' thinking, this view must seem reasonably well-founded even though Helvétius never undertakes an explicit defense of atheism as did the later Diderot and d'Holbach. In the extensive notes to *De l'Homme,* however, Helvétius reduces the charges of atheism to mere verbal quibbles and denies that there are any atheists in the world at all. But we know what strange meanings may be attached to the expressions "God" and "the Absolute" in this radical naturalism with its sociological background. Here are two significant passages. The first, expository in tone, takes its inspiration from Hume and Robinet:

"And almost all these charges of atheism must likewise be traced back to disputes about words. There is no enlightened man who does not recognize and admit a power in nature. So there are no atheists. That man is in no sense an atheist who says: motion is God; for motion is indeed incomprehensible: we have no clear-cut ideas about it, it manifests itself only by its effects and it is by it that everything is brought to pass in the universe. Nor is that man in any sense an atheist who says on the contrary: motion is not God; for motion is not a being but rather a way of being. Those men are not atheists who claim that motion is essential to matter, who regard it as the invisible and motive force pervading all parts of matter. We see the stars continually changing position, revolving perpetually upon their center; we see all bodies being destroyed and reproduced unceasingly under different forms; in a word, we see nature in an eternal fermentation and dissolution. Who then can deny that motion is, like extension, inherent in bodies or that motion is the cause of whatever is? Indeed, Mr. Hume would say, if the name of cause and effect be always given to the concomitance of two facts and if there is motion wherever there are bodies, then motion must be regarded as the *universal soul* of matter, and of the deity, pervading the very substance of them. But what of the philosophers who are not of this opinion? Are they atheists? No: *they likewise recognize and admit an unknown force or power in the universe.* What then of those who do not have any ideas of God? Are they atheists? Again, no: for then all men would be atheists, for no man has clear-cut ideas of the deity, and any obscure idea in this category is the same as no idea at all. Indeed the avowal of the incomprehensibility of God amounts, as M. *Robinet* proves, to saying in other words that the speaker has no idea of him." [31]

[30] Cf. C. N. Momdshian, *Helvétius,* Ein streitbarer Atheist des 18. Jahrhunderts, German translation (Berlin, 1959), p. 211ff. ("Helvetius' Atheism").

[31] *De l'Homme,* Sect. II, Ch. 19, pp. 142f. The editor guarantees the authenticity of these notes (cf. Preface, p. V).

The second passage, polemical in tone, comes close to the core of the problem: "There is nothing less well-defined than the meaning of this word *ungodly,* to which there is so often attached a vague and confused idea of wickedness. Is it supposed to mean an atheist? Is it to be applied to the man who has but obscure ideas of the deity? In that event, all the world is atheist: for no one understands the incomprehensible! Is the term to be applied to those who style themselves materialists? How can it be when there are as yet no clear-cut and exhaustive notions of what an ungodly materialist is? Are those men to be treated as atheists who do not have the same idea of God as do the Catholics? Then pagans, heretics and infidels must all be called atheists! Well, in that case, atheist is no longer a synonym for scoundrel or villain! It designates a man who, on certain points of metaphysics or theology, does not think like the monk or the Sorbonne. To whom in fact must this term *ungodly* or atheist be applied in order for it to call to mind some notion of wickedness? To the persecutors!" [32]

Helvétius is more closely linked than is d'Holbach to the English philosophers on which both men modelled their thinking; and so Helvétius pays more attention to the ethicosociological aspect than to the metaphysical one. It is for him an indisputable fact that all religions, without exceptions, have been the source of all the evil in human history: "The evil done by religions is real, the good imaginary." [33] This alleged fact becomes the principle on which Helvétius founds his impassioned claim that man is and should be integral and self-contained. Diderot, d'Holbach and Helvétius therefore seem to form a closely knit and inseparable trio: despite the differences in their area of investigation in their method, all three agree in finding man's deepest roots within man himself and in restrictively confining those roots within the realm of sheer experience.

Diderot's friend and editor, J. A. Naigeon, wrote a polemical essay

[32] *Ibid.,* Sect. IV, Ch. 20, p. 248.

[33] *Ibid.,* Sect. VII, Ch. 2, p. 362. The reader should not be deceived by several texts apparently favorable to religion (cf. Sect. I, Ch. 13, pp. 48ff.; Sect. II, Ch. 2, pp. 65 note). It should be remembered that the "moral law" forming the essence of the *universal religion* is not innate; it derives not from God but solely from experience (cf. especially Sect. II, Ch. 21, pp. 156ff. note, Sect. V, Ch. 3, pp. 268f. note; especially Sect. VII, Ch. 2, with the significant title: "Of the Religious Spirit destructive of the Legislative Spirit", pp. 359ff.).

There is indeed one text that seems almost a profession of faith: "Moreover with what impiety can I be reproached? I have nowhere in this work denied the Trinity, the divinity of Jesus, the immortality of the soul, the resurrection of the dead, nor even a single article of the *papist creed:* so I have in no sense attacked religion" (*De l'Homme, Recapitulation,* Ch. 3, p. 580). But principles have their own internal logic and those advanced by Helvétius have not left and do not leave any doubts as to their consequences or as to the sort of mentality to which they belong.

which bears the stamp of the ideas of Diderot, Helvétius and d'Holbach. This essay, entitled *Le militaire Philosophe,* or Difficulties connected with Religion, posed to the Reverend Father Malebranche by a Retired Army Officer (new ed., London 1768), claims to be dealing with Malebranche's notions on the knowledge of bodies; but its real aim is to demolish first the foundations of Christianity and then those of religion in general. Some have therefore seen d'Holbach, also a friend of Naigeon, as having taken a direct hand in the composition. But in contrast to the complicated and involved style of the *Système de la nature,* this little volume seeks Cartesian clarity at any price: in 18 of the 20 chapters, it claims to be expounding a truth or a principle contradictory of religion.

1. There is a rather subtle initial insinuation of Christianity into the category of the *Religions factices* (man-made religions), a term obviously anticipatory of Kant's critique of Christianity as a "statutory religion." [34] More noteworthy in this denunciation is the Enlightenment tenet admitting reason alone as principle of truth, a tenet which Lessing was to reiterate, thereby administering the decisive blow to the 19th-century notion of religious knowledge. Further there immediately leaps to the eye in this indictment Bayle's famous thesis, here stated in its positive form: "I designate as *man-made religions,* all those that have been invented by men, that are established on facts admitting other principles than those of nature and reason and other laws than those of conscience. It is not at all the wicked scoundrels, the tyrants, the extortioners, the traitors, the assassins, or the poisoners who revolt against religions; they have the same feelings about them as the majority of men do; indeed they are quite often devout to the point of superstition. It is men of solid worth who love virtue and honor, who listen to their conscience and their reason; it is such men who are horrified to see themselves entangled in ridiculous and baneful opinions" (*Introduction,* p. IIf.). There is a rather hodge-podge development of the critique of the *man-made religions* throughout the rest of the work, especially in Ch. X (*No religion can be established on facts with certainty, not even with probability,* pp. 87ff.), Ch. XIV (*No man-made religion can demand a sincere belief,* pp. 119ff.), Ch. XVII (*All the man-made religions are false,* pp. 135ff.) and the last chapter (XX) (*Every man-made religion is contrary to morality,* pp. 158ff.).

2. The author declares that no religion has any internal consistency. He contradicts Hobbes to assert that religion is a private affair and that each individual is free in the matter of religion (Ch. III, pp. 49ff.). It is up to the human reason alone to discuss and decide in the matter of

[34] Cf. Kant, *Die Religion innerhalb der Grenzen der blossen Vernunft,* IV Stück, II. Theil, Kehrbach 180ff.

religion (Ch. VI, p. unnumbered) and it would be an offense against God himself to consider reason to be a doubtful or fallible guide (Ch. VII, pp. 68ff.). In giving us reason, God has given us a clear knowledge of his will (Ch. VIII, pp. 74ff.).

3. Like Diderot, Helvétius, d'Alembert and their like, the author seems to be proclaiming the return to a "natural religion" as a universal religion: "Thus it is that on the ruins of the man-made religions there will be built the edifice of the natural religion whose precepts are the same as those of morality and are calculated to convince the minds of all men.

This universal religion affords us true ideas of the deity. It shows us the supreme Being as perfect, as infinitely powerful, infinitely just, in short, as totally free of the vices and imperfections with which his alleged ministers have been willing to tarnish his lustre. This God, creator of all things, is the author of nature which he governs, whose laws he has made, whose order he has established. Consequently, he is the author of men, he is the author of society, he loves its well-being, he binds it to order and this order depends on the fidelity with which each of the members fulfills his moral duties in the sphere he occupies" (Ch. XX, pp. 185f.).

Near the end, in the context of a reiteration of the fact that "men are creatures of God" (p. 194), there is a concomitant assertion of the coincidence without remainder of natural religion with morality: "He will thus fulfill the duties of the true religion, of the natural religion, of the universal religion, which is nothing else than the morality appointed for the whole of the human race, a morality which is beyond dispute and which cannot counsel damage to humankind."

4. The recall to the "natural religion" is addressed to everyone, including the atheists who seem to be the only ones to profit by the vehement peroration of our "soldier philosopher" who echoes Bayle, Diderot and d'Holbach: "The precepts of this religion of nature are so simple and so true that they are accessible to and cogent for Christians and pagans, Mohammedans and Chinese, Protestants and papists alike. Nay, more! The atheists themselves, whatever may be the errors of their speculations, cannot turn a deaf ear to the urgent lessons of nature and reason; they cannot but admit what they owe to their fellowmen, what need they have of those same fellowmen, what means must be used to render these fellowmen well-disposed toward them, in short, what must be done in order to live happily, to be loved and esteemed in the Society of which they are members. I go still further and maintain that an atheist, that is, a man who formally denies the existence of a God, may have more genuine and solid reasons for practicing the social virtues and

for fulfilling the duties of morality than have those superstitious persons who know no other virtues than the useless virtues of their man-made religion, no other morality than that of their priests, and who founded that morality on a false deity whom they suppose to be unjust, unfair, cruel, capricious and inconstant according as their interests demand, and whom they make so often to command men to perform the most vicious actions, in whose name they cause to be committed crimes that are most destructive of society. Yes, I repeat, it would be better not to admit a God at all than to admit the sort of God who would be wicked, grotesque, unjust; who would demand that a man sacrifice to him the reason he has given to his creatures to guide them, that a man forego the goods this God has provided for him, that a man stifle the irresistible inclinations of nature of which he is the author in order to devote himself most assiduously to making himself miserable. Were it possible to insult or offend a Being whose felicity nothing can trouble, then a man would offend him much less by doubting his existence or even by denying it outright, than by attributing to him the imperfections and the vices we are compelled to detest in our fellow human beings. The priests with their invention of a barbarous God are the real blasphemers; they are the ones who force many men to fall back upon atheism in order to try to annihilate, if possible, in their mind even the idea of a Being who cannot be thought of without trembling. It is these priests who render the existence of God doubtful or problematic, by attaching to him ideas that are wholly incompatible, which imply contradictions, which are mutually destructive" (pp. 189-191).

This passage is certainly far from irenic or pussyfooting: yet these vehement statements seem to us less radical than those of d'Holbach and of Diderot in his last years. And even these two thinkers never succeeded in freeing themselves entirely from the torment of God. That is to be the achievement of the idealist brand of immanentism as it emerges in left-wing Hegelianism. Thus we must insist that, despite these philippics, Naigeon (if he is the author of the work in question) is not the "violently anti-religious" thinker he has been labelled by one scholar,[35] even though he does show himself to be a drastic critic of positive (man-made—*factices*) religions.

[35] Cf. R. Hubert, *D'Holbach et ses amis* (Paris, 1928), p. 27.

4

Transition from Deism to Atheism in Diderot[1]

Underneath the deceptively simple surface of 18th-century Enlightenment thought there course and merge the various philosophical tributaries of the new current of thought which for a century has been swelling to the point where it will transform philosophy by an inversion of the notion of truth. French thought, which had opened the way with Descartes, returns to its pathfinder status after an invigorating bath in the overflow of the English empiricism of Bacon, Hobbes and Locke and in the critique, now placid and now wrathful, unleashed by the throng of the English Deists against the dogmas of Christianity. In the age of the Encyclopedists, however, the placid atmosphere prevails and traditional religion still enjoys respect and esteem, at least in appearance. The thrust of the polemic is against superstition

[1] The title is taken from a Soviet historian of philosophy (cf. I. K. Luppol, *Diderot,* Ses idées philosophiques, French translation by V. and Y. Feldman [Paris, 1936]). The original was published in 1924. Cf. Ch. II: "From Theism to Atheism". It has been reiterated in a study by Vartanian: "From Deist to Atheist," in *Diderot Studies* (Syracuse: Syracuse University Press, 1949). Vartanian's thesis, already mentioned, concerning the predominant influence of Descartes upon the *philosophes* can be disproved in the case of Diderot by each and every one of his writings. His profession of sensism, against all manner of ontologism, is constant from beginning to end and constitutes the submerged vein from which will germinate his atheism in his later years (cf., e.g., his defense of the *nihil est in intellectu quod prius non fuerit in sensu* [Nothing is in the intellect that was not formerly in the senses] in the *Apologie de l'Abbé de Prades,* in *Oeuvres,* ed. J. Naigeon, Vol. I (Paris, 1821), p. 435f.; ed. J. Assezat, Vol. I (Paris, 1875), p. 451). At the same time it should be noted that the empiricist epistemology is here functioning within the metaphysical framework of the One-Whole, the *Deus sive Natura* [God or Nature] of Spinoza, a framework that Diderot had assimilated preeminently (apparently) from Shaftesbury, the translation of whose *Inquiry concerning Virtue or Merit* served to launch Diderot on his philosophical career (cf. K. Rosenkranz's study, *Diderot's Leben und Werke* Vol. I [Leipzig, 1886], still a capital work on the subject, pp. 23ff. For recent studies, cf. P. Casini, *Diderot "philosophe"* [Bari, 1962], pp. 102f.).

and the tactic is that of exalting reason ever more drastically by celebrating the achievements and importance of science and the new horizons it has opened up. This trend emerges most patently in the personal writings of various collaborators of the *Encyclopédie,* especially Diderot,[2] for d'Alembert seems never to have gone quite so far as to abandon the deist stance in favor of atheism.

It would seem that two attitudes can be distinguished in the evolution of Diderot as a thinker: one a deistic stance in his youth and the other a downright atheist position in his later years; but there is here involved, in our opinion, no radical about-face but only a deepening and sharpening of the elements and demands already present and operative right from the outset. Actually Diderot's youthful work, the *Pensées philosophiques* (1746) amount to a manifesto of defiance and revolt. There is an initial claim to be writing of God [3] and Diderot is quite skillful in parrying any possible charge of impiety by a discreet mixture of humility and appeal to the snobbism of the elite. In fact he is writing, not so much about God, as about man's progressive emancipation from the constricting bonds of theology and religion.

The work begins with an overt apology for the passions as positively valuable (§ § I-VI), an apology that might well have been Thomist in inspiration had it been directed against Jansenistic rigorism. But Diderot's obvious intention was to sever God from all personal relationship with man. This prologue in fact ends on a mordantly satirical note, caricaturing the scruples and remorse of the devout for their sins against God (§ VI). And it is precisely at this point that Diderot took his most crucial step in the direction of atheism, with this disjunction or clear-cut separation in God of the metaphysical attributes from the personal ones, in the abstract conception of God as the *supreme Being* (§ IX) who is

[2] The quotations are taken from: *Oeuvres philosophiques,* ed. P. Vernière (Paris, 1961). The author prefaces each individual work with a historico-critical study, tracing the main elements in the development of Diderot's thought.

[3] "I am writing of God; I count on few readers and anticipate but a handful of endorsers. If these thoughts please no one, they may be simply poor work; but I hold them to be execrable if they please everyone" (*Oeuvres Philosophiques,* ed. Vernière, p. 9; ed. Assezat I, 127). In his "discours preliminaire" (Preface) to the French translation of Shaftesbury's *Essay concerning Virtue and Merit,* Diderot's first published work, he demolishes Bayle's thesis curtly and uncompromisingly and takes up the cudgels against the atheists in general: "The aim of this work is to show that virtue is well-nigh inseparably bound up with the knowledge of God, and that temporal happiness is inseparable from virtue. No virtue without belief in God; no happiness without virtue: these are the twin propositions of the illustrious philosopher whose ideas I am going to set forth. Atheists who preen themselves on their integrity, and men devoid of integrity: these are my adversaries" (*Oeuvres philosophiques,* ed. Naigeon I, p. 11; Assezat I, 12).

not supposed to intervene in human affairs and still less to ingress as a disturbing element into man's life. Let us inspect this step, paying more attention to the spirit of the text than to the surface expressions.

The first section of the work seems to be directed squarely *against* the atheists who are divided into three classes: *the true atheists* who say openly that God does not exist; *the skeptical atheists* who do not know what to think about this question and would remit the decision to the toss of a coin; and the *blowhards* (*fanfarons du parti*) who would prefer God not to exist and in fact give evidence by their way of life that they are persuaded he does not. Diderot expresses detestation for the blowhards as contemptible shams, sympathy with the true atheists as deprived of all consolation; and he *prays to God* for the skeptics who have not the lights they need (*ils manquent de lumières*).[4] Diderot's own contention is that "only the Deist can stand up to the atheist" (§ XIII): this is the crucial statement that ought to clarify Diderot's real position. Every positive religion is tainted by superstition which "is more injurious to God than atheism" (§ XII): [5] there is here no explicit allusion to Christianity but it is clearly insinuated to be, as a positive religion, worse than atheism.

Diderot writes in a limpid style but his work is, for all that, full of surprises. He could not be more explicit in his praise of the superiority of the Deist over the atheist and the skeptic in virtue of the Deist's adherence to the existence of God, the immortality of the soul and all that follows from this.[6] But only a few sections earlier, this same Dide-

[4] *Pensées philos.* § XXII; ed. Vernière, p. 22; Assezat I, 136. In the *Suite de l'Apologie de M. l'abbé de Prades,* Part III (1752), the term "theist" is a favorable designation for whoever accepts the whole of natural religion, while "deist" stands for whoever admits only the existence of God and the reality of moral good and evil, but denies revelation and *de facto* all religion as well (*Oeuvres,* ed. Naigeon I, pp. 449f.; Assezat I, 479). A few pages earlier, Diderot opposes the theory of innate ideas and champions the *a posteriori* origin of the proof of the existence of God the creator ". . . a consequence of man's sensations and his reflections" (ed. Naigeon, p. 442). L. Thielemann has a good recent study on the circumstances surrounding the theses of the *de Prades* work, which created an uproar among the French episcopate after having been approved unanimously by the Faculty of Theology of the Sorbonne, and on Diderot's defense of these theses (L. Thielemann, "Diderot and Hobbes," in *Diderot Studies* II [Syracuse: Syracuse University Press, 1952], p. 224).

[5] This is a restatement of the well-known thesis of Bayle with which Diderot certainly was familiar but which he here proves by a passage from Plutarch. It is therefore not surprising that these *Pensées philosophiques* were immediately condemned by the High Court ". . . as proferring to rash and restless minds the poison of the most criminal and absurd opinions of which depraved human reason is capable and as setting all religions, by dint of a feigned uncertainty, virtually on the same level so as to end by acknowledging none of them" (cf. J.-P. Belin, *Le mouvement philosophique de 1748 à 1789* [Paris, 1913], p. 25).

[6] "The Deist is firm on the existence of a God, the immortality of the soul and its consequences; the skeptic is not decided on these points; the atheist denies

rot had been making fun of the Christians in favor of the atheists! [7] We read that the time of miracles, revelations and special missions is now past and that none of these things has any cogency in establishing the true religion (§ § XLI-XLII). Investigation of the internal evidence of Sacred Scripture is then claimed to show how inferior it is to the works of Titus Livius, Sallust, Caesar and Josephus [Flavius]: and the distressingly surprising fact is adduced (a famous deist objection against Christianity) that the profane authors contemporary with Christ and the first Christians should have been virtually ignorant of the facts upon which Christianity claims to be founded (§ XLV).[8] As for miracles, they are claimed by all religions: what really counts is the complex of arguments of reason.

But what does Diderot mean here by "reason"? He discounts the proofs advanced by the metaphysicans, whose arguments against atheism have, in his opinion, gotten precisely nowhere. Atheistic materialism cannot be contained by speculation but only by scientific observation: "It is not the arm of the metaphysician that has struck the great blows dealt atheism. The sublime meditations of Malebranche and Descartes were less calculated to shake materialism than a single observation made by Malpighi. If this dangerous hypothesis of materialism is tottering in our days, the credit for this is due to experimental physics. Cogent proofs of the existence of a supremely intelligent being have been found preeminently in the works of Newton, Musschenbroek, Hartsoeker and Nieuwentyt.[9] and nowhere else. Thanks to the works of these great men, the world is no longer a god; it is a machine which has its wheels, its ropes, its pulleys. its springs and its weights." [10] Throughout the atheist

---

them. Thus the skeptic has a little more motivation for being virtuous than does the atheist and somewhat less reason than does the Deist. In the absence of a dread of the law, a certain temperamental inclination and the awareness of the prevailing advantages of virtuous living, the integrity of the atheist would be lacking in any foundation and that of the skeptic would be based on a *perhaps*" (*Pensées philos.,* § XXIII; ed. Naigeon I, 23f.; Assezat I, 137).

[7] "A certain person was asked one day if there were any genuine and thoroughgoing atheists. Do you believe, he replied, that there are any genuine and thoroughgoing Christians?" (*Pensées philos.,* § XVII; ed. Naigeon I, 17; Assezat I, 132).

[8] Diderot continues his critique of miracles in §§ XLVI-XLIX, LI-LIV (§ LIII is a drastic philippic against the miracles the Jansenists were claiming to have occurred at the tomb of the famous deacon Paris).

[9] On the significance of the work of these scientists, cf. A. Vartanian, *Diderot and Descartes,* pp. 81f. Cf. also P. Vernière's note in his edition of the *Oeuvres,* pp. 17f.

[10] *Pensées philos.,* § XVIII; ed. Naigeon I, 17f.; Assezat I, 132f. At this point, Diderot considers the argument taken from the purposiveness and finality to be observed in nature as constituting a crushing refutation of mechanistic materialism: "The subtleties of ontology have produced at very best skeptics; it took a knowledge of nature to make genuine Deists. The discovery of germs alone has

continues to be treated with all possible respect, whereas irony and sarcasm are the lot of the theologians and the apologists.

An asset in the atheist's balance sheet is the incontrovertible reality of evil, and Diderot puts into the mouth of the atheist an outspoken indictment of providence which is one of the "musts" in any work that wants to pass muster as an Enlightenment product: "I tell you that there is no God; that the notion of creation is a chimera; that the eternity of the world is no more untenable than the eternity of a spirit; that it is ridiculous to try to resolve the difficulty involved in my incapacity to conceive how motion can have engendered this universe which it so admirably displays the power of conserving, by supposing a being whom I am equally incapable of conceiving; that if the marvels that shine forth in the physical order reveal some intelligence, the disorders that reign in the moral order destroy all providence. I tell you that if everything is the

---

demolished one of the strongest negative arguments of atheism (*ibid.*, § XIX; Naigeon I, 18; Assezat I, 133). The same argument recurs in § XX which concludes: "That is my business, I replied: but agree at least that it would be madness to deny to your fellow human beings the faculty of thinking. 'It would indeed; but what is the relevance of that point?' The relevance of that point is that if the universe—indeed, why go so far as the universe? if the wing of a butterfly—offers me marks and clues of an intelligence behind that universe, marks and clues that are a thousand times clearer than the marks and clues that you have to indicate that your fellowman is endowed with the faculty of thinking, it would be a thousandfold greater madness to deny that there is a God than to deny that your fellowman thinks. Well, that being so, I appeal to your own best lights, to your own conscience: have you ever noticed in the reasonings, actions and behavior of any man whatever more intelligence, order, wisdom or purposiveness than in the mechanism of an insect? Is not the deity as clearly etched in the eye of a gnat as is the faculty of thinking in the works of the great Newton? . . . What! the physical constitution of the world is less indicative of an intelligence than is the effort to explain that constitution? . . . What a thing to say! . . . 'But,' you retort, 'I am all the more ready to admit the faculty of thinking in another because I think myself' . . . There I agree with you entirely but that is not my method of proof at all; and are not my proofs superior to yours? Is not the intelligence of a first being better demonstrated to me in nature by her works than is the faculty of thinking in a philosopher by his writings? Would I otherwise have set over against you in evidence a butterfly's wing or a gnat's eye, when I could have crushed you with the weight of the universe? Either I am sadly mistaken or else this sort of proof I have offered is more convincing by far than any dictated as yet in the schools. It is on such reasoning and other arguments of like simplicity that I admit the existence of a God, and not on these tissues of dry metaphysical ideas, less apt to reveal the truth than to make it seem like a lie" (*ibid.*, Naigeon I, 21; Assezat I, 134f.). And in the *Apologie de l'abbé de Prades,* after praising Bayle, Diderot condemns the speculations of Descartes, Clarke and Malebranche, as "powerless" against the materialists; and he concludes: "I have simply given the preference to the discoveries of experimental physics over their abstract meditations; it has been my belief that a butterfly's wing, thoroughly described, brought me closer to the deity than a whole volume of metaphysics; and this feeling of mine is shared by many persons who have no intention of insulting Descartes or of slandering Malebranche" (Naigeon I, 446; Assezat I, 477).

work of a God, everything ought to be the best possible: for otherwise God is tainted either with impotence or ill will. It is therefore for the best that I am not more enlightened upon his existence: and granted this, what have I to do with your lights?

"Even could it be proven that every evil is the source of a good, that it was good for Britannicus, the best of princes, to perish, that it was good that Nero, the worst of men, should reign; how could it be proved that it was impossible to achieve the same end without using those means? To permit vices so as to reveal the splendor of virtues is to seek a most shallow advantage at the price of a most patent disadvantage. There, says the atheist, is the gist of my objection; what have you to say in reply?" [11]

And Diderot hastens to acquit the atheist of being a scoundrel simply because he is an atheist; indeed, Diderot shows more zeal in this acquittal than did Bayle.

A theism or rather Deism, entirely science-based and amounting simply to an assertion of purposiveness in nature, such a Deism stripped of all metaphysical basis, was not likely to last long. And even in these first *Pensées,* Diderot's conviction of the existence of God is not entirely firm: he is chiefly disturbed by the problem of the "attributes of God" as traditionally stated. God seems to him to be girded with such horrifying attributes that it would be better if he did not exist.[12] And this shows Diderot's complete lack of an direct acquaintance with classical Christian theological and mystical thought on the divine goodness and mercy, and the baneful influence exerted upon him by Deism and Jansenism. The calamity is, continues Diderot, that this conception of God directly affects the behavior of those who profess religion: "I know that the somber ideas of superstition are more honored in the breach than the observance; that there are devout men who do not feel they must hate themselves cruelly in order to love God properly or that they must live a life of despair in order to be religious: their religious observance is sprightly and their wisdom strongly redolent of simple human common sense; but whence originates this disparity of sentiments among men

[11] *Pensées philos.,* § XV; Naigeon I, 15f.; Assezat I, 131f. In § XIV, there is a violent attack on Pascal, whose talent and genius is nevertheless admitted.

[12] "Judging by the picture painted me of the supreme Being, his inclination to anger, the harshness of his retribution, the numerical proportions between those he lets perish and those he deigns to reach a saving hand, the most upright soul would be tempted to wish that he did not exist. A person would be quite untroubled in his mind in this world, were he but entirely assured that he had nothing to fear in the next; nobody has ever been terrified at the thought that there is *no* God, but there is good reason for being terrified at the thought that there *is* a God like the one I have heard described!" (*ibid.,* § IX; Naigeon I, 13; Assezat I, 129f.). Vernière refers the reader to Shaftesbury as the immediate source here.

who kneel at the foot of the same altars? Shall piety be held to follow the law of this cursed temperament? Alas, how shall we say otherwise? Its influence is but all too evident in the devout man himself: depending on how he is hit by piety, he sees an avenging or a merciful God, he sees hell or heaven opened! He trembles with terror or burns with love; the syndrome is that of fever with its hot and cold chills." [13] This passage is tremendously significant: it shows how tenuous was the thread still linking Diderot's thought to the notion of the existence of God.

The whole argument about the attributes of God is a direct heritage from English Deism; but Diderot could look to a more proximate model among his contemporaries, a man like Du Marsais. Initially Du Marsais asserts that faith has no justification for existence when reason can know the existence of God and of his attributes; he then proceeds to effect an implacable indictment of all divine revelation claiming to be superior to reason: here we have the central thesis of Deism en route to atheism, a thesis which in turn will lead to the famous thesis of Lessing as we shall be pointing out.

Du Marsais' starting point is explicitly Cartesian: "All that has just been said suffices to show us what is contrary to reason. It will be seen that everything that is obviously repugnant to the clear and distinct ideas or to the common notions we have is repugnant to reason and is inadmissible for beings who have only evidence and reason as ways to discover the truth." The status of positive divine *faith* is thus radically prejudiced because God can certainly not teach truths opposed to the evidence of reason and expect man to accept them: "Hence it is seen to be nothing but madness or bad faith that could tell us that reason is opposed to divine revelation, that this revelation could teach us things *above reason,* that God demands that we believe mysteries, things contrary to reason, miracles or works contrary to the laws of nature, of which laws God is supposed to be the author." And if it is precisely by reason alone, as even the theologians admit, that we know the existence and the attributes of God, then it will be up to reason likewise to judge

[13] *Ibid.,* § XI; Naigeon I, 13f.; Assezat I, 130. The same sentiments exactly are reiterated in the brief essay "De la suffisance de la religion naturelle," published in 1770 (Rosenkranz dates it shortly after the *Pensées philosophiques*) under the name of Vauvenargues (who had died 25 years earlier!) and attributed by Naigeon to Diderot. The dominant element in the critique of all positive religions and of the mysteries of Christianity in particular is the Cartesian principle of the clear and distinct idea: "Is not all truth calculated by nature to be clear and to clarify? And revealed propositions can have neither of these qualities. No one will say that they are clear: they do indeed clearly contain (or it is clear *that* they contain) a truth, but they are themselves obscure; from this is follows that everything that is inferred from them must share the same obscurity; for the consequence can never be more lucid than the principle" (§ 5. I am quoting from the volume *Recueil philosophique* Vol. I [London-Amsterdam, 1770], pp. 110f.; Assezat I, 264. Cf. Rosenkranz, *Diderot's Leben,* Vol. I, p. 55).

of revelation: thus reason which holds firmly to the concept of God as supremely wise and omnipotent, creator of all things, cannot admit that God "should have need of men to instruct other men", that man could hinder or impede the plans of God, nor "that a good and just God would punish man for weaknesses and ignorances which he could have prevented by giving man more strength and more light".

Here we have arrived at the crucial point where Du Marsais' thought meshes with that of Diderot: "Reason will never be able to conceive that a wise God should permit man by his follies to disturb his divine plans; that a good and just God would punish man for weaknesses and ignorances which he could have prevented by giving man more strength and more light. Reason cannot conceive that a God full of equity and benevolence should suffer man, whose well-being he desires, to render himself eternally unhappy by the abuse of the freedom which he accorded to him. A God who has given man reason cannot do or say things contrary to reason, or make it incumbent upon man to believe things opposed to this reason or above this reason. A God who was desirous of rendering the human race more enlightened by revelation could not have expressed himself in that revelation in an obscure fashion nor yet have required man to believe mysteries incomprehensible to him. A just God cannot become angry with men for not being convinced of what they cannot understand. An all-powerful God cannot be troubled in his bliss by the actions and the thoughts of men whom he himself molded to be what they are. A supremely happy and self-sufficient God has no need of men or of their acts of worship in order to be glorified. A perfectly good and omnific God knows and foresees the needs of his children whom he loves without waiting for them to come begging. Finally, reason will never conceive that a good, just and wise God could punish eternally with uttermost torments passing faults committed in time by creatures whom he could have made quite different beings had he but wanted to." [14]

[14] Du Marsais, "De la raison," in *Recueil philosophique,* Vol. I, pp. 44-46. The same author makes similar remarks likewise in *Réflexions sur les craintes de la mort:* "To bolster men's persuasion of goodness, it suffices to lead them back to true ideas of the diety. They will feel that the idea of God necessarily includes the idea of perfection, of goodness, of justice, of power, of reason: they will see that these qualities are incompatible with those we ourselves judge to be imperfections and hateful dispositions in the individuals of our own species: they will be convinced that a good God cannot strip himself of his own goodness in order to proceed to a harsh chastisement of creatures he has created weak and subject to propensities, creatures whose sole and perpetual object is well-being and whose ignorance is the usual cause of their aberrations. A just God cannot inflict eternal punishment on fleeting faults of limited effect. An all-powerful God cannot be cruel or implacable, for cruelty and implacability always presuppose fear and weakness. A reasonable God cannot demand that his creatures be different than he has made them, or that they exercise faculties he had not given

The negative theology of this passage must be said to characterize the new frame of mind: it is a synthesis of Cartesian mechanism and English Deism, with a strong dash of Baconian and Lockeian sense-perceptionism, which is in process of gaining the upper hand in the boiling ferment that is the world of the French *philosophes.*

Was it then not only Diderot's theism but even his Deism that was in crisis even from the time of the *Pensées philosophiques?* He is persuaded that he has attacked only the protagonists of superstition and bigotry and he therefore expects their wrath, which they have already displayed in condemning Descartes, Montaigne, Locke and Bayle. He makes an apparently (!) candid profession of Catholicism: "I tell them frankly that I do not preen myself on being a more upright man nor yet a better Christian than the majority of these philosophers. I was born in the Catholic, Apostolic and Roman Church; and I submit myself with all my power to its decisions. I wish to die in the religion of my fathers, and I believe that religion to be good as far as it is possible so to do for one who has never had direct communication with the deity or been witness of any miracles. There is my profession of faith." [15]

But this is an empty gesture indeed, for Diderot hastens to declare that he cannot believe in the truth of Christianity nor yet accept the infallibility of the Church nor even the divine inspiration of Sacred Scripture which he insists must be subjected to the laws of criticism like any book (§ § LIX-LX). And after asserting that the final stance a man must obviously take is that of a "forced skepticism" caused precisely by the use of those books that were supposed to provide certitude, he shows the deep perplexity of spirit in which he finds himself: "It is in seeking for proofs that I have found difficulties. The books that contain the motives for my belief provide me simultaneously with reasons for unbelief. They are arsenals open to all. I have seen the Deist arm himself from them

---

them in the first place. Since the idea of God necessarily includes infinite perfection, it amounts to a dissolution of this idea to attribute to God qualities that would be downright imperfections, necessarily incompatible with the attractive and agreeable qualities that are of the essence of the deity. Thus to make God unfair, unjust, cruel and inexorable amounts to making him into a being whose qualities would be mutually destructive and could not be reconciled in the same subject; to make God spiteful amounts to reducing him to nothingness, to dread his judgments is tantamount to distrusting his wisdom, his justice and his mercy; to believe that he could push his retribution beyond all reasonable bounds or to think that he has created the greater portion of mankind but to be the playthings of his tyrannical whims—all such notions simply indicate that the man who holds them has false notions about God" (in *Recueil philosophique,* Vol. I, pp. 145f. Author's name not listed in index).

[15] *Pensées philos.,* § LVIII; Vernière, 46; Assezat I, 153. In Note 2, Vernière refers to a similar profession of faith made by Shaftesbury, on whom Diderot patterned himself.

against the atheist; the Deist and the atheist fight against the Jew; the atheist, the Deist and the Jew ally themselves against the Christian; the Christian, the Jew, the Deist and the atheist come to grips with the Moslem, and the plethora of sects of Christendom pouncing upon the Christian and the skeptic alone against everybody else." After many vacillations, Diderot brings the scales down in favor of the Christian and repeats: "I call God to witness to my sincerity." [16] No wonder that a web so fragile should ere long come apart in the hands of him who had woven it.

In fact this had already occurred barely three years later: in the famous *Lettre sur les aveugles* (1749) theistic finalism is abandoned to give place to a matter in perpetual motion in whose evolution there come into play chance, spontaneous generation, natural selection and the like: Diderot is adhering more and more resolutely to sheer experimentalism and materialistic sensism.[17] Theism and Deism have now both been abandoned and Diderot has arrived at atheism even though he is not overtly professing it.[18]

Experimentalism is defended right down the line in *De l'interprétation de la nature* (1753-54) but in a brief postscript (to the dedication) Diderot warns against all manner of atheism and materialism: "P. S. One more word and I have finished. Bear always in mind that *nature* is not *God;* that a *man* is not a *machine;* that a *hypothesis* is not a *fact:* and be assured that you will not have understood me at all at any point where you believe you perceive in what I have written anything contrary to these principles." Diderot's growing interest in "experimental philosophy" was due primarily to the influence of Buffon and Maupertuis.[19] The Naigeon edition inserts immediately after this work (*De l'interprétation de la nature*), a prayer colored by ascetical agnosticism, like the prayer of d'Holbach: "I have begun with Nature which has been called Thy work; and I shall end with Thee, whose name upon earth is God.—O God. I know not if thou art; but I shall think as though thou lookedst into my soul, I shall act as though I were before thy face. If I have sinned sometimes against my reason, or against thy law, I shall be for that reason less satisfied with my past life; but I shall not for that reason be less tranquil about my fate to come, for thou hast forgotten

[16] *Ibid.*, § LXI; Vernière, 48; Assezat I, 154f. The last section (LX) aims at a critique of religious relativism or deism.

[17] Cf. the Vernière edition, especially pp. 119ff.

[18] In a letter of June 11, 1749 to Voltaire, Diderot writes: "I believe in God, although I get along very well with the atheists" (cited by P. Vernière, *op. cit.*, p. 124, n. 2; Assezat XIX, 422). At the beginning of this same letter, we read: "It is usually during the night that the vapours rise that obscure in me the existence of God; sunrise always dispels them" (Assezat XIX, 420).

[19] Ed. Vernière, p. 249; cf. Vernière's note on pp. 249f.; Assezat II, 7.

my fault as soon as I have admitted it.—I ask nothing of thee in this world; for the course of things is necessary of itself, if thou art not; or else it is necessary by thy decree, if thou art.—I hope for thy rewards in the world to come, if such a world there be; yet all that I do in this world, I do for myself.—If I follow the good, it is without effort; if I refrain from evil, it is without thinking of thee.—I could not help but love truth and virtue and hate lying and vice, whether I knew that thou didst not exist or believed thou dost exist and art offended by wrong-doing.—Here I am, such as I am, a portion of an eternal and necessary matter, myself organized according to the dictates of necessity, or, it may be, thy creature.—But if I am charitable and good, what doth it matter to my fellows if this is by a good fortune of organization, by the free acts of my will, or by the assistance of thy grace?—And as often as you shall recite this creed of our philosophy, you shall read likewise what follows: Since God has permitted, or the universal mechanism called Fate has willed that we should be exposed, during our life, to all manner of events; if you are a wise man and better father than I, you will persuade your son betimes that he is master of his own existence, so that he shall not complain of you who have given it to him." [20]

Here once again we see how taxing and virtually indecipherable was the problem of God and religion in that century that has been designated as the "Age of Enlightenment"; the difficulty of the problematic emerges not only in the disagreements and difference of opinion between the *philosophes* but even within the works of one and the same author.

Thus, for instance, his vigorous attack on final causes, an attack which is the prologue to Enlightenment atheism, Diderot intends to be, precisely in this work, a defense of the presence of God in nature: "Who are we to explain the aims and goals, the ends of nature? Do we not perceive that it is almost always at the expense of its power that we praise its wisdom; and that we take away from its resources more than we can ever concede to its designs? This way of interpreting nature is bad, even in natural theology. It is to substitute human conjecture to the work of God; it is to link the most important of theological truths to the fate of a hypothesis." [21]

Atheistic materialism seems to be explicitly professed in the famous *Entretien entre D'Alembert et Diderot,* in which it is asserted with Toland that motion is essential to matter, that life is in continual evolution, that positive science must neglect God and leave him out of ac-

[20] Ed. Naigeon, Vol. II, pp. 223f.; Assezat II, 61f. In his last years, Diderot seems to have taken refuge in outright skepticism and sought peace of mind in study (cf. H. Dieckmann, *Cinq leçons sur Diderot* [Geneva-Paris, 1959], p. 83).

[21] *De l'interprétation de la nature,* § LVI; Vernière, 235f.; Assezat II, 53. Vernière remarks: "Diderot's Spinozism is nowhere so evident as in this attack on final causes" (note 1).

count and that any recourse to God is a sign of impotence and ignorance: God is quite simply called ". . . an agent contradictory in his attributes, a word devoid of meaning, unintelligible." [22] The dilemmas of the divine attributes which Diderot had been encountering in the *Principes philosophiques* have borne their bitter fruit and materialism now reaches the point of an explicit denial of the distinction of soul and body, impelled to the Spinozan-type conception of a universal vitalism and evolutionism in the great Whole: "There is but one great individual and that is the All, the Whole." [23]

The most radical critique of Christianity and an open profession of atheism are to be found in the *Entretien d'un philosophe avec la Maréchale de D**** (1774); this work can be considered to provide the definitive expression of Diderot's moral and religious convictions. At the outset of the dialogue, the independence of morality from religion is expressly asserted by Crudeli (who is meant to be Diderot himself): man has a natural inclination to the good; this inclination can be reinforced by education, without any appeal or recourse to any sort of faith. The direct attack is initiated by a violent indictment of religions generally, including that of Christ, as responsible for the disorders and discords that divide men and inflame quarrels among peoples; [24] there

[22] *Entretien,* Vernière, 269; Assezat, II, 112. In his meticulous analysis of Diderot's transition from theism to atheism, the Marxist historian of philosophy Luppol describes the following stages, while noting the uncertainties and fluctuations in the evolution of Diderot's thinking: in the *Discours* and the notes to his Shaftesbury translation, Diderot is certainly, as of 1745, abandoning Christianity and fluctuating on the razor's edge between theism and deism; in the *Pensées philosophiques* of 1746, he is accepting without reservations Bayle's thesis on the relations between religion and virtue, a thesis which could be fleetingly glimpsed in the notes to the Shaftesbury translation, in contradistinction to the *Discours,* but which was not yet atheistic (as opposed to the thesis of Canon Marcel); two works of 1747, the *Promenade d'un sceptique* and *De la suffisance de la religion naturelle,* give quite clear evidence of Diderot's sympathy for atheists; and in the *Lettre sur les aveugles* and subsequent writings from 1749 on, Diderot explicitly embraces atheism, ranging himself ever more openly with Spinoza (Cf. J. K. Luppol, *Diderot,* pp. 107ff. Luppol argues against the "bourgeois stand and interpretations" of Rosenkranz in the latter's *Diderot's Leben und Werke*).

[23] *Le rève d'Alembert,* Vernière, 312; Assezat II, 139. Later, in 1770, this rigid mechanism comes out in synthetic form in the *Principes philosophiques sur la matière et le mouvement,* Vernière, pp. 393ff. In the *Réfutation suivie de l'ouvrage d'Helvétius intitulé 'L'homme',* of 1774-75, Diderot specifies his own sensism and materialism as having a distinct Hobbesian bias: " 'I sense, I think, I judge; therefore a piece of matter organized as I am can sense, think and judge' " (Vernière, 564; Assezat II, 301).

[24] Consider that it [religion] has created and perpetuates the most violent antipathy between nations. There is not a Moslem who would not imagine himself to be performing an act pleasing to God and his prophet by exterminating all Christians; and these Christians, in their turn, are hardly more tolerant. Consider that it has created and perpetuates in the one and the same country divisions which are rarely composed without bloodshed. Our own history does but offer us

follows the invariable mention of the imcomprehensibility of the attributes of God, on which men have never succeeded in reaching agreement. The ethic of the Gospel is declared to be impossible in practice; the moral code common to humanity suffices for man and the hope of a life after death, i.e., of a life in conditions which are the exact opposite of this present life—such a hope makes no sense: "I do not cherish this hope because the desire for it has not in the least managed to conceal from me the vanity of such a hope; but I do not snatch it away from anyone. If a man can believe that he will see when he no longer has eyes, hear when he no longer has ears, think when he no longer has a head, love when he no longer has a heart, feel when he no longer has any senses, exist when he is no longer any where, be something without extension and without position, I leave him to it." [25] The dialogue concludes with an irony that is a categorical profession of atheism, unbelief and fatalism; this profession is without reservations or vacillation.[26] Undoubtedly the Diderot's work, still more than the more immediately apparent contributions of d'Holbach, La Mettrie and Helvétius, constituted one of the most crucial elements in the modern world.

Diderot's life was a complex and a tormented one and there seems no doubt that he ended it as an atheist: [27] he is caught in an intellectual current, or more exactly in a complex of streams of thought which may

too recent and baleful examples. Consider that it has created and perpetuates the most intense and abiding hatreds in society among citizens and in families among relatives. Christ said he had come to set husband against wife, mother against children, brother against sister, friend against friend; and his prediction has been all too faithfully fulfilled" *Entrétien d'un philosophe* (Vernière, 533; Assezat II, 512f.).

[25] *Ibid.*, Vernière, p. 542; Assezat II, 519.

[26] In the *Entrétien d'un philosophe,* Diderot makes fun of the stories of the saints (St. Bruno, the Jesuit Bohola (i.e., Bobola), defends the unbelievers and ends with the following sally: "And if you were at the point of death, would you submit to the ceremonies of the Church?" "I most certainly would." "O, you scurvy hypocrite!" (ed. P. Vernière, p. 553; Assezat II, 528).

It is therefore no surprise to read that the latest Marxist critic finds that Diderot ". . . remains, of all the great 18th century French materialists, the one who contributed more directly to preparing the ground for the socialist thinkers of the 19th century" (I. Szigeti, *Denis Diderot,* Une grande figure du matérialisme militant du XVIIIe siècle [Budapest, 1962], p. 94).

[27] A Diderot expert is of the same opinion: "Religion is for him the end product, not the beginning of knowledge, but on the basis of his philosophy of science he built an ethics and an aesthetics which included the whole realm of what we call the good life, the invisible and the 'supernatural': terms more synonymous with religion. He can be classified as a communist only through his materialism, and communists can find little comfort in his view of science, with his emphasis on heredity, genius and the power of creative imagination to transform man's destiny. The biologically-minded Engels, not the sociologist Marx, understood Diderot and felt a real kinship to him—at a time when science was free" (N. L. Torrey, Introduction, *Diderot Studies* II, p. 12).

go back to Descartes-Spinoza on the one hand and Bacon-Locke on the other; and this tidal wave impelled Diderot to a radical choice, a crucial option. And his option eventually was entirely for man: for a vision of the world that he felt to be adequate to the infinite living reality of experience and for a moral conception that responded to the inexhaustible impulses of nature and to the bent of reason. In this sense, Diderot's outlook is a synthesis of Cartesian mechanistic materialism and Leibnizian dynamic monism; this synthesis represents a convergence that became much more pronounced in the conception of the materialist atheist d'Holbach, of whom Diderot wrote: "I like a philosophy that is clear, sharply outlined and candid, like that presented in the *Système de la nature* and still more in the *Bon Sens* . . . The author of the *Système de la nature* is not an atheist on one page and a Deist on another; his philosophy is all of a piece." [28] In Leibniz notoriously, the unity of the cosmos is conceived in terms of force and process, of forces and processes which are identified with the reality of the individual monads. This activistic disintegration of the classical concept of substance as undifferentiated essence led to the elimination of God and his resolution into the activity of the individual existents.[29] Thus, by rejecting in his turn Leibniz's substantive God and retaining only the self-sufficient monads, Diderot was able to overcome the deadlock and impasse of classical mechanism by means of a vitalistic conception which anticipates some of the motive principles operative in the subsequent course of modern thought right down to and including the most novel movements of present-day philosophy.

In this sense, Diderot may well be the most typical figure of an 18th-century Englightenment philosopher, precariously holding in balance the multiple aspects of the human mind, expressing himself in a style free of syntactical complexities, revelling in a frame of mind that avoids the bottomless labyrinth of theoretical problematic, contents itself with what life can give and finds in the solitude of the scholar the authentic expression of its own mission and basic assignment, that of educating and training man up to freedom.

[28] *Réfutation de l'ouvrage d'Helvétius intitulé 'L'Homme'*, Assezat II, 398.

[29] Cf. Marx W. Wartofsky, "Diderot and the Development of Materialist Monism," *Diderot Studies* II, pp. 286ff.

5

Baron d'Holbach's Materialistic Atheism

The most cursory glance at d'Holbach's *Systéme de la nature,* the bible of 18th-century atheistic materialism, suffices to show the book as an all-out development, in its basic outlines, of the new dynamic materialism.[1] The extensive agreement with its theses on the part of present-day atheists and indeed, throughout the whole development of European materialism in the centuries following its publication, as well as the alarm the book produced not only in religious circles but even among the Deists (like Voltaire, Rousseau and their like) show that this work closed one age and opened another.

Basing itself on Descartes, Bayle and the new outlook of English Deism, especially Toland's theory of the motion of matter, the *Système* elaborates an overall picture of reality.

Motion is the principle of all alterations in nature and man, the principle of their properties and of their reciprocal relationships.

Every object is capable, in virtue of its essence and of its particular nature, of stimulating, receiving and communicating various motions; therefore some things are capable of making impressions on our sense organs and of modifying those sense organs by their presence; those things that cannot, either immediately by themselves nor yet mediately

[1] Cf. *Le Système de la nature,* P. I, Ch. 2: *Du mouvement et de son origine,* pp. 13ff. On the fundamental characteristics of the work, cf. the new essay of Y. Belaval, serving as preface to the new reprint of the 1821 Paris edition (Hildesheim, 1966): "D'Holbach is the most typical, straightforward, frank, all-of-a-piece representative (to use Diderot's expressions) of that philosophic bias that leans toward the world (Physics) and society (Political Sociology) and is unwilling to admit being anywhere except within the bounds of immanence. He thus proffers us a humanism hostile to any world beyond. Man is to live in and for this world right here" (Vol. I, p. XXVII). This conclusion of Belaval seems to us to accord perfectly with the line of interpretation of modern thought followed in our own investigation into the speculative continuity of the principle of immanence in that thought and into the consequent inevitability of its bias toward and eventual lapse into atheism.

by the action of other bodies, act upon any of our sense organs, do not exist for us, because they do not set us in motion and consequently cannot give us ideas, i.e., cannot be known or judged by us. "To know" an object means to have sensed it; "to sense" it means to have been set in motion by it. "To see" means to have been set in motion by the organ of sight; "to hear" means to have been stimulated through the channel of the organ of hearing. In short, we have awareness and knowledge of a body from the way in which it can act upon us via some alteration stimulated in us by it.

Nature is thus understood as being the sum total of all the things and all the motions that we know (are aware of) and of many other things as well which we cannot know because they are not accessible to our senses.

D'Holbach distinguishes between two species of motion, declaring flatly that it is our senses which show us that there are two generic forms of motion in the things that surround us. One is the [external] motion of mass, whereby a body is transferred as a whole from one place to another; motion of this sort can be perceived by our senses: e.g., the fall of a stone, the rolling of a ball, the motion or action of an arm. The other form of motion is a hidden internal one depending on the energy of the body itself, i.e., on its essence, on the action and interaction of the imperceptible molecules of the matter of which bodies are composed. The motions governing the growth processes of animals and plants, processes which escape our observation, are of this same sort; and so, says d'Holbach grandly, are the motions accomplished within man which we call the *intellectual faculty, thoughts and passions,* whence proceed our ideas. Motions are passive (imparted) and spontaneous, depending on whether their cause lies outside the subject or within that subject; and d'Holbach insists that man's will belongs to the first category of motion (passive or imparted), even though we believe it to be self-moved.

Motion is transferred according to precise and necessary laws governing the transition of the action of one body into another. And d'Holbach concludes that everything in the world is motion. The essence of nature is action and if we attentively consider its various parts we shall see that there is not a single one in a state of absolute rest; those parts seeming to have no motion are in reality only in a state of relative or apparent rest; they are experiencing a sort of motion which is so imperceptible that we do not succeed in perceiving it.[2] D'Holbach remarks in a note

[2] "Everything is motion in the universe. The essense of nature is to act; and we shall see that there is not a single thing that enjoys an absolute state of rest: those things that appear to us destitute of motion are in fact but in a state of relative or apparent rest; they are experiencing a motion that is so imperceptible

that this truth has been demonstrated by the famous Toland at the beginning of the century, in his work entitled *Letters to Serena,* which d'Holbach finds gratifyingly definitive on this whole point. D'Holbach himself expands his symphonic poem on the effects of motion to embrace all the extrinsic and intrinsic modifications of bodies in a world wherein nature functions as a *universal agent.*[3]

To the question as to where matter came from, d'Holbach calmly replies that it has always existed. To the further question as to where matter got its motion, he asserts, in contradistinction to Locke who posited matter as inert, that a matter that has always existed must have been self-moved from all eternity because motion is a necessary consequence of its existence, of its essence and of its primordial properties which are weight, impenetrability, shape (or figure), etc.: thus Descartes asked only for matter and motion [4] to explain the formation of the universe, but in this section of d'Holbach's theorizing it is Toland's notion that is most influential. D'Holbach considers the Aristotelian air, earth, fire and water to be basic elements of bodies but he admits we know very little about them, only a few properties in terms of the modifications they produce in our senses.[5] But d'Holbach is here not returning to the physics and metaphysics of antiquity but rather interpreting reality solely in terms of experience or of the sensory modifications produced in our sense organs. The notion of matter is thus altered:

---

and unpronounced that we cannot perceive their changes" (*Système de la nature,* P. I, Ch. 2, Vol. I, p. 18. For this theory of universal motion in matter, d'Holbach refers to Toland's *Letters to Serena* which he had translated and published, with the usual laconic identification: "A Londres 1768").

[3] In support of his idea of an "active nature", d'Holbach cites the theologian Bilfinger: "Nature is an active or motive power; thus nature is likewise called the power of the whole world, or the universal power in the world" (*De Deo, anima et mundo.* Cf. *Système de la nature,* P. I, Ch. 2, Vol. I, pp. 26f., note). He would have done better to cite and properly comprehend the Aristotelian concept of nature, a concept which is much more positive and constructive (cf. *Phys.* II, I, 192b 21; *Metaph.* V, 4, 1014b 16ff.).

[4] *Système de la nature,* P. I, Ch. 2, Vol. I, p. 31.

[5] Here is d'Holbach's own deductive process used to establish this "phenomenological physics", showing its obvious origin from English empiricism and especially (I think) from that of Hume: "We have no acquaintance with the elements of bodies but we do know certain of their properties or qualities by the effects or changes they produce upon our senses, that is to say, by the various motions their presence engenders in us. We find them to be the consequence of extension, of mobility, of sensibility, of solidity, of gravity, of the force of inertia. From these generic and primary properties flow others such as density, figure, color, weight, etc. Thus, so far as we are concerned, matter in general is everything that affects our senses in any fashion whatsoever; and the qualities we attribute to different matters are based on the differing impressions or on the changes they produce in us ourselves" (*ibid.,* P. I, Ch. 3: De la matière, de ses combinaisons différentes et de ses mouvements divers, ou de la marche de la nature [on matter, its different combinations and varying motions, or on the course of nature]; Vol. I, p. 35).

matter is no longer a passive, motionless raw material (as in Descartes, Locke); rather it is pervaded by motion and endowed with the properties requisite to it, properties that are unceasingly producing, at intervals, new effects and modifications in nature, in terms of elements and bodies.

All of this process d'Holbach delights in describing in meticulous detail before passing to a description of the laws of motion, common to all things (attraction and repulsion, sympathy and antipathy, affinity and relations) and explanatory of motion's causality. It is this causality, says d'Holbach, which is at the basis of our knowledge, although he admits that he is entirely in the dark about the ways of nature, the essence of things and their properties.[6] All the laws are themselves governed by the principle of self-preservation which holds both for the physical and the moral realm: it is that "gravitation upon the self which Newton called inertia and the moralists have termed 'self-love' in the human dimension." [7] Thence originates the harmonious order of the universe.

The behavior of these laws is governed by the most rigid *necessity,* both in the physical and the moral world. Causality is, for d'Holbach, synonymous with necessity: every cause produces an effect and there cannot be an effect without a cause. Every impulse is followed by some more or less sensible motion, some more or less perceptible change or modification, in the body that receives it: all motions, all forms of action, are, as we have seen, determined by their nature, essence, properties and combinations. The inescapable conclusion is, therefore, that all phenomena are necessary and that every being of nature in given circumstances and with given properties is compelled to act exactly as it does. Necessity is the infallible and constant nexus of causes with their effects. And we must assert that there is no independent energy, no isolated cause, no detached action in nature, wherein all beings act uninterruptedly upon one another. And nature itself is but an unending circle of motions imparted and received according to necessary laws.[8]

Man himself is no exception to this necessity, either in his physical or in his moral life: just as his physical life results from the action and

[6] *Ibid.,* Ch. 4, Vol. I, p. 48.

[7] D'Holbach appeals to St. Augustine's *De Civitate Dei* for support for this principle (*ibid.,* Vol. I, p. 53).

[8] *Ibid.,* P. I, Ch. 4, Vol. I, pp. 55f. To this "necessity" d'Holbach sings a panegyric that is a mixture of Stoic-sensist materialism and Spinozan geometric trenchancy: "This irresistible force, this universal necessity, this prevailing energy, is thus but a consequence of the nature of things in virtue of which everything acts unremittingly according to constant and immutable laws; these laws no more vary for the whole of nature than for the beings that nature encompasses. Nature is an acting or living whole, whose every part necessarily cooperates, and everything it contains necessarily conspires to the perpetuation of its acting being" (Vol. I, p. 59).

interaction of the causes or forces of his internal and external physical environment, so his moral life and what is called the social order is dependent on the ideas, the movements of will and passions operative in a certain environment. D'Holbach's treatment of this area is quite businesslike and will be taken over, albeit in somewhat softened form, into the materialistic conception of Feuerbach-Marx, as we shall be pointing out. It comes down to this: initially man claimed for his own thinking and acting (his intuitions, notions and acts of willing) a quite unique character that made him the center of the universe; in a second stage of his development, man proceeded to conceive the complex of phenomena and the order of the universe as the effect of a first intelligent cause (God), which cause is nothing but the extrapolation or projection of man himself. But both these ways of looking at the universe are (for d'Holbach even as for Feuerbach, Marx and their like) entirely unjustified because they are the result of naive anthropomorphism.[9] The only world-picture that corresponds to reality, to the facts, is that of a chain of phenomena linked together by the inflexible law of necessity, to which are subject all the actions of man even as those of any other being.[10]

"O man!," cries d'Holbach, "has it never occurred to you that you are an ephemeral being? Everything changes in the universe; nature holds no constant form, yet you claim that your species cannot disappear, that it must form an exception to the generic law that wills that everything shall change. Alas! are you not subject in the whole of your actual being to continual alterations? You, who in your folly arrogate to yourself the title of *Monarch of Nature!*" [11]

[9] "Man always makes himself the center of the universe; it is to himself that he relates all that he sees in that universe; as soon as he believes he has glimpsed a way of acting which has some points of conformity with his own or certain phenomena which are of interest to him, he attributes them to a cause that resembles himself, that acts like him, that has faculties identical with his own, the same interests, the same plans, the same bias, in a word he models this cause after himself" (*ibid.,* P. I, Ch. 5, Vol. I, p. 72).

[10] "In all the phenomena [or changes] presented to us by man from his birth to the end of his life, we see nothing but a succession of causes and effects which are necessary and in conformity with the laws common to all entities of nature. All man's faculties of acting, his sensations, his ideas, his passions, his options, his actions, are necessary consequences of his properties and of those entities that affect these properties and stir them up" (*ibid.,* P. I, Ch. 6, Vol. I, p. 79). Later this procedure is called a "vicious circle" (Vol. I, p. 99, note 22).

[11] *Ibid.,* P. I, Ch. 6, Vol. I, pp. 93f. D'Holbach is ruthless in this stand: "We conclude, thus, that man has no reason to believe himself a privileged being within nature; he is subject to the same vicissitudes as all her other products. His alleged prerogatives are based simply upon an error. Let him but use his power of thought to attain a perspective higher than that of the globe he inhabits and he will view his own species in the same way as all other beings: he will see that, even as every tree produces fruits after its kind and according to its species, so every man acts in virtue of his peculiar energies and produces fruits, actions, works, that are equally necessary. He will become conscious of the fact

Yet at the outset d'Holbach had admitted that, in terms of his action and therefore of his structure (organization), man belonged in an order, a system, a class apart and differing from that of the animals in which man does not see the same properties as in "himself." [12]

Thus in d'Holbach Spinozan pantheistic metaphysical materialism intersects sense-perceptionist materialism derived from Locke. D'Holbach, together with La Mettrie, Diderot, d'Alembert, Helvétius and the circle of the Encyclopedists carried Deism to its ontic extreme, as modern philosophical terminology would have it, an extreme of sheer and total materialism which is just as drastic in those other Encyclopedists as it is in d'Holbach and La Mettrie, even though the others may be more reserved and moderate in their expression.

The enthusiasm of the Marxists for these representatives of the French Enlightenment may therefore be admitted to be entirely justified. And it may also be admitted that ". . . 18th-century French materialism represents one of the most important ages in the history of progressive philosophical thought" and that it directly prepared the way for the revolution,[13] as modern historians of philosophy generally admit. But this simple historical judgment still does not penetrate to the core of the problem, which is to investigate the causes of the deep-cutting transformation effected by French Enlightenment thought in the life and culture, religion and politics of the modern world. We can agree entirely with the insistence of Feuerbach, Marx-Engels and the Marxists generally, that French materialism is the inevitable logical conclusion of the immanentist principle, even though it could be objected that there are quite a few thinkers and writers who, despite their prejudice against traditional thought, refused to go the whole way with materialism: men like

---

that the illusion that prejudices him in favor of himself derives from the fact that he is at one and the same time spectator and part of the universe. He will recognize that the notion of excellence he attaches to his own being has no other foundation that his proper interest and the predilection he feels for himself" (Vol. I, pp. 95f.).

[12] The relevant passage is specially important as a clarification of the "method" used in this technique of leapfrogging the difficulties: "Thus nature, in its widest significance, is the great whole resulting from the concatenation of the various kinds of matter, from their various combinations and from the various motions we see in the universe. Nature in the more restricted sense in which it is applied to each being is the whole resulting from the essence, i.e., the properties, the combinations, the motions or ways of operation distinguishing this being from other beings. It is thus that man is a whole resulting from the combinations of certain kinds of matter, endowed with peculiar properties, whose arrangement is called *organization,* and whose essence is to sense, to think, to act, in a word to move themselves in a way distinguishing them from the other beings with which they are being compared: in terms of this comparison, man fits into an order, a system, a class apart, differing from that of the animals in which he does not see the same properties that are in himself" (*ibid.,* P. I, Ch. 1, p. II).

[13] C. N. Momdshian, *Helvétius,* p. 7.

Hume in England, Rousseau and Voltaire in France, who declined to make an explicit and overt profession of materialism and atheism, continuing to admit in some sense the freedom and spirituality of the soul and the existence of God. But I find no difficulty in agreeing with the Marxist historians of philosophy that the attitudes of these men are simply instances of inconsistency, granted the modern immanentist principle they obviously professed.

The unconvincing point about Marxist philosophizing and historical interpretation is the same point that is unconvincing in d'Holbach: it is the bemusing aplomb with which they all assert man to be a privileged being, emerging from nature with needs and behavior patterns distinguishing him from other beings, and then go on to declare man to be a material being like any other, thought to be a secretion of the brain and human behavior the result of physical forces governed by the laws of the physical world in accord with the most rigid deterministic necessity. Thus does the extremist materialist conception plunge itself into the identical difficulties encountered by the idealist position; and in both cases the motivation is so opposite as to be identical, a point to which we shall return later. This does not mean that we are discrediting either Enlightenment materialism or dialectical materialism: quite the contrary, we consider them to be in fact one of the most thoroughgoing and radical forms of the forcing of the *cogito* principle to its logical conclusion which is its disintegration. The Marxist historians of philosophy [14] may well be justified in their complaint that many historians of French materialism who are themselves liberals, idealists, neo-Kantians or the like, have shown open hostility and aroused the suspicion of a definite lack of objectivity. As for our own interpretation, we feel it does justice to such distortions in a fashion more radical even than Marxist history of philosophy itself, by showing the essential adherence of atheism to the immanentist principle.

Hegel set the tone for this sort of distorted interpretation with his scorn for Locke: Hegel admits that he Lockeian philosophy has been much praised and continues to be, generally speaking, the philosophy of the English and the French and in a certain sense even of the Germans; he likewise gives Locke credit for "having abandoned the method of simple definitions adopted by Descartes, Spinoza, Leibniz . . ." and for having made an effort to deduce universal concepts, for having posed the problem of the "origin of ideas" as against the protagonists of "innate ideas". But Hegel finds Locke's method exclusively psychological and "devoid of even a suspicion of what speculation might be." [15] Hegel

[14] Cf. G. W. Plechanov, *Beiträge zur Geschichte des Materialismus* (Berlin, 1957), pp. 18f.

[15] "This is the Lockeian philosophy, wherein is contained no faintest hint or idea of the speculative" (Hegel, *Geschichte der Philosophie,* Vol. III, p. 389).

shows himself to be ignorant or neglectful of the "metaphysical mediation" effected by Toland in "linking back up to its basis" the new principle of experience which is, as we have seen, at the center of d'Holbach's dynamic materialism.

Proceeding now to the discussion of the problem of God as such, d'Holbach claims that it is the great natural calamities, the destruction and horrors of war, the continual physical ills and the terror in the face of death that lead man to conceive of a hidden and unknown power escaping and dominating all these ills. D'Holbach admits that this idea of God is found among all peoples and in all parts of the world in every age of history; the reason, he says, is that man's conditions of life are virtually universally identical and thus all know distress and pain. In place of the physical causes he does not know, man has posited God as universal cause: believing himself to be unhappy, man has exchanged the specter of his own unhappiness for God.[16] By the term "God" then, men cannot and do not intend to be indicating anything other than the most secret, remote and unknown cause of the sensible effects they experience; and it is an interim term, to be used for such time as, and to the extent that, they do not know the interplay of natural causes. The admission of the existence of God is therefore simply an effect of ignorance and laziness,[17] a mere name to which no reality corresponds. God cannot be meaningfully called "the cause of phenomena".

Nor is it really meaningful to call God "spirit" (*esprit*) or "incorporeal substance", for these ideas have been dredged up by man out of his own intimate experience, modelled on his own soul and cognition which are what he means by "spirit". They are the result of an anthropomorphic process whereby man enlarges to the dimension of infinity the perfections of his own intelligence and will. In actual fact, man has always seen and will always see in his God simply a man, no matter how great efforts he may make and no matter how drastically he may extend the power and perfections of his God; the result will always be that man will be thinking of a man, a gigantic overlifesize man to be sure, and one endowed with irreconcilable properties pushed to infinity. The idea of the *unity of God* is a further consequence of God's being conceived as the soul of the universe.[18] Just as the Deists delivered a global critique of all positive religions and all Christian confessions, so does d'Holbach deprecate indiscriminately all conceptions of the deity; he does not examine either their form or their content, and he places mythology, religion, demonology and theology on exactly the same level. His subse-

[16] *Système de la nature,* P. II, Ch. 1, Vol. II, pp. 10f. Later d'Holbach admits the existence of a natural "disposition" impelling man to this conception (Vol. II, p. 12).

[17] *Ibid.,* P. II, Ch. 1, p. 17.

[18] *Ibid.,* P. II, Ch. 2, Vol. II, pp. 43ff.

quent reduction of the reality and the idea of "spirit" to the sensible experience of mind and knowledge and to the representation of its dynamic totality is just as arbitrary and oversimplified as his reduction of thought to the physiological activity of the brain.

D'Holbach devotes special attention to the ideas theology has formed of God. The theological or metaphysical attributes of God are in reality merely negations pure and simple of the properties found in men or in other entities men know: by means of these attributes, God is divested of everything that man calls weakness or imperfection in himself or in the things that surround him. Thus, to say that *God is infinite* amounts to saying that God, as distinct from man and other things, is not confined within spatial limits; to say that *God is eternal* amounts to saying that God, as distinct from ourselves and everything that exists, has never had a beginning and will never have an end; to say that God is *immutable* amounts to saying that God is not subject to change as we and all other things are; to say that *God is immaterial* amounts to saying that his substance or his essence has a nature that we do not understand but which must be completely different from everything that we do know. Infinity, immensity, spirituality, omniscience, order, wisdom, intelligence and unlimited power—such are the vague terms used to indicate notions still more confused, which constitute the content of the metaphysical notion of God.[19]

D'Holbach devotes a special critique to the notion of God as "principle of order", i.e., to the argument drawn from "final causes" [20] and considered the most cogent for a proof of the existence of God. It is taken for granted that God created the world exclusively for man and that man has been constituted monarch of nature. Miserable monarch, exclaims d'Holbach, it takes but a grain of sand, a minor dysfunction in your bile duct or another of your physical systems to destroy your existence and your dominion! You lay claim to hegemony over the whole of nature and cannot manage to protect yourself against its slightest blow! And you are so sure that you have been created by a God who, you are convinced, watches over you to preserve you in all your ways and concerns himself with your happiness. Do you not see how the

[19] *Ibid.*, P. II, Ch. 3, pp. 62f.

[20] *Ibid.*, P. II, Ch. 3, pp. 62f. In all probability d'Holbach's allusion is to Voltaire, who claimed that the argument from the purposiveness of the universe was decisive for the assertion of the existence of God (cf. *Traité de métaphysique*, Ch. 2, *Métaphysique de Newton*, Ch. 1; *Le philosophe ignorant*, Ch. 15 and fol.; *Dictionn. philos.: Fin, Causes finales; Questions sur l'Encyclopédie: Dieu, Nature*). This is therefore a theory to which Voltaire remained faithful to the end and which may have inspired this harsh passage of d'Holbach.

There is another critique of the argument from final causes later on (cf. P. II, Ch. 5 and Ch. 7, pp. 160f. and p. 245), in the critique of Newton and theism or Deism.

beasts you believe that God to have put in subjection to your rule often tear and rend your fellows, even as fire burns them, the sea swallows them up, and they fall victim to those terrifying disorders of the elements whose order you are always admiring? . . . What indeed is man in comparison with the earth, his home planet? What is that planet in comparison with the sun? What is our sun in comparison with the throng of suns that fill the vault of heaven at astronomical distances from it? Disorder and pain and man a mite in the face of the world—that is the actual state of affairs. Such a world is ruled, not by any principle, good or evil, but solely by "fate" or the necessity of things.[21] If God is infinitely good, as he is claimed to be, why then does he not use his infinite power to make all men happy? Rather, for everyone who is joyful there are millions who suffer; for everyone who is wallowing in luxury there are millions of poor people lacking the necessities of life; whole peoples languish in poverty to satisfy the passions of a handful of princes, a little clique of moguls.

In a word, under an omnipotent God whose goodness knows no bounds, the tears of the wretched flood the whole face of the earth. An appeal to the life to come merely serves, in d'Holbach's opinion, to complicate matters instead of resolving them; and furthermore, it is a vicious circle because the life to come is asserted on the word of that God whose existence is precisely in question and up for proof. Nor does it help any more to appeal to man's "freedom" in general and in his relationship with God in particular, because this freedom, as we have seen, is likewise an illusion. And d'Holbach concludes that the modern theologians are ill-advised indeed to persist in these endless discussions about the attributes of God and end by smashing their idol with their own clumsy hands.[22]

Nor is the argument from the "consensus of the human race" more solid: such an agreement on a matter that no one has ever succeeded in understanding would prove nothing whatever even if it could be shown to exist.[23] All the theologians' proofs of the existence of God start from the false premise that matter does not exist of itself, that it cannot itself initiate its own motion, and that it is not therefore capable

[21] *Ibid.,* P. II, Ch. 3; Vol. II, pp. 67ff.

[22] *Ibid.,* P. II, Ch. 3; Vol. II, pp. 88f. D'Holbach then proceeds (pp. 89ff.) to consider the possibility of a "revelation" of the deity; but this, far from being a demonstration and proof of his goodness and good will towards man, is rather a proof of the contrary!

[23] *Ibid.,* P. II, Ch. 4; Vol. II, p. 95. The most that the argument proves is the existence in nature of "mysterious and hidden forces" (Vol. II, p. 102, note 23). D'Holbach has a critique in this chapter of Clarke's proofs of the existence of God (pp. 110ff.), based on the notion of eternity and infinity; in Ch. 5, d'Holbach attacks the proofs of Descartes, Malebranche and Newton (pp. 148ff.), noting Descartes to have been accused ("and quite rightly so") of atheism (p. 150).

of producing the phenomena we see in the world about us.[24] But it does and it can and it is; and therefore it is entirely superfluous to have recourse to an invisible spiritual *Agent*. Both the notion of absolute Spirit and the notion of the creation of matter out of nothing are incomprehensible, for in such a hypothesis God would have had to pluck matter out of himself and that means pantheism. Despite all their mental gymnastics in asserting God and his attributes, the theologians are always falling into anthropomorphism.[25]

The origin of the idea of God is explained in terms of ignorance of causes operative in our world and anxiety and distress at the ills of the life in which man actually finds himself: all of these problems are held to impel man to seek an explanation of events and a comfort for the misfortunes of his life by having recourse to a First Cause outside the world; the existence of evil in particular impels man to imagine a Being who is absolutely good and powerful and who can deliver him from his physical and mental sufferings.[26] But all this amounts simply to a subjective psychological projection: as the old saying has it, "Fear was the father of the gods." In short, had there been no evil in this world, man would never have thought of the deity.[27]

Worse still, the existence of God as conceived by the theologians is self-contradictory because the notion of God includes attributes that stand in contradiction one to another: God is supposed to be everywhere, even in material things which have extension, without himself having extension; God is called immutable, omnipotent and omniscient, yet religion inconsistently makes prayer an obligation; as omnipotent, God is called the author of miracles or infractions of the laws of nature, without regard to the fact that such an intervention by God to amend his own work is a sign that he bungled it in the first place and failed to foresee all eventualities.

A century before Feuerbach, d'Holbach is thus asserting that it was not God who created man in his own image but rather man who created God as a product of his own imagination.[28] The "natural theology" of the theists and Deists is thus an intellectual gymnastic which is totally pointless and even harmful and disrespectful: it involves several impermissible admissions: that man can offend his God, disturb the order of the universe, partake of the bliss of the supreme Being and cross up the

[24] D'Holbach refers back to P. I, Ch. 2, where he has given a proof of the thesis (of Locke-Toland and the rest) that motion pertains essentially to matter.
[25] *Ibid.*, P. II, Ch. 6, Vol. II, pp. 179ff., p. 195.
[26] *Ibid.*, P. II, Ch. 1, Vol. II, pp. 1ff. The Second Part is devoted entirely to the critique of the existence and the idea of God, with the aim of opening up to man the way to true happiness on this earth.
[27] *Ibid.*, P. II, Ch. 10, p. 345 and Ch. 1, p. 4.
[28] *Ibid.*, P. II, Ch. 7; Vol. II, pp. 207ff.

plans of this omnipotent Being. Nor is the proof drawn from the *order* of the universe any more cogent than the other ones: discord and confusion is rampant in the universe, and the world is often the cause of temptations and agitation for man; not to mention the fact that a melancholy temperament will see as toxic and evil what the more robust temperament sees as salubrious. The conclusion is that God exists only in man's imagination and is therefore bound to take on the coloration of man's own character and temperament, to be subject to man's changes of mood, etc. In short, God is but a chimera; and this chimera on balance does more harm than good.[29] Nor will d'Holbach allow God to be requisite as a basis for morality.[30] First of all, the concept man has of God is so vague and amorphous that nothing can be derived from it at all; then, the picture of a God who is always angry at man tends to paralyze action and virtuous living rather than to stimulate them; and finally, the alleged goodness of God encourages the knaves, even as his severity discourages the virtuous. Morality had need of a basis that is stable and universal and this stable and universal basis is provided by human nature itself; thus we can base morality and our moral obligations exclusively on the nature of man and on the relations prevailing between intelligent natures. In a word, it is the necessity of things that must serve as basis of morality and it is precisely this necessity which constitutes genuine moral obligation.[31] For religion-based morality must be substituted *a natural morality:* and this morality of nature is clear for all, even for those who offend against it, and need not wait until the theologians and metaphysicians reach agreement among themselves.[32] Nature imposes on man the demands of self-love, self-preser-

29 *Ibid.,* P. II, Ch. 7, Vol. II, pp. 233f.

30 Cf. *ibid.,* P. II, Ch. 9, significantly entitled: "The theological concepts cannot be the basis of morality. Comparison of theological morality and natural morality. Theology prejudices the progress of the human mind" (Vol. II, pp. 284ff.).

31 (*Theism and Morality*). "Supposing God to be the author of all things, there is nothing more ludicrous than the idea of pleasing or irritating him by our actions, our thoughts, our words; there is nothing more inconsistent than to imagine that man, or man's works, could be meritorious or blameworthy in his sight. It is obvious that man cannot injure an omnipotent being whose sovereign happiness derives from his own essence. It is obvious that he cannot displease the one who has made him what he is; his passions, his desires, his inclinations are the necessary consequences of the organization he has received; the motivations determining his will to good or evil are obviously due to the qualities inherent in him and to the beings God has placed around him. If it is an intelligent being who has placed us in the circumstances in which we find ourselves, who has given their properties to the causes acting upon us, modifying our will, how can we offend him?" Everything depends on the physical structure of the subject, a structure given by God (*ibid.,* P. II, Ch. 10, p. 332).

32 This is a reiteration of the famous thesis of Bayle, which can be seen likewise in the final chapter (Vol. II, pp. 371ff.: *Is atheism compatible with morality?*) where d'Holbach expressly cites the *Pensées diverses* (Vol. II, pp. 380, 390).

vation and a continual augmentation of the sum total of his own happiness; it obliges him to take counsel with his own reason and let himself be guided by it, to seek for truth, to be sociable, to love his fellowmen, to practice magnanimity and to acquire fame by illustrious works, etc. In short, d'Holbach saddles religion with all evils and defects, while crediting nature with all good things and all meritorious impulses: religion is the source of all slavery, in private and in public life, nature is the fountainhead of all freedom and well-being. In a word, religion is the path of all error, nature is the path of truth.

The whirligig of this antimetaphysical metaphysics stops on the note of an apology for atheism.[33] The masses, claims d'Holbach, remain slaves to religious prejudices and atheism is the attitude of a handful of free minds who are preparing the future of mankind. D'Holbach freely admits that no label is, in his own day, more full of opprobrium than that of atheist. But what *is* an atheist in sober fact? An atheist, replies d'Holbach, is a man who destroys the specters that are harmful to the human race in order to recall man to nature, to experience, to reason. He is a man whose reflection upon matter, its energy, its properties and the variety of its effects does not lead him to have recourse, for an explanation of the phenomena of the universe and the processes of nature, to any power of an immaterial order, to any purely imaginary intelligence, to any abstract notion, all of which serve not to make nature intelligible but simply to obscure it and render it still more incomprehensible and futile. If, of course, the term "atheist" be intended to indicate those who deny the existence of a force or power moving matter from within and called "God," then there are no atheists and the term "atheist" has no meaning.

Atheists, in the positive sense, are those who fight against every brand of fanaticism; they are the investigators of nature, the natural scientists who are convinced that the phenomena of nature can be explained in terms of the laws of movement of nature; they are those who can make no sense out of the entity called "spirit" and do not understand the negative attributes ascribed by the theologians to spirit and to the deity.[34] A discordant note in this hymn to atheism is d'Holbach's invocation of the example of Socrates who was condemned by the Athenians for being a worshipper of the one true God.

D'Holbach then proceeds to question whether there is any truth in the accusation that atheism makes any morality impossible, "that an atheist cannot be virtuous, that virtue is for him a daydream and nothing more, that moral probity is but an eccentricity and candor merely naivety, . . . that the only law the atheist admits is that of his own interest, that

[33] *Ibid.*, P. II, Ch. 11, Vol. II, pp. 350ff.
[34] *Ibid.*, P. II, Ch. 11, Vol. II, pp. 364ff.

conscience for him is but a prejudice, the natural law an illusion, and positive law and justice a sad mistake from beginning to end. It is really true that for the atheist good will has no basis in fact, social relations simply melt away as insubstantial, all idea of loyalty disappears, friend is always ready to betray friend, citizen to defame and revile his country, and son to kill his father in order to come into possession of his holdings?" [35] No, D'Holbach retorts, the actual picture is exactly the reverse. The atheist is a man who is well aware of nature and her laws, of his own nature and all that it involves. The atheist holds with experience and experience shows him at every moment that vice can be harmful to him, that his most carefully concealed missteps and his most hidden tendencies may one day come to light, that society demands that its own well-being be respected, that it is in his own interest to maintain his loyalty to his country which defends him and puts him in a position to enjoy securely the goods of nature. It is indeed true that the atheist has but few principles but these few are solid, not plucked out of thin air but directly tied in with the duties of this life here and now. The atheist does indeed deny the existence of God but he does not deny his own existence nor yet that of those around him nor the fact of his relations with them. It may be that some men vow themselves to atheism in order to give free rein to their passions: but such men are deceiving themselves because atheism rightly understood recalls man to nature and to reason, both of which highlight the difference between good and evil and neither of which will ever justify crimes or vices.

As for Deism's claim that the errors and horrors charged to religion should in fact be blamed on superstition, d'Holbach counters that superstition is the direct consequence of the vague and confused ideas serving as basis for religion.[36] Deism claims to conceive the deity in his pure essence, free of the contradictions of popular religion and superstition, i.e., as pure Intelligence, Wisdom, Power and Goodness, as endowed with infinite perfections, as pure spirit distinct from nature; it claims his existence is attested by the order and harmony of the universe and that his providence rules and governs the course of this universe, etc. The Deists are critical of miracles and revealed religion but they defend natural religion. They stop halfway, charges d'Holbach, and are no more consistent than those who defend superstitious religions. What sort of a God can this God of theirs be who contents himself with creating the world and ordering it according to a generic and overall providence, leaving the individual causes to operate on their own, careless of the subsequent fate of that universe he has created, indeed unable to inter-

[35] D'Holbach cites l'Abbadie, *De la vérité de la religion chrétienne* Vol. I, Ch. 17 (*Système de la nature,* P. II, Ch. 12; Vol. II, p. 371).

[36] *Système de la nature,* P. II, Ch. 13, Vol. II, p. 396.

vene in individual cases, indifferent to the evil that poisons and corrupts life? [37]

Thus there is nothing baneful or suspicious about atheism; it is not a secret sect but rather the search for truth pure and simple. The Enlightenment insisted, however, that this sort of search for truth was never the business of the broad masses; rather it is the privileged purlieu of a small group of the elite, to which group is reserved atheism, philosophy and all the deep-going and abstract sciences. But this elite labors on behalf of the entire human race. Even as the astronomer is the theoretical back-up man for the sailor, the mathematician and technologist for industry, even as every science is a theoretical back-up for some practical endeavor, so too philosophy is a task reserved to a few persons capable of delivering man from the pointless and pernicious prejudices of religion.[38] Far from being a dubious character, the atheist is therefore a perfect gentlemen. And even supposing God to exist, challenges d'Holbach, if God is a reasonable, just, good being and not a bloodthirsty, phrenetic, noxious spirit, as he has too often been presented by religion, what would a virtuous atheist have to fear from this God whom he had misunderstood and underestimated, even disdained all his life long and before whom he would find himself at the very moment of death, even as the atheist was composing himself for his eternal sleep? Here is an extract from the atheist's prayer toward the end of the *Système de la nature:*

"O God and Father, who hast not rendered Thyself visible to this, Thy son! Inconceivable and hidden mover whom I have not succeeded in discovering! Do thou pardon me if my limited intelligence hath not succeeded in recognizing Thee in a nature wherein all did seem to me the offspring of necessity. Do Thou pardon me if my heart of flesh hath not succeeded in distinguishing the noble features of Thy countenance beneath the mask of that ferocious tyrant so fearfully and tremblingly adored by the superstitious. I have not succeeded in seeing aught but an outright chimera in the piled-up brush strokes of irreconcilable properties wherewith imagination hath sought to limn thee.

"How could my dull eyes ever have perceived Thee in a nature wherein all my senses could but know material things and transitory forms? How could I ever have traced with these senses the outline of Thy spiritual essence which those senses could never fence within the bounds of experience? How could I have found the cogent proofs of Thy goodness in Thy works which bore bitter fruit or none for the beings of my own species? How could my weak brain have judged of itself of the plan

[37] The critique of Deism is presented in P. II, Ch. 7; Vol. II, pp. 207ff.
[38] *Ibid.*, P. II, Ch. 13; pp. 402f.

[of Thy Providence], of Thy Wisdom, of Thy Intelligence, when Thy universe did present itself to me as a continual mixture of order and disorder, of good and evil, of creations and destructions? Could I perchance have rendered homage to Thy justice, when I so often did see crime triumphant and virtue in tears?

"Yet, O God, hear me a little: if Thou dost love Thy creatures, I too have loved them even as Thou; in the sphere of my life on earth I have tried to make them happy. If Thou art the author of reason, this reason I have ever hearkened to and followed. If virtue doth please Thee, I have ever held it in esteem; I have not disdained it and have ever practiced it to the extent that my powers suffered me so to do: I have been an attentive husband and father, a candid friend, a loyal and zealous citizen. I have comforted the afflicted; and if on occasion the weakness of my nature hath hurt my proper self or made me somewhat of a burden to others, yet have I never made the wretched to weep and groan under the weight of my injustice nor ever devoured the substance of the poor. I have not shut up the bowels of my compassion against the tears of the widow, nor stopped my ears to the plaint of the orphan.

"Could I forsooth have ever recognized Thy voice as that of a being full of wisdom, in those ambiguous, discordant, callow oracles blazoned abroad by the imposters in Thy Name, through all the regions of this earth I now am leaving? If I have refused to believe in Thy existence, it was because I knew not what manner of being could be Thine, nor where Thou couldst be ensconced, nor what qualities could be attributed to Thee. My ignorance merits pardon because it was invincible; my spirit could not bow to the authority of certain men who would not admit themselves less enlightened than myself upon Thy essence and who, ever cavilling among themselves, did agree but on this one thing, to bellow at me the blunt command to sacrifice the reason that Thou hadst given me.

"If Thou dost render man sociable, if Thou hast willed that society should subsist and know happiness, I have ever been the foe of all those who did oppress and deceive society to draw private profit from its misfortunes. If I have thought ill of Thee, do Thou remember that my intellect could not comprehend Thee; if I have spoken ill of Thee, lay it to the account of my too human heart that did rebel against the too hateful picture that was painted for it. My deviations have been the result of the temperament Thou hast given me, of the circumstances wherein Thou hast placed me without asking my counsel, of the ideas that have penetrated into my mind without my compliance. If Thou art good and just, as Thou art claimed to be, Thou canst not then punish me for the errors of my imagination, for the errors that stem from my passions, necessary consequences of the bodily structure Thou Thyself hast given me. Wherefore I need not fear nor contemplate with any anguish the fate Thou art preparing for me. Thy goodness could not permit that I incur a punishment for transgressings that could not be avoided.

"Why didst Thou not deny me life outright rather than elevate me to the rank of intelligent beings only so that I might possess the fatal freedom that would render me unhappy and wretched? Shouldst Thou punish me severely and eternally because I have adhered to the Reason Thou hast given me; shouldst Thou be pleased to chastise me for my illusions; wert Thou to be inflamed with anger at my falling into the net Thou hast spread everywhere for me; then Thou wert verily the cruelest and most unjust of tyrants, then wert Thou not a God but a demon, a noxious devil to whose orders and savageries I would be constrained to submit but whose insupportable yoke I should rejoice to have cast off for a little space." [39]

This is a strange but significant profession of atheism, clothed of course in the guise of an apology, wherein God himself sits in the dock as culprit and man arraigns him as public prosecutor—man, or more exactly the philosopher who sees in the immediate presence of sensible objects the sole pledge of the presence of the real and in the principle of identity of formal logic the only law of thought.[40] European thought (and not the political thought only) has come a long way since d'Holbach's day: in Kant and the idealist tradition, it has endeavored to spread the verdure of this thought over the desert created by the absence of God; but having lost the fountain of living water, it has seen this desert spread ever more menacingly, desolate and deadly.

[39] *Ibid.,* P. II, Ch. 10, pp. 329-331 (fol. III). The work ends with a hymn of praise to Nature, fountainhead of everything: "O Nature! Sovereign of all beings! And you, her daughters, virtue, reason, truth, to whom all reverence and homage is due; be forever our only deities; it is to you that earth's worshipping incense ought to rise. Show us, then, O Nature! what man must do to obtain the happiness you make him desire. Virtue! warm him again with your salutary fire. Reason! guide his faltering steps into the ways of life. Truth! let your torch enlighten him" and much more of the same! (*ibid.,* P. II, Ch. 14; Vol. II, p. 453).

[40] There seems to be no possible doubt about d'Holbach's atheism. Helvétius and Diderot are also presented by the Marxists as being atheists; but Helvétius' stand is not entirely clear even though the logic of his principles seems to favor atheism. But we read that Helvétius is criticizing religion, as he himself maintains, not in order to destroy it but rather in order to purify it: "All religions are false, with the exception of the Christian religion" (*De l'Homme,* sect. I, Ch. 2 [Paris, 1818], p. 49). Then too, there is his concluding declaration which has the ring of absolute sincerity: "At no point in this work have I denied the Trinity, the divinity of Jesus, the immortality of the soul, the resurrection of the dead, nor even a single article of the *papist Creed:* so I have not attacked religion at all" (*ibid.,* Récapitulation, Ch. 3; p. 609).

6
Abbé Meslier's Radical Atheism

The fact that three abbés (Gassendi, Condillac and Meslier) should have been outstanding figures in modern French thought of sensist and materialist tendency is symptomatic and highly significant; but the significance has not yet been thoroughly investigated. Meslier is the least known of the three but at one point he was exalted by representatives of 18th-century unbelief and atheism virtually to the status of a founding father.[1] From his biography as compiled by a recent editor [2] we learn that he was born in 1678 and spent his whole priestly life as pastor of the parishes of Etrépigny and But in Champagne. He was diligent in all his religious duties; his way of life was edifying: he was stern with himself, firm against the arrogant and generous to the poor, to whom he left the little he had at his death in 1729 at the age of 55.

Among his papers were found three copies of a thick manuscript, entitled *Mon Testament,* which soon became several hundred copies that sold like hot cakes and caused an enormous uproar. In a letter of May 31, 1762, to the Count d'Argental, Voltaire has preserved a statement Meslier had directed to be communicated to his parishioners after his death. It seems to have been intended to serve as preface to his *Testament* and it explains the reasons for his defection from religion and likewise for his silence about this defection while he had been still alive. On a separate sheet, he expresses himself still more concisely: "I have seen and recognized the errors, the abuses, the vanities, the follies and the wickednesses of men; I have hated and detested them; I have not

[1] In his extremely thorough and erudite *Freydenker Lexikon,* Trinius ignores Meslier completely.

[2] I refer to the anonymous edition of the two compilations of the *Testament* made by d'Holbach and Voltaire, *Le bon sens du curé Meslier suivi de son Testament,* now in the collection *Scripta manent* whose managing editor is Constantin Cartera; this edition dates from 1930 and was published at Dijon. The biographical information on which I have drawn is to be found on pp. 251ff.

On the title-page, the Editor states: "Since the end of the 18th century, *Le Testament du Curé Meslier,* revised and published by Voltaire in 1762 and *Le bon sens du Curé Meslier* published by d'Holbach in 1772, have often been published together under the title: *Le bon sens du Curé Meslier suivi de son Testament.*

dared to say this while I was still alive but I shall at least say it in dying and after my death; and it is in order to make it known that I am composing and writing down this memorandum, so that it may serve as witness to the truth to all such as shall see it and read it, if it seem good to them so to do." [3]

Meslier stands out as a case apart in the history of 18th-century unbelief. He shows some similarities, in the contrast between his dissembling and the generous devotion with which he served an ideal whose principles and content he hated in secret, with certain early 20th-century Catholic Modernists. But in Meslier, erudition is inversely proportional to the virulence of his language against God, Jesus Christ, and the miracles and prophecies on which is based Christianity's claim to a divine origin. There is no direct connection in Meslier's outbursts with the theoretical discussions of rationalism or Deism; rather there is a splenetic eruption against everything sacred, a bitter diatribe that spares nothing and no one: all the ills and oppressions that exist in the world are blamed by Meslier on one single cause, the Christian religion. No one, not even among the pagans, has inveighed so drastically against Jesus Christ and his teaching: the invectives of the rabid opponents of religion and Christianity [4] pale before Meslier's stubby peasant prose, with its constant note of vehemence, bitterness and obtuseness. The overall impression of Meslier's writing is tedium and monotony. He manifests a degree of naiveté in the most elementary problems of thought that has few equals in the whole group of anti-religious pamphleteers, not only in modern times but even in the days of Porphyry, Celsus, Iamblichus, Julian the Apostate himself, and the most rabid foes of Christianity in ancient times.[5]

The surprising element in this diatribe, for anyone with the patience to read the patchwork of invective, is the total absence of any discussion in depth either from the theological or from the philosophical point of

[3] Extract from the *Testament,* p. 253.

[4] The most recent historians of thought are entirely in agreement with this view: ". . . A will and testament animated by such foaming rage that it cannot be read without a shiver even after the passage of two hundred years: wave upon wave of bitterness; a mass of rancor and hatreds exacerbated by their own powerlessness; a call to a revolt that Meslier had not dared to launch openly himself; the reproach of cowardice he levels against himself is a partial explanation of the frenzy of the insults he hurls at religion and God. Fury at having let himself be brought to the clerical state, at having presented the appearance of an orthodox-thinking priest, at having been oppressed and downtrodden, at having repudiated the faith and yet kept silence. He had been a hundred times on the verge of exploding, he explains, of letting this anger burst out that had been bottled up for the whole of a lifetime; but he had been unwilling to expose himself to the indignation of the priests and the cruelty of the tyrants who would have felt that the worst tortures were not harsh enough to punish his temerity" (P. Hazard, *La pensée européenne au XVIIIe siècle,* Vol. I [Paris, 1946], p. 71).

[5] Cf. *Testament de l'abbé Meslier,* p. 256.

view; yet through those interminable chapters of the *Testament,* crammed with exegetical, historical and philosophical howlers, there echoes an unfathomable and disturbing cry, the cry of disillusion, torment and racking agony of a mind that has never succeeded in grasping the spirit of Christianity, a spirit driven to the breaking point by the faults of some representatives of Christianity. The fact that Voltaire on the one hand and d'Holbach and the other Enlightenment thinkers on the other, should have taken this book so seriously, albeit from quite different points of view, is a measure of the influence this work exercised, despite its paltry insignificance from the scientific point of view, upon the development of 18th-century atheism, and explains why it enjoys such a reputation among atheists in our own day.[6]

In early February of 1762, Voltaire informs d'Alembert of the *Testament* and shows himself horrified by its content, to the point of calling it *Testament de l'Antichrist;* [7] but shortly thereafter (on the 25th of that same month), he writes to the same d'Alembert that there is "good grain" in it, and a few months later (July 12) he praises it to the skies in another letter to the same friend, to the point of calling it a new "Gospel" destined to convert the world. Why did Voltaire change his opinion so drastically? In a letter to the Count d'Agental, written about the same time as the first letter to d'Alembert, the *Testament* is branded by Voltaire as "a work most needful to the angels of darkness, a most admirable catechism of Beelzebub"; but in a later letter (October 8, 1762) to the same Count, Voltaire declares that the book "ought to be in the hands of everyone" and praises it highly in a still later letter (December 6, 1762). Voltaire likewise brings Helvétius up to date on the whole business, repeating the high praises of the Meslier patchwork (letter of May 1, 1762).[8]

It is true that, in the *Extrait* and especially in the conclusion, as

[6] Cf. German translation of the Soviet *Geschichte der Philosophie,* Vol. I, pp. 475ff.

[7] "The *Testament de Jean Meslier* has been published in Holland. It made my hair stand on end to read it. The witness of a parish priest who, on his deathbed, asks pardon of God for having taught Christianity, could tip the scales heavily in favor of the free-livers. I shall send you a copy of this *Testament de l'Antichrist* since you want to refute it" (Extract from the *Testament,* p. 257). In the matter of this edition published in Holland, d'Alembert adopts, in his reply of March 31, 1762, the hypothesis (or the expedient to cover himself?) that it is an "extract made by a Swiss" who understands French perfectly, even though he pretends to speak it badly: "It is clear-cut, concise and compact; and I bless the author of the *Extrait,* whoever he may be" (p. 258). May it not rather have been the abridgement made by d'Holbach, entitled *Le bons sens du curé Meslier?* This abridgement, however, is dated 1772, ten years later than the Voltaire-d'Alembert correspondence.

[8] "I have been sent the two extracts of Jean Meslier; it is true that it is written in the style of a braying ass; but the ass kicks up his heels to good purpose" (*ibid.,* p. 263).

reported by Voltaire, Meslier does not profess himself an outright atheist, but rather a vigorous champion of natural religion in opposition to the Christian religion: "I shall end by imploring God, so outraged by this sect, to deign to recall us to the natural religion of which Christianity is the declared enemy; to this holy religion that God has put into the hearts of all men, that teaches us to do nothing to others save what we would have done unto ourselves. Then will the universe be filled with good citizens, just fathers, obedient children, affectionate friends. God has given us this religion in giving us reason. May fanaticism cease to pervert it any longer! I am dying full of these desires rather than of hope" (Etrépigny, March 15, 1732).[9]

Voltaire's extract is skilfully chosen and captures the substance of Meslier's work while deliberately covering up the most tawdry shortcomings of this patchwork product. D'Holbach's meticulous summary is more faithful to the original, but that was the limit of the luck of this poor priest who went wrong.

Meslier's *Testament* was published in full a century ago[10] but little light has been shed on it as yet: Voltaire's summary and d'Holbach's fuller outline reveal how many points of interest there were in this chaotic conglomeration, crammed full of repetitions, parallel passages and unbelievable naiveté; at times, it can be diverting and striking, despite its exasperating prolixity. The most surprising feature of the entire situation is the undeniable fact that minds who called themselves enlightened and worshippers of reason should have seen this turgid tenth-rate effort as a veritable flash of salvific reason. Almost equally surprising is the gross ignorance displayed by this parish priest of the Christian religion and of its foundations, an ignorance that is more amazing by far than Meslier's incompetence in the field of philosophy.[11] In sum, this work of Meslier's is of cardinal importance, from many points of view for an analysis of an age so crucial as the age of the Enlightenment. We

[9] *Ibid.*, pp. 322f.

[10] *Le Testament de Jean Meslier,* ed. Charles, in 3 volumes (Amsterdam, 1864). The original title is: "*Mémoire des Pensées et Sentiments* of J. M., parish priest of Estrépigny and But, on a portion of the abuses and errors in the guidance and governance of men, wherefrom emerge clear and evident proofs of the vanity and falsity of all deities and all religions of the world, to be delivered to his parishioners after his death and to serve as a witness of truth to them and all their fellows" (Vol. I, p. 1).

[11] One of the main sources is certainly Montaigne, who is cited constantly throughout (Cf. Vol. I, p. 23: "The discerning Montaigne"; 31, 37, 58, 59f., 71, 88, 89, 94, 213, 215, 216, 217, 276; Vol. II, 6, 22, 29, 82, 111, 130, 279, 301, 386, 390, 391; Vol. III, 95, 115, 270, 305, 310, 363 and *passim!*). Less frequently cited is a work of dubious title, *Espion Turc* or *Esprit Turc* (Vol. I, p. 34) which the editor of the 1715 edition indicates to have been probably purloined from Montaigne (cf. Appendix 5 to this Chapter).

therefore here attempt to highlight a few of the typical elements of the *Testament.*

1. As its very title suggests, the *Testament* (or *Memoires*) is less a piece of objective study and research than a spiritual autobiography of a man who has spent a whole lifetime of personal grief and torment without ever having penetrated to the depths of the reality that is Christianity or even thoroughly comprehended the phenomenon of natural religion: a kind of bewildered rebel, concealing for a whole lifetime his vexation at a mistaken choice without ever having the courage to be honest with himself or others.[12] The whole case exudes a grotesque aura calculated to arouse more pity than disdain or amazement.

Meslier's faith in God and religion was shaken primarily by *the spectacle of evil and injustice* [13] of which the world was full: "I have known so much spiteful and mischievous wickedness in the world that even the most perfect virtue and the purest innocence were not exempt from the malice of the slanderers. I have seen and there can still be seen every day an innumerable multitude of unfortunate and wretched innocents persecuted without reason and unjustly oppressed, without anyone being touched by their misfortune, without any charitable protector being moved to succor them. The tears of the afflicted righteous and the miseries of such a host of peoples tyrannically oppressed by the rich and the powerful of the world have given me such a disgust and contempt for life that I have held with Solomon that the state of the dead is happier than that of the living, and that those who have never existed are a thousand times more blessed than those who do exist and groan still under the weight of such dismal miseries."

Judging by Meslier's vehement distribes, he must have considered the assignment of religion and of Christianity in particular to be that of eliminating from this world every evil, every injustice, every inequality

[12] Meslier had nothing but detestation for the total sham that his life as a priest had been and he excuses himself for having refrained from making a clear statement of his convictions "being unwilling to expose myself, while still alive, to the indignation of the priests or to the cruelty of the tyrants" (Vol. I, p. 25). His confusion of mind becomes still more evident in his constant appeal to Scriptural texts to bolster his critique of religion in general and Christianity in particular!

[13] *Introduction,* Vol. I, p. 5. The Jeremiad continues with a charge of indifference against those in authority: "The source of all the ills that are crushing you and of all the impostures that are holding you unhappily captive in error and in the vanity of superstitions, as well as under the tyrannical laws of the great ones of the earth, is none other than this detestable human politicking of which I have just been speaking; for some want unjustly to dominate their fellows and then others again want to acquire some sort of vain reputation of holiness and sometimes even of divinity; and both sorts have cleverly made use, not only of force and violence, but of all kinds of subtle wiles and tricks" (p. 7).

and of transforming life on this earth into a perennial Paradise. No wonder that a man with such premisses, which would have brought a smile to the lips of the most minor philosopher of antiquity, should have felt free, nay obliged, to dip his pen in gall and let it race across the paper. At the end of the dreary Odyssey, we read a sentence that expresses the nub of Meslier's entire rebellious objection: "Now it is neither credible nor even possible that an all-powerful, infinitely good, infinitely kind and infinitely wise being should ever have willed, in creating the world, to make such a jumble of good and evil." [14]

2. The same charge is levelled against all religions indiscriminately, but especially against the Catholic religion: all religions are human inventions, not one of them has been instituted by God. The Christian faith especially is entirely inane and fatuous, mysteries and revelation are empty meaningless prattle.[15] Moreover, Meslier is persuaded of the absolute incompatibility of faith and reason: "Hence it comes about that they consider it mandatory to renounce all the lights of reason and all the apparent evidence of the senses in order to enslave their mind under the yoke of their faith. In a word, they hold that believing faithfully necessarily involves believing blindly, without reasoning, without seeking for any proofs. Now it is evident that a blind belief in everything proposed in the name of God and on his authority is a source of error, illusion and deception." [16]

It is easy to imagine how such a man would treat the basic teachings and doctrines of Christianity and the main arguments elaborated by the Fathers and later particularly by St. Thomas (of whom I find no mention in the *Testament*) in an effort to cope with the enigma of good and evil, life and death, in human existence.

No less drastic is Meslier's condemnation of Christian morality, starting with its very foundation, the doctrine of original sin. Meslier

[14] *Testament,* Ch. XCVI; Vol. III, p. 367. This was the miracle Jesus Christ was supposed to work (cf. Vol. I, Ch. XXI, pp. 185f.).

[15] "Nevertheless this belief is always blind; for the Religions do not and indeed could not give any clear, certain and convincing proof of the truth of their alleged sacred mysteries, nor of their alleged divine revelations. They want a person to believe absolutely without entertaining the slightest doubt, but also without investigating at all, without even desiring to know the reasons: for this would be, according to them, an impudent temerity and a crime of high treason against God" (*Ibid.,* Ch. X; Vol. I, p. 68).

[16] *Ibid.,* p. 69. The next Chapter (XI) is entitled: "It [the Faith] is likewise nothing but a source and fatal cause of disorders and eternal divisions among men" (p. 70). There follow: a critique of the arguments of Catholic apologetics (pp. 73ff.), of the value of Sacred Scripture (pp. 102ff.), of miracles (pp. 138ff.), of the divinity of Jesus Christ (p. 174), of revelations (pp. 187ff.) and prophecies (pp. 231ff.), of the Roman Church (p. 313). A special critique is devoted to St. Paul (pp. 335ff.).

adduces two reasons why this doctrine is in contradiction with the very concept of God as expounded by theology:

I. "For, firstly, how is it possible to reconcile in one God such a great excess of goodness and such a great excess of love for men with such a great defect of concern as the original sin doctrine would ascribe to him in the matter of preserving man in a state of innocence once he had created man thus, and with such a great weakness and such a great frailty as God would be supposed, on this hypothesis, deliberately to have left man in, so that man could fall into sin so easily and so soon as he did in fact do?"

II. "Is it credible that an infinitely good God, full of such tenderness and benevolence for man, would have willed to reject, ruin and damn the entire human race, not only to all the sorrows and afflictions of this life but to the frightful eternal flames of hell as well, for such a slight fault as that committed by Adam in eating in a garden some fruits that he had been forbidden to eat? For the sort of fault that did not deserve even a rap on the knuckles! It is disgraceful even to harbor such a thought about a God supposed to be supremely good and supremely wise." [17]

Meslier keeps up the barrage: "if God knew that Adam was going to sin, why did he not stop him from doing so? And when once the sin had been committed, why did God get so worked up over such a negligible occurrence as to send his Son down to earth?" In the light of all this, it is no surprise to find Meslier, in his rationalistic hedonism, condemning as errors the fundamental precepts of Christian ethics: seeking virtue in suffering after the example of Jesus Christ, denouncing the pleasures of the flesh, loving one's enemies.[18] Meslier's critique of Christian morality concludes with the traditional Deist and Enlightenment charge that Christianity tolerates and even favors the abuses of the powerful: "This enormous disparity everywhere to be seen between the different estates and conditions of men, with some apparently born to tyrannize others while always enjoying their pleasures and satisfactions in this life; and others, on the contrary, born to be miserable, wretched, lowly slaves and to groan their whole life long in pain and misery—such a disparity is altogether unjust because it is in no wise based on the merits of the ones nor yet on the demerits of the others; and it is hateful because it serves on the one hand only to inspire and nourish pride, haughtiness, vanity, arrogance and conceit in the ones

[17] *Ibid.*, Ch. XL; Vol. II, pp. 149ff.

[18] "These maxims of Christian morality tend not only to the subversion of justice; they tend moreover manifestly to favor the wicked" (*ibid.*, Ch. XLI; vol. II, p. 164).

and on the other hand only to arouse in the others that hate, envy, anger, lust for vengeance, complaining and murmuring, which are the source and cause of a plethora of ills and wickedness done in the world; which ills and wickednesses would surely not occur, would men but establish among themselves a just proportion and division of power, allowing to those in command the bare minimum needed to ensure a just subordination of the governed and not enough to permit or encourage some to tyrannize the others." [19]

Meslier's hail of charges aim at battering Christianity into accepting responsibility for all the evil, all the injustices, all the hateful and most deporable aspects of human life on this earth. It is enough to make one wonder if Voltaire, d'Holbach, d'Alembert, Helvétius and associates were not counting a little too heavily on the stupidity of their fellowmen in touting such stuff abroad so diligently!

3. The latter part of the work is devoted to a demolition of belief in God [20] and Meslier's polemical weapons are especially interesting, not, to be sure, from the speculative point of view, but rather as a documentation of a culture which had reached the point of reckoning with its own principle and its own Christian tradition. This attack on Deism and the "God-worshippers" is most instructive and can be useful, in a way not intended by its author, in strengthening the foundations of genuine monotheism: for Meslier, like the other and more famous protagonists of unbelief and atheism, makes a practice of basing himself, in his attacks on religion as such and faith in God, upon the often not very edifying spectacle of the horrors and errors of State religions, polytheism, fetichism, etc.

I. *Religion is purely political in origin.* God was invented by a handful of ambitious scoundrels to paralyze their fellowmen with awe once these scoundrels had themselves laid their hands on power and wealth: "Moreover it appears quite clear that the first belief in the Gods comes simply from the fact that certain men, shrewder, craftier, subtler and perhaps even more wicked and more malicious than the others, and motivated by the ambitious desire to rise above those others and perhaps also ready to take advantage of the ignorance and stupidity of

[19] *Ibid.,* Ch. XLII; vol. II, pp. 169f. Other abuses: defending appropriation of and greed for the goods of the earth, instead of holding them in common (in which case, however, why has Meslier derided the Beatitudes, Vol. II, p. 37?), proclaiming the indissolubility of marriage instead of allowing free love, supporting the tyranny of the powerful (Ch. XLV-LIV). Meslier concludes with a violent attack on the Court of France.

[20] Meslier claims that all the scholars, learned men and scientists of antiquity were atheists or accused of atheism: Aristotle, Diagoras, Pythagoras, Pliny, Rabelais, Spinoza, and even two Popes, Julius II and Leo X! (*Ibid.,* Ch. LXI, Vol. II, p. 290).

those others, took it into their heads to assume the name and status of God and sovereign Lord, to make themselves the more feared and respected, and the others, out of fear or stupidity or misplaced courtesy or fawning obsequiousness, allowed them to do it; so did these enterprising scoundrels become masters and as masters they retained the name of God and the status of sovereign Lord as we see today . . ." [21]

II. *Polytheism and idolatry discredit religion.* For Meslier, the transition from polytheism to monotheism is not an advance in the concept of religion but a proof of its patent absurdity:

"But if our Christ-worshippers and the other God-worshippers were unwilling on that account to reject all belief in God, they were compelled to restrict themselves at least to belief in a single God, one in substance and nature, but triple in persons, as our Christ-worshippers claim him to be; well, that certainly got rid of a gaggle of Gods at one fell swoop; for out of the swarm of deities the superstitious God-worshippers had been admitting and worshipping in ages gone by, their descendents were reduced and restricted to believing in and worshipping but one single God and an invisible, incorporeal and immaterial God, at that, a God who consequently has neither flesh nor bones, nor belly, nor arms nor legs nor feet nor hands, nor eyes nor head nor mouth nor tongue nor ears nor teeth nor nails nor claws nor any other bodily part; who, therefore, likewise has no form nor shape nor color without nor yet any frame or structure within, or rather who has no inside nor yet outside, no top nor bottom; yet a God whom they claim to be everywhere, to see everything, to rule and govern everything, to sustain everything, to be quite entire in every place and quite entire in every part of every place, to be all powerful, infinitely good, infinitely wise, infinitely just, infinitely kind, in short infinitely perfect in all species of perfection, whose nature is immutable, immobile and eternal, whose nature is his power, his wisdom, his goodness and his will itself; and whose power, wisdom, goodness and will are conversely his very nature and essence. This is certainly a quite surprising sort of being; but it can certainly likewise be said to be the idea of a totally imaginary and altogether fantastical being . . ." [22]

Patently, with this sort of logic, a writer can prove anything.

III. *Critique of the proofs of the existence of God* and of creation. This critique is bemusingly disorderly, for Meslier keeps going off on tangents to such an extent that the reader loses the thread of the exposi-

[21] *Ibid.,* Ch. CXII; Vol. II, pp. 298ff., "Whence comes the first belief in and knowledge of the gods".

[22] *Ibid.,* Ch. LXIII; Vol. II, pp. 302f., "The God-Worshippers were finally obliged to admit the inconsistency of a plurality of Gods."

tion. He begins with the critique of the proofs of "one of our most noted arch-God-worshippers, Mons. de Fénelon." [23]

There follows the only specifically metaphysical remark of this entire parcel of twaddle; and it explodes with the force of a mind-staggering squib: Being cannot be created!

"Since therefore Being is and it is evident that it is, it must also necessarily be admitted always to have been . . . but it must again necessarily be admitted that it is Being which is the first principle and the prime foundation of all things. For it is evident that all things are only really and truly what they are because they have Being, and because they are themselves participations of Being, and it is clear and certain that nothing would be if Being were not. Whence it obviously follows that Being in general is that which is primary and chief and basic in all things; and consequently that Being is the first principle and prime foundation of all things. And as Being has never begun to be but has always been, as has just been proven, and as, moreover, all things are but modifications of Being, it clearly follows that there is nothing created and consequently there is no creator." [24]

The argument here touched on is traditional in Christian Platonism and is amply treated and developed by St. Thomas himself.[25] But Meslier has succeeded here in hashing things up beyond recognition; he has committed metaphysical mayhem with materialistic malice aforethought!

Quite obviously it is not Being as such that needs to be created for this would be contradictory; what needs to be created is finite participated being, i.e., the world of beings. But Meslier must present this whole argument in the way he does because of his prior commitment to place matter at the root and basis of all things, of all reality.

IV. *Matter as reality and fundamental cause of beings.* Matter is supposed to take the place of God and of his attributes, i.e., "be eternal and independent of any other cause, just as that one would be who is claimed to have created it." [26] And Meslier continues with a series of assertions whose extreme candor and forthrightness is not entirely

[23] *Ibid.,* Ch. LXIV, pp. 304ff., "They are no better founded in the belief they have in the existence of one single God." The critique of Fénelon is resumed again further on in Ch. LXXVIII; Vol. III, pp. 116ff., 134ff., 139ff; Ch. LXXXIII; Vol. III, pp. 162ff., critique of the ontological argument. For Meslier the chief representatives of theism are the ontologists Fénelon and Malebranche.

[24] *Ibid.,* Ch. LXVIII; Vol. II, p. 326.

[25] *S.T.,* Ia, q. 44, a. 1. Cf. our own *La nozione metafisica di partecipazione* (Turin, 1963 [3]). Also: *Participation et causalité* (Louvain, 1960); I do not believe that Meslier ever cites St. Thomas, though he does cite St. Augustine a few times (Vol. III, pp. 221, 223).

[26] *Testament,* Ch. LXX; Vol. II, p. 313.

equalled by their apodictic cogency: "For simply the idea of a universal matter, which is self-moved in various senses and ways, and which by these various configurations of its parts is able every day to modify itself in thousands and thousands of different manners, makes it perfectly clear to us that everything that there is in nature can be effected by the natural laws of motion and by the mere configuration, combination and modification of the parts of matter . . . And since it is certain that matter does move itself and that no one can deny this nor yet doubt it . . . matter must necessarily have its Being and its motion from itself, or else have received them both from another source. It cannot have received them from another source . . . it therefore follows that it has its being and its motion from itself; and consequently it is futile to seek outside of matter the principle of matter's being and motion." [27]

Meslier thus identifies the fact of becoming with its principles and its causes and gives to the complex of nature in its multiple articulation the name of matter; then takes the fact itself for the explanation! Matter is thus accepted unreservedly as "true being" and identified outright with being itself; [28] motion is the fundamental act of matter and thus the law(s) of being. Meslier is as glib as ever on this point: "It is patent, clear and evident that matter, or at least extension, exists necessarily, and even that it is infinite." [29]

In the light of all this, it comes as no surprise to hear Meslier assert the materiality of the human soul and its dependence on the body.[30]

And death ends all. This is the conclusion of the *Testament:* "The dead whom I am on the point of going to join trouble themselves about *nothing*, rack their brains about *nothing*. My last words in this work shall therefore be about nothingness, even as I am even now scarcely more than *nothing* and soon I shall be nothing . . ." [31] and so on with the lugubrious tale.

The consummation devoutly to be wished, the already incipient movement to which Meslier gives his unreserved approbation, is that emergence of proud and resolute men, like Ravaillac, who will deliver the world at long last from the tyrants.

[27] *Ibid.,* Ch. LXVI and LXVII; Vol. II, p. 318, 320. But he admits that there is no necessary nexus between the idea of matter and the idea of motion (p. 323).

[28] Cf. *ibid.,* Ch. LXIX; Vol. II, pp. 328ff. Cf. also: pp. 338ff., 346ff., 381f.

[29] *Ibid.,* Ch. LXXXII; Vol. II, p. 172.

[30] *Ibid.,* Ch. LXXXIX; Vol. III, pp. 273ff.

[31] *Ibid.,* Ch. IC; Vol. III, p. 398.

Appendices

I. D'Holbach—Supplementary Marginal Notes

1. From His Own Works

(a) *Call for a Return to the Study of Nature and to Experience*

"Man is unhappy only because he misprizes Nature. His mind has been so infected with prejudices that you would believe it condemned to error forever: the bandage of opinion bound upon him from earliest childhood adheres so tightly that it can be gotten off only with the greatest difficulty. A dangerous leaven is mixed in to all his knowledge, rendering it inevitably frothy, obscure and deceptive: he has tried, to his own undoing, to get out of his proper realm; he has attempted to soar beyond the visible world and his cruel and repeated falls have warned him of the folly of his undertaking, but to no avail: he desired to be a metaphysicist before being a physicist: he despised experience, to batten on systems and conjectures; he did not dare to cultivate his own reason, against which he had been early warned most drastically; he pretended to have knowledge of his destiny in the imaginary regions of another life, before even dreaming of making himself happy in the abode wherein he was then tarrying. In a word, man disdained the study of nature, to run chasing after phantoms, which like those *fata morgana* the traveller encounters by night, frightened him, dazzled him, and made him quit the straightforward path of the true, by which alone he can attain to happiness" (*Le Système de la Nature,* Preface 2nd ed., pages not numbered).[1]

(b) *Atheist and Atheism*

"What in fact is an *atheist?* A man who destroys chimeras harmful to the human race, in order to lead men back to nature, to experience, to reason. A thinker, who, after contemplating matter, its energy, its properties, and its method of operation, finds that, in order to explain the phenomena of the universe and the operations of nature, he has no need

[1] This is included in an Appendix of *Le Système de la nature,* Vol. II, pp. 464ff.

to imagine ideal powers, figmentary intelligences, beings of reason, who, far from rendering this nature better known, do but make it capricious, inexplicable, unintelligible and of no use to man's happiness. Thus it is that the only men capable of having straightforward and true ideas about nature are regarded as absurd theorizers and in bad faith to boot!

"If the word *atheist* be used to designate a man who denies the existence of a power inherent in matter, without which nature cannot be conceived, and to which motive power the name *God* is given—then there are no atheists at all.

"But if by *atheists* are understood men not given to raptures, guided rather by experience and the evidence of their own senses, not seeing in nature anything but what is really there or what they are able to know in it, perceiving and capable of perceiving in nature nothing save *matter essentially active* and in motion, combined in various ways, enjoying of itself various properties, and capable of producing all the beings we see; if by *atheists* are understood convinced physicists, persuaded that everything can be explained simply by the laws of motion, without any recourse to a chimerical cause . . . if by *atheists* are understood men who know not what a *spirit* is and who see no need to *spiritualize* corporeal causes or render them incomprehensible . . . if by *atheists* are understood men who agree in good faith that their minds can neither conceive the negative attributes and the theological abstractions not yet reconcile them with the human and moral qualities attributed to the deity . . . if by *atheists* are understood men who reject a phantom whose hateful and ill-matched qualities are calculated only to perplex the human race and plunge it into a most pesky madness—if, I say, it is thinkers of these sorts that are being called *atheists,* there can be no doubt about their existence; and there would be a very great many of them, were the light of sound physics and right reason more widespread" (*Le Système de la Nature,* Part II, Ch. IX; pp. 353, 364-366).

(c) *Intolerance Breeds Atheism*

"There are said to be fewer atheists in England and the Protestant countries, where tolerance is an established practice, than in the Roman Catholic countries, where the princes are commonly intolerant and hostile to freedom of thought. Many atheists are to be found in Japan, Turkey, Italy, and especially in Rome. The more power superstition enjoys, the more does it revolt those minds it has not managed to crush and cow. Italy was the country that produced Giordano Bruno, Campanella, Vanini, and the rest. There is every reason to believe that Spinoza would never have elucubrated his system had it not been for the persecution and ill treatment he received at the hands of the synagogue authorities. Hobbes can likewise be presumed to have been pushed into atheism because of the horrors let loose in England by the fanaticism which cost Charles I his life. The indignation Hobbes conceived for the power of the priests may well have put into his mind those principles so favorable to the absolute power of kings. He believed it to be more fitting for a State to have a single civil despot, sovereign arbiter even of religion, than to have a host of spiritual tyrants, always ready to interfere. Seduced by the ideas of Hobbes, Spinoza fell into the same error, in his *Tractatus Theologico-Politicus,* and likewise in his treatise *De Jure ecclesiasticorum*" (*Système de la Nature,* Vol. II, p. 392, note). One wonders if the second Spinoza work here referred to by d'Holbach is the *Tractatus Politicus.*

2. Warning against Modern Unbelief

La nouvelle Philosophie dévoilée, et pleinement convaincue de Lèse-Majesté Divine et Humaine au premier chef.

(*The New Philosophy Unmasked* and convicted utterly of High Treason, against God and Man).

In France. M. DCC. LXX. (1770).

First mention goes to d'Holbach, *Système de la Nature,* "which can be regarded as his masterpiece, London [actually Rouen] 1770".

"A vestige of weakness led him to ascribe this important work to a man [Mirabaud] dead these ten years. But sources claiming to be well-informed insist that this is the work of a self-styled Philosopher, presently alive and very well known. What is quite certain is that the work cannot be attributed to the deceased *Mirabaud,* under whose name it has been brought out" (p. 4).

"This would-be *Système de la Nature . . . this abominable book* is but the end product and recapitulation of a plethora of others that have been flooding Paris and the whole of France for 30 years now. It differs from the others only in this sense that those who brought it out have had the audacity to say quite clearly and with no equivocation what they themselves and their fellows had not dared to say hitherto, save by masking themselves as Deists. They appeared to be acknowledging the existence of God in all their Works. They even affected sometimes to chant the most magnificent praises of this Supreme Being. But this God they vaunted themselves upon acknowledging was for them but an idol without voice or laws, without providence or mercy, without justice, without mysteries, without wisdom and without fertility; a God to whom it is a matter of utter indifference if men adore him or adore others than him; or even adore none at all; a God to whom it matters nothing whether men acknowledge and worship His Son or whether they blaspheme Him and together with Him all the truths that He has taught us; a God to whom are equally pleasing lying and truth, error and faith, the Mohammedan, the Jew, the Heretic, the Idolator, the Christian, the

Catholic; a God who is pleased to see before him in his glory men who have repudiated, denied and striven against him, and who have had his faithful Worshippers cruelly strangled. Such had been up to now the God of the authors of the *Essai sur l'Histoire générale,* of the *Lettres philosophiques,* of the *Poème sur la Loi Naturelle,* of the *Dictionnaire Philosophique* [all these are by Voltaire], of the *Pensées sur l'interprétation de la Nature* [Diderot], of the *Pyrronisme du Sage,* of the *Philosophie du bon sens,* of the *Analyse de Bayle* [Recherches sur l'origine-M. de Boulanger, p. 5 note], *of the Despotisme Oriental,* of the *Lettres de la Montagne,* of *Emile,* of the *Contrat Social* [Rousseau], of the *Discours sur l'inégalité des conditions,* of *l'Esprit* [Helvétius], of the *Lettres Persanes* [Montesquieu], of the *Roman de Bélisaire,* of *Christianisme dévoilé* [par le feu Mr. Boulanger], of the *Militaire Philosophe* [Naigeon], of the *Histoire de l'Ame,* of a spate of articles in the *Dictionnaire Enciclopédique,* and of an avalanche of other similar products of the new philosophy".

3. Indictment of Modern Irreligion by the French Advocate General

(a) Acted upon by the High Court of Paris in a Decree of August 18, 1770, condeming various books or Pamphlets to be burned, to wit:

1. *La Contagion sacrée,* or *Histoire Naturelle de la Superstition,* a work translated from the English, London 1768.
2. *Dieu et les hommes,* a probing theological work, London, 1770.
3. *Discours sur les miracles de Jésus-Christ,* translated from the English of Woolaston, XVIII century.
4. *Examen critique des Apologistes de la Religion Chrétienne,* by Mr. Freret, 1767.
5. *Examen impartial des principales Religions du monde.*
6. *Le Christianisme dévoilé,* or *Examen des principes et des effets de la Religion Chrétienne,* 1787.
7. *Système de la Nature,* or *des loix du monde physique et du monde moral.*

Printed by Express Order of the King

"(a) Gentlemen, how long shall our patience be abused? cried the Roman Orator at a time when the Republic, exposed to all the furies of a faction ready to erupt, was counting among the conspirators its most illustrious citizens, conjoined with the ragtag and bobtail.

"Can we not today address the same words to the Writers of this century, in the face of this League that conjoins well-nigh all the writers of every style against Religion and the Government? There can be no more blinking the facts: this criminal league is itself betraying its own secret. Its chief aim and goal is the destruction of the established harmony between all classes of the Realm, that harmony that is maintained by the close relation that has always subsisted between the teaching of the Church and the laws of the body politic.

"Yes, Gentlemen, since the extirpation of the heresies that used to trouble the peace of the Church; we have seen emerge from the shadows a system more dangerous in its consequences than the errors of old that were ever dissipated in proportion as they were spawned. There has reared itself in our midst an impious and audacious sect; it has frilled its false wisdom with the title and style of philosophy; under this imposing title, it has claimed to hold a corner on all knowledge. Its partisans have set themselves up as teachers of the whole of mankind. *Freedom of thought*—that is their slogan and this slogan has resounded from one end of the world to the other.

"With one hand they have tried to shake the Throne; with the other, to overturn the Altars. Their aim was to relax the firmness of belief, to put men in another mind about religious and civil institutions; and their revolution has, in a manner of speaking, taken hold. Converts have been made in ever larger numbers: Kingdoms have felt their ancient foundations tottering, and Nations, amazed to find their mainsprings of operation annihilated, have asked themselves what dire fate has so estranged them from their former condition.

"It is to Religion, above all, that these Innovators have sought to administer the deadliest blows; they have worked incessantly to root out faith, corrupt innocence and stifle in souls all feel for virtue . . .

"No, we are no longer justified in keeping silence in the matter of this deluge of writings which has for several years now been being spewed forth by irreligion and contempt for the law. We were busy collecting all these baleful products when we were informed that this same disorder had roused the righteous indignation of the General Assembly of the Clergy of France. The King himself certified to us that the Bishops of his Kingdom had brought to the very foot of the throne complaints as lively as they were respectful concerning the unbridled audacity of the irreligious Writings.

". . . Women themselves are being initiated into these counsels of impiety and skepticism; and, neglecting the duties which properly devolve upon them and which they alone can perform, they are spending a life of indolence in the meditation of these scandalous works.

"Scarcely had they been made public in the Capital when they were spreading like a torrent through the provinces, devastating everything in their path. There are few sanctuaries untouched by the infection; it has invaded the workshops and even the quiet cottages: and the speedy result has been no more faith, no more piety, no more morality; the innocence that used to be has been corrupted; the scorching breath of impiety has parched and withered the souls of men and has burnt up virtue. The common folk used to be poor but they did at least have consolation; now they are overwhelmed by their toil and their doubts: they used to look forward in hope to a better life to come; now they are overburdened with the afflictions of their state and see nothing beyond them.

"Nor is it simply a multiplication of the wretched homegrown fruits of the impious frenzy of our own writers that we have to contemplate; there has also been set up a traffic in poison with foreign parts. National hatreds are hushed by this all-encompassing impiety; it has become a deadly bond uniting minds otherwise altogether divergent: nor does it even boggle at desecrating the ashes of the dead, of slandering their poor ghosts, in the belief mayhap that it is yet honoring their memory . . .

"You will apprehend this vile trickery, Gentlemen, in two of the works on which we are going to report.

"The seventh and last of the works we are haling into court is the acme of ignominy and scandal and crowning outrage of impiety against state and religion. It has seemed to us deserving of a thorough analysis, not only because it joins together all the blasphemies and absurdities of the six former into an attempted systematic corpus . . . but moreover because the clique of philosophers who have made it their Gospel proudly announces that this new *Système de la Nature* is calculated to destroy all prejudices, recall the whole scheme of things to its primordial state, and restore to the race of men all their rights.

"The unknown author of the *Système de la Nature*, using the name of M. Mirabeau [1770 . . .], does but reiterate the system of Epicurus (the first part). As basis for his atheism, he seems to have made it his business to destroy all accepted principles and revive all those that had been outlawed. His work is divided into two parts; in the first, he examines what is matter and what motion; then he treats of man, his origin and his end; thence he proceeds to the nature of the soul. This discussion leads him to churn up again the notorious controversies of freedom, immortality, the dogma of the life to come, fatalism, necessity, and suicide; he ends with an appraisal of man's duties to his fellows, a specification of the origin of society, and a definition of all the rights of the supreme authority.

"In his second part, the Author treats of religion, of the existence of God, of the proofs of this existence; of Deism and of optimism, of the uselessness of theology, and of the pointlessness of speaking of man's moral duties toward God: and he ends with an apology for the law of nature.

"(b) He concludes that atheism as a system presents no dangers for society; that a natural ethic, laws, politics, a wise government and education suffice to curb the passions; in a word, irreligion is according to him but a vague and figmentary charge and the superstitious man merits the name of *atheist* more than does the materialist.

"The Author ends by characterizing himself in this impious statement, *that the friend of men cannot be the friend of the Gods, who time out of mind have been the real scourges of the earth* (Ch. 14, p. 410) and he rounds off his work with a prayer to Nature which we would do out diligence to adopt were it but addressed to Nature's Author.

"Such, Gentlemen, is a summary of the *Système de la Nature,* this book which a haughty clique is presenting as the masterpiece of the human mind.

"You will tremble with horror, I doubt not, at the mere reminder of the chain of principles of this author and the baneful consequences therefrom deriving . . . he sees nothing, he conceives of nothing beyond physical objects and consequently he disallows all the objects of the intellect. It is by the physics of nature that he wishes to judge of the Author of Nature Himself; and since he so blinds himself as not to conceive a God who would be Creator and beneficent, he does not scruple to conclude that what cannot be conceived cannot exist: a conclusion as weird as it is senseless and inevitably destined to entangle him thereafter in sophism after sophism, blasphemy after blasphemy, until by such a parcel of outrages he sets religion and the law in some sort in plain defiance.

". . . Savagely does he glory in surpassing in audacity Epicurus, Spinoza and all the Philosophers, or rather all the atheists of ages past. These latter did, indeed, wrap up their hateful theories in form symbolic; sometimes even going no further than to express doubt about the existence of the supreme Being, which doubt in itself was a sort of avowal of the Deity. The author of the *Système de la Nature* declares openly and in the most pointed fashion that there is no God and could not be one. His avowed aim is to substantiate materialism and absolute fatalism.

"He wishes to persuade the peoples of all realms that kings have not or can have any other authority over them than that which they have entrusted to them themselves; that these peoples are justified in balancing, moderating and restraining that power and authority, of calling kings to account for their exercise of it, and even of despoiling them of it if they judge it in accord with their own interests so to do. He urges the peoples to make brave use of these alleged rights, and he solemnly warns them there will be no real happiness for them until they shall have set limits upon the power of their Princes and compelled these Princes to be but representatives of the people and executors of the people's will" (Abbé Nonnotte, *Dictionnaire Anti-Philosophique* [Avignon, 1767], pp. 488-492).

The Advocate General concludes on a brave note: "Religion fears only the aberrations of reason, not reason's sincere exertions. It is not opposed to the improvement and perfection of the sciences nor to the development of knowledge in the domain of physics . . ." (*ibid.,* p. 497). And he ends with a prophecy, which sounds somewhat banal against the background of the thunderheads so plainly visible, to the effect that if this sort of thing keeps up there will soon be a revolution (p. 498).

4. *Les Réflexions philosophiques sur "Le Système de la Nature,"* by M. Holland (Paris: Chez Valade, Libraire rue Saint Jacques, 1773).

This work effects a closely-reasoned analytical critique of d'Holbach which seems to us to be still of interest today, being the work of a scholar and scientist (in the Preface, Holland introduces himself as "foreigner and geometrician"). Holland words scrupulously through d'Holbach's two volumes, chapter by chapter, including in text and margin extensive quotations from the original, to which he refers with the meticulosity of a man of science in order to develop his own critique. Here are the main points of that critique:

(I) Critique of the notion of active matter, endowed with necessary motion (Vol. I, pp. 4-17; cf. also Vol. II, pp. 52f.).

(II) Defense of order and finality in nature against "chance" (Vol. I, pp. 25-47) and fatalism (Vol. I, pp. 149).

At the end there is a reference to Locke's hypothesis "that God might have communicated the faculty of thought to matter" (p. 46).

(III) Defense of the spirituality of the soul (pp. 60-101).

On p. 66, Holland reveals himself to be a follower of Descartes "who was the first to attempt to reinstate evidence in philosophy". On p. 77 Holland cites "the author of the book on the Spirit" [Helvétius: *L'Esprit*] whom Holland alleges to have purveyed radical sense-perceptionism even before d'Holbach, on whom Holland has the penetrating remark: "The author simply enunciates the thesis, without adducing even a shadow of a proof. Instead of deducing all the intellectual acts from physical sensibility, he surreptitiously introduces into the brain a new faculty . . . Thus does he deceive his readers" (p. 77f.).

(IV) Critique of an ethic without God and without sanctions (Vol. I. pp. 192-230).

(V) Caveat concerning the critique of the idea of God (Vol. II, pp. 1-19). Here is the nub of Holland's argument on this point: "He claims that by the word GOD we are simply designating the most hidden, remote, unknown cause of the effects that affect our senses. According to him, we make use of this word only when the interplay of natural causes ceases to be visible for us. Whenever we say that God is the author of some phenomenon, claims d'Holbach, it simply means that we do not know how this phenomenon could have been effected by the help of the powers or causes that we know in nature.

"It is not on such bases at all that we establish the existence of God. We designate by this word a necessary and intelligent being, on whom all the other beings depend; the first cause, not only of the metamorphoses of nature but of its existence and its properties as well. It is not at all because we could not explain an event naturally that we say that God is its author: he is the author of all and the cause of the more familiar causes. The point is not that, unless we admit his existence, we would be unable to explain naturally this or that phenomenon; the point is that without him we do not conceive of anything at all. It is not simply that we claim not to know how unintelligent matter and blind motion could produce intelligence and order: it is that we find this positively contradictory and consequently impossible. Even were we to comprehend perfectly the powers of nature, the properties of all the beings nature encloses, the effects that may result from all their possible combinations, this comprehension, far from making us atheists, would but bind us the more firmly to the deity by revealing to us daily new traces of an intelligent, ordering and governing cause of the universe. The author can be challenged to name a single great atheist physicist; yet he would have us believe that advance in the study of nature brings men closer to atheism" (pp. 15f.). On p. 18 are listed as theist scientists Newton, s'Gravesande, Muschenbroek, Haller, Buffon, Bonnet whose defense of Christianity is reported later in the work (Vol. II, p. 153, note; cf. also p. 211).

(VI) Caveat on the abuse of the modern notion of the infinite (Vol. II, pp. 21-47): here Holland the "geometrician" defends against Fontenelle and d'Holbach the purely conventional character of the modern notions of "infinitely large and infinitely small". Holland says he agrees with Locke that the idea of God is not innate but rather derives from reflection and reasoning" (Vol. II, pp. 75f.).

In this refutation of the critique of the proofs of the existence of God, Holland has an interesting remark on a d'Holbach reference to the work of "a famous author" whom he calls Dr. Baumann and of whom he says "after claiming that all the proofs advanced hitherto for the existence of God prove nothing, he substitutes for them his own proofs which are no more convincing". Holland remarks: "I do not know this work at all and I should be quite inclined to believe that the author has mistaken the name and intended to speak of a book by Mr. Kant, professor at Koenigsberg in Prussia" (Vol. II, p. 80).

The author of this work is now known to have been Maupertius, who incidentally was likewise criticized by Voltaire (in the articles Athée, Athéisme, in *Questions*). This vague quotation of Kant, perhaps the first in France, presents a certain interest. The allusion is probably to Kant's *Der einzig mögliche Beweisgrund zu einer Demonstration des Daseins Gottes* (The Only Possible Arguments to Prove the Existence of God) (1763).

(VII) Reference to bad faith and lack of proper understanding in d'Holbach's critique of Clarke (Vol. II, pp. 103f.), of Descartes (p. 109), of Malebranche and of Newton (pp. 110ff.).

(VIII) Reduction of Deism to a sect of atheism (Vol. II, p. 151).

(IX) Mention of impossibility of substantiating a morality or ethic without religion (Vol. II, pp. 177ff.): of note is the correction of d'Holbach's speculation on the Galileo case (pp. 203ff.).

(X) Critique of the thesis of Bayle on the relations between religion and morality (Vol. II, pp. 231ff.), without however any explicit reference to Bayle by name.

II. Condemnation by the French Episcopate

This formal condemnation, promulgated by the French Episcopate in 1763 is noteworthy for the close connection between religion and politics which it expressly professes from beginning to end: religion is throwing its full support to the *status quo*.

Condemnation

Of divers Books against Religion; drawn from the Proceedings of the 1763 General Assembly of the Clergy of France.

Such is the wonderful relation established by Providence between Religion and Society, that the happiness of States doth depend of necessity on the observance of the laws of God: the spirit of submissiveness and obedience which doth fashion the children of God doth likewise fashion loyal Subjects; and the same freedom and looseness of thinking that doth spawn the systems of irreligion doth shake the foundations of the Throne and of authority.

The History of all ages doth witness to this truth and our own age doth feel it but all too sharply. The same spirit that hath dared to question the All-Highest and demand of Him an accounting of his ways, his Judgments and his Oracles, hath right soon commenced to question the Masters of the Earth, to scan the titles of their power, to debate their rights and the principles governing the obedience due them.

A herd of rash writers have trampled under foot the laws of God and man; they have obfuscated the most sacred truths and unsettled the grounds of the Monarchy; they have shown deference for nothing, either in the civil or the spiritual order; they have called in question facts supremely incontrovertible; they have disparaged the wisest Institutions; they have combatted the simplest maxims; they have posed as seeing everywhere only ills to be rectified, changes to be effected, abuses to be reformed. They have presumed to begrudge to the People that pious ingenuousness that guaranteed their faith and their happiness; under pretense of enlightening the common folk, they have striven to seduce them; they have corrupted men's composure by flattering their passions and on the empty pretext of destroying their prejudices. They have been at pains to wipe out of men's minds the faintest trace of reverence and piety, of fear and love of their God, of trust and subjection to their Pastors, of respect and loyal obedience for their Sovereign; in a word, every shred of honor and virtue.

In the midst of this host of enemies, the holy City has not wanted for defenders. Bishops have put the Peoples on their guard by salutary instructions against the enticement threatening them. Able Theologians have written works discomfiting the sophistries of irreligion and civic revolt; the Paris Faculty of Theology has stigmatized with an itemized

Censure several of these impious products; the rights of the Altar and of the Throne have been vindicated; the ill is plainly not past curing; but it is pressing enough to put both Church and State on the alert; nor can it be concealed that the time-honored maxims are flagging in power of persuasion; that the bonds of obedience are slackening; that the majesty of the supreme Being and that of Kings have been and are being scurrilously insulted; that the ardor of piety and patriotism is well-nigh snuffed out in all but a few hearts, and that in the order of the faith, of morals, yea, even of public and civic order, the spirit of the age doth seem to threaten a revolution presaging utter ruin and destruction on every side.

Now therefore it is as Pastors and as Citizens, as Bishops of the Church of God and as members of a body politic of which we have the honor to constitute the first estate, that we deem ourselves obliged to raise our voice against this plethora of impious Works that hath for several years already been being brazenly hawked abroad; nor would we hold ourselves less renegade to the troth we have plighted to our Sovereign than to the vow we have sworn at the foot of our several Altars, were we not to use all the means that are in our power to counteract these felonious folios and the calamities they herald.

Mindful, however, that among such a plethora of devil's spawn there are a parcel most mortally effective, whether because gilded with greater glamor on account of the charm of novelty or the magnetism of style or the lamentable fame of their Authors, or whether because replete with principles more perverse and marks of an impiety more shocking; and that such works are for that very reason deserving of a special branding.

Mindful, moreover, of the fact that these Works are not merely blemished here and there with propositions worthy of condemnation, but are rotten to the core, and that they are entirely permeated with the sole aim of attacking the Christian Religion, the grounds of morality and the foundations of the fabric of States;

WE Archbishops and Bishops delegated by the Clergy of France and assembled in the Couvent des Grands-Augustins, edified and prompted by the examples of the venerable men who have gone before us in the Episcopate, having maturely examined the matter and invoked the holy Name of God, have condemned and do condemn all the Works that have been writ in these latter times against the Christian Religion, the rule of right conduct, and the foundation of the obedience due the Sovereign; and especially the books entitled, L'ANALYSE DE BAYLE, LE LIVRE DE L'ESPRIT, LE DICTIONNAIRE ENCYCLOPEDIQUE, EMILE AND THE WORKS WRIT IN DEFENSE THEREOF, LE CONTRAT SOCIAL, LES LETTRES DE LA MONTAGNE, L'ESSAI SUR L'HISTOIRE GENERALE, LE DICTIONNAIRE PHILOSOPHIE, LA PHILOSOPHIE DE L'HISTOIRE, LE DESPOTISME ORIENTAL . . . as containing principles respectively false, injurious to God and his majestic attributes, calculated to promote Atheism, full of the poison of Materialism, destructive of the rule of right conduct, studying to confound vice and virtue, potent to breach the peace of families, to snuff out the sentiments that unite them, sanctioning all passions and disorders of every ilk, destructive of revelation, calculated to instill scorn and contempt for Holy Writ, to topple their authority, to strip the Church of the power she hath received of JESUS CHRIST, and to discredit her Ministers, apt to rouse Subjects to revolt against their Sovereigns, to foment seditions and uproars. We do brand these Works scandalous, temerarious, impious, blasphemous, and do declare them to be as offensive to God's Majesty as they are harmful to the well-being of Empires and Societies.

And in consequence, we forbid, under the penalties of the law, to all the Faithful committed to our care and charge, to read or retain the said books and any others like them, exhorting them to remember that this prohibition is less a salutary warning than a necessary information concerning an essential duty of their calling; that he who flirts with danger will perish in it; and that it is already to incur the guilt of sin to allow themselves, out of simple curiosity, to read things capable of snuffing out faith, corrupting morals, and breaching the peace of the State.

III. Condemnation of Helvétius' De L'Esprit

The great echo that must have been roused by Helvétius' first work and the great influence it must have exerted are witnessed to by the condemnation promulgated by the Archbishop of Paris, the zealous Christopher de Beaumont, on November 22, 1758. We here present the most notable excerpts from this document:

SUMMONS *of His Excellency the Archbishop of Paris, bearing Condemnation of a Book entitled* DE L'ESPRIT.

"Such things, my dear Brethren, are the black fumes of Hell, the works of the Prince of Darkness; and we sorrow to see their traces all too clearly in a Book in wide circulation among the flock committed to our charge and care. The great distance that separates us from our Diocese hath not allowed us to raise our voice the moment that this mischievous Work, entitled *De l'Esprit,* saw the light. We got to know of it only in the wake of the scandalized uproar it occasioned in the Capital and in the chief towns and cities of the Realm. Then was our pastoral heart sore stricken and we desired the tears of *Jeremiah* to render satisfaction to the Divine Majesty outraged by so bold a thrust against Him.

But our sorrow would fall short of the mark were it to remain bottled up within our proper bosom. We must share it with you, dear Brethren, and at the same time forewarn you against the enticement. The ill being one that presseth sore and there being need for instant remedy to avert the danger, we shall not undertake a detailed instruction on the matter. We shall but speak out the main points that make the book *De l'Esprit* reprehensible in the extreme, and then we shall hasten on to pronounce upon it the anathema it hath so justly deserved.

Saint Augustine doth observe that the Enemy of our salvation is at one and the same time a roaring Lion attacking head-on and a tortuous Serpent setting ambushes. Such too are his emissaries. *Celsus* fought Christianity openly, *Hobbes* disguised his abominable system. The book *De l'Esprit* useth alternately boldness and cunning against the holy Religion we profess. Now it doth seem that the desire is to subjugate the Reign of JESUS CHRIST by force and to establish upon its ruins the Passions, purely human Laws, profane Philosophy; now a more circumspect course is pursued, respect is shown to the Gospel, a pretense is made to acknowledge its gentleness and beauty, a claim is made of being able to *raise the soul to sanctity* (*De l'Esprit,* in 4, p. 232). This is insidious talk, my dear Brethren! Fundamentally this book doth breathe but hatred for Christianity, but the fixed purpose of snuffing out in all minds the Divine light of which JESUS CHRIST Himself is the Author.

. . . The Author of the Book that doth this day stir up our pastoral zeal to combat it is a professed Partisan of the *Philosophy* of the age. He often complaineth, and with all the liveliness of a personal interest, of what he doth call the *harangues against the Philosophers* (Page 180). He accuseth the *Devout* of hating Philosophy and taxes them on this count with *bigotry* and *Fanaticism* (Pages 560, 561, 564). He doth not doubt a whit but that the Philosophers of today be *men of genius;* he defendeth them, flattereth them, heapeth praises upon them. He protesteth violently against them that hold back the *progress* of Philosophy, etc.

. . . Thus when the Author of the *Book De l'Esprit* doth promise us to widen our lights, to develop for us the principles of morality, to acquaint us with the springs of good lawgiving, to open up to us the road of happiness, to make us useful to society, and the rest, let us see if these instructions he would give us do agree with the deposit whose preservation ought to be infinitely dear to us; let us try if this proferred knowledge doth square with the Gospel. But what indeed could be imagined more altogether contrary?

It sufficeth for you to be persuaded of this that you call to mind that this pernicious Work (*De l'Esprit*) doth but proclaim and breathe forth a drastic indifference to all Religion. How often are not Religions in general, and consequently that only true one, spoken of therein as mere *opinions!* What pains are not taken to exalt the alleged wisdom of those who pass for Atheists or Materialists! What care is not devoted to giving the Reader to understand that *the hope or the fear of temporal pains or pleasures are as apt to mould virtuous men as are the eternal pains and pleasures!* (pp. 58, 68, 109, 233).

But are we not mistaken, my dear Brethren, if we think such features do but evidence an indifference toward Religion? Do they not rather comprise principles in formal opposition to all manner of religious practice? And if one but placeth beside these several passages those wherein the Author cometh out strong for universal tolerance, those wherein he inveighs indiscriminately and unrestrainedly against all who are Intolerant, those wherein he doth plainly show a mighty store of spite against the Ministers of the Church, those wherein he sniggeringly reports choice tidbits most insulting of Religion, those wherein he subverteth, so far as in him lies, the whole ethic of the Gospel, can one refrain from acknowledging that this Book *exalteth itself against the knowledge of God?* (2 Cor. 10, 5).

. . . It is indeed surprising, my dear Brethren, that the Unbelievers of today, jealous as they are of the title of Philosopher, should attach themselves to a theory so monstrous as is Materialism. A hundred times hath the horror and absurdity of this system been expounded. The spirituality of our soul hath been proven by the consciousness that we have of thought; by the faculty that dwelleth in us to make judgments, to effect reasonings, to entertain desires, doubts, resolutions; by the liveliness wherewith we compare our ideas, our sensations, our memories; by the advantage we possess of being able to raise ourselves to the knowledge of God, of virtue, of the law, of merit, and of all the purely intellectual objects altogether; by the freedom of will and choice inseparably attached to our nature. And this necessary love of existence, this overriding eagerness we have for glory, this fierce cry of all our faculties for the possession of a happiness without bounds and without vicissitudes—are they not so many earnests and pledges of a life to come, so many sensible and substantial witnesses to the immortality of the soul? Arguments infallible in themselves and which did always present themselves to the human understanding, even unto the midst of the darkness of Idolatry! With what joy do they not inundate those hearts that grace hath detached from the world!

Yet doth this Book *De l'Esprit* (pp. 5, 32, 2) come to rob us of this potent bulwark and this sweet consolation. It commences by calling in question the spirituality of the soul; it seemeth to admit only accidental differences of build and conformation of organs between man and beast: a fancy that fifteen centuries ago did enter the mind of the great adversary of the Christian Religion, the impious *Celsus.* He used to say that there was no essential difference between man and bee and that this could be judged from their respective labors. To which *Origen* did reply that man operates by reason and the beast by instinct: (*Orig. Lib. IV contr. Cels.*), which doth signify that man hath within him the consciousness of his purely spiritual action, whereas the same thing cannot be asserted with certainty of the beast whose nature is unknown to us.

The Author of the *Book De l'Esprit* soon passes from pure problematic to positive assertions: he speaks always of the soul as a being that hath but *physical sensibility* (page 293.328. 371); he admits only force and motion in this power; he makes it subject like the body to *attractions* and *inertias;* he showeth himself not to believe it capable of loving God nor yet of possessing Him, for he advanceth this strange proposition; *that man being by his nature sensible only to the pleasures of the senses, these pleasures are consequently the sole object of his desires* (page 326). What a notion, my dear Brethren! It doth destroy altogether at once the spirituality of the soul and its immortality; it debaseth man to the state of the animals; it doth limit all his prospects to the goods of his life. And what goods moreover! They will not be either the beauties of virtue, nor the riches of scientific knowledge, nor yet the delights of friendship, nor the glory of service to country, nor any of the like. All will be limited to the *pleasures of the senses,* the satisfaction of earthly desires.

. . . . It is not, my dear Brethren, that human Laws, Politics, Jurisprudence and the like cannot and ought not to co-operate in the governance of men; but these means ought always to be sub-ordinate to Religion: without Religion, these means are but a tissue of artifices, useless and even dangerous in a thousand ways. Take away Religion and all the power of the Law-makers is limited to the external forum, as the Author of *De l'Esprit* doth indeed likewise claim.

But the principles of his Book go further still: they are those of *Hobbes;* they tend to destroy all the foundations of Justice and probity; to wipe out all notions hitherto entertained concerning virtue and the duties virtue doth impose. According to this dangerous Moralist, *Physical sensibility and personal interest have been the authors of all justice; interest is the sole Judge of probity and of merit among men: if personal interest be lost sight of, there remains no clear idea of probity: the moral Universe is subject to the Law of personal interest even as the Physical Universe is subject to the Laws of motion: before the foundation of Societies, there was no Law . . . nor consequently any injustice: virtue is the desire for the general happiness; Justice consists in the meticulous observance of the conventions established by the common interest* (pp. 276, 48, 55, 127, 53, 279, 134, and 278).

Thus, my dear Brethren, there will subsist no primordial distinction, based and grounded on the eternal Law of God itself, between the Just and the Unjust; there will be no natural obligation to practice certain duties and to avoid certain faults. All lawgiving with regard to men will depend upon their union into society and on the will of the first Chiefs who will have brought them thus together. If anyone incurreth the guilt of some injustice, he will be able to be subjected to the penalties assigned by the Lawgivers; but for the rest, there will be no cry of conscience, no fear of falling into the hands of the Supreme Judge of all things. If he find any motives of integrity, of charity, of magnanimity, for undertaking virtuous actions, these will consist in knowing if the private or public interest doth display itself in his enterprises; this interest will be the driving power of everything, the sole judge of merit, the absolute cause, and the whole springboard and motive of these actions.

. . . . What weapons yet would not be furnished to us by the sacred memorials of Christianity against the pernicious rules of Morality proclaimed by this Work? As we have already hinted, my dear Brethren, in the Book *De l'Esprit,* the basis of morals is *pleasure* (Pages 361 ff.), not excluding the most fleshly, the most shameful, the most unworthy of man. The Author doth propose profane love as the great mainspring of virtues; he doth recall, in this connection, under the eyes of his Reader, the licentious practices of certain idolatrous peoples; nor doth he blush at all to string together a parcel of obscene Anecdotes, indecent Pictures, scandalous Maxims. O execrable Philosophy of our poor century; this is then your term, say rather this is the precipice whereto you lead men! What, my dear Brethren, these passions that JESUS CHRIST and the Holy Apostles have commanded us to fight, to curb, to mortify, are going to be represented to us as the very soul of all the great and heroic actions? This unhappy fruit of sin, this seed of corruption, that makes the greatest Saints to weep, is being touted before us as the universal mainspring of the governance of men? Nor is this held to be enough; reason is even in some sense condemned to be silent in the presence of the passions, to cede to them the Dominion, at least during the greater part of our days.

For here, my dear Brethren, are the astonishing propositions to be found in the book *De l'Esprit. That reason should govern and direct us in the important actions of life, this I wish to see; but let a man give over the details of his tastes and his passions. He who would consult reason on everything, would be incessantly busied calculating what he ought to do and would never do anything* (p. 618). And in the matter of elementary training, of education of youth, the Author findeth of great advantage the method of *not opposing the passions at all* (p. 337) that belong to this first age of man. Those *who do not cease to recommend the moderation of the desires* (p. 373), he doth brand as *Pedants, Haranguers, Men without Wit* (p. 164). He pretendeth that *he who, in order to be virtuous, would ever have to be mastering his inclinations, would of necessity be a honest man;* and instead of conserving due respect for the sex whose finest ornament is modesty, he seems to invite them to jump all barriers, he furnishes them with examples, he arms them with pretexts, he maketh the apology of excesses in this kind. How many of his lines, my dear Brethren, we are obliged to suppress, so as to spare your ears the danger-full details, expressions apt to effect a lesion of public decency.

Likewise must we needs be silent on those passages in this Book where the Realm is affrighted and the Citizens set on edge. How now! Was there any need, in conscience, in treating of *the power of the passions* (Page 298ff. and Page 223) to conjure up men *defying Heaven* and in arms against their Sovereigns? Was there any need to seek out of Antiquity acts better consigned to the eternal oblivion they merit, heinous crimes whose Authors were but madmen or ungodly? But behold, my dear Brethren, yet this further operation of the proud Philosophy of our age: it doth accustom those who give themselves over to it to call in question the rights of the Powers That Be, after having contended against those of the Deity. The same Writers who deny the immortality of the soul, the life to come, the foundations of morals, do undertake likewise to break asunder the ties that bind Subjects to their Masters. The attack is not launched openly, it is true, upon the immediate Superior; objects of criticism are sought in Religions far distant; the remarks, or say better the invectives, seem to be limited to governments which are passing away or which are branded as allegedly despotic. But in these temerarious discussions, there is all too much manifest evidence of sentiments of independence and even of rebellion, for which a prepossession has been allowed to burgeon, against anyone who doth bear the insignia of the Supreme Power. Soon boldness is pushed to the point of presenting in a favorable light such men as have mournfully distinguished themselves by shocking thrusts and politics of daggers. Without scruple, such are represented as uncommon titans, as mighty minds: and what impressions may not such pictures make upon Readers too gullible or already inflamed!

The book *De l'Esprit* is deserving of strong reproaches on a point we do but indicate here. It contains a doctrine right opposed to that of the great Apostle, who teacheth us that *there is no power but from God; that it is He that hath established all those powers that be on earth; that therefore he that resisteth the Powers That Be resisteth the ordinance of God and doth draw down upon himself damnation; . . . that it is therefore necessary to be subject to these Powers, not merely out of fear of chastisement, but also for conscience' sake.* (Rom. XIII, 2.5.)

Such, my dear Brethren, are the true rules of conduct; nor can we too insistently recommend to you a regard for them and the practice of them; but to abide within the bounds of this humble and Christian subjection and submissiveness, it must be well apprehended that the peace and well-being of States doth thereon depend, that even the safety of the Individual is bound up therewith; that JESUS CHRIST, the model of all the virtues, hath set an example of the most perfect submission with respect to all the Powers That Be; that the Apostles and Martyrs obeyed the most unjust commands and the cruellest persecutors; that it never belongeth to Subjects to judge their Masters and that any deviations of this sort are sheer usurpations of the authority of God Himself, Who alone can demand of Princes an accounting of their stewardship.

Beware likewise, my dear Brethren, in all your reflections on what doth touch the Realm and the Government, of adopting a right pernicious principle of the Book *De l'Esprit. What matters to the General Public,* says this Book, *the probity of a Private Person? This probity is well-nigh pointless so far as the General Public is concerned.* (Page 81). What, my dear Brethren, is not every Private Person a Member of Society, and consequently of the General Public, of the Body Politic? If each Private Person is without probity, can the Body Politic be without vice? And if each Private Person is a decent man, can the Body Politic fail to be virtuous? When JESUS CHRIST and his Holy Disciples did recommend the virtues, and the greatest of these which is charity, did they not profess to be establishing the foundations of the public weal? and when *St. Augustine* voucheth that *what constitutes the righteousness and justice of any society whatsoever is simply obeying God,* doth he not signify that if all Private Persons practice this holy obedience, the whole of the Society will be deemed faithful to those things God wills, and will thereby possess *Justice?*

This sufficeth, my dear Brethren, upon this all too famous Book *De l'Esprit.* We repeat that the present Instruction is neither a detailed analysis nor yet a sustained analysis thereof: much less is it a complete refutation thereof. There are in this deplorable Work a host of other points that would merit the strict attention of our zeal. There are utterances wanting in truth and wanting in propriety concerning certain passages of Scripture, concerning the Fathers and the Councils: there are reckless or malicious slurs on the Sacred Vows and Monastic commitments: there are panegyrics accorded certain Books and certain opinions which are most suspect, to say the least, in matters of Religion: there are subtle and cunning efforts to distinguish the function of the Philosopher from that of the Theologian: efforts whose aim is to provide a pretext for attacking Christianity while seeming to remain within the bounds of pure Philosophy. And a thousand other points, altogether reprehensible, might give rise to a large-scale Theological Work, whose structure, scope and utility we can but adumbrate in most general outline.

. . . Finally, my dear Brethren, forget not, I charge you, before our Lord CHRIST, the Author of the Book that gives us occasion to speak to you. Though the duty of our Ministry doth compel us to raise our voice against his pernicious Work, his person remains ever most dear to us, and we cherish a most particular interest in his salvation. He has indeed, by his retraction, taken a step which we must reckon to his credit: a step nevertheless which could and ought to have been more clear-cut and unstinting. Let us fervently desire that he may add all the marks and all the works of a sincere and edifying conversion. The Book whereof he is the Author doth render him most culpable in the eyes of God and men. By publishing it, he hath sown into the world the seed of a seduction whose further course it is not even in his power to arrest. The consequences of a Work that doth injure Religion and Morals are as it were eternal; such a work is a charnel smell that doth infect the whole of posterity; it is a weed accursed that doth choke out from age to age the good grain sown in the field by the Master of the Household. But, my dear Brethren, the great mercies of the Lord do burst forth in splendor when the fault is great. By coming to himself again and giving public marks and evidence of a humble and submissive, constant and zealous faith, the Author of the Book *De l'Desprit* will fill with joy the true Faithful, confound the stiff-necked Unbelievers, disabuse those who shall have had the misfortune to allow themselves to be seduced.

. . .

For His Excellency
DE LA TOUCHE

(Included as Appendix in the *Dictionnaire Anti-Philosophique,* pp. 395-413).

The text of Helvétius' recantation of the theories of *De l'Esprit,* spoken of in the 1763 Decree, has been preserved. This text is recorded in the *Dictionnaire Anti-Philosophique* in the article *Helvét:* "M. Helvét **, being informed that the High Court was proceeding to the condemnation of his book, felt obliged to present a Petition which was submitted to the Office of the Clerk of the Court. In it he said that 'the more he reflects on the misfortune he has had of composing his book entitled *de l'Esprit,* the more he must fear that he has not sufficiently explained himself by his previous recantations and declarations; that in consequence he feels himself obliged to seek to dissipate, as much as in him lies, even the faintest vestige of doubt upon the sincerity of his sorrow and his repentance. That he petitions that it may please the Court to take cognizance of the fact that he disavows, detests and retracts formally and exactly all the errors with which his Book is filled; to take cognizance likewise of the fact that he professes and will always profess the truths contrary to the said errors, submitting himself in all things to the judgment which shall be pronounced by the Court, beseeching It most humbly to be pleased to consider that his fault came rather from an aberration of the mind than from an aberration of the heart' " (p. 132).

A statement along the same lines was submitted to M. Tercier, censor of the book. The posthumous publication of *De l'Homme* was to show that Helvétius' opinions had remained unchanged in every particular. The only thing lacking had been the courage to profess them openly.

IV. Decree of the High Court

The condemnations promulgated by the Paris High Court are official documents on unbelief and atheism. We here present some excerpts taken from the Appendix of the *Dictionnaire Anti-Philosophique:*

DECREE OF THE HIGH COURT *of 6 February 1739, condemning divers Books to be torn up and burned by the Lord High Executioner.*

". . . The Court doth order that the Books entitled *De l'Esprit, le Pyrrhonisme du Sage, la Philosophie du bon sens, la Religion naturelle, Lettres Semi-philosophiques, Etrennes des Esprits forts,* and *Lettre au R. P. Berthier sur le Matérialisme,* shall be torn up and burned in the Palace Courtyard, at the foot of the grand staircase of the same, by the Lord High Executioner; doth forbid all persons, of whatsoever quality and condition, to compose, approve, print or cause to be printed and distributed, any Books, Writings or Pamphlets under any title whatsoever, against Religion, the State of morality, on pain of extraordinary prosecution and punishment to the extreme limits of the law; doth order that it be informed, on demand of the Prosecutor of the Realm, before the Recording Magistrate as regards the Witnesses there shall be in this City, and before the Bailiffs Lieutenant of the Bailiwicks and local Seneschal's Courts and other Judges of crown cases, at the instance of the Deputies of the Prosecutor of the Realm, as regards the witnesses there shall be in the aforesaid places against the Authors, Printers and distributors of the said Books having as titles: *le Pyrrhonisme du Sage, la Philosophie du bon sens, la Religion naturelle, Lettres Semi-philosophiques, Etrennes des Esprits forts,* and *Lettre au R. P. Berthier;* doth enjoin upon all such as shall have Copies of these Works, together with the one entitled *De l'Esprit,* to submit them forthwith to the Office of the Clerk of the Court, there to be suppressed; doth most expressly prohibit and restrain Durand Libraire and all others from reprinting, selling or retailing the Said Books, and all Hawkers and Distributors from vending or distributing them, all such restraints being under pain of extraordinary prosecution and punishment to the extreme limit of the Law. And having regard to the petitions of the said Helvétius and Tercier, and exercising leniency in their regard, doth take cognizance to the said Helvétius of the fact that he doth disavow, detest and retract formally and exactly all the errors with which his Book is filled, and doth likewise take cognizance to him of the fact that he professes and will always profess the truths contrary to the said errors, submitting himself in all things to the judgment which shall be pronounced by the Court, beseeching It most humbly to be pleased to consider that his fault came rather from an aberration of the mind than from an aberration of the heart; and to the said Tercier, of the fact that he disavows and detests all errors with which the said Book (*De l'Esprit*) is filled, and retracts formally the approval he did subjoin to the said Book, declaring that he doth make and will make his whole life long profession of the truths contrary to the said errors, and that it was by inadvertence that he did approve the said Book, and was the occasion of its being printed, that he doth most humbly beseech the Court to exercise leniency in his regard, declaring moreover that he doth so repent him of his fault that he hath the firm intention nevermore henceforth to undertake the examination or approval of any Books whatsoever" (pp. 417f.).

(There follows the condemnation of the first seven volumes of the *Encyclopedia,* to be dealt with in a special Decree a month later that same year, on 8 March. Cf. pp. 419f.). Among the Decrees of the same year are likewise the condemnation of Voltaire's abridged commentary on Ecclesiastes and the Song of Songs (*Précis de l'Ecclésiaste et du Cantique des Cantiques,* par M. de Voltaire, imprimé à Genève, chez les Frères Cramer, 1759), which is branded ". . . an unfaithful, misleading and licentious version . . . composed in a spirit contrary to that of Religion" (p. 421).

The condemnation of Rousseau's *Emile* deserves to be quoted in full (pp. 422-425):

DECREE OF THE HIGH COURT, Condemning *Emile* or *de l'Education,* by *Jean Jacques Rousseau,* to be torn up and burned by the Lord High Executioner.

This day, the Officers of the King did come in, and M. Omer-Joly de Fleury, Counsel of the said King's Majesty acting as spokesman, did say:

That they were submitting to the Court a printed work in four volumes, *in-octavo,* entitled *Emile, or de l'Education,* by J. J. Rousseau, Citizen of Geneva, described as printed in the Hague, in M. DCC. LXII (1762):

That this Word seemeth to have been composed with the sole purpose in mind of reducing all things to natural Religion, and that the Author is at pains to develop this criminal system in the plan of Education which he doth pretend to give his Pupil;

That he doth pretend to instruct this Pupil only according to nature which is his sole guide, in order to mould him into a moral man, that he doth regard all Religions as equally good and as severally able to be explained in terms of the atmosphere, Government, ethnic genius or other such considerations of time and place;

That he doth limit man to the knowledge that instinct doth lead him to seek out, doth flatter the passions as the chief instruments of our preservation, doth advance the thesis that a man may be saved without believing in God in that he doth admit an invincible ignorance of the Deity that can excuse man; that according to his principles reason alone is judge in the choice of a Religion, to which faculty of reason he doth leave the choice of the nature of the worship that man ought to render to the supreme Being Whom this Author thinketh to honor by speaking irreverently of the external worship He hath established in Religion or which the Church hath prescribed under the direction of the Holy Spirit Who doth govern her;

That in consequence of his system that doth admit only natural Religion, whatever it may be among the various Peoples, he doth presume to attempt to destroy the truth of Holy Scripture and of the Prophecies; the certainty of the miracles delivered in the Sacred Books, the infallibility of revelation, the authority of the Church; and that, by reducing everything to this natural Religion, wherein he doth admit but a worship and laws that shall be at the discretion of each one severally, he doth undertake not only to justify all Religions, all of which he doth pretend to be equally efficacious to salvation, but even to vindicate unbelief and recusancy as fitting for any man faced with an attempted proof of the Divinity of JESUS CHRIST and of the existence of the Christian Religion, which alone hath God as its Author, and in regard to which the writer doth carry his blasphemy to the point of making it out to be absurd, and contradictory, and of instilling a sacrilegious indifference for its mysteries and for its dogmas, the which he would fain be able utterly to destroy;

That such are the impious and detestable principles that this Writer doth set himself to establish in this Work, wherein he doth subject Religion to the examination of reason, establishing nothing more than a purely human faith and not admitting of any truths or dogmas in matters religious than such as it shall please the mind given over to its proper lights, or rather to its aberrations, to receive or reject;

That to these impieties he doth add indecent details, explanations that offend propriety and modesty, propositions calculated to make the sovereign authority seem other than what it is, and odious to boot, to destroy the foundation of the obedience that is due to that authority, and to weaken the respect and love of the Peoples for their Kings;

That they, the King's Officers, are persuaded that these marks suffice to give the Court an idea of the Work they are denouncing before it; that the maxims that are scattered through the Work amount as a whole to a fanciful system, as impracticable in its execution as it is absurd and damnable in its conception. For what would Subjects educated in such maxims amount to, if not men engrossed in scepticism and indifferentist tolerance, given over to their passions, surrendered to the pleasures of the senses, self-centred in conceit and self-esteem, recognizing no other voice than that of nature, and supplanting the noble desire of solid fame and well-founded honor by the pernicious mania for eccentricity? What rules for good conduct! What total losses for Religion and the State, the poor pupils trained in principles as appalling to the Citizen as to the Christian!;

That the Author of this Book having brazenly blazoned forth his proper name cannot be too promptly prosecuted; that it is important, since he hath made himself known, that the Law set about forthwith making an example both of the Author and of such as it shall be able to discover to have co-operated either in the printing or in the distribution of such a Work worthy, like them, of the full rigor of the Law;

That this is the purport of the findings in writing the which they are leaving with the Court together with a copy of the Book.

And the King's Officers withdrew.

They having withdrawn:

After an inspection of the Book in four Volumes in-8° entitled: *Emile, ou de l'Education, par J. J. Rousseau, Citoyen de Genève. Sanabilibus aegrotamus malis; ipsaque nos in rectum, natura genitos, si emendari velimus juvat. Senec. de Irâ. Lib. XI. cap. XIII, tom. 1. 2. 3. et 4. A la Haye, chez Jean Neaulme, Libraire, avec Privilége de Nosseigneurs les Etats de Hollande et Westfrise:* and having heard the summing up of the Prosecutor of the Realm and the Report of M. Pierre-François Lenoir, Magistrate; and having taken the matter under advisement:

The Court doth order that the said printed Book shall be torn up and burned in the Palace Courtyard, at the foot of the grand staircase of the same, by the Lord High Executioner; doth enjoin upon all such as shall have Copies of this Work to submit them forthwith to the Office of the Clerk of the Court, there to be suppressed; doth most expressly prohibit and restrain all Publishers from printing, selling or retailing the said Book, and all Hawkers as Distributors or other person or persons from vending or distributing them, under pain of extraordinary prosecution and punishment to the extreme limit of the Law; doth further order that it be informed, on demand of the Prosecutor of the Realm, before the Recording Magistrate as regards the Witnesses there shall be in Paris, and before the Bailiffs Lieutenant of the Bailiwicks and local Seneschal's Courts, as regards the Witnesses there shall be outside of the aforesaid City, against the Authors, Printers or distributors of the said Book; in regard to the intelligences made, reported and communicated to the Prosecutor of the Realm, being by him demanded and the Court, this Court doth ordain what shall be needful; and in the meantime doth order that the said J. J. Rousseau, named on the Frontispiece of the said Book, shall be seized and arrested and taken to the Cells of the Palace Keep, to be heard and questioned before the said Examining Magistrate upon the facts of the said Book, and to answer to the proceedings that the Prosecutor of the Realm doth intend to take against him; and in the event that the said J. J. Rousseau be not able to be seized and arrested, after search having been made for his Person, he being summoned to appear within the fortnight, his goods shall be seized and impounded and sequestered to the members of this Commission, until such time as he shall have obeyed the summons of the Law; and to this end doth order that a Copy of the said Book shall be deposited in the Office of the Clerk of the Court, to be used in the Institution of Proceedings. And the Court doth further order that the present Decree be printed, published and posted up on display in all places needful wheresoever. Done in the High Court, the Ninth of June, 1762.

Signed: DUFRANC

At the beginning of the *Dictionnaire Anti-Philosophique* (pp. XV-XX), we find the condemnation of Voltaire's *Dictionnaire* and of Rousseau's *Lettres de la Montagne,* against which the whole of the *Dictionnaire Anti-Philosophique* is directed. Here is the text of the condemnation of Rousseau's *Lettres de la Montagne:*

DECREE OF THE HIGH COURT, Condemning *le Dictionnaire Philosophique portatif;* and *les Lettres écrites de la Montagne,* by *Jean Jacques Rousseau, First and Second Part,* to be torn up and burned by the Lord High Executioner.

This day, all the Chambers being assembled, the King's Officers did come in, and M. Omer-Joly de Fleury, Counsel of the said King's Majesty acting as spokesman, did say:

GENTLEMEN,

If the erroneous Philosophy that doth presently cast so much depravity upon morals hath not been sufficiently enlightened or hath not enough good faith to abjure its errors, it yet ought at least to batten in silence upon its chimeras and its absurdities. That it might grow insensibly and make Converts, it had first walked by murky byways and used expedients not all the world could fathom; you have nonetheless stopped it in its tracks; and its sallies capable of deceiving your vigilance have not escaped your shrewd eye; it is strange that today it doth shake off shamelessly the veil under which it had hitherto disguised its progress and lift its head brazenly to show itself for what it is; that it doth loudly utter iniquity, open its mouth against Heaven, and study to disseminate the more readily throughout the whole earth the poison of the unbelief of its mind and the libertinage of its heart. This is the only goal that could have been envisaged by the *Dictionnaire Philosophique portatif,* and this excess is the presumptuous advantage taken of the reign of a Prince who doth but seek, in his governance of his Peoples, to strengthen in their heart true doctrine and sound morals.

Were the Author known, this Work would not seem to you any the more worthy of the strictest penalties. What madness hath not taken possession of some minds in our days? What fruit do they think to cull from their impious teaching, lashing even man's common humanity? What is the point of this Dictionary? It presents the dogmas of Religion as mere novelties insinuated by the changing seasons; it derides the discipline and usages of the Church; it destroys the Sacred Scriptures and the whole of Revelation; it attempts to sap the very foundations of the Catholic Religion; it denies the Divinity of JESUS CHRIST; it does not tremble nor blush to treat as pure fable what the Gospel Writers report of Him, nor yet to give out as a mere human institution the faith and discipline of the Church; nor yet to make over into mere superstition the Sacraments and the cult of the Saints. It reports the allegories and figures that are to be met with in the Sacred Scriptures but it hides from the Readers the object of the allegories, the truths and the facts reported thus allegorically and rendering the report and its accuracy patent to every reader.

It lays bare the contradictions between the sacred Writers, concealing most assiduously the while those explanations that reconcile most satisfactorily these apparent contradictions. It presumes to falsify the Texts of Scripture, and it gives inaccurate versions of the same; it even makes additions calculated to deceive the inattentive Reader; it shows no respect for the Writings of the Fathers and carries boldness and rashness to the limit of presuming to cast a film of ignorance and absurdity and even imbecility over such renowned and famous men as the *Augustines* and the *Chrysostoms.,* etc.

No more miracles; the Author holds that it is an insult to God even to presume them. No more original sin in man; no more freedom for his will; no more Providence, general or particular: matter is eternal in its own right: there is no certitude saving that of Physics and Mathematics: the hope of a life to come is but an illusion, man perishing altogether; abuse heaped upon acts consecrated by Religion; Divine and human Laws equally scorned; Religions presented as climatically conditioned. All the Laws of Physics are reckoned out for the meridian inhabited by the Individual, and the Rites of Religion are held to be of the same nature. There is a superifical admission of a natural Religion wherein some sort of God, yea any sort, is admitted; but what religion and what God, one may well inquire, forasmuch as the Author claims that man has no idea of God and cannot know Him, nor yet ought to give Him any worship, on the pretext that He has no need of us?

Mysteries, Dogmas, Morality, Discipline, Worship, Truth of Religion, divine and human Authority, all alike are at the mercy of the sacrilegious pen of this Author, who glories in classing himself with the brutes by lowering man to their level through his refusal to admit any happiness saving that of the senses and his insistence that man perishes altogether, just like the brutes.

And what means are used to tempt men to adopt these errors? Ridicule, jesting, doubts, sophisms, objections, difficulties, blasphemies even, repeated a thousand times over by the impious and the irreligious for eighteen centuries now and a thousand times refuted, resolved so powerfully and patently as to lend to that refutation the genuine mark of truth, incapable of making any real impression save on such as neglect to inform themselves properly or such as have some sort of personal interest in allowing themselves to be seduced and in deluding themselves.

Such is the Work which the Republic of Geneva has already condemned to the flames, and which no civilized State, even such as hath not the advantage we have of being within the bosom of the Catholic

Church, can fail to proscribe, there being no Society with whose interests licence, civic revolt and irreligion stand not in contradiction. Can one wonder that the Laws governing the various States are not any longer respected by this Author, and that that law especially which for so many centuries doth assure the Sceptre and Crown to the eldest son of our Kings should likewise be the object of his mocking banter?

To this first Work we shall join another entitled: *Lettres écrites de la Montagne,* etc. in two Parts. In the first Part, the Author is at pains to defend his former Works, and especially his *Emile,* against the ban pronounced by the Council of the Republic of Geneva: unhappily stiff-necked in the system he hath adopted, far from profitting from the censures passed upon him, from making candid avowal of the errors of which he hath been convicted and from detesting those errors, he doth rather reiterate all his impious and detestable principles against the Catholic Religion and against JESUS CHRIST Himself, its founder, against Revelation and the Sacred Scriptures, against the Miracles, and indeed all the other errors which, taken severally and together, have so justly shocked and aroused the indignation of all such as have read *Emile.* To these impieties he doth add new blasphemies which we dare not repeat and which do advertise one of these pound Philosophers who resist the truth by opposing to it their own illusions, men corrupt in mind and perverted from the Faith, but whose forward march will have its limits, for their folly shall be known to the whole world.

What more heinous and shameful abuse of mind and talents can be imagined! Religion will always have its *Celsuses,* its *Julians,* its *Sociniuses,* its *Bayles,* in a word those madmen who will blaspheme against Religion and against its divine Author: but woe to these men, who puffed up with their project of erecting a school of error and iniquities and therein perpetuating the race of the impious, do heap upon themselves the horror and the execration of wise and virtuous men of all ages and all Lands.

[Such Philosophers, says one of the great Orators of Holland, are the very ones who preen themselves most on their *distinction and good manners* and it is often simply the wrong ideas they have conceived on this score that propel them into the system of unbelief: they find, says he, that reason is too redolent of the Schoolmen and that faith is pedantic: they believe that, in order to distinguish themselves in the world, they must affect not to believe at all and not to reason at all. Let them learn of this famous man that they are regarded by the work as madmen: they are living with persons who believe in a God and a Religion, with persons who have been brought up in these pinciples: moreover they are living in a Society whose foundations are going to collapse together with those of Religion; so that if they manage to undermine these latter, they are going to be undermining, by that very fact, the former as well: all the Members of Society are interested in the maintenance of this edifice *they* want to destroy . . . The whole World doth conjure them not to establish this system, the mere acquaintance wherewith is going to be deadly to that world: thus surrounded by so many voices, so many earnest entreaties, so many solicitations, so many men interested in the institution of Religion, is it not the acme of brutality and madness to claim that Religion is a chimera, to work unceasingly to combat it, to do every diligence to destroy it and glory in so doing?]

We submit to the Court these Books, together with the findings in writing which we have made in this matter. And the said King's Officers withdrew: They having withdrawn:

After an inspection of the two Printed Books in 8°, the first bearing as title: *Dictionnaire Philosophique portatif. Londres 1764,* beginning with the article *Abraham,* and ending with the article *Virtue,* comprising 344 printed pages, with no name of Author or Printer being given; the second entitled: *Lettres écrites de la Montagne,* by Jean-Jacques Rousseau, first and second Part, printed at Amsterdam, chez Marc-Michel Rey, 1764, containing 334 pages the first Part and 226 pages the second Part; and having heard the summing up of the Prosecutor of the Realm and the Report of M. Joseph-Marie Terray, Magistrate; and having taken the matter under advisement:

The Court doth order the said two printed Books to be torn up and burned at the foot of the grand staircase of the Palace by the Lord High Executioner; doth enjoin upon all such as shall have Copies of this Work to submit them forthwith to the Office of the Clerk of the Court, there to be suppressed; doth forbid all Printers, Publishers, Hawkers and other person or persons whatsoever to print, sell, retail, or otherwise distribute them, under penalties as the Law shall provide; doth order that it be informed, upon Demand of the Prosecutor of the Realm, and before the Recording Magistrate the Court doth appoint, as regards any who shall have composed, printed, sold, or otherwise distributed the said two Printed Books; in regard to the intelligences made, reported and communicated to the Prosecutor of the Realm, being by him demanded and the Court, this Court doth ordain what shall be needful; And the Court doth further order that the present Decree be printed, published and posted up on display in all places needful wheresoever. DONE in the High Court, all the Chambers being present, the nineteenth of May One Thousand Seven Hundred and Sixty-Five.

Signed: DUFRANC

V. Cartesian Inspiration of the Espion Turc

Meslier, who is to my knowledge the only one to cite this work, says nothing of its author. The first edition carries a title somewhat different from that used by Meslier, namely: *L'Espion dans les Cours des Princes Chrêtiens, ou Lettres et Memoires d'un Envoyé secret de la Porte dans les Cours de l'Europe, où l'on voit les découvertes qu'il a faites dans toutes les Cours où il s'est trouvé, avec une Dissertation curieuse de leurs Forces, Politique et Religion* [The Spy in the Courts of the Christian Princes, or Letters and Reminiscences of a Secret Envoy of the Sublime Porte (Constantinople) in the Courts of Europe, Wherein Doth Appear the Discoveries that he Made in all the Courts in the Which he Tarried, Together with a Careful Commentary upon their Military, Political and Religious Power Structures], 8 volumes. (Cologne [actually Rouen]: Chez Erasme Kinkius, 1696). The frontispiece carries a portrait of the anonymous author with the inscription: *Mehemet Espion Turc* [Mahomet, Turkish Spy], Aet. Suae LXXII [At Age 72] which inscription eventually came to be used as the title of the book itself, a book that merits a detailed study in view of Meslier's dependence on it. The author has been identified as the Genoan Gian Paolo Marana, on whom P. Toldo has written a study entitled "Dell' 'Espion' di Gian Paolo Marana e delle sue attinenze con le 'Lettres Persanes' del Montesquieu," [On the *Espion* of Gian Paolo Marana and its Connection with Montesquieu's *Lettres Persanes*], in *Giornale storico della letteratura italiana,* XXIX (1897), pp. 45-79. Cf. also S. Cotta, *Montesquieu e la scienza della società* (Turin, 1953), p. 133 note 41. I am indebted to Prof. Cotta (University of Rome) for the above details and I wish here to express my sincere thanks to him.

In the *Préface particulière* (pages not numbered) to the first volume, we are informed about the composition of the work and about its author. This literary fiction speaks of an Italian scholar (*un savant italien*) who goes to Paris and is so smitten by the beauty of the city that he decides to stay there. Forced to change lodgings, he is offered accomodation by a hospitable elderly Italian. His curiosity leads him to rummage through a closet in his rooms in this house and his eyes suddenly fall upon a large package of papers with Arabic script upon them. He knows Arabic perfectly, the pardonably bemused reader is informed, and sees that the papers deal primarily with emergent political problems of the day; this impels him to devote himself forthwith to translating them into Italian; the first Italian edition is sold out almost as soon as it is published and arouses enormous interest in Italy. An English traveller passing through Italy chances upon the book, is fascinated by it and hastens to translate it into English and publish it in London ". . . and it is from this English translation that the present one has been made" (i.e. the French translation here presented as the end product of a veritable saga of translations!). Thus far the literary fiction.

In the first extensive *Préface générale,* we are furnished much more solid fare: especially important are references to the Cartesian inspiration of the work, references which shed considerable light on what might be called "Leftist Cartesianism" a la Bayle, Spinoza and their like. Since the text is not readily available, it will be worthwhile to cite here the most significant passages:

"I feel further that, considering our Spy to have been brought up in the Moslem religion, he could take no better path to rid himself of the foibles of education and the fables of the School (to use the terms applied by a great man to the Childish Ideas we form for ourselves of things) than to follow the advice of his beloved Descartes, the Philosopher of France, whom he so much admired; and that he advises those who wish to perfect their own Reason and arrive at the knowledge of the truth unalloyed, to rid themselves of the prejudices of Childhood and youth and to purge and clean their Mind of all the dross left in it by the first impressions received from others. The understanding so purged becomes like a *tabula rasa* equally susceptible to good or bad impressions. And this is the first step of Free Will: for before this, man is altogether a Slave, carried about by every new wind of doctrine. But he commences to feel in himself a certain power and strength when he becomes capable of saying firmly within himself, *cogito, ergo sum;* basing himself on this principle, and building on this foundation, he rears a Fortress wherein he is sheltered from all the attacks of his declared Enemies and all the wiles of his hidden Enemies. Nothing can thenceforth deflect him from the right path. Nothing can corrupt him, neither the sacrilege of the Atheists and the Free-Livers, nor yet the ridiculous Enthusiasms of the Fanatics and the Bigots. This is how our Spy appears to have behaved when once he had arrived at the age at which a man usually begins to examine the foundations of Religion and to cast the teachings and traditions received from his Fathers into the crucible, so to speak, of common sense and Reason. It is therefore no surprise to find him writing more freely of this sort of thing in letters to his close personal friends than in his reports to the Mufti, to his Vicar, to the Seraglio Preachers or to the other illustrious figures of the Ottoman court. He does not hesitate, however, on occasion to take the liberty of posing questions and revealing his own doubts to these men as well, which clearly shows him not to have been entirely satisfied with several of the Principles of the Mohammedans.

"Writing to the Jew who is his counterpart in Vienna, he tries to wean him from the blind and excessively mulish confidence accorded by those of his Race to the Jewish Rabbis whom our Spy calls pious wags. He ridicules their Fables and their vain observances and advises his Friend not to be a Bigot but to devote himself to the cheerful fulfillment of the duties of his commission and to be zealous in the service of the Great Lord; he likewise exposes to this Jewish colleague on frequent occasions the vanity and superstition of certain Christians: such exposes are quite lively writing but bear no trace of malice or gall. On the contrary, he has nothing but praise for Jesus Christ Our Savior and confines himself to condemning the vices and errors of his Worshippers; and herein he does only what a Christian theologian would do whose duty obliges him to censure and reform all the bad traits he sees in those who profess the Christian faith.

"Generally our Spy seems free of Superstition and Bigotry and the only partialities and quirks he seems to show are in connection with abstinence from certain meats and the doctrine of Transmigration of Souls. It can be concluded from this that he was a Pythagorean, which is nothing novel or out of the ordinary among the Turks, since there is a special Sect of Mohammedans entirely devoted to the precepts of this Philosopher; and Pythagoreanism is known to enjoy great esteem throughout the East.

"It should not surprise us therefore that our Author shows such fondness for the Indians who are the most rigid observers of Abstinence to be found anywhere in the world, and the most zealous partisans of the Doctrine of Pythagoras, as we learn from travellers in our own day.

"Though he cannot be said to be an antiquarian, he seems nonetheless a great Lover of Antiquities and a great Admirer of new discoveries provided they are important and worthy of the diligence of a wise man: but he does not approve that sort of curiosity which simply seeks to amass Medallions, Pictures and Portraits, and a thousand other trifles that cannot serve either to enrich our knowledge of History nor to settle problems of Chronology, nor to shed light on any problem of any consequence to which the passage of so many centuries has given rise; and whose only claim to fame lies in their antique quaintness, their well-nigh obliterated characters and their weird shape! Nor is he in favor of those petty advances of the Arts and Sciences which redound to the advantage of but one specialized branch and serve only to distract the Mind from more solid subjects. He aspires to something greater: he loves relics of the distant past but only those useful for purposes of lifting the veil from the first ages of the earth, of showing the world in its Cradle, if I may so put it. This is why he relies so heavily on the records of the Chinese and the Indians. He admires new discoveries but only such as are calculated to contribute to a knowledge of those parts of the world not yet known, or can provide us with a more accurate and perfect Idea than we have hitherto had of the design of Heaven" (This section is not paginated either but the passage we have quoted extends from the 19th to the 24th page of the *Préface générale*).

Later, in a passage dealing with women's passion for philosophical studies, there is another reference to "the famous Monsieur Descartes, whose brilliance surpasses by far the Peripatetics of antiquity and eclipses Aristotle and all the ancient Lights of Greece and Italy" (Vol. I, letter 113, p. 353).

I was surprised and interested to dicover in the Biblioteca Nazionale Vittorio Emanuele in Rome the first (and possibly only) volume of what may have been the first edition of this work. Its title is a little different and it specifically mentions Marana (as translator, of course). The title reads: *L'Espion du Grand-Seigneur et ses Relations secrètes envoyées à Constantinople, contenant les événements les plus considérabes pendant la vie de Louis le Grand.* Traduit de l'Arabe, Par le Sieur Jean Paul Marana [The Spy of the Great Lord (Sultan) and his Secret

Reports sent to Constantinople, containing the most noteworthy events during the life of Louis the Great, Translated from the Arabic by Mr. Jean Paul Marana] (Amsterdam: Chez Henry Weltstein, 1688). The fact that the last letter in the 1742 edition is dated 1693 gives clear indication that this 1688 edition is definitely the first edition. It differs from the one from which we have quoted above (which we may agree to call the second edition) in several important points. It opens with a dedication to the King of France (Louis the Great), dated January 1, 1684, and specifying the name of the alleged author as Mahmut, who is said to be ". . . Arab by nationality, concealed himself in Paris for 45 years, where he served as Spy for the Emperor of the Turks; and did so cautiously comport himself that it was never discovered that he had been there; and he died at a very advanced age. He left many Reminiscences written in Arabic, containing the most important things he observed among the Christians, and especially during the Reign of Your Majesty". On the question of the translation saga, no mention is made at all of the English and Italian versions and Marana calls French his own "native tongue" although clearly stating his Genoan origins: "I do not tell Your Majesty to what Nation I belong nor what is my estate, for Men who are not blessed by fortune have no homeland. But I beg Your Majesty, on learning that I was born in Genoa, to deign to honor me with Your Royal Protection."

A rapid comparison of this (presumably) 1st edition with the later one cited above shows the following differences: (1) A different order of the letters; (2) an absence of dating in the 1st edition, whereas the letters in the later edition are dated; (3) the absence of both General and Special Prefaces in the 1st edition. This indicates the author to have revised his work. The Biblioteca Nazionale Vittorio Emanuele in Rome has a copy of the entire work in this revision; it comprises seven volumes and is labelled "15th ed., London, Published at Company's Expense, 1742." A comparison with the two volumes of the (presumed) 2nd edition cited above, which are at our disposal, shows the text, order and dating of the letters to be identical in both editions; however, the two Prefaces in the 15th edition are paginated (in Roman numerals).

The briefest glance at the other volumes of this later edition clearly reveals the anti-Christian and anti-Roman nature of this work, a feature that undoubtedly contributed to Meslier's attraction to it: Christianity is described as diametrically opposed to Islam and the practices of the Christian religion a superstition (Vol. I, lett. 12, pp. 30ff.); abuse of Papal power by the Popes is deplored (Vol. I, lett. 117, p. 366; Vol. II, lett. 28, pp. 82ff.; Vol. VII, lett. 9, pp. 51ff.); so is the want of dignified demeanor displayed in the churches (Vol. II, let. 1, pp. 2ff.); although no arguments are adduced against the Incarnation of the Word (Vol. II, lett. 9, pp. 29f.), the author shows a clear overall preference for Islam and Mohammedans over Christianity and the Christians (Vol. II, lett. 77, pp. 238ff.); he deplores sectarianism and the wars waged everywhere by Christians against one another (Vol. IV, lett. 19, pp. 81ff.; Vol VII, lett. 6, pp. 39ff.); he attacks the scandalous conduct of several Popes and accuses Leo X of unbelief (Vol. VII, lett. 4, pp. 25ff. and cf. Vol. II, lett. 66, p. 204); but he is favorably impressed by the Quietists and defends them against the attacks of the Inquisition, the Dominicans and the Jesuits (Vol. V, lett. 108, pp. 424ff.). He professes himself to favor religion (Vol. I, lett. 41, pp. 117ff.) and is vigorously opposed to atheism which he considers the most serious malady of the West: "There are in the West a multitude of men who scorn and slander not only our Law but even their own, and who openly mock at all the Religions of the world. They are known as Atheists and Free-Livers; that is to say declared Enemies of belief in a God; infamous and dumb brutes they are, who do not dare to be alone, for fear that the very thought of themselves might prod them to greater wisdom" (Vol. II, lett. 66, p. 200: he mentions Dionysius of Syracuse as among the more famous atheists).

Atheists and Free-Livers are classed together in this critique which outlines their basic traits: "These latter are veritable Monarchs of Atheism, whose godlessness no one has dared to call in question. The Free-Livers of today are more restrained and prudent. They do not dare to violate the Temples nor publicly to profane the Altars of the Christians; but they do try to ruin surreptitiously everything that resembles Religion, and to increase the number of their supporters. . . . They are the declared Enemies of the Resurrection of the good and the bad Souls, of the Day of Judgment, of Paradise and Hell. They regard Religion simply as a political invention to subjugate the world to one single form of Government, and do not scruple to call Moses and Jesus, Son of Mary, Imposters, as well as Mahomet, our own Holy Lawgiver. They make fun of miracles and ridicule the prophecies; and it is as useless to speak to them of the apparition of one dead as to tell them there is a man in the Moon" (pp. 203ff.). The Roman court itself is, according to the author, tainted with atheism, as it traffics in indulgences and spiritual favors: "The traffic in things spiritual which is being practiced in the Highest Court of Christianity has no little contributed to plunging a multitude of men into Atheism, for it brings religion into contempt; religion is now regarded as nothing more than a piece of political trickery, as a stratagem invented by the Churchmen to keep gulls and dupes in respectful subordination. Thus those who have a better opinion of themselves and would like to pass for men of a certain intelligence take advantage of this to score the fundamental principles of all Religions and to argue against the existence of God. Instead of submitting quietly to Dogmas they claim to regard or do in fact regard as obvious impostures, they shake off, like wild and untamed colts, not only the yoke of natural Religion but even that of common Morality. And even as they have too much sense to be the dupes of a shadow Religion, so too they have not enough faith to swallow all the pious frauds of the Church as being so many

Oracles of Heaven not to be doubted on any account. They prefer to be Sceptics in all things, and to apply themselves solely to satisfying their own passions. And they believe no time to be so misspent as that spent on thinking of the life to come" (pp. 205f.). Nor does the author hesitate in the final analysis to accuse everyone in the Christian West of atheism, ". . . that the Christians are enemies of the true God, of the Emperor and of Religion" (Vol. I, lett. 41, p. 117), either because of their proclamation of the dogma of the Trinity (Vol. V, lett. 23, p. 89), or because they are the chief culprits in the spread of unbelief (Vol. VII, lett. 43, pp. 237f.).

The charge is explicitated in a letter in Volume VII: "He inveighs against the Christians for making open profession of Atheism and for publicly denying the existence of God, and he rejoices that this crime is unknown among the votaries of Mohammed" (Vol. VII, lett. 24, p. 125). This serious charge is based on the Christian faith and on Christian crime of having obscured the concept of God with the disputes of Scholasticism: "In a word, they have so subtly philosophized upon their God and reasoned so closely about the name they ought to give Him, that they have ended by losing sight of Him entirely and they keep asking one another every day if there really is any entity of this sort in the world" (p. 126). And finally comes the statement that will be repeated in various forms on many an occasion by atheists of the succeeding century: ". . . for, after all, it is only among them [i.e., the Christians] that there are Atheists, it is only among them that there are Men endowed with a mind so strong and faculties so extraordinary as to be able to deny the existence of Him from whom they get their being" (p. 128). One curious passage is that in a letter dated 1656, which speaks of a new star appeared in Europe which is supposed to have excited a Messianic expectation and enthusiasm among the Jews (Vol. IV, lett. 30, pp, 113ff.). Considering that the comet treated in the famous *Pensées* of Bayle appeared in 1680 and that the presumed 1st edition of our *Espion* dates from 1684, one is tempted to wonder if the letter in question is not in fact speaking of this 1680 comet, with the date of the letter being a mere literary expedient.

In conclusion, however, it must be stressed that the religious arguments and comments are scarcely more than parentheses in the letters, which are chiefly devoted to the political affairs of the Europe of that day.

VI. Voltaire and the Système De La Nature

One of the most exhaustive judgments on d'Holbach's major work is certainly that of Voltaire who finds it stylistically superior to Spinoza: even though the critique is limited to a few points from the first part of the first volume, it is sufficiently indicative of the highly unfavorable reaction of Voltaire. The passage we present here is certainly of a later date than the article *Athées, Athéisme,* in the *Dictionnaire Philosophique,* an article that had been inspired entirely by Bayle, as we have seen; this passage is taken from the *Questions sur l'Encyclopädie* (Sect. IV): the quotations from the *Système* are taken from the 1st edition, first part.

OF THE *SYSTÈME DE LA NATURE*

The author of the *Système de la Nature* has had the advantage of getting read by scholars, by the unlettered, by women; so he does have stylistic merits that Spinoza did not have: often of clarity, sometimes of eloquence, although he can be reproached with repetitiousness, strident ranting, and contradiction like all the others. As to the content, there is reason for most frequent distrust of the author in matters of physics and morality. What is here at stake is the interest of the human race. So let us examine whether his theory is true and useful, and let us be brief if we can manage it.

"Order and disorder do not exist, etc." (Part I, p. 60).

What! In the physical order, an infant born blind or legless, a monster —is that not contrary to the nature of the species? Is it not the ordinary regularity of nature that makes order and irregularity that is disorder? Is it not a very great disturbance and derangement, a deadly disorder, that nature should have given a child hunger and blocked up its gullet? Evacuations of all kinds are necessary and yet often the channels lack outlets and this has to be remedied: this disorder certainly has its cause. No effect without a cause; but this is a most disordered effect.

Is it not a great and horrible disorder in the moral area to kill one's friend, one's own brother? The slanders of a Garasse, a Le Tellier, a Doucin, against the Jansenists and those of the Jansenists against the Jesuits—are they not minor disorders? Like the impostures of the Patouillets and the Paulians? The St. Bartholomew massacres, the Irish massacres, etc. etc.—are they not execrable disorders? This sort of crime has its cause in passions; but the effect is execrable; the cause is deadly; this disorder makes one shudder. Discovering the origin of the disorder is another matter, of course; but it does exist!

"Experience proves that materials that we regard as inert and inanimate take on action, intelligence, life, when they are combined in a certain fashion" (Part I, p. 69).

That is just the difficulty. How does a seed come to life? Author and reader know nothing of this. Hence the two volumes of the *Système;* and are not all the systems of the world but dreams?

"Life ought to be defined, and this is what I deem impossible" (Part I, p. 78).

Is not this definition quite well-known? Is not life organization with feeling? But that you draw these two properties of motion from matter alone—that is what it is impossible to give any proof of; and if it cannot be proven, how can it be asserted? Why shout: *I know* to all the world, the while one is whispering to oneself: *I know not?*

"It will be asked: what is man, etc." (Part I, p. 80).

This article is certainly not any clearer than the most obscure passages of Spinoza, and many readers will be indignant at the peremptory tone it assumes while at the same time explaining nothing.

"Matter is eternal and necessary; but its forms and combinations are transient and contingent, etc." (Part I, p. 82).

It is difficult to understand how there would be anything contingent, seeing that matter is necessary and there exists no free being. By contingent is understood that which can be or not be; but since everything must be with an absolute necessity, every manner of being, which he here inopportunely calls *contingent,* is just as absolutely necessary as being itself. On this point, the maze is still as intricate and no way out is visible.

When you presume to assert and insist that there is no God, that matter acts by itself, by an eternal necessity, you must prove it like a proposition of Euclid; otherwise you are basing your system on a mere perhaps! What a basis for the business that is of supreme interest to the race of man!

"If man is compelled by his nature to love his own well-being, he is compelled to love the means thereto. It would be useless and perhaps unjust to ask a man to be virtuous if he cannot be so without making himself unhappy. As soon as vice makes him happy, he must love vice" (Part I, p. 152).

This maxim is still more execrable in the moral order than the others are false in the physical. Were it to be true that a man could not be virtuous without suffering, it would be necessary to encourage him to be so. The proposition here advanced would patently be the ruin of society. Besides, how will he know that a person cannot be happy without having some vices? Is it not on the contrary proven by experience that the satisfaction of having overcome vices is a hundredfold greater than the pleasure of having given in to them? Does not that pleasure always have poison in its tail, does it not lead to misfortune and unhappiness and misery? By overcoming vices, man gains tranquillity, the consoling witness of his conscience; by giving oneself over to vices, one loses peace of mind, one loses physical health; one risks everything. And the Author himself in a score of passages expresses the desire that everything be sacrificed to virtue; and he advances this proposition only to furnish in his own system a new proof of the necessity of being virtuous.

"Those who so rightly reject innate ideas . . . ought to have felt that this ineffable intelligence that we place at the helm of the world and of which our senses cannot ascertain nor certify either the existence or the qualities, is a being of reason" (Part I, p. 167).

Really, how does it follow from the fact that we do not have any innate ideas that there is no God? Is not this consequence absurd? Is there any contradiction involved in saying that God gives us ideas via our senses? Is it not on the contrary most patently evident that, if there is an almighty being from whom we take our life, we owe to Him our ideas and our senses, like all the rest? It would have had to be proven already that God did not exist; and this is just what the Author has not done; it is indeed what he has not even tried to do up to this page in Chapter X (*Dictionnaire philos.,* ed. R. Naves, pp. 513-515).

Voltaire goes on to argue against the atheism of the *Système* by an analysis of the main argument for the existence of God in deist writings, i.e., purposiveness in nature, especially in the biological order: the atheist stand of the *Système* is described as "an unheard-of folly" (p. 516). Section V has as its argument: *Of the Necessity of Believing in a Supreme Being* and in it Voltaire says that the *Système* is inferior to Spinoza inasmuch as the latter admits an intelligence in the world.

In a Note written in 1770 to the article *Causes finales,* Voltaire reports in full the *Système's* critique of final causality purposiveness (Part II, pp. 158ff.), with the following quite flattering introduction: "There comes, in 1770, a man much superior to Spinoza in some respects, as eloquent as the Dutch Jew is dry; less methodical but a hundred times clearer; perhaps a geometrician like Spinoza but not a man to commit the ludicrous folly of reasoning geometrically in the area of metaphysics and morals: this is the Author of the *Système de la Nature;* he took the name of Mirabaud, Secretary of the Académie française. Alas! our poor Mirabaud was not capable of writing a single page of the book of our redoubtable adversary. All you who would make use of your reason and instruct yourselves, read this eloquent and dangerous passage of the *Système de la nature*" (*Dictionn. philos.,* p. 539).

In the case of the atheistic elements with which the d'Holbach text fairly teems, Voltaire never fails to clarify his own disagreement in brief but effective notes and refers the reader to the refutation he had given of this atheism in the articles *Athéisme* and *Dieu.* So it seems to us that there is exaggeration in the charge of atheism levelled against Voltaire in the *Dictionnaire Anti-Philosophie,* which classes him with Helvétius: "The brand of atheism that is evident in the book *De l'Esprit* triumphs in the *Dictionnaire Philosophique*" (cf. the word *Athéisme,* p. 36. The *Dictionnaire Anti-philosophique* is attributed to the Abbé Nonnotte, but this article is by Abbé Troublet).

VII. Judgment of Laharpe and Diderot on Helvétius

For his radical sense-perceptionism or sensualism, Helvétius was violently attacked both by Jean-François Laharpe (1739-1803) in his *Réfutation du Livre De l'Esprit* (1788, but published in Paris chez les merchands de nouveautés, in 1797), and by Diderot, who also treats of

De l'Esprit but mainly effects a thorough analysis of Helvétius' other major work in his *Réfutation de l'ouvrage d'Helvétius intitulé l'Homme* (Cf. *Oeuvres philosophiques,* ed. P. Vernière, pp. 563ff.). Both accuse Helvétius, though for different motives, of failing to adhere to the principles of Locke, and especially of failing to respect the capital distinction between sensation and reflection.

Laharpe begins vigorously: "Helvétius could have been classed among writers properly called philosophers only in an age where everything had been confused: men, facts, ideas and even words. If Condillac is a philosopher, Helvétius cannot be one" (*op. cit.,* p. 9). Despite appearances, *De l'Esprit* belongs cheek by Jowl with *L'Homme Machine* of Lamettrie, who is called "The King of Prussia's atheist" and whose work is branded as ". . . outburst of a mad and brutal perversity" (p. 16ff.): "We have seen that Condillac distinguished himself by extending 11). Helvétius is admitted to have taken Locke as his starting point but is accused of diverging from him forthwith and on crucial points (pp. 16ff.): "We have seen that Condillac distinguished himself by extending and deepening the principles of Locke. Helvétius simply misuses these principles and by exaggerating the truths discovered by Locke, he draws from them the most erroneous conclusions" (p. 18). A patent example is the famous problem posed by Locke as to whether God can impart to matter the capacity of thinking: ". . . Locke proved as far as any man can, i.e., by the principles of analogy between the known and the unknown, that the soul must be a simple and indivisible and consequently an immaterial substance. However, he adds, that he would not presume to assert that God cannot endow matter with thought. Condillac agrees with Locke on the first point and joins issue with him on the second. I am entirely in agreement with Condillac, and all the good metaphysicians agree that this is the only inaccuracy that can be discovered in Locke's work . . . This man who proved against all comers the essential immateriality of the thinking principle, was no longer really at liberty to admit on any hypothesis whatsoever the possibility of this principle being rendered material" (pp. 28f.). And the entire essay is a vindication of Locke's point of view: cf., e.g., the discussion of the problem of freedom (pp. 72ff.), the refutation of the notion that pleasure and pain are the sole motive principles of morality (pp. 92ff.) and the theory of the passions in general (pp. 102ff.).

Diderot, not content with a critique of *De l'Esprit* (ed. Naigeon, Vol. III, pp. 251ff.), devotes one of his last works to a thorough examination of *De l'Homme:* this late work of Diderot may well be an indication of the old philosopher's hesitation in declaring himself for a radical materialism as Helvétius had done. Diderot's most recent editor and critic thinks that ". . . the *Réfutation d'Helvétius* marks a crucial date in the evolution of Enlightenment philosophy" (P. Vernière, in Diderot, *Oeuvres Philosophiques,* p. 560). Diderot's critique is directed mainly against the following points of Helvétius' work:

I. *To Feel is to Judge,* in connection with which contention Diderot reproaches Helvétius with having substituted for Descartes' "I think, therefore I am", the exaggerated version: "I feel, therefore I want to feel agreeably", and concludes on a vigorous note: "I prefer Hobbes who claims that in order to draw any really meaningful conclusion the line of reasoning had to be: 'I sense, I think, I judge; therefore a piece of matter organized as I am can sense, think and judge' " (p. 564).—

II. *Fame and physical pleasure* as motives of morality come in for criticism by Diderot who alleges that Helvétius has wrongly deduced a radical sensualistic eudaemonism from sense-perceptionist principles which were accurate in their own right (cf. especially p. 576, comparison with Rousseau).

III. *Nature and Genius,* pp. 576ff.

IV. *What is the mind?,* in which critique Diderot defends, against Helvétius, the thesis that the mind is a natural quality, pp. 581ff.

VI. *Truth and Tautology,* where Diderot rejects Helvétius' theory that truth can be reduced to the statement of such a fact as "White is white, black is black", pp. 598ff.

IX. *Discovery of Truth:* Diderot disagrees that truth is found as soon as glimpsed; he insists it remains always more or less hidden from man and requires unceasing search, pp. 616ff.

X. *Enlightened Despotism:* Diderot insists that it is not true that the best government is, as Helvétius quotes Frederick II of Prussia as saying, that of a prince who is despotic but enlightened, pp. 619f.

VIII. Anonymous Defense of Helvétius' "De L'Esprit"

Among the replies to the avalanche of criticism and accusations levelled against Helvétius' work and the condemnations passed upon it was an anonymous essay written by someone who must have been quite close to Helvétius; indeed the work may have been inspired by Helvétius himself, such is the similarity of style and thought in this essay with that of Helvétius. This is the essay *Examen des critiques du livre intitulé "De l'Esprit"* (London, 1760).

In the Foreword, the author, while admitting the good faith of the critics, expresses his alarm at the fact that "the charges of materialism, atheism, etc., are not being levelled only against the *De l'Esprit* but rather constitute a blanket accusation directed against the greater part of the scholars of France" (p. 5). Should someone or other have really fallen into such errors, let him be indicted; but it is not philosophy that is at fault; it has indeed performed the meritorious function of freeing religion from prejudices and making it "a matter of conviction". Thus there can be no ascent to the level of revealed truth if there is not first present the evidence of natural truths: "Nothing is therefore more dangerous than an obscuring of the natural truths, since they are the sole legitimate foundation that can ensure the consent due to the others. This is the point too often neglected by such as entangle Philosophy in fanciful ideas against which our own inner awareness clearly witnesses, would we but heed it." And he enters the indignant protest: "Nor is divine Religion less wronged by such unconsidered charges of unbelief against men whose talents are an honor and service to their Country, and whose virtues render them dear to society. The aim seems to be to prove that all the Learned are Atheists or Deists, and that the gift of faith has been accorded only to the unlearned and the half-witted. But the height of blasphemy is to employ in the defense of the eternal truth weapons proper to falsehood, a disingenuous cunning, reckless accusations and the crowning outrage of persecution" (pp. 9f.).

Therefore, says the author, he wishes, with all due respect to the judgment of the courts, the pastors and doctors of the Paris Theology Faculty, to point up the fact that the basis and object of the book *De l'Esprit* is the truth basic to the preservation of any society, i.e., the observance of the duties imposed upon man by nature and good order in society (pp. 16f.). Instead of clearing matters up, the Theology Faculty's censure has confused the situation greatly, with the obvious aim of "setting the sovereign authority against the Philosophers" (p. 21).

This cannot but be extremely harmful because "the truths of philosophy are, after those of the true Religion, the most sacred deposit that can be preserved for men. It can even be said to be the Philosophers' assignment to lead us to the foot of the altars, to prove to us with evidence the necessity and certainty of revelation, to dispose all reasonable men by reason to submit themselves to the dogmas of the faith" (p. 28f.). The essay is directed against the attacks on Helvétius in the *Journal de Trévoux* and the anonymous author, while disagreeing with Helvétius on some points, expressed his conviction that the book under fire "does not teach either materialism or contempt of holy Religion" (p. 31).

In his own indictment of the strict rigorist Sorbonne censors, the author takes two main lines: First he initiates a trenchant critique of the theory of "innate ideas" derived from Descartes, a theory to which these censors subscribed. He turns their own accusation against them, citing in his own support the Protestant, Barbeyrac: "The Theologians," says M. Barbeyrac, "themselves give much purchase to the Atheists, when, not contenting themselves with the incontestable proofs available for the great truths of Religion and Morals, they persist, in an imprudent zeal, in sustaining certain reasons which are, to say the least, highly doubtful, and then go on to exclaim that all is lost if these be not admitted like the former" (p. 182; cf. pp. 190ff.). Secondly, the anonymous author acquits the book both of the charge of having neglected to treat of the natural Law and of the duties of man towards God, and of the indictment of not having taken into account the problem of immortality: the theologians, he says, have done little or nothing to clear these matters up, indeed they have introduced much confusion into them. And he concludes: "It is therefore unjust to reproach the Philosophers for holding quite simply to the decision of the Church on the nature of our soul. If our body, as the Church teaches, is endowed with a sensitive passively receptive faculty which we hold in common with all the other animals, the inner awareness of the natural Law and of the immortality of the soul distinguishes man essentially from the brute. He cannot fail to recognize or disregard the divine light that enlightens him, constituting within him intelligence, reason, and showing him the code of his duties" (p. 168).

In the matter of the charge levelled by the Jesuit review (*Journal de Trévoux*) to the effect that the thoughts expressed by the author of *De l'Esprit* would result in materialism, the anonymous writer deems the ideal reply to be a quotation of the theory of the Jesuit P. Buffier who served as direct inspiration for the theory of knowledge contained in the work now on trial: "He [P. Buffier] teaches that our thoughts and knowledge come only from using the senses which are a part of the body" (p. 110. Cf. especially pp. 171ff.).

And so it is strange to read in the Trévoux article a judgment which amounts to saying: "P. Buffier is orthodox because he has referred all human understanding to the use of the senses, and the author of *De l'Esprit* is a materialist because he refers only the *indistinct feelings and awarenesses* to the use of the senses" (p. 175). While admitting that the gnoseology of *De l'Esprit* (and that of Buffier) comes from Locke, the Helvétius apologist insists it does not amount to a reduction of everything to a *"perpetually indistinct feeling or awareness: . . . for discerning*, adverting, deliberating, willing, reasoning, judging and deciding—all these operations in the natural order are effected by our affective and representative sensations. In fact all our knowledge goes back to these two sorts of sensations, feelings and ideas" (p. 183).

Let each group then confine themselves to their own area of competency: "The Theologians are judges of revealed faith, and the Philosophers of reasoned faith. Theologians and Philosophers do indeed often go astray on matters which are within their competency: But the certainty of the dogmas of revealed faith is assured by the infallibility of the Church, and the certainty of the philosophical truths is guaranteed by evidence. It is the evidence of natural Theology which leads to the certainty of the revealed faith and of the infallibility of the Church. Evidence is thus the principle and source of certainty of truths human and divine. Now evidence consists in the observation of our own sensations" (pp. 186f.). It is along the lines of this "frank sensism" that the anonymous author undertakes to defend the new philosophy of *De l'Esprit,* which he considers to be much better grounded than the "innate ideas" rationalism of the theologians. Despite the gaps and shortcomings that may be evident in *De l'Esprit* (cf. pp. 236ff.), the final judgment on this work cannot but be favorable: ". . . The *Author of De l'Esprit* has followed in his work the plan that a Philosopher must adopt who has law-giving in mind; and he has hewed to that plan and given a good account of himself, always excepting those deviations and errors that we have mentioned" (p. 241).

The work, whoever may have been its author, is a document indicative of the state of Christian philosophy in the Age of the Enlightenment; and it shows the blind alley into which it will stumble in the subsequent centuries, torn and rent in turn by rationalism and sense-perceptionism, by idealism and empiricism.

IX. Catholic Apologetics and Enlightenment Philosophy

Catholic apologetics sallied forth at once into the lists against irreligion and atheism, especially in France which was the chief battlefield; but it is not difficult to discern in all this heady writing a jarring note: not always, indeed, is it improvised and excessively oratorical; but almost always there is a drastic want of insight into the deep-seated principles of the whole Enlightenment movement. Instead of going to the root of the matter, as speculative analysis demands, it tended to highlight the "consequences" in the practical and moral order, often going so far as to disregard Bayle's famous polemic. We here present only a few examples:

1. The *Pensées sur la philosophie de l'incrédulité ou Réflexions sur l'esprit et le dessein des philosophies irréligieux de ce siècle,* by a certain Abbé Lamourette, Doctor of Theology (Paris, chez l'Auteur, 1786), inspired by Bossuet, hews to the standard we have mentioned, both in style and in content. The author has, however, noticed that, in contrast to the external attacks against religion in ancient times, the modern philosophers are demolishing religion's foundations (pp. 33ff.). The truly virtuous among the unbelievers will not take long, says Lamourette, to return to religion and to Christianity. (p. 51). And he here interpolates an extensive polemical reference to d'Holbach's stand: "But the author of the *Système de la Nature,* in his precipitous reduction of all philosophical systems to atheism, has rashly outrun and anticipated the intentions of his sect, which had no desire for such a speedy eruption of their momentous intrigues. For it has been discreetly agreed not to startle the world by ideas so extraordinary. There had even been the pretense of hurling the most crushing anathemas at the atheists of antiquity and of proving the necessity of a God and of a providence. Prudence had gone even farther. Let us bear in mind, it had been said, that there are some extremely frail and fearful souls who have an insurmountable fear of God and of the future. Let them then go on believing that God wants to be worshipped, that there are virtues and duties in this life, punishments and rewards reserved for the next: for all these

points are inconsequential provided we can get all revelation rejected. If in fact it comes to be accepted that God speaks to men only from the depths of their own conscience, then the individual is no longer accountable except to himself for his actions and his conduct. Your conscience will never give you more illumination than you want from it, will never trammel your inclinations and will always be at the command of your heart. And there you are, absolute and unruffled judge of good and evil, sole creator of your own principles and morality. What more could be needed? Would freedom be better safeguarded even in the tents of Spinoza? And so let us but succeed in rendering Christianity hateful and ludicrous: and then all the rules that trammel total independence will vanish like smoke" (pp. 55-57).

The *Système de la Nature* (called "the Bible of atheism") is subjected to a rather hurried examination later on (pp. 119ff.) and is squelched by a couple of quotations from Bossuet. Still later there is the same sort of critique of Helvétius' *De l'Homme* (pp. 145ff.). There is a note which is priceless in the matter of the critical perspicacity of the good Abbé: in this note he admits to uncertainty about the identity of the Author of the *Système* but contends that it is patent that *De l'Homme* is not the work of Helvètius: "Certain persons have assured me that the writer whom I seem here to have in mind is not at all the author of the *Système de la Nature* and that this work owes its origin to a philosopher presently fled to Prussia. Others, equally reliable, assert the contrary, and even claim to know it from the best source. I do not wish to be unjust to anyone and I declare that on this point, which incidentally is a matter of total indifference for the subject-matter I am treating, I accuse no one in particular and make no definitive finding. But it must be agreed by anyone who has read the books with a little reflection that the book *De l'Homme* is not by M. Helvétius; that the *Code de la Nature,* the *Pensées Philosophiques,* the *Système Social* and the *Système de la Nature* so entirely cohere in a unity of principles, a likeness of outlook, and a harmony of outcome, as to quite excuse the error, if so it be, of seeing throughout the stamp of the same brummagem shop" (p. 97).

2. Perhaps first in order of time and more impressive from the cultural point of view is the monumental *Examen du matérialisme ou réfutation du Système de la nature,* by the famous theologian, Abbé Bergier, embellished with a Papal Brief from Clement XIV dated 5 July 1769 (I quote from the Tournai edition, Typ. J. Casterman, 1838). The work follows through the *Système* almost chapter by chapter, citing it accurately and centering it within the ambit of several anti-religious writings of the time, such as the *Contagion sacrée,* published under the name of Trenchard but today attributed to d'Holbach himself, the *Essai sur les Préjugés*, attributed to Du Marsais, and the *De l'Esprit*. Bergier gives no evidence of knowing who the author of the *Système* may be and shows no concern about this point; but he is certain that this same author has

published other works already which prepared the way for the *Système.* He writes in the Preface: "In the various Works which the author of the present one has already published he has concentrated mainly on combatting Deism, which was in those days the hypothesis taught in almost all the books written against religion. Several principles which we had occasion to notice in those other books gave pretty clear warning that the philosophers were not going to stop there, that they would not long delay to profess formal atheism and sheer materialism. This line of development had been foreseen and the publication of the *Système de la Nature* should come as no surprise to us" (p. V).

Bergier is most monolithic in his critique: when once the materialistic basis of the *Système* has been pinpointed, he charges, its theories are nothing but a mass of contradictions. Thus, e.g., on the initial assertion that man is the work of nature, Bergier has this to say: "This language is less that of a reasoning philosopher than of a sick man with fever-dreams" (p. 4). Bergier immediately falls upon the basic theory of the *Système,* the Toland principle that "motion is essential to matter" inasmuch as it is no longer being supposed, as in the Cartesian and Spinozan conception of extension, that matter is homogeneous but rather that it is composed of heterogeneous particles (p. 11): in the controversy among the physicists as to whether the attraction between bodies is an effect of gravitation or vice versa, Bergier takes refuge in mystery and attributes the cause of the two phenomena, like Newton and d'Alembert, to a special will of the creator (p. 25). In his refutation of "spontaneous generation", maintained by the *Système,* Bergier does not miss the opportunity for irony: "A curious business, this. In the past, Aristotle and his followers used to be laughed at when they said that plants and animals are born out of putrefaction; thanks to the new philosophy, Aristotle was right." And in refutation Bergier appeals to Diderot in his deist phase: "The discovery of germs alone, according to the author of the *Pensées Philosophiques,* has done away with one of atheism's most powerful objections" (p. 30). On p. 32 he cites, certainly from Diderot, Needham as being in favor of the theory of germs (Needham based himself on the famous researches of Spallanzani). On the *Système's* appeal to Descartes who "required only matter and motion in order to mold the Universe", Bergier makes the dry retort: "But this is not the most sensible thing that Descartes wrote" (pp. 39f.). A little farther on, he cites Shaftesbury's *Letter on Enthusiasm* (sect. 3) against atheism: "A very well-known writer, more than a little suspect himself of unbelief, says that atheism comes from a bedrock of ill humor" (p. 45). Still farther on, Bergier credits Descrartes with the discovery of the modern notion of "mind as spirit" but says Descartes was merely again taking up a traditional concept: "It can be convincingly shown that Plotinus, the disciple of Plato, St. Augustine, and Claudius Mamertus spoke of the spirituality of the soul in the same terms as Descartes, gave the same proofs as did he, established as he did that *what thinks cannot be matter*" (p. 131). The authority of Bayle is appealed to in the defense of the spirituality of the soul (p. 120f.); Bergier is at pains to show the complete agreement of the *Système* with the *De l'Esprit,* step by step, in the sensualistic conception of knowledge and of morality (pp. 139, 142, 152, 153, 163, 165, 166, 168 f., 174, 177, 184 and *passim*). Later there is an appeal to Aristotle as reiterated in modern times by Locke: "The appeal is first to the principle held by Aristotle: *nothing enters into our mind except by way of the senses.* Thus Aristotle, worshipped at first by the Philosophers, then despised and regarded as a dreamer, is today rehabilitated to a position of honor by the materialists" (p. 197). The decisive word in defense of freedom is left solely to the witness of conscience and the authority of d'Alembert (p. 210).

It must be said to Bergier's credit that he has really ransacked the actual text of the *Système* from beginning to end, centering it in its immediate, if somewhat restricted, historical ambit. But his philosophical stature is trammelled by the apologetic concern with finding contradictions everywhere, a concern which overrides dispassionate critique, further marred here by eclecticism and oversimplification of tenets: the new materialism is, for Bergier, nothing but a simple return to Epicurus and Lucretius!

3. The best informed and solid catholic apologist seems to us to have been the Dominican Antonio Valsecchi, whose capital work was *Dei fondamenti della religione e dei fonti dell'empietà,* three volumes (Padua, 1768; I have access to the 2nd ed. of the Latin translation [Venice: Pezzana, 1770] and the 7th Italian edition [Padua: Stamperia del Seminario, 1805]).

The precise scope of this work is the refutation of the *Philosophers.* Atheism is mentioned as early as Book I on the foundations of natural religion (brief exposition in ch. II, § 3, Maupertuis, Diderot; § 5, Toland, also ch. X, § 6; § 8 Helvétius, already attacked in ch. I, § 6, § 10 and 13 and Part II, ch. V, §§ 5-12 for Rousseau). Helvétius is perhaps the author most discussed, after Bayle and together with Spinoza: ch. IV § 12 and 13; ch. VI, § 8 and ch. VII, § 2 and 3; refuted in ch. III especially § 6 on the *Lettres persanes* of Montesquieu and ch. XIV, § 9 on *L'esprit des Loix* of the same author. Valsecchi does not know Diderot from whom he does, however, cite anonymously the *Pensées philosophiques;* here he neither knows nor (so far as I can see) cites anything from d'Holbach. But he is familiar with many other anonymous texts, such as: "*Épitres sur la Religion essentielle de l'homme, Lettres Juives, Les Moeurs, Le traité de la Raison humaine, L'examen de la Religion, La Religion des Dames, La Princesse de Malhabar* and the famous *Le Telliamed . . .*" to which can be added the two poets Pope and Voltaire, Helvétius, Rousseau, and several others, whose writings are falling even into the hands of women since they are masked under such titles as

Journals, Tales, Satires and Romances." In § 8-12 we find the refutation of the atheist system of Spinoza. Criticism of Spinoza together with Hobbes recurs in Book III, ch. IV, § 5 and *passim*.

The frontal attack on atheism comes in Book III, which begins with the thesis: "The source of impiety is not in the intellect but in the heart." The treatment is based on the Fénelon contention that "there is no middle way between Catholicism and atheism" (which had been the thesis of Campanella in his day!). In his exposition of atheism, Valsecchi follows to the letter the Bayle of the *Penseées* and the *Dictionnaire* (in the De Maizeaux ed.), citing at length from the original text (pp. 315a ff.). Valsecchi shows himself to be familiar with the names and almost always likewise with the works of the chief protagonists of Enlightenment atheism (in addition to those already mentioned, there is mention of De La Mothe le Vayer, Saint Evremond, Shaftesbury [Mylordus Shaftsburgius!], Tindal, Locke, Collins, Woolaston, Pope, Voltaire, Rousseau, Montesquieu (p. 317 and *passim*), La Mettrie whose *L'homme machine* is cited (p. 321). Pascal is vigorously defended against the well-known attack of Voltaire (Book II, ch. V, § 2). There is an exposition of Bayle's thesis on the relations between religion and morality in ch. 3-9 (pp. 326-365).

There follows a discussion of Deism in ch. X and in ch. XI the refutation of the thesis of Bayle is reiterated (*the system of the libertines is pernicious to society,* pp. 347ff.), there is a special discussion of most important arguments of Bayle with which Toland associated himself (ch. XII-XVI). The second part treats of the second source of impiety and irreligion, to wit the disturbance of reason. The apologetic intent of the work is evident in its very arrangement which puts first the of the Christian religion (Book II), and discusses the problem of atheism only at the end (Book III). But Valsecchi is compelled as early as Book I to encounter some of the main representatives of atheism, as we have seen. There is no faintest sign of any advertence to, or even suspicion of, the novelty of the modern *cogito* and both the exposition and the critique follow the facile and convenient method of reducing atheism to materialism and scepticism. The chief objective piece of apologetics in the work is undoubtedly the refutation of the thesis of Bayle, of which we have already spoken; and the Author is true to the main intent of the book in never missing an opportunity of showing that the atheist never has been and never can be anything but a profligate and a felon. For Valsecchi, the distinction between deism and atheism is well-nigh negligible (Cf. Book III, ch. X, § 6). "There is little or no distinction between the Atheist who denies God and the system of the Deist who, if he does confess God, nonetheless holds that he does not govern human affairs" (*ibid.*, p. 370b): deists and atheists are both labelled as *"libertins"* (Free-Livers) and *"spiritus fortes"* (Free-Thinkers).

We therefore feel this work of Valsecchi to be of capital importance for an understanding of the attitude of late 18th-century Catholic theology toward modern thought and for an estimation of the merits and limitations of a method that has come down almost unchanged to our own days.

4. Valsecchi has presented still another critique of d'Holbach's *Système de la Nature* (which Valsecchi calls "the Code of Atheism") in his *La Religione Vincitrice* (Genoa, 1776). Expressly cited are Bergier and Holland. Part I treats d'Holbach's *Système,* which Valsecchi takes to be the work of Mirabaud (d'Holbach's pseudonym, as we have said); Part II treats of Freret's *Examen critique des Apologistes de la Religion chrétienne*. This critique of Valsecchi's excells Bergier's in knowledge of sources, tightness of reasoning, wealth of textual references and familiarity with English Deist writings, as evidenced also in Valsecchi's chief work. The oratorical tone is somewhat annoying. Valsecchi's interpretation of d'Holbach is quite simple and straightforward (and unidimensional!): the *Système* merely restates to the letter the materialistic system of Lucretius (cf. table of contents of Ch. I, p. 53). In the Introduction ("To the Reader"), Valsecchi distinguishes betwen the ancient and the new adversaries of religion: whereas the former "were and showed themselves to be well-trained and subtle in metaphysics, with a broad-based erudition . . . men who reasoned, who knew how to bring into the fray difficulties worthy of being examined and discussed", the output of the modern Philosophers or "the stock of such endless Books with which we are flooded today is and can be nothing but the refurbishing of the ancient follies" (P. IIIf.).

The refutation of the *Système* is preceded by the Essay: *Of the Line of Reasoning Rife in the Group of the Philosophers,* which presents a three-section survey of the attack on religion by the "Philosophers". Valsecchi hits first at the critique of revealed Religion: "The vaunted following of a natural Religion is but an illusion, since such Naturalism degenerates into a Deism which doth then with brief delay end in Atheism" (p. 7). After an initial reference to d'Alembert, there are cited the Books of the Socinians, of Bayle, *Le Christianisme raisonnable, La Religion essentielle* (Rousseau, Boulanger, Voltaire, Mirabaud [= d'Holbach], Helvétius and others and there is a sympathetic reference to the Galileo case, p. 47).

There is a description, cast in Biblico-mythical style, of the situation created by the Free-Liver Philosophers, "a war of the giants against heaven" but a complete blind alley: "The Spinozas with their Pantheism, the Helvétiuses with their Materialism, the Woolastons with their Allegorism, the Bayles with their Pyrrhonism, the Boulangers with their Despotism, and in the train of these Chieftains all the rest of the Legion of Free-Livers with their Essays, Miscellanies, Poems, profane and sacrilegious Romances, have been put to shame, given the lie to and convicted with most just refutations by zealous Prelates or men most learned. So that there is no System, not even a single argument against Religion produced by the disbelievers, but has been treated to the glory of truth and to their dishonor". The *Système* is here assigned doubtful pride of place and the judgment of magistrate Seguier in the *Indictment* submitted at the Paris High Court in 1770, with which we are already familiar, is reported. As refutation of the basic thesis that "motion is essential to matter", Valsecchi mentions Wollaston's critique in the French translation: *Ebauche de la Religion Naturelle* (The Hague: chez Jean Swart, 1756), Sect. V, Prop. 13: "There is nothing better proven in the whole of physics than this inaction and this inertia of matter". I have not been able to find such a passage in the original English. Wollaston's Thesis runs thus in the original: "It is so far from being true that God is corporeal, that there could be no such thing as either matter or motion, if there was not some Superior being, upon whom they depended. Or, God is such a Being, that without him there could be neither matter nor motion" (*The Religion of Nature delineated* [London: reprinted by Sam. Palmer, 1724]. The English edition is anonymous; my copy has "William Wollaston" in full, in handwriting, at the bottom of p. 218, near to the symbol N. N.) Valsecchi bolsters his outline of the contents of the *Système* with continual references to the French original but his apologetic scope and predominantly theological approach preclude his grappling with the bedrock of his adversary's position, Lockeian sense-perceptionism in the Toland version. Valsecchi, like Bergier, feels he has said everything when he has reduced his adversary to materialism, a reduction which it in no way embarrasses the adversary to admit: what was called for rather was a clarification of the sort of materialism involved here and the road of thought that had led to it (the new empirical meaning given by Locke to the *cogito* of Descartes with the theory of the "idea" as reflection upon experience).

Another corpus of apologetic works in the tradition of Valsecchi, who is expressly cited, and of other 18th century apologists (Concina, Moniglia, Del Giudice, Ansaldi and the rest) is that of St. Alphonsus Liguori, comprising the *Breve Dissertazione contra gli errori de' moderni increduli oggidí nominati Materialisti e Deisti,* the *Riflessioni sulla verità della divina Rivelazione contra le principali opposizioni dei Deisti,* and the *Verità della Fede* (2 vols.). We quote here from the Marietti edition (Turin, 1825-1826).

The main "impious ones" are Spinoza, Bayle and Hobbes; and the writer is familiar with the position of Locke who ". . . in a sly fashion, to say the least of it, questioned whether thinking and discursive reasoning suit with matter" and to whom "M. Voltaire associated himself in his Letter 13, saying: 'I am a body and I think. *I know no more*." (*Breve Dissertazione,* pp. 52f. This stand is also attributed to Hobbes, in *Verità della Fede,* Vol. I, p. 81). Among the Deist and Enlightenment philosophers cited are Collins, Toland, l'Argens, Tindal, Montaigne, Woolaston, l'Evremond, Shaftesbury (always written bemusingly enough "Schanfrerbury"!), Le Moine (*Breve Dissertazione,* p. 4.—Cf. the list of the chief works in French taking their inspiration from Enlightenment philosophy, in *Verità della Fede,* p. 8, which lists only Helvétius as author of *De l'Esprit:* the main works cited are by Montesquieu, Voltaire and Rousseau).

Bayle is named as their grand master: "The impious Pierre Bayle is the one who gives backing to all these detestable writers, collecting into one corpus all their impiety which he now defends and now impugns, so that his intention is none other than that of putting everything in doubt, both the errors of the unbelievers and the truth of the faith, so as to arrive at the ultimate conclusion that there is no thing certain to be believed nor yet any religion we are under obligation to embrace" (*Verità della Fede,* Vol. I, pp. 9f.—Cf. later, pp. 239f., note, the discussion of Bayle's thesis on the possibility of atheists observing the moral law).

PART IV

DISINTEGRATION OF IDEALISM INTO ATHEISM

1

The Spinoza Controversy (*Spinozasstreit:* Lessing-Jacobi) as Catalyst of the Disintegration of Rationalism into Idealist Atheism

It is one of the basic terms of reference of the present study to consider idealism as the most fully developed form of modern thought and as the most drastic theoretical and systematic expression of the principle of immanentism: for idealism attempted and achieved, unexpectedly but entirely consistently with its own internal logic, the synthesis of Spinozan metaphysics which enunciated a monistic (and naturalistic) principle of being and the Kantian *Ich denke* which articulated the new conception of the radical creativity of mind. The constitutive elements of this synthesis may today appear disparate and mutually alien; but the synthesis itself has shown a power of attraction virtually unequalled in the history of thought and now represents one of the basic structural ingredients of the Western mind.

In idealism, the most salient demands and aspirations of modern thought combined to kindle the flame of a hope for the long-awaited solution of the riddle of freedom and for the solution of the mystery of existence in terms of a thorough grasp of the meaning of history. Among these demands and aspirations were: the insistence that truth belonged essentially to the mind; the striving to conjoin into a dynamic unity nature and man on the one hand and nature and the Absolute on the other; the determination to surprise and seize the One and the All in the manifold and the discrete; the longing to tether the eternal in the temporal dimension and to achieve union with the primordial fountainhead of life; and finally the stress on the synthetic creativity of the mind, coiled for the leap that would absorb the sublimity of historical religion [1] into the anthropocentric confines of the speculative act.

In pinpointing Spinozan monism and the Kantian *Ich denke* as the two deepest and most operative motive forces in idealism, we have no intention of excluding other springs and influences, such as the mystical currents of Eckhart, Böhme, Bengel and Oetinger; the still longer-range influence of classical philosophy itself (Plato and Aristotle and especially neo-Platonism); and Christianity itself—springs and influences evident to anyone with even a passing familiarity with the works of Fichte, Schelling and Hegel. Nor are we forgetting that metaphysical idealism arose in the loosely-knit and heterogeneous Protestant world, in a religious atmosphere devoid of any external authority or any strong sense of historical continuity, a world where religious feeling could aspire, virtually without let or hindrance, to legitimation in the greatest variety of religious experiences: a state of affairs quite different from that in which Vico operated in a Catholic atmosphere, taking a diametrically opposed tack, that of a clear-cut and progressive surmounting of the barbarically primitive and inchoate in the thrust toward the refinement and polish of the higher forms of civilization.[2]

The surface feeling must have been that Kant's *Vernuftsglaube* (religion of reason) and, following that, especially the explicit theological bent of the idealists, Hegel in particular, had brought about a lull in the controversy between theism and atheism which had convulsed Enlightenment Deism. But Hegel was precisely the philosopher, in the wake of the more or less successful containment or mastery of the Fichte problem, to "crystallize" the henceforth inescapable demand for "instant atheism" contained in the principle of immanentism. Kant had in fact deprecated "statutory religion" or "established religion", founded on historical reality and bound up with external worship and authority; he thought such deprecation would serve to shore up the internal affirmation of God, of freedom and of immortality in the minds of individual believers.

Jacobi, who denounced Lessing's atheistic Spinozism, as we shall

[1] Thus we can agree entirely with Groos's slogan-type judgment: "Was die Idealisten gewöhnlich unter Christentum verstehen, ist kein Christentum" (What the Idealists usually understand by Christianity is not Christianity at all!) (H. Groos, *Der deutsche Idealismus und das Christentum* [Munich, 1927], p. 18); and we would extend it to read, still more drastically: "What the Idealists understand by God is not God at all!".

[2] G. Zart has gathered together the scanty elements of these influences upon German rationalism down to Jacobi and Kant in his *Einfluss der englischen Philosophen seit Bacon auf die deutsche Philosophie des. 18. Jahrhunderts* (Berlin, 1881). Cf. especially pp. 207ff.: *Die Glaubensphilosophen*—Hamann, Jacobi; and pp. 215ff. *Der systematische Kritizismus.*

soon be pointing out, exaggerated Kant's resolute theism.[3] In substantiation, Jacobi cites two significant texts, one from Kant's pre-critical period and the other from the critical period. In the first, Kant vigorously asserts that the concept of God should not stop at the Absolute, at the supreme Being; rather, he maintains, that intellect and will[4] must be constitutive elements of such a concept, i.e., that God must be endowed with a personal character and have effective freedom in his action with regard to the world and to man: thus providence is a constitutive element of God. The anti-rationalist and anti-Spinozan thrust is still more evident in the second passage cited by Jacobi. We shall also here cite this Kantian passage at length:

"Strictly speaking, the Deist could be denied to have any belief in God and be held to be maintaining only the existence of a primordial Being or supreme Cause, since the concept of God is not customarily understood to signify merely a blindly operating eternal Nature as the root cause of things, but rather a supreme Being Who is supposed to be the free and rational creator of things, and such a concept alone is of interest to us. However, since no one should be accused of intending a total denial of something simply because he does not venture to maintain it forthrightly, it is more lenient and just to say that the Deist believes in a *God* whereas the Theist believes in a *living God* (*summam intelligentiam* = supreme intelligence)."[5]

And Jacobi goes on to maintain in one of his latest works that Kant deserves credit for having righted the balance of the human mind and spirit: in opposition to the post-Aristotelian tendency in the philosophical schools to subordinate immediate cognition to mediate, primordial perceptive activity to reflection, being to the word, and especially reason to the understanding, Kant again promoted reason and interior perception to the first place of honor.[6] Jacobi excuses, indeed even approves

[3] Cf. *Von den göttlichen Dingen und ihrer Offenbarung, C. W.*, Vol. III (Leipzig, 1816), pp. 342ff.

[4] Jacobi quotes from a Kant essay which is important as showing his progressive estrangement from the Spinozan and Wolffian position: this is Kant's 1763 essay: *Der einzig mögliche Beweisgrund zu einer Demonstration des Daseins Gottes* (Cf. I, Part IV, Beitr. I. *Das notwendige Wesen ist ein Geist* [The necessary Being is a Spirit], where the anti-Spinozan thrust is evident; *C. W.*, ed. Cassirer, Vol. II, pp. 92ff.). On the anti-Spinozan stand of Jacobi and his significance in the development of German thought and especially of idealism, cf. the meticulous analysis of B. Magnino, *Romanticismo e Cristianesimo*, Vol. I (Brescia, 1962), pp. 149ff. Cf. also: L. Lévy-Bruhl, *La philosophie de Jacobi* (Paris, 1894), pp. 139ff.; F. A. Schmid, *Friedrich Heinrich Jacobi* (Heidelberg, 1908), especially pp. 248ff.

[5] *Kritik der reinen Vernunft*, Transz. Dialektik, II Buch, III: Hauptst. 7 Absch.; A 633, B 661; Reclam 495f.).

[6] Cf. *Vorrede zugleich Einleitung; C. W.*, Vol. II, pp. 11f.

of, Kant's theoretical agnosticism in finding insufficient all the proofs hitherto presented by speculative philosophy for the existence of God, of immortality and freedom; this loss, claims Jacobi, was more than compensated by Kant's bestowing on the practical reason a primacy over the theoretical reason, his consequent substantiation of the three *a priori* metaphysical truths serving as basis for morality and his insistence that the acceptance of these truths is a function of "pure rational faith". In this way Kant delivered philosophy from the sterile polemic between dogmatism and skepticism and brought philosophy to true adulthood (the age of criticism). But Jacobi taxes Kant with internal inconsistency: although the Kantian theory presupposes tacitly the existence in the human soul of two specifically distinct sources of direct cognition, sense and intellect, Kant actually only admits one such source, the senses, converting intellect or understanding into something less than a second source of cognition, into a mere faculty of judging, a faculty conditioned by the data of sensible intuition, whether that intuition be pure or empirical.

The consequences of this Kantian inconsistency are grave: sensible intuition in Kant cannot be said to be "perception" in the true sense of the word; it is not a direct and immediate presentation of reality but rather a "phenomenon"; furthermore any apprehension of suprasensible reality is rendered impossible in the absence of any intuition properly proportionate to it; and finally sensible reality itself is rendered present only as "phenomenon" and not as "thing-in-itself". Kant thus begins by an appeal to natural and rational faith [7] but subsequently abandons it to put his whole trust in the understanding which, in his system, explains nothing, destroys everything and ends in sheer subjectivism, as opposed to the Jacobian faith which leads to complete objectivity because it is founded, as we have seen, on reason, which has the function not of explaining but rather of revealing immediately the reality of the suprasensible world.[8] Kant, on the other hand, subsequently even loses the

[7] Jacobi recalls Kant's famous statement in the preface to the 2nd edition of the *Kritik der reinen Vernunft:* "Ich musste also das *Wissen* aufheben, um zum Glauben Platz zu bekommen" (And so I had to abolish *knowledge* in order to get room for *faith*) (B XXX.—Jacobi cites the text slightly differently: *C. W.*, II, 30 note).

[8] This may well be the crucial turning point as between the convergence and divergence of Jacobi and Kant. Jacobi notes it in passing, but he speaks forcefully about it. The difference is that Kant remains attached to the traditional conception that belittles and even denies outright immediate perception, asserting that ". . . via his *senses,* man receives only representations (*Vorstellungen*) which *may* indeed be referred to objects existing in themselves and independently of these representations, but which (representations) do not really contain anything of what belongs to these given objects independently of the representations". Kantianism therefore presents a closed circle, wherein everything is predetermined

very reality presented by sensible intuition inasmuch as he proclaims the purely ideal character of the forms of space and time. Thus Jacobi finds unavailing all Kant's efforts to defend himself against charges of idealism.

Jacobi thus finds the entire Kantian critique of the idealism of Descartes, Malebranche, Berkeley and the rest, to result in a total and global idealism which evaporates both the material and the spiritual world: Kant then swings round against idealism,[9] once he is not in a position to show the effective correspondence between representations and reality, and so both the world of matter and that of spirit are lost completely. Jacobi admits that there does still remain in Kant the positive assertion of "faith" which takes the place of the metaphysics he has destroyed: this faith is based on knowledge of one's own life and one's own freedom and man's truest knowing flows from his own will. With freedom, continues Jacobi, there is necessarily connected providence (*Vorsehung*), since an omnipotence without providence is blind fatalism: but these two realities are unintelligible for the Kantian or idealist kind of understanding where freedom is preceded by necessity and concived in a mechanistic fashion; such freedom is not the freedom as such which operates *intentionally,* which is the *primordial* principle of works and deeds, the only freedom worthy of the name. Although it is true that man does, in this conception, have a direct knowledge of this activity via faith as activity of the reason, man is also aware that he has here before him a nature in continual process of transformation according to necessary laws; he thus has an awareness of not being omnipotent and thus understands that above nature there is an Omnipotent, of which man is a copy (*Nachgebild*).[10] But all this, laments Jacobi, has passed entirely unobserved: even in the idealist theory of "absolute reason" the notions

---

a priori on the part of the subject, beginning with the *a priori* forms of space and time and including the twelve categories of the understanding and even the three ideas of reason. Such representations, concludes Jacobi, end up ". . . manifesting nothing but themselves" and thus do not represent anything at all; they are called "phenomena" (*Erscheinungen*), to be sure, but in reality they are but "empty phantasms" (*leere Gespenster*) that leave us completely in the dark about reality. (*Vorrede,* pp. 35f.). Here Jacobi has touched upon (without developing it) the old Aristotelian-Thomist concept of knowledge as assimilation and "ontological presence", a basic contention against the nominalist and modern principle of ideas as representations only.

9 Jacobi claims himself to have originated the argument used by Kant in the 2nd ed. of the *Kritik der reinen Vernunft* against idealism: "Without the 'You', there is no 'I' " (*Ohne Du kein Ich*), pointing out that it is to be found in the Jacobi *Briefe über die Lehre des Spinoza.* The same principle will be reiterated by Fichte who, however, will use it to merge into absolute idealism which is, for Jacobi, nihilism and atheism, as we shall see.

10 *Vorrede,* pp. 44f.

of freedom, rationality and necessity, simply merge in the final analysis into the single concept of the "unconditioned" or the "eternal essence of things" and the "eternal primordial power" of this essence. Spinoza is the thinker responsible for this identification of freedom and power; and this is the reason why Jacobi considers Spinoza the chief culprit in the matter of modern atheism, which is in substance blind fatalism and materialism.

I. Disintegration of Spinozan Pantheism into Atheism

Jacobi's entire thought, both in its negative aspect as critique of the philosophy of "representations" and in its positive aspect as a theory of faith, remains at the initial level, the "level of principle", as opposed to Kant who applied himself to the investigation of the structures of the human mind and to the idealists who went on stolidly to elaborate a "theory of knowledge" (*Wissenschaftslehre*). An occasional writer and a systematic thinker, Jacobi often touches on crucial and ultimate aspects of problems, but his penetration stops short at the level of immediacy and intuition, so that his work is rather that of a contemplative than of a speculative philosopher. Nor did Jacobi ever want to be a speculative thinker, because in his opinion pure speculation, like all pure philosophical thinking, leads inevitably to atheism: this is the point behind his famous anti-Spinozan polemic with his friend M. Mendelssohn in the letters Jacobi wrote Mendelssohn on the theory and teaching of Spinoza.[11]

The charge of pantheism and atheism against Spinoza is nothing new: [12] what spurred Jacobi to it was the entirely fortuitous discovery that Lessing was a Spinozan, but the polemic is aimed not at Lessing but at Spinoza.[13] The charge could be taken in two ways: as meaning that Spinozism is contained without remainder within (or disintegrates into) pantheism, or, vice versa, that pantheism is a component part of Spinozism, in which latter case there could be excogitated a pantheism which would free itself from the limitations and traits of the Spinozan type and could then be called a "purified Spinozism". Jacobi took up the cudgels for the first interpretation while Mendelssohn, with Herder and Goethe

[11] *Ueber die Lehre des Spinoza, in Briefen* (Leipzig, 1785 [1], 1789 [2]). On the background and circumstances of the controversy, cf. L. Lévy-Bruhl, *op. cit.*, pp. 140ff.

[12] Jacobi was certainly aware of Bayle's charge.

[13] Cf. *Jacobis Spinoza Büchlein,* nebst Replik und Duplik, publ. by Fritz Mauthner (Munich, 1912); H. Scholz, *Die Hauptschriften zum Pantheismusstreit zwischen Jacobi und Mendelssohn* (Berlin, 1916), p. XII.

and followed later by the transcendental idealists, entered the lists for the second interpretation.[14] For Jacobi, Spinozism is the most consistent and total form of pantheism, the only possible pantheism; for the others, on the contrary, there is the possibility of a Spinozan-type metaphysic purged of the unfortunate consequences of Spinoza's position: that is the context in which Mendelssohn took up the defense of Lessing and later Hegel himself undertook a direct defense of Spinoza. In any event, Jacobi's "capital indictment" was a crucial storm signal hoisted against the metaphysical and religious nihilism of modern thought and he unquestionably deserves the rank of chief public prosecutor of atheism in purely speculative philosophy.

The indictment itself is contained in a few terse and pithy propositions near the end of Jacobi's correspondence with Mendelssohn: these amount to a synthetic interpretation of rationalism, ancient and modern, whose principles in each case are destined to suffer the same fate.

1. *Spinozism Is Atheism* [15]

Jacobi entertains no doubts whatever on the meaning and significance of this statement, a meaning and significance entirely independent of the testy personal humor of some of the Spinozan commentators and critics who have made it: for Jacobi and for every theist, God is conceived as being endowed with the power of thought and free will and is consequently the fountainhead of providence with respect to the world and especially man—endowments of the deity which are entirely lacking in Spinoza and in all forms of pantheism. In a footnote, Jacobi urges Spinozism to make open and honest profession of its inherent atheism, approves Hardouin's charge of atheism levelled against Pliny against Malesherbes' defense of him, and rejects firmly the use of the term "cosmotheism" coined by Malesherbes and later reiterated by Kant, Tiedemann and Tennemann who held that Spinoza could not be charged with atheism. Jacobi insists that a God who is only the supreme Being, the One, the Single Substance, and the like, who amounts to a sort of universal restrictive mechanism, who is blind fate, whose Life (if he be granted to be alive at all) is blind and impersonal, is simply not God, is not that entity which can and ought to be understood by God. The nub of this whole position is the principle of

[14] A recent work outlining the biographical and theoretical points in this famous Spinoza controversy, in the critical period of transition from Lessing to Kant, is A. Pupi's essay *Alla soglia dell'età romantica* (Milan, 1962). V. Verra has an especially thorough analytical reconstruction of the various phases of the controversy, in his *F. H. Jacobi,* Dall'illuminismo all'idealismo (Turin, 1963), cc. 3-5, pp. 69ff.

[15] *Ueber die Lehre des Spinoza, C. W.;* Vol. IV, Part I, p. 216.

antiquity, ἓν καὶ πᾶν (One and All) which Jacobi claims Spinoza to have held in common with that same Bruno from whom Descartes, Gassendi, Leibniz [16] and their like also drew their metaphysical ideas; and this is the formula which serves as prototype for all subsequent speculative metaphysics.

The mechanistic and materialistic philosophies of antiquity had been faced with two main difficulties: that of deriving the qualities of a thinking and intelligent essence or nature from the qualities of the corporeal essence or nature (impenetrability, shape, position, size, and motion); and the impossibility of providing any *natural* existence for motion itself or its modifications. Far from resolving these difficulties, the Cartesian system had actually intensified both difficulties. Then appeared Spinoza's solution of the ἓν καὶ πᾶν which reduces the two principles to a single unity: "Matter without form and form without matter are equally unthinkable: their unification must therefore be, in all cases, essential and necessary." [17] This amounts to the identification of the elements and attributes in the one single substance: it is the theory of the One-and-All (*All-Einheitslehre*); and Spinozism comes down to this basic "foundation", Jacobi repeatedly insists.

In his letter to Hemsterhuis, Jacobi highlights the fact that the unity of being serves as that principle from which its modes, extension and thought, are derived: "Being is not an attribute nor yet derived from any faculty; it is that which sustains all the attributes, all the qualities and faculties whatsoever; it is what is designated by the term substance, than which nothing more basic can be imagined and which is in turn presupposed by all else. Among the various energies deriving from being, there are those which pertain IMMEDIATELY to substance. Such are the absolute and real continuum of extension and that of thought. Thought is simply an ATTRIBUTE, a QUALITY of substance; it can in no sense be the cause of substance. It is dependent on that which makes it to be; it is the expression and action of this substance and it is impossible that thought could be that which makes substance act." [18]

The point which Jacobi finds specially arresting in this analytical conception of being is the absolute status accruing to thought and the secondary status attributed to will: "Will is posterior to thought because it presupposes self-awareness. It is posterior to idea because it presupposes awareness of a relation. It does not, therefore, pertain immedi-

[16] *Ibid.*, 1, pp. 10f. Jacobi gives a summary of the thought of Bruno at the period of the *De la causa, principio e uno* in the first Appendix (2, pp. 5ff.).

[17] *Ibid.*, Beylage VII; 2, p. 134. It is the point on which Lessing insists and which revealed his own Spinozism (cf. 1, pp. 54, 89).

[18] *Ibid.*, pp. 127f.

ately to substance nor even to thought; it is but a derivative effect of relations and could never be a principle of action, a pure out-and-out cause."[19]

Above all, the notion of freedom is made to coincide with being itself and this gives rise to a new type of fatalism which might be called rational fatalism: "I am far from denying all freedom and I know that man has received his share. But this freedom does not consist in an imaginary faculty of being able to will; for willing can be only in a will that is, and attributing to a being a power of being able to will is like attributing to that being a power of being able to be, in virtue of which it would be the business of that being and of it alone to give itself actual existence. Man's freedom is the very essence of man, it is the degree of his power or of the strength with which he is what he is. Inasmuch as he acts in accord with the laws of his own being alone, he is acting with a perfect freedom. God who does not and cannot act except by the same power as that whereby he is, and who exists through himself alone, thus possesses absolute freedom. These are my ideas on freedom. As for fatalism, I do not reject it out of hand, only to the extent that it is founded on materialism, or on the absurd opinnion that thought it but a sible that thought should proceed or arise out of extension as that extension should proceed or arise out of thought."[20]

Since Jacobi felt that Mendelssohn, to whom he had addressed these explanations, had not yet penetrated into the speculative kernel of Spinozism, he followed up with a second exposition. This exposition was more analytical and embraced a good forty points. It can be considered one of the milestones of the penetration of Spinoza into German thought and the point of departure for the metaphysic of transcendental idealism. Here are the main points:

(a) (*Unity, immutability and eternity of being*)—"As the basis and foundation of all becoming there must stand a Being which has not itself

[19] *Ibid.*, pp. 129f. A little further on, we read the following specifications: "The will is but a secondary, derivative and relational being, even as directed motion. Just as the why of the direction of motion could not be in the direction itself, for then it would have existed before existing; even so the why of the direction of the will could not be in this direction, for then it would have existed before existing. Your velleity determined by the will is precisely an effect which produces its own cause. You grant me, for you have just said it yourself, that the will is posterior not only to thought but even to idea. Now thought, considered in its essence, is but the feeling of BEING. IDEA is the feeling of being inasmuch as it is determined, individual and in relation with other individuals. WILL is but the feeling of determined being acting as individual" (pp. 133f.).

[20] *Ibid.*, pp. 150f. In his summing up, Jacobi makes Spinoza say that ". . . in all things, action precedes reflection which is but the continuation of action. In a word, we know in proportion as we do; that is the whole point" (p. 157).

become; as the basis of all beginning, something which has not itself begun; as the basis of all mutability, something eternally immutable."

(b) (*Unity, immutability and eternity of becoming*)—"Becoming must be as eternal as being, for if ever the static in itself, the eternally immutable, the permanent in the changing, had been simply by itself without the changing, it would never have produced any becoming, either within itself or outside itself, for both would presuppose equally a beginning from nothing."

(c) (*Eternal coexistence of finite and Infinite*)—"From all eternity, therefore, the changing has been with the immutable, the temporal with the eternal, the finite with the Infinite; and anyone who admits a beginning of the finite admits a beginning from nothing." [21]

From the eternal coexistence of the finite with the Infinite, continues Jacobi, Spinoza derives at once the inseparability of the finite from the Infinite and its inability to exist apart from the Infinite, since otherwise the finite would have been produced out of nothing (Prop. IV and V): this is a critique of the biblical Christian notion of creation and it will be the main thesis of idealist metaphysics, according to which only the Infinite is and the finite is but fortuitous, but appearance. Thus, all finite things taken together form a single reality with the Infinite, not in the sense of a composition but as a "Whole" (*ein Ganzes*) (Prop. VI and VII).[22]

(d) (*God as the reality of all things*)—"That which is First in all things, in things extended as in thinking entities, in like manner (*auf gleiche Weise*), the primordial Being (*das Ur-Seyn*), the omnipresent immutable real of which each individual thing is but a property (*nur Eigenschaft*), this single infinite essence of all essences Spinoza calls God or substance." [23] Thus, particular things as such are *non-entia* (non-beings, nonentities!) and Jacobi notes in Letter L the famous principle that is to become one of the pillars of idealism and to be especially dear to Hegel: [24] "Determination is negation, in other words determination does not pertain to a thing in like manner as does its being" (Prop. XI, XII).

(e) (*God as unitary plexus of the infinite and immediate attributes, infinite extension and infinite thought*)—"Both constitute together an inseparable essence, so that it matters not at all under which of these

[21] *Ibid.*, pp. 172f. For the third principle, Jacobi quotes Spinoza's Letter XXIX.

[22] *Ibid.*, pp. 173ff. Jacobi refers to Spinoza, *Ethica,* P. I, Prop. XXVIII, Demonstr. and Scholion, and illustrates in a note using the Kantian theory of the (ideal) infinity of space and time according to the *Critique of Pure Reason.*

[23] *Ibid.*, pp. 180f.

[24] Cf. Hegel, *Geschichte der Philosophie,* ed. Michelet, Vol. III (Berlin, 1844), p. 347.

two properties God be considered, for the order and connection of concepts is identical with the order and connection of things, and all that results *formally* from the infinite nature of God must result *objectively* from that same nature, and vice versa." [25]

Each and every one of these crucial principles is substantiated by constant references to Spinoza's works, not only the *Ethics* but the letters as well, so as to strengthen the force of Jacobi's main charge that "Spinozism is atheism" because it is panentheism, pantheism, cosmotheism and the like, i.e., not because it openly denies God but rather because it identifies him with the whole of the real or with Being, with the Real as such. And both God and the concept, concludes Jacobi, must, according to Spinoza, be found both in the whole and in each of its parts and in each and every particular thing, completely and perfectly *(vollständig und vollkommen)*.[26]

(f) In order to understand Jacobi's critique properly, the reader must pay special attention to the *real identity* of motion and rest, the immediate modes of *infinite extension,* and of the infinite and absolute *thoughts,* intellect and will, inasmuch as the latter contain *objectively* what the former contain *formally;* and likewise to the *real identity* of the *Natura Naturans,* which is God, and the *Natura naturata,* infinite will and intellect (Prop. XVIII, XIX and X).[27] In a kind of absolute conjunction, extension and thought, although two different essences, are together *unum et idem* (one and the same) in the single and *indivisible* Substance; and they are likewise one and the same in each and every individual thing.

(g) The real identity of extension and thought in Substance emerges on the human level as the real identity of body and soul: actually the body is the external integument and the soul the inside of the envelope, so that the soul can become aware of anything only via the affections and modifications of the body. This means that the soul is nothing but the immediate concept (*unmittelbare Begriff*) of the body, so that the excellence (*Vortreffichkeit*) of the soul is nothing but the excellence of its body.[28] The essence of the soul coincides *objectively* and is *objectively* identified with the essence of the body.

(h) Particular things are therefore immutable in their *eternal* existence: they are indeed produced by God via the affections (*Affektionen*)

[25] *Ueber die Lehre des Spinoza,* pp. 183f.

[26] *Ibid.,* pp. 204f.

[27] *Ibid.,* pp. 184ff. The real identity (in one entity only, to wit God) of nas sion and thought is explained further in Props. XXIV and XXV. Prop. Xnsion, the definitive formulation: "Since thought is inseparably conjoined witb all that is in extension must likewise be in thought" (p. 193).

[28] *Ibid.,* pp. 196f.

or dispositions (*Beschaffenheiten*) of his own essence. *But these are as infinite and eternal as God himself and he is cause of himself* in a way that is neither transitory or finite (Prop. XXXVI).

(i) As for the connections between particular things—and this is one of the points of affinity Jacobi sees between Spinozan pantheism and Leibniz's *harmonia praestabilita*—these particular things mutually presuppose each other and are referred one to the other in such a way that any one of them could neither be nor be thought or conceived without the others nor could all the others together be or be conceived without that one: i.e., they form together an inseparable and indivisible whole (*ein unzertrennliches Ganzes*); or, more accurately and properly, they exist and cohere in an entirely indivisible infinite entity, and in no other way do they exist at all (Prop. XXXIX).[29] Whatever may be said of Jacobi's own solution or of the status and cogency of his *Glaube* (faith), there is no doubt that he was the first 18th-century thinker to trace Spinoza's whole subtle system ruthlessly back to its principles and to expose its deepest meaning and significance.

Jacobi is specially struck and shocked in Spinoza's thought by the denial of life and personality to God, of any independent reality to the infinite, of the distinction between soul and body, of free will and final causes: [30] in a word, that very *determinism* in the life of spirit that will prompt Jacobi to level the same charge against Leibniz and his school as well.

2. *Leibniz's and Wolff's Dynamism Is Atheism*

The indefatigable investigator, Jacobi, soon finds that the philosophy of Leibniz and Wolff is no less fatalistic than that of Spinoza and indeed can be reduced to the same principles as those governing the Spinozan articulation. Thus Jacobi in most forthright manner! Now the curious thing is that both Leibniz and especially Wolff had made a closely-reasoned and meticulous critique of Spinozism and come to exactly the same conclusions about it as did Jacobi! [31]

[29] *Ibid.*, pp. 202f.—The second principle or point, in which Jacobi asserts that "the philosophy of the Cabala is nothing but a confused Spinozism" (pp. 217ff.) of no particular interest to us here.

[30] Recent critics and commentators maintain that Jacobi does indeed accuse [illegible]zism of atheism but at the same time admits and recognizes the deep reli- *He*[illegible]sentiments that animated Spinoza himself (Cf. A. Hebeisen, *Friedrich* 28ff., *Jacobi*, Seine Auseinandersetzung mit Spinosa, Diss. Bern, 1960), pp. *und F.* —Also H. Hölters, *Der spinozistische Gottesbegriff bei M. Mendelssohn*

[31] A. F[illegible]*cobi*, Universitas-Archiv 97, Emsdetten, 1938, pp. 64ff.

sents a re[illegible]er de Careil, *Descartes et Spinoza* (Paris, 1863). An appendix pre- *Ethics* and o[illegible]n by Leibniz of Spinoza, a new Leibniz commentary on the [illegible]ne Spinoza letters. Jacobi was probably prompted to extend the

In fact, Jacobi's critique of the Leibniz-Wolff system seems a little forced, especially the bracketing of the Spinozan single-Substance metaphysic and the pre-established-harmony metaphysic which presupposes the pluralism of the monads; in this sense, Jacobi's critique of Lessing, the convinced Leibnizian, needs a certain modification. Leibniz's insistence on the primordial "power" and energy of the monads, which makes each of them a center of activity, is diametrically opposed to Spinoza's monistic conception. Leibniz's trenchant and indeed excessive profession of spiritualism contrasts with the destructive identity asserted by Spinoza between thought and extension, soul and body, a point on which Leibniz reproached Spinoza.

Then we also have Leibniz's express critique of Spinoza. He reproaches Spinoza with having taken a naturalistic conception as point of departure: *Spinoza starts where Descartes ended, in naturalism.* In Leibniz's detailed critique of Spinoza it can be said that there is not a single Spinozan proposition of any importance which is not vigorously rejected: the notion of substance; the denial of the possibility of creation (*ex nihilo nihil fit*); the identification of the life of God with the derivation of creatures and of the power of God with the power of creatures and the consequent inescapable pantheism; the denial of the freedom of God in the matter of creation (and consequently of providence as well) and of the individual freedom of men as well as the immortality of the individual soul; and finally, the absolute split and even opposition introduced by Spinoza between reason and faith, between philosophy and theology.[32]

Yet it cannot be denied that Leibniz felt himself quite close to Spinoza and Leibniz's comment on Spinoza's remarks in a letter to Oldenburg is revealing. Spinoza had written: "For I in no way subordinate God to fate; rather do I conceive all things to follow by inevitable necessity from the nature of God in the same way as all feel that it follows from the nature of God himself that God knows himself, which no one, of course, denies to follow necessarily from the divine nature; and yet no one holds God to be compelled by any sort of fate; rather they hold him to know himself entirely freely, albeit necessarily." And Leibniz's only comment is: "This ought to be interpreted as follows: The world could not have been produced otherwise, because God cannot but operate in the most perfect fashion. For since he is most wise, he makes the best possible choice. But it is not in the least to be thought

---

charge of atheism to include Leibniz and his school by the discovery of Spinozism in Lessing whose notion of history took its inspiration directly from Leibnizian rationalism.

[32] *Ibid., passim* and especially pp. 196ff.

that all things follow from the nature of God without any intervention of the will. The example of that operation of God whereby he knows himself seems less than apposite, because this occurs without any intervention of the will." [33]

In the final analysis, Leibniz thus identifies necessity and freedom in God and it is hard to see how he can make any meaningful distinction between the freedom with which God is asserted to know himself and the freedom of the *creatio ad extra:* Leibnizian optimism thus manifests itself as the critical twin of Spinoza's *ordo rerum est idem ac ordo idearum* (the order of things is identical with the order of ideas), despite Leibniz's sharp distinction between *truths of reason* and *truths of fact.* The absolute rationalism that links together the series of the greatest thinkers of the modern era, from Descartes through Malebranche and Spinoza to Leibniz, proceeds by stages that are indeed distinct but at the same time strictly interconnected; and transcendental idealism will furnish a definitive interpretation of these stages by considering them to be but aspects and elements of a single solution.[34] Thus whatever doubts may have subsisted, especially at the outset, in Spinoza-criticism, concerning Leibniz's disapproving attitude to Spinoza, it would seem that no doubts can now be entertained.[35] Yet I find no mention of the atheism charge nor even any express mention of the charge of pantheism, unless the charge of "naturalism" is to be understood in this sense.

In his charge of atheism, Jacobi brackets the philosophy of Wolff with that of Leibniz, but he here presents no detailed or precise proof or exposition.[36] It is a matter of record that Wolff showed himself a vigor-

[33] G. W. Leibniz, *Die philosophischen Schriften,* ed. C. J. Gerhardt, Vol. I (Hildesheim, 1961), pp. 123f.

[34] Leibniz also defends, against Spinoza, the reality of Christ's resurrection and ascension and consequently of his divinity (*ibid.,* p. 124).

[35] Cf. G. Friedmann's proof of this, against L. Stein, B. Russell and L. Brunschvicg, in Friedmann, *Leibniz et Spinoza* (Paris, 1946), pp. 197ff. In the *Confessio naturae contra Atheistas,* Leibniz makes express mention of Hobbes but says nothing of Spinoza. (*C. W.,* ed. Gerhardt, Vol. IV, pp. 105f.). The charge of atheism was first launched all-out against Spinoza by Bayle (*Dict. hist. et crit.,* Vol. IV [Basle, 1738], pp. 253f.: "He was a systematic Atheist with an entirely new method". In lengthy footnotes, Bayle presents extensive reports on anti-Spinozan writings, especially on the point of the atheism charge). The charge was accepted virtually without demur by the English deists who could claim Spinoza, in various ways, as their own forerunner (cf. G. Bohrmann, *Spinozas Stellung zur Religion,* Appendix: Spinoza in England [Giessen, 1914], pp. 59ff.).

Leibniz explicitly brackets Spinozism and deism: "I believe . . . that the group called *Socinians,* and in their wake the thinkers called *Deists* and *Spinozists* have greatly contributed to the spread of this teaching" (Leibniz, *Opera Omnia,* ed. Dutens, Vol. I [Geneva, 1768], pp. 690f.).

[36] Jacobi has a brief note referring to and citing Kant, but the passages to which Jacobi refers (in the two *Critiques* of Pure Reason and Practical Reason) seem rather vague. The charge of atheism originated from the pietists of the Faculty of Theology, led by a certain Lange, who wrote *Prüfung der vernünftigen*

ous champion and defender of the existence of God and a most resolute critic of the contrary errors: atheism, fatalism, deism, naturalism, anthropomorphism, materialism, paganism, Manicheanism and Spinozism. And he subjects Spinozism to a detailed and meticulous critique from beginning to end, his chief criticism being that of Spinozism's "fatalism" with its consequent denial of all religion and all morality.[37] Wolff even goes on to accuse Spinozism directly of impiety and to brand it as more baneful than explicit and professed atheism: Wolff indeed reiterates Bayle's phrase and stigmatizes Spinozism as the only brand of atheism reduced to a system.

In § 716 of the *Theologia naturalis,* we find the pith of Wolff's atheism charge. The thesis is: *"Spinozism is not far removed from atheism and it is equally baneful, indeed in a certain respect it is even more baneful than atheism"*. There follows the proof:

(a) "For even though Spinoza admits God as the first and only cause of all things (§ 672): nevertheless, because he denies him to be intelligently wise (note, § 712) or to operate by free will (note, § 709) and govern this universe (note, § 714), and because he posits bodies and souls and other thinking entities, if such there be, to be in that God as parts in a whole (note, § 708), he is in fact fabricating a God wholly diverse from the true God who is endowed with supreme intelligent wisdom (§ 640. part. I *Theol. nat.*) and a supremely free will (§ 431. part. I *Theol. nat.*), who governs this universe by his wisdom (§ 902. part. I *Theol. nat.*) and in whom souls and bodies and other thinking entities, if such there be, do not exist as parts in a whole (§ 708). It is therefore just as if he denied that the true God exists. Wherefore, since that man is an atheist who denies God to exist (§ 411), Spinozism obviously is not far removed from atheism. *Which was the first point.*"

(b) "Moreover, Spinozism takes away all religion (§ 714) and all divine obligation to do certain actions and refrain from others (§ 715), even as does atheism (§ 516, 539). Since therefore atheism is baneful

---

Gedanken des Herrn Wolf von Gott, der Welt . . ., in two parts (Halle, 1723, 1724): the charge resulted in Wolff's removal from the University of Halle (cf. K. Erdmann, "Das Treiben der hallischen Pietisten gegen Christian Wolf und die Philosophie überhaupt," in *Die theologische und philosophische Aufklärung des sechzehnten und neunzehnten Jahrhunderts,* Appendix I [Leipzig, 1849], pp. 333ff.). A historico-critical study of this whole matter is that of E. Zeller, "Wolff's Vertreibung aus Halle; der Kampf des Pietismus mit der Philosophie," in *Vertrage und Abhandlungen,* Vol. I (Leipzig, 1865), pp. 108ff. Wolff himself claimed that the charge had been ultimately motivated by academic jealousy and ranked the case in a line going back to the trials of Socrates and Anaxagoras and coming down to Descartes and Campanella (cf. "De peccato in Philosophum," in *Horae subsecivae Marburgenses,* a. 1731 [Frankfurt and Leipzig, 1731], pp. 371ff.).

[37] Wolff, *Theologia naturalis,* §§ 671-716, (Frankfurt and Leipzig, 1741), pp. 672ff., especially 709-710, 721ff.

inasmuch as by it is taken away all religion and all divine obligation to do certain actions and refrain from others, it can in no wise be doubted that Spinozism is equally baneful with atheism. *Which was the second point.*"

(c) "Certainly a universal fatalism is inextricably bound up with Spinozism (§ 709). Wherefore, since a fatal and lethal necessity is extended to all actions of men whatsoever by universal fatalism, while universal fatalism is not necessarily involved in atheism (§ 531); therefore Spinozism stands more in the way of moral practice than does atheism considered in itself, as entailing universal fatalism only by accident. Inasmuch therefore as atheism is baneful in the degree to which it stands in the way of moral practice, as we shall be pointing out on several occasions in due course; it is entirely evident that Spinozism is, in a certain respect, more baneful than atheism. *Which was the third point.*

(d) Final judgment: "And if any one should wish to come to a yet clearer knowledge of the great gulf separating the true God and that one that *Spinoza* fabricates and adorns with a specious definition (§ 672) that does but warm and encourage the snake hiding in the grass; then let such a one compare with Spinozism what has been proven concerning the true God, both in our system and in the first section above. So will it, of a surety, be evident what points there developed are in contradiction with Spinozism and what things must be denied of God if once Spinozism be admitted; and it will then be clear how meager is the number of those dogmas which are allowed to stand in the Spinozist system. And this is the reason that it has come about that Spinozists are considered atheists by the common and unanimous consent of all and Spinozism is held to be an impious and godless system; and while other authors who have been branded with the stigma of atheism have chanced upon defenders, no one has hitherto come forward bold enough to try to exculpate *Spinoza* of this charge of atheism. Rather is the Ethics of *Spinoza* recognized to be the single system of atheism being publicly touted abroad; whence we have judged it to be our business to overturn its foundation." [38]

It is certainly not in virtue of such explicitly anti-Spinozan passages nor indeed even in terms of the wider context that the philosophy of Leibniz-Wolff can be accused of being fatalistic and thus atheist like that of Spinoza; it is rather in virtue of the fundamental methodological principle, i.e., philosophical and theological rationalism or the claim to deduce the reality of the Infinite from the finite, i.e., the approach that denies that man has any apprehension of God, properly speaking, and

[38] *Ibid.*, pp. 729f. Wolff has been called "the last really great expert in Spinozism prior to Jacobi in Germany" (H. Scholz, *Die Hauptschriften des Pantheismusstreites*, p. XLI).

asserts that God must be attained solely via the mediation of proof: "Every method of proof leads to fatalism." [39] Now, if there has ever been a philosophy that repeats the Spinozan method of demonstrative proof, with its claim to rigor, almost geometrical precision, with continual cross references, to the point of exasperation, to preceding sections, treatises and works, a philosophy that functions like a well-oiled mechanical device modelled on the Spinozan *Ethics,* it is the monumental compilation produced by Wolff, a work without parallel in our opinion except for the *Disputationes metaphysicae* of the Jesuit Francisco Suarez, with whom Wolff gives clear evidence of having much in common.[40] These basic observations on the question of Wolff's atheism are enough for our present purpose.

Jacobi's stand thus embraces two mutually related elements which he integrates with a brusque straightforwardness: pure philosophy, of which Spinoza is the classic illustration, leads to atheism and fatalism; therefore the existence of suprasensible realities must be discovered by another route, which is that of "revelation", whose adequate principle is faith, as has already been said. Jacobi concentrated on proving the first point in his polemic with Lessing: [41] Jacobi's whole argument comes down really to the fundamental methodological observation that pure

[39] Jacobi, *Ueber die Lehre des Spinoza,* p. 223.

[40] Cf. M. Wundt, *Die deutsche Schulphilosophie im Zeitalter der Aufklärung,* Heidelb. Abhandlungen 32 (Tübingen, 1945), p. 159. Leibniz himself was dependent on and in the tradition of Suarez and mediated his influence to Wolff: P. Mesnard, "Comment Leibniz se trouva place dans le sillage de Suarez," *Arch. de Philos.* (1959), pp. 7ff. The theologian Budde accused Wolff of having likewise denied the freedom of man by separating the soul completely from the body and denying any physical influence, thus ". . . abolishing all morality and religion" (cf. Hans M. Wolff, *Die Weltanschauung der deutschen Aufklärung* [Bern, 1949], pp. 152ff.). On Wolff's fate at the hands of Catholic critics as well, cf. F. Valjavec, *Geschichte der abendländischen Aufklärung* [Vienna-Munich, 1961], pp. 140ff.

[41] *Ueber die Lehre des Spinoza,* Beylage VII, pp. 125ff. In this connection, Jacobi cites the famous passage of Spinoza: "Woe and alas! things have come to such a pass that those who openly profess themselves not to possess an idea of God and to know God only through created things (of whose causes they are ignorant) do not blush to accuse Philosophers of atheism" *Tract. theol.-politicus,* c. 2 (Jacobi, *Wider Mendelssohns Beschuldigungen in dessen Schreiben an die Freunde Lessings, C. W.,* Vol. IV, 2, p. 239). Spinoza's lament probably refers to the accusation levelled against him by the Dutch physician, van Velthuysen: "Therefore I deem myself not to go far astray of the truth nor yet to do any injury to the Author, if I denounce him as teaching simple and downright Atheism by means of disguised and counterfeit arguments" (Epist. 42; ed. Gebhardt, Vol. IV, [Heidelberg, 1924], p. 218). Spinoza's defense of himself is an evasion but it is typical and revealing: "For atheists are wont to seek above measure honors and riches, both of which I have ever scorned as all who are acquainted with me know full well" (Ep. 43, p. 219). This is indeed a somewhat thin defense when what is at stake is nothing less than the transcendence and freedom of God in the act of creation and in the governance of the world. It is this point on which Jacobi likewise insists.

philosophy resolves itself into simple reflection on the sensible and proceeds solely in accord with the principle of identity applied in the sphere of the finite in such a way as to make it impossible ever to transcend that sphere. And Jacobi makes the penetrating observation that there is connected with this rationalism a typically rationalist identification of the notion of cause (*Ursache*) with the notion of foundation or principle (*Grund*): this approach empties the notion (and reality!) of "cause" of its genuine content, dissipates its true tang and reduces it to a purely logical essence.

The notion of cause is real, it is an "experiential concept" (*ein Erfahrungsbegriff*) and therefore cannot be deduced from or reduced to the purely logical notion of principle. Consequently, the principle of sufficient reason and that of cause cannot be absolutely identified; therefore there can be no demonstrative transition from the finite to the Infinite. In this whole polemic against rationalistic pseudo-theology, Jacobi is clearly seizing upon one essential aspect of the drama of modern thought, i.e., its circling in a vacuum from the moment at which thought is conceived as a mere reflection upon sensible experience. The assertion is made that the only sort of representation possible for us is one that can be produced in accord with the laws of our own intellect. The laws of the intellect are referred subjectively and objectively to the laws of nature, so that we are not capable of forming for ourselves any concept or notion of anything that is not simply natural: what cannot become real according to nature cannot even be rendered possible, i.e., thinkable, by us in representation. To get out of this labyrinth, Jacobi asserts that the supernatural, the existence of God, is grasped prior to the natural and that the former serves as basis and foundation for the latter, that creation is at the basis of natural causality which is no longer in the thrall of strict fatalistic necessity as is demanded by the principle of sufficient reason.

Jacobi insists that man has the generic principle of knowledge in reason (*Vernunft*) which is the spiritual mental principle (*Geist*) by means of which man exists.[42] Now, when I consider the whole man, I find that his consciousness is composed of two primordial representations, that of the *conditioned* and that of the *Unconditioned*. (This is Jacobi's methodological tenet of the dual primary immediacy, as opposed to the nominalism of rationalism, Kant and idealism). The two

[42] Note also the new notion of reason, understood by Jacobi as a feeling (*Gefühl*) which apprehends the existence of the suprasensible: "As there is a sensible intuition, an intuition *via* the *senses*, so there is also a rational intuition via the reason" (*Vorrede*, p. 59). And a little further on: "The faculty of feeling . . . is the most exalted faculty in man; it is the faculty that specifically distinguishes him from the animals . . .; this faculty is, we maintain, one and the same as reason" (p. 61).

are inseparably linked, but in such a way that the representation of the conditioned presupposes the representation of the Unconditioned and can only be given together with it. Thus we have no need of any preliminary search for the Unconditioned; rather we have the same evidence, indeed a greater certainty, of its existence (*Dasein* = thereness) than we possess of our own conditioned existence. Consequently the Unconditioned, subsequently identified with God, cannot be grounded in or deduced from nature because it is outside of nature and not susceptible of any merely natural nexus with nature; thus Jacobi calls it the supernatural (*das Uebernatürliche*), from which the natural, i.e., the universe, is then derived in exclusively supernatural fashion rather than in the natural fashion [43] propounded by Spinoza and philosophical thinkers generally.

This noetic priority of the Unconditioned, vigorously identified by Jacobi with God (*Der Gott*), brought Jacobi's own view much closer to the rationalist and Spinozan view and to the later full-blown idealist view: while there did indeed remain the absolute and drastic distinction between the two orders of reality and between the two cognitions, but even this distinction is substantially attenuated, if not entirely eradicated, by the subordination of the cognition and knowledge of the conditioned to that of the Unconditioned. Jacobi is extremely reticent on this whole problematic, later to become so crucial. The further fact that Jacobi considered Spinozism irrefutable at the level of the logical understanding [44] is evidence of the clear-cut distinction posited by Jacobi between the understanding as such and the reason; and this stance will recur with renewed Spinozan overtones in idealism, especially in Hegel. It must further be borne in mind that, despite Jacobi's insistence on the distinction between cause and principle or foundation, the causality principle is limited, as in Kant, to the sphere of the finite. If the finite is to be transcended, then the principle of causality must likewise be transcended, for it does not admit of an action originating from itself.[45] Jacobi's conception of the understanding coincides with the idealist no-

[43] *Ueber die Lehre des Spinoza,* Beylage VII, especially pp. 151ff.

[44] "My letters on the theory of Spinoza were not written in an attempt to supplant one system by another, but rather to point up the invincibility of Spinozism to any attack stemming from a merely logical use of the understanding" (*Vorrede,* p. XXXVII).

[45] "The principle of causality of the understanding does not lead beyond Nature, beyond the quintessential embodiment of the finite. Indeed the principle of causality goes to show that there cannot be any such reality as a quintessential embodiment of the finite, that the concept of nature divorced from the concept of the supernatural is a fabricated and fictitious concept. And so in order to get beyond the finite, we must likewise get beyond the law of causality, which is the law of the finite and precludes any action or operation beginning itself" (*ibid.,* pp. XXXIIf.).

tion: for Jacobi the understanding amounts to no more than the power of reflection upon the finite; in no sense does it involve that deep-probing apprehension of primordial concepts and first principles with which the mind gazes out upon the world and takes bearings on the Absolute, as propounded by Parmenidean-Thomist philosophy. Neither Jacobi nor idealism, in fact, presupposes any First Principle for the understanding; both presuppose merely a something, this or that entity. The understanding posits an end to the indefinite series of conditioned realities and calls this end the beginning or the totality; and Jacobi scoffs at the very idea of calling this fabricated beginning God, insisting that such a procedure would be the height of anthropomorphism, the very anthropomorphism which holds all pantheists in thrall, including Spinoza, whose universe is the same today, yesterday and forever. The flat level ground of this universe is whirled up into a muddled dust of natures which *are* not, each one of which and the overall sum total of which are but a chameleon nothing. It could indeed be contended that Spinozism does not deny the existence of a God nor yet the existence of a genuine and real world; but in the final analysis this comes down to a mere play on words. The point of departure is the existence of a real world and the posing of the question as to whether there exists, above and beyond that world, another Being, or whether that world as a closed whole is the All, all that there is with nothing beyond it whatever.

This steady refusal of Jacobi to establish any ascendent nexus between the finite and the Infinite has deeper roots than might appear at first glance. He does, of course, appeal to his own interpretative acceptance of Humeian *Belief,* an interpretation amounting to a complete inversion, according to which contact with the real, apprehension of existence, is held to be something immediate and primordial, applicable both to the perception of natural reality and, above all, to the apprehension of the transcendent reality which Jacobi calls "supernatural", a term that is not very appropriate and can create confusion, as we have seen. But Jacobi's refusal to establish the transcendent nexus between finite and Infinite has deeper roots in his neglect, or at least his relegation to a level of secondary importance, of that central primordial experience which is the only one capable of imparting cohesion and structural solidity to the external perception of the world or to the apprehension of the transempirical and transcendent, i.e., the experience of the individual and personal ego, an experience which is intrinsic and inalienable for every knower. The admission of such a central primordial experience of the individual and personal ego by no means signifies an acceptance of the Cartesian *cogito* nor yet of the *Ich denke überhaupt* of Kant and idealism; it involves rather the admission and recognition of the elements or principles productive of the radical tension which is the constitutive and motive force of the activity of knowing: there is not nor can there be any experience in the absence of that principle of coherence provided by the deep-lying ego to whom are presented and referred the contents of experience in some sort of unified form; furthermore, in the absence of the coherent continuity of the spiritual life, of the experience-dominating focal point of the inviolable ego in its continuous self-transcendence in relation to a world which ineluctably conditions it in its practical life, there is not even the possibility of recognizing the reality of that higher object which Jacobi attributes to the "revelation" of reason, nor yet of recognizing the superiority of the personal ego over the world in that relationship with the Absolute into which this alleged revelation is supposed to bring it. I cannot conceive of God as spirit, thought, freedom and providence, unless I have first had experience and direct knowledge, in my own human reality, of what these terms signify. To have recourse here to the Jacobi *Leap* is a meaningless business; or rather it amounts, as Jacobi's own term precisely signifies, to a *mortal leap;* it is indeed not even a leap at all, it is a mere nothing, because any talk of something that man is incapable of recognizing comes down, in the final analysis, to nothing.

Jacobi's error, and it is an incurable error, at least as bad as the one with which he reproaches Spinozism, lies not so much in his critique of mediated thought and systematization, but rather in Jacobi's own failure to admit that primordial vital nucleus which is the only possible center and fulcrum of the entire cognitional and practical sphere upon which his own *Lebensphilosophie* must necessarily be based. This philosophy, in the absence of that incorruptible spiritual individual nucleus which is the singular, the human individual, evaporates into thin air or into a Spinozistic version of pietism which sets over against the Absolute of reason an Absolute of feeling and over against rationalistic dogmatism a dogmatism of the irrational. Jacobi's further statement that Spinozism is irrefutable on the level of formal logical thought serves merely to confirm the fact that Jacobi's own critique has not even touched Spinoza: any critique which does not dispute the theoretical validity of Spinoza's very principle is simply snapping in a vacuum. Of the exact relation (amounting to equivocation) between Jacobi's *faith* or *belief* and Christian faith we shall be speaking soon, when we come to discuss Jacobi's connection with religion and in particular with Christianity.

First we must mention the notion of atheism propounded in Jacobi.[46] He disagrees with Hume and asserts that it is an historical fact that

[46] Cf. *Ueber die Lehre des Spinoza,* Beylage II, Diokles an Diotima über den Atheismus, pp. 47ff. (Dated September 7, 1787).

atheism came on the scene after belief in God and religion, inasmuch as belief in God corresponds to a natural impulse whereas atheism supposes a reflection; but in reality we have arrived at the basic pillar of Jacobi's own philosophy: "Faith in a supreme Being as such who is the fountainhead of all being and all becoming, and faith in a God who is a *spirit,* are both for man data of the unfathomable reality of his own spontaneity and freedom, without which not even the first postulate of Euclid could be conceived. Therefore faith in God as such is natural for man and all the more natural is faith in a *living* God." [47]

The cult of the dead and even the fear excited by natural causes may be admitted to have contributed to the initial emergence of the idea of God; but the radical and ultimate origin of this idea lies in the spectacle of the world and the shock of emotion it produces in the soul and the imagination, calculated to raise man up to the recognition of a supreme being. This approach to the question is clearly desirous of avoiding at once the Scylla of sheer a priorism and the Charybdis of sheer a posteriorism; it recalls and echoes the position of Vico. Here polytheism is posterior to theism and it stems from man immersing himself in natural things and grappling with a cognition of their powers, with the consequence that he conceives God in anthropomorphized fashion and thus arrives at a plurality of Gods. Philosophy then administers the *coup de grâce:* it addresses itself to the ordering of everything in signs and concepts and reduces the presence of the truth to the determination of simple objects which are linked with the physical world; consequently it ends by neglecting man's own internal, interior feelings (*Gefühle*) in order to busy itself solely with concepts.

The fruit of this insistence of philosophy on the data of the external world has been the objectification of the instinctive demand for knowledge which impels man to find the "cause" of everything in the universal concept of *matter*. And the final step Jacobi alleges to have been taken by this purely abstract philosophizing, based upon the data of the external senses, is the elaboration of the notion of an "active matter" whereby man attributes to matter the principle of an internal motion bound up with its very nature; this hidden power of matter is believed to render virtually visible the foundation, evolution and eternity of the

[47] *Sendschreiben an Ehrard O., C. W.,* Vol. I, p. 251. In the conversation with Lessing: "*I believe in an intelligent personal cause of the world*" (*C. W.,* Vol. IV, I, 59). In this connection, Jacobi also cites Kant with obvious relish as an ally against Spinozism. The Kantian passage in question is: "The concept of God is not customarily understood to signify merely a blindly operating Nature as the root cause of things, but rather a supreme Being Who is supposed to be the free and rational creator of things; and this concept of a *living God* is the only one that is of interest to us" *Kritik der reinen Vernunft,* A 633, B 660f. (cf. Jacobi, *Vorrede,* p. XXIV).

world, eliminating any necessity of preoccupation with its ultimate origin or with the source of its properties. This is *simple and total atheism* as such can be designated the whole of pre-Socratic philosophy, in which the deity had become superfluous and its place in nature had been taken by the *anima mundi*. Jacobi maintains that it was only with Socrates and his disciples Plato and Aristotle that a real and genuine philosophical knowledge of God began in antiquity; but their effort was overturned and brought to nothing by politics which, precisely for political reasons, accepted into religion the notions of the most dissimilar philosophies, thus reducing the deity to a monstrosity (*Ungeheuer*) of internal contradictions. Thus, classical philosophy ended in a *second atheism*.

The third atheism was the result of modern thought, initiated by Descartes with the excellent intentions of avoiding the errors of the old philosophy; soon this philosophy adopted the geometric method, which led men to see the main aim and object of knowledge as being the cognition of matter and its properties. This led to the establishment of such an intimate connection between physics and metaphysics that the whole of the universe acquired the most fascinating homogeneity and a simplicity that precluded any other principle except self-determining matter, as being superfluous and pointless.

Jacobi holds that the third atheism is intimately connected with the first, inasmuch as both are based on the acceptance of matter as the principle and foundation of the real; but the third is more cunning and insidious because it is outfitted with the perfected method of mathematics. The second atheism, which is rather unbelief (*Unglaube*) derived from rational deductions which are justified as such, can be cured by being brought within the range of influence of true wisdom. But the third, which Jacobi calls the "gigantic spawn of our doltish pride" (*diese riesenhafte Geburt unseres thörichten Stolzes*), will be overcome only by admitting as an undeniable truth that matter is merely a word whereby we designate the sum total of real beings and their relations with our sense organs, on which our conception of matter consequently depends.

The absence of any explicit reference to pantheism in general and Spinozan pantheism in particular is not the only surprising element in this "deduction" of the forms of atheism just as surprising is the reduction of atheism to materialism in the first and third forms; and the second form, whatever may have been Jacobi's intention, really becomes devoid of any meaningful theoretical status inasmuch as it is considered to be simply the product of syncretism. But this oversimplified interpretation has deep roots in Jacobi's theoretical approach: it corresponds to his theory of cognition in terms of the two direct sources of perception, the external sense and the interior sense. The philosophy which bases itself on the former ends by identifying reality with matter; only that philosophy which, like Jacobi's own, follows Socrates and the Socratics in addressing itself to the moral world and appealing to the interior sense, is in a position to find God. This is an interpretation of the whole history of human thought in terms of atheism, with a very simple guiding thread but one which proved inadequate to cope with the case of Spinoza and was to show itself even more inadequate to cope with the new forms of atheism which were already emerging in modern thought after the revolution effected by Kant.

Another outstanding witness, of a quite different temper from Jacobi, to the destructive power of the Kantian critique was Heine who called Kant "this great destroyer in the realm of thoughts", and claimed Kant had far outdone Robespierre in terrorism. Heine accuses Kant of preparing the way for atheism primarily by his distinction between "noumenon" and "phenomenon" and his relegation of God to the status of an unknowable noumenon: "God is, according to Kant, a noumen. Kant's argument is directed to proving that that transcendental ideal being we have hitherto called God is nothing but a fabrication, product of a natural illusion. Kant indeed shows that we can know nothing at all about that noumenon, God, and that any proof of his existence is impossible for all time to come. Over this section of the *Critique of Pure Reason* can be inscribed the words of Dante: 'Abandon hope all ye who enter here!' " (H. Heine, *Zur Geschichte der Religion und Philosophie in Deutschland,* in *Ausgewaehlte Werke,* Vol. IV [Munich, 1957], p. 187). The climax of the *Critique of Pure Reason* is the critique of the traditional proofs of the existence of God and therewith of "all manner of speculative theology"; this critique totally dissipates the cloud castles (*Luftgebilde*) of deism: "Here is shown in ruthless clarity their impotence, the groundlessness and untenableness of their outlook, of their idea of the nature of God. So we are not much distressed to see this idea toppled to the ground; and that is just what Kant did, by destroying their proofs of the existence of God" (p. 189). As a good Spinozist, Heine contends that the ontological proof is valid, although it is an object of meditation rather than of demonstration. Such a highly qualified contemporary as Heine must be taken seriously and his witness may well be considered a judgment on the *Atheismusstreit* and on the entire immanentist current from beginning to end: "In his appeal to the public and his defense in court, Fichte has followed in the tradition of all contumacious men, using expressions that wound our deepest feelings. We who believe in a real God who reveals himself to our senses in infinite extension and to our mind in infinite thought; we who worship a visible God in nature and hear his invisible voice within our own soul—we are disagreeably impressed by the strident words in which Fichte declares our God to be but a figment of the brain and even makes fun of him. It is doubtful, to be sure, whether it be irony or simple madness that drives Fichte to liberate the good God so totally from all sensible accretions as to deny him even existence, on the grounds that existence is a sensible concept and only possible as a sensible reality. Science, he says, knows no other being than sensible being; and since being can be ascribed only to the objects of experience, this predicate is unsuitable for God. And so the God of Fichte has no existence, he is not, he manifests himself only as pure operation, as an order of events, as *Ordo ordinans,* as the law of the universe. In such fashion has idealism been constantly filtering the deity through all manner of abstractions until at last nothing more is left of that deity whatever. Law now holds sway among us in the stead of a God, even as among you in the stead of a king . . . Fichtean idealism is one of the most colossal errors ever concocted by the mind of man. It is more godless and damnable than the crassest materialism. What is called here in France the atheism of the materialists would show up well, as I could easily prove, when compared with Fichtean transcendentalism; it would be more edifying and more piously religious" (pp. 203f.). However, Heine condemns the court judgment against Fichte and the police action undertaken against him for his atheism.

2

Chiaroscuro of the Atheism Controversy ("Atheismusstreit")(Forberg-Fichte)

The charge of atheism levelled by Jacobi against Lessing and the reduction of Spinozism to atheism remained a private controversy between Jacobi and Mendelssohn; but the case of Fichte was to burst forth into the external forum and become a public scandal: the historical details are well-known,[1] and we shall here limit ourselves to the strictly theoretical dimension of the controversy. We contend that it is of crucial significance in our research, as showing the onward march of the principle of immanentism as it batters down, like a great juggernaut, the fragile props of rationalistic and romantic theology. The fact that subsequently Jacobi was likewise, as we shall see, to take a direct part in the controversy and back up the atheism charge[2] made by the political authorities, albeit with great restraint and sincere admiration for Fichte the man, confirms our suspicion that there was an inevitable "rhythm" in operation in modern philosophy, even though its protagonists fought with all their power not to be caught up in it. Therefore, it is difficult to exaggerate the importance, in the public and cultural life of Germany and later in the whole of European thought, of this controversy which began to transfer onto the theoretical plane as well the message of absolute freedom proclaimed by the *cogito* and actualized by the 1789 revolution: the most typical documents of the *Atheismusstreit* date from

[1] Cf. J. H. Fichte, *J. G. Fichte's Leben und literarischer Briefwechsel,* Vol. I (Sulzbach, 1830), pp. 350ff.; H. Lindau, *Die Schriften zu Fichte's Atheismus-Streit* (Munich, 1912); F. Medicus, "Fichtes Leben," as "Introduction" (*Einleitung*) to his edition of Fichte, Vol. I, (Leipzig, 1908), pp. 111ff.; W. Lutgert, *Die Religion des deutschen Idealismus und ihr Ende,* Vol. I (Gütersloh, 1923), especially pp. 47f.; W. Steinbeck, *Das Bild des Menschen in der Philosophie J. G. Fichtes* (Munich, 1938); K. Leese, *Die Religionskrisis des Abendlandes und die religiöse Lage der Gegenwart* (Hamburg, 1948), especially pp. 55ff.; E. Hirsch, *Geschichte der neuern evangelischen Theologie,* Vol. IV (Gütersloh, 1952), pp. 337ff., where the author synthesizes the results of his preceding monographs.

[2] Especially in the *Brief an Fichte* of March 1799 (Jacobi, *Werke,* Vol. III [Leipzig, 1816], pp. 3ff., 9ff.).

1798,[3] but Fichte had already by that date studied and welcomed the ideas of the revolution and had laid the basis for his own monistic-moralistic transformation of Kantianism.

As early as 1790, Fichte's thought is moving in the direction of that synthesis of Spinozism and Kantianism that will constitute the central axis of idealist speculation: [4] but it is no easy matter to effect an analytical diagnosis of this process because it presents, often pushed to a state of drastic tension, the paradox of the most fervid and intense religious feeling combined with the most explicit declaration of the dissolution of God into the active reality of human freedom and action. In this tension we find the key to the innermost and crucial significance of Fichtean speculation, as distinct from other subsequent idealist thought: the tension between the Spinozan cosmic infinite, which here becomes the infinite realm of the values of human action and history, and the assertion of Kantian freedom, which is the new landfall whereon man can safely plant his feet, the beachhead here destined not to crumble beneath him but to hurl him forward with the impetus of a youthful Columbus, certain that there can no longer be any turning back. Not only Fichte's typically forceful and original style but also his insistence on those few but crucial elements of speculative reflection, and his very vagueness in the matter of terms and even of basic concepts, combined with his titanic will to identify thought with action, speculative reflection with political campaigning, conspire to make his work the flash-point of the whole of modern idealism and to give his themes an aura of topicality every time that the question is posed concerning the quintessence of modern immanentism.

Fichte's atheism controversy has the further merit and interest of having demonstrated the priority of the metaphysical element or assumption within idealism over the epistemological element and, at the same time, the impossibility of bringing this assumption to its term because of the immanentist prejudice, the constitutive priority of mind over being, as we shall be pointing out.

The same controversy demonstrates further (and it is of capital importance for our purposes to note this most carefully) the collision in Fichte, as later in Schelling and Hegel, of the Brunonian-Spinozan prin-

[3] Cf. the list given by Fr. Meyer, *Eine Fichte-Sammlung* (Leipzig, 1921), numbers 30-88, pp. 8ff.

[4] "Before 1790, when he was moved to embrace the Kantian philosophy, Fichte's philosophical stance was that of *fatalism* with a strong admixture of *Spinozism*. He conceived of *God* as an eternally necessary being that thinks the world and thereby posits it as it is, in virtue of an eternal necessity . . . The quintessence of the Spinozan concept of the All that is God recurs in Fichte in somewhat intellectualized and spiritualized form" (E. Hirsch, *op. cit.*, Vol. IV, p. 340).

ciple of substance (the demand for the immediate presence of the All, for the resolution of the many and the different into the One and the Same), with the Kantian principle of active freedom which was supposed to transfigure that All and that Same or rather to sublimate it as a process of itself which is at once act of itself and of the other. And here again there will be manifest the mutually nullifying effect of the two opposing principles, the Spinozan principle tending to nullify the Kantian one in order to enclose the truth in the ἓν καὶ πᾶν, and the Kantian principle, incapable, even in its transfiguration into the absolute and creative Monad, of abandoning that area of generic human awareness, the human mind, which it expresses in its essence and in its function.

Thus there was in Fichte a combination of the atheistic panentheistic principle proper to Spinozism and the personalist principle derived from the a priori of that practical reason which in Kant was supposed rather to strengthen and consolidate the affirmation of transcendence. As has already been pointed out, the a priori of the Kantian practical reason as pure "ought" (*Sollen*) is no less intrinsically and deliberately atheistic than the theoretical *Ich denke*: the reconciliation attempted by Kant between virtue-freedom and the bliss of an ultramundane immortality via the justice and omnipotence of God implies a whole series of syntheses or schemata taken from the empirical sphere of pious desires and wishes (*pia desideria*) which, far from jibing with the basic principle, the practical a priori, dissolve and fragment irreparably at the first contact with that principle. And this total fragmentation of the reconciliation is precisely what Fichte effected, thus exposing himself to a dual charge of atheism, as Spinozan and as Kantian.

The pretext that sparked the charge was an article by Fichte's colleague, Forberg, concerning the "evolution of the concept of religion". This essay, entirely Kantian in its inspiration, had proceeded to void religion (God, the soul, the life to come) of all content and reduce it to a practical belief in the moral government of the world or in its rationality; or, in other words, a living faith in the kingdom of God that will come upon earth.[5] This amounts virtually to a secularized millenarianism already proclaimed by Lessing and to be more explicitly developed in the sequel by Schelling and Hegel. There can be no doubt, adds Forberg, as to what is meant by a "moral government of the world" (*moralische Weltregierung*): when things are occurring in the world in

[5] "*Religion* is nothing but a *practical belief* in a *moral world government;* or, to express the same notion in one specific sanctified language, *a living faith in the kingdom of God that will come upon earth*" (Forberg, *Entwicklung des Begriffs der Religion,* ed. Lindau, *op. cit.,* p. 37; also: *Fichtes Werke,* ed. Medicus, Vol. III, p. 137).

such a way as to guarantee the final triumph of the good, then there is a moral government of the world. If, on the other hand, virtue and vice are matters of total indifference so far as man's fate is concerned, then there is no moral government of the world. There is here highlighted and posited at the center of the new bent of mind the concept of man as "task" (*Aufgabe*), which replaced, in virtue of the principle of immanentism, the notion of man as essence or content, typical of Platonic or creationist conceptions. The principle that underwrites this "task", the exalted spirit that governs the world in accord with the moral laws, is the deity, and Forberg hastens to assert that this is the only concept of God of which religion has any need, or rather in terms of which religion itself becomes possible in the first place. Thus all metaphysical notions of God as most real, infinite, absolutely necessary Being [6] are automatically called in question. Noteworthy is the substitution of the abstract deity (*Gottheit*) for the concrete God; this is a patent indication of the change of course in the handling of the whole God-problem.

Forberg makes short work of the problem of religion: it is possible to be religious either in polytheism or in monotheism, since both are simply antithetical conceptions, and thus religion as such is of no importance. When it is admitted, continues the Kantian Forberg, that morality alone is the rule of the government of the world, it becomes a matter of total indifference whether the constitution of the world be thought of as monarchical or aristocratic; and there would be no objection to those ultramundane men whom the ancients conceived of as being gods, provided only they had acted morally. Thus in order to have a religion it suffices to admit that there exists a moral government of the world and a deity governing the world in accord with moral laws: anyone believing this has a religion. But now there arises the question: "on what is this belief founded?" (*worauf gründet sich dieser Glaube?*) Forberg points to three sources of our convictions in this matter: experience, speculation and conscience (*Erfahrung, Spekulation, Gewissen*). We learn that there does exist a moral government of the world—i.e., we see with our own eyes in our experience that good does triumph in the end and evil does founder. But anyone who seeks the deity outside of himself in the flux of things, will never find that deity. He will encounter on all sides the "works of the devil" (*Werke des Teufels*) and only rarely, and always timidly and doubtfully at that, will he be able to say: "Here is the finger of God" (*hier ist Gottes Finger*).

Speculation seems, or is held by some, to have better chances of success in proving the existence of God: it is considered capable of affording a convincing proof of the existence of a moral governor of the

[6] Forberg, *op. cit.*, ed. Lindau, pp. 37ff.; ed. Medicus III, p. 137.

world. Forberg refers to the ontological proof which claims to conclude from the very concept of the most perfect Being to his existence; to the proof from contingency which presupposes something absolutely necessary; and to the proof from the order observable in the universe, which would not be possible in the absence of an ordering principle. But all of these proofs, claims Forberg, fall short of the mark. The concept of the most perfect Being as such does not contain (and therefore does not prove) the existence of such a Being, inasmuch as being, i.e., existence, is a de facto datum, not a quality or perfection. This is the famous Kantian critique which has a certain similarity (though an equivocal one) with St. Thomas' no less famous critique of the ontological proof of St. Anselm.[7]

Nor will speculation have any better luck, continues Forberg, with the proof from *contingency* (*of the world*), which is claimed to presuppose and prove the existence of the necessary Being. For what, in fact, is the contingent (*das Zufällige*)? Is it to be understood as that which can be thought of as not being, i.e., not existing? In that case, there is no concept of an absolutely necessary Being within the entire range of the human understanding, for nothing can be found which it is impossible to think of as not existing! Is the contingent, then, to be understood as that which has not always existed, which has begun at some point to exist, and which consequently presupposes a cause that has given it existence? But, in that case, why was it that this cause which, as absolutely necessary, must have always existed, did not give existence to the contingent sooner? Was it because it could not? In that case, what was preventing it? Or was it because it did not choose to do so? In that case, what made it change its mind later on? The whole drift of these questions is gradually transforming the absolutely necessary Being into something contingent. The clear boundaries between the necessary and the contingent are being effaced.

Finally, there is the proof drawn from the *order* of the universe: such order is impossible in the absence of an ordering principle. The concept of order is drawn from our own human understanding and it has not been proven that the limits of our knowing are likewise the limits of the possible; nor has it been proven that the order of the universe is so evident as to permit any certain conclusion from it to the existence of a deity. Are we here arguing from the order observable in the physical world? Well, in that case, it must be said that a skilled architect is not by that very fact a moral governor, nor is a first-class craftsman the same thing as a god! Or are we arguing from the order observable in the moral

[7] Cf. St. Thomas, *S.T.*, I, q. 11, a. 2 and Kant, *Kritik der reinen Vernunft*, Tranz. Logik, II Abt., II Buch, 3. Abschn. §§ 3-4, A 584ff., B 612ff.

world? Then we are in still more perilous case, for the existence of evil would compel us to conclude to the existence of an evil principle just as cogently as the existence of good would compel us to conclude to the existence of the good principle! It would indeed be a bizarre procedure to conclude from a perverse world to the existence of a holy God. And so the deity is just as inaccessible to speculation as to experience.

But we still have one method open to us and it seems at last to be the right one: *conscience*. Religion, claims Forberg, is simply and solely the fruit of a "good heart", and Forberg recalls the words of the Gospel: "Blessed are the pure in heart, for they shall see God." [8] But why and how does religion emerge in the heart of a morally good human being and only in such a one? Here we are at the very heart of Forberg's theory: religion takes its origin solely and simply from the desire or the firm conviction of the pious and good heart that good can and should get the upper hand over evil in the universe.[9] Faith in the decline and defeat of good in this world, faith in the kingdom and reign of Satan on earth, would be a hellish religion. And here Forberg presents a kind of blueprint for the idealistic religion without God, a religion simply of the "man of good heart." [10] It would consist in aiming at an accord of all men on all points of moral judgment so as to bring about the advent of the "golden age for good minds" (*das goldne Zeitalter für Köpfe*). Clearly, admits Forberg, this "reign of truth" (*Reich der Wahrheit*) represents an ideal that can never be completely realized: the assignment, therefore, is to set all one's forces and powers against error and to spread truth everywhere, i.e., to behave as if (*als ob*) error could never die out entirely nor the absolute reign of truth ever come to pass. The men of good heart, banded together for the arduous struggle on behalf of truth and goodness against evil and error, constitute the "church" (*Kirche*) which is the true "Communion of Saints on earth" (*die Gemeinde der Heiligen auf Erden*).

Forberg presents several precepts of the moral code that would govern this "religion without God": to do good without wearying; to believe in virtue as winning out in the end; to hope manfully that right will triumph over injustice and the cause of good over that of evil; to work while the daylight lasts, missing no occasion to kindle and plant firmly aloft the torch of good according to your powers, ever mindful that after you may come a long night in which no one will desire or be able to will the good, and that the torch you have lighted will be the only star of

[8] *Matt.* 5, 8.

[9] "Religion arises solely and simply from *the wish that good might get the upper hand over evil in the world*" (Lindau, p. 42; Medicus III, p. 138).

[10] We are here summarizing Forberg's vigorous peroration: Lindau, pp. 42-53; Medicus III, pp. 140-147.

hope for "the upright in the land" (*die Redlichen im Lande*); [11] to do what you can to ensure that there will be more goodness and lucidity and enlightenment and great-heartedness and uprightness and peace and justice, so that your end (*Ausgang*) may find you at peace; to believe that no tiniest or most insignificant good act or resolution of yours will go to waste; to believe that the kingdom of God, the reign of truth and right will come on earth and to commit yourself unreservedly to bring it to pass.

Here we have to do with a religion that is identified with duty (*Pflicht*), the duty not of believing that there exists a God who is moral governor of the universe, but rather simply of *acting as if one believed this* (*Pflicht zu handeln als ob man es glaubte*). The theism-atheism controversy henceforth makes sense only to the man who still has confidence in speculation.

Forberg ends his essay with a brief catechism of this new religion of the atheist. This list of questions and answers on certain "insidious questions" sheds light on Forberg's entire theoretical position which is anything but transcendentalist: [12]

Q: Is there a God?—A: That is and always will be uncertain (it is but a conundrum of the speculative sphere).

Q: May a man believe in God?—A: No, for that would involve an illicit transfer to the practical sphere of faith of an object of the theoretical sphere.

Q: Is religion a conviction of the intellect or a precept of the will?—A: A precept of the will. Were it a conviction of the intellect, it would be superstition.

Q: How will the religious man act?—A: He will never weary of promoting the cause of truth and goodness in the world.

Q: Can any and every man have religion?—A: Of course, just as any and every man can act in accord with conscience. Unbelief (despair of the cause of goodness without sufficient reason) is a lack of conscience.

Q: How many articles of faith are there in religion?—A: Two: faith in the immortality of virtue and faith in the kingdom of God on earth.

Q: Is uprightness (*Rechtschaffenheit*) possible in the absence of religion?—A: No, it would be an uprightness in the absence of any interest in uprightness, just as religion without uprightness would not be religion, being an interest in uprightness without uprightness!

[11] The expression recalls that most famous of pietistic expressions: *Die Stille im Lande* (the quiet hush in the land), to which Kierkegaard likewise often alludes.

[12] Forberg, *loc. cit.*, Lindau, 54ff.; Medicus III, pp. 147ff. Forberg is reported to have confessed, in maturer years, that the questions were written in "a spirit of youthful waggery ("*in jugendlichem Mutwillen*"—Medicus I, p. 112).

Q: Can a man be upright without believing in God?—A: Yes, because here it is merely a case of theoretical faith (as has been said already above).

Q: Can an atheist have religion?—A: Certainly. Of a virtuous atheist it can be said that he is recognizing with his heart that God he denies with his lips: thus practical faith and theoretical unbelief can very well coexist.

Q: In what relation does religion stand to virtue?—A: In the relationship of the part to the whole.

Q: Can religion be learned?—A: Yes, like the other virtues: by the practice of it.

Q: Is religion an aid to virtue?—A: Not to virtue as such but to the display of virtue or to the phenomenon (*Erscheinung*) of the virtuous character.

Q: Is religion a deterrent to vice?—A: True religion cannot be, although superstition may be. The fact that a person fears the deity is a sign that that person has not yet found him. The bliss of virtue lies in finding a deity and the misery of vice in not finding any deity.

Q: Will the Kingdom of God as the reign of truth and justice on earth one day come to pass?—A: That is uncertain and, if we base our estimate on the experience of the past, the balance is in favor of improbability.

Q: Could the kingdom of Satan come instead of the kingdom of God?—A: This likewise is just as uncertain.

Q: Would the religion of the Satanist not then be just as well founded as that of the good man on this earth?—A: So far as the little we can gather from speculation is concerned, the one is no better founded than the other.

Q: Is religion in any sense a worship of the deity?—A: In no sense. There can be no duty toward a being whose existence is and always will be uncertain: anyone who would worship such a being is superstitious.

Q: Is the notion of religion expounded in this theory the true and exact notion?—Beyond a shadow of a doubt, if we are speaking of a concept of religion as something rational and not as something irrational, on the order of an incomprehensible mystery.

And the final question: Is not this notion of a practical faith rather a pointless concept than a serious philosophical concept?—The reply to this "insidious" question Forberg says he is leaving gladly to the qualified reader, and with it the judgment as to whether the author of the essay has been simply playing with the reader all along!

This essay, to which historians of thought may not have devoted the thorough study that is its due, insofar as its detailed content and main sources are concerned, is indisputably of major theoretical and historica interest, despite its apparently rather tenuous speculative content. I succeeds in summarizing quite adequately the main converging stream of modern atheism from Spinoza to Kant. It integrates into this summary a vigorous restatement of Bayle's thesis on the relation betweer virtue and atheism and sketches the blueprint of religion without God i.e., that pure religion of the moral ideal, so cherished by moderr laicism.

Forberg's atheism remained anchored to a basically skeptical anc decidedly pragmatic Kantianism. It anticipated by a century Vaihinger's famous "as if" theory.[13]

Forberg's essay left Fichte in a state of puzzled and hesitant embarrassment and he resolved to preface his colleague's essay with an article of his own, with the carefully chosen title: *"On the Basis of Our Belief in a Divine Government of the World"*. The aim of this article was to show the points of agreement between himself and Forberg, while at the same time putting the entire problem on a more integral and coherent footing. Fichte likewise repudiated any claim that the existence of God was susceptible of proof (*Beweis*), whether by way of experience or by way of speculative deduction,[14] and asserted that the only certainty that

[13] Cf. A. Vaihinger, *Die Philosophie des "Als ob"* (Leipzig, 1913[7-8]), where he writes on the relation of Forberg to Kant: "None of the well-nigh innumerable contemporary and subsequent Kant scholars had such a good basic grasp of Kant's *ultimate* purpose in his philosophy of religion. This man [Forberg], with his incisive understanding and his intellectual courage, went to the heart of the matter" (p. 736f.). One Fichte commentator, however, disagrees: "The Kant-Forberg theory of the 'As if' takes it origin entirely from the Kantian spirit, from which Kant never entirely freed himself. As for Forberg, he was only superficially influenced by Kant (or, for that matter, by Fichte)" (F. Medicus, *Fichtes Leben,* p. 113). In his overt profession of atheism, Forberg must therefore be admitted to have freed Kant and Kantianism from contradiction: "Forberg is the one who adopts consistently, consequentially and exclusively, the theoretical thought pattern of the master" (cf. Hauter, *Essai sur l'objet religieux* [Paris, 1928], p. 187).

[14] Prior to his encounter with Kant's philosophy in 1790, Fichte was a fatalist with a strong dash of Spinozism, probably under the influence of Lessing and in his tradition: "He conceived of *God* as an eternally necessary being that thinks the world and thereby posits it as it is, in virtue of an eternal necessity. Consequently this world can be nothing else than an internally concatenated whole, whose modifications are determined by the principle of sufficient reason" (E. Hirsch, *op. cit.,* Vol. IV, p. 340). The first documentary evidence of this encounter with Kant, which was crucial for the evolution of Fichte's thought, is the fragment published by Fichte's son (*J. G. Fichte's Leben und literarischer Briefwechsel,* Vol. II, pp. 18ff. Cf. Vol. I, p. 143). It would seem, however, that at this point Fichte knew only the *Critique of Pure Reason* and not the *Critique of Practical Reason,* which latter he began to read only at the end of August 1790 (cf. J. G. Fichte, *Nachgelassene Schriften* 1780-1791, ed. R. Lauth & H. Jakob, Vol. II [Stuttgart, 1962], 1, p. 286).

can be had of God is that of faith and of conscience: or in other words, that the conviction of the existence of God did not come to mankind from the proofs of philosophy but from earlier and deeper roots.

There are in fact two ways of considering the world, from the point of view of ordinary knowledge, which is the method proper to natural science, and from the transcendental point of view. In the former case, the reason is constrained to stop at the being of the world as something absolute: the world is simply because it exists and it is as it is simply because it exists that way. Thus, the point of departure is an absolute Being and this absolute Being is the world: world and being are identical concepts. The world becomes a self-grounded whole, complete in itself, and consequently an organized and self-organizing whole containing within itself and within its own immanent laws the foundation of all the phenomena occurring within it.[15] Any explanation of the world in terms of a finality implanted by a supreme Intelligence is extraneous to this approach, which is the approach proper to the physical sciences. If, however, the sensible world be regarded from the transcendental point of view, all these difficulties evaporate: there is no such thing as a world standing on its own; in all that we see, we are seeing simply the reflection of our own interior activity. Fichte therefore at once refers to his own theory of the ego, and expounds it in a long note. This exposition was later developed in his *Theory of Knowledge:* that principle which is the ego is not an object of proof but of intuition. It is an immediate truth and as such cannot be an object even of "explanation" in the strict sense, for "every explanation makes dependent" (*alle Erklärung macht abhängig*).

Fichte agrees with Forberg in asserting that the organ of apprehension of the suprasensible world is faith (*Glaube*): faith is the actuation of freedom, specifies Fichte in accord with Kant but aiming considerably higher than him. By faith I effect a self-liberation from any influence on the part of the sensible world, like a power rising above the whole of sensible reality; at the same time, this freedom is not indeterminate: it

[15] "In this point of view, the starting point is an absolute Being and this absolute being is precisely the world; the two concepts are identical. The world becomes a self-grounding whole, complete in itself, and precisely for this reason an organized and organizing whole, which contains within itself and within its own immanent laws the foundation of all the phenomena occurring within it" (Fichte, *Ueber den Grund unseres Glaubens an eine göttliche Weltregierung,* Lindau, p. 24; Medicus III, pp. 123f.). On the relation of this article to previous writings of Fichte and especially the *Sittenlehre* of 1798, cf. W. Ritzel's analysis in his *Fichtes Religionsphilosophie* (Stuttgart, 1956), pp. 76ff., 88ff. In studying Fichte, special attention must be paid to the exact significance of his terms, especially the most basic ones, such as *Wissen* (knowledge), *Glaube* (faith), which are retained from beginning to end, but with notably different if not entirely opposed meanings.

has a purpose, that of "positing itself via itself". My ego and my necessary purpose, that is what constitutes the world of the suprasensible; this is the mainspring of Fichte's assertion that the constitutive of all certainty is faith rather than logical deduction. This is the proper order of procedure: not starting from the possibility to arrive at the reality but vice versa. The proper phrasing is not: I ought, therefore I can; but rather I can, therefore I ought. The first and most immediate principle is that I ought and what I ought; this stands in no need of further explanation or justification, it is known as such and is true as such; it is neither grounded in nor determined by any other truth; on the contrary, every other truth is grounded in it. This is the world of moral action (*Moralität*), the content and purpose of freedom, to which we are borne by the transcendental point of view.

The "world" (*Welt*) is no longer being seen from the outside as a reality that is simply given, set over against the mind and in a sense doing violence to it; it is being seen from the inside as a reality arising from that interior and in function of our freedom: this is that reality concerning which no man can doubt without thereby stifling and eliminating his very self. This is the unifying and harmonizing focus of thought and will in my essence; it is the node wherein I feel myself free and open to the infinite, free in my phenomenal manifestations and capable myself of setting my own limits via my will. Faith is this primordial conviction of freedom, the persuasion that our own moral determination proceeds from our interior moral stamp. And Fichte concludes with Forberg: faith is the constitutive element of all certitude.[16] From the transcendental point of view of freedom, therefore, our world is the material rendered sensible by our duty: this is the true reality of things, the true element (*Grundstoff*) of every phenomenon. The constraint wherewith faith binds us to the reality of such a phenomenon is a moral constraint, the only constraint possible for a free being. At this point, Fichte seems to be approaching Jacobi's concept of revelation: the principle of this faith in the reality of the sensible world considered as the result of a moral order of the world can well be called "revelation" (*Offenbarung*). Our duty is what is revealed in it.

[16] "The conviction of our moral determination thus proceeds as such from a moral frame of mind and disposition and is *faith;* and to this extent it is right to say that the element of all certainty is *faith*" (Fichte, *Ueber den Grund unseres Glaubens an eine göttliche Weltregierung,* Lindau, p. 28; Medicus III, p. 126). A remark which seems obvious at first reading but does not penetrate to the deeper level of the problem is that of Fischer: "The difference between him and Forberg was the difference between a sceptical atheism and a religious pantheism" (K. Fischer, *J. G. Fichte und seine Vorgänger* [Heidelberg, 1899 [2]], p. 285). For Jacobi and indeed for every theist, pantheism is in any event at rock bottom simply atheism.

But then Fichte forthwith returns to the terminology of Forberg, going indeed even farther and using the semantically still vaguer term, "the divine" (*das Göttliche*) instead of Forberg's "the deity" (*die Gottheit*). The divine that we accept is this moral order. It is built up via the actuation of justice. This is the only profession of faith possible: to fulfill gladly and simply what duty prescribes from case to case, without doubts or scruples about the consequences. Thereby the divine becomes living and real in us: every one of our acts is accomplished on the foundation of the divine, and only in it can all the consequences of these same acts be preserved.[17] True atheism, genuine unbelief and godlessness, protests Fichte in self-justification, lies in mulling unduly over the consequences of our actions, in refusing to obey the voice of our own conscience until we know we are betting on a sure thing, in putting our own counsel above the counsel of God, in making ourselves God. Any man willing to do evil that good may come of it is a godless man. Nothing good can come of evil in a moral government of the world, and only the man who doubts the latter could for an instant believe the former.[18] No man ought to lie, even to prevent the whole world from going to pieces.

Fichte seems to us to develop loyally and consistently his own transcendental activism in terms of this concept of faith which is the fulcrum of the mind's determination of the real. This faith is a derivative faith but it is faith in the fullest and truest sense of the word. God is simply that very moral order, vital and operative: we need no other God nor would we even be in a position to comprehend him. There is no basis in reason for casting off that moral order: as soon as a man retires into himself, this moral order is that absolutely primary principle of all objective knowledge, even as freedom and the moral determination of each individual is the absolutely primary principle of all subjective certitude.

[17] "This is the true faith; this moral order is the *divine* that we accept. It is built up by the actuation of justice. This is the only possible profession of faith: gladly and ingenuously to fulfill on every occasion what duty dictates, without doubts or scruples about the consequences. Thereby does the divine of which we have spoken become vital and real for us; every one of our acts is accomplished on the presupposition of this divine reality and all the consequences of these same acts are preserved in it alone" (*Ueber den Grund* . . ., Lindau, pp. 31f.; Medicus III, p. 129).

[18] "Real atheism, outright unbelief and godlessness consists in mulling unduly over the consequences of our actions, refusing to obey the voice of our conscience until we believe we can espy a happy issue, and thus setting our own counsel above the counsel of God and making ourselves God. The man who is willing to do evil that good may come of it is a godless man. In a moral government of the world, good can never follow out of evil, and as surely as you really believe in that moral government, you will find it impossible to believe that good ever could follow from evil" (*ibid.,* Lindau, p. 32; Medicus III, p. 129).

Every subsequent objective cognition must be grounded in and determined by that primary principle, but it cannot itself be determined by anything else because there is nothing more basic than it.

At this point, Fichte makes an extremely important specification which exposes the real significance of all his speculations up to this point: the moral order of the world, of which he is speaking, cannot, he says, be conceived in the shape of a particular being (*ein besonderes Wesen*),[19] endowed with personality and consciousness; these are actually predicates and attributes taken from our finite empirical life and would therefore transform God into something finite, modelled on us men, and thus God would no longer be God. He is in fact a God beyond any concept or comprehension: we are finite and the finite cannot conceive of the Infinite nor yet comprehend it. The immediately given is and remains, consequently, the immediate and unshakeable certitude: if this were to depend on concepts, it would become wavering and uncertain for the concept of God is impossible and full of contradiction.

In the wake of such premises, anyone would expect a profession of agnosticism much more radical than that of Forberg. On the contrary, Fichte presents us with an unreservedly theistic manifesto, perhaps in an effort to soothe those minds exacerbated by the expressions of Forberg or, better still, to clarify his own new transcendental concept of God. It would, he writes, be a misunderstanding to say that it is doubtful whether there is a God or not: "It is not in the least doubtful; it is the most certain fact of all; indeed, it is the ground of all other certitude, the single absolutely valid objective fact, that there is a moral order of the universe, that every rational individual has been assigned his specific place in this order and has had his task measured for him, that each and every element of his destiny which is not caused by his own behavior is the result of this plan; that apart from it, not a hair falls from his head nor, within the sphere of influence of that plan, a single sparrow falls from the roof." [20] Yet, Fichte forthwith returns to his previous insistence that the "concept of God as a particular substance is impossible and contradictory" for anyone who allows himself a moment's reflection.[21]

[19] In the conclusion God is identified with the "divine" (*ibid.,* Lindau, p. 31; Medicus III, p. 129).

[20] *Ibid.,* Lindau, pp. 34f.; Medicus III, p. 131. The last phrase is an allusion to the Gospel (Luke 21, 18). Cf. above Forberg's diametrically opposed statements (pp. 522f.).

[21] *Ibid.,* Lindau, p. 35; Medicus III, p. 132. The article ends with two quite significant quotations from the poetry of Goethe and Schiller. Thus Fichte dissociates himself not only from the Spinozan conception but from the Christian as well: "*There is no personality, no self-awareness, apart from that of a finite individual Ego*" (E. Hirsch, *op. cit.,* Vol. IV, p. 352).

Compared with Forberg's forthright, univocal article, entirely devoid of all dialectical or transcendental subtleties, Fichte's essay may be considered a faithful self-portrait and one of the most significant documents of his genius at one of the most crucial moments in the cultural and political evolution of the German mind. Nothing more vigorous can be imagined than the assertion of theism contained in this essay; yet nothing vaguer or more problematic can be imagined than the content of this theistic manifesto in which God is reduced to the laws or order inherent and immanent in the practical reason. Nothing more decisively anti-Spinozan can be imagined than Fichte's proclamation of human freedom; yet nothing more deterministic can be imagined than the strict bonds of the law of this freedom as an interpolation into the universal order which is valid *in se* and *per se*. Hence the controversy that erupted almost at once.

The sequel to the publication of these essays is well-known: their authors were charged with atheism, the government confiscated the essays themselves and Fichte was dismissed from the University of Jena. But Fichte was not the man to bow meekly to disgrace, all the more so since he seems to have been persuaded that he had been the victim of a glaring error of fact, that his philosophy was not in fact atheistic but that, on the contrary, it was furnishing religion with the only valid and cogent foundation possible, by removing it from the competency of philosophy and entrusting it to faith. The polemical writings [22] that followed do not, however, present anything substantially new, if we abstract from the bitter thrust of the peroration, which generates more heat than light. These writings simply restate Fichte's main contentions. We shall here highlight only the main ones.

1. The distinction of the theoretical sphere from the practical one; the former has as its object the sensible sphere of the finite; the latter has as its object the suprasensible sphere of moral feeling (*sittliches Gefühl*), constituting the primary element, the absolutely immediate in human experience. Morality and religion are absolutely identical: both are expressive of a confrontation of the suprasensible and a seizure of it,

[22] Chief among these are the *Appelation an das Publikum* of 1799 and *Rückerinnerungen, Antworten, Fragen,* written that same year but not edited and published until 1845 in the complete edition of Fichte's works. Forberg for his part replied at length to the charge of atheism levelled against him with his *Friedrich Carl Forbergs Apologie seines angeblichen Atheismus* (Gotha, 1799), a volume of 181 pages; cf. H. Vaihinger, *op. cit.*, pp. 740ff., for a summary of the principal points Forberg makes in this publication: he sustains point by point his previous position and especially his contention that the problem of God is extraneous to philosophy which is consequently intrinsically atheistic and that the essence of religion is faith actualized in the "ought". Every form of "natural theology" comes down in the final analysis to mere anthropomorphism.

the former by action, the latter by faith.[23] There is a reiteration of the absolute priority, especially in the noetic sense, of the suprasensible over the sensible: far from being necessarily uncertain, the suprasensible is the only thing that is certain and every other thing is certain only because of it; far from the certainty of the suprasensible necessarily depending on the certainty of the sensible world, it is rather the theoretical necessity that follows from the necessity of the suprasensible, so as to maintain this sensible world in existence and to sustain the moral obligation of giving to that sensible world the respect due it as a means and medium. The suprasensible world is our birthplace and our only solid foundation: the sensible world is but a reflection (*Widerschein*) of the suprasensible.

2. "*I hold,*" writes Fichte, "that the *relation* of the deity to us, as moral beings, is the immediately given; a particular being of this deity comes to be conceived solely as a result of our finite imagining and in this being lies nothing else than simply those immediately given relations, which are merely collated in the unity of the concept." [24] He charges his opponents with insisting that these relations of the deity to us are supposed to derive and be deduced from a knowledge of the essence of God *in se* and *per se,* known as independent of these relations. And Fichte adduces a somewhat unexpected (but quite significant) example: he says that he himself professes to know what heat and cold is inasmuch as he experiences hot and cold, whereas his opponents apparently know heat and cold without once in their entire lifetime having had any sensation of this sort; they trust entirely and exclusively to the power of their syllogisms. And Fichte's own incapacity to concoct syllogisms of this sort is what they call his atheism!

3. Fichte readily admits that he has denied that God can be called Substance. He is also perfectly willing to concede that he has insisted that God's existence cannot be proven from sensible things, that this existence cannot be designated as "being". But all this, he claims, has been done solely in order to preclude anthropomorphism and to safeguard the transcendence of God. Actually it would be contradictory to call God "substance": substance necessarily signifies an essence that exists sensibly in space and time, and this is certainly inappropriate to assert of God. For the same reason, Fichte has denied that there can be proven from sensible things the existence of a God clothed in sensible

[23] Cf. *Appellation an das Publikum,* Lindau, p. 112; Medicus III, p. 168f. In the *Rückerinnerungen, Antworten, Fragen* (§ 32), however, Fichte is at pains to draw a distinction between morality and religion, asserting that religious faith is linked to moral conscience and fulfills it (Lindau, pp. 315ff.; Medicus III, p. 228).

[24] *Appellation an das Publikum,* Lindau, p. 119; Medicus III, p. 174.

qualities and service as principle and fountain of bliss and sensible satisfactions for man (eudaemonism).[25] But a God who is supposed to serve sense desires is a despicable being; any man of stature would be ashamed to fulfill such an office; such a God would be an evil being, sustaining and perpetuating human perdition and the debasement of reason. Such a God is quite simply the "Prince of this world",[26] already judged and condemned long ago out of the mouth of truth. So Fichte's opponents are the real atheists who have created perverse idols for themselves.

My refusal to admit such idols in the place of the true God, cries Fichte—that is what they call atheism, that is what has triggered their persecution. And Fichte's style becomes still more vehement: "What *they* call God is *to me* an idol. For me, God is a being entirely free of all sensibility and all sensual admixture, to whom I therefore cannot even ascribe the attribute of existence, accessible to me only as a sensible concept. For me God is simply and solely the ruler of the suprasensible world. Their God I deny, and I warn all men of such a spawn of human corruption; and this makes me in no sense an atheist but rather a defender of religion. My God they do not know nor are they capable of rising to any concept of him. He is simply not there for them even to deny and in this sense they are not atheists." [27]

4. Fichte writes one pungent sentence that virtually sums up his entire system: "In the matter of true religion, its sole purpose and aim is to wrest from man all supports of his laziness and all pretexts he might use to whitewash his own viciousness, to stop up all access to any sources of false consolation and to leave both man's understanding and his heart but one bulwark, that of pure duty and faith in the suprasensible world." [28] Fichte then proceeds to push Kant's idealization of space and time to its ultimate metaphysical consequence and declare himself to be denying the reality of all that is temporal and transitory in order the better to reinstate the eternal and the immutable: and so Fichte finds it strange that the charge of a denial of God should be levelled against this philosophy which rather denies the existence of the world in the sense in

[25] He alludes to the puny philosophy of his opponents, whose roots go back to rationalism (*Popularphilosophie*); and he piles on the insulting adjectives: ". . . eudaemonic, superficial, belletristic, mealy-mouthed philosophy" (*ibid.*, Lindau, p. 130; Medicus III, p. 182. Cf. also Lindau, pp. 134f.; Medicus III, pp. 186f.).

[26] This Biblical name for Satan (*John* 12, 31) is but one of Fichte's many scriptural allusions in these essays.

[27] A little later, Fichte writes: "Our philosophy denies the existence of a sensual God who would be a mere pander" (*Appellation* . . ., Lindau, p. 131, Medicus III, p. 183).

[28] *Ibid.*

which that existence is asserted by dogmatism. And as far as Christianity is concerned, adds Fichte, it is not a philosophical system at all: [29] it addresses itself not to speculation but to the moral sense of man and therefore has the same aim and purpose as his own philosophy!

5. Fichte admits that it is no easy task to clarify and pinpoint the point of disagreement between the contending parties but he will not allow the controversy to turn upon an equivocation. It is nothing but prattling nonsense, he observes disdainfully, to talk of a God of Fichte, of Jacobi, of Spinoza and the like. Fichte, Jacobi, Spinoza and the rest are not identical with their philosophy. The philosopher has no God, nor can he have one: he has only a "concept of the concept" or the idea of God. God and religion exist only in life whereas the philosopher as such is not the whole man but only that man in a state of abstraction; thus it is impossible for a man to be only a philosopher.[30] This remark reminds one of the anti-Helegian polemic of Kierkegaard! The crucial point therefore is to oppose to arid rationalism a "philosophy of life", a vital philosophy but in a transcendental sense; and here the opposition is irreconcilable. Fichte insists on distinguishing the philosophy of religion from religion itself in just the same way as he distinguishes philosophy from life. And so he finds the real point of disagreement with his opponents in this relation between thought and action, between philosophy and life: whereas they make cognition the principle of life, his philosophy, on the contrary, makes life, the vital system of feelings and aspiration, supreme and leaves to cognition merely the role of spectator. This system of feelings is therefore clear-cut in the mind and contains an immediate awareness and cognition not deduced by argumentations and chains of reasoning.[31] Fichte's position could be perfectly expressed in the contradictory formula: it is the transcendent nature of feeling (*Gefühl*) which serves as basis for the assertion of the existence and the transcendence of the suprasensible and faith (*Glaube*) expresses the immediate certainty of this.

The two points of view were absolutely irreconcilable. Fichte admir-

[29] *Ibid.* Cf. also *Rückerinnerungen, Antworten, Fragen,* § 16, Lindau, p. 296f.; Medicus III, pp. 213f.

[30] *Rückerinnerungen, Antworten, Fragen,* § 15, Lindau, p. 295; Medicus III, p. 212. Fichte is still more explicit in a letter to Reinhold, dated April 22, 1799: "The attempt to identify a mentality and attitude in philosophy makes no sense to me. Such a question as: 'Is philosophy as such atheistic or not?' is simply unintelligible to me, on a par with the question: 'Is a triangle red or green, sweet or bitter?'" (*J. G. Fichte's Leben und literarischer Briefwechsel,* Vol. II, pp. 273f.).

[31] "The opposing systems make cognition the vital principle . . . Our philosophy, on the contrary, makes the vital system of feelings and aspiration supreme and allows cognition merely the role of spectator" (*Rückerinnerungen, Antworten, Fragen,* § 20, Lindau, pp. 299f.; Medicus III, pp. 215f.).

ingly cites on his behalf the authority of Pastor Spalding, author of the essay entitled *The Definition of Man* (*Bestimmung des Menschen,* 1748),[32] a title soon to be appropriated by Fichte himself; of the court chaplain Reinhard, who was also his judge in this scandal; and above all of Jacobi, for whom Fichte evinced the deepest respect and devotion, despite their differences in the area of pure theory, and whose striking phrase about religious knowledge Fichte cites approvingly.[33]

Fichte's good faith in this whole controversy is attested not only by his ardor but preeminently by his own notion of the method and content of his own transcendental philosophy: hence, his recourse to faith (*Glaube*), not only as a new source of knowledge, but especially as a primordial source of value calculated to break the closed circle of the finite. Jacobi had in fact proceeded in much the same way; and Fichte was not without justification in invoking Jacobi to whom we must now again return.

I—*The Implicit Atheism of the "Theory of Knowledge"*

Jacobi's first remark about Fichte's position concerns the obvious contradictions into which he falls by positioning the God-problem in the field of knowing, instead of leaving it, as did Kant, in the area of ignorance. Thus Jacobi feels that Fichte himself is responsible for the charge of atheism brought against him. Jacobi agrees with Fichte that the charge is unfounded: transcendental philosophy is neither atheist nor theist, inasmuch as it is reflection upon the finite. Indeed, were such a philosophy to pretend to be theistic, it would by that very fact brand itself as atheistic, inasmuch as God would become real for the mind only insofar as he was conditioned by "argumentative" philosophy, or in other words, insofar as God would be seized "in the act of not-existing-as-such" (*auf der That des 'an sich nicht Daseyns'*). Jacobi is quite firm on this point which involves fidelity to Kant and to the transcendental method: he insists that no sane and honest man could possibly reproach transcendental philosophy for knowing nothing of God, for it is universally admitted that God cannot be the object of *knowledge* but only of *faith.* A God who could be *known* would no longer be God.[34]

Going straight to the heart of the controversy, Jacobi centers Fichte's

[32] Cf. H. Stephan, *Spaldings Bestimmung des Menschen und Wert der Andacht,* Studien zur Geschichte des neuern Protestantismus 1 (Giessen, 1908).

[33] "A godly life leads to the awareness and perception of God" (Jacobi, *Ueber die Lehre Spinozas;* Fichte cites the 2nd ed., pp. 234ff.).

[34] ". . . that God cannot be *known* but only believed. A God who could be consciously known would not be God at all" (Letter of Jacobi to Fichte 1799, Preface; *C. W.,* Vol. III, p. 7).

position in the direct tradition of modern philosophy, remarking that it combines the two main components of this philosophy, Spinozism and idealism: it is an idealist or "inverted" Spinozism (*umgekehrte Spinozismus*) as compared with Enlightenment materialism, a synthesis of materialism and idealism; and so Jacobi dubs it "the King of the Jews of speculative reason". Jacobi goes on to admit freely that "science", i.e., the pure philosophy of Fichte, is an interior action, productive of its own object in the form of thoughts springing from the primordial form of the Ego, which is thus the principle and analytical base of every object of knowledge. And this is the parting of the ways between Fichte and himself, specifies Jacobi: whereas Fichte is set on proving that the basis for all truth is to be found within the science of knowing, Jacobi himself aims at showing that this basis, i.e., truth itself, is necessarily located outside the ambit of that science.[35] This is for Jacobi the real point of tension, of identity and difference of opinion, between himself and Fichte. Fichte's philosophy is a pure philosophy, i.e., an absolutely immanent philosophy, a true system of reason, wherein everything must be given solely in and by means of reason, in the Ego as such, in this pure "selfhood", and must be contained within it; hence the reason alone must deduce everything from itself alone. Obviously Jacobi's critique is aiming straight for the heart without any detours!

Jacobi presents a masterly exposure of the new Fichtean method of sheer operationalism and of the new "principle of active negation" as constitutive act of the being of the mind; and he shows how these principles effected that breakaway, in the philosophy presented in Fichte's "theories of knowledge" (*Wissenschaftslehren*), from both dualism and realism, and initiated that new intellectual Odyssey which was to bring man, step by step, to the positive or constructive atheism of the philosophy of our own century. Jacobi does not stop at the comparatively superficial level of the atheism controversy as such nor does he refer explicitly to the works of Fichte that had been condemned. He looks much deeper, going back to the systematic philosophy that Fichte had been elaborating and expounding since 1790, in order to assess Fichte's full responsibility. Fichte's philosophy is monistic from the outset: it is based on pure reason, whose act is a perceptual grasping (*Vernehmen*) which perceives or grasps *only* itself. We are therefore dealing with a "productive process" wherein reality is constituted in the reason via the reason. "This philosophizing of the pure reason must

[35] "And so we are both desirous that the science of knowing—which is one and the same in all sciences, the very universal soul of the cognitional world—shall be perfect. The only difference is that *your* reason for so desiring is that the ground of all truth shall be clearly shown to lie within the science of knowing, whereas *mine* is that this ground be seen manifestly to lie outside that science" (*ibid.*, Lindau, p. 165; Jacobi, *C. W.*, Vol. III, p. 17).

therefore needs be a chemical process, whereby everything outside of the pure reason is transmuted into nothing and the pure reason alone left over, such a pure spirit that it cannot itself be in this rarified state but can only bring forth everything; but again it can effect this production in so sheer a fashion than the product likewise cannot be but only be contemplated as present in the productive act of the mind: the whole process and its content is a sheer act of an act (*Tat-Tat*)." [36] Thus, in Fichte's theory, cognition is indeed a production and a construction, but predicted upon a previous destruction: in order for any being to become for us an object *completely* understood by us, we must in thought destroy and annihilate it as *object,* as a reality *subsisting in itself,* in order to transform it into something subjective, into a creation of our own, *into a sheer design,* something that resolves itself in our action (*Handlung*) at this present moment (*jetzt*) into a sheer manifestation and phenomenon of our creative imagination. The consequence is inevitable: the human mind becomes the creator of the world (*Weltschöpfer*) and thus the creator of itself. But it can be its own creator only on condition of annihilating itself in its own essence in order to come into being and to possess itself in the *concept* alone, in the concept of a sheer absolute radical procession and ingression—*out of* nothing, *toward* nothing, *for* nothing, *into* nothing,[7] an oscillation (*Pendel-Bewegung*) having in the law of its own motion its own unconceptualizable and incomprehensible limitation (*eine unbegreifliche Einschränkung*).

We know already that for Jacobi philosophy as a science is self-enclosed and thus intrinsically atheistic. Now Fichte has precisely shown that philosophy is a science in itself inasmuch as it has as object the mind itself, the Ego. Thus the Ego is a science in itself, a self-contained science, and it is the only real knowledge there is; it knows itself and contradicts its own concept, that it does not of itself know or apprehend anything, etc. Thus the Ego is necessarily the principle of all the other sciences and an infallible measuring-rod and solvent, with which all things can be resolved and dissolved into the Ego without leaving behind even a *corpus delicti,* the non-Ego! Philosophical reflection is accom-

[36] *Ibid.,* Lindau, p. 167; Jacobi, *op. cit.,* p. 20.

[37] The relevant passage in Jacobi is extremely tightly-packed and penetrating: "Inasmuch as the philosophical understanding of the human mind positively cannot transcend its own production, that mind must become a world-*creator* and the creator of its own self, in order to penetrate into the realm of beings and conquer it by the instrumentality of thought. Only to the extent to which it succeeds in so becoming a creator will it experience any progress in this conquest. But the mind can be its own creator only on the mandatory condition that it annihilate itself in its own *essence and being* in order to arise again in the *concept* alone and to possess itself in this concept of a sheer absolute radical procession and ingression, *out of* nothing, *toward* nothing, *for* nothing, *into* nothing." (*ibid.,* Lindau, p. 168; Jacobi, *op. cit.,* pp. 21f.).

plished via a total abstraction whereby every being is resolved into knowing; and Jacobi speaks of a process of "progressive annihilation" (*progressive Vernichtung*). But, asks Jacobi, in view of the fact that all of this is nothing but a work (or play!) of the imagination, how can a true and real being be distinguished from an imaginary one, how can waking life be distinguished from dreams? He says that he has himself followed the opposite path, as we have already seen, i.e., the one which posits God as being outside of man and of the world and as being primary object of reason: In this sense, if you will, says Jacobi, he is "godless" (*Gottlose*) and an atheist, but after the fashion of Desdemona, Pylades, Epaminondas, Jan de Witt (Spinoza's murdered friend), i.e., out of loyalty to the true God, and he scorns the (pantheistic) philosophy that declares him an atheist.

Therefore, Jacobi has an answer and justification against the charge of atheism levelled against him by transcendental philosophy, but this philosophy has no avenue of escape from the hermetically closed circle of the Ego: "If the highest reality that I can contemplate, that I can regard, is my sheer and simple, naked and empty, Ego, with its autonomy and freedom, then self-intuition and rationality is a curse to me and I execrate my very existence." [38]

With this, Jacobi realizes he has said enough: courteously, certain of being understood by a correspondent of such intelligence, he introduces an explicit reference to Spinozism, that system which idealism (and Fichte himself!) had hoped would lead beyond Kant. While Jacobi cannot approve the teaching, he seeks to save the man: "And even though I would have to call his theory atheistic, even as that of Spinoza, I *personally* could not consider him an atheist nor yet a godless man." [39] Jacobi's alarm about the new philosophy stems from a horror of the void, a dreadful horror of nothingness, of the absolutely indeterminate. He confesses that in scrutinizing the mechanism of nature, whether from the point of view of the Ego or of the non-Ego (in the fashion of Fichte's theory of knowledge, the *Wissenschaftslehre*), he ends up with a sheer nothing-as-such which stretches beckoning, grasping, seductive hands toward his own transcendental being, so that in order to void the Infinite, he must fill it as an infinite void, a *sheer-and-simple-in-se-and per-se.*[40] And so Jacobi poses to Fichte, Spinoza and every sort of pure philosophy, the alternative that embraces that of Fénelon: either God or nothingness and the void. If man chooses nothingness and the void, he makes himself God and reduces God to a *specter,* for it is impossible, in the absence of a God, for man and everything that surrounds him to be

[38] *Ibid.,* Lindau, p. 181; Jacobi, *op. cit.,* p. 41.
[39] *Ibid.,* Lindau, pp. 184f.; Jacobi, *op. cit.,* pp. 45f.
[40] *Ibid.,* Lindau, pp. 182f.; Jacobi, *op. cit.,* pp. 43f.

more than a mere specter or phantasm. Fichte had indeed himself likewise posited the foundation of truth in the assertion of the reality of God, as we have already seen,[41] and to this end had denied to the world the attribute of reality; but Jacobi is here attacking the internal logic of Fichte's principles and so seems to neglect the writings of the *Atheismusstreit* to concentrate on the theory of the *Wissenschaftslehre*.[42] That is why he equates transcendence and God. His own position is embraced in the dual assertion: (pure) philosophy leads on principle to atheism because it dares to debase God into the categories of finitude; the immanentist philosopher, however, who cultivates an immaterial idolatry by positing a concept, a mental fact, a universal (for instance, Fichte's moral order of the universe) in the place of the *living* God, is not thereby denying morality and the true interior religion inseparably linked to such a morality. The living God can be and is here being denied "only with the lips" (*nur mit den Lippen*).

Among the unedited papers of Fichte, published by his son, there is a fragment devoted to the philosophy of Jacobi; in it, Fichte declares himself in agreement with Kant in declaring an irredeemable failure any metaphysic conceived as a system of real knowledge deduced from pure thought. He goes on to pinpoint the opposition between life and speculation in the sense that life constitutes the aim and purpose while thought is but the means and the instrument for knowing life. Thus there is a perfect antithesis and no point of contact between the two elements.[43] Fichte is known to have planned a reply to the Jacobi *Letter* which was to be rather a sort of compendium of his own philosophy as contrasted

41 "By choosing the void and nothingness, he makes *himself* God, which means he makes a *specter* God; for it is impossible, in the absence of God, for man and all that surrounds him to be more than a specter. I repeat: God is and is *outside of me, a living Being, existing on his own,* or else I am God. There is no third possibility" (*ibid.*, Lindau, p. 189, Jacobi, *op. cit.*, p. 49).

42 There is one fleeting quotation in passing from the *Appellation* (*ibid.*, Lindau, p. 190. Jacobi, *op. cit.*, p. 61).

43 *Fichtes Leben und Briefwechsel,* Vol. II, pp. 187ff., Medicus III, pp. 203ff. Fichte's faithful adherence to the principle of Kantianism even in his effort to go beyond Kant into a metaphysical realm is clearly pointed out by Rickert: "Then the validity and recognition of an absolute 'Ought' is likewise the foundation of purely theoretical knowledge, and a way is opened to the reconciliation of knowledge and faith by an *insight into the nature and essence of thinking itself.* Religion considered as faith in a principle of good objectively operative in the world can be deduced as necessary precisely because the absolutely necessary categorical imperative and the equally necessary subjective volitional response to it, both of which demand the possibility of their realization with precisely the necessity they themselves possess, are accepted as being the basis of every certitude, even for the theoretician. And this is precisely Fichte's stand. This is the reason why there can be a Kantian, i.e. critically grounded and operationally efficient philosophy of religion, on Fichte's interpretation or development of Kant." (H. Rickert, *Fichtes Atheismusstreit und die kantische Philosophie,* Kant-Studien IV [Berlin, 1900], p. 151).

with that of Jacobi. Fichte's key assertion is that "the Ego begins with freedom", that "absolute freedom is the absolute phenomenon", that "the freedom of freedom is and remains in all things simply a self-surrender to the *real* in the absolute intuition which is seized upon" and "what is given is no whit of an independent truth; it is located exclusively in intuition and not in itself". Man must therefore ascend forthwith via his understanding to the true reality, to the divine life, which offers the supreme primordial synthesis as the unity that is at once totalty and infinity. God is the moral order of the universe—*ordo ordinans absolute, eoque ipso creans* (the absolute ordering principle of order, and by that very fact creating)—and exists only in the phenomenon (*Erscheinung*) of nature and in the system of the Ego: our happiness lies in being faithful followers of the divine in us.[44]

So Fichte does not seem to have been very appreciative of this intervention of his old friend; yet not only the extreme courtesy of Jacobi's style but also the relevance of his reasoning imposed upon Fichte not merely an invitation but even a moral duty to take account of what Jacobi had written and return his courtesy by a re-examination in depth and an updating of the entire controversy: but Fichte must be admitted not to have known how to profit from the lesson he had been given by a true gentleman. This does not mean that Fichte's stand was entirely inexcusable: Jacobi himself had tried to save the man while condemning the theoretical position. And we must further bear in mind the ambiguity of Kant's position and of the theoretical atmosphere he had radiated, in which it was no longer possible to speak of a creator God and perhaps scarcely even of a God who would be a supreme Principle, *free and personal*—and this was, as Jacobi had pointed out, the crux of the whole controversy. And a final weighty consideration is the ambiguous state of Protestant theology which had suffered, in the person of Pastor Goeze of Hamburg, a slashing attack on the part of Lessing, whose *Anti-Goeze* is known to have molded the young Fichte's attitude, in the matter of religion,[45] to a greater extent perhaps even than the writings of Kant.

II—*Fichte's Self-Defense*

More elaborate and officially phrased is the defense or justification addressed by Fichte to the Pro-Rector of the University of Jena in

[44] *Zu 'Jacobi an Fichte'; C. W.*, ed. Medicus, Vol. V, pp. 359-363.

[45] Fichte himself refers and appeals to Lessing in the course of his *Atheismus-streit* (cf. Lindau, pp. 202ff., 326, especially p. 203.).

1799.[46] In regard to the question of fact, Fichte admits to having written the first of the denounced essays and to having published the second (that of Forberg) in his capacity as editor of the *Philosophisches Journal.*

In regard to the question of law, or the permissibility of the publication of the two essays, he poses two questions:

1. *Is there a blanket prohibition against the printing of irreligious or even atheistic articles which combat the Christian religion or even the natural religion?* An affirmative reply to this question could come either from the principles of reason, or from the accord of all the experts, or from a positive law. Now, in order for the affirmative reply to be founded on the principles of reason, it would be necessary to suppose that the constitutive essence of the single true immutable and perfect religion is beyond discussion and consequently likewise what goes against this religion.

(a) It is not easy to answer in the concrete: perhaps a greater scandal would be given to the one who was in error, and Fichte cites the witness of Tertullian and Luther. But can even this assumption be made unconditionally, i.e., can the true religion be established with absolute certainty? And Fichte replies that two religions can be spoken of, one taught by God in scripture and one founded on the princpiles of reason; and these two religions can have differing principles. Jesus in his own day also taught against religion—against the religion of his contemporaries—and was crucified. Luther likewise taught and inveighed and wrote against religion—again, the religion of his contemporaries—and was not crucified because he was protected by princely patronage, even though there are those [47] who find it a miscarriage of justice that he was not at least burned at the stake. Furthermore, to go no further than the recent history of the Protestant world, in the controversy between Goeze and Lessing, it was Pastor Goeze himself who admitted that it was permissible to raise objections against religion, and Lessing was in fact neither punished nor even subjected to any trial for writings that explicitly attacked religion. Thus, Lessing was allowed to publish books against religion and yet Fichte himself is not being allowed to do the same.

[46] It is entitled: *Der Herausgeber des philosophischen Journals gerichtliche Verantwortungsschriften gegen die Anklage des Atheismus,* publ. J. G. Fichte, 1799; Lindau, pp. 196ff. This work is not included in the Medicus edition. It is directed chiefly against Fichte's colleague Gruner (cf. Lindau, p. XI); the second part refers to the anonymous documents: *Schreiben eines Vaters an seinen studierenden Sohn über den Fichtischen und Forbergischen Atheismus* (1798), which Fichte attributes to the theologian Glaber.

[47] Kierkegaard among them (cf. *Diario,* under "Luther"; Italian tr. C. Fabro, Vol. II [Brescia, 1962 [2]], pp. 926ff.).

(b) But even though the publication of writings against religion cannot be condemned on the basis of the natural law, does there not exist at least a positive law against such publication? Of course there does, replies Fichte: but this law applies not to the *author* but to the *government officials.* It is a *constitutional* not a civil law. And while Fichte admits that every writer as such is subject to government censorship, he contests the right of the State to judge of the compatibility of a chain of reasoning with a decree: [48] the State cannot say "these expressions are atheistic", it simply *decrees.*

2. *But are the denounced writings really atheistic?* Fichte notes that the accusers have not taken the trouble to specify what atheism is and what they understand by it, whereas he himself has given a very definite notion of it. It appears especially from the writing of his head-on accuser (Gruner) that it is precisely his own concept of God that is equivalent to atheism and idolatry; [49] but, adds Fichte, since both are interested parties, neither should be allowed to speak the last word on the other. Fichte then proceeds to propound several "logical axioms" in order to prove that the theory expounded by himself and Forberg cannot be denounced as atheistic:

Axiom I: *The man who (in a concept) denies certain specifications of a thing, does not thereby necessarily abolish the thing (the concept) itself.* Now in these writings of Fichte there are certainly denied certain specifications in the concept of the deity, but this does not imply that the deity as such is being denied in such a way that the writings can be held to be atheistic. Fichte amazingly enough considers the major premiss in this statement to be self-evident and goes on to prove the minor.[50] In those writings, there has been denied:

(a) The extension of God in space (*die Ausgedehntheit Gottes im Raum*), or his "corporeity", and Fichte has no trouble in proving by an appeal to the very principle (*auf das Innere*) of the transcendental philosophy—an appeal we shall make ourselves in the conclusion of this chapter—that God cannot be conceived within the compass of corporeity; rather, he belongs to the suprasensible world (*das Uebersinnliche*).

(b) The comprehensibility (*Begreiflichkeit*) of God: in fact, were God to be comprehensible, he would by that very fact be something finite, because to comprehend is to define (*bestimmen*) and to define is

[48] Cf. *Gerichtliche Verantwortungsschrift,* Lindau, pp. 205ff.

[49] Fichte refers the reader to all that he has written on this point in *Appellation an das Publikum.*

[50] "We have only to discuss the minor premiss of our syllogism" (Lindau, p. 217).

to delimit (*beschränken*) with a delimitation effected by the understanding within the compass of finite experience. Thus, were God to be comprehended, he would no longer be God; he would be an idol.

Axiom II: *The man who denies certain proofs of a thing does not necessarily deny the thing itself.* Now, declares Fichte, we do deny certain proofs of the existence of God; but it does not follow from this that we are denying the existence of God himself. Here again Fichte proceeds to prove the minor only: his proof actually comes down to a repetition of the assertion already made in the denounced article, to the effect that the existence of the suprasensible world is not an object of proof but rather of faith (*Glaube*) in the sense of immediate awareness via the "internal sense" which can grasp the "in-itself" (*An-sich*) while the external senses only present the "phenomena" (*Erscheinungen*). A "proof" (*Beweis*) of the existence of God makes no sense because every proof of existence is based on the connection of something stable and in repose with something accidental and mobile. But this certainly cannot be the world of the suprasensible; nor can the causal argument possibly be used to prove the existence of God from the existence of the sensible world, because the existence in question cannot be said to be something that begins. The charge of atheism is thus nothing but a conspiracy of the "obscurantists" (*Obskuranten*) against the "friends of light" (*Freunde des Lichts*) who are the glory of the great University of Jena! The concluding section of the essay, which even evokes the specter of Vanini,[51] represents an effort on Fichte's part to attribute the whole uproar to political motives, to an attack triggered by the animosity of the conservatives and reactionaries against Fichte's own Jacobin and democratic ideas. Fichte's self-defense must be adjudged on balance to be a mere repetition of previous statements, weak and feeble on the theoretical side, and so full of skittish lamentations as to arouse the suspicion that the author is afraid he may indeed be on very thin ice.

Fichte's last apologetic piece is somewhat more serene in tone and really comes to close grips with the central point of the controversy, Fichte's identification of God with the moral order.[52] The objection had been this: supposing that all of us are the members constituting this moral order and that our mutual relations constitute the *order* of this world, then either we are ourselves God or we are the ones who make him day by day, and that leaves nothing even faintly resembling God, except ourselves.

This was a cogent objection, but Fichte makes short work of it by

[51] Lindau, p. 264.

[52] "Auf einem Privatschreiben" published in 1800 in the *Philosophisches Journal,* IX; Lindau, pp. 318ff.; Medicus III, pp. 319ff.

simply denying that he is conceiving God in anthropomorphic fashion as *living, active, powerful,* etc., or, indeed, that his God is an "out-and-out concept" (*Durch-und-durch-Begriff*).

The order of which Fichte is speaking is, says he, an "active ordering" (*tätiges Ordnen*), an *ordo ordinans,* and thus it is an order that does not belong to the world of nature and finite reality but rather subsists outside of that world, in the intelligible world. And Fichte clinches his point: "Any and every belief in a divine *that contains more* than this concept of the moral order is to that extent fiction and superstition, which may be *harmless* but is nevertheless always *unworthy* of a rational being and *suspect* in the extreme." [53] But all this is mere rhetoric: neither here nor elsewhere does Fichte ever reply to the objection that a God reduced to the moral order and thus to the compass of the rationality of human actions is not and cannot be God. In such a context God could not be without man and this is certainly what Fichte thought and Hegel was later to assert. But Fichte was right in insisting that his accusers judge the controversy from the inside of his own system and his own terminology: for this would have given the proper emphasis to the serious charge of atheism levelled against him and better brought out the true meaning of that charge.

It is the whole drift and the animating spirit of Fichte's new philosophy which should have caused alarm, more than the denounced writings themselves. Fichte's *Wissenschaftslehre* represents a more radical banishment of theistic notions than did Spinoza's philosophy; and Fichte's critique of Spinoza is but a sign of Fichte's own theologico-philosophical radicalism. Fichte utterly rejects the God of religion, the Absolute conceived as subsistent and transcendent Being, creator of the world and of man; he likewise rejects the God of Christianity who created the world in time and saved and is saving man from sin in time for eternity.[54]

The "systematic" significance of this critique of Fichte against Spinoza lies in the identification of the Kantian pure Ego with the Absolute, the substitution of the *Ich denke überhaupt* for substance as Spinoza conceived substance. Then there is the further detachment of the Kantian *Denken* (thinking) from any reference to the thing-in-itself; and finally the transformation of the Kantian *denken* into pure spontaneity, into act (*Tat*) as such and in itself. In simpler terms, Fichte's contribution to the Odyssey of modern philosophy consists in the transition from the functional Ego to the constitutive Ego, via a reconstitution of a higher or "purified" Spinozism (*geläuterte Spinozismus*), in which

[53] Lindau, p. 352; Medicus III, pp. 248f.

[54] The transcendental deduction of the pure Ego is expounded systematically in ten points in the *Grundlage der gesamten Wissenschaftslehre,* of 1794 (Medicus I, pp. 286ff.).

the Kantian Ego emerges freed of every limitation both in the speculative and in the practical sphere.

Consequently, for Fichte and later for the whole idealist school and, it might be said, for all the subsequent articulations or variants of the principle of immanentism, the Ego is the "in-itself" and the Ego-in-itself (*Ich an sich*) is the first principle. The Ego-in-itself is not some hidden occult quality but rather the real, sheer and simple, and the real that is presented effectively to the mind in reflection or as a development of self-awareness. The Ego-in-itself is therefore immediate self-awareness (*Selbstbewusstsein*); it is given in an "intellectual intuition" (*intellektuelle Anschauung*), which posits itself in producing itself.

This self-awareness or Ego-in-itself takes the place of the Kantian noumenon; intellectual intuition breaks down the barrier between the phenomenon and the noumenon: self-awareness becomes the absolute subject: "That whose being consists simply in this, that it posits itself as being and the Ego as absolute subject", which sustains every act of knowing and makes possible knowledge as such; it is that from which everything is deduced and which cannot itself be deduced from any other thing, and it is by definition removed from all multiplicity, diversity and variation. Self-awareness, self-consciousness or the pure Ego is thus identified with transcendental apperception, but freed from the drawbacks that trammelled this transcendental apperception in Kantianism and identified with the freedom of the Ego, or better still with the Ego as freedom in act, which is always the "positing" and therefore always presupposed, however the mind is moved in theory or in practice. Fichte is thus proclaiming the overcoming of all dualism in the assertion of the identity of intuition and reason, of subject-object, of finite and Infinite, of parts and Whole. The revolutionary element in Fichte's philosophy is not merely the elevation (*Erhebung*) of the Ego to the status of a noumenon, but preeminently the definitive abrogation (*Aufhebung*) of truth as contemplation and its transfer into action, into aspiration (*Streben*), into the operational freedom of the Ego, with the consequence that the practical Reason is attributed a constitutive priority over the theoretical Reason. This is the heart and the crux of the *Wissenschaftslehre* [55] throughout all its tortured reformulations.[56]

[55] In a note that seems to me to be an addition, in the later editions, to the *Atheismusstreit,* Fichte sets his own conception over against the Stoic conception: in Fichte's conception absolute Being (*absolutes Seyn*) is carefully distinguished from real existence (*wirkliches Daseyn*), whereas in the Stoic conception the infinite Idea of the Ego and the real Ego coincide, making this Stoic conception an atheistic one (*ibid.,* P. III, § 5; Medicus I, p. 470; ed. Lauth-Jakob I, 2, 410).

[56] "The theory of knowledge arises, to the extent that it is supposed to be a systematic science, in exactly the same way as do all possible sciences, to the extent that they are supposed to be systematic, through a functional definition of

From this we can clearly see, let it be noted forthwith, how Fichte could have conceived God as "the moral order of the universe", reducing him to moral rationality or rational morality in its self-actuation and thus eliminating God as a metaphysical Absolute. It is true that Fichte does posit God as the conditioning Unconditioned, but it is no less true that his God is not God, is not even conceivable, without man, without the world of freedom. Thus God can no longer exist without man. Without the Ego, God is not God. This formulation is our own but it is the clear-cut expression of Fichte's teaching.

III—*Structural Pattern of Fichtean Atheism*

Returning to the *Wissenschaftslehre,* we must note that the Ego is characterized not only by priority and centrality of position but also by "totality" (*Ganzheit*), not in the quantitative but rather in the qualitative sense, inasmuch as the Ego proceeds to the "construction" of the real via the positing of the non-Ego. Fichte explains this reduplication of the identical with itself in terms of a "fall", in terms of that negative element or that negative pull inherent in mind which will be the mainspring of the idealist dialectic. Actually the positing of the self via the Ego is synonymous with positing something *within* the Ego. But by this positing, it is setting over against itself something which is not, and therefore is limiting itself. The absolute Ego has therefore lowered itself, in and via its infinite and immediate activity, to the status of understanding and its determined and finite activity; we have here to do not with an *a*scent (*HERAUFsteigen*) but rather with a *de*scent (*HERABsteigen*).[57] By lowering itself to the status of understanding, as that which can be delimited and, as something finite, can have something set over against it, the Absolute Ego is positing a reciprocal opposition of Ego and non-Ego, in terms of which the Ego posits the negation in itself by positing the reality of the non-Ego and vice versa. Hence, the dual formula, each part of which must always be taken in conjunction with the other: (a) the Ego posits the non-Ego as limited by the Ego, and (b) the Ego posits itself as limited by the non-Ego.[58]

---

freedom which is also a determination on the part of that freedom itself; and here the definition and determination is quite specific, geared to promote the operation of the intelligence generically; and the theory of knowledge is only distinguished from other sciences by the fact that the object of these other sciences is a free operation, whereas the object of the theory of knowledge is necessary operations" (*Ueber den Begriff der Wissenschaftslehre,* II Abschn., § 7; Medicus I, p. 202).

[57] *Grundlage der gesamten Wissenschaftslehre,* § 3, p. 313.

[58] *Ibid.,* § 4, pp. 320f.

The ultimate issue of this transcendental deduction is that the human reason is derived from the infinite by an internal process of delimiting opposition; the human reason can therefore be called a limited divine reason, distinguished from that divine intellect only by a difference of degree.[59] This is the new "dynamic Spinozism" introduced by Fichte into modern thought via the self-positing and self-determination of the Ego, which is subsequently a process of active positing negation, as we have said. Throughout this whole operation, Fichte is conceiving of the Ego not as in "being" (*Sein*) but rather as in "becoming" (*Werden*), as a process of self-determination. "The statement that 'the Ego *becomes* determined' means that reality becomes abrogated in it. When the Ego posits in itself only a part of the reality of an absolute totality, it removes the rest of that totality from itself and posits it in the non-Ego . . . Thus, the Ego posits negation in itself to the extent that it projects reality into the non-Ego, and reality in itself to the extent that it projects negation into the non-Ego. The Ego thus posits itself as *self-determining* inasmuch as it is *becoming* determined, and as *becoming* determined inasmuch as it is *determining* itself."[60] In other words, in this self-negation and self-limitation into the particular of the non-Ego there is accomplished the relating of the Ego to the empirical realm of experience and of history which is no longer a reality external to the Ego, as in Kant, but is rather conceived of likewise as a self-producing negation within the Ego itself when that Ego is at the debased level of understanding (*Verstand*). Here we are obviously dealing with a relative negation that refers us back to the presupposes the "total negation" which is God himself, posited (or postulated) by the reason (*Vernunft*) in the act proper to it, the act of "faith" (*Glaube*).

For Fichte and for us, this is the real crux of the controversy. In the *Wissenschaftslehre 'nova metodo',* which dates from 1798, and so is contemporary with the *Atheismusstreit,* Fichte already explicitly reduces knowledge to willing and action; knowing, truth, becomes an acting and a tending: willing is the transcendental element of the mind which posits itself as a determination (*Bestimmtheit*), partly in terms of its very form which we can consider as a tendency whereby something is demanded outside the willing subject, partly as a being (*Sein*), as a quality of myself inasmuch as I am a willing subject. And in this context the will is the object of a possible intuition which we must assume simply in order to be able to think anything whatever. It is by this willing that I am what I am; this pure willing is my being and my being is my willing:

[59] In a letter of May 25, 1789, to M. Herz, Kant protested vigorously against this reduction, already attempted by Maimonides (*C. W.*, ed. Cassirer, Vol. IX, p. 416).

[60] *Grundlagen der gesamten Wissenschaftslehre,* II Teil, § 4, pp. 324f.

this is the primordial reality (root) of the Ego; and actually it is only this pure willing that is capable of becoming the immediate object of the mind.

Even though willing relates to something that is external and seeks that something and indeed demands and requires it, *pure* willing as such has no object to which it can relate: the object, as we have said already, is found via *feeling*. Thus a *discrete* apprehending (and that is what immediate experience is!) is called feeling (*Gefühl*).[61] And the Whole (*das Ganze*) in this context is the *Synthesis* of willing and being. Fichte sums up thus: "My true *being* is determination of willing. This is my whole being. This is comprehended in time and thereby I *become* although I am even previously to this. The whole is *a being* determined by willing; this is my whole state. But only parts thereof can be and are comprehended, and this comprehended is thus only something limited." [62]

Fichte immediately adds that this is not a limitation that is empirical in origin. No, we must probe more deeply, going back to the very origin of the activity in question. With the awareness of willing is primordially connected a consciousness of a *being*. The will as such is to be considered as a quality of my Ego, my whole state (*Zustand*). I will, therefore I *am* a willing principle. Thus with my reflection on a willing there is connected the reflection on a being. But a *being* is something objective. Therefore an object is the nexus of the two: *willing* and *being* are the same, distinguished only by their relation to different powers of knowledge of the mind, pure willing and pure thinking; being, on the other hand, is related to an intuition connected with a thinking, but not with a sheer and simple thinking, rather with an *objective* thinking, and so being is related to an object. *Pure thought* and intuiting are united and this necessarily initiates the unification of willing and being. Yet willing and being are different. When something is simply *thought*, it is a willing; but if it be *intuited*, then it becomes an object, a being. And this being is then the will itself which is an empirical will inasmuch as it is intuited and to which is connected an empirical being—and we have arrived at empirical intuition.[63]

[61] But how can feeling apprehend the real which is its "material"? Via intuition (*Anschauung*). And Fichte specifies still further that feeling (*Gefühl*) is an "affection" of our very selves and is determined by our "action" (*Handeln*) which is intrinsically limited (J. G. Fichte, *Wissenschaftslehre 'nova metodo'*, § 13; *Nachgelassene Schriften,* ed. Jakob, Vol. II, p. 483).

[62] *Ibid.*

[63] It is beyond our present scope to follow through the further evolution of Fichte's thought. In the *Darstellung der Wissenschaftslehre vom 1801,* we find the following passage: "The Absolute is neither Knowing nor yet Being, nor is it the identity of the two, nor is it both indifferently; rather it is quite simply and

We thus have in Fichte an instance of radical idealism, a tracing back of everything to the Ego and a positing of its activity as pure willing as the source and fountainhead of being and of its determinations. But the source of these determinations is taken from empirical intuition and so being is linked with particularity and exteriority which is subject to empirical space and time. The sphere of empirical intuition, of the immediate "givenness" of sense-contents, constitutes Being (*Sein*): "All being is for it necessarily a *sensible* being, for it deduces the entire concept from the form of sensibility in the first place; and so the problem of a bridge to the sensible simply does not arise for this approach. Intellectual intuition in the Kantian sense is a monstrosity, a mirage that vanishes when we try to think it, an insubstantial figment not worthy of being assigned a name. The intellectual intuition of which the *Wissenschaftslehre* is speaking, focuses not on a being but rather on an *acting*. [64] Fichte admits that Kant rejected intellectual intuition; but he asks whether the categorical imperative may not be an immediate object of consciousness?

And here we are back at our old problem: we have at our disposal two intuitions, one sensible and the other intelligible; and these two link us with the two areas of experience, external and internal. The first of these areas constitutes the sphere of being and to it are appropriate the predicates of being, such as permanence and subsistence, and the inte-

---

solely the Absolute" (Medicus IV, pp. 12f.). But in the same work there is an explicit assertion of the mutual subsumption of being and freedom: "Whether you deduce being from freedom or freedom from being, it is always simply the deduction of the same from the same, only from a different point of view; for freedom or knowing is *being* itself; and being is knowing itself, and there is no other being whatsoever" (Medicus IV, p. 34).

This is a new concept of *being* (*Sein*), more consistent with the principle of immanentism, which provides Fichte's idealism with its explicit formulation, explaining such terminology as *Seinskonstruktion* (construction of being), *Seinsproduktion* (production of being) which recur later on (Medicus IV, pp. 292ff., 299, 307, 339, 350, 387 and *passim*). *Being* actually becomes synonymous with Life (*Leben*) in the 1804 *Wissenschaftslehre* (Medicus IV, p. 283); cf. in this connection the second lecture in *Ueber das Wesen des Gelehrten* (Medicus V, p. 16). Thus in the *Anweisung sum seligen Leben* (1806), Life (*Leben*) stands for ". . . what is from all eternity and to all eternity", and so for God (Medicus V, pp. 150 and especially 159f.): this Being (*Sein*) is in no sense to be confused with the Dasein (*existence*) of immediate experience. In Fichte's late work *Staatslehre* (1812), he writes: "*Only God is.* Outside of Him, only *his Appearance* (*Erscheinung*). In the Appearance, only the exclusively genuinely real, freedom . . ." (Medicus VI, p. 479). Being has thus been promoted to the status of the name of God, but now only God is being: and so the Spinozan monism remains intact and consequently, according to Jacobi, so does the atheism.

64 *Zweite Einleitung in die Wissenschaftslehre,* § 6; Medicus III, p. 56. On this point of the dissolution of the *cogito* into the *volo,* the reader might consult my *G. F. W. Hegel, La dialettica* (Brescia, 1960), Introduction, pp. LXXXIVff.

rior determinations of this being such as substantiality and causality, etc. Only the object of experience *is* and there *is* nothing outside of experience; *and* "is" is here being used in a sense quite different from that of the logical copula.[65]

God then certainly cannot belong to the sphere of being, of sensible intuition, but only to the sphere of intelligible intuition, the sphere of action: "Purely philosophically speaking, it would have to be said of God: He is (logical copula) not a being but rather a pure acting (operation), life and principle of a suprasensible universal order, just as I, too, a finite intelligence, am not a being but a pure acting (operation), a duty-motivated operation, as a member of that suprasensible universal order." [66] Hence it must likewise be admitted that God cannot be said to be substance or cause or person or providence or anything of this sort, for these are all categories that refer to the sphere of sensible intuition and would therefore reduce God to a material substance.

There has recently been published a brief entitled "To the Germans, In Defense of Fichte", dated 1799 and written by F. Schlegel, one of the few men who spoke up on Fichte's behalf against the avalanche of accusations precipitated by the controversy over his alleged atheism. Schlegel begins by charging the Germans with not having understood anything whatever of Fichte's philosophy; he reckons with the very good possibility of their not understanding anything of this defense he is about to write either; but this is not going to deter him from speaking out. In the society to which all belong, he observes, everyone ought to aspire to the Eternal in truth and virtue: everyone therefore who feels himself called to speak out on what is of interest to all ought to enunciate his own opinion as "the voice of one individual" (*als Stimme eines Einzelnen*). "If everyone's aspiration is to be as an individual, as he should be, then the same Spirit will become manifest of itself universally."

Schlegel claims that there has been an incomprehensible misunderstanding of the whole point at issue in the controversy: "Actually both Fichte and those moderates who oppose him are in agreement that man ought to refer everything he does and everything from which he refrains (*Thun und Lassen*) to the will of God. The point at issue is "existence" (*Daseyn*) in general: not the existence of God, about which there has been so much talk, but all existence in general and its value or lack of value for action and the relation of both to the Infinite and the finite."

[65] "Manifestly *being* is not a real predicate, i.e. a concept of something which could in any way supplement the concept of a thing. It is simply the positing of a thing or of certain determinations. As used in logic, it is simply the copula of a judgment" (Kant, *Kritik der reinen Vernunft,* Transz. Dialektik, II Buch, 3. Hauptst., A599).

[66] *Gerichtliche Verantwortungsschrift,* Lindau, p. 221.

Fichte asserts that pure act is the primordial and primary element from which proceeds existence, and that it is contradictory to derive act from a primordially given existence, as philosophers have been in the habit of doing in the past. Every existence is finite and sensible and only in act (acting, action) can man grasp the Infinite and acquire the right of citizenship in the suprasensible world. Therefore the philosopher as such cannot think of infinite Reason except in its eternal act (action, operation) and as that very action; nor can he ever attribute to it an existence apart from that. In a word, what is here at issue is the srtuggle between idealism and realism. Schlegel feels that Fichte's philosophy is in perfect accord with Christian philosophy: ". . . not in virtue of any arbitrary rapprochement but in virtue of the internal necessity of its own principles. For this philosophy likewise holds that there is in the world an eternal struggle between good and evil. There exist in man two tendencies, primordially divergent, one toward the finite and the other toward the Infinite: thus it is no mere diversity of degree or shading that distinguishes virtue from vice; rather it is an absolute opposition of direction, of the road that every man is free to travel." [67] The voice of Schlegel adds a weighty confirmation of Fichte's good intentions, but it likewise underscores and highlights Fichte's principles and the impasse into which those principles had forced him.

Every philosopher is read, like music, in the key in which his work is written, i.e., in the context of his own terminology; and Fichte often recalls to his critics this *Sprachgebrauch* (terminology) of his wherein God is not only asserted but posited at the center, and in a certain sense, as we have seen, at the beginning of man's search for truth. But in another sense, which is to become more and more explicit with the evolution or dissolution of the principle of immanentism, this God is not and cannot be God: this God is but the transcendental X, the moral order of the universe, the basis and term of human action and aspiration, rationality in its self-actuation as fulfillment of man's moral perfection. And on his own presuppositions, Fichte could not say anything else.

[67] F. Schlegel, *Werke,* Kritische Ausgabe (Munich, 1963); Vol. XVIII, Appendix III: *Für Fichte. An die Deutschen,* pp. 521ff.

3

Disintegration of Idealism into Atheistic Pantheism (Schelling-Hegel)

The intimate nexus between Kantianism and the crisis of atheism triggered by idealism with certainly not Kant's deliberate intention, nor did anyone have any inkling of it when the three Kantian *Critiques* first appeared. Jacobi, for his part, seems to absolve Kant of all responsibility and make Fichte the main culprit, as having abandoned the "pure rational faith" (*reiner Vernunftsglaube*), i.e., the theory of the postulates of practical reason, in order to create a more drastically immanentist system of ethics. And no one was in a better position than Jacobi, after a good decade of the tumults of the *Atheismusstreit,* to formulate the crux of the charge. In Jacobi's opinion, the error of the *Wissenschaftslehre*, "the daughter to be expected from such a mother as critical philosophy" (*die leibliche Tochter der kritischen Philosophie*), lay precisely in the fact that the "vital functional moral order of the universe became God himself," [1] a God expressly deprived of consciousness and selfhood (personality), a God who is not a particular and identifiable being, distinct from the world and man, nor yet the cause of the moral order of the universe, but simply that moral order itself which has outside of itself neither foundation nor condition of its own activity, which exists in a purely and absolutely necessary fashion. "To attribute to God consciousness and simply that highest degree of consciousness which we call 'personality' (*being-in-itself and appearing-from-itself*); in a word, to attribute to him a selfhood or a knowledge and will of his own, is tantamount, for the *Wissenschaftslehre,* to making God a finite being, since consciousness and personality are bound up with limitation and finitude. The concept of God as a particular being or, in Kant's phrase, as a living God to whom should pertain in the highest degree the

[1] Jacobi, *Von den göttlichen Dingen und ihrer Offenbarung,* p. 346. Jacobi is clearly reporting to the letter Fichte's expressions from the "*Ueber den Grund unseres Glaubens an eine göttliche Weltregrierung*" of 1798.

perfection of self-consciousness, personality—such a concept is contradictory and impossible. And this can be said in all frankness, taking no account of the jabbering of the Schoolmen, for only thus can the true religion of the kingdom of joy arise." This philosophy could have but one outcome.

But Jacobi himself, for all the admiration he cherished for Kant, declares that Kantian criticism, when developed with rigorous consistency, was bound to give rise to the *Wissenschaftslehre* and this in turn was bound, upon rigorous development and enucleation, to lead to the monistic theory (*Alleinheitslehre*) of Schelling, which theory Jacobi calls the second daughter (*zweite Tochter*) of critical philosophy and which he labels as an inverted or glorified Spinozism, idealist materialism (*ein umgekehrter oder verklärter Spinozismus, Idealmaterialismus*).[2]

1. *The Jacobi-Schelling Polemic*

Jacobi reiterates the stand of Bouterwek and Fries in defense of Kant, admitting the good faith of the author of the *Critiques* in subordinating the speculative reason to the understanding (*Verstand*) and entrusting the practical reason with the task of transcending the limits of the understanding: Kant was clear on the point that fundamental truths, such as freedom, immortality and God, could not be deduced from other more fundamental ones; but Jacobi charges Kant with having made the error of wishing to make the knowledge of these fundamental truths into a science, i.e., to transform the immediate consciousness of them into a mediate knowledge and the immediate object into a mediate one. The understanding, Jacobi explains, was supposed to provide a basis for the reason on the one hand, while the reason was supposed for its part to build on the foundation of the understanding in accord with that understanding. The result was that the understanding annihilated the reason and the reason showed the void of the understanding, thus reducing philosophy to a mere "theory of nature", to a natural philosophy. And that is the position of Schelling.

Jacobi refers to Plato and Aristotle as the main champions of theism in the ancient world: they followed Anaxagoras in positing as principle what is most perfect. Jacobi contrasts with them the materialist philosophers of antiquity, the pre-Socratics, the ancient poets, the Pythagoreans, who had posited as principle the less perfect. Whereas Plato and Socrates had posited the will a principle, these others had posited fate, uncaused and purposeless fate. The first integral form of philosophy was

[2] Jacobi, *Von den göttlichen Dingen,* pp. 347, 354.

theism, since naturalism got a foothold only with the development of science. The aim of naturalism as a philosophical system was to trace the universe back to a single Principle, starting from which everything could be explained: this is the All or Whole of nature which then takes the place of God. Therefore, concludes Jacobi, it is in the interests of the *Naturphilosophie* of a man like Schelling that God should not exist, that there should not exist any supernatural, transcendent and supramundane being. Only on condition that there exists nothing else than nature, that nature is subsistent and all in all, can science attain its goal of perfection; only then can it flatter itself that it can become itself, like its object, all in all.[3] It is not naturalism as science that is opposed to God; it is only that naturalism which claims to identify itself with philosophy; the pure and simple science of nature, natural science, is ignorant of God, for its object belongs to the compass of sensible things; but it does not deny God nor is it averse to theism. Natural science can coexist with theism, whereas naturalism cannot.[4] For naturalism as a philosophy asserts that nature is entirely independent and sufficient unto itself: it is the One, the All, and apart from it or beyond it there is nothing. But this is an empty and totally inconsistent and groundless notion.

Naturalism actually presents no definite concept of nature: to say that nature is the "sum total" (*Inbegriff*) of every being, of every operation and becoming, of all that begins and occurs, is not to present any kind of precise or accurate philosophical notion: it is to do no more than simply to set nature over against nothingness, the void, the empty negative. In order to escape the absurdity of such a conception as would reduce nature to a rigid and immobile mass (Spinoza), the new philosophy conceived nature as the creative operation as such, sheer creating without any purpose, absolute productivity.[5] But it is only to this sort of productivity, notes Jacobi, that is devoid of subject and object and is anteriorly and posteriorly unconditioned, that there can be attributed a true and proper being; such can never be attributed to what is produced by that productivity, the infinity of particular beings which, for such a philosophical system, do not really exist at all as such. Therefore, there does not even exist a sum total of all beings; there can be only one

[3] *Ibid.*, pp. 384f.

[4] In this connection Jacobi cites Schlegel's reproach to the "philosophy of nature" for having abrogated the distinction between good and evil: "The system that teaches that all is one (let it call itself naturalism, pantheism, Spinozism or what it will) inevitably abrogates the distinction between good and evil, no matter how loudly it may protest that it does not do so.—For if everything is simply one, then everything is good, and every semblance of what we call unjust or evil is but a hollow delusion" (F. Schlegel, *Ueber die Sprache und Weisheit der Indier,* in Jacobi, *C. W.*, Vol. III, p. 387 note).

[5] Jacobi, *Von den göttlichen Dingen,* p. 389.

single, eternal and immutable Being, i.e., the Being of absolute productivity. Again, then, we have a "dynamic Spinozism": but whereas Fichte had set up the moral consciousness as Absolute, Schelling has conferred this status and dignity upon "nature" by proclaiming nature or absolute productivity to be "the holy, eternally creating primordial power of the world, which engenders and operatively brings forth all things out of itself, the only true God, the Living One".[6] But this Nature-God is in reality the God of the totality of being self-enclosed and immutable, wherein all is annihilated: Therefore, exclaims Jacobi, it is the antithesis of the God of the creationists who has rather created beings by drawing them out of nothing, out of the void. Thus, in this conception of a Nature-God, there can be no avoiding the absurdity of identifying being with nothingness in the sense of the identity of the Unconditioned with the conditioned, of necessity with reason, of reason with the absurd, of good with evil. And so this philosophy destroys what is at the very root of man's dignity, the freedom of the reason, and leaves man superior to the brute beast only in virtue of his capacity for error and falsehood.[7] Such a charge was serious indeed.

At the root of all such aberration has always lain the error of giving the understanding priority over the reason,[8] the mad ambition of constructing an analytic philosophy as a pure and simple reflection on sensible reality. Thus, whereas theism refers the world and all finite beings to the Absolute as first Cause, naturalism dissolves the whole reality of the world into that infinite ground and abyss (*unendlicher Grund und Abgrund*), the One-Whole. This inversion is quite indicative and serves to unmask the true face of the new philosophical systems in their pantheistic variants.[9] Jacobi therefore repeats to Schelling, against transcendental materialism, what he had said to Fichte, against Fichte's transcendental moralism: "Reason without personality is an absurdity just like that *substrate matter* (Grundmaterie) of that *primordial ground* or *first cause* (Urgrund), which is all and not one, or one and none (no-

[6] *Ibid.*, pp. 390f.

[7] *Ibid.*, pp. 394f.—With his solid grounding in and devotion to fideism, Jacobi distrusts any metaphysical proof of the existence of God or of creation, because his theory of faith (*Glaube*) holds that, in man, the immediate consciousness of the freedom of his nature is at once the consciousness of his likeness to God and of his dependence on God (cf. pp. 400f., 412ff.).

[8] "One becomes a naturalist or a theist depending on whether one subordinates the reason to the understanding or the understanding to the reason" (*ibid.*, p. 412).

[9] Jacobi rightly makes quite a point of the difference between cause (*Ursache*) and foundation (*Grund*) and refers the reader to *Idealismus und Realismus* and to Appendix VII of the *Briefe über die Lehre des Spinozas*. St. Thomas was equally vigorous in his insistence on the distinction between cause and principle (cf. *S.T.*, I^a, q. 33, a. 1).

one), the perfection of the imperfect, the absolutely indeterminate, and is called God by those who want nothing to do with the true God but who yet eschew any outright denial of him in so many words." [10] The crucial slogan in this battle of the giants being waged by the elderly Jacobi against the atheistic pantheism of transcendental idealism is to be found in a lengthy passage taken from the *Jenaische allgemeine Literaturzeitung* of 1807 (the year that saw the publication of Hegel's *Phenomenology of the Spirit!*): " '*Without* the world, no God!' is the formula most simply and clearly expressive of naturalism. But all the religions have from time immemorial inverted this proposition and asserted: '*without God, no world!*' Faith in God is given to us prior to any intuition of the world; with our own ego is given a primordial Ego. In the depths of our own soul we intuit the primordial form of life and we see that form reflected in the unveiled face of nature and at the sight we stand amazed, we love and we pray. This is religion; this and not any chemical process if identification wherein we merge with nature to be reduced into a chaotic mass, throwing to the winds our own life and that of nature and God together with it." [11]

This fiery profession of Jacobi's own philosophic faith clearly betrays echoes of, and allusions to, mysticism, ancient and modern, from Eckhart right down to Böhme and Schleiermacher; but it would be easy to show how the same crypto-mystical motivations catalyzed the speculations of the transcendentalist philosophers in their efforts to reduce to the One-Whole the variegated manifold of experience and the insistent vibrations of freedom. So this is not the point on which realism and idealism diverge; it is rather in a deeper-lying attitude to the very meaning of the knowing operation, a problem Jacobi felt he had solved with the positing of faith (*Glaube*). Therefore, the controversy remained open.

Schelling's reaction to Jacobi's charge was immediate and violent: Schelling himself was not subjected to any ban on his writings, removal from office or other harassment on the part of the government and was able to write this reply [12] referring only to the theoretical demands of the problem raised by the "chief prosecutor" or "Grand Inquisitor", as Schelling dubbed Jacobi. First Schelling refutes the main points of the

[10] Jacobi, *Von den göttlichen Dingen,* p. 419.

[11] *Ibid.,* p. 419 note.—Hegel will repeat to the letter, in his *Philosophie der Religion,* this phrase "Ohne Welt kein Gott" ("Without a world, no God") (*C. W.,* ed. Lasson, Vol. I [Leipzig, 1925], p. 148).

[12] The full title is: *Denkmal der Schrift von den göttlichen Dingen etc. des Herrn F. H. Jacobi und der ihm in derselben gemachten Beschuldigung eines absichtlichen täuschenden, Lüge redenden Atheismus,* 1812 (manuscript completed, however, on December 13, 1811); *C. W.,* Abt. I, Vol. 8 (Stuttgart and Augsburg, 1861), pp. 19ff.

charge (eight in all); then he goes into an extensive discussion of the atheism that had been presented as being the essence and constitutive element of transcendental philosophy in particular and of the whole of speculative philosophy in general. We shall first inspect Schelling's refutation of the eight points adduced against him:

1. Schelling deplores the part played by Jacobi in the Fichte affair and still more Jacobi's impudence in the sequel, washing his hands of the whole business and protesting his innocence. As for Jacobi's exposition of Schelling's own theory and teaching ("the second daughter of critical philosophy"), Schelling at once reproaches Jacobi with not having produced any evidence that he had abrogated the distinction between natural philosophy and moral philosophy (p. 24).

2. To the main charge that in his philosophy "there is nothing above nature and that nature is everything", Schelling replies with the positive statement that neither this assertion nor anything equivalent to it is to be found in any of his writings; [13] nor *could* it possibly be there to be found, adds Schelling, for such an assertion goes against the nature and the fundamental concept of the whole of his system. In fact he is asserting precisely the opposite of what Jacobi is attributing to him: "We understand nature as being absolute identity when it is considered not as being (existing) but rather as the ground of its own being." [14] This means that nature is distinct from existing absolute Identity in that this Identity is simply the "ground" of its existence. The existing absolute Identity is God preeminently, God as Subject and ground of being (*als Grund des Seyns*), above nature, which is non-existing or purely objective absolute identity. "Nature" here simply indicates all that is "this side of" (*diesseits*) existing absolute identity, i.e., this side of the absolute (subjective) Being who is God. It is clear that in this reply Schelling is not repudiating Spinozism; he will presently bear witness personally on this point.

3. The further assertion that ". . . the aforementioned theory of unicity [15] aims at doing away with God, immortality and freedom, to remain simply a theory of nature, a pure philosophy of nature", Schelling dismisses as simply totally false.

4. As for the charge of Spinozism ("The system of absolute identity

[13] "This sounds as though the reader would be encountering the phrase '*above* nature there is nothing and it *alone* is' everywhere in my writings. I can state positively that *it is not to be found in a single one of my writings*" (*ibid.*, p. 25). Later Schelling points out that Jacobi is liable to prosecution under the *Lex Cornelia* for publishing this false and libellous statement (p. 35 note).

[14] *Ibid.*, p. 25.

[15] This theory is described as *Alleinheitslehre* (monism), *Identitätslehre* (theory of identity), *Naturphilosophie* (naturalism), the three terms being used interchangeably (*ibid.*, p. 23).

is really and truly identical with Spinozism" which Jacobi had been branding for 25 years as atheism), Schelling does not actually deny the charge and even says that Spinozism "in a certain sense" (not, of course, as interpreted by Jacobi) is the only real aspect of any true philosophy; but Jacobi has yet to demonstrate, insists Schelling, that the "philosophy of identity" is reducible without remainder to Spinozism (pp. 25f.).

5. "The *Naturphilosophie* recognizes only *One supreme Principle* and to this extent abrogates *all* dualism except that in the supreme Principle itself". This is Schelling's loyally Spinozistic reply to the Jacobi charge that "the *Naturphilosophie* asserts that all dualism must be eliminated and thus is really (a favorite adverb of Jacobi's throughout) asserting the identity (unicity) of reason and non-reason, of good and evil". And Schelling merely adds that Jacobi should consult Schelling's essay on freedom to see that Schelling does admit moral values.

6. Jacobi has further charged that in Schelling's theory ". . . the coral that produces the islet in the sea is more like God than is man who aspires to virtue and holiness". Here Schelling accuses Jacobi of having doctored the Schelling text so as to falsify its thought. The passage in question in Schelling had said simply: "Nature is for the enthusiast of research simply *the holy, eternally creating, primordial power of the universe, which engenders and operatively brings forth all things out of itself.* The principle of imitation had a different meaning when it taught the emulation of the art of this creative force, etc." [16] Schelling puts his own text and that of Jacobi in parallel columns to show that Jacobi has added, on his own, after the phrases italicized in Schelling's original, the following phrase, which Jacobi has also put in italics: "the only true God, the Living One". And, charges Schelling. Jacobi has continued in a way that makes it sound as if Schelling were speaking: "The God of theism, on the contrary, is but a fatuous idol, a chimera insulting to reason." These additions prove only, says Schelling, that Jacobi has not understood the Schelling system at all: the only really atheistic phrase is the one added by Jacobi himself!

8. (Schelling himself presents no No. 7.) The final point of the charge seems the most serious and amounts to a drastic summary of the preceding ones: "The naturalist who asserts dogmatically: *'Everything* is nature, and there is nothing above or beyond nature,' . . . uses such terms as God, freedom, immortality, only to deceive." A man who does this sort of thing (i.e., the naturalist) is branded a deceiver and a liar (*Betrüger und Lügner*). Schelling here appeals to Spinoza and objects against Jacobi that Book I of Spinoza's *Ethics* was entitled *De Deo* (Of God) and the next chapter *De libertate* (Of Freedom), as Jacobi must

[16] *Ibid.*, p. 2.

very well know! Spinoza, concludes Schelling, was no deceiver. Schelling finds Jacobi's last attack simply unspeakable.

The crucial problem, to Schelling's mind, is whether the assertions attributed to him by Jacobi are really to be found in Schelling's works: "We have here to do with a simple question of scientific history: *what I have really maintained, and what now; whether the assertions attributed to me are truly my assertions or not; whether the passages presented as literal quotations from my writings are really to be found in my writings or not.*" [17] If this cannot be done, and Jacobi has not been able to do it, then the accuser is deserving neither of sympathy nor pardon. Especially the last charge (No. 8) that Schelling has ignored the notion of moral freedom and the notion of the Personality of the supreme Being, overlooks entirely everything that was contained in Schelling's essay on human freedom,[18] which had been written in 1807 and aimed precisely at substantiating human freedom. Jacobi has therefore committed a basic perversion of fact and even his critique of statements Schelling actually did make is not cogent.

Schelling now goes over to the offensive himself, attacking Jacobi's central thesis as expressed in the three points: (1) Spinozism is atheism. (2) The Leibnizian-Wolffian philosophy is no less fatalistic than the Spinozan, and forces any consistent and consequential researcher back to the principles of that Spinozan philosophy. (3) (And this is the main point): *Every method involving proof leads to fatalism.* Schelling has an easy time proving that by such a statement Jacobi is effecting a blanket condemnation of all philosophy and cites against him Bacon's famous contention to the effect that only superficial philosophizing leads man away from God, while profounder thinking leads him back to God.[19]

Schelling further cites against Jacobi a clearcut and powerful protest of Kant in defense of the capacity of reason in the area of suprasensible truths; and Schelling turns the charge of atheism back upon Jacobi himself: "When anyone contests the right of the reason to have the first and chief say in matters pertaining to suprasensible objects, such as the existence of God and the life to come, then *the gates are thrown wide open* to every kind of *fanaticism, superstition* and even *atheism.* And yet it seems that, in the Jacobi-Mendelssohn controversy, everything is bent upon just such a subversion at least of the power of ontological penetration of reason and knowledge, and perhaps even of rational faith (*Vernunftsglaube*); and the whole aim is the establishment of another faith

[17] *Ibid.*, p. 33.

[18] This is the essay entitled *Philosophische Untersuchungen über das Wesen der menschlichen Freiheit und die damit zusammenhängende Gegenstände* (*C. W.*, I, 7, pp. 331ff.).

[19] *Denkmal . . .*, p. 40. The Bacon passage is also cited in the fragment: *Ueber das Wesen deutscher Wissenschaft* (*C. W.*, I, 8, p. 9).

which each man can trim to his own measure. It would indeed seem that the intention must be to go to the whole way, when the Spinozan notion of God is posited as the only one in accord with all the principles of reason and yet is branded as a notion to be repudiated. For, even though it may be quite compatible with rational faith to grant that the speculative reason is not in a position even to apprehend the possibility of such a being as we must think God to be, it is certainly not compatible with ANY *faith* or with any acceptance of a being whatsoever, for the reason to apprehend nothing less than the IMPOSSIBILITY of an object and yet to be able to perceive the reality of the same object from other sources."[20] The Kantian passage to which Schelling refers and which is a kind of echo of the clearcut distinction made by Aquinas between reason and faith and of the priority of reason over faith is nevertheless expressive precisely of the Kantian teaching on "rational faith" which Jacobi had used as such an important weapon in his fight against theological rationalism.

Thus, the controversy is gradually penetrating into the very heartland of the evolution of modern thought and is evidence of the deepening criteriological crisis facing modern thinkers. Schelling proceeds, as had Fichte, to take up the defense of Lessing against Jacobi and especially to defend Lessing's Spinozan ideas against Jacobi's theory of the "leap" (*Sprung*): "Lessing behaved, in a word, like a true philosopher, who is not ashamed of his profession, even though he was known to be competent in several other professions; he preferred to accept the ill-famed Spinozan ideas rather than the orthodox ones, if these latter are not made plausible to the understanding. No true thinker can blame him for this."[21] Jacobi simply has atheism on the brain and sees atheists under every bed! Now has it profitted him a whit to have put himself under the patronage of Kant and adopted Kant's terminology: the net result of Jacobi's identification of *Gefühl* (feeling) in his own theory with *Vernunft* (reason) in Kant's has been to degrade the Kantian concept of "reason" and to create a great confusion.[22] Schelling deplores especially Jacobi's letter to Fichte with its charge that Fichte's philosophy was atheistic simply because it did not teach a personal God.

Schelling follows up with the charge that nothing could be imagined

[20] *Denkmal . . .*, p. 41. Cf. Kant, *Was heisst sich im Denken orientieren?*, ed. Cassirer, Vol. IV, p. 352. This essay is a reply by Kant to the Mendelssohn-Jacobi controversy on Spinozism and we shall be referring to it shortly in our summing up at the end of this chapter.

[21] *Denkmal . . .*, p. 45. But in the note to the following page (46), Schelling will be at pains to absolve Lessing of the charge of Spinozism!

[22] Schelling cites in his own support the severe judgment passed by Hegel, whom he calls "a well-grounded and competent judge" (*ein gründlicher Beurtheiler*), on Jacobi's "distortions and misquotations" (*ibid.*, p. 49).

more inconsistent or tenuous than Jacobi's *Glaube;* so it is Jacobi's philosophy that really leads to atheism! Schelling proceeds to a ten-point confrontation of Jacobi's philosophy with his own; this exercise is aimed at showing which is atheistic and which theistic. We here indicate only some of the main points of this confrontation. When Jacobi posits the essence of God as lying in what the philosophers have termed *aseitas* in order to indicate the most deeply-hidden secret of the divine being, he is actually opting for the concept of substance a la Spinoza! Can this *aseitas* ever be a consciousness? Can it ever be the conscious God? Does Jacobi ever succeed in combining *aseitas* with consciousness, with mind? [23]

Jacobi is entirely arbitrary when he sets naturalism and theism over against one another as antithetical systems: "I understand by naturalism not a system that bears upon external nature but rather the system *that asserts one nature IN GOD."* [24] Theism and naturalism are essentially mutually complementary: theism by itself, without naturalism, can get nowhere: it is a feckless, fruitless folly to be willing to entrust the certitude of the existence of God to such expedients as presentiment, longing (*Sehnsucht*) or feeling. The error of such theism is that of starting from God and trying to reach nature, whereas the proper procedure is the exact opposite: the starting point should be the tenet that (a) nature is in God. Schelling's philosophy is thus a "dynamic Spinozism" like Fichte's, but one which aims at transfiguring the sensible world and filling it with God, as did Goethe.

This direct confrontation of the two theories yields little appreciable result except a further clarification of the contrast and irreconcilable opposition between them, as is highlighted in the conclusion: "Jacobi asserts an unconditioned knowing of God (probably a *personal* God) deriving immediately from reason (*Vernunft*). In this I cannot agree with him and his apparent agreement with me is far in excess of my demand! The pure immediate knowing of the reason must function in accord with the absolute law of that same reason: it must be a perception and recognition of *contradiction, or absolute identity of the Infinite and the finite, as the supreme Reality.* This perception is certainly likewise a perception of God to the extent that the being of that absolute identity is already implicitly God, or more exactly, *the same being* which is transfigured into the personal God. But it cannot be called a knowing or a perceiving of the personal God." [25] There follows a train of explanation which seems to us entirely in the line of "dynamic Spinozism",

[23] *Ibid.,* p. 62. Cf. also further on in the same work (pp. 73f.) the charge that Jacobi himself is in no position to assert the "personality" of God.

[24] *Ibid.,* p. 69.

[25] *Ibid.,* p. 81.—Schelling protests that he has said exactly the opposite and refers again to the essay *Ueber das Wesen der menschlichen Freiheit* (*C. W.,* I, 7, p. 412).

i.e., a transition from an "implicit God" to an "explicit God": "I posit God as First and Last, as Alpha and Omega,[26] but he is not as the Alpha what he is as the Omega, and to the extent that it is only as Omega that he is God *sensu eminenti,* he cannot be God in that same sense as Alpha, nor, in the strictest sense, can he be called God as Alpha, unless he be expressly said to be, as Alpha, the larval (*unentfaltet* = not-yet-unfolded) God, *Deus implicitus,* as distinct from the *Deus explicitus* which he is as the Omega." And Schelling ends with a profession and statement of position amounting to an explicit admission of Jacobi's main charge against idealism: "Nor can an immediate knowing of a personal God be anything but a personal knowing, based, like all such knowledge, upon personal association (*Umgang*), upon real experience. But this has no place in philosophy; it is an affair of the reason . . . But precisely this existence of God as a personal being is the object of *science,* and not merely in some vague, generic sense; no, it is science's supreme and ultimate object, the *goal* of its strivings, toward which it has striven in all ages and which science is *just in process of attaining* at the moment when Mr. Jacobi wants to snatch it away from before your very eyes; and science is in process of attaining this supreme ultimate object precisely through the instrumentality of that philosophy which the aforesaid fine gentleman is accusing of atheism." [27]

The last part of Schelling's reply is a renewed attack on Jacobi's *Glaube* (faith): despite Jacobi's passionate professions of theism, his system leads to no knowledge of God and leaves the reason completely empty.[28] Schelling sums up his contemptuous anger at Jacobi in the single word "sycophant!" hurled as a final thunderbolt at his adversary.[29]

This reply of Schelling's has not helped us much further ahead with our problem but it is nonetheless of great importance for a proper understanding of the new wave of "dynamic Spinozism" which was to crest in Hegel.

[26] *Apoc.* 22, 13.

[27] *Denkmal* . . ., p. 82.

[28] This third part of Schelling's reply is entitled *Das Allgemeine* (*Eine allegorische Vision*) (The Broader Context [An Allegorical Vision]) and is a remorseless tweaking of Jacobi by the nose, using his own texts on *Glaube* (faith) against him (*ibid.,* pp. 83ff.). In a note to p. 93, Schelling cites F. Schlegel's critique of Jacobi: "Since, *despite all his fine songs of praise to some alleged freedom,* he denies the *will,* by declaring it to be partly identical with the rational instinct . . . partly an 'expression of the divine will', 'a spark from the eternal pure light', a 'power of the omnipotence' . . . his morality can only be love or grace". Further on, in a note to p. 121, Schlegel is cited again to the effect that the ". . . famous *mortal leap* is . . . nothing but a false alarm. . . . a Don Quixote ride through the air on the wooden horse". In two notes to p. 133, Lessing and Schlegel are cited as accusing poor Jacobi of literary immorality!

[29] *Ibid.,* p. 135.

2. *The Emergence of Hegelian Pantheism*

From all the uproar excited by Jacobi, Hegel seems to maintain a lofty absence. He was just beginning to make a name for himself in the world of thought at the beginning of the new (19th) century and preferred to reply to the problems raised by the *Atheismusstreit* from the calm Olympian heights of the dispassionate investigator of the problems themselves, far above the noise and dust of polemical battle. There is no doubt that both Jacobi on the one hand and Fichte and Schelling on the other emerged from the fray somewhat battered and Hegel burst into the field as the bearer of a new approach involving "reconciliation" (*Versöhnung*) of opposed views by an overcoming of the mutual oppositions. At the time of Jacobi's death in 1819, Hegel had already published the *Phenomenology of Spirit* (1807), the *Science of Logic* (1817) and the *Enzyklopädie* (1817): in the first of these, the unity of substance conceived as Whole, absolute Concept, Spirit, absolute Idea, already pervaded the whole "system" proposed by Hegel. Hegel did for Spinoza something similar to what Aquinas did for Aristotle, whose works had been notoriously on the blacklist of ecclesiastical authority as dangerous to the faith at the beginning of the 13th century, yet were being commented in the second half of that same century by Albert the Great and especially St. Thomas Aquinas, neither of whom saw any problem about spreading the Aristotelian teachings.[30]

The parallel between the Aristotle-Aquinas and the Spinoza-Hegel relationship is multidimensional and highly interesting, especially since Aristotle is the ultimate source of Hegel's conceptual technique as well, that technique which distinguishes him from Fichte and Schelling; and both Hegel and Aquinas took from neo-Platonic dialectic the inspiration for their own leap from the realm of the existence to that of *Esse ipsum*.[31] Both men seem to be motivated by the same desire to effect a reconciliation between philosophy and religion, between reason and faith, to solve the problem of the relationship of the finite and the Infinite, of man and God; but they manifest radically divergent interpretations of being and its measure, they are separated from each other by the drastic and irreconcilable antithesis between immanentism and transcendentalism. Indeed, it is precisely this antithesis that is the very core of the modern atheistic approach, an approach whose chief inspiration goes back to Hegel: yes, Hegel rather than Feuerbach or Marx or Darwin or Haeckel or Sartre, all of whom are second-echelon thinkers

[30] Cf. M. Grabmann, *I divieti ecclesiastici di Aristotele sotto Innocenzo III e Gregorio IX* (Rome, 1941), n. 63 and 72ff.

[31] Cf. in this connection, our *Partecipazione e causalità* (Turin, 1961), pp. 9ff., 64ff., 72ff., 99ff. and *passim*.

compared with Hegel and downright insignificant apart from him. As a radical and total articulation of the *cogito* principle, modern atheism derives from one thinker above all others, and that thinker is Hegel!

For our own investigations, it suffices to note that no thinker has been more insistent than Hegel in proclaiming and defending the existence of God; not only did he devote to this problem a famous course of lectures, he even posited God as beginning, middle and end of the search for reality and truth. Thus he was able to refute indignantly all charges of atheism, as we have seen already. Nor has any other thinker asserted more vigorously than Hegel the perfect accord between reason and faith, between (his own!) philosophy and Christianity: Hegel was more outspoken and drastic in this regard even than Jacobi and Fichte, those two doughty champions of faith, even than his adversary, the theologian Schleiermacher himself. But we must note forthwith that this Hegelian approval was the kiss of death for faith, theology and theism!

Certainly Hegel is everywhere dealing with the Absolute and equally certainly he calls this Absolute God: but this is not the transcendent God; it is the God immanent in the finite as Reality and Truth, Idea and Whole *of the* infinite, Infinite Circle of circles, a "God who without the world is not God;" [32] and never has a single phrase so frighteningly and so felicitously characterized the abyss of emptiness and desperation of the modern age!

Furthermore, it is true that Hegel did indeed positively bend double in homage to religion in general and to Christianity in particular, to which latter he attributed the discovery of man as "spirit" (*Geist*); but it is no less certain that Hegel subordinated religious knowledge to philosophical knowledge and considered the dogmas of the Christian revelation (Trinity, Incarnation, Original Sin) to be mere myths and provisional representations of what the pure concept expresses absolutely, as imperfect articulations of the mind which pale into nothingness in the bright light of philosophy. Hegel's whole philosophy—in its weird combination of extreme simplicity and extreme complexity—is a perpetual oscillation, transferring the finite into the Infinite which is considered as its only reality and the Infinite into the finite which is considered as its manifestation to such an extent that "if the divine being were not the being of man and nature, it would simply be a being that would be nothing." [33]

[32] *Philosophie der Religion*, p. 184.

[33] *Philosophie der Weltgeschichte*, Einleitung; ed. Lasson, Vol. I, p. 38. Such turns of phrase recur throughout, e.g. in connection with the knowledge of God: "The fact that man knows of God is, in virtue of the essential community, a common knowing: i.e. man only knows of God inasmuch as God in man knows of Himself; this knowing is a self-knowing, a self-awareness of God; but it is equally a knowing of God by man; and this knowing of God by man is a

Totally pervaded as it is by religion and Christianity, the Hegelian philosophy should surely not be presented as atheistic; and yet it is almost more atheistic than even Marxism or existentialism, in terms of its principles and of the very respect it shows for religion in general and Christianity in particular. In Marxism and existentialism, religion is no more, it has been utterly discarded; but in Hegel, religion is still retained in the degraded status of herald or "handmaid" of philosophy! And Hegel can calmly conclude that "there is simply no place here for problems of human freedom, the nexus of human knowing and of the individual mind with that knowing wherein man is in community with God, the knowing of God in man". The reason is simple: "Only the Infinite is, the finite is not, for it is that whose definition and determination (*Bestimmung*) and nature it is to pass away, so that it cannot be thought or represented apart from the determination of non-being involved in transcience." [34] Whatever else may be said about this passage, it is exemplary in its clarity and consistency!

Hegel's intention was certainly not to anthropomorphize God, but rather, if anything, to divinize man. In his crypto-atheism there merge metaphysical Spinozism, Enlightenment thought, Kantian critical philosophy, Lessing's rationalism, the "dynamic Spinozism" of Fichte and Schelling and still other philosophical currents as well—but all of these currents are raised and fused into a unity at a level above the contradictions and defects proper to each of these systems considered separately in itself. Hegel gives credit to Jacobi (in the only reference I have found in Hegel to the famous controversy) for having demonstrated that all scientific knowledge leads to Spinozism as to the only consistent form of thought and thus is (for Jacobi) a worthless detour into a blind alley. This is true, says Hegel, only if the thinker stops at Spinoza, imprisoning himself in the "method of intellectualistic cognition", i.e., an abstract and static method, "devoid of concept". Spinoza has proven that only "Substance is" and that the finite is not: Spinoza has enunciated the major proposition that "every determination involves a negation" and this is a definitive confirmation of the truth that only God is; for everything can be said to be something determined, even thought insofar as it is opposed to extension. But even here, in Spinoza, we are still dealing with an assertion which is an abstract statement of limitation or negation: the negative element is not flowing from thought in act: this comes into play only with the new (Leibnizian-Kantian) principle of activity as

---

knowing of man by God. The mind or spirit of man that knows of God is but the mind or spirit of God Himself" (*Philosophie der Religion,* Anhang, *Beweise für das Dasein Gottes;* ed. Marheineke, Vol. II, p. 496; ed. Lasson, Vol. III, 2, p. 117).

[34] *Ibid.,* Marheineke, II, p. 494; Lasson III, 2, p. 115.

self-consciousness or transcendental subjectivity which Hegel also calls "the principle of individuality and personality." [35]

It should be carefully noted that it is by means of the insertion of the principle of self-consciousness (self-awareness, self-knowledge), that the God of Hegel (i.e., Substance, the One) becomes individuality and personality as opposed to the substance of Spinoza: but this God is not "person", either in the simple monotheistic sense or in the sense of the Christian dogma of the Trinity. The former sense in fact demands the absolute transcendence of the Being of God with reference to the world and man (God as *esse subsistens*), whereas we have already seen Hegel to be asserting the exact opposite. The latter sense demands, according to Christian doctrine, an expansiveness of such fullness and perfection within the identity of the same divine nature that the divine Persons shall arise *ab aeterno* solely in virtue of the interior opposition of the divine relations.

For Hegel, on the contrary, the trinitarian dogma has its true meaning in the dialectic of the "concept" via the triads of "universal", "particular", and "singular" so far as content is concerned, and "concept" "judgment" and "conclusion" so far as functions are concerned; and clearly these elements correspond in rank and order to the thesis, antithesis and syntheisis of the dialectic itself. For Hegel, the Christian statement of the divine Trinity as "a relation of Father, Son and Spirit" is a "childish attitude" (*ein kindliches Verhältnis*), a natural childish approach which does not see the Spirit clearly, whereas only the Spirit, declares Hegel, is the True (*das Wahrhafte*); [36] and here is Hegel's

[35] Cf. *Geschichte der Philosophie,* Vol. III, pp. 332f., especially 360f. (charge of atheism, Jacobi), 366f.

[36] The derivation (or "overcoming") of the Christian Trinity in the dialectic of the concept is already fully expounded in the *Phenomenology of the Spirit,* Die offenbare Religion; ed. Hoffmeister (Leipzig, 1937), pp. 534ff., to which we shall return later in the conclusion.

In his youthful writings sometimes dubbed "theological" (but wrongly so, for they are drenched in Enlightenment thinking), Hegel protests that the "pure (i.e. rational!) ethic" of Jesus has been neglected by the Church in favor of a "dogmatic" one and that in the disputes on the nature of God (unity, trinity, sin, etc.), the "moral perfection" of man himself in whom dwells the deity has been forgotten. Here is a text directly inspired by Fichte, unless we are badly mistaken: "From the ideal of perfection, the only place where the holy was preserved, there vanished likewise the moral, or at least this moral element was consigned to oblivion. Instead of the moral, the truly divine, from the contemplation of which there would have been reflected warming rays into the heart of man, the mirror showed nothing more than the picture of his time, of nature, to what purpose soever the pride and passion of men saw fit to propose, for we see the whole interest of knowledge and faith focussed on the metaphysical or transcendent aspect of the idea of the deity" (*Die Positivität der christlichen Religion,* in *Hegels Theologische Jugendschriften,* ed. H. Nohl [Tübingen, 1907], p. 226). —At this period, moreover, Hegel found the terms of the Trinitarian doctrine (Father, Son, Holy Spirit) to be "felicitous expressions" (*glücklichen Ausdrücke*)

"explanation" (which we present preeminently in order to clarify the fact that with this explanation Hegel has highlighted the *profanum essentiale* (drastic and essential desacralization) to which the principle of immanentism was tending; and secondly, in order to point out that the constitutive atheism of modern thought peters out into this explanation without any hope of recovery).[37] God is for Hegel the absolute, eternal Idea: God expresses the ultimate "result" of the Logic, of the integral and perfect reflection of the mind. Therefore:

(a) The task of the speculative Logic is to consider the Idea God in-and-for-itself in its eternity, prior to the creation of the world.[38]

(b) The moment of *creation of the world* and of finite spirit is the one in which the Idea "negates itself" and what is thus created is something other (*ein Anderes*) which is posited preeminently outside of God, a "fall" (*Abfall*) from God. The essence of God is to take away this particularity and separation and thus to recover the Idea in its truth.

(e). This is the goal of that process of "reconciliation" (*Versöhnung*), whereby the Spirit reunites itself and is the Holy Spirit.

Hegel warns that this is no mere question of external distinctions; rather we are here dealing with three elements or moments, constitutive of the act (*Thun*), the very vital action of the Spirit itself in its development that is likewise an eternal life, a development and a return of this evolution into itself. A first and more precise (*nähere*) explanation is the following: Universal Spirit, the All that this Spirit is, posits itself in its three determinations, develops itself, realizes itself and is fulfilled at the end, which fulfillment and end is likewise its presupposition. For

---

as indicative of "living relations of the living, identical life, modifications solely of that same life, not oppositions of essence, not a plurality of absolute substances; thus the Son is the same essence as the Father but for every act of reflection and for a single one of such acts is something particular" (*Der Geist des Christentums und sein Schicksal,* in *Theologische Jugendschriften,* p. 308). In this sense, G. Lucacs' remarks seem to us more acceptable as an interpretation of the "objective content" of these youthful pieces (cf. G. Lucacs, *Der junge Hegel* [Zürich-Vienna, 1848], especially pp. 31ff.) than the kind of interpretation initiated by Dilthey which would make them theological in character.

[37] I am following here the already cited *Philosophie der Religion,* Vol. II, pp. 218ff. It is indicative that Hegel prefaces this dissolution of the Christian Trinity by the exposition of the ontological proof of St. Anselm (pp. 214ff.). This Anselmian proof always enjoyed special favor with Hegel (cf. *Enzykl. der philos. Wissenschaft,* § 193).

[38] As early as the introduction to the Logic, we read that it "*is the delineation of God as He is in His eternal essence before the creation of nature and of a finite spirit*" (*Wissenschaft der Logik, Einleitung;* ed. Lasson, Vol. I, p. 31; italics Hegel's).—The last chapter of the *Wissenschaft der Logik* ("The Absolute Idea"), which is virtually a word-for-word equivalent of the exposition we have presented from the *Philosophie der Religion,* is a very powerful synthetic exposition of the dissolution of the Christian dogma of the Trinity into the dialectic of the "Concept" or "Idea".

Christian revelation,[39] the fullness of the divine nature is present and equal in all three divine Persons; for Hegel, on the contrary, the processions of the divine Persons are processions from the essence and are presented as a transition from the implicit to the explicit.

But we are barely at the beginning of the Hegelian "desacralization". Hegel continues to make a direct parallel between the divine Persons and the modes of the Idea: "These are the three forms (*Formen*) in question: the eternal Being in-and-with-itself, the form of *Universality;* the form of the appearance or phenomenon, the form of *Particularization,* being-for-another; (and finally) the form of the return (*Rückkehr*) of the appearance into itself, absolute *Singularity.* In these three forms does the divine Idea explicitate itself. Spirit is the divine history, the process of self-distinction, self-negation and self-recovery, and this divine history is to be considered in each of these three forms." Hegel does nothing throughout the entire sequel but repeat in other words what he has already said about the three moments or elements of the deity; but I think that these variations on the theme of immanentism, wherein immanence is positioned at the very vortex of theology, really trace out the curve of disintegration of modern thought, as I shall point up later. So we must resign ourselves to following Hegel in his exasperating Scholasticism. He first expounds the "forms" of the Idea within the compass of *subjective consciousness* or subjective mind. The first form is the element of *Thought.* God is manifest in pure thought as in-and-for-himself but he has not yet reached the stage of appearance or phenomenon; this is God in his eternal essence with himself but manifest. The second form is that he is in the Representation (*Vorstellung*), in particularization, so that mind is hemmed into relation to the other, i.e., is appearance or phenomenon. The third element (one may wonder parenthetically why Hegel does not say "form" again this time!) is that of *subjectivity as such.* This subjectivity is partly immediate subjectivity, feeling (*Gemüth*), representation, sensation; but it is also partly a subjectivity which is the concept, thinking reason (*denkende Vernunft*), the thought of the free spirit which is *free* in itself only via the return into itself.[40]

To complete the description in terms of the a priori forms, let us now look at the distribution of the three forms in space and time. *In terms of space:* the first divine history (note the identity of divine essence, nature, etc., with "history") is *outside the world, without space,* outside

[39] Hegel is vigorous in his defense of the basic value of the trinitarian dogma of Christianity against the negligent indifference to that dogma on the part of his adversary, the pietistic theologian Tholuck (cf. *Enzykl. der philos. Wissenschaft,* Preface to 2nd ed., ed. Hoffmeister, [Leipzig, 1949], pp. 16f.; cf. also the reference to Hamann: *Berliner Schriften,* ed. Hoffmeister [Hamburg, 1956], p. 259).

[40] *Philosophie der Religion,* Vol. II, p. 220.

the finite, God as he is in-and-for-himself. The second is the divine history as real *in the world,* God in perfect existence.[41] The third is the "inner region" (*innere Ort*), the community, preeminently in the world but at the same time raising itself to heaven as a Church which already has heaven within itself but, though thus full of grace, is nonetheless active in the present world.

In terms of time: in the first form or element, God is *outside of time,* as eternal Idea, in the element of eternity insofar as this element is posited over against time. Thus is unfolded this time that is in itself and for itself and displays itself in past, present and future. In the second place, the divine history is as appearance or phenomenon (*Erscheinung*), as "past" (*Vergangenheit*); it is, has being, but a being which is at the same time also negated, is past, as that which constitutes the historical reality properly speaking (*als das eigentlich Geschichtliche*). The third element here is the present (*Gegenwart*), but only the limited present, not the eternal present, i.e., the one which separates by itself the past and the future, the one which is the element of feeling, the "spiritual nowness' (*geistiges Jetztseyn*) of immediate subjectivity. But Hegel adds that the present must also be the third (and the context here seems to demand that this mean "the future"): the community raises itself to heaven, so that there is also a present which rises essentially reconciled, fulfilled in universality via the negation of its own immediacy, a fulfillment that is not yet and is to be conceived as a future. We thus have a "now" (*Jetzt*) of the present which has fulfillment still before it, a fulfillment diverse from this "now" and posited as a *future.* It is obvious that we are no longer dealing here with the Christian dogma of the Trinity nor even with the concept of God proper to theism, but solely with the reality of the human being, of human existence elevated to the realm of necessity of the concept and displayed in accord with the categories of immanence, as can even here be read between the lines and as Hegel himself gives us still more clearly to understand in the sequel of his persistent and consistent exposition.

Passing to a loftier level of consideration, to that of the Idea as a "divine self-revelation" (*als göttliche Selbstoffenbarung*), Hegel uses biblical terminology (probably taken, however, from Joachim of Fiore) to describe the distinction between the three forms of the Idea: he speaks of the three Kingdoms appropriated to the individual divine Persons.

According to the *first* form, which is the *Kingdom of the Father,* God is for the finite spirit, man, solely as thought: this is *theoretical consciousness* in which the thinking subject is not yet posited in this relation

[41] Here Hegel uses the term *Dasein* (lit: "thereness"), which he usually uses to express existence in its immediate exteriority, as opposed to *Existenz* which presupposes mediation and reference to the "ground" (*Grund*).

as such, not yet posited in process, is free of all relation in the entirely immobile quiet and repose of the thinking Spirit, for God is being thought by this repose and God is in the simple mode of conclusion in such a way that he is concluding himself with himself in terms of his difference, which difference is still at this point within the pure *identity* and does not penetrate to exteriority but rather is immediately with itself. This is the first relation that is only for the thinking subject which is occupied exclusively with pure and sheer content.

The *second* determination is the *Kingdom of the Son,* in which God is for representation, in the element of representation in general, solely the element of "particularization" (*Besonderung*) in general (!). In this second point of view, there is thus maintained what *was* in the first the *Other than God* (and Other *of* God) but which in that first point of view was not in possession of this *determination* of Otherness. In the first point of view, God as Son is not distinct from the Father but is expressed only in the manner of *sensation:* in the second element, on the contrary, the Son receives the determination and is transferred from purely ideal status into that of representation. Whereas in the first stage God only engenders a Son, here he produces *nature;* here the Other is nature, difference comes into its own; the distinct is nature; the world in general and the Spirit which relates to this is the natural spirit, corresponding to the already-mentioned *object.*

Inasmuch as man relates to nature, he, too, is natural; and this he is only within the ambit of religion: this gives us Hegel's view on the religious *consideration* of nature and man. The Son enters the world, this is the beginning of *faith:* we are already speaking the language of faith when we speak of the entry of the Son into the world.

All of this serves to foreshadow what will be the transition to the third (and definitive) *Kingdom of the Spirit.* The finite spirit tends to reconcile itself with the infinite Spirit. But the finite spirit, asserts Hegel, is posited as "fall", as separation from God and inimical separation at that; thus he is in contradiction with this, his object, with his own content, and this contradiction is preeminently the requirement of his own supersession. This requirement is the beginning (*Anfang*) and the sequel is that God becomes for the spirit, the divine content represents itself to that spirit; but because the spirit is at the same time in one sense *empirically* finite, it is consequently in empirical form that there appears to that spirit what is God. But since the divine in this history is presenting itself for and by and to spirit, that history likewise loses its character of a merely exterior history, becoming a *divine* history, the hisotry of the manifestation of God himself. And this, concludes Hegel, is what constitutes the transition to the *Kingdom of the Spirit:* that Kingdom is constituted by the consciousness, the awareness, the knowledge that man is in himself reconciled with God and that the reconciliation (*Versöhnung*) is for and the via man; the process of reconciliation itself is contained in the cult which is the complex of acts of worship. All of this has brought us to the triad of *concept, figure* (*Gestalt*), *cult* (worship).[42] The trinitarian process is therefore simply the process of self-objectification of the concept; it expresses the transition from the abstract to the concrete. Upon this notorious and boring theme, Hegel plays variation upon variation and for him th Christian Trinity is nothing but this eternal Idea [43] which philosophy has finally presented in its speculative form. But religion communicates to men the mystery of this dogma, continues Hegel, so that they shall believe and accept it in their imaginations without being aware of its necessity, without *understanding,* without *comprehending* it—for that is the task of philosophy! And Hegel refers explicitly to the Aristotelian concept of Pure Act. Pure Act is to know (the *Actus purus* of the Scholastics, notes Hegel) but in order to be posited as pure act it must be posited in its moments or elements. To thought there pertains something of the Other—and we are launched on still another round of Hegelian triadic mumbojumbo.

But there is another point deserving of stress. And to this Hegel makes only scanty reference. It is the correspondence between the norms of subjective thought (*concept, judgment, conclusion*) and the terms of the trinitarian dogma. The concept (*Begriff*) in its universal, abstract truth, is the Father, about whom Hegel is always quite close-mouthed. In the judgment (*das Urtheil*) is the Other, what is opposed to the universal, the particular, *God,* as distinct from the universal but in such a way that this very distinct particular is the *integral Idea* of that universal in itself and for itself. As thought can be said to assume the form of "pure intuition" in the indistinct concept, so we can speak of an "absolute scission" (*absolute Diremtion*) in the judgment,[44] that crucial element in that dialectic and in the Hegelian obfuscation of the Christian dogma. For Hegel, the Christian formulation of the Trinity as relation of Father, Son and Spirit, is simply childish, not rising above the level of the imagination.

Hegel never tires of the merry-go-round of the dialectic, and we shall find it rewarding to follow him one last time: for we shall see the explicit application of the triadic dialectical rhythm. For Hegel the Father is the abstract God, the Universal, the eternal, all-embracing, total particularity. We are here in the Stage of the Spirit: here the Universal includes everything in itself; the Other, the Son is the infinite particularity, the

42 *Philosophie der Religion,* Vol. II, p. 223.

43 "Now this eternal idea, expressed in the Christian religion as what the Holy *Trinity* means, is God Himself, the eternally *triune*" (*ibid,*. p. 227).

44 *Ibid.,* pp. 225, 237, 240 and *passim.*

appearance or phenomenon; the third, the Spirit is singularity as such, but the Universal as totality is also spirit, they are all three spirit! In the third stage we say God is Spirit but the third is also the first! This is quite crucial to Hegelianism and to any right understanding of it. When we say that God *in se* according to his concept is the immediate power that splits itself and returns to itself, this is only as *the negativity which immediately relates back to itself,* i.e., absolute reflection as such is already the determination and definition of spirit. But because we want to speak of God in his *first* determination, according to his concept and want to penetrate from thence to the other determinations, we here already speak of the *third: the Last is the First.* Either because we want to avoid this when we commence abstractly or because the imperfection of the concept neglects to speak of the First *solely according to his own determination,* therefore this First is the *Universal* and that *Activity* of generating, of creating, is already a principle distinct from the abstract Universal, so that there appears as a second Principle the self-extrinsicalization (λογος, σοφία), even as the first is the abyss.[45] And Hegel himself refers to the gnostic speculations: the First, the Father, is the ὄν, the abyss, the void, the indeterminate, the incomprehensible, the negative of the concept because having this negative determination of being this negative. Therefore he is the abyss, βυθός, the depth, ὄν, the eternal who dwells in the ineffable heights, αἰών, the Beginning and Principle, before every beginning. Similarly the second, i.e., in Hegelian terms the being-other (the self-scission), in general the activity of self-determination is the most universal and generic determination as in a λογος or word, as σοφία or wisdom which Hegel explains as "the primordial, entirely pure man" (*der ursprüngliche, ganz reine Mensch*); it is an ὅρασις or seeing of God; it is also called the archetype of man, Adam Kadmon, the Only-Begotten (*der Eingeborene*).

At the end of this immanentistic deduction of the Trinity, Hegel reveals his sources: the principle of Böhme that the Trinity must be born "in the heart of man" is the Kantian principle which purified the mystical naturalism of Böhme. This principle asserted that the cogni-

[45] Here is the crucial section of this passage which is a felicitous summary of the entire Hegelian process: "The abstract God, the Father, is the Universal, the eternal, all-embracing, total particularity. We are at the level of the spirit, *the Universal here includes everything in itself.* The Other, the Son, is the eternal particularity, the phenomenon. The third, the Spirit, is singularity as such; but *the Universal as totality is itself Spirit;* all Three are the Spirit. In the third, we say, God is the Spirit but this is likewise presuppositious, the third is also the first. This it is essential to maintain: to wit, when we say that God is, by his very concept, the immediate power that splits itself and returns into itself, we must bear in mind that He is this only as *the negativity which immediately relates back to itself,* i.e. absolute reflection as such is already the determination and definition of the *Spirit*" (*ibid.,* p. 240).

tional process must contain the true or all that is in the particular.[46] And now we feel it will suffice for our purposes to pass a judgment on Hegel's theism.

The most striking feature of this "a priori geneology" of the divine Trinity is the fact, strange enough in all conscience at first glance but not so strange upon deeper and more attentive consideration, that this mystery which extolls the infinite exuberance of the divine life within the most absolute immanence of the divine essence is reduced by Hegel to a process of "becoming-other" wherein the origin of the Son and the creation of the world belong to the same process. Furthermore and consequently, the fulcrum of the trinitarian processions is not, for Hegel, the constitution and distinction of the divine Persons in terms of the opposition of the relations and the positioning of each as subsisting by itself within the identical divine nature, but rather the restitution of the unity of the Concept or Absolute Idea, the inverse process of return to the unity of the absolute Spirit as identity of finite and Infinite.

This involves the third basic observation we have here to make: it is meaningless to speak, in the context of the Hegelian explanation, of three Persons in God: even the very concept of "person" itself and of "personality"—the concept so dear to Jacobi—cannot be applied to God.[47] Hegel is quite explicit on this point: personality is that which is founded upon freedom, the first, deepest, most interior freedom, but likewise the most abstract form of freedom's manifestation in the subject: for Hegel "I am a person" means "I am for me" (i.e., myself); it is the sheerly introverted (*das schlechthin Spröde*). Person therefore stands for being-for-oneself, something rigid and unyielding, autonomous, one; but the category of the one is, according to the Logic, a pejorative category, it is the one of the utterly abstract, Hegel conceives the trinitarian distinction as a dialectical development of the divine essence and thus understands the three Persons as "elements" or "moments" of the Absolute Idea; he is therefore held to deny drastically and totally any signifiance of their own to the three Persons and to the very concept of personality: indeed, were personality in God to be insisted upon, in the context of the dogma of the Trinity, one would end up with three Gods, forgetting the *absolute negativity,* losing the unity of the

[46] *Ibid.,* p. 246.—On the Trinitarian process in Böhme, cf. *Geschichte der Philosophie,* Vol. III, pp. 278ff.—Hegel continues his exposition with a treatment of the Kingdom of the Son (*Philosophie der Religion,* pp. 247ff.: here he also treats of Christ and of original sin) and of the Kingdom of the Spirit which for him is the Absolute present in the "Community" (pp. 308ff.).

[47] To be exact, Hegel proceeds, in virtue of the principle of immanentism, in a fashion diametrically opposed to the Christian Trinitarian doctrine, denying all consistency to the term "person" in the Trinitarian process and then granting consistency to the term in the abstract, in the sense of "personality" as applied to God as Spirit and absolute Idea.

divine essence. In fact the personality that does not dissolve itself in the divine Idea is the evil (*das Böse*): "In the divine unity the personality is posited as distinct from that whereby it is dissolved." [48] And finally, far from considering the Christian Trinity notion to express the most exalted conception of God, Hegel finds it outmoded and needing to be dissolved in the simple concept of Absolute Spirit; and this concept of the Absolute as Spirit, in its turn, cannot even be articulated as a Person, but must rather be dissolved into the elements or moments of the dialectic. Hegel writes: "God is Spirit; the self-objectifying and self-knowing in this objectification, that is concrete identity." [49] Similar phrases permeate the *Philosophy of Religion.*

The whole Hegelian conception can thus be summed up in the concept of Spirit (*Geist*), which permits Hegel to execute the dual (annihilating!) movement of "unfolding" God from the interior of the immanence of the human mind and exalting this same human mind to a status and position within the very manifestation of God. Let us read one more text which seems to be among the most exhaustively univocal: "God, according to Aristotle, is Act. Pure Act is to know . . . but being posited as activity it must be posited in its elements or moments: to knowing belongs an Other and inasmuch as knowing knows that Other it is appropriated to it. Hence, we see how God, being in-itself-and-for-itself, eternally generates himself as his Son, distinguishes himself from himself—the absolute judgment. But what is thus distinct from itself does not have the shape of a being-other; rather the distinct is immediately only what has been separated from it. *God is Spirit:* no darkness, no coloration or admixture, enters into this light. The relation of Father and Son is taken from organic life and used within the sphere of the imagination: this natural relation is but an image and as such does not correspond entirely to what is here to be expressed. We say: God eternally generates his Son, God distinguishes himself from himself; thus we begin to say of God that he does this and is in the other which is posited absolutely in himself (the form of love); but we must also be aware that *God is this entire process.* God is the beginning; he does this, but he is equally the end, the totality: thus, as totality God is the Spirit. God simply as

[48] "In the divine Unity, personality is posited as resolved; only in the phenomenon is the negativity of personality distinguished from that whereby it is dissolved" (*Philosophie der Religion,* p. 239). More succinct expositions of this dissolution of the dogmas of Christianity are given by Hegel, always couched in the same terms, in the works of the last Berlin period (*Geschichte der Philosophie,* Vol. III, pp. 86ff., *Philosophie der Geschichte,* ed. Gans [Stuttgart, 1961], pp. 387ff.).

[49] *Philosophie der Religion,* Vol. II, p. 236. Therefore a Danish theologian, a contemporary of Kierkegaard, concluded that there can be no real question of any category of personality in the Hegelian philosophy (P. M. Stilling, *Den moderne Atheisme* [Copenhagen, 1844], p. 33).

the Father is not yet the Truth (thus, without the Son, is he known in the Jewish religion), he is rather the *beginning and the end,* is his own presupposition, makes of himself the presupposition (this is but another form of distinguishing). He is the eternal process . . . the absolute truth. Here there is nothing to be done, there is no help for it, there is simply no way of showing that the dogma, this reposeful mystery, is the eternal truth: this truth, as we have said, is to be attained in philosophy."[50] This text is complete in its essential elements; there is no need to comment on it!

The crux of the method whereby Hegel initially guts the dogma of the Trinity and then proceeds to a denial of God himself conceived as a free Person, creator of the world and of man, last end, etc., is the reduction of the trinitarian process to the logical process of the subjective concept (concept, judgment, conclusion = Father, Son and Holy Spirit). This subjective process is "objectified" in the three moments or elements: the (abstract) universal, the particular and the concrete, where the Real and the True become the Whole. And so, even as the Christian Trinity is "profaned" or "desacralized" in the (first) subjective process, so God is eliminated in the (second) objective process, by being conceived—be it well and truly noted!—as the "totality" of being, of life, of truth.[51] This is precisely the point, and again be it noted with all possible precision: God is the concept that comprehends itself or that develops dialectically, i.e., via the negativity of the finite and the consequent return to itself; he is the infinite virtuality of the Concept, Being as fulfilled, as intensive Totality.[52] The truth of Christian theology ends up being "proven" by the Hegelian logic whose evolution expounds the self-manifestation of the Idea and of history *in fieri,* in process.[53] Thus, the Hegelian logic constitutes the most radical and drastic mystification and desacralization, even profanation of the problem of God in the entire history of human thought. No wonder that all the forms of modern atheism hark back and appeal more or less directly to Hegel!

[50] *Philosophie der Religion,* Vol. II, pp. 228f.—And further on: "God contemplates himself in the differentiated, is linked but with himself in his Other, is only in presence of himself therein, united only with himself; he contemplates himself in his Other" (p. 233). And again: "God, the Spirit, is *likewise precisely himself* the one who *resolves these contradictions.* He does not first wait upon this understanding, these determinations that contain the contradiction . . . this scission" (p. 237).

[51] "The absolute Idea alone is *Being,* everlasting *life,* self-knowing *truth,* and is *all Truth*" (*Wissenschaft der Logik,* Book III, Ch. 3; ed. von Henning III, p. 328; ed. Lasson II, p. 484).

[52] "But it is likewise now *fulfilled Being,* the *self-conceiving concept,* being as the *concrete,* sheerly *intensive* totality" (*ibid.,* ed. von Henning III, p. 352; Lasson II, p. 504).

[53] In this sense, the last chapter of the *Logic* ("The Absolute Idea") offers a compendium of impressive evidence of this "detheologization" of thought in the sheer reduction of God to Being as a concrete universal.

4

Idealist Theologizing and Immanentist Atheism

From Kant to Hegel there is a continuous intensification in the assertion of God as Absolute, but only at the price of losing him as a transcendental Person without hope of recovery. The intensification stems primarily from the unification of, the overcoming of, the dissociation between, the theoretical reason and the practical reason: thus the assertion of God, which in Kant and the early Fichte was somewhat tangential and entrusted to *Glaube* (faith), coincides in Schelling and especially in Hegel with the speculative activity of which God becomes beginning, middle and end, form and content, inception and result (of himself!). The wildest ambitions of the Cartesian *cogito* seem finally to have been satisfied: the *cogitare,* the thinking process, the actuation of the Spirit, the Mind (*Geist*), is realized as the self-manifestation of God himself to man in nature and in history. But because the *Geist* here in question cannot be anything but the presence of human activity to itself and must dissolve into that activity, this maximal affirmative theological statement of modern thought which is the Hegelian can be readily seen to coincide, at rock bottom, with the irremediable negation of transcendence, i.e., with radical atheism.

Modern atheism does not begin with Feuerbach as a "theoretical plot": it is there in Kant himself and even before him, wherever the *cogito* is taken in all its theoretical rigor, as we have seen.

Jacobi had focussed his charge of atheism upon Spinozism, identifying with atheism that inflation of the Absolute which is pantheism, and he had hit directly first at Lessing and later at Fichte and Schelling. The same charge is even more applicable to Hegel and even to Schleiermacher, the chief theologian of modern Protestantism.[1] For Schleier-

[1] Cf. E. Brunner's excellent study, *Die Mystik und das Wort,* Der Gegensatz zwischen moderner Religionsauffassung und christlichem Glauben dargestellt an der Theologie Schleiermachers [The Opposition between the Modern Concept of Religion and Christian Faith, Illustrated with Reference to Schleiermacher's Theology] (Tübingen, 1924), especially pp. 358ff.

macher, too, the "spirit" (*Geist*), in the sense of the activity of the human mind, is but a modification, an appearance, of the Absolute. It is true that none of the great modern philosophers has spoken so much about "individuality" as did Schleiermacher, but it still remains a fact that the subject of ethics is no longer, as in Christianity and even in the theology of Kant himself, the individual human being, but rather "the" reason, Reason understood as a cosmic organism. And so Schleiermacher remains on the level of the great transcendentalist idealists. He goes so far in the *Ethik* as to speak of a "split of human nature into the manifold of individuals" in such a way that ". . . each singular is a particular individual posited as in-itself by reason and nature solely as an organ and a symbol" (§ 157). Thus for Schleiermacher, too, real being belongs to the Whole, to Reason and to nature; to the singular individual is attributed nonbeing, reality being constituted by the unification of reason and nature. For the "mystic" Schleiermacher, the Ego of the individual is but a "product of reality" (*Werk der Dinglichkeit*), a "terrestrial phenotype" (*irdische Erscheinungsform*), and consequently nothing but an "organ and symbol" (§ 50).

Schleiermacher has as little concept of the free personality as does Hegel or metaphysical idealism; and his theory of universal Reason, on which is founded his ethic, conceives the relation of finite to Infinite in just the same way as does his adversary Hegel. Jacobi's charge ought to be extended to include Schleiermacher as well, whose Spinozism and pantheism is indisputable, even though his formulations of both do seem to evolve from work to work. In the *Reden* (1798), the terms "God" and "universe", "God" and "world entity" are used to indicate identical concepts, with the impersonal "universe" being preferred to the personal "God" and the question of the "personality of God" being relegated to the background.[2] In subsequent works there is some effort made to distinguish between God and the world; but even in the *Erläuterungen* to the *Reden* (1821), the world is thought of as "the true Whole that includes God withint itself," [3] even though Schleiermacher is here trying to defend himself against the charge of pantheism. In the *Dialektik,*

[2] The diversity of the points of view defended by Schleiermacher and Fichte seems to indicate that Hirsch's contention (*Geschichte der neuern protestantischen Theologie,* IV, 515) that the *Reden* were written under the impulsion of the *Atheismusstreit* is not well-founded (thus Mertel, *Das theologische Denken Schleiermachers* [Zurich, 1965], pp. 195f.); but what is to prevent the *Reden* from having been a reply to Fichte's stand?

[3] E. Brunner, *op. cit.,* pp. 323ff. Brunner shows especially the influence on Schleiermacher of Fichte (activism), Herder, Goethe, Schelling (vitalistic pantheism), all tending to make the individual as a person evaporate into an empty name. Schleiermacher thus becomes, like Hegel, the protagonist of the universal, of the genus, of the mass, against the individual, as opposed to Kierkegaard whom Brunner here most properly evokes against Schleiermacher (pp. 329f.).

Schleiermacher shows that "a being of God outside of the world" can neither be given to us nor comprehended by us: the two terms are so mutually conditioning that Schleiermacher is moved to repeat involuntarily the formula of his adversary Hegel: "No God without the world, even as no world without God." [4] He speaks of the two parts of this statement not as identical but as dialectical "correlates". The deep-seated reason for this new pantheism is that Schleiermacher's *Glaube* (faith) is not really related to the biblical faith of Christianity but rather to the principle of immanentism realized as subjective *Gefühl* (feeling). Hence, the denial of the doctrine of creation which is judged to be "devoid of religious interest" since our "immediate sense and feeling of dependence" (*unmittelbares Abhängigkeitsgefühl*)—which is Schleiermacher's basic principle even as is intellectual intuition for the transcendental idealists—does not find in the creation doctrine "any plainer satisfaction than in the supposition of an eternal creation of the world". Thus creation evaporates, for Schleiermacher as for Hegel, into a sort of eternal dialectical relation and nexus between finite and Infinite, so that there can be no question of a theistic-type distinction between the world and God. For Schleiermacher as for Hegel "we cannot speak of a creator or fashioner of the world, but" only "of a Spirit of the world." [5]

The same ultimate pantheism permeates Schleiermacher's treatment of the crucial problem of the "personality of God". He does indeed often apply the term and concept of "living" (*lebendig*) to God, as Fichte, Schelling and Hegel had done before him; but he is most careful *not* to apply the idea of "person" to God; indeed he is prevented from so doing by his own theological semantic principle which assserts: "None of the properties we attribute to God are supposed to indicate anything particular in God, but only some particular way of referring and relating back to him the sheer feeling of dependence." [6] God thus evaporates into the "unity" (or, as Schleiermacher says, the "indifference") of contraries: God is pure, indeterminate being, the *απεῖρον* (boundless, unbounded), corresponding to the absolute indeterminacy of feeling (*Gefühl*); he is the *Seyn* (Being) of immediacy, according to the Hegelian terminology, revealed by the immediate feeling of dependence.

Spinoza and Kant are therefore mighty and operative from the depths in Schleiermacher as well. And Schleiermacher's *Glaube* (faith) as im-

[4] Schleiermacher, *Dialektik,* § 218, ed. R. Odebrecht (Leipzig, 1942), p. 303.

[5] For Schleiermacher's teaching on creation, cf. *Der christliche Glaube, C. W.,* ed. Redeker, Vol. I (Berlin, 1960), §§ 36, 2 and 49, 3. The last phrase above is from H. Scholz, reported by E. Brunner, *op. cit.,* p. 366, note 4) and is the dominant key phrase of the *Reden über die Religion,* as we pointed out in the Introduction.

[6] *Der christliche Glaube,* I, § 50, p. 255.

mediate perception of God, cause of the world, seems not far removed from Jacobi's *Glaube*. Now Mendelssohn had not been without justification in accusing Jacobi himself of atheism, for this "Grand Inquisitor" of modern atheism had entrusted everything to faith, denying the possibility of a rational proof of the existence of God.[7] Mendelssohn's charge is more in the order of allusion than of exhaustive adjudication: for Jacobi, says Mendelssohn, every philosophy involving proof is bound to lead to, indeed already constitutes, atheism and fatalism; now the necessary implication is that not only Lessing but even Leibniz, Wolff and all the "proof-adducing philosophers" are atheists and fatalists! Furthermore Aristotle would have to be admitted to have had revelations on Jacobi's principle that "every proof presupposes the proven, whose principle is revelation"; and Spinoza would have to be admitted to have been a hero of faith on Jacobi's other principle that "the element of every human cognition and activity is faith."[8] In discussing Jacobi's anti-Spinozism, Mendelssohn finds Jacobi to be as much a determinist as Spinoza, in that Jacobi does not grant to the Infinite the character of individuality and hence renders it impossible to attribute to the Infinite any will or any freedom, since both presuppose real and individual substantiality.[9]

Mendelssohn speaks out even more sharply on Jacobi's manifesto of "realism" contained in the passage: "Thought is not the source of substance; rather substance is the source of thought. Thus there must be prior to thought something nonthinking and this must be the content of our primary admission; and this something must be thought, if not absolutely in potency, yet as the absolutely first according to its inner nature in imagination, in essence." Now this, says Mendelssohn, is but a leap into the void, this thinking something that precedes all thought and is thus incapable of being thought even by the most perfect intellect! And Mendelssohn pursues Jacobi still further on this point of thought: Jacobi, says Mendelssohn, recognizes as matter and object of thought only extension and motion, to which he reduces all sense qualities, even as Locke reduced the secondary qualities to primary ones; but there is no need for a Spinozan to do this, because Spinoza held extension to be a property of the single infinite Substance.[10]

No less trenchant and pertinent is Mendelssohn's critique of Jacobi's notion of the relation between being and thought, as Jacobi expressed that notion in his letter to Hemsterhuis, where he makes Spinoza say:

[7] M. Mendelssohn, *An die Freunde Lessings,* in *C. W.* (Vienna, 1838), pp. 502ff.

[8] *Ibid.,* p. 509. Cf. the remark on Jacobi's "mortal leap" on p. 514.

[9] *Ibid.,* p. 513.

[10] *Ibid.,* p. 515.

"Thought considered in its essence is but the feeling of *being,* to the extent that it is determined, individual, and in relation with other individuals. Will is but the feeling of the determined being acting as an individual." [11] Mendelssohn confesses that he understands nothing of all this: neither Jacobi's reason or justification for appealing to Kant in order to explain the phrase "the feeling of being" nor his identification of the will (in Spinoza) with this feeling of being, since for Spinoza there can be concepts without mind, "a thinking without being" (*ein Denken ohne Seyn*).[12] So we have reached the very heart of the controversy and the principle of immanentism is levying its demands on both the rival antagonists, with neither succeeding in coping with those demands, both seeming to end in a blank void.

The *Atheismusstreit* was an essentially ambiguous situation and the result could be nothing but confusion: Jacobi's anti-Spinozism may well have been deep-seated and profoundly sincere; he may indeed have intended to hit straight for the heart; but he missed the mark entirely for the very simple reason that neither he nor his antagonist had any adequate conception of the nexus and relation between being and thought. Spinoza conceived this relationship geometrically in terms of the absolute necessity of identity; Jacobi, for his part, vacillated between a realism of feeling and a realism of faith (*Glaube*). Neither stand is either realism or idealism but both are immanentism inasmuch as being is mediated by feeling or by faith. But Jacobi was a beaten man in the controversy because his feeling is beginning (principle) and end at once and therefore explains nothing of the becoming of mind in the processes of science and nature or in the problems of history: *Glaube* is a lazy man's expedient, a contamination of a religious category which ought to follow upon the exercise of reason, not ground and precede it. Spinoza is therefore the winner, and transcendental idealism will take over his principle of the unity of being. Hegel will thus reproach Jacobi with having halted at the immediate, at the empirical finite of the *Verstand* (understanding), not even penetrating to the true nature of thought, missing the crucial requirement which is to attain freedom from mediation, to make the transition from the finite to the Infinite. The sciences of the finite are ignorant of God; and the most accurate notion of God is precisely that which Jacobi attributes to Spinoza, i.e., that God is "the

[11] Jacobi, *C. W.*, IV, 1, p. 134. Cf. p. 152.

[12] M. Mendelssohn, *An die Freunde,* pp. 519f. In the Letter to Emilia Reimarus, (May 24, 1785), Mendelssohn confesses that the more explanations Jacobi keeps sending him the less he understands of what the man is trying to say (p. 323). Jacobi's reply, *Wider Mendelssohns Beschuldigungen in dessen Schreiben an die Freunde Lessings* (*C. W.*, IV, 2, pp. 171ff.) seems to me to bear this out!

principle of being in all existence" (*das Prinzipium des Seins in allem Dasein*). The primary definition of the Absolute is precisely that the Absolute is "Being"; this is the most abstract definition, to be sure, but it is the finite from which abstraction is being made and so this definition signifies that God is the "quintessence of all realities" (*Inbegriff aller Realitäten*), the real of every reality, that which is most real (*das Allerrealste*).[13] Spinoza could not therefore be taxed with atheism, concludes Hegel, and least of all could transcendental idealism!

Fichte's stand in the *Atheismusstreit* incident is indicative; indeed it serves virtually as a key to the whole evolution and significance of modern thought. As we have seen, Fichte (as opposed to Forberg) is an unreserved theist, considering the certitude of the existence of God to be the foundation of every other certitude;[14] nor is there any reason to doubt his sincerity, once granted the identification of the Absolute with the moral foundation of the life of the spirit. Indeed the divergence between Fichte and Forberg was deeper-cutting than Fichte's accusers and opponents supposed. The *Wissenschaftslehre* asserts the existence of two antithetical worlds: the world of action and duty and the world of reflection or thought, the world of value and the world of reality and being. The first is the world of the absolute Ego or of freedom and spirituality; the second is the world of necessity and sensible immediacy, of "dead being". Hence, the insistence of the early Fichte on the untenability of the concept of God as a substantial and personal reality and the refusal to apply to God the concept of being. Anyone presuming to

[13] Cf. Hegel, *Enzykl. der philos. Wiss.*, especially §§ 50, 62 and 86. The reader is also referred to the exhaustive exposition by Hegel of Jacobi's critique of the Kantian a priori synthesis in the Logic (the Jacobi text is the Essay: *Ueber das Unternehmen des Kriticismus, die Vernunft zu Verstande zu bringen, C. W.*, Vol. III, pp. 61ff.). Hegel accepts Jacobi's critique of intellectualist abstraction, from which it is impossible to arrive at a concept or a "synthesis": from *one* (abstract) space, *one* time, *one* mind, it is impossible to arrive at a synthesis; everything is *one* and not *other,* an *is-, ea-, id*-identity without *hicceitas, haecceitas, hocceitas* (i.e. an itness without any thisness). Here three abstracts remain lost in the indeterminate; not even the "pure spontaneity" of the *Ich denke* (I think) can be of any help, for the sheer vowel cannot of itself become a consonant! Very fine, purrs Hegel. But there is another synthesis, not purely extrinsic as Jacobi thought it to be, i.e. the a priori synthesis of the diverse, of being and nothingness, which is given in "becoming" and for this synthesis, Jacobi's question as to "how?" there can be a transition from the abstract to the concrete no longer has any meaning. Jacobi's error has been to stop at the start. He has stopped at the "is-is-is" of the copula which precludes the possibility of any synthesis by its very emptiness (*Wissenschaft der Logik,* Book I, Abschn. I; pp. 81ff.).

[14] "It is no whit doubtful but rather the most certain certainty there is; indeed it is the ground of all other certitude, it is the only absolutely valid objective fact we have, that there is a moral order of the universe" (*Ueber den Grund unseres Glaubens,* Lindau, p. 34; Medicus III, p. 131).

apply to God the concept of "being" and of substance would be tying him down to finitute and to sensible reality; such a one would indeed be God-less and anti-God, a perfect atheist, because the world of being is the void of nothingness.[15] The world of pure act(ion), the realm of the absolute Ego, constitutes the moral order of the universe. It is, in Fichte's terminology, the *ordo ordinans* and the absolute Ego is God, realizing and actualizing himself, so to speak, on two fronts: it is primarily the pure act of the Ego that posits or proves the new world of values; and moreover the act of the Ego objectifies itself and thus descends into the lower world of reality, without merging with that lower world. This conception was the one that had alarmed the public authorities and resulted in the famous condemnation; but it earned Fichte the defense of some theologians who even ranked him with none other than St. Thomas Aquinas! [16] The problem was therefore the high level one of the determination of being and of the constitutive nexus of being with the mind. Fichte was already thinking in terms of the idealist Absolute; but he was still operating within the Kantian dualism between the Pure Reason and the Practical Reason. He therefore assigned being to the phenomenal reality witnessed by sense-experience and expressed by the barren copula-type "is" (*ist*). Fichte's condemnation and the charge of atheism against him represented the price he had to pay to Wolffian rationalism which had essentialized the act of being and had not found any other basis of certitude for existence than the witness of the senses. But this is the drama of the whole of modern thought, tied as it is to the principle of immanentism; Fichte, who was a less sober thinker than Kant but indubitably profounder, realized this problem and decided to posit the Absolute in an assertive and categorical form, rather than in the postulartory form of Kant, and to exalt the practical realm to the status of the primary foundation of truth and certitude.[17]

[15] Cf. the statements already mentioned in the *Appellation an das Publikum* (Medicus III, pp. 168f.).—In 1797, Fichte wrote: "[For the Wissenschaftslehre], all being is necessarily *sensible* . . . The intellectual intuition of which the *Wissenschaftslehre* speaks is directed not to a being but to a doing (an action)" (*Zweite Einleitung in die Wissenschaftslehre,* Medicus III, p. 56). And in a comment on Platner, in 1797: "One is bound to misunderstand the critical philosophy until such time as one becomes clearly aware that it is not dogmatism but idealism, whose starting point is the Ego, action, and not being" (*Logik und Metaphysik,* § 756, in *Nachgelassene Schriften,* Vol. II, p. 243).

[16] Cf. F. Herweck, *Die Giessner Beteilung an dem Fichteschen Atheismusstreit* (Leipzig, 1913), pp. 18f. and p. 41; Thomistic texts are cited declaring God to be First Principle and Pure Act! The theologian Johann Ernst Christian Schmidt and the theologian and philosopher Johann Christian Gottleib Schaumann came to Fichte's defense at Giessen.

[17] "But Fichte's immanent idealism, which did indeed take its initial impetus from Kant's theory of the postulates but then advanced to the notion of the "determinations of self-consciousness", remains within the limits of the mental

The mischance of the *Atheismusstreit* caused Fichte to proceed to a more unitary and coherent arrangement of his thought in order to clarify the essential function of philosophy: for Fichte philosophy was no longer an objective rational consideration *of* something given (in experience), as dogmatism, rationalism, and the *Popularphilosophie* of the later German Enlightenment would have it; rather it was, in the most drastic sense, "a philosophy of philosophy". For Fichte, the whole of speculative theory, philosophy, "science", as expository of the nexus of being, action and value, this mutual relation-link between the two worlds, was a self-objectifying and self-expository process: there is no complete break between the early and the later Fichte;[18] the *Atheismusstreit* simply provoked a further evolution and development, attenuating the initial Kantian dualism and bringing to the fore the unity of life, morality and religion in the absoluteness of the pure Ego.[19]

---

life: he speaks of God not as of a Being in Himself, but only in terms of his "relations to us", i.e. inasmuch as He is the sustaining and fashioning principle of and in our own lives!" (H. Heimsoeth, *Fichte* [Munich, 1923], p. 17). In the later Fichte, however, the inverse is true, as we shall be showing directly.

Initially Fichte brusquely and stubbornly replied to his critics with a renewed insistence upon his own ideas, those very ideas which had been denounced in the first place; but later (in the *Rückerinnerungen*), apparently under the influence of Jacobi's critique, he reopened the whole question and advanced a more clear-cut distinction between knowledge and faith in the sense of a distinction between the philosophy of religion as knowledge and religion itself as life and power, between a sensible feeling and an intellectual one which has in it the certitude of a moral duty and the foundation of religion. Thus the metaphysical predicates can, albeit with some reservations, be attributed to God: "Since the moral world from which our duty originates and the natural world in which we are to realize our rational purpose are thus combined into a unity in God, Fichte no longer has any objection to the usual predicates of creator, sustainer and ruler, being transferred to God" (M. Wundt, *Fichte* [Stuttgart, 1927], p. 272). This process of speculative decanting of the *Atheismusstreit* continues in *Aus einem Privatschreiben* and the more extensive *Bestimmung der Menschen* (1800) and is completed in the last works.

18 This is the thesis presented and well defended by F. A. Schmid, in his *Die Philosophie Fichtes mit Rücksicht auf die Frage nach der "veränderten Lehre"* (Freiburg im Br., 1904), especially pp. 13ff.

19 "The *Atheismusstreit* inevitably imparted a powerful impulse to Fichte's religious thought, concentrating the whole power of his mind more and more upon the religious question . . . The *Theory of Knowledge* becomes itself a Theory of Religion: that is a measure of the strength of the impulse Fichte received from the *Atheismusstreit.*" (M. Wundt, *J. G. Fichte,* pp. 268 and 277). W. Ritzel, in his *Fichtes Religionsphilosophie,* pp. 88f.), has an incisive exposition and study of the vacillations and involutions of Fichte's thought in this crucial period of the evolution of his religious and metaphysical stance. It will be useful to note that for Fichte the problem of the existence of God is extraneous to philosophy and belongs to the behavior of man as such: "The philosopher has no God nor can he have any; he has but a concept of the concept or of the idea of God. God and religion can be found only in life; but the philosopher as such is not the whole man; he is man in the state of abstraction; nor

Yet the problem seems to me not to have advanced a single step beyond Fichte's rough outline of the crucial point: in his conception of being, God is not, and cannot be, a mind or a person; and this in turn subverts the status of the human mind. It is true that neither Jacobi nor any of his contemporaries were able to return to the attack on the problem at the level on which Fichte had posed it in order to escape the scandal that ensued from it. But the plain fact of the matter was, and is even today, that a quite new approach is needed: thought must be brought back to its constitutive element, to that crucial moment at which being presents itself in its primordial nakedness to man; he who would cut this Gordian knot must get back behind the fatal fork in the epistemological road that leads either to pure objectivism or pure subjectivism. In his last years, Fichte overcame his bitterness of the days of the *Atheismusstreit* and concentrated with increasing insistence and intensity on the problem of God; thus Fichte moved further and further away from Forberg who remained stubbornly in his skeptical atheism.[20] In the subsequent editions of the *Wissenchaftslehre* (1801, 1804), the concept of the Absolute as infinite Will is predominant: both the moral and intelligible world and the sensible world are traced back to and derived from the Absolute. One must admire Fichte's struggle to free himself from the vice of pantheism and derive the truth of the finite spirit from the fullness of the absolute Life. Although this effort was doomed to the same failure that was to stalk all subsequent forms of idealism which were to fall under the hammer and sickle of the Hegelian Left, it does indicate the most inspiring element in the whole of modern idealism and represents the summit of the tension of that idealism.

A further element that sheds light on this effort of Fichte in his later years is the complete inversion of the Kantian concept of being (*Sein*), a concept that had played a notable part in the period of the *Atheismusstreit*. The critics have paid scant attention to this point: during the *Atheismusstreit*, as we have seen, *Sein* (being) was identical with *Dasein* (existence, "thereness") and signified sensible existence, the

---

is it possible for a man to be *only* a philosopher" (*Rückerinnerungen,* § 15, Medicus III, p. 212). And near the end of the same work, Fichte speaks out even more clearly: "Just as little is God's being to be defined, to be characterized, or the specific sort of his existence to be indicated; for this our thinking cannot do. What is to be done is simply to speak of His deeds and to stir up and strengthen belief, faith in these deeds, to keep them ever present in consciousness. The concept of God cannot be defined at all by existential phrases, only by action-predicates" (*ibid.,* § 41; Medicus III, p. 235).

[20] On the increasing differences between the position of Fichte and that of Forberg, as a result of the *Atheismusstreit,* cf. H. Rickert's already cited article, "Fichtes Atheismusstreit und die kantische Philosophie", pp. 148ff.

empirical immediacy of the manifold and the differentiated; therefore *Sein* could not be applied to God; yet Fichte in his later years, like Schelling and Hegel after him, was to make *Sein* the proper distinguishing mark of God [21] who is described in rigorously metaphysical terms:

1. True and genuine Being is One and does not become, does not begin, does not derive from anything; for were it to derive from something else, then a being would have to be presupposed as its foundation and another being in turn as foundation of this being and we would have an infinite regress.

2. Within this unique, single and simple Being, nothing new ever happens nor does any change occur: it is and remains immutable for all eternity.

3. Being (*Sein*) is distinct from existence (*Dasein*): the former is the object of intellectual intuition, the latter of sensible imagination and representation.

4. Being is therefore the actuality of a mind immanent in knowing; it is the life of the mind.

5. The divine Being is hidden, absolute; it is perfect and eternal life.

6. Everything derives from this Absolute Being as its manifestation and is related back to it: "The real life of knowing (knowledge) is therefore radically the inner being and essence of the Absolute as such, and nothing else." [22]

The first consequence of this theory is that we, rational beings, are not this Absolute Being, yet are linked with him in the most intimate root of our existence inasmuch as we are knowers; other things, on the contrary, who are not possessed of consciousness or mind, are not except insofar as they are known and thus located in (a) mind. In this theory, God has a Being and an intimate "private" Life, hidden within himself, but he also has an existence, a *Dasein,* i.e., his own self-manifestation in the life and becoming (process) of the manifold; yet this transition from *Sein* to *Dasein* involves no change in God.[23] Thus in God being is identical with existence and there is in God no distinc-

[21] Cf. especially *Die Anweisung zum seligen Leben oder auch die Religionslehre* (1806), lect. 3-4, Medicus V, pp. 143ff.

[22] *Ibid.,* Lect. 3, p. 155. In Lecture 4, Fichte seems to be attributing the origin of this notion of being to religious training (pp. 159f.).

[23] In these last writings, Fichte transcends Kant by denying the dead "thing-in-itself": "In rejecting Kant's concept of the thing-in-itself, Fichte is not taking exception (as did epistemological idealism) to the in-itself element, the element of "absolute" existence; he is rather objecting to the conception of this Absolute as a "thing", i.e. as something dead, inanimate, neuter; for, according to Fichte the Absolute (God) = Life" (A. Messer, *Fichtes religiöse Weltanschauung* [Stuttgart, 1923], p. 97).

tion between Being and existence; but for this very reason there must never be any confusion of Being with existence, Being must be maintained *as* Being and the Absolute as Absolute. The faculty that apprehends all this is the "firm and unshaken faith" that asserts that there exists but the One, the Immutable, the Eternal, and nothing outside of or apart from him; the whole of the mutable and changing *is not* in fact and its appearance is but an "empty sham" (*leeres Schein*)! [24] The key to the inversion is thus the identification of *Sein* (being) with Absolute Mind, the overcoming of that methodological dualism which had plagued the first theory when *Wissen* (knowing, knowledge) and *Glaube* (faith) were distinct and *Glaube* had as its object action as an aspiration to the Absolute in the practical realm. But now immanence is all-embracing; there is no remainder! It is surprising to read as early as the *Wissenschaftslehre* of 1801 the identification of the Absolute with Being, conceived as the summit of knowing and identified with knowing: it is discovered or revealed via intuition which is an act of freedom.[25]

The Being here spoken of is certainly the act of knowing, being as "presence" *of* and *to* mind, as is most explicitly asserted in the 1804 *Wissenschaftslehre,* so that there is no being without thought and no thought without being and all distinction between being and thought has been completely dissipated.[26] Within this new definition, with which Fichte seems to be taking a new step forward, away from the Kantian dualism and in the direction of Schelling and Hegel, *Being* is subjected to a complicated elaboration which would reward more thorough examination from various points of view that are outside our present scope. The central crux of the business can be expressed by saying that Being is the content, the datum, the element of objectivity, whereas freedom (*Freiheit*) is the act, the production, the element of subjectivity; and the

[24] *Die Anweisung zum seligen Leben,* lect. 4, p. 162. The change of which we are speaking is indicated right from the first lecture and consists in the identification of Being and Life (Mind): "Being, *Being,* I say, and Life is once again one and the same. Only life can be there independently, of itself and by its own instrumentality. And again Life, as surely as it is Life, carries Being with it". If being is life, continues Fichte, non-being is dead; we are no longer at the stage of the Hegelian "active negativity" but rather we are here seeing a transcendental Parmenidean vision of the real: "Being is altogether simple, not manifold: there are not several beings, but only One Being" (*ibid.,* lect. 1, Medicus V, p. 116).

[25] *Darstellung der Wissenschaftslehre,* 1801, especially § 17; Medicus IV, pp. 34f.

[26] It follows that . . . the difference between being and thinking, as valid in itself, utterly vanishes. To be sure, everything that can occur in it [i.e. the *Wissenschaftslehre*] is, in the *Phenomenon* (*Erscheinung*) that we accomplish in ourselves, in the insight that no being is without thinking and vice versa, absolutely thinking and being *simultaneously*" (*Die Wissenschaftslehre,* 1804; Medicus IV, p. 179).

Absolute is the synthesis. Fichte did, indeed, remain faithful to the end to "intellectual intuition (*intellektuelle Anschauung*); but at the stage of which we are now speaking, he talks also of Reason (*Vernunft*), which is described as the "pure light" (*reines Licht*) and constitutes the inner being and consequently the summit of the cognitional activity and ultimately Absolute Being: [27] and this is something new in Fichte and not a mere terminological progress.

This turning to being on Fichte's part in his last years seems to have been due to the influence of Jacobi. primarily to the principle that in philosophizing we "can only construct by imitating the original and primordial being" (and the *Wissenschaftslehre* shows the process as such, whereas the principle was but a postulate in Jacobi's thought system) and to the further principle that "philosophy must discover and manifest *Being in itself* and *from itself*." [28] These two principles propounded by Jacobi are held by Fichte to be of capital importance for philosophy; but Fichte does not accept Jacobi's third principle, that there cannot be any philosophy properly speaking. So on balance the *Atheismusstreit* was not without value for the new stream of thought.

The last editions of the *Wissenschaftslehre* are even more outspoken on this primacy of being, thus conceived. In the 1806 critique of Schelling, *Sein* (being) is not only the point of departure of Life (*Leben*) but its point of arrival as well, not only its beginning but its goal; and Fichte accepts Schelling's formulation to the effect that the goal of philosophy is the "knowledge of the unity of every being with the divine Being". In the 1810 *Wissenschaftslehre*, God is proclaimed to be Absolute Life (and Being), nothing is outside of God and the world is the manifestation, appearance or phenomenon (*Erscheinung*) of God, the "plan and outline of the divine life" (*Schema des göttlichen Lebens*).[29] In the posthumous *Transcendental Logic*, published in 1812, we find an exposition of the relation between Being and Life, Being and Image (*Bild*),

27 "It is therefore clear that the light or the reason or absolute being, which is all one, cannot posit itself as such without constructing itself and vice versa; that, therefore, both coincide in their essence and are absolutely one, Being and Self-Construction, Being and Self-Knowing" (*ibid.*, p. 312).

28 *Ibid.*, p. 314.—The eulogy that now follows seems quite explicitly to praise Jacobi's work above that of Schelling and Hegel: "By his doughty defense of these two principles, this writer [Jacobi] has earned great praise from his age and has shown himself in a very favorable light as against all those philosophers who are quite uninhibited in their reconstruction of nature [Schelling!] or reason [Hegel?], a reconstruction that is often a botched job at that!" (p. 315. In 1804 Hegel was just beginning his philosophical Odyssey, so the second allusion may be aimed at Reinhold).

29 *Bericht über Wissenschaftslehre*, Medicus V, pp. 320ff., 355; *Wissenschaftslehre* 1810, Medicus V, pp. 615ff.). This seems to be the final formulation: "Only God is. Outside of Him, His appearance (manifestation)" (*Angewandte Philosophie*, 1813; Medicus VI, p. 479, cf. p. 577).

Being and Concept (*Begriff*). Here we are told that Being is the ground (*Grund*) of the image and of the concept: Being is thus the actuality of Life that proceeds to the construction and comprehension (*Verstehen*) of its higher forms. This ultimate phase of the evolution of Fichte's thought, which shows a complete supersession, via the notion of comprehension (*Verstehen*), of the primitive notion of *Glaube* (faith), sees the triumph of God; but this is a God who is the only being enjoying the status of being, while all else is but appearance. Therefore this God is neither a person nor a free creator nor a providential God; both man and the world have but the status of an appearance or phenomenal manifestation of him and have no hope whatever of immortality.[30] The picture is exactly that which we see in Hegel and Spinozism generally, against which the good Jacobi had set forth with such apostolic zeal!

It is usually possible, if one but probes deeply enough, to isolate the deepest roots of a theory and the principles that have presided over its molding and evolution; but it is never an easy task to show the inner dynamic or the part played by each one of these roots and principles in the evolution of the various systems. Thus, first-echelon names in the molding of the "atheistic" theology of idealism are certainly Lessing, Kant, and still earlier Böhme, Spinoza and the very guiding notion of the Reformation itself, the notion of an immediate relationship of the individual human being to God, without any mediation of positive authority (the visible Church).

When Reimarus, Lessing, Kant and their like were presenting their critiques of historical (revealed) religion, German culture had already been thoroughly penetrated by the principles of Enlightenment thought, especially via Wolff and his school. But the transcendental idealists likewise take their inspiration directly from English and French Enlightenment thought and there are good grounds for admitting that the intervention of the Enlightenment principle played a notable part in occasioning the second "precipitation" of the principle of immanentism into atheism. But the paths and channels of this influence are often hard to detect and sometimes seem even to run at cross-purposes. But a consideration of Hegel's stance will help us here, for that stance is most revealing, despite the odd dialectical caper.

In his critique of positive historical religion, Kant is well-known to have been under the influence of English Enlightenment Deism (Locke, Shaftesbury, Mandeville, Hume, *et al.*) and of the French Enlighten-

[30] Cf. the pantheistic uncompromising denial of immortality in the *Wissenschaftslehre* of 1804: "The *Epistemology* can establish nothing concerning the immortality of the soul: for according to the Epistemology there is no soul and no dying nor mortality; there is only Life and this is eternal in itself and whatever is . . . is as eternal as this Life" (Medicus IV, p. 236).

ment (Voltaire, Montesquieu, Rousseau *et al.*) [31] Less well-known is Fichte's enthusiasm for the libertarian ideals of the French Revolution, to which he dedicated a lengthy work in his early years.[32] This work amounts to a complete political ethic, influenced mainly by the Rousseau's theory of the *volonté générale*. The basic points of this theory may be summarized as follows:

1. The value of the French Revolution is epitomized in the motto: "human rights and human dignity" (*Menschenrecht und Menschenwert*), and in the consequent proclamation of the rights and duties of man.
2. Religion is a product of morality (*Sittlichkeit*).
3. Freedom is the seal of the deity upon our forehead.
4. God is identified with Reason and is the executor of the moral laws, he is the "Father of Spirits" (*Vater der Geister*).
5. Conscience is therefore most binding law (*das Bindendste*) for man.
6. God is the universal moral judge.

On the function of the "visible Church" we read that it is "the sole legislator and judge in place of God, and that no article of faith is to be believed because it is credible as such but rather because the Church commands that it be believed". Therefore, whoever does not believe in the Church does not believe in any article of faith.[33]

Hegel's attitude toward the Enlightenment is at once more drastic and more complex: here, too, as in the case of every spiritual problem or phenomenon, Hegel goes to work highlighting the contrasts and contradictions, the positive and the negative aspects, so as to throw light on

[31] Cf. *Die Religion innerhalb der Grenzen der blossen Vernunft,* especially for the critique of the doctrine of original sin and the concept of the "Kingdom of God on earth" and of the Church.

[32] The full title is: *Beitrag zur Berichtigung der Urteile des Publikums über die Französische Revolution,* in *J. G. Fichte Werke, Erster Ergänzungsband,* ed. R. Strecker (Leipzig, 1922). Another early work of a quite different sort, however, is the brief dithyrambic eulogy of Enlightenment religious thought and its interpretation of Christianity, *Einige Aphorismen über Religion und Deismus* (1790); in the latest new edition, the editors remark that this work shows scarcely even a beginner's acquaintance with Kantian thought (*Nachgelassene Schriften,* Vol. I, p. 286).

[33] *Beitrag zur Berichtigung,* pp. 10, 40, 47, 77f., 82, 95f., 110f., 217, 224ff. (discussion of the Church and the churches with obvious allusions to the chaos of the Protestant and Reformed Churches and to the superiority of the Catholic Church: pp. 226ff. This text merits detailed special study). There is an explicit reference to Rousseau's notion of the *volonté générale* on p. 47. References to Enlightenment thought in the systematic works are rare and, in the main, disapproving (Cf. *System der Sittenlehre* of 1798: Enlightenment thought makes happiness consist in knowing [Medicus II, p. 668]; *Die Grundzüge des gegenwärtigen Zeitalters* of 1806, especially Lectures III and IV, Medicus IV, pp. 428ff., 472ff.).

the emergence of a higher truth.[34] Hegel sees the positive kernel of the Enlightenment in the call for freedom, especially in French Enlightenment thought upon which Hegel dwells; thus, in the context of the destruction of self-consciousness of the traditional concepts as rigid essences, the truth of any concept (good or evil, power or riches, the very representations of the faith on God and his relation to the world and the relation of self-consciousness, i.e., man, to him) has no value in and of itself but only to the extent that it is in this self-awareness. In other words, Hegel accepts the elimination of positive (i.e., Christian) morality and religion as truths in and of themselves. But Hegel cannot stop at this void which remains divorced from the "concept": God is in fact conceived by the Enlightenment as "the supreme being" standing by himself and having no relation any longer with the world or with man. Indeed, in its extreme form, Enlightenment thought conceived the Absolute Being as "matter" and the result was materialism and atheism. Thus Enlightenment thought has, for Hegel, two possible end-points: it can end in the abstract conception of God (Voltaire, Rousscau) as supreme being, the absolutely unknown, an ultimate X, and this Hegel claims cannot be called Atheism both because it retains the name of God and because it refers to God the necessary relations of ancient science, the duties of man, etc. Yet, this sort of Enlightenment thought comes in the end pretty much to the same fate as the other sort, namely, materialism, because God remains the Unknown even as does matter; and since God is the Unknown, relations with the Absolute are as good as non-existent or abolished so far as self-consciousness is concerned. Thus Hegel identifies—and not without justification—the two sorts of Enlightenment thinking in their ultimate practical outcome.

This will also be the contention of the Hegelian Left and of Marxist historiography. Hegel is thus in agreement with the negative kernel of the Enlightenment, i.e., the destruction of all positive morality and religion; and it is this negative element which is given free rein and drastic expression in his concept of *Geist* (which here as throughout Hegel has overtones of both "mind" and "spirit"), which expresses at one and the same time the liberation of man from all religious faith and the complete autonomy of self-consciousness. Now Hegel of course could and did claim to have combatted and overcome Enlightenment thought by restoring God and swinging again into line with Christianity; but the fact remains that in Hegel God is the absolute Concept of the Reason (*Vernunft*) and thus is immanent in *Geist,* while Christianity is presented as the religion of *Geist* whose total content has already been expounded in Hegel's own idealism. Thus, under the guise of a critique of the implicit

[34] Cf. *Geschichte der Philosophie,* pp. 456ff. Schelling is well known to have turned in his later years to a form of realist theism which he tended to harmonize with Christianity.

or explicit atheism of Enlightenment thought, Hegel has at the deepest level presented the principles of an atheism which has passed the point of no return. The extensive section in the *Phenomenology* devoted to the Enlightenment critique of positive religion [35] (designated as *superstition, Aberglaube,* the terms used by the Enlightenment thinkers themselves) is brilliant and preeminently instructive as a positive evaluation of this critique; but an analysis of any section of this work would suffice to show how God's absence is palpable throughout and how man is increasingly coming forward to take his place. For this reason, we consider this work to be not only Hegel's most brilliant but, moreover, the most radical and drastic proclamation of the *kingdom and rule of man* as involving this banishment of God.

Hegel thus anticipated Feuerbach in reducing the divine to the human and substituting anthropology, in its transcendental aspect, for theology, thereby resolving the conflict between faith and knowledge (*Glaube und Wissen*). This was in fact the very title of an important essay published by Hegel in 1802, a critique of the theory of faith of Kant, Jacobi and Fichte. This early Hegelian essay already shows how the Reason (*Vernunft*) overcomes the conflicts created by abstract intellectualism between reason and faith. This passage from the introduction is highly significant: "In recent times, culture has risen so far above the old opposition between faith and reason, between faith and knowledge, that this opposition has acquired an entirely new meaning and has been transferred into the area of competency of philosophy itself. As against the old slogan about philosophy being the handmaid of theology, philosophy has invincibly asserted her own absolute autonomy to such an extent that all such slogans and phrases have disappeared and reason . . . has asserted itself and its competency in religion so forcefully that any conflict between reason and miracles or things of that sort has come to be considered outmoded and sheer obscurantism." [36]

Hegel gives the Enlightenment more credit than Kant for this change of course, for it is to the Enlightenment that reason owes its triumph over faith. But Hegel goes on quite incisively to observe that in fact the real situation is rather a draw or stalemate between reason and faith than a clear victory for either: the Enlightenment has indeed dethroned religion for all time to come but it has not yet succeeded in giving reason

[35] *Phänomenologie des Geistes,* VI, Book II, pp. 383ff. The expositions in the *Philosophie der Geschichte* (ed. Gans, pp. 526ff.; ed. Lasson, pp. 915ff.) and in the *Geschichte der Philosophie* (pp. 456ff.) are brief specifications of this first really powerful exposition. Were we to present it here, however, we should be compelled to enter into a detailed study and explanation of its principles; therefore we have preferred to present above, in place of this lengthier exposition, the summary of the concrete process of dissolution of God and of the mysteries of Christianity effected by the Hegelian *Vernunft* in the *Philosophie der Religion.*

[36] *Glaube und Wissen,* Introduction I; *C. W.,* ed. Lasson, Vol. I, p. 223.

a firm basis in itself. There is no real victor and the result has been this plethora of "philosophies of faith" of Kant, Jacobi, Fichte, for which systems God remains inaccessible in himself. Hegel could not have made a better choice of a point of departure for his own drive to restore a philosophy of absolute Reason than precisely this paradox of those philosophies of faith which rule out any *knowledge* of God. For this paradox clearly indicated the need for a new approach which would transfigure the negative critique of the Enlightenment into one stage in the evolution of Absolute Reason; and this new approach was to be the aim and purpose of the new objective idealism in its drive to reconcile the contraries. Thus does a regressive inspection of Hegel's thought show us its substantial continuity, the absence of the sacred and of the divine that is palpable in every stage of that thought, the increasingly clear revelation by that thought of the identity of the real and the rational, of knowledge and happiness, of objectivity and truth.

The young Hegel gives no evidence of any other ideal than that of pursuing to its logical conclusion the course set by the Enlightenment, removing the roadblocks thrown up by the various "philosophies of faith" which have not succeeded in overcoming or passing beyond the purely negative stage of the knowledge of the Absolute. And it is precisely in this "static negativity" of Enlightenment thought and indeed of modern thought in general that the young Hegel incisively pinpoints the bewilderment and perplexity of the modern mind, which he describes in the concluding section of this essay. This modern mind has lost God and manifests in this bewildered perplexity of abstract thought the secularized version of the Christian Good Friday event. The wild ardor of the relevant passage in this essay foreshadows the Bacchic exuberance and intoxication of the *Phenomenology:* "The pure concept, infinity as the abyss of nothingness into which every being is plunged, ought to indicate as one of its component elements the infinite sorrow of that persuasion which hitherto has been but an historical fact in culture and is now the very persuasion on which rests the religion of this modern age, the persuasion that 'God himself is dead' (that persuasion which Pascal likewise expressed in purely empirical form when he wrote: 'Nature is such as to point everywhere to a God who has been lost, both in man and outside of man'); [37] but it ought not to treat this infinite sorrow as

[37] Pascal, *Pensées et opuscules,* ed. Brunschvicg (Paris, 1917), p. 536. Pascal speaks of a "loss" not a death of God and he attributes this loss, in accord with Christian doctrine, to the corruption of sin: "I confess, for my part, that as soon as the Christian religion reveals this principle that man's nature is corrupted and has fallen away from God, my eyes are opened to see everywhere the mark of this truth; for nature is such as to point everywhere to a God who has been lost, both in man and outside of man, and to a corrupted nature" (n. 441).

more than one element of the supreme Idea, so that the pure concept can impart a philosophical existence (*Existenz*) to what would still be the moral prescription of empirical being or the concept of formal abstraction and accordingly furnish philosophy with the idea of absolute freedom and consequently the absolute Passion, the Good Friday of speculation, which was once historical and which must be thus reestablished in the full truth and harshness of its impiety and godlessness; for the serener, less warranted and more bizarre marks of the dogmatic philosophies and of the natural religions must disappear so that the supreme Totality may, as it must, arise again in all its austerity, from its most hidden ground, embracing everything at once in the supremely tranquil freedom of its form." [38]

It is indicative that the *Phenomenology* likewise uses the same figure to speak of the new road and the triumph of the speculative Reason from the summit of absolute Cognition, both as history and as science of cognition, which together ". . . constitute the memorial and Calvary of Absolute Spirit, reality, truth and certitude of its throne." [39] Thus did Hegel commence from the innermost core of the basic themes of religion and the fundamental dogmas of Christianity and hasten to invert the relative status of philosophy and religion; but an inversion, or indeed even a displacement of the metaphysical location of an essence, amounts to a denial of the essence itself and the attribution of being and truth to its opposite!

But Fichte had already expressly proclaimed metaphysical monism with his "turning to being" (*Wendung zum Sein*) in the second series of the *Wissenschaftslehre*, subsequent to the *Atheismusstreit*, and had thus substantially arrived at the same result that Hegel was to reach later, undoubtedly under the combined impulsion of Fichte himself and Schelling. The *Wissenschaftslehre* of 1804 openly proclaims: "The essence of philosophy would consist in reducing every manifold . . . without exception . . . to an absolute Unity," [40] and goes on to stress that any effort to introduce distinction would amount to a contradiction of the whole system. All philosophies prior to Kant, observes Fichte, had posited the Absolute in Being in the sense of "thing" (*Ding*), "dead thing" (*das todte Ding*); and even after Kant, not a few Kantians and not a few epistemologists had stuck fast at the stage of that same notion of the

[38] *Glaube und Wissen*, pp. 345f. The tragic character of this "death of the sacred", proclaimed so that the new world of Reason may arise, recurs in the essay of 1802: *Ueber die wissenschaftlichen Behandlungsarten des Naturrechts*, in *Hegel Schriften zur Politik und Rechtsphilosophie, C. W.*, ed. Lasson, Vol. VII, pp. 384f.

[39] *Phänomenologie des Geistes*, VIII, *Das absolute Wissen*, p. 564.

[40] *Wissenschaftslehre*, 1804; Medicus IV, p. 171. Cf. also p. 177.

Absolute Being, i.e., at the static conception of Spinoza. With the new Fichtean turn given to epistemology, however, God is conceived as dynamic Being, as Life, Thought and Consciousness (Mind). The convergence in absolute unity of Light, Concept and Being, is the definition of God. If God be called the absolutely subsistent One, being arising in itself, then the intuition of God is the only true existence. But then, insists Fichte, God is not to be posited in dead being, the being corresponding to the static Kantian predicate "is" so indicative of immobility and death; rather God must be posited as "the living Light" (*das lebendige Licht*). And here there does indeed emerge, Fichte confesses, the difficulty that philosophy is not willing to be a dualism, that it is serious about this unity drive. It would seem that either we or God must perish: we do not want to, God must not! In Spinoza's system every individual being does indeed perish and retains only a phenomenal existence; but he likewise killed his own Absolute, because Substance is Being without life or consciousness (lifeless, mindless Being), without precisely that life (of consciousness) to which the *Wissenschaftslehre*, as a transcendental philosophy, introduces man.

And here Fichte inserts an extensive digression on the charge of atheism levelled against the *Wissenschaftslehre*.[41] It was Spinoza who was the atheist, not himself, claims Fichte. Only the thinker who wanted a dead God could accuse the *Wissenschaftslehre* of atheism, only a thinker who would be satisfied with a God dead at the very roots within, even though subsequently caparisoned with apparent life, with temporal existence, will and often even blind arbitrary autocracy. But this is no help in making anything more intelligible, neither his life nor our own; it only adds to the already excessive plethora of finite beings in the phenomenal world one further entity, just as limited and finite as they and not even generically different from them.[42] Thus for Fichte as for the young Schelling and for Hegel, the only solution is to be found in that "dynamic Spinozism" or vitalistic monism of the transcendental "I think", which identifies being with thought or with the being of mind in general, consciousness in general, which has its truth in the Absolute, the sole and single being.

In thus carrying the principle of immanentism to the point where it sapped the very foundations, Fichte and Hegel emerge as the true founders of positive and constructive atheism; the so-called "elaborations" of the Left-Wing Hegelians and of the philosophies of our own

[41] *Ibid.*, p. 225.

[42] *Wissenschaftslehre,* 1804; Medicus IV, pp. 224f. This is the whole point of that "inverted Spinozism" or "transfigured Spinozism", i.e. the dynamic Spinozism which traces its roots to Kant (Cf. the quotations in W. Steinbeck, *Das Bild des Menschen in der Philosophie J. G. Fichtes,* p. 140).

day are but simple—and often simplist—corollaries! And this point deserves to be underscored because it seems to escape many minds these days!

The 18th century first, and the 19th century in its wake, accordingly encompassed, each in its turn, the entire parabola of the adventure of atheism: the theological spasm with which Descartes and the right wing of modern philosophy had effected the new beginning in thought left no doubt about the goodness of their intentions; but the alarm signals were not long in making themselves evident: the warning was soon sounded from many sides that the human mind, once left entirely to itself, was exposed to frightening fluctuations between being and non-being. Once the mind had been uprooted from being and left with no more solid "foundation" than its own primordial vacuum, it was compelled to begin over and over again at this zero-point of itself and of the other. Now this vacuum, this mighty zero, can suffice to prevent the particular and the transient from imposing itself as truth and to keep the mind accordingly in its state of openendedness or potency, whichever you prefer. But the "forward step" toward the assertion of the Absolute can certainly not be taken on the basis of that void from which the *cogito* takes its origin; indeed the first crucial point that must here be made is that from radical doubt there flows no *cogito* whatever, not even the thought-act of doubt nor yet any act of the mind. The only prospect with any promise whatever that opens out of this modern starting point of all thinking is that of thinking as "sheer presence" of experience, sheer experential "thereness" as the spectacle of the forms and contents that succeed one another in the evolution of time and the convolution of life. In this sense, the *Deus sive natura* of Spinoza is an expression at once of the first definitive formulation of modern atheism not only and not primarily on the metaphysical level as rather on the very phenomenological level itself! And with the advent of the Kantian *ich denke* (I think), there will be a merger of this Spinozan formula and the Feuerbachian motto, *Deus sive homo* (God or man) ("the secret of Theology is anthropology"), which expresses the other extreme of the principle of immanentism.

The 18th-century atheists, like d'Holbach, could with full justification be called disciples of Spinoza who was God-intoxicated because he was nature-intoxicated;[43] but it is equally true that the 19th-century atheists, like Feuerbach and Marx, and 20th-century atheists, like Sartre and Camus, have stayed with or returned to Spinoza, even though they do not say so. The only difference is in the different value assumed by being (of the mind): for the 18th century atheists (as for Spinoza), it claims

[43] For d'Holbach, it need scarcely be mentioned, Spinoza's pantheism or panentheism is sheer out-and-out atheism (Cf. *Système de la nature* (London, 1774), P. II, Ch. 4; Vol. II, pp. 117f.; note 83).

to be positive; for the 19th- and 20th-century atheists it becomes steadily more negative, thanks to the dialectical principle which more and more explicitly, from Hegel right down to Heidegger and Sartre, traces being back to the ground of nothingness. The *cogito ergo sum* is but the first link in a chain-reaction involving the total transformation of man, a process whose definitive and crowning epilogue is the *principle* of Sartrian atheism: "existence is prior to essence". The delay in this process was caused by the illusion that there could still be talk of a human nature or essence once the existence of God had been denied: "In the philosophic atheism of the 18th century, the notion of God is suppressed, but not, for all that, the idea that essence is prior to existence; something of that idea, we still find elsewhere, in Diderot, in Voltaire, and even in Kant. Man possesses a human nature. that 'human nature' which is the conception of human being, is found in every man; which means that each man is a particular example of a universal conception, the conception of Man. In Kant, this universality goes so far that the wild man of the woods, man in the state of nature and the bourgeois are all contained in the same definition and have the same fundamental qualities. Here, again, the essence of man precedes that historic existence which we confront in experience." [44]

Between the atheism of d'Holbach and his circle and that of Sartre there intervene two of the most tightly-packed centuries in the history of human thought: they are full of the emergence and development of idealist thought down to its definitive fragmentation; but, above all, they teem with the various and opposing efforts to elaborate that "discovery of man", to metaphysicize (*"metaphysiquer"*) human nature in itself, to use d'Holbach's own term. It is this allegedly positive thrust that powers first Deism and then the Left Wing of Enlightenment thought in their critiques of Christianity and all religion in general. The subtlest element in this return to the foundation of the principle of immanentism derives from Bayle's separation of morality from religion. Bayle's thesis is as important as the *cogito* for the evolution of atheism; and this for two reasons: it asserts that man can find a basis within himself for the rationality of his own action; and preeminently it sees the *telos* and perfection of man, the reconciliation of his conflicts, the happy issue of his impulses and desires, precisely in this conformity of man's action with the norms of reason.

Kant's *categorical imperative,* that "ought" which is valid in itself and by itself, liberated from all grounding in the Absolute, is substantially

[44] J. P. Sartre, *L'Existentialisme est un humanisme* (Paris, 1946), pp. 20f. English translation: *Existentialism from Dostoevsky to Sartre,* ed. W. Kaufmann, (Cleveland: Meridian Books, 1956), p. 290.

the stance of Bayle inverted into a positive formulation, the better to highlight its real negative significance. Thus, the *Sollen* (Ought) of the *Critique of Practical Reason* was much more crucial for the evolution of 19th-century atheism than was materialistic sense-perceptionism's hostile critique of religion. For this *Sollen* was the expression of the new thust man was channelling out from within himself to power the sustainer-booster of his freedom, the precious nose-cone of his spiritual being. Kant does indeed outline in the same *Critique of Practical Reason* a proof, which he considers irrefutable, of the existence of God conceived as the indispensible powersource to weld together the two poles of rationality, to effect the union of immortality and felicity. But this desperate expedient is doomed to failure: man is left alone in the universe.

It is certainly indicative that in the *Religion innerhalb der Grenzen der blossen Vernunft,* Kant should have undertaken the championship of a universal religion that would preclude sectarian wrangling and theological squabbling, a religion without any public worship, prayer or sacrifice, yet committed to overcome the "principle of evil" and institute the "Kingdom and Reign of God" on earth by the simple exercise of freedom.[45] The implication is clear: man is capable of himself closing the circle of truth.

The fact that Kant the "pietist" was in turn accused of atheism and that the same charge was subsequently levelled, with greater reason and force, against the main idealists, such as Fichte, Schelling and Hegel, bears witness to a state of affairs which had long been coming to a head within modern thought.[46] Moreover certain other prestigious 18th-and 19th-century figures, such as Lessing, Schiller and Goethe himself, were holding to a view of life devoid of any metaphysical or theological commitment and were elaborating that "pure aesthetic outlook" which Kierkegaard is to categorize as sheer atheism and radical despair.

It might here be mentioned, by way of summing up and preview, that even as Bayle, in the atmosphere of Cartesian rationalism, was taking the first steps in the headlong rush of atheism down the slippery slopes of the principle of immanentism, the great Vico in Italy was thrusting, in

[45] Cf. especially Ch. III: Of the Triumph of the Good Principle over the Evil and of the Establishment of a Kingdom and Reign of God on Earth (ed. Reclam, pp. 96ff.).

[46] K. Löwith, the distinguished expert on the evolution of modern idealism, writes in this regard: "One of Fichte's contemporaries who was a believer in Revelation wrote to Fichte, pointing out quite justifiably that Fichte's idealism was 'nihilism' inasmuch as the Ego's consciousness of its own autonomy annihilates everything that constitutes the world; and God likewise vanishes into the moral order of the universe of the self-positing Ego" (K. Löwith, *Dio, uomo e mondo da Cartesio a Nietzsche* [Naples, 1966], p. 48).

his *Scienza Nuova,* in the diametrically opposed direction, asserting that the whole of history, even in the midst of its abysmal aberrations, was thrusting upward to God and witnessing to his presence in man's ascendant progress from barbarism to the dawn of civilization. The exceptional importance of Vico's thought derives from his intuition that there was an urgent need to strike out in the opposite direction from that charted by Descartes, i.e., that of pure rational evidence. For Vico the crucial thing was to garner the real not simply as it is expressed in pure and rarefied concepts but rather as it presents itself in the vital luxuriance of the imagination, which alone can impart real content and truth to concepts. Hence, Vico's call, in direct polemic with Descartes himself, for a picturing of man, not in terms of the easy sport of the clear and distinct ideas, but rather by means of an adventurous effort of mental penetration into the depths of time and history back to man's first origins in order to follow and trace, with attentive prudence, the vaulting arc of his steep and laborious ascent. But Vico did not have the good fortune that attended Descartes, Spinoza and Bayle; he was not listened to even in Italy.[47]

[47] "Would not our intellectual fate have been different if Italy had listened to Giambattista Vico and had taken the lead in Europe as in Renaissance times? Our 18th century forbears would not then have believed that everything that is clear is true; but would, on the contrary, have seen that clarity is reason's vice rather than its virtue. They would not have believed that reason is our primary faculty, but rather that imagination is . . ." (P. Hazard, *La pensée européenne au XVIIIe siècle* Vol. I [Paris, 1946]; p. 46).—On Vico's relations with the Lucretian and Gassendian style "Neapolitan atheists" of his day, cf. F. Nicolini, *La giovinezza di G. B. Vico* (1668-1700) (Bari, 1932), pp. 125ff. On the trial of the Neapolitan atheists by the Inquisition and the effects of this trial on Vico, cf. F. Nicolini, *La religiosità di G. B. Vico* (Bari, 1949), especially pp. 23ff.

Appendices

I. Forerunners of Atheism in Germany in the Age of the Enlightenment

Marxist historians of thought find totally inadequate and distorted the bourgeois historians' presentation of the history and evolution of modern philosophy in the Western world as the progressive emergence and consolidation of idealism. They consider Ueberweg's famous *Outline* (*Grundriss*), which in 1958 reached its 14th edition, to be the most flagrant example of this tendency to distortion: they accuse it of a deliberate neglect, on principle, of materialism and atheism. Following the advice and example of Marx-Engels-Lenin, they aim to correct this distortion and vindicate the honor of the forgotten heroes. Thus, they draw attention to the fact that at the time of Leibniz, the idealist outlook was being opposed by men like Knutzen, an anonymous writer called the atheist of Magdeburg, Gabriel Wagner, Stosch, Lau, Bucher and others.[1]

Very little is known of Mathias Knutzen: he was a revolutionary fanatic who founded a sect styled the *Conscientiarii* which numbered but a few hundred adherents and disappeared immediately after his death. In the autumn of 1674, in the university towns of Jena and Altdorf, he circulated leaflets in which there stood the following statement: "I do not believe in any God; I put no stock in your Bible; and, to show you how utterly opposed I am to you, I tell you further that priests and magistrates ought to be banished from the world, for we can get along quite well without them." [2]

The only work attributed to the "atheist of Magdeburg" has been lost and his tenets have come down to us only via the refutations of them on the part of two pietist theologians, S. J. Arnold and J. W. Petersen. According to Arnold, this unknown writer not only attacked Jesus and Christianity but even went beyond the excesses of the Epicureans and

[1] Cf. G. Stiehler, *Vorbemerkung* to the anthology edited by him to which we have here had reference throughout this Appendix: *Beiträge zur Geschichte des vormarxistischen Materialismus* (Berlin: Dietz Verlag, 1961), p. 6.

[2] This quotation is taken from W. Heise's article "Mathias Knutzen" in the *Beiträge* cited above; p. 28. Heise considers that Knutzen may have been directly dependent on Spinoza, especially in the matter of Biblical criticism (p. 37).

pagans, teaching that the world is eternal, that God does not exist, that the soul of man perishes with the body, that Moses was an intriguer and swindling cheat, that the state of matrimony is sheer fornication and has nothing sacred about it, that preachers are knaves and imposters. Petersen says that "in that work there was a furious and savage attack on the holy and triune God, Father, Son and Holy Spirit, a denial of the very existence of God (may I be pardoned for even mentioning it!), an assertion that the soul was mortal, that holy scripture is a cheat and the holy men of God seducers and deceivers". As the original source of his atheism, the unknown author cites Seneca who knew no God apart from nature; he also mentions, as more recent sources on which he has drawn, Spinoza with his doctrine of God as *causa sui* and *causa immanens,* English Deism with its denial of a personal God and any providence in the universe, and especially Toland as already professing clear-cut materialist and atheist tenets.[3]

Gabriel Wagner (or Realis de Vienna,) is known chiefly for his correspondence with Leibniz and for the vast extent of his cultural interests, which range from philosophy to natural science and from the new Logic to philosophy in the strict sense.[4] He often takes his cue from Chr. Thomasius who was his close friend. He was a doughty foe of Scholasticism, Catholic or Protestant alike; he criticized Leibniz's *Theodicy* and the doctrine of Providence, as involving physical determinism. Though he never openly professed atheism, he implicitly asserted it by identifying the Supreme Being with necessity (*Die Notwendigkeit ist sein Wesen*=necessity is his essential nature), in an obvious echo of Spinoza as his theologian opponents were quick to point out. Wagner arrogantly asserts that reason contradicts faith; in the question of the relation between matter and mind, he rejects Cartesian dualism and asserts the primacy of matter, claiming that "spirit" or "mind" simply

[3] G. Stiehler, "Der Magdeburger Atheist" in *Beiträge,* cited above, especially pp. 53ff. Stiehler claims that Enlightenment atheism in Germany was mainly influenced by Bayle and mentions one Chr. Thomasius (1655-1728) as having accepted without reservation Bayle's thesis as presented in the *Pensées sur la Comète.* Another all-out materialist was the physician U. G. Bucher. Stiehler thinks that the atheist of Magdeburg drew on both these men.

A twin source for all atheist writings prior to Lessing and Kant was a pair of pamphlets with the common blasphemous title *De Tribus Impostoribus* (Of the Three Impostors): the first of these pamphlets was of medieval Arabo-Christian origin (its author being styled Spinoza II) and accuses Moses, Jesus and Mohammed of being impostors; the other was by Kortholt (we have already cited this one) and it identified the impostors as Spinoza, Herbert of Cherbury and Hobbes. (Cf. J. Presser, *Das Buch 'De Tribus Impostoribus'* (*Von den drei Betrügern*) [Dissertation, Amsterdam, 1926] and especially *De Tribus Impostoribus* Anno MDIIC, Bilingual Edition (Latin and German), published with an introduction by G. Bartsch [Berlin: Akademie Verlag, 1960]. Bartsch's important critical Introduction is reported likewise in the *Beiträge* cited above, pp. 9ff.)

[4] G. Stiehler, "Gabriel Wagner (Realis de Vienna)" in *Beiträge,* pp. 63ff.

expresses the complex of the active powers of matter endowed with feeling.

The Marxist historians of thought have done well to reduce from oblivion these thinkers neglected by the official idealist historiography; but at least in the case of Wagner (as also in that of the famous mathematician, J. H. Lambert), the uncompromisingly materialist interpretation seems somewhat bemusing, even though our lack of original texts precludes any definitive judgment. But the mere fact of opposition to Cartesian dualism, Scholastic formalism and Leibnizian idealism by no means constitutes a profession of (psychological) materialism; nor indeed is any such profession implied in the designation of the soul as "an essential piece of the living man" (*ein wesentliches Stück des lebendigen Menschen*).[5]

Another thinker whom the Marxists claim to have been directly influenced by Spinoza and Gassendi is Friedrich Wilhelm Stosch (1648-1704), who was accused of atheism by the Brandenburg theologians because of his work *Concordia rationis et fidei sive Harmonia Philosophiae moralis et Religionis Christianae.*[6] As the title indicates, Stosch does not, like Wagner, set reason and faith over against each other in opposition; rather he conceives the two areas as being in harmony, albeit claiming for reason a complete freedom within its own area of competency. We should need access to the original texts to judge of Stosch's alleged Spinozism; but here the Marxists' interpretation is even less convincing than in the case of Wagner: the fact that God is imma-
and in God" (*von, aus und in Gott*) is still not pantheism and could even be Thomism, if the trouble be taken to isolate the original kernel of Aquinas' speculation. And when Stosch is criticizing the theory of "innate ideas", he is not, as the Marxists claim,[7] criticizing the Christian doctrine of the knowledge of God, certainly not the doctrine of Aquinas on this point nor yet that defined by the First Vatican Council and generally taught by Catholic theology.

[5] Aristotle and indeed Aquinas himself would find quite acceptable such statements as Lambert makes in the *Phänomenologie oder Lehre von dem Schein:* ". . . that the system of thoughts depends on the physical condition of the brain" and in the *Neues Organon:* ". . . that our cognition always begins from the senses and the sensations and that we must abstract the basis of our abstract concepts from individual instances presented to us by our own personal experience and by history and the witness of others" (*ibid.,* pp. 137f.). The crass error of these Marxist historians of thought is the same one committed by the Marxist theoreticians, i.e. the error of not seeing or not admitting any alternative other than idealism or materialism.

[6] Cf. G. Stiehler, "Friedrich Wilhelm Stosch," in *Beiträge,* pp. 139ff.

[7] *Ibid.,* p. 148. In the matter of moral problems, Stosch likewise remains true to the theist conception and the reader can judge for himself the inconsistency in Stiehler's comment: "These duties as moral commands have their origin in the human reason and in no sense in God. Stosch sets up the following ethical norm: Whatever you do, do it with an eye to God, yourself and society" (p. 151).

A more complex picture is presented by the personality and writings of Theodor Ludwig Lau of Königsberg (1670-1740) among whose teachers were Chr. Thomasius, Bodinus and Budde (whom I believe to be the famous Buddaeus, the historian of atheism, mentioned already). But his protracted journeys and residence in Holland, Brabant and Flanders, England, France and Italy undoubtedly contributed substantially to the molding and evolution of his thought.[8] His chief work is entitled *Philosophische Untersuchungen über Gott, die Welt, den Menschen* (Philosophical Researches on God, the World and Man), published in 1717, which echoes the complex Enlightenment and Deist influences absorbed by Lau: thus, on the one hand there is the Deist-type critique of the dogmas of historical religion (Christianity) and of the authority of the Church and of revelation in general; but there is an equally explicit assertion of the existence of God, proven from nature, God being termed *natura naturans* and the world *natura naturata.*[9] Now, although this is certainly rationalism, it does not seem to us to go as far as pantheism, let alone atheism; and when Lau makes an explicit profession of faith in God there is no reason to doubt his sincerity. Even his thesis concerning the eternity of the world, which the Marxists take to be a profession of atheism, is neither contradictory nor absurd as such and is termed a "possible" philosophical opinion by a theologian like St. Thomas who asserts that creation in time is known only by faith. Balked in their efforts to make Lau, like the other rationalists, into a professing atheist, the Marxist historians speak scornfully about "compromises". Incidentally, Lau himself opposes to the charge of atheism levelled against him the following three principles which are the very basis of deism: (1) The existence of a First and Supreme Being, who exists *a se* and *per se.* (2) The acknowledgement of a Providence higher than man. (3) Some kind of worship of God. Furthermore, Lau seems to have been accused rather of indifferentism than of atheism, as can be seen from the text of his recantation on December 17, 1728.[10]

The Marxist historians of thought have thus done well to restore to their proper place in the history of thought those thinkers who have hitherto been too much neglected for the simple reason that they did not square with the criteria of the idealist ideology; but the Marxists must themselves beware of an opposite extreme of distortion and arbitrary

[8] G. Stiehler, "Theodor Ludwig Lau," in *Beiträge,* pp. 164ff.

[9] Lau developed these points in his reply to the attacks of Thomasius, entitled: *Meditationes, Theses, Dubia, etc.* (Freistädt, 1719) (*ibid.,* pp. 186f.).

[10] "I, Thodorus Luduvicus Lau, Doctor, do confess that I have committed, in my published writings, especially in the treatise *De Deo, Mundo et Homine,* errors involving an Indifferentismus religionis (indifferentism in matters of religion). The aforesaid errors I do retract, detest and recant anew even as I did already confess and repudiate them before the tribunal, in the appendices *En, Ecce* and *Vide* attached to the *Status causae,* as also in the disputation holden before that same tribunal. Promise further to guard myself to the best of my ability and power against such disordered opinion" (*ibid.,* p. 211).

interpretation.[11] Every philosopher, like every student of the human phenomenon, lives and works in the world of his day and cannot safely be uprooted from that world and that environment. Indeed, every philosopher worthy of the name has in addition to this external world a further world of his own, fruit of his own reflection and his own intrepid commitment to the perennial search for the ultimate meaning of things; and it is ultimately only in the context of that inner world that he can be properly understood and interpreted. We feel that the greatest service that could presently be rendered would consist in the integral publication of these rare texts, so as to render them ever more accessible and fill the enormous gap still remaining in the history of thought.

II. Forerunners of Forberg

Marxist histories of thought charge that the real significance of the *Atheismusstreit* has been minimized by bourgeois historiography in a deliberate attempt to parry the attacks implicit in it upon the *status quo.*[12] Incidentally we have seen that this same complaint was made by Fichte himself. Yet, claim the Marxists, there can actually be no doubt about the real meaning of this *Atheismusstreit:* it is one link in the chain of polemics between the protagonists of the ecclesiastico-religious ideology and the champions of anti-ecclesiastical, anti-religious ideas in 18th-century Germany. Forberg's own essay, the Marxists claim to be clearly atheistic in form and content, even though Forberg does attribute some meaning (i.e., a psychological meaning—wherein Forberg is considered a forerunner of Feuerbach) to religion; actually, as we have seen. Fichte considered Forberg's position atheistic and opposed it vigorously in his own essay. Forberg replied with a defense of his own point of view; but the Marxists tax him with not having had the courage at this point to profess himself openly an atheist.[13] In fact, they say, he was: in the *Apology,* he unreservedly asserts freedom of conscience and claims that even if he were an atheist this would still be no infraction of the laws then in force, since atheism does not constitute any danger either for the

[11] The cautions we have given above concerning the problem of God can be repeated for O. Finger's exposition of the doctrine of the soul held by the 18th century Enlightenment thinkers (Michael Hissmann, Melchior Adam Wieckard and Johann Christian Lossius) (cf. O. Finger, *Von der Materialität der Seele* [Berlin, 1961]).

[12] Cf. A. W. Gulyga, "Der 'Atheismusstreit' und der streitbare Atheismus in den letzten Jahrzehnten des 18. Jahrhunderts in Deutschland," in *Wissen und Gewissen,* Beiträge zum 200. Geburtstag Johann Gottlieb Fichte 1762-1814, ed. M. Buhr (Berlin, 1962), pp. 205ff.

[13] Gulyga gives the title: *Friedrich Carl Forbergs der Philosophie Doktors und des Lyzeums zu Saalfeld Rektors Apologie seines angeblichen Atheismus,* Gotha 1799. H. Vaihinger refers to and gives details of this Apology in his *Die Philosophie des 'Als ob'* (pp. 740ff.).

State or for society. Forberg agrees with Bayle that faith is not the cause of morality, that it is a mistake to equate atheism and amorality,[14] that morality should rather be called the basis of religion. It is, of course, another matter if the State sees atheism as its foe because atheism is demolishing that religion that Voltaire wanted to preserve in order to intimidate the common herd; but in this event, religion is simply a police affair, a business of gallows and scaffolds. The State then has no other option than to liquidate atheism as a teaching, beheading the atheists or sending them into exile. But such measures could not fail to have bad consequences since they would succed in catching only those men of honor who were willing to pay the supreme penalty for their convictions. The only effective means of eradicating atheism is that of spiritual influence. This is the province of Church and schools. Every educator who is in the service of the State has the duty of educating and training his students to be good citizens at the service of the State; and Forberg declares that he has always been punctilious in so doing, in his capacity as a teacher. As for his essay on the "concept of religion", he cannot see that it represents any malfeasance because it falls within the sphere not of his teaching activity but rather of his writing career, and here only his reading public and the reviewers are competent to judge.

For the rest, also in this *Apology* Forberg holds fast to the skeptical notions expounded in the former essay, the one that had been denounced. With Kant he denies the possibility of man knowing anything about God. Faith in God amounts simply to the acknowledgement of the fact that the universe moves in accord with moral laws: the mere acknowledgement of the existence of God is not yet, in Forberg's opinion, a matter of religion; it is simply speculative theology. Faith in God becomes religion only when it is transformed into a moral principle governing man's actions. For Forberg this conception of religion is identical with the Christian conception. God is for him the "Supreme Intelligence" but this notion of "Supreme Intelligence" involves no real knowledge of God because the only intelligences I know are merely human ones. This man is the original and God the copy; God is a deified man; and if the person who says this sort of thing is not willing or ready to become an atheist, says the Marxist commentator, he ought at least to make up his mind to become a pagan.[15] But Forberg's atheism is basically agnostic rather than metaphysical; it has no special doctrinal atti-

[14] "That atheism *as such* by no means does away with morality, that on the contrary the heart can still be full of the purest moral sentiments and attitudes even when the head is full of atheistic principles; and that consequently the state has no cause whatever to be unduly concerned about the possible spread of a speculative atheism, considered simply as such" (Forberg, *Apologie*, p. 209).

[15] "This statement," comments Gulyga, "brings Forberg close to the Feuerbachian explanation of God" (*op. cit.*, p. 210). And the Marxist Gulyga also reports Forberg's profession of faith (or rather, of unbelief!) of 1821: "I have never had need of faith in any circumstance of my life and intend to stand fast in my resolute unbelief to the end, which is for me a final end" (*ibid*).

tudes as will, on the contrary, the post-Hegelian atheism of Feuerbach-Marx, as we shall be pointing out below.

The most valuable contribution of Gulyga's study is its information on the immediate forerunners of Forberg: an anonymously published treatise of Johann Heinrich Schulz, *Philosophische Betrachtungen über die jüdische Insonderheit* (1786), whose author published in 1788 an essay of harsh criticism against the notion of spirit, in which among other things he opposed any identification of religion and morality and defended the right of any man to be an atheist; other atheist writings, such as *Spinoza der Zweite* (Spinoza II) (1787) and *Spinoza der Dritte* (Spinoza III) (1790), by Karl von Knoblauch, containing a profession of radical materialism and rejecting the idea of God as a mere chimera. The immediate source on which both Schulz and Knoblauch drew seems to have been the *Philosophische Geschichte des Aberglaubens* (Philosophical History of Superstition), translated from the English and published in Hamburg in 1709.

The rural pastor Schulz (1739-1823) [16] seems to have been the most important of these forerunners of Forberg. His chief sources were Spinoza, d'Holbach and Helvétius, but he is also quite familiar with the Deist and Enlightenment critique of religion and Christianity. The origin of religion is to be sought exclusively in ignorance, immaturity (*Unmündigkeit*) and primitive man's fear in the face of the irruptions of the elements and the powers of nature. In view of his own ability partially to resist and utilize these natural forces, he promptly goes on to "imagine" a power dominating them completely: so the idea of God is simply a product of the imagination. In place of God, Schulz proposes the "source of the world", the "cosmic source" (*Weltquelle*), a notion expressive not only of the "sufficient reason" (*zureichender Grund*) of the existence of the world, but likewise of the steadfast, eternal and immutable laws of nature governing the unfolding pattern of all the changes of that world: this cosmic source is immanent within the world and so is not a transcendental "spirit". God conceived as spirit is therefore a vain illusion; Schulz even cites Fathers of the Church in support of this view.[17] The very notion of "spirit" is meaningless. In his defense of atheism, Schulz distinguishes between an atheism "in the strictest sense" (*im allerstrengsten Verstande*) and a "moderate atheism" (*ver hältnismässiger Aheismus*): he denies that there are any atheists in the former sense, it being impossible to deny the "sufficient reason" of the world; in the latter sense, all men are atheists for one another, for the religious or philosophical concept that one man makes for himself of

[16] Cf. O. Finger, "Johann Heinrich Schulz, ein Prediger des Atheismus," in Stiehler, *Beiträge,* pp. 213ff.

[17] "God is All and Nothing . . . The man who would make himself a clear picture of the Deity is like to the man who would grasp a shadow with his hand . . . The more a man seeks for God the more convinced he becomes that He is not to be found" (*ibid.,* p. 221).

the *Weltquelle* is different from that which another man makes for *him*-self and each considers his own notion to be true and that of the other man to be false.[18] Therefore, either we are all atheists or nobody is an atheist. Mendelssohn had held atheism to "undermine the foundation on which rests the well-being of social life" and had therefore claimed that it was society's duty to eradicate atheism and prevent its spread. Schulz retorts with the French Enlightenment thinkers that atheism in no way damages the well-being of social life, only that of the ruling classes who appeal to a wise divine dispensation (*Fügung*) in defense of their own domination; and there is the further fact that "all known atheists have shown themselves to be as a group the most serious-minded and zealous moralists" so that the more atheism would spread, the purer would morality become! [19] In his peroration, Schulz sets religion and morality in sharp contrast, proclaiming the superiority of the latter over the former, inasmuch as morality derives its duties and obligations directly from the nature of man: thus for our atheist pastor, as for the 18th-century French materialists, man becomes the measure of man and the sole source of his own morality and it becomes entirely pointless to try to base morality upon religion.

Of equal interest for purposes of clarifying the context of the *Atheismusstreit* is the stance of Karl von Knoblauch (1756-1794),[20] another category is "substance" which he develops in his work *Nachtwachen des Einsiedlers zu Athos* (1790). There is one single substance that embraces within itself the "sum total of the real" and of which all other

[18] "Each and every man is an atheist for the other man: for his imagination, which is and must be different from that of the other man, molds for him his own Almighty God, different from the God of the other man" (*ibid.*, p. 236).

[19] *Ibid.*, pp. 237f. The text of Mendelssohn to which this critique is directed seems to us to be this one: "The state does indeed have to see to it long-range that no doctrines are disseminated which are incompatible with the common good and general well-being, which like atheism and Epicureanism undermine the foundation on which rests the well-being of the life of society. It is all very well for Plutarch and Bayle to investigate the question as to whether the state might not be better off with atheism than with superstition; they may calculate the vexations and compare one with another the evils that have thus far poured forth from these two springs to torment the human race; they may reckon and compare the vexations and evils that threaten man from these two sources in the future. But it all comes down to the silly question as to whether a creeping fever or an acute fever is more fatal! No-one in his right mind would wish either on his friends. And so any civil society will do well not to allow either fanaticism or atheism to strike roots and spread" (Mendelssohn, *Jerusalem oder über religiösen Macht und Judenthum,* in *C. W.* [Vienna, 1838], pp. 238f.). On the relation between morality and religion, Mendelssohn had asserted a little earlier in the same work: "There is no special bracket within the system of human duties for duties to God; at rock bottom all man's duties are obligations to God" (p. 235).

[20] Cf. O. Finger, "Der Kampf Karl von Knoblauchs gegen den religiösen Aberglauben," in *Beiträge,* p. 255ff. Knoblauch expressly appealed to Spinoza in another essay: *Ueber das Denken der Materie.* Knoblauch was immediately influenced in the direction of materialism by the psychologist Michael Hissmann of Göttingen and the French physiocrat and critic of religion, J. Mouvillon.

things and individuals are but modifications (*Modifikationen*); The properties of this single substance are, as in Spinoza,[21] extension and thought, making it the "basis of all possibilties" (*Basis aller Möglichkeiten*). Therefore, it is matter itself which has in itself the principle of motion and thought itself, for there is no thought without sense perception and sensation demands the body. In his *Anti-Hyperphysik zur Erbauung der Vernünftigen* (1789), Knoblauch draws the conclusion that the notion and concept of God is absurd: God is conceived as being an incorporeal and spiritual substance, but without a body there can be no senses or sensations, without these there can be no concept, without a concept there can be no spirit, therefore God does not exist! Knoblauch likewise maintains that it is the ignorance of causes, the feeling of weakness and impotence, the evils of life and the resultant preoccupation and dread of future evils which give rise to fear and concomitant superstition. In his critique of positive religion (Christianity) as based on miracles, Knoblauch appeals to Hume, Voltaire, Rousseau and especially to his own master, Spinoza.[22]

III. Schlegel, Goethe, Herder and Spinoza

Spinoza's place in 19th-century German culture owes much to the Lessing-Jacobi controversy. It is interesting and pertinent to note how F. Schlegel vigorously took up arms against the famous charge of Jacobi, a charge calculated to hit at the roots of speculative philosophy as such, accused of atheism and concluded to a distinction between scientific branding this speculative philosophy as pantheism and consequently atheism. Schlegel defended the high moral stature of the philosophers (i.e., speculative) atheism and moral atheism: "Men like Spinoza and Fichte, whose morally strict, austere and outstanding qualities of mind and spirit could serve as model for many a man who criticizes them, ought not to be lumped together with the vulgar mass of the crass materialists; and generally speaking a careful distinction must be maintained between speculative and purely scientific atheism which is compatible with a strict morality and ethic, of the Stoic sort at least if not of the Christian, from the moral atheism, properly so-called, of all those whose thought and life is ensnared in the slime of matter and egotism, without God or even any trace of the divine. Many of these latter sort would not even be able to rise to the level of that speculative error which is not always based on a resistance to the very idea of God nor yet on a total incapacity for the notion of the divine, but rather, as was the case with these above-named men, on a thoroughly false understanding of this idea from a false point of view" (F. Schlegel, *Neue Philosophische*

21 Knoblauch here appeals not only to Spinoza, Boscovich, Buffon, Diderot but to Hume and Kant as well (*ibid.*, p. 289).

22 *Ibid.*, p. 293.

Schriften, ed. J. Körner [Frankfurt a. M. 1935], n. 279). In his introduction, the editor, Körner, distinguishes two lines in the evolution of German philosophy in the latter 18th century: Kant, Reinhold, Aenesidemus-Schulze, Maimon, Fichte, under the banner of Plato and Lessing, Herder, Jacobi, Goethe (p. 24) under the banner of Spinoza. He attributes to S. Maimon the synthesis of Kant and Spinoza. In point of fact, as we have seen, Fichte himself was the most resolute protagonist of this synthesis.

For Schlegel, Spinoza's system represents the loftiest peak of human thought: "Spinoza is thus the most consistent and consequential realist ever to have lived; and he is the most fascinating from the speculative point of view, since pantheistic realism can be most easily learned from him and he can be taken as the most signal representative of the entire breed" (F. Schlegel, *Die Entwicklung der Philosophie; C.W.*, ed. J. J. Anstett, Vol. XIII [Munich 1964], p. 270). In his brief critical introduction, Schlegel points up the vagueness of the notion of substance compared with the rigid and static parallelism of the attributes. This work dates from 1804-05 and was obviously influenced by the early Schelling.

Goethe and Herder were mainly responsible for the penetration of Spinozan pantheism into the wider area of literature and theology, at least according to Marxist historians who adduce many solid arguments for this contention (cf. H. Lindner, *Das Problem des Spinozismus im Schaffen Goethes und Herders* [Weimar: Arion Verlag, 1960]). Lindner does indeed confess to (nay, boast of!) a methodological dogmatism in his selection of criteria for his interpretation. His statement is nothing if not candid: "The line we shall take derives from the application of Marxism-Leninism. It alone can guarantee a final solution for Marxism-Leninism is the only scientific basis on which can be judged the processes and mechanisms of human society. The application of Marxism-Leninism results in a relentless critique of the rotten bourgeois ideology" (p. 21). A veritable heavy artillery barrage (and diplomatically embarrassing at that!) to shoot down sitting ducks! For the Spinozism of Goethe and Herder can scarcely be contested. What can be contested, if not in the case of the crypto-pagan Goethe, then at least in the case of Herder the theologian, is whether this Spinozism resulted in a total dissolution of the religious element and of the very idea of God into the cosmic totality. Lindner can point to two declarations of the famous thinkers in support of his contention: Goethe writes to Jacobi, standard-bearer of anti-Spinozism: "He [Spinoza] does not prove the existence of God, existence is God. And if others find this a reason to reproach him with *atheism,* I for my part would give him the laudatory title of *most theistic and most Christian;"* [23] and for Herder, Spinoza is a "divine man", a "St. John" (*ibid.*). The Spinozan formulas *Deus sive natura*

[23] *Briefwechsel zwischen Goethe und Jacobi,* cited in H. Lindner, *op. cit.*, p. 8.

is common to both Goethe and Herder and forms the basis of their respective interpretations of the world: An acknowledgement of this influence on Goethe and Herder is primarily a warning against approaching the Absolute in that particular form, which is certainly not claculated to produce a solid and consistent theism.

The present writer admits without any reservations the crucial importance of Spinozism for the evolution of modern materialism and modern idealism alike; and there appears to be no doubt that Spinozism gained a foothold not only in Germany but in France and elsewhere as well, primarily through the efforts of the bourgeois class which was liberal-inclined. But to state, as Lindner does (p. 22), that ". . . the evolution of Spinozism is to be explained, like every intellectual phenomenon in a class society, in terms of the evolution of the classes and of the class struggle" is sheer historicist fetishism, as bad as that of bourgeois individualism. It is a shrieking *deus ex machina* which can be used to explain everything and really explains nothing. Our Marxist historian of thought would have to explain in this case how, on his own suppositions, Spinoza gained most favor precisely within the most speculative and metaphysical trend in idealism, that trend that was most obviously and diametrically opposed to materialism (Fichte, Schelling, Hegel, Schleiermacher and their like), even though Kant had elaborated his notion of the ideal character of space and time precisely as an alternative to Spinozism (as Lindner himself admits, p. 176).

In an effort to preclude any possibility of a religious or metaphysical implication in the acceptance of Spinozism by a great part of modern philosophy, Lindner storms against the "neo-Platonic" interpretation of Spinoza's thought, as if Platonism did not represent a gamut of interpretation so vast as to be able to embrace everything from the sublime spiritualism of St. Augustine to the pantheistic depths of Duns Scotus Erigena, Leo Hebraeus, Giordano Bruno and, for that matter, Spinoza himself! It may well be that Goethe and Herder did in fact lay the foundations for the Spinozism of Schelling's *Naturphilosophie;* and the statement that "Jacobi's offensive against Spinozism ended in defeat" may be reasonably correct from the historical point of view. The fact remains that the usual Marxist explanation of intellectual evolution in terms of the sociologico-economic base is a confusion of the part with the whole, or more precisely of cause with effect. Since we accept the core of the thesis concerning the mandatory atheism of modern thought as such, it seems to us that Spinozism was a factor in the evolution of materialistic monism and of spiritualistic monism alike; [24] but neither interpretation captures the whole of Spinozism which less precisely in the contradiction of these two opposed extremes.

[24] Lindner is compelled to admit that in Goethe and Herder the inert Nature of Spinoza is supplanted by an evolutionary conception of the real with man standing at the summit of this evolutionary process (*op. cit.*, p. 192). And this is already an admission of the fallacy of this historicist apriorism!

IV. Spinozan Atheism and the Structural Pattern of Transcendental Idealism (Fichte)

The unity of being asserted by Spinoza notoriously sustains and links the complicated structures of transcendental idealism, beginning with Fichte and his first draft of the *Wissenschaftslehre* in 1794. Fichte took over Spinozism, considered the definitive form of dogmatic realism, side by side with critical idealism in its "most consistent, consequential and definitive form" (*am konsequentesten und vollständigsten*) as presented in Kant.[25] Fichte himself is at pains to draw a precise parallel between Spinoza's speculations and his own.[26] Spinoza, he says, has one absolute Substance just as he did; Spinoza's arbitrary division of that Substance into two modes is peripheral; for Spinoza as for Fichte—and Fichte cunningly adds that he is here giving Spinoza the most benign interpretation possible, extending Spinoza to cover not only the *sapere* (knowing) but the *knower* as well!—the finite *sapere,* insofar as it is in this truth and reality, is an accident of this substance. And Fichte insists further that for Spinoza, as for Fichte himself, it was an absolute accident, immutably determined by Being itself. Thus Spinoza acknowledges, quite as much as Fichte, the supreme absolute synthesis as essential to the very notion of an absolute substance, and Spinoza's definition of substance and accident is basically identical with Fichte's own.

The point on which the two systems diverge, says Fichte, is the "transition point" (*Uebergangspunkt*) from substance to accident. Spinoza simply does not pose this question of such a transition and so he never really pinpoints such a transition point, neither from the side of substance nor yet from the side of accident; and so, in order to ensure some distinction between substance and accident, Spinoza proceeds to allow being as accident to be fragmented into infinite modifications, modes, and consequently never succeeds in arriving at any stable, closed system. Fichte, for his part, is desirous of correcting this weakness and addresses Spinoza in these terms: "And now I ask myself: is Being necessarily split into these modes or does it not rather exist differently from the way in which you manage to think it; in which case what truth or validity can you ascribe to your thought? Or, supposing, on the contrary, that you have hit the mark and your conception of a fragmented Being corresponds to the actual state of affairs, whence then derives this split and *opposition* between a world of extension and a world of thought? In short, you would then unwittingly be steering in a direction that would culminate in a denial of your whole system: the formal unity of being

[25] Fichte, *Grundlage der gesamten Wissenschaftslehre,* Medicus I, p. 351. Later in the same work, Spinoza is mentioned as the only thinker providing a solution to the contradiction of conceiving the Ego as at once finite and Infinite (pp. 448f.).

[26] Cf. *Darstellung der Wissenschaftslehre* (1801), § 32, 3; Medicus IV, pp. 88ff.

and non-being, the fundamental form of knowing wherein lies the necessity of a split . . ." But the *Epistemology,* specifies Fichte, posits this formal unity as a transitional link and proves that the split it produces is not a split of absolute Being but rather the fundamental concomitant form of the knowing operation of absolute Being or of absolute Knowing, which is the same thing. The Absolute thus imposes determination sheerly but not absolutely; rather it imposes determination in the context above outlined and its accident is not within itself (for that would involve for the Absolute a loss of substantiality); rather this accident is *outside of* Substance, in that which is *formally* free. Existence is grounded solely in knowing, in cognition and depends simply on that same knowing, not on its primordial determinant. Thus, even the accident of Absolute Being remains simple and immutable as such and a quite different source is established for mutability, namely, the formal freedom of *knowing,* of the cognitional act. The *Epistemology* thus takes the following stand on the business of holistic monism (ἓν καί πᾶν) and dualism: it professes an ultimate and ideal holistic monism, with its contention that the eternal One (determinant) lies at the basis of all knowing, i.e., beyond all knowing; and it professes a real dualism in respect of knowing posited as real. Thus the *Epistemology* has two principles: absolute Freedom and Absolute Being (*absolute Freiheit, absolutes Sein*);[27] and it is well aware that the Absolute One cannot be attained in any *effective* cognitional sense by pure thought alone. Knowing now stands in the position of equilibrium point between these two conceptions, and it is now nothing but knowing. In the awareness of unattainability, which knowing comprehends as eternally continuous but likewise precisely as unattainable, lies the very essence of cognition, knowing, as knowing, its eternity, infinity and—incompleteness! Knowing is only to the extent that there is infinity in it, as Spinoza himself indeed wished to maintain; but it is only inasmuch as knowing rests together with this Infinite in the One that it can be protected against dissolving into itself in the restrictive sense, a fate from which Spinoza himself could not protect knowing. The Spinozan system and interpretation of reality gave rise to a closed world of knowing, a universe of

[27] As Fichte had said some years previously, it is impossible to see how, in Spinoza's system, the transition can be effected from the Many to the One or how the Many can be deduced from the One. (Cf. *Die Wissenschaftslehre von 1804,* Medicus IV, p. 194). In his *Vorlesungen über Logik und Metaphysik* (1797), Fichte speaks out even more strongly: "There is the following objection against this system: It contains something inexplicable and incomprehensible; there is no possibility of explaining how the infinite Substance makes the transition into the determinations which it has in finites. This is the crux of all metaphysic. In the *Epistemology,* the transition is clearly shown" (*Nachgelassene Schriften,* p. 243). Fichte's strong feel for teleology and activism place him nearer to Leibniz than to Spinoza (Bruno Wagener, *Ueber die Beziehung Fichtes zu Spinosa und Leibniz,* Dissertation [Borna-Leipzig, 1914], pp. 68f.).

cognition, side by side with or within infinity. Thus, in Fichte the two conceptions of being, Kantian and Spinozan, seem now to move parallel to one another, now to merge and now to diverge; but it is clearly Fichte's desire and aim to integrate and weld them into a unitary conception, even as Schelling and Hegel will be at even greater pains to do in the sequel.

A little later in the same work,[28] Fichte again takes up the theme of the parallelism, as he himself calls it, between his system and Spinoza's: For Spinoza, he continues, as for me, knowing (*Wissen*) is an accident (*Akzidenz*) of Absolute Being. But the crucial difference is this (and the Kantian element I have introduced is responsible for it); for Spinoza, there is no mediating node between substance and accident, they coincide. For me, the "mediation" (*Vermittlung*) is interpolated in the shape of the concept of *formal freedom*. This is quite independent in itself; only *materially* is it determined by the condition that in general it reaches fulfillment: even the material determination pertains only to the form (knowing cannot be without being bound, i.e., relational), not to the matter (quantity and relationship) which is already a result of this formla freedom. Spinoza's freedom is static, whereas Fichte's is dynamic since it is in tension toward the synthesis of knowing and Being, so that it is the determinate character of the content which proceeds from Absolute Being, rather than the matter of knowing which is that in which freedom is actuated and realized.

Fichte is therefore aware of the rigid circle of Spinozism wherein the unity of Being sweeps God away into creatures and creatures into God: "This," asserts Fichte, "is the difficulty of every philosophy that is unwilling to be a *dualism* but is rather totally committed to the search for unity, so that either God or we ourselves must perish. We are unwilling to perish, God must not!" [29] In Spinoza's system, individual being, as valid in itself and subsistent by itself, is lost and retains but a phenomenal existence. And Fichte readily admits Spinoza's atheism. But Spinoza has killed his own Absolute or God, Substance conceived as *Being* without *Life,* only because of a lack of awareness and consciousness of his own human knowing. It is precisely this life that is introduced by the *Wissenschaftslehre* as a transcendental philosophy. Atheist, then, Spinoza may be and indeed most definitely is, but not Fichte! Only that man could accuse his *Wissenschaftslehre* of atheism who desired to have a dead God, dead at the very roots within, even though subsequently caparisoned with blind arbitrary autocracy which is no help toward a better understanding either of his life or of our own. And so Fichte's desire and aim is to overcome Kant with Spinoza and Spinoza with Kant; but he is well aware that this cannot be achieved simply by maintaining the two in symbiosis; they must be so thoroughly mutually

[28] *Darstellung* . . ., § 36, 4; Medicus IV, pp. 108ff.

[29] Fichte, *Die Wissenschaftslehre von 1804;* Medicus IV, p. 225.

compenetrated as to overcome their respective limitations.[30] Spinoza, insists Fichte, is simply lacking in that "transcendentality" thanks to which man has access to the Infinite and which serves as a basis for freedom and man's consequent dignity as a moral subject.

Anyone attentively reading Fichte's impassioned outpourings of philosophical thought and rhetoric (and Fichte is certainly the most emotional idealist on record) can have no doubt that Fichte's whole mind was devoted in total, clear-headed and obstinate commitment to the salvation of the individual and his value. Fichte's motto could well have been: Start with the Ego and hold fast to the ego at all costs! He therefore reproaches Spinoza with the fact that his One is rigid and exclusive, that it is not transcendental and therefore Spinoza has completely forgotten *himself* in his own philosophizing.[31] The further progressive evolution of idealism, in Fichte himself as we have seen, but especially in the metaphysic of Schelling and still more in that of Hegel, will lead precisely to that insidious triumph of the Spinozan principle of the unity of Being and to that relegation to oblivion of the individual which will deprive all morality of any real meaning. The inexhaustible interest of classical transcendental idealism derives entirely from this tension between the Spinozan metaphysical a priorism (Substance) and the Kantian transcendental a priorism of conscience in their mutual indispensability and incompatibility. When, therefore, idealism has run its course, we have arrived at the end of philosophy as synthesis and the field is left free to analysis; or, again it may be said that with the end of idealism we have reached the end of the philosophical saga of the *cogito* adventure as such; we have come to the end of the line, that line that seemed endlessly open and proved to have curled round into a closed and constricting circle!

V. Evolution of Fichte's Philosophy of Religion

Recent researches have shown that there was a drastic evolution in the conception of the religion-problem and of the relations between morality and religion in Fichte's thought from his first works down to those of the *Atheismusstreit*. Thus in his *Versuch einer Kritik aller Offenbarung* (1792), Fichte fully suports the Kantian stand that faith

[30] Cf. the critique of Spinoza's dualistic pair, *natura naturans* and *natura naturata*, in the *Wissenschaftslehre 1798 'Nova Methodo'* (p. 601). In the *Vorlesungen über Logik und Metaphysik* (§ 748), atheism is linked with materialism: "The materialist is also an atheist; for something that had arisen via matter certainly cannot be called God" (p. 237). And in the preceding section (§ 747): "Materialism denies the possibility of a ground or reason for the world" (p. 236).

[31] "The only defect in this system is that it is not transcendental, that Spinoza has forgotten himself in his philosophizing" (*Vorlesungen über Logik und Metaphysik*, Deduktion des Glaubens an Gott; p. 318).

in God can be based on the demand for happiness on the part of man, the moral agent: moral man has the right to a felicity that nature as such is in no position to ensure him.

This stand has been completely abandoned in the writings denounced during the period 1798-1800. These works appeal solely to the intrinsic value of the moral laws against all forms of eudaemonism which is castigated as "radical blindness" (*radikale Blindheit*) and "alienation" (*Entfremdung*) from the law that comes from God, as idolatry and fetishism, as a denial of all religion. This comes out clearly in the following passage: "The man who wants pleasure and enjoyment is a sensual, fleshly man, who has no religion nor is capable of any; the first truly religious perception mortifies lust within us forever. The man who expects beatitude is a fool, unacquainted either with himself or with his entire disposition; there is no beatitude possible; the expectation of such beatitude and a God accepted as a result of such expectation are but figments of the brain. A God who is supposed to service lust is a despicable being" (*Appellation an das Publicum,* Lindau, pp. 125f.; Medicus III, p. 179).

In the denounced work of 1798: *Ueber den Grund unseres Glaubens an eine göttliche Weltregierung,* Fichte had already abandoned and indeed inverted the Kantian stand whereas Kant starts from the order of the universe and on this basis posits a supreme Orderer, Fichte on the contrary identifies God with the order of the universe. Thus in Kant, God is still conceived as substance, whereas in Fichte the concept of substance is identical with that of substrate and thus cannot transcend the material order: "For in Kant the order of the universe is present still as a Substance-God or absolute ideal of reason, whereas in Fichte it is but a law, a fact with no substrate. Kant maintains that God can only be known as mediated by the moral order of the universe; but Fichte goes so far as to make the two notions "God" and "moral order of the universe" interchangeable (cf. C. F. Krause, *Zur Geschichte der neueren philosophischen Systeme* [Leipzig, 1889], p. 235). Kant, for his part, agrees with the charge of atheism levelled against Fichte by Heusinger (*Ueber das idealistisch-atheistiche System Fichte's,* 1799).

The way seems to have been prepared for this resolute and drastic transition to moral Transcendentalism in several little known works of Fichte, among them the two unpublished lectures: *Ideen über Gott und Unsterblichkeit, Zwei religionsphilosophische Vorlesungen aus der Zeit von dem Atheismusstreit* (which were published later by Fr. Büchsel [Leipzig, 1914]). Here we can read the new definition of *Glaube* (faith) which was at the root of the controversy and of the new twist Fichte had given to his philosophy: "The true faith is the belief in the possibility of a realization of the moral law: there is no other faith and it comes automatically from the effort and striving to realize the kingdom and reign of God . . . Any faith which does not flow from moral conviction and persuasion is a pseudo-faith, a superstition (*Aberglaube*)

. . . The true believer says: I believe in the possibility of the realization of the moral law" (p. 49). This is a crucial shift of position: duty now has a validity of its own, apart from any reference to God (cf. H. Scholz, "Ein neues Dokument zu Fichtes religionsphilosophischer Entwicklung," *Kant-Studien* XXII [1918], pp. 398ff., especially pp. 404ff.).

In a letter of November 5, 1799, to his wife, Fichte acknowledges that the polemic of the controversy has impelled him to make a more thorough investigation of the religion-problem and to clarify its significance: "In the course of the composition of this present work, I have taken a closer look at religion than ever before. I am emotionally moved only by total clarity; the clarity I have here attained could not fail to grip my heart. Believe me, darling, this elation has contributed substantially to my unshakeable good spirits and to the indulgent benevolence with which I regard the injustices being perpetrated upon me by my opponents. I do not believe that I would ever have achieved this emotional balance without this grim controversy and its even grimmer consequences; and so, you see, my dear, the outrages perpetrated upon me have already had a result neither of us would wish to expunge" (*Fichtes Briefe,* ed. E. Bergman [Leipzig, 1919], p. 111. The work here referred to by Fichte is in all probability *Die Bestimmung des Menschen,* written between mid-July and mid-November 1799 and published in Berlin in early 1800.

Fichte seems to have been influenced in this shift of position by Schelling's *Vor der Idee des absoluten Ich,* which, Wallner claims, gave Fichte a powerful impulsion in the direction of the Spinozan doctrine of Absolute Being (cf. N. Wallner, *Fichte als politischer Denker* [Halle/Saale, 1926], pp. 140f., especially note 3. Wallner here draws on M. Horneffer, *Die Identitätslehre Fichtes in den Jahren 1801–1806* [Leipzig, 1925]). But there is ample evidence of Fichte's interest in and acquaintance with Spinoza's thought in the *Vorlesungen über Logik und Metaphysik* of 1793, which are an extensive commentary on Platner's *Aphorismen,* § 754 (cf. *J. G. Fichtes Nachgelassene Schriften,* Vol. II, pp. 238ff.). The exposition is divided into four points and pervaded with an obvious sympathy, with a clearcut preference for Jacobi's interpretation as opposed to Kant. Spinozism had no place for freedom ("There can be no thought of freedom in this system," p. 241) and Fichte refers to his own critique in the *Wissenschaftslehre,* to the effect that Spinoza does not show how infinite Substance makes the transition into its finite modes or modifications (p. 242). In his conclusion, Fichte makes an explicit reference to the incorporation of Spinozism into the new transcendental philosophy: "There is a system like the Spinozan in critical philosophy but the critical philosopher knows that he is thinking in this way. In this philosophy, Spinozism acquires transcendental validity; it is the necessary being of reason. In Spinoza it is transcendent and that is the essence of the thing-in-itself" (p. 243). A further point of interest is the comparison and contrast of Leibniz and Spinoza in § 762, no. 10, where Fichte explicitly repeats Jacobi's judgment: *Only Spinozism is atheism;* Leibnizianism is not, although it is not logical (p. 249).

We know that the early Fichte was entirely taken by Spinozism and that it was his acceptance of Kantianism which triggered his transcendental activism. It is from the interior of the Spinozan unity of being that Fichte will proceed in later years to effect the definitive development of his own theory of freedom as actuation of the individual in the plenitude of life within the All; in the process, Fichte will again find his way to the *Glaube* (faith) concept of his early years but it will not be transfigured in the light of his new metaphysic. It will amount to a "universal religion" which will integrate the individual into society and smooth out the conflicts of institutionalized religion: "It is definitely possible for every man to see the part of the great overall picture that he has to represent and bring to realization. He needs only to make his own primal life free so that it can unfold in purity and unadulterated. And if it be but a tiny point, it is yet a part of the whole. And it is a living part of the whole, a vital part, with the strength and power of that whole. The stronger and more intimate is the link and nexus with the whole, the greater likewise is the ability to arouse the other parts, i.e., the other human beings who have not yet attained to a life of their own deriving from that whole . . . This is the most radical individualism that can be imagined. The realization of the ultimate goal of all life is given over into the hands of the individual. Not, to be sure, to the individual as he lives under the influence of external circumstances and in their thrall—this is not vital life, this is but passive existence—but only to such individuals as have made their own life the manifestation of the divine life peculiar precisely to themselves. Herein lies the tremendous radicalization of this individualism and simultaneously the core of its deep-seated union with the idea of community. For it amounts to saying that these individuals stand in the most intimate, necessary connection with the Whole and that in them this Whole is operating to make itself manifest upon earth" (F. Gogarten, *Fichte als religiöser Denker* [Jena, 1914], pp. 112f.).

Solidly accepting, then, the Kantian principle that God cannot be known theoretically nor yet thought of as substance, mind, person or the like, Fichte proceeds to launch himself upon the *Critique of Practical Reason,* in an effort to deepen and consolidate the foundations of moral action and consequently of the reality being lived in the moral order; in this way he "believed" God could be attained: the moral order in its absoluteness, apart from all eudaemonistic motivations, is the deity. Therefore, in an inversion and radicalization of Bayle's thesis, Fichte makes morality again coincide with religion (cf. J. Wirth's excellent analysis in *Der religionsphilosophische Gehalt der Atheismusstreitschriften Fichtes,* Dissertation [Neustrelitz, 1926], pp. 26ff.).

Another expert in this field, E. Hirsch, came to this same conclusion and summed the matter up in two reciprocal propositions: "There is no moral obedience without religious faith," and "There is no religious faith without moral obedience." Insisting that Fichte opts for the latter,[32] Hirsch cites in this connection a significant phrase of Fichte: "Even were a man to doubt God and immortality, he would still have to do his duty." The knowledge of God is thus effect rather than cause or ground of moral action which is the only possible means of transition to transcendental reality: "The sense of duty is not based on belief in God and immortality; rather, on the contrary, it is the belief in God and immortality that is based on the sense of duty." [33]

In the definitive outline of Fichte's system, when he no longer admitted the substantiality of individuals but rather thought in terms of the infinite "kingdom of minds (spirits)", there had to be a common bond for this plurality of intellectual-spiritual beings to ensure their fulfillment of the moral ideal. This bond (*Band*), source of reason and of being, could be nothing other than a derivative of the infinite Will or Reason: "The Will is the vital principle of the Reason, is itself the Reason, absolute unconditionality. To say that the will is active of itself means that the will, simply as such, operates and dominates." [34] Yet, as C. A. Thilo well puts it, the charge of atheism was a valid charge not only against Fichte but against idealism as a whole: "For the strict consequence of idealism taken as a consistent system must be that only my own Ego has the status of an existent . . . If I am the only existent, I am my own God. Even the 'moral order of the universe', which Fichte substituted for the real God, could only amount, in Fichte's rigid and drastic idealism, to the concept of the necessity that the Ego had to produce the moral. Therefore the charge of atheism was entirely justified, to the extent that it was levelled against strict and rigid idealism as a closed and integral system. For such an idealism not only discovers no God but even makes belief in him impossible." [35]

Another curious and interesting document of this period is a collection of letters from a group of German "parish priests" (who may well have been Catholic though this is not certain) to the German "propagators and adherents of the Kantian philosophy" bearing the subtitle: "On How Urgent is the Necessity of Exterminating the Kantian Philosophy From Within the Borders of Germany". These letters express the conviction that Kantianism, which they consider to derive primarily from English sense-perceptionism, contains the germs of a transition to mate-

[32] "He is alienated from the interior uplift above everything sensible which occurs from a sense of duty in obedience to the voice of duty" (E. Hirsch, *Die Religionsphilosophie Fichtes zur Zeit des Atheismusstreites in ihrem Zusammenhang mit der Wissenschaftslehre und Ethik* [Göttingen, 1914], p. 34).

[33] *Appellation an das Publikum,* Medicus III, p. 170.

[34] *Die Bestimmung des Menschen,* III; Medicus III, p. 384.

[35] C. A. Thilo, *Die Religionsphilosophie des absoluten Idealismus* [Laugensalza, 1905], p. 5).

rialism, skepticism and atheism, even if the Kantians themselves are not aware of this: "But do not imagine, gentlemen who are followers of Kant, that we are so enraged at you as to wish to reckon you among the impious herds of the materialists, skeptics and atheists. You do indeed admit the principles but we know quite well that right many among you deny the consequents" (*Epistulae nonnullorum Germaniae Parochorum ad Germanos Kantianae philosophiae propagatores et asseclas,* seu quam sit urgens kantianam philosophiam a Germaniae finibus extermi-nandi necessitas [Frankfurt, 1799], p. 4). No names of alleged Kantians are mentioned nor is there any reference to Fichte's difficulties in 1798. At the outset there is a mention of the scandal triggered by the defense staged, under the protection and patronage of the King of Prussia, at the Sorbonne, of the theses of De Prades, who had died some years previously in exile. (p. 1).

Our perusal of the volume has revealed its bemusing ignorance of the Kantian writings.

Krause, who attended and faithfully transcribed Fichte's lectures at Jena, finds that Fichte's readings in philosophy in this initial period were quite restricted, not going beyond the German Kantians; hence the almost total absence of the God-problem from these first writings of Fichte. It was, says Krause, precisely the atheism charge and the subsequent influence of Schelling's doctrine of the Absolute (and the Spinozism therein implied) that impelled Fichte to read the mystics like Tauler, Böhme, Madame de la Mothe-Guyon and the like, all of whom exercised a profound influence on his later conception of God. Krause acknowledges that this later Fichtean God-notion amounts to an inversion of the earlier one denounced by the censor; Krause finds even the later God-notion not entirely satisfactory: "Ficthe had been cornered by the atheism charge, unsettled by his own religious feelings, enlightened by his reading of certain mystics. As a result he had come to see that his *Wissenschaftslehre* lacked and needed God; at the same time he realized full well that the acceptance and acknowledgement of God would reduce that same *Wissenschaftslehre* to a mere nonentity outside of God. This he would not, or rather could not, admit. Hence this artificial gymnastic . . . especially here [i.e., in *Die Tatsachen des Bewusstseins* (1813), pp. 210ff.; cf. *Nachgelassene Werke,* ed. J. H. Fichte, Vol. I (Bonn, 1834), pp. 407ff.] and this vain effort to bring his earlier speculations at least to some extent into alignment with the God-notion" (Krause, *op. cit.,* p. 277).

VI. Ambiguity and Crypto-atheism of Hegel's Theology

A further step along the allegedly positive path of the later Fichte was attempted by his son Immanuel Hermann (1796-1879). The younger Fichte was devoted to the philosophy of his father but sensitive likewise to the advances effected by Hegel whose lectures he attended. He attempted a synthesis of the two conceptions to the point of conceiving of God as Absolute and as Person. This he felt was rendered possible in speculative thought which conceives God as Being (*Sein*) as the Absolute which or who is living Personality (*lebendige Persönlichkeit*), primordial Personality (*Urpersönlichkeit*), as absolute Spirit (*absoluter Geist*). Hence the concept of personality, banished by Fichte, is reconciled by his son with that concept of Being wherein there meet the thought of Fichte and that of Hegel, in both cases in definitive form. (Cf. C. Chr. Scherer, *Die Gotteslehre I. H. von Fichte,* Theologische Studien der Leo Gesellschaft 9 [Vienna, 1902], especially pp. 32f., 36f. Cf. on pp. 76f. the polemic against Trendelenburg's critique of Hegel.) The younger Fichte was convinced that Hegel was by personal persuasion not a pantheist but a sincere adherent of the Christian faith in a personal God, even in the face of his own Spinozism and its logical claims (Cf. A. Hartmann, *Der Spätidealismus und die Hegelsche Dialektik,* Neue Deutsche Forschungen 163 [Berlin, 1937], n. 173f. Hartmann cites in note 31 to p. 174 the thesis of T. Dieter in *Die Frage der Persönlichkeit Gottes in Hegels Philosophie* [Tübingen, 1917], where Dieter defends Hegel's "theism" on the basis of his doctrine of prayer. Cf. *Philosophie der Religion: C.W.,* Vol. XI [Berlin, 1840], p. 285 and especially on the famous review of Göschel's *Aphorismen*). But Hegel limited prayer to the realm of "immediate religion" and religion is notoriously a degree below philosophy in the Hegelian system. In the review of Göschel, Hegel is not expounding his own thought but rather Göschel's critique of Jacobi. Hegel begins thus: "In the first section, the author presents, following in the main Jacobi's *Von den göttlichen Dingen,* the answers that *Unknowing* gives to the ultimate question: *What is God?*. In its reply to this question, *Unknowing* displays itself in full candor: *God is,* that is its first point. *God is God,* that is its second point and its *last*. He is *like unto himself only* and like unto nothing outside of himself (in accord with the understanding's principle of abstract identity). Here the truth is *immediately* certain; and from this follows the rest: God is—*all that we cannot know;* He is *toto coelo* divorced and diverse from what he is not himself; he is extramundane and transcendent—*and yet* likewise in and with us; he is real, not an individual, not a singular—*and yet* Person, indeed Personality itself; he is Person *and yet* sheerly eternal, infinite, everywhere and nowhere. It does not escape Unknowing that these statements are mutually contradictory; but the conclusion is quite simply that God is incomprehensible, unutterable, as was implied in the first phrase of the effect that God is like unto himself only" (Hegel, *Berliner Schriften,* pp. 301f.).

Göschel's critique, which Hegel clearly indicates he finds entirely cogent, claims this stand leads to nihilism and pantheism (p. 303). It is quite beyond our scope here to trace the history of the interminable and pointless squabbles about Hegelianism after Hegel's death, its fragmentation into a Right Wing of would-be theists and an atheist Left Wing insisting that the internal logic of Hegel's principles demands the denial of God as transcendent person and of any personal immortality for man, i.e., that the logical term of the Hegelian dialectic is atheism. (Cf. J. E. Erdmann for the basic points here involved, especially his *Grundriss der Geschichte der Philosophie* [Berlin, 1878 [3]], for the most complete and informative overall view of the dissolution of Hegelianism: pp. 603ff., especially pp. 644ff.: §336, Problem of Immortality, §337, Christological Problem, § 338, Theological Problem; cf. also Erdmann, *Die Entwicklung der deutschen Spekulation seit Kant* [reprinted Stuttgart: H. Glockner, 1931, Abt. III, Vol. 3, especially pp. 539ff.).

The most obvious criticism to which the theology of the Hegelian school was exposed on account of its Spinozan background was that of pantheism. (Cf. J. P. Romang, *Der neueste Pantheismus oder die junghegelsche Weltanschauung nach ihrem theoretischen Grundlagen und praktischen Konsequenzen,* Allen Denkenden gewidmet [Bern-Zürich, 1848], pp. 5ff., pp. 25ff., p. 35). Hegel is considered to be in the line of Parmenides and Spinoza and Romang launches his bitterest attacks against Strauss, Biedermann and Zeller. The same sort of charge is levelled in the *Kritik des Gottesbegriff in den gegenwärtigen Weltansichten,* an anonymously published work attributed to F. Rohmer (Nördlingen, 1857 [3]); cf. p. 38 the reference to Feuerbach's critique of the Hegelian theology; cf. also Rohmer, *Gott und seine Schöpfung* (Nördlingen, 1857).

The Spinozan-pantheist and atheistic undertones of metaphysical idealism have been highlighted, in a further development of Jacobi's charge, by Gottlob B. Jäsche, editor of Kant's *Logik,* in his monumental: *Der Pantheismus,* especially in Vol. III: *Allheit und Absolütheit oder die alte kosmotheistische Lehre des ἓν καὶ πᾶν in ihren modernen idealistischen Hauptformen und Ausbildungen* (Berlin, 1832). Cf. on p. 77, the remark on Fichte: "The God of the idealist ethic of the *Epistemology* is thus . . . not a genuinely existing and real entity but rather one caught and held in sheer becoming!" Jäsche considers Fichte to profess a "practical realism of faith" (p. 81) in his *Die Bestimmung des Menschen;* but, from the time of the *Anweisung zum seligen Leben* Jäsche finds that Fichte conceives of God as the one and only and necessary Being, total life; in the lectures on the "Mission of the Scholar", says Jäsche, Fichte is already presenting the world as immanent in God, inasmuch as ". . . the relation of God to the world is defined as the relation of the divine life, hidden in itself, purely in itself and perduring in itself and thus immutable in its extrinsication or extension in exterior existence" (p. 114). In Schelling's Spinozism, God generates himself from and in himself and as Spirit-Life, as supreme Living Mind, effects within himself the unity of nature and spirit (p. 154f.). This subverts the Christian doctrines of creation and personal immortality (pp. 177f.). In Hegel, pantheism takes the form of a *Cosmotheism,* conjoining God and the world in the identity of a single Whole or All (p. 216) and the thought of man is identified with the thought of God (pp. 301f.). Jäsche's work is the most informed and coherent study of this problem from the viewpoint of speculative theism.

An explicit charge of atheism is levelled against metaphysical idealism (and against Hegel in particular) in the anonymous *Ueber die Wissenschaft der Idee,* Part I: *Die neueste Identitätsphilosophie und Atheismus oder über immanente Polemik* (Breslau, 1831). Cf. on p. 234 the generic judgment on Hegelian philosophy: "The standpoint of that alleged freedom of thought which abstracts from everything and then claims that this abstraction is a being which is nothing, definition of God, and that it is itself the knowing truth, united with God's own absolute knowing—this freedom of thought, to which faith is supposed to be a subordinate representation, is not a rational standpoint at all: it has no faith and no real knowledge. It is a negation of negations, a self-contradiction, an interior controversy. History shows falsehood to represent within itself a contradiction of itself: from time immemorial sounds the contradiction: You shall be as God, knowing good and evil (*Eritis sicut Deus, scientes bonum et malum*)" (The author mentions a previous study he has written on the Hegelian philosophy, entitled *Absolutes Wissen und moderner Pantheismus* [Leipzig, 1829]). In the preface, the author shows Hegel's dependence on Schelling and Fichte's on Schlegel (p. V ff.); and toward the end of this preface, he extolls the superiority of "religious faith" over all human knowledge. The author shows a thorough knowledge of Hegel's main works (the *Phenomenology,* the *Logic,* the *Philosophy of Right* and the *Encyclopedia*) and his critique is inspired by Jacobi (cf. pp. 133ff.). He derives the atheism of the Hegelian system from Hegel's Spinozism (pp. 194ff.) and isolates the real crux of the entire Hegelian system: "Here the atheism of the Hegelian philosophy shows up in its true light, its pitiable feebleness and turbid complexity. The human Ego is the ultimate positive stronghold; abstraction is generality, generic knowing and again concrete individuality and subject; trivialities are cloaked in abstract combinations of words; and nowhere is there any real intellectual life or vitality. This made it possible to perpetrate this shrieking contradiction of positing a self-consciousness alleged to know itself in itself as absolute yet defined as being far too perishable even to be styled corruptible; and to compound the impudence by maintaining, precisely at the point where philosophy wants to identify itself with the eternal Spirit that this Spirit, this eternal Mind, can likewise be taken as being just such a nonentity, just such a *nihil negativum*" (pp. 200f.).

The same explicit charge of atheism was levelled against the Hegelian philosophy by the Danish theologian, Peter Michael Stilling, in his *Den moderne Atheisme eller den saakaldte Neohegelianismes Consequenser* (Copenhagen, 1844). The author refers explicitly to Feuerbach's famous critique of Hegel and Hegelianism (pp. 3f., 10). Stilling refers to the lack or denial of all singularity, individuality and, above all, "personality" (pp. 32f.) and the consequent denial of individual (personal) immortality (pp. 45f.). We shall be speaking in our next Chapter of Stilling's exposition and critique of the philosophical thought of the Left Wing Hegelians and especially of Feuerbach.

Another critic of Hegel in this same tradition was H. M. Chalybaeus. His *Historische Entwicklung der spekulativen Philosophie von Kant bis Hegel* (Dresden, 1837) presents a particularly thorough exposition of the progressive complication of the problem of religion, especially in Fichte, Schelling and Hegel; and his later essay, *Philosophie und Christenthum,* Ein Beitrag zur Begründung der Religionsphilosophie (Kiel, 1853) begins with the thesis: "The speculative systems of contemporary philosophy have led to naturalism and atheism" (p. 2).

The collapse of the notion of God as Supreme Being and transcendent Person is paralleled in idealism, especially in Hegel and the theology of the Hegelians, by the collapse of the basic truths of Christian dogmatic theology, Trinity, original sin and Incarnation. The Hegelian Left, as we shall soon be seeing, is to have the curious but significant function of setting itself against the "letter" of Hegelianism in order to enucleate more thorougly the spirit and the logical implications of the principles of the Hegelian system. In his controversy with D. F. Strauss, Carl Friedrich Göschel himself saw the basic problems from this point of view in his *Beiträge zur speculativen Philosophie von Gott und von dem Gott-Menschen* (Berlin, 1838). But we shall be having occasion later to treat of the relation between modern philosophy and Christianity.

VII. F. Von Baader's Critique of Hegelian Spinozism

Hegel can be said to have been the chief contemporary stimulus and object of Baader's entire critical work. We have seen already that Baader's esteem for Hegel's philosophical endeavor does not blind him to the insufficiencies and dangers of the system and that he is a trenchant and deep-probing critic of Hegel. An appendix to a letter of Baader to a certain Dr. S., dated April 29, 1829 (and thus written while Hegel was still alive), contains some interesting points of Hegel-criticism, which we present here not because they add anything really new but because of the thoroughness with which they cover the entire problematic of the religious life:

1. Hegel's spiritualism is a creature-exalting Spinozism and pantheism, for Hegel holds that the Universal Spirit or the Spirit of the World obtains and maintains his (its!) own consciousness only with the help of (*durch Hilfe*) of individual (creaturely) personalities.

2. As for Baader's own works, anyone finding them to contain pantheism against Tauler and Meister Eckhard; such charges would then in Baader's opinion. It would be just as wrong to level such charges of pantheism against Tauler and Meister Eckhart; such charges would then

be legitimate at least in part against Scotus Erigena and the author of the *Theologia deutsch.*

3. A truly philosophical conception and vision of things is possible only on the admission that God knows himself and his creatures. But God can know and cause creatures (the world, creation) only insofar as he is distinct from them. A God separate from creatures and knowing them as relations in the very act whereby he relates to them, is, to be sure, unknowable to those relations as such; but he is not deprived of the power freely to render himself knowable to those relations.

4. The notion of the relation of Spirit to nature as to that which owes its origin to the self-initiated withdrawal of Spirit can be found in J. Böhme; but there it accords with religion rather than standing in opposition to it.

5. The principles of agents producing matter are the Elohim. Hence the Gnostics' erroneous approach with their notion of the Demiurge.

6. Baader points out that he has often come out against the Hegelian denial of the Church and will be even more outspoken on this point in his forthcoming *Philosophy of Society.* Generally speaking, Hegel has pushed the negativity of Protestantism to the ultimate extreme. But this consequentiality of Hegel has had a salutary effect: cf., e.g., the recent syncretistic retreat of Schelling, who after having given lectures here [at Munich?], wants to put new wine in old bottles and patch the old (pantheistic) garment with new cloth.[36]

Hegel is known to have been early acquainted with the work of Baader and to have been influenced by it; he held Baader in high esteem and managed to meet him in person in Berlin about 1823-24. Their conversations made Hegel acquainted with the work of Eckhart and gave him a deeper and more thorough understanding of Böhme. From this period at which the two philosophers met in Berlin dates an unpublished letter of Hegel to von Baader, in which Hegel tries to disarm the criticism Baader had addressed to him in his *Fermenta cognitionis:* "I think," writes Hegel, "that we agree on the main point; and the few criticisms you may have had of some of the points I made can easily be cleared up." The letter would seem to be a prelude to a personal conversation. On the problem of the relation between religion and philosophy, Hegel minimizes the deep-cutting difference of viewpoint: "As to the way in which I speak of the difference between religion and philosophy, I am really bringing everything down simply to a difference in the *Form* of knowledge and cognition; and in view of the fact that the *content* of the truth is not only common to but identical in both, to which the (Holy) Spirit bears *witness,* i.e., in view of the fact that the Reason is *in itself, free,* I prefer to indicate the form of the religious [reality] by the term *imagination* or *representation,* to show that this religious cognition and knowledge has to do with something *external,* something *given,* etc.;

[36] F. von Baader, *Biographie und Briefwechsel C. W.,* Vol. XV (Aalen, 1963), pp. 454f.

for religion is and should be for all men, not only for trained thinkers; and so its content should, so to speak, penetrate into the heart from the *imagination* (*Vorstellung*), as does our habitual knowledge, without any intervening elaboration into a scientific concept; and it is *from this aspect* that I say that in such a content thinking Reason is not in itself, inasmuch as it is only imagined." [37] Hegel will repeat these declarations of basic agreement in the preface to the 2nd edition of the *Encyclopedia* (1827) but Baader will retort that ". . . we are still not in agreement on the main theoretical point (*Hauptlehre*)".

VIII. A Modern Interpretation of Hegel's Anthropological Atheism (Kojève)

The basic atheistic bias of the Hegelian dialectic comes out most clearly in the *Phenomenology of Spirit*. A. Kojève, in his *Introduction à la lecture de Hegel* (Paris, 1947) has a very incisive analysis of this dimension of Hegel's thought. We here present the crucial paragraphs of Kojève's analysis of the concluding section of the *Phenomenology of Spirit,* the one devoted to "absolute Knowing (Knowledge)" (*absolutes Wissen):*

"In the philosopher, 'truth' (*Wahrheit* = the comprehensive revelation of *objective* reality) coincides with 'certitude' (*Gewissheit* = *subjective* certainty), or with the knowledge the philosopher has of himself. That is to say: on the one hand, the philosopher effectively realizes, in and through his concrete and active existence, the idea that he constructs for himself of himself, i.e., the 'ideal' that he is supposed to realize; and, on the other hand, the knowledge that he has of himself is a total knowledge, in the sense that it is a knowledge of the Totality of Being. And the philosopher *knows it*. In him, *Wahrheit* (truth) assumes the form and shape (*Gestalt*) of *Gewissheit seiner selbst* (certainty of his self), i.e., he knows that he *is* himself the real Totality that he is *discovering and revealing* by his knowing. Or better still, as Hegel says: Truth (*Wahrheit*) has an empirical existence (*Dasein*), for it is the real philosopher, i.e., a flesh-and-blood human being, who is realizing Absolute Knowing (the Absolute Knowledge). And this Absolute Knowledge exists for this real philosopher as a 'knowing-of-him-*self*' or a "knowledge-of-him*self*" . . . In theological knowledge, truth reveals a reality essentially *other* than that of the knowing itself or of its empirical base. God is *other* than the theologian or theology. In the knowledge and knowing of the philosopher, on the contrary, the object of knowledge, the knowledge itself and the subject possessing it are all one. And Hegel says that this *coincidentia oppositorum* occurs because 'the con-

[37] The text has been published by H. Grassl, in *Hegelsche Studien* II (1963), pp. 108ff. Grassl announces an extensive study on this whole matter and meanwhile gives the main points of his interpretation in the introduction and notes.

tent has received the form of the personal Ego'. Now, the content of theological knowledge is God: the philosopher can then be said to be the man who has been wise enough and strong enough to identify himself with God in the sense that he refers the totality of his Knowing (Knowledge) not to a Being partially other than himself, but rather to the Being he himself is, this Being being the *Whole of* Being.

"There is of course no question here of a mystical union and the term God is here nothing more than a metaphor. There is no Being to Whom (or Which) the philosopher *unites himself* for he *is* total Being: and he is 'God' only in the sense that the whole of *his* Knowing (Knowledge), which is the whole of truth, is but a development of the *sum qui sum.* He *is* in effect *all* that is; and he *says it;* and he *is* all that he *says.* In other words, his Being is his Knowing (knowledge) of his being; he *is* the revelation of being because he *is* (the) Being revealed. Or again: the Knowledge he has of his being *is* his very Being; he is the Knowing (knowledge) and it is in *being* Knowing that he is what he is, i.e., the philosopher" (pp. 325f.).

In this context and against this background it becomes clear how Hegel, in his progressive liberation of man from transcendence, refuses to attribute death to man (as *Spirit*) and attributes it to God as transcendent Absolute instead: "It is this transcendence of death in and through history which is the *truth* (= revealed reality) of the subjective certitude of 'survival': Man 'transcends' his death to the extent that his very being is nothing else than his action and that this action of his propagates itself throughout history (which, incidentally, is itself finite!). But man attains to this truth only very late in life and always regretfully. At the outset he believes (or better: he would like to believe) in his own personal survival after his death, and in his imagination he denies his own definitive annihilation. But man is human only to the extent that he lives in a world. And so he can only imagine himself as living humanly after his death on this earth by the device of imagining a transcendent world or a 'beyond' which he calls 'divine' (the divine or the 'sacred' being nothing else than the 'natural habitat' of deceased human beings). But we have seen that where there is *eternal* life, and consequently God, there is no longer any room either for human freedom or individuality or historicity. Thus the man who asserts himself to be immortal always ends (if he transcends the contradiction here involved) by thinking of himself as a purely natural being, determined once for all time in his purely individualized and in no sense existence. And if he has any idea of historical free personality it is to God that he attributes it, thereby attributing to God that very death which he refuses to attribute to himself. But man cannot be satisfied short of realizing his own individual personality and *knowing* that he is realizing it. Thus the man who believes himself immortal, or (which is the same thing) believes in God, never reaches satisfaction and lives always in contradiction and conflict with himself. As Hegel says, such a man is '*ein un-*

glückliches Bewusstsein' (an unhappy consciousness) and lives in a state of dissension (*Entzweiung*). The definitive satisfaction of man as the man who makes history necessarily implies the *consciousness* of realized individuality, individualized personality (via the universal acknowledgement of particularity, individuality). And this consciousness and knowledge necessarily implies, in turn, the awareness of death. And so, if the complete satisfaction of man is the aim and purpose of history and its natural end, this can be said to be achieved by the perfect comprehension by man of his own death. Now it is by and in terms of Hegelian science that man has for the first time fully understood the phenomenological, metaphysical and ontological sense of his own essential finitude. And so, again, if this science which is wisdom was only able to come onto the scene at the end of history, it is because history is perfected and definitively accomplished only in this science. For it is only by understanding himself, in the light of this science, as mortal, i.e., as a free historical individual, that man arrives at the plenitude of the knowledge of a self that has no longer any reason to deny itself to itself nor yet to become other than it is. The Hegelian science culminates in the description of man understood as a whole or dialectical being. Now to say that man is dialectical means to say that he 'appears' to himself as mortal (phenomenological level) or (which amounts to the same thing) that he exists necessarily in a natural world which has no beyond, i.e., where there is no place for a God (metaphysical level); or again (which once more amounts to the same thing), that man is essentially temporal in his very being, which is thus, rightly considered, simply *action* (ontological level)" (p. 524).

This Kojève critique comes down, in the final analysis, to the *resolutio ad hominem* of Hegelianism already effected a century earlier by Feuerbach. It is not difficult to see why it did not meet with the approval of such an Hegelian survivor as J. Wahl (cf. Wahl, "A propos de l'Introduction à la Phénoménologie de Hegel par A. Kojève," in Deucalion 5, *Etudes Hégéliennes* [Neuchatel, 1955], pp. 77ff.).

Hegel and Heidegger: Convergent Atheistic Disintegration of 'Sein' (Being) into 'Dasein' (Thereness, Being There, Empirical Existence)

Heidegger's *Sein und Zeit* deserves exceptional credit for having brought clearly out into the light of day the inescapable atheistic bias of modern *Bewusstsein* (consciousness), of that modern attitude, stance and approach to reality in its most drastic form, as developed in Hegelian thought. Heidegger has taken the obfuscating wraps of Hegelian systematization off that atheistic bias:

"God and human survival have been denied by some men time out of mind. But Hegel was the first to attempt an integral atheistic and finitistic *philosophy* of man (at least in the *Great Logic* and the earlier writings). Not only did he present an accurate description of *finite* human existence on the phenomenological level, which enabled him to utilize without contradiction the basic categories of Judeo-Christian thought; he went further and attempted (not entirely successfully, it must be admitted) to supplement this description by a metaphysical and ontological analysis which was likewise radically atheistic and finitistic. Few of his readers, indeed, grasped the point that the dialectic signified, in the final analysis, nothing short of atheism. Since Hegel, atheism has never again been raised to the metaphysical and ontological level. In our own days, Heidegger is the first to have undertaken the enucleation of an integral atheistic philosophy. But he does not seem to have pushed it beyond the phenomenological anthropology developed in the first volume of *Sein und Zeit* (the only one to have been published). This anthropology (undoubtedly a remarkable and authentically philosophical one) adds nothing substantially new to the anthropology of the *Phenomenology of Spirit* (which, incidentally, would probably never have been understood, had Heidegger not published this book of his); but Heidegger's own ontological atheism or finitism are implicitly asserted in this book in a perfectly consistent, trenchant and consequential fashion. This has not prevented some readers with a *prima facie* claim to competency from speaking of a Heideggerian theology and from claiming to have found in his anthropology a notion of survival and immortality" (Kojève, *op. cit.,* p. 525 Note 1).

Heidegger's treatment of the God-problem in his later writings have, as we shall see in due course, in no way invalidated Kojève's analysis, which pursues the logical implications of principles and strives to get rid of all equivocation. On the contrary, they have simply confirmed the cogency of that analysis.

IX. Charge of Atheism Against Herbart

This charge was expressly levelled by the theologian Anton Günther in his *Die Justemileus in der deutschen Philosophie gegenwärtiger Zeit* (1838) and renewed in a still broader context in his essay: "Ueber Atheismus in metaphysischen Systemen," *Zeitschrift für Philosophie und speculative Theologie* Vol. III, No. 2. Herbart's most illustrious pupil, M. W. Drobisch, came to his defense n *Grundlehren der Religionsphilosophie* (Leipzig, 1840); cf. pp. vff., 18ff. Günther denounces, in virtually Kierkegaardian terms, the "atheistic" character of modern metaphysics in its divorce from theology ("And so metaphysics is divorced from theology and to this extent *atheistic*"—in Drobisch, *op. cit.,* p. viii). Günther insists that the theological argument of Kant and the Kantians (Herbart and Drobisch included) comes down to a purely aesthetic and practical postulate: "The presupposition of a higher Being to which he is forced by the purposiveness of the external world is not much better than the practical postulate in the rational theology of the older critical philosophy; for it can at most be an aesthetic postulate where the postulate of critical philosophy is a practical one. Kant postulated God and immortality under the compulsion of the *disharmony* in the *moral* world; and Drobisch postulates God under the compulsion of the *harmony* in the *physical* world. But monadology can subsume such a postulate just as well under the category of aesthetic postulates. For it designates as aesthetic all thinking which dissolves into relations and sets this relational thinking over against metaphysical or ontological thinking that deals *exclusively* with relationless thoughts and their content, Being *as such,* which is *eo ipso* assigned a character of *absoluteness.* But monadology has banned this aesthetic from any place or status in ontology" (pp. xf.).

Günther further draws attention to the strict nexus between the way of considering and approaching the God-problem and the basic question of the relations between reason and faith for any "Christian conscience" (*christliches Bewusstsein*) worthy of the name: "What is at stake is nothing less than the reconciliation of faith with knowledge, positive theology with philosophy, historical authority in State and Church with the authority of human reason" (p. xviii).

Drobisch on his side replies, as was to be expected, with an exposition of the difference in viewpoint, in the approach to these points and others therewith connected, on the part of the Catholic tradition on the one hand and the Protestant tradition on the other, which latter starts from and remains within the sphere of immanence.

PART V

EXPLICIT AND CONSTRUCTIVE POST-HEGELIAN ATHEISM

Prefatory Note

The fact that the explicit atheism of the 18th century, in its effort at consolidation, appealed predominantly to the principles of sensism and materialism could give rise to the impression that (materialist) atheism was a foreign body, in conflict with the primordial and system-founding spirit of the *cogito* itself. How does this square with our repeated contention (substantiated by numerous textual references) that the Cartesian *cogito* as such can be designated as radically atheistic, as can likewise its rationalistic variants, empiricism, Deism and Enlightenment thought? The plain fact of the matter is that Descartes himself was accused of atheism and, even more to the point, the most brilliant of all Cartesians, Spinoza, came to head up the new forms of atheism, masked or overt, to which the Deists, Freethinkers and explicit atheists of pre-revolutionary French Enlightenment atheism appeal.

The *cogito* then had created a whole atmosphere involving the explusion of the sacred and the transcendent. The crucial component element of this atmosphere was really quite a simple one: the *cogito* had transferred first the basis and subsequently the content of truth to the interior of the mind, making the act of consciousness, of awareness, of knowing and the structures of the mind in its intuitive, predicational and discursive functions, the very basis of the presence of being and the structures of being, not simply from one restricted point of view, but from a drastically exhaustive and all-inclusive point of view, resolving the very act and structures of being into the act and structures of mind. The metaphysic of being had been supplanted by the metaphysic of mind. Mind had been made "self-moving" and self-constitutive and therewith had been abolished any real constitutive nexus outside the mind, whether the immediate nexus with being or the mediate nexus with God. Mind and knowing will henceforth be defined not with reference to being but rather with reference to the "phenomenon" of being of which the mind and the knowing act constitutes the ultimate truth.

Whatever may be said of the priority of function (of which we shall come to speak later on in the course of our critical discussion), the priority of *foundation* and *constitution* of the mind over being acquires its definitive formulation in the Kantian transcendental, starting point of the "battle of the giants" of transcendental idealism against the transcendence and the personality of God. Kant was himself accused of atheism,[1] not only by the apologists of Christianity but even by Fichte himself,[2] in the heat of the *Atheismusstreit.* Fichte had tried to elevate to the status of a system the Ego of Kant's practical philosophy; and this effort had brought him to the realization that the Kantian philosophy lacked any primordial certainty of God.[3] And the result was that it was precisely with Fichte that the constitutive atheism of the new transcendental principle came to light unequivocally for the first time and Fichte's own protests served only to highlight still further the abysmal and unfordable moat modern thought had dug round the Ego: "A God who cannot say: 'I am', a God devoid of personality and deprived of existence, a God who creates nothing and imparts nothing—such a God is no God, as truly as there lives a God who is a spirit, free of all shadow of darkness and full of a life that is love. To play with mere empty magic formulae in the matter of that which is most holy—this is a most unholy game." [4] The charge against Fichte we have seen to have been based on quite specific statements of Fichte who understood and interpreted the Kantian categories within the strict (and restrictive) limits of sensible reality, and consequently as circumscribed by the forms of space and time. Accordingly, in the strict sense, God cannot be an "object" (*Gegenstand*) of cognition nor can the notions of substance or

[1] The atheism charge against Kant occurs frequently and in various forms (Cf. e.g., Kant's contemporary Miotti, *Ueber die Falschheit und Gottlosigkeit des Kantischen Systems* [Vienna, 1801]; and the most thorough historian of idealism, O. Willmann, *Geschichte des Idealismus,* Vol. III [Braunschweig, 1879] pp. 494f.). Willmann speaks of a "Kantian cynicism" and says: "Kant believed in the immortality of the soul as little as he believed in God" (p. 494). The postulates of the Practical Reason are reduced, in the wake of the demolition of the Pure Reason, to mere useful "functions" suited to serve the less erudite. And Willmann concludes: "This is what makes the *Kantian atheism* so much more repulsive than, for example, the undisguised Humean brand" (p. 495).

[2] Cf. the letter of April 22, 1799, to Reinhold (*Fichte's Briefwechsel,* ed. Schulz, Vol. II, p. 84), in which Kant's philosophy is called "sceptical atheism". Paulsen's objections to Willmann's strictures (cf. preceding Note) are therefore unjustified (*Philosophia militans,* Gegen Klerikalismus und Naturalismus [Berlin, 1908 [3-4]], p. 14). B. Bauer also accuses Kant of atheism, in the words: "Kant had denied God in theory, preached atheism and opposed to the Gospel a stiffnecked resistance" (*Die Posaune des jüngsten Gerichts,* 1841; in *Die Hegelsche Linke,* ed. K. Löwith [Stuttgart, 1962]).

[3] On the somewhat confused relations between Spinozism and Kantianism at this point, cf. E. Hirsch's remarks in his *Die idealistische Philosophie und das Christentum* (Gütersloh, 1926), pp. 144ff.

[4] *Lavater an Reinhold,* in H. Maier, *An der Grenze der Philosophie* (Tübingen, 1909), p. 260.

cause, nor even indeed the notions of Unity, Reality and Actuality be applied to Him without internal contradiction.[5]

Anyone familiar with the classical works of modern thought, anyone who has followed through the elaboration of its problems from the interior of its principles, will be well aware that we have here to do with much more than a mere academic question of terms. Between the two parties, accsuers and accused, there was already no possibility of compromise or reconciliation. The confusion and entanglement deepened, however, with the further evolution of idealism: efforts at compromise and expedients without end threatened to postpone indefinitely any fundamental clarification, any real definitive clash of principles, in that extremely fluid intellectual world that was German post-Enlightenment Protestantism. After the clamor of the *Atheismusstreit* had died down, and Jacobi's charges with them, the equivocal myth of the reconciliation between idealism and theism, and even between idealism and Christianity, reached such an incredible climax that the University of Berlin actually presented Hegel with a medal bearing the laudatory inscription: *Defensor Christianismi!* And the Right-Wing Hegelians, the conservative theologians of this school, kept up the myth!

[5] "The concept of God as *Unity, Reality* and *Actuality* would be impossible and contradictory. He [Fichte] will, in a word, be likely to maintain that God must not be conceived of under categories at all" (I. H. G. Heusinger, *Ueber das idealistisch-atheistische System des Herrn Prof. Fichte,* [Dresden and Gotha, 1799], pp. 78f.—Cf. the explicit charge of atheism on pp. 57ff.).

A recent demonstration of the basic atheism of Hegelian thought as seen in the dynamic of the evolution of idealism is that of R. Garaudy, *Dieu est mort,* Etude sur Hegel (Paris, 1962).

1

The Hegelian Dialectic: A Bridge to Atheism (Bauer-Strauss)

The equivocal myth of Hegelianism's capacity for reconciliation with Christianity and theism was attacked head-on by the Left-Wing Hegelians, to whom beyond all doubt belongs the credit of having pushed the principle of immanentism a decisive step further toward its foundation, nothingness. At virtually the same moment, Feuerbach, B. Bauer and Kierkegaard attacked the Hegelian fortress on various flanks; all three converged on the same conclusion, the explicit charge that the imposing Hegelian metaphysic of Absolute Spirit amounted to a mythologization of Christian theology and concealed in its foundation, as its "truth and essence", a radical atheism.[1]

Although Feuerbach's critique preceded that of Bauer (1809-1882) by a few years, we shall deal first with Bauer, since his critique was more straightforward, less subtle, less thorough and more analytical and descriptive.

The Preface (*Vorrede*) warns the reader not to let himself be taken in by the appearance of "worthiness and Christianity" of this philosophy which is always murmuring the word "reconciliation" (*Versöhnung*)

[1] *Die Posaune des jüngsten Gerichts über Hegel den Atheisten und Antichristus* (The Trumpet of the Last Judgment Upon Hegel, Atheist and Antichrist), published anonymously in November 1841. The critics esteemed the title an ironical one. It was included in the excellent anthology by K. Löwith, *Die Hegelsche Linke* (pp. 123-225) from which our quotations here are taken. The work aimed at burlesquing and protesting the Hegelian Right and the adoption of Hegelianism by official Prussian circles. It bristles with Scriptural quotations and, despite its tedious prolixity, represents a document of prime importance for our purpose here.—From a letter of December 24, 1841, from Jung to Ruge, we learn that the work was a joint effort of Bauer and Marx (MEGA, I, 1, 2, p. 262); a letter of the same date from Bauer to Ruge tells us that Marx's contribution had been cut to a minimum by illness (MEGA I, 1, 2, p. 265).

but "hides an asp's venom beneath its tongue" (a reference to Ps. 140, 4). The chief error of the previous opponents of this philosophy, notes Bauer, even of the philosophically erudite opponents, was that of not having recognized the true depth of the error of the original system, i.e., its atheism; and this error of believers is, claims Bauer, still being nurtured today by the cleverness and craftiness (*List*) of the Young Hegelians who, in the hope of putting their adversaries off the track and keeping their axe from the roots of the tree, keep chattering about the fact that their starting point is not the same as that of the Old Master, Hegel, himself (p. 124). But the moment of truth has arrived. The Old Hegelians (v. Henning, Gabler, Rosenkranz) have disowned the Young Hegelians and brought pressure to bear on the government to ban them entirely from teaching and all positions of trust on the pretext that they have betrayed Hegel. Actually exactly the opposite is true: the Young Hegelians are in fact the true, the authentic Hegelians (p. 128).

Next there is warning against the "Center Hegelians" (Fichte Jr., Weisse, Sengler and K. Fischer) [2] who have applied themselves, in conformity with the Christian truth, to the defense of the personality of God, the truth and historical reality (*Facticität*) of revelation and the immortality of the soul, aiming primarily at a rebuttal of pantheism, as a hereditary foe of Christian truth, and proclaiming the irreconcilability of the Hegelian philosophy with Christianity. This does not, of course, prevent these Center Hegelians from accusing one another of remaining still attached to Hegel: Sengler accuses Fichte Jr. and Weisse of teaching a pantheism which is simply ". . . an *intensification* of the Hegelian one" (p. 131). Nor is it any use for them to appeal to Schelling to strike down Hegel, because Schelling is a cipher. Their claim that their philosophy chews directly on the cud of the real simply indicates that this philosophy is a "philosophy of animals" (*eine Philosophie der Thiere*—p. 137).[3] Leo, designated as the "public prosecutor" of Hegelian

[2] Fichte's son pinpointed the exact purpose of the little work which he called a "farce": "We mention, as a comic postlude, and briefly at that, the Trumpet sounded not against Hegel or the atheists but rather against the Old Hegelians, the Schleiermacherian theologians, against all those who wish to disseminate religion and scientific knowledge, especially against the shape of philosophy presented and maintained by this journal [this was the *Zeitschrift für Philosophie und spekulative Theologie*], and intended to bring us all down as once the walls of Jericho". And Fichte concludes incisively: "This is the work of a resolute Young Hegelian" (I. H. Fichte, *Ueber die christliche und antichristliche Spekulation der Gegenwart* [Bonn, 1842], p. 53).

[3] Bauer reproaches the third class of anti-Hegelians, the Schleiermacherians, for their ambiguity and vacuousness: they are neither flesh nor fowl, neither philosophers nor theologians, neither Christians nor secularists and all their fine zeal evaporates in wisps of ineffectual smoke (p. 139). On pp. 140f. there is

atheism, is likewise castigated for having seen only the externals while missing entirely the bases and spirit of Hegelian atheism.

Plunging now into the mainstream of the argument, Bauer makes the basic point that Hegel's philosophy, for all its alleged recognition of the value of religion and of the agreement between Christianity and philosophy, actually contains within itself the dissolution and destruction of religion and the perversion or radical deformation of the basic dogmas of Christianity. The fatal germ in Hegelianism which kills all piety and religion lies in its *pantheism,* whereby religion or the religious relationship "is conceived in terms of the 'relation of substantiality' and as the dialectic wherein the individual spirit gives itself in holocaust to the universal Spirit, which has power over it, inasmuch as this universal Spirit is Substance or *Absolute Idea,* and takes away the individuality of the individual spirit, uniting such spirits to itself". This amounts to an assertion of the dissolution of the individual into the (Spinozan) unity of Absolute Spirit. And there is yet another more horrifying feature in Hegelianism: the conception (and this is what gives Hegelianism its distinctive flavor) that the religious relationship is nothing but an internal relation which exists within *self-consciousness,* so that all the forces and powers which, as Substance or Absolute Idea, seem still to be distinct from self-consciousness are in fact merely elements proper to that self-consciousness and which are simply objectified in religious imagination. In simple terms and as everyone knows, religion is for Hegel an element inferior to philosophy, inasmuch as the Absolute is conceived by religion simply in the limbo of imagination. "Whoever has tasted of this germ is dead for God for he considers God as dead; whoever ingests this germ has fallen lower than Eve when she ate the apple and led Adam astray; for Adam did yet hope to become as God, whereas the adherent of this system lacks even this ambitious pride, complimentary at least to God even though sinful; for such a one does not in the least want to become as God, he wants only to be I-I (I-am-I) and to attain and enjoy the blasphemous infinity, freedom and self-sufficiency of self-consciousness. This philosophy wants no God, no gods

---

presented a lengthy passage from the Schleiermacherian, Nitzsch (*System der christlichen Lehre,* 3rd edition, § 206) on Church-State relations and St. Augustine's teaching (from *De Civ. Dei,* XIV, 4; XIV, 28 and XV, 2, 4, 5) is set over against it as a model to be followed by anyone whose aim it is to overcome modern atheism: "Augustine knew what ecclesiasticism is. He had and knew but one true Church. He knew what State means" (p. 143). This solidarity or at least affinity between Schleiermacher and Hegel is asserted again later in the same work, but here it is more accurately admitted that Hegel had already expounded his whole system in the *Phenomenology of Spirit* and had taken his inspiration for his notion of faith as "immediacy" rather from Jacobi, while at the same time arguing bitterly and sharply with his colleague from Berlin (p. 152).

even, like the heathen; it wants only men, only self-consciousness and everything in it is sheer ostentatious self-consciousness."[4]

Bauer presents a lengthy development of this thesis in individual points, of which we shall merely touch briefly on the main ones:

(a) *The religious Relation as a Relation of Substantiality*[5] i.e., Spinozism in the sense of the absorption of the individual into the substance of the Universal as the Objective Whole. The point of departure is the dissolution (*Aufhebung*) of the finite into the Infinite, of the Ego in its particularity into the Universal which is "absolute fulfillment" (*absolute Erfüllung*). Everything, every particularity and therefore the Ego likewise belongs to the Universal: this Universal is supercomprehensive in my regard and by its own motion shows me as infinite; but since I am also finite, I am for now a "moment in this life, a mere element of this life, an element that has its particular being, its subsistence only in this substance and in its essential moments or elements" (p. 157). The finite mind is thus a form of appearance assumed by the Universal, substance; it is an internal distinction posited within itself by the Universal as a mandatory precondition for self-knowledge, since the Universal can only communicate itself via finite mind or spirit and can attain self-knowledge accordingly only by means of this self-finitization. Hegel's praise of religion is so much dust thrown in the eyes of believers; the hard fact is his dethronement of the mind of man: "Even the relation of substantiality is allowed status by Hegel only for a moment, the moment in which the finite consciousness renounces its finitude: substance is but the momentary spur of flame wherein the Ego sacrifices its finitude and limitation."[6] The end of this motion is not substance but self-consciousness which has posited itself in reality as infinite and has received and accepted into itself the universality of substance as *its own* essence. This philosophy of religion truly reveals the depths of Satan of which the Apocalypse speaks (Apoc. 2, 13): for it only the Ego is substance, it is All, but the Ego has the diabolical pride to posit itself as universal, infinite self-consciousness. A satanic philosophy indeed, which, under hypocritical expressions of respect, conceals a scorn and degradation of religion, of the divine essence and of revelation.

(b) *The "Specter of the Spirit of the World"* (*Das Gespenst des Weltgeistes*). This is the "factotum" of the real and of history and thus the

[4] *Die Posaune,* p. 151.

[5] The terminology here used comes from Hegel: "This notion [of God as the One-Absolute and the Absolute-One] some have wanted to designate by the name *Pantheism;* it would be more accurate to designate it as the notion of substantiality. God is initially determined only as Substance; the absolute Subject, the Spirit, likewise remains Substance but he is not only Substance but further determined within himself as Subject" (*Philosophie der Religion,* ed. Marheineke, Vol. I [Berlin, 1840], p. 93).

[6] *Die Posaune,* p. 161.

usurper of God's rightful status. And Bauer has no trouble documenting this with the most explicit assertions of Hegel.[7] This *Weltgeist* must be the most astute and diabolical of demons. It is his place and not that of Jesus Christ to effect the perfect "reconciliation" of man. Hegel in fact finds that in Christianity the reconciliation has not yet been achieved: for in Christianity that reconciliation is imagined and represented only as being accomplished outside of man, i.e., in a transcendent God and via Jesus Christ, so that the spirit remains unreconciled in itself and has its world divided into a beyond (*Jenseits*) in which the reconciliation must be effected, and a here (*Diesseits*) in which the subject lives with its griefs and sufferings. Hegel sings generous praises of the most important steps that the human spirit has accomplished in the direction of godlessness and unbelief (e.g., the French Revolution). But what is this "Spirit of the World"? None other than universal humanity, mankind as a whole in the dynamic of its historical evolution: the Spirit of the World has its "Actuality" (*Wirklichkeit*) preeminently in the spirit and mind of man, i.e., it is really nothing, like the "concept of the spirit" which evolves and perfects itself in the Spirit of History and in its self-consciousness. The human self-consciousness is thus the only real power in the world and in history; and history has no other meaning than that of the *fieri* and evolution of self-consciousness [8], the Ego come full circle upon itself!

Bauer concludes that the "Spirit of the World" is but a front-man, mask-type idol which Hegel trots out every so often to lavish upon is the attributes of the deity and the scepter, crown and purple robe. But this idol, which amounts really to no more than a figure of speech, a mere metaphor, really stands for self-consciousness, to which Hegel does not scruple to consign the throne of God, the scepter of the Most High, and his royal robe of purple. This can only indicate the hate (*Hass*) that Hegel cherishes for God.

(c) *Hatred of God* (*"Hass gegen Gott"*).[9] Hegel loses no opportunity to heap scorn upon the faith which, starting from the immediate, thrusts upward toward God. He treats it as sheer superstition, pseudo-faith (*Aberglaube*). And any theological stance considering the world to be a creation of God falls for Hegel in this category. He is, on the other hand, very quick with his praise for those philosophies which, like atom-

[7] Taken with preference from the *Geschichte der Philosophie* (ed. Michelet [Berlin, 1840²]).

[8] Here Bauer mentions (p. 164) Hegel's quotation of the Virgilian text: *Tantae molis erat, seipsam cognoscere mentem* (Such an effort it was for the mind to know itself—actually this represents a particularly non-Virgilian rewrite of the actual line to which reference is given in Hegel, *Geschichte der Philosophie,* Vol. III, p. 618, namely Aen. I, 33: *Tantae molis erat Romanam condere gentem*).

[9] *Die Posaune,* pp. 165ff.

ism for instance, demolish the very idea of creation; he is outspoken in his delight every time he finds a system that has no need of the deity in order to explain the world, whereas he is not at all at home with those philosophers who pay homage to God and derive the creation of the world from his holy will. He is really at home only with those philosophers who derive everything exclusively from reason: Hegel apportions praise and blame to all philosophers, from Descartes on, in terms of their ability to get along without God or their attempt to assert God. For him "every philosophy is pantheistic" and the summit of philosophy is represented by the atheist Spinoza: either Spinozism or no philosophy at all! "Spinozan being is the indispensable beginning of all philosophy" inasmuch as Spinoza asserted the unity of substance.[10] The primordial starting point was the unity of being proclaimed by the Eleatics; the second stage was Christianity with its contribution of the notion of the concrete individuality of the spirit; [11] but still more concrete is the demand of the unity of substance levied by Spinoza and Hegel does not scruple to proclaim the superiority of the Spinozan ethic over that of the Gospel. The theistic philosophers become the favorite targets of his ironic barbs: Malebranche is mocked for his pious style and Hegel charges that in Malebranche's writings there can be found nothing but ". . . vacuous litanies to God, a catechism for eight-year-olds on the goodness, justice, omnipresence [of God], on the moral order of the world—and the theologians never get beyond this their whole life long", they remain perpetual eight-year-olds! [12] Hegel derides the "boring thoughts" (*langweilige Gedanken*) of Leibniz on optimism as vulgar playing to the galleries and haughtily proclaims that "real understanding is quite a different thing again": the Leibnizian philosophy is an unbroken succession of "arbitrary contentions" (*willkürliche Behauptungen*), sheer metaphysical romancing which can best be appreciated in the light of that truth which these contentions were trying to avoid.[13] As for the postulate of the existence of God in Kantian ethics, it deserves nothing better than the reply once given by that French astronomer to Napoleon: "I have had no need of this hypothesis"; the "kernel of truth in Kantianism lies . . . in the recognition and admission of freedom." [14] Fichte is showered with praise for having removed the inconsistencies in Kant by achieving absolute unity via an elimination of

[10] Hegel, *Geschichte der Philosophie,* Vol. III, p. 337.

[11] In the final summary of the main stages of the evolution of the human mind and spirit, however, Christianity no longer figures at all (cf. *Geschichte der Philosophie,* Vol. III, pp. 619ff.): there is an immediate leap from the Neo-Platonists to Descartes-Spinoza-Leibniz.

[12] Hegel, *Geschichte der Philosophie,* Vol. III, p. 374.

[13] *Ibid.,* p. 408.

[14] *Ibid.,* p. 501.

all reality other than the mind: he has done away with God entirely, putting the Ego in his place and denying him even the value of a hypothesis. This Fichtean notion of the Ego is, for Hegel, the necessary complement to that equally necessary starting point of speculative philosophy, Spinoza's notion of the one single Substance: "He posited the Ego as an absolute principle, from which, from whose simultaneous immediate certainty of itself, the whole content of the universe must be derived as a product: the Reason is therefore in itself the synthesis of concept and reality."[15] Now man has no more need of God: he is dead for philosophy and the Ego alone, as self-consciousness, lives and operates and is All (p. 169).

(d) *Atheism Integral to Hegel.* Hegel's sympathy and even solidarity with the materialism and atheism of the French Enlightenment thinkers,[16] contemporaries or followers of Spinoza, is for Bauer a revelation of the innermost spirit of the radically atheistic Hegelian philosophy. This association, usually neglected by the older historians of modern thought, jibes perfectly, of course, with Bauer's charge against Hegel. The spirit of the youthful writings of Hegel, called theological writings (wrongly, as we have seen) had undoubtedly been molded along the lines and under the influence of the French atheists and materialists who were partisans of *l'esprit.* French philosophy was more lively, more mobile, more spirited (*geistreich*) than the English empiricism of Locke and Berkeley or the static and negative skepticism of Hume. It was permeated by the absolute Concept turned against the whole world of existing notions and fixed and established thoughts, destroying the whole of the establishment in every sense and revelling in the awareness of sheer freedom. This idealist drive is powered by the certitude that what is, what has value in itself, is to be referred without remainder to self-consciousness: neither the concepts of good and evil (those singular essences that govern the operational self-consciousness, nor the notions of power and riches, nor yet the fixed notions of belief in God and in his relation to the world, his hegemony and the consequent duties of the self-consciousness to him—none of these are truths with an objective subsistence in themselves, apart from self-consciousness.[17] And Hegel sees the assertion of an integral atheism in its definitive theoretical form in

[15] *Ibid.,* p. 555.—Bauer makes the incisive observation that ". . . Hegel's atheism becomes more and more patent and manifests itself in its full crassness, when we notice how this Antichrist has such a high respect for the French who rebelled against God and despises the Germans for not having had the courage to deny God and not having been able, even in the Age of the Enlightenment, to forget God and Religion completely" (*Die Posaune,* p. 173).

[16] To this point Bauer devotes the entire § 5 (*Bewunderung der Französen und Verachtung gegen die Deutschen* [Admiration for the French and Contempt for the Germans], pp. 174ff.).

[17] Hegel, *Geschichte der Philosophie,* Vol. III, pp. 456f.

this philosophy: "All these forms, the real-in-itself of the actual world, the in-itself of the suprasensible world, are eliminated in this spirit conscious of itself." Hegel may well have been reading back some of his own ideas into this French Enlightenment materialist atheism; yet his reading is instructive for a thorough grasp of the inescapable bias of the principle of immanentism to atheism in the dynamic of modern thought. For Hegel, French Enlightenment atheism's sweeping away of all static and rigid structures amounted to a radical actuation of the negativity of the spirit, inasmuch as ". . . self-consciousness transforms those structures into something other than what they were as immediately given, in order to assert in turn the principle of positivity, namely, that . . . it is precisely via this molding and motion in terms of, and by the instrumentality of, its own self-consciousness that Spirit gives form and value to its own interests". La Mettrie, Diderot, d'Holbach, Helvétius and the rest are thus credited with the discovery and comprehension of the "concept proceeding from the elimination of the Absolute or *Etre suprême* and its replacement by 'matter' as empty bare objectivity," and Hegel goes on to comment on the necessary connection between a proper understanding of self-consciousness and this phenomenon in French Enlightenment thought called atheism and/or materialism.[18] The incisiveness of Hegel's analysis lies in his having bypassed the better-known aspects of crass empiricism in this philosophical current, in order to highlight the speculative progress and even revolution represented by this philosophy in regard to the clarification and development of the principle of immanentism. In that development French Enlightenment thought of the materialist-atheist stripe represents a major stage: the elimination of all the notions of faith and of every product of tradition and authority and the exclusive assertion of the present and actual essence, inasmuch as "self-consciousness recognizes the In-Itself only as that which is for it as self-consciousness, in which it knows itself real", i.e., matter, for this philosophical current.

With the scornful phrase: "Of *this* French positive philosophy, there is no need to speak", Hegel disposes of the other wing of French Enlightenment thought, the deistic trend, including Rousseau and Voltaire. For Hegel this wing has one insuperable defect: it lacks the principle of (dialectical) negativity quite simply because it still maintains absolute principles and truth(s). The sole positive aspect Hegel sees in this theistic wing of the French Enlightenment is the uncompromising war waged by the French Enlightenment theists as well ". . . against existence (*Existenz*), against faith, against the age-old power of authority". But Hegel's eulogy of the materialist wing of the French Enlightenment

[18] "We here see, therefore, nascent so-called *materialism* and *atheism*, as the necessary result of the pure comprehending self-consciousness" (*ibid.*, p. 458).

deserves to be cited in full: "French atheism, materialism and naturalism demolished all prejudices, winning out over the aconceptual assumptions and orthodoxies of the religious establishment associated with the habits, customs, opinions, juridical and moral norms of bourgeoisiedom; with the common sense of natural reason and with a spirited earnestness of purpose, free of all pettifogging demagoguery, it rebelled against the established order, against the constitution of the State, against the administration of justice, against the form of government, against political authority, even against art." [19] And as if this were not enough, Hegel goes still further (and here Bauer finds his remarks to be even more applicable at the time when Bauer himself is writing, in the wake of the ruin of the Protestant schools of theological thought, preeminently at the hands of Schleiermacher, theological liberalism and especially Hegelian atheistic pantheism): "The French expounded and espoused precisely as the conviction of the individual in himself those general ideas concerning freedom of the spirit which Luther had begun to inculcate merely in man's soul and feelings. This freedom was as yct unaware of its simple root and so it did not grasp the universal but it was already that universal itself whereby all content vanishes into thought which fills itself with itself." Thus the French atheist materialists proclaimed freedom in its purity, in the Luther tradition and in a more perfect and radical form: "Freedom becomes a universal state (*Weltzustand*), joins with universal history and becomes an age of that history; it is the concrete freedom of the mind and spirit, a concrete universal. Basic principles pertinent to the concrete now come in to take the place of the abstract metaphysic of Descartes." [20] Here Hegel shows exemplary clarity and logical consistency and his explicit alliance of the principle of immanentism with atheistic materialism ought not too readily to be overlooked or forgotten! Bauer's exposition of this point ends with an ironical reference to theism, warning theists to be careful not to raise their voices too drastically against materialism, atheism and naturalism. Bauer's denunciation of Hegel as Antichrist may well seem a paradox, however sincerely meant on the one hand and however ironically pre-

[19] *Ibid.*, pp. 460f.

[20] *Ibid.*, pp. 461ff.—A little later, Hegel notes with satisfaction the struggle of the French Enlightenment ". . . against the Catholic religion, against the fetters of superstition and the hierarchy" (p. 462). In his exposition Hegel relies more on Robinet's uninspired *De la nature* than on d'Holbach (pp. 469ff.). For confirmation of the present exposition of the Hegelian position, cf. Hegel's chapter on the Enlightenment and the French Revolution, in the *Philosophie der Geschichte* (ed. K. Hegel (Berlin, 1840), pp. 526ff.; ed. Lasson, pp. 915f.). Hegel had already spoken about Luther's contribution to the development of the concept of freedom (*Geschichte der Philosophie*, ed. cit., p. 230. Cf. also *Philosophie der Geschichte*, ed. K. Hegel, pp. 501f.; ed. Lasson: p. 916. There is a notable divergence between the two editions at this point in the text.

sented from the tactical point of view on the other; but surely no one can deny that it is both stimulating and pertinent.

Bauer continues his interminable accusation with a denunciation of the "destruction of religion" in general, which seems entirely superfluous in the light of what has gone before.[21] He expounds at length on Hegel's scarcely surprising preference for the naturalistic religion of the Greeks (pp. 190ff.). More incisive and pithy is Bauer's exposition of the origin of religion as a "product of self-consciousness" (*als Product des Selbstbewusstseins*), entirely dominated and outclassed by the Idea or Concept proper to philosophy, since the area of religion is entirely restricted to the sphere of the imagination (*Vorstellung*). Thus, concludes Bauer, whereas religion still maintains that reflection of God in history and in human life, philosophy does away with this illusion and shows that behind that mirror there is no one and nothing—nothing, that is, but a mirrored image of the Ego!

Hegel's atheism, concludes Bauer, is indisputable: [22] it is so patent and explicit that all Hegelians ought to have recognized and exposed it long ago; the fact that a large percentage of them still insist on maintaining that Hegel is a theist can be explained only in terms of their self-deception as a result of their own religious commitments. Bauer then proceeds to lament the fact that the Hegelian Left has likewise maintained Hegel to be a theist, despite the atheistic notions of this Hegelian Left itself: these Left-Wing Hegelians have based themselves primarily upon Hegel's *Philosophy of Religion,* bemusingly oblivious to the fact that Hegel's respectful attitude to religion in that work is nothing but a stratagem (*List*) to mask his fundamental atheism which is subsequently asserted, more or less directly, in other works, especially the *History of Philosophy.* Bauer's critical attitude in this matter toward the Hegelian Left is surely carping punctiliousness, for Strauss, Feuerbach, Marx and their like certainly expressly declared that Hegel's philosophy was atheistic and that his initial principles logically led to atheism, even though they considered the man himself to have been personally a theist. If Bauer is right in his indictment (and the passages he cites seem to prove his case!), then Hegel was undoubtedly a hypocrite of the first order: but we are not here interested in any biographico-historical judgment or moral stricture upon the person of Hegel; our only interest lies in the meaning and internal logic of those principles themselves and their

[21] B. Bauer, *Die Posaune,* pp. 180ff. There follows an interesting section on Hegel's hatred of Judaism (pp. 186ff.) and his hatred against the Church (pp. 192ff.), his contempt for Sacred Scripture and sacred history (pp. 199ff.), even on his hatred for *Quellenforschung* (research on sources) and writing in Latin (pp. 222ff.). On Hegel's critique of the Latin of the Scholastics, cf. *Geschichte der Philosophie,* Vol. III, p. 122.

[22] B. Bauer, *Die Posaune,* p. 202.

operational influence upon the molding of the modern mind right down to our own day. From this point of view, Bauer's little work may be fairly conjectured to have been intended to be, not so much a critique of Hegel, as rather an attack on the inconsistency of the Right-Wing Hegelians who pretended they could reconcile Christian supernaturalism with Hegel's philosophy. Besides, Bauer is well-known to have become one of the most committed adherents of the Hegelian Left, applying the very principles of his man whom he had branded as "Antichrist", to the demolition of Christianity as a religion and even of the historical reality of Jesus Christ himself,[23] initiating contemporaneously with Strauss the "mythical" method of interpretation of the Gospels and consequently himself crossing over to swell the ranks of the new "anthropological atheism" initiated by Hegel.

The transition to atheism via the bridge of the Hegelian dialectic, in the case of D. F. Strauss (1808-1874), is less complicated and can be dealt with more briefly. He is credited with the paternity of the "myth theory" as a key to the interpretation of the Gospel story and thus of Christianity itself and of religion in general.[24] The Enlightenment criticism, so praised by Hegel, now acquired its definitive basis with the elevation of human subjectivity to the status of a transcendental principle: the human reason is the power which creates history by its own evolutionary thrust. Basically Christianity—just like the pagan religions [25]—expresses this fundamental idea that history is the incarnation of God, the unity in evolution of the divine nature and human nature, i.e., in philosophical terms, the idea that cosmic or universal reason finds its most perfect realization as historical Reason in the historical life of mankind. Thus the dogmas of religion must be resolved, in terms of

[23] Cf. H. Stephan, *Geschichte der deutschen evangelischen Theologie seit dem deutschen Idealismus* (Berlin, 1960 [2]), pp. 160f. Cf. also G. Runze, *Bruno Bauer, Meister der theologischen Kritik* (Berlin, 1931), p. 21.

[24] Its most sensational upshot was the denial of the historical reality of Christ, in the early work *Das Leben Jesu* (Tübingen, 1836; ed. Zeller, *C. W.*, Vol. IV [Bonn, 1877]) which made Strauss famous. His overall interpretation of the truth of Christianity is to be found in his systematic work: *Die christliche Glaubenslehre in ihrer geschichtlicher Erscheinung und im Kampfe mit der modernen Wissenschaft*, 2 vols. (Tübingen-Stuttgart, 1840-41). On the "Hegelian" origins and evolution of Strauss' atheism, cf. especially the two essays of H. Maier: "D. F. Strauss," in *Verhandlungen des III. Internationalen Kongress der Philosophie* (Heidelberg, 1908), especially pp. 179ff.; and "D. F. Strauss," in *An der Grenze der Philosophie*, pp. 268ff.

[25] On this point, Strauss is critical of Hegel for having conceded Christianity a special status, higher than that of the other religions (cf. *Die christliche Glaubenslehre*, Vol. I, p. 15). The so-called "historical Christ" whose reality is enveloped in "myth" must yield to the "ideal Christ" and this "ideal Christ" is, for Strauss as for Hegel, the ideal human type; and thus we have a "transformation of the religion of Christ into the religion of humanity" (K. Barth, *Die protestantische Theologie im 19. Jahrhundert* [Zurich, 1947], p. 501).

their kernel of truth, into philosophical truths and philosophy must take the place of faith: exactly as Hegel maintained, what dogmas and religious myths are expressing in sense images and sensible terms comes to be expressed by reason by the instrumentality of the universality of the concept, or, in plain words, is brought back to the limits of the human reality in its historical flux and evolution.

Strauss himself confesses at the outset of his writing career [26] that his point of departure is the demolition of Christianity and religion by the Spinozan principle, in the tradition of Reimarus, Lessing, Kant, etc.: to attain to his true happiness, man must fulfill his eternal nature, i.e., must apply himself to developing the powers innate in himself rather than clutching at contingent facts. Thus the really important assignment for every human being consists not so much in coming to know "historical Christianity" as rather in trying to realize within himself "ideal Christianity", which is simply generic humanity in its complete and infinite perfection. This is the transition from the religion of Christianity to the religion of humanity. The idea of human perfection Strauss holds to be, like the other ideas given to the human Spirit, an embryonic idea that germinates little by little under the influence of experience and proportionately to the aptitudes of the various peoples and civilizations and the spiritual riches of the individual personalities of history. Christ's life and teaching certainly make him one of the most outstanding personalities of human history but even in this towering personality there were gaps: family life and political activity, art and artistic enjoyment, are all missing from his life and teaching; and these are "substantial gaps" (*wesentliche Lücken*) that have to be filled in. Jesus cannot therefore be conceived as the God-Man, as what God has introduced into humanity; accordingly he cannot be pointed to as an ethical model (*Muster*) to be imitated and believed in by man as a condition for man's felicity. It is impossible to admit that the whole perfection of the species is exhibited in a single individual; only the "genus" as a whole corresponds to the Idea. Only the genus (*Gattung*), therefore, is the bearer of the fullness of humanity. Man and God are essentially related: mankind is the Son of God, the deity itself effects in man the consciousness of this essential unity by attaining to knowledge of itself. At death, the individual loses his own autonomous personality to return into the Absolute which is the One Whole.

This is the hard core of the new "atheistic" theology.[27]

It is mankind as a whole, not the single individual, that accomplishes the union of the two natures, the incarnate God, the infinite God who

[26] Cf. *Das Leben Jesu,* Schlussbetrachtung; pp. 386ff.

[27] G. C. B. Punjer, *Geschichte der christlichen Religionsphilosophie seit der Reformation* Vol. II (Braunschweig, 1880), pp. 264f.

alienates himself in finitude and recalls his own infinity. It is the genus, mankind as a whole, that continually dies, rises again and ascends to heaven—thus actualizing the Gospel "myth"—in its unceasing effort to rise above its material conditions in order to attain ever higher goals of its own civilization. With one bound, the young Hegelian had leaped directly from Christology to atheism by the intermediary of the Enlightenment-Hegelian notion of the species or humanity, mankind.[28]

Strauss' work has a significance, therefore, similar to Feuerbach's: the "anthropological disintegration" of religion. But Strauss effects this disintegration, paradoxically enough, in even a still more negative way than Feuerbach.[29] Although Feuerbach did indeed invert the Hegelian view and put man in the place of God, he at least continued (as we shall note below) to attribute a positive heuristic value to religious ideas as hints, albeit quite inadequate imaginatively distorted ones, of the content and value of universal humanity. Strauss on the contrary stresses that religious knowledge is positively blemished: it is not even worthy of the status of a "popular metaphysic". Strauss always sees the root of religion in the reason, in the cognitive impulse, in the need the spirit feels to know its own identity (*Wesensgleichheit*) with universal Reason. But philosophy and religion have nothing but their starting point in common for they diverge forthwith: religion into the aberrations of the imagination and the blind aspirations of instinct, philosophy into scientific and speculative investigation.[30] And so Strauss stigmatizes as false the Hegelian formula of the identity of content and diversity of form of knowledge as between religion and philosophy. This removes not only all possibility of reconcilation between religion and philosophy but even any relevance or significance of the dogmas of theology for the knowledge of the real. Religion, says Strauss in a close approach to Schleiermacher, is purely affective and not rational in origin; it arises from the "feeling of dependence" and the desire for happiness pushed to infinity: this thrust impels man to extend his causal conclusions beyond the sphere of experience and to conclude to the existence of God and of divine powers. Thus Strauss, too, like Feuerbach, Bauer, Marx and Engels, was liberated by Hegel and in turn liberated himself from Hegel

[28] A historian of Protestant theology has therefore remarked: "Strauss cannot be said to have deviated substantially, by this step, from the tenor of the Hegelian philosophy, even in its Christological dimension" (F. H. R. von Frank, *Geschichte und Kritik der neueren Theologie insbesondere der systematischen seit Schleiermacher* [Erlangen and Leipzig, 1894], p. 171).

[29] Strauss himself confessed in this connection: "Indeed theology itself is only productive to the extent that it is destructive" (*Die christliche Glaubenslehre,* p. 264).

[30] Cf. H. Maier, "D. F. Strauss," *Verhandlungen,* pp. 188f.

by the instrumentality of Hegel[31] to swerve in his later years to positivistic materialism.

From the critique of the divine person of Christ, the God-Man, Strauss proceeded resolutely to the critique of the concept of God as a goal of modern philosophy.[32] The "philosophical concept" of God as Absolute of itself destroys the (Judeo-Christian religious concept of God as Father of men. Actually, as Kant has demonstrated, not one of the traditional proofs (ontological, cosmological, moral and the rest) can stand up to the criticism of an illicit extrapolation, and Kant is known to have built up his *Critique of Pure Reason* without any reference to God. And Fichte, says Strauss, went even further in the systematic period of his philosophical career, when he defined God as the moral order of the universe, rejecting the notion of a personal God as contradictory. The God-notion we find in the younger Schelling is derived from Spinoza's notion of substance and amounts to the notion of God as the absolute identity of the real and the ideal. Schelling, therefore, had no idea whatever of a personal God apart from the world. And finally, Hegel with his principle that (Spinozan) Substance is to be conceived as subject or Spirit left his commentators an enigma (*Rätsel*) and his followers an escape route (*Ausflucht*). Some of these followers saw in this precisely the acknowledgement of a personal God, while others, appealing to Hegel's clearer formulations and to the whole spirit of his system, proved that this amounted merely to positing becoming and evolution as an essential element of the Absolute; moreover, they saw the thought, the knowledge of the deity in man being contrasted, as the knowledge of the ideal existence of God, with the knowledge of nature as real existence.

Schleiermacher has been still more outspoken and unanswerable on this point, continues Strauss, in his atheist estimate of modern thought.[33] Schleiermacher's *Reden über die Religion* already showed that it was to him a matter of small importance whether the Being we feel ourselves simply to be dependent upon be conceived as personal or impersonal; and even the assertions in his *Glaubenslehre* were not exactly calculated to dissipate the impression of pantheism that hangs over

31 "Hegel's philosophy had liberated him; it had clarified for him the relation between idea and reality, brought him to a deeper understanding of speculative christology and opened his eyes to that mysterious interpenetration of finitude, God and man" (A. Schweitzer, *Geschichte der Leben-Jesu-Forschung* [Tübingen, 1926 4], pp. 80f.).

32 I am here following the exposition in *Der alte und der neue Glaube,* §§ 36ff.; *C. W.*, ed. E. Zeller, Vol. VI, pp. 70ff.

33 Strauss' special predilection for Schleiermacher is well known (Cf. *ibid.*, §§ 17-19, pp. 27ff.).

his whole way of thinking. He does indeed say that the two ideas, God and the world, are not identical from one point of view. When we think God we posit a unity without plurality; when we think the world we posit a plurality without unity. Thus the world is the sum total of opposites, and God the negation of all oppositions. Yet, from another point of view, it is impossible to conceive one of these two ideas without the other. As soon as we try to conceive God prior to the world or without the world, we realize that we have before us only an empty image created by the imagination; nor are we able to posit any other relation between God and the world except their coexistence (*Zusammensein* They are not the same thing but they are "simply two values for the same thing". Moreover, both ideas are but empty thoughts, blank notions (*unausgefüllte Gedanken*), mere outlines, which we can only fill up and bring to life by restricting them to the scope of the finite, as when we conceive of God as a conscious and absolute Ego. Schleiermacher is therefore in agreement with Fichte. And we can add, concludes Strauss, that these principles contain the net result of the whole of modern philosophical speculation on the God-problem. The God-concept depends on the operation whereby, to employ Schleiermacher's formulation, in the conception of being, the element of unity is separated from that of multiplicity, the unity is posited as the cause of the multiplicity and consciousness and intelligence is attributed to that unity in view of the fact that the multiplicity here in question appears as a totality structured in terms of an end or purpose. But since the precise conception of being demands only that being be conceived as unity in multiplicity and *vice versa,* the supreme Idea ultimately emerges simply as the idea of the universe.[34] This can be enriched and will in fact be enriched and filled out with everything that we recognize in the natural and moral world as power and life, as order and law; but we shall never be able to transcend that world and any effort or desire to imagine an author of the universe as an absolute personal being will only result in our creating for ourselves a mere picture of the imagination. The whole of what has been thus far said, i.e., the whole of modern philosophical thought, clearly indicates and confirms this sobering reflection. And any effort to conceive of personal immortality will inevitably meet with the same fate.[35]

This puts an end to all rational theology; nor is there any justification for invoking the "feeling of dependence, as does Schleiermacher. This feeling of dependence is not, in fact, the only path followed by man in his approach to God. Feuerbach has shown, declares the atheist theolo-

[34] *Ibid.,* § 39, p. 80.

[35] *Ibid.,* §§ 40-41, pp. 81ff. Cf. O. Pfleiderer's severe denunciation of Strauss' superficiality in his *Die Entwicklung der protestantischen Theologie seit Kant und in Grossbritannien seit 1825* (Freiburg i. Br., 1891), pp. 131ff.

gian Strauss, that man has through the ages fashioned for himself a religion and lifted himself up to God likewise and preeminently because of his desire to assert himself, because of his need to react against the state of dependence and oppression he feels in the face of nature, and to recover his freedom.[36]

It is in the return from this "positive alienation" that modern thought has "overcome" the God-problem and finally laid the foundations for the edification of the new man: the place of God is not left vacant, it is taken over by the "world," [37] not the worst of all possible worlds, but the best!

This last work of Strauss is known to have suffered a ruthless and savage critique at the hands of Nietzsche in the first of his *Unzeitmässige Betrachtungen* (Thoughts Out of Season).[38] Nietszche castigated Strauss for his slovenly and muddled style and accused him of a total failure to understand the capital products of modern thought or to appreciate the way in which that thought has been linked with religion in general and Christianity in particular; and Nietzsche lashes out at what he feels to be the reason for this dereliction of Strauss, namely, his compliant acceptance of a most unwholesome and morbid realism (an allusion to Strauss' acceptance of Darwinism!). Strauss, cries Nietzsche, has not the faintest suspicion of the basic antinomy between idealism and the drastic relativity of all science and rational articulation: he is no longer in any position to understand Kant because he has been corrupted by Hegel and Schleiermacher. But the worst example of the infamous vulgarity of Strauss' entire mental attitude is, for Nietzsche, his inability to offer any other explanation of the dreadfully serious instinct of negation and the dreadfully serious thrust toward an ascetic sanctity in the first centuries of the Christian era than a piffling allusion to an alleged surfeit of sexual pleasures in the immediately preceding period and a consequent malaise and nausea. This stupid approach accounts for Strauss' distorted picture of the ancient anchorites and saints and indeed of Jesus himself, whom Strauss describes as a fanatic whose resurrection Strauss is unwilling to accept because, snaps Nietzsche, it conflicts with that "universal history humbug" (*welt-historischer Humbug*)! Despite his theological past and his pretended transition to

[36] "To this extent Feuerbach is right in saying that the origin and indeed the very essence of religion is the wish. Had man no wishes he would not have had any Gods either" (*Der alte unde neue Glaube,* § 42, p. 90).

[37] *Ibid.,* pp. 96f.—This represents an all-out transition on Strauss' part to scientific positivism (Cf. Ch. III: *Wie begreifen wir die Welt,* especially pp. 103ff.).

[38] F. Nietzsche, *Unzeitmässige Betrachtungen,* Erstes Stück. David Strauss, der Bekenner und der Schriftsteller (1873); *C. W.,* Vol VI (Munich, Musarion, 1922), pp. 129ff.

philosophy, Strauss has never really understood Christianity;[39] and the pitifully small amount that he has learned from philosophy can be deduced from his identification of philosophy, in his old age, with science and his designation of it as "the new faith". Much better the old faith, snorts Nietzsche. None of the modern investigations into history or nature bring an ounce of grist to the mill of that pantheistico-materialistic faith professed by Strauss in the All, the Whole, about which, unlike the ancient Stoic, he has nothing intelligent or even intelligible to say! Most reprehensible of all is Strauss' way of speaking of God and of Jesus Christ and his total ignorance concerning the origin of religion. Strauss is a sad and typical example of the "Philistinism" and degeneracy of Germanic culture which is producing creatures with the courage of a lion on paper (*auf dem Papier*) but not before witnesses where a Christian or indeed any believer generally shows his mettle.[40] These wretched Philistines are the victims primarily of a theology already contaminated to the core by a vacuous and decadent philosophy.

Before concluding this section on Strauss, the first instance of a public precipitation of the atheism latent in Hegel, we must recur to a remark already made and to be repeated in the sequel: the atheism that transformed the whole cultural pattern and the generic conception of life in the Western world, from the death of Hegel (1831) to our own times, derives from manifold factors and influences, negative and positive, but the most operative of them all and the one that at a certain moment clearly got the upper hand is indubitably the Hegelian interpretation of religion. The efforts of the Hegelian Right to contain the thought of the master within the limits of a tolerable orthodoxy were obviously doomed to failure. This does not mean that Hegel's approach and attitude was free from ambiguity. In season and out of season Hegel lavishes the most passionate eulogies upon religion[41] and especially on Christianity for having brought the world the certainty of the unity of God and man, the bridging of the gap between the finite and the Infinite and for having simultaneously clarified the basic notion of freedom, whose principal forms he claimed, as we have seen, that Christianity's dogmas expressed as elements of the very activity of the human mind. Christianity, there-

[39] In the first rough copy of the work, sketched out in the form of letters, we read in No. 10: "He has no concept of Christianity" and again in No. 18: "No philosophy" (*ibid.*, p. 224).

[40] Cf. *Der Wille zur Macht,* § 841; *C. W.*, ed. Musarion, Vol. XIX, p. 239; *Was den Deutschen abgeht,* Vol. XVII, p. 101. And elsewhere, under the heading "The Impious of the Land" (*Die Unfrommen vom Lande*), we read: "Strauss. Philistinism is the real impiety (*die Philisterei ist die eigentliche Unfrömmigkeit*)"; *Gedanken,* Vol. VII, p. 234.

[41] Cf. *Philosophie der Religion, C. W.*, ed. Lasson, Vol. I (Leipzig, 1921), p. 1ff. Cf. also *Philosophie der Geschichte,* pp. 270ff.

fore, differs quite drastically from all other religions and philosophies of antiquity, and its distinctive feature is a notion which, even in the Hegelian pantheistic philosophy, ought to have been recognized and acknowledged as being operative within the whole evolution of the Western mind. Yet, when he is summarizing the main stages of the evolution of human thought, which led to the formation and molding of modern thought, Hegel entirely forgets Christianity. He mentions specifically Parmenides' notion of being, Plato's universal, Aristotle's concept, the abstract subjectivity of the post-Aristotelian systems (Stoics, Epicureans, Skeptics), the Neo-Platonists' conception of thought as a whole or totality; but then he overleaps a thousand years to come immediately to Descartes-Spinoza-Leibniz and to Kant, ending with the Absolute Idea of transcendental idealism wherein all the oppositions are so beautifully resolved.[42] This provides the Hegelian Left and the atheists of our own day with a new argument, and one of the most cogent ones, for their contention that they have on their side the man who was the most controversial, but likewise the most radical and committed philosopher of immanentism.

[42] Hegel, *Geschichte der Philosophie,* Vol. III, pp. 619ff.—Yet in his exposition of Spinoza's thought, Hegel had asserted: "The only difference between our standpoint and that of the Eleatic philosophers is that because of Christianity, concrete individuality is quite present to the mind of the modern world" as opposed to the still abstract Spinozan Substance (*ibid.,* p. 337). And again: "But the content of Christianity, which is the truth, has as such remained unchanged and therefore has no further history or as good as none" (*Geschichte der Philosophie,* Introduction, ed. J. Hoffmeister [Leipzig, 1944], p. 17).

2
From Hegelian Theology to Anthropology (Feuerbach)

Although the Hegelian Left was unanimous in its drastic enucleation of the atheism implicit in Hegel, it followed no clear or coordinated plan. The theological wing, including Bauer and Strauss, concentrated more directly on the consequences of Hegel's philosophy of religion for the whole method of theology and of the historical treatment of the initial emergence and shaping of Christianity. Meanwhile the philosophical wing, including Feuerbach, Marx and Engels [1] proceeded to a drastic clarification of the new meaning of man in the wake of the "death of God". Marx gives Strauss the credit for having begun the "process of decomposition" of the Hegelian system and is sharply critical of the "limitations" of the critique effected by these theology-prone Young Hegelians. The "Old Hegelians" had resolved "everything", including the religious categories, into abstract logical categories; but the Young Hegelians *criticized* everything by substituting religious categories or by considering everything to be theological. Thus the Young Hegelians agree with the Old Hegelians in their belief in the hegemony of religion, of concepts, of the universal in the existent world. Their critique accordingly produced nothing more than a certain elucidation (and an imperfect elucidation at that!) of the origins of Christianity.[2] They never even had an inkling of the crucial problem that was crying to be dealt with after the death of Hegel, namely, the investigation of the connection (*Zusammenhang*) of German philosophy with the

[1] There seems to me no evidence in Marx's own writings that he attributes *Die Posaune* to Bauer. Marx does indeed devote himself (together with Engels) at great length to Bauer's historico-philosophical ideas which he subjects to a ferocious criticism. Cf. *Die heilige Familie* (MEGA, P.I. Vol. 3; *K. Marx-F. Engels Werke,* Vol. II [Berlin: Dietz Verlag, 1958]; English translation, *The Holy Family* [Moscow: Foreign Languages Publishing House, 1956]).

[2] K. Marx-F. Engels, *Deutsche Ideologie,* I, Feuerbach; *K. Marx-F. Engels Werke,* Vol. III (Berlin: Dietz Verlag, 1958), pp. 18f.

German situation, the connection between their criticism and their material environment. Feuerbach is one of these young dreamers but Marx and Engels agree [3] in crediting Feuerbach's critique with having taken the crucial step in the radical liberation from religion which is the first step on the road to the "building of the new man". Marx specifies that both Strauss throughout all his writings and Bauer in his 1841-42 essay on the Synoptic Gospels, as also in *Das entdeckte Christentum* (1843) still remained, at least potentially, sheer prisoners of the Hegelian logic. Thus, for instance, in this latter work of Bauer, Hegel's own expressions can be read word-for-word; and Bauer seems entirely oblivious to the fact that his attitude to the Hegelian dialectic has remained entirely unaltered, despite his material criticism of Hegel.[4] Elsewhere Marx specifies that the Strauss-Bauer controversy about *substance* and *self-consciousness* is a controversy *within the framework of* Hegelian speculation. In Hegel there are two elements, the *Spinozan substance* and the *Fichtean self-consciousness;* and these two elements Hegel tries to fuse into the necessarily contradictory Hegelian notion of *Absolute Spirit.* The first element is that metaphysical travesty of nature resulting from a *separation* of nature from man; the second element is that metaphysical travesty of Spirit resulting from a *separation* of Spirit from nature. The third, specifically Hegelian element is a metaphysical travesty of the unity of the two, *real man* and *real mankind.* Strauss is consistent in his development of Hegel from the *Spinozan point of view;* Bauer is equally consistent in his development of Hegel from the *Fichtean point of view.* But both remain within the framework of theology. Both criticize Hegel for having used one of the two elements to *falsify* the other; and then each goes on to develop one of these two elements *unilaterally* and therefore logically! Both go beyond Hegel but both remain *within the framework of* his speculation and simply represent respectively the one or the other aspect of his system.

Quite different, observes Marx, was the attitude of Feuerbach who

[3] As is amply proven by the famous statement in the 1844 Manuscript: "Positive humanistic and naturalistic criticism dates only from Feuerbach. His writings have exercised an influence that is all the solider, profounder, wider-ranging and more lasting for being so unobtrusive. They are the only works since Hegel's *Phenomenology* and *Logic* to embody a genuine theoretical revolution" (K. Marx, *Zur Kritik der Nationalökonomie,* MEGA, Part I, Vol. 3, p. 34; ed. H.-J. Fueter & P. Futh, Vol. I [Darmstadt, 1962], p. 508). A few paragraphs earlier, Marx refers to the haughtiness of the theological wing of the Hegelian critics and reports a series of expressions typical of Bauer, without actually mentioning him by name (*ibid.,* p. 33; ed. Fueter-Futh, p. 507).

[4] If *Die Posaune* is indeed Bauer's work, as claimed by many experts, then this judgment of Marx seems to us inaccurate. Yet Marx seems to have actually collaborated with Bauer in this work, at least to some small degree.

was the first to achieve a thoroughgoing critique of Hegel *from the Hegelian point of view.*[5] Feuerbach resolved metaphysical *Absolute* Spirit into "real man who has nature for foundation". He pushed the *critique of religion* to its extreme by laying down, in brilliant and imposing fashion, the principles for *the critique of Hegelian speculation.*[6] Thus the evolution of explicit and constructive, i.e., positive atheism is more than simply the most striking historical fact of the modern age, in the political and sociological fields; it is an event which necessitates a thorough and uncompromising retrospective examination of the essence of modern thought in terms of that *principle of immanentism* which constitutes its main axis and has given rise to the new definition of man by inverting the relationship between being and thought, between the mind and reality. Dialectical materialism is not the only historical end product of this principle; but few of its rivals are as radical as it is. And this is all the more significant when it is taken into consideration that the "atheism" of dialectical materialism flows precisely from the disintegration and denunciation of the gratuitous and unfounded assumptions, not only of the conservative Hegelian theologians, but of the pseudo-revolutionaries as well.

The chief artisans of this spiritual revolution knew what they wanted. And the fact that their opponents were so surprised and scandalized by their atheistic and materialistic conclusions serves merely to highlight the lassitude of an age and a culture buried forever by the harsh reality of its own spiritual tension.

The transition from Hegel to Feuerbach, which marked the crucial point in the expulsion of God from the modern world, is therefore no mere bolt from the blue. Rather it resembles that lightning bolt that hits and splits open the trunk of a tree already dead and rotten within. It signals the inevitable end of a whole era, an end prepared and precipitated by the tilting bias of a whole civilization and culture.[7] The transi-

[5] Feuerbach himself declared: "I consider myself to be more intimately related to Hegel and more indebted to him than to any other thinker" ("Feuerbach Verhältnis zu Hegel," in *Nachlass,* ed. K. Grün, Vol. I [Leipzig-Heidelberg, 1879], p. 387; *C. W.,* ed. Bolin-Jodl, Vol. IV [Stuttgart, 1905], p. 147).

[6] Marx-Engels, *Die Heilige Familie,* MEGA, p. 147. Later, amid the ironical castigation of Bauer's "absolute Criticism" there are indications of a greater regard for Strauss' work (p. 150). In *Deutsche Ideologie,* the thought of Strauss is designated as "pantheism" (p. 159), and it certainly represented a force no less corrosive of religion and deism than was Feuerbach's. Engels informs us that Strauss' *Leben Jesu* was in circulation, in English translation, in proletarian circles, together with Proudhon's *La propriété* (Cf. *Die Lage der arbeitenden Klasse in England* [Leipzig, 1845]; *Marx-Engels Werke,* Vol. II, p. 455).

[7] For an up-to-date overall exposition of Feuerbach's thought on religion, cf. W. Schilling, *Feuerbach und die Religion* (Munich, 1957). Feuerbach's relation to Hegel is dealt with quite superficially and Schilling seems to miss the origin-

tion to an open declaration of atheism and Feuerbach, as opposed to Bauer, is a positive affair: what Hegel had said of God is attributed to man, the qualities and properties of perfection declared by Hegelian theology to be exclusively those of God are here declared to be a reality simply the "perfections of the human species"; the "species" is the reality, not the alleged essence of God. The new principle is therefore not so much an inversion of the Hegelian outlook as rather what I think might be fairly called its transference from the sphere of the metaphysical Absolute to the existential sphere of humanity in act. This reading is bolstered by a consideration of the second element or principle of positivity in the "reform of the Hegelian dialectic" undertaken by Feuerbach, namely, the Feuerbachian treatment of Christ as intermediary between the abstract Absolute and existent man: in Feuerbach still more than in Hegel and Strauss and in contradistinction to the Deist-Enlightenment tradition, the Christian "dogmas" of the Trinity, the Incarnation and sin are vehicles, adumbrations and "myths" which contain and manifest the kernel of real truth about the human being. Thus Christ and Christology become indeed "mediators" but no longer in order to lift man to a knowledge of the life of God and of his relation to man, but rather to lead man to the knowledge of the truth of his own natural being. The third positive element in this resolution or dissolution of the divine into the human is precisely the "transition" from the abstract (the Absolute) to the concrete (man),[8] but man still considered in the

---

ality of Feuerbachian thought. On this point, the Catholic author G. Nüdling has been more successful in culling the essential elements. Cf. his article "Die Auflösung des Gott-Menschenverhältnisses bei Ludwig Feuerbach," in the anthology, *Der Mensch vor Gott,* Festschrift Th. Steinbüchel (Düsseldorf, 1948), pp. 208ff. This article is a summary of Nüdling's longer work, *L. Feuerbachs Religionsphilosophie,* Die Auflösung der Theologie in Anthropologie, first published in 1936, now in its 2nd edition, Paderborn 1961. On the transition from Hegel to Feuerbach, cf. our: *Feuerbach-Marx-Engels: materialismo dialettico e materialismo storico* (Brescia, 1962), pp. xxiff., to which we likewise refer the reader for Feuerbach's epistemology and especially for his strange theory of "mediate sensibility".

[8] Fichte Jr. likewise acknowledges this transition or "resolution": "It [Hegelian philosophy] loses entirely the real character of religion; subjectively it can only admit a bare minimum of the religious consciousness, and objectively it must put forward a specifically different concept of that consciousness. If the Absolute is actualized *only* in man's self-consciousness, if man, mankind, is God positing Himself into consciousness and realizing Himself there and there alone, then religion is *objectively* nothing more than this divine-human mental process of the ingress of the Idea into a finite self-consciousness to assume there a personal form" (I. H. Fichte, *Ueber die christliche und unchristliche Spekulation der Gegenwart,* p. 21). This seems to us the very crux of Feuerbach's own critical stance in his examination of *The Essence of Christianity.* Fichte sums it up excellently, a little later on in the same work, in these words: "Religion, man's consciousness of God is man's consciousness of himself" (p. 30).

Hegelian sense of the universal in act; the concrete is not the individual but the species, humanity inasmuch as it is always and everywhere.

This is the obvious sense of the principle: "The secret of *theology* is *anthropology,* but *theology* is the secret of *speculative philosophy,* i.e., speculative theology which is distinguished from *common* theology by the fact that it posits in the "here", i.e., makes *present, determined and definite, realized,* that divine essence, that divine nature which common theology, out of fear or incomprehension, had posited in the remote beyond." [9] Feuerbach's theoretical importance in the disintegration of Hegelianism and the shaping of present-day atheism lies entirely, in my opinion, in this self-confinement within the dimension of the immanent. He is therefore significant, not so much for his lapse into sensualism and materialism (as both idealist and positivist historians of thought have maintained), as rather for his elucidation of the crucial point that, in the wake of the *cogito,* the being of the world is the limiting horizon for the existent who is man. Thus, paradoxical though it may sound, it is essential to understand Feuerbach's continuity with Hegel in order to grasp the significance of the violent blow administered by Feuerbach to 19th-century European philosophy. Feuerbach, too, is faithful, after his own fashion, to the principle of the transcendental: he, too, insists that the real must be understood as being that which is rendered present by the *cogito,* i.e., the *human mind in its act of knowing;* Feuerbach's modification (amounting indeed to an inversion) of the Hegelian position lies in Feuerbach's insistence that we are here dealing at rock bottom with an act of sense knowing, of sense awareness. Feuerbach remains faithful to Hegel likewise in his interpretation of religion and especially Christianity,[10] both of which he still continues to interpret positively (as opposed to Marx-Engels, as we shall soon note below). They are expressive of a real, albeit imperfect, stage of the progress of the human spirit, a stage whose imperfection is eliminated by Hegel via the *Aufhebung,* the ascendent movement toward the absolute Concept (*Begriff*), but by Feuerbach via the return to sensible man, man as a sensing being. For both, then, Christianity with its symbols and its dogmas expresses the structure of the communal human consciousness of the "species" wherein is actualized the truth of the being of man. The Christian religion is a still mythical and mystical sociology and anthropology.

[9] Feuerbach, *Vorläufige Thesen zur Reform der Philosophie,* 1843; *C. W.,* ed. Bolin-Jodl, Vol. II (Stuttgart, 1904), pp. 222f.; *Kleine philosophische Schriften,* ed. M. G. Lange (Leipzig, 1950), p. 55.

[10] Cf. in this connection Ch. I of *Das Wesen des Christentums* where Feuerbach treats of the "essence of man" (*C. W.,* ed. Bolin-Jodl, Vol. VI [Stuttgart, 1906], pp. 1ff.).

Unquestionably Feuerbach was carrying on, on this crucial point, the approach of Strauss, who in his *Das Leben Jesu* (1836) had introduced that concept of "species" (*Gattung*), as ultimate truth of the human being, the concept which was via Feuerbach to function in Marx-Engels as the final catalyst of the transformation of the metaphysical Absolute into sheer and pure immanence. Feuerbach makes the Christian dogma of the union of the two natures, divine and human, in the divine person of Christ into a mythical representation of the relation between the individual and humanity, in the sense that humanity is that whole which has need of unfolding itself in an infinite succession and number of singular individuals: thus, the Incarnation becomes the "myth" of this relationship and Christology the key of philosophy.[11] The following passage from Strauss gives in a nutshell the idea that Feuerbach was to make central to his own exposition:

"Can this attribution of reality to the idea of the unity of the divine and the human natures by any stretch of the imagination be made to mean that this divine nature has actualized itself but once in one single individual as never before and never afterward? But the idea does not actualize itself by pouring into one single individual the fullness of its reality and scrimping with all the others, by expressing itself perfectly in that One and never more than imperfectly in all the others; rather the idea loves to exhibit its wealth in a plethora of copies mutually complementary, mutually positing and mutually exclusive. And must not this be the true reality of the Idea? Will not the Idea of the unity of the divine and human natures necessarily be a real Idea in an infinitely more lofty sense if I comprehend the whole of humanity in its actualization rather

[11] In a letter dated November 22, 1822, which Feuerbach sent to Hegel together with the text of the thesis *De ratione una, universali infinita* (Cf. Feuerbach, *Briefwechsel und Nachlass,* ed. K. Grün, Vol. I [Leipzig-Heidelberg, 1874], pp. 214ff.), Feuerbach explicitly states his intention to criticize Christianity as a religion of the beyond and consequently a denial of the sensible world of intuition. In the early part of this long letter, Feuerbach extols the power of religion, but only insofar as it is manifested in the intuition of the senses and incarnate in the world. He then goes on to assert the need for a new age of the autocracy of the reason (*Alleinherrschaft der Vernunft*) which is calculated to impart at last to philosophy the comprehension of the All, the Whole: all will become Idea and Reason, a new history and a new creation. The letter concludes with a specific attack on religion in general and Christianity in particular, charging that Christianity is simply and solely (*nur*) the antithesis of the world of antiquity and that Christianity's chief dogma does not succeed in redeeming the reason, being directed rather to the person: "*It* [the reason] *lies there uncomprehended, mysterious, not taken up or incorporated into the unity of the divine being. Only the person* (*not nature, the world, the spirit or mind*) *celebrates its redemption . . . And so reason is surely not redeemed in Christianity*" (p. 218; italics Feuerbach's).

than singling out individuals as such? Is not an incarnation of God from all eternity truer than one single such incarnation at a definite point in time? The key to the whole of Christology is that the subject of the predicate which the Church assigns to Christ is posited not as any one individual, but rather as an Idea; a real Idea, however, not an unreal one as in Kant. If you try to think of the properties and functions which Church teaching attributes to Christ as being present in one individual, a God-Man, then you are faced with a contradiction. But there is no such difficulty if instead you think of them as present in the Idea of the Species.[12] Humanity is the unification of the two natures, God made man, the infinite Spirit which becomes infinite in finitude in his alienation and mindful of his infinitude: Son of the visible Mother and the invisible Father, of Nature and Spirit; Wonderworker, inasmuch as Spirit in the course of human history assumes ever more power than nature in man as outside of him so that nature becomes subject to his activity as inert material reality. Humanity is sinless inasmuch as the course of its evolution is without stain, immaculate, for contamination attacks only the individual; humanity is he who dies, rises again and ascends to heaven, inasmuch as it derives an ever more exalted spiritual life from the negation of its own maturity and its own unity with the infinite Spirit in heaven from the transcendence of its own finitude as

[12] The famous Catholic theologian and contemporary of Feuerbach, F. A. Staudenmaier, likewise accepts the inevitability of the disintegration of idealist pantheism first into materialism and then into atheism. There are, he grants, two forms of pantheism, one which dissolves the world into God (acosmism, Berkeley) and the other which dissolves God into the world (transcendental idealism). But the first of these forms evaporates into an illusion, leaving only the second which is atheism sheer and simple: "And with this atheism is already present and pantheism's unwillingness to allow the world to subsist side by side with and outside of God as an Other, a distinct entity, created and ruled by a personal supramundane God, has already identified that pantheism as atheism. Hegel's phrase, *Without the world God is not God* is soon converted into the contention: *God is nothing but the world,* and this in turn soon takes the final form: *only the world is and God is not.* And if there lingers inconsistently any God whatever, it is a shadowy God, a God devoid of truth, reality, and life, a God amounting to nothing more than an empty word or name". And Staudenmaier continues with a scarcely flattering evaluation of the German philosophers: "Germans, scions of a pious and religious-minded nation, have thus denied *God* and *immortality* with an *impudence* and *shamelessness,* such as the world has perhaps never seen, even in the pagan age of antiquity; and in an effort to wrest the palm of atheism from the French, these Germans have articulated their denial with a boldness, ruthlessness and insolence, calculated to make Voltaire, Diderot and the most wanton of the Encyclopedists truly appear as innocent children" (F. A. Staudenmaier, *Die Grundfragen der Gegenwart* [Freiburg i. Br., 1851], pp. 37f.). For the further elaboration of this critique, the author refers the reader to his *Darstellung und Kritik des Hegelschen Systems* (Mainz, 1844), especially pp. 845ff.

personal, national and global Spirit. By faith in this Christ, in his death and resurrection, man is justified before God, i.e., by the revival of the Idea of humanity as such, the individual likewise becomes a sharer in the divine-human life of the species via the negation of negation, i.e., the negation of the natural and sensible state which is itself already a negation of the Spirit. This and this alone is the absolute content of Christology." [13]

Here, then, the implicit atheism of Hegel is rendered explicit, demanding and inescapable; and Feuerbach is one of the first to take this line, transmuting Strauss' theological anthropology into a naturalistic anthropology.

Feuerbach succinctly expresses the basic elements of this transmutation in these words: " 'Pantheism' [idealist pantheism, especially that of Hegel] is the *necessary consequence* of theology (or theism)—it is *consistent and consequential* theology; *'atheism'* is the *necessary consequence* of 'pantheism'—it is consistent and consequential 'pantheism' " [14]

This diagnosis seems to us quite oversimplified and more relevant to the "content" than to the "form" of thought: the atheism that stems from the Hegelian pantheism or panentheism has its real roots in the acceptance and radicalization of the principle of immanentism, as we have seen already and shall be discussing in greater depth in our conclusion. In Hegelian speculation, the theological element serves two purposes: that of providing an absolute status for the content and then further that of providing a schematic representation of the dialectical transitions or elements. Feuerbach cannot sustain his accusation against theology as such of having provided the principle of pantheism; the most he can do is to sustain, perhaps, as will Kierkegaard, this accusation against a certain type of theology like the Hegelian which is, as Bauer so aptly branded it, a synthesis of Spinozan Substance, the active Ego of Fichte and the dialectic of contraries of Proclus-Böhme. And Feuerbach simply develops the Straussian principle and inflates it into a system, especially in his major work, which bears the felicitous title *Das Wesen des Christenthums* (1841), a title perfectly indicative at once of what Feuerbach was aiming at enucleating and what he has utterly failed to express with his erroneous and underhanded approach and his weirdly mottled end product. The whole of the Hegelian duality-tension between finite and Infinite is downgraded and bowdlerized into a synthesis of I

[13] D. F. Strauss, *Das Leben Jesu,* Vol. II (Tübingen, 1836), pp. 734f. (Cited in M. Reding, *Der politische Atheismus* [Graz-Vienna-Cologne, 1957], pp. 98f. Reding presents an accurate review of the evolution of the anthropological principle by the Hegelian Left.)

[14] Feuerbach, *Vorläufige Thesen,* p. 223; ed. M. G. Lange, p. 55.

and Thou in human relations; for the Hegelian tension Feuerbach substitutes human sympathy, which he pompously and pretentiously designates as a dialectic or "dialogue of I and Thou." [15]

We are presently interested less in a detailed investigation of the Feuerbachian articulation of this transcendental sensistic anthropology than in a depth-probe into Feuerbach's establishment of a new type of transcendental—"man as the object of man"—which constitutes the original element, what we have also designated above as the positive and constructive element, of the new "atheism" derived from the *cogito* and above all from the burrowing into the very germ plasm of the Hegelian Absolute. We shall limit ourselves to the Introductory chapter of *The Essence of Christianity,* which contains the exposition of the pith of the whole work. But this chapter we shall dissect with a thoroughness dictated by the seriousness of the subject matter and the undeniable interest of the new method.[16]

Feuerbach begins by asserting that religion presupposes the essential distinction between man and animals. He pinpoints this essential difference as being "consciousness" (*Bewusstsein*), not in the generic sense of that word, for then it would apply to animals as well, but rather in the strictest sense, in which it connotes a being having as its object its own "species" (*Gattung*), its own essence (*Wesenheit*).[17] Only in this latter sense is consciousness the capacity for science and science is the "consciousness of species" (*Bewusstein der Gattungen*). In everyday life we have to do with individuals, in science with species. It is only a being who has for object its own species, its own essence, who is able to have as objects other things or beings according to their essential nature. We

[15] "The true dialectic is not a monologue of a *solitary thinker with himself; it is a dialogue between I and Thou*" (*Grundsätze der Philosophie der Zukunft,* § 62; *C. W.*, Vol. II [Stuttgart, 1904], p. 319; ed. M. G. Lange [Leipzig, 1950], p. 169; English translation by Manfred H. Vogel, *Principles of the Philosophy of the Future* [Indianapolis-New York-Kansas City: The Library of Liberal Arts, Bobbs-Merrill, 1966], p. 72). It is probable that the title of Feuerbach's most famous work is itself of Straussian origin. Feuerbach saw in Strauss ". . . the man who had finally spoken a word to his age, a word in season, a frank and free word" and Feuerbach castigates the heads of the German Universities, "men stupid and spiteful as beasts, who had attacked him" (Letter of November 1, 1837 to his friend Chr. Kapp; *Ausgewählte Briefe; C. W.*, ed. Bolin, Vol. I [Leipzig, 1904], p. 313).

[16] Cf. the English translation by George Eliot, *The Essence of Christianity,* (New York, Evanston and London: Harper Torchbooks, Harper and Row, Publishers, 1957), pp. 1-32.

[17] Feuerbach reproaches traditional materialism with its failure to recognize that man is a new kind of being: "The obtuse Materialist says: 'Man is distinguished from the brute *only* by consciousness—he is an animal with consciousness superadded;' not reflecting, that in a being which awakes to consciousness, there takes place a qualitative change, a differentiation of the entire nature" (*Das Wesen des Christenthums,* p. 3 Note; English translation, p. 3 Note 1).

have here the same old principle of immanentism, as is patent, with its content the universal mind of man, universal human knowledge; but this is an immanence-horizon much narrower and more constricted than that of Hegel's all-embracing Concept (*das Allumfassende*). But right here at the outset, Feuerbach trips over his own feet: immediately after attributing to man, as distinct from animals, the capacity of speaking with himself, and performing on his own the functions of the species, he proceeds to assert that individual man in fact exercises these functions of the species via the I-Thou dialectic!

If religion arises in man in virtue of his nature, then, says Feuerbach, it arises inasmuch as man knows himself and inasmuch as this knowing-himself is not merely the basis but also the object of religion, as Strauss had maintained. Religion arises as "consciousness of the infinite" (*Bewusstsein des Unendlichen*), and since this consciousness is nothing more than self-consciousness, religion is the consciousness that man has of himself, of his own essence (as species), yet again not of that essence as finite and limited but rather as *infinite*. Feuerbach indeed proceeds to insist, as a good Hegelian, that consciousness in the strict and proper sense and consciousness of the Infinite are inseparable and that consciousness is essentially infinite and all-embracing in nature. But since the object of consciousness is here that consciousness itself, what is called consciousness of the Infinite is nothing more than consciousness of the "infinity of consciousness" (*Unendlichkeit des Bewusstseins*). Precisely in the case of man, his peculiar consciousness of the Infinite has as its object the *infinity* of man's *own* essence.[18] There is the crux of the new transcendental anthropology. Feuerbach throughout makes every effort to be consistent with this realistic immanentism and we have good reason to follow him attentively, even though the issue seems vitiated from the outset.

Not only does man develop himself; the very constitutive powers of man, reason, will, affection (*Vernunft, Wille, Herz*) are made to develop themselves for their own sake (*um seiner Selbst willen*). Thus, the "divine trinity" which Hegel evaporated into the abstract dialectic is in fact the operational unity of reason, will and love. These are the powers that operate in man and dominate him; yet this unity transcends the individual man and is his transcendental constituent (this last term is ours, not Feuerbach's) whose power no individual human being can resist; it is an absolutely irresistible power that sweeps all obstacles away before it (and this Feuerbach does expressly say). Love, will, reason are therefore not individual, personal principles, pursues our

[18] Hence the constantly recurring critique, already mentioned, of the notion of man as an "individual" (cf. *ibid.*, pp. 8ff.; English translation, pp. 8ff.).

"naturalistic" Hegelian; rather they are powers of the species which dominate and ought to dominate the individual, his passions and his impulses. Hence, he says, we can understand how the *object* of man is man himself, i.e., his own objective essence; and Feuerbach actually writes "consciousness of the objective is the self-consciousness of man". The objectivity of being is therefore nothing more than the projection of consciousness, of the mind (Hegel had called it the "result"): "We know the man by the object, by his conception of what is external to himself; in it his nature becomes evident; this object is his manifested nature, his true objective *ego*." [19]

The religious sublimation or alienation results from the failure to distinguish between the individual and the species, the failure to attribute those constitutive forces of love, will and reason, to the species of their transfer instead outside of man into an imaginary Being independent of man: religion simply excises man's powers, properties and attributes and then divinizes them as an independent being or nature.[20] Here again we see the Straussian principle still at work, this substitution of the *Gattung* for the deity; this is the appeal to Hegel in order to transcend Hegel by invoking humanity above and beyond and superior to the individual: "The *absolute* to man is his own nature. The power of the object over him is therefore the power of his own nature." [21] In Feuerbach, the Hegelian *Bewusstsein* (consciousness) becomes *Selbstbewusstsein* (self-consciousness), focus and principle of truth. For Feuerbach as for Hegel finitude and non-entity coincide and truth henceforth can only be present as a concrete universal, as infinity in act. Thus the self-actualization of consciousness is "the immediate verification and confirmation, corroboration of itself" (*die unmittelbare Bewahrheitung*

[19] *Ibid.*, p. 6; English translation, p. 5.

[20] A recent critic remarks: "He [Feuerbach] believes himself to be defending against Hegel the truth of Hegel's own dictum that the species precedes the individual" (K. E. Blockmühl, *Leiblichkeit und Gesellschaft*, Studien zur Religionskritik und Anthropologie im Frühwerk von L. Feuerbach und K. Marx [Göttingen, 1961], p. 33). In his earlier critical essay *Ueber Philosophie und Christenthum* (1839), written under the inspiration of Strauss to acquit Hegel of the charge of being un-Christian (*Unchristlichkeit*), Feuerbach asserts that the notion of *Species* (*Gattung*) goes back to Kant rather than Hegel (*C. W.*, ed. Bolin-Jodl, Vol. VII, p. 69); this essay already contains the basic principles developed in the major work *The Essence of Christianity.*

The fact remains, however, that Hegel was the one to dissolve the individual into the concrete Universal as a mere element, moment or appearance of that Universal; and this dissolution of the individual is likewise absolutely basic to the Strauss-Feuerbach notion of *Gattung* (Species). Feuerbach is quite justified, however, in his contention that, if Hegel be accused of atheism for having reduced God to the *Gattung* and thus destroyed Christianity, then the same charge must be levelled against Kant, Fichte, Herder, Lessing, Goethe, Schiller et al. (p. 77).

[21] *Das Wesen des Christenthums*, p. 6; English translation, p. 5.

und Bekräftigung ihrer selbst). We are, for all practical purposes, in an atmosphere of existential phenomenology; and certainly in a *Lebensphilosophie* of the first order, something really quite new to the philosophic mind and tradition of the West.[22] Thus the conclusion, so far as religion is concerned, is quite inescapable: religion, as the assertion of an infinitely perfect Being outside of man and called God, is nothing else than the extrapolation or severing, the "alienation"—(*Entäusserung, Entfremdung*) to use the terminology of Hegel which will be taken up again by Marx—of man from his own perfection. Thus the denial of God is the crucial step toward the vindication and authentication of the being of man.

The extrapolation which gives rise to religion Feuerbach attributes to the power of feeling for feeling is *the* constitutive element of the essence of religion and of Christianity in particular. But in fact (and, indeed, likewise according to traditional Christian belief) feeling as such is atheistic because it is an essentially subjective attitude: it denies an *objective God;* feeling is God unto itself. If feeling then is the essence of religion, religion collapses of itself inasmuch as it becomes a direct and apodictic argument in favor of the "atheistic structure" of the human mind, of human consciousness.

This remark we accept entirely if it be referred to the consciousness of the *cogito,* of the *volo* (as it is both by Feuerbach and the whole of modern and present-day philosophy), i.e., to the principle of immanentism. Feuerbach's definition of religion, thus considered, is quite in line with the one given by that very Hegel whom he wanted to transcend: "Consciousness of God is self-consciousness, knowledge of God is self-knowledge." [23] And what has hitherto been called "atheism" is in reality simply the most positive negation that can and should be made, the reintegration of the universal consciousness of man in its proper place as "subject" of its own infinite perfections. We cite Feuerbach's concluding definition in this matter verbatim for it is of special importance for our own investigation: "Religion, at least the Christian, is the relation of man to himself, or more correctly to his own nature (i.e., his subjective nature); but a relation to it, viewed as a nature apart

[22] "Consciousness is self-manifestation, self-affirmation, self-love, joy in one's own perfection. Consciousness is the characteristic mark of a perfect nature" (*ibid.,* pp. 7f.; English translation, p. 6. [We have departed from the Eliot translation by one word: "self-manifestation" where Eliot had written "self-verification"; her rendering seems to stem from a misreading of *Selbstbethätigung* in the original as *Selbstbestätigung*—Translator's Note.]).

[23] *Ibid.,* p. 15; English translation, p. 12. And later in the same work we read: ". . . in the nature and consciousness of religion there is nothing else than what lies in the nature of man and in his consciousness of himself and of the world" (p. 27; English translation, p. 22).

from his own. The divine being is nothing else than the human being, or, rather, the human nature purified, freed from the limits of the individual man, made objective—i.e., contemplated and revered as another, a distinct being. All the attributes of the divine nature are, therefore, attributes of the human nature." [24] Religion is therefore quite simply an instance and phenomenon of anthropomorphism. This is Feuerbach's fundamental critique of it.

But Feuerbach likewise assigns special importance and devotes a special consideration to the term "existence" (*Existenz*) and to the problem of the existence of God. The certitude of the existence of God, he remarks, depends on the certitude of a certain quality of God and is therefore not an immediate certitude. But what does the predicate indicate? What does "existence" signify? The concept of being, of existence, is the primary and primordial concept of truth. Thus, like the good immanentist he is, Feuerbach equates "being" and "existence". Now, since in religion man is simply "objectivizing", *separating from himself* his own attributes and conceiving God as "abstracted" from the world, nothing more than an abstract existence belongs to God; and this cannot have any meaning, not even for believers.[25] Infinity or the divine essence, continues Feuerbach, is the spiritual nature or essence of man, but isolated from man and represented as a nature or essence subsisting by itself. In fact, to say that "God is spirit, really means to say that spirit is God . . . God is not this or that spirit, mine or thine . . . as an individual spirit: God is spirit in general and yet is individualized or personified like the concept of humanity, which as species (*als Gattung*), in contradistinction to the individuals, exists as a thought species [i.e., has the mental being of a universal idea]". Feuerbach reduces the difference between monotheistic Christianity and polytheistic paganism to the simple fact that paganism distinguishes between being and thought, whereas Christianity unifies the two; this is the real and only meaning of the Thomist concept of pure act.[26] God, then, is not this or that spirit, yours or mine; he is Spirit sheer and simple but he has been thought and represented as an individual, single, independent man (*als ein singulärer, einzelner, selbstständiger Mensch*). God is generically precisely as the concept of individual or personified species, which, as

[24] *Ibid.*, p. 17; English translation, p. 14.

[25] Feuerbach's conclusion: "Existence, being, varies with varying qualities" (*ibid.*, p. 25; English translation, p. 20).

[26] *Das Wesen des Christenthums,* Erläuterungen, Bemerkungen, Belegstellen, p. 338. These Erläuterungen (Explanations) are catenae of Patristic and Scholastic texts, with preference given to St. Thomas, with almost all of whose works Feuerbach demonstrates his familiarity. [In the Eliot translation, these appended sections have been severely curtailed and rearranged. We have therefore made our own translation—Translator's Note.]

species, is thought as the species existing distinct from the individuals. God is the totality and quintessence of all realities means that God is the totality and quintessence of all species and all concepts of species. The difference between paganism and Christianity in this regard is that for the pagans the species was a thought essence [i.e., a "being of reason"] which has existence only in the real sensible individuals, whereas for the Christians the species as such has as thought essence an autonomous existence of its own! The pagans distinguish thought and being, the Christians identify the two. Polytheism rests upon the distinction of thought and being, of species and individual; monotheism rests upon the unity of these two pairs.[27]

Religion therefore is lacking in an object, or better, in a "subject"; it is a totally deserted temple, an illusion, an empty mirage. But Feuerbach seems not at all pleased at the prospect of being called an atheist and seeks rather to turn the charge back upon his accusers: "The negation of the subject is held to be irreligion, nay atheism; though not so the negation of the predicates. But that which has no predicates or qualities, has no effect upon me; and that which has no effect upon me has no existence for me. To deny all the qualities of a being is equivalent to denying the being himself . . . The denial of determinate, positive predicates concerning the divine nature is nothing else than a denial of religion, with, however, an appearance of religion in its favor, so that it is not recognized as a denial; it is simply a subtle, disguised atheism." For Feuerbach the concept of God depends on the concepts of justice, goodness, wisdom, which can therefore be conceived by themselves and independently of God; accordingly the denial of the subject (God) does not actually involve the denial of the predicate. In fact we know that such predicates, indeed the predicates in general, are sustained solely by the common consciousness (or mind) of man as universal Subject. And inasmuch as "divine" means the excellence of qualities which transcend the limitations of the individual and belong to the "species" as such, these predicates of universal value and infinite perfection can perfectly well be said to be "divine" even without God; indeed they emerge as truly and really divine only with the suppression of the fictitious and unreal subject and the substitution in its place of the only real and true subject, which is man. In this sense it is possible to speak of a "transformation of the sacred" in the work of Feuerbach, but only "so to

[27] *Ibid.*, p. 341. This thesis is bolstered throughout with texts of Aquinas, taken from the *Summa contra Gentiles* and the *Summa Theologica.* In his brilliant *Das Wesen des Glaubens im Sinne Luthers* (1844), Feuerbach shows how the theological God-man antithesis has been exacerbated in Protestantism, which has taken it to involve a veritable affirmation-negation tension, as opposed to Catholicism, which grants a positive status and value to human nature as such.

speak".[28] The proper way to designate Feuerbach's accomplishment seems to us to be quite simply to speak of his obfuscation, his mystification and his mythologization of the sacred!

Conclusion: God, as he has been conceived by philosophy and theology, is nothing but the psychological projection of the infinitized human consciousness or mind. For Feuerbach, God is not a physiological nor yet a cosmic being but a psychological being. Hence, in religion, man is seeking himself or is himself as object, an object serving the purpose of a God. The *mystery of the Incarnation* is said to be the mystery of God's love for man; in fact it is the mystery (i.e., mythical expression of the love that man bears to himself. The *mystery of the Trinity* is the mystery of participated social life, the mystery of I and Thou. The creation out of nothing expresses the non-divineness (*Ungöttlichkeit*), the non-essentiality, i.e., the nothingness of the world. The nothingness out of which the world was created is its own nothingness. And after his review of the fundamental truths of Christianity, Feuerbach declares—as opposed to Hegel who saw in the Incarnation the theological expression of his own speculative thesis on the dialectical unity of the divine and the human—that "The Christian religion is a contradiction. It is at once the reconciliation and the disunion, the unity and the opposition, of God and man. This contradiction is personified in the God-man".[29] Thus Feuerbach has been rightly charged with a total and radical anthropologization of Christ.[30]

The orthodox Hegelianism of this Feuerbachian approach and attitude leaps to the eye of the most casual observer. And it robs the much-touted atheism of the Hegelian Left of any claim to real originality.[31] For Feuerbach, just as for Hegel, it is man who knows himself and that self is consciousness in the modality of self-consciousness, the absolute truth as the true absolute identity of all oppositions and contradictions; for consciousness that becomes self-consciousness cannot be anything but man, human consciousness, the human mind; and so there is no

[28] Cf. H. Arvon, *Ludwig Feuerbach ou la transformation du sacré* (Paris: P.U.F., 1957).

[29] *Das Wesen des Christenthums,* pp. 345ff.; English translation, p. 332.

[30] "Feuerbach retains all the predicates and functions of the Christ of ecclesiastical Christology and ascribes them to man" (K. E. Blockmühl, *Leiblichkeit und Gesellschaft,* p. 34).

[31] There is a patent influence of the strictest Hegelian semantics in this latest of Feuerbach's long line of definitions of religion as man's self-objectification of his being and the transformation of this object into a Being distinct from himself: "Man—this is the mystery of religion—projects his being into objectivity, and then again makes himself an object of this projected image of himself thus converted into a subject; he thinks of himself, is an object to himself, but as the object of an object, of another being than himself. Thus here. Man is an object to God" (*Das Wesen des Christenthums,* p. 37; English translation, pp. 29ff.).

need for us to follow the complicated gymnastic whereby Feuerbach attempts to reduce the religious activity in all its truths and actions, and the dogmas of Christianity in particular, to mere inflations, exteriorizations, extrapolations and alienations of the universal human consciousness, the generic human mind.

It will be useful to return at this point for a moment to Hegel, the chief if not the only culprit in this "atheism complaint". For Hegel it is not Being but Life, Truth in itself and by itself and the whole manifold that is displayed in nature as exteriority and in (finite) spirit as history, which is a manifestation or "appearance" or "phenomenon" (*Erscheinung*) of the Absolute. Thus Hegel seems from one point of view to be neglecting sensible reality and man himself, considered in his particularity and individual personality, for both are relegated into the sphere of the phenomenon and fated to "disappear" in the course of time. But, from another and no less important point of view, the Absolute, in virtue of that very principle we have already mentioned ("without the world God is not God" [32]), has no activity of his own but rather accomplishes his activity in the world and in history and can be said virtually to breathe only with the breathing of history which is solely human history. And this is the most serious ambiguity in Hegel and the one that split his school into the two opposing wings. And Hegel himself explains his own meaning in this matter so clearly as to preclude any equivocation or misunderstanding, e.g., in the following closely-packed and significant passage:

"The fact that man knows God is, in virtue of the essential community, a common knowing: i.e., man only knows God inasmuch as God in man knows of himself; this knowing is a self-knowing, a self-awareness of God; but it is equally a knowing of God by man; and this knowing of God by man is a knowing of man by God. The mind of spirit of man that knows of God is but the mind or spirit of God himself. And that

[32] Feuerbach certainly has in mind likewise the following text of the *Enzyklopädie* in which Hegel extols the superiority of philosophy over religion and of reason over faith. Hegel remarks that the knowledge of God cannot be satisfactorily attained in the poor-quality imaginative pictures of faith (*schlechte Vorstellungen des Glaubens*) but requires an advance to conceptual thought and is therefore the business of the philosophers rather than of the amateurish and slipshod theologians, who are content to conclude simply that we know nothing of God. Hegel continues: "There is need for painstaking and accomplished speculation in order to put into a clear-cut and adequate thought what God is as Spirit. The following principles are involved, in the first instance: God is God only insofar as he himself knows himself; this self-knowledge of his is further his self-consciousness (awareness of himself) in man, and it is man's knowledge of God progressing to man's knowledge of himself (self-knowledge) in God" (*Enzyklopädie der philos. Wiss.*, § 564, ed. J. Hoffmeister [Leipzig, 1949], p. 472). Hegel refers to Göschel's *Aphorismen,* which we have already mentioned.

disposes of all the questions about man's freedom, about the connection between his knowing and his individual consciousness or mind, on the one hand, and the knowing in which he is in community with God, the knowing activity of God in him, on the other." [33]

The transition from the Hegelian *Geist* (Spirit) to the Straussian and Feuerbachian *Gattung* (Species) was already inherent in the very bias of the speculative cast proper to and indeed absolutely essential to Hegelian thought, i.e., the dialectic nexus between the finite and the Infinite. Strauss, as we have seen, swung from idealism to anthropological materialism along the arc of the theological problematic of the shaping of Christianity and the structure of the faith. Feuerbach effects the same leap or swing but on a much deeper level and within the very framework of the theoretical tension of idealism, freeing from the superstructure of pseudo-theology the genuine content of a consciousness whose backdrop and scaffolding is exclusively the world of nature and man.

The real significance of that "doubt" wherewith Descartes initiated modern thought lies in thc distinction between confused ideas and clear and distinct ideas and the consequent demand for a critique of the knowing act in order to arrive at certitude. This instituted the "genetico-critical" method in philosophy. This line of approach was adopted, insists Feuerbach, by Kant, Fichte and Hegel too, whose *Logic,* despite the mystical image he uses in his Preface,[34] is the purest product of his free philosophical spirit. The Hegelian philosophy is the restoration of philosophy from its decline *within* the very age of that decline. The grandeur and the genuine philosophical treasure in Hegel's *Logic* is to be found precisely in that for which the majority of his opponents reproached him, namely, the effort he there made to mold a Logic and a Metaphysic *in se et per se,* cut loose from any grounding in a subject or an Absolute. But apart from the particular historical idiosyncrasies and

[33] *Philosophie der Religion,* ed. Marheineke, Vol. II, p. 496. This passage is a restatement of § 564 in the *Enzyklopädie.*

There can be no doubt that Feuerbach had in mind this Hegelian conception and indeed this precise passage when he made his articulation of the crucial point in his own dissolution of God into man: ". . . if in the consciousness which man has of God first arises the self-consciousness of God, then the human consciousness is, *per se,* the divine conciousness. Why then dost thou alienate man's consciousness from him, and make it the self-consciousness of a being distinct from man, of that which is an object to him? Why dost thou vindicate existence to God, to man only the consciousness of that existence? God has his consciousness in man, and man his being in God? Man's knowledge of God is God's knowledge of himself? What a divorcing and contradiction! The true statement is this: man's knowledge of God is man's knowledge of himself, of his own nature. Only the unity of being and consciousness is truth" (Feuerbach, *Das Wesen des Christenthums,* p. 278; English translation, p. 230).

[34] Feuerbach does not specify whether this is the Preface to the 1st edition (1817) or to the 2nd (1831).

personal antipathies that exercised a disturbing influence on Hegel, he was even more seriously still under the domination and in the thrall of that very spirit that had led to the "decline of philosophy" and consequently to the return of all the ancient superstition in the area of theory and practice alike, in a word, to all the barbarities of the 19th-century world. There is, cries Feuerbach, but one foundation and one law for philosophy: freedom of spirit, freedom of mind, freedom of consciousness, freedom of conscience are synonomous designations for that spirit.

What need is there, he protests, of systems? What we need is investigation, free inquiry, genetico-critical research. Instead of speculating on the Trinity, on the Incarnation and on the dogmas of the Church in which we have been born and brought up, in order to demonstrate and prove them to be the only true and rational ones, we ought rather to investigate the essence of religion, the essential peculiarity of its doctrines and their origin, not merely the historical origin that rationalism was always seeking, but rather the interior spiritual origin. Descartes' philosophy thus gave philosophy a genuine foundation by basing it upon the act of criticism, the act of self-conscious and self-knowing thought, clear and distinct. It threw out, first of all, the obscure, irrelevant, immaterial and meaningless qualities and the substantial accidents of the Scholastics; and therewith it shattered the foundations of the dogma of transubstantiation, despite Descartes' own efforts to reconcile it with his philosophy. In general, the spirit of Descartes' philosophy, as a critical philosophy, is totally opposed to the spirit of Catholicism. The subjection of the believer and the autonomy of the doubter cannot live together under one roof: hence can be seen how unhappy was the attempt of philosophers like Huet, La Mothe la Vayer and their like to reconcile piety with skepticism.[35]

When he wrote these remarks, Feuerbach's Hegelian loyalties may well have still been strong and his sensist bias barely nascent; but his decision in favor of atheism was, on the contrary, already mandatory, as a corollary to his loyalty to the "principle of freedom" instituted by Descartes in modern thought, elaborated by Kant's categorical imperative, and taken to its extreme conclusion in Fichte's *Sittenlehre*.[36] Nie-

[35] L. Feuerbach, *Pierre Bayle*, ch. III; *C. W.*, ed. Bolin-Jodl, Vol. V, pp. 134ff.; and especially ch. VII, pp. 256ff. with the pertinent notes on pp. 413ff.

[36] "Atheism, which met with so much scorn and contempt, was nothing else than the necessary and therefore salutary transitional step from the empirical God, the God objectively standing over against the thinker as an external thing, from the God about whom the vulgar question could be asked: Is there a God?, from the God who precisely for this reason was a *controvertible* and *disputable,* far from divine (*ungöttlichen*) God, to idealism, to the notion of the Spirit, to the concept of *the divine in and of itself,* to the autonomous, unalloyed comprehension of the essence of nature as the essence of the moral Idea" (*ibid.*, ch. V, p. 210). Cf. also the pertinent Note 10 on pp. 400f.

ther anthropologism nor sensism nor materialism, those successive way-stations of Feuerbach's philosophical saga, were the real basis of his atheism; this atheism flowed immediately from the principle of consciousness, being but the outright acceptance of the *cogito,* an acceptance disencumbered of all superstructures, theological or systematic. The Hegelian concept of man as *Gattung* (Species) is far more important and operative in Feuerbach's philosophical endeavor [37] than are the materialistic overtones which, despite their consistency, represent a confusing and complicating element and a source of ambiguity and equivocation which we shall find again in Marxist atheism.

Feuerbach considered himself to be the liberator of modern thought and modern man from the internal contradictions of the idealist philosophy and from the metaphysical and theological fetters in which that philosophy was entangled. He held the identification of thought and being, which he said was the central doctrine of the philosophy of identity, to be nothing but a necessary consequence and development (*Ausführung*) of the concept of God, whose concept or essence includes being in the sense of *esse.* The identity of thought and being is simply the expression, said Feuerbach, of the divinizing of reason, of the persuasion that thought or reason is the absolute Being (*das absolute Wesen*), the totality and quintessence of all truth and reality. But the identity of thought and being actually expresses simply the identity of thought with itself.[38] And it is in this thought, understood as reflection on the sensible or "sensible consciousness" [consciousness of the sensible], that the essence of freedom and consequently the essence of man consists, for Feuerbach as well. Hegel pretends to effect the reconciliation of irreconcilables: faith and unbelief, theology and philosophy, religion and atheism, Christianity and paganism; thus his negation or denial of God, his atheism remains within the framework of the synthesis and God is defined as a process (*Prozess*) and as an element of this

[37] In the Appendices to the *Grundsätze zur Reform der Philosophie,* we find we find a perfectly clear-cut statement on the concept of "Spirit": "What is the 'Spirit'? How is it related to the senses? As the genus is related to the species. The senses are universal and infinite, but only in their own field, in their own species, the Spirit on the other hand is limited to no definite field, is sheerly universal; it is the compendium, the unity of the senses, the embodiment and sum (*Inbegriff*) of all realities, whereas the senses are but the embodiment and sum of definite, limited, exclusive realities. The Spirit is therefore non- and supra-sensible, inasmuch as it is over and beyond the particularity and limitation of the senses, blending their provincial spirit into a common spirit; but the Spirit is at the same time simply the essence of sensibility, inasmuch as it is simply nothing other than the common and generic unity of the senses" (*Grundsätze zur Reform der Philosophie,* II; *C. W.,* ed. Bolin-Jodl, Vol. II, p. 354).

[38] *Grundsätze der Philosophie der Zukunft,* § 24; *C. W.,* Vol. II, p. 282; ed. M. G. Lange, pp. 128f.

process of atheism; this Hegelian God is therefore a contradictory God, an atheistic God (*ein atheistischer Gott*).[39] This is the contradiction inherent in all idealist metaphysics.

From this point, Feuerbach proceeds, even before Marx, to the transcendence of atheism itself: to speak of atheism makes sense only so long as it makes sense to speak of theism; but when God and theism have lost all meaning and become mere nonsense syllables, atheism likewise no longer has any meaning, or at most a historico-cultural meaning referring to ages in which the human race was still in a stage of arrested development. That synthesis attempted by modern philosophy, charges Feuerbach, disintegrates into the negation of both the elements which it claims to have unified: actually modern philosophy is the denial of rationalism just as much as it is the denial of mysticism, of pantheism just as much as of personalism, of atheism just as much as of theism; or rather it is the unity of all these antithetical truths, being itself an absolutely clear and autonomous truth.[40] And Feuerbach claims—with good reason, it seems to us—that this dissolution or "precipitation" he has effected of the *cogito* into the sheer presence in act of reality thanks to sensible consciousness (*nur das Wirkliche, Sinnliche, Menschliche ist das Wahre* = only the actual, sensible, human is the true)—that this constitutes the final assignment of modern thought.

Religion and the religious consciousness thus disintegrate of themselves, like an empty rind, like a long-outmoded and irrelevant survival. The real question of the day is no longer the discussion about the existence or nonexistence of God but rather the discussion of the existence or non-existence of man. It is not whether God is essentially homogeneous with or heterogeneous from us but rather whether we human beings are homogeneous with or heterogeneous among ourselves; not how man shall get justice before God but rather how man shall get justice before men; not whether we are tasting in the bread of the altar the body of the Lord but rather whether we are getting the bread we need for our physical bodies; not the old conundrum of rendering to God the things that are God's and to Caesar the things that are Caesar's

39 *Ibid.*, § 21, p. 277; ed. M. G. Lange, p. 123. And earlier in the same work Feuerbach says: "Pantheism connected, therefore, atheism with theism, the negation of God with God . . . Pantheism is theological atheism" (*ibid.*, §§ 14-15, p. 264; ed. M. G. Lange, p. 108; English translation, p. 22). And in another work: "'Atheism' is inverse pantheism" (*Vorläufige Thesen ueber Philosophie; C. W.*, Vol. II, p. 224; ed. M. G. Lange, p. 56).

40 *Vorläufige Thesen,* p. 241; ed. M. G. Lange, p. 75. Löwith can therefore say with full justification: "Feuerbach's philosophy is thus a new start, a recommencement in the wake of the irrevocable end, not of *philosophy as such,* but certainly of *classical* German philosophy" ("L. Feuerbach und der Ausgang der klassischen deutschen Philosophie," *Logos* XVII [1928], pp. 327ff.).

but rather the imperious summons to render to man at long last the things that are man's; not the question of whether we be Christians or pagans, theists or atheists, but rather the business of proclaiming that we human beings, sound of mind and body, are, or are in process of, becoming free and active partners in everyday life. The man who knows and says nothing more about me than that I am an atheist, concludes Feuerbach, knows and says exactly nothing about me. The question as to whether there is a God, the tension between theism and atheism, was a matter for the 17th and 18th centuries; it is no longer relevant or meaningful in the 19th. I deny God. For me, this means that I deny the denial of man; for a celestial, illusory, imaginary status for man, which in real life inevitably degenerates into the negation, the denial of man, I substitute the status of sensible and real man, a status inevitably involving political and social consequences. For me, the question of the existence or non-existence of God is simply the question of the existence or non-existence of man.[41] Feuerbach can certainly not be faulted for any lack of determination and consequentiality in carrying a principle to its ultimate conclusion.

Let us here endeavor, in the light of Feuerbach, to pinpoint even more closely the sense and significance of the principle of immanentism as a lapse into atheism, for this has been and will continue to be the specific aim of our present study. In Feuerbach's precipitation of the atheistic sediment of that principle of immanentism there was effected a lesion basic for Marx, Engels, Lenin, for the existentialism of Sartre, Merleau-Ponty, Camus, and in general for all the brands of atheism that swarmed forth out of the decomposing carcass of idealism. The vital point is the profound difference between the speculative idealism of preceding centuries and this new denial of God.[42] And this point is so absolutely vital to our purpose that I crave indulgence for so insisting upon it. Actually, says Feuerbach, the notion of atheism, taken in its strictest sense, i.e., as speculative atheism, consists exclusively in the denial of the *existence* of God. Although the atheist does indeed likewise deny the essence of God, this latter denial is not the root of the evil but is merely a derivative ill. And so the specific concept of the atheist, his typical status in the history of thought, is that of a man who is taking away the existence of God, taking away existence from God. It is not that the atheist takes away God's existence by taking away his essence; rather it is that he takes away that essence only indirectly by taking

[41] Feuerbach, *Aus dem Vorwort zur ersten Gesammtausgabe; C. W.*, Vol. II, p. 403.

[42] I am here following Feuerbach's own exposition in Note 10 to chapter V of his *Pierre Bayle* (pp. 400f.).

away the existence. The being of God, the question of the existence of God, takes us into the *empirical* world. The existence of God, when affirmed, creates and gives rise to an *empirical* concept at most. The question: Does God exist? was identical, in conformity with the concept of being, in other situations which are not of immediate interest to us here, to the question: Do spirits exist? Does the devil exist? The whole question concerning the being (existence) of God was thus a question concerning the existence of a pluralizable being, a being of whom there could be many, a being which could be manifested by the things outside of us—in short, an exterior, objective, particular, *empirical* being. And this God-being was a being who had in him the essence of sensible being without any of the signs (*Zeichen*) of that sort of (sensible) being. And the fact that this being, whose very concept made him to be an object of experience, conflicted with real experience which did not give any sign or evidence of this God-being—this was the basis of atheism. Atheism doubted and denied, therefore, a being suitable and appropriate, by his very concept and nature, to be an object of *doubt,* of denial, of negation. It denied not the divine as such but simply an *atheistic* concept, as in fact the concept of being was! Thus far the amazing and instructive Feuerbachian apology for atheism.

Now, quite obviously, for Feuerbach and his philosophical kind, all efforts to prove or demonstrate the existence of God (all the efforts, that is, which had been made by modern philosophy with thought as their starting point) are bound to be vain and pointless: for they wish to conclude from the *interior reality* of reason to an exterior reality, to pluck from the thistledown of mental reality (spirit, mind) the full-blooded rose of an extra-mental reality, to derive from the concept a nonconceptual reality, a factual reality.[43] But thistles yield roses as little as they yield figs, and the only refuge from contradiction was atheism. Feuerbach called in question the principle of immanentism as little as did any of the others; and so he never saw that the first and fundamental contradiction, nay impossibility, is that of deriving being from consciousness and making being a function of consciousness. And in Feuerbach himself this impossibility was rendered still more patent by the fact that his appeal was exclusively to sensible consciousness.

[43] Cf. in this connection K. Löwith's essay, "L'achèvement de la philosophie classique par Hegel et sa dissolution chez Marx et Kierkegaard," in *Recherches philosophiques,* IV (1934-1935), pp. 232ff.

3

Anthropological Atheism to Naturalistic Atheism (Engels)

Engels was virtually self-taught in the field of philsosophy; and his philosophical work usually appears as inextricably bound up with, and even submerged in, that of Marx, with whom he collaborated, from earliest adult years, on several major works, such as *The Holy Family* and *The German Ideology,* both published in 1845. But the publication of his youthful writings [1] has revealed an Engels, who in his youth had lived through his own personal religious crisis, within the framework of that wider crisis that was unfolding in Germany in the first decade after Hegel's death and who was, at the time of his meeting with Marx, already much further along the same road. Engels had been fevered by the flame that was licking the whole of the German youth of that day, the flame lit by Strauss, Bauer and Feuerbach. Engels' forward march is a resolute one, free of all nuances, hesitations and equivocations; and he shows on occasion an incisive grasp of the problems and

[1] These are included in the *Marx-Engels Gesamtausgabe* (MEGA), I Abt., Vol. 2: *F. Engels Werke und Schriften bis Anfang 1844,* published for the Marx-Engels Institute, Moscow, by D. Rjazanov (Berlin: Marx-Engels-Verlag, 1930). H. Ullrich has made a study of the social and cultural environment of Engels' youth in his *Der junge Engels* (Berlin: VEB Deutscher Verlag der Wissenschaften, 1961, 2 vols.). Of the tangled politico-religious situation, Ullrich writes: "Orthodox Protestantism was a rabid enemy of political and intellectual progress. It defended the outmoded existence and hegemony of the already doomed feudal class and declared it to be inviolable, as willed by God. Its champions gave no quarter to any ideas or actions that went beyond or contradicted the dogmas of the Bible and were therefore in direct or indirect conflict with the feudal system. Each and every attempt of the progressive minds of the time to break the fetters in which orthodoxy had shackled human reason and to propogate the freedom of the human mind and spirit was condemned and every criticism attacking the allegedly God-given hegemony of the princely aristocracy or, still worse, religion itself, was decried as arch heresy" (Vol. I, pp. 66f.). But Engels' own religious crisis seems to us to have matured and been resolved under the pressure of quite personal reflection within the framework of the speculative religious problematic and under the combined impulsion of Strauss and Hegel (cf. Note 2 immediately below).

a remarkable power of consistency with principles: whoever starts from Hegel, Engels testifies, (and no one can start anywhere else at this period) can only end in atheism.

Strauss had been the chief influence in bringing Engels to Hegel,[2] and the young Engels expresses unqualified esteem for the author of the *Leben Jesu.* But the work of Bauer and later still that of Feuerbach as Feuerbach progressively clarified his own distinctively Feuerbachian principles and aims [3] exercised a profound influence on Engels' mind and helped impel him to that new interpretation of man disencumbered of any reference, positive or negative, to religion or theology, which Engels himself was later to carry to its logical extreme in collaboration with his famous friend Marx.

Initially Engels plunged headlong into reflections on theology, which netted him nothing but a mass of doubt and torment concerning the basic teachings of religion in general and Christianity in particular (providence, sin, redemption, inspiration of scripture, the life to come, etc.).

Here is how he describes his state of mind and soul in July 1839: "My religion was and is a blessed quiet peace and if I retain it after my death as well, I am content. Nor have I any reason to believe that it will be deliberately taken from me. Religious persuasion is an affair of the heart and its only relation to dogma is the extent to which this latter does or does not conflict with feeling. Thus can the Spirit of God bear

[2] Cf. in this connection Engels' 1839 correspondence with the Graeber brothers, conservative Protestants. For example, Engels calls the *Leben Jesu* ". . . an irrefutable work" (MEGA I, 2, p. 525) and hails Strauss, together with Theodor Mundt and Karl Kutzkow, as the standard-bearers of the new Germany: ". . . I know of only *one man* among our present generation who has such a mind, such power and such courage, and that is David Friedrich Strauss" (p. 532). He is Engels' hero and a sheer genius: "For I have pledged myself to the banner of David Friedrich Strauss and am a first-rate 'mythicist'; I tell you Strauss is a wonderful fellow and a genius and sharp-witted as they come" (p. 546). And Engels speaks of his conversion to Hegelianism: "For I am on the point of becoming a Hegelian; whether I will go the whole way I don't know yet, to be sure; but Strauss has shed so much light on Hegel for me as to make the whole business pretty plausible, I must say" (p. 552). On December 2, Engels writes: "I have now been brought by Strauss onto the straight and narrow road to Hegelianism" (p. 554).

[3] Any attempt to reduce Feuerbach to a mere old-fashioned romantic out-of-season or a synthesis of Fichte and Hegel, as do certain Marxist historians of thought who desire jealously to guard the absolute originality of Marx-Engels (cf. e.g. J. Vuillemin, "L'humanisme athée chez Feuerbach," *Deucalion* 4 [Neuchatel and Paris, 1952], pp. 22f.), involves a failure properly to understand Feuerbach's progressive discovery of "sensible being" within the framework of the principle of immanentism in the course of his increasing divergence from Hegel. Feuerbach shows ever greater penetration into this new discovery, climaxed by his *Summa* of post-Hegelian atheism, the *Essence of Christianity* (1841).

witness to you by means of your feeling that you are a son of God, but that it is the death of Christ which makes you so—that is not yet certain; were it otherwise, then feeling would be able to think and your ears to see. I pray every day, nearly the whole day, for truth, for *the* truth; I have been doing so ever since I began to doubt and yet I am not coming back to your faith. After all, it is written: ask and you shall receive. I am seeking the truth everywhere where I have any hope of finding even a vestige or a semblance of it. Well, I simply cannot acknowledge your truth as that which is eternal. But again it is written: seek and you shall find. Who is there among you who if his son ask him for bread will give him a stone? How much more your Father in heaven . . . The tears are flowing from my eyes as I write this; I am in great turmoil; but I feel that I shall not go down to perdition, I shall win through to God to whom my whole heart aspires. And this, too, is a witness of the Holy Spirit, upon which I wish to live and die, even if the Bible should say the opposite ten thousand times over." [4]

But at this period in the life of the young Engels, Schleiermacher's new theology, with its softening of the severity of the bible, is still acting as a counterbalance to the Straussian bias: "If you obey the bible," he writes to his friend Graeber, "then you would not be able to have anything more to do with me. In the Second Epistle of John (if I am not mistaken) it is written that one should not even greet the unbelievers, not even to say, "Hail"! to them. There are a plethora of such texts and they have always scandalized me. You must not go on doing what is written in the bible. Moreover, to call orthodox evangelical Christianity the religion of love seems to me the most stupefying irony. According to your Christianity, Fritz, nine-tenths of mankind will be unhappy and one-tenth happy; and that is supposed to be the infinite love of God? Think a

[4] Letter of July 12 to F. Graeber (MEGA I, 2, pp. 530f.). Engels was by nature religious-minded to an even greater extent, perhaps, than Feuerbach and in sharp distinction from Marx. Engels' religious-mindedness comes out clearly in his youthful writings: cf. in this connection the letter to F. Graeber of which we have just spoken. Among Engels' youthful writings is a poem to Jesus Christ (dated by Rjazanov in early 1837, at the time of Engels' Confirmation) which is an ardent profession of faith (MEGA I, 2, p. 465, lines 3-32). But Engels' father was already expressing concern about the boy in a letter to his wife Elisa: "Once again, may the good God be pleased to take the boy under His protection that his mind may not be corrupted. So far he has been developing an alarming thoughtlessness and lack of solid principle, side by side with his otherwise gratifying qualities" (MEGA I, 2, p. 463). Concerning the sincerity of his faith and of the sentiments expressed in his poetry, he was to write two years later to his friend F. Graeber who had completely misunderstood the whole situation: "You have misunderstood me in that matter of the poem of belief. I did not believe for the sake of the poem; I believed because I saw that I could not go on living without believing, because I repented my sins, because I needed communion with God" (MEGA I, 2, p. 530).

moment how mean and petty God must be if that were his infinite love. It is clear, on the contrary, that if there does exist a revealed religion, the God of that religion would be indeed greater than what reason shows us but could not be in contrast or conflict with the voice of reason. Otherwise the whole of philosophy would be not only pointless but downright sinful; but without philosophy, there is no culture (*Bildung*), without culture there is no humanity, without humanity there is in turn no religion . . . I can still go along with men like Schleiermacher and Neander, for they are consistent and they have a heart . . . For Schleiermacher especially I have a tremendous esteem."

And Engels goes on in an excited tone, baring his soul completely; and that soul emerges as profoundly different from Marx's who never had a single stirring of religious feeling. Engels at once tells his friend that he has been scandalized at the scorn (*Verachtung*) with which he speaks of the union with God and the religious life of the rationalists. Poignantly and powerfully he exclaims: "You rest easy in your warm bed of faith and have no idea of the struggle of us men outside on this question of whether or not there is a God. You do not know the pressure of the weight that we feel with the first doubt, the weight of the old faith in the moment of decision *pro* or *con,* whether to go on carrying it or shrug it off your back . . . Religion is an affair of the heart and whoever has a heart can be pious; if, on the contrary, a man's piety has its roots in the intellect or even in the reason, then such a man has no religion. The tree of religion grows out of the heart and gives protecting shade to the whole man and sucks its nourishment from the air of reason; but its noblest fruits are the dogmas; whatever is over and above these is from the evil one.[5] This is the teaching of Schleiermacher and I hold to it myself." [6]

But this Schleiermacherian buttress proves fragile indeed and under the implacable blows of Strauss' demythologization Engels sees all the main dogmas of Christianity collapse (inspiration of scripture, original sin, Trinity, Incarnation, virgin birth and the rest). And Engels confesses openly to his friend that he has leapt over the wall: "I have pledged myself to the banner of David Friedrich Strauss and am a first-rate 'mythicist'; I tell you Strauss is a wonderful fellow and a genius and sharp-witted as they come. He has cut the ground from under your theories, the historical foundation [of the Christian religion] is irremediably undermined and the dogmatic foundation will collapse on top of it. This Strauss is irrefutable." [7]

[5] Matt. 5, 37.
[6] Letter to F. Graeber; postscript of July 27 (MEGA I, 2, pp. 531ff.).
[7] Letter to F. Graeber, October 29, 1839 (MEGA I, 2, p. 546).

Hence, Engels' inevitable conversion to Hegel; unlike Feuerbach who turns to the philosophy of religion and the young Marx who will latch onto the *Philosophy of Right* and the *Phenomenology,* the young Engels finds his favorite fare in Hegel's *Philosophy of History,* but always as seen from the Straussian point of view.[8] Henceforth, Engels feels freed from every encumbrance and marches resolutely down the new road side by side with the neo-Hegelians.

From his new vantage point, Engels proceeds to show the consistency of Hegel's atheist stance as against the uncertainties of Kant-Fichte and the theistic deviation of Schelling on the one hand and against the fatuities of the conservative Hegelians on the other. The principle according to which philosophy must always fluctuate between two poles, seeking certainty now in the thing and now in the Ego, Engels ascribes to the effects of the Ego of Fichte on the "thing-in-itself" of Kant. This principle is certainly applicable to Schelling but never to Hegel.[9] Engels' commitment to Hegel grew rapidly in extent and profundity during the next two years, 1841 and 1842, athwart a violent polemic[10] against Schelling's attempt, upon his arrival in Berlin, to stake an exclusive claim to the new course of thought proclaimed by Hegel. Everything

[8] "His (Hegel's) *Philosophy of History* at any rate is just what I would have wanted to write myself. Be sure to get hold of Strauss' Sketches and Critiques, the treatment of Schleiermacher and Daub is wonderful. No other man can write so thoroughly, so clearly and so interestingly as Str(auss)" (MEGA I, 2, p. 552). In the last letter to F. Graeber (February 22, 1841), Engels teases his friend about the futility of his anti-Straussian polemic in the face of the new course philosophy has taken (pp. 562f.).

[9] Engels, *Immermans Memorabilien,* MEGA I, 2, p. 115. The General Staff of neo-Hegelianism has already been picked (cf. the article "Ernst Moritz Arndt," of January 1841, MEGA I, 2, p. 102, where we read: "Strauss will be permanently epoch-making in the field of theology, Gans and Ruge in the field of politics").

[10] Comprising three articles, two published anonymously and one under the pseudonym of Friedrich Oswald. Rjazanov has grouped them under the general title *Anti-Schelling.* One is a newspaper diatribe published in late November 1841, written under the strong impression made on Engels by Schelling's Inaugural Lecture (November 15) and entitled "Schelling über Hegel". The other two are longer and more elaborate articles: "Schelling und die Offenbarung," (written in late 1841 and early 1842); and "Schelling der Philosoph in Christo" (1842).

Kierkegaard, too, it will be remembered, had been in Berlin to hear Schelling and had also been deeply disillusioned, after an initial enthusiasm (Cf. Papirer 1841, III, 9, 179: "I am so happy to have heard Schelling's second lecture . . ."; and then in a letter to his brother Peter in February 1842: "Schelling chatters insupportably . . .", *Breve og Aktstykker vedrorende S. Kierkegaard,* ed. N. Thulstrup [Copenhagen, 1953], Vol. I, p. 109). Kierkegaard took notes on these lectures from November 1841 to February 1842 (as is shown by a reference in *Papirer* III, C, 27) and these notes have been published in a German translation by A. M. Kortanek, *Schellings Seinslehre und Kierkegaard* (Munich, 1962), pp. 98ff.—Kierkegaard's notes show none of the critical and polemical intensity of Engels and break off at the discussion of revelation and the Christian religion.

good in Hegel is Schelling's personal property, flesh of his flesh, is it? What a distortion, cries Engels. And that new edition of Schelling's *Identitätsphilosphie,* with his weird elucubrations on existence and "potencies" is destructive of the entire positive element in modern thought. Kant has freed rational thought from space and time and Schelling is taking existence from us now. What have we left? Engels brusquely observes that this is not the time to prove against Schelling that existence falls within thought, that being is immanent to spirit and that the basic principle of the whole of modern philosophy, the *cogito ergo sum,* cannot be so unceremoniously subverted simply by blustering words. Schelling's recourse to the fact of revelation is a lapse into the empirical sphere and Engels consoles himself with the assurance that, despite the exalted position Schelling has managed to obtain, the issue of the struggle is not for a moment in doubt, for never has there been such a rush of youth (and even the adversaries are constrained to admit this) to the banner of the neo-Hegelians; never has the thought that dominates this neo-Hegelian group been displayed with so much courage, feeling and talent on their part as just at this moment. And this strengthens our hearts, cries Engels, and stiffens our sinews against this new enemy; it assures us that the sword of enthusiasm is as trusty as the sword of genius.[11]

War had now been declared; and soon Engels, encouraged by Schelling's scant success in Berlin, was carrying the attack directly to the fundamental idea of the new attitude which his opponent, Schelling, had exhibited in his monumental *Philosophie der Mythologie* and *Philosophie der Offenbarung.* This was the idea of the reconciliation (*Versöhnung*) of faith and reason, of philosophy and revelation wherein was supposed to consist the second phase of his allegedly "positive" philosophy. In point of fact, says Engels, Schelling has here succeeded only in obfuscating and mythologizing the very essence of philosophy itself. Hitherto, philosophy had always set itself the task of comprehending the world as rational. What is rational is also free and necessary; what is necessary must be or become real. This principle is the bridge of the imposing achievements of modern philosophy in the practical sphere. Schelling, instead of following this straight road, swerves off on a curve, elects compromise, and, instead of asserting the rationality of the world, denies the rationality of philosophy. He introduces the distinction between reason (*Vernunft*) and non-reason (*Unvernunft*) and calls the rational the comprehensible (*begreiflich*) a priori and the irrational the comprehensible a posteriori.[12] He assigns the former to the "pure

[11] Cf. "Schelling uber Hegel," MEGA, I, 2, pp. 173ff.

[12] The original here has "begreiflich" repeated, which obviously makes no sense in the context (*ibid.,* p. 188, line 33).

science of reason" or negative philosophy, and the latter to the "positive philosophy" newly founded by himself. This is the first great dangerous break between Schelling and all the other philosophers, Engels hastens to comment: this is the first attempt to smuggle authoritarian faith into the free science of thought and together with that authoritarian faith the mysticism of feeling, the fables of gnosticism, fracturing the unity of philosophy and the integrity of any conception of the world by means of the supreme contradiction of making Christianity likewise the principle of philosophy. But all to no avail!

How, in fact, does Schelling go about his nefarious and impossible task? By refurbishing and trotting out again the Scholastic distinction of essence and existence, of the *quid* and the *quod,* the *Was* (what) and the *Dass* (the fact that), and then proceeding to assert that reason (*Vernunft*) teaches the *Was* of things, whereas experience demonstrates the existence or the *Dass*. But this, pursues Engels, would necessarily limit the field and scope of thought to the possible and entirely exclude from it the real world. Reason would be powerless to demonstrate or prove the existence of anything and would be constrained to accept as sufficient in this regard the witness of experience. But philosophy must deal with objects which, especially on the principles of a theist like Schelling, transcend experience, e.g., God; can reason then forget about existence? Schelling does indeed trot out a long discussion but it proves exactly nothing. To the question: Does God exist?, we must, on his own premises, reply most definitely No (*Nein!*). Schelling's principle is that reason should not occupy itself in pure thought with really existent things but rather with possible things; thus its object is indeed the essence of God but in no sense his existence. For the real God, then, there must be found another sphere than the purely rational one; the premise of existence must be things, which show themselves only in a second dimension, *a posteriori,* to be possible and empirical (*erfahrungsmässig*) in their consequences, i.e., real. Here the real difference between Hegel and Schelling comes out: Hegel asserts: "What is rational must also be real," [13] whereas Schelling says that "what is rational is possible".

Engels' critique penetrates implacably into the very heartland of the new "positive philosophy". Reason is proclaimed to be the *infinite potency* (*die unendliche Potenz*) of knowing. Now potency is the same as "capacity" (*Vermögen*): it seems as such to be entirely devoid of any content; yet it has a content and has it precisely without any cooperative act (*Aktus*) on its own part, otherwise it would cease to be potency,

[13] Hegel, *Philosophie des Rechts,* Vorrede; ed. J. Hoffmeister (Hamburg, 1955), p. 14. Cf. *Enzykl. der philos. Wiss.,* Einleitung § 6; ed. Hoffmeister, p. 36. The original is: "Was vernünftig ist, das ist wirklich; und was wirklich ist, das ist vernünftig".

because potency and act are opposed the one to the other.[14] This content then becomes of necessity immediate, innate; and since to every knowing there corresponds a being, only the infinite potency of being, corresponding to the infinite potency of knowing, can be. This potency or power of being, this infinite power-to-be (*Seinkönnen*) is the substance from which we must derive our concepts. It is the constitutive function of pure thought, immanent in itself, to deal with this substance. This pure power-to-be is not simply a preparation to exist; rather it is the concept of being itself, being which according to its nature passes eternally into the concept, or rather into the concept in order to pass into the existent (*Seiende*) which is not separated from being but nonetheless passes from thought into being. This is the mobility of thought which makes it impossible to stop at pure thought and necessary, on the contrary, to pass eternally into being. But in this whole exposition, observes Engels, there is no transition, no passage into real being, only into logical being. Thus in place of pure potency there appears a logical Being (Existent). But since the infinite potency now behaves and functions as the *prius* or premise of what in thought itself begins by the passing (transition) into being, and since it is only the whole of real being that corresponds to the infinite potency, reason as the content co-expanding with that potency, possesses the power a priori to grasp being and thus to attain to the content of any and all real being without any recourse to the aid of experience. What actually happens, reason has known as a possibility, logically necessary. Reason does not know *that* the world exists; it only knows that if the world exists, it must be made thus and so.

The conclusion in the God-problem is then inevitable: since reason is a potency, its content can therefore only be in the order of potency. Therefore, God cannot be an immediate object of reason, for God is something real, not simply something potential, possible. In the potency of being we now discover primarily the possibility of passing into being (existence); but this is precisely what is understood by "matter". Being is therefore, in Schelling, only able to be thought of as matter, *hyle*, chaos, empty; and he indicates this with various terms such as "limitless being" (*schrankenloses Sein*), "tranquil being" (*gefasstes Sein*), "pure being" (*reines Sein*), "logical being" (*logisches Sein*), "imperturbable being" (*gelassenes Sein*), "immemorial being" (*unvordenkliches Sein*), "untameable being" (*konträres Sein*).[15]

But these basic categories of act and potency derive from an age of confusion and Hegel was right in banishing them from logic. Schelling

[14] According to the teaching of Aristotle (*Metaph.* IX), reiterated by Schelling.
[15] F. Engels, *Anti-Schelling,* p. 194. On God as "immemorial being" cf. below, pp. 219ff.

has simply compounded the confusion by his use of this act-potency opposition as a synonym of the Hegelian pairs: "being-in-itself" and "being-for-itself" (*Ansichsein und Fürsichsein*), ideality and reality (*Idealität und Realität*), power and expression (*Kraft und Aeusserung*), possibility and actuality (*Möglichkeit und Wirklichkeit*).[16] Potency constitutes for him a special sensible-suprasensible being (*ein apartes sinnlich-übersinnliches Wesen*) connoting chiefly "possibility" (*Möglichkeit*); so we have here a philosophy founded on possibility. And the Germans are supposed to be grateful to Schelling for having led them *into* the wilderness of possibility! Thus "the impotence of this philosophy of potencies" is obvious: its claim to pass from possibility to reality simply will not stand up! It cannot prove that anything exists, only that if anything does exist it must be thus and so. This is the exact opposite of Hegel for whom real existence was likewise given in thought.

The logical conclusion of modern philosophy, says Engels, is quite a different one, inclining rather to the early Schelling stand or at least to the premisses of that stand: reason is absolutely only as "spirit" (*Geist*) and spirit can exist only in-and-with nature. Feuerbach's incisive mind was the first really to clarify this philosophical approach and attitude. As soon as and as long as existence is abstracted from it it is no longer possible to speak of it in general; but if a contact be maintained with something existent, then there can be a progress to the existence of other things which, if the logical process be accurate, must also exist. Granted the existence of the premises, the existence of the consequence is likewise evident. Now the basis of all philosophy is the existence of reason; and here Engels repeats his profession of faith in the principle of immanentism. This existence of reason is proven by its activity (*cogito ergo sum*). If one starts therefore with the reason as existing, then the existence of all its consequences follows automatically: it was thus that Hegel was able to prove the existence of nature from the existence of reason. It is interesting to remark how at this point Engels is merging the Hegelian a priori elements with the sensistnaturalist elements of the Feuerbach of the *Essence of Christianity;* but Engels' denunciation of the blind alley into which Schelling had blundered was the *coup de grâce* with which the Hegelian Left intended to strike down at once Schelling's equivocal theologizing and the equally ambigious theological position of the Hegelian Right. What did Schelling ever really achieve in Berlin, exclaims Engels. Why did he not write a refutation of Strauss' *Leben Jesu* and of Feuerbach's *Essence of Christianity?*[17] Hegel, therefore, has won the day: this is the emphatic conclusion of the neophyte philos-

[16] *Ibid.*, p. 195.

[17] And Engels launches into a lengthy tangential criticism of Schelling's conception of Christianity and of its chief dogmas (pp. 211ff.).

opher Engels.[18] Hegel is the man who has opened up a new age of the mind by bringing the older age to its fulfillment. It is interesting (and a sign of the atheistic bias of immanentism) that Hegel should now be attacked both by his successor Schelling and by his most recent disciple Feuerbach; but Feuerbach's critique is constructive: he has consciously and deliberately unified the old and the new in Hegel. And the young Engels concludes that Feuerbach's critique of Christianity is a necessary complement to that speculative theory of religion founded by Hegel.

This critique had reached its high point in Strauss who contended that dogma was in process of *objective* self-dissolution and disintegration into philosophical thought. Feuerbach was leading the attack at the same time on another front, reducing the religious attributes, definitions and predicates to human *subjective* relationships; and this Feuerbachian reduction in no sense involved any rebuttal of Strauss' conclusions, but rather provided for the first time a really cogent proof of them. And both Strauss and Feuerbach in fact arrive at the same conclusion: the secret of theology is anthropology. And so Hegel is indisputably the innovator among the traditionalists and the traditionalist among the innovators.[19] Thus, Engels, even before he had begun to collaborate with Marx, had already conceived the idea of the transcendence of (the theological) Hegel by (the speculative dialectical) Hegel. Engels grieves over the miserable ultimate fate of Schelling's philosophy, which ends up ensnared in faith and un-freedom (*Unfreiheit*). How different was the young Schelling! How many radiant Athenas sprang full-fledged from his seething brain as from the forehead of Zeus, to be encountered as inspiring champions even in the later battles! How freely and boldly did he sail the open sea of thought in search of that Atlantis, the Absolute, whose image he saw so often rising in a mist of dreams from the far-off

[18] Actually Engels remarks somewhat more accurately that Hegel's "principles" had won out over the pseudotheological and pseudohistorical inconsistencies Hegel had perpetrated in the *Philosophie der Religion* and the *Philosophie des Rechts:* "Everything that seems too orthodox in the *Philosophy of Religion* and everything that seems too pseudohistorical in the *Philosophy of Right* is to be taken from this point of view. The principles are always independent and liberal, the conclusions no one would deny to be here and there repressive and illiberal. And this was where some of his pupils stood up and held fast to the principles, repudiating the conclusions when these were unjustifiable" (*ibid.,* p. 184).

[19] This is a crucially important Engels text: "Thus Hegel is indeed the innovator among the traditionalists and yet the traditionalist among the innovators. And so Feuerbach's critique of Christianity is a necessary complement to the speculative theory of religion founded by Hegel. This speculative theory reached its summit in Strauss: dogma disintegrates *objectively* throughout the course of its own history into philosophical thought. Simultaneously Feuerbach reduces the religious attributes to *subjective* human relationships. This amounts in no sense to a rebuttal of Strauss' results; rather it furnishes for the first time a really cogent proof of them. And both reach the same conclusion, that the secret of theology is anthropology (*ibid.,* p. 225).

horizon of the sea! How fiercely there then burst forth from him the fire of youth as in a flaming enthusiasm, like a God-intoxicated prophet he prophesied of a new age! How often, rapt by the spirit that had fallen upon him, he did not even realize the meaning of his own words! How vigorously did he fling wide the door of philosophizing, so that the fresh breeze of nature was wafted out of the crabbed room of abstract thought, the warm spring sunshine fell upon the seedbed of the categories and awakened all the slumbering forces. But, alas, the fire burned itself out; the Odyssean courage faltered; the fermenting juice changed into vinegar before it had become wine! [20]

Then Schelling was in agreement with the "so-called pantheism" of Hegel, that divinization of the world and of himself. That is the thesis of all the books of his first period; in those works it shines forth clear as day. The tragedy was simply this, that the young Schelling did not have a clear overall view and did not know exactly where this road could have led.[21] And so the sad sequel could follow. But the result is that Schelling is now neither in a position to attack atheism nor yet to defend Christianity or religion in general.

Since man with Hegel, as the Hegelian Left saw it, had taken the place of God and the "self-consciousness of mankind" (*das Selbstbewusstsein der Menschheit*) had become the fountainhead of being and value, the new Grail, behold truth had at last found its meaning and its foundation (and this we might add is the definitive and fully-developed significance of the *cogito* and the principle of immanentism) to which new and definitive truth Engels wishes to pledge unqualified "faith" as to the only salvific Truth, the Phoenix of Araby that rises ever and again rejuvenated from the flames.[22] This ingenuous picture-

[20] *Schelling und die Offenbarung*, pp. 226f. And a little further on, Engels writes in an obviously ironic vein: "And so *Schelling* was only now able to arrive at a proper evaluation of his erstwhile comrade in godlessness, the ill-famed and disreputable *Hegel*. For this *Hegel* had such a pride in reason that he went so far as to declare it God when he saw that he could not arrive via it at another, true God above and beyond man. And so *Schelling* made open declaration of his desire to have nothing more to do with this fellow or his teaching and ceased to bother about him at all" (p. 234).

[21] Cf. *ibid.*, pp. 204ff.

[22] One illustrative text among many: "And this faith in the omnipotence of the Idea, in the triumph of the eternal Truth, this firm confidence that it will always stand firm as a rock even if the whole world rise up against it, this is the true religion of a genuine philosopher, this is the basis of true positive philosophy, the philosophy of universal history. This is the supreme revelation, that of man to man, wherein all the negation of criticism is positive . . . The Idea, the self-consciousness of mankind, is that wondrous phoenix that builds its own pyre out of the most precious stuff there is in the whole world and rises again rejuvenated from the flames that destroy an old former age" (*Schelling und die Offenbarung*, p. 227).

postcard mentality and attitude is a patent evidence of the unusual euphoria animating the new generation of philosophers in Germany in the wake of Schelling's Berlin fiasco: "Was not the overthrow of Hegelianism predicted as due by Easter 1842, and with it the death of all the atheists and non-Christians? Everything has turned out differently. The Hegelian philosophy continues to survive as before in the universities, in the literary world, among youth. It knows that none of the blows thus far delivered to it have done it any damage whatever and awaits its own further evolution with equanimity . . . When Hegel, at his death in 1831, left the heritage of his system to his disciples, they were few indeed in number. The system had been presented by Hegel only in its rigorous and rigid form, the severity of which was subsequently so often censured . . . Hegel for his part had such a haughty confidence in the power of the idea that he had made little effort to win popular sentiment over to his teaching. But hardly was Hegel dead when his philosophy began its real life. In the mouth of his pupils, it assumed a more humane, more intuitive form; opposition in official philosophical circles became steadily weaker and more negligible and finally petered out entirely. Youth took possession of the heritage of novelty offered it . . . And a new dawn broke, a dawn of worldwide significance, like that dawn on which there arose out of the mists of the East the free Greek mind." [23]

And Engels continues his dithyrambic narration of the passionate fervor, the romantic and messianic zeal animating himself [24] and all the other youthful parricides who were ready to deliver the death blow to Hegelian theological idealism in order to save the essence of Hegelianism.

[23] *Ibid.*, pp. 182f., p. 225.

[24] In that same year (1842), Engels wrote the little poem "The Triumph of Faith" (*Der Triumph des Glaubens*), a satire, in four cantos, of Bauer's *Die Posaune* against Hegel. (Cf. MEGA I, 2, pp. 253ff. for the text of this satiric poem.) Engels shows no hesitation or reservations in attributing *Die Posaune* to Bauer (cf. "O let the judgment trumpet soon be sounding!", p. 254, line 15). The scene of action in the poem is Hell where Hegel and Voltaire, together with Danton, Edelmann, Napoleon and others have formed a circle around the Devil who is about to pass judgment on Bauer; after the others have spoken their piece to the Devil, Hegel himself speaks up as follows:

> "All of my life to science I devoted,
> And atheism with all my power promoted.
> Self-consciousness onto the throne I prodded,
> Hoping to see the old-time God ungodded".

And Hegel goes on to lament the fact that his teaching has been misunderstood:

> "Lo, in these latter days one man arisen,
> Named Strauss, and he half understood my vision,
> Only to throw it overboard completely
> When Zurich's siren song sounded so sweetly"

(pp. 257, lines 6-17).

The third canto names "a blackguard from Trier", an obvious allusion to Marx, and "the fearful Feuerbach" (pp. 268f.).

Engels thus shows a keen sense for the logical implications of the situation: the landfall of modern philosophy is atheism, the liberation from all metaphysics, the restoration of man to himself; and the standard-bearer of this definitive discovery of man, the Messiah of the new mankind is Hegel, not the Hegel of Rosenkranz and the Hegelian Right which is swiftly dying out nor yet the Hegel of the muddled humbug of the "Young Germany" (A. Jung), but the Hegel of Strauss and Feuerbach: the "war of principles" is in full swing and Christianity itself is at stake.[25] It is simply no use to make solemn declaration of acceptance of the principles and then refuse the conclusions, to accept Hegel and Strauss and then extol Christianity and march arm-in-arm with religion, with the established order.

In the latter part of 1842 Engels arrived in Manchester, England, to work in his father's business there; his thought broadened and matured: as we have mentioned, he had already had a first meeting with Marx and their friendship was soon to be cemented in common devotion to a single ideal. Engels' contact with the English world sharpened his interest in the problems of labor, but the religious problem still continued to be in the foreground of his thoughts, as is evident from his letters to a Swiss newspaper.[26] This was the period during which Engels' own thought was crystallizing; and his collaboration with Marx can definitely be considered to have been a collaboration of equals, with Engels perhaps even having a slight edge over Marx, in the sense that he saw many points sooner albeit less profoundly and incisively.[27]

[25] In an essay published in June 1842 under the pseudonym of Friedrich Oswald, Engels writes: "The Young Germany movement is a thing of the past, the Young Hegelian School has arrived: Strauss, Feuerbach, Bauer, the *Annals* (*Jahrbücher*) have attracted everyone's attention; the war of principles is in full swing; it is a matter of life and death; Christianity is at stake; the political movement is pervading everything" (*Alexander Jung, Vorlesungen,* MEGA I, 2, p. 324). This Alexander Jung declares himself to be a disciple of the new Schelling brand of theism (p. 332).

[26] Cf. *Briefe aus London,* III, June 9, 1843. The letter begins by stressing the vigor with which the English Socialists are fighting the various Churches and religion in general (". . . they want nothing to do with religion"): they are polemicizing against Christianity and in favor of atheism; this is usually presented, to be sure, in an agnostic form (". . . that the existence or non-existence of God can be treated as a matter of indifference to man"), but there is no lack of radical atheists (*ganze Atheisten*) among the theoretical socialists, such as the agitator Charles Southwell (MEGA I, 2, pp. 370ff.). In this same correspondence, Engels laments the fact that he has not been able to find a publisher for the English version of Strauss' *Leben Jesu* which has had to be brought out in installments; the same thing, he says, has happened to Rousseau, Voltaire, d'Holbach and even Byron and Shelley who are only read by the lower classes (*ibid.,* pp. 366, 372f.).

[27] Cf. e.g. the Essay "Umrisse zu einer Kritik der Nationalökonomie," written about the end of 1843 and published in the *Deutsch-Französische Jahrbücher* of

The problem of religion emerges again in Engels' essay *Die Lage Englands,* a critical study on Thomas Carlyle's *Past and Present,* from which Engels cites an extensive excerpt containing Carlyle's quite perceptive analysis of the spiritual crisis of Europe. Carlyle had written: "To speak in the ancient dialect, we 'have forgotten God'; . . . We have quietly closed our eyes to the eternal Substance of things and opened them only to the Shows and Shams of things . . . There is no longer any God for us! . . . in our and old Johnson's dialect, man has lost the *soul* out of him . . . and vainly seeks antiseptic salt . . . we, for the present, with our Mammon-Gospel, have come to strange conclusions. We call it a Society; and go about professing openly the totalest separation, isolation. Our life is not a mutual helpfulness; but rather, cloaked under due laws-of-war, named 'fair competition' and so forth, it is a mutual hostility" (Cf. Carlyle, *Past and Present,* Everyman's Library, pp. 131, 132, 141). But even Carlyle has underestimated the total depravity of these rich English Malthusians, cries Engels: Carlyle merely has their representative, the "humane physician", deploring their failure to give any aid to the poor Irish widow who finally succumbed to typhus-fever and infected seventeen other people—deploring that failure with the remark: "Would it not have been *economy* to help this poor Widow? She took typhus-fever, and killed seventeen of you!" (Cf. Carlyle, *op. cit.,* p. 143). In fact, says Engels, these monsters would rejoice at the fact that this multiple death had eased the overpopulation problem by 18 head! [28]

Carlyle distorts the whole question of atheism, charges Engels. According to Carlyle, all will be sterile and purposeless so long as mankind remains plunged in "atheism", so long as mankind does not recover its "soul". He is not suggesting, of course, any restoration of Catholicism to its old vitality nor even a preservation of the present religion of England, but rather a return to religion as such (perhaps to the old English Deism?). Carlyle maintains that it is evident for all to see with their own eyes to what a pass England has been brought by two centuries of atheistic government and how worn and tattered this atheism is becoming. But for Carlyle, observes Engels, atheism signifies not simply the denial of a personal God but rather the denial of the whole fabric of the universe, of the infinity of that universe, the denial of reason, despair of spirit and truth. Carlyle's war is being waged not against the denial of

---

January 1844 (MEGA I, 2, pp. 379-404). Marx expressly cites this article in his famous *Zur Kritik der Nationalökonomie, Oekonomisch-philosophische Manuskripte* of that same year (1844) with the significant remark: ". . . in which I likewise indicated in quite general form the first elements of the present work" (MEGA I, 3, pp. 33).

[28] *Die Lage Englands,* MEGA I, 2, pp. 412f.; *Karl Marx-Friedrich Engels Werke,* Vol. I (Berlin: Dietz, 1961), pp. 525ff.

the Christian Bible but rather ". . . against the more appalling unbelief, against the denial of the bible of universal history".

This is the eternal Book of God wherein every man can see the finger of God, so long as that man's soul and the light of his eyes be not spent. Carlyle's new religion, continues Engels, is not aimed at the salvation of man but rather at the restoration of a new aristocracy, at "hero-worship". And this is evidence of the skepticism of the English mind, its despair or reason, its innate inability to resolve contradictions. Carlyle is a prize example of this sort of mind.[29]

Engels does not hesitate to go over to the counterattack. His new analysis introduces us to that critique of religion which its protagonists style as constructive and positive and which dialectical and historical materialism is soon to raise aloft as its own banner. Carlyle laments the vacuum and the inner void of our age, the rottenness at the core of all the institutions of society; he is right in his diagnosis but such laments do no good whatever. To cure the ill, the would-be physician must first find the root cause behind the mere symptoms. Had Carlyle really devoted himself to a search for that cause, he would have found that this confusion and this emptiness, this "lack of soul" and this irreligion and "atheism" have their deepest roots in religion itself. Religion by its very nature involves the emptying of man and nature of all content and the transfer of this content into the phantom specter of a transcendent God who deigns to grant to man and nature a morsel of his own surplus! "Now as long as faith in this transcendent phantom specter is still lively and operative, man will at least attain via this detour to some sort of content." And Engels reiterates the new "positive" explanation of religious deviation or alienation, launched by Feuerbach: the energy shown by religious ages and religious-minded men is simply the psychic energy that man ought to put to work in the interests of his species but which religion squanders by applying it to the phantoms of an alleged beyond. And so man, faced with this religious alienation, looks to atheism as the guarantee of the recovery of his lost freedom: "The strong faith of the Middle Ages did indeed, in this way, confer upon this era a remarkable energy, but it was no energy streaming in upon man from outside; rather it was an energy that lay already in man's own nature, albeit still unrecognized,

[29] Carlyle is therefore a pantheist in the idealist sense but leans more to the early Schelling than to Hegel; his "hero-worship" or "genius-worship" he has taken from Strauss' pantheism. But, says Engels, the critique of pantheism has been so exhaustively accomplished in recent times in Germany that there is very little left to be said. The really vital points in this connection are to be found in Feuerbach's thesis in what Engels calls the *Anecdota* (this is the *Vorläufige Thesen zur Reform der Philosophie* of 1842) and in Bauer's writings (*Die Lage Englands*, p. 424).

still undeveloped. That faith gradually weakened little by little; religion crumbled before advancing culture. But still man did not come to the realization that he had worshipped and deified his own being as an extraneous being".[30] In his state of lack of knowledge and simultaneous lack of faith, man cannot have any content. He is *compelled* to despair of reason and nature; this void and lack of content, this despair of the eternal facts of the universe will continue to persist until mankind comes to see that the being he has been adoring and worshipping as God is simply his own nature which he has thus far failed to recognize.

Carlyle accuses our age of lying and hypocrisy. Good! So do we, when we attack the hypocrisy of the Christian situation, the Christian posture in our age. But our attack is launched in terms of the development of philosophy, for, thanks to the work of Feuerbach and Bruno Bauer, we know that it is religion that is responsible for this whole lamentable situation, insists Engels. Carlyle is wrong in decreeing the decline of Catholicism and of Christianity in general and then outlining a new religion, the pantheistic "hero-worship" of which he is so fond, the worship of labor. Impossible, for religion has exhausted all its powers and so has pantheism, whether that pantheism be tailored in the style of Spinoza, Schelling, Hegel or Carlyle himself. We wish to do away with atheism, declares Engels; we, too, wish to make an end of atheism as Carlyle describes it; but we want to do this by restoring to man the value that he has lost through religion. We want to restore to man not a divine content of value but a human one; and this restoration (*Wiedergabe*) amounts simply to the awakening in man of self-consciousness. We are therefore not much concerned about this charge of atheism levelled against us. If, however, Carlyle's pantheistic definition of atheism were accurate, then it would not be we but our opponents who would be the real atheists.

In the matter of "history" (*Geschichte*) too, the Christians introduce the doctrine of the "history of the kingdom of God" (*Geschichte des Reiches Gottes*), denying all substantial status to real history and claiming such a substantial status for their own abstract, transcendent (*jenseitige*) history which is to attain its consummation in terms of the recapitulation of the human race in their Christ. As for us, we do defend the claim of history to a substantial status but we see in history not the revelation of "God" but rather the revelation of man. We aim at the transcendence and eradication of everything allegedly or apparently superhuman (*Ueberwindung alles scheinbaren Uebermenschliches*). It is only the *human* origin of all the religions that saves them and confers

[30] *Ibid.*, p. 425; *Marx-Engels Werke,* Vol. I, p. 543.

upon them some little claim to respect: only the awareness that even the most besotted superstition contains, at rock bottom, the eternal attributes of the human being—only this awareness saves the history of religion and especially the Middle Ages from meriting total repudiation and everlasting oblivion.[31] This whole attitude of the young Engels still amounts simply to the anthropological disintegration of religion effected by Feuerbach. But already Marx was burrowing deeper, aiming at the ultimate and definitive accomplishment, the final catalysis of the principle of immanentism that would result in the disintegration of that principle itself!

[31] "It is only the *human* origin of the content of all religions that preserves for them here and there some claim for respect; only the awareness that even the maddest superstition does indeed contain, at rock bottom, the eternal attributes of the human being, albeit in grotesque and distorted form,—only this awareness preserves the history of religion and especially of the Middle Ages from that blanket rejection and *everlasting* oblivion, which would otherwise be the fate of this 'God-filled' record" (MEGA I, 2, p. 427; *Marx-Engels Werke,* Vol. I, p. 546). "The godlessness (*Gottlosigkeit*) of our age is precisely its 'God-fullness' (*Gotterfülltheit*)." The antithetical terms are deliberately chosen by Engels to indicate the inversion of values. So it is not proper to say that "man has lost his soul and is beginning to become aware of his loss"; it must rather be said that "it was in religion that man had lost his soul, alienated his humanity, and he is becoming aware of the fact that the only way to salvation lies in the transcendence of all imaginations and a resolute return not to 'God' but rather to himself" (*ibid.,* p. 428). Pantheism, which is the end state even of Carlyle, is but "the last preliminary step prior to a free human outlook" (*die letzte Vorstufe zur freien, menschlichen Anschauungsweise*) (MEGA I, 2, pp. 428f.; *Marx-Engels Werke,* Vol. I, p. 547).

4

The Atheism of Dialectical Materialism (Marx)

The critique of religion and the liquidation of God had been exhaustively accomplished by the Young Hegelians in the course of the first decade after Hegel's death. Marx simply takes this for granted and pushes on to pioneer in the area of the new definition of man. This meshes ideally with the aspirations of the young Engels who was soon to become Marx's collaborator; the two were bound together by a community of thought so intimate and functional as to render their intellectual partnership indissoluble. Marx's own contribution lay in the ideological and constructive order and was to lead to the new leap forward, already glimpsed by the young Engels, beyond the negative anti-theistic propaganda of Strauss-Bauer-Feuerbach, which marked an important milestone for modern philosophy, until then unaware of its real atheistic and materialistic kernel, and served as a point of departure for the transcendence and supersession of atheism itself, no longer by means of complicated theological discussions but rather by a pioneering thrust into the horizons of the real life of man.

Marx's original contribution, when compared with that of the Young Hegelians, seems to us to lie in his having transformed what in them had been a simple dissolution or disintegration into atheism of Hegelian idealism into an outlook and approach which embraced or aimed at embracing, as an interpretation of human thought, the whole arc of the history of philosophy. It provided—on the basis of the new principle holding consciousness to be equivalent to sensibility, to sense-perception and sensory activity—an explanation of the evolution of human civilization in terms of the movement of the Hegelian dialectic. Marx's new method can only be expressed in such paradoxical terms as "The critique of critical critique" (the subtitle given by Marx-Engels to *The Holy Family*), indicating the transcendence and supersession of the dross of theology and of the impasse at which the Young Hegelians (Feuerbach included) had stopped short; and "the dialectic of the dialectic", indicating the revival of the Hegelian method functioning no longer in the context of a tension of two worlds or two spheres or elements of consciousness but rather exclusively within the finitude of sensible consciousness, sense-awareness. We shall limit ourselves, as we have throughout, to following the essential thread of the central idea.

The End of the Feuerbachian Critique of Religion

1. As opposed to Engels, who was brought up in a pietistic environment, and had had an intensely religious or religion-oriented childhood and youth, Marx seems to have been totally untouched by the problem of the three Kantian transcendentals (God, freedom, immortality). Marx's mind seems to have had but one interest and bias, that of sensible being, whose theoretical underpinning had been provided by Feuerbach. And this bias to the sensible drove Marx relentlessly his whole life long. As early as his thesis on the natural philosophy of Democritus and Epicurus (1841),[1] Marx was formulating and vigorously expounding his own historiographical criterion, to the effect that the constructive line of human thought generally and of Greek thought in particular was not the spiritualism or idealism initiated by the Socratic systems, but rather the materialism of the atomists. And Marx's mind was one of those resolute and unwavering minds that elect one option and stick to it remorselessly. Judging by the several extensive notes to the last two chapters (IV and V) of the first part of his early Thesis,[2] Marx was probably aiming at showing the continuity or affinity between the explicit atheism of Epicurus' materialism and the implicit atheism of modern idealism. He reproaches Hegel's disciples, for instance, with having failed solidly to penetrate the spirit of Hegel's thought, and recommends in this connection the attitude of the liberals as that which is most faithful to the "concept and principle of philosophy" and thus most truly critical, starting from the concept and arriving at real advances.

More important is Marx's critique of Schelling, for this allows us to compare Marx on this point with Engels whose attitude in this matter we have already studied. Marx considers Schelling's famous phrase from

[1] Critics find that this Thesis tends to rehabilitate the idealism of Epicurus as against that of Democritus. In Epicurus Marx found substantial analogies with the philosophy of nature of Schelling and Hegel (cf. A. Cornu, *Marx,* l'homme et l'oeuvre [Paris, 1934], p. 125).

[2] I am here following the text of H.-J. Lieber & P. Furth: K. Marx, *Frühe Schriften,* Vol. I (Darmstadt: Wissenschaftliche Buchgesellschaft, 1962), pp. 70ff. The Editors have given these notes the significant sub-titles: *Das Philosophisch-Werden der Welt als Weltlich-Werden der Philosophie* (The 'Philosophization' of the World as Secularization of Philosophy).

the *Philosophische Briefe über Dogmatismus und Kritizismus* of 1809: "The term *'weak'* should be applied not to the reason that does not acknowledge any objective God but to the reason that *is willing to* recognize one." [3] "Weak" is surely far too mild a word, insists Marx. Schelling should remember what he himself had written in his earlier works. For example, in the essay on the "Ego as Principle of Philosophy" we read: "If it be admitted, for instance, that God, insofar as he is defined as an Object, is the real ground of our being, then he himself surely falls, insofar as he is an object, within the sphere of our knowing and so cannot be for us the ultimate point on which this whole sphere is suspended." [4] And again Marx reminds Schelling of the last phrase of the letter mentioned above: "It is time to proclaim to the better mankind the *freedom of the mind* and no longer to tolerate its weeping for the loss of its own chains." [5] Now in simple prose, these expressions mean that if you want to start from the constitutive autonomy of the Ego or the immanence of being within consciousness, which is the new concept of freedom, then there is simply no place whatever for God. And that was written in 1795! What cannot be expected of the intelligent man of 1841?

To bolster his case, Marx makes a brief digression on idealism's proofs of the existence of God. Hegel actually stood these theological proofs completely on their head: he repudiated them in order to justify them! But woe to the clients, scoffs Marx, whose lawyer can do nothing better to save them from death than to murder them himself! Hegel, for instance, interprets the deduction of God from the world in the following formula: "Since the fortuitous does *not* exist, God exists," whereas the theological proof reads exactly the opposite: "Since the contingent (fortuitous) has a true being, God exists." God is the guarantee of a contingent world (*zufällige Welt*). Obviously the inverse conclusion is likewise hereby asserted. We have here, says Marx, an alternative either arm of which leads to a negative conclusion. Actually, Marx pursues, either these proofs of the existence of God are meaningless tautologies, like the "ontological proof", and then even Kant's critique with his example of the hundred thalers is superfluous and even beside the point; or else the proofs of the existence of God are nothing but proofs of the existence of substantial human self-consciousness, logical explanations of this self-consciousness; and this is the new principle of Feuerbach.

[3] In the preceding period Schelling had remarked that ". . . if you want to act freely, you must act *before* there exists an objective God; it matters little that you believe in him when you have acted. But weak reason must be pardoned" (Schelling, *Philosophische Briefe über Dogm. und Krit.; C. W.*, Abt. I, Vol. I [Stuttgart & Augsburg, 1856], p. 290).

[4] Schelling, *op. cit.*, p. 165.

[5] *Ibid.*, p. 292.

Take, for example, the ontological proof. What being is immediately, as soon as it has been thought? Self-consciousness. In this sense, concludes Marx, all the proofs of the existence of God are proofs of his non-existence, refutations of all the notions that have been formed of God. The true proofs ought rather to say: "Because nature is poorly organized, God exists"; "Because there exists an irrational world, God exists"; "Because there is no thought, there is God". But what does this signify, demands Marx, except that God exists for the man who considers the world irrational and thus gives evidence of his own irrationality? Or that the existence of God is unreason, a mere piece of nonsense? And Marx's indictment ends with two other significant quotations from Schelling: "If you suppose the *idea* of an *objective God,* how can you thereupon speak of laws which reason produces of itself, since autonomy can belong only to *an absolutely free being?"* and "Is it not a crime of high treason against humanity to hide principles that are universally communicable?" [6]

From the very moment at which he first took a stand on the matter, then, Marx saw to the very depths of the atheistic nature of the principle of immanentism. He saw that that atheistic core was not simply a consequence of the thought of the two most popular representatives of the elder generation of absolute transcendental idealists, Hegel and Schelling, but was rather already fully present in their very systems of thought.[7]

2. The Thesis on Epicurus and Democritus was an important milestone in Marx's thought: it was the end product of those youthful aspirations that had led Marx to abandon the study of law so as to devote himself to philosophy with the aim and object of freeing the culture of his age from the last theological encumbrances [8] and of proclaiming the absolute freedom of man. Public enemy No. 1 of this freedom was religion; but modern philosophy had dissolved God and every other transcendental (the soul, immortality and the rest) into empty mirages of the imagination. The climax of this first period of Marx's writings, dominated by the Feuerbachian critique, is certainly the *Introduction* to

[6] Marx, *Frühe Schriften,* Vol. I, p. 76; MEGA, I, 1, pp. 80f.

[7] Marx's increasing conviction that Feuerbach is more significant and important than Strauss in the dynamic of modern thought is mirrored in the enthusiastic reaction of Marx to *The Essence of Christianity* on its first appearance: "There is no other path for you to *Truth* and *Freedom* than through this Fiery-Brook [a pun in the German on the etymological significance of Feuerbach's name which Marx here hyphenates thus: "den Feuer-bach"—Translator's Note to this English edition—A. G.]. This Feuerbach is the purgatory of our present age" ("Luther als Scheidsrichter zwischen Strauss und Feuerbach," in K. Marx, *Frühe Schriften,* Vol. I, p. 190).

[8] Marx's youthful Hymn to Prometheus (MEGA I, 1, pp. 30-31), inspired by Goethe, may be taken as his signal profession of atheism.

Marx's *Contribution to the Critique of Hegel's Philosophy of Right.*[9] This Introduction is certainly the classical text of Marxian atheism. It is to this text that recourse must always be had for any judgment on the effective genesis and theoretical consistency of Marxism, on its deepest motivating principles, even though this Introduction is written rather in journalese than in the lean, dry style of the Critique itself, which seems to have been composed before it. The strictly philosophical element in this Introduction is confined to the first few paragraphs, but it is remarkable for its allusions and suggestions, which present an impressive picture of the unbroken progress and intensification of the process of disintegration of the sacred in the modern mind.

(a) "For Germany the *criticism of religion* is in the main complete, and criticism of religion is the premise of all criticism . . . *Luther,* we grant, overcame bondage out of *devotion* by replacing it by bondage out of *conviction.* He shattered faith in authority because he restored the authority of faith. He turned priests into laymen because he turned laymen into priests. He freed man from outer religiosity because he made religiosity the inner man. He freed the body from chains because he enchained the heart." [10] This, Marx readily allows, was a step in the right direction, the direction of the final solution; but it stopped halfway. To be sure, it did emancipate the lay popes, the princes, into autocrats in their own houses, able to play fast and loose with the no longer sancrosanct persons and goods of the Church, able in the Protestant countries to confiscate Church estates at will. But the real and definitive liberation will come only when man has been delivered from his inner "priest", from religious-mindedness as such. In one short sentence Marx passes from the *de facto* to the *de jure* assertion of the claim of radical atheism to be the only genuine logical conclusion of the Reformation as he sees that Reformation in the dynamic of modern man's evolution to perfect freedom: "The criticism of religion ends with the teaching that *man is the Supreme Being for man.*" [11]

[9] *Zur Kritik der Hegelschen Rechtsphilosophie, Einleitung,* in Karl Marx, *Frühe Schriften,* Vol. I, pp. 488-505; *Marx-Engels Werke,* Vol. I, pp. 378-391. English translation in K. Marx and F. Engels, *On Religion* (Moscow: Foreign Languages Publishing House, 1955), pp. 41-58. Pagination is identical in the Schocken Books (New York, 1964) edition reprinted from the 1957 Foreign Languages Publishing House edition.

[10] *Frühe Schriften,* Vol. I, pp. 488, 497f.; *Marx-Engels Werke,* Vol. I, pp. 378, 386; English translation, pp. 41, 51.

[11] *Frühe Schriften,* Vol. I, p. 497; *Marx-Engels Werke,* Vol. I, p. 385; English translation, p. 50: we have here departed from this translation by rendering the original German "*das hochste Wesen*" as "the Supreme Being" rather than retaining the translation "the highest essence", since we feel that the former rendering, while being entirely faithful to the original, better highlights the atheistic bias—Translator's Note to this English edition—A.G.

(b) Marx considers the religious alienation to be the basis and ground of every other alienation and consequently posits the critique of religion as the premise of all criticism and the emancipation from religious-mindedness as the premise of all emancipation. The optimum aim and goal is no longer the coexistence of the three elements of consciousness Hegel had identified (art, religion, philosophy) within the totality of the spirit; it is rather the total recovery of the human mind and consciousness as a sensible reality. Marx proceeds in rigorously Feuerbachian fashion: "The *profane* existence of error is discredited after its heavenly *oratio pro aris et focis* (plaidoyer for the altars and hearths) has been rejected. Man, who looked for a superman in the fantastic reality of heaven and found nothing there but the *reflection* of himself, will no longer be disposed to find but the *semblance* of himself, the non-human where he seeks and must seek his true reality." The liberation consists primarily in the exposure of the ultimate root of religious alienation: "The basis of irreligious criticism is: *Man makes religion,* religion does not make man". This principle is interpreted in the style of Hegel-Strauss-Feuerbach, not in the classical sense according to which religion is the actualization of a moral virtue. Religion is judged to be an arrested or perverted development of consciousness: ". . . religion is the self-consciousness and self-feeling of man who has either not yet found himself or has already lost himself again" and consequently abstracted himself from his real world which is the world of man, the state, society.

(c) Clearly, then, religion is not simply a speculative error; rather it is responsible for all the ills of real life and constitutes the greatest single obstacle in the way of man's attainment of freedom: by postulating a life and a felicity in the beyond, religion makes man indifferent and passive in relation to the here-and-now, a docile tool in the hands of the mighty, an easy prey for the clever and the unscrupulous. True, *"religious* distress is at the same time the *expression* of real distress and the *protest* against real distress"; but this is precisely because ". . . religion is the sigh of the oppressed creature, the heart of a heartless world, just as it is the spirit of a spiritless situation. It is the *opium* of the people". This famous phrase seems to us to be a conclusion rather than a principle, a historico-phenomenological statement of fact rather than a point of argumentative departure; besides it is simply a figure of speech. The assertion-conclusion pair immediately preceding it, on the other hand, do have the status of principles. Religion is *"a reversed world-consciousness"* (*ein verkehrtes Weltbewusstsein*), the *"fantastic realization* of the human essence". And this in turn leads Marx to the drastic and unmistakable conclusion: "The struggle against religion is therefore mediately the fight against *the other world,* of which religion is the spiritual *aroma . . . the criticism of the vale of woe,* the *halo* of which is religion."

(d) Arguing against the "declaration of the Rights of Man" which guaranteed to every citizen "freedom of worship," [12] Marx asserts that the separation of Church and State, the emancipation of the State from religion, even the proclamation of an official State atheism means nothing so long as the State does not simultaneously proclaim its own independence of religion, constituting itself in its universality above all the particular elements, as Hegel had given precise directions for doing.[13] Political emancipation is not enough, argues Marx against Bauer who had favored simple "separation" (in the case of the Jewish question) of the conscience of the citizen from that of the believer; what must be achieved is the emancipation of man as such: "Even the emancipation of the State from religion still leaves intact religion as such, even if it be no longer a privileged religion. The conflict besetting the adherent of a particular religion in the matter of his civic duty is but *a part* of the generic *secular contradiction between the political State and bourgeois society.* The perfect Christian State is the State that confesses Christianity as a State and abstracts from the religion of its members. The emancipation of the State from religion is not the same thing as the emancipation of the real individual human being from religion." [14]

Every emancipation is a leading of man back to himself. The French Revolution started out as an emancipation of the State and stopped halfway, at mere separation rather than supersession; so it did not achieve the emancipation of man: "Human emancipation is achieved only when man as a real individual absorbs into himself the abstract citizen and when as a real individual he has become a generic being (*Gattungswesen*),[15] in his empirical life, in his individual personal labor, in his personal relationships; only when man has recognized and organized *his own powers* as *social* powers and therefore no longer divorces these social powers from himself by making them into *political* powers." At this point begins Marx's supersession of Feuerbach, his transition from static anthropological atheism to dynamic constructive atheism, an atheism beyond negation, an atheism which is quite simply humanity, mankind in act in its historical manifestation.

[12] Cf. *Zur Judenfrage, I,* in *Marx-Engels Werke,* Vol. I, pp. 361ff.

[13] Marx actually cites Hegel's *Philosophie des Rechts.*

[14] *Zur Judenfrage, I,* p. 361.

[15] Cottier, the well-informed critic of the dynamic of the Hegel-Feuerbach-Marx development, thus shows brilliant insight in noting: "The Marxian *Gattungswesen* (generic being) is a scion of the Hegelian christology" (M. M. Cottier, *L'athéisme du jeune Marx,* ses origines hégéliennes [Paris, 1959], p. 24; cf. p. 135 for Feuerbach).

In this light does Marx see the limitations of Feuerbach's anthropology and of his atheism. Feuerbach deserves credit mainly for having shown that traditional philosophy is nothing but religion reduced to thought and developed in terms of thought and is therefore likewise to be condemned as simply one more form and mode of existence of the *alienation* of human existence.[16] The chief defect of Feuerbach's approach, according to the definitive balance sheet cast in the *Theses on Feuerbach,*[17] lies in his having forgotten the deeper notion of the Hegelian philosophy and the quintessence of modern philosophy, and having conceived of reality as a static "object", as a sensible intuition, instead of considering it as in process, "as human sensuous activity" (*sinnlich menschliche Tätigkeit*), as practice (Thesis I). But practice lies at the origin of thought, not *vice versa* (Thesis II). Feuerbach, moreover, is always stopping halfway: he did really reduce the religious essence into the secular human essence; but he went no further because he considered the human essence as " 'genus', as an internal, dumb generality which merely *naturally* unites the many individuals" (Thesis VI). Feuerbach's approach thus remains bourgeois, like that of the old classical and 19th-century materialism. Consequently he does not see that " 'religious sentiment' is itself a *social product*" (Thesis VII). He is a prisoner of the old philosophical prejudice: "The philosophers have only *interpreted* the world, in various ways; the point, however, is to *change* it" (Thesis XI). Feuerbach has regressed to old-style philosophy and so his atheism is still an abstract atheism, wherein it is only man in the abstract that has taken the place of God, not yet man in the concrete. Feuerbach has superseded Hegel by reducing being to sensible consciousness, sense-awareness; now Feuerbach himself must be superseded by an interpretation of this sensible consciousness as action or practice.[18] Thus, there must be a return to Hegel in order to supersede Hegel definitively.

[16] *Oekonomisch-philosophische Manuskripte,* Kritik der Hegelschen Dialektik und Philosophie überhaupt, § XII; MEGA I, 3, p. 152; *Frühe Schriften,* Vol. I, p. 639.

[17] *Thesen über Feuerbach,* in *Marx-Engels Werke,* Vol. III, pp. 5ff. English translation in *On Religion,* pp. 69ff. Written in 1845, they were published by Engels in 1888, after Marx's death. A year previous to the composition of these *Theses on Feuerbach,* Marx had given Feuerbach unqualified credit for the "establishment of *true materialism* and of *real science,* since Feuerbach also makes the social relationship 'of man to man' the basic principle of the theory" (*Oekonomisch-philosophische Manuskripte,* MEGA I, 3, p. 152; *Frühe Schriften* I, p. 639; English translation published by Foreign Languages Publishing House (Moscow, 1961), as Karl Marx, *Economic and Philosophic Manuscripts of 1844,* p. 145.

[18] Cf. the brief note: *1. ad Feuerbach,* published under the title *Marx über sein Verhältnis zu Hegel und Feuerbach,* in *Marx-Engels Werke,* Vol. III, p. 356.

Constructive Atheism: The Dialectic (Return to Hegel)

It does not suffice, therefore, to reduce being to man and conceive of becoming as the relation of man to the world and of man to man; rather it must be explained how this occurs. Feuerbach did indeed see that religious alienation lies at the basis of the *alienation* [19] from which man suffers in the Hegelian speculative scheme of things; but Feuerbach did not succeed in showing how man proceeds to the appropriation (*Aneignung*) of his own substantial powers, how man is to be conceived as the "result of himself". Yet Hegel was the very man who asserted, above all in the *Phenomenology* (1807), which is for Marx "the true birthplace and mystery of Hegel's philosophy" that "The True is the Whole, the All. But the Whole is only the being that has fulfilled and perfected itself by and through its own development. Of the Absolute it must be said that it is essentially a *result,* that only *at the end* is it what it really and truly is; and herein we see its nature as a real subject or a becoming-itself." [20]

The grandeur of the *Phenomenology* lies in its discovery of the dialectic of things, in having conceived the "dialectic of negation" as the chief motive force of history. Hegel's merit is therefore that of having understood man's self-production as a process (*Prozess*), objectification as desubjectification, as alienation and supersession of this alienation; and of having therefore understood the essence of labor (*Arbeit*) and true objective man (true because real) as the result of *his own labor.* The defect in Hegel here is that he considers work as the essence (*Wesen*) that actualizes itself in man: i.e., he sees only the positive aspect of labor, not the negative one; he considers abstract spiritual intellectual labor, philosophy! Real concrete labor is the becoming-for-himself of man (*Fürsichwerden des Menschen*) within the framework of alienation. So this dialectic, this struggle of negation, must be brought down from the rarefied world of concepts into the real world of things, into that framework of actual conflicts within the world of labor. The dialectic of negation must be switched on seriously in the real world. At its very core, then, Marxist atheism is distinguished from Feuerbachian atheism by the transition from the notion of "sensible man" to the

[19] Marx uses the Hegelian terms *Entäusserung* and *Entfremdung* almost interchangeably to signify "alienation". The German *Entäusserung* would convey the somewhat more juridically nuanced sense of an active seizure and sequestration, whereas *Entfremdung* would convey rather the simple state of alienation itself. Cf. the remark of J. Hyppolite, in his *Genèse et structure de la Phénoménologie de l'esprit de Hegel* (Paris, 1946), p. 372.

[20] *Phänomenologie des Geistes,* Vorrede; ed. J. Hoffmeister (Leipzig, 1937), p. 21.

notion of "economic man" and from the love-dialectic of the I-Thou to the strife-dialectic of the "class struggle". And Marx can conclude: "Here we see how consistent naturalism or humanism distinguishes itself both from idealism and materialism, constituting at the same time the unifying truth of both. We see also how only naturalism is capable of comprehending the act of world history." [21] Once again it is a question of superseding Hegel by means of Hegel, of really applying the dialectic of negation to the human process of labor, thereby converting the alienation itself into the mainspring of the restitution and vindication of the authentic human being.

Hence, it can be seen that Hegelian idealism and crypto-atheism are an abstraction, a flight from the real. And the reason for this is not far to seek: the *Aufheben* in the Hegelian dialectic took on no real sense of "abolition" and retained altogether the other meaning, "conservation"; and so nothing really new occurs in reality and the contraries are reduced by thought to mere "moments of movement" (*Momente der Bewegung*). Actually, in the *Philosophy of Right, "aufgehobene"* private right is equal to morality, *aufgehobene* morality is equal to the family, the *aufgehobene* family is equal to civil society, *aufgehobene* civil society is equal to the State, and the *aufgehobene* State is equal to universal history. Thus, in reality, private right, morality, family, civil society and State continue to subsist; it is simply that they have lost their isolated status and become modes of being of man, modes which reciprocally produce and disintegrate one another. The dynamic of negation remains hidden and inoperative. It manifests itself only in thought and more specifically in philosophy, insofar as philosophy is the higher moment or element in the life of the Spirit.[22] But in this conception, even though the higher moment (philosophy) does indeed overcome and supersede the lower, it does not really negate it, indeed it must conserve it as basis and "phenomenon" (*Erscheinung*), as indispensible preliminary to the transcendence and supersession. Hence it can be seen how Hegel is basically a radical atheist inasmuch as he holds the truth of religion not to be found in religion itself but rather in philosophy and in philosophy alone. "If, however, the philosophy of religion, etc., is for me the sole true existence of religion, then, too, it is only as a *philosopher of religion* that I am truly religious, and so I deny *real* religious sentiment and the really *religious* man. But at the same time I *assert* them, in part within my own existence or within the alien existence

[21] *Oekonomisch-philosophische Manuskripte,* MEGA I, 3, p. 159; *Frühe Schriften,* I, p. 650; English translation, p. 156.

[22] Notoriously, for Hegel the Spirit manifests itself as art, religion and philosophy as the Absolute is referred respectively to exteriority, interiority or the dialectical synthesis of the two.

which I oppose to them—for this *is* only their *philosophic* expression—and in part I assert them in their own original shape, for they have validity for me as merely the *apparent* other-being, as allegories, forms of their own true existence (i.e., of my *philosophical* existence) hidden under sensuous disguises." [23] Marx's line is thus that of an all-out mobilization of the Hegelian negation aimed at an all-out salvaging of the human being estranged and alienated in labor.

Marx can thus be said to have clarified the exact significance of his atheism, of communism and communist atheism. Communist atheism is the abolition, annulment, abrogation (*Aufhebung*) of God; communism is the abolition, annulment, abrogation of private ownership of the means of production; both represent the staking of a claim on behalf of man to a really human life. And thus we here have a positive Humanism, a Humanism proceeding positively from itself. Therefore, concludes Marx, "atheism and communism are no flight, no abstraction; they are not a losing of the objective world begotten by man . . . they are but the first real coming-to-be, the realization become real for man, of man's essence, of the essence of man as something real." [24] Marx has much more to say about and in criticism of Hegel but for us in our present study the crux of the whole matter lies in this claim staked for the reality of the human being, a claim entailing the alternative: either God or man, the salvaging of man based on the negation and denial of God. Hence, the Marxist formulation of religious alienation as the basis of the other alienations and consequently the fight against religion for the affirmation and consolidation of atheism as the prime and principal task of the Marxist conception of life, as the ABC of dialectical materialism (Lenin). At the same time it must be noted what a great store Marx sets upon the presentation of his own communism and atheism as an integral Humanism, as the goal of the whole of preceding history. Communism does indeed begin from the outset with atheism,[25] but that atheism is at first far from being communism; it is still mostly an abstraction, still mired in the spiritualism-materialism antithesis, not yet totally committed to the search for that basis it requires in order to come forward as a strong operative force. This basis can, according to Marx, be found only in Marxist socialism.[26] For this Marxist socialism, the entire sweep of universal history is nothing but the production of man via human

[23] *Oekonomisch-philosophische Manuskripte,* §§ XXIX-XXX; MEGA I, 3, pp. 164ff.; *Frühe Schriften,* I, pp. 655ff.; English translation, p. 162.

[24] *Oekonomisch-philosophische Manuskripte,* § XXX; MEGA I, 3, p. 167; *Frühe Schriften,* I, p. 658; English translation, p. 164.

[25] Marx cites Owen as an example here.

[26] Cf. *Oekonomisch-philosophische Manuskripte,* § V; MEGA I, 3, pp. 114ff.; *Frühe Schriften,* I, pp. 594ff.; English translation, pp. 103ff.

labor, the dynamic evolution of nature via man. This is plainly the radical Marxist version of the principle of immanentism, which furnishes man the evident and irrefutable proof of his own genetic process (*Entstehungsprozess*), of his own birth as a self-effected nativity. In Marx, the substantial status of man and nature has become (via labor) practically palpable and visible: man has become for man a nature-bounded existent, a being of nature (*Dasein der Natur*); nature has become for man a man-conditioned existent. And the consequence is an impossibility in practice of even putting the question concerning the existence of an extraneous entity above and beyond nature and man; for this very question would as such entail the admission of the fact that neither man nor nature enjoys substantial status. And in this reasoning Marx is being perfectly consistent with the immanentist principles from which he started: if being is grounded primordially upon consciousness and man is defined essentially as sense-consciousness, as a relation with the sensible world, then clearly no entity transcending sense-consciousness can either exist or even, if the pun be pardoned, make any "sense"!

Marx has no difficulty whatever in asserting socialism to be the positive self-consciousness of man no longer even needing to deny or negate religion since socialism starts directly from the *theoretical and practical consciousness and knowledge* of man and nature as being a consciousness and knowledge of man's own essence and nature and very being. Thus atheistic communism can well be presented as being the "negation of negation", i.e., the negation of religion insofar as religion, according to consistent immanentism, is itself the negation of the substantial status of man or a negation of man's relation to nature as the only source and criterion of value. Hence, the formulation which can serve likewise as a summary of the development of the principle of immanentism in Marxism: "Atheism, as the denial of this insubstantial status, no longer has any meaning, for *atheism* is a *negation of God,* and postulates the *existence* of *man* through this negation." [27] Atheism has no longer any meaning because to be a man means to be aware of oneself as in a sensible and sense-perceived world, to be pressured by sense interests that announce themselves irresistibly in temporally-textured living: there is no longer any need for a formal denial of the suprasensible, for every act of consciousness, every act of human awareness is, by its very occurrence, a recurrent existential denial of that suprasensible.

[27] *Oekonomisch-philosophische Manuskripte,* § XI; MEGA I, 3, p. 125; *Frühe Schriften,* I, p. 607; English translation, p. 114. We have here preferred the rendering "insubstantial status" for the original "*Unwesentlichkeit*" to the rendering "inessentiality" of the English translation.

5

The Socio-Political Atheism of Lenin

Lenin's outstanding contribution to Marxist ideology lies in his deepening of the meaning and significance of the new "atheism" in its structural value and its revolutionary impetus, motivated by one simple and clear-cut notion that aims at putting an end once and for all to every misunderstanding and every compromise.[1]

Lenin highlights preeminently the continuity and the simultaneous difference between Marxist atheism and the atheism of the Enlightenment thinkers and of Feuerbach.[2] The philosophical foundation of Marxism, as Marx and Engels have repeatedly insisted, is dialectical materialism, which has entirely taken over the historical tradition both of 18th-century materialism in France and of Feuerbach in Germany. And this dialectical materialism is a materialism that is unqualifiedly atheistic and resolutely hostile to all religion. This explains, observes Lenin, the charge of inconsistency levelled by Engels in his *Anti-Dühring* (which Marx had been able to read in manuscript form) against the atheist and materialist Dühring for having left an opening for religion and religious philosophy. As for Feuerbach, the same Engels reproaches him (in his famous Essay on Feuerbach) with having combatted religion not in order to annihilate it but rather in order to renew it, in order to "concoct" (*erdichten*) a new "higher" religion. There must rather be a tenacious adherence to Marx's principle that "religion is the opium of the people": this is the bulwark of the whole Marxist outlook on the problem of religion. Hence derives likewise the Marxist principle for

[1] The pith of Lenin's writings concerning the subject of religion and Marxist relation to it has been published by the Little Lenin Library in an excellent translation from the official text provided by the Institute of Marxism-Leninism. We cite throughout from the Little Lenin Library edition of 1933 (New York: International Publishers). The translation was entitled *Religion*.

[2] Cf. the article "The Attitude of the Workers' Party Towards Religion," presented as Chapter II of *Religion* (pp. 11ff.).

interpretation of the sociology of religion: it considers all religions and all Churches today, each and every one of the religious organizations, to be agencies of bourgeois reaction in the service of capitalist oppression.

Feuerbach's psychological interpretation must yield to the sociological interpretation, and this sociological interpretation in its turn must be much more radical both from the ideological and from the pragmatic point of view. Hence, Lenin is drastic in his criticism of Gorky for continuing to toy with the God-idea and the God-picture.[3] For Gorky "... God is a complex of those ideas, worked out by tribes, by nations, by humanity at large, which arouse and organize social emotions, and which serve to unite the individual with society, and to curb zoological individualism". This whole notion Lenin sees as being patently false and just as patently reactionary: it is sheer idealism.

And Lenin lashes back at Gorky in an outrage all the keener because of Lenin's solid, deep and continuing friendship with the great writer: "God is (historically and socially) first of all a complex of ideas engendered by the ignorance of mankind, and by its subjection, firstly beneath the forces of nature, secondly by class oppression—ideas that *perpetuate* this ignorance and blunt the class struggle. There was a time in history when, in spite of this origin (and this is the real meaning of the idea of god), the democratic and proletarian struggle took the form of a struggle of *one religious* idea against another. But this time has long been passed. Now in Europe, just as in Russia, *every* defence or justification of the idea of god, even the most refined and well-intentioned, is a justification of reaction". And Lenin goes on to brand Gorky's definition as both reactionary and bourgeois: reactionary because the God-notion Gorky has enunciated, far from organizing social emotions, has lulled and blunted them by preaching slavery, far from uniting the individual with society, it has always bound the oppressed classes by faith in the divinity to submission to their oppressors; bourgeois because the God-notion Gorky has enunciated is unscientific and unhistorical, "because it deals with general, 'Robinson Crusoe' conceptions—and not with definite *classes* situated in a definite historical epoch".

Lenin saw the Hegelian dialectic as the ideal instrument for the elimination of the God-idea and therefore insistently recommends to his fellow workers on the staff of the magazine, *Under the Banner of Marxism,* "a systematic study of Hegelian dialectics from the materialist point

[3] This letter is the second of two presented as Chapter VII of *Religion,* pp. 41-47, "Two Letters to A. M. Gorky". The second letter, the one here cited from, extends from p. 44 to p. 47. Near the end of this letter (p. 46) Lenin ironically observes: "It is not true to say that philosophical idealism 'always has in view only the interests of the individual'. Did Descartes have the interests of the individual more in mind than Gassendi? Or Fichte and Hegel more than Feuerbach?".

of view, i.e., the dialectics that Marx applied concretely in his *Capital* and used in his historical and political works." [4] And he goes on to give concrete suggestions in this matter: ". . . we can and must work out these dialectics from all sides. The magazine must publish excerpts from the principal works of Hegel; must interpret them materialistically, and give examples of how Marx applied dialectics, as well as examples of dialectics from the field of economic and political relations. Modern history, particularly modern imperialist war and revolution, provide innumerable examples of this kind."

On the relations between Marxism and religion, Lenin is outspoken and to the point, always the perfect combination of practical organizer and intransigent ideologist: he declares that religion must be regarded as a private matter but instantly specifies exactly what he means by this: "The State must not concern itself with religion; religious societies must not be bound to the State. Every one must be absolutely free to profess whatever religion he likes, or to profess no religion, *i.e.,* to be an atheist, as every Socialist usually is." [5] But just a few lines earlier he has repeated Marx's expression that religion is the opium of the people [6] and proceeded to make the point even more crudely: "Religion is a sort of spiritual booze in which the slaves of capital drown their humanity and their desires for some sort of decent human existence." And he underscores heavily the responsibility of Party members to be militant atheists: "To the party of the Socialist proletariat, however, religion is not a private matter. Our party is a league of class-conscious, progressive fighters for the liberation of the working class. Such a league cannot and must not be indifferent to lack of class consciousness, to ignorance or insanity in the shape of religious beliefs . . . One of the objects of our organization, the Russian Social-Democratic Labor Party, is precisely to fight against all religious deception of the workers. For us, the ideological struggle is not a private matter but one that concerns the whole Party, the whole proletariat." [7]

Anti-religious and atheistic propaganda is thus an essential part of the program of Marxist agitation and indoctrination. But Lenin calls for a special method of conducting such indoctrination. Marxists must proceed quite differently from bourgeois-type atheists and anti-clerical agitators. Marxists must take a "positive" and not merely a negative atti-

[4] *Religion,* p. 34.

[5] "Socialism and Religion," which appears as Chapter I of *Religion,* p. 8. One of the points of the Erfurt Program of 1891 was that religion should be made a "private matter".

[6] This phrase is repeated three times in the article "The Attitude of the Workers' Party Towards Religion," *Religion,* pp. 12, 18, 20.

[7] *Ibid.,* p. 9.

tude in the face of religion. This extremely practical point constitutes Lenin's original contribution to the consolidation of political atheism.[8]

Marxism, insists Lenin, is materialism. And as such its opposition and hostility to all manner of religion is every bit as drastic and trenchant as that of the 18th-century Encyclopedists or of Feuerbach. But Marx-Engels materialism is also dialectical and goes beyond the Encyclopedist and Feuerbach in applying materialist philosophy to the field of history and the social sciences. Lenin, we have already mentioned, was preeminently the shrewd practical organizer; yet he was not a sheer opportunist with no sacred principles: the key to the entire man and to his dynamic lies in the fact that he was and strove to act as a convinced *dialectical* materialist. In his famous essay, "The Attitude of the Workers' Party Towards Religion", Lenin sketches in masterful and most revealing fashion the whole gamut of this dialectical technique. We therefore cite at some length:

"We must combat religion—this is the A.B.C. of *all* materalism, and consequently of Marxism. But Marxism is not materialism which stops at the A.B.C. Marxism goes further. It says: We must be able to combat religion, and in order to do this we must explain from the materialist point of view why faith and religion are prevalent among the masses. The fight against religion must not be limited nor reduced to abstract, ideological preaching. This struggle must be linked up with the concrete practical class movement; its aim must be to eliminate the social roots of religion . . . In modern capitalist countries the basis of religion is primarily *social.* The roots of modern religion are deeply embedded in the social oppression of the working masses, and in their apparently complete helplessness before the blind forces of capitalism, which every day and every hour cause a thousand times more horrible suffering and torture for ordinary working folk than are caused by exceptional events such as war, earthquake, etc. . . . Fear of the blind force of capital . . . this is THE *tap-root* of modern religion which, first of all, and above all, the materialist must keep in mind, if he does not wish to remain stuck for ever in the kindergarten of materialism . . . The Marxist must be a materialist, *i.e.,* an enemy of religion. But he must be a *dialectical* materialist, *i.e.,* one who fights against religion not in the abstract, not by means of abstract, purely theoretical propaganda, equally suited to

[8] Lenin therefore trenchantly opposed all those who seriously wanted to make Socialism into the new religion. In "The Attitude of the Workers' Party Towards Religion," he lashes out against "our Lunacharsky and Co." (*ibid.,* p. 18) for this weakness and his "Two Letters to A. M. Gorky", especially the first (pp. 41-44), are diatribes against this same sort of "god-creating". "There is as much difference between god-seeking, god-building, god-creating and god-begetting, *etc.,* as there is between a yellow devil and a blue devil." (p. 42).

all times and to all places, but concretely, on the basis of the class-struggle actually proceeding—a struggle which is educating the masses better than anything else could do. The Marxist must be able to judge the concrete situation as a whole. He must always be able to determine the boundary between anarchism and opportunism." [9]

The main point is the total "subordination" (*Unterordnung*) of the fight *against* religion to the fight *for* socialism. Lenin was concerned lest the overt campaign against religion might backfire; in order to forestall such an undesirable possibility, he insisted strongly that this anti-religious campaign should always be intimately tied in with the class struggle, avoiding any direct assault on the ticklish area of religious feeling and aiming rather at mobilizing the feelings of class interest by championing and headlining demands for the rights of the working classes.

Lenin deals with several quite specific practical instances in which this proper hierarchy of values and this salutary flexibility must be adhered to:

1. *The Policy To Be Followed in a Strike:* Supposing the economic struggle to have culminated in a strike in a locality in which the union is the Christian Workers' Union, composed of a vanguard of fairly class-conscious Social Democrats who will obviously be atheists and a rather backward mass of believers, many of whom are even church-goers. "A Marxist must place the success of the strike movement above all else, must definitely oppose the division of the workers in this struggle into atheists and Christians, must fight resolutely against such a division. In such circumstances the preaching of atheism is superfluous and harmful . . . To preach atheism at such a time and in such circumstances, would only be *playing into the hands* of the church and the priests, who would desire nothing more than to have the workers participating in the strike movement divided in accordance with their religious beliefs" [10]

2. *The Policy To Be Followed on Admission of the Clergy into the Party:* Here again the dialectical approach is absolutely essential in the specific situation prevailing in Russia at the time at which Lenin writes. He rejects out of hand the traditional Social-Democratic policy of unreserved approbation of clergy membership in the Party. This "traditional" policy was elaborated in terms of the situation in Western Europe and the situation in Russia is quite different: "We must not say once and for all, that under no circumstances can priests be allowed to join the Social-Democratic Party; but neither should we categorically affirm the opposite. If a priest comes to cooperate with us in our work—

[9] *Ibid.*, pp. 14, 15, 16.
[10] *Ibid.*, p. 16.

if he conscientiously performs party work, and does not oppose the party program—we can accept him into the ranks of Social-Democracy . . . But if, for example, a priest joined the Social-Democratic Party, and made it his chief and almost exclusive business to propagate religious views, then, of course, the party would have to expel him" [11]

3. *Attitude to Religious Feelings of Lay Party Members:* "We are absolutely opposed to the slightest affront to these workers' religious convictions. We recruit them in order to educate them in the spirit of our programme, and not in order to carry on an active struggle against religion." [12]

4. *Should a Party Member Be Allowed To Declare That Socialism Is His Religion?* That, again, all depends, insists Lenin, on what he means and what are the specificities of the situation: "It is one thing if an agitator or some one addressing workers speaks in this way in order to make him understood, as an introduction to his subject, in order to present his views in terminology to which the backward masses are more accustomed. It is quite another thing when a writer begins to preach "god-creating" . . . Socialism . . . To pronounce censure in the first case would be mere quibbling, or even misplaced restriction of the freedom of the propagandist. . . . In the second case censure by the Party is necessary and obligatory. For the former, the statement 'Socialism is my religion' is a step *from* religion *to* Socialism, for the latter it is a step *from* Socialism *to* religion" [13]

Unity of the worker movement is of capital importance for Lenin; but of equal importance for a proper understanding of his technique of flexibility in matters of religious convictions and atheist propaganda is his profound conviction that religion is but an epiphenomenon at best (or worst!) and that the economic struggle is the true lever of human history. In his 1905 article, "Socialism and Religion", he articulates this entire complex of convictions with lapidary clarity and precision: "It would be bourgeois narrow-mindedness to lose sight of the fact that the oppression exercised by religion on humanity is only a product and reflection of the economic oppression in society. No books, no preaching, can possibly enlighten the proletariat, unless it is enlightened by its own struggle against the dark forces of capitalism. The unity of that genuinely revolutionary struggle of the oppressed class to set up a heaven on earth is more important to us than a unity in proletarian opinion about the imaginary paradise in the sky." [14]

[11] *Ibid.*, p. 17.
[12] *Ibid.*, p. 17.
[13] *Ibid.*, p. 18.
[14] *Ibid.*, p. 10.

And the crucial point is echoed in his article, "The Attitude of the Workers' Party Towards Religion", written four years later (1909): "... the class struggle ... in the conditions of modern capitalist society, will convert Christian workers to Social-Democracy and to atheism a hundred times more effectively than any bald atheist sermons." [15] And Lenin drives his point even further in the earlier article, "Socialism and Religion". Again the dialectical approach, again the twin and equally trenchant insistence on the indispensibility of atheism to dialectical materialism and consequential political socialism, on the one hand, and on the need for flexibility and a situation-oriented, constantly changing practical policy on the other: "We shall always preach a scientific world conception; we must fight against the inconsistencies of the 'Christians'; but this does not mean that the religious question must be pushed into the foreground where it does not belong. We must not allow the forces waging a genuinely revolutionary economic and political struggle to be broken up for the sake of opinions and dreams that are of third-rate importance, which are rapidly losing all political significance, and which are being steadily relegated to the rubbish heap by the normal course of economic development." [16]

The great centripetal whirl of the principle of immanentism is becoming patently clear in Lenin, whose tactical shrewdness should not obscure his deeper philosophical convictions. For throughout Lenin is preaching much more than simply a purely practical approach to concrete situations in abstract from theory or with disregard for theory. Practice, the inevitable and inevitably changing pull of the here-and-now, the concrete situation, *is* ultimate reality for this arch-immanentist. It is pointless to take even the long view (even if that view be soundly Marxist) in a revolutionary situation. One must absolutely concentrate on that focus where and where alone true reality exists: the *present moment* of the revolutionary situation. Any analysis of religion in general is fruitless and can be deleterious; what counts is assessing properly the place of religion *today* and *from day to day* as the situation steadily changes. Then proper tactics can be worked out which will inescapably change themselves as rapidly as the situation. Consistency in the purely theoretical sense is for Lenin not only stupid but actively ontologically ludicrous and therefore deleterious, because it inevitably issues in a jelling, a kind of freezing of categories that were never meant to be so

[15] *Ibid.*, p. 16.

[16] *Ibid.*, p. 10. The concluding sentence of this same article well sums up Lenin's whole theoretical and practical attitude and simultaneously pinpoints his ecology of religion: "And then, under a régime cleaned of mediaeval mustiness, the proletariat will wage a great open struggle for the abolition of economic slavery, the real source of the religious deception of mankind" (p. 11).

frozen: since reality-to-be-transformed changes constantly, categories and tactics must as well! Practically in the revolutionary situation that will yield best and profoundest results which is in fact most deeply bedded in reality; and there is nothing (not human knowing, nor speculation, nor certainly religion) which is even nearly so deeply-bedded in reality as the forces of economic man which must initially be mobilized. Any sane hierarchy of values will take this into account and, while not forgetting the religious question and engaging in proper amounts of discreetly disseminated anti-religious propaganda,[17] will concentrate preeminently on the mobilization of the economic forces of the proletariat which alone, properly mobilized, can ensure that transformation of reality which *is truth* for Lenin.

In his address to the Third All-Russian Congress of the Young Communist League of the Soviet Union, delivered on October 2, 1920, Lenin exhorted these young people to mold their character according to the Communist ethic which is an ethic totally subordinated to the interests of the working class and utilizing as its instrument the class struggle. This ethic must deny and actively opposed the bourgeois ethic which preaches a morality derived from the commandments of God: "Of course we say that we do not believe in God. We know perfectly well that the clergy, the landlords and the bourgeoisie all claimed to speak in the name of God, in order to protect their own interests as exploiters. Or, instead of deducing their ethics from the commandments of morality, from the commandments of God, they deduced them from idealistic or semi-idealistic phrases which in substance were always very similar to divine commandments. We deny all morality taken from superhuman or non-class conceptions. We say that this is a deception, a swindle, a befogging of the minds of the workers and peasants in the interests of the landlords and capitalists." [18]

It is essential, therefore, to transcend and supersede, not only every form of theism and belief in God, but even the Enlightenment type of atheism, to which Lenin reproaches Feuerbach likewise with having remained attached.[19] The significance of Lenin's theoretical contribution lies therefore in a most drastic restitution of the Marxist dialectical

[17] ". . . we must necessarily explain the actual historical and economic roots of the religious fog. Our programme necessarily includes the propaganda of atheism. The publication of related scientific literature (which up till now has been strictly forbidden and persecuted by the autocratic feudal government) must now form one of the items of our party work." (*ibid.*, p. 10).

[18] *Ibid.*, pp. 47f.

[19] Cf. Lenin, *Aus dem philosophischen Nachlass* (Berlin, 1958), p. 320, where Lenin writes concerning the last (30th) lecture of *Das Wesen der Religion* that "it can be presented as a typical example of Enlightenment atheism with a socialist coloring" since Feuerbach is still conceiving of man abstractly.

process and of Marxist atheism to the spirit of Hegelianism; thus, he rebukes Plekhanov for having "criticized Kantianism (and agnosticism generally) more from the point of view of vulgar materialism than from that of dialectical materialism . . ." and the Marxists of the early 20th century for having "criticized the Kantians and the followers of Hume more in the style of Hume (and of Büchner) than in the style of Hegel"; and Lenin warns: "It is impossible to have a full understanding of Marx's *Capital,* and especially the first chapter, without a thorough study from beginning to end and a real comprehension of the *whole logic* of Hegel. Consequently, for half a century, none of the Marxists has understood Marx!" And Lenin specifies exactly why Hegel is of such capital importance: he proved that "the laws and forms of logic are not empty husks, but rather the reflection of the objective world. Or, to be more precise, he did not prove it but rather *brilliantly surmised* it." [20]

It was by means of this integration of Feuerbach's anthropological materialism into the Hegelian dialectic that Marxist atheism, in its Leninist form, desired to express the content and demand of the principle of immanentism, freed from all the theological, moralistic and pscyhological shackles in which it had continued until Lenin's time to be bound throughout the evolution of modern thought. The integration was calculated to provide simultaneously the "content" for the Hegelian dialectic and the "form" for the content of Feuerbach's Humanism, supplying to each in this way from the other respective element that each had lacked. The actual fact of the matter is that first Feuerbach and then still more drastically Marx simply brought to light the basic atheism of the Hegelian ideology, an atheism both of form and of content. This is fully borne out by the following crucial passage of Marx's own critique of Hegel: "It is now time to lay hold of the *positive* aspects of the Hegelian dialectic within the realm of estrangement: (a) *Annulling* as an objective movement of *retracting* the alienation *into itself*. This is the insight, expressed within the estrangement, concerning the *appropriation* of the objective essence through the annulment of its estrangement; it is the estranged insight into the *real objectification* of man, into the real appropriation of his objective essence through the annihilation of the *estranged* character of the objective world, through the annulment of the objective world in its estranged mode of being—just as atheism, being the annulment of God, is the advent of theoretic humanism, and communism, as the annulment of private property, is the justification of real human life as man's possession and thus the advent of practical

[20] *Aus dem philosophischen Nachlass,* pp. 98f. And a little further on, we read: "Logic is epistemology. It is a theory of knowledge. Knowledge, cognition is the reflection of nature by man" (p. 101).

humanism (or just as atheism is humanism mediated with itself through the annulment of religion, whilst communism is humanism mediated with itself through the annulment of private property). Only through the annulment of this mediation—which is, itself, however, a necessary premise—does positively self-deriving humanism, *positive humanism*, come into being."[21] This whole thrust is a relentless *reductio ad principium* of the entire philosophy of immanentism: atheism is proclaimed as the basis and ground of humanism, the expulsion of God as a condition of the assertion of man, for if God exists, man is not free!

In a being-oriented philosophy, on the other hand, in an ontological rather than an anthropological metaphysics, as Marx's contemporary Kierkegaard demonstrated against Hegel, it is only in virtue of the divine omnipotence that a true and genuine created freedom can be conceived.[22]

[21] Marx, *Economic and Philosophic Manuscripts of 1844*, English translation, p. 164.

[22] Cf. the chief text n. 1017 in the *Papirer* 1846, VII A 181; Italian tr. by C. Fabro, Vol. I (Brescia, 1962 [2]), pp. 512f. Cf. also: C. Fabro, *Tra Kierkegaard e Marx* (Florence, 1952); C. Fabro, *Storia della Filosofia*, Vol. II (Rome, 1959 [2]), pp. 810ff., 917ff.

6

The Positive Atheism of Marxist Humanism

We have contended that Marxist atheism is no mere isolated phenomenon nor simple deviation in the process of modern thought, but represents rather a decisive step in the disintegration of that thought, a disintegration ineluctably contained within the very principle on which that thought is founded. We have found Marxist atheism to be the most convulsive episode of the apocalypse that is presently shaking the foundations of human coexistence. It must also be borne in mind that the essence or theoretical kernel of Marxist atheism is not actually bound up in any way with the sociological and economic outlook of Marxism: Marx takes his stand at the very outset on the denial of God via Hegel and the neo-Hegelians Strauss, Bauer, Feuerbach, Hess and their like, i.e., via the assertion of the *Gattungswesen* and *Naturwesen* of man and its substitution for the deity. The sociological explanation of the origin of religion from capitalist oppression is secondary and derivative,[1] whereas the denunciation of religious transcendence, of the "beyond" (*Jenseits*), as the root of all human alienation and the assertion of immanence and immanentism, the exclusive reality of the here-and-now (*Diesseits*) as a prerequisite for and principle of the salvaging of the alienated human being, is primary and essential to Marxist atheism. Paradoxically, Marx was an atheist before he was a Marxist! Certainly from the time of his Thesis and his first contacts with philosophy (Kant, Hegel, Schelling) and perhaps even earlier. And if such a way of speak-

[1] Moses Hess seems to have been the man to show that religious alienation, as presented by Feuerbach, finds its proper application in the economic and social situation. (Cf. A. Cornu, "L'idée d'aliénation chez Hegel, Feuerbach et K. Marx," in *La Pensée*, 17 [1928], p. 72. Cf. also Cornu's *Moses Hess et la gauche hégélienne* [Paris, 1934]: "Hess was the first to underscore the necessity of transforming the Hegelian philosophy into a philosophy of action and, foreseeing the failure of the liberal movement, to set a social rather than a political goal for this action" [p. VII].)

ing can be tolerated in an approach and attitude like the Marxist which definitively rejects the whole world of ideas and degrades it to the status of a mere "alienation", Marxist atheism might be said to be the congealed merger of the main streams of modern thought. Prior (temporally and logically) to its being or aspiring to be a social revolution or a system of political economy, Marxism aspires to be an interpretative reading of the history of philosophy and of philosophy as such, it aspires to be a philosophy of non-philosophy, a dephilosophizing philosophy. To that ambiguity of atheism which derives from the idealist heredity there is here added the ambiguity of a sensist and materialist heredity. The vigorous and decisive acceptance of the materialist principle combines and conspires with the acceptance of the Hegelian dialectic within the framework of that same materialism to cut short the vacillations of the Hegelian Left which was still tinged with theology (Strass, Bauer) or anthropology (Feuerbach, Stirner). And Marxism was hereby bringing to light another deep-seated element of Hegelianism, namely, the fact that its crypto-atheism was intimately bound up with its crypto-materialism.

Marx makes Descartes [2] far more responsible for Enlightenment materialism than Spinoza. Descartes had, in his Physics, granted to matter a self-creative power (*selbstschöpferische Macht*), holding the vital act to be reducible to mechanical motion. He completely separated his *physics* from his *metaphysics*: within the limits of his physics, *matter* is the only *substance* and the sole ground of being and of knowing. French mechanical materialism therefore harks back to the Physics of Descartes, as opposed to his Metaphysics; and his disciples Le Roy and La Mettrie and Cabanis were, by profession, anti-*metaphysicians,* being as they were *physicians.* Le Roy transposed the Cartesian notion of the structure of animals to the human soul and concluded that the soul is reducible to a mode of the body; he even accused Descartes of having concealed his own real opinion on this point. Cabanis brought Cartesian materialism to its perfection in his *Rapport du physique et du moral de l'homme.*[3] This Cartesian metaphysics forthwith encountered its chief opponent in Gassendi, who restored Epicurean materialism; and English

[2] For the next stage of our exposition, cf. K. Marx-F. Engels, *Die Heilige Familie,* Ch. VI, d) "Kritische Schlacht gegen den französischen Materialismus" in *Marx-Engels Werke,* Vol. II, pp. 131ff.; English translation, pp. 167ff. Cf. also Marx-Engels, *Ueber die Religion* (Berlin, 1958), pp. 45ff.; English translation, *On Religion,* pp. 59ff.

[3] It should, however, be noted that when Cabanis comes to compile the list of his own ideological antecedents, he begins with Locke, ". . . the greatest and most useful revolution of philosophy" and goes on immediately to Helvétius and Condillac without even passing mention of Descartes (*Rapports du physique et du moral de l'homme,* Vol. I, Preface, [Paris, 1815 [3]], p. IX).

and French materialism was notoriously always closely related to Democritus and Epicurus.

Another important opponent of the Cartesian spiritualistic metaphysic was the English materialist, Hobbes; Hobbes and Gassendi succeeded in triumphing over their opponent precisely at the moment at which his philosophy was the officially dominant one in all the French schools. This metaphysics of the Cartesian school was dealt a substantial blow by Voltaire's anti-theological activity and especially by that of P. Bayle, concerning whom Marx writes: "As Feuerbach was driven by the fight against speculative theology to the fight against *speculative philosophy* precisely because he recognized in speculation the last prop of theology, because he had to force theology to turn back from pretended science to *coarse,* repulsive *faith,* so Bayle, too, was driven by religious doubt to doubt about metaphysics which was the support of that faith. He therefore critically investigated metaphysics from its very origin. He became its historian in order to write the history of its death. He mainly refuted *Spinoza* and *Leibniz.*"

But after the demolition of metaphysics there was need of a positive system to fill the void left by that demolition. And this was precisely the work of Locke with his treatise on the origin of human reason; but the foundations of materialism had already been laid in England by Bacon and, above all, by Hobbes, who slashed all the theology and theism out of Bacon and proclaimed "exclusive materialism".

Sensuousness lost its bloom and became the abstract sensuousness of the *geometrician. Physical* motion was sacrificed to *mechanical* or *mathematical* motion; *geometry* was proclaimed the principal science. Materialism became misanthropic (*menschenfeindlich*). In order to strike down the *misanthropic* and *disincarnate* spirit in its own field, materialism was obliged itself to mortify its own flesh and become *ascetical.* It became a *being of reason* (*Verstandeswesen*); but it also developed its own theology of reason. The materialist reasoning of Bacon and Hobbes goes as follows: if man's senses are the source of all his knowledge, then intuition, thought, imagination, etc., are nothing but phantoms of the material world, more or less divested of the sensuous form of that world. Science can only give a name to these phantoms. One name can be applied to several phantoms. There can even be names of names. But it would be a contradiction to say, on the one hand, that all ideas have their origin in the world of the senses and to maintain, on the other hand, that a word is more than a word, that besides the beings represented, which are always individual, there exist general beings, i.e., universals. An *incorporeal substance* is just as shrieking a contradiction as an *incorporeal body. Body, being, substance,* are one and the same idea.

Thought cannot be separated from matter *which* thinks. Matter is the subject of all changes. The word "infinite" (*unendlich*) is meaningless (*sinnlos*) unless it simply indicates the ability of our mind to go on adding idea to idea without end. Since only what is material is perceptible and knowable, we consequently know *nothing* about the existence of God. I am sure only of my own existence. Every human passion is a mechanical motion ending or beginning. The objects of impulses are what is called good. Man is subject to the same laws as nature. Power and freedom are identical.

Now to this materialism Locke gave the epistemological basis with his sense-perceptionism. In France, Condillac went still further, asserting that not only the soul, but the senses too, not only the art of creating ideas, but also the art of sense-perception are matters of *experience* and *habit* (*Erfahrung, Gewohnheit*). The whole development of a human being and of man as a species depends, therefore, on education and environment. It was Helvétius who achieved the explicit synthesis of Cartesian materialism and sensism, in his *De l'homme,* in which the omnipotence (*Allmacht*) of education is extolled. Marx sees another such explicit synthesis of the two materialisms in La Mettries's *L'homme machine,* and still another in d'Holbach's *Système de la nature.* A point of interest in this context is Marx's mention, in his panoramic outline of his materialist antecedents, of Robinet and his *De la nature:* Marx calls Robinet "the French materialist who had the most connection with metaphysics and was therefore praised by Hegel",[4] and Marx highlights Robinet's own explicit reference to Leibniz. At the end of this combined investigation of his own antecedents and sincere profession of his own materialism, Marx states categorically and explicitly: "There is no need of any great penetration to see from the teaching of materialism on the original goodness and equal intellectual endowment of men, the omnipotence of experience, habit and education, and the influence of environment on man, the great significance of industry, the justification of enjoyment, etc., how necessarily materialism is connected with communism and socialism." [5] These declarations serve

[4] Cf. Hegel, *Geschichte der Philosophie,* ed. Michelet, *C. W.*, Vol. XV, pp. 470ff. Hegel finds Robinet's theory "still more dangerous" (*noch gefährlichere*) than that of d'Holbach: he does indeed admit the existence of God, but denies that we can form any idea whatever of his attributes on the grounds that this would amount to sheer anthropomorphism. I must say, after a comparison of the texts translated by Hegel with the edition of *De la nature* cited by him (Amsterdam, 1766, Vol. I, Part I, ch. 3-4, not pages 16-17 as Hegel says, but rather p. 23) that Robinet's is a vigorously theistic position, comparable perhaps to that of Voltaire.

[5] K. Marx-F. Engels, *Die Heilige Familie, Marx-Engels Werke,* Vol. II, p. 138; *Ueber die Religion,* p. 52; English translations, *The Holy Family* pp. 175-176; *On Religion,* p. 67.

as a better introduction into the spirit of Marxist atheism than any critical interpretation.

(a) First of all, it is not a skeptical negation but rather a constructive affirmation, starting from the structure of man as active practical "sensuousness": it is from the dynamic materialism of Epicurus, the Stoics and, above all, the 18th-century French thinkers, that Marx borrows, via Feuerbach, the critique of metaphysics, on the one hand, and, as a sort of rebound, the new "content" of being and the expulsion or trivialization of God.

(b) Yet it must be borne in mind that the acceptance of dynamic materialism is not a direct heritage as in the case of the Utopian communism of Fourier and Owen, who therefore take atheism as their point of departure,[6] but rather is mediated by Feuerbach's humanism; and this mediation is in turn filtered through the atmosphere of Hegel, especially of the Phenomenology, the Logic, the Philosophy of Right and the Philosophy of History as evolution and actualization of the species.

(c) For Marx and his followers, this actualization of the species is immersed, as it was not in Hegel, in practical interests and more especially economic ones, to such an extent that economics constitutes the base and the key to the understanding of history; yet even on this point, where he is most explicitly materialistic, Marx remains bound to the Hegelian conception of man, not only as species (Strauss, Bauer, Feuerbach) but also as "becoming" and tensional evolutionary phenomenon.

(d) Finally it is preeminently from Hegel that Marx takes the "form" of this becoming which is the *dialectic* or struggle to transcend oppositions. This formal element might seem indeed superfluous in a sketch of the foundations of Marxist atheism, whose deepest foundations might seem to have been amply articulated in the three preceding points. Actually, however, the situation is not quite so simple: Marxist atheism must of course be called "dynamic" but it must not be understood to be dynamic in just any sense, neither in the "physicistic" sense of classical materialism, nor yet in the metaphysical or even epistemological sense of Cartesian, Leibnizian and Enlightenment materialism, which speaks of a self-moving matter and a sensuousness that develops by itself into thought. The man of Marx who takes the place of God and of the Hegelian Absolute constitutes himself his own content: [7] thus the "content" does not subsist apart from and still less does it precede the dialectical form; rather it is the result of the self-actualization of the form, it *becomes* together with that form and via that form. Thus it is not strictly true that atheism is for Marxism, as Marx and Marxist

[6] K. Marx-F. Engels, *Die Heilige Familie,* p. 139; *The Holy Family,* p. 176.

[7] "Marx's humanism is the transcendence of abstract humanism and of theological atheism" (J.-Y. Calvez, *La pensée de Karl Marx* (Paris, 1956), p. 542).

Scholasticism declare it to be, a simple point of departure, to be considered as a "past" moment, devoid of meaning or relevance. Rather the contrary is true: the God-problem is always involved in each and every one of the moments or elements of the Marxist conception, for the simple reason that at every step and stage of the assertion of "dialectical historical sensible being" man is posing explicitly or implicitly the goal of supersession of the corresponding metaphysical, i.e., theological moment or element. Thus the God-problem continues to be very much alive, even though in the negative form of the campaign against God and the negation and denial of God, and dominates even the practical dimension of Marxism.[8]

In the Hegelian conception, God was plainly on display as the master design of the whole; in Marxism, man has become the master design but God remains in the background as the fretwork tracery of the generality of life, justice, and freedom, in process of evolution toward a terrestrial *eschaton* of a classless world. Marx tries to evade this troubling presence, but without success; and none of his followers has ever succeeded in evading it nor indeed can any of them ever hope to succeed: they all assert initially that the critique of religious alienation is the first and fundamental step in all criticism, the very basis of all ensuing criticism and activity; then they proceed to declare that atheism has become "meaningless" (*sinnlos*). But this amounts to an affirmation of the dialectic followed by an immediate denial and negation of it, for the dialectic is the revolutionary tensional interplay of thesis and antithesis; and the reciprocal member in the triad including man as a sensible being is clearly man as a finite spiritual being and ultimately God as an infinite spirit whose place man claims to take over. In other words: there can be no meaningful talk of tension, of vindication or of dialectic, until the "quality of being" of the goods being disputed and of man who lays claim to them have been brought onto the same ontological plane; nor can there be any meaningful talk of tension, of vindication or of dialectic, if it is a question of a simple difference of degree, as e.g., in the relation of the animal to sensible goods.

In this case the result will be the tyranny of the stronger which is just what Marxist socialism makes its key reproach to capitalist materialism. Incidentally, this capitalist materialism can declare itself entirely in agreement with Marx's historical materialism and, precisely in virtue of it, repudiate dialectical materialism, until such time as dialectical materealism appeals to some ideal and ceases to signify simply the triumph

[8] Cottier is therefore right in saying: "The Marxian reply to the God-problem is the practical suppression of the need for God. Life settles out of hand the questions of the human mind . . . The genuine and the spurious needs" (M. Cottier, *L'athéisme du jeune Marx*, p. 360).

of the stronger. But to what ideal can dialectical materialism appeal? Moreover, in giving to the terms "matter" and "material" one meaning and value when applied to things and a different meaning and value when applied to man (namely, the new meaning of antithesis as foundation of the dialectic), Marxism is transgressing not only the ground rules of philosophy but even those of the human mind itself which always tends to give to its terms of discourse a meaning which cannot—even according to Marxism—be indifferent with respect to its contradictory! The appeal to the "living substance", i.e., to Hegel's dialectic followed by the refusal to recognize the "power behind the throne", i.e., the Absolute (which Hegel placed at the foundation not simply in the midst and at the end of the dialectic) amounts to a curious double-talk and clouds all communication in hopeless ambiguity. In this sense, the champions of theism have no need to refute Marxist atheism: it refutes itself in its very effort to characterize itself as dialectical with the consequent dissolution and disintegration of its own terms into meaninglessness; it is caught between the Scylla of trivialization of the dialectic [9] and the Charybdis of the admission of the Absolute, of spirit, of God.

In its own characterization of consciousness as having fundamentally material attributes, is not Marxism perpetrating the same absurdity as it, in company with the Hegelian Left, accuses theists of perpetrating by their characterization of God as having purely human attributes? Indeed, Marxism is in a much worse pickle than Hellenistic Christian spiritualism ever was: for Hellenistic Christian spiritualism has, in it ascent to God, a means of keeping distinct the levels of being and with them the characteristic differences of the beings involved; whereas dialectical materialism's atheism has no option but to refer all its distinctions to the immediate empirical sphere, a sphere to which Marxism simply cannot keep clinging if it wishes to avoid the company of capitalism. Yet there seems to be no escape route open for Marxism out of this immediate empirical sphere so long as it clings to its radical materialistic sensism.

This point is important; indeed, it is *the* crucial point, both from the speculative and from the practical point of view, in a consideration not

[9] And the "dialectic" is plainly just as essential to Marxism as are its much-touted materialism and atheism; indeed the dialectic gives Marxism its specific character and constitutes its primordial kernel, both as regards the epistemological element (the "reflection theory", *Widerspiegelungstheorie*) and as regards the economico-socological element (the "class struggle", *Klassenkampf*). And so, though Marx may well be said to have consummated the inversion, initiated by Feuerbach, of the theology-prone Hegel (cf. G. Dicke, *Der Identitätsgedanke bei Feuerbach und Marx* [Cologne and Opladen, 1960], p. 23), it must be added that Marx accomplished this process of "naturalization" of man by means of the principles of the Hegelian Logic and primarily by means of the *Aufheben* (conserving annulment, annulling conservation) of the dialectic.

only of Marxism but of the position of a man like M. Reding who, himself a "spiritualist", yet claims that "Marx's materialism is not essentially atheistic." [10] To such a statement, the initial reaction is surely stupefaction! But let us examine Reding's stand: he admits that for Marx the actualization of the socialist State will, inevitably, lead to the suppression of religion, for this State will represent the realization of those social relationships which render superfluous any projection of our desires into a heaven somewhere in the beyond. But it does not follow, he contends, that atheism is identical with Communism. But what should be said about the relationship between materialism and atheism in Marx? That is the question that must be answered here. And Reding tries to answer it in a chain of reasoning, involving seven points, each of which he believes to be or be founded upon Marx's own exposition of his dialectical materialism: [11]

1. Marxist materialism is primarily *empiricism,* i.e., observation of experience.

2. Consequently, Marxist materialism is essentially *realism,* making thought dependent on experience.

3. Thence the transition is effected to historical "economism", i.e., realism in respect of the economic facts and values, insisting that the economic realities are indeed real.

4. Since the economic values (concept of property, labor) are in continuous development and evolution, Marxist materialism is a *historical realism.*

5. Inasmuch, further, as history is subordinated to the dialectic, Marxist materialism is a *dialectical materialism.*

6. Marxist materialism characterizes itself as materialistic because Marx believed that philosophy had reached its summit with Hegel and further advance was possible only on condition of an abandonment of theory and an assertion of (revolutionary) *practice.*

7. Thus Marxist materialism is, according to Marx, nothing but the *simple study of reality,* as opposed to abstract philosophy. Thus Reding concludes, against the common interpretation that the materialism of Marx is the basis of his atheism, saying that it is rather the atheism which is the motive for the materialism.

Far from clarifying the consistency of Marxism, this exposition seems to us to aggravate the perplexity of the neutral observer. The seven points, far from meshing into an integral whole, seem rather to bark and bite at one another, or at very best to run together into a mottled blotch.

[10] M. Reding, *Der politische Atheismus,* p. 349. On the points we are here discussing, cf. Reding's exposition "Atheismus und Materialismus," pp. 170ff. which we here summarize.

[11] Cf. *ibid.,* pp. 172ff.

Thus, the transition from empiricism to realism, i.e., the specification of realism from below, is not really justified: realism (e.g., that of Aristotle) is just as much opposed to empiricism (e.g., that of Democritus) as to idealism (e.g., that of Plato). Nor can the author have recourse to the claim that this is an economic realism and thus specified from above, for then, either the economic factor and value is left in the crude state of simple fact and we are back in empiricism again, or else the economy is being considered in its historical process as the development and evolution of a reality regarding the process of production, distribution and use of sensible goods. The author seems, indeed, to be taking this latter line, because he proceeds to characterize Marx's stand further as historical realism and dialectical materialism. The problem here lies in this appeal to history which is really nothing but a docketing of isolated facts. Such facts can, of themselves, bear no effective witness whatever; an interpretation of them is necessarily presupposed. And when this interpretation is presented, as Marx presents it, within the framework of the Hegelian dialectic, the confusion must be admitted to be worse confounded. It is as bad as an attempt to drive a train along two diverging rails: the train must either split or go off at least one of the rails! Empirical realism and dialectical immanentism are mutually incompatible approaches. And there is a further problem: revolutionary practice is clearly a foreign body within the organic framework of either empiricism or immanentism; and yet revolutionary practice is precisely supposed to effect the synthesis of the opposites. Another quite bemusing action of the author is that of characterizing as "a simple study of reality" a system so complex and internally tortured [12] as Reding himself indicates Marxism to be when he uses the dual identification tag "dialectical materialism or historical materialism". And this characterization of Marxism as a simple study of history is all the more surprising in the light of Marx's own assertion of the absolute primacy of practice.[13]

But Reding has still more surprises in store for us: he asserts that the last two characteristics, the "activist character" and the "study of reality" do not really conflict with belief in God or even, indeed, with Christianity [14] now, either this remark must be taken within the context and framework of the Marxian system (as would certainly seem to be the author's actual intention, in which case it does not jibe with his own

[12] The complexity and ambiguity of Marx's system is amply confirmed by the fact that discussion is still going on, even in countries with a Marxist regime, concerning the nature of the dialectic whereby Marx aims at actualizing the human being (cf. C. Fabro, *Feuerbach-Marx-Engels,* especially pp. XCVIIIff.).

[13] As in his Thesis XI on Feuerbach: "The philosophers have only *interpreted* the world, in various ways; the point however, is to *change* it" (*Marx-Engels Werke,* Vol. III, p. 7; *On Religion,* p. 72).

[14] M. Reding, *Der politische Atheismus,* p. 175.

admissions concerning Marx's eschatological humanism; or else the remark must be taken in abstraction from that whole Marxian context, in which case, however, it is entirely beside the point, since the activism and reality-study involved are obviously those occurring within the framework of Marxian immanentism! The fundamental error in Reding's interpretation, as in that of so many other interpreters of Marx who talk about his "realism", is that they ignore or at least pass too lightly over the distinction of degree and form within the principle of immanentism between immanentism and idealism. We have seen how Marx remained an immanentist despite his opposition to, and critique of, Hegel's idealism and how, in the final analysis, he retained much more of Hegel than he rejected. Any assertion, therefore, that Marx's materialism is not essentially atheistic stands in patent contradiction to text and context. Likewise the contention that Marx's emphasis on the economic element over the other elements need not be interpreted atheistically involves a neglect of the principle which is basic to "historical materialism", i.e., the principle that it is the economic base (*Basis, Unterbau*) which conditions the existence and development of the other values, as Reding himself admits. Reding should also remember that Marx holds the existence of religion to be conditioned by, and predicated upon, the existence of an antagonistic economic situation and to be therefore fated to disappear as soon as man has attained the freedom that is his due.[15]

Any attempt, therefore, to interpret Marx in the light of Aristotle and St. Thomas or *vice versa,* as proposed by Reding (and already undertaken by Hohof) [16] involves a clutching at fortuitous and superficial resemblances and a neglect of the essential, namely, the primordial relationship between being and consciousness, being and mind, being and

[15] Another statement which is entirely false if applied directly to the two systems as they stand is J. Schumpeter's assertion: "Marx's philosophy is no more materialistic than Hegel's" (cited in M. Reding, *Der politische Atheismus,* p. 349). Marx himself, as we have seen, made no bones about his own materialist sensism. We, too, consider Hegel's spiritualism to be indefensible; but that only aggravates the indefensibility of Marxism.

[16] "For this reason, we have subjected Marxism to a comparison with Aristotle and Thomas, with both of whom it is intimately connected. Marx cannot simply be replaced by Aristotle, but we are persuaded that the Marxist picture of man, especially his ethics and politics, would only stand to gain from an enrichment with Aristotelian-Thomist ideas" (M. Reding, *Der politische Atheismus,* p. 354). I believe G. W. Plekhanov, the theoretician and historian of Marxism, was the first to call for a synthesis of Marx and St. Thomas: "No attempt has thus far been made to complement Marx by Thomas Aquinas" (*Grundprobleme des Marxismus* [Berlin, 1958], p. 13). Rjazanov, in his Introduction to MEGA I, 3, corrects Plekhanov and mentions the studies *Die Bedeutung der Marxschen Kapitalkritik* and *Warenwert und Kapitalprofit* by the Catholic author W. Hohof; the pertinent note appears in the Italian translation (Milan, 1945, pp. 163ff.), but has been omitted in the German edition.

knowing. As we have seen, the definition of man as a *Naturwesen* and a *Gattungswesen* involves the extirpation of any and all metaphysical transcendence because it makes man essentially a "being-in-nature" and a "being-for-society", thereby evicting any genuine freedom of the human person which rests solely on the foundation of the Absolute. Reding indeed acknowledges that the idea of God reactivizes man's authority to the same extent to which it supports and sustains that authority. Human authority is not absolute, is not the final court of appeal; that authority cannot decide according to its own whim; it takes its justification from a supreme authority outside itself. Thus religion involves a dual limitation of political power. The Church limits the absolute power of the State from the institutional point of view, while belief in God limits that absolute power from the ethical and juridical point of view.[17] But this is precisely what Marx himself does not and will not admit; and indeed it is ruled out entirely by his thought, no matter how that thought be interpreted, whether materialistically or Hegelianly, or worse still as a synthesis of the two approaches. Marxist "political atheism" flows from the ontological and anthropological atheism involved in the Hegelian-Feuerbachian inversion of the whole notion of immanence,[18] an inversion theoretically not unlike that effected by atheistic existentialism, as we shall note below. Any talk of a "political atheism", prescinding from a fundamental atheism rooted in the very notion of the structure of the human being, is meaningless both in the light of Christian teaching and of the principles of Marxism. This materialism is the only possible foundation of those Marxist principles!

Let us try to pinpoint the issue here still more exactly.[19] The issue is a burning one and all misunderstanding must be meticulously precluded. In any theoretical discussion of the distinction between and separability of materialism and atheism in Marxism, there must be a *drastic and total* abstraction from the question of the degree to which socialism and Christianity are opposed and the degree to which they may be reconcilable on the ethico-economic level. More specifically, there must be a total abstraction from the question of the fundamental compatibility of the socialist notion of property and ownership with natural law and Christian morality. Here there may well be a possibility of evolution and dialogue, precisely in the light of the principles of Christianity and

[17] M. Reding, *Der politische Atheismus,* p. 355.

[18] We cannot therefore agree with Reding's statement: "If we understand Marx's philosophy of religion in terms of the basic intent of the whole system, then it must be emphasized that man is supposed to be liberated in the religious sense as well as in the political, moral and philosophical" (*ibid.,* p. 354).

[19] We are here thinking particularly of Reding's teacher, T. Steinbüchel, the resolute champion of the synthesis of Christianity and Socialism (cf. Steinbüchel's *Sozialismus* [Tübingen, 1959]).

Thomism on the nature and use of material goods in human society. Indeed, the recent documents of the magisterium of the Church on the social question openly acknowledge and even advocate such a dialogue: a socialism that asserts man's transcendence and safeguard's his spiritual dignity and the rights of the human person, cannot but arrive at an understanding with Christianity and be integrated into it. But this socialism can never adhere to the line of Hegel-Feuerbach-Marx-Engels-Lenin, for they all deny the transcendence and the theological foundation of the human person in his being and his operation.

What then does it mean to call Marx a realist? [20] The mere fact of a certain opposition between Marx and Hegel does not justify this unequivocal characterization of Marx. Marx's opposition to Hegel is considerably less drastic than his opposition to Feuerbach, as is proven, on Steinbüchel's own [21] admission, by Marx's resumption of the dialectical method. Marx himself and the impeccably orthodox Marxist theoreticians even reproach Feuerbach with the persistence of "theological remnants" in his static and consequently absolutistic conception of man as "the God of Man" (*Homo homini Deus*). Marx could indeed be said to be a realist in the cultural sense and Marxism could be called an economic, political and historical realism, in the sense of accommodating to the course of history and practicing realistic policies (*Realpolitik*); but Marx's principal sources, Hegel's Philosophy of History and especially his Phenomenology of Spirit positively teem with this sort of "realism". Thus Marxist materialism is every bit as much a *monism* as is Hegelian idealism: the latter is a monism of Absolute Spirit, the latter a monism of "economic man"; and for both the world of nature and history is the "battlefield" (*Kampffeld*) of man's progress.

This basic immanentist monism was the only condition on which Marx was able to take over from Hegel, as against Feuerbach, the "dialectical method" which is the alpha and omega of Marxism, to an even greater extent than it is of Hegelianism itself. Actually for Hegel the dialectic has to do with the *Erscheinung* (phenomenon, appearance) rather than with the *Wesen* (being, essence, inner core) or the Absolute. It indicates the process of "transition" and of reference of the empirical reality to the Absolute; and Hegel precisely calls the supersession and transcendence of this empirical reality the "baneful infinity" (*schlechte Unendlichkeit*), this endless transition from finite to finite, or again the "transition from the first to the second immediacy," [22] which happy turn

[20] T. Steinbüchel, *Sozialsmus,* p. 47.

[21] "His taking-over of the dialectical method is what is typical of *Marx's* position in the history of sociology and philosophy of history" (*ibid.,* p. 49).

[22] Hegel uses the expressions: "*Wiederherstellung der Unmittelbarkeit*" (restoration of immediacy) (*Enz. d. philos. Wiss.,* § 122; ed. Hoffmeister, p. 132), "*Herstellung der ersten unmittelbarkeit . . . das Unmittelbare durch Aufhebung der*

of phrase on Hegel's part has almost escaped the notice of the numerous and vigilant band of champions and critics of Hegelianism. But the Absolute which is in-itself-and-by-and-for-itself does not become;[23] rather it is the motionless center of convergence of all the evolutionary rays. Thus does Hegel's Logic coincide with his Metaphysics: whatever may be said about the internal consistency and strength of the Hegelian system, there is one point on which there can be no doubt whatever: that system definitely thought (and quite rightly so!) that dialectical progress demanded the foundation of a bias and a goal; otherwise the gates are wide open for all solutions (including the capitalist one!) and for all sorts of mad adventures (including the total destruction of the human race, an eventuality which is beginning to seem a distinct possibility in our own days, not so much on account of the power of the new weapons as on account of the refusal to accept any overriding criterion for their use).

In Marxism the notion of man as *Naturwesen* and *Gattungswesen* is that of a universal caught in suspension between the two poles of nature and history, both of which, far from providing an explanation and a foundation for anything, themselves stand preeminently in need of explanation and foundation:[24] thus in Marxism everything is left up in the air and entrusted to the mere chance of "baneful infinity", as the result of a "practice" which is posited as the law of its own development and is

---

Vermittlung, das Einfache durch Aufheben des Unterschiedes, das Positive durch Aufhebung des Negativen" (production of the first immediacy . . . the immediate by annulment of mediation, the simple by annulment of the difference, the positive by annulment of the negative) (*Wissenschaft der Logik,* Book III, Ch. 3; ed. Lasson, Vol. II [Leipzig, 1934], pp. 497f.).

[23] "The essence, as we have just said, is nothing else than thought itself. Over against the essence we set the appearance, change and modification etc. It is therefore the essence, the aggregate, the universal, the eternal, which is always thus. God is pictured in various ways but the essence of God is the universal, the everlasting, that which permeates all and transcends all imagination (*das durch alle Vorstellung Hindurch-dringende*" (Hegel, *Vorlesungen über die Geschichte der Philosophie,* Introduction: System u. Geschichte der Philosophie; ed. Hoffmeister [Leipzig, 1944], pp. 83f.).

[24] The error in Steinbüchel's approach, as in that of the "Catholic concordism" that champions a Marxist realism, lies in the uncritical acceptance of Marx's famous principle: "It is not men's consciousness that determines their being; it is rather, on the contrary, their social being that determines their consciousness", on which Steinbüchel comments as follows: "This insight amounted to a definitive supersession of idealism, in that it acknowledged all idea-fashioning in law and custom, in politics and science, in philosophy and religion, to be a social product and thus always something secondary. It likewise served as the basis for an epistemologically grounded system of socialism, now itself considered as a social ideal, a content of consciousness, a necessity which is derived from the social structure which in its turn is conditioned by economic relations" (T. Steinbüchel, *Sozialismus,* p. 32). But Steinbüchel is here simply accepting from Marx without any reservations the circular dialectic of economics and knowledge, a complete blind alley.

always open to question and consequently to supersession. What have the Marxists replied, what indeed can they reply to this charge of a fundamental equivocation and ambiguity in their system? It is difficult to see how the Marxists can shatter or at least badly dent the internal consistency of their system so as to bring even a minimum of order into the dust of battle of history and guarantee a definitive bias to its evolution: any such effort, even without recourse to the Hegelian *Aufheben* in its peculiarly shrivelled Marxist interpretation, always involves some sort of ascendent movement; but the Marxist philosophy of history, making the economic reality, as it does, the content of the human being, is unidimensional. Not only does the Marxist dialectic preclude the possibility of any fulfillment of the prophesied abolition of classes; strictly speaking, it cannot even manage to establish itself as a dialectic, unless it be the violence-prone and explosive dialectic of the "qualitative leap". Therefore, it is hopeless, from the outset, to try to salvage a piece of this system, whether in its Hegelian or in its Marxist variant, by excising it from the system as such in order to insert it into another and opposite conception. The transplant, like every blood transfusion, must be of the same biological type as the host; and it is precisely the furious struggle of Marxist atheism against religion which forms a great part of the history of our day.

Steinbüchel himself admits as much in substance when he agrees that both Marx and Hegel utterly destroy the freedom and consequently the personality of the individual and conceive of freedom as an historical and collective and necessary activity, since they champion the necessity of historical evolution, which, in Marxism, is the necessary evolution of the economic forces and laws. But what or who is the responsible subject of this whole movement? Hegel and his disciple Marx reply: the great man of a given age. Very well, but in virtue of what principle do these VIPs and VVIPs arrogate to themselves such an assignment? And what is the argument in favor of such a handover of power which, as Steinbüchel himself admits, inevitably ends in the suppression of the most intimate and personal node of the human being in his distinctively human nature, by reducing him to a mere instrument of an alleged necessity of historical evolution.? [25]

Steinbüchel even considers whether the conceptions of Marx and

[25] "Within the *Marxian* conception of history, man is at the deepest level merely the executive organ of social necessities and mechanisms, any configuration of consciousness is the exponent and indicator of apersonal and suprapersonal mechanisms, and man becomes, if we may again quote Hegel, a mere accident of the universal, the natural. In this last point of the Marxian philosophy of history we again encounter the bias of Hegel's pan-logosism. The universal (in Hegel, the Idea; in Marx, the mechanism of economic development and evolution) ultimately annuls personal independence, autonomy and freedom" (T. Steinbüchel, *Sozialismus,* pp. 54f.).

Engels can be said to be "materialism" at all! He does indeed acknowledge and report the explicit declarations of materialism made by Marx and Engels, their choice of the terms "dialectical materialism" (Marx) and "historical materialism" (Engels), their appeal to the 18th-century French materialists against the still abstraction-prone Hegelian Left; and he criticizes their naive realism and especially the superficiality of Engels' critique of the Kantian "thing-in-itself". But Steinbüchel proceeds to find an entirely anti-materialistic element embedded within this "materialistic conception" of history, inasmuch as history is conceived as a self-moving dialectical unfolding, entirely permeated by reason and teleological in nature (*die vernunftvoll-teleologische . . . sich bewegende dialektische Entfaltung*); and this, says Steinbüchel, would surely exclude any purely and exclusively mechanical or mechanistic explanation of historical development. Let us admit (and we feel that such an admission is possible) that this was indeed Marx's intention. The hard fact remains that this intention is simply not supported by, nor will it jibe with, the premisses of Marx's whole system: in a materialist or crypto-idealist world—dominated by the laws of economics in accord with the necessity of historical development and evolution, wherein the individual is absorbed into the universal [26]—rationality and teleology coincide with necessity.

Of the antithetical pair, materialism-spiritualism, Marxism has beyond a shadow of a doubt chosen and chosen unequivocally materialism, a materialism which is a total inversion of the idealism of Hegel, an immanentistic materialism not a physical materialism, a dialectical sensism, a dialectical economism if you will, but always materialism; a materialism that clashes with Hegel, yes; but not in function of the principle of immanentism which is common to both! And this collapsing of the principle of immanentism into phenomenological materialism [27] by means of a sense-perceptionist, sensist epistemology as in Marx, is

[26] Steinbüchel repeats most trenchantly within a few pages what he has already said on this point: "All individuality is, to be sure, *as Hegel* would have it, an accident of a universal substance; or, to follow Marx in his abandonment of this metaphysical basis, it is an incidental and subsidiary outcome and outgrowth of the universal economic mechanism. The individual has value and meaning only in terms of the universal which achieves a break-through in him. This is the ultimate *monistic* bias, which is likewise at the root of the materialist conception of history, which can leave neither place nor meaning for the ineffably personal" (*ibid.*, p. 59). A little later, Steinbüchel cites the Thomist principle: *Omne agens agit propter finem* (every agent acts in terms of an end) (p. 66); but the end here mentioned supposes the order and hierarchy of ends which in turn supposes a transcendent supreme End.

[27] "But *metaphysical* materialism and *historical* materialism sets out only to be a *positivistic* view of history, making the economic reality, rather than the Idea of Hegel's idealist conception of history, the principle of interpretation of all historical phenomena, even including the cultural-intellectual phenomena of the historical life of society: law, morality, religion, philosophy" (*ibid.*, p. 58 Note).

perhaps the most remarkable feat of heroism in modern thought, for it is truly the ultimate in taking seriously the basic principle involved. Any restriction, then, to "political atheism" flies in the face of text and context. Steinbüchel speaks of "metaphysical materialism" but this term seems to us less than accurate: the radical sensism which serves as the basis and inspiration for Marxist epistemology admits of no metaphysics whatever; moreover, the whole controversy between the Hegelian Left and the Hegelian Right revolved around the status of metaphysics, with the Left refusing it any status at all. And the controversy of Marx-Engels in *The Holy Family* with the speculative wing of the Hegelian Left is once again anti-metaphysical in tone and inspiration, coming out in favor of sheer economic historicism, without remainder. And finally, the sacrosanct terms, "dialectical materialism" and "historical materialism", themselves are anti-metaphysical.

Reding's assertion that atheism is for Marx a "combat weapon" (*Kampfmittel*) involves no denial but rather a presupposition that atheism constitutes the inner core of the explanation of the world and man: [28] politics is the decision taken by man with regard to history and its evolution; but this sort of decision presupposes the decision or specification man makes of himself and of nature and of his relation to nature.[29] Nor is any escape route afforded by the mere fact that the Marxist concept of "matter" embraces all the degrees of the real and thus likewise the activity of the spirit, that we are consequently not here dealing with the insensible and impenetrable matter of rationalist metaphysics; this merely *aggravates* the atheistic stance of Marxism, rendering it radically irretrievable. The Marxist conception, remaining faithful to the principle of consciousness, assumes the sphere of sense appear-

[28] Even Reding acknowledges it to be the first point or level (*Schicht*) in this explanatory interpretation: "Like many of his contemporaries—David Friedrich Strauss and the young Nietzsche, to name but two—Marx decided in favor of a knowledge without faith. The world is to be explained and can be explained without God. There need not be any God" (M. Reding, *Der Sinn des Marxschen Atheismus* [Munich-Salzburg-Cologne, 1957], p. 15). And so the question raised by Steinbüchel and his pupil and disciple Reding is undercut from the outset: "From the time of his Thesis on two Enlightenment-type thinkers of antiquity, atheism always lies in the background of Marx's concept of 'materialism'. The specification of his own, economic, atheism takes the form of the delimitation and distinction of his own thought from the classical materialism of the French Enlightenment and from the 'humane' but merely 'contemplative' materialism of Feuerbach. All three brands of materialism presuppose 'scientific' atheism" (K. Löwith, *Nietzsches Philosophie der ewigen Wiederkunft des Gleichen* [Berlin, 1935], p. 180, Note 48).

[29] Categorically "there must not be any God, otherwise man is dependent upon him, owes his being and life to him and is under obligation to him. Rather is man the autocratic demi-urge of his own fate. Marx crowns his theoretical atheism with the idea of the self-creation of the earth and man" (M. Reding, *Der Sinn des Marxschen Atheismus*, pp. 15f.).

ances and of the sensible products of human activity to be the fundamental "reality". Not only therefore does it rule out as inconceivable any transcendent Absolute as in Hegel; it excludes by definition any spiritual reality as such. The atheism scoffed at in Hegel by Bauer and Marx in their *Die Posaune* has now taken a step backward and is strictly solidary with the "new" materialism, precisely because it expresses the inverted Hegelian pseudo-spiritualism. Reding himself writes: "Matter is the Absolute for Marx, as Man was for Feuerbach, Spirit for Hegel, the Indeterminate for Schelling. And just as the Spirit in Hegel gathered into itself all the degrees of being, so do matter and nature in Marx embrace both purely material reality and spiritual phenomena as well. Marx must be taken seriously in his claim to have turned Hegel right side up; and the inevitable implication is that, just as the Hegelian Spirit included matter, so Marxian matter likewise includes spirit." [30] The net result of all this is simply that the closed circle of finitude and consequent atheism has been doubly sealed: once in virtue of the principle of immanentism as such and then in virtue of the reduction of the sphere of immanence to sensible reality and the material and sensible practice (practical activity) of man. Of the ambiguity inherent in this disintegration and reductive resolution we shall be speaking in our concluding chapter, when we discuss the principle of immanentism in detail.

For the moment, we conclude that, if there is one clear point in the whole evolution of Marxism, from the young Marx right down to the Marx of *Capital* and from the classical Marxist triad (Marx-Engels-Lenin) right down to contemporary Marxism of any economico-political stripe, it is this fundamental atheism and materialism. And our analysis has shown that atheism and materialism in Marxism end up being "physical materialism" or skepticism, in virtue of the *humanism* to which Marxism lays claim.[31] Any effort, therefore, to rebut the charge of atheism levelled against Marxism by talking of "economic materialism" and the like, simply aggravates that charge itself, inasmuch as the economic reality constitutes the flash-point of the *physical* matter-spirit antithesis and binds man hand and foot to nature and historical so-

[30] M. Reding, *Der politische Atheismus*, p. 78. Hence the Engelsian Marxists, like Lenin, include the concept of "spirit" and of "society" within that of nature (cf. Lenin, "Zur Frage der Dialektik," in *Aus dem philosophischen Nachlass*, (p. 285).

[31] In this connection, Engels, e.g. in an important letter of November 19, 1844, to Marx, declares his preference for Stirner's atheism derived from egotism over that of Feuerbach which starts from God in order to arrive at man: "Stirner is right in repudiating Feuerbach's "Man" (at least that of the *Essence of Christianity* Feuerbach); this Feuerbachian "Man" is derived and deduced from God. Feuerbach finally arrived at 'Man' and so 'Man' is still crowned with a theological halo of abstraction. The proper way to arrive at 'Man' is exactly the opposite" (*Briefwechsel zwischen Marx und Engels*, MEGA III, 1, p. 7).

ciety in a relationship of material reality that defines him without remainder. Thus, for orthodox Marxism, a human relationship that is not economico-political in nature, is simply unthinkable: everything in human history occurs and unfolds in virtue of conflicts and tensions of an economic nature. We are not here interested in the internal ambiguities of the Marxist theory and teaching, nor yet in the dubious mixture in Marxism of realism and idealism; rather, our point of interest here is the clarity and consistency of Marx's "plan for man" which he himself advanced in controversial contact with Hegel's pseudo-spiritualism. Marx himself proclaimed that plan in a classical passage: "In the social production that men carry on, they enter into definite relations that are indispensable and independent of their will; these relations of production correspond to a definite stage of development of their material powers of production. The sum total of these relations of production constitutes the economic structure of society—the real foundation, on which rise legal and political superstructures and to which correspond definite forms of social consciousness. The mode of production in material life determines the general character of the social, political and spiritual processes of life. It is not the consciousness of men that determines their existence, but, on the contrary, their social existence determines their consciousness." [32]

It is so obvious as to need no detailed proof, that the adjective "spiritual" here used to qualify the phrase "process-of life" has a purely cultural meaning, being conjunctive and not disjunctive with respect to the fundamental substantive, life, which is economic in nature. It is not man's consciousness, i.e., any autonomous quality of man which raises him above socio-economic conditioning, which determines his existence, but on the contrary, his social existence determines his consciousness.[33]

[32] Marx & Engels, *Basic Writings on Politics and Philosophy,* edited by Lewis S. Feuer (New York: Doubleday Anchor, 1959), p. 43.

[33] It has been noted that Engels, as opposed to Marx, ends in a cruder form of materialism, Darwinian in stripe (cf. G. Wetter, "Marxismo e ateismo," in *Il problema dell'ateismo* [Brescia, 1962], pp. 139ff.). But another expert has noted that this slight difference between the two men is entirely irrelevant to the basic problem: "Marx's anthropology should not, as sometimes happens, be considered in isolation from or even in opposition to Engels' ontological declarations. Engels rightly understood his friend's anthropological ideas to be not only unequivocally anti-theistic but moreover built up on the anti-idealist conception of sensible nature elaborated by Feuerbach. And Marx's retention of the dynamic dialectic of Hegel made no difference here. It was in this conviction that Engels tried to provide, with his own dialectical materialist ontology, the appropriate metaphysical foundation for Marx's anthropology" (P. Ehlen, *Der Atheismus im dialektischen Materialismus* [Munich, 1961], p. 179). And Ehlen concludes: "In order to bring about a 'more peaceful co-existence between Marxism and Christianity', Marxism would have to give up its fundamental sustaining idea. But what would then be left would no longer be Marxism. Our chief reason for this more

The formula can be admitted to reveal an Hegelian structure, inasmuch as it posits the demand for mediation of immediate consciousness on the part of the human universal (*Gattungs-Naturwesen*); but it must be added that this universal is constituted by the sum total of the processes of material production. Marx's materialism has therefore advanced a stage beyond that of Strauss-Bauer-Feuerbach, which was theological in origin, or that of Stirner, which was psychological in origin. And we can speak interchangeably of humanistic materialism, naturalistic atheism, atheistic humanism and the like permutations, because what is understood in each and every case is the bilateral and reciprocal dialectic of man and nature. This dialectic is not understood in any indeterminate sense, but rather, as it were, raised to the second power, inasmuch as the nature here spoken of is not simply that stable nature of abstract objectivity but rather the world in which man finds himself and which man himself must create with his own labor. Engels and Marx were thus entirely in agreement on the essential point. A conciliatory extension of dialectical and historical materialism in the direction of Christianity is just what the Marxists want; but their aim and goal is one quite different from that envisaged and understood by the naive Christian appeasers.

In conclusion, it must be said that the profound and truly revolutionary significance of Marxism, viewed from whatever angle, manifests itself in terms of this double imprisonment of nature in man and of man in nature, with the consequent double estrangement of man from God:[34] the alienation of alienation and the disappearance of classes, which is the function and goal of the dialectic and the τέλος of history, becomes in the end that transcendental *Weltgericht* (Doomsday) spoken of by Schiller and Hegel, which assigns to man his definitive place in nature, no longer simply as a piece or element of nature but rather as that "result" of which Hegel speaks in the Preface to the Phenomenology, when he refers to man having taken the place of the True Absolute.

One further clarification is in order on the relations between religion and materialism in Marxism. One critic has seen fit to view Marxism as a kind of "Messianism" dedicated to the liberation of the proletariat;

---

thorough treatment of the above-mentioned interpretations of Marx has been our conviction that they represent an attenuation of the harsh reality of Marxist atheism. The dialectical materialism founded by Marx is anti-God to the core and consequently likewise anti-human, anti-man" (*ibid.*).

[34] Cf. on this point the remarks of E. Thier in his *Das Menschenbild des jungen Marx* (Göttingen, 1957), pp. 30ff. The strongest confirmation of our own line of interpretation is to be found in the semi-official anthology prepared by the Institute of Marxism-Leninism, which we have here cited in the English translation, *On Religion*. Cf. also J. Lacroix: "This attitude involves and implies in Marx an atheism which is no mere superstructure of his theory but rather essential to it" (*Le sens de l'athéisme moderne* [Tournai-Paris, 1958], p. 33).

and this in a double sense: first, inasmuch as Marx felt that Christianity had fallen short of its assignment of liberating man from capitalist oppression, the Church having instead become the ally of bourgeois capitalism; and secondly, and more pretentiously, inasmuch as Marx had taken over from his Jewish heritage the Messianic idea of the liberation of man by means of the vicarious sufferings of the chosen proletariat. Marx is thus held to have preserved the central point of the Judeo-Christian conception of history as "salvation history" (*Heilsgeschichte*) and interpretation of history as a "doctrine of salvation" (*Heilslehre*). Marx presents this idea in the form of the eschatological notion of a revolutionary transformation of history into socialist society, a "classless society" (*klassenlose Gesellschaft*). Thus the proletariat is not a class within this present society but rather stands outside of it, providing the foundation for the possibility and hope of a classless society. For this reason, the proletariat is the key to the problem of the whole of society globally considered. Only from this universalist and eschatological point of view can Marx assert that the proletariat is the "heart" of the society of the future and that the Marxist philosophy is the "head" of that society.[35] Thus, even as human labor is catalyzed by, and takes the place of, the idea of God, so too the idea of the coming of the "classless society" is hastened by, and takes the place of, the "kingdom of God"; but it is a kingdom of God without God! [36] This interpretation is not without its power of attraction: even as in Hegel the Absolute Spirit is being realized and actualized in historical mankind, so in Marx the "proletariat" embodies in itself the aspiration and mission of the liberation of man. The proletariat is the protagonist of the history of the future.

Yes, this interpretation is indeed attractive; but it runs into serious difficulties within the framework of the absolutely fundamental ideas of Marxism. First and foremost, it contradicts the fundamental principle of the Marxist ideology, which is expressly sensist and admits of no religious admixtures whatsoever; this was precisely the error with which Marx and Engels reproached the theological Hegelian Left (Strauss, Bauer and Feuerbach himself). Religion is the basic alienation; it is the alienation responsible for all the other alienations. And there can be no question in Marxism of a Feuerbachian kind of conserving annul-

[35] K. Löwith, *Weltgeschichte und Heilsgeschichte* (Stuttgart, 1953), p. 42.

[36] Cf. H. Rohr, *Pseudoreligiöse Motive in den Frühschriften von K. Marx* (Tubingen, 1962), pp. 42ff. In addition to Löwith, Rohr cites the following authorities as favoring this thesis: A. J. Toynbee, the famous English historian; W. Philipp, J. Taube and G. Wunsch who calls Marx a "Godless Luther" and his revolution a "prophetic passion" (*prophetische Leidenschaft*) and a "secularized eschatology".

ment (*Aufheben*); rather there must be ruthless extermination all along the line: the very name of God, the very words "immortality" and "religion" must be made to disappear. No one who is at all familiar with the writings of Marx and Engels can fail to discern the radical and total phobia and hatred they display for everything even faintly redolent of religion.

Moreover, the sacred writings of Marxism fully bear out the contention that the concept of the *proletariat* is not derived in these writings from scriptural sources or texts; no one has ever found a single such reference in the Marxist writings. It originated rather, as Popitz observes, from Marx's sociological investigations and observations and from his interest in the proletariat of the French Revolution: Marx holds that the political revolution is possible only when one definite class produces within society, on the basis of its own historical situation, the emancipation of society as such.[37] Thus, the origin of the notion of the "emancipation of the proletariat", of the advent of the new classless society, has no historico-sociological connection whatsoever with the liberation of the Jewish people from bondage in Egypt. Nor does this Marxist notion represent in any sense an inversion of the Christian doctrine of redemption from sin and the Last Judgment. Rather it is a frankly and patently sociological notion, with a very clear historical nexus with the ideals of freedom of the French Revolution and with the conditions of the day in Germany; and with a theoretical nexus primarily with the Hegelian dialectic of the "unhappy consciousness (*unglückliches Bewusstsein*) of the "master-slave" relationship.

It is to man, to mankind in general, that Marx like Hegel addresses himself: any positive or negative reference to any religion whatever, except for the call for the alienation of alienation, the negation of negation, is entirely absent not only from Marx's written works but from his aspirations and plans as well; and, above all, it is entirely absent from his conception of man as a *res naturae et historiae* (an entity of nature and of history), the sole artificer of his own adventure. Engels is no less explicit, and his complete agreement with Marx is one of the bulwarks of present-day Marxism as authoritatively expressed in Soviet Leninism. The shades of difference, such as they may be, between Marx and Engels on this point pale into total insignificance in the case of the fundamental problem of the assertion or denial of God.

It is certainly open to discussion whether Marxist-Leninist atheism is the crucial disintegrative event of "our age"; but it seems to us indisputable that Marxism *is* "structurally" an atheism, in the deepest sense and

[37] Cf. H. Popitz, *Der entfremdete Mensch, Zeitkritik und Geschichtsphilosophie des jungen Marx* (Basel, 1953), pp. 92ff.: "The Emancipation Idea".

in every single dimension of the phenomenon of Marxism which may be being surveyed. Radically Marxism is atheism because it is immanentism and consequently sensism and anthropologism; it is atheism whether considered as dialectical and historical materialism, as scientific or technological or economic humanism; it is atheism, in short, however it be considered. Lenin's drastic expressions are perfectly consistent with Marxism and are still Gospel in Communist countries.[38] Our own exploration of the foundations (for there are more than one) of Marxism has convinced us that Marxism may well be able to modify, even quite drastically, its economic teachings (and, indeed, it seems to be doing this already, e.g., in regard to the right of ownership), but it can never renounce atheism, because atheism coincides and is identical (as a "negative formulation") with the new conception of man which is positive and constructive humanism. The basic principle of modern thought, which posits truth and value as originating from man rather than from being as such, has been pushed to many extremes in the last hundred years. These extremes have been as varied as rationalism, empiricism, idealism, materialism, positivism and neo-positivism, pessimism, titanism, pragmatism and existentialism. The great variety of these terminal states derived from the principle of immanence witnesses to the fundamental ambiguity of the principle itself and the consequent antithetical polyvalence of its possible developments. But *all of them are atheistic,* as is the principle itself in the deepest sense. The principle and, above all, its various end-states are an assertion of man's *exclusive and total appropriation of himself*. Atheism is not a problem either for Marx and the young Hegelians or for present-day thought; it is an accepted fact and point of departure.[39]

The scope of our present study does not include the problem of the practical attitude of Marxist governments to believers: Lenin himself, as we have seen, strongly recommended an initial "tolerance" but only as a situational tactic aimed at quite unequivocal ultimate extirpation of religion. A problem of a quite different kind, of course, is the question as to whether Marxism's critique of religion may have hit on certain symptoms of degeneracy and inconsequentiality among believers, certain instances of failure of believers to live up to their own beliefs. Marxism may well have nosed out these weak spots and the Christian community

[38] Cf. the statements of Stalin and Khrushchev on this point, on which they are in complete agreement, as reported by H. Gollwitzer in *Die marxistische Religionskritik und christlicher Glaube,* Marxismus IV (Tübingen, 1962), p. 69, n. 1. This "loyalty to atheism" is one of the fundamental points of Leninism, as we have seen.

[39] "Atheism is no problem for him [Marx]; he takes it for granted" (L. Landgrebe, "Das Problem der Dialektik," *Marxismus-Studien,* III [1960], p. 42).

may therefore well profit from attention to the Marxist reproaches. But we are deeply persuaded that this entire problematic (and it is a tormenting one!) is exclusively of phenomenological interest; it is relevant only to specific individual and collective situations and totally irrelevant to the structure of the Marxist (and Modernist) conception of the world in general. Any other interpretation is mere quibbling or vain and dangerous daydreaming!

Two questions arise from the Gollwitzer [40] exposition of Marxist criticisms of religion: (1) Is it true that Communism as a Party is and always must be essentially atheistic and anti-religious? (2) Is it true that religion is and always must be a superstructure (*Ueberbau*) of the class society?

To the first of these questions we have no hestitation in giving an unqualifiedly affirmative reply: yes, Marxism is intrinsically, essentially atheistic, in value of the two strands, idealism and materialism, which merge in that essence.

To the second of these questions our reply must be less forthright and more nuanced, because the religious fact manifests itself in quite complicated forms in human life and history.

In the first place, "religion" as such is not and cannot in any sense be a superstructure of the class society: it expresses the fundamental relationship of man to God as last end and consequently figures as a radical principle of all man's conduct, not only in regard to nature and society, but toward himself as well.

Secondly, those actual instances throughout history in which a religion became subservient to a ruling class must be attributed to an unfortunate preponderance of politics rather than to religion as such, let alone to the Christian doctrine on the whole matter, which clearly teaches man to "render unto Caesar the things that are Caesar's and unto God the things that are God's", thus making a clearcut distinction between the two levels of human life and relationships of establishing an unmistakeable hierarchy of values.

Thirdly, and this is the heart of our reply; even though Christianity has been proclaimed a "State Religion" by some States, this has not caused it to cease to be the "historical religion" of man, of every being and every society. Thus, even in those States where religion and specifically Christianity have been denied recognition, they yet maintain intact their own institutions and channels transcending the temporal interests of individuals and even of States. This does not imply any denial, indeed, if anything, it affords a confirmation of the possibility that the gigantic and explosive clash emerging from Marxism's open declaration

[40] Cf. H. Gollwitzer, *Marxistische Religionskritik,* p. 114.

of war upon religion in general and Christianity in particular may well contribute—by its direct and indirect provocation of the decline and fall of the closed capitalist society—to a revival and renaissance of the virtue of genuine religion and piety and to a renewal of Christendom. This would be more in accord with Christian principles and closer to the spirit of the Gospel because it is freed from the distortions and deformations of complex and recurrent historical entanglements. The cardinal tactical error of Marx and Marxism of every stripe lies in the failure to realize the hopeless incongruity of commencing a drive to defeat and overcome capitalism on the basis of the very same materialistic conception of man as an exclusively sensible economic being which capitalism itself professes! To have any hope of real success, Marxism would have to start from man as autonomous and consequently from the Being who sustains that autonomy; but that would be highly inconvenient for Marxism. In this whole area, therefore, Marxism has no ideological advantage over capitalism; nor will it ever gain any such advantage so long as it persists in professing materialism and the class struggle; for in this struggle the law of the jungle prevails and victory goes to the stronger. For Marxism, therefore, the battle is lost before it even begins.

Marxist atheism is anthropological rather than theological: God exists *through and by the instrumentality of man;* God owes his existence to man inasmuch as man perceives and apprehends himself as "spirit" and free subject or person, and consequently poses to himself the problem of being, truth, social justice and the like, in contradistinction to the animal, which is not spirit and for which the jungle law of the strongest prevails. And so Kant was right in insisting that the entire interest of both the speculative and the practical reason centers in three questions: What can I know? What can I do? What can I hope? as preliminaries to a reply to the basic question: What is man? [41] This must be answered unless everything is to be left hopelessly up in the air.

The second methodological error of Marxist atheism stems from its Feuerbachian heritage: it is to consider the concept of God as a psychological illusion and to reduce monotheism to a mere "precipitate" of polytheism, whereas the only sensible initial drive must be geared to establishing the first Principle of being and the ultimate Foundation of truth and of justice, without which man cannot be man. It is strange but significant that Marx's whole teaching on religion evolved out of and is substantially contained within the solid kernel of his youthful polemic against Plutarch's teaching that God punishes the wicked and rewards the good and of his reiteration of the Epicurean-Lucretian reduction of

[41] *Kritik der reinen Vernunft,* Methodenlehre; A 805, B 833, ed. Reclam, p. 610.

the origin of religion to "fear", from which two points Marx deduces the basic identity of Plutarch's religion with that of Epicurus.[42] Nevertheless, we feel that certain Protestant theologians are operating too hastily and highhandedly in skipping the speculative stage entirely in order to confront modern and Marxist atheism directly with the "living God of the Christian conscience" as a logical and methodological antecedent and thus to rule entirely out of court the very problem of the existence of God.[43] Prior to the God of faith there is the God of reason and reason must itself purge itself of the errors of Epicurus, of Kant, of Hegel and the rest, in its bracing and taxing ascent toward God.

[42] Cf. K. Marx, *Dissertation,* Aus der Vorarbeiten [Fear and the Extramundane Being]; Karl Marx, *Frühe Schriften;* ed. Lieber-Furth, Vol. I, p. 91 and p. 956 with the first and significant quotation taken from d'Holbach's *Système de la nature.* For an analysis of these texts, cf. K. E. Blockmühl, *Leiblichkeit und Gesellschaft,* pp. 115ff.

[43] Two such formulas: "*Einen Gott den 'es gibt', gibt es nicht*" (A God who 'exists'—there is no such God) (D. Bonhoeffer). "God's existence is therefore not susceptible to denial, because it would first have to be comprehended in order to be denied. It cannot be proven that God exists, but it can be proven that the statement 'God does not exist' is absurd" (in H. Gollwitzer, *Die Marxistische Religionskritik,* p. 139). And Gollwitzer argues along the same line as Barth to the naive conclusion that atheism does not exist: "Now what is this atheism in actual fact? Patently a denial and a negation which has no substance whatever, which is an impossible possibility" (p. 140). These Pickwickian theologians simply execute a blanket repudiation of all shades of realist or idealist philosophy; nor are they the only ones thus unwittingly to open the gates to the God-deniers with this convenient assertion that atheism is impossible!

Appendices

I. Carlyle, Engels and Atheism

Engels' essay "Die Lage Englands," published in the *Deutsch-Französische Jahrbücher* of 1844, is of such capital importance that we here append all the pertinent excerpts from this critique of Carlyle's *Past and Present*. The Carlyle book had been published in London in 1843. In his critique, Engels shows himself to have been profoundly influenced by Bruno Bauer and especially by Feuerbach: "In his critique of Carlyle's notions on the philosophy of history, a critique which occupies the latter portion of the essay, Engels is clearly still following Bruno Bauer and especially Feuerbach. It is well-known what an enthusiastic 'Feuerbachian' Engels became after the appearance of *The Essence of Christianity*. In the period between 1843 and 1845, the anthropological principle was, for Engels, the Alpha and Omega of philosophy." [1] The original German text of this Engels essay is available in MEGA I, 2, pp. 412-428 and in the later *Karl Marx-Friedrich Engels Werke* (Berlin: Dietz Verlag, 1961) Vol. I, pp. 525-549. An inspection of the German text will show that Engels' translation of Carlyle is remarkably faithful to the letter and the spirit of the English writer in those excerpts which Engels puts in quotation marks and sets off by indentation from his own commentary; he is substantially less faithful and accurate in those paraphrases which he unhappily introduces by such phrases as "Carlyle says", "Carlyle continues", "Carlyle maintains". In the case of the former type of quotation, we have preferred to insert here the exact wording of Carlyle from the English original, indicating by *** any instances of a total omission by Engels of a word or phrase of the Carlyle original; where Engels himself indicates such an omission or immediate transition to another part of the text we have indicated this by the usual . . . within the already indented Engels' quotation from Carlyle. In the case of the paraphrase, we have simply translated Engels' German rendering, which often departs quite substantially from Car-

[1] D. Rjazanov, Introduction to MEGA, I, 2, pp. LXXIIIf. There are explicit references to Engel's debt to Feuerbach and Bruno Bauer in the text we are here presenting in translation. These references occur in MEGA, I, 2, pp. 424 and 425; in *K. Marx-Friedrich Engels Werke* [Berlin: Dietz Verlag, 1962], Vol. I, p. 543.

lyle's actual text. We append in square brackets the page references to Carlyle *Past and Present* (New York: John W. Lovell Company, no date), a service Engels did not himself provide for his readers. We have indicated in parentheses the point at which a new page of Engels' text *begins:*

"(532) We have, continues Carlyle, thrown away the religious sentiment of the Middle Ages and have gotten nothing in its place; we have

> ' "forgotten God" ***. We have *** closed our eyes to the eternal Substance of things, and opened them only to the Shews and Shams of things. We quietly believe this Universe to be intrinsically a great unintelligible PERHAPS; extrinsically, clear enough, it is a great, most extensive Cattleford and workhouse, with most extensive Kitchen-ranges, Dining-tables,—whereat he is wise who can find a place! [Engels here translates: ". . . he who is wise finds a place!"] All the Truth of this Universe is uncertain; only the profit and loss of it, the pudding and praise of it, are and remain very visible to the practical man.
>
> 'There is no longer any God for us! God's Laws are become a Greatest-Happiness Principle, a Parliamentary Expediency: the Heavens *** an Astronomical Time-keeper; a butt for Herschel-telescopes to shoot science at, to shoot sentimentalities at: —in our and old Johnson's [2] dialect, man has lost the *soul* out of him; and now *** begins to find the want of it! This is verily the plague-spot; centre of the universal Social Gangrene [Carlyle, *op. cit.,* pp. 133f.] . . . There is no religion; there is no God; man has lost his soul, and vainly seeks antiseptic salt. Vainly: in killing Kings, in French Revolutions, Manchester Insurrections, is found no remedy. The foul *** leprosy, alleviated for an hour, reappears in new force and desperateness next hour.' [Carlyle, *op. cit,* p. 134]

"But since the place of the old religion could not remain entirely empty, we have come by a new Gospel in its stead, a Gospel that sits well with the emptiness and meaninglessness of the age. It is the Gospel of Mammonism. The Christian heaven and the Christian hell have been abandoned, the former as doubtful, the latter as senseless—and you have a new hell; the hell of present-day England is the consciousness of "not succeeding, of not making money!'

> " 'True, it must be owned, we for the present, with our Mammon-Gospel, have come to strange conclusions! We call it *Society;* and go about professing openly the totalest separation, isolation. Our life is not a mutual helpfulness; but rather, cloaked under due laws-of-war, named "fair competition" and so forth, it is a mutual hostility . . .' [Carlyle, *op. cit.,* p. 143]

[2] Engels here writes "old Ben Jonson's".

"(537) . . . This is the state of England, according to Carlyle. An idle, land-owning aristocracy, that 'has not even learned to sit still and at least to foment no mischief'; a working aristocracy, sunken in Mammonism; an aristocracy that is nothing but a band of bucaneers and pirates, where it ought to be an assembly of chieftains of labor and captains of industry; a parliament elected by bribery; a philosophy of sheer spectatorism,[3] of Donothingism, of *laissez-faire;* a worn-out, crumbling religion; a disintegration of all common human interests; a global despair of truth and humanity and a consequent global isolation of men within the confines of (538) their 'brute individuality'; a chaotic, riotous confusion of all human relations, a war of everyone against everyone else; an all-embracing spiritual death, a want of 'soul', i.e. of genuine humanity: a disproprotionately strong working class, in insupportable oppression and misery, in a state of angry disaffection and rebellion against the old social order and consequently a menacing, irresistibly advancing democracy—everywhere chaos, disorder, anarchy, disintegration of the old bonds of society; everywhere an inner vacuum, inanity and debility.—That is the state of England . . .[4]

"What are the prospects for the future? The present state of affairs will not and cannot continue. We have seen that Carlyle, on his own admission, has no 'Morrison's Pill', no panacea for the ills of society. And he is right on this point, too. Any social philosophy that sets up a brace of principles as its upshot, that keeps administering nothing but Morrison's Pills, is still very inadequate; it is not so much bare conclusions that we need as rather *study;* results and conclusions are nothing without the evolution that has led to them, that we have known since Hegel's day. And the conclusions are worse than useless if they are made to jell, rather than being used, as they should be, as premisses for further development. But the conclusions must likewise temporarily assume a definite form, must be structured out of vague indeterminateness into clear thoughts; and in the wake of this structuring, in a nation so drastically empirical as the English, the conclusions cannot escape the form of Morrison's Pills. Carlyle himself, even though he has absorbed a good deal of the German spirit and is fairly far removed from vulgar empiricism, would probably be touting a few pills of his own, were he less vague and wooly on the subject of the future.

"As things stand, he declares that everything will be pointless and to no avail, so long as mankind remains plunged in atheism, so long as it

[3] Cf. Hegel: ". . . while the consciousness is inspecting itself, we have no other option than pure contemplation from this side either" (*Phänomenologie des Geistes,* Introduction, ed. Hoffmeister, p. 72).

[4] As an indication of this inanity of the England of those days, Engels here notes that, when the Strauss work *Das Leben Jesu* appeared, there was no respectable man found in all of England who was willing to translate it nor yet any editor of repute ready to publish it. It was finally translated by a Socialist lecturer and published serially by a minor Socialist printer. Sold at a penny a number, it was read only by the workers of Manchester, Birmingham and London (MEGA I, 2, p. 407; *K. Marx-F. Engels Werke* [Dietz], Vol. I, pp. 527f.).

does not recover its 'soul'. Not that the old Catholicism is to be restored in its vitality and power nor even that the present religion is to be preserved. Carlyle is well aware that rituals, dogmas, litanies and Sinaitic thunder are all to no avail, that not all of the thunder of Sinai can make the truth a whit truer or any reasonable man at all afraid, that the religion of fear (539) has been mightily superseded. But he does insist that religion itself must be restored, for he claims it is patent to what a pass England has been brought by 'two centuries of atheistic government'—since the 'blessed' Restoration of Charles II—and that we shall gradually be compelled to see that this atheism is beginning to become worn and tattered. But we have seen what it is that Carlyle designates as atheism: it is not so much the disbelief in a personal God, as rather the disbelief in man's inner nature, in the infinity of the universe; it is the disbelief in reason, it is despairing of spirit and truth; Carlyle's war is being waged not against disbelief in the revelation of the Bible but rather against the 'frightfulest disbelief, disbelief in the Bible of Universal History'. This is the Eternal Bible, the Eternal God's-Book, which every born man, till once the soul and eyesight are extinguished in him can see God's Finger writing. To scorn and discredit this is an infidelity like no other, an infidelity which you would punish, not with fire and the stake, but certainly with the most peremptory order to hold its peace till it got something better to say.[5] . . .

"(542) His whole view is basically a pantheism and indeed a German pantheism. Englishmen know no such thing as pantheism, only skepticism; the net result of the whole of English philosophizing is a despair of reason, an admission of inability to resolve the contradictions into which reason has ultimately been driven, and consequently a relapse into faith on the one hand and a surrender to sheer practicality and utilitarianism on the other hand, without any further concern with metaphysics and the like. And so Carlyle is a 'prodigy' in England and a pretty incomprehensible prodigy at that for the practical-minded and skeptical Englishmen. People there stare at him and mumble of 'German mysticism' and tortured English; others maintain that there is really something in it, when all is said and done, that his English is indeed peculiar but beautiful nonetheless, that he is a prophet and the like. But nobody quite knows what to make of it all.

"For us Germans, who know the presuppositions of Carlyle's standpoint, the matter is clear enough. Remnants of Tory Romanticism and humane insights out of Goethe on the one hand; skeptical-empirical England on the other—these factors suffice for a deduction of Carlyle's whole view of the world. Like all pantheists, he has not yet overcome or transcended the contradiction; and the dualism is all the worse in the case of Carlyle because of the fact that he *is* familiar with German

[5] At this point, Engels makes a considerable disgression to show that Carlyle was directly dependent on Goethe, the poet of the religion of the future with its cult of "labor" which is the slogan of the new gospel (Cf. MEGA I, 2, pp. 421, 423. Also 428; *K. Marx-F. Engels Werke,* [Dietz], Vol. I, pp. 540f. Also p. 547).

literature but *not* with its indispensible complement, German philosophy, so that all his insights and views (543) are immediate, intuitive, more Schellingian than Hegelian. With Schelling Carlyle really does have a plethora of points of contact—with the old Schelling, not with the 'Revelation'-Schelling [6]; with Strauss, whose philosophy is likewise pantheistic, Carlyle agrees in the matter of 'hero-worship' or 'genius-worship'.

"The critique of pantheism has recently been so thoroughly effected in Germany that little more remains to be said. Feuerbach's theses in the 'Anecdotes' [7] and the writings of Bruno Bauer contain all the pertinent material. We shall therefore be able to confine ourselves simply to drawing the consequences from Carlyle's standpoint and to showing that this standpoint is basically nothing but a preliminary to the standpoint of this Review.

"Carlyle laments the vacuum and the inner void of our age, the rottenness at the core of all the institutions of society. The lament is justified; but laments alone do not meet the case. To cure the ill, the would-be physician must discover the root cause. And had Carlyle done this, he would have found that this confusion and emptiness, this 'soullessness' this irreligion and this 'atheism' have their root in religion itself. Religion is by its very nature the emptying of man and nature of all content, the transfer of this content into the phantom specter of a transcendent God, who then deigns to grant to man and nature a morsel of his own superfluity. Now as long as faith in this transcendent phantom specter is still lively and operative, man will at least attain via this detour to some sort of content. The strong faith of the Middle Ages did indeed, in this way, confer upon this era a remarkable energy, but it was no energy streaming in upon man from outside; rather it was an energy that lay already in man's own nature, albeit still unrecognized, still undeveloped. That faith gradually weakened little by little; religion crumbled before advancing culture. But still man did not come to the realization that he had worshipped and deified his own being as an extraneous being. In this state of lack of knowledge and simultaneous lack of faith, man cannot have any content. He is *compelled* to despair of reason and nature; and this void and lack of content, this despair of the eternal facts of the universe will continue to persist until mankind comes to see that the being it has been adoring and worshipping as God is simply its own, hitherto unrecognized, nature, until—but why should I continue to paraphrase Feuerbach?!

"The void has been there within for a long time already, for religion is the act of self-inanition on the part of man; and you wonder that, now

[6] An allusion to Schelling's *Philosophie der Offenbarung* [Philosophy of Revelation].

[7] The reference here is to Feuerbach's *Vorläufige Thesen zur Reform der Philosophie,* which appeared in 1843 in the second part of the collection *Anekdota zur neuesten deutschen Philosophie und Publicistik.*

that the purple robe that covered it up has faded and tattered, now that the miasma that enveloped it has been dissipated, this void should emerge so terrifyingly before you into the light of day?!

"(544) Carlyle further accuses our age of lying and hypocrisy; this charge is the immediate consequence of the preceding one. Naturally, the void and the emasculation must of course be decently cloaked and propped up with tinsel, padded garments and hoops of whalebone! We too attack the hypocrisy of the Christian posture of our age; the fight against it, our own liberation from it and the liberation of the world from it, are ultimately our sole assignment. But because we have come to a recognition of this hypocrisy through the evolution of philosophy, and because we conduct our campaign scientifically, the inner nature of this hypocrisy is no longer so strange and incomprehensible to us as it certainly is for Carlyle. We too trace this hypocrisy back to religion whose first word is a lie—or does not religion, then, begin by showing us something human and maintaining that it is something superhuman, divine? But because we know that all this lying and immorality follows from religion, that the religious hypocrisy, theology, is the archetype of all other lies and hypocrisy,[8] we are therefore justified in extending the name of theology to the whole of the falsehood and hypocrisy of the present, as was done first by Feuerbach and Bruno Bauer. Let Carlyle read their works if he wants to know whence comes the immorality that is poisoning all our relations.

"A new religion, a pantheistic hero-worship or cult of labor ought to be founded or must be expected to arise? Impossible! religion's entire potential has been exhausted. After Christianity, after the absolute, i.e., abstract religion, after 'religion as such', no further form of religion can possibly arise. Carlyle himself appreciates the fact that Catholic, Protestant or any other kind of Christianity you want to name is irrevocably approaching its downfall; did he but understand the nature of Christianity, he would realize that after it no other religion is any longer possible. Not even pantheism! For pantheism as such is a consequence of Christianity, inseparable from its premisses, at least modern, Spinozan, Schellingian, Hegelian and Carlyleian pantheism! Here again, Feuerbach relieves me of the need of presenting any proof of this statement.

"As I said, we too are concerned with and committed to doing battle against the unsteadiness, the inner void, the spiritual death, the mendacity and insincerity of the age; against all these things, we are waging a life-and-death struggle, just like Carlyle; and we have far more probability of success on our side than does Carlyle, because we know what we want. We want to make an end of atheism, as Carlyle describes it, and we want to do it by restoring to man the content (545) he has lost through religion. We want to restore to man not a divine content but a

[8] Cf. H. Gollwitzer's remarks on this charge levelled by Engels against theology (Gollwitzer, *Die marxistische Religionskritik und der christliche Glaube,* French Translation [Tournai, 1965], pp. 189ff.).

human one; and this restoration amounts simply to the awakening in man of self-consciousness. We want to get rid of everything proclaiming itself to be supernatural and superhuman and thereby clear away the mendacity and insincerity, for the pretense of the human and natural to be superhuman and supernatural is the root of all falsehood and lying. Consequently we have declared war once and for all upon religion and the religious notions; and we are not much concerned about whether we are called atheists or some other name. If, however, Carlyle's pantheistic definition of atheism were accurate, then it would not be we but our Christian opponents who would be the real atheists. *We* do not dream of attacking the 'eternal intrinsic facts of the universe'; on the contrary, we have been the first to substantiate them firmly, by proving their eternity and shoring them up against the almighty whim of a self-contradictory God. *We* do not dream of declaring 'the world, man and his life to be a lie'; on the contrary, it is our Christian opponents who commit this immorality by making the world and man dependent on the grace of a God, who was in reality nothing but a misbegotten creation brought about by the mirroring of man in the turbulent matter of his own undeveloped consciousness. *We* do not dream of doubting the 'revelation of History' nor yet of despising that revelation; history is our One and All and is accorded by us a higher status than it is granted by any other former philosophical school, even by Hegel, for whom history was supposed ultimately to serve merely as a proof of his logical paradigm.

"Scorn for history, contempt and disregard for the evolution of mankind, is exclusively the purlieu of our opponents. It is again the Christians who, by positing a special 'History of the Kingdom of God', deny all substantial status to real history and claim this substantial status for their transcendent, abstract and, moreover, fabricated history; it is the Christians who set up an imaginary goal for history in the consummation of the human species in their Christ; it is the Christians who interrupt history in mid-course and are consequently compelled, for consistency's sake, to brand the following 1,800 years as nothing but downright foolishness and sheer meaninglessness. *We* do not stand up for the substantial status and meaningfulness of history; but we see in history not the revelation of 'God' but rather the revelation of man. For our part, in order to see the magnificence of the human being, in order to recognize the true greatness and nobility of the evolution of the species in history, its unceasing progress, its ever-certain triumph (546) over the folly of the individual, its transcendence and eradication of everything allegedly or apparently superhuman, its arduous but successful battle with nature to the victorious issue of the ultimate attainment of free human self-consciousness, the realization of man's unity with nature, the free autonomous creation of a new world founded upon purely human, moral living conditions—in order to be able to see and recognize all this, we have no need of any preliminary invocation of the abstraction of a 'God' or the ascription to that abstraction of all that is beautiful, great, noble and truly human. We have no need of this digression; we have no need of stamping over the genuinely human the seal of the 'divine' in order to convince ourselves of its grandeur and magnificence. On the contrary, the 'more divine', i.e., the more inhuman, something is, the less will we be able to admire it. It is only the *human* origin of the content of all religions that preserves for them here and there some claim for respect; only the awareness that even the maddest superstition does indeed contain, at rock bottom, the eternal attributes of the human being, albeit in grotesque and distorted form,—only this awareness preserves the history of religion and especially of the Middle Ages from that blanket rejection and *everlasting* oblivion, which would otherwise be the fate of this 'God-filled' record. The more 'God-filled' the more inhuman, the more bestial; and the 'God-filled' Middle Ages certainly did produce the ultimate in human bestiality, serfdom, the *ius primae noctis,* etc. The god*lessness* of our age, about which Carlyle laments so much, is precisely its God-*fulness.* And all of this likewise makes it clear why I presented man above as the solution to the Riddle of the Sphinx. Hitherto, the question has always been: What is God? and German philosophy has arrived at the answer: God is Man. Man has only to come to know himself, to measure all vital relationships against himself, to judge them according to his own nature, to organize the world in genuinely human fashion according to the dictates of his own nature—and he will have solved the riddle of our time. It is not in non-existent transcendent regions, not beyond space and time, not in a 'God' permeating the world or set over against it—it is not in any of these that the truth is to be found; no, it is much nearer, in man's own heart. Man's own nature is much more splendid and noble than the imaginary nature of any conceivable 'Gods' which are themselves nothing but the more or less confused and distorted image of man. Carlyle is therefore mistaken in saying with Ben Jonson that man has lost his soul and is now beginning to become aware of his loss; the correct thing to say would be (547) that man has lost his own nature, estranged himself from his own humanity in religion and is beginning to notice his own emptiness and instability, now that religion has begun to totter with the progress of history. But there is no other salvation for him, he can reconquer his humanity, his true nature in no other way than by a radical overcoming of all religious notions and a resolute, whole-hearted return not to 'God' but rather to himself."

II. Reason and the Existence of God: Marx, Schelling, Hegel

We here append the complete text of Marx's remarks on Schelling and Hegel, to which we had reference at the beginning of Section 4 of this Chapter:

" 'The term "weak" should be applied not to the reason that does not acknowledge any objective God but to the reason that *is willing to* recognize one.' (Schelling, *Philosophische Briefe über Dogmatismus und Kritizismus,* Erster Band, Landshut 1809, p. 127, Brief II.) Mr. Schelling would be well advised, generally speaking, to reflect upon his own early writings. Thus, for example, in his essay on 'The Ego as Principle of Philosophy', we read: 'If it be admitted, for instance, that God, insofar as he is defined as an Object, is the real ground of our being, then he himself surely falls, insofar as he is an object, within the sphere of our knowing and so cannot be for us the ultimate point on which this whole sphere is suspended', *loc. cit.* p. 5.

"Finally, we remind Mr. Schelling of the closing words of his abovementioned Letter: 'It is time to proclaim to the *better* mankind the *freedom of the mind* and *no longer to tolerate its weeping for the loss of its own chains.', loc. cit.* p. 129.

"If it was high time in 1795, how much more so in 1841?

"To take one notorious case, the *proofs of the existence* of God, Hegel stood these theological proofs completely on their head, i.e., refuted them and repudiated them in order to justify them. But of what use to his clients is that lawyer who can save them from being condemned to death only by murdering them himself? Hegel interprets, for instance, the deduction of God from the world in the following formula: 'Since the contingent does *not* exist, God or the Absolute exists,' whereas the theological proof reads exactly the opposite: 'Since the contingent has a true being, God exists.' God is the guarantee of a contingent world. Obviously the universe conclusion is likewise hereby asserted.

"The proofs of the existence of God are nothing but *empty* tautologies—e.g., the ontological proof means nothing more than: 'what I really imagine to myself is a real notion for me', it exercises an influence upon me; and in this sense all the gods, whether pagan or Christian, have possessed a real existence. Did not Moloch of old dominate his votaries? Was not the Delphic Apollo a real power in the life of the Greeks? Nor is Kant's critique here at all to the point. If someone imagines he is in possession of a hundred thalers, if this notion is not for him an arbitrary one, if he believes in it, then for him those hundred imaginary thalers have the same value as a hundred real thalers. He will, for instance, write a cheque with his imagination, acting *just as the whole human race has acted, in writing a cheque on its gods!* But Kant's critique could have weakened the original ontological proof. A hundred real thalers have the same sort of existence as the imaginary gods. Has a real thaler any existence elsewhere than in the imagination, albeit a generic or common imagination? Take a banknote into a country that is not familiar with this sort of use of paper and everyone will burst out laughing at your subjective notion. Come with your gods into a country where there live other gods and you will have proven to you that you are suffering from fits of abstraction and flights of fancy. And rightly so. Anyone bringing to the ancient Greeks a mutable God would have found the proof for the non-existence of this God. The land of reason is for God generically what a foreign land is in a given region for specific gods; it is a region in which his existence ceases.

"Or again the proofs of the existence of God are nothing but *proofs of substantial human self-consciousness, logical explicitations of that self-consciousness.* Take, for instance, the ontological proof. What being is immediately, as soon as it has been thought? Self-consciousness. In this sense, all the proofs of the existence of God are proofs of his *non-existence, contradictions* of all the notions of a God. The true proofs ought rather to say: 'Because nature is poorly organized, God exists'. But what else does this say than *that God exists for the man for whom the world is irrational, for the man who therefore is himself irrational? Or that unreason is the existence of God,* i.e., that the existence of God is a piece of nonsense?

" 'If you suppose the *idea* of an *objective God,* how can you speak of *laws* which reason produces itself, since autonomy can belong only to an absolutely free being?', Schelling, *loc. cit.,* p. 198.

" 'Is it not a crime of high treason against humanity to hide principles that are universally communicable?', *idem,* p. 199.

We have translated the above excerpt from "Aus den Anmerkungen zur Dissertation," in *K. Marx Frühe Schriften,* (Darmstadt: H. J. Lieber & P. Furth, 1962) Vol. I, pp. 74-76.

PART VI

THE RELIGIOUS ATHEISM OF ANGLO-AMERICAN EMPIRICISM

Prefatory Note

The philosophy of the Western world in modern times can indeed be said to have developed as an interacting system of mutual influences. This is particularly true of the development of the problem of the Absolute. Yet it is no less true that each specific culture has stressed one particular attitude or approach, has absorbed the influences from abroad through the filter of that attitude, has assimilated these influences, tinged them with its own specific cast, and then retransmitted them to others, including precisely those from whom it received them.

English thought, as we have already seen, effected a most vigorous and resolute disintegrative catalysis of the principle of immanentism into the immediacy of experience. Thus English thought effects, in a radical and yet surreptitious form, the transition from medieval to modern thought, with a continuity which is at once obvious and enigmatic. This precise enigma is not encountered in any other stream of modern speculative thought. And the most surprising point about this superficially bewildering English thought stream is the extreme and persistent reluctance of all its philosophers, despite their attitude and stance of empirical subjectivism, to make any profession of atheism. Hume himself, as we have seen, refused to make any such profession, limiting himself to expressing his own doubts about the positive "definition" of religious doctrine and practice. But Hume, by his denial of causality as a relation of ideas and his simultaneous assertion of that same causality as a natural impulse and belief, was able to sow doubts likewise about the rational proofs and indeed even about the demonstrability by reason of the existence of God, and at the same time to maintain that some sort of persuasion concerning the supreme Being lay in the depths of the mind as a basis to which the whole movement of experience could be referred or to which it could aspire.

Thus, we have neither intuition nor proof of the existence of God; but neither do we have any dialectical exaltation of finite reality to the status of Absolute, with its consequent submersion of the Infinite in the finite.

Rather we have a persistence within the mind, within human consciousness, of a demand for a foundation in a Principle, immanent, to be sure, within the self-constituting act of experience, yet consolidating that fluid act in its manifold articulation. This is what explains the persistence of the problem of God in English empiricism and the tenacious resistence offered by that empiricism to the flood of positivism and atheistic Hegelianism sweeping in from the continent. It is to that strange saga with its somber ending that we now turn our attention.

1

The Problematic of the "Empirical Principle"

The empirical principle is more demanding than either the rationalist or the idealist development of the principle of immanentism gave any indication that it would be; and at the present moment that empirical principle is revenging itself in no uncertain terms on both rationalist and idealist. Present-day Marxism, existentialism, phenomenology and neo-positivism are all proclaiming the impossibility or "supersession" (*Ueberwindung*) of all metaphysics; and this insistence bears eloquent testimony to the perennial vitality and long-range efficacy of the empirical principle, whose basic insistence is that the concrete must precede the abstract, that truth must be given in the form of "presence" and consequently be reducible to some form of immediacy which cannot be attained either in the abstractive sphere of the understanding nor in the discursive sphere of the reason. Rationalism has found it quite easy to reproach empricism, as did Hegel, with the fact that "instead of seeking truth in thought, it rushes off to seek it in external or internal experience".[1] But empiricism has always been able to retort that idealism itself cannot get along without experience and must likewise start from experience. Thus the problem is not here one of dissolving experience into thought or thought into experience. It is rather the problem of clarifying which of the two, thought or experience, subsumes the other and which is more basic for an existent like man. Although it may indeed be the case that man can think only according to generic and universally valid laws, it is no less patently true that he is always thinking in terms of a reality which is given or presented to him and with respect to which he initially always feels himself to be a spectator and to which he only later relates as an active agent. Therefore, Hegel himself was compelled to acknowledge: "Empiricism does indeed contain this great principle, that what is true must be in reality and must

[1] Hegel, *Enz. d. philos. Wiss.*, § 36, ed. J. Hoffmeister (Leipzig, 1937), p. 63.

be 'there' (i.e., accessible) for perception . . . Philosophy agrees with empiricism in acknowledging only what is; it has no place for *what merely is to be and therefore is not now there"*.[2]

It is important fully to grasp Hegel's own attitude to empiricism and the empirical principle, not only in order to attain a better understanding of the development of this principle but likewise in order to acquire a better appreciation of the coexistence in Hegel's own thought of the most divergent and even diametrically opposed lines of modern thought. This understanding is essential to a proper grasp of the feasibility of Hegelianism being transplanted into a speculative soil so completely antithetical as that of empiricism. Hegel takes note of empiricism's clarion call for a moratorium on empty abstractions, a deflection of interest and concentration to the here-and-now of man and nature; and Hegel readily admits that there is a hard core of reasonableness and cogency in this demand. The present, and here-and-now, must take the place of the empty beyond, of the nebulous forms and gossamer strands of the abstract understanding. This understanding grasps only finite attributes that are groundless and unstable; reason alone has the generic impulse to discover an infinite attribute, and reason's pioneering thrust is aimed not into time but rather into thought. This impulse, therefore, conceives the present, the here-and-now; but it does not succeed in conceiving it in its true existence. The external is *as such* the true, because the true is in reality and must exist. That infinite which reason is seeking is, therefore, in the world, even though it is not present in its infinite truth in every single individual sensible form.

Now it is precisely such individual and transitory sensible forms that the perception (*Wahrnehmung*) grasps. True cognition and understanding cannot, therefore, stop short at simple perception; rather it must seek in the individual perceived objects for the universal and the permanent (*das Allgemeine und Bleibende*). This search represents the transition from sheer and simple perception to experience (*Erfahrung*); and the crucial defect of empiricism lies in its failure to make this transition at all or, at least, to make it properly and effectively.

Empiricism attempts to effect the transition by having recourse to *analysis*. In perception, says empiricism, there is a concrete manifold whose attributes have to be enucleated by division, separation and fragmentation. This fragmentation, therefore, has the effect of dissolving and separating the attributes from those connnections forged between them by experience, while adding simply the subjective activity of the separation itself. Analysis is therefore the progress from the immediacy of perception to thought. In the sphere of thought, the attributes which

[2] Hegel, *Enz. d. philos. Wiss.*, § 38, ed. Hoffmeister, p. 64.

the analyzed object contained within itself in unified form obtain the form of universality by the simple fact of their being separated. But it is precisely here that empiricism makes its fatal error: it imagines that this analysis to which it elects to subject objects leaves those objects fundamentally unscathed, whereas in actual fact this analytic process transforms the concrete into something abstract. It kills what was alive for only the concrete, the One, is truly living. The split and separation here involved cannot, of course, be avoided: it is mandatory for a proper understanding of the fact that the spirit is separation in itself. *But* this separation is but *one* aspect of the toal process and the main thing is to unify what has been separated.

Hegel then proceeds to show the relations between empiricism and abstract thought in the metaphysics of antiquity: this ancient metaphysics had as its content those universal objects of reason such as God, the soul and the world in general; this content was taken from imagination (*Vorstellung*) and it was philosophy's assignment to reduce the universal objects to the form of thought. The same general approach held good for Scholastic philosophy, for which the dogmas of the Christian Church represented the content and the assignment was a more precise specification and systematization of these dogmas by the instrumentality of thought. Empiricism starts with a quite different content, the sensible content of nature and the content of the finite spirit. In the metaphysics of antiquity the initial content was infinite and that metaphysics proceeded to make it finite by means of the finite form of the understanding. In empiricism, we have the same finitude of form and the added finitude of content!

Both ancient metaphysics and modern empiricism use the same method in the sense that both proceed from unquestioned presuppositions. For empiricism in general the true is the external; and even if the *existence* of something suprasensible may be known, no knowledge of it can be attained otherwise than in the sphere of perception. Hence, empiricism has come to be identified with materialism, for which the objective reality is matter as such. But matter is something abstract which cannot, as such, be imagined or represented at all and can therefore be said not to exist as such, inasmuch as it only exists as something concrete and determinate.

This is bad enough; but there is worse to come: for empiricism is compelled to make this abstract matter the foundation of every sensible object; the result is a drastic and absolute individualization and singularization of reality, for the ultimate foundation is an abstract something whose existence can only be in the form of a concrete singularized individual. This introduces an element of ultimate fragmentation which is a brute datum and thus makes empiricism a theory of "un-freedom" (*Unfreiheit*), since freedom consists in my having absolutely no alien Other over against me but rather in my depending upon a content which I myself constitute. Empiricism is further constrained to assert that reason and unreason (*Vernunft und Unvernunft*) are sheer objective data which I must accept as they storm in upon me; I must abdicate all right even to pose the question as to whether and to what extent my experience reveals something which is rational in itself, much less to levy the demand that that something *shall* be rational in itself.[3]

Empiricism's error, therefore, lies in its "rationalism", in its drastic isolation of the particular contents, moments and elements of experience, in its continual interruption of the current of the spirit and its splitting and fragmentation of the forms and manifestations of the life of the spirit. It dissociates these forms and manifestations and consequently falls into *skepticism* inasmuch as immediate experience, which empiricism assumes to be the only criterion and source of truth, is not in a position to substantiate and serve as foundation for necessary and universal truths. Empiricism conceives of the necessary and the universal simply as features of the content; it has not yet penetrated to the conception of the necessary or the universal as features of the act of thought; hence empiricism must necessarily lapse into skepticism.

Hegel's highhandedness[4] with the empiricists is somewhat surprising, for Hume had certainly glimpsed the unique status of the *a priori* categories, as Kant quite properly certified. Hegel damns empiricism with faint praise: he admits that empiricism had indeed seized upon the principle that "truth" is in some sense "a presence in experience"; but Hegel proceeds to position this principle in the lowest stage of the Phenomenology, namely, "sense certitude"; and Hegel's own aim is to transfer certitude entirely from the content and concentrate it exclusively in the act of cognition, in the Ego as principle of assertion and as that which posits being. The Hegelian Logic commences in exactly the same drastic manner, but it sticks to the pure form, i.e., to sheer empty Being.

[3] Hegel, *Enz. d. philos. Wiss.*, § 38, Zusatz; ed. L. von Henning (Berlin, 1840), pp. 80ff.

[4] Hegel refers to his 1802 review of Schulze's *Verhältnis des Skeptizismus zur Philosophie* (cf. *Erste Druckschriften,* ed. Lasson [Leipzig, 1928], especially pp. 175ff., 193ff.). But there is no explicit reference to Hume in this article and Hegel gives him credit, in the Encyclopedia, for having set up "the truth of the empirical, of feeling and of intuition" as a firm foundation against Greek skepticism; Hegel equates this Humean principle with the principle of the sheer activity of the mind. Whereas the skepticism of antiquity involves the sort of reversion to the individual mind that denies the possibility of finding truth even there, modern skepticism, on the contrary, has "faith" in the reality of self-consciousness and can already be considered as a stage of idealism (Cf. *Geschichte der Philosophie,* III. Theil; ed. Michelet, [Berlin, 1844], p. 440).

Despite idealist influences and feedback, empiricism subsequently continued to remain faithful to its own primordial principle, that of referring and reducing truth to the presence of the immediately perceived within the sphere of perception. The continuing and persistent dualism of this form of immanentism was probably the main reason why the God-problem persisted in empiricism and sturdily resisted the abrasive solvent of immanentism as such.

The Flux of Experience and the Finitude of God (J. S. Mill, W. James).—The theistic position did continue to be sustained in modern thought, even though it was no longer consistent, after Hegel, that it should be. It was bound up with a conviction of the necessity of some efficient nexus of the Infinite and the Absolute with the flux of becoming of the contingent. Such a nexus had shown itself to be indefensible in the wake of Hegel, and atheism was actively embraced as the only consistent position by the Hegelian Left. But a different state of affairs prevailed in those empirical philosophies which considered the flux of becoming and the truth deducible from it in terms of the object itself rather than of the subject. These philosophies viewed this flux from the standpoint of nature and history as subsuming man the knower; and they postulated God as the ground of order in this finite reality. Consequently, this God was thought of as being just as finite as the horizon within which he was present to the mind.[5] It could almost be said that, even as for Hegel God is the Whole of the real which is conceived as infinite, so for theistic empiricism, God is the whole of the real which is conceived as finite. This theistic empiricism may conceive this finitude either in sheer and simple static form or in evolutionary dynamic form. In the latter conception, there may even be some overtones of an infinite "divine". And precisely "the divine" rather than God, properly so called, is the proper term of reference in these approaches which absorb or subsume God into the finitude of the world. As usual, we shall limit ourselves here to an outline of the main line of development of the principle at issue.

For John Stuart Mill (1806-1873), the meaning and value of religion is in direct proportion to its utility, to its capacity for having a beneficial effect on human behavior. He held religion to be quite obvi-

[5] The finitist theory seems to be of long standing: "The theory of a finite God is not a recent invention but is adumbrated throughout the history of philosophy. The Platonic demiurge, the Aristotelian prime movers, and the Averroistic first cause are more remote examples in the finitist tradition, and the problem becomes a steady concern during the modern period. Locke was well aware of the finitist implications of the rationalistic, deductive approach to God, providing him with one of his strongest reasons for rejecting the a priori method in philosophy. Within the empiricist line itself, Hume and Voltaire deemed a finite Deity to be probably the safest inference from the order in nature" (J. Collins, *God in Modern Philosophy* [London: Routledge & Kegan Paul, 1959], p. 286).

ously the source of profound personal satisfaction and of noble and exalted feelings for man. Thus faith in God or the gods, and the belief in a life after death becomes the woof into which each individual mind can weave, according to its own capacity, its own images of ideals it can copy or fabricate. Everyone hopes to find in the after-life the good that he did not succeed in finding on earth, or else he hopes for something still better than what has been intimated to him by the good that he has seen or known in part on earth. As long as man's life here on earth is inadequate to satisfy man's aspirations there will always be a yen for higher things and more lasting consolation; and this longing will always find its most obvious satisfaction in religion.[6] The Epicurean attitude of "Let us eat and drink, for tomorrow we die" cannot be the last word.

Mill is evidently here speaking of a fabrication of the imagination, or more exactly, in his own words a "hope of imagination". But he does not treat it as an "alienation", as do the Hegelian Left and contemporary philosophy; rather he treats it and interprets it in terms of a growing consolidation and strengthening of the human being. Mill agrees with Hume in asserting that polytheism was the first stage of religion and of theism, wherein each one of the various deities had his own portion of reality to rule and govern. But monotheism, with its assertion of the absolute unity of the deity, Mill feels can be better reconciled with the results and conclusions of science. He notes that we are accustomed to find, in proportion to our means for observation and research, a definite and specific beginning for every individual fact. Yet, wherever there is a beginning of this sort, we always find that there has been an antecedent fact (which we call a cause), without which the phenomenon thus beginning would not have been. Consequently the human mind was bound to ask whether the whole of which these particular phenomena are a part did not likewise have a beginning, whether there was not an antecedent for the whole series of causes and effects that we call Nature. The only satisfactory reply to this question is theism.[7]

It should be noted at once, as of considerable importance for our present investigation, that here in Mill the Humeian *Belief* is again being taken up in a positive sense, after its further explicitation by Hamann and especially Jacobi and Kant himself, as a weapon for the reconquest of that metaphysical world which the reflexive *cogito* had lost by its

[6] John Stuart Mill, *Nature, the Utility of Religion, Theism,* Being Three Essays on Religion (London, 1874), p. 104. In virtue of the utilitarian principle that inspires the whole of Mill's theory, it is but natural that that theory should immediately establish a sharp contrast between the God of nature and the God of Revelation; nor is it at all surprising that Mill should entirely agree with deism in proclaiming the superiority of the God of nature over the God of revelation (p. 112f.).

[7] *Ibid.,* pp. 133f.

pale cast of doubt.[8] In the wake of the demands levied by the scientific inspection of the world, the theistic approach must restructure itself into an adequate alignment with this scientific view and the generic truths it has succeeded in establishing; theism must banish any and every anthropomorphic notion of a God with a mutable will, who successively alters his own decrees. The phenomena of nature must be firmly maintained to occur in accord with generic necessary laws. They take their origin from quite definite natural antecedents. And if their ultimate origin goes back to a will, then this will must have established those generic universal laws and willed those antecedents. If there is a Creator, his intervention must have been such as to make the events to depend on the antecedents and to be produced in accord with fixed laws. But once this is granted, concludes Mill, there is nothing in scientific experience which is opposed to the faith, the belief that these laws and sequences were, for their part, due to the divine will. Nor is there any need to suppose, Mill insists in criticism of the more rigid deistic position, that the divine will should have operated once for all or that God, having once set the system in motion, should have stood aside to allow it to continue to develop on its own: science has no objection to the contention that each and every event is the result of a special act of volition of the supreme governing Power, provided only that this power abide by the universal laws He has established in each and every one of his particular acts of will.[9]

Were this condition imposed by Mill to have been absolute, then it would have excluded that direct and special intervention of God which is miracle and then Mill's position would have simply relapsed into that deism that reduces God to the status of the notion of universal Reason, refusing to accord him any status as *person*—a stage which we have already seen to have been crucial in the evolution toward modern atheism. But Mill speaks rather of "evidences of theism" adapted to the various cultural states of men; his main contention is that all *a priori* arguments must be criticized and rejected as invalid.

The first and best known of these is that of the First Cause; it is entirely devoid of any value for the substantiation of theism. And the reason is that there is no need for any cause for the existence of that which has no beginning; and matter and energy, which comprise nature, have not had any beginning so far as our experience can judge. Every change in the visible world is conditioned by a preceding change and no

[8] On the development of this concept of *Belief,* cf. Mill's controversy with Hamilton who spoke of "Belief without Knowledge", confining *Belief* to the apprehension of first principles and *Knowledge* to the conclusions derived from these principles (J. S. Mill, *An Examination of Sir William Hamilton's Philosophy* [London: Longmans, Green, Reader, and Dyer, 1872 [4]], pp. 74ff.).

[9] J. S. Mill, *Three Essays on Religion,* p. 136.

inspection of phenomena as we see them entails any need to admit or presuppose a primal and primordial will or act of volition: the world does not, by the simple fact of its existence, bear any cogent witness to God. And this holds true both in the material realm of nature and in the realm of minds that have had their beginning in time. Experience does indeed bear witness to the fact that each and every one of them has been caused, but there is no necessity that their cause should have been a first Intelligence.[10] This is once again the notion of causality proposed by Hume, under evident Kantian influence: the causal nexus holds only for the sensible world.

Nor does any kinder fate await the argument drawn from the "general consent of Mankind". It involves the existence in men of a special natural faculty for knowing God; and this no-one has ever succeeded in observing or proving, even though certain people can very easily be conceived as being definitely endowed with such a belief or faculty. Equally inadequate are the ontological arguments proposed in modern thought beginning with Descartes and thoroughly demolished by Kant.[11] As for Kant's own new argument drawn from the existence of the moral law, necessarily requiring a supreme lawgiver, it is not convincing either, because the feeling of moral obligation is to be observed equally well in those who do not admit the existence of God or make any use of it in their ethic.[12] The still more famous and widespread argument drawn from "marks of design in Nature" seems no more cogent. This Mill claims to be an inductive argument, inasmuch as it begins with the products of human art and intelligence and attributes the whole complex of nature to the operation of a universal Intelligence or a supreme Intelligent Will. Here Mill's critique shows a clear Darwinian influence: the finality observable in the realm of nature and especially of the phenomena of life can easily be conceived as being the result of the "survival of the fittest", once the existence of a few elementary laws of organic life is admitted; the rest could well be conceived as occurring as a result of processes of adaptation whose effects are subsequently transmitted by heredity so as to perfect the species in this way.[13]

Mill does however incline to see this argument as the one worthy of

[10] *Ibid.*, pp. 153f. Hence, likewise, the impossibility of miracles; cf. pp. 219, 232 (explicit reference to the critique of Hume). Mill is quite outspoken: "Accordingly when we hear of a prodigy we always, in these modern times, believe that if it really occurred it was neither the work of God nor of a demon, but the consequence of some unknown natural law or some hidden fact" (p. 230). Cf. on p. 238 the attack on the Catholic teaching, denied by the Protestants, concerning the continuing presence of miracles in the Church.

[11] *Ibid.*, pp. 613ff.

[12] This is the famous thesis of Bayle.

[13] J. S. Mill, *Three Essays on Religion*, pp. 172f.

the greatest respect, even though it does not amount to more than a "probability" argument having the value of an analogy. But this argument is greatly strengthened, concludes Mill, by deep-cutting inductive considerations which establish the fact that there is a certain definite causal connection between the origin of natural structures and the functions they perform. The argument has particular force in the realm of vegetative life. But, here again, Mill denies that it can transcend the bounds of mere probability. Once the foundation of natural religion has been removed, the supernatural type of religion collapses as a necessary consequence.

Mill aims at being quite explicit in his own conclusions.[14] The first and basic conclusion is that there exists absolutely no categorical evidence in favor of theism; therefore the proper attitude, whether on the natural or the supernatural plane, is *skepticism.* Mill feels this skepticism to be distinct both from belief and from both types of atheism, the dogmatic denial of God's existence (negative atheism) and the denial that there is cogent evidence either pro or con in the question of the existence of God (skeptical atheism). The net result, however, is still a denial of the existence of God. All the arguments adopted in favor of the existence of a Supreme Mind have no higher status that the lowest degree of probability. The power of this Mind over material things cannot be absolute; his love for creatures cannot have been the only motive for creation even though he may have taken their good into consideration. The notion of providence is to be abandoned entirely;[15] so is the notion of the continued existence of the creator, which is not really certain, even though we cannot conceive of him as being subject to the death from which terrestrial things suffer; the other attributes of the deity are equally indefensible as apodictic certainties, even as the possibility of his being able to intervene in the course of nature. Equally devoid of apodictic certainty is the belief in a life God might grant to man after man's death. On all these points, Mill sees man as unable to raise himself even into the realm of "belief" or natural faith, let alone into that of knowledge.[16] We have here to do, says Mill, with "simple

[14] Cf. *ibid.,* pp. 242ff.

[15] "The notion of a providential government by an omnipotent Being for the good of his creatures must be entirely dismissed" (*ibid.,* p. 243).

[16] The empirical principle does not admit of exceptions: ". . . the meaning of the abstract must be sought for in the concrete, and not conversely" (*An Examination of Sir William Hamilton's Philosophy,* pp. 296f.). But God as Absolute and Infinite is an abstract entity and by definition cannot be concrete; Hamilton was entirely right in rejecting Cousin's contention that man can have an intuition of God as Absolute and necessary Cause of things ("In this contest it is almost superfluous for me to say, that I am entirely with Sir W. Hamilton. The doctrine, that we have an immediate or intuitive knowledge of God, I consider to be bad

Hope", And man must resign himself to remaining forever at this level, which is "a region of imagination merely" devoid of any basis for really confident expectation. Nevertheless, remarks Mill, philosophers have hitherto devoted too little consideration and attention to this realm of imagination: it is of great importance in the structure of human life and therefore merits being cultivated at least as much as does reason, with which it collaborates most intimately.

Imagination exercises its most important function precisely in the field of religion, says Mill. For imagination is familiar with the notion of a morally perfect Being and is habituated to taking the approval of such a Being as the *norm* or rule against which our characters and lives are measured and by which they are governed. This personification of our standard of excellence is in no way inhibited by conceiving of this Person as purely imaginary. Mill attributes to Christianity the dubious credit of having fostered the belief that our highest notions of a synthesis of wisdom and goodness are actually concretely realized in a living Being; Mill's extensive and obvious *caveats* on thc score of this Christianity-fostered belief make it clear that he considered it to have contributed more to a regression than to a genuine progress of man's reason and his morality. Although Mill admits that belief in God has a certain efficacy and beneficial effect on moral feelings which a purely and exclusively rational approach does not have, he nevertheless finds the rational approach, with its admission that the power of the creator is limited, to be a considerably truer and more consistent conception of Ideal Goodness. In further explanation of this finitistic conception, Mill declares that modern man looks not so much to a metaphysical notion of a God who would be an omnipotent creator as rather to Christ, to God Incarnate, idealized by Christianity, first by the enthusiasm of the disciples and subsequently by the speculations of Alexandrine philosophy. For skeptical rationalism, Mill avers in conclusion, there is a possibility that Christ was really what he believed himself to be: not God, of course, for he never advanced the slightest claim to be God nor did the idea ever even enter his head, but *a man who had from God* a quite special assignment, that of guiding mankind to truth and justice. And this is the beneficent effect of religion. Yet, one must ask what real meaning this whole exposition can have, if God has been confined within the realm of imagination as Hegel, Feuerbach and Marx had confined him. Mill himself admits it can have none at all or very little. He closes

metaphysics, involving a false conception of the nature and limits of the human faculties, and grounded on a superficial and erroneous psychology"; p. 47). But in this case, argues Mill, the concepts of Absolute and Unconditioned which Hamilton wishes to continue to use in order to designate God are no longer valid, losing all meaning if they be applied beyond the field of experience.

his peroration with a summons to the "Religion of humanity" and sometimes to the Religion of duty.[17] This is the religion preached in France by Comte; but it goes back to Deism, to Enlightenment thought and to idealism, to Kant and to immanentism, i.e., to the unbroken thread of the modern principle of immanentism!

The philosophy of *Belief* made a notable advance toward a clearcut theological stance and posture in the brilliant work of William James (1842-1910), who was entirely faithful to the now established line of Anglo-Saxon philosophy, holding to a "finite God", capable of being conceived solely as involved in the experience of nature and human activity.[18] Three distinct periods or stages can be identified in the evolution of James' thought, in which there is a progressively stronger declaration and articulation of James' theological outlook.

In the first period, God is conceived primarily as a catalyst of man's moral energy, as an indispensible stimulus of the most vigorous and exalted spiritual power. God becomes the postulate for moral action: he frees and brings into play our latent energy. God expresses the realm of the ideal to which human life and action must tend; he is the expression rather than the object of our faith in ideals. God is thus conceived in his "commensurability" with the goals of human action. In this period, James is quite forthright in declaring that he can perfectly sympathize with the most radical detestation of the very idea of God, considering the use that has been made of him in history and philosophy as a "starting point", as a premiss for allegedly well-founded deductions. But James finds a real and meaningful place for God as an ideal to be attained and rendered probable. This stand corresponds exactly to Mill's. James sees no reason why this God must be "the ALL-including subjective unity of the universe." He feels that it suffices that there be *some sort of* subjective unity in the universe having goals commensurable with those of the philosopher himself and being, at the same time, big enough to be the strongest among all the powers that may exist; and *this sort of* subjective unity he feels there must be in the universe. He refuses outright to accept the position that denied the existence of finality in the subjective world. Nor can he see how a goal can exist apart from a Mind. Yet, he is unwilling to go too far: in saying that "God exists", he means simply that his own goals are somehow supported by a mind powerful enough to control and govern the whole course of the universe. This, James specifies, is neither monotheism nor polytheism, because it is less a speculative position than a practical and emotional faith, akin to a "Promethean Gemüth". All of the difficulties theism has

[17] J. S. Mill, *Three Essays on Religion*, pp. 255f.

[18] Evidently even the Scottish school of Hamilton and Mansel remained faithful, in spite of Mill's critique, to the anti-intellectualist conception of *Belief*.

encountered stem from the gratuitous dogma that God is the all-inclusive reality. Once one succeeds in thinking of a primordial pluralism of which God may be a member, once that single subjective synthesis is abolished, then piety ceases to be incompatible with manliness and religious "faith" with intellectual honesty.[19]

In this stage of James' thought, therefore, God is the guide of our vital power but he cannot be conceived as a principle of theoretical explanation or as "a moral and intelligent Contriver of the World". James is therefore contending that God, whether he exists or not, is the most adequate possible object of our mind. And James' contention is that, granting a *certain* exterior reality to this hypothetical being, that being must be defined as God for he is the only ultimate object which is, at one and the same time, rational and possible for the human mind to contemplate. God expresses the intelligibility for man of the universe and of nature, according to the formula: "Anything short of God is not rational, anything more than God is not possible." [20] This means that, in the chapter dealing with the natural history of our mind, God can be called the normal object of our mind. God thus constitutes an infinite prospect and an ideal guarantee for the mind's self-motion and operation. In the absence of God, the appeal to man's moral energy falls short of its maximal stimulating power, the note of infinitude and mystery. The idea of God is so efficacious that, even in the absence of the metaphysical and traditional reasons for believing in God, men would have to postulate him simply in order to go on "living hard, and getting out of the game of existence its keenest possibilities of zest. Our attitude toward concrete evils is entirely different in a world where we believe there are none but finite demanders, from what it is in one where we joyously face tragedy for an infinite demander's sake." [21] God, therefore, constitutes the fountainhead of energy and power in the moral realm of human action.

In the second stage, James undertakes a deeper and more thorough treatment of the concrete realization of religious experience and activity

[19] Cf. the hitherto unpublished letter of James to Thomas Davidson, dated January 2, 1882, included by J. S. Bixler, in his *Religion in the Philosophy of William James* (Boston, 1926), pp. 125ff. The most representative work of this first period is *The Will to Believe and other Essays,* which includes various articles by James, written between 1880 and 1892. We have consulted this and shall cite from it in the sequel in the new Dover edition first published in 1956 but presented as "an unabridged and unaltered republication of the first edition of 'The Will to Believe and Other Essays in Popular Philosophy' and the second edition of 'Human Immortality'" (New York: Dover Publications Inc., 1956).

[20] William James, *The Will to Believe,* p. 116. Italics are in the original.

[21] *Ibid.,* p. 213. There is an evident fusion of empiricist and idealist elements in this postulation of God as a surety of action (James actually cites by name his idealist colleague Josiah Royce: p. 214).

in general and points up the liberating and salvific effects it has on man, exposed as he is to that evil that surrounds us on every side.[22] The best criterion of James' progress in pragmatism in this second stage as compared with the first would seem to us to be the following: in the first stage, the value of the concepts was conceived in function of their practical results; in the second, the truth of the concepts themselves is defined in terms of their value, so that the practical results no longer serve merely to clarify the concepts but become the criterion for establishing the truth of those concepts.

In a vigorous attack on the traditional theology manuals, Catholic and Protestant alike, James remarks that the various arguments these manuals advance can, at best, serve as a sort of confirmatory evidence for those who already believe in God, but that they can do no good whatever to the atheist. Modern philosophy, James insists, has made a clean sweep of these worthless antiques, this whole collection of bric-a-brac, that succeed only in emptying the religious life of all its élan. Even as the existence of God flows from the pragmatic significance it represents in human existence, so, too, the significance of his metaphysical attributes must be reinterpreted. God is certainly a good deal more than the mere tedious enumeration of these attributes provided by traditional metaphysics. James insists that the value of principles is to be sought in facts and since every fact is a particular fact, the whole interest of the question of the existence of God would seem to consist in the consequences that existence can bring about for particular cases or the advantages it can procure in individual instances. Thus, God is more and more insistently designated as the "ideal power" with which we feel ourselves in connection but which it would be an error to think of as infinite or to endow with infinite attributes. All that we can say in this regard is that we can experience a union with *something* larger than ourselves and in that union find out greatest peace. Philosophy with its passion for unity and mysticism with its monotheistic bent both "pass to the limit" and identify the something with a unique God who is the all-inclusive soul of the world. James' pragmatic position makes God the foundation of a dynamic monism of action, though he quite specifically calls in question and virtually rejects the rigid traditional monistic view that unless there be one all-inclusive God, our guarantees of security are not perfect.[23]

Considerable light will be shed on James' whole position by an inspection of his replies to a questionnaire sent out in 1904 by Professor

[22] This stage is represented primarily by *The Varieties of Religious Experience* (New York, London and Bombay: Longmans, Green, and Co., 1902), which can legitimately be considered to be James' chief work. The Chapter "Philosophy" (pp. 430ff.) is especially pertinent to our present purpose.

[23] William James, *The Varieties of Religious Experience,* pp. 552ff.

James B. Pratt of Williams College, to which James filled out a reply at an unascertained date in the autumn of that year:

"2. What do you mean by God?—A combination of Ideality and (final) efficacity.

(1) Is He a person—if so, what do you mean by His being a person? —He must be cognizant and responsive in some way.

"(2) Or is He only a Force?—He must *do*.

"(3) Or is God an attitude of the Universe toward you?—Yes, but more conscious. 'God', to me, is not the only spiritual reality to believe in. Religion means primarily a universe of spiritual relations surrounding the earthly practical ones, not merely relations of 'value', but agencies and their activities. I suppose that the chief premise for my hospitality towards the religious testimony of others is my conviction that 'normal' or 'sane' consciousness is so small a part of actual experience. What e'er be true, it is not true exclusively, as philistine scientific opinion assumes. The other kinds of consciousness bear witness to a much wider universe of experiences, from which our belief selects and emphasizes such parts as best satisfy our needs. . .

"3. Why do you believe in God? Is it (1) From some argument? —Emphatically no.

Or (2) Because you have experienced His presence?—No, but rather because I need it so that it 'must' be true. . .

"4. Or do you not so much believe in God as want to *use* Him?—I can't use Him very definitely, yet I believe.—Do you accept Him not so much as a real existent Being, but rather as an ideal to live by?—More as a more powerful ally of my own ideals." [24]

God thus belongs to the context of human action, to the world in which man has to live out his life. Actually, remarks James in the most representative work of this second period, we live in a pluralistic universe, crisscrossed by a plethora of results, positive and negative, such as to make the monistic solution of the transcendental ideal evaporate into a sheer abstraction. God is a part of this pluralistic universe and so he is finite. God is not outside of us, is not extrinsic to us: "We are indeed internal parts of God and not external creations, on any possible reading of the panpsychic system. Yet, because God is not the absolute, but is himself a part when the system is conceived pluralistically, his functions can be taken as not wholly dissimilar to those of the other smaller parts,—as similar to our functions consequently." [25] Yet,

[24] This is reported by J. S. Bixler, in his *Religion in the Philosophy of William James,* p. 135.

[25] William James, *A Pluralistic Universe* (New York, London and Bombay: Longmans, Green, and Co., 1909), p. 318.

James' final judgment is that pantheistic monism has more profoundly grasped the problem here involved than has Catholic dualistic realism: pantheistic monism has entitatively unified man and God.

In this critique, which is of capital importance for a proper understanding of a further stage in the progressive disappearance of God from modern thought, James reproaches theism with having conceived God and his creation as entities distinct one from the other, thus leaving the human subject outside of the deepest reality of the universe. God is complete and perfect in himself from all eternity; he produces the universe outside of himself by a free act and as an extraneous substance; and He produces man as a third substance, extraneous to Himself and the world. According to Scholastic theology, God says "one", the world says "two," and man says "three"; God has no real or substantial relation to creatures; they are *toto genere* distinct and have *nothing* in common. God can affect creatures with his action, but he can never be affected by their reaction. Strictly speaking, theism does not allow for any real relation of a social sort between God and man and everything is consequently pervaded by a character of externality. God is no longer heart of our heart and reason of our reason; rather he is our magistrate and our sole duty consists in mechanical obedience to his commands. Thus the capital error of theism is a lack of intimacy. It is strange that James should have had such a foreshortened and ludicrously distorted idea of creationist theism as to prefer Hindu pantheism to creationist orthodoxy: "God as intimate soul and reason of the universe has always seemed to some people a more worthy conception than God as external creator. So conceived, he appeared to unify the world more perfectly, he made it less finite and mechanical, and in comparison with such a God an external creator seemed more like the product of a childish fancy." [26]

He therefore makes a sharp and accurate distinction between the Absolute of the pantheistic and monistic systems and the creator God of orthodox Christian theology and insists, for his own part, that the God of philosophy is an essentially finite being, himself encompassed within the cosmos rather than encompassing the cosmos within himself. A God worthy of the name must be finite and only thus can those mischiefs and contradictions be avoided that arise from the concept of the Absolute which by definition can have nothing outside of itself. James specifies that the God whom he contrasts with the absolute might conceivably

[26] *Ibid.*, pp. 28f. And so the innermost "common and generic" trait of genuine religious experience seems to be "the fact that the conscious person is continuous with a wider self through which saving experiences come" (*The Varieties of Religious Experience,* p. 515); and "the whole interest of the question of God's existence seems to me to lie in the consequences for particulars which that existence may be expected to entail" (p. 522) and again "God's existence is the guarantee of an ideal order that shall be permanently preserved" (p. 517).

have *almost* nothing outside of himself; he might already have triumphed over and absorbed all but the minutest fraction of the universe; but that fraction, however small, reduces him to the status of a relative being. And James contends that in principle this saves the universe from all the irrationalities incidental to absolutism.[27] In order to be accessible to human experience, God must be neither Absolute nor infinite. God is thus constitutive of human experience and consequently belongs to human reality as an attribute of that reality.

The third stage in the development of James' theological thought sees him committed to merging and blending the two preceding notions of God as a power and God as the catalyst of our powers. He makes a sweeping condemnation of the theistic (in James' view, the dualistic) conception of God: this conception is abstract and sterile on principle. The Absolute thus conceived is of no assistance either to nature or to our own human living, although, of course, this conception takes good care of God who is declared to be immutable in himself. Pragmatism, on the other hand, points to the middle way between the extremes of materialism and theism. For both of these latter everything is anteriorly drastically conditioned in the world, by God in the theistic conception and by the material physical forces in the materialistic view. Thus, these two extreme approaches ultimately come down to the same thing, both maintaining the universe to be set once and for all on an unalterable course. In the pragmatic approach, God emerges at once as practically superior to the God of the other two approaches: in the pragmatic view, God is the guarantor of an ideal order that will be preserved in perpetuity. A world with a God in it to say the last word may indeed burn up or freeze; but we would then think of that God as still mindful of the old ideals and sure to bring them elsewhere to fruition. Thus, if God is there, tragedy is only provisional and partial, and shipwreck and dissolution can never be the absolute end.[28] The need of an eternal moral order, says James, is one of the deepest needs of the human spirit; and the extraordinary tonic and consoling power of the verse of such great

[27] William James, *A Pluralistic Universe,* pp. 125f. Cf. the later evaluation and critique of Fechner's conception of God as the universal Soul containing the world (pp. 145ff.) and the sharp comments on Hegel, Royce and Bradley, for their inept introduction of God as Infinite and Absolute to resolve the manyness-in-oneness problem ("Hegel, Royce, Bradley, and the Oxford absolutists in general seem to agree about this logical absurdity of manyness-in-oneness in the only places where it is empirically found. But see the curious tactics! Is the absurdity *reduced* in the absolute being whom they call in to relieve it? Quite otherwise, for that being shows it on an infinitely greater scale, and flaunts it in its very definition": p. 296).

[28] William James, *Pragmatism,* A New Name for Some Old Ways of Thinking (New York, 1908), pp. 19, 70f., 96ff.

poets as Dante and Wordsworth is due precisely to the fact that they lived on the conviction of such an order.

James sharply contrasts the laborious study of God by the attempted deciphering of his creation with the *enjoyment* of God as an inner personal experience. It is precisely in such innerpersonal experiences that the prime evidence for God must be said to lie. When such experiences have seized upon God, "his name means at least the benefit of the holiday". As for the more cumbersome business of the truth of God, we must make our peace with the fact that it can be attained only when all our other truths, now in process of violent collision, have somehow straightened themselves out together, a consummation devoutly to be wished! [29]

The final conclusion and essence of this Jamesian pragmatic position is that the idea of God has a practical significance and importance: it is useful in human experience. But it is useful solely as an idea or a prospect of action; it has no objective reality whatsoever. This notion of God's involvement in human activity and his consequent finitude expresses the very paradox it would like to resolve: the paradox of considering the deity from within human life and experience and consequently finding him to be infinite; and of subsequently inconsistently positing God as the foundation and propulsive force powering human life and action. For God must have no attribute that would create any gulf between him and man or render him inaccessible or unattainable. Above all, there must be no descendent continuity of consciousness as between God and man. The net result is a radical empiricism in the shape of vitalism and panpsychism, with the contention of a universal mind and consciousness, embracing in man the entire reality of the universe.

In one of his last statements of position on this whole problem, James confessed himself to be in substantial agreement with the "ideal" God of his friend Charles A. Strong, to whom James writes in 1907: "The 'omniscient' and 'omnipotent' God of theology I regard as a disease of the philosophy-shop. But, having thrown away so much of the philosophy-shop, you may ask me why I don't throw away the whole? That would mean too strong a negative will-to-believe for me. It would mean a dogmatic disbelief in any extant consciousness higher than that of the 'normal' human mind; and this in the teeth of the extraordinary vivacity of man's psychological commerce with something ideal that *feels as if* it were also actual . . . and in the teeth of such analogies as Fechner uses

[29] ". . . we can *study* our God only by studying his Creation. But we can *enjoy* our God, if we have one, in advance of all that labor. I myself believe that the evidence for God lies primarily in inner personal experiences" (*Ibid.*, p. 109).

to show that there may be other-consciousness than man's. If other, then why not higher and bigger? . . . What harm does the little residuum or germ of actuality that I leave in God do? If ideal, why (except on epiphenomenist principles) may he not have got himself at least partly real by this time?" [30]

From James' reply to the Pratt questionnaire of 1904, we can conclude that for James God is a combination of ideality and reality (actuality) and that he virtually amounts to the totality of universal human consciousness ". . . from which our belief selects and emphasizes such parts as best satisfy our needs." [31] James freely admits the existence and uniqueness of that religious experience which is the fountainhead of the various religions, of philosophy and theology: we can and must admit that "Something, not our immediate self, does act on our life!" [32] But three years after this letter to Henry Rankin, James is writing to James Henry Leuba in a most cautious vein: "Now, although I am so devoid of *Gottesbewusstsein* in the directer and stronger sense, yet there is *something in me* which *makes response* when I hear utterances made from that lead by others. I recognize the deeper voice." [33]

Though this statement may indeed reveal a laudable continuing openness and absence of negative dogmatism, it is perilously close to the famous exasperated final thrust of the clergyman in conversation with the recalcitrant and trenchant atheist: "But dammit, man, there must be a something somehow somewhere!" In any case, James is quite outspoken on the point that God cannot possibly be conceived as absolute: "I myself read humanism theistically and pluralistically. If there be a God, he is no absolute all-experiencer, but simply the experiencer of widest actual conscious span . . . Ethically the pluralistic form of it [humanism] takes for me a stronger hold on reality than any other philosophy I know of—it being essentially a *social* philosophy, a philosophy of 'co', in which conjunctions do the work." [34] The last phrase serves as an ideal introduction to our next two finitizers in the Anglo-American tradition, Bradley and Royce.

[30] *The Letters of W. James,* Vol. II, ed. by his son Henry James, (Boston, 1920), pp. 269f.

[31] *Ibid.,* p. 213.

[32] Letter to Henry W. Rankin, *ibid.,* pp. 149f.

[33] *Ibid.,* Vol. II, p. 211.

[34] William James, *Essays in Radical Empiricism* (New York, 1938), p. 194.

2

Conjunction of the Absolute with the Finite in Empirical Idealism (Bradley-Royce)

Hegel had indeed praised empiricism's "great principle" of the identity of truth and reality; but he would never have expected and certainly did not foresee any possible synthesis of empiricism and idealism, such as that which was in process of development toward the end of the 19th century in English philosophy, with the tension between James and Bradley. We have seen that, for James, the only access route to God is the experience of actual human living. James was always firm in opposing the slightest concession to pure speculative reason of any capacity to open up an access route to God, for the very simple reason (and here James was quite right) that every idealist conception was fated always to end in monism. Bradley (1846-1924) had initially treated the problem in his major work,[1] and he returned to it in the context of a fundamental critique of the whole speculative attitude of the pragmatism of his adversary, James.[2]

The "emotional way" pioneered by Hume and further explored and pursued by the Scottish school and subsequently by Mill and James, is simply not adequate, with its search for the ultimate foundation of truth in action, aspiration and the like: "If indeed . . . there were no force in the world but the veiled love of God, if the wills in the past were one in effort and substance with the one Will, if in that Will they are living still and still are so loving, and if again by faith, suffering, and love my will is made really one with theirs—here indeed we should have found at once our answer and our refuge. But with this we should pass surely beyond

[1] F. H. Bradley, *Appearance and Reality* (London, 1893 [1], 1897 [2] [we here follow the 9th Impression of 1930]), especially Chapters XXV and XXVI.

[2] F. H. Bradley, *Essays on Truth and Reality* (Oxford, 1914). The early chapters, especially Chapter 4 and Chapter 5 with its Appendices, constitute a closely-reasoned critique of James' pragmatism.

the limits of any personal individualism. For this we must have more than a mere accumulation of several efforts. We cannot rest in a God who is no more omnipotent than one of ourselves, and who, though animated, I dare say, by the best intentions, cannot answer for the unknown force that confronts himself and us," [3] that is, the anthropomorphic God of pragmatism is not God at all, because he is made to man's own measure and thus is a pure illusion.

Christian theology, remarks Bradley, has the concept of God as the Infinite, Omnipotent and Omnipresent Being. This is a complete fusion of the metaphysical "quality" of Being and the anthropomorphic "qualities" of intellect and will; and it gives rise to the well-known difficulties: presumably Bradley is here alluding to the difficulties of conceiving the freedom of God's intervention in creation and in the contingency of human history, of reconciling divine providence with the existence of evil and the pre-motion of God with human freedom, etc. For Bradley, who here agrees with James, the only avenue of escape from these difficulties is to remove or renounce one or more of the "troublesome attributes". If God is made finite and presumably to some extent ignorant and impotent, in short, if he is reduced on principle to the status and level of one creature among others, certain objections obviously lose their force. Thus, again, if one wants to treat God as a person over against others, the easiest way is to deny that he is infinite. And if you wish to relieve a person of moral responsibility, it is a well-known expedient to deprive him either of knowledge or of power.[4] But Bradley readily admits that there are difficulties in the other position as well, i.e., the idealist monist one. These he undertakes to resolve.

When Bradley comes to treat directly of the God-problem,[5] he makes a clear-cut and drastic distinction (agreeing here with idealism and especially with Hegel) between God and the Absolute. God has no meaning outside of the religious consciousness and that consciousness is essentially practical. The Absolute as conceived by philosophy cannot be God because the Absolute as such is related to nothing, and there cannot be any practical relation between it and the finite will. When a man begins to worship the Absolute or the Universe, and to make it the object of religion, he has by that very fact transformed it utterly. From this there follows likewise for Bradley the fundamental inconsistency of religion: in any but an imperfect religion, God must be perfect because he must

[3] *Ibid.*, p. 82. In Note 1 to that page, we read the important specification: "Instead of 'a God' I should perhaps have written 'a God or a set of gods'. Our new gospel seems not to have decided at present whether monotheism or polytheism is to be the creed of the future. I should be inclined to agree that from a religious point of view the difference in this case has no importance."

[4] *Ibid.*, p. 100 Note.

[5] *Ibid.*, ch. XV: "On God and the Absolute," pp. 428ff,

be the complete satisfaction of all finite aspiration; but at the same time God must stand in relation with my will. Thus, the object of religion is supreme goodness and power. Consequently, religion consists in the relation between the perfect will and our finite will. Now if perfection is actually realized, then what becomes of my will which is over against the completely Good Will? On the other hand, if there is no such Will, what becomes of God? This is the root of the difficulty experienced in substantiating the religious notion of God: "Religion naturally implies a relation between man and God. Now a relation always (we have seen throughout) is self-contradictory [because, for Bradley, a relation demands that its two terms shall be independent one of the other and at the same time be connected one with the other!] . . . This general conclusion may at once be verified in the sphere of religion. Man is on the one hand a finite subject, who is over against God, and merely 'standing in relation'. And yet, upon the other hand, apart from God man is merely an abstraction. And religion perceives this truth, and it affirms that man is good and real only through grace, or that again, attempting to be independent, he perishes through wrath. He does not merely 'stand in relation', but is moved inly by his opposite, and indeed, apart from this inward working, could not stand at all. God again is a finite object, standing above and apart from man, and is something independent of all relation to his will and intelligence. Hence God, if taken as a thinking and feeling being, has a private personality. But, sundered from those relations which qualify him, God is inconsistent emptiness; and, qualified by his relation to an Other, he is distracted finitude." [6] He who would avoid Scylla falls into Charybdis.

One easy way out would be to renounce the perfection of God, let him remain good still but in a limited sense. This Bradley feels to be substantially the finitist position of Mill and James. God is reduced to the status of a being who will do the best he can but whose knowledge and powers are limited. Although sufficiently superior to us to be worshipped, God will nevertheless remain imperfect; and this very imperfection will be the salvation of religion! The aim and goal of religion will be to aid God in the struggle against evil, an aim and goal undoubtedly worthy and noble, capable of inspiring man to heights of heroism. But a closer look at the whole situation shows us that this conception has degraded God without thereby ensuring any real salvation. Once it is admitted that the deity is limited and thus contains imperfection, it is an illusion to imagine that the downward pull can be arrested at the appropriate limit. Thus, anyone who asserts the imperfection of God finds

[6] F. H. Bradley, *Appearance and Reality*, p. 394. On the difficulties involved in this conception, cf. the recent study by H.-J. Schüring, *Studie zur Philosophie Francis Herbert Bradley* (Meisenheim an Glan, 1963), pp. 121ff.

himself in a desperate dilemma: he must either try to show that the rest of the universe, extrinsic to his limited God, is known to be still weaker and more limited; or else he must incite us to follow our leader blindly and, for all we know, into an overwhelming common catastrophe. The result in either case is bound to be the loss of religion. Thus, every avenue of escape is closed. If God is perfect, religion becomes inconsistent as we have seen. Indeed it was this very inconsistency that led us to the admission of a limited God in the first place. Now that we have seen the insoluble dilemma posed by a limited and finite God, we have reached a total dead end. We must conclude that it is impossible to find any *theoretical consistency* for religion; and this is a cardinal point for Bradley.[7]

The first step toward a clarification of the concept of "theoretical consistency" is to admit that every truth must be considered to be imperfect. Nor does Bradley hold at all with the notion that truth will in the end become consistent and definitively true; it will simply be satisfactory to various degrees and the idea that we dispose of absolute truths in science and in practical life, he rejects as an illusion. Every truth in these areas has an approximate significance and value in relation to the needs and questions to which it is supposed to respond. Such truths cannot therefore pretend to any theoretical consistency. The same holds true, according to Bradley, for the truths of religion. Certainly the ideas that best express our supreme religious needs and their satisfaction must be true; but they do not possess any ultimate truth because we are not in a position to know that which ultimately is supposed to render them perfect. From this point of view, the religious truths are like any other particular truth attainable by man or by any other finite being operating as we do or indeed operating in any other way whatsoever. To pretend that they have any "theoretical consistency" would be ridiculous; they are in exactly the same situation as all other particular truths. The only thing that can be demanded of these truths is that they satisfy our religious needs and practice and in this sense and in this realm they are certainly true. It would thus be an error to demand for religious truths that theoretical consistency which would only result in a fundamental mutilation of religion.

On the basis of these premisses, Bradley proceeds to discuss the two fundamental problems of religious knowledge: the personality of God and the immortality of the soul.[8] A personal God cannot, Bradley insists, constitute the ultimate truth about the Universe, for in that ulti-

[7] Cf. F. H. Bradley, *Essays on Truth and Reality*, ch. IX: "On Appearance, Error and Contradiction," pp. 245ff.

[8] On the immortality of the soul, cf. F. H. Bradley, *Appearance and Reality*, pp. 444ff.; *Essays on Truth and Reality*, pp. 438ff.

mate truth such a personal God would be included and superseded by something higher than personality.

There is throughout Bradley a strange mixture of idealist terms and themes with references to empirical reality and experience. This should be noted most attentively because it is common to a great percentage of the English-speaking philosophers of the last hundred years. They seem blissfully unaware of any tension here, to say nothing of any contradiction or irreconcilability.

Thus, Bradley continues vigorously and serenely: "A God that can say to himself 'I' as against you and me, is not in my judgement defensible as the last and complete truth for metaphysics." [9] But religious consciousness cannot imagine God's will except as being in relation to mine. Much more necessary than the "personality" of God is the real presence of God's Will in mine, our actual and literal satisfaction in common: this is the idealist principle of immanentism. Properly speaking, the notion of God as a "person" belongs to mythology; it is an illicit extrapolation to want to make a subjective feeling the center of the real: [10] the individual as such has neither truth nor consistency.

What are individual human beings when they are divorced from the community? For Bradley the entire universe is wrecked if the individual by himself is anywhere a fact! The reality of the immanent Will in the universe therefore cannot possibly be personal; that supreme reality which religion calls God is and must be held to be super-personal. Yet, practical religion seems to call for the belief in God as a separate individual. Well, such a belief, however justified and true it may be, simply must be supplemented by other beliefs which really seem to contradict it but are in fact even more vital for religion. It is certainly one-sided, to say the least, to think that a God should have made this strange and glorious Nature and then placed himself outside of it. If we shut ourselves up within the confines of this idea we lose large realms of what is beautiful and sublime. Even our notion of religion itself suffers. Until the Maker and Sustainer becomes also the indwelling Life and Mind and the inspiring Love, how impoverished the universe remains! That is why "pantheism" is essential as the only solution enabling us to avoid both crude polytheism and the anthropomorphic and externalistic notion of a

[9] F. H. Bradley, *Essays on Truth and Reality,* p. 432. In a footnote to this page, Bradley writes: "The doctrine that there cannot be religion without a personal God is to my mind certainly false"; and in his major work, he asserts: "To begin one's work by some bald assumption, perhaps about the necessity of a 'personal' God, is to trifle indecently with a subject which deserves some respect" (*Appearance and Reality,* p. 401).

[10] Cf. F. H. Bradley, *Essays on Truth and Reality,* the fascinating Chapter XIV: "What is the real Julius Caesar?" pp. 409ff.; *Appearance and Reality,* Chapter X: The Reality of Self," pp. 89ff.

personal God. The definitive formulation must therefore be: ". . . the reality of God means his own actual presence within individual souls, and, apart from this presence, both he and they are no more than abstractions."[11] And the only alternative is an individualism that reduces God to one finite person among others, a person whose influence remains utterly and exclusively external. And this in turn leads to the ruin of religion.

The crux of the question is this: religion must, on the one hand, rule out any identification of God with the Absolute, for then he would have no relation with man; but religion must, on the other hand, tend to conclude that man's relation to God is a relation to the Absolute, i.e., conceive God first as a "person" and partner of man and then as a cosmic principle having no relation whatever to man. The contradiction inherent in religion is that of founding itself on this relation (of man to God and God to man) and then trying to perfect itself by the rupture or supersession of this very relation.[12] God is therefore contradictory: "The falling apart of idea and existence is at once essential to goodness and negated by Reality. And the process, which moves within Reality, is not Reality itself. We may say that God is not God, till he has become all in all, and that a God which is all in all is not the God of religion. God is but an aspect, and that must mean but an appearance, of the Absolute."[13]

In order, therefore, to thrust beyond the finitism of Mill and James, Bradley reiterates the Spinozan principle as filtered through the monistic conception of self-consciousness as universal Intelligence and Will, of which the individual subjects and events are the "appearances". Religion and philosophy, for their part, are but "appearances"; neither of the two can really be called the perfection of the other and the real completion and perfection of both can be found only in the Absolute. The essential problem, therefore, remains for Bradley that of the (Hegelian) relation

[11] F. H. Bradley, *Essays on Truth and Reality,* p. 437.

[12] "If again you separate them, God becomes a finite factor in the Whole. And the effort of religion is to put an end to, and break down, this relation—a relation which, none the less, it essentially presupposes. Hence, short of the Absolute, God cannot rest, and, having reached that goal, he is lost and religion with him" (*Appearance and Reality,* pp. 395f.).

[13] F. H. Bradley, *Appearance and Reality,* pp. 396f. Bradley claims that it is precisely the efforts to capture and confine the Absolute within religion that endangers religion itself: "It leads to the dilemma, If God is, I am not, and, if I am, God is not. We have not reached a true view until the opposite of this becomes self-evident. Then without hesitation we answer that God is not himself, unless I also am, and that, if God were not, I certainly should be nothing" (p. 398 Note 1). This is an obvious reference to what Bradley considers to be the only possible escape from the atheistic thrust and bias of, e.g., Nietzsche and Feuerbach.

of existence and essence, of the finite with the Infinite as of parts to the Whole in the form of the relation of the Absolute with its appearances,[14] wherein is expressed the ultimate meaning of reality. We feel that Bradley's *Appearance* derives directly from Hegel's *Erscheinung,* including as its first moment or element the *Schein.*[15]

The appearance consists in the dissociation or "looseness" of content and existence; because of the resultant self-estrangement, every finite aspect is called an appearance. Everywhere the finite is self-transcending, alienated or estranged from itself and in the act of passing over from itself into another existence. In this Bradleyian assertion, there is an obvious reference and appeal to the first stage of consciousness in Hegel's *Phänomenologie des Geistes.* Hence, the finite is an appearance because, on the one hand, it is an adjective of reality and on the other hand it is an adjective which is not itself real. It is only the Whole, the All, which is real in metaphysical idealism. And this Whole, this All, is the Absolute.

But the truth of the Absolute cannot be expressed in any one formula. On the one hand, we must say that "everything is appearance" and no appearance nor yet any combination of appearances is identical with Reality. This is half of the truth and taken by itself it constitutes a dangerous error. We must correct it with the other half of the truth: "The Absolute *is* its appearances", is really each and every one of them and all of them together; but if the appearances be taken individually or even all together and it be asserted without qualification that they are the Absolute, the position becomes untenable and hopeless. The appearance cannot become the Absolute nor can the Absolute be identified with the appearance. Bradley believes he has found a way out of the impasse with his theory of the degrees of reality. This theory holds that the Absolute is indeed identified with each and every appearance and with the sum total of them, but not equally! For some appearances are more real than others. Thus, each and every thing is essential and yet one thing is worthless in comparison with others. Nothing is perfect as such and yet every thing contains to some degree a vital function of perfection. Every posture of experience, every realm and level of the universe constitutes a necessary factor in the Absolute. Thus, while it can be granted that every appearance, taken in itself, is an error, not every error is an illusion.[16] There is no province of the universe wherein

[14] Cf. *Ibid.,* Chapter XXVI: "The Absolute and its Appearances," pp. 403ff.

[15] Cf. Hegel, *Wissenschaft der Logik,* Buch II, 1. Abschn., 1. Kap; ed. Lasson, Vol. II, 7ff.

[16] On the difference between error and illusion, cf. F. H. Bradley, *Appearance and Reality,* Chapter XXVII, especially pp. 486ff. On p. 488, Bradley writes: "The positive relation of every appearance as an adjective to Reality, and the

the Absolute does not dwell. There is a truth in every idea, even a false one; there is a reality in every existence, however tenuous. And where we succeed in attaining reality and truth, there we find is the one and undivided life of the Absolute. The appearance without the Absolute would be impossible: by what could it possibly appear? And reality without appearance would be nothing for there is certainly nothing outside of appearance. Yet, once again it must be repeated that the Absolute is not the sum total of things. It is the unity in which all things, coming together, are transmuted, in which they are changed all alike, though not changed equally. In this unity, all relations of isolation and hostility are affirmed and absorbed, entirely reconciled in the harmony of the Whole. Even the ugly and the evil, even falsehood and error belong to the Absolute; but they are subordinate aspects; they have meaning only when applied to the Absolute's appearances, for the Absolute as such is good. The relation of Absolute and appearance is here dialectical in the extreme, more so even than in the Hegelian conception. For in the Hegelian system, thc Absolute is ultimately defined in terms of perfection; whereas in Bradley the relation has no perfecting or eschatological sense whatsoever, being defined solely in terms of that conjunction, that "togetherness", that is typical of post-Hegelian "actualism". Ugliness, error, evil—all these negative aspects belong to the Absolute and all essentially contribute to the riches of the Absolute. The Absolute would not only be impoverished were its appearances taken away from it; it would be bankrupt! [17] It is the function of metaphysics to investigate the realm of the appearances, to measure each one of them against the idea of perfect individuality in order to arrive at an understanding of its "degree" of reality,[18] and to arrange the appearances in an order and a system of gradated reality and merit.

In the end, Bradley makes a sober but resolute profession of Hegelian orthodoxy, as opposed to the philosophers inspired by emergent and organic evolution, which admit the infinite progress of the real. He asks:

---

presence of Reality among its appearances in different degrees and with diverse values—this double truth we have found to be the centre of philosophy." And shortly thereafter: "The Reality itself is nothing at all apart from appearances. It is in the end nonsense to talk of realities—or of anything else—to which appearances would appear, or between which they somehow could hang as relations" (pp. 488f.).

[17] "Ugliness, error, and evil, all are owned by, and all essentially contribute to the wealth of the Absolute. The Absolute, we may say in general, has no assets beyond appearances; and again, with appearances alone to its credit, the Absolute would be bankrupt" (*ibid.*, p. 433).

[18] Bradley considers this the central point of his whole philosophy: "It is because the Absolute is no sundered abstraction but has a positive character, it is because this Absolute itself is positively present in all appearance, that appearances themselves can possess true differences of value" (*ibid.*, p. 488).

Is there in the end and on the whole, any progress in the universe? Is the Absolute better or worse at one time than at another? And his reply is unconditionally negative. He admits that there is progress and retrogression in the world; but he holds it to be unthinkable that the Whole as such moves either on or backwards. The Absolute has no history of its own, though it contains histories without number. But these are merely partial aspects in the region of temporal appearances. Their truth and reality may vary much in extent and in importance, but in the end it can never be more than relative. "The Absolute has no seasons, but all at once bears its leaves, fruit, and blossoms." [19]

This ultimate specification of Bradley's conception of the universe is aimed at clinging to the most orthodox Hegelianism in the sense of championing the most rigid identity of being and knowing. "The Reality comes into knowledge, and, the more we know of anything, the more in one way is Reality present within us. The Reality is our criterion of worse and better, of ugliness and beauty, of true and false, and of real and unreal . . . And Reality is one Experience, self-pervading and superior to mere relations . . . Outside of spirit there is not, and there cannot be, any reality, and, the more that anything is spiritual so much the more is it veritably real." [20] Thus, for Bradley, Reality is the referend establishing the degrees of reality, of good and evil, and the likc. In thc second-last sentence we have cited above, there is an overt and drastic profession of what might be called "empirical actualism". And the last sentence cited, which is the concluding sentence of the main text of *Appearance and Reality* is an express reference and appeal to Hegel's own essential message. But the Hegelian conception seems to us to be in one sense less static, inasmuch as it asserts that the Whole (*Ganze*) is a Result (*Resultat*) and thus tends to admit "progress" into the interior of the Spirit. But this conflicts with the principle of Act and Bradley may have been intending to remove this contradiction. The net result was a successful divorce of the concept of God from that of the Absolute and a naked presentation of the essentially atheistic nature of the principle of immanentism.

Josiah Royce (1855-1916) made a significant and important effort at mediation between the Jamesian "philosophy of life" and the Bradleyian metaphysics of the Absolute, between the personal God and the all-encompassing unity of the reality of consciousness. Aside from an obvi-

[19] The image is borrowed from Strauss (cf. *Appearance and Reality*, p. 442, Note 2). Bradley holds the evolutionary-progress notion to be incompatible with Christianity: "You cannot be a Christian if you maintain that progress is final and ultimate and the last truth about things" (p. 443).

[20] *Ibid.*, p. 489.

ous influence stemming from Hegelian idealism, there can be noted in his works the insistent note of mysticism, deriving especially from Eckhart and Indian philosophy; but all these notes and echoes tend to be founded in and tempered by that peculiarly cautious English empiricism which never loses vital contact with experience, even in its boldest thrusts to unify the real via the Absolute conceived as Spirit.[21]

In his critique of the realist conception of the Being and consequently of the transcendence of God, Royce closely follows Bradley: *realism* cannot offer any solution for the problem of evil, for once God has been conceived as a supreme Power creating and conserving the world, then God must either be admitted to be incapable of preventing evil, in which case he is imperfect, or else he must be admitted to be unwilling to prevent it, in which case he becomes responsible for the evil itself. The apparently diametrically opposed conception, *mysticism,* with its assertion of the immediate intuition of Being and the Absolute, is little better, for it suffers from the opposite defect, that of unwillingness to admit the finite and of a reduction of the world of appearances to the point of annihilation.[22] Royce certainly considers the Kantian critical approach to be superior to both the aforementioned conceptions: it professes "total reflection" and thus conceives the real as a whole, thus avoiding the extrinsicism inherent in realism, and simultaneously championing the conjunction of appearances to Reality, defending their status against the inanition foisted upon them by mysticism. But Kantian criticism is but a transitional, not a definitive position: the dualism of "thing-in-itself" and "appearance" must be overcome, as must likewise the resulting dualism between real and possible being, for these dualisms impede that pursuit of total and concrete truth substantiated and demanded by the idealist principle.[23] We have here reached the crucial point of confluence of the theoretical considerations that are operating to exacerbate the God-problem at its innermost node: realism, in virtue of its

[21] "Royce combines that typically English empiricist prudence, that telling and ingenious psychological penetrations, with an entirely un-English metaphysical boldness and adventurousness" (G. Marcel, *La métaphysique de Royce,* [Paris, 1945], pp. 8f.). His idealism could be called a synthesis of James and Hegel mediated by Bradley; the description is somewhat empirical but was suggested by Royce himself (cf. Josiah Royce, *The Philosophy of Loyalty* [New York, 1920], p. 325).

[22] Cf. Josiah Royce, *The World and the Individual,* Vol. I (New York, 1899, which 1st edition we have consulted in the Dover edition of 1959), Lectures IV (pp. 141ff.) and V (pp. 185ff.).

[23] *Ibid.,* pp. 47ff., 77ff., 196ff. The crucial point here is that metaphysics directs its main attention to seeking proofs (*a priori* and *a posteriori*) of the existence of God and then proceeds to profess agnosticism concerning his essence; idealism, on the other hand, concentrates exclusively on the essence of God which absorbs the problem of his existence and constitutes the comprehensive formula of truth itself (cf. in this connection especially the long and pithy note on the distinction between *esse essentiae* and *esse existentiae:* (pp. 51f.).

radical pluralism, cannot attain to the Absolute One; mysticism, in virtue of its radical monism, cannot substantiate the manifold of appearances; Kantian criticism posits the lively and concrete dialectic of the many and the One, only to inhibit and arrest its progressive development.

The only valid solution, therefore, is the idealist one, with its unification in distinction (as parts in the whole) of the many in the One and its consequent identification of Reality with the Idea. But in contradistinction to German idealism, which had demoted natural and revealed religion to a status inferior to that of philosophy, Royce conceives of a nexus of strict conjunction between religion and philosophy, ascribing signal importance to the values religion proposes for man's life. The chief of these are the person and freedom. He readily acknowledges that the higher ethical religions have attained in general outline the absolute truth: these religions have taught that the higher universal life of the cosmos is rational and good, that it is all around us and intimately close to us despite our ignorance of it, that it is meaningful in the extreme, despite the fact that we may presently be far from experiencing the fullness of that meaning, that this universal life has a real interest in our personal destiny as moral beings, and, finally, that our own human loyalty can bring us into an intimate face-to-face encounter with the true will of that universal life.[24] This is in substance the creed of what Royce agrees with Hegel in calling the "absolute religion", the religion of the "absolute truth" or of the absolute human Reason. Ultimately it coincides with absolute or essential Christianity, i.e., Christianity freed from dogmas and specific credal statements. Royce agrees with the Spinozists that the vital element of Christianity is not the "historical Christianity" of the Church but rather the "essential Christ" of Reason, independent of any historical event. From this principle flows the conception of God which Royce holds to be the only valid alternative atheism.[25]

This approach holds that God must be primarily acknowledged to be a spirit and a person; but he is not a being who exists in separation from the world, simply as its external creator. God expresses himself in the world and the world is simply his own life in the conscious activity which he externalizes. Royce has recourse to the metaphor of God expressing himself in the poems and portraits, the music and other

[24] "First, the rational unity and goodness of the world-life; next, its true but invisible nearness to us, despite our ignorance; further, its fulness of meaning despite our barrenness of present experience; and yet more, its interest in our personal destiny as moral beings; and finally, the certainty that, through our actual loyalty, we come, like Moses, face to face with the true will of the world, as a man speaks to his friend" (Josiah Royce, *The Philosophy of Loyalty*, pp. 390f.).

[25] I am here following particularly the synthetic exposition Royce presents in *William James and Other Essays*, p. 167ff.

artistic creations that arise in the mind of the artist and consciously incorporate his will. Or again, God is the whole world seen from a lofty vantage-point and in its totality as an infinitely complex life incorporating in a series of endless temporal processes a single divine idea. The reader is immediately struck by the operative influence, in this formulation, of the Hegelian formula: "Without the world, God is not God", a formula Royce aims at disentangling from its systematic and semantic complexity in order to bring it closer to actual human living and immerse it therein.

You can and must distinguish, specifies Royce, between the world as seen by common sense, in a true and real but fragmentary fashion, and the world as studied by our sciences. You can and must distinguish between the world of phenomena and God who is infinitely more than can be expressed by any finite system of natural facts or human lives. But this distinction between God and the world does not signify any separation of the two. The world is the fragmented accumulation of phenomena that we see. God is the conscious meaning expressing himself in and through the totality of all the phenomena. Considered as a simple accumulation of natural processes, individual lives and events in time, the world is at no time or place a complete expression of the divine will. But the entire world or universe, of which our world is a fragment —the totality of what is, past, present and future; the totality of physical reality and mental reality, of the temporal and the permanent—this whole universe is present primarily to the eternal divine Mind as a single Whole and this Whole is what the Absolute chooses as its expression of itself and is conscious of choosing as its own life. This world taken in its totality is primarily the object of the divine knowledge and the act in which it is incorporated is the divine will. And Royce makes a reference to that same biblical text which Spinoza used as a point of departure to eliminate positive revealed religion. He compares the totality of the world to the divine Logos as not only being with God but being God.[26]

[26] "Like the Logos of the Fourth Gospel, this entire world is not only with God, but is God" (*William James and Other Essays,* p. 169). Royce is fully persuaded that he is here in accord with the spirit of the Church's teaching, if not with the letter of its formulation; and he feels he is expressing the vital essence of this teaching better than it is expressed in such official formulas: "I believe, however, that this is the view of the divine nature which the church has always more or less intuitively felt to be true, and has tried to express, despite the fact that my own formulation of this doctrine includes some features which in the course of the past history of dogma have been upon occasion formally condemned as heresy by various church authorities. But for my part I had rather be a heretic, and appreciate the vital meaning of what the church has always tried to teach, than accept this or that traditional formulation, but be unable to grasp its religiously significant spirit" (p. 170). Royce's approach is quite in line with "Johannine Christianity" as derived from Spinoza and developed by Lessing and transcendental Idealism.

This is the essential meaning of God's immanence, says Royce, and this is the meaning of modern idealism.

The essential bulwark of this whole conception, Royce hastens to specify, is that "God and his world are one". And this unity is no mere inert natural fact. It is a unity of a conscious life, wherein, in the course of an infinite time, a divine plan, an infinitely complex yet perfectly definite spiritual idea is expressing itself in the lives of innumerable finite beings and yet in the unity of a single universal life. Royce is therefore parting company with speculative idealism and aligning himself rather with Schopenhauer in conceiving the unity of the real not as speculative Reason or Idea but rather as will; Royce speaks expressly of "a world will". This means that he is admitting a single temporal process for the whole world and acknowledging that the world will articulates and unfolds itself as "a single volitional process", wherein all our lives are conjoined. We are but different modes of willing, continuously linked one with another and with the total will of the world, a will that pulses and thrusts in all of us equally but, with infinite variety, seeks now one special goal and now another, accomplishes now one particular enterprise and now another, presupposes an infinity of events as its own past, proceeds to an infinity of enterprises as its own future, is content not to be any one of us but shows in our social life the community of our varied infinite aspirations, even as it presents in our individual lives an infinite variety of differentiations and directions in its goals. There is one single will in all of us. Royce points out that he has elsewhere [27] attempted to show that this does not deprive us of our own proper individuality. We are neverthless one, even though many of us think we are entirely separate entities. We are one as God sees us: "I mean by the term 'God' the totality of the expressions and life of the world will, when considered in its conscious unity." [28]

Royce proceeds to explain that God is the consciousness that knows and understands the entire life of the world; but he is a consciousness that contemplates this life with a single glance, as his own life, as himself. Therefore he not only wills but attains, not only seeks but possesses, not only passes from one expression to another but is eternally the entire temporal sequence of his own expressions. Royce's whole conception can virtually be said to constitute a climax in the centripetal ascendant scale of equation of being with life, life with consciousness, consciousness with self-consciousness and self-consciousness with the will of the Whole.

Royce resolutely rises to the metaphysical outlook of a vitalist and pragmatist monism, having a Hegelian-Schopenhauerian background,

[27] Cf. e.g., *The World and the Individual,* Vol. I, pp. 462ff.
[28] Josiah Royce, *William James and Other Essays,* p. 285.

even though Schopenhauer would have shuddered at such a bracketing of himself with his most detested adversary Hegel. Royce proclaims that God has and is will; and this will, if it be considered as a temporal sequence of actions, is identical with what Royce had earlier called the world will. Considered from the inside, however, as a divine will, this world will is no longer merely an infinite sequence of volitional actions, but is "one whole of life" in its eternal unity.

This likewise gives us the key to the true meaning of the divine attributes. Thus, God is *omniscient* because his glance comprehends and finds unified in a single eternal instant the totality of the temporal process with all its contents and meanings. God is *omnipotent* because all that is done is seen in his own unity, in his deed, and this despite the variety and the endless struggles that are involved in the freedom and variety of finite individual expressions. God is *immanent* in the finite, because nothing is that is not a part of his self-expression. He is *transcendent* of all finitude because the totality of the finite processes is preeminently present to him, because no finite being possesses a true totality. These attributes seem clearly to come right out of the *Summa Theologica* of St. Thomas Aquinas (with whom, moreover, Royce, on several occasions shows himself to be quite familiar [29]), but the whole Thomistic thrust and system is stood entirely on its head: being realizes itself via mind, not vice versa; and so the infinite God actualizes himself in and through the finite. And we must also bear in mind—Royce is quite insistent in repeating this—that the transition between finite and Infinite is likewise here an inversion of that transition as conceived by realist metaphysics: true and concrete perfection can only be expressed by the supervention of imperfections. An absolute result can be attained only by means of an infinite series of temporal aspirations. And the absolute personality itself can exist only as mediated by the unification of the lives of imperfect and finite personalities. The infinite life cannot live unless it becomes incarnate in a finite form and regains its global significance by a conquest of finitude in its total expression of life and reality. Moreover, in the very logic of this dynamic Spinozism, no ra-

[29] Royce's principal work, *The World and the Individual,* has several references to and quotations from St. Thomas: cf. especially, Vol. I, p. 6, where Hegel and St. Thomas are represented as expressing the two antithetical forms of speculative theology; Vol. I, p. 78, which has a comparison of St. Thomas and Meister Eckhart; Vol. I, pp. 85f., where Royce detects a mystical and even pantheistic vein in Thomist theology in view of its contention that God receives nothing from creation but remains unchanged and perfect in Himself both prior to, during and subsequent to the creative act; Vol. I, pp. 230ff., where Royce gives a careful and penetrating exposition (considering the date at which it was written and the fact that Royce was an idealist) of the Thomist notion of the relation of God to creatures, a notion which Royce incisively designates as an original synthesis of mystical, Platonic and Aristotelian elements.

tional satisfaction can be attained except by a victory over irrational dissatisfactions. Consequently, the supreme good logically requires the conquest of evil. The eternal has need of the expressions in a temporal series of which the eternal is the unifying principle. The divine will, as world will, must differentiate itself into individual series, forms of finitude, aspirations, ignorant quests for the light, beings hagridden by the doubts and errors of the wanderer; only thus can the perfection of the spirit be attained.[30]

At this point, Royce poses most emphatically the *problem of evil:* how can the existence of evil be reconciled with that principle of conjunction or "togetherness" [31] of which Royce has just given so many incisive and vigorous articulations? With a profoundly troubled humaneness, Royce calls this problem "the most tragic question of our present human existence". Why, he asks, if the world is the embodiment of the divine life, why in that case is there so much evil in it, so much darkness, ignorance, misery, dissatisfaction, war, hate, disease and death: in brief, why is the world as we know it so full of the irrational? Are these sad and painful facts perhaps but illusions, bad dreams of our finite existence, unknown to the very God who is and knows the whole truth? No, is Royce's honest and forthright reply, which cannot be the answer for it still leaves us with the problem: how could God permit all this?

Royce confesses that the problem of evil is the great problem that stands between our ordinary and finite way of seeing life on the one hand and our consciousness of the reasonableness and the unity of the divine life on the other. But this seems to us a typically idealist way of posing the difficulty; and from the idealist approach there came, as we have seen, a strong incentive for the "precipitation" of the principle of immanentism into outright and professed atheism in present-day philosophy, even in the Anglo-Saxon world, as we shall be saying and showing very shortly. Royce, for his part, attempts a solution that is virtually Nietzschean: so as not to be overpowered by the existence and the pressure of evil, we must look to the values represented by the higher religious consciousness of our race. But he does not present his solution in the abstract; it is to be understood concretely, inasmuch as it is expressed in the wisest and best heroes of morality of all the races and nations of mankind.

This moving peroration can scarcely be called a solution. But it does have its own poignancy. Suffice it here to note Royce's final formulation: the absolutely necessary and binding law of the most exalted spiritual life is to become perfect through suffering. This is a law that holds for God and for man alike, for those among men who have already been

[30] Cf. Josiah Royce, *William James and Other Essays,* pp. 286f.
[31] Cf. *Ibid.,* pp. 171f.

enlightened by learning the true lessons of their own sufferings, and for those who are still looking forward, full of hope, to a life animated by the anticipation of joys to come and worldly success. The goal of a high-minded life, concludes Royce, consists not in gaining good fortune but rather in transmuting all the transient values of fortune into eternal values. This we shall better do when we learn by experience how even the greatest misfortune can be turned to good account by wise resolutions and the grace deriving from our conscious union with the divine, so as to raise us to the level of something much better than any mere good fortune can give us: we can come to understand how God himself endures evil and triumphs over it, raising it and liberating it from itself, overcoming it by transmuting it into the service of the good. Royce seems to dwell with special preference on such considerations as these. He has a great interest in and attachment to the doctrine of Atonement, that major theme in Anglo-Saxon theology, Catholic and Protestant alike.

It is in this context that Royce sees the supreme relevance of the Christian dogma of the Incarnation: [32] the doctrine of Incarnation and Atonement is in its essence simply the notion of God which demands this solution of the problem of evil. In actual fact, this Roycean approach to Atonement serves merely to confirm the unavoidable demand of the principle of immanentism. The chief point about the Incarnation, says Royce, is that God is expressing himself in this world of finitude, is incarnating himself within the narrow scope of human imperfection, but is doing this in order to win his spiritual victory over evil in the eternal world (i.e., in the conscious unity of the whole of his life) by means of finitude and imperfection, through pain, suffering and temporal loss. And this victory constitutes God's supreme good and ours. But Royce is careful to specify that the doctrine of the Incarnation by no means teaches the natural divinity of man; rather it teaches that the world will desires our unification with the universal end, that God will be born in us (an echo of Eckhart) in and through our own consent, that the whole meaning of our lives lies in transmuting transitory and temporal values into eternal meanings. Mankind becomes aware of the Incarnation of God only to the extent to which mankind looks toward God, i.e., toward the complete unity of the rational life of the spirit.

In this context likewise the real meaning of the doctrine of the Atonement becomes clear: since we are in time and in a state of transition, we are destined to attain to our union with the divine life only to the extent that we learn to triumph over the evil that is in us, the

[32] Cf. *Ibid.*, pp. 179f.

afflictions of misfortune, irrationality and sin that now hold sway over us. This is why it was said even of Christ that he had to suffer! Thus, in Christ, God-Man, God suffered once for all, to save us: in him alone "the Word was made flesh and dwelt among us". The forms of religious imagination are transitory, says Royce, but the truth lying behind these symbolic forms is eternal. And that truth is twofold: first, God attains to perfection by expressing himself in a finite life and triumphing in and through his own finitude; then, our sadness and sorrow is the sadness and sorrow of God. God's aim is to express himself in winning for us, by the sure victory over evil, a union with the perfect life; and consequently we owe our fulfillment, even as our existence, to the suffering and the triumph of God himself.

In this twofold truth, claims Royce, there is summed up the vital element of Christianity.[33] The Hegelian line is plainly visible in this "transcendental reduction" of religious consciousness and this "resolution" of the God-problem. It makes Christianity's doctrine of the Incarnation and Passion of God in time to be the supreme religious expression of that "negation" which is the propulsive force of human progress in history. For this reason, Hegel called Christianity the "absolute religion".[34] But Hegel held the "absolute truth" of Christianity to be expressed in absolute form only by philosophy which maintains that there is no other life, truth, goodness or reality except that which man brings into being in his own history, so that "without the world and without man, God is not God". God is the static and the dynamic unity of the world, the world will; he lives only in and through the world; and he is the all-inclusive synthesis of the world's evolution.

The theoretical foundation of this unique form of dynamic immanentism is drawn from the very structure of the "Idea" itself: the idea, as the proper and proportionate act of the spirit, seeks itself alone and therefore "can be judged only by itself"; the idea is the absolutely primordial point of the mind for Royce as opposed to St. Thomas who asserts that the mind is directed primarily to the object and that it is only by the apprehension of the object that the mind can apprehend itself and reflect upon itself. For Royce, on the contrary, it is always the Idea that is of prime significance, whether I am thinking of God or of current gossip, of my own death or of the fate of mankind, of the truths of mathematics, of the physical world or of the world of business or of the problem of Being. Moreover—and this is the second step in Royce's immanentist disintegration of thought—my idea is a cognitive process

[33] Cf. *Ibid.*, p. 183.
[34] Cf. Hegel, *Phänomenologie des Geistes,* VII, C. 2; ed. Hoffmeister, pp. 525ff.

only to the extent that it is, at the same time, a volitional process, an act, the partial accomplishment of a goal. The object signified by the idea is an object because it is willed to be an object and the will in question is the will that incorporates the idea. Royce specifies quite precisely: "In seeking its object, any idea whatever seeks absolutely nothing but it's own explicit, and, in the end, complete, determination as this conscious purpose, embodied in this one way. The complete content of the idea's own purpose is the only object of which the idea can ever take note. This alone is the Other that is sought." [35]

Reality is indeed expressed in the idea but this expression consists in a total referral of the reality to the idea. Thus the essence of the idea is activity: its activity is will, the very structure of the idea lies in the realization of a goal. Royce stresses that when he speaks of "will" he does not mean any mere abstract psychological power but rather the primordial essence and structure of consciousness as act: "What the idea always aims to find in its object is *nothing whatever but the idea's own conscious purpose or will, embodied in some more determinate form* than the idea by itself alone at this instant consciously possesses. When I have an idea of the world, my idea is a will, *and the world of my idea is simply my own will itself determinately embodied*". [36]

Being and life, and the idea that sustains both, thus flow from the will. It can be clearly seen that the transition from this to the Marxist formula concerning consciousness as liberation from alienation or even to the existentialist formula concerning the priority of existence over essence involves only a tiny step if any at all. The principle of immanentism has effectively undermined the traditional formulations, which have irremediably lost all genuine content and meaningful reference; it is now simply a question of shaking off the shackles of these outmoded formulations. The principle of immanentism is pressing toward its ultimate actuation, disencumbered of all content save that of the act itself and its self-formation.

In his major work, Royce takes a step that brings him very close indeed to the disintegration of being into the individual act of consciousness that will be effected in Italy by Gentile. For Royce here defines being and truth in terms of sheer presence: "True Being is essentially a Whole Individual Fact, that does not send you beyond itself, and that is, therefore, in its wholeness, deathless. Where death is, Being in its wholeness is not." [37] But Royce found himself faced, within the frame-

[35] Josiah Royce, *The World and the Individual,* Vol. I, p. 329. Italics are in the original.

[36] *Ibid.,* p. 327.

[37] *Ibid.,* p. 380.

work of his own position, with the specifically metaphysical question of the relationship between the finite and the Absolute, between man and God, a question which Royce designates as being "of essential importance".[38] It is, he says, at this point and at this moment that man recovers the true sense of Being and of himself in it. It is indeed true that the individual human being is a mere grain of sand, an utterly insignificant element in the great complex of the physical world and the relentless flux of time; but that human individual alone can know all this! And all this can be real only by virtue of an ontological relation which, properly considered, links man, despite all his weakness, to the very life of God, and the whole universe to the meaning of every individual. It is perfectly consistent with the principle of immanentism for Royce to assert that it is in God that man possesses his individuality;[39] and this Royce does assert with his customary fervor. This dependence is the condition of man's freedom and unique significance.

Royce himself proclaims that his whole philosophy has been the lesson of the unity of finite and infinite, of temporal dependence and eternal significance, of the World and all its Individuals, of the One and the Many, of God and of man. Not only in spite of our finite bondage, but precisely because of what it means and implies, we are full of the presence and the freedom of God. Thus, does Roycean idealism actualize the personality of God, which for Royce is an ethical category and signifies ". . . a conscious being, whose life, temporally viewed, seeks its completion through deeds, while this same life, eternally viewed, consciously attains its perfection by means of the present knowledge of the whole of its temporal strivings".[40] Thus, it is that God is a Person. Temporally viewed, his life embraces the entire realm of consciousness insofar as, in its temporal strivings toward perfection, this consciousness of the universe passes from instant to instant of the temporal order, from act to act, from experience to experience, from stage to stage. Eternally viewed, God's life is the infinite whole that includes this endless temporal process, and that consciously surveys it as one life, God's own life.

Thus God is a Person because he is self-conscious, and because the Self of which he is conscious is a Self whose eternal perfection is attained through the totality of these ethically significant strivings, these

[38] *Ibid.*, Vol. II, p. 440.

[39] Immanentism identifies the relation of conjunction with that of dependence. This, indeed, is what distinguishes immanentism from theistic realism. But this identification amounts to an eliminaton of dependence as such, which no longer signifies distinction but rather unification and dissolution into the great sea of Being which is consciousness in its totality.

[40] *The World and the Individual*, Vol. II, p. 418.

processes of evolution, these linked activities of finite Selves. God's perfection or self-consciousness is not the temporal result of any process of evolution nor is it an event occurring at the end of time, or at the end of any one process, however extended, that occurs in time.[41] Royce has recourse here to a metaphor that would have been the making of Gestalt psychology: this perfection of God, this self-consciousness of his, says Royce, is a melody which does not come into existence contemporaneously with its own last note, but is, on the contrary, a whole whereof the notes are but abstracted fragments. God in his totality as the Absolute Being is conscious, not *in* time, but *of* time, and of all that infinite time contains. In time there follow, in their sequence, the chords of his endless symphony. For him, this whole symphony of life is present at once. But there is no single temporal instant that can pretend to have attained such a status of totality or such a terminal position: there is no single temporal event to which the whole creation moves.

This conception overcomes all the self-contradictions to which the idea of the Infinite has usually been exposed.[42] And Royce sums up thus: at every instant, in the temporal order, the will of God is in process of expressing itself. Now since this is true of every instant of time, it follows that every stage of the world-process, viewed as God views it, stands in an immediate relation to God's whole purpose. Hence, there is, indeed, always progress in the universe insofar as at any instant some specific finite end is nearing or is winning its temporal attainment. Yet Royce is entirely too firmly committed to his metaphysical bias of dissolving the many into the One to admit that there can be any question of progress in the strict finite sense of that word, any progress, that is, simply in virtue of succession in the temporal sphere. He entirely repudiates the idea that whatever comes later in time must be in all respects better or be in every way nearer to God's perfection than is what comes earlier in time. The only true progress is that which is seen from the point of view of eternity; such progress is present in every instant of time, inasmuch as every instant is seeing the realization of some goal not previously realized: "Every age therefore has, as the historian Ranke once said of the ages of human history, its 'unmittel-

[41] C. von Ehrenfels, a disciple of Bolzano, cites it with an incisive analysis, in his article "Ueber Gestalt-qualitäten," in *Vierteljahrschrift fuer wissenschaftliche Philosophie* XIV (1890), pp. 249ff. Cf. our *Fenomenologia della percezione* (Brescia, 1961 [2]), pp. 195ff.

[42] A special investigation of this problem is made by Royce in a Supplementary Essay appended to the lectures published in Vol. I of *The World and the Individual* (pp. 473-588). Here Royce examines the theories of the Infinite advanced by Bolzano, Dedekind, Cantor, Couturat, Schroeder and others, especially Royce's own colleague Bradley. In this Essay, Royce shows that the axiom that "the part cannot be equal to the whole" is not applicable to an infinite collection of objects.

bare Beziehung auf die Gottheit' [immediate nexus with the deity]".[43] In the light of these premisses, the relationship between God and man can be better understood.

Man, too, is a Person; but man is not an absolute Person. He needs his conscious contrast with his fellows and with the whole of the rest of the universe, to constitute him what he is. It is because each individual human being stands thus in contrast to all other individuals that each can speak of "my intention, my meaning, my task, my desire, my hope, my life"[44] as something unique. This is the finite Ego or Self, considered in the flux of the individual instants of time. But it is only from the point of view of God, that the genuine Self, an Individual, can be seen in its internal meaning. The Self of this instant's longing has its true and conscious relations to all the rest of the infinite realm of Being, for the true individual meaning of this passing moment becomes conscious in God, even though we men are not wholly conscious of it. In fact, the principle of conjunction demands that this instant find the complete and individual expression of its whole meaning only in the entire life of God. The temporal brevity of the instant is no barrier to its eternal significance so far as God is concerned. Each such instant, seen from the point of view of eternity, is always and completely in God; and there the true meaning of this temporal instant's deed wins its eternal and self-conscious expression. Hence, we see how neo-Hegelianism united the bad and good Infinities into a dialectical systolic-diastolic process, making them interacting and intercommunicating, instead of leaving them divorced and hostile as had Hegel. This is of great importance for our investigation of the atheistic bias of the principle of immanentism. "It follows that the same considerations which imply the intimate union of every temporal instant's passing striving with the whole life of God, equally imply that an individual task which is ideal, which is unique, and which means the service of God in a series of deeds such as can never end without an essential failure of the task, can only be linked with God's life, and can only find its completion in this union with God, in an individual life which is the life of a conscious Self, and which is a deathless life. And thus at length we are led to the first formulation of our conception of human immortality. We ourselves and not simply other individuals become conscious in God of what we are, because in God we become aware of how our wills have attained their fulfillment by union with him and how his Will obtains its satisfaction only in virtue

[43] *The World and the Individual,* Vol. II, p. 425.

[44] *Ibid.,* p. 430. Royce's 1899 Ingersoll Lecture, *The Conception of Immortality* (Boston and New York, 1900) is devoted to this problem. Cf. especially pp. 48ff. and Note 5 to p. 83.

of our participation in the Whole, in the Absolute Individual who is God.

Royce's gallant effort expresses the summit of what can be called the English-speaking Hegelian Right and the ultimate bulwark of that liberal optimism that had already been forced into a crisis on the continent at the end of the 19th century with the first thrusts of Marxist materialism, but which was to receive the final blow only from the double crisis of the two World Wars that between them virtually wrote the history of the first half of our own 20th century. Along with much other bric-a-brac, this God was likewise bound to perish who was but an anthropologized version of the Hegelian Absolute and who takes on the lineaments of God only to the extent that he descends and realizes himself in history and in the far from splendid reality of human existence. Royce was convinced that he had solved the problem left unresolved by Bradley, namely, the problem of showing how individuals or particular appearances find their unity in the Absolute.[45] As a matter of actual fact, Royce's work contributed substantially to the "precipitation" of the principle of immanentism into its most radical form as assertion of the finitude of man's being and the temporal meaning and fate of his freedom.

[45] Cf. *The World and the Individual,* Vol. I, pp. 473f.

3

The Demotion of God to the Status of an Emergent Cosmic Ideal (Morgan-Alexander)

European philosophy slipped serenely unheeding, after the death of Hegel, in the direction of that explicit and declared atheism we have already seen in the Marxists. In Anglo-American philosophy, on the other hand, there was a gallant effort at "theological resistance" and God was considered to be the foundation of the ideal sphere and of the world of values. The alliance of Hegelian idealism with English empiricism caused no convergence of the antimetaphysical features of the two parent philosophies; rather it imparted a theological impulse as unexpected as it was lively and effective in a goodly number of the best representatives of Anglo-American thought. The first point of convergence, or at least the most obvious, was in the notion of "evolution" that Darwin had applied within the sphere of biological forms in such a way as to suggest that evolution was clearly a progressive and perfective process. In the wake of an ever closer conjunction and collaboration between science and philosophy, Anglo-American thought interpreted reality straightforwardly and without complicated dialectics or abstruse conceptual gymnastics as "emergent evolution".[1]

The whole of the real was conceived as in motion, as a thrust to the actualization of more perfect forms; and it was held to be shot through with forces that ensured this thrust of success. Man with his intelligent mind is at the center of this expansive activity; but he does not express the totality of that activity (as Hegel eventually came to hold him to do), nor is man the only active principle nor yet the ultimate goal of that activity, for man himself is co-involved not only as mover but also (and perhaps even more so) as moved, in this continuous ascendent expansion of the real. Thus, the divine and God become a "quality" and

[1] The term is from Lloyd Morgan, *Emergent Evolution* (New York: Henry Holt and Company, 1923).

soon come to be a quality of consciousness rendering possible to the world and to the naturalistically conceived consciousness a new avenue of approach for the comprehension of the new science and the new social categories from which the European Hegelian schools had cut themselves off in their rigid epistemology and their sterile battles and formalistic discussions about "reforms" of the Hegelian dialectic. Perhaps one element of notable importance contributing to this "theological resistance" in Anglo-American philosophy should be sought in the specific character of English Protestant religious attitudes, always strongly conservative in bias and apparently still stoutly resisting the skeptical and materialistic corrosion that is so extensively undermining European philosophy today. But this point merits a special study which goes beyond the scope of our present investigation, devoted as it is exclusively to showing the atheistic bias of the principle of immanentism.

A more obvious element directly operative in the structuring of this "philosophy of progress", which is a unique synthesis of realism and idealism, is to be found in the recourse to Spinoza. This enabled the Anglo-American philosophers to keep the two realms of matter and spirit distinct and to make them both converge in a deeper and more primordial unity which is not confined without remainder to pure consciousness and cannot be adequately expressed in terms of mind alone. This Spinozan approach is of course present in Bradley and Royce as well; but it takes on a new meaning and significance in the trend of modern science we have just referred to in the figure of Alfred North Whitehead. The road was opened up for Whitehead to this unique convergence of advanced science and deep philosophy by a solitary and meticulous thinker, Samuel Alexander (1859-1938).[2] Alexander likewise held firmly to the empirical principle in his treatment of reality; but he understood it in a very precise way which shows how deeply he had been influenced by idealism: the world is not the amorphous mass of Lockeian sensations or of Humeian impressions; it is intrinsically unified

[2] Whitehead mentions Alexander together with Morgan in the Preface to A. N. Whitehead, *Science and the Modern World* Lowell Lectures 1925 (New York: 1929), p. XI ("I am especially indebted to Alexander's great work"). In his principal work *Process and Reality,* The Gifford Lectures, Edinburgh 1927-28 (New York: Harper Torchbooks, 1960), Whitehead makes more specific acknowledgement of indebtedness to Alexander for the "principle of unrest" (*Process and Reality,* pp. 42f.) and for the term "enjoyment" (p. 65), which latter suggested to Whitehead his key theory of "feeling" as we shall see in due course. Alexander's major work is *Space, Time, and Deity,* The Gifford Lectures at Glasgow 1916-1918, 2 vols. (London 1920 [1], 1934 [2]). The 2nd edition, identical in pagination with the 1st, contains an important new Preface, on which we shall draw heavily for our introduction of Alexander's notion of God. Donald B. Kuspit has a lengthy treatment of the relations between Alexander and Whitehead in his "Whitehead on Divinity" (*Archiv für Philosophie,* XI, 1ff.) pp. 74ff.

in space and time. The Kantian summons is here taken most drastically to heart and Alexander appeals at once to that basic principle of all actualism, the unity of experience. He specifies that "the world does not exist in Space *and* Time, but in Space-Time, that it is a world of events".[3] Space and Time cannot exist apart from one another, because either taken by itself is a mere abstraction. Alexander himself indicates his recourse to Spinoza in this process of unification of experience: the paired attributes of extension and thought here become the Space-Time pair and time is synonymous with mind, i.e. with experience in act and in process, in irreversible evolution. The stuff of the universe considered as a unity of Space-Time is motion, pure motion which is prior even to the generation of matter itself. This the real anterior ultimate is neither act nor potency but rather motion which sustains both, actuating and developing them. The notion of rest is therefore merely relative. Nothing can escape the irresistible flow of the Space-Time unity: if, indeed, anything could come to rest, then everything would stop and Space-Time would lose all meaning.[4] The reality of experience thus resolves itself into motion and what we call rest is likewise motion: every body is involved in this universal motion. We are seeing the return of the Heraclitan conception, mediated by Spinozism which we have already indicated to be the kernel of Whitehead's whole view of reality: even though an object is not in motion with reference to its immediate environment, it is always being moved by the motion of the earth, etc.

[3] "The hypothesis of the book is that Space-Time is the stuff of which matter and all things are specifications. That the world does not exist in Space *and* Time, but in Space-Time, that it is a world of events, has and had, even when I wrote, become common property through the mathematicians, with whom, as I suppose, the conception was a piece of scientific intuition." S. Alexander, *Space, Time, and Deity,* 2nd ed., Vol. I, p. VI). On the same page, Alexander declares that his own conception "has nothing in common with the great mathematical or logical constructions, such as that of Mr. Whitehead". And a little later, Alexander specifies that he wishes to follow a method different from that of Whitehead and to confine himself rigorously metaphysical analysis (pp. VIIf.).

[4] "Now, strictly speaking, all existence is local motion or locomotion, and there is no such thing as rest, except as a relative description of such things as are not in motion relative to each other, like myself and the table at which I write. If anything were at rest, everything would be at rest, and Space-Time would lose its meaning" (*Space, Time, and Deity,* 2nd ed., Vol. I, p. XII). In the light of such a statement of principle, it is not difficult to grasp the metaphysical bias of Alexander's philosophy: it is filtering being and even the Absolute through the components of space and time, in what might be called a second-echelon derivation from Descartes, mediated by a certain synthesis of Spinoza and Kant, and of course by English empiricism: "Alexander always said that his doctrine of space-time—i.e. of a matrix in which space, interpreted as space-stuff like Descartes' *extensio* but never timelessly (since it was motion and time was its 'mind') —had been reached *metaphysically,* that is to say, by intellectual experiments with the 'ultimates' " (J. Laird, "Memoir," in S. Alexander, *Philosophical and Literary Pieces* [London, 1939], p. 63).

Another cardinal Spinozan element which is basic to Alexander's outlook is the priority of metaphysics over epistemology, a priority so pronounced as to convert the latter into a sub-heading of the former. This Alexander calls "naturalism".[5] This naturalism conceives the union of soul and body in a strictly dynamic fashion and it defends the absolute correspondence between the two, as also between the respective acts, such as *enjoyment* and *contemplation*. We are of course not conscious of the neural process which conditions our knowing; but Alexander (and English neo-realism with him) insists that our cognitive acts do not consist in the presentation of an object in the form of a picture produced by the thing in my mind; we here have rather the thing itself or a selection from it, so that the mental process is and "act" of the mind of which I as a living being take possession. Alexander here specifies his relation to Spinoza: the fundamental act of *enjoyment* [6] is articulated in Spinoza's proposition that the mind is the idea of the body, so that the idea that Paul has of Peter indicates rather the constitution of Paul's body than the nature of Peter.[7] In other words, cxplains Alcxander, the idea that Paul has of Peter is a mental condition whose other aspect is a bodily condition of Paul and this differs depending on whether the idea

[5] To which Alexander has no objection if it be thus understood: "The mind is a thing which has its proper place assigned to it in the scheme of things. If such a doctrine is called naturalism, I am content to be with Spinoza, and can claim that such naturalism, like his, admits all the human things of worth" (*Space, Time, and Deity,* Vol. I, p. XIII).

[6] "Enjoyment" as used by Alexander goes beyond the limit of simple pleasure to indicate "satisfaction" in the sense of goal-attainment, and corresponds in this self-actualization of experience to the primordial actuation of consciousness. Book IV, Chapter I of Alexander's *Space, Time, and Deity* deals with God as object of contemplation of speculative reflection; Chapter II of the same Book deals with God as object of the religious sentiment (Vol. II, pp. 373ff.).

[7] The proposition in question is Proposition XVII of the Second Part of Spinoza's *Ethics: "If the human body is affected in a way that involves the nature of some external body, the human Mind will contemplate the said external body as existing in act, as present to it, until such time as the body is affected in a way that precludes the existence or presence of that body."* The Scholion contains the explanation: "Nor do I believe myself to be far wrong, seeing that all those points which I have assumed contain scarcely a single postulate that is not patent from an experience concerning which we have no right to doubt, after we have shown the human body, as we sense it, to exist (cf. Corollary after Prop. 13 of this Book). Moreover (from the preceding Corollary and Corollary 2 to Proposition 16 of this Book), we have clearly seen what is the difference between the idea, e.g. of Peter which constitutes the essence of the Mind of Peter himself, and the idea of that same Peter which is in another man, say Paul. For the former idea directly displays the essence of the Body of Peter himself and involves the existence only so long as Peter exists; whereas the latter idea indicates rather the constitution of Paul's body than the nature of Peter, and Paul's Mind will go on contemplating Peter as present to itself, even though Peter has ceased to exist" (Vol. II [Heidelberg: Gebhardt, 1924], pp. 104, 105f.). Later in *Space, Time, and Deity,* Alexander presents a critique of Spinoza's pantheism as eliminating the sphere of values (Vol. II, pp. 392f.).

is the one corresponding to Peter, to John or to someone else. Thus Alexander substitutes his terms "enjoyment" and "contemplation" for Spinoza's ambiguous use of the genitive in the phrase "idea corporis" (idea of the body) and "idea Petri" (the idea of Peter). Alexander wants to avoid the possibility of a misunderstanding like that of Spinoza's in conceiving that there is an idea of the mind which is united to the body and then again an idea of the idea and so on to infinity; it is true that the mind is an idea, but an idea of an idea is sheer redundancy. I can think the idea of an idea, concludes Alexander, only insofar as an idea (of an external thing) is included in a larger whole of ideas which is the mind. And this larger whole is always a whole within the environment of experience; and it is structured within that environment by powers of the knowing subject. Thus the notion of "consciousness" has no mysterious overtones whatever: the activity of consciousness is considered to be the simple and result of central neural processes.[8] Alexander thus admits that consciousness, the mind, does not constitute a new "quality" of being, but rather amounts simply to a *relation,* a relation of "reference" between the perceiving body and its object. The mind vanishes from the scene as a level or stage distinct and different from life: man and leaf differ only in complexity; everything is conscious of other things insofar as they can enter into its environment and it would seem that for Alexander being and life on the one hand, life and consciousness on the other, are really identical. This would moreover be consistent with Alexander's Spinozan naturalism which recalls Fechner's universal animism or panpsychism.[9] The theory of God is therefore for Alexander simply a part of the overall theory of "emergent evolution"

[8] "The real question raised in my mind is whether the physiological process, I mean as described physiologically, is not enough, and whether I have done rightly, as I still feel I have, in making consciousness a 'quality' of the brain-process. Enjoyment for me was always identical with the brain-process and its connections. Now I find it not so easy to recover my mind of seven years ago, and I may have expressed myself and perhaps really thought in a way which led to misapprehension. But all that I mean now by various enjoyments is brain-processes with their quality of consciousness, a quality which they do not have unless the process is of a certain sort, which is therefore intrinsic to them" (*Space, Time, and Deity,* Vol. I, p. XVI). And a little later, Alexander elaborates: "First, with me mental happenings are dynamic from the outset, being identical with certain physiological processes. Second, no mental event is a 'content'; the characters of green or sweet or being a tree do not belong to the mental process which apprehends, but to the physical object which is apprehended" (p. XXI). This theory of the direct correspondence between the cerebral processes and the mental states has been reiterated in the Berlin School *Gestalt* psychology (cf. C. Fabro, *La fenomenologia della percezione,* pp. 367ff.).

[9] Fechner is considered to be one of the founding fathers of this "physical theology" and of the dissolution of God into "the divine" understood as an ascendent thrust of the real (cf. C. Hartshorne, *Philosophers Speak of God* [Chicago: University of Chicago Press, 1953], pp. 15b, 23a, 140b, and especially 254bff.). Cf. also *The Letters of William James,* Vol. II, p. 269.

pioneered by Lloyd Morgan,[10] who was thus responsible for the first thrust in the direction of the naturalistic transformation of Spinozan pantheism into an evolutionary dissolution of the Absolute.

In his treatment of the specific problem of God as such, Alexander seems to go farther and speak more strongly than Whitehead.[11] The object of religious feeling is identical with the object of philosophical reflection. In the approach to God, religious feeling constitutes the original and primordial drive, like Spinoza's intellectual love; and speculation provides the theoretical justification. Thus the two areas, religion and philosophy, prove to be complementary. Alexander dismisses as less than cogent the multitude of traditional metaphysical arguments, a priori and a posteriori, for all have tended to conceive God as an Absolute divorced from the real; Alexander contends that the only proper approach is that which describes God as a "quality" of the real, as being within that reality conceived as the Space-Time unity, of which God then expresses the ever-emerging forward rim. Alexander is here articulating with considerable precision that fundamental thesis of a God in continual process of becoming via the evolution of the world. This is the quintessence of the metaphysic and theology of this whole Anglo-American school, in their supreme effort to save God for philosophy within the limits of the principle of immanentism. Alexander quite sharply denies that he has ever said or meant to say that God never is but is always yet to be. He specifies that his meaning is quite different: God as actually possessing deity does not exist; God *thus* considered is indeed an ideal, is always becoming. But there is a sense in which God really exists: as the universe, the whole universe tending toward deity. And Alexander makes a crucial distinction, basic to his entire system: Deity is a quality, God is a being. And actual God is a kind of forecast or foreshadowing of ideal God.[12] Thus, for Alexander, God is a cosmological content and can claim, so to speak, two birthplaces: the first is ultimate quality toward which the dynamic unity of Space-Time is moving.

Within the all-embracing stuff of Space-Time, the universe exhibits an emergence in Time of successive levels of finite existences, each with its characteristic empirical quality. The highest of these empirical qualities known to us is mind or consciousness. Deity is an empirical quality and

[10] There is an explicit reference to Morgan in the Preface to the 2nd edition (*Space, Time, and Deity*, Vol. I, p. XXIII).

[11] I am here following Alexander's exposition in *Space, Time, and Deity*, Book IV, ch. I: "Deity and God"; Vol. II, pp. 341ff.

[12] "What I say is that God as actually possessing deity does not exist, but is an ideal, is always becoming; but God as the whole universe tending towards deity does exist. Deity is a quality, and God a being. Actual God is the forecast and, as it were, divining of ideal God" (*ibid.*, Vol. I, p. XXIII).

will at any given moment indicate precisely the next higher empirical quality to the highest we know. This quality the universe is bound to bring to birth but at the moment it is spoken of by us as deity it is still unknown to us; therefore our altars are erected to the Unknown God! In the Space-Time unity there is an innate *nisus* or thrust, an ascendent drive, in virtue of which creatures thrust athwart matter and life to the realm of mind. Deity is therefore, at each and every stage of the real, the actual activity of the self-transcendence of that real into a new quality. Thus deity is not to be identified exhaustively with "mind" nor yet with "spirit". God, the being which possesses deity, must be *also* spirit or spiritual, in the same way as he must be living and material and spatio-temporal; but his deity is not spirit.

Clearly Alexander aims at rising from the quality of the "divine", to which evolution bears witness in its positive ascent, to an eventual recognition and acknowledgement of God as the subject and bearer of this quality. God, he says, is the entire universe insofar as it possesses the quality of deity. The whole universe is the "body" of this being and deity is the "mind". But the possessor of that deity, the subject and bearer of it, is not actual but ideal. If God be considered as an actual existent, then He is simply the infinite world with its thrust towards deity. Alexander approvingly inserts here the Leibnizian phrase concerning the world as big or in travail with deity.[13] These are figures of speech, of course, but we have no better way of expressing this truth.

Deity as a real "empirical" quality is the goal of the whole universe; yet the deity of God remains entirely within the world and he is in no sense outside it. Since God's deity depends on mind, and this in turn on finites of a lower order, until ultimately in this descendent regress we reach the simple primordial matrix of Space-Time, therefore there is no part of the universe that is not used up to sustain the deity of God. And all the things of the universe are parts of his body.[14] Pursuing the thread of this dialectic, Alexander next declares that God is creative, not precisely as God but rather as the Space-Time unity and specifically in

[13] "God is the whole world as possessing the quality of deity. Of such a being the whole world is the 'body' and deity is the 'mind'. But this possessor of deity is not actual but ideal. As an actual existent, God is the infinite world with its nisus towards deity, or, to adapt a phrase of Leibniz, as big or in travail with deity" (*ibid.*, Vol. II, p. 353). And shortly thereafter: "Now the body of God is the whole universe and there is no body outside his" (p. 357). "Universe" here clearly stands for the whole of the unified field of Space-Time.

[14] The statement is formulated dialectically but it always remains on the level of the reciprocal concreteness of the two terms: "God is immanent in respect of his body, but transcendent in respect of his deity" (*ibid.*, Vol. II, p. 396). And this body of God is the latest and current unity that has been attained in the process of cosmic evolution.

virtue of Time which is the moving principle. God's constitutive quality, deity, is at any stage the next empirical quality. As such it owes its being to the pre-existing finites with their empirical qualities and is their outcome; and so it is created. The Creator, in the strictest and truest sense, therefore is Time, not God. And Alexander's conclusion is that God, like all things in the universe, is in the strictest sense not a creator but a creature. It is here important to note that, for Alexander, God *is* a thing in the universe, whereas Space-Time is *not in the universe* but rather itself constitutes the universe and the body of God. Certainly, Alexander hastens to add, God is not a creature of our imagination or of our thought; he is an infinite creature of the universe of Space-Time; and what makes him God is the finite empirical quality of deity. It is not God, therefore, who precedes the world; rather it is the world that precedes and produces God. Whitehead used approximately the same formula in a somewhat more elastic form.

For this approach, the serious problems connected with the origin of evil in the world, those problems that have been tormenting mankind through all the ages, those problems that have seemed so completely insoluble, simply cease to exist, cease to have any meaning.[15] Deity in itself is finite and cannot be otherwise; only when it is considered as being in God as the whole of Space-Time, can deity be said to be infinite, i.e., omnipresent and eternal; and in this sense it differs from all the other empirical qualities.

This totality, Alexander hastens to note, cannot be identified, properly speaking, with our mind, because the activity of our mind cannot be infinite, since it is conditioned by and dependent on the neural processes as we have seen.[16]

Alexander now has no difficulty in drawing the logical conclusions of his whole approach, the most important of which for the purposes of our

[15] In Book IV, Chapter III: "Deity and Value," Alexander insists on the cosmological character of his God, asserting that "deity is not itself a value, for values are human inventions and deity is ultra-human" (Vol. II, p. 409). God can therefore be called the Supreme Being: He is beyond good and evil and can therefore use evil to bring good out of it. Deity on the other hand is a positive value and "since God's deity 'represents' his whole body, evil which forms a part of that body is contemplated by God as a part of that body on which also his deity, in which there is no evil, is based" (p. 419). And Alexander concludes on a Spinozistic note: "Evil is, therefore, redeemed as part of God's being, of the matter of him" (*ibid.*).

[16] Alexander distinguishes two sorts of infinity, internal and external: "An inch is internally infinite in respect of the number of its parts and corresponds to an infinite line of which it forms only a part. But it is itself finite in length. In the same way, our minds, though finite in space-time, may be infinite in respect of their correspondence with the whole of things in Space-Time" (*Ibid.*, Vol. II, p. 359).

present investigation is this: deity can in fact be said to "exist" for it is an empirical quality; but God "does not exist" and cannot be said to exist in the hypostatic form of an actual infinite, only in the sense of an infinite tendency.[17] This is the God of the Spinozan unity, but conceived as a unity in the infinite evolution which is the result of and the very nature of Time.

A further important specification must be made at this point. The reason why God cannot, in Alexander's view, be conceived either as individual or as actual existent infinite, is because the true primordial infinite is the Space-Time unity from which derive all the other infinities, God included, all of which are less than that primordial Space-Time unified field. Deity must always be conceived as being in process of becoming, as being "in nisus" and, in this sense, Alexander himself admits that his view cannot be called unqualifiedly "theistic".[18] In the light of this, there is really no reason for surprise at the torrent of statements, disconcerting enough in their trenchant and drastic frankness, that submerge God completely in becoming, in process, to such an extent that he can properly be said only to become, not to exist. The point is that the world is really the only constitutive infinite reality and the world, in its infinity, is tending to infinite deity, is pregnant with it; but infinite deity does not exist and, it should be added, if it did, then God (i.e. the actual world as possessing infinite deity) would cease to be the infinite God and would crumble into a plethora of finite gods! God, then, can be infinite only on condition that deity does not exist as infinite. Alexander's stand on this whole matter is entirely consistent provided the crucial principle be kept always in mind that the infinite has meaning and value as an ideal and can be called a value precisely and only inasmuch as it is an ideal. This is the crucial principle of an "evolution-of-God theology".

Infinite deity incorporates and embodies the conception of the infinite world in its straining after deity. But the attainment of deity makes deity

[17] "But the infinite God is purely ideal or conceptual. The individual so sketched is not asserted to exist; the sketch merely gives body and shape, by a sort of anticipation, to the actual infinite God whom, on the basis of experience, speculation declares to exist. As actual, God does not possess the quality of deity but is the universe as tending to that quality. This nisus in the universe, though not present to sense, is yet present to reflection upon experience. Only in this sense of straining towards deity can there be an infinite actual God" (*ibid.*, p. 361).

[18] Theism, as ordinarily understood, is for Alexander an imaginative and mythical conception: "The actual reality which has deity is the world of empiricals filling up all Space-Time and tending towards a higher quality. Deity is a nisus and not an accomplishment. This, as we shall note, is what prevents the conception from being wholly theistical" (*ibid.*, p. 364).

finite. Deity is an empirical quality like mind or life. Before there was mind, the universe was straining towards infinite mind. But an infinite mind cannot exist; there are only many finite minds. Deity is subject to the same law as other empirical qualities, and is but the next member of the series. God as an actual existent is always becoming deity but never attains it. He is the ideal God in embryo. The ideal when fulfilled ceases to be God, and yet it gives shape and character to our conception of the actual God, and always tends to usurp its place in our fancy.[19] It is clear, then, that the deity of God, as an emergent quality of the world of Space-Time in process, is different in different things and varies with the passing of time: The Space-Time universe is always one as such and it is the "body of God" but it still varies in its empirical constitution and hence in its deity.

We can therefore say that God pertains to the ideal realm of speculation and deity to the realm of the real flux and becoming of experience: thus God is ideal and not actual, and deity is a real quality and not an ideal one; it is, as it were, the soul of the real. If the ideal God could be actual, and his deity realized, then deity would truly be the soul of the world in strict analogy with the human soul; but, in actual fact, the world-soul is a "variable quality", according to the level for which it is the next in the hierarchy of qualities. But it is never realized and remains prophetic only. Deity is a quality not yet realized but in process of realization; it is future rather than present and therefore becomes (for Alexander as for the whole empiricist tradition) an object of "faith" in the proper sense of that word. Actually we do not directly experience any act or effect of God within ourselves; we have only our feeling, aroused by our devotion to God or worship of him. At this point, however, Alexander agrees with Berkeley that we nevertheless do know God with an evident certainty surpassing in some senses even our certainty of the existence of other minds. In religion the contact with the object is effected by feeling alone and so "our faith in God is nearer to simple sensation than our assurance of each other's minds"; it is simpler than our assurance of one another's existence. Our certainity of other minds is based solely on a specific experience, "intercourse" with those minds, whereas we have a twofold foundation for our conviction of the reality of God: both the specific experience (religious feeling) and the speculative evidence derived from this experience itself.[20] The speculative evidence clearly pertains, in any conception which is basically an immanentist

[19] *Ibid.*, pp. 365f.

[20] It is a somewhat surprising conclusion: "Thus we are sure of other minds only on the ground of specific experience; we are assured of God's reality on the ground both of specific experience and speculative evidence, derived from experience itself" (*ibid.*, p. 381).

Spinozan one,[21] solely to the One and to the Whole as Idea, also called God by religion.

Alexander's overall view of reality is of capital interest because it merges and conjoins the basic motifs and nuances of the modern principle of immanentism: the constitutive priority of experience or the act of consciousness, the Spinozan unity of the contraries as one Whole, the Kantian structural transcendentality of the *a priori* forms of space and time and the primordial and constitutive actuality of becoming as emergence (Hegel) are combined in Alexander by the instrumentality of the intentional efficacy of feeling and the foundation of belief (Hume) into a unitary interpretation of the real. Although aimed at obviating the deficiencies of the other solutions taken in isolation one from the other, the real actually serves merely to reinforce the conviction that the principle of immanentism, no matter how developed, cannot avoid swinging back to its initial point. English thought could almost be said to have played, at crucial moments in the process of the molding of modern thought, the role of a "mediator of immediacy", a salvager of experience as the primordial and ultimate element. Even as the Cartesian *cogito,* initially firmly tied to theological mediation, becomes in time the *empirical principle* of Locke-Hume, founded on the identity of presence and truth in sense-perception, so, too, the transcendental of German idealism eventually strains forward and upward to the status of an eschatological and trans-historical Whole, only to find itself at the end being conceived simply as the Whole of the world of experience as reality in flux of becoming, with deity expressing in successive situations, to an infinite degree but always in finite forms, the *vis emergendi* (power of emergence), conceived, however, as an "empirical property". God is described as the *vis a tergo* (propulsive power), the possibility of possibility, the power guaranteeing progress to infinity, a power that, in a certain sense, cannot become real except at the price of inhibiting and finitizing even itself. Whereas Whitehead, impelled by his drive to "realize" God, does not boggle at all at finitizing him, Alexander prefers to keep God scaled to infinity and therefore confines him to the realm of the ideal. Both Whitehead and Alexander and, indeed, the whole school of English neo-idealism, see traditional theism as stopping at an empty God-notion and atheism as overexerting itself, in pointless pother, to combat their notion.

To cite Alexander's own clear and incisive exposition: "God . . . is

[21] In an explicit reference to Spinoza, Alexander observes that Spinoza's option in favor of the static being of thought, to the complete exclusion of time, entails for the Spinozan system a major difficulty: ". . . no satisfactory account can be given of how finite things come into existence. We understand why they are resolved into God but not how they issue from him" (*ibid.,* p. 401).

both body and soul, and his soul is his deity. Since God's body is the whole of Space-Time, God in respect of his body is all-inclusive, and all finites are included in him".[22] According to this conception, which Alexander holds to be the only plausible form of theism, God cannot be said to have been or to be or to be about to be realized in an infinite "qualitied" being; rather he is in a continuous process tending toward this quality of deity.[23] And this quality is emerging everywhere in the flux of becoming of the real, from the lowest forms of life right up to and including mind (and beyond!). The distinctive quality of God (and this is the crux of the "cosmologism" of Alexander's theology) is not mind but rather "the next higher quality". Therefore, God is not a being on the level of man, with personality and mental powers like man's, raised only to a higher pitch. Rather God transcends all finites, because he is the whole world as tending to a higher order of finites. In this sense, Alexander contends that his conception can properly be called theistic, a contention with which the theist will not be at all ready to agree. Rather this is sheer and outright pantheism, or if you prefer panentheism; it is consequently sheer atheism, on our interpretation, an atheism still more radical than the explicit slogan-type atheism we have already encountered. For this conception holds God to transcend all finites in quality for the obvious and drastic reason that God, for it, no longer exists, in view of the fact that the world is creator and God has been reduced to the status of a creature.

In his effort to reconstitute God starting from the world, an effort that ends quite simply in the dissolution of God into the world, Alexander is trenchant and uncompromising: God himself, as actual God, does not possess realized deity, but only the Spinozan *nisus* or *conatus* (striving) toward it; and Christian theism, with its admission of the God-Man, redeemer and mediator between God and man inasmuch as he is more than man, mounts for Alexander to a limitation of the perception of deity to man and a denial of it to the cosmos as a whole in the infinite expansion and flowering of its many forms. In this way, Alexander snaps shut from the theoretical point of view the ring opened by James in the hope of a synthesis of empiricism and idealism, of immediacy and mediation, of experience and reflection, a synthesis articulated as a process of consciousness in the idealism of Bradley and Royce, both of whom can easily be seen by any perceptive reader to have influenced Alexander's *Space, Time, and Deity*. Now Alexander closes the "ring of the world" making reflection cede pride of place to experience, man to

[22] *Ibid.*, p. 394.

[23] This is Alexander's overriding principle, succinctly stated thus: "In reality, God is never thus realised in the contradictory form of an infinite qualitied individual, but he is in process towards this quality of deity" (*ibid.*, p. 394).

nature and God to man and the world. And because God is the infinite ideal and synthesis of body-soul or of Space-Time and inasmuch as he includes within his body all creatures that suffer, there is suffering and pain in God as well. Yet the deity of God as emergent quality indicates precisely the overcoming of all grief and anguish. Therefore, we can say with Aristotle [24] that God enjoys an infinite pleasure. This is emergent evolution with a vengeance!

The originality of Alexander's conception lies mainly in his reiteration of the Spinozan paired attributes of Being, with the substitution of Time for Thought as the drive-powering process. This substitution is intended to avoid both the impasse of rationalism's static Absolute and the idealist reduction of God to Absolute Mind, a reduction that makes thought the point of departure, whereas it is only one of the points of destination, albeit the highest. Alexander consequently produces a system that is tightly woven and closely reasoned; his terminology is perfectly consistent and he seems to feel that this consistency suffices to defy all other risks. Everything flows from the nisus (push, striving, impulse) which Time impresses upon Space even as the soul impresses an impulse on the body; Time is called the Soul of Space; all the qualities that arise in experience (cognition, freedom, values and the like, including even mind itself) are but functions and "complexities of Time". "In the hierarchy of qualities the next higher quality to the highest attained is deity. God is the whole universe engaged in process toward the emergence of this new quality, and religion is the sentiment in us that we are drawn toward him, and caught in the movement of the world to a higher level of existence." [25] The great drawback is that, in this system, deity as such never becomes real.[26] That is the drawback that Whitehead strove to eliminate with his notion of the bi-polar God, of the conjunction, "togetherness" and mutually complementary relationship of God and the world.

[24] Cf. *Metaph.* XII, 7, 1072b. 16.

[25] These are the concluding words of *Space, Time, and Deity* (Vol. II, p. 429). Man's immortality therefore consists in preparing the way for deity and producing enjoyment for the being of God.

[26] Cf. C. Hartshorne, *Philosophers Speak of God,* p. 372a. Deity is, in Alexander's system, a "futuribile"; thus, the precise relation between actual and real is obscured and there is rather the tendency to equate ideal and real!

4

Concrescence or Dispersion of God into the World (Whitehead)

A new and still more crucial advance in the disintegration of the principle of immanentism into its sheerly atheistic residue was accomplished, along a different and unusual line, by A. N. Whitehead (1861-1947), with his return to the finitistic conception of God. He entangled deity in the infinite flux of the becoming of the real, thereby wrenching it free of the sterile tension of the formalistic dialectic and of the staticism of the systems of metaphysical idealism. From idealism Whitehead retained the impulsion to conceive truth as the Whole and in the Whole and consequently to see the Absolute from the interior of this Whole and in function of its self-realization. On the other hand, Whitehead's God seems almost as intimately linked as Aristotle's to the process of evolution of the world. And this new theology and teleology is presented in the form of a speculative "cosmology".

In this new variant of English empirical idealism, the chief focus of interest is not God's existence nor the problematic of the proof of that existence, but rather the description of the Absolute and the Whole, the problem of how God is interpolated into the world and the world into God. Whitehead's philosophy amounts virtually to a reiteration of neo-Platonism within the framework of the idealist principle of conjunction or "togetherness" which is likewise the central point in Whitehead's theological cosmology.[1]

His thought has been called "a philosophy of organism", not only because of his strongly unitary conception of the real but also and primarily because of his drastic insistence on the mutually comple-

[1] "His interest in 'togetherness' is not only metaphysical but religious in its stress on the need for fellowship with other living centers of experience and with the mysterious universe as a whole" (J. S. Bixler, "Whitehead's Philosophy of Religion," in *The Philosophy of Alfred North Whitehead,* edited by P. A. Schilpp [New York, 1951], p. 490).

mentary nature of the world and God, time and eternity; this insistence is expressive of the principle of togetherness as an essential law of reality and as a creative process, always in act.

The surprising and often perplexing fact about Whitehead, the fact that makes his thought so original, is that he should have first distinguished himself as a brilliant mathematician and then transferred his attention to philosophy and metaphysics, not in order to subject them to the mathematical method but rather to approach the human mind from the opposite side, in its continual process of transcending and "transgressing" identity. Thus, for Whitehead, in a very real sense the world is *not* God and God is *not* the world; and not only must the world be said not to be without God, so too in virtue of the principle of essential conjunction and togetherness, God for his part must be said not to be without the world. The world does not strictly "enter into" the concept of God, e.g., have God as its essential referend as in the Thomistic notion of analogy; rather it serves in a certain sense as the foundation of the reality of God and of his self-realization and self-assertion.

From this point of view, Whitehead's philosophy is a sort of bemusing "Aristotelian" re-evaluation of the reality in act of nature, in the tradition of the whole modern trend toward disintegration of idealism as instanced especially in Nietzsche, positivism, Heidegger and their like. It is still more precisely a reassessment of the capacity of this nature to manifest and, in a certain sense, to "sustain" God or rather what should be called deity and the divine. The relationship is not, however, a clear-cut nexus of causality or derivation: Whitehead is by no means saying, with traditional metaphysics, that God is the cause and the world the effect; nor yet is he saying with Alexander that the world is the cause and God the effect; rather he is speaking of a unique and well-nigh inexpressible sort of correlation which must be understood as a corporate and mutual substantiation and foundation, though Whitehead never succeeds in making this crucial point entirely clear.

In a somewhat oversimplified but, we believe, entirely defensible interpretation of Whitehead, it could be said that, although critics of Whitehead have not yet adverted to this point and Whitehead himself never mentions it, we have here a new variant of the Spinozan principle of *Deus sive natura* (God or nature). But here the "or" does not indicate straightforward identity or direct correspondence, but rather a certain function of constitutive complementarity, along the lines of the Aristotelian bipolarity of act and potency, or perhaps more accurately along the lines of the Hegelian pairing of *Schein* and *Sein* (seeming and being), *Erscheinung* and *Wesen* (appearance and essence), *Endlichkeit* and *Unendlichkeit* (finitude and infinitude.[2] In any case, Whitehead's approach to Aristotelian dualism is asymptotic at most and only in the realm of teleology; in the matter of the Aristotelian Unmoved Mover, Whitehead's position is diametrically opposed to that of the Stagirite and entirely in the tradition of Mill, James, Bradley and the rest, who shaped the very essence of the deity in terms of "finitude". All due credit must be given to this branch of English neo-Hegelianism for its depth of penetration and its serious effort to investigate the God-problem so as to find an avenue of escape both from positivistic materialism and from the impasse of the idealist dialectic, not by a process of pseudo-simplification but rather by an intensification of the most valid elements that human thought has developed and perfected in the whole of its long history.

The highest tribute that can be paid to this thrust of modern English speculation is to say that what was for the Greeks the "gigantomachy of being" has become in Whitehead and his school the "gigantomachy of the becoming of God" by the definition of his "attributes". This tremendous question of the "attributes of God", dramatically raised in medieval Arab philosophy and cheerfully forgotten by European idealism (from which has stemmed the impudent and impertinent denial of God on the part of modern philosophical systems) is here again posed as the only key to salvation for man.

This new God-notion can be designated, especially in the intellectual Odyssey of Whitehead himself, as an "emergent synthesis" of Greek, Hebrew and medieval notions.[3] Whitehead believes that there was a continuity of evolution among these different cultures and ages which is much more real and operative than the contrasts and conflicts among them that can so easily be identified. Not only are the ties between scholastic thought and Greek philosophy patently evident; modern thought and science itself are incomprehensible and unthinkable in abstraction from Greek thought and especially from Christian thought.

Among Greek thinkers, Plato deserves, in Whitehead's opinion, pride of place for having arrived, late in life (Cf. the *Sophist* and the *Timaeus*), at the conviction that the divine element in the world must be conceived as operating as a persuasive agency and not as a coercive

[2] The sole approving reference to Spinozism (and an indirect one at that) is Whitehead's acceptance of Alexander's *nisus* theory, which seems to me to be extremely important in Whitehead's thought. (Cf. D. B. Kuspit's masterly study, "Whitehead on Divinity," *Archiv für Philosophie,* XI, 1-2, pp. 74ff.)

[3] ". . . this tone of thought in Europe . . . must come from the medieval insistence on the rationality of God, conceived as with the personal energy of Jehovah, and with the rationality of a Greek philosopher" (A. N. Whitehead, *Science and the Modern World,* p. 18). For our subsequent exposition, cf. especially *Adventures of Ideas,* (New York: The Macmillan Company, 1952), pp. 213ff.

agency,[4] a doctrine that must be considered one of the greatest discoveries of the human mind, inasmuch as it asserts that ideals are effective in the world and that forms of order evolve.

The second phase is the supreme moment in religious history, according to the Christian religion. The essence of Christianity is the appeal to the life of Christ as a revelation of the nature of God and of his agency in the world. At this point, Whitehead gives his own variant of the long series of versions of "Johannine Christianity" or a Christianity of reason, outlined by Spinoza, later elaborated by English Deism and launched anew on the continent by Lessing. All these versions speak of the total mutual interpenetration of faith and reason, religion and philosophy. For Whitehead, the power of Christianity lies in its having shown the revelation in act of what Plato had divined in theory. Plato had never succeeded in giving any positive meaning to the God-world relation. The World, for Plato, includes only the image of God, and imitations of his ideas; it never contains God and his ideas themselves. Therefore his solution is weak in the extreme. What metaphysics requires is a solution exhibiting the plurality of individuals as consistent with the unity of the universe, and a solution which exhibits the world as requiring its union with God, and God as requiring his union with the world. Sound doctrine also requires an understanding of how the ideals in God's nature, by reason precisely of their status in his nature, are thereby persuasive elements in the creative advance. In the collision-encounter between Christianity and Platonism, Whitehead opts for the Christian theologians as the first consistent artificers of a direct doctrine of immanence and a rational account of the role of the persuasive agency of God.

But Whitehead immediately proceeds to a most trenchant critique of Christian theology, a critique which is of importance to us here primarily as a revelation of Whitehead's own bias: for his objection to Christianity is that it asserted the absolute transcendence of God after having proclaimed his immanence:

"Unfortunately, the theologians never made this advance into general metaphysics. The reason was this check was another unfortunate assumption. The nature of God was exempted from all the metaphysical categories which applied to the individual things in this temporal world. The concept of him was a sublimation from its barbaric origin. He stood in the same relation to the whole World as early Egyptian or Meso-

[4] It is a fundamental theory of the freedom of God as foundation (and not obstacle) for the freedom of man. Plato and Aristotle express it in the polemical phrase (against Empedocles) "the gods are not jealous" and in the contention that philosophy as the science of truth is the only "free" science (cf. Aristotle, *Metaph.*, I, 2, 983a 2ff.).

potamian kings stood to their subject populations. Also the moral characters were very analogous. In the final metaphysical sublimation, he became the one absolute, omnipotent, omniscient source of all being, for his own existence requiring no relations to anything beyond himself. He was internally complete. Such a conception fitted on very well to the Platonic doctrine of subordinate derivations. The final insistence, after much wavering, on the immanence of God was therefore all the more a fine effort of metaphysical imagination on the part of the theologians of the early Christian ages. But their general concept of the Deity stopped all further generalization. They made no effort to conceive the World in terms of the metaphysical categories by means of which they interpreted God, and they made no effort to conceive God in terms of the metaphysical categories which they applied to the World. For them, God was eminently real, and the World was derivatively real. God was necessary to the World, but the World was not necessary to God. There was a gulf between them.

"The worst of a gulf is, that it is very difficult to know what is happening on the further side of it. This has been the fate of the God of traditional theology. It is only by drawing the long bow of mysticism that evidences for his existence can be collated from our temporal World. Also the worst of unqualified omnipotence is that it is accompanied by responsibility for every detail of every happening. This whole topic is discussed by Hume in his famous Dialogues," [5] which we have already considered.

What distresses and repels Whitehead in the God of traditional theology is precisely that point which is cardinal for that theology in its definition of God: his real transcendence and absolute independence of the world. Incidentally, Whitehead is just as reproachful of Greek philosophy on this same point.[6]

Faithful to, and consistent with, the principle of conjunction or togetherness as foundation of the true concretion of God, Whitehead con-

[5] A. N. Whitehead, *Adventures of Ideas,* pp. 216f.

[6] Cf. e.g. A. N. Whitehead, *Essays in Science and Philosophy,* (London: William Brendon & Son, Ltd., 1948), p. 64.

But Whitehead openly acknowledges the beneficial influence of the medieval conception upon the evolution of modern physics itself, e.g. in Lagrange and especially in Maupertuis: "We find in Maupertuis a tinge of the theologic age which preceded his birth. He started with the idea that the whole path of a material particle between any limits of time must achieve some perfection worthy of the providence of God. There are two points of interest in this motive principle. In the first place, it illustrates the thesis which I was urging in my first lecture that the way in which the medieval church had impressed on Europe the notion of the detailed providence of a rational personal God was one of the factors by which the trust in the order of nature had been generated" (A. N. Whitehead, *Science and the Modern World,* pp. 89f.).

tends that the distinction of an independent God from the world, with the consequent ascription to him of priority, separateness and subsistence, must be repudiated, on pain of leaving God in thrall to abstraction. Both of the ways in which traditional theology has hitherto presented God must therefore be rejected as abstract and inadequate. The first of these ways is the one that conceives God as pure perfection. As such God has been conceived by the theologians in terms of value, as completeness and fullness of reality, so total that no perfection could be conceived in which he would be wanting; this entirely excludes from God any form of potency; every being, on the contrary, receives from him every act and every perfection. This conception pictures perfection statically, abstracting from the temporal character inherent to every process and prescinding from the real contrasts, conflicts and relations that are operative in all such processes. This insight was Locke's contribution in his critique of the metaphysic of substance. The second way in which traditional theology has wrongly conceived God is in terms of causality. It has identified God with the sheer power of causality as "cause of all things". But this divorces God from the real context of the world. That insight was Hume's contribution in his critique of causality. Whitehead conceives of God as a cosmological principle and prescinds from any ethical or religious function.

Whitehead's position can be most conveniently specified and its significant context pinpointed by means of symbols.[7] Let us symbolize the doctrine of sheer independence as CC, indicating with the first C an exclusion of all causal dependence and with the second the contention that independent activity describes all aspects of the divine being. The opposite extreme may then be indicated by WW, with the first W signifying that there is a world-aspect of God and the second indicating that there is nothing independent of the world in God. The median position will then, obviously, be CW, indicating that there is indeed an independent factor, which is cause but not effect, and also a dependent or, as Whitehead calls it, a "consequent" factor, which itself has causes. Now it is clear that, if God be nothing but sheer absolute perfection, a doctrine we can symbolize as AA, there would then be no basis, from the standpoint of perfection, for the distinction, from the standpoint of causality, which CW involves. For simple perfection is—simple! But suppose perfection has two aspects, one absolute (A), and the other not absolute and hence in some sense relative (R). Then the C in CW might be the A in AR, and the W in CW might be the R in AR. It is likewise apparent that CW is to CC and WW as AR is to AA and RR. In each

[7] Cf. C. Hartshorne, "Whitehead's Idea of God," in *The Philosophy of Alfred North Whitehead,* pp. 513ff. I shall adhere to Hartshorne's scheme of letter-symbols.

case we have a positive synthesis which excludes only the negative or abstract aspect of the extreme positions.

We may now pursue still more specifically this "physical idealism" of Whitehead. What is crucial both in A and in R is not precisely their quality of A or R which distinguishes and opposes them on the formal level, but rather the way in which they relate to perfection. A-Perfection means the property of surpassing all others while not surpassing self, whereas R-Perfection means the property of surpassing all others while also surpassing self. Hence R-Perfection permits, if it does not indeed require, growth in the R aspects of a being. Thus R is a richer conception than A, since it includes the relation of universal superiority to others, which is the only positive feature of A, and includes likewise the equally positive relation of self-transcendence, self-superiority, self-enrichment. But it is more intelligible for a being to transcend self in some respect and others in all respects, to be AR, than to transcend both self and others in all respects, to be RR, or than to transcend others in all respects and self in none, to be AA. These and similar reflections always return to the same key point: perfection ought to be conceived, not in terms of static identity, but rather in terms of the active synthesis of contraries, as process. It is not motion that has to be explained in terms of immovable principles; rather *perfection is motion and in motion* and it is meaningless to acknowledge a fixed term as terminal of the process itself. Whitehead is quite outspoken in insisting that whatever perfection be conceived, there is another beyond it; and the reason is that all realization is finite and therefore there is no perfection which represents the infinitude of all perfections.[8]

For Whitehead, then, even as for the Hegelian Left (strange as the bracketing of the two may seem at first glance), the dialectic operating is solely that of finitude or of "baneful infinity". It is precisely the feeling of imperfection and the adventure of evil that provides the stimulus for that progress, wherein the synthesis of beauty and evil is realized and transcended ad infinitum: "The intermingling of Beauty and Evil arises from the conjoint operation of three metaphysical principles:—(1) That all actualization is finite; (2) That finitude involves the exclusion of alternative possibility; (3) That mental functioning introduces into realization subjective forms conformal to relevant alternatives excluded from the completeness of physical realization."[9] Thus mental activity

[8] "Progress is founded upon the experience of discordant feelings. The social value of liberty lies in its production of discords. There are perfections beyond perfections. All realization is finite, and there is no perfection which is the infinitude of all perfections. Perfections of diverse types are among themselves discordant" (A. N. Whitehead, *Adventures of Ideas,* p. 330).

[9] *Ibid.,* p. 333.

breaks the montony of physical repetition and overcomes the disharmony of reality.

Therefore, there can be no absolute maximum of harmonious contrasts, since possible contrasts are inexhaustible and mutually exclusive by the very meaning of possibility as a field of open alternatives. Similary there can be no greatest possible happiness of all things other than God. Hence God's knowledge cannot be absolute in its aesthetic value and sympathetic joy. Yet that knowledge certainly can be complete in its accuracy and adequacy to what is actual and what is possible at any given stage of cosmic development. Thus, God's knowledge must be A in its cognitive perfection or truth, and R in its concrete self-value as enjoyment or bliss. This reasoning necessarily involves the admission that there must be an independent causal factor which, like cognitive adequacy, is abstract and neutral to the distinction between potential and actual, and that there must also be a dependent or consequent factor which is concrete and varies with *de facto* actualization of potency. In other words, recurring now to our symbols, AR-CW [or better perhaps, A(C)-R(W), in order to show that A and C, R and W, are the same factors considered from two points of view, those of value and causality] is the most promising formula for the divine nature, although the idea it defines is one whose possibilities have only recently begun to be taken really seriously and explored in depth.

What, now, in the light of all this, is Whitehead's idea of God? Is it a case of AR-CW, or is it one more abstract extreme (such as AA-CC, or AA-CW, or RR-WW, or some other of the eight logically possible cases), involving the fallacy of misplaced concretion which Whitehead has been at such pains to avoid? Certainly God is, for Whitehead, the chief exemplification of the metaphysical principles and these metaphysical principles form a set of contraries or "ideal opposites". Thus, in the case of God, whom Nicholas of Cusa had already called the *coincidentia oppositorum,* Whitehead contends that: "The final summary can only be expressed in terms of a group of antitheses, whose apparent self-contradictions depend on neglect of the diverse categories of existence. In each antithesis there is a shift of meaning which converts the opposition into a contrast.

"It is as true to say that God is permanent and the World fluent, as that the World is permanent and God is fluent.

"It is as true to say that God is one and the World many, as that the World is one and God many.

"It is as true to say that, in comparison with the World, God is actual eminently, as that, in comparison with God, the World is actual eminently.

"It is as true to say that the World is immanent in God, as that God is immanent in the World.

"It is as true to say that God transcends the World, as that the World transcends God.

"It is as true to say that God creates the World, as that the World creates God." [10]

Such expressions, as can clearly be seen, represent a sharp and drastic break both with the realist and the idealist tradition. In this dialectic, which sets out to be the transcendence and supersession of all dialectic, God is no longer the pure empirical concrete (direct immediacy) nor yet the abstract Absolute (formal mediation), but rather the concreteness of real perfection, where the terms "perfection" and "reality" are mutually substantiating: perfection is, as we have seen, always finite but it is likewise always open and in process of continuous ascent, and reality lies precisely in this infinite progress.

Whitehead can therefore be said to have made a supreme effort, in his own way, like St. Thomas before him, to overcome and supersede Platonism with Platonism, to unite transcendence to immanence and to substantiate each by means of the other, by having recourse to the Aristotelian principle of concretion.[11]

We must now return to our symbolic formulation to ask the crucial question: Granted that God is unequivocally A and C, though not AA and CC, is he AR and CW? We have already seen quite clearly that God is certainly A plus a relative aspect, and that he is C plus the world as

[10] A. N. Whitehead, *Process and Reality,* pp. 527f. The inescapable conclusion is that God's nature (at least his consequent nature) must be said to be relative, incomplete and in flux. Whitehead makes this abundantly clear: "The vicious separation of the flux from the permanence leads to the concept of an entirely static God, with eminent reality, in relation to an entirely fluent world, with deficient reality" (p. 526); "The consequent nature of God is the fluent world become 'everlasting' by its objective immortality in God . . . The first half of the problem concerns the completion of God's primordial nature by the derivation of his consequent nature from the temporal world" (p. 527).

[11] Whitehead's position can thus be said, in a certain sense, to remain in the Aristotelian tradition, like that of Hegel: "It is sheer and simple being that is an element of becoming, not becoming that is an element of being . . . The convertible form is something abstract and universal, that is contained in the concrete particular. As applied to God (an application which Aristotle unfortunately overlooked) this theory signifies that God's immutable form is not his concrete individual actuality but rather an abstract feature of the Deity. The concrete God would be a becoming and the eternal form an abstract property belonging to each and every phase of this becoming. Whitehead calls this abstract form of God his 'Primordial Nature,' and designates the concrete divine actuality as 'The Consequent Nature of God' " (C. Hartshorne, "Das metaphysische System Whiteheads," *Zeitschrift für philosophische Forschung,* III [1948], p. 573; cf. p. 567). Only thus, maintains Whitehead, can God have a real relation (e.g. of love and providence) with the world in general and with man in particular.

internal to his complete nature: thus God is not so much Being by his essence or a free subsistent Person as rather the Primordial Nature which is the First or Prime Perfection, everywhere present to unfold his hidden and inexhaustible potentialities. God is therefore a sort of *Anima mundi,* a world-soul, possessing the properties of Aristotelian Act; but the whole Aristotelian conception has here been recast within the framework of the modern notion of science and according to the dictates of the principle of immanentism, as we shall be seeing directly. In point of fact, God becomes here the All-Inclusive, since the content of every other individual, if and when it exists, is and must be contained in God, whereas God in his turn surpasses every particular value. He is R-Perfect, surpassing all others in all possible circumstances.

We are here at the very heart of Whitehead's conception. The first principle, which is the essence of actual reality, of that which is completely real, is *process.* Every actual form is understood solely in terms of its becoming or its perishing. There is no static point to arrest activity as Platonism tried to do with its principle of the Idea, stable in its "separateness", and as Aristotelianism likewise attempted to do with its principle of the Primary Substance, stable in its fundamental determinations and attributes, a doctrine that was reiterated, according to Whitehead, in Locke's notion of Mind as an "empty cabinet" passively receiving the impressions of the ideas, so that for Locke, too, reality consisted not in a process but in the static recipient of the process.

Whitehead, on the contrary, insists that process itself is the basic reality, in no need of any antecedent static substance. Hence the processes of the past, in their perishing, are themselves the energizing principle of every new occasion: the past is the reality that is at the basis of every actual present event. The process is its absorption into a new unity with ideals and with anticipations, by the operation of the creative Eros. The Eros is, of course, in Plato, the primordial power that sustains the dialectic of the Ideas.

The second metaphysical principle, for Whitehead, is the doctrine that every occasion of actuality is in its own nature finite. There is no totality which is the harmony of all perfections. Were God to be such a totality, totally in act, then the "social nature" of God would have to be denied, whereas on the contrary God must be said to be love in the sense clarified by Spinoza and previously propounded by the Scholastics (who would be somewhat surprised to hear this!),[12] with the important

[12] It is therefore somewhat surprising to find Hartshorne maintaining: "Whitehead's God is as much, nay more, the supreme Being as is the God of the Thomists". Thomism designates God as transcendent *actus purus,* whereas Hartshorne expressly rules this out for Whitehead's God (cf. "Whitehead's Idea of God," pp. 523 and 527).

difference that, whereas Spinoza's God-Substance is static, Whitehead's God is indissolubly linked to motion.

In this connection, it must be remembered that Whitehead distinguishes two elements in his di-polar God-notion: a Primordial Nature which he calls "conceptual" and may well conceive (though he is not clear on this point) to be not yet conscious; and a Consequent Nature, which is conscious of its own progress; and it is in the conjunction or "togetherness" of these two elements or moments that our knowledge of God is expressed.[13] This conception seems to avoid the reef of the "finitude" of God, for God can be called both finite and infinite. But this apparently dextrous gymnastic serves eventually only to tie Whitehead's conception in inextricable knots.

Whitehead calls his own thought a "philosophy of organism" [14] and he means this in a metaphysical sense rather than a physical or biological one. His doctrine of God is not so much a theology as a cosmology; not, however, the sort of cosmological theology that would reduce God to crass physical form, but rather a transcendental cosmologizing of God in the sense that the world is grounded in God and God in the world, with God remaining, nevertheless, at once the beginning and the end. This meticulous precision on our part may seem tediously pedantic, but it is absolutely essential in order to preclude two equally baneful errors: the ingenuous characterization as theism of a doctrine that is especially insistent upon the very points that threaten the very foundations of theism; and the temptation to consider as atheism one of the last and most vigorous efforts of modern thought to evade the atheistic bias of the principle of immanentism. Whitehead's intention, in his conception of God, was to avoid the "static God" of the Greco-Judaeo-Christian tradition, to wrench God free from the realm of abstraction, to preclude the twin error of abandoning the world to endless motion and positioning God in self-subsistent immobility. There is, for Whitehead, no such thing as the simple problem of fluency and permanence. There is rather a double problem: actuality with permanence, requiring fluency as its completion. The first half of the problem concerns the completion of

[13] Whitehead refers this knowledge of God to the realm of "feeling" with a recurrent explicit appeal to Hume (cf. *Process and Reality,* pp. 520ff.), as we shall be seeing below.

[14] For the immediately following exposition, cf. *Process and Reality,* Part V, ch. 2: "God and the World," pp. 519ff. It can be said at once that, in Whitehead's philosophy, God in no sense occupies a teleological anchor-position, let alone a status of sheer transcendence; rather He is involved as a part in the structure and definition of the real: "God is not to be treated as an exception to all metaphysical principles, invoked to save their collapse. He is their chief exemplification" (*Process and Reality,* Part V, ch. 2, p. 521, cf. Donald B. Kuspit's thorough treatment in "Whitehead on Divinity," pp. 98ff.).

God's primoridal nature by the derivation of his consequent nature from the temporal world. The second half of the problem concerns the completion of each fluent actual occasion by its function of objective immortality, devoid of "perpetual perishing", that is to say, "everlasting". It is not hard to see that this new Principle of Act, to which we have already referred above, is simply a new version of the principle of immanentism.

We have, therefore, in Whitehead's opinion, to do with a double problem which cannot be separated into two distinct problems. The consequent nature of God is the fluent world becoming "everlasting" by its objective immortality in God. Thus, the objective immortality of actual occasions requires the primordial permanence of God, whereby the creative advance ever re-establishes itself endowed with initial subjective aim derived from the relevance of God to the evolving world. It is as if we were encountering a filtered, dialecticized neo-Platonism, within the environmental framework of the Lockeian empirical principle, which in turn is being given a new and much deeper meaning. In Whitehead's conception, God and the world confront one another, stand over against each other, expressing the final metaphysical truth, which neither can express in isolation or taken onesidely or when pretending to any haughty priority over the other: each is all in all.[15] Thus each temporal occasion embodies God, and is embodied in God. In God's nature, permanence is primordial and flux is derivative from the World; in the World's nature, flux is primordial and permanence is derivative from God.

Whitehead is aiming at nothing less than a total articulation of the mutual conjunction of God and the world. Thus, he says, the World's nature is a primordial datum for God; and God's nature is a primordial datum for the world. Creation achieves the reconciliation of permanence

[15] This is directly suggestive of Neo-Platonism's πάντα ἐν πᾶντα (cf. Proclus, *Elem. Theol.*, Prop. 103 [Oxford: Dodds, 1933], p. 13; cf. C. Fabro, *Participation et causalité* [Paris-Louvain, 1960], p. 425). For any proper grasp of the internal thrust of Whitehead's thought, it is indispensable to realize how agilely he adapts the principles of various other systems to his own. Specifically, he declares himself to be following in the line of Descartes, Locke, Hume and Kant, in conceiving the act of knowledge or cognition as an apprehension of the flux and the structure of reason as a reflection upon the "eternal objects" and possibilities of process (cf. his outspoken essay: *The Function of Reason* [Princeton, 1929], especially pp. 48f., 67ff.).

A. H. Johnson admirably pinpoints the change in Whitehead's notion of God between *Religion in the Making* and *Process and Reality:* in *Religion in the Making,* Whitehead rules out any possibility of considering God as the end point of the evolution of the world. The modification of this approach in *Process and Reality* is of crucial importance for our present problematic (Cf. A. H. Johnson, *Whitehead's Theory of Reality* [New York, 1962], p. 235).

and flux when it has reached its final term which is everlastingness. The respective demands of the two elements, though opposite in kind, are equally stringent in intensity: God is the infinite ground of all mentality, the unity of vision seeking physical multiplicity. The World is the multiplicity of finites, actualities seeking a perfected unity. Therefore neither God, nor the World, reaches static completion. Both are in the grip of the ultimate metaphysical ground, the creative advance into novelty. Either of them, God and the World alike, is the instrument of novelty for the other.

In this Whiteheadian philosophy as perhaps likewise in the earliest Greek philosophy, God and the World move conversely to each other in respect of their process. God is the primordial unity of relevance of the many potential forms: in the process he acquires a consequent multiplicity, which the primordial character absorbs into his own unity. The World is the primordial multiplicity of the many actual occasions with their physical finitude: in the process it acquires a consequent unity, which is a novel occasion and is absorbed into the multiplicity of the primordial character. Thus God is one and many and the World is one and many in this transcendental cosmology: [16] the Whole as truth is the synthesis in act.

God must be conceived as a unity proceeding in the direction of multiplicity and the World as a multiplicity converging in its actualization towards unity. At this supreme point of his system, Whitehead, despite his cosmologism, meshes with Royce's doctrine of atonement and comes close to a cosmic eschatology of being. In the later phases, the many actualities are one actuality, and the one actuality is many actualities. Each individual actuality lives out its life and then passes into novelty, which novelty, however, is by no means equivalent to death for that individual actuality; it is not a passage into non-being. It is what Whitehead calls the passage into the divine nature which is ever enlarging itself. And this passage effects a total adjustment of the immediacy of joy and suffering which is the final end of creation.[17] It is in this way that the immediacy of sorrow and pain is transformed into an element of triumph. This is the notion of redemption through suffering, which haunts the world. Therefore—and this is the final formulation by White-

[16] "The theme of Cosmology, which is the basis of all religions, is the story of the dynamic effort of the World passing into everlasting unity, and of the static majesty of God's vision, accomplishing its purpose of completion by absorption of the World's multiplicity of effort" (*Process and Reality,* p. 529f.).

[17] "Each actuality has its present life and its immediate passage into novelty; but its passage is not its death. This final phase of passage in God's nature is ever enlarging itself. In it the complete adjustment of the immediacy of joy and suffering reaches the final end of creation" (*ibid.,* p. 530).

head of this cosmic God of his—the consequent nature of God is composed of a multiplicity of elements with individual self-realization. It is just as much a multiplicity as it is a unity; it is just as much one immediate fact as it is an unresting advance beyond itself. Thus the actuality of God must also be understood as a multiplicity of actual components in process of creation. This is God in his function of the kingdom of heaven.

Whitehead's formulations are impressive, even though they are unsatisfactory and inadequate, either as theism or as atheism or as pantheism. In this conception of Whitehead's, each actuality in the temporal world has its reception into God's nature. The corresponding element in God's nature is not temporal actuality, but is the transmutation of that temporal actuality into a living, ever-present fact. An enduring personality in the temporal world is a route of occasions in which the successors with some peculiar completeness sum up their predecessors. The correlate fact in God's nature is an even more complete unity of life in a chain of elements for which succession does not mean loss of immediate union. Thus, even as in temporal succession, there is here too a continual passage of the past into the future. This is the principle of "universal relativity" which is not to be stopped at the consequent nature of God. This nature itself passes into the temporal world according to its gradation of relevance to the various concrescent occasions.

This advent of the "Kingdom of Heaven" passes through four creative phases in which the universe accomplishes its actuality. There is first the phase of conceptual origination, deficient in actuality, but infinite in its adjustment of valuation. Secondly, there is the temporal phase of physical origination, with its multiplicity of actualities. In this phase full actuality is attained; but there is deficiency in the solidarity of individuals with each other. Thirdly, there is the phase of perfected actuality, in which the many are one everlastingly, without the qualification of any loss either of individual identity or of completeness of unity. In everlastingness, immediacy is reconciled with objective immortality. In the fourth phase, the creative action completes itself. For the perfected actuality passes back into the temporal world, and qualifies this world so that each temporal actuality includes it as an immediate fact of relevant experience.

In this sense, it can truly be said that the Kingdom of Heaven is among us. It is with us today. For God's love for the world is operative in this fourth phase, transforming what is done on earth into a reality in heaven and then causing that celestial reality to pass back into the world. In this living tidal phenomenon, the love in the world passes into the love in heaven and then floods back again into the world. This makes it licit to speak of God as the great companion and sympathetic fellow-sufferer.[18]

Herein, too, we find the exhaustive meaning of objective immortality. Every particular fact, occasion and actuality returns in eternal process into God, into the Being of God, but only so that God himself shall return in an equally eternal process in and into every particular moment of the world and every instant of time.

Whitehead's philosophy is among the most sustained and complex of modern systems of thought; but this concept of God which constitutes its dominant theme is presented with an explicit and unmistakable dialectic which will meet with a spirited repudiation on the part of theist and atheist alike. A God who has a necessary and constitutive nexus with the evolution of nature is not God, but simply one of the two moments or elements of the real as it presents itself to reflection. Similarly, a nature which, in its process of evolution, flows back into God and acquires unity in him, is no longer nature, at least not the nature that is encountered in experience, in the technological sciences and in everyday life. In Whitehead's scheme, God and nature do indeed substantiate each other; but they also obfuscate each other quite hopelessly. And the reason for their mutual substantiation in Whitehead is a deep-seated systematic one: the demand for the sort of God Whitehead has presented flows from the very transcendentality of Whitehead's own cosmology.

The name that comes immediately to mind is that of Bradley, with his paired opposites, appearance and reality. And indeed Whitehead specifically refers his reader to Bradley.[19] But Bradley's paired opposites indicate only the two elements of contrast present in the objective content of experience. But the fundamental and primordial opposition professed by the modern *cogito* principle is that between subject and object, between the object apprehended and the mode of apprehending it, between the physical pole and the mental pole; and this very opposition is constitutive of the metaphysical act. From Descartes, Whitehead's "philosophy of organism" takes the assertion of the "plurality of actual entities"; but Whitehead's "ontological principle" is simply a develop-

[18] "For the kingdom of heaven is with us today. The action of the fourth phase is the love of God for the world. It is the particular providence for particular occasions. What is done in the world is transformed into a reality in heaven, and the reality in heaven passes back into the world. By reason of this reciprocal relation, the love in the world passes into the love in heaven, and floods back again into the world. In this sense God is the great companion—the fellow-sufferer who understands" (*ibid.*, p. 532).

[19] In *Adventures of Ideas,* Whitehead entitles Chapter XIV: "Appearance and Reality" with obvious reference to Bradley. Despite his methodological differences, Whitehead declares himself to be in agreement with Bradley on the final outcome and considers his own work to be a "transformation of some main doctrines of Absolute Idealism onto a realistic basis" (*Process and Reality,* p. viii).

ment of the principle that Locke expounds in his *Essay* II, XXIII, §7, when he declares that "power" is a "great part of our complex ideas of substance".[20] This Lockeian notion of substance is transformed by Whitehead into the crypto-idealist notion of "actual entity" and the notion of power into the principle that the reasons of things are always to be found in a nature composed of specific actual entities (the nature of God, as we have seen) and/or in a nature of actual entities bounded by time. The reasons of supreme absolute value are to be sought in the former sort of nature; the reasons relevant to a particular environment, in the latter. But the full complement of reasons cannot be exhausted in either the one or the other of these two natures. The "actual entity" is the *res vera* in the Cartesian sense of the term; it is true with the evidence of presence in act and is therefore a "substance" in the Cartesian sense (of a content of consciousness) and not in the Aristotelian sense (of a primary substance); but whereas in the Cartesian conception, the category of "quality" was dominant over that of "relatedness", in Whitehead, "relatedness" dominates "quality".[21]

The "ontological principle" Whitehead describes as asserting that "everything is positively somewhere in actuality, and in potency everywhere". It constitutes, he explains, the first step in the description of the universe as a solidarity of many actual entities, where each actual entity is to be conceived as an act of experience, a process, not describable in terms of the morphology of a "stuff". And here Whitehead introduces as a third and basic element, after Descartes and Locke, the appeal to the Humeian doctrine of "feeling". It is by the instrumentality of "feeling" that the many data are absorbed into the unity of one individual "satisfaction". This use of the term "feeling" Whitehead likens to Locke's use of the term "idea", but still more closely to Descartes' use of *sentire* (to feel, feeling), in the Second Meditation, to indicate immediate apprehension by the act of cognition of the idea itself.[22] In the constructive genesis of his own "philosophy of organism" Whitehead evinces a capacity of assimilation which may well be peerless, in its vastness of range and depth of penetration, in the whole of modern-day thought. Darting from Descartes to English empiricism,

[20] For Whitehead's attitude to Locke, cf. especially: *Process and Reality,* Part II, Chapter I, Section 6 (pp. 80ff.) and Part II, Chapter IV, Section 2 (p. 173): "This conception, as found in the philosophy of organism, is practically identical with Locke's ways of thought in the latter half of his *Essay*".

[21] Cf. *Process and Reality,* pp. viii-ix.

[22] This Second Meditation of Descartes always figures in the foreground of Whitehead's thought and references: cf. *Science and the Modern World,* pp. 202, 210; *Process and Reality,* pp. 77f.; *Adventures of Ideas,* p. 270. But Descartes' influence on Whitehead goes deeper and affects his very conception of sensible reality as process in act (cf. *Essays in Science and Philosophy,* pp. 174ff.).

from rationalism right over to Kant and idealism, Whitehead collates and purifies the "principle of act" with the object of inverting it into the principle of neo-realism as an assertion of the presence of the act itself. The inversion amounts to a drastic reiteration of the principles proper respectively to the various philosophies Whitehead has inspected and their elevation to the level required by the essential demand levied by the *cogito* principle: thus, e.g., Whitehead retains Descartes' recourse to God as foundation for the truth of the judgment, in the sense that the notion of God is necessary in order to explain (as we have seen) the mutual conjunction and togetherness within the opposition of the many and the One, or to effect the mediation between the physical prehension or perception (of the many) and the conceptual prehension (of the One).[23] In thus pinpointing the real significance of the *cogito,* throughout his summary but incisive survey of the whole development of modern thought, Whitehead is aiming at an exposure of the inconsistencies of that thought, wherever they occur; he is determined to denounce all the inhibitions and obstructions that have resulted from the static conception of being and to forge resolutely forward, with his pioneering doctrine of the convergence and coincidence of actuality, truth and the coexistence of the World and God, of death and immortality.

Whitehead's "philosophy of organism" takes the Humeian doctrine of feeling as its starting point for a resolution of the God-problem. Feeling is, according to Hume, the observation of a presence of the acts of consciousness and cognition; it is therefore, concludes Whitehead, the "germ of the mind" and by "mind" he here understands the complex of mental operations involved in the constitution of an actual entity: in the multiplicity of the conscious and unconscious mental acts, feeling clothes the dry bones with the flesh of a real being, emotional, purposive, appreciative. In virtue of the binding force of feeling, there arise "entities in act", unified and held in act by the backlog of past experience in their creative process of concrescence. But Hume holds the conceptual feelings to be derivative in character, inasmuch as they suppose the experience of the past and are therefore inapplicable to the primordial actual entity, which is God, since in him there obviously is no past.

The "philosophy of organism" can trace its derivation primarily along the dual axis, Descartes-Spinoza-Locke-Hume and Descartes-Locke-Hume-Kant; and the evolution of the Whiteheadian philosophy involved a purification and speculative integration of the heritage of all these

[23] *Process and Reality,* Part II, Chapter I, Section 5, p. 78. "The philosophy of organism is the inversion of Kant's philosophy" (Part II, Chapter III, Section 1, p. 135. Cf. also pp. 172f.).

philosophers, effected within the framework of the principle of presence and of actual entities.[24] But Whitehead declares that his very loyalty to this speculative line makes him determined to resist its tendency to dissolve being into the abstract quality of simple immediate content; Whitehead, on the contrary, insists on asserting concretion and concreteness and it is in terms of this that the demand for God arises. God is, as we have seen, the mediator between sensible prehension, the utmost bounds of sense-perception of the abstract qualities which Whitehead calls "eternal objects" within the Lockeian-Humeian-Kantian Whole, and intellectual prehension: God is the principle (as Primordial Nature) and the term or fulfillment (as Consequent Nature) of the objectivity and transcendence of cognition.[25] Only thus can the defect of Hume's position be overcome: the subjectivist principle must be reformed and corrected by the notion of process as a Whole, a notion which Whitehead feels is, in turn, simply the extension of the Hegelian notion of the real.

Here is Whitehead's summary of this point: "The universe is at once the multiplicity of *res verae* and the solidarity of *res verae.* The solidarity is itself the efficiency of the macroscopic *res vera,* embodying the principle of unbounded permanence acquiring novelty through flux. The multiplicity is composed of microscopic *res verae,* each embodying the principle of bounded flux acquiring 'everlasting' permanence. On the one side, the One becomes many; and on the other side, the many become one. But *what* becomes is always a *res vera,* and the concrescence of a *res vera* is the development of a subjective aim. This development is nothing else than the Hegelian development of an idea." [26] This is a restatement of the notion of truth as a Whole, which Whitehead conceives as always in flux. In a certain sense Hegel, likewise, did think along the same line, but not in the same way.

The philosophy of organism can justifiably be designated as a return

[24] Whitehead's truly masterly development of this whole point is most instructive concerning the disintegration of modern thought (*ibid.,* Chapter V: "Locke and Hume"; and Chapter VI: "From Descartes to Kant," pp. 198ff.).

[25] "Transcendent decision includes God's decision. He is the actual entity in virtue of which the *entire* multiplicity of eternal objects obtains its graded relevance to each stage of concrescence. Apart from God, there could be no relevant novelty" (*ibid.,* Chapter VII, Section 4, p. 248).

[26] *Ibid.,* Chapter VII, Section 5, p. 254 and cf. Preface, p. viii-ix. Whitehead has important remarks on the influence of Hegelian philosophy upon the emergence and development of the philosophy of organism in his *Essays in Science and Philosophy* p. 88; obviously Whitehead absorbed Hegel's thought as mediated by the English Neo-Hegelians (Haldane, McTaggart and especially Bradley). Another major influence was, of course, Samuel Alexander, as Kuspit has so admirably demonstrated (Donald B. Kuspit, "Whitehead on Divinity," p. 71, pp. 104ff. especially the quite important Note 8).

to Heraclitus,[27] both in the sense of an explicit articulation of the πάντα ῥεῖ of incessant flux and in the sense of an assertion of the λογος as contentual principle, imparting consistency and meaning to the whole process. Perhaps it could better be described in Whitehead's own terms as a synthesis of Aristotle and Hegel [28] via Descartes-Locke-Hume and with the mediation of Bradley. The nature and very essence of truth is defined in terms of the relation of conformity between appearance and reality; this definition is consciously intended as a substitute for the Aristotelian doctrine of the distinction between primary and secondary substance: "In a general sense, the Appearance is a work of Art, elicited from the primary Reality. Insofar as the Appearance emphasizes connections and qualities of connections which in fact reside in the Reality, then the Appearance is truthful in its relation to Reality. But the Appearance may have effected connections, and have introduced qualities, which have no counterpart in Reality. In that case, the occasion of experience contains in itself a falsehood, namely the disconnection of its Appearance from Reality. In any case the Appearance is a simplification of Reality, reducing it to a foreground of enduring individuals and to a background of undiscriminated occasions." [29] This perception of enduring individuals belongs to the final Appearance wherein the occasion of experience terminates. In the primary phase, the past is initiating the process in virtue of the energizing of its diverse individual occasions. This is the Reality from which the new occasion springs. This is a first-order reality of the sensible pole. The process is urged onward by operation of the mental pole which provides conceptual subject-matter for synthesis with the Reality. This is a second-order or reflexive Reality.

It is at this point that there finally emerges the Appearance, which is the transformed Reality after synthesis with the conceptual valuations. This transition from the first to the second phase of the Appearance and the Reality is substantially a reproduction of the Hegelian transition

[27] Cf. John F. Gates' spirited summary in *Adventures in the History of Philosophy* (Grand Rapids, 1961), p. 210.

[28] Whitehead has an explicit and comprehensive statement on this point: "Almost all of *Process and Reality* can be read as an attempt to analyse perishing on the same level as Aristotle's analysis of becoming. The notion of the prehension of the past means that the past is an element which perishes and thereby remains an element in the state beyond, and thus is objectified. That is the whole notion. If you get a general notion of what is meant by perishing, you will have accomplished an apprehension of what you mean by memory and causality, what you mean when you feel that what we are is of infinite importance, because as we perish we are immortal. That is the one key thought around which the whole development of *Process and Reality* is woven, and in many ways I find that I am in complete agreement with Bradley" (*Essays in Science and Philosophy*, p. 89).

[29] *Adventures of Ideas*, pp. 362f.

from the first to the second immediacy, from the abstract exterior immediacy of the *Schein* to the constitutive essential immediacy of the Idea. It pushes beyond the impasse of the *Critique of Pure Reason,* with the doctrine of the phenomenon; it denies all meaning to the problem of synthetic *a priori* judgments [30] and then proceeds to pose the God-problem in the manner of Hegel.

But Whitehead's God, as distinct from Hegel's, is not the Absolute, because he expresses himself in terms of a relation to the world (AR) and is immanent in the world, although dynamically rather than statically: both as Primordial Nature and as Consequent Nature, God is always referred to the world as a function of its process of evolution. Whitehead also speaks of a third nature in God, the "superjective nature"; and he defines this as "the character of the pragmatic value of his specific satisfaction qualifying the transcendent creativity in the various temporal instances".[31] But always we have, in Whitehead, a God immanent in the world, a principle of limitation in the form of concrescence and concretion, a God who is in turn positioned on the crest of the endless evolution or process, as the outcome of creativity, as the foundation of order, and as the goal towards novelty.[32]

And it should further be noted that every actual entity, God included, is something individual in its own right and therefore transcends the rest of actuality; but at the same time, every actual entity, God included, is a creature and therefore transcended by the very creativity it qualifies.[33] Whitehead is inclined to grant to this God the Spinozan attribute of *causa sui;* [34] but this does not jibe at all well with Whitehead's trenchant

[30] Cf. *Adventures of Ideas,* p. 378. Cf. also *Process and Reality,* Part II, Chapter III, Section 1. The title of Chapter XIV of *Adventures of Ideas* ("Appearance and Reality") is most indicative. The appearance-reality nexus defines the problem of truth (*Adventures of Ideas,* pp. 309ff.), of beauty (pp. 324ff.) and of peace (pp. 366ff.). On the Hegelian theory of the "primary and secondary immediacy", cf. *Wissenschaft der Logik,* ed. Lasson (Leipzig, 1934), Vol. II, pp. 9, 11, 94, 97, 106f., and especially 352ff., 497. For a discussion of this theory, cf. C. Fabro, *Hegel: la dialettica* (Brescia, 1960) Introduction, pp. LXXIVff.

[31] *Process and Reality,* Part II, Chapter III, Section 1, p. 135.

[32] The clear and conclusive passage on this point is: "God is the ultimate limitation, and His existence is the ultimate irrationality. For no reason can be given for just that limitation which it stands in His nature to impose. God is not concrete, but He is the ground for concrete actuality. No reason can be given for the nature of God, because that nature is the ground of rationality" (*Science and the Modern World,* p. 257).

[33] "It is to be noted that every actual entity, including God, is something individual for its own sake; and thereby transcends the rest of actuality. And also it is to be noted that every actual entity, including God, is a creature transcended by the creativity which it qualifies" (*Process and Reality,* p. 135).

[34] This Spinozan notion of God as *causa sui* will be combined with the other Whiteheadian notion of the *nisus* or interior thrust, a notion basic to the philosophy of organism; and the result will be the notion of the two natures in God,

insistence, in the immediately preceding section, on the fact that God is "a creature transcended by the creativity" which He qualifies.

The elimination or implicit denial of God in this Whiteheadian system is in direct proportion to the effort expended to defend and preserve him. In this respect Whitehead's philosophy is exactly parallel to that of Hegel and of the Hegelian Right. As opposed to Hegel, however, Whitehead ties God without remainder to the world of experience, in virtue of the empiricist shading of Whitehead's philosophical thought-scheme, which causes him to lay stress on the appearance of being and on the strict conjunction of God with the world, to such an extent that God can be said to be an attribute of the world, even as the world can be said to be an attribute of God.

The generic principle of empiricism, according to Whitehead, is based on the tenet that there is a principle of concretion which cannot be discovered by the abstract reason. What further can be known about God must be sought in the region of particular experiences, and therefore rests on an empirical basis. If he be made into the Absolute and the Perfect, then he is likewise made responsible for evil. If, on the contrary, God be conceived "as the supreme ground for limitation, then it stands in his very nature to divide the Good from the Evil, and to establish Reason 'within her dominions supreme' ".[35]

Whitehead's undeviating commitment to the spirit of the modern *cogito* principle, his steady determination to adhere consistently to the empirical principle of concreteness (concretion, in Whitehead's own terms), and his keen sense of the values operative in human life—all this makes Whitehead's conception of God (or, rather, his implicit and indeed virtually explicit denial of God) and consequently his whole philosophical system of capital importance as a clarification of the significance, structure and inevitable destination of the principle of immanentism, in one of its most brilliant and drastically articulated variants.

A thoroughgoing and exhaustive judgment on Whitehead's method of positing his intracosmic God would require an extensive exposition of the whole complex structure of his system, a system strongly reminiscent of his severe mathematical training. But a judgment on the crucial features of that system is possible simply on the basis of the principles

---

the primordial and the consequent. Whitehead makes specific acknowledgement to Samuel Alexander: ". . . I think the universe has a side which is mental and permanent. This side is that prime conceptual drive which I call the primordial nature of God. It is Alexander's *nisus* conceived as actual" (*Essays in Science and Philosophy,* p. 89). Donald Kuspit has a good treatment of this whole point in his "Whitehead on Divinity," pp. 74ff.

[35] *Science and the Modern World,* pp. 257f. And a little earlier: "In the place of Aristotle's God as Prime Mover, we require God as the Principle of Concretion" (p. 250).

already expounded and their inevitable further specification. Our repeated assertion that Whitehead's thought remains faithful to the principle of immanentism will seem strange only to those who identify immanentism with idealism, i.e., confuse the genus with one of the species. It is quite true that Whitehead's avowed aim and goal is to shatter the bounds of the rigid alternative as between realism and immanentism, or theism and atheism. But the heart of his thought and the explicit development of that thought bears witness at every step to his unqualified adherence to the modern principle of consciousness or mind, of which his philosophy presents a new and brilliant variant. The "World" of this philosophy is an integral dynamic web of relations between contents of consciousness: the building-blocks of this edifice, in continuous process of construction, are the acts of "prehension" which exhibit the "actual entities" in the fashion of the Humeian *impressions*.[36] The only difference is a systematic one, not a real one in our opinion: Whitehead conceives, with Plato, of a realm of "eternal objects" (as possibles) as a background against which the "actual entities" emerge as a selection from among these objects. The act of constitution of such "actual entities" is called "satisfaction" and it involves the positive prehension of the objects. In this first moment of prehension, called by Whitehead "a process of concrescence", the satisfaction which is the constitution of the appropriate act of consciousness is based on "feeling", exactly as in Hume, on the emergence and mysterious yet ever-present self-articulation of feeling, which is therefore identified with prehension. Thus, the primordial cognition of the real is identified with the dynamic of feelings,[37] a dynamic which consequently expresses the meaning and foun-

[36] Cf. the explicit reference to this notion of Hume in *Process and Reality*, Part III, Chapter V, Section 4, p. 411. We have here the transformation of the Cartesian *cogito* into the Humeian *feeling:* "Descartes' 'Cogito, ergo sum' is wrongly translated, 'I *think*, therefore I am'. It is never bare thought or bare existence that we are aware of. I find myself as essentially a unity of emotions, enjoyments, hopes, fears, regrets, valuations of alternatives, decisions—all of them subjective reactions to the environment as active in my nature. My unity—which is Descartes' 'I am'—is my process of shaping this welter of material into a consistent pattern of feelings. The individual enjoyment is what I am in my role of a natural activity, as I shape the activities of the environment into a new creation, which is myself at this moment; and yet, as being myself, it is a continuation of the antecedent world. If we stress the role of the environment, this process is causation. If we stress the role of my immediate pattern of active enjoyment, this process is self-creation" (A. N. Whitehead, *Modes of Thought* [New York: The Macmillan Company, 1938], pp. 227f.).

[37] Whitehead distinguishes two feelings, physical and conceptual, even as Hume had previously distinguished two kinds of impressions, impressions of sensation and impressions of reflection: feeling is therefore at once the cohesive principle (synthesis) and illuminating principle (evaluation, judgment) of experience, conferring on the act of cognition its status of being *causa sui*, even though deriving from past experience. This is how Whitehead presents the dynamic of the

dation of truth, in such a way that the conscious knowing subject can be called *causa sui*. The world actually stems from the emergence of the meaning of the world and its structures, of their differentiation, relation, elevation and unification (in the One) under the impulse and thrust of the underground current of feelings powered by that "belief" or "faith" which they generate. It is not surprising, therefore, that the God required by the philosophy of organism as the principle of unity of such a world should be a function of the creativity of the world itself as it presents itself to the human mind and therefore a dimension of the eidetic horizon of the mind as it addresses itself to the world.

This Whiteheadian formula of the "di-polarity" of God has been further developed and studied by Charles Hartshorne (1897—). Whitehead had started from the interpretation of reality as motion or becoming, a "principle of unrest" according to which reality is the "actual entity" in the sense of experience in continual process of becoming; he had concluded that the traditional concept of substance as an unchanging subject of change had to be entirely abandoned.[38] Although Whitehead designated his own system as a "philosophy of organism,"

---

cognitive act, a dynamic dominated by the feelings: "A feeling—i.e. a positive prehension—is essentially a transition effecting a concrescence. Its complex constitution is analysable into five factors which express what that transition consists of, and effects. The factors are: (i) the 'subject' which feels, (ii) the 'initial data' which are to be felt, (iii) the 'elimination' in virtue of negative prehensions, (iv) the 'objective datum' which is felt, (v) the 'subjective form' which is *how* that subject feels that objective datum." (*Process and Reality,* Part III, "The Theory of Prehension," Chapter I: "The Theory of Feelings," pp. 337f. This entire chapter, pp. 334-360, will be studied most intensively as constituting the real theoretical back-bone of the philosophy of organism; it has been somewhat neglected by Whitehead experts and critics.) It should be noted, at the outset, that for Whitehead, as for Bradley, Royce and the other English neo-Hegelians, the metaphysical problem of God consists in the definition of his being and his nature in terms of the categories of the real and the ideal and on the basis of primordial experience: God as Primordial Nature is the realm of the "eternal objects" (the possible) and as Consequent Nature he is the realm of the "actual entities" (the real). The existence of God therefore in no sense constitutes a speculative problem: the experience of the existence of God is a private affair of each of the individual particular consciousnesses or minds, connected with the becoming, the fluent thrust of its own "concrescence" (cf. Donald B. Kuspit, "Whitehead on Divinity," pp. 130 and 157f.). Whitehead's insistence on the immediacy of presence of feeling (as in Hume) takes us back to Hegel's own penetration of the deep-cutting significance of empiricism on which we commented at the outset of this chapter.

[38] *Process and Reality,* Part I, Chapter II, Section 4, p. 43. The other basic notion Whitehead takes from Alexander is that of "enjoyment" which Whitehead, however, prefers to term "feeling" as more faithful to the tradition of empiricism and which Whitehead himself defines as "the term used for the basic generic operation of passing from the objectivity of the data to the subjectivity of the actual entity in question" (*ibid.,* II, Chapter I, Section 1, p. 65).

the physico-metaphysical bias seems to predominate in Whitehead over the biologico-metaphysical bias of an Alexander: instead of bringing into play the God-deity tension as content of the expansion and process of Time, Whitehead insists outright on the God-World tension. This tension, it should be most carefully noted, is no longer held to be sustained solely by the passage of time; it is understood rather indivisibly as the act recurrently emergent from the fullness of the relations that subtend it. God's inextricable connection with the world thus becomes even more intimate: for both Alexander and Whitehead, God expresses the ideal and has the status of reason, principle and end or term (or indeed "effect" if you will) of the emergence of the real in its process of becoming; but in Whitehead's conception, which makes no distinction between God and deity—the God-World relation is presented as more intimate "togetherness" [39] or conjunction. There is a greater stress on the act itself as emergence, in the sense that it is itself process in act, a process of which the world and God constitute two elements or moments.

In order the better to express this conjunction or togetherness as constitutive of the experience of the real, Hartshorne has recourse to the "Law of Polarity" formulated by Morris Cohen (1880-1947), which takes us back to the ancient conception of the coexistence of contraries in every process of the real, a conception formulated in theory by Heraclitus himself.[40] This law asserts that ultimate contraries are correlatives, mutually interdependent, so that nothing real can be described by the wholly onesided assertion of simplicity, being, actuality, and the like, each in a pure form, devoid and independent of complexity, becoming, potentiality, and related contraries. As Cohen formulates it, this law or principle of polarity asserts that ". . . the empirical facts are generally resultants of opposing and yet inseparable tendencies like the north and south poles." [41] Cohen insists that this Principle of Polarity is of capital importance and value in intellectual research, "like the principle of causality, against the abuse of which it may serve as a help. If the principle of causality makes us search for operating causes, the principle of polarity makes us search for that which prevents them from produc-

[39] I do not believe that Whitehead's distinction between Primordial Nature and Consequent Nature in God can be held to correspond to the God-deity tension in Alexander, because God as Primordial Nature precisely serves to resolve the space-time tension.

[40] Cf. C. Hartshorne, *Philosophers Speak of God,* pp. 2ff. and the concluding study: "The Logic of Panentheism" (pp. 499ff., especially 504).

[41] "The last example suggests that to make logic applicable to empirical issues, we must employ the principle of polarity. By this I mean that the empirical facts are generally resultants of opposing and yet inseparable tendencies like the north and south poles" (Morris Cohen, *A Preface to Logic* [London: George Routledge & Sons Ltd., 1946], p. 75).

ing greater effects than they do. In physical science the principle of polarity would thus be represented by the principle of action and reaction, and the principle that whereever there are forces there must be resistance. In biology it has been expressed by Huxley, in the aphorism that protoplasm manages to live only by continually dying. This finds its ethical analogue in the mutual dependence of the concepts of self-sacrifice and self-realization. Philosophically it may be generalized as the principle, not of the identity, but of the necessary copresence and mutual dependence of opposite determinations. It warns us against the greatest bane of philosophizing, to wit: the easy artificial dilemma between unity and plurality, rest and motion, substance and function, actual and ideal, etc." [42]

Cohen finds most felicitous Felix Adler's use of the figure of the scissors to stress the fact that the mind can operate really effectively only by using both unity and plurality, like the two blades which move in opposite directions. The same figure, Cohen points out, has been used by Marshall in his analysis of economic problems to stress the mutual dependence of the economic factors of supply and demand. In fact the principle allows of the most varied and extensive applications. His conclusion is that what might be called "twilight zones" or "regions of indetermination" may be encountered in the realm of psychical and physical existence; and that these zones or regions may have a reality and a consequent intelligibility of their own.[43] For these zones or regions, the logical principles of contradiction and excluded middle are simply not adequate, with their sharp antitheses and rigorous dichotomous divisions: either black or white, soft or hard, warm or cold, virtuous or sinful. For there may well be things that belong to neither alternative. We may be the most vigorous anti-Hegelians, says Cohen; we may realize the intellectual suicide involved in denying or even softening the distinction between opposites; yet we must grant that, in the case of things in transition, there are times when opposite predicates may be equally true. We cannot, in fact, draw an absolutely sharp dividing line between day and night, or say when a man ceases to be alive and becomes dead. No distinction seems sharper than that between the visible and the invisible. Yet actually there is no sharp line dividing what we see from what we do not see. Our field of vision in fact tapers off from the illumined focal regions of attention to the region of the invisible.

[42] Here is the crucial Cohen passage: "Philosophically it may be generalized as the principle, not of the identity, but of the necessary copresence and mutual dependence of opposite determinations. It warns us against the greatest bane of philosophizing, to wit: the easy artificial dilemma between unity and plurality, rest and motion, substance and function, actual and ideal, etc." (*ibid.*, p. 76).

[43] *Ibid.*, pp. 73f.

Thus, in all these twilight zones, there occurs precisely that "coexistence of opposites" to which the Principle of Polarity refers. The point is that the laws of logic apply to the realm of essence, i.e., to natural existences only in so far as they are determinate. If nature means the realm of the determinate, then obviously all the indetermination exists in another realm, which we may call *maya,* mind, or something else, if we will, but which must in any case be viewed as non-natural. But if nature includes both determination and indetermination, our empirical view of things can be explained and so can the growth of scientific knowledge. There is nothing in logic or nature to prevent the existence of complexes in which contrary tendencies are conjoined. The law of contradiction does indeed assert that nothing can be *a* and *not-a* in the same relation. But it does not veto the existence within the same essence of opposite determinations. All that it demands is the existence of a distinction of aspects or relations wherein the contraries hold.[44] This whole approach can thus lead us to the assertion that lies at the basis of the philosophies of emergence and especially the philosophy of organism, namely the assertion that reality and life in all its forms and degrees can be said to be dialectical, but in a constitutive sense, not merely the methodological sense of Hegel: progress occurs not by way of the supersession of opposition in a third reality distinct from the two opposites, but rather in the intensification of their opposition and the mutual conservation of the opposites themselves. This is the law of all the concepts referring to reality as such.

Twilight zones are characteristic of reality. The principle of polarity properly applied to such zones requires that all the concepts referring to such zones, such as reality, existence, experience, the universe, etc., shall be essentially indefinite in meaning. It is only in the realm of formal or strictly logical concepts that there can be no twilight zones. But such zones are always present in the realm of psychical and physical existence.[45]

Hartshorne takes this dipolar conception and applies it rigorously, in order to refute and overcome the monopolar conception most typically expressed in the Thomist conception of God as *actus purus,* or in the notion that the Absolute is, by implication, a uniquely actual, completely unrelated Being. Hartshorne is persuaded that the Principle of Polarity is the only alternative which is capable of breaking out of the

[44] "The law of contradiction does not bar the presence of contrary determinations in the same entity, but only requires as a postulate the existence of a distinction of aspects or relations in which the contraries hold" (*ibid.,* p. 75).

[45] Cohen feels he can thus avoid not only nominalism and conceptualism, but also two types of unsatisfactory realism, atomistic and organic, and likewise the two opposite approaches of rationalism and mysticism (*ibid.,* pp. 78ff.).

impasse into which the God-problem has been forced by the antithetical positions of theism-atheism or theism-pantheism. The irreconcilability of these positions is primarily due to their divergent and opposed interpretation of the concept of cause: for the theists, God is cause of the world, but since he is perfect in himself, he always has been and still remains independent of the world; for the pantheists, God is cause inasmuch as he is in himself comprehensive of the world and holds it within his own being. Here we are faced with a radical *either-or*.

Modern thought, maintains Hartshorne, is in a position to offer an alternative view, which will break the closed circle of the "radically asymmetrical" conception of causal necessity, which dominates the two types of solution just mentioned. This new solution consists in an application of the principle of polarity, articulated in the becoming of being according to Whitehead's scheme. As applied to the God-problem, this principle asserts that God as supreme (in the sense of universal) cause is what is required by other things and which itself requires only that the class of other things be not null. There is thus established between God and other things a relation of interaction, making it possible for God to impart an influence to the world and receive an influence from the world in turn. Such a reactive being could not, of course, be identified with the supreme cause; but it still might be this cause, *in an aspect of itself*.

A man as a power is not a single cause but a stream of causes, each of which is also an effect. God, too, as an agent or power is not *a* or *the* cause of all things; rather he is to be conceived as a (or *the*) *supreme stream* of causation which at the same time is the supreme stream of effects. Thus the new solution mediates between the apparently irreconcilable notions of God as all-inclusive reality and God as a transcendent Reality: it satisfies both the demand for God as First Cause and the demand for God as all-inclusive reality; and it can be expressed in the formula: *God is CW*.[46]

This formula, which Hartshorne designates as the assertion of "panentheism", can indeed be held to express the heart of the theology of all the thinkers of the school with which we are here dealing, a school of which Hartshorne himself is a vigorous exponent and an incisive investigator. Hartshorne is convinced that this solution of mutual inter-

[46] The new formula reads: "Thus the positive content of theism and pantheism can be consistently combined in *God is CW;* for the contradiction between theism and pantheism arises only from the denial of any possible distinction between God as independent cause and God in his total actuality" (C. Hartshorne, *Philosophers Speak of God,* p. 504a). Later the formula assumes the form AR, i.e. unity of Absolute and relative, always understood in the light of the principle of polarity (Cf. pp. 507bff.). Therefore the full-fledged formula of pantheism is the synthesis AR-CW (Cf. pp. 512a-513a).

dependence of God and the world is the only one capable of saving the reality of God.

It is not enough to say that God is immanent as well as transcendent. The cause is of course in the effect, since it is logically necessary to that effect. Only thus could the cause, in fact, be inferred from the effect. "But is God merely cause, merely C, or is he CW? This is the critical question; and it is not answered by asserting both world immanence and world transcendence of God. The important question, as Fechner remarked, is whether the world is immanent in God." [47]

This seems to clarify the position entirely and Hartshorne is able, in the light of his premisses, to interpret the other attributes of God (eternity, simplicity, perfection, and the rest) just as Whitehead had already done. Hartshorne devotes a specially closely-reasoned discussion to the problem of a reconciliation of the divine knowledge of contingent facts in a way calculated to save at once the immutability and perfection of God (and of the divine knowledge) and the contingency of a certain fact *x*, which, precisely because it *is* contingent, could *not be* and could thus render the divine knowledge of fact *x* false.[48] Theism, concludes Hartshorne, can therefore be saved only in the form of panentheism, not separating God from the world but rather making the world the receptacle of God, along the line of that panpsychism which has been developed from Leibniz down to Fechner and Whitehead.

Nothing, Hartshorne assures us, can be extraneous to God, not even matter: many philosophers have categorically repudiated the notion of dead matter and made life to be the universal reality; Leibniz is but the most illustrious representative of this approach. As for human freedom, the Fechnerian principle justifies us in conceiving it, too, as a part of God.

Thus the truth of theism can be expressed solely in the formula AR-CW. The absolute, nonreflexive or merely identical factor in God, God as A-C, is the pure cause which neither is nor contains any effect; the unmoved mover which, in the words of Jacob Böhme, is *in* God but is not God (in his concreteness). "The superrelative or reflexively transcendent perfection of God is the fulness of his being, his wholeness as always self-identical, but self-identical as self-enriched, influenced but never fully determined by (and never fully determining) others—in short, a living, sensitive, free personality, preserving all actual events with impartial care and forever adding new events to his experience. The absolute is the One merely as One; the superrelative is the many as also one, or the one as also many. The world as not God is the many merely

[47] *Ibid.*, p. 506a.
[48] *Ibid.*, p. 510b.

as many—an abstraction from the many as one, as the integrated, active-passive content of omniscience." [49]

All other conceptions are, for Hartshorne, pure abstractions making impossible any proper consideration of God's fundamental attributes: life, consciousness and knowledge, freedom. We thus have in this conception, which is almost indistinguishable from panpsychism, simply another variant of the principle of immanentism. This comes out most clearly in its identification of the notion of substance with the notion of cause, by which is effected the "decantation of attributes" between God and the world through the mediating instrumentality of the human mind.

The notion of "emergent evolution" is therefore bound to be maintained with increasing intensity in this type of philosophy which lays claim to an unequivocal and explicit assertion and affirmation of God, which indeed insists it is effecting a last-minute salvage operation upon the God compromised by the antithetical positions of theism and atheism: Morgan, the chief proponent of this emergent evolution, recalls that Bergson too had spoken of a "creative evolution".[50] The conception of emergent evolution can be considered the heir of the initial speculation of the English Enlightenment, which attributed to matter, as against the Cartesian notion of dualism, the intrinsic capacity for self-motion and thus for life, sensation, perception (Toland) and possibly even of thought (Locke). This initial approach was further deepened by Hume's theory of "faith" as opposed to the rationalist notion of causality.

This new "naturalistic idealism" or "realist idealism" became more and more explicit in the later and more elaborated forms of this approach. It had recourse to the Hegelian conception in this modified form with the aim and object of welding to a solid consistency, with the aid of the dialectic, the mutual functional relation of the Spinozan Whole or All with the parts, and of guaranteeing the endless march of "progress" presented to the human mind in its relation to the world. This conclusive encounter between empiricism and idealism is of capital theoretical interest to us here, because of its effective intensification of what must be termed the quintessence of modern thought and the true meaning of the principle of immanentism, which in our interpretation is the only principle that excludes any opening whatever onto transcendence and is therefore capable of substantiating a positive and constructive atheism which

[49] *Ibid.*, p. 514b. Hartshorne repeats in another work this basic idea of the new synthesis of theism and pantheism: "God includes the lesser subjects, but so that their freedom is preserved and his responsibility for the details of their acts is not unlimited. This involves an aspect of passivity and process toward novelty in God, despite the eternal necessity of his existence and essential character" (C. Hartshorne, "Panpsychism," in *A History of Philosophical Systems,* edited by Vergilius Ferm [New York, 1950], p. 452).

[50] Cf. L. Morgan, *Emergent Evolution,* p. 287.

is at the same time an absolutely dead-end atheism. For certainly the emergent evolution of a world that "is making itself" God cannot constitute or substantiate any such possibility of an opening onto transcendence; it is sheer cosmic process and nothing more.

"Emergent evolution works upwards from matter, through life, to consciousness which attains in man its highest reflective or supra-reflective level . . . The most subtle appreciation of the artist or the poet, the highest aspiration of the saint, are no less accepted than the blossom of the water-lily, the crystalline fabric of a snow-flake, or the minute structure of the atom.

"Emergent evolution urges that the 'more' of any given stage, even the highest, involves the 'less' of the stages which were precedent to it and continue to coexist with it. It does *not* interpret the higher in terms of the lower only . . . It does not interpret the lower in terms of the higher. . . .

"But if [and here the Spinozan element emerges in Morgan] we may acknowledge on the one hand a physical world underlying the phenomenal appearances with which we are acquainted by sense, and, on the other hand, an immaterial Source of all changes therein; if, in other words, we may acknowledge physical events as ultimately *involved,* and God on whom all evolutionary process ultimately *depends,* then we may . . . accept both causation and Causality without shadow of contradiction." [51]

The crucial point to be realized, insists Morgan, is that causality as such is always "emergent" for it is a production, in each instance, of a higher "quality of being". In this synthesis of causation and Causality [52] there is a real place for faith in God but there is also a place and indeed an absolute demand for a "full and frank acceptance of the naturalistic interpretation of the world which is offered by emergent evolution." [53] A God in isolation from the world would be simply meaningless.

This relation of God to the world is conceived by Morgan in a thoroughly realist fashion: and we must have a firm grasp of this "realism" in order properly to appreciate the profoundly immanentistic character of this entire school of "naturalistic theology". Morgan's own example of the "lowly plant" is an ideal instance of his line of argumentation:

In this plant, there are physico-chemical events, and there is emergent vital relatedness. If we deal with the plant's materiality in abstraction from the supervenient life or with its life apart from a physical basis, then in either case we are concerned not with the concrete whole in

[51] *Ibid.,* pp. 297ff.

[52] On this distinction and its supersession, cf. *ibid.,* Lecture X, pp. 274ff.

[53] Here Morgan declares himself to be completely in agreement with Alexander's notion concerning the God-Deity relation (*ibid.,* p. 299).

accordance with its level of emergence, but with a *res incompleta.* The *res completa* is the living organism, nothing less but also nothing more. Similarly, man, the highest natural system that we know, is a *res incompleta,* if considered in abstraction from those emergent qualities which give him, in alliance with all that is involved, his status as *res completa.* Now the highest of these emergent qualities, for Morgan as for Alexander, is deity. And in the matter of the God-World tension, Morgan insists that it is not the world without God, but the world with God that is grasped from within this concept of the *nisus* in Causality manifested in all natural events.

Immanence is thus the absolutely basic feature of this theological empiricism. Morgan insists that such expressions as "within the system", "within the organism", "within the mind" ought not to preclude the recognition of what exists and subsists beyond the confines of our mind: the physical world, other minds, and God. "We acknowledge God as above and beyond. But unless we also intuitively enjoy his Activity within us, feeling that we are in a measure one with him in Substance, we can have no immediate knowledge of Causality or of God as the Source of our own existence and of emergent evolution."[54] And this is the real crux of the matter: even though a God "above and beyond" is indeed admitted, still his proper place is within man, within man's life and mediated by man's consciousness, i.e., that feeling which is the deepest principle of the conservation and continuous presence of what is in process of actualization. And this actualization essentially involves a garnering of the past, a past of cosmic memory extending likewise into the future and making itself present in the actual moment and event. And in this *nisus,* man is the sole witness to God, because man is likewise the only genuine subject and proper tabernacle and receptacle of God.

For Anglo-American naturalistic idealism, philosophy ought most certainly not to succumb to the finite, limit itself to describing the simple event, narrating transient episodes; but if philosophy wants to be faithful to its mission as unveiler of being, then it must seek out the vantage point at which the many are inserted into the One, the divergent stand at gaze in the Identical, and the changeable rest within the Unchanging.

[54] *Ibid.,* p. 301. And Morgan almost immediately thereafter makes a forthright and vigorous profession of faith in this evolutionary naturalism: "In such credal terms I believe in a physical world at the base of the evolutionary pyramid and involved at all higher levels; I believe that throughout the pyramid there are correlated attributes and that there is one emergent process of psycho-physical evolution; and I believe that this process is a spatio-temporal manifestation of immanent Activity, the ultimate Source of those phenomena which are interpreted under evolutionary naturalism" (p. 309).

Strange as it seems, this very conception of the finite and evolving God constitutes, in a certain sense, the apodictic proof of the radical despair into which modern thought has fallen in its efforts to provide a really substantial foundation for truth. This finite-God conception likewise represents the supreme effort to avoid a total sell-out to Marxist and existentialist historicism. Whitehead has, in fact, served as one of the chief antidotes, in English-speaking countries, to the speculative breakdown invading those countries from the European continent. His thinking on God aims to be a kind of Gospel of Salvation, mediating between the atheism of present-day, and the allegedly restrictive transcendentalist conceptions of traditional, theology. The following excerpt from a Whitehead essay brings out the Whiteheadian stand with special poignancy:

"If you ask me what God is, I can only answer he is a being whose body is the whole world of nature, but that world conceived as actually possessing deity, and therefore he is not actual as existent but as an ideal, and only existent in so far as the tendency towards his distinctive character is existent in the actual world. God, you will say, is on this showing an ideal being, whose deity does not yet exist, but is the next quality due to emerge, and cannot therefore be known by us. He exists only in the striving of the world to realize his deity, and to help it as it were to the birth. Moreover, he is not a creator as in historical religions, but created." [55]

There we have an honest and forthright statement of the Whiteheadian God-notion: the cosmic power and energy, the eternal and everlasting *nisus* of the world, of the whole universe, in its infinite and endless expansion.

[55] *Science and Religion* (New York: Charles Scribner's Sons, 1931), p. 136. W. Mays has likewise based his interpretation of the God of *Process and Reality* on these and similar passages (Cf. W. Mays, *The Philosophy of Whitehead*, [London-New York, 1959], pp. 56ff., especially p. 73). But Hartshorne has expressed reservations about this interpretation (Cf. *The Relevance of Whitehead*, edited by J. Leclerc [London-New York, 1961], p. 23).

5

Truth as Action and the Vanishing of God in Dewey

The empiricist principle of Anglo-American philosophy eventually precipitated explicit atheism with the pragmatism of John Dewey (1859-1952), for this pragmatism eliminated the problem of God and religion from the theoretical area.[1] The pragmatism, which in William James had been confined to the bounds of a research and investigation method, now becomes a conception of reality and truth resulting from the processes of the practical reason in its efforts to resolve the problems of life. Ideas and reflective procedures are now simply the instruments man uses in order to transform the reality that surrounds him in accord with the requirements of his own goals. Dewey's pragmatism has, for this reason, been called *instrumentalism*; and it can be considered at once the most radical and the most representative attitude in present-day American thought.

On the God-problem, Dewey admits no compromises whatsoever: God is a name devoid of content, a sheer psychological illusion. Indeed, the very fact of religion and the religious consciousness generally are reducible to a psychological illusion for the very simple reason that religion in all its forms asserts the existence of a supernatural being who is an unseen Power, creator of the world and man, to whom man owes subjection, the offering of prayers and sacrifices. A man who lives in this sort of psychological environment is called religious. But Dewey distinguishes sharply between the substantive and the adjective, between religion and religious: religion[2] always signifies a special body of beliefs and practices having some kind of institutional organization, while the

[1] Dewey's theory of religion is to be found in his essay: *A Common Faith* (New Haven: Yale University Press, 1934).

[2] Religion is for Dewey a strictly sociological term always having the same basic meaning whether it be used of naturalistic or spiritualistic religions, for pure natural religion or historical supernatural religion: religion always involves the admission of a supernatural Being and thus clashes with experience (cf. *ibid.*, pp. 2ff.).

adjective "religious" prescinds from any institution or system of beliefs, indicating only attitudes that may be taken toward every object and every proposed end or ideal.

Since religion, thus conceived, is a simple historical product, it falls as such entirely outside the area of philosophical knowledge. But the category of the "religious" must be restored to its original purity by clarifying what is really meant by what Dewey calls the "religious elements of experience."

James had maintained, with admirable openness that there could be no denying the religious experience that serves as the basis for religion. Dewey takes a quite different approach. Having excluded religion as irrelevant to his purposes by his very definition of religion, Dewey proceeds to ask what the adjective "religious" really means, as applied to experience. His aim is precisely to divorce religious consciousness and awareness from all connections it has hitherto had in the various religions with the belief in a supernatural Being and with the dogmas and cultic practices with which the various religions have surrounded it. He wants to show that these are all simply encumbrances that presently smother or limit the religious quality of experience, so that that quality will be restored to its genuine purity only when it has been emancipated from all such superstructures. It can readily be seen that this critique of religion is not far removed from that of positivism or of the Hegelian Left. It is especially reminiscent of Feuerbach and his cult of mankind.

Can a genuine "religious experience" be admitted at all? Dewey readily admits that there is much talk, in his day, especially in liberal circles, about religious experience as vouching for the authenticity of certain beliefs and the desirability of certain practices, such as particular forms of prayer and worship. It is even asserted, he grants, that religious experience is the ultimate basis of religion itself. But this claim that religious experience is something unique and specific, that it is a *kind* of experience which can be contradistinguished from aesthetic, scientific, moral and political experience—such a claim Dewey finds to be groundless and even meaningless. Rather "religious" indicates a quality of experience that may belong to any and all of these experiences. It is the exact opposite of that sort of experience that can exist by itself! And nowhere does this come out more clearly than when the intelligent investigator notes that the defenders of religious experience as precisely this distinct and identifiable *kind* of experience proceed forthwith to use *their* definition of religious experience as a justification of belief in a special kind of object and as a basis for a special kind of practical behavior.[3]

[3] "But 'religious' as a quality of experience signifies something that may belong to all these experiences. It is the popular opposite of some type of experience that can exist by itself. The distinction comes out clearly when it is noted that the

It is true, admits Dewey, that certain men claim to have had genuine religious experiences, especially within the Christian religion; it is further true that these men attribute to such experiences effects of crucial importance for the whole orientation of their own lives. The only problem, he retorts, is that if this proves anything, it proves far too much: such experiences are a universal fact, extending to all religions, even those which do not admit a personal God; indeed such experiences are claimed even by men who admit no God at all and have no religion! Such an experience, therefore, cannot be said to provide any experimental proof of the existence of God: "In reality, the only thing that can be said to be 'proved' is the existence of some complex of conditions that have operated to effect an adjustment in life, an orientation, that brings with it a sense of security and peace. The particular interpretation given to this complex of conditions is not inherent in the experience itself. It is derived from the culture with which a particular person has been imbued." [4]

Dewey does not intend to deny the genuineness of this "religious" quality nor yet its importance in life. His aim is simply to contest the interpretation that the religions of the world have given to this quality and this experience: it does not, in fact, prove the existence of a supernatural Being and it admits of a purely naturalistic explanation. The actual religious quality in the experience described by such religions and set apart as something special and *sui generis* is, in actual fact, the *effect* produced, the better adjustment in life and its conditions, *not the manner and cause of its production.* The religious experience could be described as derivative and collateral: it takes place in different persons in a multitude of ways. It is sometimes brought about by devotion to a cause; sometimes by a passage of poetry that opens up a new perspective; sometimes it is the result of philosophical reflection, as in the case of Spinoza who was held in his own day to be an atheist.

The essence of religious experience is a process of adaptation: it belongs within the class of those phenomena of accommodation man effects in the face of changes in his environmental conditions. This process of "accommodation" has two main features: first of all, it affects *particular* modes of conduct, not the entire self; secondly, the process if

---

concept of this distinct kind of experience is used to validate a belief in some special kind of object and also to justify some special kind of practice" (*ibid.*, pp. 10f.). Thus "religion" and "religious" are irreconcilable and there can be nothing in common between the two realms: "The opposition between religious values as I conceive them and religions is not to be bridged" (p. 28). In order to save the religious values, man must free himself from all religion, inasmuch as the religious values can exist and be found solely in the exercise of human experience.

[4] *Ibid.*, p. 13.

mainly *passive*. But, as distinct from the natural processes of adaptation, the religious attitude includes a note of submission. This submission is voluntary, not externally imposed; and as voluntary it is no mere Stoical resolution to endure unperturbed the vicissitudes of fate and fortune. It is more outgoing, more ready and glad, and likewise more active. Dewey specifies that, in calling it voluntary, he does not mean to imply that it depends on a particular resolve or volition. It is a change *of* will conceived as the organic plenitude of our being, rather than any special change *in* will.

It is not *a* religion that brings this change about; but when it occurs, from whatever cause and by whatever means, there is a religious outlook and function. In his description of the origin of religious consciousness and awareness, Dewey reiterates the idealist theory of the creative imagination; but he gives this theory a broadly empirical base, in conformity with the pragmatic method and theory of the origin of religion from the unconscious, proposed by James. As for Schleiermacher, religious consciousness originates from the contemplation of the Universe; but Dewey is considerably more precise and specific. The point of departure is the admission of a considerably more intimate connection than is usually admitted between the imagination and the behavior of the human self as a whole. The idea of the Whole, both of our own personal being and of the universe, is the work of the imagination rather than an idea, properly speaking. Dewey presents a stagewise description of the phases of the process. First, the limited world of our observation and reflection becomes the Universe only by way of the extension and amplification produced by the imagination; it cannot be apprehended in knowledge nor realized in reflection. The complete unification of the self as a Whole is equally impossible of attainment by observation, thought, or practical activity. The *whole* self is an ideal, an imaginative projection. Hence the idea of a thoroughgoing and deep-seated harmonizing of the self with the Universe (here used as a name for the totality of conditions with which the self is connected) operates only through imagination. An "adjustment" possesses the will rather than being an express product of that will. Religionists, says Dewey, have been quite right and entirely justified in thinking of it as an influx from sources beyond conscious deliberation and purpose; this fact, indeed, helps to provide a *psychological* explanation of why this sort of adjustment has so generally been attributed to a supernatural source. Obviously the unification of the self throughout the ceaseless flux of what it does, suffers and achieves, cannot be attained in terms of the self itself! The self is always directed toward something beyond itself and so its own unification depends upon the idea of the integration of the shifting scenes of the world into that imaginative totality we call the Universe.

At this point Dewey has recourse to the synthetic principle of "faith". In this he is operating in the line of empiricist Anglo-Saxon thought and especially in accord with Hume, even as was Whitehead. Faith is not only a principle with a religious value, as the Christian religion asserts; it has a moral and practical import as well. But even apart from any theological context, a distinction must be made between a "speculative" or intellectual belief and a 'justifying faith"; for there is a crucial difference between belief that is a conviction that some object or being exists as a truth for the intellect and belief that is a conviction that some end should be supreme over one's own conduct. Conviction in the moral sense signifies being conquered, vanquished, in our active nature by an ideal end; it signifies the acknowledgement of the rightful claim of that ideal end over our desires and purposes. Such an acknowledgement is practical and not primarily intellectual. Long and arduous reflection may indeed have been involved in arriving at the conviction, but the intellect may still remain unsatisfied. The authority of an ideal over choice and conduct is the authority of an ideal, not of a fact; it is the authority of a truth guaranteed to intellect, not the authority of the status of the one who propounds the truth.

Dewey presents a very extensive analysis of this moral faith, the *Common Faith,* from which his famous essay took its title. It is, in his eyes, the initial psychological nucleus of the origin of religion. It is not easy to grasp the true nature of this faith; it seems to have been still harder for philosophers and theologians to admit that its object is and must remain in the ideal realm; instead they have degraded this ideal by building vast intellectual schemes to prove that such an ideal is real not as an ideal but *as an antecedently existing actuality*. They have failed entirely to observe that in converting moral realities into matters of intellectual assent they have evinced lack of *moral* faith themselves! Faith that something should be in existence as far as lies in our power is changed into the intellectual belief that it is already in existence. And when physical existence does not bear out the assertion, then the physical is subtly changed into the metaphysical. And already the game is up: moral faith has been inextricably tied in with intellectual beliefs about the supernatural. And this is the origin of religion!

Dewey stresses that all he has thus far said does not imply that all moral faith in ideal ends is by virtue of that fact religious in quality. The religious is "morality touched by emotion" only when the ends of moral conviction arouse emotions that are not only intense but are actuated and supported by ends so inclusive that they unify the self. The inclusiveness of the end in relation to both self and the "universe" to which an inclusive self is related is indispensable. And this jibes well with the etymology of "religion" as coming from a root meaning "bound" or "tied". Originally, says Dewey, it meant being tied or bound by vows to a particular way of life; from the Deweyan philosophical point of view, the religious attitude generically signifies being bound through imagination to a *general* attitude, much broader than anything indicated by the adjective "moral" in its usual sense.

But, says Dewey, if we apply the overall conception he has expounded to the dictionary definition of religion as "recognition on the part of man of some unseen higher power as having control of his destiny and as being entitled to obedience, reverence and worship," [5] then the terms used in that definition take on a new significance. The unseen power controlling our destiny then becomes that ideal which in the rational realm takes the place of God. All possibilities, as possibilities, are ideal in character. (Incidentally, these "possibilities" of Dewey seem to us to be quite closely related to the "eternal objects" of Whitehead.) The artist, the scientist, the citizen, the parent, as far as they are actuated by the spirit of their callings, are all controlled by the unseen and sustained by a faith. "For all endeavor for the better is moved by faith in what is possible, not by adherence to the actual." [6] Nor does this faith depend for its moving power upon intellectual assurance or belief that the things worked for must surely prevail and come into embodied existence. The authority of the object to determine our attitude and conduct is based on the intrinsic nature of the ideal. The inherent vice of all intellectual schemes of idealism is that they convert the idealism of action into a system of beliefs about antecedent reality; and from this it is but a short step to the admission of a supernatural Principle. And at this point religion intervenes, exacerbating the grim facts of existence in order subsequently to placate the fear and anguish and the pessimistic and despondent attitudes deriving from them by recourse to this supernatural Being as a refuge and escape from the stern laws of Fate and implacable destiny. Hence the recourse to practices of expiation and propitiation. And, at the other extreme, there arises the irreligious attitude which attributes human achievement and purpose to man in isolation from the world of physical nature and his fellows. But our successes are dependent upon the cooperation of nature. The sense of the dignity of human nature is as religious as is the sense of awe and reverence when it rests upon a sense of human nature as a co-operating part of a larger whole. Thus, natural piety is not necessarily either a fatalistic acquiescence in natural happenings or a romantic idealization of the

[5] This definition Dewey takes from the *Oxford Dictionary* (cf. *A Common Faith*, p. 3).

[6] *A Common Faith*, p. 23.

world; it may rest upon a just sense of nature as the whole of which we are parts, while also recognizing that we are parts that are marked by intelligence and purpose, having the capacity to strive by their aid to bring conditions into greater consonance with what is humanly desirable. Such piety is an inherent constituent of a just perspective in life. This piety can, we must here parenthetically observe, only be defined as a religious stance without any religion behind it, indeed a stance forthrightly against any religion!

The principles entering into this religious perspective are understanding and knowledge. And Dewey makes the downright claim that faith in the continued disclosing of truth through directed cooperative human endeavor is more religious in quality than is any faith in a completed revelation, given once and for all. Faith in the possibilities of continued and religious inquiry does not limit access to truth to any channel or scheme of things. It does not first say that truth is universal and then add there is but one road to it! It does not depend for assurance upon subjection to any dogma or item of doctrine.

This Dewey description of faith as he sees it as a genuinely positive force is quite close to the "philosophical faith" of the Kant-Jaspers tradition and to the religion of humanity proposed by Comte: a religious attitude, divested of all "mythology", and identified with the worship of humanity and science; [7] an attitude that relies on human collaboration to resolve on this earth the problems of truth and existence.

In this positivistic sociology culminating in the ideal goals of a continuous process of mankind, the idea of God and the conviction of his existence are explained as the effect of a misunderstanding and of an illicit extrapolation, to wit, the *identification* of the ideal with a particular Being, especially when that identification makes necessary the conclusion that this Being is outside of nature. It emerges, insists Dewey, when the imagination idealizes existence by laying hold of the possibilities offered to thought and action and projecting them beyond the bounds of nature and human society. But in point of fact the artist, scientific man, or good citizen depends upon what others have done before him and are doing around him; he is an integral part of a process whose advantages he enjoys. The idea of God or of the divine is simply one of the ideal possibilities unified through imaginative realization and projection. But this idea of God or of the divine is also connected with

[7] "It trusts that the natural interactions between man and his environment will breed more intelligence and generate more knowledge provided the scientific methods that define intelligence in operation are pushed further into the mysteries of the world, being themselves promoted and improved in the operation. There is such a thing as faith in intelligence becoming religious in quality" (*ibid.*, p. 26).

all the natural forces and conditions, including man and human association, that promote the growth of the ideal and further its realization. We have here, therefore, neither ideals completely embodied in existence nor yet ideals that are mere rootless, utopian fantasies. For there are forces in nature and society that generate and support the ideals. They are further unified by the action that gives them coherence and solidity. And Dewey proposes, apparently perfectly seriously, that the name "God" be applied to this active union of the ideal and the actual.[8] But he hastens to add that the name is of little importance and is a matter for individual decision. But the fact remains, he insists, that the *function* of this dynamic union, operative in the realm of thought and the realm of action, is identical with the force that has in fact been attached to the conception of God in all the religions that have a spiritual content.

It is this Idea of the dynamic union between the ideal and the actual realm which Dewey wants to see asserted and championed. It is an active and practical union; it is a *uniting,* not something given ready-made in advance. Dewey must be given full credit for his good faith in choosing this strange notion of the unifying principle between the ideal and the actual realms as the best description of God: he is persuaded that atheism and theism (which latter he calls "supernaturalism") share the common fault of considering man in a state of isolation. For, says he, in spite of supernaturalism's reference to something beyond nature,[9] it still conceives of this earth as the moral center of the universe and of man as the apex of the whole scheme of things. It regards the drama of sin and redemption enacted within the isolated and lonely soul of man as the one thing of ultimate importance. Apart from man, nature is held to be either accursed or negligible.

Dewey likewise finds militant atheism to be tainted with a lack of natural piety. It passes far too lightly over the ties binding man to nature that poets have always celebrated. It all too often takes up the stance of man living in an indifferent and hostile world and uttering blasts of defiance. A religious attitude, however, needs the sense of a connection of man, in the way both of dependence and support, with the entire enveloping world that the imagination feels is a universe. And Dewey feels that the use of such words as "God" and "divine" in this whole

[8] "It is this *active* relation between ideal and actual to which I would give the name 'God' " (*ibid.,* p. 51).

[9] It is clear from the entire context of Dewey's thought that the term "supernatural" stands simply for theism in the traditional sense, the theologico-philosophical position that conceives God as a perfect Being, cause of the world and distinct from it and thus "above" or "superior" to it. In no sense does "supernatural" signify for Dewey what is does for traditional Catholic theology when used, e.g. of the gratuitous order of grace.

context may serve a useful function of protecting man precisely from this sense of isolation and from the despair or defiance that could result from it and condemn man to a paralyzed sterility.[10]

It must be noted at once that for Dewey "God" is a functional and symbolic term, with no real antecedent referend. It serves simply to indicate the convergence of those factors of existence that generate and sustain our ideas of the good as a goal and an end to be striven for and exclude a multitude of forces and impulses that at any given time are irrelevant or deleterious to this striving. We are here dealing, therefore, with a psychological expedient, an ideal projection and emergent in the area of value, fulfilling a function of selectivity and concentration.[11]

In Dewey's approach, too, God, or rather the divine, comes into being with man and through man. God is introduced as the principle of that nexus man must actualize with the world and with the society in which he lives in order to realize ideal values. We can see in Dewey still another modification of the Spinozan theme, more specifically a modification of that theme under the influence of Hegel, who seems to have cast a long shadow over the early Dewey.[12] Although Dewey does indeed operate within the framework of the humanistic demands levied by the James-Bradley-Royce tradition, the Deweyan scheme scarcely suffices to afford man any refuge from the corrosion of his ideal ends or to guarantee the substantiation of those values without which man loses all proper meaning and lapses into the status of a mere part of nature. Dewey's assertion of God is based on a foundation far more tenuous than that of his predecessors. It is closer to Fichte's assertion of the moral order of the world as absolute, an assertion which brought down on Fichte's head the charge of atheism, from which he tried in vain to escape by falling back, like Hegel, on a conception of God as *Sein selbst* (Being itself, Being as such). The root cause of Dewey's dilemma is exactly the same

[10] "Use of the words 'God' or 'divine' to convey the union of actual with ideal may protect man from a sense of isolation and from consequent despair or defiance" (*A Common Faith*, p. 53).

[11] Dewey expressly warns against taking this conception as a religion of humanity: "The 'divine' is thus a term of human choice and aspiration. A humanistic religion, if it excludes our relation to nature, is pale and thin, as it is presumptuous, when it takes humanity as an object of worship" (*ibid.*, p. 54).

[12] On Dewey's familiarity with and affinity for the European tradition of philosophy and on the influence upon his thought of German philosophy in particular, cf. E. Baumgarten, *Der Pragmatismus,* R. W. Emerson, W. James, J. Dewey (Frankfurt a. M., 1938), p. 207; "Dewey, on the contrary [as opposed to Emerson and James], was a professional philosopher in the German style. His school was that of Leibniz, Kant, Hegel. He grappled with this European tradition, especially the tradition of German idealism, in the fashion of a self-assured expert, sure of his instruments and of how to use them". Cf. also p. 221; "He did undeniably give a substantially new bias to the Hegelian mentality by his drastic simplification and conventionalization".

as that of the impasse into which Fichte and Hegel likewise worked themselves at a point in their philosophizing quite anterior to any discussion of the God-problem as such: God can be the sure foundation of all else only if being has previously been recognized and admitted as the founding bulwark and sustaining principle of consciousness, only if being has been made the basis of mind. A God who has been reduced to the status of a function of the process of history, which process has in turn been founded upon the human mind,—such a God is a consequent, no longer moving being from its very depths but merely offering a projection of a desire for that unity of the real which man lacks and desires but to which he has forever lost the key by placing being at the mercy of consciousness, of mind.

The root of this "humanistic inversion" of the God-problem is closely related to the vein of English empiricism with its idealist coloring already indicated. But Whitehead had sought in his own way to return to the conceptions of Plato and Aristotle and restate them within the framework of the principle of immanentism. Dewey, on the contrary, vigorously asserts the basic identity of these two philosophies and their common irreconcilability with modern thought. Moreover, he indicts all metaphysical philosophies, right down to and including Hegel and Bradley, for having taught that Ultimate Reality is either perfectly Ideal and Rational in nature, or else has absolute ideality and rationality as its necessary attribute. Hence, Dewey contends, they were all bound to belittle and depreciate sensible reality, becoming and motion. They all thought of change as introducing deficiency and incompleteness and consequently concluded that perfect Being, true and complete Reality, must be changeless and fixed forever.[13] He cites Bradley, "the most dialectically ingenious Absolutist of our own day", as expressing this whole approach perfectly in his phrase: "Nothing that is perfectly real moves." And he insists that Plato and Aristotle were in substantial agreement on the changelessness of the fully realized reality, the divine and ultimate, even though Plato may have taken a pessimistic view of change as mere lapse, while Aristotle took a more complacent view of change as a tendency to realization. Though Aristotle called this fully realized reality Activity or Energy, the Activity knew no change, the energy did nothing. In a waspish figure, Dewey calls it the activity of an army forever marking time and never going anywhere. Immutable, One

[13] "Wherever there is change, there is instability, and instability is proof of something the matter, of absence, deficiency, incompleteness. These are the ideas common to the connection between change, becoming and perishing, and Non-Being, finitude and imperfection. Hence complete and true Reality must be changeless, unalterable, so full of Being that it always and forever maintains itself in fixed rest and repose" (J. Dewey, *Reconstruction in Philosophy* [New York: Henry Holt and Company, 1920], p. 107).

and Self-Identical, this ultimate reality is Total, All-Comprehensive and therefore enjoys complete and eternal Good. It *is* Perfection.

In this metaphysical conception, degrees of knowledge and truth correspond with degrees of reality point by point. Therefore only the Supreme Reality is a totally worthy object of knowledge; hence only pure contemplative knowing is true in itself and sufficient unto itself; and so it is the highest and indeed the only attribute that can be ascribed to God, the Highest Being in the scale of Being. In other words: the abstract ideal has been substituted for the concrete real, the One for the manifold, the divine for the human, the Changeless for the evolving, intelligible abstraction for sensible experience; and the chief function of philosophy becomes that of detaching man from the real world of nature and history, of the things and events that arise and perish, in order to turn his gaze to the intuition of the supernatural and eternal Being. Dewey attributes this conception to Greek and Christian philosophy and accuses it, together with idealism in general, of having gravely distorted man's awareness and notion of the real and likewise of having put all possible obstacles in the path of the progress of science. But science finally triumphed over the traditional ideal that held truth to be found in contemplation. Today, says Dewey the pragmatist, every intelligent human being is entirely persuaded that truth is action, operation, experiment in the various fields of knowledge. The scientist has not to depend on the philosopher; rather it is from science that philosophy itself must take its problems, its concepts and its method. It was under the pressure of modern science and the experimental method that Dewey, to an even greater extent than Whitehead, who still remained a metaphysician after his fashion, severed the last ties with the idealist Absolute to circumscribe the universe within the exclusive bounds of human experience.[14]

Change in the sensible world is no longer conceived, as in Whitehead, as coexisting side by side with the Supreme Being, as a transient and manifold aspect of the One and Changeless Reality. Rather, change becomes itself the ultimate reality in its progressive self-realization and it is upon this reality that the scientist operates, transforming it in conformity with his own plans and goals. And it is only in this process of transforming things by science and technology that man comes to the knowledge of reality: an active organizational conception of knowledge has been substituted for the passive and contemplative attitude of Greek thought and of the various religions, completely sterile all of them, including Christianity itself. And to the degree to which this active conception of knowledge gains the upper hand, men are fired with

[14] On the critique of the metaphysical conception, cf. also J. Dewey, *Experience and Nature* (New York: W. W. Norton & Company Inc., 1929), pp. 412ff.

courage and an aggressive attitude to nature.[15] This is in sharp contrast with the metaphysical and aesthetic conception which is purely passive. Nature now becomes plastic, something to be subjected to human uses. Change is no longer looked upon as a fall from grace, as a lapse from reality, truth and being; it comes to be seen as reality in process of self-perfecting evolution. In the wood and stones and iron which he observes, man is concerned with their fitness to effect certain special changes that he wishes to see accomplished. His attention is directed to the changes they undergo and the changes they make other things undergo so that he may select that combination of changes which will yield him the desired result. Change thus becomes significant of new possibilities and ends to be attained; it becomes prophetic of a better future.

Dewey castigates intellectualist metaphysics as a sourgrapes attitude on the part of men too pusillanimous to make their knowledge a factor in the determination of the course of human events. These men have sought a refuge of complacency in the notion that knowledge is something too sublime to be contaminated by contact with things of change and practice. But the ordinary man has shown a complete disregard for their philosophizing in their ivory towers so totally divorced from reality and life; and they have been banished from any effective participation in public life or the world of affairs, a fate which they have richly deserved.

The proper attitude is exactly the opposite of that adopted by these intellectualists: the objectivity of knowing is a function solely of practice and of action. This is the basic principle of Dewey's theory of education, which has now penetrated into virtually every non-Communist country, especially in the post-World War II period, in the wake of the infiltration of American culture and the American way of life. This theory holds that the structures and objects which science and philosophy set up in contrast to the things and events of concrete daily experience do not constitute a realm apart in which rational contemplation may rest satisfied; it insists rather that they represent the selected obstacles, material means and ideal methods of giving direction to that change which is bound to occur anyway. But Dewey is careful to specify that this change of human disposition toward the world does not mean that man ceases to have ideals, or ceases to be primarily a creature of the imagination. It signifies rather a radical modification in the character and function of the ideal realm which man shapes for himself.

In classical philosophy, the ideal world is essentially a haven in which

[15] "But in the degree in which the active conception of knowledge prevails, and the environment is regarded as something that has to be changed in order to be truly known, men are imbued with courage, with what may almost be termed an aggressive attitude toward nature" (*Reconstruction in Philosophy*, p. 116).

man finds rest from the storms of life. It is an asylum in which he takes refuge from the troubles of existence with the calm assurance that it alone is supremely real. But for Deweyan pragmatism, which holds knowledge to have real existence and validity only to the extent that it is active and operative, the ideal realm ceases to be a kind of Platonic Empyrean and becomes simply that collection of imagined possibilities which serves as inspiration for man's efforts to achieve ever new and higher goals.[16] This "collection of imagined possibilities" again recalls Whitehead's "eternal objects". The idea and the ideal are thus not expelled from the picture nor entirely repudiated or denied; they are conserved as an operative principle in reality. It is simply that the idea is brought down from the suprasensible noumenal world where it previously eked out its abstract existence; it is converted into an "instrumentality of action", a suggestion of something to be done or of a way of doing it. The possibility or idea is employed as a method for observing actual existence; and in the light of what is discovered the possibility takes on concrete existence. It becomes less of a mere idea, a fancy, a wished-for possibility, and more of an actual fact, stimulating invention so that the concrete environment is transformed in the desired direction, idealized in fact and not merely in fancy. The ideal is realized through its own use as a tool or method of inspection, experimentation, selection and combination of concrete natural operations.

It can easily be seen how this approach entirely abolishes all that dualism and conflicting contrast between theory and practice which had plagued both realist and idealist metaphysics. In the pragmatist conception, the sole criterion of knowledge is experimental. With the advent of modern science, says Dewey, a tremendous change has occurred in the interpretation of knowledge. For the experimental sciences, knowledge means a certain kind of intelligently conducted doing; it ceases to be contemplative and becomes in a true sense practical. Hence philosophy too must alter its nature if it wants to survive: it must assume a practical stance; it must become operative and experimental. And this transformation of philosophy entails an enormous change in the conceptions of the "real" and the "ideal". The "real" ceases to be something ready-made and final and becomes that which has to be accepted as the material of change, as the obstructions or the means of certain specific desired changes. "The ideal and rational also cease to be a separate

[16] When the belief that knowledge is active and operative takes hold of men, the ideal realism is no longer something aloof and separate; it is rather that collection of imagined possibilities that stimulates men to new efforts and realizations. It still remains true that the troubles which men undergo are the forces that lead them to project pictures of a better state of things. But the picture of the better is shaped so that it may become an instrumentality of action" (*ibid.*, p. 118).

ready-made world incapable of being used as a lever to transform the actual empirical world, a mere asylum from empirical deficiencies. They represent intelligently thought-out possibilities *of* the existent world which may be used as methods for making over and improving it." [17] Therein lies the essence of the conversion of philosophy from a contemplative to an operative discipline. Dewey indeed contends that a thoroughly and habitually active and operative conception of philosophy would emancipate philosophy from the epistemological puzzles that have so long perplexed and plagued it: [18] for all these puzzles arise in the first place from a conception of the relation of mind and world, subject and object, in knowing, which assumes that to know is to seize upon what is already in existence.

Idealism would be far from ready to accept this panacea of Dewey. For idealism, at least from Hegel on, knowing is identical with thinking.[19] And indeed Dewey himself made considerable use of this identification, even though he did drastically simplify and dilute it.

In any case, Dewey explicitly declares that philosophy cannot "solve" the problem of the relation of the ideal and the real. That is the standing problem of life. And we have seen above that it is, for Dewey, the assignment of the "religious" man as that man sets himself resolutely against both atheism and the religions that cling to the metaphysical Absolute and the supernatural God. Philosophy's first function is the negative and preliminary one of emancipating mankind from the errors which philosophy itself has fostered; but it likewise has the positive assignment of making it easier for mankind to take the right steps in action by making it clear that a sympathetic and integral intelligence brought to bear upon the observation and understanding of concrete social events and forces, can form ideals, that is aims, which shall not be either illusions or mere emotional compensations.[20] This is the final

[17] *Ibid.,* p. 122.

[18] "If knowing were habitually conceived of as active and operative, after the analogy of experiment guided by hypothesis, or of invention guided by the imagination of some possibility, it is not too much to say that the first effect would be to emancipate philosophy from all the epistemological puzzles which now perplex it" (*ibid.,* p. 123).

[19] Cf. e.g., Hegel, *Phänomenologie des Geistes,* Einleitung, especially pp. 71f.

[20] Santayana therefore judges philosophy in Dewey to be an idolatry of an empty symbol, having a purely pragmatic value (George Santayana, "Dewey's Naturalistic Metaphysics," in *The Philosophy of John Dewey,* edited by P. A. Schilpp [New York, 1951], p. 261). And Collins remarks, from the realist point of view: "He accepts at face value the identification between the Hegelian absolute and the God of theistic philosophy. Hence he overlooks the sharp and radical difference between the idealistic *contrast* of the absolute and its relative modes and the theistic distinction of God and finite things" (J. Collins, *God in Modern Philosophy,* p. 274).

conclusion, in the practical order, of this Deweyan philosophy which aims to be a reconciliation of the Baconian principle with the idealist principle, of immediacy and mediation, of experiment and reflection, of the real and the ideal, of the individual and the universal, of fact and value, of experience and reason, of nature and freedom. It is this set of reconciliations that every philosophy worthy of the name should provide and desires to provide; and Dewey tried to do it by pushing both principles to their ultimate extreme in order to make them meet. And they do meet in an unexpected way, but a way that for all that has deep roots in Anglo-Saxon philosophy; for it is, or at least appears to be, the religious realm which is entrusted with the function of bringing them together: God is assigned the role of expressing and making possible the reconciliation. But precisely this ethical postulation of God, like the Kantian one, is nothing but an appearance: [21] in reality, it is man himself who tends in various ways to assign substantiating priority to one dimension of his own disposition over the others; and it is most often the utilitarian dimension!

Any more extensive and multi-dimensional investigation of the "forgetfulness of God" in Anglo-American philosophy would transcend the limits of our present purpose. What we have thus far seen is quite enough to enable us to conclude that the problem of God and immortality, of freedom and value, has never been attacked in any school of European philosophy with the zeal and commitment shown by these last heirs and scions of Baconian and Lockeian empiricism. When empiricism was transported into the European setting, together with rationalism and positivism, it took on its atheistic bias quite speedily and readily, even as it penetrated into the neo-Kantian and even the Hegelian schools. But in the Anglo-Saxon cultural environment, penetrated as it was and is by a deep-seated moralism, empiricism allied itself almost automatically with the idealist principle and posited in God the foundation and substantiation of truth and value. And it should be most carefully noted that, in attributing belief in God to the realm of the imagination (Bergson's *fonction fabulatrice* [myth-making faculty]) or to the Humeian power of "feeling", these philosophers have no intention of belittling the value of that belief nor have they any desire to reduce God to the arid and formalistic Jasperian *Umgreifende* (Encompassing, the

[21] Indicative in this regard is Dewey's rider appended immediately after his statement cited above in Footnote 8 to this section. He adds: "I would not insist that the name *must* be given. There are those who hold that the associations of the term with the supernatural are so numerous and close that any use of the word 'God' is sure to give rise to misconceptions and be taken as a concession to traditional ideas" (*A Common Faith,* p. 51).

Encompassing One); rather they intend to position Him at the very center of life and accord him the status of guarantor of human progress. And by a strange paradox, in this empirically-inspired philosophical approach, it is the ideal that gains the upper hand over the real; and it is feeling rather than abstract reason or the dialectic that discovers the presence and the foundation of the real. It is true, on the other hand, that, as a result of its positioning God in the realm of existence or as a complement of a real that conditions him in the realm of existence, this philosophy likewise was bound to end by confining God, as we have seen it do, within the Hegelian tension of essence and existence, and conceiving Him as immanent in the identity of act and potency, powerless to detach himself from the world and stand out over against it. What is continually emerging is the world itself and man within that world, in a ceaseless striving after new goals. Thus, there was the serious risk that God would eventually be identified, in whole or in part, with matter which would be conceived as the primordial source of every form and power.[22] In any case, to speak of an "existence" of God would amount to a reduction of God to exteriority and particularity and would no longer have any real meaning. It is patent that this desperate effort to salvage God was not going to be able to succeed long range; and the proof of this is that today Anglo-Saxon philosophy (especially the schools of neo-positivism, pragmatism, and their like) has finally aligned itself with the atheistic stands of continental European philosophy.

Dewey's thought can thus be said to represent the culminating balance sheet of Anglo-American philosophy in its effort to keep the empirical principle radically and unflinchingly faithful to the principle of immanentism, an effort which leads to a misunderstanding of the theological dimension, no less inevitable and no less strident than in the metaphysics or rationalism and idealism. The drastic terminal stance of Dewey comes out most clearly in the direct comparison of his own

[22] This is the explicit position, e.g., of Charles Hartshorne: "I hold the doctrine (called 'crazy' by Aquinas) that prime matter, the ultimate potency which all change whatever actualizes, is an aspect of God" (C. Hartshorne, "Santayana's Doctrine of Essence," in *The Philosophy of George Santayana,* edited by P. A. Schilpp [New York, 1951], p. 153). The Aquinas judgment here referred to occurs in *S.T.,* I, q. 3, a. 8. In fact, Santayana makes the basic point about matter: "It is all things in their potentiality, and therefore the condition of all their excellence or possible perfection" and he explicitly accuses idealism of being crypto-materialism (Cf. G. Santayana, *The Realm of Matter; Book Second of Realms of Being* [New York: Charles Scribner's Sons, 1930], p. v. pp. 190ff.). Santayana moreover intends to draw a perfectly clear-cut distinction between the concept of "pure Being" and that of the God of theism (Cf. G. Santayana, *The Realm of Essence; Book First of Realms of Being* [New York: Charles Scribner's Sons, 1927], pp. 58ff.).

philosophy with that of Whitehead which Dewey repeatedly instituted.[23] Dewey is not, in these comparisons, attempting a critique of Whitehead, properly speaking; rather he is paying homage to the common principles and ideals of a fellow-journeyer on that ideal road which has been opened up to man by modern thought.

The following excerpt from one such comparison is instructive and revealing: "Mr. Whitehead says that the task of philosophy is to frame 'descriptive generalizations of experience.' In this, an empiricist should agree without reservation. Descriptive generalization of experience is the goal of any intelligent empiricism. Agreement upon this special point is the more emphatic because Mr. Whitehead is not afraid to use the term 'immediate experience'. Although he calls the method of philosophy that of Rationalism, this term need not give the empiricist pause. For the historic school that goes by the name of Rationalism (with which empiricism is at odds) is concerned not with *descriptive* generalizations but ultimately with *a priori* generalities from which the matter of experience can itself be derived. The contrast between this position and Mr. Whitehead's stands out conspicuously in his emphasis upon immediately existent actual entities. 'These actual entities,' he says, are the final real things of which the world is made up. There is no going behind actual entities. They are the only *reasons* for anything.' The divergence is further emphasized in the fact that Whitehead holds that there is in every real occasion a demonstrative or denotative element that can only be pointed to: namely, the element referred to in such words as 'this, here, now, that, there, then'; elements that cannot be derived from anything more general and that form, indeed, the subject-matter of one of the main generalizations, that of real occasions itself." [24] Whitehead had in fact insisted that "actual entities" and "real occasions" were synonymous.[25]

[23] I am here thinking particularly of Dewey's two essays: "Whitehead's Philosophy" (in John Dewey, *Problems of Men* [New York: Philosophical Library, 1946], pp. 410ff.) and "The Philosophy of Whitehead" (in *The Philosophy of Alfred North Whitehead,* ed. by P. A. Schilpp, pp. 641ff.). Dewey confines his references to Whitehead's works in the latter article almost exclusively to *Adventures of Ideas*: "But in view of the simplicity and completeness with which the gist of Whitehead's doctrine is set forth in this book, I do not regard this limitation as of especial importance in respect to my interpretation and criticism" (John Dewey, "The Philosophy of Whitehead" in *The Philosophy of Alfred North Whitehead,* p. 644, Note 1).

[24] John Dewey, *Problems of Men,* pp. 410f.

[25] Cf. A. N. Whitehead, *Process and Reality,* p. 27. The notion of "actual entity", reminiscent of (but not entirely identical with) the Humeian notion of *impressions,* is further developed by Whitehead in the "twenty-seven Categories of Explanation" (pp. 33ff.).

In order properly to understand this notion of experience, Dewey insists, it must be borne in mind that it is not restricted to the human realm but embraces the whole of nature: everything that characterizes human experience is found in the natural world; conversely, what is found in the natural world is found in human experience, by a kind of transfer or intentional decantation. As examples of the strict correspondence between the two areas, Dewey cites the following: (1) Change is such a marked trait of conscious experience that the latter has been called, somewhat exaggeratedly, a mere flux. Every actual entity in the universe is in process; in some sense *is* process. (2) No two conscious experiences exactly duplicate one another. Creativity and novelty are characteristic of nature. (3) Conscious experience is marked by retention—memory in its broadest sense—and anticipation. Nature also carries on. Every actual occasion is prehensive of other occasions and has objective immortality in its successors. (4) Every conscious experience involves a focus which is the center of a determinate perspective. This principle is exemplified in nature. (5) Every conscious experience is a completely unitary pulse in a continuous stream. The continuity of nature includes atomicity and individualizations of the ongoing stream.

Dewey maintains that this correspondence between the two areas is fundamental to Whitehead's method and system. Whitehead himself has said (and Dewey quotes him verbatim): "Any doctrine that refuses to place human experience outside nature must find in the description of experience factors which enter also into the description of less specialized natural occurrences. If there be no such factors, then the doctrine of human experience as a fact within nature is mere bluff, founded upon vague phrases whose sole merit is a comforting familiarity. We should either admit dualism, at least as a provisional doctrine, or we should point out the identical elements connecting human experience with physical science." [26]

This is a new kind of attempt to find not merely a simple correspondence between knowledge and reality but rather a correspondence between two forms of knowledge, between the experience of the psychical realm and that of the physical: indeed, the very terms used by physics (electron, proton, photon, wave-motion, velocity, hard and soft radiation, chemical elements, matter, empty space, temperature, energy-radiation, etc.) are indicative of qualitative differences between the "occasions" in regard to the way in which each one of them actuates its energy; and these differences are constituted exclusively by the flux or flow of energy, i.e. by the way in which the occasions in question have

[26] A. N. Whitehead, *Adventures of Ideas,* Part III, Chapter XI, p. 237.

inherited their energy from the past. In Whiteheadian terms: in the ideal-real duality, there can be no question of separation or "bifurcation" but only of "dipolarity" of the two orders or areas.

Which of these two aspects, asks Dewey, is primary and leading, and which is secondary and auxiliary? In Whitehead's lengthy systematic analysis, the treatment of this point is a highly complicated one; but Dewey feels that the crucial point is the Platonically-inspired theory of the "eternal objects" and of their relation to the "actual entities", a relation which Whitehead designates by the term "ingression". Now ingression, warns Dewey, suggests an independent and ready-made subsistence of eternal objects, the latter being guaranteed by direct intuition, according to the mathematical model followed by Whitehead. It is at this point that Whitehead speaks of the ingression of the eternal objects into the "actual occasions" or "actual entities".[27] And for this ingression, there is need of a principle that would act selectively in determining what eternal objects ingress in any given immediate occasion; this principle is God.

Dewey remarks, justifiably we feel, on the difficulty of bringing into meaningful relation the order of the "eternal objects" conceived according to the mathematical pattern and the real order which is in flux. He recognizes the positive merit of Whitehead's effort at least to introduce the rather complicated and cumbersome intermediary apparatus of God, harmony, mathematical relations, natural laws, that is required to effect the interweaving of eternal objects and immediate occasions. Dewey feels that the chief difficulties in Whitehead's system arise from precisely this intermediary apparatus required in the interweaving of elements, the interweaving being required only because of the assumption of original independence and not being required if they emerge to serve functionally ends which experience itself institutes. It is precisely because Whitehead has begun by a mathematical method of generalization which implies the primacy of the static element over the dynamic, over process, that he has worked himself into this difficulty.[28]

[27] This is the first of the Categories of Existence: "Actual Entities (also termed Actual Occasions), *or* Final Realities, or *Res Verae*" (A. N. Whitehead, *Process and Reality,* p. 32), to which corresponds the first of the Categories of Explanation: "That the actual world is a process, and that the process is the becoming of actual entities. Thus actual entities are creatures; they are also termed 'actual occasions' " p. 33).

[28] "There is, without doubt, a certain irony in giving to Mr. Whitehead's thought a mathematical interpretation, for that implies, after all, the primacy of the static over process, the latter, upon this interpretation, being limited to immediate occasions and their secondary reactions back into what is fixed by nature; as in the case of the change in Primordial God" (John Dewey, *Problems of Men,* p. 418).

Dewey himself, as we have seen, positions the ideal in the ethico-social realm, thus referring it from the outset to the formative process of human reality. In Dewey's own system there is no longer the split or gulf between the real and the ideal order, from the methodological point of view, that there was in his Anglo-American predecessors, and especially in Whitehead.[29]

But for us there here appears a gulf that is bottomless and unbridgeable, between Dewey's philosophy and even a minimum theistic position. Dewey excludes God entirely as a transcendent Principle. In Dewey's whole system, more drastically than in that of any one of his predecessors, Being has meaning, beginning, evolution and end or goal solely and without remainder within the human reality. And the name of God is but a remnant, a survival or a nostalgic echo from an Age of Gold irretrievably forfeited and gone beyond recall.

[29] Here is Dewey's definitive judgment on Whitehead: "Of one thing I am quite sure. He has opened an immensely fruitful new path for subsequent philosophy to follow, and has accomplished this task by wedding observable facts of physical experience to observable facts of human experience. The result is an almost incomparable suggestiveness on all sorts of topics—in case a mind is not closed to suggestion from a new source. But I am not sure that he does not frequently block and divert his own movements on the road he is opening by subjecting his conclusions to a combination of considerations too exclusively derived from a combination of mathematics with excessive piety toward those historic philosophers from whom he has derived valuable suggestions" (John Dewey, "The Philosophy of Whitehead," in *The Philosophy of Alfred North Whitehead,* edited by P. A. Schilpp [New York: Tudor Publishing Co., 1951], pp. 659f.).

Appendices

I. English Personality Atheism (McTaggart)

The incisive exegete and interpreter of Hegel, Ellis McTaggart (1866-1925), himself a thinker with a strongly developed speculative turn of mind, takes a quite different line from that taken by the predominant group of English idealist protagonists of the finite and created God. He holds that the admission of the existence of God is based on the "desire" that God shall exist; it proceeds from the desire to attain to a good and is thus linked to an attitude toward "change": to the desire that something shall change or else to the desire to preclude a change that is being or may be experienced. This may not be true for all desires, he admits, even though it is true for many of them. It seems that there are some cases in which desire has no relation to change.

McTaggart discusses the problem as to whether desire has a necessary relation to change. In the course of this discussion he makes the following dialectical analysis of the desire for God: "Take the case of a man who believes that God exists. If he accepts the usual theistic view of God's existence, he will believe that it is impossible that God should ever cease to exist. A desire for God's existence cannot, for such a man, be a desire for a change, since he believes that God exists. Nor can it be a desire to resist change, since any change in the fact of God's existence would be impossible. But cannot such a man have a desire for God's existence? It seems to me that he certainly can. If he holds God's existence to be good, or to be advantageous to him, and if he desires whatever is good, or whatever is to his own advantage, then he will desire God's existence. Or, again, he may desire it ultimately, and without a reason" (Ellis McTaggart, *The Nature of Existence,* ed. by C. D. Broad [Cambridge, 1927], Vol. II, ch. XL, § 448, p. 137).

Thus far, McTaggart's discussion of the God-problem has been merely in the order of a phenomenologico-ontic example, indirectly cited. But later in the same work, McTaggart treats expressly of God and immortality. He asserts that neither God nor immortality can enter into the intentional complex of "existence" since the qualities or characteristics proper to God (*personality, transcendence* and *goodness*) are in conflict with the requirement of existence. And he proves this as follows:

"Personality is the quality of being a self, and we have already discussed what is meant by a self. In including supremacy in the definition of the quality of deity, I do not mean that a being should not be called a God unless he is omnipotent, but that he must be, at the least, much more powerful than any other self, and so powerful that his volition can affect profoundly all else that exists. In including goodness, I do not mean that a being should not be called a God unless he is morally perfect, but that he must be, at the least, more good than evil" (p. 176). And McTaggart insists that it is entirely illegitimate to say that God can be conceived impersonally: personality is an essential attribute of that reality that is called God; impersonal conceptions are but verbal surrogates of God and the idea of God.

Such is the current meaning of God in theology and in ordinary language; in philosophy, however (by which we must take McTaggart to mean modern philosophy), the meaning of God has a much broader scope. In "philosophy" (McTaggart specifically mentions Spinoza and Hegel) everything that exists is said to be God, provided only that it possesses some sort of unity and is not a mere aggregate, conglomerate or sheer chaos. If the term "God" be given this meaning, then everyone, except perhaps the skeptics, admit the existence of God. But in the event, McTaggart protests, the God-problem becomes trivial. His conclusion: "The important question is not whether there is a God, but what sort of nature he, or it, possesses" (p. 177). This meaty observation we draw to the attention of all those—and they are legion—who claim to be writing philosophy and the history of philosophy but whose good intentions are by no means equalled by the consistency of their principles.

McTaggart's overall conclusion is that there is a drastic difference between the theological conception of God and the philosophical one: for philosophy God is the Whole, the All and the Absolute, hence modern philosophy is intrinsically atheistic, because, remarks McTaggart, the Whole and the Absolute can be simply the World itself in its complex totality.

Resuming his analysis, McTaggart sharply contests, against the claims of the finitistic theists, the possibility (from the point of view of modern thought) of any relation between God and the world, especially the relationship of creation in the sense in which theology understands creation (pp. 178ff.) or the relationship of Providence (p. 181). As for the famous argument for God's existence drawn from the order of the universe, McTaggart dismisses it as meaning only that the cosmos is not a chaos, a statement surely not requiring for its substantiation the positing of a personal transcendent and independent God (pp. 184ff.). The denial of personal immortality is a necessary consequence of all this: immortality is simply the eternity, the everlastingness of the universal mind.

McTaggart's conception is thus perfectly orthodox Spinozism or Hegelianism (On McTaggart's complete agreement with Spinoza, cf. his own statement on p. 187 and the pertinent note 1. On his agreement with Hegel, cf. his brilliant analyses: "The Personality of the Absolute," in *Studies in Hegelian Cosmology* [Cambridge, 1901], pp. 56ff.; and *Studies in the Hegelian Dialectic* [Cambridge, 1896], especially pp. 135ff.).

Knudson is therefore quite justified in designating McTaggart's orthodox Hegelianism as "atheistic personalism". Knudson sums up thus: "There is therefore, according to McTaggart, no God. Nothing exists but persons connected in a unity. Beyond them and independent of them there are no real beings of any kind . . . Such a view of the world is manifestly personalistic in spite of his atheism" (A. C. Knudson, *The Philosophy of Personalism* [Boston University Press, 1949], p. 22). And McTaggart's atheistic personalism foreshadows some of the main contentions of the atheistic humanism of our own days.

II. The Finite God and Catholic Theology

The attempt of the Catholic, W. E. Stokes, to effect a synthesis of Whitehead's absolute evolutionism and Thomist theism seems to us more unwarranted than daring (Cf. W. E. Stokes, "Whitehead's Challenge to Theistic Realism," *The New Scholasticism* 38 [1964], pp. 3ff.). Stokes claims that the synthesis is easy enough to effect provided it be admitted that God, even while remaining immutable and transcendent, can yet have a "real relation" to the world; and such a real relation is in turn possible, if only the naturalistic Greek notion of God as *esse* be abandoned and the notion of God as loving freedom be adopted instead.

Others, such as Daniel W. Williams, have taken the opposite line and remarked that, according to Whitehead, God's first relation to the world (i.e. his relation as "primordial nature") is "by *not acting*": God acts by being. He is the order to which everything must conform if it wants to be at all. The Primordial Nature is simply what is and nothing can be anything in particular without conforming to that order. No specific action is accomplished by the primordial nature, it simply sets the limits to what any action can be. God's action as "Consequent Nature" is to be apprehended in feeling. Thus the specific response of God to the world becomes a constitutive function of the world. (Cf. Daniel W. Williams, "How Does God Act?: An Essay in Whitehead's Metaphysics," in *The Hartshorne Festschrift, Process and Divinity,* edited by William L. Reese & E. Freeman [Lasalle, Illinois, 1964], pp. 170ff.).

W. A. Christian reduces the quite complex elements entering into Whitehead's conception of God to three main points, as follows:

1. Our experience is considered as being a succession of moments.
2. This complex of experience is a chain of actual occasions.
3. The source of the subjective aspirations of these occasions is an

actual primordial and eternal entity, whose true and proper name is God. (Cf. W. A. Christian, "The Concept of God as Derivative Notion," in *The Hartshorne Festschrift,* p. 193. In this essay, Christian further specifies and amends the interpretation of Whitehead he presented in his major work: *An Interpretation of Whitehead's Metaphysics,* [New Haven: Yale University Press, 1959], pp. 292ff., 353.).

But we are persuaded (and Christian himself seems to admit it) that Whitehead's position, whether understood within the framework of that overall complex of Anglo-Saxon philosophy to which it belongs, or interpreted in terms of its own internal structure, ends by binding God to the world not only in the logical order of knowing (as does St. Thomas) but also in the real order as a mutual relation with the world. Both God and the world are self-transcending and each is involved (immanent) in concresence. (Cf. W. A. Christian, "Whitehead's Explanation of the Past," in *A. N. Whitehead, Essays on his Philosophy,* [Englewood Cliffs, N.J.: Prentice-Hall, 1963], pp. 99f.).

We consider Andrew Reck to have been entirely justified in characterizing this conception as "panpsychism" and "panentheism", inasmuch as the fundamental metaphysical attributes can in some sense be predicated interchangeably of God and the world alike. Both can be said to be eternal, temporal, conscious, cognitive, inclusive of the world, possessing all things as constituents (Andrew J. Reck, "The Philosophy of Charles Hartshorne," in *Studies in Whitehead's Philosophy,* Hague, 1961] pp. 101f.).

It is not difficult to trace the dominant attitude of this panpsychist, panvitalistic conception through the increasingly complex forms it assumes in James, Royce and Bradley, right up to and including the impressive edifice of Whitehead-Hartshorne: always it is the same metaphysic of English deism, historicizing God, immersing Him in the world; always there is present, too, the drastic evolutionistic principle of the infinite progress of the cosmos and of life.

III. The Humanist Manifesto of American Atheism

Parallel to the sociologico-politically based atheism that spread over Europe under the impulse of idealism and Marxism, there developed in the English-speaking countries and more especially in the USA a cultural movement of broader scope, called Humanism or Neo-humanism. Starting from the position of pragmatism, it ended in a denial of God and immortality substantially as radical as that of the other (European) atheism and proclaimed the *Kingdom of Man* as the only ultimate reality. The difference between Marxist-Leninist atheism and this American atheism lies mainly in the fact that the Neo-humanists held that the religion of man and humanity should be substituted for the religion of God. This was precisely the serious inconsistency for which Lenin had reproved Gorky and with which Marx had earlier reproached Feuerbach.

Religion is presented by this Neo-humanist school "as consciousness of the highest social values". God is relegated to the status of a mere "symbol" of such values and faith in God is nothing but faith in man. It is therefore not surprising to read the following definition of God by E. S. Ames, one of the most zealous protagonists of the Neo-humanist movement: ". . . God is not a superhuman personal or superpersonal being, but simply the reality of the world, in certain of its aspects and functions, *personified and idealized*—that is, the world, or the good in the world, treated *as if* it were an ideal Person" (cited by Douglas C. Macintosh, "Contemporary Humanism" in *Humanism, Another Battle Line,* edited by William P. King, [Nashville, 1931], p. 46).

In 1933 there was published in the USA a *Humanist Manifesto,* which is substantially a profession of anthropological atheism. This Manifesto is an important document even today, despite the obviously dated insistence on the retention of the term "religion" used in a way and a context that can only arouse, in 1968, a queasy but well-founded suspicion of a combination of hypocrisy and ingenuousness. This *Manifesto* should serve as a salutary warning to those American Christians (Catholics in particular) who would still like to find some point of contact between neo-evolutionism and Christian thought. We present here the most important sections of the text of this document, as published by A. H. Dakin, in his *Man the Measure,* Essay on Humanism as Religion, Princeton University Press, 1939, pp. 50-55:

"The time is come for widespread recognition of the radical changes ni religious beliefs throughout the modern world. The time is past for mere revision of traditional attitudes. Sciences and economic changes have disrupted the old beliefs. Religions the world over are under the necessity of coming to terms with new conditions created by vastly increased knowledge and experience. In every field of human activity, the vital movement is now in the direction of a candid and explicit humanism . . .

"There is great danger of a final, and we believe fatal, identification of the word *religion* with doctrines and methods which have lost their significance and which are powerless to solve the problem of human living in the Twentieth Century. Religions have always been means for realizing the highest values of life. Their end has been accomplished through the interpretation of the total environing situation (theology or world view), the senses of value resulting therefrom (goal or ideal), and the technique (cult) established for realizing the satisfactory life.

"Today man's larger understanding of the universe, his scientific achievements, and his deeper appreciation of brotherhood have created a situation which requires a new statement of the means and purposes of religion. Such a vital, fearless, and frank religion capable of furnishing adequate social goals and personal satisfactions may appear to many people as a complete break with the past. While this age does owe a vast debt to the traditional religions, it is none the less obvious that any religion that can hope to be a synthesizing and dynamic force for today must be shaped for the needs of this age . . . We therefore affirm:

"1. Religious humanists regard the universe as self-existing and not created.

"2. Humanism believes that man is a part of nature, that he has emerged as the result of a continuous process.

"3. Holding an organic view of life, humanists find that the traditional dualism of mind and body must be rejected.

"4. Humanism recognizes that man's religious culture and civilization . . . are the product of gradual development due to his interaction with his natural environment and with his social heritage . . .

"5. Humanism asserts that the nature of the universe depicted by modern science makes unacceptable any supernatural or cosmic guarantees of human values . . . Religion must formulate its hopes and plans in the light of the scientific spirit and method.

"6. We are convinced that the time is passed for theism, deism, modernism, and the several varieties of new thought. Religion consists in those actions, purposes and experiences which are humanly significant. Nothing human is alien to the religious. It includes labor, art, science, philosophy, love, friendship, recreation . . . The distinction between the sacred and the secular can no longer be maintained.

"8. Religious humanism considers the complete realization of human personality to be the end of man's life and seeks its development and fulfillment in the here and now.

"9. In place of the old attitudes involved in worship and prayer the humanist finds his religious emotions expressed in a heightened sense of personal life and in a cooperative effort to promote social well-being. . . . It follows that there will be no uniquely religious emotions and attitudes of the kind hitherto associated with belief in the supernatural.

"11. Man will learn to face the crises of life in terms of his knowledge of their naturalness and probability . . .

"12. Believing that religion must work increasingly for joy in living, religious humanists aim to foster the creative in man and to encourage achievements that add to satisfactions of life.

"13. Religious Humanism maintains that all associations and institutions exist for the fulfillment of human life . . . Certainly religious institutions . . . must be reconstituted as rapidly as experience allows, in order to function effectively in the modern world.

"14. . . . The goal of Humanism is a free and universal society in which people voluntarily and intelligently cooperate for a common good.

"15 and last: We assert that Humanism: will:

"(a) affirm life rather than deny it.

"(b) seek to elicit the possibilities of life, not flee from it;

"and

"(c) endeavor to establish the condition of satisfactory life for all, not merely for the few . . .

"So stand the theses of religious humanism.

"Though we consider the religious forms and ideas of our fathers no longer adequate, the quest for the good life is still the central task of mankind.

"Man is at last becoming aware that he alone is responsible for the realization of the world of his dreams, that he has within himself the power of its achievement. He must set intelligence and will to the task."

The definition of "Humanism" given by C. F. Porter, the drafter of the *Manifesto,* is rather wooly: "Humanism is faith in the supreme value and self-perfectibility of human personality" (*ibid.,* p. XI). Among the signatories were: John Dewey, E. A. Burtt, John H. Randall, Roy W. Sellers.

The first heralds of this movement were W. James and C. S. Schiller and perhaps F. C. Peirce. Two University groups belong to the movement: the Columbia Family and the Chicago Family. Both seem to have or at least show more horror at the term "atheism" than at the reality behind that term. This atheistic humanism takes as its point of departure Protagoras' principle: "Man is the measure of all things." In modern thought, it borrows chiefly from the system of Fichte, attributing to the Ego the assignment of positing itself, an assignment which many humanists consider to be the essential task of man (J. A. Fagginger, *Humanism States its Case* [Boston, Mass., 1933], p. 4). This individualistic conception is somewhat artifically set over against Marxist collectivism as human culture in opposition to machine culture! (p. 128).

A more recent account by C. Lamont fully bears out our own diagnosis: the new Humanism (which is proclaimed as "the real American philosophy") is presented as a synthesis of scientism, materialism and vitalism, which makes aesthetic experience the cardinal human experience. It leaves no dualisms of any kind whatever: thinking is as natural a process as walking or breathing; science has eliminated the problem of God and immortality (Cf. C. Lamont, *Humanism as a Philosophy* [New York, 1949], pp. 19ff., 28ff., 145ff.).

America, too, has thus seen the transition from an ambiguous theism to a radical humanism which is the stance proper to that positive atheism which stems from the theoretically more consistent tradition of European philosophy. It is therefore not surprising to find a philosopher of liberal leanings, like Morris R. Cohen, making an explicit profession of atheism at a convention of the American Philosophical Association (Cf. E. S. Brightman, *The Problem of God* [New York, 1930], p. 21). Cohen is devastatingly consistent in his rebuke to those who would desupernaturalize religion, especially Christianity, and then try to reconcile this desuperaturalized remnant with modern philosophy: "In the first place, I cannot subscribe to your view, now fashionable, which associates religion with something vaguely philanthropic divorced from supernatural dogmas. That seems to me a woeful confusion which honest men should reject with all their might. The great historic religions cannot be divorced from their supernatural teachings. No one, it seems to me, can rightfully say that he does not believe in the divinity of Christ or in the efficacy of prayer, baptism and other historic rituals. To say that, it seems to me, involves a method of interpretation of historic documents which would make anything mean anything else. I see no earthly advantage in pursuing such a method" (Letter of December 16, 1934, to Fred Reustle, cited in L. Cohen Rosenfeld, *Portrait of a Philosopher:* Morris R. Cohen, in Life and Letters [New York, 1962], p. 213).

One of the most brilliant and well-known expositions of this Humanism is the famous 1929 essay of Walter Lippmann, *A Preface to Morals* (new edition, Boston: The Beacon Press, 1960), in which the name of God is still retained but only as a "supreme symbol" of the supreme beatitude: "as the highest good at which they [modern man] might aim" (p. 325).

Dewey's disciple, C. Lamont, has presented the best philosophical analysis of this atheistic humanism in his *The Illusion of Immortality* (New York, 1958 [3]). He urges a forthright and candid acceptance of death as an inevitable fact (echoing, on this point, the famous Italian philosopher Benedetto Croce). In the conclusion of this book, to which Dewey himself gave his approval in a Preface, Lamont insists that this straightforward acceptance of death reduces death to a triviality unworthy of our concern: "It liberates all our energy and time for the realization and extension of the happy potentialities of this good earth. It engenders a hearty and grateful acceptance of the rich experiences
It engenders a hearty and grateful acceptance of the rich experiences attainable in human living amid an abundant Nature" (p. 278. Cf. p. IX).

PART VII

FREEDOM AS AN ACTIVE DENIAL OF GOD IN EXISTENTIALISM

Prefatory Note

That existentialism which might be called the "latest style in philosophy" must be credited with having defended freedom as such against the frenzy of exteriority and collectivism into which positivist naturalism and Marxist dialectics have plunged. The existentialists have in fact traced freedom back to, and buttressed it upon, the radical demand of the *cogito* itself for total spontaneity. Therefore, this existentialist philosophy is structurally atheistic from the outset—whatever some of its mystically inclined protagonists may think [1]—and in this respect French existentialism must be credited with model consistency as opposed to the systematic inconsistencies of German existentialists who are still tied to Kant and idealism. Moreover, the French existentialists have been stimulated to this very consistency by their own national tradition of philosophy that goes back from Bayle to the giants of 18th-century Enlightenment thought, who had already roughed out a substantial amount of the outline of the modern world and of man living in that world as alone responsible for his own destiny. It is French existentialism that has effected, by its explicit return to the *cogito* of Descartes, a greater radicalization of the atheist bias of Hegelianism than has German existentialism which seems to commence with Schopenhauer and especially with Nietzsche.[2]

But the trenchant clarity of the French and the tormented problem-pondering of the Germans converge and merge into that Janus-faced countenance that is the visage of so much of the present-day world. And the ambiguity of present-day existentialism lies primarily in the overt and deliberate obfuscation of Kierkegaardian existence, which as such

[1] We here have in mind the philosophies of Le Senne and Lavelle. Both have an idealist background and have remained substantially extraneous to the Kierkegaardian notion. So has Marcel, despite his great literary renown. Marcel seems to have been inspired and influenced by the "realist idealism" of the later Schelling. Hovering perpetually on the border-line between phenomenology and ontology, Marcel's thought can never really settle down.

[2] For an exposition of existentialism as derived from Kierkegaard and an explanation of where it deviates from him, the reader is referred to C. Fabro, *Dall'essere all'esistente* (Brescia, 1957). Cf. also C. Fabro, *Storia della filosofia,* Vol. II (Rome, 1959 [2]), pp. 839ff.

was totally anchored in God. This existence is submerged in the finitude of historical consciousness in the Kant-Hegel-Nietzsche tradition in Jaspers, in the Kant-Hegel-Nietzsche-Hölderlin tradition in Heidegger, and in the Descartes-Hegel-Feuerbach-Marx-Freud tradition in Sartre and the restless tidal flux of French existentialism. Atheist existentialism with its centrifugal displacement of being and freedom into the radical contingency of the individual, constitutes to an even greater and more drastic extent than dialectical materialism the ultimate and total disintegration of the principle of immanentism and the manifest proclamation of the meaningless triviality of man's being and his destiny.

The history of the development of the modern *cogito* principle is precisely this self-certification of human freedom, appropriating its own spheres of power and entrenching itself resolutely within the confines of its own primordial generative force. This thrust or inclination to disintegrate the *cogito* into the *volo* had been inhibited or masked by the *Begriff* (concept) and the Absolute Idea in Hegel; but it came out full force in the absolute voluntarism of Schopenhauer and of Nietzsche who is the forefather of existentialism or more precisely of the actuation of the atheistic bias of modern existentialism. Existentialism does indeed claim descent from the "great Christian" Kierkegaard and it insists that it is attempting to restore to the individual the freedom that had been conferred by metaphysical idealism upon the Whole or the All in the flux of history; but equally obviously this existentialist philosophy plunges the new category of existence totally into the confining bell-jar of immanentism; and it has in it as much of the old as the new, more in fact, especially the dialectic of consciousness variously compounded from Kant and the idealists (especially Hegel) and freed from all theological tether.[3] The *Lebensphilosophie* was of crucial importance in this new and decisive phase of the "atheistic decantation" of the modern *cogito*. It is no mere coincidence that the twin giants of German existentialism, Jaspers and Heidegger, distilled their own inquiry into being out of reflection upon the person and works of Nietzsche. And Nietzsche continues in a direct line from Schopenhauer in his disintegrative conversion of the *cogito* into the *volo*.

The real meaning and importance of Schopenhauerian atheism has been brought out expertly by Nietzsche in a famous passage of *The Joyful Wisdom*, a passage that ought to give the racist fanatics pause, Nazi and post-Nazi alike! [4] Nietzsche is trying to clarify what is the

[3] On the obfuscation of Kierkegaard's Socratico-Christian "existence" notion on the part of German speculative existentialism, cf. our *Dall'essere all'esistente*, pp. 337ff.

[4] F. Nietzsche, *Die fröhliche Wissenschaft*, Book V, § 357; *Gesammelte Werke*, Musarionausgabe, Vol. XII (Munich, 1924), pp. 285ff.; *Nietzsche's sämmtliche*

innermost essence of the German soul; and his conclusions are not flattering. First of all, he insists that the main positive contributions of the great German thinkers (Leibniz, Kant, Hegel) were not original but rather had been current in European thought even before them. Then he accuses the Germans of having tried instantly to attenuate and impede the development of everything new and positive that they had thus inherited. Nietzsche asks: Were the German philosophers really *German* philosophers? And the pith of his reply is that they were only partly so: first of all, because the master-ideas of a Leibniz, a Kant or a Hegel, could easily have been discovered by non-German thinkers and some of these ideas had in fact been discovered already by non-Germans; then, furthermore, because the German thinkers above-named had not yet probed the German soul to its depths. Therefore, as philosophers, they were not really German.

The same must be said, Nietzsche contends, about Schopenhauer. And it is here that we encounter the leitmotif of atheism: "The event *after* which this problem was to be expected with certainty, so that an astronomer of the soul could have calculated the day and the hour for it—namely, the decay of the belief in the Christian God, the victory of scientific atheism—is a universal European event, in which all races are to have their share of service and honor. On the contrary, it has to be ascribed precisely to the Germans—those with whom Schopenhauer was contemporary—that they delayed this victory of atheism longest and endangered it most. Hegel especially was its retarder *par excellence,* in virtue of the grandiose attempt which he made to persuade us at the very last of the divinity of existence, with the help of our sixth sense, "the historical sense". As philosopher, Schopenhauer was the *first* avowed and inflexible atheist we Germans have had: his hostility to Hegel had here its motive. The non-divinity of existence was regarded by him as something understood, palpable, indisputable; he always lost his philosophical composure and got into a passion when he saw anyone hesitate and beat about the bush here. It is at this point that his thorough uprightness of character comes in: unconditional, honest atheism is precisely the *preliminary condition* for his raising the problem, as a final and hardwon victory of the European conscience, as the most prolific act of two thousand years' discipline to truth, which in the end no longer tolerates the *lie* of the belief in a God." [5]

Nietzsche therefore praises Schopenhauer as a thinker of heroic integ-

---

Werke, ed. K. Schlechta, Vol. II (Munich: Hanser, 1956), pp. 225ff. English translation by Kurt F. Reinhardt, *Joyful Wisdom* (New York: Frederick Ungar Publishing Co., 1964), pp. 305ff.

[5] *Ibid.,* ed. Musarion XII, p. 287; ed. Schlechta II, p. 227; Reinhardt, pp. 307f.

rity, who did not hesitate to go to the ultimate extreme of that pessimism which is atheism in act, radical and irreparable. But even Schopenhauer, insists Nietzsche, raised this question as a good European, not as a German. And Nietzsche expresses open distrust of all nationalism in philosophy.[6]

The point of chief interest to us in this Nietzsche passage is the unique position ascribed by Nietzsche to Schopenhauer in the evolution of modern thought, in the explicitation of the essential atheism of the principle of immanentism. For this purpose, Schopenhauer was satisfied simply to take Kant, paying no attention to the dialectical maunderings of transcendental philosophers such as Fichte, Schelling and Hegel, all of whom he heartily detested. Kant was enough if only Kant were forced back to the very core and center of his own principle and freed from internal contradictions. The only reality of which we can speak is the universe of sensible phenomena; such phenomena, which constitute the world as our *idea* (*Vorstellung*), are to be taken for what they are or appear to be, without posing any questions about the *whence,* the *whither* or the *why.* There is no thing-in-itself except the will, which mirrors itself in the Idea, remaining in itself unconscious: it is a blind and irresistable thrust appearing first in vegetable and animal life and then unfolding itself in the world of the Idea. Will is thus essentially a *Will-to-Life,* the thing-in-itself, the integral substance, the essence of the world, whereas sensible life, the visible world, the phenomenon is but the mirror of the will. Thus, since the phenomenon is the correlate of the thing-in-itself, so is the body the correlate of consciousness, of the mind as will, in a relationship of mutual and inseparable conjunction. The basic error of all systems hitherto has been the refusal or failure to recognize that will and matter are correlative, that the former exists only for the latter and the latter is only the reflection of the former, that they are in fact the same thing but viewed from opposite sides.[7] Nietzsche was thus perfectly right in designating Schopenhauer the real and radical exponent of the atheism of immanentism.

The Will assumes in Schopenhauer's system that "foundation" status which it had implicitly in Kant and which became explicit in transcendental idealism, especially in Schelling (as Heidegger often recalls), but which had always been inhibited by the system and frustratingly imprisoned in a metaphysics of the Aboslute. And it must also be borne in mind

[6] Here Nietzsche expressly denounces the "Deutschland über alles" as "a principle sufficiently unphilosophical" (Musarion XII, p. 290; Schlechta II, p. 229; Reinhardt, p. 310).

[7] Cf. A. Schopenhauer, *Die Welt als Wille und Vorstellung,* Book IV, 54; *C. W.,* ed. Frauenstädt, Vol. II (Leipzig, 1916), pp. 325ff.; *Ergänzungen zum ersten Buch,* Ch. I; ed. Frauenstädt, Vol. III, pp. 18f.

that, with the total disintegration of immanentism into atheism, the Schopenhauerian "Will" becomes in essence "cosmic", consciousness comes to be equivalent to "worldliness" and is defined substantially as a relation to the world, in a surprising anticipation of the Heideggerian *In-der-Welt-sein* (being-in-the-world). This means that consciousness, the mind, in its self-actualization as Will, must resolve itself into, and become identified with, the World as Will and Idea; and this resolution and identification must be a total one, without any remainder whatsoever. It must dissolve the cognition of self into the cognition of the other: "The only total knowledge of itself that the Will possesses is the Idea in its totality, the totality of the world of intuition. This world is its own objectivity, its own revelation, its own mirror." [8]

This in turn means that the act of awareness, the act of knowledge is reduced to a simple "standing at gaze" (Hegel's *reines Zusehen*); and the mind is the "camera blind spot" in this whole operation, for man simply takes cognizance of the Will which is the essence of the world. This is the only thing that counts: hence the denial of any world proper to the spirit and of every form of transcendence, which is repudiated under the generic pejorative designation of Platonism. We are persuaded that the crux of the whole matter is this: the principle of immanentism can be catalytically metamorphosed at any moment (and has been several times, as we have seen, in the evolution of modern thought) into radical atheism. It does not matter at all what line is being taken in the development of the principle; the catalysis occurs and the metamorphosis follows as soon as the principle of immanentism is forced back to its foundation and conceived as primordial and therefore exclusively and absolutely unconditioned. And this is precisely what is done by the *cogito* or the *percipio* or the *volo,* or indeed any other mental act, when that act is taken as primordial.

[8] A. Schopenhauer, *Die Welt als Wille und Vorstellung,* Book II, 29, p. 196.

1
The "Death of God" in the Vitalistic Irrationalism of Schopenhauer and Nietzsche

As long as it had remained faithfully submissive to the *cogito,* as a principle of cognition and guarantee of certitude, the principle of consciousness had had to have recourse to auxiliary hypotheses in order to recover that content of the act of cognition which the initial doubt had crippled or banished. This ambiguity had enabled rationalism even to delude itself that it was recovering God and reinstating him as the foundation of the processes of thought. But this very ambiguity clamored for a clarification, a clarification which Kant provided by his unflinching attribution of the realm of certitude to the Practical Reason or the active Ego (Freedom); and this, exalted to the status of the Absolute, was variously developed in the idealism of Fichte, Schelling, Hegel.[1]

Feuerbach opened the way for the transition of the Hegelian absolute Concept (= Will) into the will of sensible man (who in turn becomes collective economic man in Marx). In a parallel thrust, Schopenhauer and Nietzsche in his wake, proclaimed pure will to be the essence of being and thing-in-itself and to be the transcendental assignment of man: being metamorphoses into a will-to-life, a will-to-will, a will-to-power (*Wille zum Leben, Wille zum Willen, Wille zur Macht*). The objectivization of being as "primordial will" (*Urwille*) thus resolves itself into the forms and modes of this will, in accord with the title of Schopenhauer's chief work, *Die Welt als Wille und Vorstellung* (The World as Will and Idea).[2] The Will thus becomes the "primordial being" (*Urwesen*) and the "primordial source of that which is" (*Ur-*

[1] Cf. C. Fabro, *Hegel; la dialettica* (Brescia, 1960), pp. LXXXIVff.

[2] H. Hasse, *Schopenhauer* (Munich, 1926), pp. 212ff. presents a quite knowledgeable and objective exposition from the theoretical point of view.

quelle des Seienden), the prime mover of all activity. This Will has neither goal nor end outside of itself and its action. It is henceforth pointless and even meaningless to try to discover the "why", the "whence" and the "wherefore" of this activity. Its becoming is the everlasting flux of its action in the world, its striving to transcend itself in ever more perfect forms and to entrench itself as a "will-to-life" in the world. It is therefore "the supremely real, the innermost nucleus of reality itself" (*das Allerrealste, der Kern der Realität selbst*). And so we have here a return to the cosmic monism of the ἓν καὶ πᾶν (the One and All), in terms of the total compenetration of mind and being in the Will. Not only is theism henceforth untenable; even transcendental pantheism is rendered meaningless. Schopenhauer accepts the substance of Feuerbach's critique of theological idealism, with a slight modification: theology is, for Schopenhauer, not anthropology but rather anthropologism! The conscious and professed destination of this radical immanentism is *atheism,* which must be here understood not as a successor to theism but rather as claiming the "right of prior occupancy"! Thus the *cogito,* having become sheer Will and willing, is here in process of transformation into the "dynamic character of the essence of the world",[3] which is the version of the modern principle of immanentism propounded by Schopenhauer.

For Nietzsche, in turn, atheism becomes the point of departure: [4] it is in fact the starting point of the new thrust of the principle of immanentism; modern man has lost the sense of the reality of God and the imposing but arrogant Hegelian theology represents simply the "final obstacle" in the way of the advent of forthright and radical atheism. Nietzsche's thought unfolds within the framework of this special "experience" that he felt within himself and proclaimed to the point of self-laceration. Consequently this Nietzschean thought develops not in deductive form but rather in the form of an analysis of the drama of the modern mind which has condemned itself to self-motion and self-structuring, to positing the denial of God as the basis for the assertion of man.

Nietzsche thus begins from Schopenhauer, but his avowed aim is the formation of the new man who in turn will mold the future. For this reason, Nietzsche constitutes the definitive moment of transition, not to

[3] Cf. G. Siegmund, *Der Kampf um Gott* (Berlin, 1957²), pp. 228f.

[4] M. Reding claims that the reading of F. A. Lange's famous *Geschichte des Materialismus* induced in Nietzsche a profound change of heart toward the influence of his predecessor Schopenhauer (cf. M. Reding, "Nietzsches Verhältnis zur Religion, Christentum und Katholizismus," in *Festschrift K. Adam* [Düsseldorf, 1952], pp. 282ff.). But it is Heidegger, as we shall see, who has done most to clarify the divergence between Nietzsche and Schopenhauer.

genuine existentialism, which had been expounded almost a half century previously by Kierkegaard in controversy with Hegel and the bumptious Schopenhauer himself, but rather to that present-day atheistic existentialism which, as we shall be pointing out in due course, has betrayed the genuine existential demand by interpreting and positioning the being of existence within the confines of the principle of immanentism. The decay of the belief in the Christian God, the victory of scientific atheism, is for Nietzsche a universal European event, in which all races are to have their share of service and honor. Schopenhauer, as we have seen, is, in Nietzsche's eyes, the first avowed and trenchant atheist Germany has produced; he was a man who regarded the absence of God from existence as something understood, palpable, indisputable. And Schopenhauer, according to Nietzsche, held honest and unconditional atheism to be the very preliminary condition for further philosophical advance, in that it freed European thought, after so many centuries, from the lie of the belief in a God.[5]

The slogan and formula of Nietzschean atheism is to be found in the Hegelian declaration: "God is dead".[6] This motto permeates and sustains the whole Nietzschean position. It is articulated in most concentrated form in the famous § 125 of *The Joyful Wisdom* (1882). This section is entitled "The Madman" and reads:

"Have you ever heard of the madman who on a bright morning lighted a lantern and ran to the market-place calling out unceasingly: 'I seek God! I seek God!'—As there were many people standing about who did not believe in God, he caused a great deal of amusement. Why! is he lost? said one. Has he strayed away like a child? said another. Or does he keep himself hidden? Is he afraid of us? Has he taken a sea-voyage? Has he emigrated?—the people cried out laughingly, all in a hubbub. The insane man jumped into their midst and transfixed them with his glances. 'Where is God gone?' he called out. 'I mean to tell you! *We have killed him,*—you and I! We are all his murderers! But how have we done it? How were we able to drink up the sea? Who gave us the sponge to wipe away the whole horizon? What did we do when we loosened this earth from its sun? Whither does it now move? Whither do we move? Away from all suns? Do we not dash on unceasingly? Backwards, sideways, forewards, in all directions? Is there still an above and below? Do we not stray, as through infinite nothingness? Does not empty space breathe upon us? Has it not become colder? Does not night come

[5] Cf. F. Nietzsche, *Die fröhliche Wissenschaft,* Book V, § 357; Musarion XII, p. 287; Schlechta II, p. 227; Reinhardt, pp. 307f.

[6] The expression comes originally from Plutarch and recurs in Pascal and in Hegel himself, as Heidegger notes (cf. M. Heidegger, "Nietzsche's Wort 'Gott ist tot,'" in *Holzwege* [Frankfurt a. M.; Klostermann, 1950], p. 197).

on continually, darker and darker? Shall we not have to light lanterns in the morning? Do we not hear the noise of the grave-diggers who are burying God? Do we not smell the divine putrefaction?—for even Gods putrefy! God is dead! God remains dead! And we have killed him! How shall we console ourselves, the most murderous of all murderers? The holiest and the mightiest that the world has hitherto possessed, has bled to death under our knife—who will wipe away the blood from us? With what water could we cleanse ourselves? What lustrums, what sacred games shall we have to devise? Is not the magnitude of this deed too great for us? Shall we not ourselves have to become Gods, merely to seem worthy of it? There never was a greater event—and on account of it, all who are born after us belong to a higher history than any history hitherto!'—Here the madman was silent and looked again at his hearers; they also were silent and looked at him in surprise. At last he threw his lantern on the ground, so that it broke in pieces and was extinguished. 'I come too early,' he then said, 'I am not yet at the right time. This prodigious event is still on its way, and is travelling—it has not yet reached men's ears. Lightning and thunder need time, the light of the stars needs time, deeds need time, even after they are done, to be seen and heard. This deed is as yet further from them than the furthest star—*and yet they have done it!*—It is further stated that the madman made his way into different churches on the same day, and there intoned his *Requiem aeternam deo*. When led out and called to account, he always gave the reply: 'What are these churches now, if they are not the tombs and monuments of God?' ".

Four years later, in 1886, Nietzsche added a Fifth Book to *The Joyful Wisdom*. This new Book was entitled: "We Fearless Ones"; and in it Nietzsche again takes up the same theme, at the beginning of § 343 ("What our Cheerfulness Signifies"):

"The most important of more recent events—that 'God is dead,' that the belief in the Christian God has become unworthy of belief—already begins to cast its first shadows over Europe."

Nietzsche compares this event to a solar eclipse and proceeds to a quite forthright statement:

"In fact, we philosophers and 'free spirits' feel ourselves irradiated as by a new dawn by the report that the 'old God is dead'; our hearts overflow with gratitude, astonishment, presentiment and expectation. At last the horizon seems open once more, granting even that it is not bright; our ships can at last put out to sea in face of every danger; every hazard is again permitted to the discerner; the sea, *our* sea, again lies open before us; perhaps never before did such an 'open sea' exist."

Nietzsche's denial is here, beyond all question, an absolutely radical one: God is dead, not only the God of Christianity, although this God is specially pilloried; Buddha is dead, too; and all the gods of every age and of every religion are likewise dead. Nietzsche's statement amounts to a proclamation of a fact in the history of the human spirit: it asserts that this modern age has rid itself of God and religion, that modern man has effected a radical exorcism of the divine. Nietzsche is casting a balance sheet of modern thought and is proclaiming, even as did Feuerbach and the Hegelian Left, even as did Schopenhauer, that there is no room for God any more in the mind and heart of modern man. But Nietzsche parts company entirely with the quietistic pessimism of Schopenhauer. Nietzsche intends to fill the void left by the disappearance of God: the place of God cannot be left vacant. And this is the point of his doctrine of the "Superman" which forms the main theme of *Thus Spoke Zarathustra* (1883-1885).[7]

When he has greeted the old hermit of the mountain, Zarathustra expresses his amazement (at the end of § 2) that "this old saint has not yet heard in his forest that *God is dead!*"; and on his arrival at the nearest of the towns, Zarathustra immediately announces (in § 3) to the people assembled in the market square: *"I teach you the Superman.*[8] Man is something that should be overcome. What have you done to overcome him?" The Superman is defined as "the meaning of the earth" (*der Sinn der Erde*) and the people are warned to remain true to the earth and not to believe those who speak of superterrestrial hopes: "Once blasphemy against God was the greatest blasphemy, but God died, and thereupon these blasphemers died too. To blaspheme the earth is now the most dreadful offense, and to esteem the bowels of the Inscrutable more highly than the meaning of the earth." Now that God is dead, man must simply turn his back on the traditional values: happiness, reason, virtue, justice, piety. The Superman insists Zarathustra, is the only acceptable alternative, now that man can no longer become God; for the Superman is the upper limit, set over against the lower limit which is brutalization. And in the following § 4, we read the definition: "Man is a rope, fastened between animal and Superman—a rope over an abyss." And soon afterwards the specification: "What is great in man is that he is a bridge and not a goal; what can be loved in man is that he is a *going-across* and a *down-going*" for man is a going-across toward the Superman and a down-going or perishing for those who must sacrifice themselves and be sacrificed in order to make possible the advent of

[7] *Also sprach Zarathustra,* ed. Musarion, Vol. XIII, pp. 8ff. English translation R. J. Hollingdale, *Thus Spoke Zarathustra* (London, 1961).

[8] And in the rough draft we read: "God is dead and it is now that the Superman lives!" (ed. Musarion, Vol. XIV, p. 134).

that Superman. Superman thus takes the place of God, as we read Part II, § 2: ("On the Blissful Islands"): "Once you said 'God' when you gazed upon distant seas; but now I have taught you to say 'Superman' ". The truth of being is transferred into willing, so that value is a creation of man; but man certainly cannot create God: "God is a supposition; but I want your supposing to reach no further than your creating will. Could you *create* a God?—So be silent about all gods! But you could surely create the Superman . . . God is a supposition: but I want your supposing to be bounded by conceivability. Could you *conceive* a god?—But may the will to truth mean this to you: that everything shall be transformed into the humanly-conceivable, the humanly-evident, the humanly-palpable! You should follow your own senses to the end!"

The dynamic immanentism of the Will-to-Truth is nurtured and sustained here too by the denial of God: "God is a thought that makes all that is straight crooked and all that stands giddy . . . Willing liberates: that is the true doctrine of will and freedom . . . In knowing and understanding, too, I feel only my will's delight in begetting and becoming; and if there be innocence in my knowledge it is because will to begetting is in it. This will lured me away from God and gods; for what would there be to create if gods—existed!" [9]

Nietzsche can justly be called the anti-Kierkegaard: the Danish son of a businessman made everything else defer to, and depend on, the stance of man "before God"; the German son of a Protestant minister protests that in the new conception of man this "before God" signifies a renunciation on man's part of the value that the Superman is supposed to create: "Before God! But now this God has died! You Higher Men, this God was your greatest danger. Only since he has lain in the grave have you again been resurrected. Only now does the great noontide come, only now does the Higher Man become—lord and master!" Hence the Nietzschean conclusion that is diametrically opposed to Marxism: "How shall man be *overcome?* The Superman lies close to my heart, *he* is my paramount and sole concern—and *not* man: not the nearest, not the poorest, not the most suffering, not the best." And Nietzsche repeats straight-forwardly the Hegelian dictum: evil is necessary for the realization of the Superman: "The most evil is necessary for the Superman's best." (*Das Böseste ist nöthig zu des Uebermenschen Bestem*).

At first the process of the Nietzschean reductive transformation of human ideals may seem confused and cumbersome; yet the stages are

[9] Jaspers maintains that this is the crucial and most radical passage of Nietzsche as herald of the definitive expression of the modern principle of self-consciouness: "Only when there is no God, will man become free" (K. Jaspers, *Einführung in die Philosophie* [Zurich, 1950], p. 111).

tolerably evident: nihilism, death of God, will to will, will to truth and Superman, and finally Will-to-Power (*Wille zur Macht*) [10] which is the best-known formula for this transfer of the Absolute from God to the Superman: an expression that witnesses at once to Nietzsche's radical atheism and his reductive transformation of the Christian ideal which states that man must become more than man, like to God. The Will is substituted for the Intellect as the being of consciousness; thus value (*Wert*) must necessarily be substituted for God and man becomes the creator of values in the Superman by way of the Will-to-Power. This is the origin of the "Philosophy of Value" (*Wertphilosophie*) and of subsequent atheistic existentialism, as we shall be pointing out directly.

Nietzsche's importance for the dissolution of the liberal bourgeois world is therefore equal to that of Feuerbach-Marx; but whereas their thrust was toward proletarianism, Nietzsche's was in exactly the opposite direction. The Will-to-Power is the true "essence of the world", the "essence of life" which actualizes itself and must actualize itself as self-transcendence, emergence, domination, in ever-ascending forms.[11] This doctrine of the Will-to-Power seems to constitute the final level of Nietzsche's thought, to which he devoted the last of his energies before the shadows of madness descended upon him. It expresses at once the radical atheism of the principle of immanentism, inasmuch as being is left in man's own power and man initiates everything in-and-from-himself; and again inasmuch as the foundation of existence is identified with the impulse of human subjectivity which is the Will-to-Power, unencumbered, uninhibited: that Will-to-Power can be said to impel ahead of itself by its own power the being it creates as value.[12] Death of God, Superman, Will-to-Power and Eternal Recurrence are the stages whereby Nietzsche asserts being as the self-manifestation of the human mind in the form of its primordial impulse.

[10] The first texts relevant to the transformation of the *Wille zur Wahrheit* (Will-to-Truth) into the *Wille zur Macht* (Will-to-Power) go back to the years 1884-85. The Will-to-Power is made the basis of the doctrine of the "Eternal Recurrence of the Identical" (*ewige Wiederkunft des Gleichen*) and thus constitutes the very essence of existence (cf. *Die neue Aufklärung*: ed. Musarion, Vol. XIV, pp. 283ff.).

[11] Cf. the references in *Jenseits von Gut und Böse* (ed. Musarion, Vol. XV, p. 111) and *Zur Genealogie der Moral* (1887) (*ibid.*, p. 343). The posthumously published *Wille zur Macht* is held by Schlechta to be a compilation by Nietzsche's sister Elizabeth and P. Gast, from Nietzsche's papers (cf. K. Schlechta, *Der Fall Nietzsche* [Munich, 1958]. In his new edition of Nietzsche's works, Schlechta has rearranged this material [*Nietzsche's sämmtliche Werke,* Vol. III, pp. 1393-1423]).

[12] "The innermost entity of the Will-unto-Power can be nothing else than that Will itself. It is the way in which the Will-unto-Power pro-poses itself as Will to itself" (M. Heidegger, "Nietzsche's Wort 'Gott ist tot'," p. 224). For Schopenhauer's "pessimism of the weak," Nietzsche has substituted the "pessimism of the strong" (*ibid.*, p. 207).

For Nietzsche God is dead because man has killed him. And man's motive?—God's shameless pity for man. God saw all man's secret failure and baseness and man cannot allow such a witness to live. Or more directly: modern man has conceived freedom and the existence of God as antithetical; they are mutually exclusive and man has chosen freedom. Thus has Nietzsche carried the principle of immanentism back to its ultimate origin which is also its definitive term: if the *cogito* is the principle of being and being is the becoming of consciousness, then the *cogito* is identified with the *volo,* which is no mere abstract willing nor yet a willing of self-annihilation. Rather it is a willing of the actualization of the Superman who is to take the place left vacant by God; and this actualization is willed via the annihilation of the Other—God first, and then the herd (*Herde*), the mass, the scum of inferior humanity.

What is the real significance of this cathartic "atheism", this expulsion of God so that the Superman may live? It is no easy matter to find a clear-cut answer in the dense mass of Nietzschean thought, presented in aphorisms, metaphors and paradoxes that overarch one another like the waves of a stormy ocean. Nietzsche interpreters are still wrestling with this problem even today.[13] But it seems certain that Nietzsche was aiming at an elimination of the old metaphysic and of Christian theology, in order to make room for the new conception of being as "life" (*Leben*), a conception which emerges precisely from the transformation of all values by the Superman in whom is realized and actualized the Will-to-Power.[14]

A further vexed question is that of Nietzsche's subsequent specification of the precise quality of the being that Superman is to realize. Did Nietzsche put the main stress on the values of the progress of history and the emergence of great men? Or was it his intention rather to conceive of man in function of the blueprint of an ever more intimate unity of man's will with Nature? [15] It is difficult to arrive at a definitive

[13] Jaspers insists that Nietzsche's thesis must not be oversimplified into "banal godlessness." Cf. K. Jaspers, *Nietzsche* (Berlin, 1950 [3]), p. 250; English translation *Nietzsche,* An Introduction to the Understanding of his Philosophical Activity, by Charles Wallraff and Frederick Schmitz (Tucson, Arizona: The University of Arizona Press, 1965), p. 245.

[14] Heidegger therefore classes *Thus Spoke Zarathustra* with Schelling's *Untersuchungen über das Wesen der menschlichen Freiheit* (1809), Hegel's *Phenomenology of Spirit* (1807) and Leibniz's *Monadology* (1714), all of which are purely metaphysical works (M. Heidegger, "Nietzsche's Wort. . .", p. 233).

[15] For a discussion of the Heideggerian interpretation, cf. E. Fink, *Nietzsches Philosophie* (Stuttgart, 1960). Heidegger evinces a constantly mounting interest in Nietzsche: cf. *Sein und Zeit* (Tübingen: M. Niemeyer Verlag, 1927), § 76 (English translation by John Macquarrie & Edward Robinson, *Being and Time* [New York and Evanston: Harper & Row Publishers, 1962], pp. 444ff., especially 448); the Essay cited from *Holzwege;* the volume of lectures *Was heisst Denken?* (Tübingen, 1954), which is a commentary on the enigmatic Nietzschean text: "Deserts grow:

answer and it is our personal conviction that both interpretations are defensible, constituting in fact a new facet of the ambiguity and incurable malaise of the principle of immanentism. In view of this ambiguity, it is not surprising that Nietzschean atheism could have served as inspiration for such opposing trends as D'Annunzian hedonism, the race frenzy of National Socialism and the opaque morass of present-day German existentialism. From an overall point of view, Nietzsche can be considered, even as Engels considered Feuerbach, as the definitive term of German philosophy (and of the principle of immanentism together with it) in the tradition Kant-Goethe-Lessing-Herder-Fichte-Hegel-Schleiermacher, as an exaltation of the life realized in man.[16] Nietzsche's polemical fury of denunciation of religion, and more especially of any notion of a personal God who creates man and a Providence preparing a future life for man, would then amount to an "historical judgment" on the process of modern culture: "In Nietzsche we see a man whose acute sensitivity identifies the hidden destiny of his own age with his personal fate, with his own destiny as a thinking being. By his trenchant taking upon *himself* of this destiny, Nietzsche becomes, as it were, a prophetic voice or an apocalyptic sign of this event which obscurely agitates many and which he calls the death of God." [17] It might be more accurate to say that Nietzsche's campaign against religion and Christianity was the result of a "psychic trauma" and that Nietzsche's denial of God hid a deep religious feeling, a feeling that had been played false and frustrated and was seeking to vent its outrage in the proclamation of the Will-to-Power as the fullness of life. This whole point deserves very special attention.

The anti-religious outbursts against Christianity in particular and against the person of Christ, in Nietzsche's famous *Antichrist,* may well bear a similar interpretation. In this connection, Jaspers has collected an impressive list of phrases from Nietzsche exalting the person of Christ and Christianity; these phrases certainly ought to be cast into the balance against the better-known hostile ones.[18] The denial of

woe to him who harbours deserts!" (*Also sprach Zarathustra,* p. 385; English translation, p. 319). Cf. also K. H. Volkmann-Schluck, *Nietzsches Gedicht: "Die Wüste wächst, weh dem, der Wüsten birgt"* (Frankfurt a. M., 1958), another commentary in the Heideggerian tradition.

[16] Cf. W. Ter-Georgian, *F. Nietzsches Stellung zur Religion,* Dissertation (Halle a. S., 1914), pp. 84f. Ter-Georgian refers likewise to Lange, Ueberweg and Eucken, all of whom were, like Nietzsche, protagonists of a sort of "religion of humanity".

[17] B. Welte, *Nietzsches Atheismus und das Christentum* (Darmstadt, 1958), pp. 19f. In a deeper sense, contends Welte, Nietzsche's atheism is expressive of the free "possibility" man has to deny God (p. 37): the opportunity afforded man to fight against God.

[18] K. Jaspers, *Nietzsche und das Christentum* (Hameln, 1948), pp. 5ff.

Christianity in Nietzsche is a consequence of the denial of God, from which primordial denial likewise flows the denial of all truth, all morality and the whole traditional interpretation of world history; hence the need to begin all over again. Nihilism and despair are in Nietzsche as in Kierkegaard the point of departure for a new effort to recover that being that has been lost; but Nietzsche's dialectic is the exact opposite of that of Kierkegaard.

Nietzsche set up the pagan god Dionysius with predilection over against Christ; but he admired in Christ the repudiation of the official (Pharisaical) morality. Jaspers thinks that Nietzsche was aiming at a new synthesis of the pagan ideal with the Christian, in the appearance of that unique prodigy, the Superman: "A Roman Caesar with the soul of Christ." [19] But we cannot help feeling that this alleged religious sentiment in Nietzsche was rather a kind of cultural memory of a world still too close at hand to be entirely forgotten; for a genuine and effective religious demand can only be posed and actualized in the framework of transcendence.

[19] *Ibid.,* p. 75.

2

The "Death of God" as a Structural Judgment of the Modern "Cogito"—the End of the Metaphysic of Essences (Platonism)

In order to arrive at a judgment on the content and form of Nietzsche's atheism and its significance, we must adopt his own point of view, which is that of an interpretation of being, existence, on the basis of life (*aus dem Wesen des Lebens*). Life exists, i.e., lives as referred and referring to itself: it has within itself the principle of being, of existence, and therefore expresses the essence of being in its totality. The life of which Nietzsche is here speaking is not solely and indeed not, properly speaking, in any sense life as immediately preceptible and naturalistically conceived; rather this "Life" refers to the fountainhead and primal origin of being, of existence, so that existence is conceived as an unceasing ascendent motion, as "becoming" (*Werden*). From the point of view of the subject, this ever-intensifying being is conceived as "Will-to-Power" which is actualized in and through the Superman. From the point of view of the object, i.e., history as a Whole, it is designated by the Heraclitan formula, current in the classical world, "the Eternal Recurrence of the Identical". Real human knowledge or the truth of being is to be found in a plunging into this becoming wherein is realized that Life which Western civilization, corrupted by Platonic idealism, has forgotten in a perverse effort to actualize the empty world of the ideas and the categories.[1] It is this empty world and the illusory values proper to it that must be denied, re-evaluated, turned upside down, so that Superman may live.

[1] "*Faith in the categories of reason* is the root cause of nihilism,—we have measured the value of the world by categories *which refer to a purely imaginary and fictitious world*" (F. Nietzsche, *Aus dem Nachlass der Achtzigerjahre,* ed. K. Schlechta Vol. III [Munich, 1957], p. 678).

The crucial point here at issue is the significance that should be assigned to Nietzsche's "nihilism" and consequently to his proclamation of the "Death of God". In proclaiming life as basic, one Nietzsche interpretation insists, he was animated by the desire to eliminate the dualism of the Platonic-Christian conception of the intelligible world as principal and real and the sensible world as secondary and apparent.[2] He felt this must be done in order to give to life its full expansiveness and self-affirmation. Nietzsche's attack on Christianity is an attack on the conception of God as the Supreme Being in the sense of the one who supremely is (*das Seiendste*), i.e., in the sense of First Cause, and of the world as created by God and dependent on his Will.

Nietzsche is thus represented as attacking a very definite theologico-philosophical tradition and his proclamation of the "Death of God" is held to be pure polemics rather than actual "atheism". Nietzsche is held to be denying or repudiating belief in the existence of God or belief in a "be-ing God" (*an einen "seienden" Gott*) in the sense in which these Nietzsche interpreters insist God has always been thought, proven, imagined and believed. Nietzsche's protest is that if God is to be a true God he must be true Being. Therefore the Divine (*Das Göttliche*) henceforth becomes a condition (*Zustand*) of life, of that life that is, in conformity with the conceptions of the Eternal Recurrence of the Identical, the true Being of every being, amounting to unconditioned and unconditional self-affirmation. But this approach, argue such interpreters, is not "atheism" but the exact opposite. And they argue that any definitive judgment on Nietzsche's alleged atheism would require a preliminary clarification of two questions: (1). How is being itself conceived, once the being of the existent is transferred into the essence of life or interpreted in function of life? and (2). How is the nature of God conceived, when the divine becomes the supreme condition of life? [3] If the norm and the exegetical context be properly grasped, they contend, Nietzsche's atheism disappears entirely.

But it is precisely in terms of this norm and this whole context that Nietzschean atheism is at once an operative part and the ultimate term of his nihilism. It is true that Nietzsche is rebelling against a specific type of culture and civilization which is that of Platonic intellectualism, for which he aims to substitute his own *Lebensanschauung*. But it is

[2] "The supreme goals, the causes and principles of the existent, ideals and the suprasensible, God and the gods—all this is conceived in advance as value. We therefore arrive at an adequate understanding of Nietzsche's concept of nihilism only when we know what Nietzsche understands by value. Only in the light of such an understanding do we grasp what Nietzsche really meant by his phrase 'God is dead'" (M. Heidegger, "Nietzsche's Wort . . . ," p. 209).

[3] This is the thesis of K. H. Volkmann-Schluck (cf. his article "Zur Gottesfrage bei Nietzsche," in *Anteile, M. Heidegger zum 60. Geburtstag* [Frankfurt a. M., 1950], pp. 232f.).

equally certain that Nietzsche is starting his whole critique and "substitution" maneuver from the modern principle of immanentism, from the *cogito* as that cogito has disintegrated into the *volo*.[4] Thus the essence of the Nietzschean "Life" is the "Willing" which is its own principle and therefore excludes any other principle, even as does the *cogito*. And because in modern philosophy the mind begins from and with itself, the *cogito* is in effect a *volo* (a *volo* which we hold to be just as much a vacuum as is the *cogito,* preceded by the nothingness of doubt). It must therefore be admitted that for modern metaphysics the being of the existent appears as sheer and simple "Will". This is already implicit in Descartes, but it becomes explicit in Leibniz and constitutes the essence of modern metaphysics. And we must remark at once that this dissolution of being into "willing" or into the assertion of self-consciousness as "Life" can only constitute the leitmotif[5] of a metaphysic and philosophy of immanentism, which will disintegrate and effectively inter real and genuine metaphysics. And so Nietzsche can indeed be said to be effecting the "critique of the times". But his diagnosis is not that of a physician; rather it is the diagnosis of one sick, indeed sick unto death, of the same disease and committed to curing himself and others by intensifying to the ultimate extreme the virulence of the germ.

More recent criticism of Nietzschean nihilism seems to be arriving at an even greater unanimity of opinion that this nihilism represents a dissolution of the ideals of the rationalism and Enlightenment thought of the West. There seems to be considerably less general agreement on the relation between this nihilism and the basic atheism which it presupposes on the one hand, precisely as a disintegrative activity, and consti-

[4] This is also the (metaphysical) sense ascribed by Heidegger to the Nietzschean motif of "vengeance" (*Rache*) as a radical demand upon being whose essence is transposed into the "form of willing" (*Gestalt des Wollens*) and Heidegger cites as models the following three propositions of Schelling: "There is, in the final and highest analysis, no other being than willing. Willing is primordial being and to it alone suit all the attributes predicated of that original primordial being: uncausedness, eternity, independence of time, self-affirmation. The whole of philosophy is but a striving to find this supreme expression" (*F. W. J. Schelling's philosophische Schriften,* Vol. I [Landshut, 1809], p. 219). And Heidegger continues: "The word 'Willing' here designates the Being of the existent in general. This is Will . . . The Leibniz conception comes out clearly in Kant and Fichte as the rational-will, which Hegel and Schelling simply echo, each in his own way. It is what Schopenhauer means when he gives his major work the title: The World (not Man) as Will and Idea. It is what Nietzsche is thinking when he recognizes the primordial Being of the existent as a Will-unto-Power." (M. Heidegger, "Wer ist Nietzsches Zarathustra?," in *Vorträge und Aufsätze* [Pfullingen: Neske, 1954], pp. 113f.). There is an identical Heideggerian passage in the same context in *Was heisst Denken?,* pp. 35f. Cf. Heidegger's recent systematic exposition in his *Nietzsche,* Vol. I (Pfullingen, 1961), pp. 44ff. ("Das Sein des Seienden als Wille in der überlieferten Metaphysik," with the usual references to Schelling and Hegel), pp. 70ff. ("Wille und Macht"), pp. 467ff., 648ff.

[5] Again cf. M. Heidegger, "Wer ist Nietzsches Zarathustra?", p. 117.

tutes on the other hand in the shape of the "Will-to-Power." For our part, we are persuaded that it amounts quite simply to an evasion of the crucial question to interpret Nietzschean atheism simply as a polemical retort to or critique of the "God of the philosophers", the God of the Hebrews and of theology or of a moral or ontological metaphysic.[6] This crucial question is whether the human enquirer can adequately pose the problem of being or of truth or justice without being compelled to pose the problem of transcendence; and not just any sort of transcendence, phenomenological, historical or what have you, but precisely the theological transcendence constituted by the admission of God Who is Being by his very essence and principle of beings. Now any such admission is entirely absent, not only from Nietzsche but, in our opinion, from anyone who remains faithful to the tenet of the priority of mind or consciousness over being. For such thinkers, the God-problem becomes impossible, meaningless, useless (as Sartre will say); it becomes a rhetorical formula, foreign to philosophy; for philosophy may just possibly emerge as an ontology, but never as a metaphysic.

Heidegger is just as surely bypassing the central and crucial question when he insists (against Baeumler and Jaspers) that the kernel of Nietzsche's thought lies not in the Heraclitan doctrine of the "Eternal Recurrence of the Identical" but rather in the positive aspect of the Will-to-Power as a supersession of all forms of Platonism and a consequent eventual attainment to Being in its primordial requirement.[7] The crucial question is how anyone can speak of an ontology in the absence of the "foundation" of a metaphysic, unless, of course, the foundation of the ontology in question is to be simply and solely mere appearing, sheer present-ness rendering itself present as such.

It is therefore quite beyond our comprehension how several recent Nietzsche critics and interpreters can so confidently assert that Nietzsche does not oppose God as such nor yet deny his existence, but aims only at demolishing an inadequate conception of God, at fighting only the "God of the philosophers" and not the "God of Abraham, Isaac and Jacob". Such interpretations insist that Nietzsche is combatting only that Being thought out by metaphysics and presented as God; thus his proclamation of the "Death of God" signifies the abolition of this sort of God, of a particular configuration (*Gestalt*) of ontology. Such a reading of Nietzsche would make the passionate tone of his fight against Christianity proceed basically not from any hatred of God but rather from a new transformation being experienced in the thought of Being.[8]

[6] To which E. Fink seems to limit it in his *Nietzsches Philosophie,* pp. 140ff.

[7] Cf. M. Heidegger, *Nietzsche,* Vol. I, pp. 29ff.

[8] E. Fink, *Nietzsches Philosophie,* p. 147. And Fink concludes: "The notion of the Death of God is first of all a historical interpretation of the modern state of man as the advent of nihilism, and then it is a radical critique of religion, ethics

Our first remark on all these interpretations is this: it is a simple matter of fact that Nietzsche does carry the principle of immanentism to its ultimate disintegrative extreme in his proclamation of the horizon of man as the foundation of being. And this is precisely the radically atheistic stance, not of philosophy as such (Fichte) nor of any philosophy, but precisely of modern philosophy which makes being coincide with the presence *of* consciousness, in accord with the primordial demand of the *cogito,* as explained in the famous description of the structure of consciousness given by Hegel in his short "Introduction" to the *Phenomenology of Spirit.* And Nietzsche repudiated *en bloc* God, transcendence, immortality, the life to come, the Gospel of Christianity, in order to exalt exclusively the joys, the struggles and the triumphs of life in time.

It could be said that, if Nietzsche eliminates the theological or "contentual" Transcendent, he does maintain and exalt the structural transcendent, i.e., the creativity of consciousness: in the place of the Theodicy or justification of God, he puts the "apology of man" and in the place of the transcendental values, the created values of man as poet and thinker—values such as love and power. Nietzsche is quite firm on one point: after the elimination of transcendence, it would be a new error, worse than the first, to make man into the new God, the Absolute. No, man is a finite and limited being, and it would be madness to conceive of him as infinite. In the wake of the suppression of God and of the values associated with transcendence, man has a free field; he becomes the creator of new values. But man's creative activity is a finite activity, which is all the more effective as man relates, in his activity as poet, thinker and artist, to the basic foundation. Things as such are all on the same level; they play no part whatever in determining degrees or dimensions of value: only human activity, the quantum of man's will to power, is the source and norm of all value. Metaphysics yields pride of place, in this apology of man, to what later came to be called philosophical anthropology. This philosophical anthropology proposes to restore man from the passive acceptance of values to that primordial and self-generating life that projects from out of itself its own values. Man is to be helped to recover his own forgotten and concealed creativity. Once man has come to recognize himself as the creative principle and positing agency of his own values, he has won through to the opportunity of expressly positing henceforth new values. Hence, Nietzsche's attack on all morality, especially the Christian ethic, because it maintains that

---

and philosophy in the Age of Metaphysics. This critique is to complete the drama of the dying of God, so as to open up a new, fruitful and terribly beautiful, a 'tragic' view of the world" (p. 151).

morality is solidary with metaphysics. But from this there likewise follows Nietzsche's diffidence and distrust for philosophy in general, even his own philosophy, even the very notion of truth—a diffidence that is admitted even by his most benign interpreters. What is supremely important is life and the exuberant and impetuous flowering of life; and life is endangered the moment that it entrusts itself to truth, to being in general. So we have in Nietzsche, surely, not a new concept of theoretical truth to be substituted for an older one, but rather a distrust of truth as such and an exaltation of life which embraces and encompasses truth. And such a distrust of truth and such an exaltation of Life is perfectly consistent from Nietzsche's point of view; for in his defense of human freedom "Nietzsche is thinking of German philosophy and of Hegel in particular".[9] It should therefore come as no surprise that German existentialism should have found in Nietzsche the ideal bridge by which to make the transition to the new concept of freedom as existence.

We therefore believe that Nietzsche's "positive value" in our investigations is incomparably superior to that admitted by his recent apologetes who, in their desire to acquit him of the charge of atheism, impart a purely cultural content to his work and a purely historicist intent to his thought. In our eyes, on the contrary, Nietzsche has a truly definitive historical importance, at once cathartic and eschatological, in the drama of modern thought and Western formalism in general. The "nihilism" that he sees and denounces at the heart of modern philosophy beginning with Socrates, the feature that he condemns unmercifully in his critique of the "ideal world" as presented by philosophy and religion alike, is the superposition of ideal being upon real being. But we must immediately add that he launches this condemnation from within the confines of modern thought, himself a victim of the very error he wants to combat. He knows no other meaning of the word "being" than "life" because he is thinking crudely of the idea and representation[10] of being and so subordinates being to consciousness as animate being, as willing, acting, becoming.[11]

[9] Cf. *ibid.,* p. 160.

[10] "Being—we can picture it no other way than as '*living*'. How, then, can something dead 'be'?" (F. Nietzsche, *Aus dem Nachlass der Achtzigerjahre,* Vol. III, p. 483. Schlecta maintains that the posthumous publication, *Die Wille zur Macht,* which claims to be a compilation of this mass of Nietzsche jottings and which has introduced them into European culture, is not the work of Nietzsche, nor even its divisions nor the titles of the four books; rather it is in sharp contrast with the occasional and heterogeneous character and content of the original jottings. [Cf. K. Schlechta, *Der Fall Nietzsche,* p. 110 and pp. 87ff. Cf. Schlechta's proofs and documentation, in *Aus dem Nachlass der Achtzigerjahre,* Vol. III, pp. 1393-1423.])

[11] "*Being* as a generalization of the concept 'Life', 'Living' (breathing), *being animate, willing, acting, becoming.*" (*Aus dem Nachlass der Achtzigerjahre,* Vol. III, p. 548).

Nietzsche is an enthusiastic admirer of Heraclitus for having discovered the doctrine of the laws of becoming and of the play of necessity and the consequent exaltation of life in the play of contraries; but he is extremely wary of Parmenides, who thought of being as an immutable presence which knew neither "was" nor "will be" and who attributes truth exclusively to the intellect, relegating the various and changeable perceptions of the senses to the world of illusions. To this Parmenidean Being which he understands as the abstract and possible *essentia* (essence), Nietzsche opposes the critique of Aristotle and of all those opponents of the ontological argument (such as St. Thomas and Kant, etc.), the critique that insists that *existentia* (existence) cannot be derived from sheer *essentia.*[12] But in his critique, Nietzsche has totally lost sight of the Parmenidean Being that is no longer thought of as act but rather as content (*essentia*), in the tradition of Aristotelian essentialism. For Nietzsche, "being" is a completely empty concept and really means simply "breathing" (*atmen*), thus evincing even in its etymology the most wretchedly empirical origin.

Nietzsche therefore abandons the immutable truth of Parmenidean being and opts for Heraclitan becoming; he transfers truth from Being into becoming. Thus Nietzsche transfigures the world: what had been the illusory appearance of the Parmenidean δόξα (glory) becomes the world of that reality which is the Eternal Recurrence (of the Identical). And at the end we have a pure motion, without the metaphysical and theological superstructures of the idealist dialectic: existence can be only unidimensional: a presence of the present.

Nietzsche is therefore speaking from the platform of modern thought which he carries to its total disintegration-point. And so anyone speaking *with* or *about* Nietzsche must take his place on that same platform; and this will remove all ambiguity from his utterances! Nietzsche and the Nietzschean cannot possibly accept the suprasensible world or the reality of God who is the Principle of that world, because consciousness must actualize itself as life and within consciousness there cannot be conceived any other dimension than that of life or of the irruption of immediacy, the self-affirmation of the will-to-life, as a will-to-will, a will-to-power. Consciousness as will constitutes itself in its becoming by a "leap" (*Sprung*): in Marx, the *Ich denke überhaupt* became an economic will and therefore positive in its result; in Sartre, the *cogito* of freedom becomes radically nihilating activity; in Nietzsche, who wants to overcome Schopenhauerian pessimism, consciousness is under compulsion to readjust life and to conform itself to the thrust and impulse of life by grasping it before it has evaporated into the dualisms and opposi-

[12] Cf. F. Nietzsche, *Die Philosophie im tragischen Zeitalter der Greichen,* §§ 9-13; *C. W.,* ed. K. Schlechta, Vol. III, especially pp. 388ff.

tions of reflection. This is precisely that "innocence of becoming" (*Unschuld des Werdens*), which constitutes in its way a "radical modulation" of the modern principle and of formal philosophy in general. Moreover this is expressly stated in the internal reduplication evident in the formulas already indicated, all of which are summed up in the elementary formula of the will-to-will (*Wille zum Willen*) which is a direct descendent and derivative of the formula: "the truth of consciousness is self-consciousness."

In this becoming, therefore, the will is not moved to any Other: it simply becomes itself, proceeds always within itself, toward what is itself; this is what makes it the "willing of willing" and the "will-to-will", the will to self-affirmation, self-intensifying by its own effort and agency, as it strives toward an indefinite augmentation of power. The "leap" of which Nietzsche speaks is therefore not basically different from that of Hegel. The Hegelian leap is the "return" of the Absolute into itself via the dialectical transcendence and supersession of the finite, recognized as its element, moment and appearance. The Nietzschean Will (*Wille*) becomes or tends to become the *Wille zum Willen* (will-to-will), the raising to an infinite power of its own actualization of itself, whose object is neither outside of nor other than but precisely and solely that self-actualization of the will in itself,[13] secure in the conviction that this is the only self-guaranteed certitude.

The chief protagonist of a positive interpretation of Nietzschean nihilism in our own day is Heidegger himself, who makes a great point of Nietzsche's declaration: "My philosophy is an *inverted Platonism.* The further I get away from true being the better. Life in becoming is my aim." But inverting Platonism means inverting the norm of truth, positioning the sensible where the intelligible belongs, repudiating the idea and the intelligible as fictions and proclaiming the reality of the sensible in the flux of immediacy and life. And this in turn entails the destruction of metaphysics and of every effort to restore the "thing-in-itself" in favor of a total commitment to sheer appearing (*Schein*). It likewise involves the inversion of the notion of truth which is now interpreted as a "form of error".[14] Truth now has the meaning of "erring" or "straying" into the tumultuous flux of life. Such a drastically aesthetic consideration of life epitomizes the ultimate issue of Western philosophy in its dual aspect, negative and positive. Heidegger categorically states:

[13] Heidegger formulates this quite precisely in his comment: "What the Will wills, it does not strive toward as toward something it does not yet have. What the Will wills it has already. For the Will wills its Willing. Its will is its desideratum. The Will wills itself." (M. Heidegger, "Nietzsche's Wort . . . ," p. 216).

[14] "*Truth is that kind of error* without which a certain species of living being cannot exist. The value for *Life* is ultimately decisive." (F. Nietzsche, *Wille zur Macht,* ed. Musarion, Vol. XIX, p. 19).

"The proposition 'God is dead' is not an atheistical tenet, but rather the formula for the radical experience of an event of Western history." [15] He concludes that this is something that can and should be put right by the philosopher of the future or at least that such a rectification cannot be denied to be a legitimate assignment of that philosopher of the future. Well, that is perhaps something for the said philosopher of the future to decide; but there is certainly none of this in Nietzsche himself. Nietzsche condemns as Platonism any positing of transcendence whatsoever; and the expression "God is dead" is absolutely unequivocal: it is not static but dynamic, for it implies and demands the complementary declaration: "and cannot rise again!" And so, too, Nietzsche's nihilism is dynamic, even as was Marx's: its goal is the advent of the new man; it posits the proclamation of the simultaneous "de-valuation" of the values of the beyond and "re-valuation" of the values of the here-and-now, of which man alone is the foundation and the agent, the measure and the fulfillment.

Like Marx, Nietzsche retraced the path of the Hegelian phenomenology, from the realm of the reason and the understanding to the realm of the sheerly vital sensible. His ultimate destination was in no sense candid and straightforward consciousness as such; rather it was a total mobilization and a raising to the nth power of what the principle of immanentism had signified in the molding of modern man.

There can indeed still be enigmatic ambiguity in the interpretation of Nietzsche's atheism; but it stems from the ambiguity of the being that is proper to the principle of immanentism. But if this principle be traced back and forced back to its origin, as our investigation has attempted to do, then all ambiguity vanishes. If Nietzsche be read in this light, then he can readily be seen to be what Heidegger likewise implies him to be: the end term of modern thought as an "historical judgment": "Why atheism today? The 'Father' in God is thoroughly refuted, likewise the 'judge' and the 'rewarder'. Also his 'free will'—he does not hear us, and even if he heard us he could not help. The worst of it is that he seems to be incapable of communicating clearly. Is he unclear?—This is what I

[15] M. Heidegger, *Nietzsche,* Vol. I, p. 183. Jaspers' interpretation is more forthright: "Nietzsche does not say, 'There is no God,' or 'I do not believe in God,' but 'God is dead.' He believes that he is ascertaining a fact of present-day reality when he peers clairvoyantly into his age and his own nature" (K. Jaspers, *Nietzsche,* p. 247; English translation, p. 242. Cf. K. Jaspers, *Nietzsche und das Christenthum,* p. 53). In a letter written in 1866 to Baron von Gersdorff, Nietzsche makes fun of the following statements presented to him by Deussen with a challenge to refute them: "There *could* be a God, and this God *could* have revealed himself, and this revelation *could* be contained in the Bible. Oh Brahma! And a man is supposed to base the course of his own life on such possibilities!? And he even challenges me to refute them for him!" (cited in G. Walz, *La vie de Friedrich Nietzsche d'après sa correspondance* [Paris, 1932], p. 122).

have found out from many questions and conversations as to the cause of the decline of European theism. It seems to me that the religious instinct is growing powerfully but is rejecting theistic ratification with deep distrust." [16]

And then Nietzsche proceeds to a diagnosis of the anti-Christian and atheistic bias of modern thought: "What, basically, is all modern philosophy doing? Since Descartes . . . all philosophers are assaulting the old concept of soul, under the pretence of criticizing our subject and predicate concept. This means an assault on the basic premise of Christian doctrine. Modern philosophy, being epistemological skepticism, is secretly or openly anti-Christian, though by no means anti-religious. (But that is said for subtle ears only)." [17] It may well have been this passage that suggested to Heidegger the positive interpretation of Nietzsche's stance; and there is one plausible aspect in this interpretation: for Nietzsche, atheism is not a destination nor yet the conclusion of a proof; rather it is an option and a point of departure. For atheism is synonymous with nihilism, it is inextricably bound up with the abandonment of the transcendence of Being and with man's eventual recovery of himself and of the sensible world, of life on this earth, the only life made for him as opposed to the illusions of the spirit and the transcendental beyond.

Nietzsche is in the line of Feuerbach, in the matter of the dissolution of the Hegelian Absolute into the reality of man. But Nietzsche's dissolution of that Absolute has a more radical significance than Feuerbach's and is closer to Bauer and Marx.[18] For Nietzsche sees in religion in general and in Christianity in particular not a stage in the manifestation of the human being but rather a deviation, indeed the most pernicious form of alienation and the cause of man's "dehumanization" and of his unhappiness here on earth. God, as Creator and Judge of man, is the destroyer of man's freedom: the laws of God are man's chains and religion his prison. Only man can legislate for man; and this is the meaning of the modern Revolution, a restoration to man of his freedom by the denial of God. It is no longer a case, as in Feuerbach, of a simple change of sign, of a substitution of man where Hegel posits God and the Absolute. Rather man and the human is to be set over against the tendency of religion and theology-prone philosophy to speak of God: man is to be "built up" upon and by means of the negation of God.

[16] F. Nietzsche, *Jenseits von Gut und Böse,* § 53; ed. Schlechta II, p. 615; ed. Musarion XV, p. 73; English translation by Marianne Cowan, *Beyond Good and Evil* (Chicago: Henry Regnery Company, 1955), p. 60.

[17] *Ibid.,* § 54; ed. Schlecta II, pp. 615f.; ed. Musarion XV, pp. 73f.; English translation, pp. 60f.

[18] Cf. K. Löwith, *Von Hegel zu Nietzsche* (Stuttgart, 1950 [2]), p. 373.

Löwith has stressed this point: "Nietzsche's doctrines of the 'Death of God,' of the 'nihilism' deriving from it, a nihilism which demands the overcoming of Christian man and his supersession by the 'Superman', and finally his doctrine of the 'World' which, as nature, represents a 'Will-to-Power' willing itself and an 'Eternal Recurrence of the Identical'—all these are no mere doctrinal fragments in the traditional sense; rather they are part and parcel of the single drive for a 'new betrothal' with the world, from which we had been divorced in the wake of the victorious campaign of Christianity against the pagan worship and veneration of the cosmos." [19]

Nietzsche's atheism, therefore, aims to be *positive* or constructive, no less than that of Marx. And it aims to be radical: it expresses not so much a denial (of God) as rather an assertion of freedom (of man). We feel that the real significance of the Nietzschean denial, strange as it may seem, has to do, not so much with the theological realm that had been liquidated already by the Hegelian Left, as rather with the moral realm, where Nietzsche strives to remove the last and worst obstacle in the way of freedom.[20] In this sense, Nietzsche likewise ranges himself against socialism (which he considers to be a form of "secular Jesuitry"). Over against Christianity, Nietzsche sets an ethic of his own; over against the transcendent values of Christianity, he sets his own category of values, calculated to protect man against the "risk" that is his fate. Thus Nietzsche's thought likewise is saddled with a sort of historical "eschatologism", still linked, like the socialist one, to the Christian conception of a liberation of man from necessity. Like Marx, Nietzsche thinks he is asserting man's freedom from theological chains, even though he does it in a different way from Marx; and again, like Marx, Nietzsche ends by trussing and binding that freedom in still heavier and more somber chains. Marx hobbles man's freedom with the adventitious chains of economic conflict or the class struggle; Nietzsche ties it to the chariot of "becoming" driven by the unscrupulous impulse of the Superman, making it dependent on the irrational and subject to the unconditional acceptance of the "result", the *de facto* reality of the historical process.

[19] K. Löwith, *Gott, Mensch und Welt* (cited from Italian translation, *Dio, uomo e mondo da Cartesio a Nietzsche* [Naples, 1966], p. 103).

[20] "With him, rebellion begins with 'God is dead,' which is assumed as an established fact; then it turns against everything that aims at falsely replacing the vanished deity and reflects dishonor on a world which doubtless has no direction but which remains nevertheless the only proving-ground of the gods . . . Nietzsche did not form a project to kill God. He found Him dead in the soul of his contemporaries. He was the first to understand the immense importance of the event and to decide that this rebellion on the part of men could not lead to a renaissance unless it was controlled and directed" (A. Camus, *L'homme révolté* [Paris, 1951], p. 91; English translation by Anthony Bower, *The Rebel* [New York: Vintage Books, Random House, 1956], p. 68).

And so, in the end, the whole uproar of rebellion and freedom is muted to the minor-key acceptance of the Hegelian philosophy of history, to the "justification of evil", to a veritable "cacodicy" which takes the place of the Leibnizian theodicy. Thus, too, Nietzsche's *immoralism,* like his atheism, assumes a positive significance, that of an affirmation of the vital impulse. But it should be most diligently borne in mind that this affirmation is effected in Nietzsche, too, on the basis of a negation, not on the basis of the biological or psychological immediacy of the vital impulse itself, as the *Lebensphilosophie* seems to have felt it was. And this point is of no small importance for our interpretation of modern atheism. The re-valuation effected by Nietzsche with his Will-to-Power appeals (as he himself explicitly testifies) to the crucial stages of modern thought: to the Cartesian *cogito,* to the autonomy of Kantian freedom, to the Hegelian dialectic divested of its formal mechanism, and above all to the deep-running impulse of "Awareness" of Hegel's *Phenomenology*, considered as a nihilating activity. This makes it quite understandable that the Will-to-Power should have its meaning and foundation in its own self-actualization as a Will-to-Nothingness, inasmuch as the essence of the Will-to-Live is a "willing-of-nothing(ness)", a refusal to tarry or jell, a trenchant insistence on being in process of becoming and on willing the becoming in its totality as a perfectly welded chain of necessity (*amor fati*).[21] It is really no exaggeration to call Hegel and Nietzsche the twin giants (after Spinoza) of modern atheism: for both have such a trust in the "enormous power of the negative" that they proclaim the justification of force and violence and consequently of evil as a propulsive force of history; both aim at superseding the antithesis of true and false by asserting the equivalence or at least the equation of truth and error.

This we see to be the main line of modern thought; and Nietzsche is one of the crucial "waystations" or junctions on that line. The real importance of his thought, in the deepest sense, lies not so much in its having been the occasion of such phenomena of aesthetic degeneration as Titanism, absolute aestheticism, National Socialism and the like.[22] It is to be found rather in the fact that Nietzsche called the modern mind to a definitive reckoning, implacable and inexorable. And it is in the light of that reckoning that the real meaning and ambiguity of present-day existentialism can best and most readily be clarified.

[21] K. Löwith, *Nietzsches Philosophie der ewigen Wiederkunft des Gleichen* (Berlin, 1935), pp. 57ff. (The Conversion of the Will-to-Nothingness into the Willing-of-the-Eternal-Recurrence).

[22] Cf. in this connection: H.-H. Schrey, *Existenz und Offenbarung,* Ein Beitrag zum christlichen Verständnis der Existenz (Tübingen, 1947), pp. 39f. Also: J. Hommes, *Zwiespaltiges Dasein,* Die existenziale Ontologie von Hegel bis Heidegger (Freiburg i. Br., 1953), pp. 185ff.

3

The Flight from the Absolute in Jaspers

Jaspers adopts an ambiguous attitude to the God-problem; but then everything in present-day thinking on this problem is an ambiguous mixture of positive and negative attitudes. For Jaspers, the cypher-script (*Chifferschrift*) notion constitutes at once the destination and the foundation for the convergence of every reference of the mind; and God is presented as the supreme cypher, "the cypher of cyphers." [1] But precisely because the God-problem is presented as the "cypher of cyphers" it proves to be doubly inscrutable and enigmatic: it is a cypher and a cypher of cyphers, i.e., a cypher raised to the second power, the radically and essentially indecipherable cypher that any intentional entity must be which is in the order of the *sum* (I am), i.e., the existence of consciousness in the bias of its primordial and self-generating freedom, which resists and precludes any determination of "content".

In such a state of affairs, religion remains, as in the idealist tradition, a provisional stage, inferior to philosophy which has as its object the dialectic of human freedom, a freedom that is self-grounded and self-contained. That freedom originates and constitutes a new order; there is a marked cleavage between that order and the physical world and God cannot be found in the world.[2] Jaspers, like Nietzsche, rejects the idealist identification of God with the Whole or the All. But after he has

[1] The doctrine of the "cypher" understood as a sheer and simple "reference" that can never constitute itself into an "object" is the key to the entire philosophy of Jaspers (Cf. K. Jaspers, *Philosophie,* Vol. III, Metaphysik [Berlin, 1956 [3]], pp. 128ff.).

[2] "It is the stern challenge to endure, in the void of the world, the fact that God is not there as anything whatever in the world" (*Der philosophische Glaube* [Munich, 1947], p. 103). For a metaphysic of *esse,* like that of St. Thomas, God *is* present to and in the world "per essentiam, per potentiam et per praesentiam" (by essence, by power and by presence) (Cf. *S.T.,* I, q. 8, 1-3; cf. C. Fabro, *Participation et causalité* [Paris-Louvain, 1960], pp. 509ff.; Italian edition *Partecipazione e causalità* [Turin, 1961], pp. 470ff.).

removed God from the world, he finds no "room" for God, because the mind in its transcendence remains in itself the sole source of determination of being. In this conception of the "divine cypher" God would seem, in the final analysis, to have no other assignment than that of indicating the task of "continuous infinite transcending" that the mind must effect upon its object in its unending journey. God thus amounts really to a compromise term to overcome the Hegelian antithesis between baneful and benign infinity by the existential exaltation of the act (or form) of aspiring over the content of the aspiration itself. God cannot be an object, a content: being cannot be God, insists Jaspers (in agreement, here, with Heidegger). God cannot be a "person" but only a cypher and the "cypher of cyphers." [3]

[3] A most revealing passage in this regard is the following: "It is hard to reduce the personal God to his cypher-being. God as Transcendence remains remote. In this cypher that I, as man, create myself in a second language, He is brought close to me for a moment. But the abyss of transcendence is too deep. This cypher is no relaxation of the tension. It is fulfilling and dubious at once, it is and is not. The love that I direct to the deity as Person can only be called love by way of metaphor. It becomes enthusiasm for the beauty of existence (*Dasein*)". In the concrete, therefore, everything comes down to "relations with the world": "Unworldly love is love for nothing but groundless beatitude [i.e. beatitude without any solid foundation]. Only as loving transfiguration of the world is love for transcendence substantial and effectively actual (*wirklich*)" (K. Jaspers, *Philosophie,* Vol. III, p. 167). Jaspers varies the spelling of his key word in the original German: in the passage just cited and elsewhere (cf. *Vernunft und Existenz* [Groningen-Batavia, 1935], p. 75; *Nietzsche,* pp. 199, 289 and *passim*), he writes *Chiffre;* but in the later works (cf. *Von der Wahrheit* [Munich, 1947]; *Einführung in die Philosophie,* p. 35 *et passim*), he uses the spelling *Chiffer.*

[In this English rendering, we have used throughout the spelling "cypher", taken from the translation of parts of *Von der Wahrheit* by Jean T. Wilde, William Kluback and William Kimmel, entitled *Truth and Symbol* (New York: Twayne Publishers, 1959). As twice in the passage cited in this footnote (*grundlose Seligkeit*-unfathomable/groundless beatitude; *wirklich*-real/effective), so in his use of *Chiffre/Chiffer,* Jaspers reveals his dominant tendency to subtle and simultaneously multidimensional use of words, for "cypher" is patently suggestive of the dual meaning "empty" (cipher = zero and the original Arabic root from which it derives, ṣafara, means "to be empty") and "cryptic code, meant to be understood only by those who have the key to it". We have preferred the less usual spelling in order to avoid an undue tipping of the scales in favor of the first of the two meanings here mentioned. "Cipher" is altogether too suggestive of inanity and zero.

By the same token, we have throughout preferred and consistently adhered to the rendering "The Encompassing" which the above-mentioned translating team gave to the other key Jaspers term "das Umgreifende". Ralph Manheim's otherwise superb translation of *Einführung in die Philosophie* (English title: *Way to Wisdom,* An Introduction to Philosophy [New Haven: Yale University Press, 1951]) seems to us to falter drastically in rendering "Das Umgreifende" as "The Comprehensive". First of all, there is a perfectly good and usual German word for "Comprehensive", namely "Umfassend, das Umfassende"; surely Jaspers, with his keen feel for language, wanted to express something more active when he chose the much more active root "um-*greifen*". Secondly, "comprehend", both

Jaspers talks much and often about God but he never really says anything about him; and he ends by reducing him to a nonentity, to an empty name: "God is only a name. A name would seem to be most appropriate here, seeing that it is not something thought, not a category. But God can be called by a thousand names, by an infinite number of names. But to speak of him as something thought would imply a desire each time to enclose him within categories. The One God eludes thought, is unthinkable; if he could be thought he would be a finite among other finites. He eludes imagination and intuition, for they would make him into something sensible. God is for thought and intuition simply a blank point in the dynamic of transcendence, the point of reference of everything that is, but neither sustainer, goal nor fountainhead. And so God is remote and incomprehensible, so remote as to seem unattainable, so incomprehensible as to seem to vanish into nothingness." [4]

We would mildly suggest that God does indeed vanish into nothingness, in Jaspers' philosophy, because it passes comprehension how any entity reduced to a "blank point" could serve any other purpose "in the dynamic of transcendence" than that of making the void of being itself the void. Nor is it tenable that this void is merely the total absence of the finite: for, in the wake of the decapitation of the Hegelian Absolute, effected in accord with the principle of immanentism by Feuerbach and the Hegelian Left, by Marxism, by existentialism, by phenomenology and allied philosophical schools and trends, there is absolutely nothing left but the finite, the contingent, nothing but what can render itself present in space and time, in nature and history.

The key to this whole position is to be found in what we should like to call the "return to Kant" provided this "return" be understood in the sense of a "recapitulation" of modern thought, especially German thought, along the arc stretching from Kant to Hegel to Nietzsche: ". . . no being that we know is being in itself and as a whole. The phenome-

---

etymologically and semantically, conveys in English primarily the notion of "grasping hold of", whereas "encompass" conveys, both etymologically and semantically, the notion of "going round" and hence of enclosing.

While we entirely agree with the Author's judgment concerning the brilliant intuition that led one translator to render "das Umgriefende" as "The Immanent All-Enclosing"' (cf. Footnote 12 to this Section, below), this seems to us both impermissibly expansively interpretative as a translation and quite unnecessary, if the felicitous "The Encompassing" be used, since this conveys both the sense of restrictive enclosing and the sense of universal comprehensiveness!—Translator's Note]

[4] K. Jaspers, *Von der Wahrheit*, pp. 690f. [This section was not translated in *Truth and Symbol;* we have therefore made our own translation—Translator's Note.] It is meaningless, after Kant, to speak of "proofs of the existence of God": "A proven God is no God" (K. Jaspers, *Der philosophische Glaube*, p. 30; cf. *Einführung in die Philosophie*, p. 41; English translation, *Way to Wisdom*, p. 42).

nality of the empirical world was made fully clear by Kant." [5] Thus, if the cypher is, as Jasper claims, the language of transcendence, this language can, by definition, never communicate anything whatever to the human mind; therefore it has no meaning except that of cypher or symbol to which man has not and can never have the key. All the attributes apply indeed to God: being, love, creator, truth, goodness; but they fade and melt away either into nonentity or into nonsense. How, in the face of this, can Jaspers' assertions really ring true when he insists that "God exists" or that "the existence of God is an absolute mandatory postulate"? According to this same Jaspers, God can never become a "Thou" to whom man can turn to institute a personal relationship. It is probable that Jaspers, in conformity with his theory of freedom, wanted to attempt a mediation between the atheist and the religious man, between Nietzsche and Christianity, in order to show that the antithesis here was only an apparent one and to assert that the solution is to be found solely in his own "philosophical faith".

An exhaustive exposition of Jaspers' theory of religion would indeed require a meticulous reconnaissance ranging over the various works of his long career. Equally certainly, his notion of God, identified with a new notion of transcendence, cannot be fairly presented, much less disposed of, in a single definition or a pedestrian straw-man idea. The hard fact remains, however, that Jaspers' thought shows a perfectly clear bias and follows a perfectly clear line, that leaps at once to the eye of anyone who is even a little familiar with his writings and with the philosophers from whom he took his inspiration: Kant, Hegel, Nietzsche. We therefore feel justified in making the flat statement that Jaspers is not and cannot be a theist, in the classical and realist tradition to which we subscribe; but it is equally certain that Jaspers has never professed himself an atheist.

In a recent work, published in late 1962,[6] and devoted to a study of the relation between philosophical faith and revelation, Jaspers again takes up from the outset the whole problem of transcendence with an

[5] K. Jaspers, *Einführung in die Philosophie,* p. 76; English translation, *Way to Wisdom,* p. 79.

[6] K. Jaspers, *Der philosophische Glaube angesichts der Offenbarung* (Munich, 1962), In the Preface, Jaspers asserts that in a great number of human beings today the power of believing is only latent, that the prophets of the present moment are not succeeding in finding the right words, that the Christian faith in revelation has not succeeded in two thousand years in making the habit of truth effectively active in life and thought. Only "freedom", actualizing itself in an unrestricted and boundless communication, can serve as the ground for a universal understanding among men. It is "philosophical faith", or the loyalty of reason to its own boundless power and potential, as realized in philosophy, that can and must proclaim that man can still save himself (pp. 7f.).

assiduity and breadth of range bearing eloquent witness to the importance he attributes to this problem in the whole context of his thought. Yet his basic attitude seems to us to have remained exactly what it was before; and that is what really matters.

The most striking point about this new work is that the whole exposition is again based on the "cypher" theory of transcendence; and this theory seems to be still more watered down and tenuous than in the preceding works. Then, God, or rather Deity (*Gottheit*) is conceived in the shape of intentional levels: the One God, the personal God, the Incarnate God, etc., each one of which constitutes a "cypher". The God of the Bible, of Abraham, Isaac and Jacob, well reveals the abstractness of the abstract God of Aristotle; but this God of the Bible in turn becomes a "cypher", for Jaspers holds with Fichte that "person" can only be spoken of within the compass of man and can be conceived only as limitation and finitude, so that to begin by conceiving of God as person amounts to depriving transcendence of its status as the Encompassing of all encompassing. Finally, the third cypher, Christ as God Incarnate, is philosophically impossible, leaving the philosopher with a choice between the (historical) corporeal Christ and Christ as a cypher (Incarnate God-Man).[7]

Jaspers' conclusion is that man becomes that God that he has before his eyes as believer. And he insists that this does not involve any subjectivization of the "forms of God" (*Gottesgestalten*), provided only that man conceive God as a "cypher" in the mutual tension of objectivity and subjectivity and resolve in that cypher the various attributes of the deity and the dogmas of Christianity. The pith of this whole work can be summed up in this brief excerpt from it: "The cypher of God and the existence of man correspond. God's transcendence-cognate existence does not attain to man's existence moves within the cypher. That form that the individual man allows to appeal to him in his own particular cypher becomes an element of his life. He develops himself in the image of the cyphers of God which he thinks." [8] Reason is given the last word on the problem of religion and reason's definitive form of self-expression or self-realization is the situational "historicity" of the subject. For almost fifty years now, since his transition from psychopathology to philosophy, Jaspers has been writing this sort of thing; and the lengthy digressions on culture in his latest writings add nothing to what had already been said or was already known. It is now clear that Jaspers cannot write anything other or otherwise than this.

There can be no doubts in the mind of any critic who starts, as we

[7] *Ibid.*, pp. 213ff. Cf. especially pp. 235ff. for denial of the personality of God.
[8] *Ibid.*, p. 249.

have done, from a concept of God that precludes ambiguity; only one judgment is possible on Jaspers' thought: his much-touted theism resolves itself into atheism. Even a benevolent critic, like Ricoeur, admits that Jaspers' writings leave the impression of an "inchoate atheism" (*unvollständiger Atheismus*), having its origin in the effort to arrive at an unstable compromise between Kierkegaard and Nietzsche. For Jaspers, too, the old God is dead. It is consequently inevitable that the false proper name of Transcendence (i.e., God) should betray to the eyes and ears of the atheist simply a last lingering fear and an ultimate extreme of obfuscation and that the cypher of transcendence should appear to him as the heir and successor of the mediating logos. The problem as such, therefore, disappears and the tension between transcendence and existence is free to dissolve into an interior tension within the bounds of my own self, appealing to that self which responds, stretched taut as it is between the hidden depths of my own subjectivity and the actions and experiences which in everyday life utilize this inaccessible wealth in order to take ever clearer cognizance of it. This dissolution of religion by and into philosophy can give rise to a proud and haughty ethic, specifically a form of neo-Stoicism, allowing no place for "prayer" wherein the real relation between God and man is instituted and realized.[9]

On first reading, it may seem that every problem in Jaspers leads to an opening upon the infinite or transcendence and thus upon the God-problem; but a modicum of reflection will show that in every case what seems to be an opening upon the infinite is but another turn of the key in the prison-door, and that each new inspection of the horizon of transcendence ends in a new substantiation or consolidation of immanentism. This dialectic, whereby the existential opening upon the infinite invariably culminates in a form of entombment of the Self within the sphere of the finite, stems from the central notion of the *Umgreifende* (Encompassing) which dominates the whole of Jaspers' philosophical edifice.

[9] P. Ricoeur, "Philosophie und Religion bei Karl Jaspers," in *Karl Jaspers,* Philosophen des 20. Jahrhunderts (Stuttgart, 1957), pp. 635f. Ricoeur had reached substantially the same conclusions in a work published ten years earlier in collaboration with H. Dufrenne (P. Ricoeur and H. Dufrenne, *Karl Jaspers et la philosophie de l'existence* [Paris, 1947]). Here is the forthright conclusion of that work: "That is why it would be a misreading of Jaspers' peculiar genius to make his philosophy into a proto-Christian philosophy; a 'Christian existentialism' could only express an outsider's opinion on the meaning of faith in Jaspers. And the first point that would strike the believer is that Jaspers' critique of religion had entirely bypassed the specifying element of religious faith; the main thrust of Jaspers' criticism is actually directly to the conflict between authority and freedom, which is only the exacerbated form of the conflict between objectivity and existence." (pp. 391f.).

What is this *Umgreifende,* this Encompassing? [10] Its very etymology points to an action of embracing, comprehending, containing as a whole; but this whole is not a real and actual whole; rather it is a possible whole and, as such, the basis for the mind's unbounded capacity to open up. If indeed we are always living and thinking within a delimited horizon (situation), then we certainly must, from time to time, push aside this and that particular horizon, in order to be able to live and act; and so on *ad infinitum.* That is what constitutes the Encompassing. It is the homologue of the Hegelian *Vernunft* (Reason) immersed and substantiated in existence; therefore it does not itself constitute any horizon for existence; rather it is what renders possible each and every horizon. In his latest works, Jaspers recalls with predilection Nicholas of Cusa's notion of the *coincidentia oppositorum:* "I achieve—with Plotinus, Eckhart, Cusa—the sublime thoughts, wherein precisely every object is lost, while a music of abstraction yet seems to waft to me the deepest manifestation-potential of being. Disciplined speculation brings us the mystical experience of the One in all. Infinity strides to our encounter along a road cleared entirely of everything directly apprehensible. And infinity itself eschews every determinate shape and form (*Gestalt*). It is precisely in the dissolution of every structured content that infinity can be experienced. Infinity endeavors to fade out into nothingness". Being presents itself to us only as historicity and consequently within the bounds of finitude. Being shows itself to us only in the polarity of an Infinitude without history and a historical finitude; and the mediating agent is the mobile tension thrusting us into the heights and the depths of being.[11] The Encompassing is then a kind of inapprehensible apprehender, a scattering harvester, a dissolving container, simultaneously indicating being itself (*Sein selbst*) or transcendental objectivity, and referring to what we are ourselves or that wherein being from time to time assumes a determinate form. In neither case is the Encompassing conceived as a simple aggregate of particular and determinate powers of being, accessible to us; rather it is the totality in its fullness or consid-

[10] Cf. K. Jaspers, *Von der Wahrheit,* pp. 43ff., 123ff., 605ff. The term is not used in the lengthy work *Philosophie,* in which Jaspers speaks only of *Transzendenz* and *Chiffre.* The first exposition of the significance of significance of the *Umgreifende* is to be found in K. Jaspers, *Vernunft und Existenz,* pp. 28ff.; this exposition already contains all the basic elements to be more thoroughly developed later. The brief, clear synthetic account in *Einführung in die Philosophie,* pp. 28ff. (English translation, *Way to Wisdom,* pp. 28ff.) will be a helpful guide to the lengthy and tortured analysis given in Von der Wahrheit.

[11] K. Jaspers, *Von der Wahrheit,* pp. 897f. Therefore speculation on Being, the Name of God revealed to Moses ("I am Who I am", "I am Who am", "I am He Who is", "I am the Be-ing One": Exodus 3, 14) solves nothing; it merely generates an infinite tension when bracketed with the notion of God as Person (cf. *Der philosophische Glaube angesichts der Offenbarung,* p. 258).

ered as the ultimate foundation of every happening and becoming, every event and process within being, whether being-in-itself or being-for-us.[12]

And here is the crucial point in Jaspers' whole argumentation on this point: because we are positioned within the bounds of immanence, we can touch the Encompassing only by way of Transcendence or by way of a movement that effects a transcending of immanence. But this, in turn, necessarily entails our conceiving transcendence as the Encompassing of all encompassing (*das Umgreifende aller Umgreifenden*), which consequently becomes the Transcendence of all transcendences (*Transzendenz aller Transzendenzen*). In the context of such a designation of God, Jaspers' repeated assertion that "God is" (*Gott ist*) evaporates into an inapprehensible cryptogram which by definition cannot be an object of thought but only of faith; and the faith directed to such a flimsy and blurred mental presence is mightily exposed to all the assaults of doubt. The existence of God must be said to have been banished, in this philosophy, to an extraneous position at one of the poles of the dialectic where it serves as a primordial and substantiating referent; but the main point is that the God here in question is no longer the God of the theist tradition but rather the God of transcendental objectivity. And moreover Jaspers has burnt all the bridges of valid proof, electing to rely upon the inherently unstable pontoon of "philosophical faith" which, far from excluding unbelief, demands and requires it as the opposite pole needed for the actuation of the existential tension. Such a faith, of which doubt, despair and fear are integral elements, is the exact opposite of certitude.

Any indictment of atheism, such as that which Ricoeur brings against Jaspers' thought, implies that very clear God-notion which is calculated to provide man with a grasp of the meaning of his own existence and destiny. But in Jaspers' system, this meaning is achieved and revealed, not in the realm of cognition but rather in the realm of action or in the form of existence. Here again, then, as at every crucial point in Jaspers' philosophy, we find ourselves face to face with the Kantian doctrine of the hegemony of the Practical Reason over the Pure Reason, of (philosophical) faith over knowledge. God is not an object of sensible experience. God is invisible and cannot be the object of intuition but only of faith. And Jaspers maintains his loyalty to the Kantian approach by

[12] Thus we feel that a brilliant insight is shown in a recent English rendering of *das Umgreifende* as "The Immanent All-Enclosing" (Cf. R. D. Knudsen, *The Idea of Transcendence in the Philosophy of Karl Jaspers* [Kampen, 1958], p. 51). Another critic, one of a great number who could be mentioned, presents this development of the meaning of this immanence: "What must be detected and urged, in all cases, is transcendence in immanence, in other words, being in beings, truth in truths, man in men" (I. Paumen, *Raison et existence chez Karl Jaspers* [Brussels, 1958], p. 327).

declaring that this faith has its source "not in the limits of worldly experience but in the freedom of man. The man who attains true awareness of his freedom gains certainty of God. Freedom and God are inseparable."[13]

This sort of statement seems to be directly and diametrically opposed to the logic of the principle of immanentism, to which Jaspers nonetheless remains bound and which is expressed in French existentialism in the brutal but consistent formula: if God exists, I am not free (Sartre).[14] Actually, the only logical outcome of that line of argument of Jaspers which we have just quoted would be the Thomist or Kierkegaardian notion of participation: the total dependence, in terms of such participation, of the existent upon him who is Being by his very essence. But in this sort of approach, the element and moment of cognition (the presence of being) is prior to the element and moment of action; and thus freedom is the decision of the person who is already oriented to the truth of being. Consequently it is meaningless, in this kind of approach, to speak of "faith" in the philosophical realm as a principle of transcendence.

Jaspers' own line of argument proceeds as follows: I am conscious of myself; and in my freedom I am not through myself but am given to myself, for I can fail myself and I cannot force my freedom. Where I am really and authentically myself, I am certain that I am not *through* myself. The highest freedom is experienced in freedom from the world, and this freedom is a profound bond with transcendence. It is this freedom that constitutes existence: my certainty of God has the force of my existence. And I can have certainty of God not as a content of science but as presence for existence. There is therefore a necessary connection between the certainty of freedom and the certainty of the existence of God, between the denial and negation of freedom and the denial and negation of God. And there is also a connection between the assertion of a freedom without God and the deification of man.

Once again our reply must be that it is precisely the concept of freedom as autonomy in action that has accomplished the divorce of the mind from Being and thus from God, in such a way that the awareness of freedom which is posited as the radical element of the presence of

[13] K. Jaspers, *Einführung in die Philosophie,* pp. 43ff.; English translation *Way to Wisdom,* pp. 44f. In this Chapter IV ("The Idea of God") we find Jaspers' clearest account of his own position on the God-problem.

[14] Jaspers, however, quotes Nietzsche: "Only when there is no God does man become free" and limits himself to the remark: "But using the same figure we might say the reverse: Only with his eyes to God does man grow instead of seeping away undammed into the meaninglessness of life's mere happenings" (K. Jaspers, *Einführung in die Philosophie,* p. 117; English translation, *Way to Wisdom,* p. 117).

being, far from motivating and requiring a reference to God, in fact irremediably precludes any such reference. Nor does the denial or negation of God necessarily lead to the deification of man; as such, it leads only to an acceptance of man as a situational being, leaving the way open to such divergent subsequent interpretations of this situational being of man as those proposed, e.g., by historical materialism on the one hand and atheistic existentialism on the other.

At one point, Jaspers seems to be assailed by a desire to curb or ignore the mad rush of the principle of immanentism toward atheism. He tries to arrest that headlong dash with a little sermon against plunging into the abyss of the void; but the sermon fails to indicate a single foothold or even handhold to which man could cling: "To believe in God means to live by something that is not in the world, except in the polyvalent language of phenomena, which we call the hieroglyphs or symbols of transcendence. The God of faith is the distant God, the hidden God, the indemonstrable God. Hence I must recognize not only that I do not know God but even that I do not know whether I believe. Faith is no possession. It confers no secure knowledge, but it gives certainty in the practice of life." [15]

This renunciation of *all* knowledge of God in favor of the risk or wager of belief, pushed thus to the ultimate extreme of the renunciation implicit in the phrase "I do not know whether I believe", seems to us perfectly consistent with the radical bias of a freedom unmoored from being and knowing; it can be considered to be the philosophical counterpart of the *fides fiducialis* of Luther, to whom Jaspers does not fail to refer. But in this case the faith that is supposed to lead to God becomes an absolutely gratuitous act, positioned beyond choice itself, seeing that man does not know what he is choosing, does not know what he is choosing, does not know even that he has chosen!

For Jaspers, then, even as for Nietzsche and Sartre, and for Fichte before them, the *cogito* has metamorphosed into the radically naked *volo,* dissolving into Lessing's "sheer aspiration" which rejects and refuses all manner of certainty. For Jaspers, as for Kant and idealism, objective thinking is simply a matter of determining and defining by categories; but God, being infinite, is not amenable to any categorization; [16] he is utterly extraneous to and beyond all thought. This is why

[15] K. Jaspers, *Einführung in die Philosophie,* pp. 48f.; English translation *Way to Wisdom,* pp. 50f. In the immediately preceding sections, Jaspers has shown that our proper attitude towards God has been most eloquently expressed in the three biblical injunctions: "Thou shalt not make unto thee any graven image or likeness"; "Thou shalt have no other gods before me"; "Thy will be done" (pp. 46ff.; English translation *Way to Wisdom,* pp. 48ff.).

[16] Cf. e.g. K. Jaspers, *Die grossen Philosophen,* Vol. I (Munich, 1957), pp. 346f.

we cannot even know *whether* we believe in God. And this is precisely what Jaspers' critics call his "atheism"; and they seem not to be far wrong.

Jaspers' position on the problem of religion must be said, on balance, to be ambiguous in the extreme and scarcely calculated to shed clearer light on the whole question: the headlong rush precipitated by the very inherent bias of a principle like that of immanentism cannot be arrested at will by the desperate expedient of a "leap" into transcendence. Jaspers starts from the nihilism of Nietzsche and transforms the Will-to-Power into a Will-to-Believe. But even a champion is ill-advised to leap without a solid support under his feet for the take-off! In Jaspers, religion dissolves into a form (of climate or atmosphere) without content; and it remains entirely circumscribed by philosophy, of which it is at once the antagonist and the foundation, attaining to actualization and clarification solely in and through philosophy.[17] To persist in speaking of "transcendence" in this context is redolent of caricature and, above all, of equivocation; and this equivocation is common to all the trends of present-day philosophy which believe themselves to have superseded and overcome the very foundation of idealism, which is the principle of immanentism, simply by their profession of some sort of dualism or by their rejection of the pseudo-theology of Hegel.

A striking evidence of the ambiguity of Jaspers' position is to be found in the fact that his "philosophical faith" is extraneous alike to the area of faith and to that of philosophy. It is not faith, because the essence of faith, which is at the very basis of all religion, implies an assent to a witness and thus involves a personal relationship, and in the case of theological faith the relationship of man with God as God "has entered into the history of existence", especially in and as Jesus Christ (the *"Gud blev til"* ["God came into existence", a phrase cast in the same mold as that of Genesis 1, iii: "And God said: Let there be light,' and *there was light*" (i.e., light came into existence)] of Kierkegaard). Nor is Jaspers' "philosophical faith" philosophical: it obviously cannot be if it is to be faith, for faith and philosophy are mutually exclusive, unless by faith be understood simply that trust and confidence that reason has in itself as a whole and unless it be this whole in turn which is called upon to express transcendence and faith in God—which is in

[17] This is the explanation of Jaspers' aversion to revealed historical religion, in the wake of Lessing and Kant, and of his categorical rejection of it: God manifests himself from all eternity and *through the whole of mankind*, not simply in one special people (Israel) or through a few privileged persons (the Prophets, Jesus Christ). Thus mankind as a whole is the mouthpiece of God (Cf. K. Jaspers, "Antwort," in *Karl Jaspers*, Philosophen des 20. Jahrhunderts, pp. 776f. Also K. Jaspers, *Der philosophische Glaube*, pp. 74ff.).

effect what Jaspers does! Thus the circle of immanence is reinforced and closed still more tightly upn itself. Seen in this light, Jaspers' opposition to Bultmann's *Demythologization* loses all real bite; and Bultmann has not failed to take advantage of the opportunity to make this point to his theological opponent, Jaspers.[18] There is but a tenuous semantic difference between the concept of "cypher" inspired by Kant and the concept of "myth" circulated by the Hegelian Left (Strauss). The two concepts have the same essential function and serve the same essential purpose: that of conceiving truth as an existential historical process, surpassing form and content.

The impasse or blind alley involved in this position is the reduction of faith (*Glaube*) itself, in its turn, to the status of a "cypher" and a "cypher of cyphers", inasmuch as it represents precisely the mouthpiece of transcendence. It is not always easy to get one's bearings amid the luxuriant foliage of Jaspers' terminology; but one thing is certain: Jaspers' definitive stand represents a triumph of Nietzsche over Kierkegaard. For Jaspers' faith is not only a "lay" or "secular" faith, divorced from and in conflict with any Church whatsoever; it even rules out all religion on principle. In short, it culminates not in God but in man, in the inexhaustible capacities of historical reason to open out beyond itself. Paradoxically or "dialectically" speaking, Jaspers' entire system of thought could be said to be one vast tension of contraries: under the appearance of a drastic assertion of transcendence there is accomplished

[18] Cf. especially the polemical Essay "Wahrheit und Unheil der Bultmannschen Entmythologisierung," in *Kerigma und Mythos,* Vol. III (Hamburg-Volkdorf, 1954). The Jaspers-Bultmann confrontation has also been published separately, in German under the title *Die Frage der Entmythologisierung* (Munich, 1954) and in English translation by Norbert Guterman under the title *Myth and Christianity* (New York: Noonday Press, Farrar, Straus & Cudahy, 1958).

The conservative Protestant theologian, W. Lohff, has replied to Jaspers' critique of religion with a vigorous insistence that the object of faith is an event which transcends the dialectic; this amounts to a rejection of the thesis of Lessing, which had already been rejected by Kierkegaard in his *Philosophische Smuler* and in his monumental *Efterskrift*. But Lohff goes on to say that a simple option or counter-rejection must be entered against Jaspers' rejection: "Theology cannot prove the opposite; it can only witness it by a decisive option . . . All argument pro and con becomes meaningless in this context. For neither of the opposing parties can bear the burden of proof" (cf. W. Lohff, *Glaube und Freiheit,* Das theologische Problem der Religionskritik von K. Jaspers [Gütersloh, 1957], pp. 184ff.).

Thus Protestant theology confines itself to pitting assertion against assertion and denial against denial, on the authority of the Bible alone: "The uniqueness of God in the 'I AM' precludes any claim to a monopoly on the part of purely human approaches to God . . . The uniqueness of God will not be recognized or admitted by any natural man, but only in the Spirit of God revealing it." (O. Hammelsbek, "Theologische Bestreitung des philosophischen Glaubens," in *Offener Horizont,* Festschrift für K. Jaspers [Munich, 1957], pp. 30f.).

the most integral immanentism; under the appearance of an all-encompassing faith there is hidden the most radical unbelief; under the appearance of a continual reference to God there is hidden a radical denial of the possibility of any real approach by man to God and of any attempt by man to enter into a personal relationship with God; under the appearance of existential dualism and pluralism there is hidden the monism of Being, as represented by the inapprehensible marrow of the Encompassing.[19]

The root of all this ambiguity lies in the identification of God with Transcendence and in the identification of this Transcendence in turn with the Encompassing (*Umgreifende*), understood as an objective ideal that serves as the goal of the tendency of freedom toward self-realization and renders that self-realization possible. Thus there is a fluctuation between affirmation and negation; but it is the negation that gains the upper hand in the end: the Encompassing (*Umgreifende*) becomes the "Uncompassing" (Uncomprehending, *Ungreifende*) and the "Unencompassed" (Uncomprehended, *Unbegriffene*); faith emerges as the negation of all certainty; transcendence emerges as merely souped-up immanence; and the result is that this metaphysic, which is in substance a "Theory of the Cypher", a game of "symbols" that ends in "Checkmate",[20] cannot but culminate in a denial of God as the Supreme

[19] But a very shrewd critic has not let himself be taken in by appearances: "Jaspers is, like Schelling and Hegel, rather a monist than a dualist. As such, he stands in sharp contrast to the two great Danish philosophers, Grundtvig and Kierkegaard, who were both frank dualists. In the early 19th century, Grundtvig came out strongly against Schelling's philosophy of identity; in the mid 19th century, Kierkegaard launched an equally strong attack on Hegel's dialectical 'mediation' of the contraries, which in Kierkegaard's view could never be mediated in all eternity" (S. Holm, "Jaspers Religionsphilosophie," in *Karl Jaspers,* Philosophen des 20. Jahrhunderts, p. 660).

[20] "The emphasis is on foundering in the symbols and cyphers; and only very plain and modest statements (obviously only 'finite' ones) concerning the idea of God are permitted" (F. J. von Rintelen, *Philosophie der Endlichkeit als Speigel der Gegenwart* [Meisenheim/Glan, 1951], p. 391). Räber can therefore make a good case for comparing Jaspers' position to the explicitly atheistic stand of N. Hartmann (Cf. T. Räber, *Das Dasein in der 'Philosophie' von Karl Jaspers* [Bern, 1955], p. 14). Hence the crying need to get out of the impasse of the Jaspers-Bultmann controversy: "Philosophy in 'Philosophical Faith' and philosophy in theology (Bultmann) tries to capture the super-secular content with secular categories . . . What Nietzsche did not recognize or grasp was . . . that in any given age of Christendom, the pure and unalloyed proclamation of the Gospel breaks through and transcends the merely historical" (O. Hammelsbek, "Theologische Bestreitung des philosophischen Glaubens," p. 34).

In his most recent works, Jaspers seems to insist more on the positive character of Transcendence, but always with the "cypher" reservations: "This tranquillity is sustained in the Transcendence, into which we yearn to be taken up, together with our afflicted fellow-wayfarers. The immutability of God is a cypher of this repose. Thither does man strive, thrusting no longer simply forward in the world

Being, recognized as Creator of the world and Father of men. But only a God so conceived and so understood can call man and be called upon by man in a direct relationship involving the exercise of freedom. And so, for Jaspers, existence, which is the actualization of freedom, always resolves itself solely into a "transcendence of form", invariably implying in turn the immanence of the content, and consequently having neither shape nor meaning except in a finite world.

---

but upward to the Transcendence, inscrutable to our knowing mind, well-nigh unnameable" (K. Jaspers, *Kleine Schule des philosophischen Denkens* [Munich, 1965], p. 58). And in this infinite thrust of mankind to the Transcendence, it is the cypher that excells and outstrips theology which is tied to a profession of faith (p. 136).

It might be noted that in his latest works, Jaspers makes every effort to render possible, if not an agreement, at least an encounter between "philosophical faith" (*philosophischer Glaube*) and "revealed faith" (*Offenbarungsglaube*): "I am persuaded that philosophical faith and revealed faith need not engender mutual enmity, but that they can find a common meeting-ground. More than that. I hope, against all the evidence of history, that they can conclude an alliance" (K. Jaspers-H. Zahrnt, *Philosophie und Offenbarungsglaube* [Hamburg, 1963], pp. 99f.). But in any such bargain, it is always reason, with its infinite motion, that gets the lion's share. Indeed, in the major work devoted to this whole problem-complex, revelation itself becomes in turn a "cypher" of reason, with dogmatic faith renouncing all claim to hegemony or exclusive competency (Cf. *Der philosophische Glaube angesichts der Offenbarung,* pp. 477ff.).

We hope to treat of the conflicting encounter between the Christian faith and modern philosophy in a separate work, tentatively entitled *Il Problema di Cristo nel Pensiero Moderno* (The Problem of Christ in Modern Thought), on which we have been working for many years and which will be similar in scope to the present work.

4

The "Want" of God and the Inescapable God-Problem in Heidegger

There have been some, though infrequent, voices of assent to Heidegger's thought, from Protestant and Catholic circles alike, from the moment of his first appearance on the philosophical scene.[1] But the voices of dissent have been considerably more numerous and vigorous. They have tended to concentrate on two main charges: the *nihilism* and the *atheism* which they hold to be integral to, and inseparable from, Heideggerianism.

The charge of "nihilism" was based not only on the central thesis of

[1] For a positive Protestant assessment, cf. Heinz-Horst Schrey, "Die Bedeutung der Philosophie M. Heideggers für die Theologie," in *M. Heideggers Einfluss auf Wissenschaften* (Bern, 1949), pp. 90ff.; for a positive Catholic assessment, cf. M. Schmaus, *Katholische Dogmatik* [2], Vol. I (Munich, 1939), pp. 90, 223, 246 and Vol. IV, 2 (1953), p. 130, and also M. Müller, *Existenzphilosophie im geistigen Leben der Gegenwart* (Heidelberg, 1949), translated into French as *Crise de la métaphysique* (Paris, 1953). More numerous and insistent are the critical voices. Cf. among the Protestant critics: G. Krueger, "M. Heidegger und der Humanismus," in *Studia Philosophica* IX (1949), pp. 93-129, and K. Löwith, *Heidegger Denker in dürftiger Zeit* (Frankfurt a. M., 1953); among the Catholic critics: J. Möller, *Existenzialphilosophie und katholische Theologie* (Baden-Baden, 1952), especially pp. 181ff. and J. Hommes, *Zwiespaltiges Dasein,* pp. 8ff.

Among English-language studies on Heidegger, special mention should be made of Thomas Langan, *The Meaning of Heidegger.* A Critical Study of an Existentialist Phenomenology (New York: Columbia University Press, 1959), a knowledgeable but extremely benevolent interpretation; and especially the recent monumental (764-page) study by the American Jesuit scholar William J. Richardson, *Heidegger,* Through Phenomenology to Thought (The Hague: Martinus Nijhoff, 1963). Richardson, though critical, is basically sympathetic to Heidegger. His special merit is the meticulous effort at standardization of English terminology for the rendering of the semantemes of this subtle manipulator and etymological archaeologist of his own native (German) language. Throughout this chapter, we have adhered consistently to the Richardson renderings of all crucial concepts. Considerable compounding of original complexity and even chaos has resulted from the divergence and even disparity of renderings on the part of earlier translators. In Heidegger renderings, drastic precision is absolutely mandatory.

Was ist Metaphysik? (Bonn: Cohen, 1930), which posited Non-Being (*das Nichts*) as parallel to and even as the foundation of Being (*das Sein*), but likewise on the whole attitude and approach, in *Being and Time* (*Sein und Zeit*),[2] to *There-being* (*Dasein*) as Being-unto-end (*Sein zum Ende*), which ultimately emerged as Being-unto-death (*Sein zum Tode*).

I. *The Charge of "Atheism" and the Absolute Primacy of Being*

The charge of "atheism" was a subsequent and derivative charge; and Sartre presented his own atheistic existentialism as the completion and logical conclusion of the phenomenological ontology of *Being and Time*.

Heidegger's reply was speedy and could not have been more categorical: in his *Brief über Humanismus* (1947), he rejected both the "atheism" charge and the Sartrean claim; defending the positive character of his own new interpretation of Being, Heidegger vigorously disassociates his own position from Sartrean existentialism and atheism. Nevertheless, the Heideggerian position must certainly be admitted to diverge drastically from every known theological position of Western thought, both on theproblem of God and on that of Being, from which latter problem the God-problem directly derives. And the divergence manifests itself both in what Heidegger denies and in what he positively asserts.

It is indicative, not to say "paradoxical", that Heidegger, in his essay on Rilke, agrees with Hölderlin in characterizing the modern age as a "time of want" (*dürftige Zeit*) still enshrouded in the darkness of night; and this because our times are characterized by the "want of God" (*Fehl Gottes*).[3]

[2] The original German text, *Sein und Zeit,* was first published as "Sein und Zeit. Erste Hälfte," in *Jahrbuch für Philosophie und phänomenologische Forschung,* VIII (Spring 1927), edited by Edmund Husserl, and was published simultaneously in a special printing. The English translation by John Macquarrie & Edward Robinson, *Being and Time* was made from the 7th German edition published by Neomarius Verlag, Tübingen. In a Preface to the Seventh German Edition, Heidegger himself notes: "While the previous editions have borne the designation 'First Half', this had now been deleted. After a quarter of a century, the second half could no longer be added unless the first were to be presented anew. Yet the road it has taken remains even today a necessary one, if our Dasein is to be stirred by the question of Being" (Cf. English translation, *Being and Time,* p. 17).

[3] "Wozu Dichter?," in *Holzwege,* p. 284. Heidegger indicates that the worst feature of the times is that this "want of God" has not yet been heeded or recognized as a "want" in either sense of that word!

Heidegger cites the following features as typical of the deviations of modern civilization which have issued from modern thought: *science, machine technology*, facilitated by the development of applied mathematics; *art* conceived in accord with the canons of aesthetics, where the work of art comes an object of individual experience and art itself the expression of man's life; *culture* as a realization of the highest values with the transition to the "politic of culture". And finally, as a fifth phenomenon of the modern age, *desacralization* (*Entgötterung*).[4] This term (which in the original means literally "degodding") does not signify, Heidegger is at pains to point out, merely the displacement of the gods, vulgar atheism. Desacralization is a process with a dual aspect: on the one hand, the picture of the world (*Weltbild*) has been dechristianized by the positing of the Infinite, the Unconditioned, the Absolute, as the foundation of the world; and, on the other hand, Christianity has expressed its distinctively Christian character in a way-of-looking-at-the *world* (the Christian world-picture) and thus has undergone a modernization process. Desacralization is the state in which man finds himself because of a want of de-cision (*Ent-scheidung*), understood as freedom unto truth in its negativity, with respect to God and the gods. Revived Christianity has the better half of the bargain; but, Heidegger hastens to add, desacralization "is thus seen to be so little exclusive of religious feeling that it is rather by this channel that the relation to the gods is transformed into religious experience". It is not difficult to see, in this paradoxical approach, the dialectical function assigned to Non-being as parallel to Being, a function clarified in Heidegger's later writings.

These later writings pose an urgent question to the reader: "What is Heidegger's attitude to theism and Christianity?" The answer is by no means simple and the Heidegger-interpreters have not yet found any basis of agreement. The ambiguity of the Heideggerian position here stems once again from his historicizing bias: [5] on the one hand he seems to accept as inevitable for philosophy the modern trend to the expulsion of God; on the other hand, it is difficult in the extreme to know whether and to what extent Heidegger identifies the truth of Christianity with its historical manifestations, in other words whether he admits the divine status of Christianity as the only revealed religion (Kierkegaard's "Religion B") or whether, on th eother hand, he considers Christianity to be an historical modification or interpretation of the fundamental religious feeling attributed to man (Kierkegaard's "Reli-

[4] Cf. "Die Zeit des Weltbildes," in *Holzwege*, p. 70.

[5] Cf. especially the *Nachwort* to M. Heidegger, *Was ist Metaphysik?* (Frankfurt: Klostermann, 1949 [5]), pp. 40ff.

gion A").[6] Sporadic but insistent references weight the scales in favor of a negative rather than a positive attitude here on Heidegger's part.

Heidegger's judgment on Christianity is explicit in the later works, in which the influence of Nietzsche becomes more and more operative: Heidegger reproaches Christianity with having renewed and revived the Platonic cleavage of the real by the distinction between creatures as lower beings and creator as the higher Being, and with having opposed this conception to the classical conception; and Heidegger seems to approve Nietzsche's definition of Christianity as "Platonism for the people".[7] This solidarity between Christianity and the perversion of Greek metaphysics is patently insinuated and Heidegger leaves no doubt that he finds this solidarity to work against the best interests of Christianity. He even has recourse to St. Paul's words as involving a condemnation of Greek philosophy. The passage is vital to any proper grasp of Heideggerian historicism.

Heidegger notes that classical metaphysics had taken as its object τὸ ὂν and so inevitably moved within the realm of *ens in quantum ens* (being as being) in its totality. Thus it saw this totality of being as such in its most general features (ὂν καθόλου = universal being); but subsequently this totality came to be considered in the sense of the supreme and therefore divine Being (ὂν καθόλου, ἀκρότατον θεῖον). In this way, Aristotelian metaphysics perpetrated the supreme equivocation of posing at once as an ontology and a theology; this enabled it to be taken over by Christian theology. The theological character of Greek philosophy, therefore, does not depend on the fact of this Greek philosophy subsequently having been taken over by the theology of Christianity and transformed by it. It depends rather on the unveiling and revealing of being as being, from the outset in Greek philosophy. This unveiling of Being was the main element in Greek philosophy that rendered possible its take-over by Christianity. Whether this take-over was to the advantage or to the detriment of Christian theology, the theologians can decide, upon reflection on what constitutes Christianity and on what St. Paul wrote in his first Letter to the Corinthians 7, 20: "Do you not see how God has shown up the foolishness of human wisdom?" And here is the admonition to Christian theology: Is not

[6] For this distinction between natural religion and revealed religion, in Kierkegaard, cf. S. Kierkegaard, *Afslut. uvid. Efterskrift,* p. II, sect. 2 A, 3; *C. W.,* Vol. VII, pp. 456ff.; Italian translation by C. Fabro (Bologna, 1963), Vol. II, pp. 353ff.

[7] M. Heidegger, *Einführung in die Metaphysik* (Tübingen, 1953) p. 80; English translation by Ralph Manheim, *An Introduction to Metaphysics* (New Haven: Yale University Press, 1958), p. 106. Cf. "Der Spruch des Anaximander," in *Holzwege,* p. 310.

Christian theology going to have to make up its mind once more definitively to consider philosophy as foolishness, in accord with the word of the Apostle? By its ambiguous and double-faced approach, metaphysics confines itself within being and renders itself incapable of any experience of Being which hides in being.[8]

Heidegger himself never says what precisely is the essence of Christianity. But we know that he finds the Christian idea of creation inadmissible, as implying a production out of nothing and therefore denying the truth of the principle: *ex nihilo nihil fit*. Nothingness or Non-being thus becomes, in Heidegger's opinion, the concept which, in the Christian philosophico-theological tradition, is opposed to that Being that truly is, the *Summum ens,* the Supreme Being, God as *ens increatum* (uncreated being). But Heidegger holds this to be an overleaping of the crucial point, the fundamental point, because it involves a neglect of the problem of Being and Non-being, and especially the problem that "if God produces out of Non-being, he must precisely be able to relate to Non-being. But if God is God, He cannot know non-Being, since He excludes from Himself, as Absolute, all nonentity".[9] The only valid concept of "Non-being" is attainable not by setting Non-being over against being (*ens*) but rather by making it belong to the Being of beings, of the existent (*ens*) and ultimately to identify it theoretically with Being itself, in accord with the Hegelian principle that "pure Being and pure Non-being are the same".[10]

Heidegger interprets the doctrine of creation as the second typical element of the perversion of Western thought, the first being the Platonic-Aristotelian conception which made being (*das Seiende*) in its totality, as Being itself, the foundation of the opening-up of being. The second error now proceeds to transform being, thus open as a totality, into being as something created by God. This error Heidegger holds to have been perpetrated in the Middle Ages. The third error was that of transforming being into an object of imagination and representation; and this Heidegger holds to have been the work of modern subjectivism.[11]

Heidegger's rejection of the Christian doctrine of creation is rooted in his critique of the hylomorphic theory which he accuses Medieval philosophy of having transferred from the realm of exterior instrumentality into a conception of being. This point seems to us crucial for a pinpointing and resolution of the ambiguity in which the entire Heideggerian

[8] *Einleitung* to M. Heidegger, *Was ist Metaphysik?* [5], pp. 18f.

[9] *Ibid.*, pp. 35f.

[10] Hegel, *Wissenschaft der Logik,* Book I; ed. Lasson, Vol. I, (Leipzig, 1934), p. 67.

[11] Cf. M. Heidegger, "Der Ursprung des Kunstwerkes," in *Holzwege,* pp. 63f. Cf. also M. Heidegger, "Die Zeit des Weltbildes," p. 83.

apparatus operates on this essential point. From his own words, it is clear that Heidegger identifies the *ens creatum* of Christianity with the composite of matter and form; and it is equally clear that Heidegger attributes such an interpretation to St. Thomas Aquinas. But a modicum of familiarity with Christian thought would make it clear that the doctrine of creation asserted in the Bible has been taught unequivocally by Christianity since its first appearance on the scene. And a modicum of familiarity with and understanding of medieval thought would make it clear how vigorously and persistently St. Thomas fought to defend the thesis that created spiritual natures are absolutely devoid of any matter whatever and therefore simple substances, composite only in the sense of being a union of essence and the participated act of existence (*esse*). The relation of existence (*esse*) to the created essence which it actualizes is indeed a relation of act and potency like that of form and matter; but it is not realized in the same way as is the form-matter relation; rather it is realized in conformity with the dialectic of participation. The universal hylomorphism mentioned by Heidegger was indeed championed during the Middle Ages by the school that styled itself "Augustinian"; but St. Thomas fought it most vigorously during his whole life. The tragedy was that Aquinas' own solution was not followed in subsequent centuries, due to an invasion of formalism which infiltrated the Thomistic school itself and gave rise to disturbing fluctuations. The Heideggerian ambiguity should warn all Thomists (and all philosophers, for that matter!) how urgent it is to return to the genuine Thomist metaphysic of participation. The fortunes of this metaphysic are in no way tied to the fortunes of the Platonic-Aristotelian dualism, inadvertent to creation; nor yet to the fortunes of Scholastic formalism, inadvertent to real and genuine existence (*esse*) and to the ontological status of spiritual beings.[12]

The most surprising element in the Heideggerian approach to this

[12] Cf. Thomas Aquinas, *Quodlibet. De Spiritualibus creaturis.*, Art. 1. Genuine Thomism speaks of *essentia* and *esse,* not of *essentia* and *existentia,* nor yet of *esse essentiae* and *esse existentiae*. It is these latter approaches of formalistic Scholasticism which Heidegger rightly considers to be the beginning of the ambiguity of modern thought, culminating in Nietzsche (Cf. M. Heidegger, *Platons Lehre von der Wahrheit. Mit einem Brief über den "Humanismus"* [Bern: Francke, 1947]—hereinafter to be referred to as *PLBH*—p. 86; *idem, Holzwege,* pp. 219, 223, 233); but Heidegger is wrong in attributing them to Thomas Aquinas himself, as he does repeatedly (Cf. M. Heidegger, *PLBH*, pp. 57, 68f.). Heidegger posits the question of *essentia* and *existentia* as central to the whole problem of the truth of Being and he treats of it constantly, down to and including his major work *Nietzsche*. For the notions of *esse* in Aquinas, cf. C. Fabro, *La nozione metafisica di partecipazione* (Turin, 1963 [3]), pp. 187ff. On the fluctuations of the Thomistic school, cf. *idem, Participation et causalité,* pp. 280ff.; Italian edition *Partecipazione e causalità,* pp. 603ff.

whole problematic is his recent declaration that the doctrine of the Christian faith on creation not only ignores the real "question" of Being but displays "neither faith nor questioning, but . . . indifference" to the question itself. Thus, he charges, the opening words of the Bible: "In the beginning God created the heavens and the earth" constitutes no real reply to this question, because it bears no relation to it whatever. And the reason is that, for faith, this question is foolishness. Well, says Heidegger: "Philosophy is this very foolishness." Therefore a "Christian philosophy" is a round square and a misunderstanding. To philosophize is to ask: "Why are there beings at all and not much rather Non-being?" And if this question be resolutely and consequentially posed, then it signifies "a daring attempt to fathom this unfathomable question by disclosing what it summons us to ask, to push our questioning to the very end. Where such an attempt occurs there is philosophy."[13] To Christianity, there is left only theology, conceived as "a thinking and questioning elaboration of the world of Christian experience, i.e., of faith." And he remarks most severely on the "disastrous notion that philosophy can help to provide a refurbished theology if not a substitute for theology, which will satisfy the needs and tastes of the time." Such an attitude is indicative of a loss of faith in "the true greatness of the task of theology". This bastard "Christian theology", thus joined in unholy union with Greek philosophy, comes down quite simply to a metaphysic and is part and parcel of the process of secularization of the Western mind.[14]

The meaning and significance of these insinuations becomes quite clear in the light of Heidegger's contention that Christianity itself might well be a consequence and elaboration of nihilism. This nihilism stems, for Heidegger, precisely from that brand of metaphysics which he is combatting. This metaphysics, Heidegger charges, has mistakenly distinguished Being into a sensible and a supra-sensible world and then held the former to be sustained and determined by the latter. The age of metaphysics is that historical span embracing the fatal loss of all constructive and structuring power on the part of the suprasensible world,

[13] M. Heidegger, *Einführung in die Metaphysik,* p. 6; English translation *An Introduction to Metaphysics,* p. 8. The other quotations in this paragraph are from the same page in the German original, from p. 7 in the English translation.

[14] Cf. "Hegels Begriff der Erfahrung," in *Holzwege,* p. 187. Heidegger adds that medieval theology supported the very basic errors committed by the Latin translators in rendering the Greek term φύσις as *natura,* the Greek term ἐνέργεια as *actualitas,* the Greek term ουσία as *substantia,* the Greek term ὑπο-κείμενον as *subjectum* and so on; it was from these mistranslations that the precipitous decline of Western thought took its origin. The error of the Latin version lies in having omitted all reference to the appropriate primordial experience linked with each one of these Greek terms (Cf. M. Heidegger, *Holzwege,* pp. 12ff., 273, 298; *idem, Einführung in die Metaphysik,* pp. 10, 138, etc.; English translation *An Introduction to Metaphysics,* pp. 13, 139f., etc.).

the Platonic Ideas, God, the moral law, the authority of reason, progress, the happiness of the majority, culture, civilization. Heidegger concludes: "Unbelief, in the sense of a decline and fall of the doctrines of the Christian faith . . . is always merely a consequence of the nihilism implicit in metaphysics." Atheism and unbelief would then have to be attributed to Christian theology itself, as that theology has entered into an alliance with metaphysics. This would be the meaning of the phrase "God is dead", as uttered by Nietzsche (and the young Hegel before him).[15]

II. *The Eclipse of the "Sacral" and the Loss of God*

Heidegger's polemical stand on the God-problem can be expressed in the following terms, which show how that stand derives from his conception of the truth of Being: even as Western thought, especially after Plato and Aristotle, has misunderstood the problem of the truth of Being, so it has confused and jeopardized the whole God-problem as such. Actually the original terms for Being in Greek philosophy all had the same basic significance: Anaximander, with his χρεών (literally "Handing" or "Handling"), is thinking of Being as handing to beings their essence, or more precisely as handing-out beings in that by which they come-to-presence; Parmenides' term μοῖρα (literally "Portion" or "Portioning") indicates the structural character of that handing-out and the resulting presence of the "present" (gift handed out); the same can be said, claims Heidegger, for the λόγος of Heraclitus, the ἰδέα and the εἶδος of Plato, the ἐνέργεια (and even the ουσία) of Aristotle, all of them loud in their proclamation of the "open-ness" for the shining-forth of Being in beings.[16] The decline and fall of philosophy commences when the εἶδος (as such "form" but from εἰδῶ, "to see") begins to be conceived as a superadded and static form for Aristotelian contemplation, when the ἰδέα has become a μορφή (form) of a body, the σύνολον (literally "the whole together") has come to be thought of as the single

[15] M. Heidegger, "Nietzsche's Wort 'Gott ist tot,'" p. 204. Hegel is cited on p. 197 and Pascal on the following page as reporting Plutarch's saying: "The great Pan is dead."

Corresponding to the denial of creation within the limits of natural religion is the denial, within the limits of supernatural religion, of the Incarnation and the Redemption in and through Christ's Death and Resurrection as "conclusive events" of history. With his theory of Demythologization, R. Bultmann has developed, with his own principles, this denial, tacit but implicit in the thought of Heidegger (cf. R. Bultmann, *Das Evangelium des Johannes* [Göttingen, 1950 [11]], p. 38 and *passim;* cf. also *idem,* Jesus [Tübingen, 1951[13]], pp. 7 ff.; English translation: *Jesus and the Word* [New York: Charles Scribner's Sons, 1958], pp. 3ff.).
him" (Lasson, I, p. 63).

[16] Cf. M. Heidegger, "Der Spruch des Anaximander," in *Holzwege,* p. 342.

whole resulting from the combination of μορφή and ὕλη (matter), and the ἔργον (literally and primordially "deed") begins to appear in the guise of the ἐνέργεια ("operation"). This form of presence becomes the *actualitas* of the *ens actu*. The *actualitas* becomes "effective reality" (*Wirklichkeit*). "Effective reality" becomes "objectiveness" (*Gegenständlichkeit*). "Objectiveness" becomes subjective "esthetic experience" (*Erlebnis*).[17] And so the Being of beings and its truth have come to be forgotten and neglected ever more seriously; and this forgetfulness and neglect has culminated in the complete foundering of modern thought and Western civilization.

Heidegger devotes all his own efforts to a concentrated attempt to recover and render manifest again, both in ancient and in modern thought, the fundamental truth which that thought has forgotten and is concealing: it is beyond question that the most varied Heidegger essays all converge on this one crucial point: his anaylsis of Anaximander, Parmenides, Heraclitus (with the brief note on Protagoras) and Sophocles to detach the pre-Socratic conception; his study of Plato's myth of the cave; his continual references to Aristotle; his studies on Kant and Hölderlin; his masterly analysis of the Hegelian notion of "experience" in the brief Introduction to the Phenomenology; and his studies on Nietzsche. Equally evident is Heidegger's main aim: that of doing away with metaphysics and philosophy itself considered as a technique of conceptual manipulations (abstraction, dialectic) and of abolishing the monopoly of metaphysics and philosophy upon the interpretation of the truth of being, in order to make room for a "preontological experience" of that truth. For Heidegger the term "preontological" is equivalent to the term "ontological" properly used and therefore is diametrically opposed to any irrationalist, vitalist, instinctivist or other such approach and conception.

Heidegger's aim is to avoid at once both the Scylla of metaphysics which would push God back into the far distance as mere cause of being and would inevitably lead to nihilism, and the sceptical phenomenonism of Sartre which makes the denial of God the very principle of philosophy. Heidegger himself rather poses the relation to God as constitutive of human being, inasmuch as the human being related only to the finite is outside of Being and "homeless" (*heimatlos*). Heidegger aims at a supremely drastic stand, transcending all problematic and reducible to the following conditional formula: "Granted that the truth of being consists in openness to the self-presentation of the Being of beings, the problem as to whether or not God exists can only be settled on the basis of the self-presentation of Being itself". The crux of decision is therefore an experience and not any set of conceptual mechanisms. Is there such

[17] Cf. M. Heidegger, "Der Ursprung des Kunstwerkes," in *Holzwege,* p. 68.

an experience? Heidegger's main charge against the modern age is precisely that of having forgotten and neglected this experience; the greatest error of modern times and the real root of modern-day ills is precisely this consigning to oblivion of the crucial constitutive experience of humanity. This is the experience of "the sacral" (*Das Heilige*). But for Heidegger, too, the manifestation of God is the end-term of a process of which he himself indicates the following stages: "(1) Only on the basis of the truth of being can the essence of the sacral be thought. (2) only on the basis of the essence of the sacral can the essence of deity be thought. (3) Only in the light of the essence of the deity can the proper connotation of the word 'God' be thought and expressed." [18]

There is thus a progression in the ontological revelation: from being to the sacral, from the sacral to deity, from deity to God. And it is the first step here which is really crucial: it is uniquely in terms of the "dimension of the sacral" that the God-man relation can be evaluated, uniquely in terms of this dimension that it can be decided whether God is near to man or whether on the contrary God has turned his face away from man at the moment in history at which we are living. But the "sacral" manifests itself only in the revelation of Being and is therefore beyond any reflexive or conceptual thought: "The sacral is primordially simply the dimension of presence (*Wesensraum*) of deity, buttressing in turn the dimension needed by gods and God; this dimension can therefore come to light only in the wake of a long preparatory illumination and experience of Being itself." [19] This primordial and crucial experience, therefore, is not a process of discursive reasoning but rather a "process of experience."

The essence of the "sacral" is studied in Heidegger's commentary on Hölderlin and especially highlighted in the latest writings. Heidegger shows that, for Hölderlin, the terms "nature", "chaos", "the sacral", "the open" ultimately come down to the same thing. Choas too is sacral and the open indicates the *immediate,* wherein can be effected the encounter between mortals and the Immortals. The "sacral" is above and beyond gods and men and is precisely that which renders possible the presence of the former to the latter: "The sacral, as that which is more ancient than the ages and higher than the gods, constitutes in its ad-vent the basis of a new beginning of a new history. The sacral effects the primordial decision concerning men and gods, whether they are and who they are and how they are and when they are." [20] The sacral bequeaths the Word and effects its own ad-vent in this Word; this "sacral" is therefore of that cosmic nature, suggested to German idealism by Spin-

[18] M. Heidegger, *PLBH,* p. 102.

[19] *Ibid.,* pp. 85f.

[20] M. Heidegger, *Erläuterungen zu Hölderlins Dichtung* (Frankfurt a. M.: Klostermann, 1951 [2]), pp. 73f.

oza and the theosophical tradition and translated by Hölderlin into the realm of poetry even as by Schleiermacher into the realm of theology.

The secret of Hölderlin's poetry lies in its discovery of this realm of the "sacral" as the suture needed by the modern age which is the "age of the gods fled away and of the gods to come", "a time of want" (*eine dürftige Zeit*). It is the poet's assignment "to name the gods in form primordial, what Hölderlin calls *'stiften'* (origin-ate); it is the philosopher's assignment subsequently to think them after their proper essence." [21]

But what then is this "sacral"? For the poet, it is the Supreme, the Glad-some (*das Höchste, das Heitere*); it is holiness in the sense of wholeness, wholesomeness, "the angelic which is the property of the gods." There is therefore an intimate solidarity between Being and the sacral for ultimately the very re-velation of Being (i.e., the re-versal of its veiling, its unveiling) reveals itself as founded upon the sacral. Likewise evident is the solidarity between the sacral and deity; but here no static conclusion is possible, especially when we are speaking of the ultimate stage, that of the trasition from deity to God.

In his latest writings, Heidegger has introduced his own ontological picture of the self-structuring of the "thing" in combination with its own becoming in the open-ness of Being into a perfect square: the earth and the heaven, the mortals and the Divine Immortals. They converge to form a unity, but their convergence is of a sort that precludes either subsisting without the other, since each mirrors after its own fashion the essence of the other. Thus it is that there is "World" (*Welt*) and that "World worldifies" (*Welt weltet*).[22] But who are these "Divine Immortals" (*Die Göttlichen*)"? They are the messengers sign-posting toward deity; and it is their secret guidance that re-veals God in his essence, that very essence that veils him in every encounter with what is present.

Heidegger has an analysis of the poetic essence of the ontological Quadrate in the notes to an unpublished commentary on Georg Traskl's lyric poem *A Winter Evening* (*Ein Winterabend*). The wayfarer wandering on "paths obscure" is summoned into the hospitable house where bread and wine await him; but even before this, the "dawn of grace" may have prepared for the seeker a clear gold splendor of its own. From this poetic vision Heidegger is led to the crux of his own theme. Calling things by their name (the tolling of the evening bell, the snow on the window, bread and wine in the cottage) bring things nearer; thereby the

[21] *Ibid.*, pp. 37, 44.

[22] Cf. "Der Ursprung des Kunstwerkes," in *Holzwege*, p. 33. This odd Heideggerian neologism has already occurred in *Vom Wesen des Grundes:* "World never *is*, it *worldifies*" (Welt *ist* nie, sondern *weltet*") (M. Heidegger, *Vom Wesen des Grundes* [Frankfurt a. M., 1949 [3]], p. 40).

world is likewise brought nearer, that Quadrate mirrored in the world (earth, sky, Divine Immortals, human mortals). In the world thus evoked, things "tarry in some fashion". Mortals are summoned as guests into this Quadrate of the world. In the language that is granted to man there is effected nothing less than the unification of thing and world, their intimate mutual nexus, but simultaneously their persistence in their respective distinctness. Heidegger calls this a "dif-ference" which must be understood in the deepest sense of a *dif-ferre* (a bearing of each other out) and a "scission-between" (*Unter-Schied*). This scission manifests itself as "pain" and is accomplished as pain. The wayfarer who in Traskl's poem crosses the threshold petrified by pain is cor-relating what is dif-ferentiated, is effecting the transition and translation from exteriority to interiority. Thus does the man who poetizes and thinks thus to no-one ought to create himself a God by cunning in order to mask this dwell or not dwell—God".

In his commentary on Hölderlin, Heidegger had stopped at the sacral, writing: "The sacral manifestly appears. But God remains remote . . . God is wanting and the "want of God" (*Fehl Gottes*) is the reason for the want of the 'sacred names' ". In his commentary on Rilke, Heidegger seems to consider this want as irreparable, at least for the present: even though such a want of God "does not preclude either the continuation of the Christian relation to God in individuals and in the Church, nor yet any de-valuation of this relation to God," [23] it does mean that no-one ought to create himself a God by cunning in order to mask this want, that no-one ought even to appeal to the usually accepted God, for this would evince a highhanded neglect of this deep want and lack. Heidegger's conclusion is that man must "wait in the want thus compounded until from the nearness to the wanting God there be warranted the primordial word that names the Exalted." [24]

This diagnosis clearly highlights the solidary nexus between the eclipse of the sacral and modern atheism: the vanishing of God from the modern world is the direct consequence of the loss of the truth of Being, of the reduction of Being to a purely mental basis and of the act of Being to willing, to the Will-to-will, to the Will-to-power (*Wille zur Macht*). Heidegger shows that he has realized that the insecurity of the modern world is the consequence of the forgetfulness of Being in Western philosophy.[25] It is indeed the forgetfulness of Being as such which provokes and triggers the vanishing, the total eclipse of the sacral in the individual being. This melting away of the sacral inescapably involves a

[23] M. Heidegger, "Wozu Dichter?," in *Holzwege,* p. 248.

[24] Cf. "Das Ding" (written 1950) and "Bauen, Wohnen, Denken" (written 1951), both published in *Vorträge und Aufsätze.*

[25] Cf. "Wozu Dichter?," in *Holzwege,* p. 271.

closing of the open-ness to the sacral. And this closing in turn obscures and hides the want of God. The obscure want causes each and every individual being to experience an insecurity-situation, which thrusts man into the world, into the whole of being, as a homeless expatriate. The very "where" (*Wo*) of any abiding "whereabouts" (*Wohnung*) within the individual being as such seems to be annihilated, for Being itself as the principle and foundation buttressing all such abiding habitation has been rejected. It is this homelessness of man with respect to his own *essence* that has been half-admitted and half-denied, and in any case replaced by the thrust for conquest of the earth and the drive outward into outer space. It is the forgetfulness of being that impels man to deny himself in the world and to lose himself in There-being.[26]

In the face of a conception of truth as the Will-to-power, every man is defenseless and lost already. The lethal power (*das Tödliche*) in our modern world is therefore not the atom bomb as it is so often touted as being the deadly weapon *par excellence*. It is something quite different that has long been threatening man with death, with a drastic destruction of his very human nature; and that is the absolutism of sheer willing on the part of radically autonomous man.[27] It is this notion about the will which is threatening men in their very essence, this notion that the will is its own ultimate foundation and justification, and the consequent erroneous supposition that a liberation, transformation, accumulation and peaceful management of the things and objects of nature will suffice to render man's estate (*das Menschsein*) tolerable for all and more happy than miserable.

But the peace touted by this pacifism is obviously the restlessness of the frenzy of anthropocentric and ultimately inevitably tyrannocentric autocracy, a self-rule that is deliberately self-centered and self-oriented. What threatens man in his very essence is the opinion that holds that this pursuit of mere material productivity can be risked safely so long as other interests are kept in play, such as those of a religious faith: as though religious faith could subsist once man has lost the truth of being. What is threatening man in his very essence is the opinion that holds that technocracy can bring the world into line and into good shape, whereas it is in fact precisely this technocratic management which is reducing to the lowest common and uniform denominator of the production-line all hierarchies of values, thus destroying in advance the very terrain for the possible ad-vent of such a hierarchy and for its recognition, a recognition that would proceed from a true picture of being!

[26] Cf. M. Heidegger, *Nietzsche*, Vol. II, p. 394.

[27] I am here paraphrasing the passage of the essay "Wozu Dichter?," in *Holzwege*, pp. 271f.

The transition in the evolution of modern thought from the *cogito* to the *volo* has effected a tragic transformation of what claimed to be a human Enlightenment and an affirmation of freedom into an ever-increasing darkening of night over the world and an augmentation of the essential panic accruing from the felling if being defenseless and indeed of being under attack from all sides. This happy summer solstice of technology, so loudly touted, is the shortest day that ever dawned for man: for it brings him up squarely against the threat of an endless winter. Not only is man now deprived of any abiding home; the very integrity of the ensemble of beings is thrust into dark, foreboding question! The healing remedy eludes us; the world is sinking into the dismal state of an incurable. Not only is the sacral hidden from us, that sacral that could in its wholesomeness serve as a scent to lead us to deity; even the scent of the sacral, in its turn, seems to have gone cold, for there is scarcely even any human mental health in evidence, scarcely any human whole-ness. The last frail hope is that there are still mortals capable of seeing the threat of the want of health and wholeness for what it is, namely, the threat posed by the want and lack of radical salvation. They must see what a peril is hanging over man's head. This peril consists in the threat to the very essence of man in his relation to Being itself, not in any merely accidental danger. It is the radical peril of eternal perdition, of man's losing him*self* irretrievably.

III. *Hegelian "Being Itself" (Sein selbst) and Heideggerian "Being of beings" (Sein des Seienden): The God-Problem*

Heidegger identifies as follows the cardinal contributions of Nietzsche, Hölderlin and Hegel: Nietzsche clarified the essence of nihilism; Hölderlin probed more deeply than anyone before into the hidden presence of deity; Hegel, for his part, demonstrated the issue of the problem of Being in its speculative aspect. For Hegel showed that thought is not to be considered from the psychological point of view nor yet from the angle of vision of the theory of knowledge (i.e., epistmeologically), but rather in the radical dimension of the "thinkability of the thought", in the supreme freedom of its own essence, according to the principle of the "transcendental" which Hegel conceives as an Absolute.[28]

The "business" (*Sache*) of thought for Hegel is Being, understood as

[28] Cf. "Die onto-theo-logische Verfassung der Metaphysik," in *Identität und Differenz* (Pfullingen: Neske, 1956), pp. 38ff. English translation by Kurt F. Leidecker, *Essays in Metaphysics: Identity and Difference* (New York: Philosophical Library Inc., 1960), pp. 33ff.

thought thinking itself, thought coming to itself primarily in the process of its speculative development; it is Being (*Sein*) grappling with the conceivability of beings in absolute thought and as absolute thought. For us, Heidegger specifies, the business of thought is the same, i.e. Being, but Being in terms of its difference (*Differenz*) from beings. More precisely stated: for Hegel, the business of thought is thought as "Absolute Concept";[29] for the Heideggerian, the business of thought is the abovementioned difference as difference.

Hegel's "measuring-rod" (*Messgabe*) for his colloquium with the whole history of philosophy is an ingress into the power and dynamic of what has been thought by preceding thinkers; and it is no accident that he expressly applies his measuring-rod on occasion in his confrontation with Spinoza and Kant. In Spinoza, Hegel finds the acme of the "substance-approach". But he insists that this cannot be accepted as definitive, because it does not trace being back to its ultimate ground (*Grund*) as self-thinking thought; being as substance and substantiality has not yet displayed itself as a subject in its absolute subjectivity. Kant takes a different approach; and this Kantian approach has been crucial for idealism: Hegel sees in the principle of the a priori synthesis of apperception "one of the most profoundly important principles for speculative evolution". Heidegger says that his own rule for confrontation with the philosophical tradition is the same, i.e., an ingress into the thrust of the thought of the past: the difference is that Heidegger is going to seek for that thrust not in what has been thought (as do Hegel and Aristotle in order to "supercede" what has been thought),[30] but rather in something that has not yet been thought, not yet been really thought through, but which burgeons ever anew: the Being of beings.

Hegel does, to be sure, insist that he is making a drastic and radical beginning in his first determination, the simple and immediate phenomenon of "pure being". But for Hegel this beginning is something which is neither immediate nor yet mediate; and it is presented in its speculative

[29] Heidegger quotes from Hegel, *Wissenschaft der Logik,* Vol. II, p. 484: "The Absolute Idea alone is Being, imperishable Life, self-knowing truth, and the whole of truth." In his recent essay "Hegel und die Griechen," in *Die Gegenwart der Griechen im neueren Denken.* Festschrift für Hans-Georg Gadamer zum 60. Geburtstag (Tübingen: Mohr [Siebeck], 1960), pp. 43ff., Heidegger recurs to this profound agreement of his own thought with that of Hegel, as he traces the Hegelian approach to Being (*Sein*) back to the first beginnings of Greek speculative thought.

[30] This is the same line as that taken by the Neo-Hegelians with Hegel himself: we think particularly of their distinction between what was "living" and what was "dead" (i.e. what was viable and what was unviable) in Hegel's philosophy; we think also of the various and often disparate "reforms" of the Hegelian dialectic by Rosenkranz, K. Fischer, Erdmann, Weisse, right down to N. Hartmann and our own day.

nature as a "result", primarily in the sense of "repercussion" (*Rück-prall*) of the accomplishment of the dialectical motion of self-thinking thought: the product of this motion, the Absolute Idea, is the definitive and manifest Whole, the fullness of being. The repercussion of this fullness is the "void of being" (*die Leere des Seins*), which must be the starting point in science: thus beginning and end of the motion alike is being, which manifests itself as the circular motion which proceeds within its own limits from the fullness of the maximum extrinsication into the fullness of intrinsication. Thus the business of thought for Hegel is self-thinking thought as intrinsically circulating being: this serves as Hegel's justification for his contention that the beginning is given by the "result" or that the beginning in philosophy must be made from the result of the entire dialectical motion.[31] Thus, philosophy is "knowledge of God", theology in the modern sense (or perhaps more accurately in the Aristotelian sense?) rather than in the critical sense of the poet-philosophers of antiquity.[32]

The question of the "onto-theo-logical" character of metaphysics is thus transformed into the question: "How does God[33] come into philosophy, not only modern philosophy but philosophy as such?" The exact sense and significance of the question must be pinpointed before a proper reply can be given. And this leads us again to the very center of Heidegger's thought. To the question: How does God come into philosophy? we can give a proper reply only if we can clarify the nature of that focus into which God is supposed to come, namely philosophy itself.

As soon as we approach the problem of the history of philosophy in a fashion deeper-cutting and more comprehensive than the strictly historical point of view, we shall find that God has entered into it all along the line. But granted that philosophy as thought is the free total involvement in being (*das Seiende*) as such, it follows that God can contact philosophy only to the extent that philosophy, by its very nature, demands and determines the fact and the fashion of his ad-vent into it. And so the question: How does God come into philosophy? comes down to the question: Whence does the onto-theo-logical conception of the essence of metaphysics originate? Now such a statement of the question already

[31] Heidegger recurrently cites that expression from the Introduction to Hegel's *Wissenschaft der Logik,* which Hegel had put in parentheses "it would be God who would have the most incontestable right that the beginning should be made from him" (Lasson, I, p. 63).

[32] Cf. Thomas Aquinas, *Summa contra Gentiles,* I, 4: "Since the deliberation of almost the whole of philosophy is oriented to the knowledge of God" (*Cum fere totius philosophiae consideratio ad Dei cognitionem ordinetur*).

[33] Hölderlin's terminology consistently employs the definite article in all such terms: *der Gott* (the God), *die Gottheit* (the deity), *das Göttliche* (the God-like [= Divine]).

signifies a "re-view" and in this review we reflect on the origin and provenance of the onto-theo-logical structure of all metaphysics.

Returning to Hegel, we see that he thinks Being in its most radical void, in its maximum universality. Simultaneously he thinks Being in its perfectly accomplished fullness. Similarly he calls speculative philosophy, i.e., genuine philosophy (according to his mind), not "onto-theology" but rather the "Science of Logic". This Hegelian designation, Heidegger remarks, manifests the basic line of approach of philosophy as metaphysics, for which from antiquity thought is the business of "Logic"; and Hegel, faithful to this tradition, finds the business of thought in the individual being as such and in the whole, in the movement of Being from its own void to its own fully-developed fullness. And Heidegger tells us the reason why Hegel can do this: it is because for him Being manifests itself as thought.

But Hegel is not the only one who thinks this way: for Ontology, Theology, Onto-theo-logy, etc., are taken in the same sense as Psychology, Biology, Cosmology, Archaeology, etc., where the suffix "logy" indicates that it is a question of "science of", i.e., of a whole considered as that very complex which science regards and treats it as being. And so metaphysics is onto-theo-*logy* inasmuch as it thinks being (*das Seiende*) as such, i.e., universally considered. Metaphysics thinks the Being of beings as the ultimate ancestral unity of what is most universal, of what is everywhere equally valid, i.e., of the Supreme over and above everything. Thus is the Being of beings thought of as being antecedently the ancestral ground. And so we can grasp how it is that God comes into metaphysics and how God there presents himself as the ultimate Source, the "primordial Thing" (*Ur-Sache*), i.e., as *causa sui,* so that being (*das Seiende*) in general and as primordial is "un-ified with" (*in Einem mit*) Being as such in the Greatest and the Highest. The unity of this One is of such a nature that the Last (the latter, i.e., Being) functions as ground and source of the First (the former, i.e., being). The only point is (and it is here again the crucial point!) that the "difference" between the two has not yet been thought at all.

The Being of beings is basic, in the sense of being "ground" (*Grund*) only as *causa sui.* And this is the metaphysical concept of God. Metaphysics must think of God, since the business of thought is Being; but Being shows itself in manifold forms as "ground": as λόγος, as ὑποκείμενον, as substance, as subject.[34] This seems to me to clarify the speculative ambit within which Heidegger maneuvers the Being-beings relationship, within which he speaks of the Being of beings as what is indicated in terms of the "difference". The point here is—and it

[34] Cf. "Die onto-theo-logische Verfassung der Metaphysik," p. 57; English translation, *Essays in Metaphysics,* p. 59.

is the turning point in Heidegger's reversal (*Kehre*): we are only really and genuinely thinking Being when we think of it in terms of its difference from beings; and we are only really and genuinely thinking of beings when we think of them in their difference from Being. This approach is what really brings the difference into proper focus. But if we try to effect an imaginative representation of that difference, then we are forthwith seduced into conceiving the difference as a relation which our own imaginative function has added to Being and beings. This is the conception of traditional and especially of idealist philosophy. But this approach degrades the difference to a distinction produced by our own intelligence. If, on the other hand, we take the "re-view" approach, then we can say: "The Being of beings is properly designated as Being which 'is-es' those beings. The 'is-es' here represents a transitive action of Being passing over [into the beings]. Being here shows itself in the form of a passing over to beings: Being comes-to-presence by unveiling, but simultaneously hides by veiling; it is indeed present-ness but likewise hidden-ness in beings. "Ad-vent" is here a self-concealing Presence, and signifies concealment in non-concealment: Being keeps itself hidden even as it "be-s" (transitively understood) a being.

The point to which Heidegger holds firm in these later writings is the essential conjunction and indivisibility of Being and beings, and the determination and definition of the "difference" wherein is effected the "re-view" called for by Parmenides of old, in his claim of the identity of Being and thought (not in a merely epistemological sense, but rather in the ontological sense already indicated), an identity which Heidegger transfers into the problem of the "difference" between Being and beings. It is within the ambit of the "difference" and on the presupposition of that difference that Heidegger now proceeds to assert (for the first time, it seems to me) what might be called the perfect reciprocity: "That being which, in the ad-vent, the coming-to-presence that conceals itself in non-concealment, is the grounded, and as grounded can be said to be product (produced), does in fact, after its own fashion, ground, operate, cause. The issue of (produced by) the grounding and the grounded as such likewise not only maintains and sustains the two (the grounding and the grounded) separate one from the other, but even maintains them in mutual tension. The separate outcomes (grounding and grounded) are so interwoven in the out-come that not only does Being as ground ground beings, but beings also in turn and after their own fashion ground Being, cause it. Beings can manage this because they "be" the fullness of Being, because they are Be-ing *par excellence*." [35]

[35] *Ibid.*, pp. 66f.; cf. English translation, *Essays in Metaphysics*, P. 61, from which we have felt compelled to depart quite drastically, in the interests of a standardization to the Richardson terminology.

The perfect circularity here manifest shows ever more clearly the more the analysis is intensified how Being substantiates the difference and shows itself as the "different" of beings. Heidegger's statement on this point is of capital and decisive importance: "Inasmuch as Being shows itself as the Being of beings, as the difference, as the issue, it preserves the differentiation and the mutual reference of grounding and underpinning, Being grounds beings; beings as Be-ing *par excellence* ground Being, beings bring Being to pass, Being comes-to-presence in beings; there is mutual twinning between bringing-to-pass and coming-to-presence in reflection. Speaking from the point of view of reflection, this means that the issue is a circling, a mutually circular motion of Being and beings. The grounding itself appears within the clearing of the issue as something that *is,* and consequently as something that, like beings, is a proportionate substantiation, i.e., causation, and yet as such a substantiation requires in turn a grounding via the supreme Cause." [36] But, for Heidegger, the thinker who focusses on the "different" and desires to think beings in the Whole, thinks those beings in an angle of vision which fixes on the different in its difference, without properly adverting to the difference as difference. The different manifests itself as the Being of beings in general and as the Being of beings taken supereminently. Therefore Being appears as ground, beings as grounded; but the supreme Being is the grounding entity in the sense of First Cause. Hitherto, however, metaphysics has been thinking precisely of the Being of beings in those beings themselves, and allowing the "difference" to escape it whereby Being and beings are conjoined and distinguished. One possible way of answering the vexed question could derive from the question: How does God come into metaphysics?, from the essence of metaphysics as such. But the notion that metaphysics has made itself of God is, as we have said, that of *Causa sui* and Heidegger insists: "This is the proper name of God in philosophy",[37] letting it be clearly understood that he considers the Spinozan-Hegelian notion as most representative of the evolution (and of the deviation) of Western thought. It is no longer any surprise, in the light of all this, to hear him say that ". . . the God-less thinking that is contrained to forego the God of philosophy, God as *Causa sui,* is perhaps nearer to the divine God".[38] And this is

[36] *Ibid.,* p. 68; English translation, *Essays in Metaphysics,* p. 62. Again we have departed drastically for the same reasons.

[37] It would be more accurate to say "in the philosophy of Spinoza"! For Spinoza says: "By *causa sui* I understand that whose essence involves existence, or that whose nature cannot be conceived except as existing (*Ethica,* Book I, def. 1). For St. Thomas, on the contrary, God is *esse ipsum,* not mediated by essence. For Heidegger, God cannot be a Person if God is Being itself.

[38] Cf. M. Heidegger, "Die onto-theo-logische Verfassung der Metaphysik," p. 71; English translation *Essays in Metaphysics,* p. 65.

precisely the reason for and the significance of the "re-view", the regress (*Schritt zurück*) from metaphysics into the essence of metaphysics.

With this whole line of thought, Heidegger has certainly contributed to a clarification of the need for a metaphysical orientation in the probing for the truth of being.[39] Heidegger can be said to approach the formulations of Pascal, Kierkegaard, Dostoevsky and such thinkers, in his Nietzsche-inspired analysis of modern and present-day atheism; his path moves along the line of Kant and Hegel, on the other hand, but with the specific distinguishing peculiarity of the re-gress. It is the "straight and narrow path" of Being that Heidegger wishes to regain, that path from which Western thought has gone astray. This "straight and narrow" is for him the only path that offers any hope for thought (and man in thought) becoming finally what it ought to be, the sheer and simple "presence of the Being of beings." Heidegger's path is probably not yet a cul-de-sac: the nexus between Being and the Absolute, attained by the "re-view" and the re-gress into the essence of metaphysics, may well trigger other steps, calculated to bring Heideggerian thought out of its present ambiguity or at least to clarify that ambiguity.

IV. *Indifference to the God-Problem.*

Heidegger claims that the philosopher knows nothing of God and therefore knows nothing of "eternity" either.[40] The philosopher is not a believer and when he reflects on time, he has already decided to "understand time in terms of time itself" (*die Zeit aus der Zeit zu verstehen*), i.e., in terms of the indefectible beings which may well manifest themselves as eternity but which are in truth a pure derivative of temporal being. Heidegger has always remained loyal to his first conception of time, that presented in *Sein und Zeit.* The least that can be said of this position is that it is quite in line with Heidegger's youthful studies on Scotus and that it entrusts to faith the problem of God, together with all the other *praeambula fidei.*

[39] Heidegger includes Thomist philosophy in his accusation of the "formalization" of Being effected from the time of Plato and Aristotle (down to and including idealism and Sartre). (Cf. *Sein und Zeit,* § 20, p. 93; English translation, *Being and Time,* p. 126.) Disoriented by Scotus, Heidegger has not managed to notice the major and salutary upset effected by St. Thomas with his own notion of *esse,* understood as an emergent intensive act, diametrically opposed to *existentia,* understood as "actualization of an essence" (*Verwiklichung einer Essenz*); nor has Heidegger grasped the radical implications of Aquinas' concept of God as *ipsum esse subsistens,* when that concept is seen in the light of this Thomist notion of *esse.* (Cf. M. Heidegger, *PLBH,* p. 71).

[40] This statement was made by Heidegger at a conference on Time, held in 1924; it is reported by K. Löwith in his *Heidegger, Denker in dürftiger Zeit,* p. 43.

In this respect, we do not see any substantial evolution between the first and the second period of Heidegger's thought: the reversal (*Kehre*) actually has no importance in respect of the basic questions, except as making any sort of positive response drastically unlikely, at least on the God-problem. It is true that Heidegger does, in his later period,[41] make *Sein selbst* (Being itself) the condition and ground of ontology, in contradistinction to his earlier interpretation of *Sein* (Being) on the basis of the *da* (There), an interpretation which bases the presence of *Sein* (Being) upon the "existent human reality", the There-being (*Dasein*) of the human existent. Therefore it would seem that, in his later period, he has overcome the phenmoenological subjectivism of the earlier writings. Consequently he sees the thrust of man, in this later stage of his thought, as directed to *Sein selbst,* rather than to the world, as in his earlier writings: the thruster is no longer man but Being itself which refers (in the strict etymological sense of "carries back") man into existence as his proper essence. But the change is less thoroughgoing than might appear and proves entirely negligible so far as our present problem is concerned: what remains basic for Heidegger is the fact that Being coexists with There-being, with the human reality, and has no meaning beyond the horizon of that reality. We might say, in other words, that, although Heidegger has abandoned immanentistic notions of the immanence of Being in the sense of "subjectivity" (as propounded in *Sein und Zeit*), he has in no sense abandoned this immanentistic notion, but has indeed reinforced it, in the more radical sense of "finitude" of a world that projects itself via man in his historical flux of becoming: there is Being to the extent that there is truth; there is truth to the extent that there is man; and there prevails, therefore, a rigid reciprocity both between *Sein* (Being) and *Seiende* (beings) and between *Seiende* (beings) and *Dasein* (There-being). And so the circle is closed: there is no abandonment of the reference of the truth of being to the essence of man; rather is this very reference made the central determining factor of the definition of Being itself.

In the *Sein-Seiende, Seiende-Dasein* reciprocity or circularity, *Sein* (Being) must be held to express the ground, the referend, the clearing which renders possible the coming-to-presence (*Anwesen*) of the *Seiende* (beings), so that however and wherever man probes with all his might, he will always and only find beings (*das Seiende*) but never

[41] Especially since the *Brief über Humanismus* (1947) in which Heidegger declares that the *Kehre* (reversal) has been from *Sein und Zeit* (Being and Time) to *Zeit und Sein* (Time and Being). This does not signify any change of viewpoint but rather a deepening of what led to the "basic and original experience of the forgottenness of Being" (*Grunderfahrung der Seinsvergessenheit*) (cf. M. Heidegger, *PLBH,* p. 72).

Being (*Sein*). And we already know that Being is not God nor yet the divine: if then Being is a function and comes-to-presence in function of beings, it can be readily understood why Being is said to be intrinsically "finite". Being (*Sein*) as ground of coming-to-presence can thus in no sense whatever express the mode of being of the beings which are *die Seienden,* and still less can it express the Supreme Being or a Creator-God.

Heidegger stands entirely outside the Christian tradition of a Creator-God and is therefore precluded from any clear assertion concerning a creation on the part of God or on any question relating to the first origin of Being and of the spirit. After devoting the whole of his labor and energies to the denunciation of the forgetfulness of being occasioned by Western philosophy's confinement of Being into the subjectivity of essence, Heidegger has himself found no better solution than to entrust the truth to a new form of subjectivity, still more comprehensive and radical (i.e., insuperable) than that of immanentism and metaphysical realism.[42] The Heideggerian *Sein selbst* (Being itself), as distinct from the Hegelian *Sein selbst* presented as the "definition of God", is atheistic in content, structure and position, inasmuch as it is the coming-to-presence of the finite by the instrumentality of a finite being condemned to a finite destiny like man's. Heidegger's *Sein* (Being) as such does not, like Sartrian freedom, attain to realization in function of its denial of God; Heidegger's *Sein* simply affirms the finite. But it does neglect God entirely and, even though it may not exclude all open-ness to God, it certainly leaves man deprived of all real support,[43] always in suspension between Being and Nothingness, between non-concealment and concealment. Heidegger has indeed gotten beyond the God who is finite because cosmic (and cosmologized!); but Being still remains finite in its very structure, which is the structure of the phenomenal, of the coming-to-presence, of the "appearing". And so the basic question: Why is there being and not non-being?, remains unanswered.

[42] "Fundamentally, however, Hegel's constructive progress and ascent is not different from Heidegger's destructive regress and descent. Both operate within the same modern eccentricity of a metaphysical historicism, in that they both historicize the Absolute, of the Spirit and of Being respectively" (K. Löwith, *Heidegger, Denker in dürftiger Zeit,* pp. 44f.). In this event, Heidegger's denial of the Absolute emerges as much more serious than Hegel's; for Hegel makes the Absolute, at least from the purely methodological point of view, the principle operating "behind the scenes".

[43] Heidegger seems to conceive of the possibility of a recovery of God on the part of the human mind, in the wake of the decline and fall of philosophy; this recovery would take the form of a conversion (the "leap") and would be social in character (Cf. L. Schuwer, "Intorno ai presupposti della demitizzazione: 'Wie kommt der Gott in die Philosophie,'" in *Il problema della demitizzazione* [Rome, 1962], especially pp. 142ff.).

In Heideggerian terminology, we encounter the twin-pairs, Being and beings, the Divine and the gods or God. Only in this context can the God-problem have any meaning. Now we know that Being and beings subsist in an essential (reciprocal) conjunction and that Being is not God; and an equally essential conjunction prevails between the Divine, the sacral and the gods. We know also, from the famous passage in the *Brief über Humanismus,* that the two twin-pairs are strictly related: the thought of Being prepares the way for the notion of the sacral and the notion of the Sacral moves man to think of "deity"; and it is on the basis of the essence of deity that we can indicate what the name "God" means.[44] Just *what* this transition is, and above all just *how* it occurs, Heidegger does not say; but he does present it quite uncompromisingly as the task of metaphysics: "Metaphysics must think out toward God, because the business of thought is Being; and Being comes-to-presence as ground in manifold ways: as λόγος, as ὑποκείμενον, as substance, as subject." [45]

But all of this does little to help toward any solution of the problem-complex. Moreover it seems to us that the transition is radically compromised, inasmuch as Being as ground is here (as in Aristotle) expressed in many ways (τὸ ὄν πολλαχῶς λέγεται), i.e., in the four indicated, no one of which pertains to or is referred to God. And this is philosophy's aberration, according to Heidegger's charge. God thus is banished from metaphysics because Being is not God: thus, we read that in Being as beings there appear "dis-harmonies"; at the root and basis of the Being-beings tension is the Being-Non-being tension or, better, the tension between Being (in the sense of "coming-to-presence") and nihilation which is disappearing. And this takes us back, unless we are mistaken, to the Hegelian beginning of sheer and pure *Sein* (Being) in conflict with Non-being, in such a way that this conflict is not the death but rather the life of Being. And we can say that, as in Hegel, this Heideggerian *Sein selbst* has the Absolute towering behind it, not in the Hegelian dialectical form but rather in the form of the experience of the sacral: but this experience of the sacral is beyond the bounds of philos-

[44] M. Heidegger, *PLBH,* p. 102.

[45] M. Heidegger, "Die onto-theo-logische Verfassung der Metaphysik," p. 57; cf. English translation, *Essays in Metaphysics,* p. 53. Again we have made our own translation.

Thus the metaphysics of the past, as "*theo*-logy", perpetrates a "Degodding" (*Entgötterung*), that "Desacralization" of which we have already spoken; and it perpetrates this felony by means of its pseudo-Absolute and pseudo-Infinite. The Heideggerian metaphysics, as "*onto*-logy", asserts "God-*lessness*" (Gott-*losigkeit*), in terms of the "finitude of Being". But this Heideggerian position, that seems to coincide with the position of English neo-idealism, in fact derives from a diametrically opposed approach.

ophy. Heidegger's philosophy therefore crystallizes as "God-lessness (*Gott-losigkeit*), as opposed to Western "contentual" philosophy, which culminated in a process of "Un-Godding" (*Entgötterung*). This certainly does signify a radical supersession both of pantheism and of materialist naturalist, deist and rationalist atheism in general, who nullify God by reducing him to the sum total of beings: pantheism in a positive identification and the other forms of atheism in a negative rejection of the very name and concept of God as superfluous. Such a supersession could certainly make possible the search for or the presentation of the true God who cannot be identified with the sum total of the real. But this would involve a dissolution of the continuity and conjunction asserted by Heidegger between the twin pairs of Being-beings and Sacral-Divine; and the accomplishment of the "transition" promised earlier would be precluded. We are therefore left at the end with the insurmountable assertion that for Heidegger God is foreign to and banished from philosophy.

Especially in his later works, Heidegger touches parenthetically but quite explicitly on *the relations between faith and reason,* between philosophy and revelation; and we feel that the conclusion just stated above likewise flows from Heidegger's whole way of conceiving these relations. We have already made quite clear what Heidegger's stand is; here we must add that it is most important for a proper understanding of the precise import of this stand to keep constantly and clearly in mind that Heidegger accepts the angle of vision of modern transcendental idealism as the point of departure of philosophizing, as starting point for the analysis of beings. He does indeed appeal to the Aristotelian formulation of philosophy's assignment as being the investigation and definition of being as being (ὂν ᾗ ὄν); but Heidegger converts this formula into its exact opposite, by interpolating that other question which made its entry into philosophy with Leibniz: "Why is there being at all and not rather non-being?" (*Warum ist überhaupt Seiendes und nicht vielmehr Nichts?*) [46]

Heidegger is certainly well aware of the difference between the two formulas, considerably more so, in fact, than his critics. The point is that the latter (Leibnizian) formulation involves starting with a search for the foundation or ground of being, a search that is preconditioned by the reply and itself represents a prefiguring of that reply, since by its very structure the question, thus asked, already contains the reply that renders a reply pointless and superfluous. And this very fact, in turn, of

[46] M. Heidegger, *Einführung in die Metaphysik,* p. 1; cf. English translation, *An Introduction to Metaphysics,* p. 1 for another example of the confusion introduced by persistently divergent renderings of crucial Heideggerian terms. We have here again adhered to Richardson's standardization.

a reply being pointless constitutes the quintessence of transcendental philosophy, when purified of the superstructure of realist and idealist theological metaphysics and reduced to its own true ground and foundation. For to ask why there is being rather than non-being already amounts to making being dependent on the enquirer who is man and constitutes therefore an assertion that the possibility of being lies primarily in man himself, together with the foreshadowing of the meaning of the destiny of being itself in its conflicting dichotomy with non-being. The Heideggerian assertion that Being is not a product of thought but thought rather an "event" of beings,—this is not yet realism, although it is not idealism any more either, at least in the systematic sense. But it is still immanentism or loyalty to modern-style transcendentalism, in the sense that it bases truth on the a priori capacity of the subject who is man. The Heideggerian question itself already virtually contains the confirmation of this modern-style transcendentalism, drawn directly from Kant but identical with that radical doubt which forms the hidden "ground" of the principle of immanentism, from which (as we have tried to show throughout the entire course of these, our investigations) there flows the absence of God in modern philosophy.

In classical realism, Being is not the "posited" but the "positing" in relation to consciousness, to mind: consciousness is actualized by being, not just anyhow but in a fashion clearly indicating that being is the true ground of consciousness: there is consciousness *because* there is Being and *to the extent that* there is being and *in accord with* the forms of being. Thus the primordial proposition of classical realism is an affirmation of being as self-sufficient and radically primal: Being, as such, suffices unto itself and thereby is the act and ground with respect to consciousness. In this first moment, wherein Being, as ground, actualizes consciousness, there does not and cannot enter into the equation any shadow of non-being, of nothingness, for Being is light and actuality of presence and therefore self-witnessing; and it is the consciousness of being that is "posited". A "being" that would lead the enquirer back to the positing transcendentality of consciousness as its ground would necessarily be something posited by consciousness; and if being is posed by consciousness, it is already de-posed or subordinated to consciousness, to the mind as a function of consciousness, in accord with one or other of the forms of the principle of immanentism.

A further corroboration of our contention concerning the transcendentalism of Heideggerianism is to be found in the very antithesis mobilized by the question between being and non-being. The interpolation of non-being, of nothingness, into the basic question concerning Being, makes crystal clear the transcendentalistically biassed nature of the question itself: for it is only when the mind or transcendental subjectivity is the positing power with respect to Being that subjectivity can cover and embrace the entire spectrum of the possible and actual coming-to-presence of Being and call it in question. But the only way in which the mind, the "substantiating" mind, can call Being in question is to trace it back to the essence of the mind in its sheer potentiality with respect to Being; and this sheer potentiality is the antithesis of being, i.e., non-being, Nothingness. And in this fashion noth-ingness is put on a par with Being; indeed it is Nothingness which calls Being in question, lowering upon it at every moment, undermining its act and presence, emerging as much more than a simple opposite of being, acquiring the status of founding diarch together with being itself! Now no such diarchy can endure; indeed philosophically it is dissolved at the very outset in favor of one of the diarchs; and here Nothingness is initially given the status of being the ultimate ground rendering possible the self-manifestation, the coming-to-presence of Being. Anyone with a modicum of familiarity with the crucial elements of Heideggerian thought is well aware that this granting of ultimate status to nothingness is no mere arbitrary inference but rather the exact formulation of the new outlook Heidegger purveys on philosophy in the wake of the demolition of the Hegelian pseudo-theology.

This makes it easy to grasp the significance of a tightly-packed Heideggerian passage in which the Heideggerian notion of the relations between philosophy and revelation is specifically articulated. The text is so important that we take leave to cite the original at great length. Heidegger begins by saying that an acceptance of the Bible as divine revelation and truth gives the believer the answer to the question as to why there are beings instead of nothingness, even before that question is asked:

". . . everything, that is, except God himself, has been created by him. God himself, the increate creator, 'is.' One who holds to such a faith can in a way participate in the asking of our question, but he cannot really question without ceasing to be a believer and taking all the consequences of such a step. He will only be able to act 'as if' . . . On the other hand a faith that does not perpetually expose itself to the possibility of unfaith is no faith but merely a convenience: the believer simply makes up his mind to adhere to the traditional doctrine. This is neither faith nor questioning, but the indifference of those who can busy themselves with everything, sometimes even displaying a keen interest in faith as well as questioning.

"What we have said about security in faith as one position in regard to the truth does not imply that the biblical 'In the beginning God created heaven and earth' is an answer to our question. Quite aside from whether these words from the Bible are true or false for faith, they can supply no answer to our question because they are in no way related to it. Indeed, they cannot even be brought into relation with our question. From the standpoint of faith our question is 'foolishness.'

"Philosophy is this very foolishness. A 'Christian philosophy' is a round square and a misunderstanding. There is, to be sure, a thinking and questioning elaboration of the world of Christian experience, i.e., of faith. That is theology. Only epochs which no longer fully believe in the true greatness of the task of theology arrive at the disastrous notion that philosophy can help to provide a refurbished theology if not a substitute for theology, which will satisfy the needs and tastes of the time. For the original Christian faith philosophy is foolishness. To philosophize is to ask: 'Why are there essents [beings] rather than nothing?' Really, to ask the question signifies a daring attempt to fathom this unfathomable question by disclosing what it summons us to ask, to push our questioning to the very end. Where such an attempt occurs, there is philosophy."[47] The two fields, philosophy and theology, are therefore sharply contradistinguished.

This passage is echoed in another passage, just as crucial and just as explicit, which definitively established Heidegger's stance: "By its very essence, metaphysics is at once ontology in the strictest sense and theology. This onto-theo-logical essence of true philosophy (*πρώτη φιλοσ-σοφία*) is indeed well-founded in the manner in which, e.g., the *ὄν* as *ὄν* comes into open presence. The theological character of ontology does not in fact rest at all upon the fact that Greek metaphysics was later taken over by the church theology of Christianity and transformed by it. It rests rather upon the way in which from the beginning beings have revealed themselves as beings. It is this revealing and unveiling of beings that made it possible from the outset for Christian theology to take over Greek philosophy; whether this take-over has been to the advantage or detriment of Christian theology, it is up to the theologians to decide on the basis of the experience of the Christian fact, reflecting on the words written in St. Paul's First Letter to the Corinthians: *οὐκ εμώρανεν ὁ θεὸς τὴν σοφίαν τοῦ κόσμου*: Hath not God rendered foolish the wisdom of this world? (I Cor. I, 20). But the *σοφία τοῦ κόσμου* is, according to I Corinthians 1, 22, precisely what *Ἕλληνες ζητοῦσιν* (the Greeks seek after). Aristotle expressly calls the *πρώτη φιλοσοφία* a *ζητουμένη* (a search). It may be that Christian theology will decide once

[47] M. Heidegger, *Einführung in die Metaphysik*, pp. 5f.; cf. English translation, *An Introduction to Metaphysics*, pp. 6ff., which we have followed in the main, standardizing terminology.

and for all to take seriously the word of the Apostle and thus to consider philosophy a foolishness." [48]

The two passages are not identical but in a certain sense complementary. Both assert a clear-cut irreconcilable contradistinction, not merely a distinction of dimension, between reason and faith, between philosophy and theology, with the result that the God-problem is banished from philosophy, seeing that it is meaningless to speak of the Absolute in the realm of Being which comes-to-presence in origination from nothingness. While the first passage brands faith as entirely extraneous and irrelevant to the problem of the ground of being, the second expressly claims for faith a field of its own, simply putting it on its guard against the equivocation of a drastically rationalistic theology. Here again there burgeons the Nietzschean distinction between Christendom and Christianity, a distinction that restricts the genuine living of the Christian message to the first generation of apostolic times, when the first Christian community was living entirely under the direct radiation of the Spirit. If a specific historical nexus can licitly be maintained, as we believe it can, then Heidegger's position is clearly in the tradition of Scotus and Nominalism, which claimed that faith and reason were separated by a chasm and consequently denied the demonstrability of the *praeambula fidei*, such as the existence of God, the immortality of the soul, creation, etc.

Heidegger's position is particularly reminiscent of Luther; [49] but the critics have not failed to highlight the further fact it is no accident that the boldest trend in present-day Protestant theology, Bultmann's demythologization (*Entmythologisierung*) drive, should have taken its inspiration from the Heideggerian *Sein.* According to Heidegger, the molding of a theology or "world-view" in Christendom was the crucial step in "secularization" and consequent *Entgötterung* in the West; Christendom itself is therefore guilty of both! Thus, for Heidegger, Christendom's take-over of philosophy in the elaboration of theology has served not to raise reason to the service of faith, but rather to destroy faith in the interests of reason, contributing in this way to the elimination of the religious element and dimension. This shows that Heidegger sets no stock whatever in the assistance of the Spirit in the evolution of the life of the Church; and only an extreme liberal-wing Protestant could write as did Heidegger in approving commentary on Nietzsche: "Christianity is for Nietzsche the historical and worldwide

[48] M. Heidegger, *Was ist Metaphysik?* [5] Einleitung, p. 18.

[49] Birault likens Heidegger's conception of faith to Luther's (H. Birault, "La foi et la pensée d'après Heidegger," *Philosophies chrétiennes,* Recherches et Débats [1955], p. 113).

phenomenon of the Church, in its existential reality and its demands which have exercised a decisive influence on the molding of Western man and modern culture. This Christianity is not the same thing as the Christ-ianity of the New Testament faith. Even a non-Christian life can affirm (*bejahen*) Christianity and utilize it as a power-ploy (*Machtfaktor*); conversely, a Christian life has no absolute need of Christianity thus understood. Thus, debate on [and criticism of] Christianity need not involve any impugning of the Christian fact (*Bekämpfung des Christlichen*), just as a critique of theology is not necessarily by that very fact a critique of the faith which theology is supposed to interpret." [50] But the whole point is that there are various kinds of theology just as there are various kinds of philosophy; and Heidegger seems to have lumped together all philosophy in his condemnation of philosophical formalism with its forgetfulness of being and likewise to have lumped together all rapprochement between reason and faith and the very *munus theologicum* as such, in his blanket condemnation of rationalism in theology. And the results have been similar in the two realms: in the natural realm, there remains nothing but sheer Life (*Leben*) in the form of experience of Being (*Sein*); in the realm of revelation, there remains nothing but sheer Life in the form of experience of the "sacral"; nor is there any visible distinction between historical religion in general and Christianity as a specific historical religion founded by Jesus Christ who presented himself to the world as the Son of God.

The provisional conclusion (and it must be provisional for Heidegger is still thinking and writing must be that Heidegger does not "profess" atheism as such, has indeed declared explicitly that his energies have always been devoted to a radical critique of atheism, that very atheism which constitutes the fiery epilogue to Western thought. Yet Heidegger's own thought, in its strictest interpretation, both in the earlier and in the later Heidegger, is in the tradition of Kant: pure reflective thought cannot attain to the assertion of God and is powerless to decide the God-problem: God is at best solely the object of religious experience, not of philosophy.[51]

[50] Cf. M. Heidegger, "Nietzsche's Wort 'Gott ist tot,'" in *Holzwege,* pp. 202f. Cf. also H. Birault, "De l'être, du divin, des dieux chez Heidegger," in *L'existence de Dieu* (Tournai, 1961), pp. 53ff., and *idem,* "La foi et la pensée . . . ," pp. 117ff.

[51] At the period of *Sein und Zeit* and *Was ist Metaphysik?,* Heidegger declared: "Neither a positive nor a negative decision concerning a being-unto-God is contained or implied in the ontological interpretation of There-being as being-in-the-world. But it is true that the illumination and elucidation of transcendence provides primarily an *adequate concept* of *There-being,* with regard to which being it can thereupon be *asked* how matters stand with the God-relationship of There-being" (M. Heidegger, *Vom Wesen des Grundes,* p. 36, Note).

Perspicacious theologians allege that reason and faith are irreconcilably opposed in the Heideggerian conception: what Heidegger styles "openness" to *Sein* (Being), a Being which is intrinsically finite, necessarily involves and imposes its own ontologico-metaphysical "closedness" to all transcendence and revelation in the sense of religion as a doctrine of salvation (*Heilslehre*) for the world in thrall to the radically lethal powers of error and death. The Heideggerian stand, contending that the human λόγος is intrinsically atheistic constitutes the most radical inherent atheism.

Bonhoeffer writes: "Heidegger's philosophy is *a consciously and deliberately atheistic philosophy of finitude.* In this philosophy everything is biassed by the instrumentality of There-being to the 'closedness' of finitude as such. The closed conception of finitude is crucial for the existential analysis of There-being. The solidary 'closedness' here involved can no longer be separated from finitude. The existential being-potential, like all other existential features of There-being is revealed, not as a generic existential feature of finite There-being, but rather as essentially conditioned by the 'closedness' of finitude. The philosophical concept of finitude is in its very essence a concept of closed finitude. *There is therefore no room left here for the notion of revelation;* and all concepts of being must therefore be recast in the light of the recognition imposed by revelation that finitude as creatureliness is open for God. And so, despite its powerful broadening influence due to its disclosure of the existential sphere, the Heideggerian concept of being must be said to be unusable for theology." [52] And Bonhoeffer goes on to say that Heidegger's position remains substantially idealist (p. 85) and antithetical to the Christian conception, in that Heidegger simply does not take the problem of death really seriously.

Heidegger in fact declares that thought takes no sides, either with theism or with atheism. But this neutrality is not a neutrality of indifference; rather it stems from a due consideration of the limits imposed upon thought, by the very nature of thought itself and as a result of what thought assigns to itself as object of reflection, as a result of the truth of being.[53] This position is the complete antithesis of the notion St. Thomas defends, the notion of being as sheer and transcendent act. This Thomist position is impervious to Heidegger's critique of the Scholastic *essentia-existentia* pairing; indeed St. Thomas, with his original notion of *esse* (to which Heidegger never adverts at all!) had already exposed the insufficiency of that Scholastic approach and overcome its drastic

[52] D. Bonhoeffer, *Akt und Sein,* Transzendentalphilosophie und Ontologie in der systematischen Theologie (Munich, 1964), p. 50.

[53] M. Heidegger, *PLBH,* p. 103.

equivocation. However, despite this serious and incomprehensible lacuna, which gravely compromises the whole of Heidegger's basic interrogation on being, Heidegger's contribution is worthy of high esteem: first of all, for its clarification of the inevitability of an "inanition" of being as act on the part of the principle of immanentism and of the consequent structural atheism of modern thought; and further, for its demonstration of the equal inevitability with which the Parmenidean appeal to the demands of Being must lead to the overcoming of "form" or of categorial thinking and of the finite in general and to a consequent Aquinas-type stabilization in the act of *esse* via the dialectic of participation.[54] This is the sure path to an overcoming of the kind of ontology which is closed in upon the Being of beings and to a substantiation of that metaphysic which opens the gates to the *Esse ipsum* who is Creator of the world and last end of man.

[54] On the nuanced relations between Heidegger's work and the Thomist dialectic of participation, cf. C. Fabro, *Participation et causalité*, especially pp. 76ff.; Italian edition, *Partecipazione e causalità*, especially pp. 60ff.

Schrey's critical evaluation of the problem we have here mentioned should come as no surprise, showing, as it does, the opposition between Heidegger's existential hermeneutics and the Catholic position, and the congeniality of that hermeneutic with Protestant theology: "Thomism, which claims that the contemplation of Being leads to the recognition, not only of the 'truth of things', but also of the truth of God, will not be able to accept Heidegger's statement that the philosopher is hagridden by the absence of God as by the manner of his presence. For Thomism is bound by the Decree of Vatican I: 'If any man shall say that the One and True God, our Creator and our Lord, cannot be known with certainty by the natural light of human reason through those things that are made [i.e. creatures]: let him be anathema.' Heidegger's blueprint for a definition of the relation between philosophy and theology is, on the other hand, much more consonant with Protestant thinking, which bases the certainty of faith on revelation, rather than on man's natural insight. Bultmann has been the man to take most seriously the challenge of the problem of existence in theology. He sides entirely with Heidegger's definition of the relation between philosophy and theology and campaigns against the notion of theology as a philosophical system or a mythology. God is not a datum for ivory-tower speculation and philosophical manipulation." (Heinz-Horst Schrey, "Die Bedeutung der Philosophie Martin Heideggers für die Theologie," in *Martin Heideggers Einfluss auf Wissenschaften*, p. 18).

5

Patent Atheism in French Existentialism

Jaspers and Heidegger have both been called atheists and neither seems to like it. The solution of their problem is simple: they still have the opportunity of dissipating the uncertainties and ambiguities that have given grounds or at least good pretexts for the charge. On the other hand, there is an exemplary consistency with the modern *cogito* principle in the patent atheism asserted by French existentialism and particularly by Jean Paul Sartre (1906—). It is suggestive and symmetrical that modern thought, which began in France with the professing theist Descartes, should attain to its epilogue or at least to one of the most radical extremes of its own internal logic, again in France with the atheist Sartre.

The characteristic feature of French existentialist atheism is its phenomenological structure, a structure already fatally contained in its very point of departure, i.e., in the reduction of being to a phenomenon and of metaphysics to an ontology, or still more precisely to the *cogito*-powered phenomenological ontology. This amounts to a reduction of the being of the *cogito* to the *phenomenon of being* (*phénomène d'être*). It may be not unduly flippant to identify Sartre as a 4-H man in respect of the inspiration of his whole thought, for Sartre's phenomenology draws its inspiration from the three great recent thinkers: Hegel, Husserl and Heidegger and from the much earlier philosopher Hume, first not only in point of time but also in point of importance insofar as the phenomenological version of the *cogito* principle is concerned. Sartre aims not at a merger of these thinkers and their systems but rather at a supersession of all of them, in a dissolution of being into pure appearance, amounting to a simultaneous elevation of appearance to the status of being. In somewhat schematic and oversimplified form it might be said that being, which idealism had confined in Kant to the narrow compass of the copula in judgments, or absorbed, in Hegel, into the dialectic of the

Absolute Idea, becomes in Sartre the self-actualization of consciousness at its primordial stage of perception. As Ricoeur writes: "The consciousness which renders its objects present, sees them as present, effects their presence, sustains and supports the consciousness which ascribes meaning, judges and articulates. It is this shift of emphasis which marks the transition to existential phenomenology; the simple fact of the matter is that it is in perception, thus reinterpreted, that there are revealed simultaneously the meaning of the existence of things (objects) and the meaning of the existence of the subject." [1]

The influence of Kierkegaard is that of the theoretician of anguish, understood as the simultaneous inanition and isolation of the being of the Individual; but the aim is an interpretation of the being of man which is the direct antithesis of the faith of the founder of existentialism, a faith which vanquishes anguish in joy and in the hope of salvation.[2] It is true that both primordial consciousness and dialectic are actualized, in Sartre's novels and philosophical works alike, with a psychoanalytic "content" or bias; but this we feel to be a limitation or deviation of the new notion of freedom which Sartre aims to proclaim.

If the Cartesian soul-body dualism is the basis of Sartre's atheistic phenomenology, the Cartesian doctrine of *freedom* constitutes the structural principle and the real objective of the new interpretation of the *cogito*, in which the meaning of the *cogito* itself (and consequently of freedom) is totally inverted, to an even more drastic extent than Feuerbach's natural man amounted to an inversion of Hegel's Absolute Spirit. Sartre takes Descartes' tenet that thought has a being; from the Hegel-Husserl-Heidegger phenomenology, he takes over the tenet that this being is *as such* a void-of-being, that thought (and the mind which underpins thought) is not a *thing*. Sartre thus takes the mind, the *cogito* to be that absolute anterior terminal which cannot be derived from anything more basic; and we feel he is perfectly consistent in so doing. Modern philosophy, beginning with Descartes, has in fact always loudly proclaimed this absolute anterior terminal without ever being able to endow it with genuine reality; for the mind, the *cogito,* can be this absolute anterior terminal only if it be conceived as the "void-of-being" (*néant-d'être*). Once being has been reduced to appearance, this appearance is henceforth the act of consciousness: apart from this appearance, this coming-to-presence, the mind is non-being; and in the appearance,

[1] P. Ricoeur, *Phénoménologie existentielle,* in article "Philosophie-Religion," in *Encyclopédie Française,* Vol. XIX, (Paris, 1957), p. 19, 10-a.

[2] Cf. C. Fabro, *Dall'essere all'esistente,* pp. 127ff. The Nietzschean influence, highlighted by Ricoeur (*Phénoménologie existentielle,* p. 19, 10.10), seems to us rather to have been presupposed than directly suggested by Sartre himself.

in the coming-to-presence, the being of the mind, of consciousness, is the "phenomenon of being", i.e., the appearance, the coming-to-presence itself! For instance, the pen I have in my hand fills my present consciousness, my mind as of this moment; it constitutes the very fabric of that consciousness; therefore the presence of the pen constitutes the being of the mind. Were the mind, the *cogito,* to have a being of its own over and above and anterior to the *cogitare,* the actual thinking act, then we should have to posit a "consciousness of consciousness" and this "consciousness of consciousness" would in its turn presuppose another anterior consciousness in order to "be" (present) and so on ad infinitum,[3] so that the mind would never succeed in being consciousness of being, in actualizing its own freedom and attaining to the truth, i.e., in arriving at being. Existential nihilism and phenomenological ontology are thus equivalent and form the basis of that equivalence Sartre proclaims between freedom and atheism on the basis of the *cogito.*

In declaring the mind to be a "void", Sartre is setting aside the whole spiritualist tradition of the West, for which the soul (and the mind) has a reality in itself and this reality is the higher one, the body and the physical world expressing the other reality, of a lower order. In further declaring that the object of the mind is the very act of coming-to-presence, Sartre is in effect saying that the mind in act *is* the object as such, in opposition to all forms of idealism and empiricism, which filtered the reality of being via an image which was thus interposed between being and the mind, trammelling the effective union of the two. Up to this point, Sartre has interpreted the Cartesian *cogito* in the light of Heideggerian *There-being:* the complex analysis which he devotes to filling the void, both of *being-for-itself* and of *being-for-others* (which is the body as mediator of the *in-itself* which is the Other and the world of the others) serves only to strengthen and clarify the constitutive negativity of being of the human mind. In Sartrian terms, we can sum up this latest and most consistent and consequential interpretation of the *cogito* in the two definitions: The mind or *for-itself* is the *nihilating Totality* and the world or the *in-itself* is the *nihilated* or *de-totalized Totality.* The *for-itself* and the *in-itself* can be given and posited only as a reciprocal mutual negation and thus preclude any possibility of man having reality of being apart from and independently of this negation. This is the ultimate significance of the Sartrian principle that *existence precedes*

[3] Cf. H. Van Lier, *L'existentialisme de J.-P. Sartre,* in article "Philosophie-Religion," *Encyclopédie Française,* Vol. XIX, p. 19, 12-15a. This is a concise but excellently ordered account of the fundamental elements of the Sartrian phenomenological ontology, as grounded in the *cogito* and constituting the kind of disintegrative negation bound to give rise to atheism.

essence [4] (precedes it, however, in such a way as to render meaningless any notion of essence).

And it is still more meaningless to try to speak of God as the Absolute in itself and for itself or as the identity (the totality in act) of the in-itself-for-itself. Sartre does indeed admit that this has been the basic and fundamental project of human reality and he understands it (or at least expresses it) in the tradition of the Golden Age of metaphysical idealism, which exalted the human mind into the project of becoming God ("man is the being whose project is to become God" [5]). But this project is balked by the very essence of the "freedom" whereby man is supposed to accomplish such a transformation: for "freedom" as essence of the *cogito* is inextricably linked to "nihilation", so that freedom is *lack of being* (*manque d'être*) which can never actualize itself in an affirmation which transcends the presence of being in situation, i.e., of individual being. This is that fundamental bias of phenomenological ontology which Hegel had expressed in his assertion that "the mind is the negative:" [6] this Sartre takes to mean that the mind is capable of shucking off the shackles of its past and commencing again and again anew, without beginning or end. More precisely: "It is the act which decides its ends and motives, and the act is the expression of freedom" (*Op. cit.,* p. 513; English translation, p. 438). Once the principle of immanentism has been accepted, there follows the negation of metaphysics or the reduction of being to a phenomenon; and then all these Sartrian conclusions are quite legitimate. It is no mere chance that Sartre considers Descartes the classical champion *par excellence* of freedom,[7] even if critics often give preference to his phenomenological analyses and dialectical passages. Sartre in fact finds as early as Descartes two very different doc-

[4] Cf. J.-P. Sartre, *L'existentialisme est un humanisme* (Paris: Les Editions Nagel, 1946), pp. 17, 21; English translation by Philip Mairet, *Existentialism and Humanism* (London: Methuen & Co., 1948), pp. 26, 28. Cf. also *L'être et le néant,* (Paris: Gallimard, 1943), p. 655 and *passim;* English translation by Hazel E. Barnes, *Being and Nothingness* (London: Methuen & Co., 1957), p. 515 and *passim.* Sartre attributes the principle expressly to Heidegger (p. 513; English translation, *Being and Nothingness,* p. 438) and to Hegel himself as author of the phrase "Wesen ist was gewesen ist " (Essence is what has been") (p. 515; English translation, *Being and Nothingness,* p. 439).

[5] J.-P. Sartre, *L'être et le néant,* p. 653; English translation, *Being and Nothingness,* p. 566.

[6] *Ibid.,* p. 511; English translation, p. 436. With a direct reference to Sartre himself, M. Merleau-Ponty accepts the substance of the Sartrian doctrine of freedom (Cf. M. Merleau-Ponty, *Phénoménologie de la perception* [Paris: N. R. F., 1945], pp. 496ff.; English translation by Colin Smith, *Phenomenology of Perception* [London: Routledge & Kegan Paul, 1962], pp. 434ff.).

[7] I am following the Essay "La liberté cartésienne," prefaced to *Descartes* (Anthology of Texts on Freedom) (Geneva-Paris, 1946), pp. 9ff. It is reproduced in *Situations I* (Paris: N. R. F., 1947), pp. 314ff.

trines of freedom under the appearance of a unitary teaching: the one doctrine sees freedom as the faculty for understanding and judging; the other expresses man's autonomy in the face of truth, inasmuch as man is responsible for truth. It is this autonomy which constitutes the essence of the *cogito* principle and witnesses to the fact that truth is a human affair by virtue of the fact that I must actualize it for it to exist. Hence for Descartes judgment consists in the adherence of the will and the free commitment (*engagement*) of my being. For Descartes then, as for Heidegger, claims Sartre, man is the being through whom truth appears (comes-to-presence) in the world; man must think the world in his status as *There-being* or in the ontico-ontological order of *"Being-in-the-world"*. Descartes himself comes to the point of conceiving this freedom as essentially equal for every man, even equal as between man and God, and as absolute and infinite even though man is finite. It is true that man comes to be held to constitute the truth himself only with Kant: Descartes held that man simply discovers the truth because God has already established the relations that keep things in balance. But even in Descartes, there is an act of freedom at the origin of every judgment, whether that judgment be $2+2=4$ or *cogito ergo sum!* This freedom, which is purely positive and therefore creative in God, can be negative in man, inasmuch as man can choose evil and in this choice of evil realizes what is more truly his own and cannot be in God and in respect of which man certainly cannot be said to depend on God: in this ability of man to retreat, to flee, to disengage himself, Descartes was anticipating already the Hegelian active negativity.

The Hegelian non-being or nothingness thus corresponds to the will and ability to doubt everything and Sartre asserts (quite rightly, we believe) that methodical doubt becomes the very type of the free act: his two citations from Descartes are cogent: (1) "Nonetheless . . . we experience this freedom to be in us, that we can always abstain from believing those things that are not patently certain and proven" and (2) "The mind which, using its own freedom, supposes all those things not to exist concerning the existence of which it cannot entertain the slightest doubt whatsoever." [8]

Now we know that doubt can and must infect any judgment on anything that is outside of our own thought, i.e., it can "put in parentheses" (as Husserl will say) all existents: this means that I am in the full exercise of my freedom when, being myself void and naught, I *nihilate* everything that is (exists). Descartes limited negativity to the negation of error; he did not go so far as to conceive of negativity as a productive power, creative of being; this creative power he reserved to God and

[8] *Ibid.*, p. 34; *Situations I*, p. 326.

idealism, on the contrary, was to make constitutive of human subjectivity. Yet Descartes posited freedom as the ground of being, three centuries before Heidegger's *Vom Wesen des Grundes.*

This is the deep-seated reason why freedom is anterior to and productive of being (of the *cogito!*) and thus productive of the truth: because man is atheistic and authenticates his own being and his own freedom as an affirmation of the Ego, the Self, involving the negation of God. Thus Sartre can reason: if God exists, I am no longer free; but I know myself to be free; therefore God does not exist. This is the primordial moment, the constitution of the *autonomy* of the will with regard to being; and this is at once the fundamental experience and the "fundamental choice" of being what one is, in existentialist terminology. But for Sartre and for modern thought in general, from the time of Kant's *Ich denke überhaupt,* the choice is effected as a project of "Being-in-the-world" and thus the *object* of any such choice is intrinsically finite; and so God cannot exist even from the point of view of the object.[9] More correctly we may say that precisely the infinity of freedom as a form, as subjectivity, the infinite openness of existence demands to be actualized in the world each and every time in a finite fashion and thus demands a finite content: only thus can freedom realize itself as nihilation of its own being. Thus radical freedom, as (nihilating) infinity, excludes God, for otherwise God Himself would be its ground; and at the same time the finitude of freedom's being as *There-being* once again excludes God who certainly cannot be a finite entity. And Sartre's final conclusion is that man cannot synthesize the For-itself-In-itself into any comprehensive totality which would be God.

Sartre readily admits that man feels a deep-rooted desire to effect just such a synthesis; but this is a vain aspiration and Christ Himself cannot alter the situation: "Each human reality is at the same time a direct project to metamorphose its own For-itself into an In-itself-For-itself and a project of the appropriation of the world as a totality of being-in-itself, in the form of a fundamental quality. Every human reality is a passion in that it projects losing itself so as to found being and by the same stroke to constitute the In-itself which escapes contingency by being its own foundation, the *Ens causa sui,* which religions call God. Thus the passion of man is the reverse of that of Christ, for man loses himself as man in order that God may be born. But the idea of God

[9] The "origin" of the world is explained precisely from the starting-point of the Nothingness of the For-itself: "The for-itself has no reality save that of being the nihilation of being. Its sole qualification comes to it from the fact that it is the nihilation of an individual and particular In-itself and not of a being in general. The For-itself is not nothingness in general but a particular privation; it constitutes itself as the privation of *this being.*" (J.-P. Sartre, *L'être et le néant,* pp. 711f.; English translation, *Being and Nothingness,* p. 168).

is contradictory and we loses ourselves in vain. Man is a useless passion." [10]

Dostoevsky has therefore anticipated the starting-point of existentialism in writing: "If God did not exist, everything would be possible!" In actual fact, since God *does* not exist, everything is permitted and man finds no opportunity of tether, either in himself or outside himself. If existence precedes essence, there does not exist any human nature as such, which would be given and firmly fixed; and man is free, *man is freedom.* And finally, if God does not exist, there is no longer any question of "transforming" the old values into new ones, as Nietzsche wanted to do: if God does not exist, then there are no more values at all, nor yet any order of things which might legitimize man's conduct. Hence the Sartrian expression that ". . . man is condemned to be free." [11]

And when Sartre says that existentialism is atheism, he is persuaded that he had grasped and articulated the *cogito* principle in its primordial sense and dimension, as constitutive of man's freedom: "Existentialism is nothing else but an attempt to draw the full conclusions from a consistently atheistic position. . . . Existentialism is not atheist in the sense that it would exhaust itself in demonstrations of the non-existence of God. It declares, rather, that even if God existed that would make no difference, from its point of view. Not that we believe God does exist, but we think that the real problem is not that of his existence; what man needs is to find himself again and to understand that nothing can save him from himself, not even a valid proof of the existence of God. In this sense existentialism is optimistic, it is a doctrine of action, and it is only by self-deception, by confusing their own despair with ours that Christians can describe us as without hope." [12]

But surely this is whistling in the dark! How can this intrepid conclusion be reconciled with the negativity of the mind and the finitude of being which had driven Sartre in his major work to the conclusion that man is a useless passion, precisely because his being lacked the theological axis?

The other giant of French existentialism. M. Merleau-Ponty (1908-1961) is equally faithful to the slogan of "Either God Or Man"; and he has the further merit of proceeding to a "verification" of the principle of immanentism in a more immediate and direct form. Metaphysics takes

[10] *Ibid.,* pp. 707f.; English translation, *Being and Nothingness,* p. 615.

[11] J.-P. Sartre, *L'existentialisme est un humanisme,* p. 37; English translation, *Existentialism and Humanism,* p. 34.

[12] *Ibid.,* pp. 94f.; English translation, p. 56.

its origin and attains to its accomplishment as direct apprehension of "presence" as "perception of the other" than me, but this is a perception of that other precisely as referred to me.[13] Thus there can only be metaphysics when there is selfhood, *subject*ivity, i.e., only from the moment when we cease to live in the evidence of the object (whether an evidence of direct experience or of the mind matters little) and perceive indissolubly the radical subjectivity of every one of our experiences and its truth value. The mind, consciousness, the *cogito,* is not therefore mere awareness of the presence of being; it demands and requires that being always come-to-presence as being-for-me (*l'être pour moi*): hence there are already posited, as the only dimensions of transcendence, nature or the world (*monde*) which is the dissimilar Other, and human society which is the similar Other; so we have a phenomenological transcendence totally closed off against any effort at metaphysical transcendence. My own selfhood reveals itself as essentially "a capacity for the other": it is the "void" which summons and solicits the presence of the other, in a reciprocally substantiating exchange: I define myself as a relation to the other and the other can come-to-presence in experience only to the extent that I recognize the other as "mine", as my own life which is thus individual and universal at once. This is what Merleau-Ponty understands by the "metaphysical experience", which is realized in two stages or moments: first as surprise in the face of the "grappling" (*affrontement*) of contraries, then as awareness of their identity in the simplicity of action. And so we are back again with the Hegelian "standing at gaze" of pure phenomenology, which radically excludes any prospect of a "system" and any positing of an Absolute.

Indeed system, as a sheer edifice of concepts, rendering immediately compatible and compossible all the aspects of experience, ends by eliminating the metaphysical consciousness of the pure "standing at gaze" and with it likewise all morality. Anyone desirous of basing the fact of rationality or of communication on an absolute of value or of thought is forthwith faced with the following dilemma: either this absolute does not really intervene in terrestrial affairs at all and leaves rationality and communication self-grounded; or else the absolute does in fact descend into them, so to speak, in which case, however, it subverts all human means of verification and of justification. In other words, the circle of immanentism cannot be broken. Merleau-Ponty feels, as does Sartre, that the existence of God is superfluous, that it leaves all the problems just where they were before: it is of no importance whatever whether

[13] I am following M. Merleau-Ponty, *Sens et non-sens* (Paris: Les Editions Nagel, 1948), pp. 186ff.; English translation by Hubert L. Dreyfus & Patricia Allen Dreyfus, *Sense and Non-Sense* (Evanston: Northwestern University Press, 1964), pp. 93ff.

there exists or does not exist an absolute thought or an absolute value-judgment on each and every practical problem, since I have only my own opinions at my disposal in each individual instance where I must make a judgment. Worse still, this recourse to the Absolute ends by destroying the very thing it is supposed to substantiate. For as soon as I become convinced that I have patently attained to the Absolute Principle of all thought and all value-judgment and can yet keep my own speculative and practical intellect for myself, then I have the right to make my own judgments entirely independent of everyone else's control or criticism: they acquire a scaral character and in the practical order I come into possession of an escape (*fuite*) gap, which transforms all my actions. It changes the suffering I am causing into happiness, my cunning into righteous reasonableness, and I dispatch my foes with a pious dagger. It should be noted at once that we are here dealing with a hypothetical positing of God and a sense of the God-problem that revolve entirely within the orbit of the *cogito,* [14] *within the ambit of the principle of immanentism*, which holds that the certainty of consciousness, i.e., mental and subjective certitude, is the sole substantiating principle: the very positing of God is a function of the *Bewusstsein überhaupt* (mind as such, consciousness as such), along the lines of the *Glaube* (faith) of Kant-Jacobi-Schleiermacher-Fries etc.

From this angle of vision, the only one he gives any indication of recognizing, Merleau-Ponty has no difficulty in propounding his own "atheological" position in accord with the Hegelian principle that "the mind is its own measure." For he points up the fact that, as soon as a man has grasped the point that truth and value can only be, so far as we are concerned, the result of our own verifications and our own value-judgments in our contact with the world, in the presence of others and in given situations of cognition and action; and when a man has further seen that this identification is so restrictive that the very notions of truth and value lose all meaning apart from these distinctively human dimensions—then the world assumes its proper importance, the particular acts of verification and evaluation wherein I bind together a scattered experience regain their crucial importance; and we can then say that there is an aura of irrefutability surrounding cognition and action, so far as truth

[14] This point is fundamental: "The plurality of consciousness is impossible if I have an absolute consciousness of myself. Behind the absolute of my thought, it is even impossible to conjecture a divine absolute. If it is perfect, the contact of my thought with itself seals me within myself, and prevents me from ever feeling that anything eludes my grasp. . ." In place of this idealist interpretation, closed upon the Absolute (God as coinciding with the *cogito*), Merleau-Ponty substitutes the phenomenological interpretation of the opening of the *cogito* to the world (M. Merleau-Ponty, *La phénoménologie de la perception,* pp. 428ff.; English translation, *Phenomenology of Perception,* pp. 373ff.).

and falsehood, good and evil are concerned, for the very reason that I do not pretend to find absolute evidence of that truth and falsehood, of that good and evil. In other words, it must be said that the distinction between true and false, between good and evil, cannot be given absolutely but only "situationally" in terms of the coordinates of experience present in the knowledge of each individual. We read in Merleau-Ponty the explicit declaration that ". . . Metaphysical and moral consciousness dies upon contact with the Absolute, because beyond the dull world of habitual or dormant consciousness, the consciousness is itself the living connection between myself and me and myself and others." [15]

Consequently metaphysics is no longer an edifice of concepts used by us in an effort to render our paradoxes less blatant; rather it is the experience we have of all the situations of personal and collective history [16] and of actions which we take up into ourselves and there transform by rationalizing them. Their very emergence in the mind is therefore already their justification; and metaphysics no longer issues in an edifice of knowledge but rather in the awareness of the coming to presence of all the events mentioned above, in all their precariousness or "contingency" which is the very essence of their being and therefore the "condition" or foundation of a metaphysical vision of the world.

Merleau-Ponty accordingly hastens to make the superfluous declaration that this sort of metaphysics is irreconcilable with the patent content of religion or with the contention that there exists an absolute thinker of the world: the bankruptcy of Leibniz's *Theodicy,* which posits the world as being indispensable for God, seems to Merleau-Ponty to clinch this point. God is therefore no longer the Creator of this world; God is at best an Idea, in the restrictive Kantian sense of the term, a term of reference of a human reflection which considers the world as it is and proceeds to distill into this idea what it would like the world to be. This amounts to saying, with Feuerbach, that God is a creation of man's own desire. Metaphysics could not indeed create a God conceived not "for us" but in and for Himself, except as trans-mental, beyond our ideas, the anonymous power that sustains all our thinking and all our experience.[17] Religion is accordingly no longer a conceptual conclusion, but simply and solely a way of life, an inter-human experience. Christianity,

[15] M. Merleau-Ponty, *Sens et non-sens,* p. 191; English translation *Sense and Non-Sense,* p. 95.

[16] On the problem of history, Merleau-Ponty refers expressly to Heidegger's *Sein und Zeit* (Cf. M. Merleau-Ponty, *Phénoménologie de la perception,* pp. 469ff.; English translation, *Phenomenology of Perception,* pp. 412ff.).

[17] Merleau-Ponty challenges Husserl, rightly in our opinion, on the possibility of introducing a "transcendence of immanence" (*ibid.,* p. 193, Note: English translation, *Phenomenology of Perception,* p. 152, Note).

says Merleau-Ponty, achieved the distinction of setting aside the God of the philosophers to preach the God who assumes man's estate and dies for man. Christianity (or religion, thus conceived) is readily acknowledged to be a part of culture, not as a dogma or a belief, but as an "anguished cry" which cannot be anything else or anything more and resolves itself in the end into the most trenchant negation and denial of the infinite as that infinite is conceived in the various ideologies.[18]

The deepest and ultimate basis of this atheism is exactly the same as that of all the other brands we have studied, though this brand is most sharply and drastically phenomenological; and that basis is the restriction (or "opening-up"—at this point the terms are interchangeable) of being to the horizon of man taken as he is (to the phenomenological enquirer, of course!). However, Merleau-Ponty is no champion of a designation of philosophy as "humanism" in the tradition of Feuerbach, Marx, Sartre and the rest. For Merleau-Ponty insists that man is not a principle of explanation: man in fact explains nothing for man is not a power but a weakness in the heart of being. And so we are back at the notion of a radical "contingency" balking not only any religion but even any discussion of the ultimate questions.

Philosophy accordingly is to be judged and evaluated in its very beginnings, in its primordial self-constitution as reflection on the act of consciousness, on the primal act of the mind. And such an evaluation will make it perfectly clear that only one of two conclusions is possible: either that the very term "atheism" has become utterly meaningless; or else, if and when it is agreed that the mind can of itself serve as the ground and foundation of every value-judgment, that philosophy has always been equivalent to atheism and will never be able to be anything else.[19]

This position of Merleau-Ponty may indeed seem, from certain angles, to be less radical than the Sartrian dialectic of the negative; yet it

[18] And elsewhere, Merleau-Ponty argues against Maritain: "The philosopher will only ask himself if the natural and rational concept of God as necessary being is not inevitably that of the Emperor of the world, if without this concept, the Christian God would not cease to be the author of the world, and if the criticism we are now suggesting is not the philosophy which presses to the limit that criticism of false gods which Christianity has introduced into our history" (M. Merleau-Ponty, *Eloge de la philosophie* [Paris: Gallimard, 1953], p. 65; English translation by John Wild & James M. Edie, *In Praise of Philosophy* [Evanston: Northwestern University Press, 1963], p. 47).

[19] "Hence one bypasses philosophy when one *defines* it as atheism. This is philosophy as it is seen by the theologian. Its negation is only the beginning of an attention, a seriousness, an experience on the basis of which it must be judged" (*ibid.*, p. 63; English translation, *In Praise of Philosophy*, p. 46). And Merleau-Ponty proceeds to defend Spinoza as "the most positive of philosophers" (p. 64; English translation, p. 63).

is in fact no less explicit in its claim that the human horizon is definitive for and constitutive of freedom, as the absolute void serving as the ground and foundation of the very possibility of any presence whatever [20] and of any relevance of such presence in the field of being and of value.

French existentialist atheism must accordingly be credited with having probed back most expertly into the essential implications of the Cartesian *cogito* and having accepted most fearlessly the inescapable conclusions of that principle. The result has been a restatement of the ideas and ideals of the 17th- and 18th-century materialist Enlightenment thought (as instanced in La Mettrie, d'Holbach, and Helvétius); but this restatement has been buttressed with the most meticulous and incisive analysis of human experiences that could be derived from idealism, Bergsonism and especially from the phenomenology of Husserl.

The Cartesian *cogito* has given this French atheist existentialism the conviction that thought, the *act* of mind, of consciousness, constitutes and exhausts being; the *cogito* of Husserl has furnished it with the further persuasion that this being is not a "thing".[21] It would indeed seem as if these existentialists were desirous of maintaining the void gouged by methodical doubt and guarding the radical inviolability of that void. Such a void reduces the mind, consciousness, to nothing (*rein*) and frees it of the arduous and demanding constructive assignments with which it had been saddled by idealism. By accepting and making their own the phenomenological principle of being as sheer appearance, sheer coming-to-presence or self-dissolving "present-ness", these existentialists offer an iron-clad guarantee that the mind will preserve its own void, its own nothingness, will not become entangled with anything, so as to

[20] Merleau-Ponty's definition of the essence of freedom is a Sartre-dominated one: "There is free choice only if freedom comes into play in its decision, and posits the situation chosen as a situation of freedom. A freedom which has no need to be exercised because it is already acquired could not commit itself in this way: it knows that the following instant will find it, come what may, just as free and just as indeterminate." (M. Merleau-Ponty, *Phénoménologie de la perception,* p. 499; English translation, *Phenomenology of Perception,* p. 437).

Whatever may be said of the fundamental atheism of French existentialism and of Merleau-Ponty in particular, we wish to draw attention to Merleau-Ponty's essay "Christianity and Philosophy" (published in M. Merleau-Ponty, *Signes* [Paris: Gallimard, 1960], pp. 176ff.; English translation, by Richard C. McCleary, *Signs* [Evanston: Northwestern University Press, 1964], pp. 140ff.). This essay is an incisive examination of the controversial problem of "Christian philosophy" and shows a real effort at understanding.

[21] Cf. Merleau-Ponty's reference in *Signes,* p. 186 (English translation, *Signs,* p. 148). And according to a recent critic: "Sartre's *Atheism* is an expression of this Nothingness . . . for it is but the reverse side of the positive contention of a fundamentally uncommitted and unshackled freedom" (N. Noack, *Die Philosophie Westeuropas* [Darmstadt, 1962], p. 295).

keep itself infinitely open to appearance [22] and faithful to nothing (in both senses of the double meaning of that last phrase!). Thus the typical feature of this existential atheism is its consequentiality, its refusal to compromise or nuance its stand in the face of the consequences of that stand, its acceptance of the fact that immanentism, taking as its starting-point doubt as radical negation, inevitably involves the conclusion that the being of man, reducible as it is and must be to consciousness in its self-realization, is actualized as a negation in terms of the reciprocal tension of negation between the self and the other. Thus every act of consciousness, every act of the mind as a sheer "phenomenon of being" is double negative: not only is it a negation of the other (-being) of the mind, in accord with the phenomenological transposition of the Cartesian soul-body dualism; it further manifests itself, on the reound, as a continuously renewed manifestation of the void, the nothingness of consciousness, of the mind, whose very actualization and mobilization of powers within its own void serves merely to plunge it more deeply and more intensively into that void, that nothingness *which it is!* Sartre's two phrases: "Consciousness isolates nothingness" and "nothingness haunts being" are two sides of the one coin, indeed two articulations of the same fact. Existentialist atheism is far removed from the strident and blaring propaganda of Marxist atheism; the existentialists are themselves under no illusion about the fate of man who has denied God, nor do they wish to delude anyone else about it. The distinguishing feature of French existentialism lies in its phenomenological salvaging and consequential processing of the *cogito* principle, its renunciation and denunciation of the dialectic as the last bulwark of positivity and its consequent unconditional and consequential acceptance of existence as a tragic dimension.

The definitive expression of this constitutive negativity of the *cogito* principle, a negativity which seems to us to intensify with the intensification of the principle of immanentism, is to be found in the existentialist notion of freedon as sheer "letting-be" in a situational context, as what we may be permitted to formulate in the phrase "perpetual self-reduction to non-being", and in the identification of man with this freedom.[23]

[22] This openness of the mind to appearance is obviously an expression of the principle of immanence itself; it is, in fact, that principle, rather than any appeal to the essential element of the realism of antiquity, as one critic would have it (Cf. H. Van Lier, *L'existentialisme de J.-P. Sartre,* p. 12.15); we can see no reason to doubt Merleau-Ponty's substantial agreement with Sartre on the theoretical background and basis of the problems (Cf. M. Merleau-Ponty, *La structure du comportement* [Paris, 1949], Preface by A. de Waelhens, pp. V ff.).

[23] "This total freedom palpably belongs in equal measure to every human being, precisely because it does not involve any degrees. Or rather each and every human being palpably *is* freedom—for freedom is not one quality among others"

It is nonetheless significant and typical that the idea or conception of a phenomenon-type being conceived as non-being should be held to involve a mandatory negation and denial of God: "Evidently it is necessary to find the foundation of all negation in a nihilation which is exercised *in the very heart of immanence;* in absolute immanence, in the pure subjectivity of the instantaneous *cogito* we must discover the original act by which man is to himself his own nothingness." [24]

We can therefore designate this existentialist atheism as the constantly actualized historical realization of the original fatal bias, as a kinetic actuation of that bias, converting it into an unceasing "falling from being into nothingness". And so Sartre is quite right in saying that we are in such a sorry plight that God Himself could do nothing for us, even if He did exist. For the human mind is in a state of total dispossession: not only has it no claws to sink into being and to grapple onto the world; even its own self-actuation is effected solely by a dissolving of being into coming-to-presence and by a dissolving even of itself on each such occasion into that sheer void which is the only womb hospitable to the conception of such sheerly phenomenal being.

We therefore insist again that it is a mistaken approach to speak of "atheistic *conclusions*" in any of these philosophies of radical immanentism. The point is rather that *immanentism as such is already a denial of God, from the very outset, as a principle that denies primordial substantiating status to being as the ground of all else.* This has been our main point throughout, the very heart of our interpretative endeavor; and it cannot be too trenchantly stressed. Any other angle of vision on the phenomenon of modern atheism and its whole dynamic simply misses the crucial point and silts it over with peripheral accidentals.

From the very moment of the acceptance of the *cogito* principle, being is groundless and therefore cannot itself serve as a ground. We have already seen that, for Sartre, the *En-soi-pour-soi* (In-itself-For-itself) designating God is contradictory, is a futile and even harmful hypothesis, because the notion of "cause" and *a fortiori* the notion of "first cause" is the very antithesis of the notion of consciousness-freedom. This Sartrian contention is perfectly clear and intelligible on the basis of the internal logic of Sartre's own position; what is incomprehensible is how there can be any question, in such a position, of a "positive

---

(J.-P. Sartre, "La liberté cartésienne," p. 18; *Situations I* p. 318). And in Sartre's major work: "Freedom, in fact, as we have shown in the preceding chapter, is strictly identified with nihilation. The only being which can be called free is the being which nihilates its being . . . Freedom is precisely the being which makes itself a lack of being" (J.-P. Sartre, *L'être et le néant,* p. 655; English translation, *Being and Nothingness,* p. 567).

[24] J.-P. Sartre, *L'être et le néant,* p. 83; English translation, *Being and Nothingness,* p. 44.

and constructive freedom", how the Sartrian absurd can be said to be not nihilism but a possibility of salvation.[25]

Existentialism's delight in nothingness and atheism may well be simply a defiant tweaking of the nose of a world and a culture that has been cumulatively responsible for the betrayals of being and the innumerable ambiguities and equivocations which have disgraced the evolution of modern thought and which this existentialism has simply brought out into the open. But in that case, the existentialist profession of atheism assumes the significance, not merely of an end result or consequence, but rather of an integral actuation of the primordial principle and of the original plan and project! It is therefore not those forms of atheism that are in need of updating; rather it is incumbent upon the conservative philosophies to effect an updating and abandon, at long last, their tactics of compromise: "Atheism thus understood is absolutely incredibly radical. It attacks not only the Demiurge-God but the whole empyrean of intelligible Ideas, the whole notion of a Transcendental Subject, even that Eternal Recurrence and that Messianism of the Future which, in Nietzsche and Marx respectively, were still a consolation to man in the wake of the death of God. This atheism even attacks the idea of *essence.* The *cogito* of Descartes and the *cogito* of Husserl, although empirical, did at least base themselves on an essence from whence they drew their justification for existence. The *cogito* of Sartre is not only contingent but lacking in all justification, it is "absurd", "superfluous", "sheer facticity". And the same is true of the *In-itself,* to preclude any danger of it providing, even indirectly, a justification of the *For-itself.*" [26]

Sartre's system is a complete blind alley. The fluctuations or even inconsistencies inherent in the Sartrain phenomenology pale into insignificance before the consistency of his principle: "Yet we re-discover a real autonomy for man in the search for the true, even as in the pursuit of the Good. But only to the extent that he is a nothingness. It is by means of his own nothingness and to the extent that he traffics with Nothingness, Evil and Error that man escapes from God, for God Who is an infinite plenitude of being could not conceive or govern nothingness." [27] This clinches the Sartrian point that man authenticates himself

[25] Cf. J.-P. Sartre, "La liberté cartésienne," p. 21; *Situations I,* p. 320; H. Van Lier, *L'existentialisme de J.-P. Sartre,* p. 14.1b.

[26] Van Lier, *L'existentialisme* . . . p. 14.1b. Sartre's most thoroughgoing and radical phenomenological and theoretical analysis of the negativity of the mind, of consciousness, aside from his novels and comedies, seems to us to be his *Saint Genet, comédien et martyr* (Paris, 1952).

[27] J.-P. Sartre, "La liberté cartésienne," p. 33; *Situations I,* p. 325. And later in the same article, Sartre comments on how the principle of immanentism advanced by Descartes himself overturned and inverted Descartes' own would-be theological position and stand: "Descartes was perfectly well aware that the concept of freedom included the demand for an absolute autonomy, that an act of freedom was

in negativity and via negation; but this self-authentication is no longer aimed, as it was in Hegel, the founder of the dialectic of negativity, at a re-ascent to the positive; rather it is directed toward a dissipation of that positive even in the still innocent moment of immediacy and appearance. This *may* (and the conditional form is mandatory in reference to this whole area) may be the explanation of the advances and retreats executed by French existentialist atheism with respect to Marxist materialism. This existentialist atheism is indeed eager to work at the transformation of society but seems to be unwilling to accept the risks of an explicit and integrally consistent action program.

Freedom is the dominant theme in the atheistic brand of French existentialism, whose most eloquent and outspoken champion is Sartre.[28] Freedom is the beginning and end of the new modern conception of immanentism. The freedom notion carries the long and arduous Odyssey of modern philosophy back to its beginnings, to its "principle", the essentialism of Cartesian doubt which is the very essence of the *cogito*. For this freedom notion amounts to a new notion of the "gratuitousness of being", so to speak, or of gratuitous freedom: "Cartesian freedom, infinite, amorphous, nameless, purposeless, *perpetually renewed,* but sovereign because it can refuse assent." When Mauriac introduces a reference of freedom to God, from the Christian point of view, Sartre reproaches him, saying that such a freedom ". . . could *not be constructive;* a man having this freedom can never create himself nor mold his own history. Free will is but a disjointed and discontinuous power, permitting indeed brief escapes but productive of nothing but short-lived events with no real future . . . Freedom loses all its power and its indetermination; it acquires a definition and a nature, because we know *against what* it is directed, *from what* it is freedom." [29]

Sartre finds the work and thought of A. Camus (1914-1960) to be quite in line with his own, especially Camus' theory of "man the absurd", expounded in his novels and philosophical essays (*The Myth of*

---

an absolutely new product whose germ could not be included in a preceding state of the world and that, consequently, freedom and creation were synonymous and identical . . . It will require two centuries of crisis—crisis of Faith, crisis of Science—for man to recover this creative freedom that Descartes posited in God for the first wild surmise to occur at last of this truth that is the cardinal basis of humanism: man is the being whose appearance makes a world exist" (*ibid.,* pp. 47f., 51; *Situations I,* pp. 332f., 334).

[28] "We were persuaded *at the same time* that historical materialism provided the only valid interpretation of history and that existentialism remained the only concrete approach to reality. I make no pretense of denying the contradictions inherent in this attitude" (J.-P. Sartre, *Critique de la raison dialectique* [Paris, 1960], p. 24).

[29] J.-P. Sartre, "M. Francois Mauriac et la liberté," in *Situations I,* p. 49.

Sisyphus) Says Sartre: "His hero was neither good nor bad, neither moral nor immoral. These categories do not fit him: he belongs to a quite singular category which the author specifies as the *absurd.*"[30] Absurd, as here used, can have two dimensions of meaning. Primarily it indicates man's relation to the world, a relation that emerges as a divorce between man's yen for unity and the insurmountable dualism of spirit and nature, between man's thrust toward the eternal and the *finite* character of his existence, between the "solicitude" (*souci*) which is man's very essence and the futility of his efforts. The poles of tension of this absurd are death, the irreducible plurality of truth and of beings, the unintelligibility of the real, chance and the like, which are the common features of philosophical irrationalism and pessimism of all ages. This might be called the "objectively absurd" or man as a passion of the absurd.

Man the absurd does not commit suicide, like Dostoevsky's atheists. He wills to live, without renouncing a single one of his certitudes, with no future, with no hope, with no illusion, devoid even of resignation. He focusses on death with passionate attentiveness and this very enthrallment frees him: he realizes the "divine responsibility" of the condemned criminal. Everything is permitted because there is no God and death comes as the end. All experiences are of equal status and value; the sole point is to acquire them in the greatest possible quality. In the face of this "ethic of quality" all values collapse: man the absurd, cast into this world, a rebel,[31] irresponsible, has no need "to justify anything." He is *innocent*. The absurd, which is man without God, the godless man, is thus first considered as a "feeling" and then as a "notion", fruit of reflection: first, that is, as the presence and awareness of the daily and amorphous flux of reality as lived, then as the rational transposition of this kind of absurdity by the instrumentality of human reason and articulation.

Sartre most incisively observes that in this view articulation loses all color of transcendence and the verb "to be" is a simple copula of sheer limpidity, sheer passivity, confined to noting down facts.

What is the nature of this absurd? Camus effects a highly controversial transposition of the Kierkegaardian absurd and calls it "philosophical suicide" and "logical suicide"; it is "sin without God", inasmuch as this absurd, which is the metaphysical state of the conscious man, does not lead to God. It is, says Camus, a convenient way of indicating the movement by which thought negates itself and tends to transcend itself in its very negation: "For the existentials, negation is their God. To be

[30] Cf. Sartre's interpretative explanation of *L'étranger* [The Outsider], in *Situations I*, pp. 99ff.

[31] *L'Homme revolté* is the title of a volume of Camus essays published subsequent to Sartre's interpretation of his earlier book *L'étranger*.

precise, that god is maintained only through the negation of human reason." [32] The "leap" then, far from constituting an extreme danger as it does for Kierkegaard, is the sole law of life, as assertion of the absence of all law; and "absurd freedom" is its motive power. "Living is keeping the absurd alive" and is "thus revolt. It is a constant confrontation between man and his own obscurity. It is an insistence upon an impossible transparency. It challenges the world anew every second . . . It is that constant presence of man in his own eyes. It is not aspiration, for it is devoid of hope." [33]

It might however be noted that Camus proceeded to found a publication series with the overall title *Espoir* (Hope), in which there appears a number of philosophical essays with a decidedly positive bias, such as B. Parain's *L'embarras du choix* and Simone Weil's famous works, of Christian inspiration, *L'enracinement, La connaissance surnaturelle, Lettre à un religieux* and *La condition ouvrière*. The "foreword" to this Series included a declaration of aims which is worthy of serious study, as indicating something more than a mere change of style. It is a profession of faith in the value of man, despite the abyss of nihilism into which civilization has hurled him: "We are in nihilism! Is there any way out of nihilism? That is the question with which we are saddled. But we shall not slip out of it by making a show of being oblivious of the malady of the age nor yet by resolving to deny its existence. The only hope lies in calling it by its name and effecting a detailed diagnosis of it, so as to find the cure in the extremity of the disease." The aim of the Series is, therefore, to arouse and promote this hope: the individual volumes may present a confirmation of nihilism or may, on the contrary, attempt to get beyond it; but the overall program is quite clear: "They will all, however, form a common front, they will all witness to an identical effort to define or surmount the lethal contradiction in which we are living. If the time has come when we must choose, this very compulsion itself represents progress. *Let us then realize that this is the time of hope,* even if it be a hard-won and demanding hope." The aim of the Series is therefore to aid, albeit in the simplest and most modest way, "*. . . to expose the tragedy and to show that tragedy is not a solution nor yet despair a defensible ultimate stand.* It depends on us to convert these unavoidable trials into pledges of hope." [34] We have certainly not yet

[32] A. Camus, *Le mythe de Sisiphe* (Paris: Gallimard, 1942), p. 61; English translation by Justin O'Brien, *The Myth of Sisyphus and Other Essays* (New York: Vintage Books: Alfred A. Knopf, Inc., and Random House, Inc., 1955), p. 31. And Camus specifies in a Footnote: "it is not the affirmation of God that is questioned here, but rather the logic leading to that affirmation." (*Le mythe de Sisiphe,* p. 62; English translation, p. 31).

[33] *Ibid.,* p. 77; English translation, p. 40.

[34] This significant and unexpected declaration appears on the back cover of *L'homme revolté.* Italics are mine.

reached the definitively Kierkegaardian stand, but neither are we very far from it, so great is the similarity in the two writers' exposure of the *angustia* and the *presussura saeculi.* It is not easy to say whether Camus, so tragically struck down at the height of his powers, might have completed his Odyssey in a positive sense; but this declaration we have just cited bears witness to the fact that he was indeed already far along the road.

Camus does not sidestep the God-problem as does Sartre; rather Camus poses this problem lucidly and incisively: "From the moment that man submits God to moral judgment, he kills Him in his own heart. And then what is the basis of morality? God is denied in the name of justice, but can the idea of justice be understood without the idea of God? At this point are we not in the realm of absurdity?" [35]

Camus is here candidly focussing attention on the conflict between the radical immanentist stand that has been the Procrustean bed of modern thought and the demand of the innermost essence of man. And he elaborates the conflict as mirrored in the destructive atheistic thinking of such philosophers and poets as Stirner, Nietzsche ("Nietzsche's sole admiration was for the egotism and severity proper to all creators"), Lautréamont ("With Lautréamont, the rebel flees to the desert"), Rimbaud (". . . with Rimbaud, nihilist dejection prevailed; the struggle, the crime itself, proved too exacting for his exhausted mind. The seer who drank, if we may venture to say so, in order not to forget ended by finding in drunkenness the heavy sleep so well known to our contemporaries"), Breton ("Whoever refuses to recognize any other determining factor apart from the individual and his desires, any priority other than that of the unconscious, actually succeeds in rebelling simultaneously against society and against reason. The theory of the gratuitous act is the culmination of the demand for absolute freedom") and several others. Camus' final conclusion is: "Man, on earth that he knows is henceforth solitary, is going to add, to irrational crimes, the crimes of reason that are bent on the triumph of man." [36]

The whole tone of Camus' diagnosis of modern thought, certainly the most lucid diagnosis we have thus far encountered, seems to us to indicate an attitude and a bias which are no longer those of a Sartrian accomodating to the finding his delight in nothingness and the absurd. Camus seems already to have broken through to an expectant hope of something "beyond nihilism".

[35] A. Camus, *L'homme revolté,* p. 84; English translation, *The Rebel,* p. 62.

[36] *Ibid.,* p. 132; English translation, *The Rebel,* p. 104. In this denunciation of nihilism, we feel there is also implicit a criticism of the Sartre who wrote of "Freedom as a nihilation of being" (*Liberté comme néantisation de l'être*).

6

Essence and Existence: The "Forgottenness of Being"

The *essentia-existentia* confrontation, that bitter battleground on which the medieval Scholastics after Aquinas clashed so inconclusively,[1] has assumed even sharper prominence in the campaign for clarification Heidegger has undertaken with a view to finding a way out of the impasse in which Western metaphysics has deadlocked itself as a result of the preferential status it has assigned to formalism and in which modern philosophy especially is hopelessly mired. In his 1947 *Brief über Humanismus,* Heidegger is particularly concerned to point out that the term *existentia* as used by the Scholastics in contradistinction to *essentia* has nothing in common with Heidegger's own term *Ek-sistenz.* The *existentia-essentia* pairing highlights the difference between actuality and possibility, whereas the Heideggerian mention, in *Sein und Zeit,* of the *Essence* (*Wesen*) of man together with Heidegger's insistence that the Essence (*Wesen*) of human reality, There-being (*Dasein*) consists precisely in its existence (*Existenz*) is rather in the tradition of Kant-Hegel-Nietzsche: for Heidegger is proclaiming the strict conjunction of the two elements within the ambit of human freedom; and in this sense, which we consider for our part to be immanentist and actualistic, Heidegger can indeed assert that his notion has nothing in common either with the Scholastic expression *Deus est suum esse* or with the Sartrian formula that "existence precedes essence" (p. 72).[2] Heidegger's formula "The *Substance* of Man is Ek-sistence" (*"Die Substanz des Menschen ist die Ek-sistenz"*) (Cf. *Sein und Zeit,* pp. 117, 212, 314 then comes down to the simple statement: "The way in which man shows himself in his own nature to Being is his ek-static standing within the truth of Being" (*op. cit.,* p. 74). We are here dealing therefore, with

[1] On Scholastic ambiguity and confusion, cf. our studies on the Thomist notion of participation: *La nozione metafisica di partecipazione; Participation et causalité;* Italian translation *Partecipazione e causalità.*

[2] The quotations are from *PLBH.*

the "reality" of man and not with essence and existence in the traditional sense; and this reality is shaped by the mode of being and being-situated of man "thrust-into-the-world." Up to this point, there is no substantial innovation on the basic tenets of *Sein und Zeit.*

Heidegger rightly remarks that the term *existentia* in the Scholastic twin pair *essentia-existentia* is equivalent to *actualitas,* expressive of the *fact* of being realized in some thing: in Heidegger's own term *Da-sein,* on the contrary, the *Da* (*There*) signifies the mode of be-ing which is proper to man: man is in the "clearing of Being" (*Lichtung des Seins,* [which we feel can better and more pertinently be rendered in English by this recourse to the primordial object-indicating meaning of the German word than in any recourse to overtones of illumination: *Lichtung im Walde,* e.g., is a "clearing" in the forest, with all the overtones that this implies, but with a predominantly object-designating dimension—Translator's Note]). Heidegger is therefore not unjustified in his critique of the static formal definition of man as a "rational animal", whereas man's true parameter is his relation to Being; nor is Heidegger wrong in accusing metaphysics of this incomprehension: "Metaphysics repudiates the simple essential stand that man manifests himself only in his essence into which he is hailed by Being. Only by this hail. "has" he found that wherein in which his essence dwells. Only from this dwelling 'has' man 'language' as the dwelling that guards for his essence the ek-static moment [transcendence as Being-in-the-world]. This standing in the clearing of Being I call the *Ek-sistenz* of man" (pp. 66f.).

To Heidegger's mind the famous *essentia-existentia* controversy (as futile as it is famous!) all began in the Aristotelian distinction between "whatness" and "thatness" (τί ἐστιν and ὅτι ἔστιν), between *was* and *dass;* [3] and it never attained any clarity because of the preliminary blocking of all reflection on the basis. Until such time as the relation of man to Being (and *vice versa*) has been clarified, thought is impossible; we do not even know what thinking is, nor what the relation of "Being and Thought". Heidegger's entire terminology makes it clear that he recog-

[3] *PLBH,* p. 69. The following passage from a later Heidegger work is entirely along the same highly significant and suggestive line: "The term 'There-being' (*Dasein*) was chosen for the domain where Being essences (*Wesensbereich*) in which man as man stands. We have done this so as to articulate, simultaneously and in *one* word, both the relation (of drawn-ness) (*Bezug*) of Being to the essence of man and the essential relationship of man to the open-ness (*Offenheit*) ("There" ["*Da*"]) of Being as such. We have not allowed ourselves to be inhibited in our choice by the fact that metaphysics uses this name for what is otherwise designated by such terms as *existentia,* actuality, reality and object-ness, objectivity, nor even by the fact that ordinary speech tends to be permeated and dominated by the metaphysical meaning of the word when it talks of "human being" or "human existence" (*vom* "*menschlichen Dasein*")." (M. Heidegger, *Was ist Metaphysik?,*[5] p. 13).

nizes only the traditional nominalist-rationalist definition of *existentia* as "the act whereby a thing subsists, is posited outside the state of possibility:" [4] *essentia* and *existentia* are, for Heidegger and this tradition, two diverse "states."

In Heidegger's major work on Nietzsche, *essentia* and *existentia* (*Was-sein* and *Dass-sein*) are expressly referred back to ἰδέα and ἐνέργεια as to their linguistic ancestors; and Heidegger considers this distinction as the origin of the most serious equivocations in the history of thought, from the *cogito* of Descartes, right on down to the Kantian discussion of the "Proofs of the existence of God" and evolutionism's notion of the "struggle for existence".[5] Such a distinction is therefore no more academic elucubration of ancient metaphysics; rather it goes back to an event (*Ereignis*) in the history of Being. We can subscribe to this Heideggerian assertion likewise, but always with the fundamental reservation: though applicable to formalistic philsophy, both scholastic and modern, it is not at all applicable to the position of St. Thomas, who tried in vain to show philosophers the way to avoid this snare. St. Thomas' own position does not recognize the twin pair *essentia-existentia* at all; rather it distinguishes between the *quod est* (that which is) (substance) and *esse* (act of Be-ing); clearly, therefore, St. Thomas' *esse* is not the same as Heidegger's *Sein,* which latter, we feel, relapses into the principle of immanentism, inasmuch as it is pure presence (*Anwesenheit*).[6] Although the fact and notion of immanence is novel and original in its meaning as presented by Heidegger, it still remains the immanence of immanentism, because Heidegger's formulation still insists on the *essential and reciprocal* conjunction of Being and beings and consequently of being and consciousness; and this inevitably involves in turn another consequence which Heidegger readily admits: namely that the Being of beings is intrinsically finite and that our "knowledge" is likewise intrinsically finite, inasmuch as it is an apprehending, conceptual, contemplative event. Thus, in this Heideggerian context, it is meaningless from the outset to call God *esse ipsum, esse purum, esse per es-*

[4] Cf. M. Heidegger, *Kants These über das Sein* (Frankfurt a. M.: Klostermann, 1963), p. 32.

[5] "Being is distinguished into what-being(s) is (are) (*Was-sein*) and that being(s) is (are) (*Dass-sein*). With this distinction and its preliminaries, the history of Being as metaphysics begins" (M. Heidegger, *Nietzsche,* Vol. II, p. 401; Cf. also *Kants These über das Sein,* p. 32; *Vorträge und Aufsätze,* pp. 74ff.).

[6] The appeals to Old High German, on the part of Heidegger himself and by professional philologists, as substantiating the contention that *Wesen* = come-to-presence, merely serve to confirm the ambiguity of Heidegger's own position, in claiming to have found a new middle way between immanence and transcendence (Cf. E. Fraenkel, *Das Sein und seine Modalitäten,* Lexis II (1949), fasc. I, pp. 146ff. and fasc. II, p. 162; E. Schöfer, *Die Sprache Heideggers* [Pfullingen, 1962], pp. 92ff. (*Wesen*), 94ff. (*Sein*).

sentiam as *Ens perfectissimum, summum, etc.*[7] Might not Heidegger's own position itself be an effect of that very "forgottenness of Being" which he so legitimately and justifiably criticizes? [8] We think so; and we are further convinced that it even furnishes, in its extreme ambiguity, one of the most radical expressions of the principle of immanentism, in its inevitable hightlighting of the essential reciprocity and sheer circularity prevailing between Being and human There-being!

[7] Heidegger never properly distinguishes between the position of St. Thomas and that of Suarez: everything Heidegger writes on the concept of *esse* and on its relation to the concept of causality and consequently on the concept of God as *summum ens, summum bonum* (Cf. M. Heidegger, *Nietzsche,* Vol. II, pp. 415f.) is most revealing, as showing the gravity of Heidegger's oversight in this whole matter. For a more thorough treatment of this whole problematic and a rectification of the situation, we refer the reader again to our own studies on the Aquinas concept of participation (Cf. Footnote 1, above, to this Section).

[8] Heidegger quite rightly notes that the Suarezian notion of "*existentia*" (Disp. Metaph. XXXI, sect. IV, n. 6) had a profound influence on the inception of modern metaphysics (M. Heidegger, *Nietzsche,* Vol. II, p. 418); but Heidegger entirely fails, here as everywhere else in his writings, to take into account the great gulf that separates the Suarezian position and the tradition summed up in that position from the position of St. Thomas himself!

Appendices

NATURE AND THE "SACRAL" IN HEIDEGGER

Since 1929, Heidegger has steadily declared or implied the God-problem to be extraneous to philosophy. In that year, in his *Vom Wesen des Grundes,* he asserted, pursuant to his analysis of *Time and Being,* the circularity or mutual conjunction of *There-being* (*Seiende*) and *being-in-the-world* (*In-der-Welt-sein*): "Neither a positive nor a negative decision concerning a possible being-unto-God is contained or implied in the ontological interpretation of There-being as being-in-the-world. But it is true that the illumination and elucidation of transcendence provides primarily an *adequate concept* of *There-being,* with regard to which being it can thereupon be *asked* how matters stand with the God-relationship of There-being" (M. Heidegger, *Vom Wesen des Grundes,* p. 36, Note. Cf. M. Heidegger, *PLBH,* pp. 101f.). The ground of this position seems to us quite pertinent to the fundamental inspiration of Heidegger's thought with its ontico-phenomenological background: the problem of Being and of the existence of God is a problem of "presence" of what must be called the "divine reality". This divine reality is expressed by the Sacral (*das Heilige*); [1] and hence the possi-

[1] We have deliberately chosen the rendering of "*das Heilige*" as "the Sacral" rather than as the more usual and current "the Holy" against the strongly expressed advice of several experts we have here consulted. Their contention was that "das Heilige" had been virtually canonized as "the Holy" in English especially from the translations of Rudolf Otto's works on which Heidegger appears to have drawn. This argument seems to us less than cogent, especially in the context of the extreme diversity and even disparity of Heidegger renderings in English. The more serious objection raised against our rendering has been that "sacral" precisely conveys the preponderant overtone of executive and operative *human* action rather than the ontological anterior dimension or quality. Our reply is that such an impression is indeed conveyed by "sacralized" and a fortiori precisely by "hallowed" which would stem from "holy"; whereas "sacral" conveys much more the overtone of a state or permanent quality attaching to certain places and rites. Finally, we must note that we have here departed from Richardson, who renders "*das Heilige*" indeed as "the Holy." But: (a) Richardson has no special axe to grind for his rendering in this case or at least does not grind it, the rendering and the whole treatment being peripheral to his overriding purpose; and (b) he does not treat it as a *key* Heideggerian neologism (which it quite obviously is not!) nor even as an old word so surcharged with meaning as to warrant inclusion in his Glossary.

bility of the presence of God can only be estimated in terms of the possibility of an experience of the Sacral, as Heidegger himself immediately declares (cf. M. Heidegger, *PLBH,* p. 102). In the *Nachwort* to *Was ist Metaphysik?* (p. 46), we read the following distinction between philosophy and poetry: "The thinker says Being; the poet names the Sacral" (*Der Denker sagt das Sein. Der Dichter nennt das Heilige*); but we also read that the thinker and the poet "live close together on the remotest mountains" and we know nothing of their dialogue. But we do know at least that the meaning of Being comes solely from the flux or becoming-process of history.

The assignment of showing how man enters into relations with the Sacral, i.e., the exhibition of "the Open" (*das Offene*) through which the Sacral opens itself (dis-closes itself) to men and gods at once—this is rather the work of the poet who chants the festal sacral song, than it is of the philosopher. (Cf. *Erläuterungen zu Hölderlins Dichtung,* pp. 139f. Cf. on pp. 57f. the definition of the relation between the Sacral [*das Heilige*] and the Open [*das Offene*], in conformity with Hölderlin's conception of poetry, according to which Nature is "above and beyond" the gods, because it is the Sacral and thus more ancient than the ages and higher than the gods.) It is therefore no overwhelming surprise that Heidegger should define the Sacral as structurally basic to the nature of the gods: "The Sacral is not sacral because it is divine; rather, the divine is divine because it is, in its own way, 'sacral'; for, in the same verse, Hölderlin calls 'Chaos' likewise 'sacral'. The Sacral is the essence of Nature." p. 58).

The insurmountable objection we have felt to the English "holy" is that it far too strongly denotes moral perfection. As for our own rendering, we begin its justification from Webster. Here again we are well aware of the *caveat* that semantic use must always outweigh etymological status; but we are persuaded that this law applies only in dealing with conversational renderings, not with technical terms. "Sacral" is defined as "of or for religious rites or observances"; and Webster has an illuminating distinction between "holy" and the more usual conversational form "sacred" (which we have avoided precisely because it is so conversationally current and therefore weighted with too many obvious associational overtones): "*holy* suggests that which is held in deepest religious reverence or is basically associated with a religion and, in extended use, connotes spiritual purity. . .; *sacred* refers to that which is set apart as holy or is dedicated to some exalted purpose and, therefore, connotes inviolability". Our consultants exultantly proclaimed that this clinched their case against us, since "sacred" precisely connoted the human action of setting apart. But we have *not* chosen "sacred" but rather "sacral" as denoting, not the setting apart but rather the comprehensive character of that which is so set apart. Sacral is patently opposed to profane. And the opposition stems precisely from the fact that the "sacral" is positioned (not by human executive action but rather by simple recognition of an antecedent status) within the place-of-power, within the circle where man encounters the more-than-human, whereas the profane is outside that circle of powerful encounter.

Heidegger is quite gingerly in refusing to equate or even predominantly refer "*das Heilige*" to God or the divine; it is higher than man or gods; it is the utterly and inviolably anterior. "Sacral" better conveys this than does "Holy".

The "Sacral", designated by Hölderlin as the object of poetry, is the festive joy of the encounter or intimate fellowship of man with the deity, a fellowship which, however, does not submerge the difference of nature, any more than it was submerged for the demigod who was taken up among the gods. The sacral or the divine here mentioned is not theological in character, but rather phenomenologico-ontic, in the sense of Greek poetry as revived by Hölderlin. The earth and the light, the angel of the house and the angel of the year are all called deities, as principles instilling serenity and inviting to salvation. The Sacral, therefore, must not be confused with God: "The Sacral is epiphanic but God remains remote and the world (Nature), even in showing-forth the Sacral, bears witness at the same time to the Want (*Fehl*) of God" ("Heimkunft/An die Verwandten," in *Erläuterungen zu Hölderlins Dichtung,* pp. 19, 27). The Sacral thus seems bound up with nature (φύσις) and with the mysterious manifestation of nature's powers and forces to man's experience. We even read that, for Hölderlin, the Sacral is "Chaos" itself, from which emerges every experiential reality: it is the "Future", it is what is primordial, it remains sound and whole and integral in itself and imparts soundness, wholeness and integrity to everything and everyone; it remains in itself unattainable for any individual reality, be it "a God or a man". The Sacral is hidden in "mystery (*Geheimnis*) and is therefore the "de-ranging" (*ent-setzend,* Heidegger's hyphenated version of a German original usually signifying "horrifying" or "tremendous") element, which consequently emerges as the Awesome (*das Entsitzliche*) [2]; and the poets' knowing of it is a fore-boding (*Ahnen*). In this sense, it is the function of the Sacral to converse the whole in the intact and integral immediacy of its presence and present-ness: it indicates the calm present-ness of what must come, a present-ness that has its place in the soul of the poet.

The point that must be stressed and highlighted is this: it is in the Sacral that there occurs the encounter between men and the gods and between the gods and men; and this encounter is a mediated encounter (to use Hegelian terminology), mediated by the poet's verse, which effects the revelation or dis-closure, or again un-veiling, of the Sacral and makes it manifest (or dis-closed, or un-veiled) together with the poetry itself; and apart from this mediation, men would not have of themselves and by their own power any immediate relation to the Sacral. Again, the Sacral is called "interiority itself" (*die Innigkeit selbst*), and, with Hölderlin, the "heart" (*das Herz*) and "more ancient than the

[2] Richardson comments in a Footnote on the impossibility of retaining in English the word play here involved (W. Richardson, *Heidegger,* Through Phenomenology to Thought, p. 427, Note 10). The *Ent-setzliche* is that which possesses the capacity for being *ent-setzend; ent-setzend* is the executive actualization of the capacity designated as *"entsetzlich"*. Where *"ent-setzend"* is rendered as "de-ranging" (felicitously, we agree), *ent-setzlich* would be "de-ranging-ible" but English boggles at this form.

ages and higher than the gods" (Cf. "Wie wenn am Feiertage," in *Erläuterungen zu Hölderlins Dichtung,* pp. 61f., 71). To the Sacral pertains the initial decision concerning men and gods: who they are and how they are and when they are. The Sacral gives the word and comes itself in this word: the word is the e-vent (*Ereignis*) of the Sacral. Heidegger extols Hölderlin's poetry as being more powerful than that of any other poet to e-voke the Sacral with which the becoming-process of nature is permeated for the mind of man.

The absolutely radical and proper reason for the absence of the God-problem from philosophy is, for Heidegger, an even deeper one: he holds that Being (*Sein*), in its reality the Presence of that which comes-to-presence (*die Anwesenheit des Anwesenden*), neither is nor has a content, nor can it ever become an object like a being. It is therefore the Other of being; it is Non-being, that Non-being that is un-veiled by anxiety (*Angst*). We are here dealing, therefore, not with Non-being in its very essence (*das Nichten des Nichts*), but rather with that Non-being that renders possible, within the "essential anxiety", the coming-to-presence or the appearing of (a) being(s). Thus Heidegger reacted vigorously to the charge of nihilism. In the *Nachwort* to the fourth edition of *Was ist Metaphysik?* (Bonn: Cohen, 1943), he says that the Non-being that anxiety determines in its essence does not have the function of "sheer empty negation" but could be almost said to be, rather, a phenomenological transcendental, inasmuch as it is that which must emerge from the removal of all beings and which is distinct from those beings and hence "what we call Being": for Non-Being is the Other of beings, eluding representation as beings and therefore comes-to-presence (*west*) as Being (*Was ist Metaphysik?, Nachwort,* p. 41). It should here be pointed out that this 4th edition (1943) has a passage which has been slightly but crucially altered in the 5th edition (1949). The original (1943) reading was: "Being *indeed* comes-to-presence without beings" (das Sein *wohl* west ohne das Seiende); in the 5th edition, this passage reads: "Being *never* comes-to-presence without beings". Richardson has an interesting commentary on this, in a section of his *Heidegger,* Through Phenomenology to Thought, entitled "The Case of the Altered Epilogue" (pp. 563ff.). Carlini still follows the 1943 text in his Italian translation (Milan, 1953, p. 47) and comments in a footnote: ". . . which is reminiscent of the Christian concept of God who, as Creator, exists by Himself, even without the world". But in point of fact Heidegger thinks exactly the opposite, as is evident from his positing of a perfect reciprocity between Being (*Sein*) and beings (*Seiende*).

M. Müller makes an ingenious attempt to reconcile the two variants. He finds them mutually complementary: "Being does indeed (*wohl*) come-to-presence without beings (4th edition), inasmuch as it itself does not 'have' but 'is' the difference of beings and with the difference bears, together with itself, the different. Being, in this regard, has no 'outside' and therefore has no want. But it does have a history. If I consider it from this point of view as the Other of beings (as reality in tension with the real which is *distinct* from it), then it does have need of beings, then there leaps to the eye what we have called its contingency, i.e., the fact that it *never* comes-to-presence without beings (5th edition). Thus beings (*Seiende*) can be considered, with respect and reference to Being, now as what is distinct from Being, from the Being to which they are referred, now as what is not separate, what is contained in Being itself. Now if the difference be considered from the point of view of beings, then it does not disappear, for, from the point of view of beings, Being is always "above" (*über*) beings, since Being overtops and excels every such being and every That-being (*Das-sein*); and every participation of beings in Being is precisely a "having-*part*" and the difference cannot disappear; in individual beings, the "whole of Being" (*das 'ganze Sein'*) is not present . . . and its presence occurs in different ways, as required by the environment of the finite and of history. But if the difference be considered from the point of view of Being, then the difference can very well, as difference, appear as 'indifference' (undifferentiatedness, a matter of no account or importance) as well." (M. Müller, *Existenzphilosophie im geistigen Leben der Gegenwart,* pp. 50f. Note). This perspicacious explanation confirms the danger of a "closure" of Heideggerian thought to all theological transcendence, in the proper meaning of that term. But it may be pointed out that man was designated, even in the original text of the lecture, as the " 'stand-in' for Non-being" (*Platzhalter des Nichts*) (*Was ist Metaphysik?,* p. 34). This same notion was expanded and incorporated into one of Heidegger's most famous metaphors in "Der Spruch des Anaximander": "To conservation as the guarding of Being corresponds the shepherd who has so little to do with an idyllic sheepwalk and nature mystique, that he can only become a shepherd of Being to the extent that he remains a 'stand-in' for Non-being. Both are the same" (M. Heidegger, "Der Spruch des Anaximander," in *Holzwege,* p. 321).

It is in fact Non-being, the object of anxiety, that is instrumental and indispensible in accomplishing that pure experience of Being already mentioned and in overcoming and superseding There-being: Non-being is the ground and foundation of Transcendence itself. In 1947, Heidegger goes still further, with the explicit reference to the "Non" as a negation of the negation of the essence of Being: thus, in *PLBH,* Heidegger indicates that, since Being is not a being but rather conceals itself even in revealing itself, there is no way for There-being to grasp it by itself except as Non-being; but this necessity does not spring originally from There-being itself; rather it is rooted in Being *it*self; for the very simple reason that Being comports this negativing element as intrinsic to its nature. "The negativing element in Being is the essence of what I call Non-being. Thought, therefore, because it thinks Being, thinks Non-being." (M. Heidegger, *PLBH,* P. p. 114). It is in terms of the "negativity" (*Nichtigkeit*) within the depths of Being, that the problem of man's "transcendence" can and must be posed: for it is in the "thrust into Non-being . . . [that] the There of Being . . . is intrinsically negatived" (W. Richardson, *Heidegger,* Through Phenomenology to Thought, p. 535. Throughout this paragraph, we have drawn on Richardson's exposition, *op. cit.,* pp. 534f., almost to the point of paraphrase. On the critical function of "Non-being", cf. C. Fabro, *Dall'essere all'esistenzia,* p. 380).

In his still more recent work, *Kants These über das Sein,* Heidegger continues to grapple with this same problem-complex. But it could almost be said that we are here witnessing a *Kehre* (reversal), which seems to us strangely redolent of a return to Aristotle, who held that being is divided, broken up and scattered amid and in beings and has meaing (sign-ifies) in the diversity of the predicates, so that Being as such 'is not' nor does it, as such, sign-ify at all. The difference—and it is certainly an important one—is that, for Heidegger, as we have seen, Being does precisely signify Non-being (of There-being). In fact, at the end of this recent work, devoted to the meaning of Being in Kant, Heidegger expresses himself in the following terms, at the end of his treatment of the relation between Being and Thinking (*Sein und Denken*): "In the homely little word 'is', there lies concealed all that is remark-able about Being. And the most remark-able point of all is that we ponder whether 'Being', whether the 'is' itself can be, or whether Being never 'is' and it yet remains true: Being is (a) given (*Es gibt Sein*).[3] But whither comes, to whom goes the gift in the 'is given', and what is the manner of the giving? Being cannot *be*. Were it to be, it would no longer remain Being, but would be *a being!* (M. Heidegger, *Kants These über das Sein,* p. 35).

However all this is to be interpreted and whatever is the more or less recondite significance of these passages in the evolution of Heidegger's thought, there must be admitted, in any event, to be an undeniable unity of doctrine; and it is our opinion that Heidegger does well in defending this unity.

[3] Richardson has interesting observations on this *crux interpretum* on p. xx of his *Heidegger,* Through Phenomenology to Thought. The usual "There is" rendering would leave this particular passage quite bemusing! While Richardson's own "is granted" rendering is impressive, we have felt that the simpler rendering "is (a) given" is both closer to the original and more evocative of exactly what Heidegger here wants to communicate.

PART VIII

THEOLOGY OF ATHEISM DIALECTICAL THEOLOGY AND DEATH-OF-GOD THEOLOGY

Prefatory Note

Protestant theology generally has given little attention to the problem of atheism which has been spreading throughout Western culture for a century and which dominates the main trends of present-day thought. Liberal Protestant theologians, who have welcomed the evolution of modern philosophical thought as instanced in Schleiermacher, Hegel, Ritschl, R. Otto, Troeltsch and others like them, seem to be unaware of the atheism implicit in the principle of immanentism and consider atheism to be simply the result of a misunderstanding of that principle. Those conservative Protestant theologians who adhere more closely to the founding fathers of the Reformation (e.g., present-day "dialectical theology") ascribe little importance to the problem of atheism for the very simple reason that they consider it to be the issue and effect of (totally) corrupt human reason, utterly vitiated by the Fall and haughtily claiming to be able to reach God by its own powers. Thus for these theologians the existence of God is solely an object of faith. Fallen man is completely split off from God; and so to the (physical) impossibility of comprehending God that derives from the finitude of our being, there is added the moral impossibility of knowing his existence, this latter impossibility deriving from the original corruption of the intellect and the will, subverted by pride and concupiscence.

The existence of God and of his attributes is therefore believed and known in the same fashion as, and together with, the mystery of the trinity, from which, according to the statement of the Augsburg Confession, it is indistinguishable: "With broad agreement, the Churches among us teach that the decree of the Synod of Nicea concerning the unity of the divine essence and the Three Persons is true and to be believed without any reservation. To wit, that there is one divine essence which is called and is God, eternal, incorporeal, indivisible, measureless in power, wisdom, goodness, Creator and Sustainer of all things visible and invisible; and that at the same time there are Three Persons of the same essence and power, co-eternal, Father and Son and Holy Spirit." [1]

[1] *Conf. Aug.*, Pars I, art. 1: *De Deo,* quoted in J. T. Müller, *Die symbolischen Bücher der evangelische-lutherischen Kirche* (Gütersloh, 1886 [6]). The 1542 *Catechism of the Church of Geneva* seems to be less rigid. The reply to Question

Despite the explicit statement of St. Paul (*Rom.* 1, 10ff.), the rigid Lutheran notion of the *Deus absconditus* radically precludes any possibility of man approaching God apart from or prior to faith; it therefore categorically denies any natural knowledge of God, and specifies that the lack of such knowledge is the penalty of original sin: ". . . the graver vices of human nature . . . *ignorance* of God, contempt of God".[2] Atheism is thus the fullness of sin as fault and as penalty, Satanic possession of man from which there is no liberation apart from the grace of faith. Thus far, some quite well-known statements of Luther.

Especially his *Deus absconditus* (or again *Deus involutus*) is commonly agreed to have originated primarily in that nominalism in which he was trained in his youth, rather than in Greek and Christian Neoplatonism. Luther asserts: "But since these divine goods are invisible, incomprehensible and entirely hidden, nature consequently cannot attain or love them unless it be elevated by the grace of God." And Luther holds the new principle of justification to be solidary with this principle of absolute fideism: "For the same reason it is also the case that the spiritual man cannot be judged, understood, seen by anyone, not even by himself, because he abides in the most lofty shadows and darkness of God." [3]

25: "Why do you add that He is Creator of heaven and earth?" reads: "Because he has manifested Himself to us by his works, we must seek for Him in them (Ps. 104; Rom. 1:20). For our understanding is not capable of grasping his essence. But the world is unto us as a mirror, in the which we can contemplate Him according as it is expedient for us to know him." (In W. Niesel, *Bekenntnisschriften und Kirchenordnungen der nach Gotteswort reformierten Kirche* [Zollikon-Zürich: Evangelischer Verlag, 1938], p. 5). Cf. also the 1561 *Ecclesiarum Belgicarum Confessio,* art. II: "We know Him in two ways: first, through creation, conservation and governance of the whole world: seeing that this world is before our eyes like a most beautiful book, wherein all creatures, great and small, function as those signs and characters showing forth to us the invisible things of God that are to be contemplated; to wit, His everlasting power and divinity, as saith St. Paul, Rom. 1:22. All of which suffice to convince men and render (unbelief) unpardonable" (*ibid.,* p. 120).

[2] "For we desired to signify that the sin of the beginning (original sin) doth contain these ills as well: ignorance of God, contempt of God: a lack of the fear of God and trust in God, an inability to love God. These are the chiefest vices of human nature warring precisely against the first table of the Decalogue" (*Apol. Conf.,* II, 14, in J. T. Müller, *op. cit.,* p. 80). This statement implies that this lack of knowledge of God pertains to the very definition of sin: "Thus the old definition, in saying that sin is a want or deficiency of justice, doth eliminate not only the obedience of man's lower powers, *but also the knowledge of God,* or at least certainly the power of arriving at such knowledge" (*Apol. Conf.,* II, 23, in J. T. Müller, *op. cit.,* p. 81).

[3] *Luthers Vorlesung über den Hebräerbrief 1517-18,* Vol. II: *Die Scholien,* ed. J. Ficker (Leipzig, 1929), pp. 99, 13-16. One expert, however, feels that the recent crisis-theology has departed drastically from Luther who was much closer to traditional theology on this point: "Scholastic theology classed the acceptance of the existence of God among the so-called *Praeambula fidei,* which are not in

The Lutheran concept of the hidden God signals two elements or aspects of the negativity of our natural knowledge in regard to God: first there is the God who is *de facto* hidden; then there is the God who is indicated as hiding himself.[4] The first element is the Neoplatonic notion of the *Deus occultus,* the God who is mysterious because of the transcendence of his being; Luther pushes this notion to the extreme and makes God utterly unintelligible, utterly unknowable to man.[5] The second element is Luther's own contribution, and it is linked to the doctrine of "myth" and to the Gnostic aberrations. It proclaims the absolute triviality and inadequacy of human language in regard to God, so that even when God reveals himself, he is really only concealing himself. Specifically, the incarnation in Jesus Christ is the highest and definitive form of this concealment, from which follows the hiddenness of the Church and the saints (*"Abscondita est ecclesia, latent Sancti"*).[6]

Deus absconditus et revelatus: what sin has hidden from reason, God

---

the strict sense an object of faith, since they are already accessible to the natural knowledge of reason. Luther could (albeit not via this dogmatic classification as *Praeambula fidei*) ascribe to all men, by nature or in virtue of a universal tradition scarcely distinguishable therefrom, a knowledge of the Deity, a knowledge, that is, of His being, though not a knowledge of His will. More recent evangelical theology, from Schleiermacher to Karl Barth has, on the contrary, attempted with increasingly drastic bias, to eliminate entirely the very idea of a natural theology, in tempo with the *de facto* disappearance of that older self-evidence and without giving sufficient consideration to the consequences that would follow from such an elimination" (G. Ebeling, "Luthers Reden von Gott," in *Der Gottesgedanke im Abendland* [Stuttgart: Schaefer, 1964], p. 36). One of the consequences of this sort of absolute fideism in dialectical theology must certainly be held to have been the leaving of a free field for the advance of atheism in present-day German philosophy.

[4] "In the concept *Deus absconditus* lurks a double fact: first, the hidden God, and then the God Who hides Himself" (W. Köhler, "Der verborgene Gott," in *Sitzungsbericht der Heidelbergischen Akademie der Wissenschaften, Philosophisch-historische Klasse,* 1942-43 [Heidelberg, 1946], p. 4).

[5] This utter unknowability had been formulated in straightforward fashion by Ockham, according to the statement to be found in the charge-sheet indictment of Lutterell, Chancellor of Oxford: "That any statement concerning God and His attributes made in this life amounts to nothing more than the positing of conceptual relations and possesses no objective content whatsoever. Whereas in the life beyond things themselves are subject and predicate of a statement, human knowledge in this life has to do only with concepts. And so no true statements can be articulated concerning God's being and attributes" (n. 29) (F. Hoffmann, *Die erste Kritik des Ockhamismus durch den Oxforder Kanzler Johannes Lutterell* [Breslau, 1941], p. 40).

[6] Cf. W. Köhler, *op. cit.,* pp. 24f. Gogarten is equally categorical: "Nor is God anywhere more impenetrably hidden than in His revelation." (F. Gogarten, *Der Zerfall des Humanismus und die Gottesfrage* [Stuttgart, 1937], p. 16). For a study of the entire question of the *Deus absconditus* in Luther, the reader is referred to H. Bandt, *Luthers Lehre vom verborgenen Gott;* Theologische Arbeiten VIII (Berlin, 1958). This work treats of the whole evolution of Luther's thought on this cardinal point.

has revealed in Christ. Therefore there is no longer any God *extra Christum* but only *in Christo.* Hence the fierce and dogged aversion shown by Luther against the position defended by St. Thomas against the Averroist theory of double truth (a theory accepted by the University of Paris). Luther utterly refused to accept St. Thomas' assertion that a truth must be in theology if it is true in philosophy.[7]

We have in Luther a kind of "restrictive Christology" if we may put it that way: for Luther, God and Christ are embraced in a single glance; Christ is the Lord of Hosts and there is no other God apart from his manifestation in Christ. A further reason for this contention on Luther's part is his insistence that God can only be known as a *Person* and man for his own part must relate to God as a person, i.e., by way of freedom [8] which has been totally corrupted by sin and cannot accept the *Law* or aspire to God except through the mediation of Christ.

Yet, Lutheran theology has on occasion somewhat modified the rigidity of this stand. Thus, in the *Solida Declaratio* of the *Formula Concordiae,* we read that:

(a) man does have "an inkling that a God does exist" (*ein tunkel Funklein dass ein Gott ist*);

(b) this knowledge is however "but an inkling, an indeterminate and universal knowing";

(c) no sooner does man try to develop this inkling than he entangles himself in errors and arrives not at God but at the idols of paganism.

The *Catechismus Maior* asserts that all peoples, albeit they have spontaneously felt the impulse to seek God, have strayed into idolatrous polytheism: "Once again wilt thou readily see and judge how the world hath everywhere built up and doth everywhere practice nothing but the false worship of God and idolatry. For there was never a tribe of men, however savage and wild, but did build up and practice some sort of worship of God. For all did compete to assign that God for worship from whom they hoped for some reward, divine assistance or solace." [9]

[7] Cf. the documentation reported by F. Kattenbusch, "'Deus absconditus' bei Luther," in *Festschrift für J. Kaftan,* pp. 170ff.

[8] Cf. *ibid.,* pp. 213f.

[9] *Catechismus Maior,* Pars I, § 17. And an ample explanation is given in § 18: "Hence we see that the heathen who were devoted, kit and caboodle, as the folk proverb has it, to riches, domination and empire-building, simultaneously worshipped their Jove as the supreme God. Others again whose aim was money as such or business success or sport, in bed or out of it, piously venerated Hercules, Mercury, Venus and other deities. Women in childbed claimed Diana or Lucina for their deity. And so on, each person selected for worship that God to which he or she was attracted heart and soul. Thus, in the opinion of the heathen, to have a God means simply to trust and believe. But in this do they err and go astray, that their trust is misplaced and deceptive, for it neither rightly tends nor is ordered toward the true God, aside from Whom it is crystal clear that there is no other God, neither in heaven or on earth." (J. T. Müller, *op. cit.,* pp. 388f.).

It might here be remarked that Luther and Lutheran theology anticipated by three centuries the two basic theses on religion advanced by 19th-century dialectical materialism and the positivistically biassed comparative historians of religion: namely, that religion is an imaginative extrapolation of the present and visible life into a future and invisible one; and that idolatrous polytheism is to be considered the primitive form of religion, corresponding to the manifold needs of man.

This attitude explains the categorical repudiation by orthodox Lutheran theology of any "natural theology": [10] Luther and Protestant theology do not acknowledge essences in their ontological stability and immutability; they speak solely in terms of existence and thus again prepare the way, albeit indirectly, for the modern approach.

[10] Cf. the modern bibliography on Luther's attitude on this point, in E. Schlink, *Theologie der lutherischen Bekenntnisschriften,* Einführung in die evangelische Theologie, Vol. VIII (Munich: C. Kaiser Verlag, 1947^2), p. 86. The most recent and informed comparative historians of religion notoriously find inadequate the outlines of Hume, Hobbes and their 19th-century followers.

1

The Repudiation of "Natural Theology" (Barth)

Orthodox Protestantism thus holds atheism to be the universal state of man apart from faith or without faith. There is no intermediate theism possible; it is a case of believe in Christ or be an atheist. Such is the stand made famous by *dialectical theology* or *crisis theology,* the contemporary movement whose outstanding protagonists are Karl Barth, Emil Brunner, Gogarten, Turneysen, K. Heim and especially Rudolf Bultmann, Dietrich Bonhoeffer, Paul Tillich and their disciples.[1] This theology is called "dialectical" because it holds every articulation and investigation concerning God to be a speaking *with* God, not *of* God; and especially because it contends that we can only speak about God by having recourse to conflicting and mutually contrasting statements. Thus:

(a) man, left to himself, cannot arrive at the knowledge of a personal creator God;

(b) therefore it is God himself who must call man, reveal himself to man either directly via conscience or in Christ and by way of Holy Scripture. To this call, there must correspond on man's part that *faith* (*Glaube*) which consists not in an intellectual assent, but rather in a "decision" (*Entscheidung*) and a "venture" (*Wagnis*) whereby man places himself before God. This decision is held to derive entirely from the influence of God's grace.

(c) Thus man, whoever he may be, cannot properly speak *of* God, but only *with* God, for God is not an object or any sort of thing, but a

[1] For a preliminary outline, cf. J. Ries, *Die natürliche Gotteserkenntnis, im Zusammenhang mit dem Imago-Begriff bei Calvin;* Grenzfragen zwischen Theologie und Philosophie, XIV (Bonn, 1939), especially pp. 80ff. On the Protestant side, cf. P. Strauch, *Theologie der Krisis.* A brilliant overall exposition with an extensive discussion both of the problematic and of the various trends of the dialectical theology and buttressed by a meticulous bibliography has just appeared: it is B. Gherardini, *La seconda Riforma,* Uomini e Scuole del Protestantesimo moderno (Brescia, 1966); cf. especially Vol. II, pp. 81ff.

Person; God is not an It but a He. Thus the human articulations concerned with God and the thinking that precedes and fashions them ought never to be formal and abstract (metaphysical) but always concrete and personal (existential). Hence, the close ties admitted by dialectical theology to exist between itself and Kierkegaard's existentialism, a point still however in need of further clarification.

The doctrinal atmosphere of the Lutheran *Deus absconditus* renders readily intelligible the repudiation by Protestant theology of Aquinas' doctrine of analogy. That Protestant theology holds that our concepts become equivocal when applied to God. These concepts then do violence to the divine majesty and Karl Barth, for one, considers analogy to be an invention of Antichrist.[2] Thus according to the strict Lutheran tradition, there cannot be any "Natural Theology" but only a revealed theology, a theology *ex verbo Dei.* We must here note, however, a lively debate and controversy between Barth and the Zurich theologian, Emil Brunner, who seems to come close to the Thomist position, admitting a "point of contact" (*Anknüpfungspunkt*) and defending the possibility of a knowledge of God on the part of the natural reason. Brunner insists that these points constitute a doctrine not only of the Bible as such but of Reformation thinking as well.[3] Indeed, he contends, the whole field of

[2] "I consider the *analogy of being* to be the invention of Antichrist and I think it enough to prevent anyone from becoming Catholic" (K. Barth, *Die kirkliche Dogmatik,* Vol. I/1 [Zürich, 1947^{5}], p. VIII. Cf. also Vol. II/1, especially pp. 234ff.). More recently, Barth has substituted the *analogy of relation* for this *analogy of being:* "No correspondence and similarity of being, no *analogia entis;* for the being of God and that of man are and always will be incommensurable; and furthermore it is not a question of this two-fold being, but rather of the *relation* in the being of God on the one hand and the *relation* between God's being and man's on the other. Between these two relations as such there does exist a correspondence and similarity, and in this sense the second is the image of the first. There is an *analogia relationis.*" (*ibid.,* Vol. III/2, p. 262).

[3] E. Brunner, "Zum Problem der 'natürlichen Theologie' und der 'Anknüpfung' ", in *Der Mensch im Widerspruch* (Zürich, 1941^{3}), p. 541: "The recognition of rational knowledge in its own realm is a part not only of Biblical teaching but also of the teaching of the Reformation." And a little later, he adds: "Human reason and divine revelation stand not only in a negative but also in a positive relation to each other." (p. 549). Barth's stand on this matter seems to us clearly expressed in the following passage: "Revelation is God's self-exhibition and self-depiction. Revelation bursts upon man in the presupposition of the complete and utter vanity of man's own efforts to know God on his own; it comes as a confirmation of the vanity of those efforts, whose lack of success is based not, to be sure, on any fundamental theoretical necessity, but certainly on a practical and factual one. In revelation, God tells man that He is God and that as such He is man's Lord and Master. Revelation thereby tells man something radically new, something he does not know in the absence of revelation and cannot tell either himself or others without it. That man *could* in theory know and proclaim these facts is of course true, as surely as revelation articulates only the truth. And if it is true that God is God and as such man's Lord and Master, then it is also true that man is on such a footing with God as to be theoretically able to know him". And a

theology becomes a chimera unless this capacity be admitted. Brunner thus outlines the degrees of this "fitness" (*Tauglichkeit*) of reason: reason can know both the world and man, and the latter both in terms of their physical qualities and in terms of their spiritual qualities; but it cannot, apart from the Word of God, know the true being of man for this knowledge is impossible without the knowledge of the true God. Thus (as Luther also held), the reason is not entirely excluded from the knowledge of God, at least until it becomes a question of the divine essence and will: it can likewise know something of the law of God but not of the grace that pardons sin. Thus, the *image of God* has been defiled but not destroyed by sin. A "remnant" of this image has remained even in fallen man and it is this remnant that constitutes the proper being of *humanitas*.

A positive relation must therefore be admitted between reason and faith, at least up to a certain point: thus, it cannot be admitted that man is purely passive, like a stone. Faith does indeed form and fashion the "new man"; but the "old man" is the presupposition for such remarks as St. Paul makes about the "new man": from being impious and unbelieving, man becomes pious and believing; the "newness" accrues to an already existing person, whose mode of existence needs renewal; and the new creation (*nova creatura*) consists in the *cor incurvatum in se ipsum* (heart turned in upon itself) of fallen man becoming a heart open to God. In this process, insists Brunner, God is the first cause but not the only cause; man is likewise a cause, though in a different degree: man must be able to accept and respond to God's invitation, to consent to the grace God grants out of pure love. This demands a supreme activization on man's part.[4]

God's action demands acts of the human person for its accomplishment, or rather it demands the total single act of which the person is capable, to which nothing corresponds in man's integral activity except the "integral" act of sin, and this only in areas defined by faith. Bultmann is here presupposing the structure of the human being to be a

---

little farther on, Barth adds: "The truth that God is God and our Lord and Master and the further truth that we could know and recognize Him as God and Lord—this truth can only come to us by means of Truth Himself. This coming-to-us of truth is just what revelation is." (*Die kirchliche Dogmatik,* Vol. I/2, p. 329).

[4] "But it is and always will be a mystery how this supreme activation of the human heart, of the human mind, can and does occur in the divine *actio,* which engages and enlists man's *actio* as *passio.*" (p. 552). Brunner has recently likewise criticized Barth's rejection of the *analogy of being* in favor of the *analogy of faith* alone; Brunner shows the insufficiency of the latter in the absence of the former (cf. "Zur Lehre von der 'analogia entis'", in his *Dogmatik,* Vol. II [Zollikon-Zürich, 1950], pp. 50ff.).

substantial structure and man to be a responsible being obligated to decision. It is this personal structure, as an actual being, that always constitutes the quintessence of man; and this, generically speaking is what constitutes the "point of contact" mentioned above. It is true that man in separation from God is under the dominion of sin; but it is also true that man, called by grace, must deny himself and abandon sin and therefore perform acts by accepting grace and detaching himself from sin. And this is action *par excellence:* though it remains a mystery, it is the activity of response which has remained as a power in man's essence.[5]

This controversy sheds some light on Barth's own attitude to atheism, which he somewhat oddly brackets with "mysticism",[6] saying that both are radical stands, the former exaggerating the negative, the latter the positive. Mysticism signifies a self-emancipation from all mere outward expressions, manifestations and expositions of religion in the interests of a concentration on the interior impressions. Barth's notion of mysticism is thus not far removed from quietism, which is mysticism's most dangerous counterfeit and has often been condemned as such.

Atheism, for its part, signifies for Barth primarily the destruction of mystery; it is therefore "negation". Even atheism contains something positive; yes, even in its most radical forms. And this positive element is for Barth exactly the same positive element to be found in mysticism. It is the religious reality in an interior vacuum, empty of all form of activity, wherein knowledge and object are one: the Chinese *Tao,* the Hindu *Tat Tvan Asi,* Hegel's *An-und-für-sich.* And it is in virtue of this positive element that atheism attacks head-on the edifice of established religions with their dogmatic theology and their moral theology. The difference between atheism and mysticism is that, while mysticism remains silent, atheism shouts aloud to the four winds of heaven and hurls itself upon religion, proclaiming its denial and rejection of dogmas and its moral emancipation, its denial of the existence of God and of the value of the moral law.

Hence, says Barth, atheism can be seen to be more resolute and active than mysticism and on the other hand much more naive in its acceptance of authority and dogmas in the field of culture, of history and of

[5] Brunner reiterates this stand likewise in the essay "Die 'natürliche' Gotteserkenntnis, das Problem der 'Theologia naturalis,'" in *Dogmatik,* Vol. I: *Die christliche Lehre von Gott* (Zurich, 1946), pp. 137ff. On the interpretation of the famous Pauline text (Rom. 1:19ff) Brunner writes: "The responsible being, i.e. the being of man as distinct from every other creature, is his personal being. Even the sinful man does not cease to be a responsible person and responsibly a person; this personal being, grounded in creation itself, cannot be lost" (p. 139).

[6] *Die kirkliche Dogmatik,* Vol. I/2, § 17,2: "Religion als Unglaube"; (Zollikon-Zurich, 1945[3]), pp. 324ff.

the sciences, i.e., the whole phenomenon of secularism.[7] Atheism in fact thrives and sustains itself on the conviction of the existence of religion opposed to it. We can now see that Barth is confining himself to generic negative Enlightenment atheism, without taking into consideration the present-day constructive atheism of existentialism and Marxism, derived from the Hegelian dialectic and the humanism of Feuerbach and Nietzsche. He calmly surveys atheism as a derivative and a *sui generis* confirmation (by its very opposition) of religion itself, as a phenomenon originating in the same faculty: the negative that presupposes the positive! [8] The atheist is basically a disobedient rebel and therefore speculative atheism comes down to practical atheism; it is the insurrection of the wisdom of the world (*σοφία τοῦ κοσμου*: I Cor. 1, 20), of the wisdom of men (*σοφία ἀνθρώπων*: 1 Cor. 2, 5), which is foolishness (*μωρία*) in the sight of God. And philosophy, any philosophy not proceeding from the revealed Word, is irreligion. Thus Christian philosophy, which does proceed *ex verbo revelato,* is simply theology.

I believe that Barth's ostracism of modern philosophy can be accepted, for he is here criticizing a philosophy which considers faith in inferior stage destined to be surpassed and supplanted by philosophy. But Brunner's insistence on the necessity of a positive step by philosophy to prepare the ground for the faith is supported by the mainstream of theological tradition, Catholic and Protestant alike. And if Barth's critique of the *analogia entis* is really intended to be as stringent as his expressions would indicate, then it calls in question theological language itself which is taken from the realm of human life and reason (by Barth himself, who is the most prolific theological writer of our day!) Quite obviously Barth's critique of the Thomist doctrine of analogy must have exceeded his own intentions; otherwise it would ultimately give aid and comfort to atheism itself.[9]

[7] *Ibid.,* p. 351.

[8] "It is not really so totally opposed to religion as its certainly few happy and its countless unhappy devotees are in the habit of insisting. It is really no more opposed to religion than the source to the stream, the root to the tree, the unborn child in the womb to the fully grown adult. It is silent religious possession; it is the contemplation of the universe and the creative power of the individual feeling in its nameless, formless and inactive unity, grasping after such contemplation; it is the ability to be in the world and to be a human being, which always precedes the 'stammering one' but which this 'stammering one' and later any religion will certainly project out of itself quickly enough. Precisely the ability to be in the world and to be a human being is, as man's own specific ability, identical with the ability to excogitate and mold gods and to justify and hallow itself" (*ibid.,* p. 314).

[9] It is a little surprising that a Catholic theologian like Urs von Balthasar should have maintained that the difference between the position of Barth on analogy and the Catholic position is actually no greater than that prevailing between Catholic theologians in the interpretation of the Vatican I Constitution on the Catholic Faith or that prevailing between Barth and other Protestant theologians, e.g.

Barth's stand on this point has fluctuated considerably.[10] In the period down to the first edition of his *Römerbrief* (1919) inclusive, he does not seem to exclude the possibility of a knowledge of the true God that would proceed from sensible things, and it is in this sense he interprets the famous Pauline text (Rom. 1, 19-22). The bedrock of his position, fluctuating between fideism and intuitionism, comes out quite clearly in this passage: "The notion of God is given to us in a fashion as immediate as our own being. When, therefore, we resist God, we are not resisting something given from outside; rather are we suppressing something that desires to proceed from within our very selves; we are denying not something foreign but our own most intimate nature. Man cannot separate himself from his origin: in all his thinking, willing and feeling, the memory of it accompanies him, as a warning and an exhortation, as the real, familiar central point of his longings, as premise and aim of his life. In suppressing this memory, he is committing an act against nature. He is betraying not only God but himself as well" (Bern, 1919 [1], p. 14). This is the very antithesis of the Thomist position which proposes the "ways" and "fashions" in which ". . . ancient philosophers came to a knowledge of Him (God), and this is a most efficacious way": [11] a vigorous acknowledgement of man's perennial longing to seek for his own Principle!

In a second period, beginning with the second edition of the *Römerbrief* (1922), continuing through *Die christliche Dogmatik* (1927) and culminating in the first two volumes of *Die kirkliche Dogmatik* (1932-1942), Barth asserts that God can be known only by faith. Faith is a paradox, a strict mystery: even the Person of Christ and his revealing mission are concealed in paradox and we know them only by faith. There is therefore no place left for a "natural theology".[12] One of the

---

Brunner (Hans Urs von Balthasar, *Karl Barth. Darstellung und Deutung seiner Theologie* [Olten: Hegner, 1951], pp. 93ff., especially the summary on pp. 175ff. and the conclusion on p. 389). Cf. on this point W. Krech's article "Analogia fidei oder analogia entis?" in *Antwort,* Festschrift zum 70. Geburtstag von K. Barth (Zollikon-Zurich: Evangelischer Verlag, 1956), pp. 272ff.

[10] Cf. Sebastian A. Matzak, *Karl Barth on God,* The Knowledge of the Divine Existence (New York, 1962). This is a succinct but solid and informative exposition, inspired by Thomist doctrine.

[11] *Lectura super Evangelium S. Joannis,* ed. R. Cai (Turin, 1952), n. 2, p. 1, col. b.

[12] Hence the strongly polemical character of these writings: "Henceforth Barth drastically excludes any notion of the legitimacy of any natural theology whatsoever. He turns not only against the various notions of liberal Protestantism but also and primarily against that of Catholic theology. He expressly rejects the "alleged natural knowledge of God" asserted by Vatican I and the idea of a natural theology, comprising the science of the 'praeambula fidei' " (H. Bouillard, *Karl Barth,* Genèse et évolution de la théologie dialectique, Vol. I [Paris, 1957], pp. 140f.).

On Luther's conception of the *Deus absconditus,* cf. *Luthers Vorlesung über den*

chief and crucial influences responsible for this change of position is held to have been the writings of Kierkegaard, whose doctrines, however, Barth certainly watered down considerably in the subsequent volumes of *Die kirkliche Dogmatik* and in his later writings, especially *Die protestantische Theologie im 19. Jahrhundert* (1947).[13] Thus, e.g., in this work he praises Kant's clear-cut stand, as opposed to that of Rousseau and Lessing: Kant is credited with having established the limits of reason in such a way as to render possible a dialogue with a well-defined theology (p. 238). And Barth has explicit praise even for Kant's theses in *Was ist Aufklärung?* (1784) and *Die Religion innerhalb der Grenzen der blossen Vernunft* (A 1783, B 1784), as having overcome the skeptical impasse of Hume (p. 240). Barth claims that Kant never poses the question "Whether" (*ob*) but only the question "How" (*wie*), and so does not deny the ability of human reason to transcend the purely philosophical area and assist in some fashion in the work of theology. First of all, theology can take from Kant's philosophy the methodological criteria for its own assignment, as rationalist theology did not do, but A. Ritschl in the late 19th century and later his disciple W. Herrmann did do. (Barth attended Herrmann's lectures in Tübingen.) Then, further, theology can broaden the area of the necessities of reason, beyond the theoretical and practical realm, recognizing in fact a new *a priori* faculty, that of "feeling" (*Gefühl*), as did Schleiermacher, De Wette, Jacobi, Fries *et al.* (pp. 272f.).

Barth further praises Kant for having ascribed to the Practical Reason the ability to prove the existence of God, thus prefiguring the possibility even of a metaphysic.[14] Thus Barth presents a positive inter-

---

Hebräerbrief 1517-1518, Vol. II, *Die Scholien,* p. 99. For an interpretation of this Lutheran notion in its dual dimension, cf. W. Köhler, "Der verborgene Gott," pp. 5ff., and C. Fabro, "Il problema di Dio, Introduzione al problema teologico," in *Orientamenti e problemi di teologia dogmatica,* Vol. II (Milan, 1957), pp. 58ff.

[13] This monumental volume devoted to 19th-century Protestant theology omits Kierkegaard entirely, while including not only Rousseau, Hegel and Lessing, but even the outright atheists like Feuerbach and Strauss. After serving as chief inspiration for the *Römerbrief,* Kierkegaard was shelved and Hegel serves henceforth as the inspiration of "dialectical theology" as we shall be pointing out (cf. C. van Til, *The New Modernism,* An Appraisal of the Theology of Barth and Brunner [Philadelphia, 1946], especially pp. 43ff. On Kierkegaard, cf. also Sebastian A. Matzak, *op. cit.,* pp. 296ff.). In this sense, we agree with Bouillard (*op. cit.,* Vol. I, p. 107) and with Matzak (*op. cit.,* p. 307), that Barth cannot be considered a disciple of Kierkegaard.

[14] Kant is known to have written *Die Streit der Fakultäten* (1794) in order to exonerate himself from the charges of the theologians. On Kant's essentially negative attitude to theology and on Barth's quite controversial interpretation, which neglects no less a work than the *Kritik der reinen Vernunft,* cf. O. Samuel, *Die religiösen und nichtreligiösen Offenbarungsbegriffe,* Theologische Forschung 16 (Hamburg-Bergstedt, 1958), pp. 345ff.

pretation of *Die Religion innerhalb der Grenzen der blossen Vernunft,* which the theologians of Kant's own day regarded with jaundiced eye.[15] And Barth ends by ascribing to Kant an attitude toward theology not much different from that with which the Catholic Church credits St. Thomas!

In the light of all this, it is not surprising to find Barth approving of Schleiermacher's philosophy of religion (Barth, *Die protestantische Theologie,* pp. 379ff.) and seeing in Schleiermacher a model Christian theologian, rightly attuned to the modern age: "Not only does he represent modern culture, he *preaches* and *demands* it. For this reason alone, anyone desirous of really getting to know Schleiermacher must not fail to take note of his *Philosophical Ethics* and his *Christian Morality,* over and above the *Speeches* and the *Glaubenslehre,* and above all the *Sermons,* for those better known works do not bring out nearly so clearly as do these less well known ones the fact that Schleiermacher as a theologian *wanted* something quite definite from his hearers and readers, something very definite indeed, to which everything else he said and wrote was related only as a means to an end or a lever to the weight to be hoisted." [16]

Barth follows Schleiermacher in admitting the possibility of a rational defense of the propositions of the faith: "Apologetics is an attempt to prove, with the tools of thought and language, that the principles operative in philosophy, natural science and historical research, at a given time, at least assuredly do not exclude the propositions of theology, based upon revelation or faith, and may even actually require those propositions. To its own age, apologetics proves, at its boldest the *rational necessity* (*Denknotwendigkeit*), and at its most cautious, the *rational possibility* (*Denkmöglichkeit*) of the theological principles drawn from the Bible or from Church dogma or from both. Concerning the scope and content of these principles, apologists may of course disagree." [17] Barth thus makes no secret of the importance he ascribes to Schleiermacher in the development of Protestant theology and piety nor yet of the deep influence this thinker has exerted on Barth's own thought.

But Barth mentions some reservations as well, and as often happens

[15] "The critique of the knowledge of pure reason is thus supposed to have brought that knowledge not into dishonor but rather to a status of real honor: Kant feels that, by his clarification of the relation of this knowledge to the empirical knowledge of experience, he has by no means destroyed metaphysics; quite the contrary, he feels that he has for the first time substantiated its status as a science: metaphysics as knowledge from the practical reason" (*Die protestantische Theologie,* p. 247).

[16] *Ibid.,* pp. 388f.

[17] *Ibid.,* p. 392.

in the case of Protestant theologians, these reservations may be just as radical as the agreements. Thus, Barth finds this Schleiermacherian *Gefühls-Bewussteinstheologie* to be so excessively committed to the anthropological method as to risk compromising the basic truths of Christianity: the Trinity, the Incarnation itself and the absolute dichotomy between grace and sin. Here Barth finds Schleiermacher inferior to Luther and his reservations about Schleiermacher are especially pronounced in the matter of the God-problem and the God-notion: "In the face of this state of affairs, the question must at least be raised as to whether the divinity of the Logos was here as unequivocally presupposed as was the divinity of the Spirit in the case of the Reformers; and whether, in the default of this, the *divinity* of the Spirit, which apparently here constituted the central pivot, was really the divinity of the *Holy* Spirit." [18]

This generic approach probably explains the judgment Barth passes on Hegel: he unhesitatingly repudiates Hegel's reduction of the Christian dogmas to truths of Absolute natural Reason; but he acknowledges simultaneously that Hegelian philosophy may be useful to theology, especially in providing it with the principle of the dialectical method (*ibid.,* pp. 368ff.). Barth gives the impression that the Hegelian "method" as such can well accord with his own Biblical theology.[19] And so, after a series of questions which show Barth's own puzzlement on various elements of Hegelianism, it comes as no surprise to read Barth's statement that: "Defects and reservations on individual points cannot justify the abandonment of a program like this one." (p. 365). All of which is extremely disconcerting on the part of a man who has dubbed the Thomist analogy of being an invention of Antichrist!

In a third period, beginning in 1946 and continuing to the present, Barth seems to have returned to his initial stand, displaying a more favorable attitude to the ability of the reason to know God at least in a certain fashion and thus bridging the gulf between reason and faith and admitting that reason has a certain ability to present philosophical proofs of the existence of God. Barth's own efforts are worthy of respect as are likewise the acumen of his interpreters in finding a positive kind of evolution in Barth's theological negativism; but the attentive reader

[18] *Ibid.,* pp. 413f.

[19] Barth highlights the work of Schleiermacher in the field of ethics and practical action and exalts Schleiermacher, together with Fichte, Arndt, Scharnhorst—as opposed to Hegel and Goethe—as one of the motive powers of the liberation wars (*Freiheitskriege*) in the genuine spirit of Luther. He therefore opposes the contention of his colleague Emil Brunner (*Die Mystik und das Wort,* Der Gegensatz zwischen moderner Religionsauffassung und christlichen Glauben dargestellt an der Theologie Schleiermachers [Tübingen, 1924]).

will not fail to notice the continuity and unity of Barth's thought both on the God-problem and on the notion of theological faith, on both of which points Barth has always dissociated himself entirely from the solution offered by realist metaphysics and Catholic tradition.[20] That Barth's thought has developed and fluctuated we do not deny; but we feel that the development and the fluctuations have always left intact the substance of Barth's thought on the knowledge man can have of God: and that substantial Barthian position is a radically negative and negativist one, derived from the tradition of the Reformation and subsequently aggravated by the contacts indicated between Barth and modern thought.

[20] Critical evaluations have been explicit concerning the Hegelian contamination of Barthian theology: "To anyone interested in the history of philosophy, the Barthian Trinity does not fail to offer a striking analogy with the Hegelian Trinity. Being, Non-being, Becoming: do we not find that movement of truth which was Hegel's key point in a new form in the interplay of the *absconditus* and the *revelatus,* in this transition from death to life which produces *Geschichte*?" (J. Rilliet, *Karl Barth théologien existentialiste?* [Neuchatel, 1952], p. 82).

2

The Radical Bankruptcy of the Natural Knowledge of God (Bultmann)

For dialectical theology there exists only man in the concrete, ma the sinner, separated from God and incapable of establishing contact with God except by faith. Thus there can be "God-talk" onl on the basis of faith and at the level of fallen man. In the context of a repudiation of any metaphysic, capable of speaking about God from th angle of vision of being, proper to it, being must be admitted to be comprehensible only as finite and man to exist only as a sinner and in functio of his sinfulness. Thus God's only attribute is that of being the "Wholl Other" (*der Ganz-Andere*); and man's thrust is not toward an eve closer approach to God but rather toward an ever greater regressio from him, in an ever intenser awareness of sin. Dialectical theolog maintains the quite admissible thesis that man can speak of God onl "within the limits of his own humanity and that only God himself ca speak adequately of God."[1] Thus, whereas modern philosophy ha apotheosized man, orthodox Protestant theology has believed itself to b exalting God by reducing man to a ruin incapable of recognizing o acknowledging God in created reality or of aspiring to God from th springboard of man's own existence in the world.[2] Dialectical theolog

[1] "Karl Barth does not have too much confidence or trust in the cognitiv abilities of man, as is borne out by Barth's total repudiation of the rational proof of the existence of God and the solution he offers to the problem of Faith. Havin repudiated the notion of theological Faith which adheres to the Truth because i is based on a divine testimony manifested in a historical 'fact' and having don away with the rational element in the knowledge of God, Barth loses sight o the nexus of a problem belonging, at least in part, to the realm of huma potentialities, with the other problem which pertains to the sovereign liberalit of God. And everything becomes grace." (B. Gherardini, *La parola di Dio nell teologia di Karl Barth* [Rome, 1955], pp. 22f.).

[2] Cf. K. Barth, "Ludwig Feuerbach," in *Die Theologie und die Kirche,* Vol. I (Zollikon-Zurich, 1928), pp. 226ff.; English translation as "An Introductory Essay"

thus pushes the "principle of negativity" of Protestant faith to its logical extreme, holding that man receives faith not in order to speak of God but rather in order to confess his own sinfulness, his fallen state. Dialectical theology is not dialectical in the sense that it admits any *Aufhebung* in the Hegelian sense, but rather in the sense that it insists on the infinite and unbridgeable distance between God and man; and even on the impossibility of any "communication" whatsoever except mutual repulsion, almost akin to the relation between the *en-soi* and the *pour-soi* in Sartre.

This radically negative conception of dialectical theology is likewise the conclusion of Rudolf Bultmann, the theologian who has explicitly ranged himself with Heidegger's atheistically biassed existentialism, with its outlook on being as intrinsically finite and precluding the very possibility of reason's "trans-cending" (*Überstieg*) to God. Bultmann feels that articulations concerning God generically have no meaning if to speak "of God" (*von Gott*) means to speak "about God" (*über Gott*).[3] And he feels the reason is quite simple: at the moment such an articulation has been accomplished, it has lost its object, God. Bultmann's proof is typical and merits detailed exposition, in the interests of a more lively appreciation of the intimate nexus between the absence of God from the speculative context and the absence of the view of being as a possible avenue of meaningful encounter with God himself, as a possible dimension of God's inexhaustible meaning and meaningfulness. Man cannot speak *of* and *about* God who is the Almighty and the reality that determines everything, for man cannot legitimately consider God as an object of thought and thus imply him to be some sort of neutral object that I can reject or accept at will. It is impossible to speak "about God" because that would presuppose that man can find a vantage point (*Standpunkt*) that would be outside of the object of discourse, a vantage point that would provide the circumferential location justifying the very syntactical use of "about"; but there cannot be any vantage point outside of God. It is therefore impossible to speak of God on general principles, because of universal truths that are true independently on any nexus with the concrete existential situation of the speaker. The situation is the same in the case of God as in the case of love: there can be no speaking of love without this very speaking being itself an act of love, remaining exterior to love.

---

in the George Eliot translation of Feuerbach's *The Essence of Christianity* (New York, Evanston and London: Harper Torchbooks; Harper and Row, Publishers, 1956), pp. xixff.

[3] R. Bultmann, "Welchen Sinn hat es, von Gott zu reden?," in *Glauben und Verstehen,* Vol. I (Tübingen, 1954[2]), pp. 26ff.

Bultmann concludes that philosophy becomes atheistic precisely when and because it claims to be able to speak *of* and *about* God, in the same way as science. Indeed, a science would be just as atheistic if it were, as science, to assert the reality of God as if it were to deny that reality. The reason for this agnosticism is to be sought in the metaphysical nominalism of Reformation and subsequent Protestant theology: any speaking of God in scientific propositions, i.e., in generic universal truths, amounts to a speaking in propositions whose very meaning lies in the fact that they are universal, i.e., that they abstract from the concrete situation of the speaker. But any speaker who articulates this sort of proposition is placing himself outside the actual reality of his own existence and consequently outside of God; and he is speaking of anything but God.[4] God cannot be that "whereupon" (*woraufhin*) man can speak.[5]

The only way left open to man to speak of God is by speaking of

[4] "The possible *atheism* of a science would not consist in its denying the reality of God, but rather that science would be just as atheistic were it, as science, to maintain that reality. For speaking of God in scientific propositions, i.e. in generic truths, amounts simply to speaking in propositions whose very meaning consists in the fact that they are generically valid, that they abstract from the concrete situation of the speaker. But by the very fact of doing this, the speaker is placing himself outside the actual reality of his own existence, and consequently likewise outside of God, and is speaking of anything but God" (*ibid.*, p. 27). Indeed, remarks Bultmann, this claim to *disputare de Deo* (debate about God) is not only error and madness (*Wahn*), but "sin" (*Sünde*), the sign of Adam, according to Luther.

[5] This would amount to a consideration of God from the outside and a conversion of His existence into a universal truth included within a "system" of knowledge; and that is precisely the πρωτον ψεῦδος, according to Bultmann (*ibid.*, pp. 32f.). This critique of the philosophical knowledge of God is obviously directed solely against the formalistic and immanentistic philosophies which reduce even God to an object among objects by conceiving Him as a "being among beings", whereas God is, according to the Bible, the Almighty Who is the principle of the being of all things. And Bultmann appeals expressly to Heidegger who finds in the modern age the acme of the "forgottenness of being" (*Vergessenheit des Seins*): "Martin Heidegger calls the age in which man objectifies everything that comes his way the age of subjectivity. Such an understanding of reality Bultmann calls 'the attitude of a whole age to the world and history, an attitude which has come to be taken quite simply for granted'. In such an age, God is regarded and discussed on an analogy with the world" (W. Schmithals, *Die Theologie Rudolf Bultmanns* [Tübingen, 1966], p. 33). Bultmann, Heidegger and the whole of dialectic theology simply do not advert to the Thomist notion of the *actus essendi* and the absolute transcendence of God as *esse ipsum*. On the relations between Heidegger's philosophy and Bultmann's theology and especially concerning the alleged "supersession" (*Ueberwindung*) of the subject-object pattern in both conceptions, cf. the thesis of G. Noll, *Sein und Existenz,* Die Ueberwindung des Subjekt-Objektschemas in der Philosophie Heideggers und in der Theologie der Entmythologisierung (Munich, 1962) (the exposition of Heidegger's thought is based particularly on his *Sein und Zeit*).

himself, not just anyhow and still less in the indeterminate realm of being, but solely within the existential ambit of faith, i.e., not considering God as a neutral "Wholly Other" (*das Ganz-Andere*) but as a personal "Wholly Other" (*der Ganz-Andere*). Such a neutral metaphysical consideration would be tantamount to a "flight from God" and a hatred of God, that *aversio a Deo* which is at once sin and the punishment of sin, the state of sinful man. The notion of "God as the Wholly Other" and of the consequent obligation to speak thus of the Almighty, cannot however be taken to mean that God is something outside of me that I must seek above all things and that in order to seek him I must somehow get outside of myself. The fact of the matter is that the statement that God, who determines my very existence, is likewise the Wholly Other, can be meaningful only in function of a consideration of God as standing over against me, a sinner, as *the* Wholly Other, only in function of a consideration of this same God as standing over against me as the Wholly Other to the extent that I am "world" (*Welt*). It makes perfect sense to speak of God as the Wholly Other as soon as man's actual state has been seen to be that of the sinner who would like to speak of his own existence but cannot. This sinner would have to speak of that existence as one defined and determined by God, but can speak of that existence only as a sinful one, i.e., as one in which *he* cannot see God, as one over against which God stands as the Wholly Other.[6]

The existential moment is as crucial for the knowledge of God as it is for the knowledge of man; these two knowledges are reciprocally conditioned, for any articulation about reality which prescinds from the moment wherein alone we can possess the real (i.e., the moment wherein the real is seized in our own existence) is self-deception (*Selbsttäuschung*). The world must not enter into our relationship to God and so we cannot say: because God rules reality, he is also my Lord; rather it is only when we have expressed ourselves on God in our own existence that it is meaningful to speak of God as the Lord of reality. Bultmann's conclusion is that we are god-less as long as we see ourselves as a piece of world; and that God, for his part, is the Wholly Other because this

[6] "That God Who conditions and defines my existence is notwithstanding the Wholly Other can therefore only mean that he stands over against me, the sinner, as *the* Wholly Other; that he stands over against me, inasmuch as I am *world,* as *the* Wholly Other. It makes sense to speak of God as the Wholly Other when I have seen that the actual situation of man is that of the sinner who would fain speak of God and cannot, who would fain speak of his own existence and cannot do that either. He would have to speak of his own existence as one conditioned and defined by God can only speak of that existence as such as a sinful existence, i.e. as one in which *he* cannot see God, as one over against which God stands as the Wholly Other" ("Welchen Sinn hat es, von Gott zu reden?," p. 30).

world as god-less is sinful, not because God dwells somewhere outside the world.[7] We can therefore say that in this theological conception of man (and of God), existence precedes essence. This is an anticipation of the substance of the formula which Sartre will make the basis of his own atheism.[8] The conclusion already signalled above therefore stands: any speaking *of* and *about* God resolves itself into a speaking *out of* God, an articulation of faith, a speaking out of our own inmost selves and about ourselves, with the world playing no part either as object or starting point of the articulation and with the articulation proceeding from and concerning itself with ourselves only as we are sinners.

In this regard, Bultmann makes an important specification. Are we not faced with the abolition (*Aufhebung*) of man, *with downright quietism,* if the God-problem is confined to speaking of God as the Wholly Other and this in turn resolves itself into speaking of us men only as sinners?[9] Bultmann's reply is that this conclusion would be justified if the God-problem were posed in terms of knowledge and if God were an object "whereby" (*woraufhin*) to govern our behavior, as though speaking or not speaking of God were a matter left to our own discretion. But this is not the way things stand. We have an "incumbency" (*Müssen*) to speak of God, not obviously in the sense that this act is conditioned from outside (by the world), but in the sense that this speaking is a free act, proceeding from our own existential being, and that it is only in such an act that we *are* ourselves and are entire. Such an act is *obedience,* a free accomodation to an incumbency.[10] This incumbency does

[7] "If it be true that the world as seen from the outside is god-less and that we are god-less to the extent that we see ourselves as a piece of world, it is likewise true that God is not the Wholly Other inasmuch as He dwells somewhere outside the world, but rather inasmuch as this world as god-less is sinful. This world seen from the outside, in which we move as subjects, is our world, which we take seriously and thereby characterize as sinful" (*ibid.,* p. 33).

[8] When Bultmann wrote this essay (1925) Heidegger's *Sein und Zeit* (1927) had not yet appeared. Bultmann was to refer explicitly to that work later and the affinity between the two thinkers is witnessed by Bultmann's dedication to Heidegger of the first volume of *Glauben und Verstehen.* At the time of writing, Bultmann was especially attracted by liberal theology, as is brought out in this passage cited from W. Herrmann: "Where we ourselves are, there is the world. The man who tries to grasp God beyond this world is therefore attempting the impossible. When he thinks he has found God, he has in fact grasped nothing but a part of the world or the world divested of its concrete and plastic definiteness and conceived as abstractly as possible" (cf. "Die liberale Theologie und die jüngste theologische Bewegung," in *Glauben und Verstehen,* Vol. I, p. 24 note).

[9] Cf. also the essay "Die Bedeutung der 'dialektischen Theologie' für die neotestamentalische Wissenschaft," in *Glauben und Verstehen,* Vol. I, p. 117.

[10] This is the interpretation given by liberal and existential theology to the Pauline precept ". . . ad oboediendum fidei" (to promote obedience to the faith) (*Rom.* 1:5): "The only mandatory obedience that can here be meant is one which is a *free act;* for only such an act stems from our existential being, only in *such*

not originate from any evidence, objective or subjective: whether it is a reality we do not know at all, we can only believe that it is (*ob dies Müssen Wirklichkeit ist, das können wir nur glauben*). We can therefore speak of God only from the starting point of faith and by the instrumentality of faith, in virtue of what faith operates in us, revealing us as sinners before his face.[11] Whatever knowledge a man may have of the world and of himself has not any cannot have any relation to God: this relationship can be cultivated only insofar as God himself takes the initiative, within the dimension of faith, i.e., when sinful man is justified by faith (*aus Glaube*). And so we know nothing either of God or of our own real selves; we possess both solely in faith and by God's grace: we can speak of God only on the basis and foundations of grace, of the remission of sins; and this we have only by faith, i.e., by grace. And Bultmann's conclusion, after this lengthy articulation, is simply that any articulation concerning God is sinful if God exists and senseless if there is no God. None of us can decide which is the case.[12] At this point we must indeed agree with Bultmann's conclusion, as far as Protestant theology, orthodox or liberal, is concerned: for that theology has disqualified reason and repudiated metaphysics before the fact and, after

---

an act *are* we ourselves and are we entire. Such an act is *obedience;* for obedience means an accomodation, in a free act, to an 'incumbency'." ("Welchen Sinn hat es, von Gott zu reden?" p. 34).

[11] In this connection Bultmann cites W. Herrmann's expression (from *Die Wirklichkeit Gottes* [1914], p. 42): "The only thing we can say of God is what he does to us" (*ibid.,* p. 36). Recently Bultmann has returned to this point, insisting on the fact that faith is absolutely non-objective and non-objectifiable. This insistence submerges faith in the flux of existential becoming and so the circle is closed and there is no escape, no hope of grappling onto the world or history, which is closed even as the mind within the circle of individual experience. Thus Bultmann writes: ". . . what we call facts of redemption are themselves objects of faith and are apprehended as such only by the eye of faith. They cannot be perceived apart from faith, as if faith could be based on data in the same way as the natural sciences are based on data which are open to empirical observation. To be sure, the facts of redemption constitute the grounds of faith, but only as perceived by faith itself. The principle is the same in our personal relationship as persons with persons. Trust in a friend can rest solely on the personality of my friend which I can perceive only when I trust him. There cannot be any trust or love without risk. It is true, as Wilhelm Herrmann taught us, that the ground and object of faith are identical. They are one and the same thing, because we cannot speak of what God is in Himself but only of what He is doing to us and with us" (R. Bultmann, *Jesus Christus und die Mythologie* [Hamburg, 1965], p. 85; English translation, *Jesus Christ and Mythology* [London: SCM Press, Ltd., 1960], pp. 72f.).

[12] "This sort of articulation is likewise an articulation concerning God and as such sinful if there is a God and senseless if there is no God. It is not the business nor yet the competency of any of us to say whether it is meaningful and justified" ("Welchen Sinn hat es, von Gott zu reden?" p. 37).

the fact, has rejected the living teaching authority of the Church as the historical organ of faith, animated by the Holy Spirit.

In a slightly earlier essay, Bultmann presented in outline the conclusions of his critique of that liberal theology which Barth and Gogarten in particular had been in process of developing since World War I.[13]

1. God is not a datum (*Gott ist nicht eine Gegebenheit*). This statement Bultmann maintains against religion founded on natural experience and religion based on the experience of life as lived (*Erlebnisreligion*) and inclined to consider the contact with the divine object established by the simple distinction of the rational mind in terms of psychic conditions (which I take to mean in terms of external and internal experience), making God into a directly accessible datum, conceived either as creative vital force or as the irrational.

2. But neither is God the "Given-Up" nor the "Un-given" (*Gott ist aber auch nicht das Aufgegebene oder Ungegebene*). This statement crystallizes Bultmann's critique of idealist philosophy with its evolving God and its consequent *de facto* divinization of man. Rather, insists Bultmann, does God signify the total abrogation of man, his supreme jeopardy, the summoning of man to the bar of judgment.[14] And this, says Bultmann, involves no skepticism nor pessimism, which attitudes arise only when man himself is made the starting point, whereas here God is the sole point of departure. But this seems to us to be a too easy way out: anyone electing to base himself on a phrase of Luther's, as Bultmann does here, should not neglect or disregard Luther's own condemnation of reason. If faith is and ought to be everything in the mind's stance before God, Luther has already (as we have seen above) condemned reason for any claim to speak of God and then reduced faith itself to a passive acceptance of the Word of God. But this second point is denied in Bultmann's subsequent principle which articulates likewise the blind-alley conclusion of the whole dynamic of Protestant theology.

3. Faith is not a state of mind (*der Glaube ist nicht ein Zustand des Bewusstseins*) [15] the generic phenomenon is also a state of mind, comments Bultmann, or at least it can be; but to the extent that it is a state of mind, it is not faith. Protestant theology was bound to end up in this

[13] Cf. "Die liberale Theologie und die jüngste theologische Bewegung," in *Glauben und Verstehen*, Vol. I, pp. 1ff.

[14] "*But God is not the 'Given-Up' or the 'Un-given' either,* in the idealist philosophical sense that God realizes himself in the process of the revelation of reason in mankind, or is real in the Logos which lies at the root of the rational life of man. For that would amount to a deification of man. *Rather does God signify the total abrogation of man, his negation, his jeopardy, the summoning of man to the bar of judgment!*" (*ibid.*, p. 18).

[15] In this connection, Bultmann recalls that K. Barth reiterates Luther's paradoxical principle that "we only 'believe' that we believe" (*dass wir nur 'glauben', dass wir glauben*) (*ibid.*, p. 24).

maze of negations and negativity chasing one another in a vacuum. For Protestant theology is unaware of the Thomist doctrine of the (infused) habits as principles of acts, or else it rejects that theory; nor does Protestant theology make the proper distinction between faith, grace and charity, rather centering everything on faith alone. Hence, the somewhat strange phenomenon (on reflection, not all that surprising) of a professional theologian like Bultmann unhesitatingly accepting the atheistic platform of modern thought as presented today by Heidegger, and still continuing to interpret the Word of God!

An important specification of the problem of the relation between reason and faith in the God-problem is to be found in one of Bultmann's contributions to the persistent "natural theology" debate. Here Bultmann expressly admits the existentialist inspiration of his remarks. He begins by opposing to the Catholic position, which maintains the possibility of a "natural" (i.e., philosophical) theology, the Protestant insistence that the only avenue of approach to God open to man is faith and divine revelation and that everything that is styled as God prior to this faith and revelation is not God.[16] He then proceeds to demolish one by one the arguments of the traditional Catholic position. He seems to me to make three main points:

1. There is the fact of *understanding:* the Christian message offered to man must be able to be understood by him in such a way as to enable him to distinguish the stand of faith from that of unbelief. Well, says Bultmann, there may very well be admitted to be this sort of "pre-understanding" (*Vorverständnis*) but it must be considered to be a negative moment, to be exercised the moment faith appears, even as the old (sinful) man is done away with at the moment of the proclamation of justification. And so Bultmann agrees with Barth in denying the existence of any "point of contact" (*Anknüpfungspunkt*) between reason and faith: the "new man" of faith is such in virtue of his belief, not in virtue of any renovation of qualities already possessed. Faith is an existential category and transforms the existent from head to foot. Even as unbelief dominated the entire human existent as typical modality of natural man, so too faith is an existential form. Existence, remarks Bultmann (following the new set of the principle of immanentism), is not *something which* man comes to possess and which he can take into consideration at his own discretion; *it is man himself!* Thus the new existence of faith does not mean that faith understands revelation as "something" (*etwas*) new; rather it means that man in faith understands revelation only inasmuch as he understands *himself* as new in faith.

[16] Cf. "Das Problem der 'natürlichen' Theologie," in *Glauben und Verstehen,* Vol. I, p. 294.

Faith in revelation reveals to man that he is a sinner; and it is precisely as a sinner that man is enabled to reach God: existence as such, man immersed in the world, can indeed understand the difference between natural existence and the existence of faith, but only so as to refuse the latter.

We must here point out that the Catholic position here under fire is somewhat more refined than Bultmann credits it with being. It asserts categorically the distinction between the two orders of nature and grace, no less categorically, in fact, than does dialectical theology. But it goes on to remark that, even as existence presupposes essence, so too knowledge by faith presupposes that rational knowledge which renders possible man's progress to the decision of faith, so that faith may be that "reasonable homage" which St. Paul recommends (Rom. 12, 1). The believer must indeed renounce the "old man" together with his errors and lusts; but man must be admitted to have within him even before redemption at least the "potency" of that cure that comes to him by the divine initiative. This is one of the basic points of disagreement between Catholic teaching and Protestantism which emerges from this whole discussion of the "theological locus" of the act of faith.

2. There is the fact of the *witness of the heathen:* even those religions which are beyond the bounds of Christianity and the faith likewise *speak of and about God*. However they may conceive God, these religions certainly intend to designate the Supreme Being (*das höchste Wesen*), in whom man hopes for the satisfaction of his longings and the liberation from his ills, whom he names to express the origin and unity of the world, the *causa prima* with all its connotations of unconditioned primordial substantiating unity. Such religions also present God as the "guarantor of the moral law", as the source of the knowledge of good and evil, as the voice of conscience; or, again, they proclaim God to be the Non-rational, the Numinous and the Fascinating.[17] But the sum total of such witness by no means constitutes, in Bultmann's eyes, anything even approaching a proof of God *ex consensu gentium!* Even granting that these religions intended to give expression to God, it does not follow that this God is real: there can be no conclusion from the idea of God to the reality; only to faith in the God of revelation does this idea become genuinely limpid. The true recognition and acknowledgment of God is always and only that of faith, as the definitive acknowledgment of his Word proclaiming him. Bultmann's meaning is not, of course, that the Christian faith consists simply in a full flowering of the knowledge of God to be found in germ in the other religions: that would amount to an admission that there is nothing more than a difference of degree between Christianity and those other religions. Bultmann

[17] According to the idea of R. Otto in *Das Heilige*.

is throughout stressing the existential aspect: forming
does not mean having possession of God, for he become
by faith in revelation. Thus, the essence of unbelief is
(*Ungehorsam*), a disobedience (explains Bultmann in
terminology) to the "demand of the moment" wherein it
upon man to resolve to have faith, to believe.[18] This disobe
take the form either of an outright denial or of a naively
appropriation to himself of the divinely initiated event, an app
expressed either in the claim to be himself its author or in the
to a cosmic self-justification.

3. There is, finally, the fact or "phenomenon of philosoph
claiming to be able to understand man's very existence and consequ
feeling that faith can be explained, in some sense, as an "existe
motion" (*als Bewegung des Daseins*). Bultmann admits, in what see
to us to be an approach on his part to the position of the Swiss theol
gian Emil Brunner, that philosophy and theology do indeed agree o
certain points and that certain propositions (*Aussagen*) of theology seem to be prefigured in philosophy; he further agrees that an atheist like Feuerbach, for example, may be as well able to understand true Christianity as any Christian theologian.[19] But Bultmann hastens to add that philosophy is also well aware that faith considers philosophy's position to be unbelief: there is not and cannnot be any real continuity or nexus between the notion of existence proper to philosophy and that of faith. Justifying faith is not an existential phenomenon; and this for two reasons: because faith as a historical act (in the Protestant view) is always accomplished in the concrete decision of the "moment"; and furthermore, because faith as an eschatological event leads back to the primordial creation, to the possibility of primordial obedience, that genuinely creative obedience which philosophy knows to be accomplished precisely in faith.

Now this, I think, a Catholic theologian could likewise admit. And he could also admit that unbelief, in the sense of the option for freedom as substantiating parameter of the existent, is made manifest primarily from the vantage point of faith and by faith itself. If the Christian existent contains a negative knowing of God, then it contains a precognition of the Christian message; and if philosophy elaborates this un-

[18] "Unbelief is disobedience. Where faith is the hearkening to God's demand in the moment constituted by God's word of judgment and forgiveness spoken into it and by the neighbor encountering us in it, unbelief is disobedience to the demand of the moment" ("Das Problem der 'natürlichen' Theologie," p. 304).

[19] On this point, Bultmann refers to and reports on K. Barth's study on Feuerbach. Kierkegaard had been still more explicit (cf. *Papirer 1847,* VIII A 434; especially 1849, X 2 A 16, which contains the phrase *et ab hoste consilium;* cf. also 1854, XI 1 A 559).

derstanding of the existent, it must be able to elaborate likewise that precomprehension. And a Catholic theologian could further accept Bultmann's concluding assertion that "natural theology" cannot serve as the foundation of dogmatic theology nor even as a particular section of it, nor yet as a specific sub-discipline within it. The Catholic theologian could also agree that the formal structures of the existent, as displayed in ontological analysis, are "neutral", i.e., hold good for every existent: they are valid for *the existent as such,* to whom the Gospel message is addressed, be he unbeliever or believer. Existence, the existent (object of philosophy's ontological comprehension), displays the conception of the world and of the real founded on the being wherein it is constituted. And so it is unbelief, the refusal of faith as such, which is opposed to faith; it is not this analysis of existence (the existent) and of its basic neutral structures. But by this very concluding statement Bultmann has admitted at least a "potential" opening of philosophy onto and for theology! He seems to have had in mind, during this entire polemic, the rationalist-idealist position with its usurpation by philosophy of the function and status of theology and of faith.

Even Bultmann's final remark that the meaning and possibility of natural theology are legitimate subjects of theological investigation [20] can have a meaning which would be acceptable to a Thomist theologian. And does not Bultmann's own theology draw heavily precisely on the Heideggerian analysis of *Dasein* (There-being)? A "neutral" relationship is a relation of "potency" or "possibility" and not that relationship of implacable contradiction Bultmann advanced at the outset.

The dialectical theologians at this point proceed to take refuge in the existential diversion and this forces them out of their equivocation: the theologian assuredly has the right to use a technical language of his own, but he is also under obligation to bridge the gulf between this language and ordinary human discourse; [21] and only philosophy can perform that

[20] "Therewith the last question is finally clarified, namely, the status of the usefulness of ontological endeavor when once ontology has been ontically grounded. This grounding does not mean that a corresponding ontology could be drafted from just any sort of world-view. Rather it shows itself in the drafting of world-views generically speaking." ("Das Problem der 'natürlichen' Theologie," p. 312).

[21] K. Löwith, a critic with a Heideggerian but resolutely thesistic bias, remarked in this connection: "A man or even a God who spoke a language exclusively his own, could not expect meaningful dialogue nor yet the hearkening to his demand. That would require an interpreter, familiar with the language of man and the language of God alike. The phrase about the "claim" of "God's word" remains sterile and dogmatically existential, so long as no attempt is made to fit the particular language of the Christian Gospel message and theology into its radical and fundamental nexus with the generically human capacity for articulation and thought." (K. Löwith, "Die Sprache als Vermittler von Mensch und Welt," in *Gesammelte Abhandlungen* [Stuttgart, 1960], p. 210).

function. It seems to us of prime importance that the function should indeed be assigned to philosophy which is capable of performing it and not to some theory of knowledge that compromises theological endeavor from the outset. Bultmann has recurred repeatedly to this problem from such varied points of view as the relation between Hellenism and Christianity, the problem of "natural revelation" (*natürliche Offenbarung*), the encounter of Humanism and Christianity, and the like; [22] but he seems to us never to have modified substantially his negative attitude. He does indeed admit that philosophy can broach, in its own way, the problem of the existence of God and can even attack the problem of the attributes of God (omnipotence, holiness, eternity and transcendence, among others); but the knowledge involved is a reflexive knowledge, *pointing backward to man rather than forward to God.* Thus, when man speaks of God's omnipotence, he is really articulating merely his own impotence and anguish of his own limitations; when he speaks of the holiness of God, he is really articulating only his awareness of his own perennial involvement in a struggle between good and evil, together with his sense of oppression in the face of the darkness and uncertainty surrounding him; when man speaks of the eternity and transcendence of God, he is actually articulating simply the impermanence (*Vorläufigkeit*) of his own existence.[23]

All this amounts to saying that man is compelled to admit to finding nothing in this world even faintly resembling such attributes. Such is the judgment faith must pass upon the claim of a natural knowledge of God such as was advanced, e.g., by the Stoics in antiquity, in their effort to base a theology on cosmology.[24] In fact, contends Bultmann, nature is a hostile power, wrapt in in obscurity and revealing nothing whatever to us about God. Nor is even the voice of conscience (*die Stimme des Gewissens*) for man the voice of God. In no sense whatever are either nature or history the voice of God; there is but one single voice of God and that is Christian revelation. It is only as a believer, as a "new creature" that man can see in nature and history the revelation of God.

[22] Cf. "Die Frage der natürlichen Offenbarung," in *Glauben und Verstehen,* Vol. II, pp. 79ff., 117ff., 133ff.

[23] Hence the conclusion we have seen already: "The knowing of God is initially a knowing of man about himself, about his own boundedness, and God is the power breaking through this boundedness of man and thereby raising man to his true and genuine reality" (*ibid.,* p. 86).

[24] Bultmann recalls the Stoic principle ὁμολογουμένως τῇ φυσει ζῆν (*ibid.,* p. 87. Cf. also *Theologie des neuen Testaments* [Tübingen, 1954 [2]], pp. 491ff; English translation, *Theology of the New Testament* [New York: Charles Scribner's Sons, 1951]). The problem is attacked more categorically in the essay "Anknüpfung und Widerspruch," in *Glauben und Verstehen,* Vol. II; cf. especially pp. 123ff.

To the problem, therefore, as to whether there is or can be a point of contact, a nexus, between natural religion and Christianity, between reason and faith, between philosophy and revelation, Bultmann's reply must be unequivocally in the negative. The only theological stand Bultmann would find allowable is that the Christian faith is no mere generic phenomenon in the spiritual history of mankind, no mere generic religious manifestation, but rather the reply to a demand levied on man by special revelation of God. Christianity, consequently, is not the product of an evolution within the ambit of the history of religions; Christianity is not a flower that has germinated within the garden of the human spirit; rather it is a vine grown over the wall, with its roots in the beyond (*jenseits*). Only as such can it serve as link between man and the transcendent world of God. Thus, for Bultmann there is not nor can there be any "continuity" between the Christian religion and the non-Christian religions. Now the Catholic theologian can agree with Bultmann on this last point, but must part company with him when Bultmann goes on far beyond the denial of any such "continuity" between revealed and natural religion as is asserted by rationalist and idealist theology and posits a "contradiction" (*Widerspruch*) between these two forms of religion: [25] for in so doing, Bultmann is denying the existence of man of any sort of set or "organ" capable of religious development. To say that faith and grace "destroy" nature and reason, and further to present this contention as the only alternative to the rationalist solution of a "continuous process" of transition from natural to revealed religion, amounts to an abuse of the dialectic of existence, which is preeminently a struggle "in the choice of possibilities". Dialectical theology's assertion that the nexus is to be sought not in any positive point but rather in the negative point of contradiction and sin [26]—this assertion is acceptable at most in

[25] "It is therefore understandable that more recent theology answers resolutely in the negative the question as to whether there is a nexus between the Christian faith and the religious feelings and ideas of man: *there is no nexus, but only a contradiction!* There is no such thing as a religious organ in man that only needs to be educated. Even as God speaks to us does He Himself likewise create in us the organ wherewith to hear Him." ("Anknüpfung und Widerspruch," p. 119). The Catholic doctrine of grace and the infused virtues is precisely the witness to the "new life" that God grants the soul with the elevation to the supernatural order: but we must repeat again insistently that a more basic nexus between nature and grace than the existential relation of opposition is the "nexus of potency," of possibility of the elevation of nature to the supernatural order which has remained even after sin, after the Fall.

[26] Bultmann calls this a paradoxical discovery; to our mind, it is a blind alley: "Man's opposition to God is the nexus point for God's opposition to man. *Man's sin is the nexus point* for the contradicting word of grace." But a little later, Bultmann comes back to the drastic uncompromising formulation: "God's opposition is to man as such and *God* has no nexus point in man" ("Anknüpfung und Widerspruch," pp. 120, 122).

a secondary sense (as in the well-known stand of Thomism on the "motive of the Incarnation"). Understood in any other way, such an assertion amounts to an immanentist and Heideggerian positing of "nothingness" as the foundation of the coming-to-presence of Being!

Dialectical theology must face squarely the question: how can man's mind even recognize that it has a duty to accept the Word of God, if that mind is held to be structurally atheistic?

In his latest writings, Bultmann has been at special pains to pinpoint his exact stand on the God-problem. Theology must indeed, he declares, attend to its duty of saying what we mean when we speak of God and even when we say we cannot speak of God as he is in himself, for even this presupposes some notion of what God is. The dilemma is that on the one hand this notion must be expressed in concepts, which concepts themselves, on the other hand, make God an object of conceptual thought. Thus, I must, for instance, make use of such concepts as transcendence, omnipotence, futurity (*Zukünftigkeit*); and if I am going to use them, I simply have to explain them as concepts! In this sense we can indeed speak of an "abstract essence of God"; but there can be no question of any discursive articulation of the "essential structure of the divine existence" for that would involve an illegitimate introduction into the divine of a layering permissible only in the human. Indeed Bultmann proceeds to specify, against the American theologian Schubert M. Ogden, that the concept "existence" can be used in a generic sense only within the dimension of human be-ing.

The mere mention of the "existence" of God rouses the suspicion that the term "existence" is being used in the old pre-Kierkegaardian sense of "presentness" (prae = esse = being-to-hand = *Vorhandensein*) as distinct from essence (esse-nce = *Wesen* = *Essenz*). As used today, however, existence (*Existenz*) is a parameter distinctively typical of the human being inasmuch as man has shouldered his being as his own, inasmuch as he has shouldered the responsibility "of being", inasmuch as man is a temporal being (be-ing), an historical sort of being flowing from his past into his future his progress powered by decisions relative to past and future.[27] In terms of such a concept, there can certainly be no question of the "existence" of God, for God is not immersed in historicity (*Geschichtlichkeit*) like man; rather He stands firm in His own eternity.

Can we at least speak of the "essence" (*Essenz*) of God? To do so,

[27] "Zur Frage einer 'Philosophischen Theologie,'" in *Einsichten,* Vol. IV (Tübingen, 1965), p. 105. The basic elements have been assembled in a recent work by G. Hasenhüttl, *Der Glaubensvollzug,* Eine Begegnung mit Rudolf Bultmann aus katholischem Glaubensverständnis (Essen, 1963), pp. 109ff. (cf. our review in *Divus Thomas,* 1966, pp. 329ff.).

we would have to come face to face with God, or have a basis (*Grund*) in philosophy for so speaking. But whence can philosophy draw concepts adequate to speak of God? And at this point Bultmann appeals to Heidegger's final position on Being (*Sein*), a refusal to identify Being with God because of the conviction that any talk about God can be nothing other than an existential confession.

But it should be noted that when Heidegger thus disposes of the God of philosophy (or at least of that philosophy that adheres to the tradition of metaphysics and defines God as *causa sui*), he goes on immediately to maintain: ". . . the God-less thinking that is constrained to forego the God of philosophy, God as *causa sui,* is perhaps nearer to the divine God." [28] This Heideggerian contention, welcomed by Bultmann, is a perplexing oversimplification. How can there be any meaningful specification of the "God of the philosophers" as such in the face of the plethora of differing and opposed conceptions of God, of his existence and his nature, that has been typical of Western philosophy? And how can such a synthetic concept of God be equated with the Spinozan notion of *causa sui,* which can very well be taken (and has indeed been taken!) as being the formula of metaphysical atheism? The philosophers of antiquity conceived (or at least made stunning efforts to conceive) God as the Good, as Love, as Very Life (Plato, Aristotle, Plotinus, et al.) and St. Thomas eradicated all manner of essentialism root and branch by calling God *Esse subsistens,* cause not of himself but of the whole of the finite which is *ens per participationem.* The Kantian Heidegger obviously cannot call God Being because for him Being (*Sein*) is intrinsically finite, bounded by space-time. This new and specific appeal to Heidegger and to the finitude of Heideggerian Being points up the importance of the philosophical substrate in this radical agnosticism [29] of Protestant theology, a theology that borders on atheism or at least reveals the strange solidarity in present-day Protestant theology of all the areas and dimensions of modern mentalistic and epistemological negativity.

We must therefore agree with Knevels in his incisive critical remark to the effect that when Bultmann asserts that he is not speaking of an idea of God but "is concerned to speak of the God who holds our time

[28] M. Heidegger, *Identität und Differenz* (Pfullingen, 1956), p. 71; English translation, *Essays in Metaphysics: Identity and Difference* (New York, 1960). But perhaps, adds Bultmann, there might be a possibility of a formal definition of the concept of God by means of a further determination of the Heideggerian-style Being-Non-being relation ("Zur Frage einer 'Philosophischen Theologie,' " p. 106).

[29] Schnübbe's conclusion that "Bultmann is a theologian and not a philosopher," seems to me for this reason less than accurate (O. Schnübbe, *Der Existenzbegriff in der Theologie Rudolf Bultmanns* [Göttingen, 1959], p. 140).

in his hands and who encounters each one of us in our own time" he is not speaking of God at all but only of man.[30]

To the radical agnosticism of classical Protestant theology, unaware of analogy or unwilling to accept it, there has here been added the psychological set of restrictive existential philosophy, restrictive in virtue of its dual profession of the negativity of mind-and-knowing and of the consequent finitude of being. Not one of these German theologians, standard-bearers of existential theology, has taken the trouble to "go back to Kierkegaard" and capture his real point about God and Christ; rather have they preferred to bypass existence, its problematic and its demands, taking refuge in an appeal to the patron deities of German thought from Kant to Heidegger. And it comes therefore as no surprise to see Bultmann, in the fine fury of his all-out effort to despoil God of every attribute ascribed to Him by the old metaphysic, going so far as to transform God's eternity (*Ewigkeit*) into the historicity (*Geschichtlichkeit*) of his biblical manifestations. Bultmann's very formula here reeks of Hegelianism: "If God is a Person in the biblical tradition, then he is historical. The Creator *is* not without or in the absence of the creation . . ." [31] This is a sheer sophism because it is creation which presupposes Creator and not vice versa! St. Thomas well saw that in this case the real relation obtains on the part of the creature and not on that of the Creator.[32] And so it is not at all surprising to find Bultmann agreeing entirely with the contention of the Anglican Bishop John A. T. Robinson [33] and rejecting all manner of transcendence and supernaturalism. Demythologization (*Entmythologisierung*) means much more than a mere elimination of all factual concreteness; it implies likewise the total rejection of any search for the foundation of acts and phenomena and the consequent banishment of any hope of metaphysical activity. This is an uncompromisingly immanentistic theology; indeed it is properly speaking simply "theological existence" and no longer theology as such, i.e., no longer theological reflection: "There is no flight out of the world into a Beyond; rather God is encountered in the Here-and-Now. The whole point is to understand this paradox and that understanding is

[30] Cf. W. Knevels, *Die Wirklichkeit Gottes* (Stuttgart, 1964); Italian tr. (Brescia, 1966), p. 282.

[31] R. Bultmann, "Der Gottesgedanke und der moderne Mensch," in *Glauben und Verstehen,* Vol. IV, p. 125. Bultmann cites D. Bonhoeffer, E. Bethge, H. Ebeling, R. G. Smith, G. Vahanian, as being in agreement with his atheistic theology of existence (pp. 113ff.).

[32] "Creation in the active sense signifies the divine action which is His essence with relation to the creature. But the relation in God to the creature is not a real one but only a rational one. The relation of the creature to God however is real relation" (*S. T.* I[a], q. 45, a. 3 ad 1).

[33] Bultmann has an examination of Robinson's famous *Honest to God* in his 1963 essay: "Ist der Glaube an Gott erledigt?" appearing in *Glauben und Verstehen,* Vol. IV, pp. 107ff.

effected not in theological reflection but rather in real life, in the existential dimension." [34] But existence conceived as freedom-in-act and historicity of Being presupposes a subject-in-act and an object serving as reason and end of the act itself and as its transcendental foundation (*Grund*). It is indeed no wonder, then, that the whole of this "existential theology" ultimately vanishes "into air, into thin air". This "foreclosure" not only of philosophy but of existential theology to the God-problem has two chief results: it causes that theology to "precipitate" as *atheistic theology;* and it necessitates an ultimate appeal on the part of that theology (at least in its more recent forms, deriving from the latest post-Schleiermacherian liberal theology) to the principle of immanentism with its insistence on the intrinsic conditioning by the mind of every dimension of being and of the ultimate meaning of truth itself.

[34] "Ist der Glaube an Gott erledigt?" p. 112. In this essay, Bultmann also examines the position of the American theologian, G. Vahanian, who holds that religious feeling as an aspiration to transcendence is responsible for the decline of Christianity in our days (p. 111). Bultmann judges Vahanian's *The Death of God* (New York: George Braziller, 1961) to be "the most exciting theological book . . . in recent years", comparable to K. Barth's *Römerbrief*. Sympathetic interpreters of Bultmann hasten to explain that the denial of transcendence must here be understood as referring solely to transcendence conceived in spatial terms, coupled with an affirmation of God as here-and-now (*Diesseits*) or *Persona,* i.e. "accessible to man" (cf. W. Schmithals, *Die Theologie Rudolf Bultmanns,* p. 35). But no metaphysician or theologian (with the exception of the English Platonists like More, Clarke, Newton et al.) has ever conceived transcendence in spatial terms: indeed these authors, precisely by identifying God with Absolute Space, made him immanent in the world, even as present-day Protestant theology makes Him immanent in history.

3

Existential Reason Dissolved into Atheism (Tillich)

In closer accord with the demands of modern thought seems to be the stand of Tillich (1886-1966), the pioneer of the *kairos-theology*.[1] His contention is that there can be no philosophical preamble to faith nor yet any rational proof of the existence and transcendence of God prior to theological reflection. The point of departure is what Luther called *Anfechtung*[2] (temptation) and Tillich, in his American period, renders as "utter despair" coincident with the utter trivial meaninglessness to which man has been condemned by sin. Luther can thus, in Tillich's mind, be considered the forerunner of existentialism[3] (and, one might add, especially of the negative or atheistic brand of that existentialism). But over against this negative pole Luther set the positive one deriving from the first commandment that "God is God" and man knows this! Tillich points out that Thomas Münze's radical protestantism enjoys greater favor in America than Luther. Tillich himself synthesized both poles into the famous formula: "absolute faith and the courage to be".

Faith is certainly a raising of the soul above the finite toward the Infinite, tending to a union with the Ground of Being; but it is more, it is the personal encounter with the Personal God; and faith is still more, it is the state of the being who has been seized by the power that makes

[1] "Kairos is fulfilled time, the moment of time which is invaded by eternity. But Kairos is not perfect completion in time" (P. Tillich, *Die religiöse Lage der Gegenwart* [Berlin, 1926], p. 117; English translation, *The Religious Situation* [New York: Meridian Books, 1956], p. 176). For a development of this doctrine, cf. *Kairos, Geisteslage und Geisteswendung* (Darmstadt, 1926), edited by Tillich himself, who wrote two articles for the volume: "Kairos, Ideen zur Geisteslage der Gegenwart," pp. 1ff. and "Kairos und Logos, Eine Untersuchung zur Metaphysik des Erkennens," pp. 23ff.

[2] Cf. P. Bühler, *Die Anfechtung bei Martin Luther* (Zurich, 1942), especially pp. 79ff.

[3] P. Tillich, *The Courage to Be* (New Haven: Yale University Press, 1953), p. 170.

that being be itself and thus is "the courage to be." Faith is the experience of this power and in faith is realized what modern existentialism designates as "situation".

This is for Tillich a paradoxical experience: Being Itself (Himself!) infinitely transcends every finite being. God radically and implacably transcends man in the encounter with man. Faith bridges the infinite gulf that here yawns between man and God; and faith does this by accepting the fact that, "in spite of" the gulf, there is present the power of being. Thus the Separated is accepted. The acceptance effected by faith is an acceptance "in spite of" and it is from this "in spite of" of faith that there flows the "in spite of" of courage. Faith is not the theoretical affirmation of something uncertain; it is the existential acceptance of something transcending ordinary experience: it is the "state of being" of him who feels able to affirm himself, a synthesis of mystical experience and personal encounter (and, we might add, likewise, a synthesis of the Lutheran principle of faith and the modern principle of self-awareness). Existentialism, says Tillich, probably alluding here to Kierkegaard, thought it could solve the problem with the theory of the "leap". Tillich himself feels that the only real answer, granted the fact that the basic situation is the "courage of despair",[4] is the contention that the acceptance of despair is in itself faith and on a line convergent with the courage to be. In this situation, the positive includes the negative and the negative subsists upon the positive which it negates: this is precisely the dialectical aspect of faith. Faith, which makes possible the courage to despair is the acceptance of the power of being: the act of accepting meaninglessness is itself a meaningful act, is an act of faith.

Such an attitude, situation or act, Tillich calls "absolute faith", in that it has no specific content: it is faith sheer and simple. It is indefinable, because everything defined is dissolved by doubt and meaninglessness. Yet, he stresses, it is no mere outburst of subjective emotion, no mere mood devoid of any objective ground. Analysis of the nature of absolute faith reveals the following elements. First, the experience of the power to be, the power of being which is present even in the face of the most radical manifestation of non-being: there is simply no experience of negativity or even of the abyss of non-being and of meaninglessness that

[4] It is the ontological significance of this attitude, which pervades the whole of Tillich's theology, which accounts for its popularity in the Protestant world, a popularity in function of timeliness: "The reason for the attention this still incomplete dogmatic theology has attracted at home and abroad lies in Tillich's attempt, undertaken in this work, to expound and develop the Christian message in ontological categories. The crucial notions are the designations of God as 'Being-itself', of the reality of Christ as the 'power of Being' and of the reality of man within the scheme of the redemption as 'Being' under the condition of existence, separated from its 'Depth' or its 'Ground'" (Wilhelm F. Kasch, "Die Lehre von der Inkarnation in der Theologie Paul Tillichs," *Zeitschrift für Theologie und Kirche* 58, 1 [1961], p. 56).

does not reveal a hidden meaning. Secondly, there is the realization that the experience of non-being depends on the experience of being and the experience of meaninglessness on the experience of meaning. Thirdly, there is the acceptance of the being accepted. Naturally in despair there is no-one accepting and nothing accepted. But there is the power of acceptance itself which is accepted. Meaninglessness, as accepted, includes an experience of the power to accept. The conscious and deliberate acceptance of this power to accept is the religious response of absolute faith, of a faith despoiled by doubt of every concrete content, yet still persisting as faith and as the source of the most paradoxical manifestation of the courage to be.

In this way, Tillich points out (in agreement with Barth and the Protestant tradition), faith surpasses and transcends mystical experience, inasmuch as faith includes an element of scepticism, contains the apprehension of meaninglessness which is lacking in mystical experience. It likewise transcends the divine-human encounter, for if the encounter can indeed be formulated as the meeting between a definite subject (man) and a definite object (God), it can equally legitimately be formulated inversely as the meeting between a definite object (God) and a definite subject (man). Now a faith limited to this (as is faith in ordinary theology) does not escape from radical doubt nor consequently from critique and transformation. Hence the new stand, that of the "courage to be": in its radical form, it constitutes the key to an idea of God transcending the inadequacies inherent in mysticism and the divine-human encounter notion alike.

Whereas Barth works more within the framework of the sin-faith tension, Tillich attends rather to the philosophical tension of being and non-being which structures the power of being, whose affirmation reveals non-being and overcomes the negation included in non-being. For it must be admitted that being does include non-being, does encompass it. We can never think of being—and here Tillich appeals expressly to neo-Platonism, to Hegel and the *Lebensphilosophie*—without a double negation: being must be thought of as the negation of being, as has been indicated already by the very expression "power of being", affirming the ability to be against the opposition of other beings and thus claiming for itself the dynamic character proper to life. Here Tillich maintains that modern philosophy (Spinoza included!) meshes with the philosophy of the Living God, for God's own yes to himself would have been devoid of life in the absence of the no that He had to overcome in himself and in his creature; without that no, there would have been no revelation of the ground of being, there would have been no life.[5] This conjunction of

[5] In this connection, Killen quite rightly remarks: "At this point Tillich has simply adopted Hegel's triad Being, Non-being and Becoming but changed the Becoming into Power of being. It is hard to see that there is any great difference

negative and positive is constitutive of creativity itself and productive of the very structure of the "demonic" in its dual aspect, creative and destructive, as tensional unity of form-creation and form-destruction: "Where the destructive quality is lacking, one can speak of outstanding power, of genius, of creative force, not of demonry. And *vice versa,* where destruction is evidence without creative form, it is fitting to speak of deficiencies, flaws, decline or the like, but not of demonry." [6]

The "courage to be" thus stems from the divine yes which includes the no, even as God's infinity includes finitude. The self-affirmation of God is the power that renders possible the self-affirmation of the finite being, which is the "courage to be". The courage participates in the self-affirmation of being itself, it participates in the power of being which prevails over non-being. And so, concludes Tillich, the only valid proofs for the "existence" of God are these acts of courage wherein we affirm the power of being!

Tillich believes he has overcome the theism-atheism split with this doctrine of "absolute faith" as "courage to be". He holds this split to have arisen in the first place from the desire to attribute to God some special content. The content proper to absolute faith is "God above God"; and such faith, together with the concomitant courage, takes up into itself the doubt that obtrudes itself in regard to God and therefore transcends the theist idea of God. Tillich uses its own dialectical method to prove this, reviewing three forms or degrees of theism.[7]

The first is a vague affirmation of God such as exploited by the politicians, the dictators and the image-makers; at best it may be a poetic formulation but it is always inconsistent and inconsequential, even as is the atheism that is opposed to it. This brand of theism and its corresponding form of atheism are lacking in despair and so do not lead to faith.

The second form of theism, opposed to the first, formulates what we

---

between Hegel's 'becoming', at this point, and Tillich's Power of being, particularly when a study of Tillich's view of God's creativeness makes creation an inherent activity of God. If it were not for the resistance of Non-Being, God would be static like the unmoved mover of Aristotle" (R. Allen Killen, *The Ontological Theology of Paul Tillich* [Kampen, 1956], p. 128).

The weakness of Tillich's notion of creation comes out in the ambiguity of the notion of "nihil", which is the Heideggerian *Nichts* and ultimately the Hegelian Non-being, not the "nothing" or "void" of the Bible (cf. J. Heywood Thomas, "Some Comments on Tillich's Doctrine of Creation," in *Scottish Journal of Theology,* 14, 2 [1961], p. 116).

[6] P. Tillich, *Das Dämonische,* Ein Beitrag zur Sinndeutung der Geschichte, Sammlung Gemeinverständlicher Vorträge 119 (Tübingen, 1926), p. 9; English translation in *The Interpretation of History* (New York: Charles Scribner's Sons, 1936), pp. 81f.

[7] P. Tillich, *The Courage to Be,* pp. 182ff.

have called the divine-human encounter, i.e. the conception of God as "Person" in his personal relation to man conceived as person, in the line of biblical tradition and the historical tradition of Christian theology. Atheism, according to this point of view, is the human effort to dodge this encounter. It is an existential problem, not a theoretical one.

There is a third meaning of theism, a strictly theological meaning, the synthesis of the two preceding brands. This third form of theism admits, with the first form, the necessity of affirming God in some fashion and likewise develops the proofs of the "existence of God"; but its chief concern is to establish a doctrine of God which will transform the encounter of man with God into an encounter between two persons, each one of whom enjoys its own reality independently of the other. And we discover here the real kernel of Tillich's dialectic in his next contention: both the philosophical and the technological approach must be transcended, for they have led to atheism, ancient and modern, right down to and including modern existentialism, against which Nietzsche revolted with his proclamation that "God is dead" and which is responsible for the despair that has invaded virtually the whole of the modern world.[8]

The third solution, beyond theism and atheism, is the only valid solution to Tillich's mind. And it is "absolute faith", devoid not only of the foundation of visible authority (as was Luther's) but even of content, even of the revealed "Word" as such, which was typical of Barth's notion. In a word, this absolute faith has no content whatsover! Barth distrusts all philosophy, ancient and modern, as being a human word launched against God in consequence of sin; Barth thus turns back to purely biblical faith. Tillich, for his part, sees the point of departure in the alleged faith-religion and philosophy-revelation tension and proceeds to the affirmation of "absolute faith" which has no content whatever.[9] Thus God cannot even be said to be a Person; for were God a Person,

[8] "This is the God Nietzsche said had to be killed because nobody can tolerate being made into a mere object of absolute knowledge and absolute control. This is the deepest root of atheism. It is an atheism which is justified as the reaction against theological theism and its disturbing implications. It is also the deepest root of the Existentialist despair and the widespread anxiety of meaninglessness in our period" (P. Tillich, *The Courage to Be,* p. 185).

[9] To this radical Protestant conception of faith as a "tension" of contraries corresponds the assertion that doubt is inherent in faith, an assertion which Tillich himself admits to be irreconcilable with the Catholic conception of the authority of the Church: "Faith and doubt do not essentially contradict each other. Faith is the continuous tension between itself and the doubt within itself. This tension does not always reach the strength of a struggle; but, latently, it is always present . . . Faith embraces itself and the doubt about itself." (P. Tillich, *Biblical Religion and the Search for Ultimate Reality* [Chicago: University of Chicago Press, 1955], pp. 60f.). But can a faith which includes doubt ever really be faith? A fortiori, can it be the faith of the Gospel, a truly evangelical faith?

he would have to be classed in the category of "individuality" which is unfitting to God. In the wake of Kant, nature governed by physical laws is one thing and personality ruled by moral laws quite another. But God cannot be conceived as a superior-type person, separate from the world or the "realm of ends" of the human sphere. Tillich's formula is that God is certainly personal but not *a* person. The term "person" suits only to the hypostases of the Trinity, but not to God himself as such; the expression "personal God" signifies that God is the ground of all personality and that he carries within himself the ontological power of personality; and "The protest of atheism against such a highest person is correct".[10]

Just as Tillich had proposed to overcome the theism-atheism antithesis in dealing with the problem of the existence of God, so here he aims, in his definition of the nature of God, to get beyond the antithesis of naturalism and supernaturalism. And he follows the same methodological line of dialectic as in the former problem: [11] Supernaturalism is unacceptable because it applies to God the categories of the finite and thus makes him finite; but naturalism is just as untenable, because it denies the distinction between God and the world. A middle way must be found, a way Tillich claims has already been taken by theologians of stature such as Augustine, Aquinas, Luther, Zwingli, Calvin and Schleiermacher. This way agrees with naturalism in asserting that God would not be God were he not the creative ground of every being, that God is the infinite and unconditioned power or indeed, in the radical formulation, *Sein-Selbst* (being-itself). Thus God is neither "alongside" beings nor yet "above" them: he is nearer to them than they are to themselves. He is their creative ground, here and now, always and everywhere.

Tillich notes that, up to this point, this third way could be accepted by some forms of naturalism at least. But now he introduces two concepts, apparently of Heideggerian ancestry, which contradistinguish his view from mere naturalism: these are the notions "self-transcending" and "ecstatic". The term "self-transcending" has two elements: "transcending" and "self". God as the ground of being infinitely transcends that of which he is the ground and abyss.[12] He stands *against* the world insofar as the world stands against him; and he stands *for* the world, insofar as he draws the world toward him. This mutual freedom from each other

[10] P. Tillich, *Systematic Theology*, Vol. I (Chicago: University of Chicago Press, 1951), p. 245, where there is the further surprising statement: "God became 'a person' only in the nineteenth century . . .".

[11] Cf. P. Tillich, *Systematic Theology*, Vol. II (Chicago: University of Chicago Press, 1957), pp. 6ff.

[12] Critics here recognized the influence of Böhme. But Böhme used the term *Ungrund* (Ungrounded, Non-Ground), whereas Tillich likewise attributes to him the term *Urgrund* (Primordial Ground) (*Systematic Theology*, Vol. I, p. 179).

and for each other, on the part of God and the world, is the only meaningful sense in which we can understand the "super" in the term "supernaturalism."

To call God transcendent in this sense does not imply the setting up of a "superworld" of divine objects; it does mean that the finite world, within itself, points beyond itself, that it is self-transcendent. And it is the same with the syllable "self" in "self-transcending": the finitude of the finite points to the infinity of the infinite. This finite which we encounter in everyday experience goes beyond itself to return to itself in a new dimension; and this is what constitutes "self-transcendence". The immediate experience of self-transcendence is to be found in the encounter with the holy.[13] This encounter has an ecstatic character. "Ecstatic" here means that the experience of the holy transcends ordinary experience without removing it. And such an understanding of God, so acquired, is neither naturalistic nor yet supernaturalistic, declares Tillich. The divine transcendence is here equated with the freedom of the creature to turn away from the essential unity with the creative ground of its being. Such a freedom presupposes that the creature is substantially independent of its creative ground or principle; and likewise that the creature remains in substantial unity with that creative ground or principle. In the absence of this substantial unity, the creature would be unable to "be". It is not the idea of a highest being, a supreme being alongside the world that makes pantheism impossible; rather it is this quality of *finite freedom* within the creature.[14]

The most important consequence of this line of reasoning in Tillich is the "problem of the symbolic knowledge of God." Tillich is as unwilling as Barth to admit analogy. Tillich actually asserts that whatever one knows about a finite thing one knows about God, because the finite thing is rooted in God as its ground. Then he proceeds to a second equally absolute statement: anything one knows about a finite thing cannot be applied to God, because God is the "Wholly Other". The unity of these two divergent consequences is the symbolic knowledge of God.[15]

[13] Tillich often expressly appeals to the work of R. Otto, *Das Heilige* (cf. *Systematic Theology,* Vol. I, pp. 215ff.; *The Protestant Era* [Chicago: University of Chicago Press, 1948], pp. 180ff.).

[14] Tillich remarks that this idea of God restructures the whole of Christology and refers to his chapter on "Reason and Revelation" in *Systematic Theology,* Vol. I (pp. 71ff.).

[15] Tillich's "symbolic knowledge" would seem to have to do with the attribution of the predicates as such, found in creatures, and not with that of the modes: thus, "If we say that God is the infinite, or the unconditional, or being-itself, we speak rationally and ecstatically at the same time. These terms precisely designate the boundary line at which both the symbolic and the non-symbolic coincide." (P. Tillich, *Systematic Theology,* Vol. II, p. 10). The term "symbolic knowledge" comes, of course, from the Pseudo-Dionysius, who is supposed to have written a "symbolic theology."

It is worthy mentioning in conclusion of our presentation of Tillich's novel attitude to atheism his interpolation of the consideration of Being (*Sein*) into theological reflection. We have already mentioned this in speaking of the application to God of the Platonic-Thomistic-Hegelian-Heideggerian attribute of *esse ipsum* (*Sein Selbst*). In theology, says Tillich, we encounter being in three dimensions: in the doctrine of God, where God is called "Being as Being" or "the ground and power of being"; in the doctrine of man, where a distinction is usually made between man's essential being and his existential being; and finally in the doctrine of Christ, wherein he is called "the epiphany of the 'New Being' ".[16] The first impression is that Tillich has come very close to the Thomistic claim on behalf of *esse* as an intensive transcendental; and that Tillich's movement in this direction may well have occurred under the influence of Heidegger with his claim for the uniqueness of *esse-ipsum* against the formalism of the nominalist and positivist anti-meta-physical tradition. But Tillich's further treatment of the problem betrays a quite different bent of mind. *Esse-ipsum* is not for Tillich that which corresponds to the most indeterminate and abstract notion of *ens,* proper to nominalism, positivism and indeed Hegel himself, as the empty remnant of total abstraction. The "power of being" is rather a "transcendental" in the medieval sense, as that which is beyond the particular and the general alike. Tillich recalls Parmenides, the Hindu philosopher Sankhara and then with one bound arrives at the existentialism of Heidegger and Marcel.[17]

The basic error of Tillich, and of this effort to effect an immediate synthesis between revelation and modern philosophy, lies in the opposi-

[16] Cf. C. Fabro, *La nozione metafisica di partecipazione* (Turin, 1963 ^{3}), pp. 190ff. Killen also notes these points of contact between St. Thomas and Tillich, when he writes: "Both have an ontological system; both build their systematic theology on their ontology: both base theology on a philosophical system and both have a very strong rationalistic line in their thinking" (Killen, *op. cit.*, p. 111, n. 4). But Killen is entirely mistaken in stating that St. Thomas was the one to found his ontology upon essentialism while Tillich founded his on existentialism; for it was precisely St. Thomas who re-discovered the *esse-ipsum* of Parmenides and made a real distinction between it and essence!

[17] Like Heidegger, Tillich also speaks of the Hidden-ness of Being (*Verborgenheit des Seins*): "No philosophy can suppress the notion of being in this latter sense. It can be hidden under presuppositions and reductive formulas, but it nevertheless underlies the basic concepts of philosophizing. For 'being' remains the content, the mystery and the eternal *aporia* of thinking. No theology can suppress the notion of being as the power of being. One cannot separate them. In the moment in which one says that God *is* or that he has being, the question arises as to how his relation to being is understood. The only possible answer seems to be that God is being-itself, in the sense of the power of being or the power to conquer non-being." (P. Tillich, *Systematic Theology,* Vol. II, p. 11). Such statements fit Aquinas' notion of *esse* better than they do any other notion!

tion between being and person and the consequent declaration that if God is Being hc cannot be a person. Tillich is unaware of the metaphysical structure of the person as subsistence, as the actuality of the being of the spiritual substance; and he conceives personality primarily as a human psychological reality.[18] God so conceived is reduced to the universal Act, essential Life wherein every being participates and which is participated in every life. And Tillich's specification that God is not to be called "impersonal" but rather "suprapersonal" [19] is but a sop to neo-Platonic and idealist metaphysics, especially that of Hegel.

A very good illustration of Tillich's conception of God in such a fashion as to effect allegedly a resolution of the theism-atheism antithesis is to be found in a passage from his Sermon on Psalm 139. This sermon bears the title: "The Escape from God".[20]

" 'Where could I go from Thy Spirit? O, where could I flee from Thy face?' The poet who wrote those words to describe the futile attempt of man to escape God certainly believed that man *desires* to escape God. He is not alone in his conviction. Men of all kinds, prophets and reformers, saints and atheists, believers and unbelievers, have the same experience. It is safe to say that a man who has never tried to flee God has never experienced the God Who is really God. When I speak of God, I do not refer to the many gods of our own making, the gods with whom we can live rather comfortably. For there is no reason to flee a god who is the perfect picture of everything that is good in man. Why try to escape from such a far-removed ideal? And there is no reason to flee from a god who is simply the universe, or the laws of nature, or the course of history. Why try to escape from a reality of which we are a part? There is no reason to flee from a god who is nothing more than a benevolent father, a father who guarantees our immortality and final happiness. Why try to escape from someone who serves us so well? No, those are not pictures of God, but rather of man, trying to make God in his own image and for his own comfort. They are the products of man's imagination and wishful thinking, justly denied by every honest atheist. A god whom we can easily bear, a god from whom

18 Cf. especially *The Protestant Era,* ch. VIII: "The Idea and the Ideal of Personality," pp. 115ff.

19 "Supra-personal is not impersonal; and I would ask those who are afraid to transcend the personalistic symbolism of the religious language to think, even if only for a short moment, of the words of Jesus about the hairs on our head being counted—and, we could add, the atoms and electrons constituting the universe. In such a statement there is at least as much potential ontology as there is actual ontology in the whole system of Spinoza" (P. Tillich, *Systematic Theology,* Vol. II, p. 12).

20 Included in the volume of sermons with the indicative title *The Shaking of the Foundations* (New York: Charles Scribner's Sons, 1948), pp. 38ff.

we do not have to hide, a god whom we do not hate in moments, a god whose destruction we never desire, is not God at all, and has no reality."[21]

Tillich proceeds to trace the fundamental traits of modern atheism along this same theoretico-existential line. We must quote him again at some length in view of the extreme importance of this analysis and the fact that this analysis is just as significant in the modern world as that of Barth:

"The pious man of the Old Testament, the mystical saint of the Middle Ages, the reformer of the Christian Church, and the prophet of atheism are all united through that tremendous human experience: man cannot stand the God Who is really God. Man tries to escape God, and hates Him, because he cannot escape Him. The protest against God, the will that there be no God, and the flight to atheism are all genuine elements of profound religion. And only on the basis of these elements has religion meaning and power." Tillich goes on to warn of the danger represented by the abstact terms and concepts of theology. Articulations concerning the divine Omnipotence and the divine Omnipresence are still redolent of qualities of human experience; and a theology using them must not imagine it can escape from atheism: "It encourages those who are interested in denying the threatening Witness of their existence. The first step to atheism is always a theology which drags God down to the level of doubtful things. The game of the atheist is then very easy. For he is perfectly justified in destroying such a phantom and all its ghostly qualities. And because the theoretical atheist is just in his destruction, the practical atheists (all of us) are willing to use his argument to support our own attempt to flee God."[22]

But radical atheism, concludes Tillich, is impossible, as is proven by Nietzsche himself, the theoretician of idealist atheism: having killed God, man goes to prostrate himself at the feet of Zarathustra, finding God again in a man. God is always thus revived in something or somebody, for He cannot be murdered, and the story of every atheism merely serves to bear this out.

And so the origin of modern atheism, of the atheism of our own day, is to be sought in theology itself. In its desire to get beyond myth, this theology has conceived God as an object or as "the supreme Essence" so as to make him an object of the mind. Thus has a "content" been

[21] The conclusion immediately following these words is most significant: "Friedrich Nietzsche, the famous atheist and ardent enemy of religion and Christianity, knew more about the power of the idea of God than many faithful Christians" (*ibid.*, p. 42). "Presence of God created the same feeling in Luther that it did in Nietzsche" (p. 44).

[22] *Ibid.*, pp. 45f.

substituted for Act and the very meaning of Act is restrictively vitiated. For the truly transcendent *Absolute* transcends every positing of an essence, even a supreme essence! The very act of positing anything of this sort vitiates or demolishes the religious act itself. This demolition, specifies Tillich, precipitates the atheism latent in every religious act. The moment the abysmal transcendence of such a religious act is lost, there begins an objectification of the Unconditioned and the non-objective. This is destructive of religious and spiritual life. God is reduced the status of an "entity" (*Ding*) and so is degraded in fact into a "non-entity" (*Unding*). The religious function of atheism consists in a head-on attack on the religious act and a demonstration that the articulations of the Unconditioned are not objects concerning whose existence or non-existence a discussion is possible. In one of his earlier writings, Tillich had already asserted that the word "God" is indicative of a contradiction in the human mind between a spurious meaning which is a mental content and a genuine meaning represented by this content.[23]

For Tillich too, therefore, atheism is part and parcel of man's state and the indispensable dark side of man's very meaning. It does not eliminate or exclude the religious act; rather it renders that act possible and supports it. It is the negative element which is active and operative in the religious act itself, according to the modern dialectic. The religious act affirms its own truth in proportion to its elimination and transcendence of all "content", in proportion as it is posited as a sheer transcending! But surely such a "dialectic" involves and amounts to an explicit capitulation before the principle of immanentism positing the act as ground of the content! And surely the contention that faith includes doubt as a constitutive element inevitably involves an inanition of faith; such a faith can no longer be, as it was for the Reformers themselves, the invincible certitude in the struggle against the world and the devil!

[23] "The word 'God' thus causes a contradiction to appear in the mind between an improper meaning which is a mental content and a proper meaning which is represented by this content." (P. Tillich, *Religiöse Verwirklichung* [Berlin: Furche Verlag, 1929], p. 102). Tillich himself reports in this connection a discussion between the theologians Hirsch and Traub about his "atheism" (*ibid.*, p. 286, n. 14).

4

Death-of-God Theology and the End of Religion (Bonhoeffer)

The ultimate extreme and radical sense of dialectical theology is the contention that the end term of man's evolution and adult stage of his culture involves a definitive recession of man from God and of God from man, and consequently "the end of religion" in Bonhoeffer's phrase or the "death of God" with its concomitant "death-of-God theology" in the preferred phrase of the Anglo-American theologians of our day who follow Bonhoeffer's lead, beginning with the controversial character of J. A. T. Robinson.[1]

In an early essay on the Christian Idea of God, Bonhoeffer (1904-1945) makes a clear-cut distinction between the philosophical and the theological approach to God: [2] philosophy is typically "free from premises" and thus operates within the category of "possibility" which it can never transcend. But Bonhoeffer further refuses to admit any other philosophy than that of immanence, starting from the self and ending outside of God; this approach is likewise that of all dialectical theology and

[1] Among those who take their inspiration directly from the later Bonhoeffer of the *Briefe an einen Freund* (Nov. 18, 1942—August 23, 1944), translated into English under the titles *Letters and Papers from Prison* (London, 1953), and *Prisoner for God* (New York, 1962) are: Kenneth Hamilton, *Revolt Against Heaven* (Grand Rapids: Eerdmans, 1966), with its Chapter 10: "Bonhoeffer's Religionless Christianity" (pp. 169ff.); William Hamilton, *The New Essence of Christianity* (New York: Association Press, 1966), pp. 54f.; Thomas J. J. Altizer and W. Hamilton, *Radical Theology and the Death of God* (Indianapolis: The Bobbs-Merrill Company, 1966), especially pp. 113ff.; Paul M. van Buren, *The Secular Meaning of the Gospel* (New York: The Macmillan Company, 1966), pp. 1ff. and *passim;* Leslie Dewart, *The Future of Belief,* Theism in a World Come of Age (New York: Herder and Herder, 1966), especially pp. 42ff.; Gabriel Vahanian, *No Other God* (New York: George Braziller, 1966), pp. 13f., 19ff.

[2] D. Bonhoeffer, "Concerning the Christian Idea of God," in *The Journal of Religion* (1932); now included in *Gesammelte Schriften,* Vol. III, ed. E. Bethge (Munich: C. Kaiser Verlag, 1966), pp. 100ff. This study, like others included in this volume, belong to Bonhoeffer's Union Theological Seminary period.

indeed of the whole of post-Hegelian Protestant theologizing. Philosophical thinking, says Bonhoeffer, can never develop into real thinking, or more accurately reality-thinking. Philosophy can form a conception of reality but a conceived reality is not a genuine reality, for thinking is a closed circle centered upon the self and thus the ultimate "reality" for any philosophical reflection must necessarily be a self void of all objectivity and totally non-conceptualizable, a non-objective self (*nichtgegenständliches Ich*). Thus, incisively remarks Bonhoeffer, thinking does violence to reality, by wresting it from its primordial "objectivity", because thought means system and system excludes reality. Thus in thought, not only the fellow-man but God as well is subordinated to the self. Such is the inevitable result of idealist philosophy and of every exact philosophy that seeks to be autonomous. Bonhoeffer too is a prisoner of the Fichtan principle subordinating being to consciousness (*ohne Bewusstsein kein Sein*) and considers the principle of immanentism to be the indelible mark of the negativity of the human spirit, of the human mind, the sign of its fallen status. The captivity of human thought within its own prison, its inevitable autocracy and self-glorification can be interpreted theologically as a result and consequence of the fall of man. But "before" the Fall, man ought to be considered as being able to think reality, i.e., to think God and fellow-man as realities. Man "in" and "after" the Fall, on the contrary, refers everything to himself, makes himself the center of the universe, does violence to reality, makes himself God and God and other men his creatures. Man accordingly can never attain to reality, because his thought is no longer "in reality"; it remains in the category of possibility and there is no bridge between possibility and reality. Bonhoeffer analogously distinguishes between philosophy and theology, between reason and faith, as between *a priori* and *a posteriori,* immanence and transcendence. This method marks the point of departure and gives evidence of the internal coherence of the evolution of Bonhoeffer's thought within the rigid framework of orthodox Lutheranism's notion of reason as *homo curvatus in seipsum,* set over against man saved by faith.

The "anthropological" trait distinctive of modern thought had been Bonhoeffer's theme as early as 1930 [3] and this transcendental anthropologism he held to have had two divergent possibilities of development, in function of whether man sought to understand on the basis of his own activity (*Werk*) or on the basis of the *limits* (*Grenze*) he encounters in his activity. Max Scheler had taken the first line: initially, Scheler had posited a "material a priori", thereby postulating the intuition of the

[3] D. Bonhoeffer, "Die Frage nach dem Menschen in der gegenwärtigen Philosophie und Theologie," Antrittsvorlesung in der Aula der Berliner Universität am 31 Juli 1930, in *C. W.*, Vol. III, pp. 62ff.

world of values whose purest form was love by the instrumentality of which man was able to intuit God; later Scheler had spoken of man as prisoner of the world, as the being in whom the world of instincts had gotten the better of the world of values, making man the powerless prey of demonic powers.[4] To theological staticism had succeeded a-theological staticism, to the All-God of the intuition of the Absolute ("all knowledge about God is a knowledge mediated by God = *alles Wissen um Gott ist ein Wissen durch Gott*)[5] had succeeded the All or Whole of universe-man and nothingness-God, with the indeterminate disappearance of man's being as an indeterminate and indeterminable possibility or pure potential.

Man's being is, on the contrary, a dynamic or determined and self-determining potential for Heidegger, whose evolving thought Bonhoeffer incisively expounds on the paradigm of *Sein und Zeit*. Here, man's constitutive parameter, the essence of existence, is "being-in-time" (*in-der-Zeit-sein*), inasmuch as man is a being-in-the-world (*in-der-Welt-sein*) and consequently always tied to a historical situation. Yet here too man's being is explained as and dissolved into mere potentiality, in Heidegger's own phrase: man's being is primarily possibility. Man's being is thus "what it can be, and the way in which it is the possibility."[6] It is this fundamental approach that leads to the acceptance of "being-thrust-into" (*Geworfenheit*) or of a "fall" (*Verfall*) into the world and of the final being-unto-death (*Sein-zum-Tode*) as the ultimate meaning of being, so that man's existence is comprehended as a totality and as a "resolve to death" (*Entschlossenheit zum Tode*) in defiance of the threat of the inauthentic or of a dispersion in the plethora of everyday banality (*Alltäglichkeit*). Thus, each and every moment is a

[4] Bonhoeffer incisively remarks that Scheler's error lay in separating essence from existence (p. 67); but Bonhoeffer himself, like the other Reformation-style theologians, never even adverted to the possibility of calling in question the principle of immanentism, the modern *cogito* principle.

[5] Cf. M. Scheler, "Vom Ewigen im Menschen" in *Gesammelte Werke* (Bern: Francke Verlag, 1954 [4]), Vol. I, p. 278: Scheler believed he had, by means of this principle, radically precluded all manner of subjectivism. It was against this principle, which held religious experience to be primordial and undeducible (*Ursprünglichkeit und Unableitbarkeit religiöser Erfahrung*), that Bonhoeffer was to protest so sharply in his latest period. It is the material *a priori* as set over against Kant's formal *a priori*. (*ibid.*, p. 170). In this period, Scheler criticized and vehemently repudiated the pantheistic-panentheistic conception of modern thought (*immanentia Dei in mundo*), according to which man is a beam or ray (*Strahl*) of God, a "function" of the divine Spirit, in such a way that it proves to be God who thinks in man, with the result that, as in Hegel and N. von Hartmann, "God becomes aware of Himself primarily in man" (*ibid.*, p. 156).

[6] M. Heidegger, *Sein und Zeit* (Tübingen: Neomarius Verlag, 1926), p. 143; English translation, *Being and Time* (New York and Evanston: Harper and Row, Publishers, 1962), p. 183.

moment of decision between the authentic and the inauthentic; but such a man, say Bonhoeffer, has not and cannot have any relation to God.[7]

Clearly, therefore, for Bonhoeffer, who is himself no philosopher and does not wish to be one, the state of philosophy is the one he finds in his own cultural world and which the Protestant principle impels him to interpret as the final issue of the fall of man and consequently as the definitive emergence of *hybris* [8] which has abandoned God and been abandoned by God.

The early Bonhoeffer is adamant in his interpretation of modern thought (and of philosophy in general) as a flight from God, if not indeed as a rebellion against God, an attempt on the mystery and transcendence of God, an absorption of the revelation of God into the

[7] "Heidegger's man is not destined, in the final analysis, to bear divine features nor to be lord over the world as an intellectual and spiritual being (*Geist*); rather he is destined to be man existing in the world, and indeed threatened by the world, exposed to the inimical powers of death, of trivializing commonplaceness, of facelessness (*des Man*); he is destined to succumb to the world in terms of his existential potentialities and to have to seek for himself, his own identity, in perpetually renewed questing" (D. Bonhoeffer, "Die Frage nach dem Menschen . . .," p. 70). Bonhoeffer incisively identifies this conception as a return to Hegel with a Kantian strain (p. 71). In his Habilitationsschrift, published the same year, Bonhoeffer charges that the constitutive atheism of Heidegger's *Dasein* (There-being) is the result of an identification of Act and Being, rendering existential philosophy incapable of application to theology: "Heidegger's philosophy is a consciously atheistic philosophy of finitude. It relates everything to the self-incapsulation, in *Dasein,* of the finite. It is cardinal for the existential analysis of *Dasein* that finitude should be conceived as sealed-in. *Incapsulation* can no longer be separated from finitude. Like all other existential characteristics of *Dasein,* its potentiality is revealed as determined by the incapsulation of the finite, not as a general existential constant of finite *Dasein.* In its essence the philosophical concept of finitude is that of incapsulated finitude. Here, then, no room has been left for the idea of revelation, and with the knowledge in revelation that finiteness is creatureliness, i.e. is open to God, all concepts of being must be formed anew. It follows that Heidegger's concept of being, despite its powerful expansion of philosophy through discovery of the Existential sphere, cannot be adapted for the purposes of theology." (D. Bonhoeffer, *Akt und Sein,* Transzendentalphilosophie und Ontologie in der systematischen Theologie, Theologische Bücherei 5 [Munich 1964 [3]], p. 50; English translation by Bernard Noble, *Act and Being* [William Collins Sons & Co., Ltd., London, and Harper and Brothers, Inc., New York, 1961], p. 65). Later in the same work, Bonhoeffer repeats: "When we put the question of continuity, it becomes evident that Heidegger's concept of existence is useless for elucidating *being*-in-faith" (p. 76; English translation, p. 100. Cf. p. 85 [English translation, p. 112] for Bonhoeffer's identification of Heidegger with idealism and p. 126 [English translation, p. 167] for his critique of the "Being-unto-death" [*Sein-zum-Tode*] notion as frivolous in the extreme. For the Christian, death is a consequence of the sin of Adam and it is a drastic peril, not a "full-fillment", unless man is saved and resurrected by Christ).

[8] The *hybris* motif will become dominant in the *Letters and Papers from Prison* (cf. the German edition, *Widerstand und Ergebung,* p. 159 and the *Begriffsregister,* p. 323).

course of history, the denial of God as a personal being and his replacement by the impersonal Whole of history, a denial likewise of the divinity of Christ who is reduced to a simple teacher and model of mankind. In sharpest fashion does Bonhoeffer contrast God's revelation in history (Christianity) with the revelation of God in the Idea. In the former, it is Christ who reveals God to us "in hiddenness" whereas in the latter God is revealed in the activity of man "in openness". Idealism makes history into a mere *symbol.* Individual historical facts take their essence not from the fact that they *are* something, but rather from the fact that they signify something generic. Jesus becomes simply a symbol of the love of God, his cross a symbol of pardon. And when we come to comprehend that generic something so signified, we can permanently forget the facts themselves. Since the fact is but the transitory bearer or carrier of eternal values and ideas extrinsic to it, so Jesus too is but the transitory carrier of the new generic truth. In short, idealist philosophy, charges Bonhoeffer, does not take seriously the ontological status of history; and that means it simply does not take history itself seriously.[9] Pressing this critique to its extreme, Bonhoeffer can effect a return to Luther, more radical that the one effected even by the "dialectical theology" of Barth, Tillich and Bultmann,[10] no one of whom ever burnt all the bridges to philosophy.

The point is that in faith the God-man relation is itself internal to faith as such and thus God can never "become an object". I can have no other certainty relative to the act of faith than that provided in and by faith itself: "Whether I do or do not believe is therefore something I cannot learn from any reflection on my religious acts, but it is equally impossible, while I am in process of believing, to centre my attention on my belief in such a way that I would have to believe in my belief. Belief is never directed to itself, but only on Christ, on something extrinsic. And so it is only in the believing in Christ that I know that I believe, which is to say that here and now I do not know it, and in reflexion on the believing I know nothing." [11]

[9] D. Bonhoeffer, "The Christian Idea of God," in *C. W.*, Vol. III, pp. 105f.

[10] Cf. especially *Akt und Sein,* pp. 59ff. (Barth), pp. 62, 72, 74f. (Bultmann), p. 64, note 13 (Tillich) and *passim.* (English translation, *Act and Being,* pp. 81ff. [Barth], pp. 73f., 84, 96ff. [Bultmann], p. 87, note 1 [Tillich]). The precise aim of the Dissertation is to highlight the primordiality of the theological act, as against the contaminations of philosophical and theological "reflection": above all, to get rid of the Heideggerian diversion, to which Tillich and Bultmann and perhaps even Barth himself come perilously close. In these theologians, says Bonhoeffer, the error has been that of taking the concept of existence from a realm "outside of faith"; and indeed, we might add, from a philosophy opposed to faith!

[11] *Ibid.*, p. 71. (English translation, p. 95) Equally futile, therefore, are the efforts of the "I-Thou-dialectic" for they too involve reflection and objectification.

Bonhoeffer holds this to be the only way of salvaging the transcendence of faith, by freeing it from all ties with the transcendental, with a relationship to the mind. We do not agree with some critics in seeing Bonhoeffer's transition from this earlier position to his later one as a "leap" of any sort; we find in this transition simply the desire for coherence and consistency driven to its inevitable conclusion, that extreme of theological Manicheanism which is the natural and inevitable issue of the Lutheran *cor curvum in se* and which forms the basis of the Adam-Christ antithesis in Bonhoeffer's radical theology. In the earlier Bonhoeffer position, however, the negative pull to the proclamation of what will be called the *Death-of-God Theology* as conclusion from these premises was inhibited by the importance of the Christological and ecclesiological element: Bonhoeffer defined man as "Being in" and understood this as "Being-in-Christ" or "Being-in-the-Church". This latter articulation comprised the following points: (a) the Church as the site of comprehension of Christian existence, (b) the mode of being of God's revelation, (c) the mode of being of man in the Church, and finally (d) the question of the knowledge of the Church. Thus, *Sein-in-der-Kirche* (Being-in-the-Church) is substituted for *Sein-in-der-Welt* or *Sein-in-der-Zeit;* and revelation is to be conceived only in relation to the notion of the Church, considered as constituted by the preaching of the death and resurrection of Christ in the community today, by the community and for the community. This community (*Gemeinde*) notion constitutes for Bonhoeffer the contingency trait proper to revelation. Fallen man's self-realization is here likewise effected, in typical Protestant fashion, as a strictly "personal" rather than an abstract and reflexive phenomenon, in terms of the relation to Christ in the community: [12] for the Person of Christ reveals himself to the community and in

[12] "This is why the Protestant idea of the Church is conceived in personal terms, *scil.* God reveals himself as a person in the Church. The Christian communion is God's final revelation: God as 'Christ existing as community', ordained for the rest of time until the end of the world and the return of Christ. It is here that Christ has come the very nearest to humanity, here given himself to his new humanity, so that his person enfolds in itself all whom he has won, binding itself in duty to them, and them reciprocally in duty to him." (*ibid.*, p. 91; English translation, p. 121). Revelation is no longer to be referred to a lone event of the past, it is rather a continuing reality, being accomplished in the life of man which is a communal existence. Existence is a sociological category and as such is personal; it is contradictory to seek from it a "there is" (*es gibt*) apart from the existent; it is dynamic. This holds for God Himself: "There is no God that 'there is'. God 'is' in the personal reference, and . . . being is his being a person" (p. 94; English translation, p. 126). This is the exact antithesis of the Kierkegaardian dialectic of the Absolute: "God does not think, He creates. God does not exist, He is eternal. Man thinks and exists and existence separates thoughts and being, forces them apart in succession" (*Afsluttende uvidenskabelig Efterskrift* [Copenhagen, 1925], *C. W.*, Vol. VIII, p. 321). A little earlier (pp. 317ff.), Kierkegaard has expressly denied that any sort of human thought can have continuity.

the community and thus man can attain the existential encounter with Christ only by way of the community.

The later Bonhoeffer, with his insistence on the principle of the "maturity of the world" (*Mündigkeit der Welt*), is the supreme expression of the most radical form of the attitudes that have formed the subject of our investigation throughout this volume. We must therefore consider them in meticulous detail to collate the final impassioned profession, not only of a single life but of an entire era.[13] The God-problem, as we have seen, is for Bonhoeffer inextricably linked to the problem of Christ and the Church and consequently to the problem of the goal and fate of history. We feel it more appropriate here to follow the internal rhythm of Bonhoeffer's own declarations, reflections and outpourings to that friend who was certainly a theologian and perhaps a collaborator of Bonhoeffer himself.

1. *Separation of Religion and Christianity. Denial of Religious A Priori:*

"They keep on telling me that I am 'radiating so much peace around me,' and that I am 'always so cheerful'. Very flattering, no doubt, but I'm afraid I don't always feel like that myself. You would be surprised and perhaps disturbed if you knew how my ideas on theology are taking shape. This is where I miss you most of all, for there is no one else who could help me so much to clarify my own mind. The thing that keeps coming back to me is, what *is* Christianity, and indeed what *is* Christ, for us to-day? The time when men could be told everything by means of words, whether theological or simply pious, is over, and so is the time of inwardness and conscience, which is to say the time of religion as such. We are proceeding towards a time of no religion at all: men as they are now simply cannot be religious any more. Even those who honestly describe themselves as 'religious' do not in the least act up to it, and so when they say 'religious' they evidently mean something quite different. Our whole nineteen-hundred-year-old Christian preaching and theology rests upon the 'religious premise' of man. What we call Christianity has always been a pattern—perhaps a true pattern—of religion. But if one day it becomes apparent that this *a priori* 'premise' simply does not exist, but was a historical and temporary form of human self-expression, i.e. if we reach the stage of being radically without religion—and I think this is more or less the case already, else how is it, for instance, that this war, unlike any of those before it, is not calling forth any 'religious' reaction?—what does that mean for 'Christianity'?

[13] In the *Letters and Papers from Prison,* especially the *Letters to a Friend* (pp. 40ff.), covering the period from November 18, 1943 to July 28, 1944.

"It means that the linchpin is removed from the whole structure of our Christianity to date, and the only people left for us to light on in the way of 'religion' are a few 'last survivals of the age of chivalry,' or else one or two who are intellectually dishonest." There follow a torrent of staccato questions relative to the fate of Christianity: "If we do not want to do this, if we had finally to put down the western pattern of Christianity as a mere preliminary stage to doing without religion altogether, what situation would result for us, for the Church? How can Christ become the Lord even for those with no religion? If religion is no more than the garment of Christianity—and even that garment has had very different aspects at different periods—then what is a religionless Christianity? [14] . . . The questions needing answers would surely be: What is the significance of a Church (church, parish, preaching, Christian life) in a religionless world? How do we speak of God without religion, i.e., without the temporally-influenced presuppositions of metaphysics, inwardness, and so on? How do we speak (but perhaps we are no longer capable of speaking of such things as we used to) in secular fashion of God? In what way are we in a religionless and secular sense Christians, in what way are we the ἐκ-κλησία, 'those who are called forth,' not conceiving of ourselves religiously as specially favoured, but as wholly belonging to the world? Then Christ is no longer an object of religion, but something quite different, indeed and in truth the Lord of the world. Yet what does that signify? What is the place of worship and prayer in an entire absence of religion? [15] Does the secret discipline, or, as the case may be, the distinction (which you have met with me before) between penultimate and ultimate, at this point acquire fresh importance?"

At this point, Bonhoeffer finds he has to break off the letter and promises his friend that he will resume the discussion very soon in a further letter. But before closing, he adds an illuminating observation on his bitter and exasperated refusal to accept "natural theology" and natural religion:

"The Pauline question whether circumcision is a condition of justification is to-day, I consider, the question whether religion is a condition

[14] Here Bonhoeffer makes a parenthetical criticism of K. Barth: "Barth, who is the only one to have started on this line of thought, has still not proceeded to its logical conclusion, but has arrived at a positivism of revelation which has nevertheless remained essentially a restoration. For the religionless working man, or indeed, man generally, nothing that makes any real difference is gained by that." (Letter of April 30, 1944, pp. 91f.).

[15] "Religionlessness" (*Religionslosigkeit*) is absolutely equivalent to atheism; yet I have not found the term "Atheism" (*Atheismus*) used even once in all these Letters, though Bonhoeffer does use the term *Atheismus* expressly in the *Ethics* as we shall be pointing out. The reader of the Letters would do well to keep the identity of meaning firmly in mind.

of salvation. Freedom from circumcision is at the same time freedom from religion.[16] I often ask myself why a Christian instinct frequently draws me more to the religionless than to the religious, by which I mean not with any intention of evangelizing them, but rather, I might almost say, in 'brotherhood.' While I often shrink with religious people from speaking of God by name—because that Name somehow seems to me here not to ring true, and I strike myself as rather dishonest (it is especially bad when others start talking in religious jargon: then I dry up almost completely and feel somehow oppressed and ill at ease) —with people who have no religion I am able on occasion to speak of God quite openly and as it were naturally. Religious people speak of God when human perception is (often just from laziness) at an end, or human resources fail: it is in fact always the *Deus ex machina* they call to their aid, either for the so-called solving of insoluble problems or as support in human failure—always, that is to say, helping out human weakness or on the borders of human existence. Of necessity, that can go on only until men can, by their own strength, push those borders a little further, so that God becomes superfluous as a *Deus ex machina.* I have come to be doubtful even about talking of 'borders of human existence'. Is even death to-day, since men are scarcely afraid of it any more, and sin, which they scarcely understand any more, still a genuine borderline? It always seems to me that in talking thus we are only seeking frantically to make room for God. I should like to speak of God not on the borders of life but as its centre, not in weakness but in strength, not, therefore, in man's suffering and death but in his life and prosperity. On the borders it seems to me better to hold our peace and leave the problem unsolved. Belief in the Resurrection is not the solution of the problem of death. The 'beyond' of God is not the beyond of our perceptive faculties. Epistemological theory has nothing to do with the transcendence of God. God is the 'beyond' in the midst of our life. The Church stands not where human powers give out, on the borders, but in the centre of the village. That is the way it is in the Old Testament, and in this sense we still read the New Testament far too little on the basis of the Old. The outward aspect of this religionless Christianity, the form it takes, is something to which I am giving much thought, and I shall be writing to you about it again soon." [17]

[16] It might be noted that St. Paul's own work and witness (cf. *Acts* 15: 1ff. and *Gal.* 2: 1ff.) were mainly instrumental in precipitating the decision of the Council of Jerusalem to the effect that Christ has freed us from the bonds of the Law, of which circumcision is a type.

[17] Letter of April 30, 1944 (*Widerstand und Ergebung,* pp. 178ff.; *Letters and Papers from Prison,* pp. 92f.).

2. *Opposition of Religion and Christianity:*

Bonhoeffer returns again to his central point in the wake of his reading of V. von Weizsäcker's *Weltbild der Physik,* a book which evidently made a great impression on him. It provided the stimulus for a specification of his "radical refusal" of any contact or collaboration of a positive sort between faith and reason in the style of a natural religion or a natural theology:

"It has brought home to me how wrong it is to use God as a stop-gap for the incompleteness of our knowledge. For the frontiers of knowledge are inevitably being pushed back further and further, which means that you only think of God as a stop-gap. He also is being pushed back further and further, and is in more or less continuous retreat. We should find God in what we do know, not in what we don't; not in outstanding problems, but in those we have already solved. This is true not only for the relations between Christianity jnd science, but also for wider human problems such as guilt, suffering and death. It is possible nowadays to find answers to these problems which leave God right out of the picture. It just isn't true to say that Christianity alone has the answers. In fact the Christian answers are no more conclusive or compelling than any of the others. Once more, God cannot be used as a stop-gap. We must not wait until we are at the end of our tether: he must be found at the centre of life: in life, and not only in death; in health and vigour, and not only in suffering; in activity, and not only in sin. The ground for this lies in the revelation of God in Christ. Christ is the centre of life, and in no sense did he come to answer our unsolved problems. From the centre of life certain questions are seen to be wholly irrelevant, and so are the answers commonly given to them—I am thinking for example of the judgment pronounced on the friends of Job. In Christ there are no Christian problems." [18]

The notion of a "religionless Christianity" (equivalent to atheism) is at the very heart of Bonhoeffer's preoccupations and it impels him to a speedy resumption of the same theme he had promised to pursue. In the Letter of May 5, 1944, he writes to his friend:

"A bit more about 'religionlessness.' I expect you remember Bultmann's paper on the demythologizing of the New Testament? My view of it to-day would not be that he went too far, as most people seem to think, but that he did not go far enough. It is not only the mythological conceptions, such as the miracles, the ascension and the like (which are

[18] Letter of May 25, 1944 (*Widerstand und Ergebung,* pp. 210f.; *Letters and Papers from Prison,* p. 103f.).

not in principle separable from the conceptions of God, faith and so on) that are problematic, but the 'religious' conceptions themselves. You cannot, as Bultmann imagines, separate God and miracles, but you do have to be able to interpret and proclaim *both* of them in a 'non-religious' sense. Bultmann's approach is really at bottom the liberal one (i.e. abridging the Gospel, whereas I see it theologically.[19]

"What do I mean by 'interpret in a religious sense'? In my view, that means to speak on the one hand metaphysically, and on the other individualistically. Neither of these is relevant to the Bible message or to the man of to-day. Is it not true to say that individualistic concern for personal savlation has almost completely left us all? Are we not really under the impression that there are more important things than bothering about such a matter? (Perhaps not more important than the matter itself, but more than bothering about it.) I know it sounds pretty monstrous to say that. But is it not, at bottom, even Biblical? Is there any concern in the Old Testament about saving one's soul at all? Is not righteousness and the kingdom of God on earth the focus of everything, and is not Romans 3, 14ff., too, the culmination of the view that in God alone is righteousness, and not in an individualistic doctrine of salvation? It is not with the next world that we are concerned, but with this world as created and preserved and set subject to laws and atoned for and made new. What is above the world is, in the Gospel, intended to exist for *this* world—I mean that not in the anthropocentric sense of liberal, pietistic, ethical theology, but in the Bible sense of the creation and of the incarnation, crucifixion, and resurrection of Jesus Christ."

And Bonhoeffer launches into another sharp critique of Barth: "Barth was the first theologian to begin the criticism of religion,—and that remains his really great merit—but he set in its place the positivist doctrine of revelation which says in effect, 'Take it or leave it': Virgin Birth, Trinity or anything else, everything which is an equally significant and necessary part of the whole, which latter has to be swallowed as a whole or not at all. That is not in accordance with the Bible. There are degrees of perception and degrees of significance, i.e., a secret discipline must be re-established whereby the *mysteries* of the Christian faith are preserved from profanation. The positivist doctrine of revelation makes it too easy for itself, setting up, as in the ultimate analysis it does, a law of faith, and mutilating what is, by the incarnation of Christ, a gift for us. The place of religion is taken by the Church—that is, in itself, as the Bible teaches it should be—but the world is made to depend upon itself and left to its own devices, and that is all wrong.

[19] Bonhoeffer returns later to this critique of Barth, Tillich and Bultmann in the Letter of June 8, 1944 (*Widerstand und Ergebung*, pp. 218ff.; *Letters and Papers from Prison*, pp. 106ff.), of which we shall be speaking directly.

"I am thinking over the problem at present how we may reinterpret in the manner 'of the world'—in the sense of the Old Testament and of John 1, xiv—the concepts of repentance, faith, justification, rebirth, sanctification and so on. I shall be writing to you again about that." [20] And in fact he does a few days later.

3. *New Theology for a New World!*

In the Letter of June 8, 1944, there is a spirited reference to the origin of the whole problematic with which Bonhoeffer is dealing in the development and evolution of Western culture and civilization:

"I will try to define my position from the historical angle. The movement beginning about the thirteenth century (I am not going to get involved in any arguments about the exact date) towards the autonomy of man (under which head I place the discovery of the laws by which the world lives and manages in science, social and political affairs, art, ethics and religion) has in our time reached a certain completion. Man has learned to cope with all questions of importance without recourse to God as a working hypothesis. In questions concerning science, art, and even ethics, this has become an understood thing which one scarcely dares to tilt at any more. But for the last hundred years or so it has been increasingly true of religious questions also: it is becoming evident that everything gets along without 'God' and just as well as before. As in the scientific field, so in human affairs generally, what we call 'god' is being more and more edged out of life, losing more and more ground." [21]

This is precisely the constitutive parameter of the "adulthood" of modern man (*die Mündigkeit der Welt*), which Protestant and Catholic theologians agree in designating as "the great defection from God" which the Christian apologetes are vainly if vigorously trying to stop. Bonhoeffer claims to have taken as his point of departure this *de facto* edging of God out of the world, now that that world has come of age: ever since Kant, says Bonhoeffer, God has been relegated to the realm beyond experience.[22] In his Letter of July 16, 1944, Bonhoeffer proceeds to a more detailed tracing of the historical line of development:

"On the historical side I should say there is *one* great development which leads to the idea of the autonomy of the world. In theology it is first discernible in Lord Herbert of Cherbury, with his assertion that

[20] Letter of May 5, 1944 (*Widerstand und Ergebung,* pp. 178ff.; *Letters and Papers from Prison,* p. 95).

[21] Letter of June 8, 1944 (*Widerstand und Ergebung,* pp. 215f.; *Letters and Papers from Prison,* pp. 106f.).

[22] Cf. Letter of June 30, 1944 (*Widerstand und Ergebung,* pp. 229f.; *Letters and Papers from Prison,* pp. 114f.).

reason is the sufficient instrument of religious knowledge. In ethics it first appears in Montaigne and Bodin with their substitution of moral principles for the ten commandments. In politics, Machiavelli, who emancipates politics from the tutelage of morality, and founds the doctrine of 'reasons of state'. Later, and very differently, though like Machiavelli tending towards the autonomy of human society, comes Grotius, with his international law as the law of nature, a law which would still be valid *etsi deus non daretur*. The process is completed in philosophy. On the one hand we have the deism of Descartes, who holds that the world is a mechanism which runs on its own without any intervention of God. On the other hand there is the pantheism of Spinoza, with its identification of God with nature. In the last resort Kant is a deist, Fichte and Hegel pantheists. All along the line there is a growing tendency to assert the autonomy of man and the world.

"In natural science, the process seems to start with Nicolas of Cusa and Giordano Bruno with their 'heretical' doctrine of the infinity of space. The classical cosmos was finite, like the created world of the Middle Ages. An infinite universe, however it be conceived, is self-subsisting *etsi deus non daretur*. It is true that modern physics is not so sure as it was about the infinity of the universe, but it has not returned to the earlier conceptions of its finitude.[23]

"There is no longer any need for God as a working hypothesis, whether in morals, politics or science. Nor is there any need for such a God in religion or philosophy (Feuerbach). In the name of intellectual honesty these working hypotheses should be dropped or dispensed with as far as possible." [24]

We are now in a position to sum up the stages of the way to God and salvation in Christ as those stages are seen and articulated by this theologian of such imposing stature who has produced such a profound shock in modern theology, provoking spirited reactions of traditionalist assertiveness and steering other theologians toward the still somewhat misty paths of Death-of-God Theology:

(a) There is an acceptance of the irreversibility of the situation of modern man in all fields of life and thought. This amounts substantially to a recognition of the "adulthood" attained by man in our modern age by means of a total emancipation from the "holy" by the instrumentality of philosophy combined with technological and scientific progress. In the context of this new maturity of religionless man, "God" as working hypothesis, as stop-gap, has become superfluous. Thus all areas of

[23] Bonhoeffer seems to be unaware of the classical position of P. Bayle on this point, which we have expounded and commented at length above.

[24] Letter of July 16, 1944 (*Widerstand und Ergebung*, pp. 239f.; *Letters and Papers from Prison*, pp. 120f.).

human thought are restored to full autonomy and there is proclaimed an all-out resumption of a "revelation theology" (*Offenbarungstheologie*), directed rather to the "fact" (*Sache*) of the Church than to personal faith in Christ. Here we have total immanence of God in the world and in history.[25]

(b) The worldliness-God nexus thus becomes central and crucial: religionlessness is constitutive and insuperable in our world today. This makes for a tragic Christianity, epitomized in the desertion of Christ by the disciples (Mt. 26,40) and his abandonment even by the Father on the Cross (Mk. 15, 34). This is *metanoia;* the religious man is called to suffer with God, to suffer God's sufferings in a Godless world. Bonhoeffer declares impressively: "He must therefore plunge himself into the life of a godless world, without attempting to gloss over its ungodliness with a veneer of religion or trying to transfigure it. He must live a 'Worldly' life and so participate in the suffering of God. . . . It is not some religious act which makes a Christian what he is, but participation in the suffering of God in the life of the world." [26] So did Christ himself act and so his disciples and apostles: the single element common to all is a participating in the suffering of God in Christ. This is their "faith" and it is also the only biblical meaning of "conversion" (*Umkehrung*). Thus we have total immanence of Christ in the world and in history.

(c) Deriving from all this, we have the elimination of any need for transcendence and of every sort of moral and religious supernaturalism. It is this principle that is the very basis of the Death-of-God Theology: "Unlike the other oriental religions the faith of the Old Testament is not a religion of salvation. Christianity, it is true, has always been regarded as a religion of salvation. But isn't this a cardinal error, which divorces Christ from the Old Testament and interprets him in the light of the myths of salvation?" [27] Man must become totally dedicated to this worldliness and Bonhoeffer explains what he means by worldliness: ". . . taking life in one's stride, with all its duties and problems, its successes and failures, its experiences and helplessness. It is in such a life that we throw ourselves utterly into the arms of God and participate in his sufferings in the world and watch with Christ in Gethsemane. That is

[25] Bonhoeffer has left us the bare outline for a book he would have liked to write (cf. *Widerstand und Ergebung,* pp. 257ff.; *Letters and Papers from Prison,* pp. 163ff.). He intended to limit the work to not more than 100 pages and have three chapters: 1. A Stocktaking of Christianity. 2. The Real Meaning of the Christian Faith. 3. Conclusions. The tightly packed and stimulating outline he has left us sums up in two pages the whole gamut of the themes treated by his Letters.

[26] Letter of July 18, 1944 (*Widerstand und Ergebung,* p. 244; *Letters and Papers from Prison,* pp. 122f.).

[27] Letter of June 27, 1944 (*Widerstand und Ergebung,* pp. 225; *Letters and Papers from Prison,* pp. 111ff.).

faith, that is *metanoia,* and that is what makes a man and a Christian."[28] And so, finally, we have total immanence of the Christian in the world and in history.

Bonhoeffer's stand may indeed have some points of contact with "dialectical theology" and indeed Bonhoeffer himself admits this to be the case. Yet, Bonhoeffer's is a new and suggestive effort to arrive at a "radical theology" by carrying the Lutheran principle of *sola fides* to its absolute extreme. This may explain Bonhoeffer's fundamental attitude, his designation of our present-day world as the age of man's adulthood pure and simple, a designation that might have come from any Marxist or existentialist atheist. Bonhoeffer grants that modern science has led to the elimination of God from all fields of the knowable, thereby jettisoning all theological aspects of the various classical and Enlightenment "theodicies" and gouging a deep gulf between science and religion.[29]

Furthermore, Bonhoeffer is persuaded (undoubtedly under the influence of his own philosophical and theologian training) that the only issue of modern philosophy is atheism. This shows that for Bonhoeffer philosophy begins with Descartes and that the earlier philosophical systems which appealed to and culminated in a notion of transcendence constitute quite simply an already outmoded historical phenomenon. We have already said that we entirely agree that the *cogito-volo* principle inevitably pushes its champions into atheism and even nihilism; but this is not "adulthood", this is not maturity but rather radical disintegration of the human mind, which must return to Parmenidean Being as

[28] Cf. Letter of July 21, 1944 (*Widerstand und Ergebung,* pp. 247f.; *Letters and Papers from Prison,* pp. 124f.). In this letter, Bonhoeffer writes of the genesis of his impulse to treat those themes that occupied and dominated his last years: "I remember talking to a young French pastor at A. thirteen years ago. We were discussing what our real purpose was in life. He said he would like to become a saint. I think it is quite likely he did become one. At the time I was very much impressed, though I disagreed with him, and said I should prefer to have faith, or words to that effect. For a long time I did not realise how far we were apart. I thought I could acquire faith by trying to live a holy life, or something like it. It was in this phase that I wrote *The Cost of Discipleship.* To-day I can see the dangers of this book, though I am prepared to stand by what I wrote." This book, published in 1937, can be considered as preliminary to the major (uncompleted) work, the *Ethik.*

[29] "A scientist or physician who seeks to provide edification is a hybrid" (Letter of July 16, 1944: *Widerstand und Ergebung,* pp. 240f.; *Letters and Papers from Prison,* p. 121). On the Enlightenment "theodicies" based on purposiveness in nature, cf. W. Philipp, *Das Werden der Aufklärung in theologiegeschichtlicher Sicht* (Göttingen, 1957). There is lacking in Bonhoeffer that distinction, of which we shall be speaking in the next Chapter, between the specific scope and commitment of science which confines the scientist within the ambit of the laws of phenomena, an ambit to which the God-problem is definitely foreign, and the *scientist himself,* as an integral human person seeking the meaning and foundation of the Universe and the issue of his own destiny.

"ground" if it wants to save itself, not only in the realm of nature but in the realm of faith as well!

Finally and consequently the equivocation inherent in the very notion of "adult world or man" as applied to the modern world of our day in its atheistic disintegration is a product of the convergence of the theological immanentism of the Lutheran principle and the philosophical immanentism of the modern *cogito* principle. May we not see here the revenge of reason for the banishment of philosophy effected by Luther, pietism and the like? For when reason is exiled where can faith be sheltered?

How can anyone imagine that the historical issue of Christianity implies a complete rout of man's rational faculties and that the acceptance of such a state of affairs makes us real "modern Christians"? [30]

Other phenomenologists of the modern religious mind, e.g., Kierkegaard (to whom Bonhoeffer has several vague references) have had a totally different understanding of what is needed in the modern day: they have come out in favor of a downright assertion of transcendence and of theological supernaturalism: indeed Kierkegaard even rejects any notions of imitation and thus of the Church as seeming to overshadow and supplant the direct responsibility of the "individual" (as Bonhoeffer's "Church" certainly does!).

Bonhoeffer's radical denial can be taken as symptomatic of the radical passion for Lutheran consistency: apart from any consideration of theological methodology, the conclusions of a Bonhoeffer serves to confirm our previous judgment on dialectical theology. And this judgment holds good likewise for the whole of Protestant theology which takes seriously, as Bonhoeffer wishes it to do, the problem of salvation. This whole theology has declared itself incapable and even unwilling to face the phenomenon of worldwide defection from God; it has capitulated before atheism and disbelief.

Bonhoeffer was not spared to put the last finishing touches to his thought and he himself confesses that it is less than perfectly polished.[31] But he expresses the hope that it may render a good service to the Church's future. Now it can certainly be said that this form of theological extermism can and should lead to a revision of the foundations of religion and of Christianity on the part of Protestants and Catholics

[30] Bonhoeffer is certainly right in criticizing (especially in Letter of June 8, 1944: *Widerstand und Ergebung,* pp. 218ff.; *Letters and Papers from Prison,* pp. 106ff.) the rationalist equivocation of liberal theology (Troeltsch, Harnack and the like) and in denouncing the positivistic and pietistic dross in Althaus, Barth, Tillich, Bultmann and the like. The only point is that such a critique should have led its author to change course completely, swerving round at a 180° angle from Luther, as Kierkegaard well sees.

[31] "All this is very crude and sketchy" (*Widerstand und Ergebung,* p. 262; *Letters and Papers from Prison,* p. 166).

alike. But Bonhoeffer is as dubious a guide as he is a salutary gadfly. A man who denies all natural religion and asserts that Christ does not call man to a new religion but to a new life, as though religion were not the ground of our life "before God"—such a man is plunging the mind into a void. St. Thomas admitted at once the natural aspiration of man to God and thc validity of the *praeambula fidei*.[32] He did not hesitate to proclaim, in terms of his original and unique concept of *esse,* the immanence of God in the world; indeed he proclaimed it with a power and intensity surpassing any demand advanced by those theological or philosophical subjectivisms in which modern theology and philosophy have allowed themselves to be ensnared. In the context of this sort of immanence, God's transcendence no longer has the meaning which Bonhoeffer so roundly condemned. God is no longer "on the borders" as Bonhoeffer so rightly feared to see him located; rather is he closer to things than the things to themselves and closer to the soul than the soul to itself, first through creation and then through grace. Immanence and transcendence are like concave and convex, mutually grounded, mutually grounding. This is indeed subjectivism but it is a metaphysical subjectivism in the sense of a primordial and constitutive realization of freedom causing man to emerge upon the world.

Bonhoeffer could go on to write: "Just one more point for today. When we speak of God in a non-religious way, we must not gloss over the ungodliness of the world, but expose it in a new light. Now that it has come of age, the world is more godless, and perhaps it is for that very reason nearer to God than ever before."[33] But surely to call a world "come of age" simply because it has emancipated itself from God all along the line amounts to a renunciation of any effort to diagnose error and of all hope of producing a cure; surely in fact it amounts to an approving acceptance of the victory of the Beast and the universal apostasy of which Gospel and Apocalypse speak.[34] Surely the Bonhoeffer attitude amounts quite bluntly to throwing in the sponge.

It is no surprise then that Bonhoeffer, who in his earlier writings was more admired for his ecumenical interests, should have provoked in his

[32] St. Thomas speaks of the "natural inclination of man to know the truth about God" (*S.T.*, I-II, q. 94, a. 2). but this doctrine is based on the "image of God in man" which Catholic theology holds to have been defiled by sin, *but not destroyed* as Protestantism or at least Lutheranism maintains: "Man has a natural aptitude for knowing and loving God; and this aptitude lies in the very nature of the mind which is common to all men" (*S.T.*, I, q. 93, a. 4).

[33] Letter of July 18, 1944 (*Widerstand und Ergebung*, p. 246; *Letters and Papers from Prison,* p. 124). On God's immanence in the world, according to St. Thomas, cf. *S.T.*, I, q. 8, aa. 1-4; *ibid.*, q. 105, a. 5 (cf. also C. Fabro, *Participation et causalité* [Paris-Louvain, 1960], pp. 509ff.).

[34] *Luke* 18: 8; *Apoc.* 13: 1ff.

later writings a storm of "renewal" in theology as such. This storm is still blowing hard and it will suffice for our present purpose to limit ourselves to a few remarks on the issue of the God-problem. The strictly theological problems, especially those of the relation between God and Christ, Christ and the believer, faith and history, and the like, presently being debated by the Death-of-God Theology, quite transcend the scope of our present investigation which has been devoted to a strictly philosophical examination of the loping shadow of the denial of God as that shadow blots out more and more of the horizon of our age. If we would "live before God" we must never tire of seeking and finding him with all the resources of our intellect, of our mind and our will, at every moment of our life, for it is true indeed, as Bonhoeffer says, that God is in this world, that he is in all things and in the powers behind each and every happening. To this research we are impelled, in ascendant order, by the collaborating drives of the religious instinct innate in the soul of man, of reason and of religion; and this, prior to any historical revelation. This is the Catholic contention and especially the stand of St. Thomas, a stand which here again is expressive of the most adequate and complete interpretation of man when it is understood properly in terms of the profound semantic of analogy, equidistant from irrationalist fideism and anthropocentric atheistic immanentism. In this sense, a modern theologian who has not lost courage has been able to point to St. Thomas as a corrective of this new theology of bewilderment: "The being of the creature is referred in St. Thomas to its essence in such a way that the simple existence of such a creature stands out as a sheer chance, explicable only in terms of a gift of the Creator. Essentialist philosophy had to break up and Hegel to develop a new ampler and better-grounded sort of essentialism before human existence could be again represented in its inessential fortuitousness. In this sense, St. Thomas too can be considered (in his controversy with Averroes) among the forerunners of Sören Kierkegaard, the liquidator of Hegel." [35]

Bonhoeffer, on the other hand, exacerbates the tension of "dialectical theology" and pushes to the extreme the inverted Averroism implicit in it: on the one hand, the activity of reason extolling man's sufficiency in all fields and proclaiming the superfluity and indeed the uselessness of God as a working hypothesis; on the other hand, the absolute act of faith, positing God in this world, as present in history. This is to speak at once with the voice of radical atheism and radical fideism. And even Averroism never went that far, not even in its most drastic form, as

[35] E. Haible, *Schöpfung und Heil,* Ein Vergleich zwischen Bultmann, Barth und Thomas (Mainz, 1964), pp. 128f. The influence of Feuerbach himself on the Death-of-God theology has been highlighted by a theologian of that school (cf. K. Hamilton, *Revolt against Heaven,* p. 30, note 8).

taken up again in modern thought, e.g., from Descartes to idealism. Is not a denial of reason in the order of nature equivalent to a compulsion of reason in the area of philosophy and science to "bury God" as Nietzsche so poignantly put it? Is not a denial of grace equivalent to an incarceration of the Christian in a world that has "won" the struggle with God without being able to institute any other relationship with God than that of an impotent plunge before the eyes of the equally impotent God into the yawning gulf of final atheism and universal apostasy? What possible meaning can here attach to the world and God, man and the Christian mysteries, when everything is plunged in the *mysterium iniquitatis?*

Bonhoeffer admits no compromise: "And the only way to be honest is to recognize that we have to live in the world *etsi deus non daretur.* And this is just what we do see—before God! So our coming of age forces us to a true recognition of our situation *vis à vis* God. God is teaching us that we must live as men who can get along very well without him. The God who is with us is the God who forsakes us (Mk. 15, 34). The God who makes us live in this world without using him as a working hypothesis is the God before whom we are ever standing. Before God and with him, we live without God. God allows himself to be edged out of the world and on to the cross. God is weak and powerless in the world, and that is exactly the way, the only way, in which he can be with us and help us.[36]

"Matthew 8,17 makes it crystal clear that it is not by his omnipotence that Christ helps us, but by his weakness and suffering." [37] And herein, maintains Bonhoeffer, lies the difference between biblical Christianity and all other religions: these latter exalt God's omnipotence as man's surest aid, whereas the bible shows man God's powerlessness and suffering, shows man, too, that only such a powerless suffering God can help him.

Professional theological training is not required in order to be able to sense the screaming dissonance of this theology of defeatism which claims to relink the New Testament to the Old but in fact eliminates revelation by proclaiming the world victorious and Christ the dupe, irremediably defeated. To these ravings of a theology lethally infected by the German dialectic of negativity, Christ himself replies in the Gospel: "Be of good cheer; I have overcome the world!" (Jn. 16, 33).

[36] This may well have suggested to Robinson the title for his *Honest to God.*

[37] This absolutely crucial passage, revelatory of the pith of Bonhoeffer's thought is to be found in Letter of July 16, 1944 (*Widerstand und Ergebung,* pp. 241f.; *Letters and Papers from Prison,* p. 121f.). This thought is reiterated in the short poem with the significant title "Christians and Unbelievers" (*Christen und Heiden*) (*ibid.,* pp. 246f.; *Letters and Papers from Prison,* p. 174).

And the Christian can likewise overcome the world in the power of Christ, each one of us can! Kierkegaard likewise highlights the "straight and narrow" path of the Gospel, but he grounds his articulation on the triumphant Christ. He invites us to collate the various aspects of Christianity in the "straight and narrow path" of existence oriented to the halo of glory of that Ascension and final triumph which this defeatist theology relegates to the illusory penumbra of myth:

"And so on this Ascension Day we must above all remember that the way is a straight and narrow one; we must remember it, on pain of not comprehending the Ascension. Remember: the way was straight and narrow right to the end, right to the moment of death, which was the intermediate moment; and then followed the Ascension. It was not midnight when he went up to heaven; but neither was it at the end of the end of the road, for the road ended on the cross and in the tomb. The Ascension is not a continuation of the life that was, that is true! And a straight and narrow road, which even in this life becomes ever easier to tread, never leads up on high, not even when it reaches its supreme goal, victory: it never rises to such a height as to become an Ascension into heaven. But every man really on the right road, every man who has not taken a wrong road, is truly on that 'straight and narrow' path.

"So must we indeed speak of the Ascension into heaven and of the fact that Christ is the way to attain to it . . . Christ ascended into heaven: no victor has ever triumphed so! 'A cloud hid him from their sight'. No victor has ever been so taken up from the earth. 'They saw him no more'. No triumph has ever had such an epilogue. 'He sits at the right hand of the majesty on high.' So the triumph does not end with the Ascension? No, it only begins there: no one has ever had such a triumph. 'He shall come again with legions of angels'. So the triumph does not end with the sitting at the right hand of the Almighty Father? No, that was but the end of the beginning. Eternal Victor!" [38]

[38] S. Kierkegaard, *Til Selvprövelse,* 1851, No. II; *C. W.,* Vol. XII, pp. 402f.

5

Toward an "Atheistic Theology" (John A. T. Robinson)

In an essay in theological criticism examining all the dogmas of Christianity and, more basically, the basic question of faith as such, the Anglican bishop and theologian John A. T. Robinson has drawn the logical consequences of the positions of Bultmann and more especially Tillich on man's stance before God and particularly on the meaning Christian dogmatic and moral truths can have for modern man.[1]

Robinson's own stance is not at all easy to detect or detach amid the often exaggerated and bewildering play of paradox and the professedly reportorial technique of the essay. Nor is the situation helped any by the obvious parallels between the theological climate to which he refers and which he is analysing and the climate and attitudes prevalent a century ago when the Hegelian Left, especially Bauer, Feuerbach and Strauss, were aiming at nothing less than a total demolition of Christianity and religion generally.[2] Robinson's approach might perhaps be called radical theological historicism or, were the term not too vague and generic, even theological existentialism.

Robinson speaks explicitly of a "Copernican revolution" in the field of theology, involving the shaking of the twin foundations of traditional piety and theology, the *transcendence* of God and the *supernatural status* of the Christian mysteries, by modern theological and historical criticism. The second chapter is entitled: "The End of Theism?" and the

[1] J. A. T. Robinson, *Honest to God* (Philadelphia: The Westminster Press, 1963). Robinson seems to have been most profoundly struck by the thought of Lutheran Bonhoeffer and his notion of "religionless Christianity" (cf. especially pp. 36ff.). Nor does Robinson make any secret of his unreserved adherence to the evolutionist theories of the materialist Julian Huxley (p. 127), although Robinson does indeed express some reservations about Huxley's atheism.

[2] Cf. the section "Man and God" in *Honest to God,* pp. 50ff. for an explicit Tillichian appeal to Feuerbach in an argument with K. Barth and the substitution of existential anthropology for theology.

question mark might very well have been omitted: for the entire chapter amounts to a call for the abandonment of all hope of a return to or revival of the old view of reality with God at the summit as absolute and free Creator. God is conceived in frankly pantheistic terms [3] as that "ultimate reality" concerning whose existence there can be no discussion, but only concerning whose nature it can be debated whether this is best described in personal or impersonal terms. No longer can it be maintained that the notion of transcendental First Cause is a valid concept of God; the only really valid one, claims Robinson, is the Tillichian notion of God as the "ground of our being"

The chief error of the traditional metaphysical and theological conception of God has been the notion of *transcendence* and the consequent *supranaturalism* inseparable from such a notion. The mistake has been to conceive of God as somehow "outside" the world, as "out there" or "up there" in some Beyond all his own. Such a God, who is conceived as having created the world and then retired beyond it, to intervene only when he feels he must or wants to—this God Robinson holds to be not the true God but an idol. Thus the notion of God as a "Person" is a remnant of the old-style metaphysics which must be abandoned: theology must at long last be "secularized" and God built into the very fabric of our everyday lives, so that every theological statement will be existential. God must no longer be conceived as a "super-Being" beyond this world of ours nor must he endowed with personal qualities. Rather he must be conceived as being the immanent Author of this world, immanent in that world and in ourselves, able to be engaged in dialogue as the infinite subsistent Thou.

Robinson hopes to push man's thinking about God beyond theism and atheism alike; and his vision culminates in an ever deeper and more intimate immersion in the knowledge of God as love: "To believe in God as love means to believe that in pure personal relationship we encounter, not merely what ought to be, but what is, the deepest, veriest truth about the structure of reality." [4] And this, he specifies, is not an act

[3] The *Deus sive natura* of Scotus Eriugena and Spinoza is in fact invoked in forthright fashion, with an appeal to the authority of Tillich.

The evolutionist J. Huxley, cited by Robinson, has given him the logical answer on this point: Any assertion to the effect that God is the ultimate reality is ". . . nothing but a play on words and so vague in content as to be meaningless in the last analysis . . . The God-hypothesis is no longer scientifically sustainable; it has lost its explanatory value and become an obstacle for our thinking. No longer does it convince or console and the decision to abandon it is often productive of a feeling of great relief" (J. Huxley, "Der Gott des Dr. Robinson," in Club Voltaire, I [Munich, 1964], p. 42).

[4] J. A. T. Robinson, *Honest to God,* p. 49.

of cognition nor the result of the so-called "proofs" of the existence of God; rather it is "a tremendous act of faith." Belief in God is, for Robinson, equivalent to trust; and this trust is a well-nigh incredible self-abandonment to the uttermost in love, in the persuasion that such abandonment will result not in our being confounded but rather in our being "accepted" by that Love which is the ground of our being, to which ultimately "we 'come home' ".

This destructive revolution in the field of metaphysics and theology is paralleled in Robinson by an equally radical revolution in the field of ethics. This latter revolution involves the overt proclamation of "the New Morality". Its preamble is a "non-religious" interpretation of prayer as traditionally understood. This reinterpretation amounts to a critique so stringent as to be a denial.[5] Prayer is no longer a turning to God but to one's neighbor, to every man, in whom God and Christ are really present: it is to see one's personal concern for that neighbor in terms of *ultimate* concern, to introduce God into the relationship, realizing that our own relationship to God must pass by way of our neighbor, just as our relationship to that neighbor must pass by way of God Who is the eternal *Thou* and substantial *Love,* and thus the ground of every personal relationship. Morality in this context will no longer be based on absolute laws and positive sanctions promulgated by some sort of subsistent righteousness. Robinson frankly admits that this law-based ethic is the exact equivalent of the supranaturalist conception of God and is expressed in the commandments given to Moses by God upon Sinai. The most typical example of this type of morality is, for Robinson, the *corpus* of Catholic moral theology, which he admits "is magnificent in its monolithic consistency". He adds that this mentality pervades the Protestant Church as well, albeit in "more muddled form".

What, then, is the deepest pervading spirit of what Robinson himself calls *theological radicalism?* It is primarily, from the theological point of view, a reduction of the specific demands of the Christian truths, of Christianity as a revealed historical supernatural religion, to the level of natural religion or religious feeling, and of natural religion to the neutral level of potentiality, of suspension, of risk, of choice, as purveyed by

[5] A much better qualified Protestant theologian expressed himself quite differently on this whole point a few years ago: "There is no religion in which prayer does not constitute an essential part of piety and there is no piety conceivable apart from prayer. Consequently it would be expected that this importance of prayer would find expression in theology as well. And in fact it does . . . If prayer is the veritable vital nerve of all religion, then the theological understanding and articulation of religion must likewise bring out the position of prayer at the very center of religion. All theology must begin by an interpretation of prayer" (C. Stange, *Die Bedeutung des Gebetes für die Gotteserkenntnis,* Studien des apologetischen Seminars, Heft 37 [Gütersloh, 1933], p. 5).

modern philosophy.[6] We are forced to this judgment by Robinson's unremitting insistence on theology's abandoning those notions which modern man no longer finds intelligible and by his equally unremitting insistence that the mere fact that modern man finds these notions unintelligible constitutes, of itself, a sufficient reason for abandoning them! There is not a single reference, in this Christian bishop and theologian, to the obligation or at least the possibility of a critique of the modern principle of immanentism which, in combination with the Protestant principle of inwardness, has logically eliminated the very foundations of any theology, either as a development of a dogmatic tradition founded on the Bible or as an integration of man's natural knowledge of God. God is not an object of knowledge but only of vital contact.

Robinson's dilemma comes out clearly in his remarks on the sanctions of the moral law. "There can be no doubt about Christian standards . . . In any change they are unchangeable: the only question is whether men live up to them . . . But equally obviously it is a position that men honour much more in the breach than the observance. The sanctions of Sinai have lost their terrors, and people no longer accept the authority of Jesus even as a great moral teacher. Robbed of its supranatural supports, men find it difficult to take seriously a code of living that confessedly depended on them."[7] Very shortly thereafter, Robinson overtly announces the end of the *homo religiosus,* asserting that the Christian ethic ought to hold good for all men universally, even for the atheist. The problem with this stand in the Robinson context is simply that Robinson himself has already rejected (together with Bultmann and Tillich, not to speak of Bonhoeffer!) any metaphysical notion of man!

We have here, then, the indisputably interesting result of the convergence of the Protestant denial of the foundation of authority and of the modern empirical principle, two forms of immanentism, engendering two negations and merging in the affirmation of man as being "let be" in that history that he himself is building and structuring from moment to moment, in function of the forces in play in each succeeding era, within the ambit of a sort of transcendental faith or trust. It is this transcendental trust that is supposed to function as the common platform for all possible forms of human activity of believers and atheists alike. Thus

[6] Robinson feels it is important, from the theological point of view, to heighten still more the effective abandonment (or so it would seem) of the ecclesiological establishment and consequently of a living teaching authority in the Church. In this connection, Robinson takes up G. Downing's phrase about "transformer stations" (cf. J. A. T. Robinson & David L. Edwards, *The Honest to God Debate* [London: SCM Press Ltd., 1963], p. 236).

[7] J. A. T. Robinson, *Honest to God,* p. 109.

not only philosophy but even theology, at least a great part of modern Protestant theology, has deserted God and created "the desert of God" in the mind of man, preparatory to a desertion of Christ, by a diminution to the point of annihilation of there redemptive meaning of His presence in history. This sacred history which the Christian tradition had conceived as an extention of the Gospel message, as the presence of the eternal in time, as salvation history (*Heilsgeschichte*); these facts and events of the Life of Christ from the Nativity to the Crucifixion and Resurrection, that used to be held to constitute the *καιρός* of salvation from sin and the promise of our own resurrection; these promises of redemption from sin, incorporation into Christ by grace and pledges of life eternal beyond the limits of time and the narrows of our present anguished existence—all these have been relegated to the penumbra of mere allegories and myths. Such is the issue of modern "philosophy of the spirit": man is drowned in time, freedom in history and existents in the featureless ocean of temporalized being!

Here we have a theology (if it can, indeed, be at all properly called theology) tethered entirely to a negativist philosophy which is itself in constant flux on the crest of the river of history. Here we have a being characterized as a "depth at the center of life" but proving actually to be rather the metaphysical void engulfing the finite realities that are existents and swallowing up their aspirations; a terminal Nothingness antipodal to Being and replacing the primordial Nothingness out of which God drew beings to ground them in Being.

Just as the discipline of philosophy purges itself in the immanentist philosophical school of all nexus with transcendence by referring being to mind and thereafter rushes irresistibly to its issue in the positive atheism represented by radical humanism, so too, as another echo of the same drama of ungrounded freedom, the Christian discipline is purged by the principle of the subjectivity of faith in modern Protestant theology of all nexus with the mystery of the Incarnation of "God in time" (Kierkegaard) and thereafter rushes equally irresistibly to its issue in the strange incarceration of man in a freedom rendered meaningless by the mortal destiny of sin as a necessary and insuperable event of cosmic proportions. Neither purgation has been salutary, for both the philosophical rejection of transcendence and the theological plunge into the radical historicism of demythologization have left man eviscerated rather than cleansed. A transcendence-free philosophy has now been joined by a revelation-free theology, a discipline without truth has been joined by a discipline without hope; man is derelict on the great wave of the world!

Appendices

I. Kierkegaard and Dialectical Theology[1]

The relations of the 19th-century Christian Socrates with modern theology are no less ambiguous than his relation to modern existentialism. We have already seen that the contact between the official existentialist philosophies and Kierkegaard's stringent dialectic of faith (as proclaimed especially in his monumental *Postscript* and his culminating works, notably *The Sickness unto Death* and *The Practice of Christianity*), were little more than accidental and served only to goad these philosophers to "go back to the old" as Kierkegaard himself would have put it, i.e., to the voluntarism of modern immanentism. Jaspers, who considers Kierkegaard (together with Jesus and Nietzsche!) a psychopath, goes back to Kant's rational faith, Heidegger goes back to the domineering freedom of Hölderlin and Nietzsche, Sartre to the absolute freedom of Descartes, Marcel—who derives from the later pallid Schelling and never evinced any interest in Kierkegaard—loses himself in the labyrinth of a faith which he touts as being an immediate experience of the Transcendent!

About the same thing can be said about modern theology taking its inspiration from existentialism as dialectical theology does or at least claims to do: it sees the element of "clean break" in the Danish thinker, hushing up his critique of the negativity of modern thought in the wake of Hegel. Thus, Barth undoubtedly and expressly aligns himself with Kierkegaard in his *Römerbrief,* but equally clearly breaks with Kierkegaard in his *Church Dogmatics,* because Kierkegaardian theology seems to him (and with good reason!) to be tending toward Catholicism; and when Barth comes to write his *Die protestantische Theologie im 19. Jahrhundert* (1947), he accepts Lessing and Feuerbach while taking no notice whatsoever of Kierkegaard. Tillich too sees Kierkegaard in the context of Feuerbach, Marx and Nietzsche; he is more sympathetic to

[1] Thomas J. J. Altizer, "Theology and the Death of God," in Altizer and Hamilton, *Radical Theology and the Death of God,* pp. 95ff. These appendices are intended primarily as expository and informational; they do not aim at a detailed and exhaustive treatment of the Death-of-God theology, which transcends the scope of our investigations in this volume, devoted exclusively to the strictly philosophical aspect of atheism.

Kierkegaard than is Barth but he boggles at the Evangelical radicalism of Kierkegaard's critique of modern thought or Protestantism (Cf. J. L. Adams' essay, "Tillich's Concept of the Protestant Era," in an appendix to Tillich's *The Protestant Era* [Chicago, 1948], pp. 273ff.). As for Bultmann, as far as I can see, he pays virtually no attention to Kierkegaard.

Notwithstanding all this, Altizer asserts that modern theology was founded by Sören Kierkegaard; and founded not only in response to the collapse of Christianity, but more deeply in response to the advent of a reality wholly divorced from the world of faith. And Altizer refers directly to *The Sickness unto Death,* as condemning modern philosophy as outright paganism, and to the *Postscript,* as highlighting the tension of objectivity and subjectivity in faith as a dialectic. The crucial point, Altizer maintains, is that Kierkegaard could identify authentic human existence with existence in faith. And Altizer proceeds thus: "Kierkegaard knew the death of God only as an objective reality; indeed it was 'objectivity' that was created by the death of God. Accordingly faith is made possible by the negation of objectivity, and since 'objectivity' and 'subjectivity' are antithetical categories, it follows that faith can be identified with 'subjectivity'. Today we can see that Kierkegaard could dialectically limit 'objectivity' and 'subjectivity' to the level of antithetical categories because he still lived in an historical time when subjectivity could be known as indubitably Christian. Less than a hundred years later, it will be little less than blasphemy to identify the truly 'existential' with existence in faith. But in Kierkegaard's time the death of God had not yet become a subjective reality. Hence authentic human existence could be understood as culminating in faith, the movement of faith could be limited to the negation of 'objectivity', and no occasion need arise for the necessity of a dialectical coincidence of the opposites." (*Radical Theology and the Death of God,* pp. 97f.).

Kierkegaard does indeed stand at the antipodes of the latest Protestant theologizing of the Altizer sort, the theology that desists from any critique of modern atheism and indeed claims to start from it. But the reason is a matter of principle in Kierkegaard which the new theologians of defeatism persistently ignore though it is central to the whole of the Kierkegaardian dialectic. It is Kierkegaard's firm stand against the pseudo-subjectivity of the modern *cogito* principle from Descartes to Hegel and against the extrinsicism of reformation and especially Lutheran religious piety and practice.[2] Kierkegaard does indeed often assert (as Altizer claims) that "the Christianity of the New Testament no

[2] Moreover, Altizer himself considers the writings of Blake, Hegel and Nietzsche and of course Tillich (whose disciple Altizer considers himself to be, although he thinks of himself as still more radical than Tillich [Thomas J. J. Altizer, *The Gospel of Christian Atheism* (Philadelphia: Westminster Press, 1966), especially p. 10]) to be precursors and heralds of the Death-of-God theology.

longer exists" but he goes on to reaffirm forthwith not the "death" but the "majesty" of God who demands of every Christian the imitation of Christ and missionary zeal and endeavor. And Kierkegaard does categorically reject the "death of God" and he refutes the negative conclusions of Hegel and Feuerbach; and this not only from theological motives and because of his own deep religious aspiration, but primarily because of the inconsistency of the radical doubt that serves as the basis of modern thought.

Kierkegaard does indeed (as Altizer notes) operate within the framework of Hegelian terminology; but he does this precisely in order the better to strike out more directly at the error of Hegel [3] and to reiterate Greco-Christian realism: this in fact enables Kierkegaard to set the Absolute again truly in the center of reality and to re-establish the decisive status of freedom as absolute choice of the Absolute. Modern philosophies, on the other hand, almost all (neo-positivism, philosophy of language and analytic philosophy alike) circle in a veritable Hegelian orbit; they are not critics operating with the terminology of the man they criticize, but satellites forever tied to Hegel's center of gravity.

The new theologians do not even touch in passing on the basic problem of theological methodology which lies beneath all their tergiversations. This problem is the relation between reason and faith. Nor can we in this professedly philosophical investigation embark on any detailed study of the theological problematic here involved: that we must postpone for the other study on we have working for so many years already, namely the place of Jesus Christ in modern thought. This study will be all the more pertinent to the Death-of-God theology because of the fact that, beginning with Bonhoeffer, it is Christ who is at the heart of the theologians' considerations, albeit in a context fraught with tragic consequences indeed. For the moment, let it simply be said that it should be clear that Kierkegaard took an unequivocally positive stand on the question of the relation between reason and faith. A reasonably attentive and careful study of Kierkegaard's thought should indeed reveal to the unbiassed mind the fact that the Kierkegaardian stand on this problem is not substantially different from the classical stand: there is a sort of reason (the defuddled reason of modern man) which destroys faith; but there is another sort of reason (natural reason, not yet so befuddled) which lays the groundwork for faith and can assist in theological reflection. The later Kierkegaard spoke explicitly on this point.[4]

[3] "For Kierkegaard's thinking was and always remained substantially an *anti-Hegelian thinking*" (H. Wein, *Realdialektik,* Von hegelscher Dialektik zu dialektischer Anthropologie [Munich, 1957], p. 14. Cf. also Note 1).

[4] As early as the *Postscript* with its discussion of "paradox" but especially in the *Papirer:* X^2 A 354, X^2 A 432, X^4 A 635 (Italian translation, 2nd ed., Nos. 2110, 2151, 2716). Cf. especially the discussion with the theologian Theophilus Nicolaus (Magnus Erikkson), now published in: *Papirer* X^6 B 66-82, pp. 69ff. (Cf. C. Fabro, *Dall'essere all'esistente* [Brescia, 1965^2], pp. 162ff.).

One more point must be made in this connection: anyone accepting the notion of the "total fall" or "total depravation" of reason and its consequent radical irreconcilability with faith, must take exception not only to Scholasticism but even to the Fathers of the Church as early as the second century; and this seems to me to be going a little too far! [5] This is what comes of not being clear on matters of principle; and the real merit of the new "defeatist theology" is that it has brought such methodological gaps into the clear light of day.

Ogletree may indeed have some justification for his benign interpretation of Bonhoeffer's speculations as being not so much a "Death-of-God Theology" as rather an abandonment of a false conception of God in order the better to facilitate the return to the God of the Bible.[6] The fact remains that Bonhoeffer's whole stress is rather on the coming of-age of modern thought in its destruction of God than on the radical deviation of human reason in modern philosophies, from Spinoza to Hegel, Nietzsche, Heidegger and Sartre, those very philosophies that eliminated God.

II. Bonhoeffer and the Meaninglessness of Metaphysico-Theological Language

Neo-positivism seems to have produced a new articulation of the problem of the language-reality nexus. The approach of the neopositivists is not concerned with describing the subjective process occurring in our mind (for that is a psychological problematic), nor yet with describing the relations between concepts, words, propositions and that to which they refer (for that is an epistemological problem), nor even with judging the concrete truth or falsehood of the propositions (for that is the business of the individual sciences); rather the neo-positivists are here concerned solely with establishing what relations a certain fact (such as a proposition) must have with another fact in order to function as a "symbol" of that other fact. Here the two main problems are: (a) that of indicating the conditions guaranteeing that the combination of symbols will make sense rather than non-sense; (b) that of indicating the conditions required for univocity of meaning or reference of symbols or of combinations of symbols. In this connection, Wittgenstein, the admitted initiator and founder of the whole movement of linguistic analysis, states his main contention which Russell summarizes as follows: "The essential business of language is to assert or deny facts. Given

[5] This is the paradoxical thesis of W. Kamlah, *Der Mensch in der Profanität, Versuch einer Kritik der profanen durch vernehmenden Vernunft* (Stuttgart, 1949), especially p. 210.

[6] Cf. Thomas W. Ogletree, *The 'Death of God' Controversy* (London: SCM Press Ltd., 1966), p. 15. This exposition is impressive in its clarity and objectivity; the author shows first-hand knowledge of the texts.

the syntax of a language, the meaning of a sentence is determinate as soon as the meaning of the component words is known. In order that a certain sentence should a certain fact there must, however the language may be constructed, be something in common between the structure of the sentence and the structure of the fact." [7] But again there are elementary facts and other composite facts, made up of combinations of these elementary facts; to the former correspond atomic propositions, to the latter, molecular propositions. So what is crucial for the truth of propositions are the facts themselves; the foundation of the truth of propositions lies in the "verification" of the facts.

Now, judging from Paul van Buren's interpretation, it is in this climate of thought that Bonhoeffer effects his proclamation of "religionless Christianity." Bonhoeffer is represented as having no thought of withdrawing from the modern world into the old Christian ghetto of traditional formulas of the faith and of dogma; rather he is said to have behaved like a citizen of the modern world, inclined to consult the weather map and the weatherman about the changing climate than to "turn to God in prayer." So the question becomes this: what meaning can the language of metaphysics and religion have for the man of today, in the opinion of these new theoreticians of "linguistic analysis" who abound especially in the Anglo-American world.[8] To pose the question in these terms is to answer it already: no-one, be he believer or sceptic, can know ("verify") any of those things that belong or are said to belong to the sphere of the transcendent and supernatural; therefore, no-one, be he believer or sceptic, can attribute any meaning to those terms that articulate such things; and what those terms are we already know from Bonhoeffer's list.

It is not germane to our purpose to enter into detailed debate on analysis of language; but the vicious circle of the neo-positivists is evident: they start from the hypothesis that only terms referring to experience can be meaningful, and by experience they understand exclusively the sphere of "sense data". But this is an arbitrary restriction of the meaning of "experience" to the immediate sphere of the sensible, i.e., particular and material "contents". Therefore inevitably not only theology but even philosophy, as dealing with universals, is deprived of any meaning. And one might simply ask, on the neo-positivists' own terms, why the *act* whereby the content of experience is rendered present cannot iself be "given" in the very "coming-to-presence" of experience itself? And the further question can be posed (with Aristotle and

[7] L. Wittgenstein, *Tractatus Logico-Philosophicus,* With an Introduction by Bertrand Russell (London, 1922), p. 8.

[8] Paul M. van Buren, *The Secular Meaning of the Gospel.* In his own analysis, van Buren relies unreservedly on Bultmann's "demythologization", making no reference to the grave reservations this doctrine has excited even in Protestant circles. In the matter of linguistic analysis, it is van Buren himself who appeals to Wittgenstein (cf. *ibid.,* pp. 13ff., 101ff.).

Brentano) as to whether an object can in fact be given without the simultaneous presentation of the subject which is the knowing mind and without the consequent apprehension of the oppositional tension between the sensible and the non-sensible intellectual. It is perfectly true that the terms and problems of philosophy, ethics, religion and the like, transcend the scope of the physicist, the biologist, the astronomer and the like; indeed such problems and terms may even be said to be meaningless for such specialist. But this does not mean they are totally meaningless, for the natural sciences do not in fact exhaust the whole universe of meaning open to the human mind!

Wittgenstein does indeed maintain that the propositions of philosophy and of ethics cannot make any sense; philosophy should be careful to say only what *can* be said; but this means the propositions of natural science, quite unrelated to philosophy! But Wittgenstein admits another demension beyond science, the dimension of the inexpressible, the "mystical".[9] The arresting trait in Wittgenstein is his passion for clarity. Some early jottings show his lively interest in the metaphysical problem:

"What do I know about God and the purpose of life?

"I know that this world exists.

"That I am placed in it like my eye in its visual field.

"That something about it is problematic, which we call its meaning.

"That life is the world.[10]

"That my will penetrates the world.

"That my will is good or evil.

"Therefore that good and evil are somehow connected with the meaning of the world.

"The meaning of life, i.e., the meaning of the world, we can call God.

"And connect with this the comparison of God to a father.

"To pray is to think about the meaning of life." [11]

The God-problem seems here to have become the crucial problem but at the same time God seems to have come to mean the world considered

[9] Cf. L. Wittgenstein, *Tractatus Logico-Philosophicus,* 6.41-6.522, pp. 182ff. "Mysticism" seems therefore here to take the place of metaphysics (which Wittgenstein repudiates): the mystical element is that upon which it would be meaningless to make any pronouncements, which it would be meaningless to describe or even to think, since this would amount to using language for something to which it cannot be logically applied. But the mystical element is linked to a feeling and language can "point to" it (*zeigen*), though it cannot "say" (*sagen*) it. "Feeling" is thus held to be, in its own way, a source of meaning (cf. J. Hartnack, *Wittgenstein und die moderne Philosophie* [Stuttgart, 1962], p. 41). Wittgenstein's positivism comes out in his way of considering immortality which he holds can be nothing but temporal duration (cf. *Tractatus Logico-Philosophicus,* 6.4312, p. 184).

[10] These last two propositions are reiterated in the *Tractatus Logico-Philosophicus* (cf. 6.41 and 5.621, pp. 182ff.).

[11] L. Wittgenstein, *Notebooks 1914-1916* (Oxford, 1961), p. 72e.

as a whole and as the relation that things have to one another within this whole.

In any case, we may conclude that precisely the analysis of language led Wittgenstein to transcend the immediate "data" and then admit that ethics, albeit consisting of propositions which go beyond experience and consequently being transcendent,[12] yet has a valid and legitimate status of its own and something to contribute to human thought. Why then is not religion at least on a par with ethics? It is indeed hard to see why, if ethics which is transcendent has and ought to have meaning, religion and theology should not have meaning. This is not to say for a moment that Wittgenstein was a defender of metaphysics or of supernaturalism, but only that in his own definition of meaning and of the technique of the new linguistic analysis he admits the limits of this new science and sees the area of the ethico-religious transcendent as holding the key to the final meaning of life.

And a final point should here be stressed: it is not the business of linguistic analysis to decide generically on the meaning, value and possibility of the objects themselves; it deals with objects as such only in function of the various modes in which they present themselves to the senses. Any statement that there is one way and one only in which data can be presented to the mind, namely the empirical way of *In-der-Welt-sein,* is precisely one of those global propositions which transcends the data and is therefore meaningless, on the basis of the principles of linguistic analysis itself.

III. Bonhoeffer's Diagnosis of Modern Atheism

In his essay entitled "Inheritance and Decay", Bonhoeffer institutes an impressive examination of the roots of atheism in the West; this inspection of the "process of secularization" is characterized by Bonhoeffer's typically radical thrust. We find here again those cardinal features that confirm the complexity and profundity of that problematic that grips the religious mind of the West in a pincers of a disturbing and apparently dead-end quandry.

Bonhoeffer maintains that it is only in the Christian West that it is possible to speak of a historical heritage. The concept of historical inheritance is bound up inextricably with a consciousness of temporality and opposed to all mythologization; and such a concept is possible only where thought is consciously or unconsciously governed by the entry of

[12] "Ethics is transcendent" (G.E.M. Anscombe, the English translator of the *Notebooks* has "transcendental" but the original German reads: "Die Ethik ist transzendent" (*ibid.,* p. 79).

[13] Appearing in the *Ethik,* published, like the other already published and hitherto unpublished works, under the editorial supervision of E. Bethge (Munich, 1949); published in English as *Ethics* (London: SCM Press Ltd., 1955), pp. 25ff.

God into history at a definite place and a definite point of time. Here history becomes a serious matter, says Bonhoeffer, without being canonized. The 'yes' and the 'no' which God addresses to history in the incarnation and crucifixion of Jesus Christ introduces into very historical instant an infinite and unresolvable tension. Now, whereas in the traditional scheme of things (from Lessing to Kierkegaard and down to and including Cullmann) revelation has been interpreted as the entry of eternity into time in such a way that on the one hand eternity maintains its freedom and transcendence and on the other hand man can insert himself into eternity by the instrumentality of freedom, for Bonhoeffer (in a still more radical sense than for Bultmann) [14] there is nothing left but time, that new "historical time" evolving as a continuous and inevitable process of man's defection from God to the point of atheism. This is the basic meaning of historical heritage in the evolution of Western Christianity.

Bonhoeffer proceeds to distinguish two lines of development: on the one hand, that of the Western peoples who molded their own Christianity by means of a positive synthesis of the Roman heritage; and on the other hand, that of the Germans who, expecially after the Reformation, turned exclusively to the Greek world in such a way as to provoke a tension destined inevitably to reach an anti-Christian stand as the patent result of the line of cultural development stretching from Winckelmann to Nietzsche.

I shall leave to the historians, especially the historians of theology, the judgment on the cogency of this interpretation of Western Christianity. What is pertinent to our present purpose is Bonhoeffer's reference to the influence of the Reformation and to Nietzsche's link with the Reformation as unleashing initially the process of secularization and subsequently positive atheism. Bonhoeffer writes: "The reason why Germany's attitude to the heritage of antiquity differs so profoundly from that of the West European nations is undoubtedly to be found in the form assumed in Germany by the gospel as a result of the Reformation. It was only from the soil of the German Reformation that there could spring a Nietzsche. The revolt of the natural against grace contrasts sharply here with that reconciliation of nature with grace which is found in the Roman heritage. It was for this reason that, in a way which for the West European nations was quite incomprehensible, Nietzsche could win the positive approval of one school of German Protestant theology" (p. 28). Yet Bonhoeffer claims that for both groups, Germans and others alike, the reconciliation between classical antiquity and the Cross of Christ has always been a highly unstable one; and the high degree of tension involved was bound eventually to lead to a break, despite the

[14] Cf. in this connection the meticulous analysis of G. Krause, "Dietrich Bonhoeffer und Rudolf Bultmann," in *Zeit und Geschichte,* Dankesgabe an R. Bultmann zum 80. Geburtstag (Tübingen, 1964), pp. 439ff.

fact that Christianity functioned for many centuries as the only power guaranteeing to the West not only religious but even political unity.[15]

The Reformation, says Bonhoeffer, broke asunder the unity of the faith. And forthwith there began that *process of secularization* that led to the present modern situation. But this, insists Bonhoeffer, amounts to a total misinterpretation of the real message of the Reformation: this message was that there is no holiness of man either in the sacred or in the profane as such, but only that which comes through the merciful and sin-forgiving word of God. This has been forgotten and the Reformation has been celebrated as the emancipation of man in his conscience, his reason and his culture and as the justification of the secular as such. And forthwith rationalism erupts. From Catholic France, on the other hand, came the "French Revolution" which is a symbol of the modern Western world, proclaiming the emancipation of reason, of the classes, of the people.

The process that led reason, thus emancipated, to seek via technology for an absolute mastery over nature, Bonhoeffer feels to be a process of equal importance to the proclamation of the Rights of Man. Thus Bonhoeffer sees modern Western atheism as deriving directly from the emancipation of the masses effected by the French Revolution: "It is totally different from the atheism of certain individual Greek, Indian, Chinese and western thinkers. It is not the theoretical denial of the existence of a God. It is itself a religion, a religion of hostility to God. It is in just this that it is western. It cannot break loose from its past. It cannot but be religious in essence. That is why to the human eye it is so hopelessly godless. Western godlessness ranges from the religion of Bolshevism to the midst of the Christian churches. In Germany especially, but also in the Anglo-Saxon countries, it is a markedly Christian godlessness. In the form of all the possible Christianities, whether they be nationalistic, socialist, rationalist or mystical, it turns against the living God of the Bible, against Christ. Its god is the New Man, no matter whether he bears the trade-mark of Bolshevism or of Christianity" (pp. 38f.). The name that comes to mind immediately is Dostoevsky.

However suggestive this diagnosis may seem, it appears to us to be less than accurate. It is patently dominated by Protestant theological pessimism. Bonhoeffer here quite clearly proclaims his fundamental call for a return to a pure Biblical Christianity (or at least to a Christianity proclaimed to be such!), without authority (Pope), without Reformation (Luther), and consequently without hierarchical Church or any

[15] Bonhoeffer highlights the crucial importance for this process of the Papacy-Empire dualism and strife, in the wake of Christ's conversion of the West into a historical unity, pervaded by spiritual movements and where even the wars aim at the promotion of the unity of the West; simliarly, in the struggle between Pope and Emperor, Christ Himself, higher than either, is the supreme uncontested unity (*Ethics,* pp. 30f.).

point of insertion whatsoever into historical reality: "Luther's great discovery of the freedom of the Christian man and the Catholic heresy of the essential good in man combined to produce the deification of man. But, rightly understood, the deification of man is the proclamation of nihilism." (p. 39). This is atheism without hope, religious atheism, "hopeless godlessness" which has corrupted the churches; "but there is also a godlessness which is full of promise, a godlessness which speaks against religion and against the Church." (p. 39) [16] And this is precisely the atheism that Bonhoeffer, as we have seen, takes as his point of departure for the return to Christ and to Biblical Christianity. His diagnosis, as here presented in this essay, reveals all his own limitations, resulting from a theological radicalism and simplism which will surely not prove convincing either to Protestants or to Catholics, and still less to atheists themselves.

IV. Demythologization, Existential Atheism and Theism

Schubert Ogden claims that the phenomenon of modern atheism and of the religious crisis of the world of our day is much more complex than the Death-of-God theologians would have it. It admits of quite different approaches and solutions. Indeed "The claim currently being made by certain Protestant advocates of a theology *post mortem Dei*—namely that Christian faith does not require a theistic explication—is so wildly implausible as scarcely to merit consideration." [17]

First of all, maintains Ogden, both faith and "unfaith" can have two related but clearly different senses, *theoretical* and *practical.* The former assumes a more or less conceptual form and is inseparably causally linked to man's historical existence and consequently reflects the quite divergent conditions that may determine man's existence in history. In this form, "unfaith" and faith alike are tied to certain categories proper to the particular historical period in which man finds himself; both have a cognitive content which, upon explication, issues in various forms of *Weltanschauung* (atheist or theist), which however are limited to the period of history to which they belong. In the practical dimension, on

[16] Religious feeling and practice in the United States of America, on the contrary, is based on a concept of democracy, founded not on man the unrestrictedly enfranchised but rather on the Kingdom and sovereignity of God and the limitation of all worldly power by that sovereignty. This, Bonhoeffer feels, tends to prevent the American situation from gravitating toward radical anti-clericalism and to keep atheism more covert (pp. 40f.). I can myself testify, after a brief stay in the United States, that religious practice—where it exists—seems more straightforward, candid and outgoing than in Western Europe.

[17] Cf. Schubert M. Ogden, "The Christian Proclamation of God to Men of the so-called 'Atheistic Age'," *Concilium,* Vol. 16 (New York: Paulist Press, 1966), p. 96.

the other hand, we have to do with an *existential* act of concrete commitment: in theism, the integral confidence in God and Jesus Christ and in atheism a trust in man and in his destiny in the world. Therefore, argues Ogden, it is at least theoretically conceivable that there might be a certain type of "atheism" which emerges as such in virtue of its opposition to a certain definite form of theism, i.e., to a certain type of affirmation of God, and which is at least temporarily reconcilable and compatible with a genuine existential faith in God's love as promised to us in Jesus Christ.

From the existential point of view, atheism would be the act of cleaving to some earthly idol as the end and goal of personal life, taking the place of the true God, and in this sense, says Ogden, all ages can be called "atheistic" because "there is no distinction, since all have sinned and fall short of the glory of God (Rom. 3, 22f.)". There are also those who reject such and such a *specific* form of theoretical theism as traditionally presented in the preaching and teaching of the Church. And, of course, there may be those who combine both forms of atheism; yet Ogden feels it to be of capital importance that we recognize that the two forms can exist separately. "What distinguishes Western humanity today," he continues, "is not a greater existential distrust of God, but an ever more widespread theoretical dissent from the assertions of classical theism." [18] We must immediately here enter a *caveat* against Ogden's bemusing oversimplification of the problem: for he presents "classical theism" from the time of the heyday of Greek pagan philosophy down to and including the Patristic period and the age of Scholasticism as a monolithic whole; and he foregoes even the most cursory examination of the internal structure of modern thought as articulated from Descartes to Sartre to see whether such thought be even capable of tackling the God-problem. Like the vast majority of the avant-garde theologians of our day, Ogden shows not the slightest evidence of even suspecting that modern atheism stems precisely from that philosophy in which he and his fellow-theologians were trained and within the framework of which they still operate in their theologizing! Modern atheism is a positive assertive atheism, not merely a negative polemical one.

Ogden himself rejects the extremist form of the Death-of-God Theology and sets himself the task of outlining a theism conformable to the needs and requirements of our modern age: he is persuaded that the real assignment of theology today lies not in the proclamation of an "atheistic age" with the consequent admission that we are now living and will be living henceforth in a post-Christian age; rather, claims Ogden, theology's assignment today is that of giving to God and Christianity the meaning that is compatible with our present-day culture.

Bultmann's *demythologization* notion seems to Ogden to provide us

[18] *Ibid.*, p. 93.

with an excellent hermeneutical tool for this purpose.[19] For this notion of demythologization, in application to Christian theology, calls for the exclusion from the object of faith of all "mythical" elements, such as the Biblical account of creation, the eschatological prophecies, the miracles of Christ, his redemptive work and in general all those extraordinary facts and events reported in the Bible which cannot be explored by science and history. Biblical language must in such cases be taken as being "symbolical" and must consequently be interpreted within the context of the historico-cultural milieu in which these accounts were written. Furthermore, modern man, says Ogden, simply cannot accept any longer the notion of an absolute and immutable, transcendent and supernatural God; he finds it merely a bemusing combination of myth and traditional (unacceptable) metaphysics.[20] Thus, concludes Ogden, anyone really wishing to speak of God to the men of our so-called atheistic age must abandon classical theism and see if another form of Christian theism can be found.

Ogden feels, as we have said, that the new form of Christian theism includes Bultmannian demythologization, whereby the field of religion and Christianity is purged of the underbrush of unintelligible elements. He feels that the soundest metaphysical base for this new form of religion will be furnished by A. N. Whitehead's neo-classical metaphysics which will render genuine existential commitment in faith possible for modern man, in conformity with his training and his aspirations: "Whitehead is able to conceive God as the eminently relative One whose very essence is his pure unbounded love for man and the world." [21]

We have already expounded this whole notion of Whitehead's at great length and we have ourselves stressed its moving poignancy. But we must observe here again, as we pointed out in our evaluation of Whitehead then, that Whitehead's "God" is an "end result", just like Hegel's God and the God of any pantheism whatsoever; he can neither hear nor aid man here and now because he is always the Coming One, He is the

[19] Bypassing here the theological aspects, it suffices to note that Bultmann has applied to theology the absolute historicism of Heidegger, a historicism which asserts the identity of being and time and therefore cuts away all the foundations of metaphysical transcendence (cf. R. Bultmann, "Neues Testament und Mythologie," in *Kerygma und Mythos,* Theologische Forschung I [Hamburg: Herbert Reich, 1948], pp. 33ff.; English translation, "New Testament and Mythology," in *Kerygma and Myth* [New York: Harper and Row, Publishers, Harper Torchbooks, 1961], pp. 1ff. For a general exposition, cf. G. Noll, *Sein und Existenz,* especially pp. 61ff., 98ff.). One critic thinks that Bultmann's stand can be linked only to the Heidegger of the *Sein und Zeit* period (1927) and not to the later Heidegger of the *Kehre* (cf. H.-G. Gadamer, "Martin Heidegger und die Marburger Schule," in *Zeit und Geschichte,* p. 487).

[20] Ogden appeals on this point to Pascal's contradistinction between the God of the philosophers and the God of Abraham, of Isaac and of Jacob; but we feel his appeal to be misplaced.

[21] Ogden, "The Christian Proclamation . . .," p. 97.

term of history not its antecedent creator and so Bonhoeffer was quite right to reject such a God.

We have three final questions concerning the acceptability for Christian theism of Whitehead's God: Is Whitehead's God-notion not a purely philosophical one and so inadequate from the outset for true theology? Is it not moreover a pantheistic and thus implicitly atheistic notion? What is here left of the majesty of the God of Abraham, Isaac and Jacob?

As for Bultmann's new hermeneutical principle, is it not borrowed directly from Heidegger's earlier atheistic philosophy? [22]

V. From Dialectical Theology to "Radical Theology" (John A. T. Robinson)

The title of Robinson's intriguing essay *Honest to God* was, as we have pointed out, drawn from Bonhoeffer; but Tillich and Bultmann are obviously likewise co-inspirers of the content. From Tillich, Robinson takes over the notion of a substitution of depth for height in theological symbolism, designating God as the "Ground" of our being, rather than as a Being "out there", an Other who lives "beyond the bright blue sky" and whose existence can and must be an object of proof. From Bultmann, he takes over the notion of a "trans-historical" reinterpretation of the whole of Biblical history as reported in the Old and New Testaments alike, a "demythologization" in virtue of which "the entire conception of a supernatural order which invades and 'perforates' this one must be abandoned." [23]

But Robinson's chief source of inspiration seems clearly to have been Bonhoeffer, especially the Bonhoeffer of the *Letters and Papers from Prison,* with his call for the launching of a "religionless Christianity" no longer dependent on the premise of religion.[24] and therefore viable even in a world in which the traditional God is no longer relevant. The order of the day is an admission of the Copernican revolution that has occurred in the heartland of theology and a consequent effort to restate the Gospel in terms that will be meaningful to modern man.

[22] Ogden reiterates the very temerious thesis of O. Pöggeler (*Der Denkweg Martin Heideggers* [Pfullingen, 1963]) to the effect that the early Heidegger of *Sein und Zeit* modelled his historical interpretation of life on reflections garnered from an inspection of the religious practices of the early Christians and that this resulted in an extension to God of the temporality of human be-ing (existence and life) (Schubert M. Ogden, "The Temporality of God," in *Zeit und Geschichte,* pp. 381ff.).

[23] J. A. T. Robinson, *Honest to God,* pp. 21ff. Robinson has himself collated, in *The Honest to God Debate,* the key passages from critical articles and reviews on the book.

[24] J. A. T. Robinson, *Honest to God,* pp. 36ff.

Robinson is here accepting without reservation, in the line of the "New Theology", the total destruction effected by modern criticism of the old way of conceiving the relations between man and God, between the sinner and grace. Robinson agrees that this old approach presupposes a view of the world which is now outmoded and consequently this old approach is neither intelligible nor acceptable to modern man. "Our concern is in no way to change the Christian doctrine of God but precisely to see that it does not disappear with this outmoded view." [25]

Robinson is therefore accepting as an unarguable fact that the objectivist and metaphysical approach of classical theology has actually led to the radical negation presently designated as "Death of God", a negation whose long shadow has, in this last century since the death of Hegel, been loping over the whole of Western culture. Modern man simply cannot make any sense out of such terms as "nature," "substance," "cause," "relation," and the like, because these terms are bound up with a particular world-picture which is simply irrelevant today; no useful purpose can be served by a continued use of such terms in theological discourse; indeed they are positively harmful, not only to man's comprehension of God but even to man's interest in the God-question! So the "Death of God" amounts really to a felicitous event, expediting the return to the true and genuine God. It is in this context that Robinson insists that a really modern man cannot but be an atheist (i.e., in terms of the old-style terminology used to explicate the God-notion), though at the same time this really modern man cannot remain an atheist for the very simple existential reason that the encounter with the Risen Christ will constrain him to abandon his notion that there is no God at all.[26]

Robinson therefore wants to go the whole way with dialectical theology, compel that theology itself indeed to go further than perhaps some of its protagonists would have wished to take it, develop with trenchant consequentiality that theology's premises concerning the constitutive negativity of the nature-grace nexus and the reason-faith nexus; *and then make this very negativity the very basis of the new theological message to the new man,* using atheism itself as the foundation for the new affirmation of God, for the new experience of God on the part of the new man.

This new Death-of-God theology is quite simply a defeatist capitula-

[25] *Ibid.*, p. 44.

[26] Dr. Robinson in fact asks, in his recent essay *The New Reformation?* (London: SCM Press Ltd., 1965), the precise question: "Can a truly contemporary person *not* be an atheist?" and his answer is: "There is no going back to the pre-secular view of the world, where God is always 'there' to be brought in, run to, or blamed. Yet, in another sense, he may find that he *cannot* be an atheist, however much he would like to be. For on the Emmaus road, on the way back from the tomb, the risen Christ comes up with him and he knows himself constrained." (p. 116).

tion before the negations enunciated by modern thought from Feuerbach and Nietzsche right down to Heidegger and Sartre. Robinson is frank and outspoken in sketching the dimensions of this capitulation: [27]

1. *God is intellectually superfluous.* Neither science nor philosophy has any room for God these days. God has lost all meaning for man. The human intellect can get no hold on God and no-one any longer feels the need of posing the God-problem.

2. *God is emotionally dispensable.* Not only does man no longer feel any need of God or religion. He is convinced that any such ties are positively harmful to him in a desacralized world, a world whose essence is in Heidegger's phrase "to worldify", "to become world still more" (*Welt weltet*). This sort of world is a secularized world and "Secularization means that man must accept responsibility for his own destiny, neither trying to blame it on the gods nor expecting some providence to relieve him of it or see him through".

3. *God is morally intolerable.* The operative factor in Robinson's thinking here seems to be the "scandal of evil" rather than the Kantian categorical imperative (as the theoretical context would require) or the extremity of Sartrian existential freedom. Thus Robinson asserts that ". . . A God who 'causes' or 'allows' the suffering of a single child is morally intolerable." On the one hand physical and moral evil is today spreading in forms and proportions hitherto unknown; on the other hand, sensitivity to pain and suffering has been and is being constantly increased by the progress of science and culture. The resulting tension has broken man's spirit and lamed his aspiration and he prefers to be left alone with his physical pain and his mental torment.

Robinson is obviously a sensitive man, a kind man and a deeply humane man; and his ideas and theories will undoubtedly continue to stimulate salutary discussions even beyond the present impressive literature he has inspired. The problems he poses in the practical moral dimension are very real and pressing. But all of this does not alter the fact that Robinson's theological method leaves much indeed to be desired: when theology takes its point of departure from philosophy and uses philosophy's method, untoward consequences are bound to ensue, not to mention the fact that such a procedure is the very reverse of the *sola Biblia* principle so basic to Reformation thinking.[28] It therefore seems to us, on balance, that the Death-of-God Theology phenomenon represents not so much a real rebuff and challenge to classical theology

[27] *Ibid.*, pp. 107ff.

[28] And it has been rightly remarked that in the Bible God is a living Personal Being relating to man with an inter-personal relationship calculated to resolve the problem of life; He is no mere concept or "plastic idea" (*Vorstellung*) to be shucked off by modern philosophy (cf. P. Ricca, *La "morte di Dio": una nuova teologia?* [Turin, 1967], pp. 35ff.). The God who is dead in the modern mind is the debilitated and immanentized God of modern philosophy, not the true God of Hosts of the Bible.

as rather an expose of the pernicious method and missteps of liberal theology in its patent inability to forestall the dire consequences of its own alliance with modern immanentist philosophy.

This is the key point in the whole crisis of dialectical and radical theology in our day. And we feel that insufficient attention has been paid precisely to this point by a Catholic philosopher who has zealously thrown himself into the controversy: this philosopher, Leslie Dewart, finds the Death-of-God to be a real and not merely a cultural problem; and he claims that the proofs of the existence of God adduced by Scholasticism and more particularly by St. Thomas Aquinas are clearly open to the "vicious circle" objection of having been based on the real distinction in creatures between essence and existence, for which very distinction they are supposed, on the other hand, themselves to provide the foundation.[29] We must once again point out that St. Thomas considered his "ways" to represent arguments discovered by philosophers (i.e., by natural reason operating in actual existents) and therefore to be perennially valid for every age and culture, including the Christian.

VI. Meanings of and Attitudes to "The End of the Age of Religion"

Our approach to the problem of theism and atheism has been predominantly and preeminently philosophical, for we are persuaded that the nub of the problem is philosophical; and we hope we have demonstrated this in the course of this volume. Moreover, we feel that the confusing interpolation of the God-problem as such into the framework of theological problematic, as effected by dialectical theology, has led in the final analysis to a hopeless muddling of two epistemological levels, of two levels of meaning which are totally distinct, which any intelligent human thinker can and ought to hold resolutely apart, namely the levels of reason and of faith with the corresponding respective areas of philosophy and theology.

An equally disturbing mental confusion, approaching delirium, seems to us to be evidenced by such statements as those made by Gabriel Vahanian in a recent article, to the effect that we are at the dawn of a new "post-Christian" age and culture wherein theism has the status of a simple hypothesis, no less and no more valid than atheism. It seems to us grotesquely excessive to saddle the transmission of the Christian faith with the responsibility of having brought about the duoble alienation, religious and cultural, that has led modern man to place his life under the sign of the "Death of God".[30] And the author's contention that the

[29] L. Dewart, *The Future of Belief,* pp. 152ff.

[30] This is the thesis reiterated in various forms by Gabriel Vahanian, "Theology and 'the End of the Age of Religion'," *Concilium,* Vol. 16, pp. 99ff. Cf. on pp. 107ff. his critique of the inconsistency of the position of Bonhoeffer and his followers.

reason for this pernicious effect lies solely in the fact that the transmission of the Christian faith has been effected in categories bound up with a religious view of the world seems to us less than cogent, to put it mildly.

Vahanian does not boggle at lumping together Nietzsche, the standard-bearer of the "God is dead" slogan, and Sören Kierkegaard, the founder of Christian existentialism, who described himself as an "essentially religious writer": "For Kierkegaard, Christianity is dead: so dead that Kierkegaard would not call himself a Christian. For Nietzsche, God is dead." [31] The judgment on Nietzsche is of course true, but it is irrelevant because Nietzsche *accepted* modern immanentism and consequently proclaimed that it makes no sense any longer to go on speaking of God and religion, as indeed it does not for those who, like Nietzsche, accept this modern point of departure. But Kierkegaard does *not* accept this point of departure, indeed, as we have already mentioned, he expressly repudiates it and discounts entirely the validity of the critique of Christianity effected by Feuerbach and Strauss, those disciples of Hegel. Kierkegaard makes a drastic distinction between the apostasy of modern philosophy and the sane thinking of a Socrates, between the miserable and deplorable state of establishment Christianity (especially Danish Protestantism) and Christianity as such, i.e., the Christianity of the New Testament, which Kierkegaard himself considers to be the only hope of the world and for whose restoration he intends to work as a sort of undercover agent within Christendom.[32]

Vahanian is entirely right in his reservations on the score of Bon-

[31] Cf. G. Vahanian, *The Death of God,* The Culture of Our Post-Christian Era, p. 210. On the same page, Vahanian goes on to assert: "An unsuspected meaning of Nietzsche's cry is that the absence of God corresponds to Kierkegaard's view of the infinite qualitative difference between God and man." This amounts to a wrenching of the phrase to a meaning it does not have in the Kierkegaardian text or context: the "infinite qualitative difference" is the metaphysical distance between creature and Creator, as affirmed in the fundamental principle of revealed religion (not merely Christianity alone), expressed by St. Thomas in the doctrine of analogy. Kierkegaard comes substantially close to this position, whereas Barth, as we have pointed out already, rejects and repudiates analogy as an invention of Antichrist!

[32] Elsewhere Vahanian himself admits this: "Over a century ago, Kierkegaard wrote in *Sickness Unto Death* that Christianity was 'the fundamental misfortune of Christendom'. For a correct diagnosis of the contemporary situation, we need, it seems, simply reverse the terms and declare that 'Christendom' is the fundamental misfortune of Christianity. Since the time of Kierkegaard the transition to the post-Christian era has, indeed, become an everyday reality, and the 'death of God' is now the cultural 'event' by which modern man recognizes and admits this change" (G. Vahanian, *Wait Without Idols* [New York: George Braziller, 1964], p. 31). For our own part, we feel rather that Kierkegaard's diagnosis has been basically correct in attributing the degeneration of Christianity precisely to a pernicious worldliness (which dialectical theology wants to make central to Christianity) and to modern thought which has devastated all religious knowledge and even awareness!

hoeffer's project for a religionless Christianity, "anchored as it is in the conviction of the insurmountable incompatibility between faith and religion;" of this project, Vahanian perceptively remarks that it would "succeed only in substituting a new dichotomy, that of atheism and theism, for the traditional cleavage between the sacred and the profane or the religious and the secular, and in laying the foundations for an innerworldly millenarianism instead of the otherworldly and transcendental millenarianism that Christian traditionalism based on the dyad of this world and the next." [33] Vahanian accurately describes Bonhoeffer's error as that of continuing "to consider the problem of faith under the aspect of an antinomy, that of the Church and men or of God and the world, in which the roles are reversed: it is not the wretched sinner who stands before the majesty of God, but it is man in all his strength who stumbles against the weakness of God." And Vahanian crisply remarks, pinpointing the basic and radical insufficiency of Bonhoeffer's ambitious project: "I do not see the need of replacing triumphalism with a kenotic Christianity." [34]

Less convincing is Vahanian's alignment of his own master Karl Barth with St. Thomas Aquinas. Vahanian attempts to show a parity or at least a parallel between Aquinas' contention that the natural knowledge of God is "imperfect" and Barth's Calvinistic opposition of religion not to irreligion but to revelation, considering (natural) religion as the supreme expression of unbelief. Quite the contrary, St. Thomas had such a high opinion of natural religion that he asserted man's natural inclination to God and then proceeded to take from the philosophers the arguments and proofs of the existence of God, using them in a natural speculation about God which serves in Aquinas as a remote preparation for theology.

Vahanian is entirely right in his observation that St. Paul intended his apostolic endeavor to be a cooperation in the work of God and Christ, "for the sake of God" and not, as Bonhoeffer wishes his to be, "in spite of God"; and no more telling description of Bonhoeffer's own plunge could well be imagined than Vahanian's characterization of the Bonhoefferian project as a "transposition of the problem . . . from eschatology to a *mystique* of immanentism." [35] But we cannot go along

[33] G. Vahanian, "Theology and 'the End of the Age of Religion'," pp. 107ff. Cf. also G. Vahanian, *No Other God,* p. 21. (The article cited above is reprinted, with footnotes, as Chapter 2 of this book.)

[34] *Ibid.*

[35] Vahanian the Barthian, indeed, seems to find no difficulty in characterizing the Biblical transcendentalist conception as "mythological" and the modern immanentistic one as "scientific" (*ibid.,* p. 99; *No Other God,* p. 13; identical context in *Wait Without Idols,* p. 34). And Vahanian likewise seems to go on to blame Christianity for the present situation: "Thus, the emergence of radical immanentism does not mean that man has today become less religious or nonreligious. It may simply mean that Christianity, after conquering the paganism of antiquity, has in turn bred its own paganism, in the various secularistic creeds that have sequestrated traditional Christianity and neutralized it as a cultural,

with Vahanian's extrapolation from the Pauline declaration: "That we should be atheists with atheists, as Paul made himself a Jew with Jews, certainly is in accordance with the freedom which the Christian enjoys in regard to all men *for the sake of God.*" St. Paul was indeed willing to make himself a Greek with Greeks, but he never once breathed a word about becoming an atheist with atheists: this Paul would have considered quite simply the capital sin of apostasy!

Nor can we accept his contention that: "It is evident that Christianity should not attribute to itself any religious or cultural particularism." For what real meaning is left in a Christianity reduced to the common denominator of all religions and cultures? The constitutive parameter of Christianity is precisely its distinctive character of "Good News" such as "eye hath not seen nor ear heard nor hath it entered into the heart of man," such as "none of the princes of this world knew" (1 Cor. 2, 9.8).

The fundamental error of dialectical theology, bound up with the Lutheran principle of *simul justus et peccator,* is not only and indeed not primarily that of having stressed the universal inevitability of sin and consequently of atheism; rather that fundamental error lies in having asserted the solidarity and intrinsic conjunction of faith and disbelief, of theism and atheism, making faith to contain within itself unbelief and theism to conceal within itself atheism. The same error stated in speculative terms might be described as the contention that the dialectic of faith and unbelief, theism and atheism, constitutes not the "potentiality" or "possibility" of choice but the "actuality" or "reality" of the choice itself. In this sense, Death-of-God theology truly constitutes what Kierkegaard would have called the gravest "acoustical illusion" concerning God and Christianity from the foundation of Christianity to the present day, what Kierkegaard would not in fact have hesitated to stigmatize as "the triumph of Antichrist". But in the Gospel, it is Christ and not Antichrist who will judge the world and history, whatever Hegel may say to the contrary. One must almost suspect that this whole theological movement, Barth and the Barthians like Vahanian included, are in thrall to Feuerbach and accept his formula that the "essence of theology is anthropology"; indeed one must wonder if they have not further modified this Feuerbachian tenet to read: "the essence of *religion* is anthropology". The two formulations are by no means identical, either for Feuerbach or, *a fortiori,* for St. Thomas! It is not enough to condemn the Death-of-God Theology while continuing to profess and maintain its principles.

---

political, philosophical, i.e., theological ferment" (*No Other God,* p. 31). Nevertheless, Vahanian's position may be admitted to be less radical than that of Altizer, Hamilton and van Buren: for Vahanian (as for Barth) God is and remains the "Ganz-Andere" ("Wholly Other") of any cultural phenomenon; but basically Vahanian is just as destructively biassed as any of these others, as his benevolent critic Ogletree himself admits (*The "Death of God" Controversy,* pp. 21f.).

Gathering together here, then, the many threads of our argument on this problematic of capital importance, we may sum up dialectically, albeit using a dialectic quite different from that of the newest theology which has allowed itself to be sucked in entirely by the antithesis, abandoning pusillanimously the very struggle and conflict which its name "dialectical" presupposes.

(a) *Atheism exists:* this we admit and proclaim as loudly as any dialectical theologian, in opposition to that apologetic which clings ludicrously to its triumphalistic optimism. *But* in opposition to the Death-of-God Theology, we sharply contest the assertion that atheism is a *universal* phenomenon. Everywhere, in all religions and confessions, in the most varied social strata, there persists the belief in and the conviction of the existence of God, even, as we shall be seeing in our final chapter, among the most outstanding modern scientists. The rot and corruption in this area has come predominantly from modern philosophy.

(b) Christianity or more properly *Christendom is at fault:* this we admit and proclaim, in unison with Vatican II which so roundly condemned triumphalism and recognized the gravity of the phenomenon of atheism in our day.[36] *But* we challenge most sharply Vahanian's transition from the historico-anthropological dimension to a condemnation of institutions as such and to an attribution to Christianity itself of the responsibility for the atheism now rampant; [37] and we further challenge the contention that the widespread atheistic trend in our world is irreversible.

Kierkegaard, too, was wrong, then, when he declared that "Christianity no longer exists". If that were true, then God would have failed entirely: equally futile would have been God's gift of reason to man that man might find God and God's gift of redemption to man in Christ that man might be saved. But such a miserable failure of a God is simply no longer worthy of the Name of God! The Death-of-God Theology is no longer a theology at all; it is quite simply a mockery and derision of God, the final despair of an age that has lost God because it has denied, betrayed and defected from him.

[36] "Pastoral Constitution on the Church in the Modern World (*Gaudium et Spes*)," §§ 19-21, in *The Documents of Vatican II* (New York: Herder and Herder, 1966), pp. 215ff.

[37] The charge is explicit: "In other words, Christendom (and what else can this mean today but Western culture?) is the great misfortune of Christianity. And the situation would not be quite so ironical, were it not to Christianity itself that we owe this Western culture that has changed our world into a no God's land. Post-Christian man is the child of Christian man" (G. Vahanian, *Wait Without Idols,* p. 33).

PART IX

THE INNER NUCLEUS OF MODERN ATHEISM

1

The Virtual Atheism of the Principle of Immanentism

Protagonists and antagonists alike agree on the interpretation of the fundamental bent of modern thought, on the new thrust originating with the principle of immanentism: it consisted in a swing from the object to the subject, from the world to the self, from the external to the internal.

It would seem that there can likewise be ready agreement on the evolution of the meaning assumed by the theoretical nucleus of immanentism in the development of modern thought, from Descartes to our own day, from the manifold forms of rationalism to English phenomenism (Hume), Kantian criticism, the most ambitious forms of metaphysical idealism, and right down to the present-day philosophies such as Marxism, existentialism, pragmatism, neo-positivism and the like: it has amounted quite simply to an articulation of the speculative conclusions virtually contained already within that principle of immanentism, an articulation that has enabled that principle, over the course of three centuries, to return again to the primordial purity of its own speculative requirement.

Nor should there be much disagreement about the fact that the historical development of the principle of immanentism on the critico-theoretical level has been spiral rather than rectilinear; within one and the same age, disparate and antithetical interpretations of the principle of immanentism have clashed headon; the Malebranche, Spinoza and Leibniz interpretations within evolving Cartesianism; English empiricism and the German rationalism of Wolff-Baumgarten-Thomasius from which was to stem the Kantian revolution; the Fichte, Schelling and Hegel interpretations within metaphysical idealism; the divergent interpretations of the most representative existentialists within present-day thought, Jaspers, Heidegger, Camus, Marcel, Sartre.

This should certainly induce caution against hasty oversimplifications and point up the complexity and nuances of this whole development; but it should likewise serve to focus the critic's attention on the crucial problem of detecting and detaching the primordial meaning of the principle of immanentism itself, considered in terms of that basic philosphical assignment which is the discovery of *the foundation of the truth of being.* It is in this radical sense, not in any historical or polemical sense, that we maintain that the principle of immanentism is intrinsically atheistic and coincides with the *radical assertion of atheism, inasmuch as the very definition of an immanentist stand on being* can only involve a denial of *that transcendence in the epistemological dimension wherein consists the first step of theism rightly and radically understood.* In this sense we speak of the "essential atheism" of the principle of immanentism. It may well be that a substantial number of modern philosophers, beginning with the practicing Catholic Descartes, profess themselves to be theists and believers; but that does not alter the fact that the principle they start from is atheistic and is implemented in implicitly or tendentially atheistic statements *in the very course of the articulation, in terms of that principle, of the affirmation of the existence of God!* For when the act of knowing is posited as the ultimate beginning, it has no other truth than that of its naked self-positing and self-effectuation; and the content is its own sheer process of realization, its truth being dissolved into the pure historicity of (the) human be-ing (*Dasein*). This historicity (or content of the act, quality of being) may then be held to be embodied in aesthetic, scientific, economic or political activity and even occasionally in religious activity which it allegedly requires and demands (I am thinking of those Protestant theologians and the so-called Christian spiritualists, who claim to be able to bend the method of immanentism to an affirmation of transcendence); but already it is too late for such identifications to have any substantive importance or even significance: they are all but matters of personal taste and arbitrary choice, not in any sense of theoretical foundation. Thus, it is more accurate to speak of *structural or constitutive atheism* in the case of the principle of immanetism: the removal or absense of the possibility of a "presence" (existence) of God is the very essence of the *cogito,* inasmuch as the *cogito* principle asserts the truth of the act and content of consciousness (mind) on the basis of the exclusion of the act and content of being, deriving the truth of the content of being from the alleged truth of the act of mind!

Beneath the external history of the principle of immanentism, a history shot through with the clashes and contrasts of the modern systems in any one age and in their bewildering succession, there is an "internal history" which consists and is realized in the form of a growing awareness of the primordial exigency of the *cogito* itself: this is the deepest and most ultimate cause of the opposition of contemporary systems in any given age and, moreover, of the continuous "advance" to ever more essential or allegedly essential forms of the principle of immanentism. And in this sense we consider the atheism of Marxism, existentialism, neo-positivism, pragmatism, and the like in our own age as the genuine "precipitation" of the principle of immanentism. And the oddest feature of all, to which philosophical reflection ought to attend most carefully, is this: that the principle of immanentism itself goes down in the course of this development and with the disappearance or total transformation of the principle itself, philosophy as such likewise disappears as a meaningful human activity, as the above-mentioned present-day philosophies expressly admit and assert. A strange nemesis, indeed, for that principle that was touted originally as the keystone of the interiority of truth and has today led to a conception of man as completely evacuated into the historical, economic, operational reality of the space-time coordinates that restrictively define him!

In the course of this three-century-long "struggle" or "race" toward ultimate consistency and consequentiality, modern philosophy has actualized its own innermost essence, which is that of the *radical experience of doubt,* or the *experience of radical doubt,* which is the negative-historical formulation of the principle of immanentism. *Doubt* is quite simply regarded not as directed toward appearance but directed toward being; and the truth of being itself is hit by this radical doubt. Indeed appearance is asserted as stimulus and reason for a doubt calculated to serve as an instrument to attain the ultimate truth, a truth of such a strange sort that doubt exposes not simply the demand for it (as is the case in all reflective awareness and in philosophy as such) *but the very foundation of that truth!* And the further conclusion is worthy of the closest attention: *cognitional activity is conceived as active negativity,* negation being the constitutive element of affirmation which is a mediation of non-being in order to render possible the affirmation of being. This non-being (or radical doubt) can have various points of reference, can attack the object in various aspects: Descartes began by doubting immediate experience and the experience of the physical sciences, then went on to doubt mathematics itself and all acquired knowledge, until the very act of knowing itself became philosophically expendable. But he then swung over to a stabilizing principle in his trust in theological reason, to which the great representatives of rationalism, such as Spinoza, Malebranche, Leibniz, Wolff and their like, remained faithful for various and often quite disparate reasons. The non-being that substantiated doubt in rationalism and convalidated in direct proportion by its opposition the truth of its contrary was referred to immediate experience, to the "datum", to the empirical finite, to the passing moment.

Far from inhibiting English empiricism, this actually stimulated it in its affirmation—an affirmation again made precisely in virtue of the principle of immanentism and with better reason or at least consistency than the above-mentioned affirmations or rationalism—that the non-being, which was supposed to substantiate doubt, should rather be referred to the useless heavy baggage of the universals and that the principle of every valid assertion ought to be located in the *single act of experience that is the momentary impression of the act of sensing*. Here, then, are two opposing interpretations of doubt and of the *cogito,* which have concurrently sustained and corroded modern thought from within its innermost nucleus, driving it, as we shall see, outside the bounds of philosophy into sheer action or sheer inaction, as evidenced respectively today by Marxism and existentialism.

In its treatment of *content,* then, modern philosophy developed like a great theological concert, a series of variations on the theme of the ontological argument; and this development was a quite conscious and deliberate one, beginning with Descartes and continuing through Malebranche, Spinoza, Leibniz, down at least to Hegel who constitutes the summit of ambiguity, i.e., of theological extrapolation and extrinsicization of man and of anthropocosmic interpolation and intrinsicization of God, seeing that here the True is solely the Absolute, the Necessary (rationalism), the All (Kant, idealism) and the act is "*veri*fied" within the ambit of this Necessary, this All, as a coming-to-presence and being-brought-to-presence of that Absolute. This does not abolish the drastic distinction obtaining between the Olympian world of rationalism and the turbulent sea of Kantian criticism and idealism: but the difference here in question is only one of mode and method of attaining and affirming the Absolute; it is not a diffierence of opinion concernng the Absolute's noetico-ontic function as foundation for the transition from experience to metaphysics.

Therefore, it should not be surprising to see this classical line of modern thought being presented in major key in Descartes and used by him quite explicitly as a polemical weapon against atheism and materialism [1] to serve as the foundation for certitude concerning the existence of

[1] In the *Discours de la Méthode* (1637), Descartes sets himself the goal of "rightly steering reason and seeking truth in the sciences"; but the *Meditationes de Prima Philosophia* (1641) assign a quite specific competency to metaphysics: ". . . wherein is demonstrated the existence of God and the immortality of the Soul"; and Descartes provides an extensive gloss on this statement in the letter to the Dean and Doctors of the Faculty of Theology of Paris. And in the *Praefatio,* he clearly explains his aim of opposing the atheists whose positions derive

God and the immortality of the soul; nor should it be surprising to see Hegel indignantly rejecting the charge of atheism almost universally launched against Spinoza (and of course indirectly against Hegel himself, for having designated Spinoza as the forefather of philosophy: "Being a Spinozist is the essential beginning of all philosophizing" [2]).

Hegel's defense, as we have seen, was most spirited and illuminating: only those could have accused Spinoza of pantheism and atheism who attribute "a true reality", an affirmative reality, to the finite world. Of course such people could easily accuse Spinoza in this way because they themselves are moving in the "world of finite appearances" which Spinoza (and Hegel with him!) denies entirely: the world in its basic aspects, extension and thought, resolves itself into God so that in reality and in truth "only God is" (*nur Gott ist*).[3] This charge of atheism levelled against Spinozism—*and against philosophy as such*—Hegel finds ultimately more obvious (if not more convincing) than those of acosmism and pantheism, since the way Spinoza (and Hegel) must represent the Absolute (as indeed must philosophy as such, according to Hegel) is diametrically opposed to the notions of the common man and of those philosophies which base themselves on the understanding (*Verstand*) for which even the finite is true and real and therefore distinct from the Infinite.[4]

In its treatment of the *act* of knowing, on the other hand, the principle of immanentism has sought to develop itself and polish its credentials as a "principle of knowledge" by means of a demand as essential and primordial as its thrust in the matter of content, namely, the contention

---

either from excessively ingenuous notions of God or from the claim to penetrate his nature and activity: "And let me simply say in general that all the arguments bandied about by the atheists with a view to impugning the existence of God, always depend either on an ascription to God of human dispositions or on an arrogation to our own minds of such power and wisdom as to spur us on to an attempt to define and comprehend anything and everything that God can and should do; so that, if only we be mindful of the fact that our minds are to be considered as finite and God as incomprehensible and infinite, these arguments of the atheists are not going to give rise to any difficulty for us" (*Meditationes; C. W.*, Vol. VII, ed. Adam-Tannery [Paris, 1909], p. 9).

[2] Cf. Hegel, *Geschichte der Philosophie; C. W.*, Vol. XV, ed. Michelet (Berlin, 1844), p. 337.

[3] Hegel, *Enzyklopädie der philosophischen Wissenschaften,* § 50; ed. Hoffmeister, (Leipzig, 1949), p. 76. In the famous Preface to the second edition of 1827, Hegel defines the history of philosophy as "the history of the discovery of the *thoughts* about the Absolute, which is its object" and takes the occasion to associate himself with Lessing (whom, as we know, Jacobi had in his day accused of Spinozism!) in defending Spinoza (*ibid.*, pp. 12ff.).

[4] Cf. especially *Enzyklopädie der philosophischen Wissenschaften,* § 573, pp. 477ff. The allusion to "pietistic theology" is surely intended to hit at the theologian Tholuck who is expressly quoted and criticized in the Preface to the second edition (pp. 15f.) as the "enthusiastic representative of the pietistic line".

that *truth is the immediacy of the act.* The doubt that ran to seek refuge in the Absolute in the Cartesian *cogito* was held to have jumped the gun entirely: if the certainty attested by doubt is the presence of the act of doubting which is the *cogito,* the affirmation of the *cogito* cannot transcend the act itself and the very certitude of the *cogito* is proportionate to the doubt, the exclusion and negation in respect of all that "transcends" the act of the moment, i.e., in respect of any content that is not the act itself in its momentary presentness. The truth of the *cogito,* if it excludes the content in its first selfpositing (the *other* being the Absolute), must exclude it permanently if it wishes to maintain the truth of its own presence. Therefore, it is patent that immanentism cannot embrace and substantiate simultaneously act and object and that a choice must be made: the history of modern philosophy is the tension of this choice, continually renewed. And the struggle involved can be truly called a family fight because both tendencies, empiricism and idealism, claim to start from the same principle, the principle of mind, of cognition, of the consciousness or immanence of being. In actual fact the struggle is one which the very principle of immanentism is conducting with and against itself, inasmuch as it finds itself constrained to lose one pole of the dialectic (and to admit the loss!) every time it tends or tries to go radical, to delve to its own deepest roots. If it goes to the Absolute, selecting and "choosing" the content, it loses the act and with it presence (presentness) as substantiated-substantiating immediacy; if, on the contrary, it goes to the act, selecting and "choosing" the immediacy of presentness, it loses the content and with it the foundation of structure and meaning.

In any case, philosophy—to use a Hegelian term reiterated by Heidegger—"going to the bottom" of the principle of immanentism [5] is

[5] We have repeatedly stressed (and not by mere accident!) the special status accruing to Hegel in the evolution and development of the principle of immanentism which has led to the phenomenologico-pragmatic bowdlerization of present-day thought. A penetration of the deep-lying motivations of Hegelianism is the indispensable key to a proper grasp of the spirit of the culture of our time and the exact state of its structural atheism. Hegel can be said to have been the idealist who has been most criticized by the very thinkers who have been most desirous of appropriating to themselves the genuine substance of his thought; therefore Morton Price's statement seems to us in no way exaggerated: "Not only did [Hegel] influence the originators of marxism, existentialism and instrumentalism, now three of the most popular philosophies in the world, but at one time or another he dominated the founders of the more technical movements, logical positivism, realism, and analytic philosophy. The point is that Karl Marx, Kierkegaard, John Dewey, Bertrand Russell, and G. E. Moore were at one time or another close students of Hegel's thought and some of their distinctive doctrines reveal the imprint or the scars of previous contact or struggle with that strange genius" (in H. Wein, *Realdialektik, Von hegelscher Dialektik zu dialektischer Anthropologie* [Munich, 1957], p. 14).

constrained to confess and admit its own "sinking" (*Untergang*) to make way for willing and acting. And it is suggestive indeed that this admission of the end of "pure thought" (i.e., philosophy and philosophizing) today explicitly asserted by modern philosophy should have taken its origin from the elimination of God in Feuerbach-Marx's assertion that religion is the product of a psychological illusion and Hegel-Nietzsche's assertion that "God is dead" in the life of modern man.

In a theoretical interpretation of the principle of immanentism, its dissolution into the atheism of modern thought in our day is no mere fortuitous or optional event, it is inevitable and immaent, it is constitutive of the very reduction of the principle itself to its primordial element. And although the various present-day philosophies may well be divergent and even opposed in their "method", yet the structure and the content of the act remain for all on the same level, that of finitude, of a mind, a consciousness and a cognition (executive actuation of that consciousness) defined in its ontological dimension as "Being-in-the-world". The expulsion of God is therefore solidary with radical doubt, with the *cogito,* with the *Ich denke überhaupt,* all taken as basically an *actus ponens*, determining truth: in this sense Spinoza is more consistent with Descartes and Malebranche, and Hobbes more consistent with Bacon and Locke.[6] Ancient and Renaissance atheism derives its negation from *negative* elements, either materialism or the problem of evil or the providence controversy; modern atheism on the contrary reaches the atheistic posture by means of a fundamental *affirmation,* the affirmation of the transcendental human subjectivity, the act of the *cogito* as stemming from the subject and structuring and actualizing the object to which it relates as ground to grounded.

1. *Principle of Immanentism and Finitude of Being*

Immanence as a phenomenon is of course well-known to classical thought; but modern thought touts a new concept of immanence which is supposed to provide a new starting point for thought, capable in turn of providing a definitive substantiation for speculative reflection. For classical thought, too, knowing was an immanent process as was every vital process, inasmuch as every action of animate beings flows from the interior of the vital principle and is consummated therein as a perfection of its operative faculties; and such processes were called immanent in

[6] We have already seen the explicit charge of atheism launched immediately against ontologistic and Cartesian rationalism by the illustrious Jesuit historian of the Councils, J. Hardouin in his treatise *Athei detecti* (Atheists Unmasked) and by the Calvinist theologian Gisbertus Voetius.

contradistinction to the processes of becoming in the inorganic world which latter were held to be processes of simple transformation. Immanence, in classical thought, signifies "increment within the self" (*De an.*, II, 4, 417b. 7) and hence knowing is a process perfective of being, not constitutive of being.

In modern thought, on the contrary, immanence is constitutive and substantiating with respect to being. In the simplest formulation the difference between the approach of classical thought and that of modern thought to this whole question is the following: for realism, it is being, in its givenness and self-presentation to consciousness, to the mind, which substantiates and brings to act the mind itself, hence, causing the consciousness (mind) to become a consciousness of being and to mold the truth as conformity to being; for modern thought, thanks to the intervention of radical doubt, it is consciousness (the mind) which initiates proceedings by and from itself in its own act of "thinking" (*cogitare*), with the result that being expresses the being-in-act of the mind and hence is identified with the mind's own actualization; it molds itself in function of the various ways in which the mind is held to be-in-act: clear and distinct ideas (Descartes, Spinoza, rationalism), vision of God (Malebranche), monads as active centers of the All (Leibniz), the categories as actualizations and the Ideas as universalizing projections of the transcendental *I think* (Kant and idealism). The same thing can be said for the empiricist line of development, wherein a more restrictive interpretation of the *cogito* as "act" of *percipere* led to a prompter and more radical elimination of the metaphysic of the Absolute.

From one point of view, of course, it can be said that the principle of immanentism runs through its whole cycle in every one of the most representative modern philosophers, inasmuch as every system is precisely the actualization of the principle itself; but from another point of view, namely, that of the truly *consistent* enucleation of the principle, it must be admitted that precisely the system, the very notion and aim of constructing some sort of system, is what most directly counteracts and impedes the actuation of the principle in its simonpure form. And in this sense it must be admitted that only in the philosophy of our own day is there observed that radical "premiselessness" (*Voraussetzungslosigkeit*), that sheer and simple commencement of the conscious knowing mind from itself, which constitutive doubt and the sheer *cogito* as such demand. The purity of the principle of act is present in all modern philosophers and it suffices to hear their terminology in order to be convinced of this: the Cartesian *cogito,* the *entelechia* of the Leibnizian monad, the Spinozan *nisus* or *conatus* are certainly in this line, which equally and undoubtedly becomes more pronounced with Kant's *Ich denke überhaupt* and still more with the absolute metaphysical Ego

(Self) of the transcendental idealists, abstracting as we have said from the systems themselves which constitute the "downfall" of the principle itself. What is important is the elevation (*Erhebung*) of the self, the Ego, to act and the ascent (*Aufstieg*) to cull the act in its nascent state as sheer becoming and self-foundation.

An excellent example for our diagnostic purposes, indeed perhaps the crucial one, is offered by the brief *Einleitung* (Introduction) to Hegel's *Phenomenology of Spirit*.[7] It, and not the grandiose and more famous *Vorrede* (Preface) constitutes the true "introduction" into the most original if not the most powerful of Hegel's works, a work in which Hegel institutes the true concrete beginning of his own philosophizing, starting from the constitutive identity of being and thought and plunging into its dynamic. We think it pertinent to present here the most suggestive elements of this Hegelian vision, because in this text the Cartesian *cogito* and the Kantian *Ich denke überhaupt* have burst all bonds and are sweeping forward in sheer and integral freedom. But the assertion of this freedom has a difficult time coming through. In the prologue Hegel sets out in fact to clear the ground of all encumbrances and he criticizes the functional conception of thought as an "instrument" and means to attain being and the Absolute, the conception that had been systematically elaborated by Kant. To refute this conception, Hegel appeals to the object of his own "system", the Absolute, which was certainly not able to be attained by any thinking of this sort! [8] And a thought that does indeed stabilize itself in the Absolute requires that Hegelian pseudo-theology to which we have already referred and to which we shall in due course return; and it manifests the patent exchange of immanence as presence for immanence as content. Fortunately for us, Hegel here abruptly ceases to appeal to the Absolute and proceeds with a fantastically brilliant and terse analysis of the principle of immanentism, hitting its salient features with rare perceptive genius. Heidegger was not unjustified in classing this Hegelian analysis of act with Aristotle's reflections on ὂν ᾗ ὂν (being as being).

2. *Meaning of Doubt and Negation*

Still another hesitation intervenes before the affirmation of integral freedom. Hegel asserts, in the rationalist and Kantian tradition, that truth can be molded only as a system or as a *formation* of the initial or

[7] We have translated this brief Introduction in our *Hegel, La dialettica* (Brescia, 1966[2]), pp. 13-27.

[8] Although Hegel criticizes Schelling who began with the Absolute, he repeats this initial appeal to the Absolute in the *Enzyklopädie der philosophischen Wissenschaften* (§ 14).

apparent awareness: this apparent knowledge is not true, the systematized is; but it is precisely the awareness of the non-truth of the apparent knowledge, the advertence to the non-truth of every immediate phenomenon which as such resolves itself into nothingness, and consequently ultimately the *doubt* itself in its active or nihilating form which amounts to that uncovering of the negative which is the secret power of the dialectic.

The first step in reflection is that of recognizing and affirming the identity of mind and reality, of thinking and being; Hegel also calls this the overcoming of the opposition between thinking and being which opposition itself is "the supreme sundering" (*die höchste Entzweiung*). The second step is the "transition to the Absolute" which in Hegel constitutes the term and "result" of the dialectic and which he presents as the definitive metaphysical foundation and substantiation of the truth of being. The first step is the ontico-ontological element which continues as the guiding thread throughout modern neo-Hegelianism and actualism down to the Marxism and existentialism of our own day; the second step is the systematic element which falls away at once when Hegel's pseudo-theology comes under fire.

The identity of thought and being is nothing but the reflective formulation of the *cogito* considered as the autogenetic primordial act of the mind.[9] Not only, therefore, does the object of thought have no reference to any reality outside thought itself; the very concept that is truly adequate to being is in turn identical with mind. Continually rediscovering itself in every object and act, the mind "is the act of surpassing the limited and, since this limited belongs to it itself, it is the act of surpassing itself" and it is precisely this transcending of the limited (finite) which constitutes the "reason" which remains forever within itself wherever it moves, so that "the concept corresponds to the object and the object to the concept." Any would-be Beyond (*Jenseits*) of the mind ultimately finds itself ailing within the mind itself.

3. *Finitude of Being and Negation* (*Denial*) *of God*

As soon as being is conceived as presence, presentness, being-present, that being-present which is the act of consciousness (mind), the principle of act becomes possessed of an all-pervading and all-embracing hegemony: being is act in the extreme concreteness of its individuality, singularity and historical temporality, as the sheer impression and awareness of sensation and reflection as in Hume; and it is solely in this

[9] Cf. C. Fabro, *La dialettica hegeliana,* Introduction, pp. XLIf.

sense that consciousness, the mind, is concreteness and freedom, according to the principle of immanentism. Any talk of a dual world, of appearance and reality, of phenomenon and noumenon, of finite and Infinite, is now simply meaningless: if the antithesis, that opposition out of which the dialectic arises and by which that dialectic is supported, is not present from the first moment, does not constitute the very structure of that first moment, then it can only be forced upon the situation from the outside and hence invalid. In this sense philosophy resolves itself into the simple "taking account of the principle of act" which Hegel expresses in the most drastic phenomenological formulation as "sheer standing-at-gaze" (*reines Zuschauen*). Hegel, like Descartes, invokes God as the *ultimate* foundation of truth (*das Wahre ist das Ganze*): this can be explained on the basis of the spiritual training both had received, the climate of a quite specific theological situation, operative as it were "behind their backs" [10] to use another felicitous expression that Hegel laid at the basis of the dialectical advance of thought. Actually, the sole foundation of the *cogito* is the *cogitare,* the act of consciousness (of mind) in its own self-actualization, which cannot and ought not to be mediated by any content (object) but only by itself in the historical experience that impels it. On this point, Heidegger and Sartre agree, as representatives of the latest phenomenological ontology: the "Presence of that which comes-to-presence" (*die Anwesenheit des Anwesenden*) of Heidegger undoubtedly prepared the way for and suggested the *phénomène d'être* of Sartre, although Heidegger still persists in rejecting the charge of atheism. The "transference" Hegel desired to make from the finite to the Infinite with his distinction between a dialectic of true infinity and a dialectic of "baneful infinity" or the "leap" (*Sprung*) into Being-itself (*Sein selbst*) would signify that the *cogito* is not being, for it is meaningless to posit a *cogito* that is not an act of consciousness or its coming-to-presence. The formula of ontological phenomenology, expressive of the radical and utterly drastic finitude of being and the negation of God, is indeed to be found in Hegel himself: "The phenomenon is the beginning and the ending which of itself neither begins nor ends but is in itself and constitutes the reality and the motion of the life of truth." [11] The notion of phenomenon or appearance (*Erscheinung* has here lost all negative character accruing to it from its contraposition to the thing-in-itself, the noumenon and the Absolute, and has assumed that simple and irreducible character of sheer presence

[10] Hegel, *Phänomenologie des Geistes,* Introduction; ed. Hoffmeister (Leipzig, 1937), p. 74. Cf. also: *Enzyklopädie der philosophischen Wissenschaften,* § 15; *Wissenschaft der Logik,* Introduction; *C. W.,* Vol. I, ed. Lasson (Leipzig, 1934), pp. 30f.

[11] Hegel, *Phänomenologie des Geistes,* Preface, p. 39.

and coming-to-presence wherein man's mind expresses its own selfactuation in time. The identity of mind and being is therefore the identity of being and time and of being and history "without remainder". And so, though it can indeed be said that no philosopher has ever spoken so much about God or appealed so much to God as Hegel, it must also be forthwith admitted that no philosophy, not even that of Spinoza, has so incited to the negation of God as that of Hegel, the common trunk from which the branch forms of extreme modern atheism (existentialism and Marxism) diverge.

This reduction of modern philosophy to atheism (as negative formulation) and to humanism (as positive formulation) is no novelty; it goes back more than a century: but the "positivity" of this reduction is a claim of present-day philosophy inasmuch as it has aimed at appealing to the *cogito* in its primordial purity. Therefore, any effort to combat the atheism of modern philosophy within the ambit of the principle of immanentism gives evidence simply of a failure to grasp in its drastic purity the neat notions that lie at the very root of that principle: contemplation or sheer presence, as "letting-Being-be", or sheer activity, as the self-actuation of pure Will. For these indeed are the two antithetical but equally possible meanings of the *cogito*. United in metaphysical idealism, they subsequently split asunder and now confront one another in the opposing schools of existentialism and Marxism. But this is an irrelevant opposition at the ultimate level of the ground and principle which is the act of mind, the act of consciousness, even though in a pinch existentialism may justly lay claim to a greater consistency of principle, which has been lost in Marxism with its return to the Hegelian conception of truth as a "Whole" (the collective, the worker class, mankind as a "whole") and as a "result" (elimination of classes, in this world State). On the other hand, it cannot be forgotten that if the real issue of the *cogito* is realized in the perennial removal of all content or in the coming-to-presence of the Present and nothing more, as existentialism quite logically asserts, then this issue is diametrically opposed to that for which the principle was invoked in the first place, i.e., the substantiation of the existence of God and the immortality of the soul. Faced, then, with the overall phenomenon of modern philosophy, one of two choices is mandatory: either the acceptance of the annihilation of thinking (and of being) or beginning again from the very outset.

The *cogito*, therefore, has a strictly metaphysical meaning and sginificance. Thus, its developments or interpretations, whether subjectivistic in the phenomenist sense, or absolutistic in the would-be theological sense, all constitute an inhibition and drastic frustration of the principle itself: for phenomenist subjectivism implies the renunciation of that very truth in itself which the *cogito* is called upon to substantiate; would-be theological absolutism (as, e.g., in Hegel) implies no less a renunciation of comprehension of that Absolute which is the All, the Whole, whose totality consists in the very dynamic of the dynamism of the world and history. It is legitimate to speak of a "realistic" bias in the principle of immanentism, but only on condition that it be left in its most generic meaning, not specified by any reference of the act to anything other than its own self-realization.

The most radical form of this self-realization in absolute freedom is, in our opinion, solely that of "existence" or decision to be in the moment with respect to the end, death; it is not the various reform versions of the Hegelian dialectic remaining loyal to the principle of the Whole and the Absolute, neither the historicity and circularity of the Crocian Spirit nor yet the Gentile comprehension of pure Act. History and the reality of a nature standing over against man are indeed accepted and admitted; but this by no means constitutes a profession of dualism and still less of realism in the classical sense. The extreme and definitively genuine form of immanentism is precisely the constitutive reference of the finite mind to a finite world or the projection without remainder of the mind into the world, in its total and punctiform self-realization in the moment of sheer event. And this mind announcing itself as intrinsically finite by virtue of the fact that it perceives an intrinsically finite world—this is what constitutes the simon-pure formulation of immanentism: immanentism lies precisely in the finitude of this being-present of the mind to a world that defines it and renders presence possible precisely by means of the finitude which is essential for the coming-to-presence. This in turn transcendentally defines and delimits the finitude of consciousness and of freedom as a potentiality of (for) being. Sartre is therefore right in asserting, within the framework of the logic of the principle of immanentism, that existentialism is not atheism in the sense of amounting to no more than the assertion that God does not exist, but rather that immanentism declares that, even if God did exist, it would make no difference, would change nothing.[12] It suffices to appeal to the *cogito,* to determine man's being, human be-ing in terms of the *cogito,* and the game is effectively up! And this radical derivation or substantiation of atheism must be admitted to be the only really consequentially drastic one, since it is the only one analytically deduced from the principle of consciousness without any naturalistic, metaphysical or theological deviations or detours. It is much more radical than ancient or

[12] Jean-Paul Sartre, *L'existentialisme est un humanisme* (Paris, 1946), p. 95; English translation, *Existentialism and Humanism* (London: Methuen, 1948), p. 56.

Enlightenment materialism which had to engage in quite an amount of footwork to reduce thought and cognition to an activity of matter; more radical than monism or pantheism, both of which have to reduce the plurality of subjects to a mere illusion or fortuitousness; more radical than theologico-metaphysical idealism which reduces or refers the divine life to the intensive historical totality of the activity of the human spirit; more radical even than the atheism promulgated by Stirner and Nietzsche who transferred the pseudo-transcendence or emergence of the idealist God into the Superman and the Individual. We hold the whole of present-day philosophy to be more or less anti-idealist, but not because it has returned to metaphysical realism and dualism, rather because it has dared courageously to go the limit with the principle of immanentism, defining being exclusively in terms of man or of the human being (be-ing) as manifested solely in the act of consciousness as dialectic of temporal being.

4. *From Epistemological Immanence to Epistemological Immanentism to Ontological Immanentism*

The problematic of immanence as such pervades the whole of philosophy. The controversy or antithesis between Plato and Aristotle, viewed from the angle most immediately pertinent to the determination of the *locus veritatis* (the site of truth), revolves around the question of whether truth is immanent or transcendent with respect to sensible reality. Here "immanence" has an ontological but not yet a metaphysical significance. This latter significance will be approached only with the Neo-Platonic doctrine of the triads (οὐσία, ζωή, νοῦς).[13] Immanence comes to have a metaphysical connotation only with the speculation of Philo and the Fathers of the Church concerning the creation and God's omnipotence as reaching to the ultimate and definitive being of reality, dorn to matter and up to and including the human will itself and the wills of those spiritual beings standing at the summit of the marvelous *machina mundi*. This full and adequate conception of immanence receives its definitive theoretical formulation in the Thomistic speculation on participation which certainly served as inspiration for Eckhart and Nicolas of Cusa, but was initially opposed by the powerful anti-Thomist streams within Scholasticism and subsequently remained almost entirely unnoticed.

[13] On these triads, cf. J. Pepin, "Histoire de la philosophie ancienne," in *Histoire de la philosophie et de la métaphysique*, Vol. I (Paris, 1955), p. 235. Cf. also C. Fabro, *Partecipazione e causalità* (Turin, 1961), pp. 190f.

The almost total ignorance of modern philosophers, Feuerbach excepted, concerning the inner drama of Scholasticism, combined with their deception by its most flashy and superficial expositions, produced a deep cleavage in Western thought which must be bridged in the interests of both parties.

The most current meaning of immanentism as opposed to immanence as such is the epistemological meaning connoted by the modern *cogito,* i.e., the contention that the mind has itself [14] for its object and has no need of seeking that object "outside of" itself, and that consequently a reality "beyond" the mind and thought, a transcendent reality, as it is called, is unthinkable. But this meaning of epistemological immanentism has been filtered through a whole spectrum of meanings that can scarcely be maintained in the face of a rigorous speculative judgment, since the whole thrust of the filtering is to an inversion and total contradiction of the classical meaning of immanentism, an inversion culminating in the assertion of the total extrinsicization or secularization of the mind. Even immanentism itself is totally dissolved in the very process of the authentication of the principle of immanentism, and the end result is the mandatory renunciation of all philosophical speculation desirous of appealing to a principle transcending man and watching over his fate.

Epistemological immanentism goes back to Berkeley, proceeds through Hume-Kant-Fichte and can be called "the doctrine of reality as representation": it is the theme of the so-called *philosophy of immanence,* whose avowed aim was to think the *cogito* in its absolute purity of total reflection of (the) act in itself.[15] In its fight against metaphysics, in its opposition to any positing of a reality transcending the realm of consciousness and in its admission of the immanence of every content

[14] Hegel is specific on this point from the time of the *Phenomenology:* "Concept and object, measuring-rod and thing-to-be-measured are present in the mind itself and so any addition on our part is superfluous; rather are we relieved of the exertion of the comparison of both and of the very *examination,* and there remains for us from this angle, too, only the sheer standing-at-gaze (*das reine Zusehen*)". And he proceeds to identify the two elements, act and content: "For the mind, the consciousness is on the one hand a consciousness of the object, and on the other hand a consciousness of itself; a consciousness of what is true for it and a consciousness of the knowing thereof" (Hegel, *Phänomenologie des Geistes,* ed. Hoffmeister, p. 72).

An Aristotelian with realist bias thus expressed the essence of idealism as follows: "What lies outside and beyond any possible consciousness, any possible mind, is not even a possible object of thought but rather a sheer non-entity, and conversely only what is a possible object of thought can exist and it can only exist precisely through and for thought" (T. Waitz, *Lehrbuch der Psychologie als Naturwissenschaft,* [Brunswick, 1849], pp. 2f.).

[15] Cf. especially W. Schuppe, *Grundriss der Erkenntnistheorie und Logik* (Berlin, 1894); and for an overall exposition, R. Ettinger-Reichmann, *Die Immanenzphilosophie,* Darstellung und Kritik (Göttingen, 1916).

of consciousness, this philosophy is in line with the whole complex movement of Neo-Kantianism, whether idealist (Eucken, Natorp, Rickert *et al.*) or positivist (Lass, Mach, Avenarius), typical of the last decades of the 19th century. Its common feature was a fierce resistance to any effort at "metaphysicization" of the Self and an insistence on conceiving consciousness (the mind) solely as act in its immediacy. It insisted on complete abstraction from such artificial oppositions as realism and idealism, since there is neither an *outside* nor an *inside* in cognition and the reflective philosopher must stop at, and concentrate upon, the essential and fundamental character of knowing as such, which is the "immediately given" (*das unmittelbar Gegebene*), as apprehended in the knower's own reflection on his knowing, on what the mind has as immediate datum, and in analysis of this datum.

The nucleus of this analysis is as follows: the "datum" is found solely in the relation to the Self, to the subject or mind, as what that mind has, and hence solely as content of the data of the mind, of consciousness, as result of the act of mind (*als etwas Bewusstes*). This being-given with respect to the mind does not of course signify any spatial inclusion "within" the mind (*kein räumliches Eingeschlossensein*). In the being-given in general there is no outside nor inside but only a being-conditioned by the mind, only the fact that the not-self or object cannot be posited without a self or subject, that the datum, the given, cannot be received without the knower or subject and *vice versa.* Subject and object are the two elements to be distinguished in the datum as a primordial whole in which each of these elements presupposes the other so that they can be separated only in logical analysis. The precise formulation here is that of the essential conjunction (*wesentliche Zusammengehörigkeit*) of subject and object, or the correlation of consciousness and content (*Bewusstsein und Inhalt*), of self and notself. Therefore, and this is the crucial point, being (*Sein*) or existence can mean only object of consciousness (*Bewusstseinsobjekt*), content of consciousness (*Bewusstseinsinhalt*), being-conscious or conscious being (*bewusstes Sein*). Hence any transcendent reality having no relation to the mind, in the sense that it can be thought of as existing independently of the mind, i.e., as existing in itself, invariably implies a contradiction, whether or not such a reality be acknowledged as knowable. By the very fact that a reality is thought, it is no longer independent of thought, it is no longer an unthought being. Thus the concept of "transcendence" in the sense of an existing without relation to consciousness or self, in the sense of a reality independent of the mind, would signify not only the overstepping of experience but a total overstepping of the consciousness-relation (*das Ueberschreiten der Bewusstseinsbeziehung*); and this in turn would open the door to metaphysical dualism.

Now the self shows itself in immediate awareness, in immediate consciousness, as something that can *be* only a subject, that can *have* only properties, that can exercise activities, but can never have anything of which it is a substrate, which is added to it as its properties or activities; and not only does it not need anything of this sort, it simply cannot have any such thing. It is entirely futile therefore to ask what might be meant by being outside of the mind, whether there is such another being (being, way of being), or whether the two ways of being can agree as two species coordinated in certain abstract properties which would constitute the generic concept of being.[16] Being itself, as it is expressed in the act of consciousness, displays within itself the two component parts, the Ego-point and the object-world (and primarily in that world its "own" body), in such a unity that either of them without the other immediately vanishes into nothingness, that the one is posited by the very act of positing the other.[17] And this is not nor can it properly be called idealism, declares Schuppe, and still less can it be called solipsism.[18]

Proceeding, then, to the problem of "existence", the philosophy of immanence distinguishes the perception of one's own existence from the perception of the existence of other things: our own existence we have only in consciousness, in auto-intuition, in the finding-of-ourselves, in being the object of ourselves; the existence of other things is given inasmuch as they have relation to the self or inasmuch as that self finds their definitions as contents of its own consciousness, of its own mind. The point of departure for the concept of existence is therefore consistently found in the mind itself, in consciousness itself, in one's own existence.

This basic outline of the philosophy of immanence already makes it clear that the problem of the existence of God is for this philosophy entirely meaningless; it is noteworthy that Schuppe takes only the

[16] "What being is supposed to mean, aside from conscious-being, whether there is still another sort of being, and whether the former and the latter have certain common characteristics, like two species of one genus, characteristics which constitute the generic concept of being—this is the question. Such characteristics will be sought for in vain" (W. Schuppe, *Grundriss der Erkenntnistheorie und Logik,* n. 23, p. 17).

[17] "It pertains to being itself that it displays within itself the two component parts, the Ego-point and the object-world (and first of all in that object-world the Ego-point's 'own' body) in this unity, that either of them without the other immediately vanishes into nothingness, that one is posited with the other" (*ibid.,* p. 22).

[18] "I have identified consciousness with thought in general, and this means that in my philosophy the particular species and categories of thought cannot erupt out of this, their generic character. There can therefore be no doubt that I count everything that is an object of thought to belong, by that fact, to the content of consciousness" (W. Schuppe, "Bergmann's reine Logik und die Erkenntnistheoretische Logik mit ihrem angeblichen Idealismus," *Vierteljahrschrift für wissenschaftliche Philosophie* III [1879], p. 473).

ontological argument into consideration. Actually pure being has merely the office of purely functional predication, without any content whatsoever, and thus as such means nothing. The notion of being has no content and thus cannot be or constitute a predicate of any sort, as Kant has proven. Being is nothing unless it is the being (be-ing) of some thing, e.g. something perceived or thought or serving as object of a feeling or of a tendency of the will: being therefore always presents itself as something particular, of which I take cognizance as a content of my own activities of consciousness, from which God is by definition excluded.[19]

This outlook, therefore, taking its starting point from Hume as interpreted by Kant, emerges as a "transcendental phenomenology" such as was already beginning to take shape in the later Fichte when he posited "knowing" (*Wissen*) as the object-phenomenon (phenomenal object) of philosophy, that knowing, to wit, that manifests itself in itself in a new knowing. Knowing is also awareness of itself inasmuch as it is conscious of any other object. Consciousness makes the reflexive pronouncement: I simply know that I know (am knowing). It is the business of philosophy to substantiate this knowing which here is a phenomenon, i.e., an object of an actual knowing (act.) [20] But Fichte, after having posited the first fact (of thought) takes on his own the first step (as Descartes had done in his own way before him), by positing the Absolute and the whole procedure is of a disconcerting simplism which only the appeal and reference to Spinoza could somewhat explain: as only the Absolute is, so is its appearance (*Erscheinung*) and the appearance is the understanding wherein the Absolute comprehends itself and thus objectifies itself.[21] This is the nucleus of the Hegelian position, as we have seen; but Neo-Kantianism and especially the "philosophy of

[19] Cf. W. Schuppe, *Grundriss der Erkenntnistheorie und Logik,* § 153, pp. 167f.; § 159, pp. 176ff.

[20] "Philosophy specifically has as its phenomenon the *knowledge* which reveals itself in itself in a new knowledge. Knowledge is aware of *itself,* just as it is aware of any other object. In reference to itself, consciousness, the mind, likewise says: it is; I *know* precisely that I know. It is the business of philosophy to *establish and substantiate* this knowledge which in philosophy is a phenomenon, i.e. object of an actual knowledge" (J. G. Fichte, *Die Tatsachen des Bewusstseins* [1813]; *Nachgelassene Schriften,* Vol. I, ed. R. Lauth and H. Jakob [Stuttgart, 1962], p. 403).

[21] The relevant passage is in Fichte's terse and pithy style: "Aside from the Absolute, however, only the *understanding* is absolute, as God Himself, for it is His appearance. But this appearance is only in the understanding of itself, since this intelligent, i.e. self-understanding being is precisely absolutely the being of the appearance, of the phenomenon" (this is substantially Berkeley's *Esse est percipi*): J. G. Fichte, *Die Tatsachen des Bewusstseins,* p. 408. Fichte has no trouble deducing—"on paper" as Kierkegaard would say!—from this notion of "phenomenon" or appearance the manifold reality of the real (cf. pp. 418ff.).

immanence" have abandoned Spinoza to return to rigid Kantian orthodoxy. The human understanding can pronounce only by the instrumentality of syntheses effected within the area of finitude.

In the course of the development of the principle of immanentism, it has become steadily clearer that the "recourse to God" is not only superfluous and inappropriate but downright harmful to the principle itself. This "recourse to God" had been the refuge of Berkeley, the founder of epistemological idealism, and later of the idealists and of Fichte himself, though he was accused of atheism; in the case of post-Berkeleyian philosophers mentioned, the recourse had been effected, to be sure, within the framework of the principle of the Transcendental. But any such recourse is a mistake. The proper procedure is to supplement Berkeley with Kant, without any relapse into the theologism of Berkeley (or still worse of Leibniz-Spinoza-Descartes). The most drastic formulation of immanentism must face the problem of the concept of "consciousness in general" (*Bewusstsein überhaupt*), which is not in its turn a content of consciousness (*Bewusstseinsinhalt*) but simply a form of consciousness (*Bewusstseinsform*). "Reality" then is the being-given to a mind, a consciousness: to-be-real means *to be a content of a mind in general* [22] abstracting, in the act of knowing, from all the contents that form the particular elements of the self, and one is left with mind in general, universal consciousness, universal mind. The various schools of immanentism differ in function of the way in which they explain the nexus between the content and act of consciusness and in function of the nature they attribute to the "conjunction" of the content and the act that sustains it. Thus, the Neo-Kantian Baden school (Windelband, Rickert) developed the notion of the constructive a priority of practical Reason in its elaboration of the "philosophy of values"; the Marburg school worked rather with the structural apriority of the pure Reason in its effort to transform the universal Self into a Reason or Logos having the mission of generating even the material of sensation and the forms of experience in an infinite process.

The most striking feature revealed by this hasty sketch of the fortunes of immanentism is the basic continuity observable in the manifold and apparently discordant immanentistic trends. For it can be said in substance that in the direct transition from English empiricism to Kantian apriorism, to the idealist Aboslute Self or Ego, the element that falls by the wayside or is diversified is the accessory, pure auxiliary and ancillary element; that element may well vary in function of the demands of the particular cultural situation; but the essential element, the priority of

[22] "To be real *means* to be the content of a consciousness, of a mind" (H. Maier, *Philosophie der Wirklichkeit,* Vol. II, 1 [Tübingen, 1926], pp. 197f.).

act as substantiating and grounding over content as substantiated and grounded—this essential element is steadily maintained and purified in its status as foundation and ground of being. An outstanding representative of this whole tendency, Rickert, noted this in the case of the evolution of his own thought. He points, in one of his last works,[23] to a substantial alteration of terminology (*eine wesentliche Änderung des Sprachgebrauches*) with regard to the term of most interest to us in the discussion of the God-problem, namely the term "being" (*Sein*). In the 3rd edition of Rickert's *Der Gegenstand der Erkenntnis, Einführung in die Transzendentalphilosophie* (Tübingen, 1915), *Sein* has a more restricted meaning than in his subsequent works and in the subsequent editions of this work. Initially "Being" is expressly construed with "being-of-value" (*Gelten*), and Rickert explicitly warns that there can be no stopping at an "ontology" as the end point of human philosophical effort. But this terminology showed itself, in the course of Rickert's further reflections, to be inadequate and a cause of misunderstandings. In the Preface to the 4th edition of the same work, he signals a change of position on the point of the term "being": it now appears to him as the most important term of all. It is no longer used to indicate the real in opposition to the unreal, the valid or the valuable; rather it is now used to indicate, in a most generic way, everything that is an object of thought in general; therefore this term always now carries a rider indicating whether real or unreal being is meant, in any case where this would otherwise be unclear.[24] This virtually represents an advance from Kant to Hegel, at least in the semantics of Being as such. Being is now used for everything that is, for everything that "there is" or that can be thought as "something"; this therefore includes validity, meaning, value and obligation. And so "ontology" can now quite well be the "last

[23] In this work, Rickert claims to be professing a "theory of being" (*Seinslehre*) contradistinguished from any metaphysical conception. He too accepts the equation "immanence = content of consciousness, of mind"; but for him the contents of consciousness of being are matched by the higher contents of value: "There is still an 'other world' than the immanent real world; and this other world lies in the realm of value or encounters us as an *Ought* which can never be traced back to a starkly existent (*ein Seiendes*). It persists 'independently' of every real entity and is to that extent *transcendent;* indeed only in it do we have the ultimate basis of the theoretical in general or the 'object' of knowledge . . ." And he concludes that such logical relations are not relations between existents but rather between values: "But we cannot stop at *any* ontology as the ultimate. The logical does not exist, it is *valid*". (H. Rickert, *Gegenstand der Erkenntnis,* Foreword to 3rd edition, cited in 4th-5th edition [Tübingen, 1921], p. IX).

[24] "In this connection the concept or notion of 'being' was crucially important. The word 'being' is now no longer being used for the actual or the real in opposition to the unreal, the valid or valuable, but rather as a most generic expression for everything that can be thought. It therefore always has a rider wherever it would otherwise be unclear whether real or unreal being is meant" (H. Rickert, *Der Gegenstand der Erkenntnis,* Foreword to 4th and 5th edition, p. XII).

stop" in that science that aims at a knowledge of the world in its entirety and totality.[25] Hence, the speculative interest in pinpointing the various meanings of "being". And Rickert immediately notes that "being" is to be distinguished above all from "existing"; "existing" is broader in its application than is "being", for "existing" is said not only of the real realm but also of the ideal, e.g., of mathematical figures. *Das Seiende* can, in this terminology, be either real or ideal. The real can in turn possess a sensible reality (physical or psychic) or a suprasensible reality; and the real is the object of metaphysics in this latter sense.[26] And this brings us to the Whole, the All in the absolute sense, as the "thing-in-itself", starting from which this world can be spoken of as the *Diesseits*.

The actuation or expansion of immanentism, which is perhaps the most accurate descriptive designation of this further development of the Kantian principle, has its focus and center of meaning in the activity of judgment, whose self-expansion expresses the very self-actualization of being. This is a reiteration of Kant and a return to the predicative synthesis as a positing of the real, starting from Hegel and the ferment aroused by him in the subsequent philosophical systems. Hence, we can readily understand Rickert's elevation of the "proposition" (*Satz*) to the status of *ens realissimum* in every science and indeed in every knowledge accessible to any scientist. Without propositions there can be no theoretical understanding among men. As long as sciences have existed, the proposition has formed the most important and key element in the effort to make sense out of sensible reality. For in the absence of propositions, which have previously been objects of perception on the part of men working in science, there can be no mutual understanding among men and science is thus impossible.[27] On the other hand—and here the Kantian element takes the upper hand—any man forming propositions speaking of being and aiming at the knowledge of the totality of the world, really expresses only some part or aspect; hence the proposition in the very moment that it opens up the horizon of being, also closes that horizon: a statement with which Jaspers would entirely agree! The important point here is the progress that has occured in

[25] "Let it therefore be noted at this point that I am now calling everything 'being' (*seiend*) that 'there is' in any sense whatsoever or that can be thought as 'something'; this therefore includes validity, meaning, value and obligation (*das Gelten, den Sinn, den Wert und das Sollen*). To this extent, 'ontology' can now quite well be 'the ultimate' in science, that aims at a knowledge of the world in its totality" (H. Rickert, *Die Logik des Prädikats und das Problem der Ontologie* [Heidelberg, 1930], pp. 8f.).

[26] Rickert acknowledges the importance of the thought of N. Hartmann and M. Heidegger in this supersession of the neo-Kantian position on the primacy of logic and of epistemology in philosophy (*ibid.*, p. 10).

[27] Cf. *ibid.*, p. 44.

respect of "being" which has changed from being copulative as it was in Kant and has become constitutive,[28] although the Kantian overall context remains entirely intact, namely, the contention that what we render present to ourselves is concepts, not things, so that a hundred real Thalers contain no more than a hundred possible thalers.

In this ontology of knowledge (an echo of the *Metaphysik der Erkenntnis* of N. Hartmann and expressive of a more highly developed form of immanentism which Rickert himself acknowledges to have been absent from the Kantian text) there is a reaffirmation of the Kantian notion of transcendental subjectivity as actuating its own world of objects in its totality.[29] Placed at the center of the proposition, not as a simple copula but rather as a principle actuating and effecting the coming-to-presence of the world, being is essentially finite even as the point-instant actuations of consciousness are finite; it is this form of immanentism as the self-actuation and self-realization of a world by consciousness, by the mind, that takes its definitive shape as a being-in-the-world (*in-der-Welt-sein:* Heidegger) of the mind, the common denominator of the present-day philosophies, amounting to a radical secularization and finitization of being.

Rickert's effort to stress the Being of beings, an effort that in turn has stimulated the development of the new ontologies, does not overcome immanentism, indeed it simply reinforces it.[30] But immanentism is now

[28] In his later works, Rickert ascribes a crucial importance to the question of being, in order to rebut the charge of scepticism to which critical philosophy is exposed: "This leads to the further question as to what the word 'being' (*Sein*) can possibly mean in an objective knowledge. We are in the habit of speaking of a 'copula'. Does the combination of subject and predicate by the word 'is' signify merely such a 'coupling' in every case? Or is there not rather here expressed, at least occasionally, the fact that something 'is' in still another sense of that word? The very statement 'This is brown' presupposes, if it lays claim to being an objective cognition, that 'this' *is* radically speaking; and such being transcends the mere coupling of 'this' and 'brown' " (H. Rickert, "Die Heidelberger Tradition und Kants Kritizismus," in *Deutsche systematische Philosophie nach ihren Gestalten,* Excerpt [Berlin, 1934], p. 22).

[29] Very shortly thereafter, in fact, we read: "The multiplicity of meanings the word 'be' has in various judgments strongly suggests the thought that the *being of the world* for its part, is itself manifold, and that an ontology can therefore only be considered to be genuinely universal if it takes into consideration the *plurality* of the being of the world expressed in the sciences" (H. Rickert, "Die Heidelberger Tradition und Kants Kritizismus," pp. 22f.). This new notion of being as multidimensionally signifying the Totality of the world, Rickert has developed systematically in the final synthesis of his thought: *Grundprobleme der Philosophie* (Tübingen, 1934); cf. pp. 54ff.

[30] Cf. L. Nelson, *Ueber das sogenannte Erkenntnisproblem* (Göttingen, 1908), pp. 506ff., for a critique of the "first stage" Rickert (*Der Gegenstand der Erkenntnis,* 1st ed.) on the part of the leader of the voluntaristic wing of the neo-Kantian school. The critique is equally applicable to the later Rickert.

assuming a shape different to what it had in Schuppe: now it is using "Being" as a principle of objectivity and stressing this principle rather than the simple subjectivity which used to be held to realize itself in theitatic objectivity of pure representation of the "content or act of consciousness." As the dynamic in the progress of the definition of "being" has led to a swerving away from the definition of Reality as a theological Totality (as in transcendental idealism) or the projection of that Reality into the Totality of the world constructed by the new science and the new empirical techniques and technology, immanentism has reached its most radical and paradoxical meaning in the dissolution of Reality into the ceaseless self-realization of the mind in function of the real and historical world that circumscribes that mind. Now the mind, consciousness, is actually defined as "relation to the world"; and this definition is expressive of the essential finitude of being itself: for being-in-the-world can only mean for the mind, in its temporality and historicity, a being-in-terms-of-finite-plans-and-projects, a mode of being strictly delimited by the constitutive form imposed not only by historical time but likewise by the "dark wind of the future" (to use Camus' poignant phrase) that carries to each and every mortal the news of his final end, death. Thus, the term "immanence" has virtually disappeared, giving place to the term "transcendence" expressive not only of a breaking out of the "walled garden" of immanence in its transcendental meaning, but moreover its radical dissolution. But when "transcendence" is understood, as it is in these philosophies which are the ultimate precipitate of the *cogito,* to mean the being and self-actuation of the mind, of consciousness, in the world, then it signifies the exact opposite of what Transcendence meant in classical metaphysics.[31] It connotes the self-projection of the subject into a world which the mind can structure only in terms of finite forms and contents; consequently, it excludes even more stringently than ever before the faintest possibility of attaining the Absolute in any sense whatsoever; it simply solders still more tightly round my own thinking and that of any mortal those chains of finitude wherein all that thinking occurs as a miserable and pitiable process of attempted recollection vitiated by unceasing centrifugal dispersion. This means not an attainment of Being but an utter and irrevocable loss of Being, a loss so drastic as to make immanence itself lose all meaning:

[31] This equivocal coincidence of the term "Transcendence" may explain the tendency of a certain type of "Christian philosophy" and of some adherents of what they choose to call "Neo-Scholasticism" to agree, on the substance of the problem, with the very immanentistic philosophy they want to combat. Hence the incomprehension of the metaphysical significance of the principle of causality and the calling in question of St. Thomas' proofs of the existence of God on the part of these Neo-Scholastics.

derelict and defenseless man is assailed on all sides by the great brute advancing wave of the "world", powered by the tidal swell of the coming-to-presence of being.

The disastrous issue of the modern *cogito* principle should therefore not be attributed to the very notion of immanence as such, but rather to the fact that the *cogito* has assigned to that notion a status it cannot support, wrenching it away from being and then commissioning it to make being, to construct being, to be the site, the model and the limit of being.

Genuine immanence, as conceived in the classical line of Aristotle and St. Thomas, is the intentional presence of being in the mind, a presence that raises to act the particular potencies of capacities of cognitive beings as a transition from act to act in the soul's acquisition of its own perfections, a change involving no loss or destruction, but on the contrary a conservation and growth of the subject in itself.[32]

Classical Thomist realism holds a *perfective immanence,* involving a heightening in being of both the subject of the bringing-to-presence (the mind) and the object that comes-to-presence (the world), in their encounter in the cognitional act: both go up a degree in the ontological hierarchy: the mind by an intentional possession of the form of being and being itself by the spirituality of the soul to which it is conjoined.[33] In modern thought, on the contrary, it is a *constitutive immanence* that dominates the scene, resolving and dissolving being, in various ways in the various systems, into the forms and modes of self-actuation and self-realization of the mind, and ending in that total dispersion of the knower into sheer "standing-at-gaze" or into pure action, which was demanded by the *cogito* from the very outset. Baader was therefore quite right in recalling thinkers, in the full flush of transcendental idealism, to the primordial nature of knowing defined as the simultaneous positing of immanence and transcendence or as "the simultaneity and inseparability of a being-given and a being-received" (*Simultaneität und Untrennbarkeit eines Gegeben- und Aufgegebenseins*). In fact Baader virtually re-states the Aristotelico-Thomist concept of knowing: "The knower, therefore, relates to this principle as receiver, deepening himself not by positing himself but by continuing and extending himself." And turning directly to the Hegelian *Aufhebung* notion, Baader observes that since

[32] "For it is by exercise of knowledge that the possessor of knowledge becomes such in actuality: and this either is no qualitative change (for the thing develops into its own nature and actuality), or else is qualitative change of a different sort" (*De Anima,* II 5, 417 b 5). For a further development of this point, cf. C. Fabro, *Percezione e pensiero* (Brescia, 1962 [2]), pp. 48ff.

[33] This doctrine will attract the attention of Hegel in particular, among the moderns; he has a magnificent exposition of it in *Geschichte der Philosophie,* Vol. I, pp. 252ff.

knowing is primarily a receiving on the part of the knower, it demands, being the gift (*Gabe*) it is, the simultaneous admission and recognition of a Giver (*Geber*). It is of course right and proper to admit and take full cognizance of the immediate existent that enters into the mediation process subordinated to the knower; but simultaneously account must also be taken of the Immediate as such, standing above the knower and human understanding which are subordinated to the Reason of this Immediate which in turn is subject to the architectonic Intelligence of God.[34] In other words: no immanence without transcendence and the transition to Transcendence is inherent in immanence, as expressive simultaneously of the foundation (spirituality) and the consummation (the Absolute) of that immanence.

[34] F. von Baader, *Vorlesungen über spekulative Dogmatik,* Viertes Heft (Münster, 1836), pp. 94f. Von Baader was acquainted first-hand with the works and thought of St. Thomas, to whom he appealed on occasion in his debate with idealism. The *Erläuterungen zu Auszügen aus den Werken des hl. Thomas von Aquin; C. W.,* Vol. XIV, ed. F. Hoffmann (Aalen, 1963), pp. 197-384, seem to belong to von Baader's later period. On the Thomist principle that in God "the knower, the knowing power and the known are entirely identical (*intelligens et quo intelligit et intellectum sint omnino idem*) (*Compendium Theologiae*), von Baader comments vigorously: "Modern philosophy has wrongly extended this identity of the knower and the known in God to the creature and creaturely reality as well" (p. 199). And shortly thereafter, he specifies even more precisely: "The identity of the knowing and the known (being) occurs only in self-awareness and even here only in God preeminently. In us, *esse* and *intelligere* are not naturally one and our articulated word, which has only intelligible being, is distinct in nature from our understanding (which has natural being). But the opposite is true in the case of God. Wherefore the Son is called *consubstantialis Patri,* because He is not a word accruing almost accidentally to the intellect as in our own mind (*verbum prout in mente nostra quasi accidentaliter intellectui supervenit*)" (pp. 202f.).

2

Disjunction of Act and Content in the Atheistic Precipitate of Idealism (Fichte-Hegel-Von Baader)

Kant's *Ich denke überhaupt* is extremely enlightening, not only because it stands at the center of modern thought, at the watershed between the metaphysical schools of rationalism and idealism, but also because of the priority it attributes to act over content and the consequent claim of a constitutive value for the synthesis of the subject over against content, of form over against matter. In the wake of Descartes, Spinoza develops the *cogito* in terms of the content which is the Absolute of perfection and thus gives rise to the closed system of *aeterno modo* necessity. Leibniz tries, by the introduction of the monad as wholly active "microcosm", to break this closed circle by asserting the mandatory correlation or essential conjunction of act and content and so to guarantee simultaneously the absoluteness of content and the primordiality of freedom of the subject. English empiricism, initially with the Locke-Leibniz controversy and subsequently with the dissolution of causal rationalism effected by Hume, enabled Kant to free the Leibnizian dynamism from the "contentualistic" superstructure and to return the act of consciousness to its primordial constitutive function. But almost immediately the evolution of transcendental idealism accorded Spinoza a resounding victory, as it were from beyond the grave,[1] by elevating the *I* of the *I think* to the status of Absolute and treating it as Being itself, thus effecting a convergence and merger of the two elements

[1] Dilthey uses almost eschatologico-theological terms in speaking of this event: "And so Spinoza suddenly emerged, as if from his grave, side by side with the transcendental idealism of Kant which was just in process of its final evolution and its initial flush of influence. Indeed it seemed as if he was destined to become the Lord of the living!" (W. Dilthey, *Das Leben Schleiermachers,* [Berlin: Mulert, 1922 [2]], p. 183).

which had seemed hitherto mutually repellant: the Absolute of act and the Absolute of object and content.

Knowing revealed itself as a doing and doing became a knowing, just as the finites presented themselves as the moments or elements of the Infinite and the Infinite as the reality and truth of the finites. Of this "new Spinozan spring" Hegel is the most convinced protagonist; [2] but the whole of idealism is pervaded with it: transcendental idealism was a *coincidentia oppositorum* in the shape of an infinite "contraction" which was at the same time an infinite "expansion" (to put in it Böhmian terms), destined to lead very soon after the death of Hegel (1831) by its own extremity of tension to the definitive emergence of the atheistic precipitate of the principle of immanentism. We can therefore say that, even though at first glance it seems as though the various attempts to substantiate the Absolute in modern philosophy, in the post-Cartesian and post-Kantian eras, were indeed, as they aimed at being, efforts to arrest that atheistic bias; yet a closer look at the cycle of problems revolving in its ever narrowing spiral to the breaking point shows those efforts to have been the very steps whereby the principle of immanentism conquers by stages the resistance of the metaphysical tradition and prepares the definitive advent of the *regnum hominis*. It is no accident that, in this process of metaphysical dissolution of the *cogito* effected by transcendental idealism, the paradigms are the very fundamental dogmas of Christianity; they are displayed as moments in the self-realization of the transcendental human subjectivity (especially in Hegel) within the confines of the world and its history.

The metaphysical "bulwarks" thrown up by modern thought, be they metaphysical or theological, must therefore be admitted to be indefensible in the precise measure in which the *cogito* is affirmed as the "new principle" of philosophical speculation and endeavor and as the radical inversion of the axis of the speculative substantiation of being.

Efforts have been made to align the Cartesian *cogito* with St. Augustine in order to save Cartesian metaphysics and distinguish it from the subsequent Spinozan pantheism and the later evolutions of idealist pantheism. For our present purposes it suffices to note that Descartes

[2] Cf. especially, as a generic focussing of our whole problematic, Hegel, *Enzyklopädie der philosophischen Wissenschaften*, § 50 (in which, as we have seen, he defends Spinoza against the charge of atheism). According to Hirsch (*Die idealistische Philosophie und das Christentum* [Gütersloh, 1926], pp. 44f.), Spinoza's influence was crucial in the molding of the Hegelian "system" as a unity: ". . . all reality is a single great living entity, . . . there is only One in all things". This, says Hirsch, caused the Hegelian system to become the "destroyer of ethics" (*Der Zerstörer der Ethik*) because precisely its geometric "Ethics" destroyed the deep moral thrust of the Kantian *Ought* (*Sollen*).

asserts himself to be making and was fully convinced he *was* making an absolutely new start with the *cogito,* and that, in point of fact, as Hegel notes,[3] the philosophy that followed Descartes simply developed and deepened this inversion in decisive stages as it proceeded along its varied ways. There is simply no evading the stark fact that between modern philosophy and classical philosophy there is a great gulf fixed!

Descartes' salvaging of God (ontological argument) and modern metaphysics' similar efforts at recovering God (Malebranche, Spinoza, Leibniz, *et al.*) may indeed take their inspiration from Augustine and Anselm (Hegel indeed refers admiringly to St. Anselm [4]); but this is an arbitrary step that does not jibe with the internal logic of the *cogito* itself which is and can be nothing but a "situationalization" of man in the world.

The attempted diversionary maneuver of English empiricism, with Bacon, Hobbes, Locke and their disciples, far from signifying any return to realism, was in fact the first step in the explicit assertion of the priority of the act of experience, and here, again, Hegel's judgment (which we have reported above) was dead right: empiricism and English Deism have just as crucial an importance for the dissolution of the *cogito* into atheism as does the Kantian *Ich denke*. We have here immanentism and not realism: the Lockeian principle of the "idea" as a reflection upon the act of experience (or Humeian *impression*) and the famous hypothesis of "thinking matter" (Locke, Toland) are patent evidence of the staggering advance of the principle of immanentism in England as compared with its status in continental rationalism. If it had not migrated to England, the Cartesian *cogito* would never have made this drastic claim of locating the very interiority of the act in its individual singularity as sheer presence or pure experience; nor would it have consequently given rise first to the activism of Enlightenment philosophy and subsequently to the active transcendental Ego of continental idealism as initiated by Kant. The mere term "empiricism" should not deceive us concerning the deeper meaning of this whole philosophy nor yet concerning the alarming advance it represented on the road to the "atheistic precipitation" of the principle of immanentism.

The importance and the ultimate fate of the God-problem in modern thought can clearly be seen in the altered structure of the ontological

[3] "Descartes took a quite new turning in *philosophy;* with him begins the new age of philosophy . . . Descartes took as his starting point the contention that thought must begin from itself" (Hegel, *Geschichte der Philosophie,* Vol. III, ed. Michelet, p. 304).

[4] Cf. Hegel, *Philosophie der Religion; C. W.,* Vol. III, 2, ed. Lasson (Leipzig, 1930), pp. 172f. This introduction is dated 1831, the year of Hegel's death. Cf. also Hegel, *Enzyklopädie der philosophischen Wissenschaften,* § 193; *Geschichte der Philosophie,* Vol. III, pp. 147ff. We shall be returning directly to this line of argument.

argument as between rationalism and transcendental idealism: modern thought can indeed be said, in a certan sense, to precipitate out its true sediment and simultaneously dissolve its innermost essence by the instrumentality of the intrinsic dialectic of the *ontological proof*. St. Anselm can certainly not be held personally responsible for modern immanentism; but there is no doubt that his famous proof furnished a transitional bridge and point of departure for the principle of immanentism: actually doubt and even the *cogito* are propedeutic and phenomenological expedients; the real beginning, for Descartes as for Malebranche, Spinoza and Leibniz, is the *cogito Deum* (*I think God*); and rationalism as a serach for the Absolute is but a concerto that might be titled "Variations on the Theme of the Anselmian Proof". The notable difference between the form of this proof in St. Anselm and that it assumes in rationalism is this: St. Anselm starts from a fullness of experience, as shown in the *Proslogium* pervaded with mystical sensitivity and culminating in a fervent prayer preliminary to his argumentation; the rationalist starts in the vacuum of all experience and by a single act of total reflection claims to establish squatter's rights upon the fullness of the Absolute.

Hegel's repeated critique of the Anselmian proof is suggestive. Hegel makes no essential distinction between the original Anselmian form and the various rationalist forms down to Kant who demolished the proof. In Hegelian terminology, the critique asserts that the proof if valid in its content (*der Inhalt ist wohl richtig*), but defective in its form (*die Form aber mangelhaft*), because the Anselmian (and subsequent) form is developed on the level of the static and abstract understanding (*Verstand*) rather than on the dynamic and concrete level of Reason (*Vernunft*). The outstanding defects of the intellectualistic approach are: first, the constant presupposition that thought is determined by something prior to itself and somehow Supreme; next, the assumption that there are two sorts of thought entities, one sort that are and another sort that are not, so that initially only the finite is and the Infinite (which is not yet for knowledge) is subsequently deduced via the identity of essence and existence, a procedure that makes the existence of the Supreme (*Summum*) an abstract deduction. Hegel's main criticism of Anselm is that for him the Supreme must also "be" and the identity (in God) of thought and being is considered only in the realm of the understanding, which Hegel holds to be subjective.[5] For Anselm, notes Hegel,

[5] Hegel claims that the reiteration of this argument in Descartes and Spinoza does not differ much from the Anselmian form of the same argument, whose defects it shares, especially the defect of having presupposed, i.e. taken abstractly, the unity in God of being and thought, rather than having made them the "result" of the dialectic or movement of the negativity of consciousness (cf. *Enzyklopädie der philosophischen Wissenschaften*, § 193, pp. 175f.: here Hegel cites the Latin text of the *Proslogium*).

the finite likewise "is" but in it essence and existence are distinct, and thus, being remains purely extrinsic.

In his last treatise of 1831, Hegel reproached Descartes, Leibniz and Wolff with having always mentioned the ontological proof "alongside of" others, whereas in fact it is the only true and genuine one (*obgleich er allein der wahrhaftige ist*). And he launches, from the viewpoint of his own theology-oriented metaphysic, a drastic and thoroughgoing critique of Kant's critique of the ontological proof, showing that the Kantian distinction of essence and existence, of possible and real, is a function of an intellectualist limitation, of the desire to keep Being (*Sein*) distinct from the "Concept" (*Begriff*). But this is the purely accidental being (*zufälliges Sein*) of extrinsic or empirical immediacy, not that proper to the "Concept", since the truth of Being is necessity as Spinoza has shown, that necessity in virtue of which God is called *causa sui*. The Concept necessarily contains Being: it is simple self-relatedness, "immediacy" in the sense of lack of or freedom from all mediation (*Vermittlungslosigkeit*), since mediation holds only for the finite. The Concept, when we consider it, is that in which all difference has been absorbed, in which all the determinations obtain only as ideal(s). This ideality is free of mediation, free of all differentiation; it is perfect clarity, sheer luminosity and conjunction ("being-with-itself"). The freedom of the Concept is likewise an absolute relatedness-to-itself, an identity that is also immediacy, a unity without mediation. The Concept thus has being in itself. It is itself being. Negate the total coincidence and it is just your opinion that you have separated being from the Concept.[6]

The error in Kant's critique of the ontological proof is that of saying that you cannot extract reality from the Concept; but this is to conceive the Concept as finite. Yet again the finite is that which negates itself. The Concept is this eternal activity of positing being identical with itself; and now Hegel proceeds on this basis to substantiate his own position. In intuition, sensation, etc., we have external objects before us; but we assume them into ourselves and thus they are objects ideally in us. The Concept is thus this activity of negation of its own distinction. Considering now the nature of the Concept, this identity of the Concept with Being is no longer in Hegel a presupposition (as in Anselm) but rather a result. The path of the dialectic is indeed this self-objectification of the Concept which makes the Concept to be truth and thus the unity of subject and object.

And this is, for Hegel, the Christian point of view: here we have the concept of God in its full truth, this concept is identical with being.

[6] Cf. Hegel's last discussion of the ontological argument in 1831 in *Die Beweise vom Dasein Gottes,* ed. Lasson (Leipzig, 1930), pp. 172ff.

Being is the most impoverished of abstractions; the concept is not so impoverished as not to have within it this abstraction. We ought not to consider being in the impoverishment of abstraction, in the baneful immediacy, but rather being as the Being of God, as the being of the concrete whole, distinct from God. The mind (consciousness) of the finite spirit is concrete being, the raw material for the actualization of the concept of God. Here there is no question of an addition of being to the concept nor only of a unity of the concept and being. Unity is to be conceived rather as an absolute process, as the life-force of God, in such a way that the two aspects are distinct in it but it is the absolute activity of its own eternal self-production. We here have, concludes Hegel, the concrete representation of God as Spirit (*Geist*). The concept of spirit is the concept that is in itself and by itself, knowing; this infinite concept is the negative relation to itself. And so it is also judging, distinguishing; but the distinct, i.e., that which has been distinguished, which initially appears as the extrinsic, the a-spiritual, i.e., that which is outside of God, is identical with the concept. The evolution of this Idea is Absolute Truth. In the Christian religion there is a coming to consciousness, to awareness of the fact that God has revealed himself and God is precisely this self-revealing (revelation in the active sense); what is revealed, on the other hand (revelation in the passive sense) is the fact that God is manifest.[7] Religion must be for all men, for those who have purified their thought to such an extent that they know what is in the pure element of thought, those who have arrived at the speculative knowledge of what God is, and also for those who have not overcome or gone beyond feeling and imagination.

And as if to put the finishing touch to his speculative testament, Hegel most vigorously distinguishes the realm of religion from that of philosophy, in order to show the superiority of the latter over the former. Man, he continues, is not a pure thinking being; rather does thought manifest itself as intuition, as imagination; thus Absolute Truth revealed to (self-

[7] As Hegel says in the text, (*ibid.*, p. 176), "revelation" is a plunging into immanence, because "God is not jealous" (*Gott nicht neidisch ist*), as he delights in repeating. Hegel arrives at the formula that the Spirit of God actualizes and knows Itself in man, because it is "God's self-consciousness which knows itself in man's knowing" (*Gottes Selbstbewusstsein, welches sich in dem Wissen des Menschen weiss*). This is the genuine "mediation", always in act, which grounds the second immediacy, the authentic one, of the circular or reciprocal conjunction of the finite and the Infinite (cf. *ibid.*, p. 49. A little earlier, on pp. 44f., Hegel cites and praises Göschel's essay *Aphorismen über Nichtwissen und absolutes Wissen* [Berlin, 1829], for its defense of Hegel's own notion ". . . of God's self-consciousness, His self-knowledge in man, man's self-knowledge in God". There is a reference to Göschel in the same context in the *Enzyklopädie der philosophischen Wissenschaften,* § 564. This section, at the beginning of the treatise on "revealed religion," has a vigorous summary of this doctrine, so crucial for the "atheist bias" of Hegelianism).

revealing to) man must be likewise for man as an intuiting and imagining being, for man as endowed with feeling and sensation. This is the form in terms of which religion generically differs from philosophy. Philosophy thinks what is otherwise only in terms of imagination and intuition. In imagination man is also a thinking being. Only the thinking being can have religion and thought is also imagination. But the religion of the thinker is the only free form of truth. The understanding is also a thinking (entity or act) but it stops at identity: the concept is concept and being is being (*der Begriff ist Begriff und das Sein ist Sein*). And this onesidedness and partiality persists always in the understanding. In truth, however, these finitudes no longer hold as identical; they are indeed but they are only elements or moments (*Momente*) of a Whole, a Totality. And Hegel rails against religion which stops at mystery and defends philosophy which dissipates and dissolves every mystery into the process of becoming from the heights of the dialectic of reason. Those who are scandalized at philosophy for thinking religion do not know what they want. Hate and vanity have a free field here under the outer guise of a (false) humility; true humility consists in a plunging of the spirit into truth, into having the object only in itself. Thus is dispersed all subjectivity still present in sensation. We must consider the Idea only from the speculative point of view and justify it against the understanding that rebels at every content of religion. This content is called mystery, because it is something hidden for (from) the understanding which does not attain to the process that is this unity: thus every speculative content is a mystery for the understanding.

Up to this point Hegel is being entirely consistent. He is simply reiterating what he has always said: that the conception held by religion of the relation of man to God as a relation of two "distinct realities", as a relation implying a dependence of man on God, is an imperfect way of thinking; and that the true and proper way of thinking is that of philosophy, using the "Concept" in which the opposites and the distinct are unified, in which Absolute Spirit is Being and finite spirits are its manifestations. What Hegel here says in a positive formula: ". . . the mind of the finite spirit is concrete being, the raw material for the actualization of the concept of God" is equivalent to his other negative formula: ". . . without the world, God is not God." But to say that God is only inasmuch as the world is and that he thinks only inasmuch as man thinks is equivalent to denying to God being and thinking. This is just what Feuerbach in fact spots and criticizes in Hegel.

Actually then what Hegel often calls the "elevation of the human spirit to God" (*Erhebung des Menschengeistes zu Gott*) is simply degradation of God to the level of human reality without remainder; and it is in this way that, as we have seen, Hegel understood the Christian dogma of the Incarnation.

The most evident root of Hegel's catalytic atheism and of that of transcendental idealism in general lies in the dimension of *content,* and can be pinpointed as the dialectical identification of the finite and the Infinite. Franz von Baader, a contemporary of the transcendental idealists, did not hestiate to denounce this atheistic bias of Spinozan origin in Fichte, in whose system, prior to and perhaps to a greater extent than in the systems of Schelling and Hegel, the fate of the *cogito* is accomplished, in that the assertion of the Ego as the positor of being automatically involves the exclusion and expulsion of God. Von Baader charges that the new philosophy has become godless (*gottlos*), has broken loose from God (*los von Gott*) and is not without God (*ohne Gott*): it has wrenched religion from man's intimate nucleus, which is thought, in order to interpolate it into the idea or representation (*Vorstellung*) as Hegel or into feeling (*Gefühl*) as Schleiermacher.[8] Von Baader specifies three fundamental errors raging in the world of thought in his day and together consummating the corruption of philosophy.

The first (Von Baader says "one") of these philosophemes, traceable to Kant but specifically expressed by Fichte, posits a false notion of the spontaneity of intelligent natures as contrasted with non-intelligent, asserting that this spontaneity is absolute rather than potential. In place of the notion that man has in himself the law (reason, *Vernunft*) and thanks to this capacity can receive causality as the animal cannot and hence man is called intelligent, this new philosophy purveys the notion that man is himself the source and author of the law and hence not, as religion teaches, the religious organ of the law (image of God, *Gottes Bild*) but rather legislator, God Himself.[9] It is the autonomy of the categorical imperative (*Du sollst*) which we have also indicated as being a root of atheism and which Fichte transformed with his doctrine of the self-positing Ego, from the point in 1794 where he asserted: "The Ego, the self is and posits its own being by the instrumentality of its own sheer being. Being is at once the agent and the product of the action; the active principle is what is produced by this activity: action and operation are one and the same thing and therefore the *I am* is the expression of an operative activity." [10] The meaning here would be that the action of being is executive, productive and that therefore

[8] F. von Baader, *Vorlesungen über religiöse Philosophie,* im Gegensatz der irreligiösen älterer und neuerer Zeit; *C. W.,* Vol. I, p. 155.

[9] F. von Baader, *Bemerkungen über einige antireligiöse Philosopheme unserer Zeit,* 1824; *C. W.,* Vol. II, p. 445.

[10] J. G. Fichte, *Grundlage der gesamten Wissenschaftslehre; C. W.,* Vol. I, ed. Medicus (Leipzig, 1908), p. 290.

"to be" is both intransitive and transitive! All of this is already posited with the "I am I" (*Ich bin Ich*).

The Ego as subject and the Ego as predicate coincide, explains Fichte, and thus the formula can be inverted: the Ego posits itself *because* it is. It *posits* itself by its sheer being and *is* by means of this sheer *being-posited*. This means that the Ego is the pure Subject. It represents an inversion of the Cartesian and Kantian *cogito* by a Spinozan interpolation and can thus be called a Spinozan Kantianism, inasmuch as the Ego takes from Spinoza the unity of constitutive Absolute Substance and from Kant the absolute productive activity, thus implementing the dual immanence or metaphysical reduction to unity in the realm both of substance and of activity. Nothing would appear at first glance so foreign both to Kant and to Spinoza; yet nothing could be more in conformity with the deepest thrust of both, the determination to attribute to thought or to the mind, consciousness in its pure state, the foundation, the grounding (in the transitive sense) of its own activity. Thus the Ego, the Self—a Kantian term entirely absent from Spinoza's vocabulary—is here in the guise and function of the one and only Substance.[11] Being is without remainder identical to thought and the Ego, the Self as pure Consciousness (self-consciousness) is by its essence subject and object, beginning, middle and end: only the abstract intellect or understanding can distinguish them, notes Fichte. In actual fact it is absurd to think the Ego in the sense of self-consciousness as being a passive inert substance; it is impossible to abstract from one's own self-consciousness and so there is no ground for asking what is the ground or principle of self-consciousness, for it and it alone is that ground or principle. The Ego is, continues Fichte, to the extent that and inasmuch as it posits itself. Since it is only by the positing and posits only by (the) being—the Ego is by the Ego—and therefore posits itself simply as it is, it posits itself necessarily and is necessarily by and through the Ego. I am only for myself but for myself I am necessary (*Ich bin nur für mich aber für mich bin ich notwendig*).

The transcendental deduction of the identity of the self and being admits of no uncertainty: "Self-positing" (*sich selbst setzen*) and "being" (*sein*), said of the Self are entirely identical. To say: I am because I have posited myself, is the same as saying simply: I am, for the I who is posited (who posits himself) and the I who am are entirely

[11] "That entity whose being (essence) consists in the fact that it posits itself as existent is the Ego as absolute subject. Even as it posits itself, it is; and even as it is, it posits itself; and the Ego is therefore fundamentally necessary for the Ego. Whatever is not for itself is not an Ego, not a Self" (*Grundlage der gesamten Wissenschaftslehre,* p. 291). Fichte often declares his adherence to Spinozism which had been disseminated in Germany especially by Lessing and Goethe.

identical. Hence the formulas: I am *because* I am; and I am what I am. The conclusion of this whole deduction of the actual operation (*Tathandlung*), in which the *Wissenschaftslehre* culminates can be summed up in the simple statement that the Self is the primordial author of its own being.[12] And Fichte himself reminds us of the speculative itinerary of his own deduction by his recall and critique of preceding systems of philosophy: he admits that his own formulation was already present in Kant, but only as fundamental principle of all knowing, not as fundamental principle sheerly and simply (*überhaupt*) (i.e., of being); the Spinozan unity was lacking. Descartes before him had enunciated a similar principle, continues Fichte: *cogito ergo sum*. This does not represent in reality anything more than the minor premise and the conclusion of a syllogism whose major would be: *quodcumque cogitat, est* (whatever thinks, is), but which Descartes himself could well regard as an immediate fact of consciousness, of knowledge. In that case the formula says virtually: *cogitatus sum, ergo sum* (I am being thought, therefore I am) just as Fichte will say *I am therefore I am*. But here the *sum* adds nothing at all: thinking does not follow necessarily from being but being most assuredly does follow from thinking! For what *is* thinking most certainly *is*! Thought is indeed not the essence but only a particular determination of being and there are quite a few other determinations of our being besides thought.

Reinhold took a step forward with his principle of "representation" or the idea (*Vorstellung*), a principle which reduced to Cartesian terms would read: *represento, ergo sum* or still better *repraesentans sum, ergo sum*. But even this "representing", notes Fichte, can be said not to be the essence of being but rather a particular determination thereof, besides which there are other determinations of our being, even if these other determinations do indeed have to pass via the medium of representation in order to arrive at empirical consciousness.[13]

Spinoza's case is different: he is the only thinker to have gone beyond the limit at which Kant's critical philosophy stops. Spinoza produced the highest unity of the human mind and his only error was to conceive of it as something already achieved whereas it is something which is still to be produced (as will be done precisely by the *Wissenschaftslehre*). But it must be admitted that when a thinker goes beyond the psychological *I*

[12] "The Ego primordially posits sheerly its own being" (*Das Ich setzt ursprünglich schlechthin sein eigenes Sein*). (*Grundlage der gesamten Wissenschaftslehre*, p. 292). And Fichte adds the explanatory note: "The Ego is necessarily an identity of subject and object: it is a subject-object, and it is such simply, without further mediation (*ohne weitere Vermittlung*)."

[13] Fichte refers the reader to S. Maimon, *Ueber die Progressen der Philosophie*, for the proof of this.

am of Descartes, he ought necessarily to arrive at Spinozism.[14] We can therefore say that in Fichte's dissolution of being into thought and of the world into the Ego, the Self, the content comes from Spinoza (the unity-totality of being) and the form or quality of being from Kant (universal thinking selfhood). And this is what Von Baader calls "inverted Spinozism" (*ein umgekehrter Spinozismus*) and judges to be "sheer atheism" (*rein gottesleugnerisch*).[15] And Baader holds that the ultimate root of this deviation is already present in Descartes separation of the knowledge of nature from the knowledge of God, or, as Baader himself puts it, of naturalism from theism.

Indeed, charges Von Baader, Descartes has from the outset excluded any Christian philosophy by his thesis that the first requirement for orderly and proper philosophical activity and speculation is to doubt everything. This means that any philosophy must be totally independent of all revelation and all religion. And then, laments Baader, the theologians come along and, in their outrage at this rationalism, begin to claim that the first requirement for being a good theologian is to cease being rational! Descartes has carried our Solomon's judgment without Solomon's wisdom and this childish slicing (the division between naturalism and theism) has also been much touted by the French Revolution; Jacobi himself has declared that it is in the interests of reason to ignore or deny God since with the admission of God the use of reason ceases.[16] Baader sees Fichte's radical defect in his direct transition from sheer affirmation (positing) to sheer negation; this is a labor of Tantalus in the absence of a higher positive entity to serve as foundation. But the conclusion from all this should not be Jacobi's contention that speculation leads to atheism: actually there is such a thing as

[14] Fichte Jr.'s defense of his father passes over this Spinozan element or principle in silence: "Fichte's contention that brought upon him the reproach of atheism was simply the contention that God cannot be anything '*objective*', any thing able to be thought of in the (sensuous) forms of objectivity, in Fichte's own terminology a 'substance' of any sort. And he was indisputably right in this restrictive contention and in the grounds he adduced in support of it." (I. H. Fichte, *Psychologie,* Die Lehre vom bewussten Geiste des Menschen, Vorrede, § XXVI [Leipzig, 1864], p. xxv note).

[15] F. von Baader, *Bemerkungen über einige antireligiöse Philosopheme unserer Zeit,* p. 447. The second erroneous "philosopheme" is the deist position asserting that reason (*Vernunft*) is given to man as an active principle (*Anlage*) but that man is alone in the use and exercise of this principle and therefore is sole principal agent (*Alleinwirker*) and not a collaborator (*Mitwirker*) with the Divine Reason. The third "philosopheme" is characteristic of the *Naturphilosophie* (Oken, Schelling, Oersted?) and is materialistic in inspiration: it conceives the essence of the world as matter proceeding immediately and eternally from God, as God's eternal outgoing and estrangement (*Ausgang, Entäusserung*), conditioning eternally God's eternal return (as Spirit). This approach thus claims to explain everything, God included, without God (*ibid.,* pp. 445ff.).

[16] F. von Baader, *Revision der Philosopheme der Hegelschen Schule* (Stuttgart, 1839), pp. 187f.

adequate knowledge and it is a synthesis of practical and speculative knowledge. Atheism arises upon the rupture, denial or neglect of this nexus; or when, as in transcendental idealism, there is undertaken the attempt to deduce the knowledge of God, as also that of other intelligent beings and of non-intelligent beings (knowledge throughout here being understood in the transitive sense) from man's knowledge of himself, from self-consciousness, self-awareness (*Selbstbewusstsein*).[17]

Schelling went on to develop the process of the identity of being and knowing, in the Fichtean tradition, on the dual front of nature and freedom of the life of the spirit; he walked a tightrope between the two, whereas Hegel expanded the hegemony of spirit by the dialectic of negation, attributing to the transcendental Ego not only the ability simply to posit itself (as did Fichte) but also the active hegemony over every particular determination of the real, thus rendering possible the *Aufheben* of the opposites and a self-elevation, by the instrumentality of negation, to the Totality of the Absolute.

Let it be noted, in order to keep clearly in view the simultaneous complexity and rectilinearity of the evolution of the principle of immanentism, that this crucial advance of Hegel over Schelling and Fichte (an advance whose "form" seems to us to be more in the line of Fichte and whose "content" seems to be rather in the line of Schelling) is due to the complementary Spinozan principle: *omnis determinatio est negatio*. This principle, transferred to the *Ich denke überhaupt,* constitutes the mainspring of the Hegelian dialectic.[18] Thus, thanks to the mutual "intrinsicization" or necessary conjunction of the finite and the Infinite proclaimed by transcendental idealism, man himself and every other free subject (subject of freedom) is only a mode (Spinoza) or moment (Hegel) of the one and only Substance or absolute Subject-Object. Action is as unitary as being and human action is referred to the action of the Absolute not as the action of a Secondary Cause to the Primary Cause but rather as the action of a phenomenon (*Schein. Erscheinung*) to that of the one and only Reality or Being (Essence, *Wesen*), which, considered as a Whole, an All, is the realm of Spirit (*Geist*) and the proper object of the Concept (*Begriff*). Such a conception excludes God as transcendental principle of the natural order and likewise excludes any mediation by Christ in the order of the redemption

17 F. von Baader, *Vorlesungen über spekulative Dogmatik,* Zweites Heft (Münster, 1830), pp. 31, 39. Therefore, says von Baader, Fichte has not overcome "baneful spiritualism and baneful naturalism" in his refusal to attribute personality to God because of his identification of personality with finitude, in disregard of the Church's conception of the Persons in God as *proprietates* (*ibid.*, p. 82).

18 von Baader presents a thoroughgoing critique of the famous Spinozan principle which Hegel makes the basis of the dialectic, as we shall be pointing out presently.

from sin. Baader finds this to be the error of those theologies taking their inspiration from idealism: "According to these theologies, not only does man possess of himself the power to take possession of the kingdom of God; he even has the duty of doing so with his corrupt, rebellious and egotistical will; nor is there any need, or even, at least according to Kant, any way (*Mittel*) to free him and to slay this perverse will which is barring him from entry into this kingdom of God. The root of this perversion goes back to the very origins of mankind. It can be no surprise in these latter days to see those who call themselves Christian theologians intent on making us Christians without a Christ and demons without a devil [nor yet, we might add, to see philosophers professing themselves to be godless theists, i.e., theists without God], when we consider that our first parents were taught by the 'doctrinaire serpent' (*die doktrinäre Schlange*) the trick of becoming like God without God, even in defiance of God's will, and when we further recall that so many philosophers have been teaching us what amounts to the same trick (namely, that of knowing God without God), since they actually do always begin all their proofs and constructions of God from something that is not God and yet aim at bringing us through to God in the end." [19]

Baader holds the fundamental error of modern idealism to be Spinozism, the identification of the finite with the Infinite. Modern philosophy (since Kant) has lost its clear notion of the distinction between (total) central action which is cooperation and instrumental action; consequently, it has had to exalt man into the supreme region of absolute action in order to keep man above the region of purely instrumental (non-free, blind) action; it has had to make man into a God in order to keep him from being or remaining a brute beast. And as soon as man has been posited as a divine being, then there are but two alternatives: either to deny overtly man's degradation by sin or to postulate (as Kant in fact did) a self-liberation and self-elevation (*Selbstbefreiung und Selbsterhebung*) by means of the imperative of his own absolute autonomy, of his divine being. Such a philosophy must always appear simultaneously open and shut, bold and cowardly, atheist and anti-Christian. And Baader concludes: "Man is nothing if not an organ (image) of God and therefore he who denies the original likewise negates the image, even as the negation of the latter likewise denies the former." [20]

[19] F. von Baader, *Ueber die sich so nennende rationelle Theologie in Deutschland; C. W.*, Vol. II, pp. 499f.

[20] F. von Baader, *Bemerkungen über einige antireligiöse Philosopheme unserer Zeit,* § 18; p. 475. Later in the same work (§ 25), Baader accuses Hegel of materialism for having contended that matter proceed from all eternity from God and having thus made into "the eternal body of God" (*der ewige Leib Gottes*), in contradistinction to the Pauline doctrine of the "body of this death" (*Rom.* 7:

This diagnosis sees the atheism of modern philosophy as coming primarily from the monism that slips into materialism. If Baader is less overt in his criticism of Hegel than in his critique of Fichte, the reason may be Hegel's tendency to welcome and accept into his thought a certain mystical bent, derived from Eckhart and Böhme. But on the crux of the problem, Baader minces no words. The Spinozan principle: *Omnis determinatio est negatio* is false, both with respect to the *Determinans* (*Producens*) which is determining itself freely in distinguishing itself from something different from itself, and in respect of the *Determinatum,* which here likewise stems from something that is not determined as a thing, a specific entity. Just as the Self could not be without the not-Self so too the not-Self could not be without the Self. By the term "difference" can therefore be understood only the contrast between the determining and the beind determined; and it is only division or articulation (*Gliederung*), which the philosophers of nature confuse with difference, which cuts the Gordian knot of this indivisible unity and opens the birth canal to genuine variety, freely determining beings in their determinateness and freedom. For Spinoza's principle there must consequently be substituted another: Every immediate determination is a contradiction or confusion; and every mediate determination is an organization. And Baader concludes: "Mediation here occurs by way of the introduction of the Idea at the very beginning of nature." [21] This is substantially the Augustinian-Thomist principle of creation, as we shall soon be pointing out.

18, 24). Baader charges that Hegel consequently neglects the opposition of flesh and spirit and takes anguish for happiness, death for life (*ibid.,* p. 484. Cf. also § 25, pp. 488f.). The basic error goes back to Spinoza who denies the "personality of God (cf. F. von Baader, *Ueber die Notwendigkeit einer Revision der Wissenschaft natürlicher, menschlicher und göttlicher Dinge* [Erlangen, 1842], p. 5). In a lengthy note in the Preface to the 2nd edition of the *Encyclopedia* (1827), Hegel has a courteous and conciliatory but evasive reply to Baader's critique (ed. Hoffmeister, p. 16). Baader, however, was to stand firmly by this critique to the end, as we are in process of showing.

[21] F. von Baader, *Revision der Philosopheme der Hegel'schen Schule,* p. 178. Thus the Hegelian dialectic must start from a genuine positive entity in order to avoid ending up in nothingness; and the Spinozan principle must be inverted to read: *Omnis determinatio est positio* (Every determination or definition is an affirmation) (von Baader, *Ueber den Begriff des Gut—oder positiv Nichgut—oder negativ gewordenen endlichen Geistes,* § 5 [Lucerne, 1829], pp. 10f.). Cf. also § 22, where Baader shows that the Spinozan principle leads to materialism and denounces the annihilation or reduction to nothing of God in Hegelian philosophy: "The basis of the *Naturphilosophie* further developed by Hegel was the same concept of God as a positive substance, whose active causality was to be sought not in the divine Persons but rather in creaturely ones, the result of which was that God is held to sleep unless and until he awakes through, in and by means of the creature and comes to Himself as Spirit" (p. 28). In § 24, Baader returns to the same point, remarking that Hegel is right in saying that ". . . the

Although Baader makes Spinozan the chief culprit in the atheism (or atheization) of modern idealism, he does not neglect the guilt of the "identity of being and thought" which was asserted with mounting rigor by the *cogito* principle in the various stages of modern thought. Rigid consistency has been of the same service in philosophy as it is in mental illnesses: it has served to highlight the absurdity of a principle in terms of its necessary consequences. Thus, for an immanentist, the identity of being and knowing requires that "knowing God" shall mean "being God". And so this doctrine in the final analysis leaves us no hope whatever of knowing God, since God and man will never manage to get together, for where man is there God will not yet be and where God is man will no longer be! Therefore does Baader speak of the "latent madness" of this philosophy which promises man that he shall become God's equal without God and in defiance of God and which claims to teach us to know God without God.[22]

So for Baader likewise there are two main roots of the atheism rampant in modern thought: the Spinozan principle of the unity of being which submerges God in the world rather than creation in God; and the basic principle of the identity of being and thought which renders impossible any transcendence and confounds God with man.

Clearly, therefore, the principle of immanentism comes to its full flowering in the "principle of conjunction" which is the most advanced formulation of monistic pantheism and which subsequently dissolves into atheism via the much-touted actualization of God in the world: thus the Infinite is held to actualize Itself in the finite, the Necessary and Absolute in contingents, Eternity in time, the One in the many; in short, Being in beings and the Universal in the particulars. The assertion that the reality of the Infinite is constituted by its concealment in the finite, by its *relation* to the finite, is the Spinozan formulation of atheism. The assertion that the reality of God as (Absolute) Spirit is constituted by his self-actualization in human institutions, is the Hegelian formulation of atheism. The assertion that the reality of the world and man, emancipated from the Absolute, is doomed to actualize itself in the finite, is the formulation of atheism reduced to the absolutely fundamental demand of the principle of immanentism. It is encountered

---

Idea is not so powerless as not to be real" but that Hegel ought likewise to add that this Idea (as it is in God and is God Himself) is not so barren and impoverished as to have need of an actualization effected by creatures (pp. 29f.). On the "closedness" and sterility of the Spinozan principle, cf. also: F. von Baader, *Ueber die Notwendigkeit einer Revision der Wissenschaft natürlicher, menschlicher und göttlicher Dinge,* p. 17.

[22] F. von Baader, *Bemerkungen über einige antireligiöse Philosopheme unserer Zeit,* § 33, pp. 493, 495. Cf. on p. 494 the critical note on Jacobi as having fallen, albeit in a different way, into the same error charged against the "philosophers", that of reducing God to a merely mental reality.

in present-day philosophies in the wake of the contributions of Feuerbach, Kierkegaard, Marx, Nietzsche, and precludes any possibility of retreat out of utter shrieking immanentism.

For the outstanding modern thinkers and critics, an assertion of theism starting from the principle of immanentism is not only ridiculous but preeminently dishonest: there can be no *sanatio in radice* in the field of thought any more than there can be in the field of being which thought manifests. From the moment and to the extent that the self-styled theistic idealists and Christian spiritualists engage the *cogito* and hand being over to it on a leash, they are bound to fall either into the "principle of conjunction" (if they are metaphysicians) or into the "principle of act" (if they are actualists); and both the former pantheistic and the latter voluntaristic principle involve the finitude of being, which is the stand of present-day atheistic humanism.

To the whole of this philosophy of immanentism can be applied the reproach levelled by Baader against the *Aufhebung* of the Hegelian method: far from negating the finite and effecting an elevation to the Infinite, they end by negating and degrading the Infinite into the finite and consequently losing the Infinite as such and dissolving God's personality into created personalities condemend to a perpetual irremediable lethargy.[23] The atheistic character of idealism in its metaphysical aspect and of the principle of immanentism in its very essence were seen and denounced unequivocally well in advance of the Hegelian Left, by a man who had lived through the entire drama of the new philosophy.

And so, by a strange but irresistible nemesis, the much touted claim of the interiority of the principle of immanentism has dissolved into an exteriority which leaves the mind with nothing but the dimensions of time; and the new type of transcendence, which is the relation to the world, resolves itself into a continuous process of "alienation" into which the Ego itself disappears, absorbed by that finitude that is limited as content in its historical givenness and occurrence, but unlimited as a process in its givenness or occurrence in history.

[23] The passage is from von Baader at the height of his powers: ten years after the death of Hegel, von Baader prefers to address himself to the Hegelian school which had remained faithful to its founder on this essential point: ". . . after Spinoza, such specification and specificity had to be called a denial of life (*negatio vitae*); then *Naturphilosophie,* following Spinoza, has likewise conceived the reality of life solely as its finitization, i.e. as a supersession and abrogation of an infinite indeterminate non-life, which latter is not quite God but rather the prime matter for a personal God. The Hegelian school then proceeds to maintain that God acquires his personality, for this school conceives of God as a sleeper who is only awakened out of the sleep of his personality by the finite personal self-consciousness, and who forthwith abolishes this latter (finite self-consciousness) in his awakening, thereby, of course, forfeiting his own awakener; and this process between creature and creator, maintain the Hegelians, continues indefinitely" (F. von Baader, *Ueber die Notwendigkeit einer Revision der Wissenschaft natürlicher, menschlicher und göttlicher Dinge,* p. 20).

Modern thought could indeed be said to be a succession of inversions of the axis of the mind in the determination of the real: hence the originality and wealth of its analyses of human subjectivity and selfhood as analyses of the "situation of man in the world". On the other hand, in virtue of the fact that the two terms or protagonists, consciousness and self-consciousness, remain unchanged throughout all these inversions, the result likewise remains unchanged and constant: man is repeatedly "defined" on the basis of his position or situation in the world.

It is therefore no surprise that the ultimate issue of all these inversions should be a conception of consciousness, of the mind, wherein the self, the Ego, which was the point of departure, has been completely and totaly voided of itself by being dissolved, *at its own hands,* into the relation to the world: the "world" becomes in turn the complex of relations which man is in process of implementing and developing in that world, a world in which the "universals" are all winking out one after another in the wake of the eclipse of the Ego itself.

Being is henceforth dissolved into the sheer activity of man; and nothing has contributed more drastically than idealism with its pseudo-theology, to the emergence of the hegemony of the human subject in the interpretation of the real.[24] The mind, for its part, has been voided of all solid being and hurled down from the pinnacle of its pseudo-elevation to the level of the divine; and now it has become nothing but a stage for the spectacle of the world or an arena for the gladiatorial combats of private or public history. The "ought-to-be" at which the philosophy of immanence was aiming in Kant has for more than a century now (since Feuerbach and Nietzsche and indeed even in Hegel himself) been being actuated as the brute facticity of occurrence, of "happening". And freedom no longer constitutes the intensive center of the subject's structure and status but serves merely as the dispersal point for the fortuitous propulsion of the subject into sheer occurrence: it *is* indeed quite simply this propulsion and this constant readiness for sheer occurrence. And this can be called a new nemesis; actually it is the same old nemesis all over again, the judgment on the spirit that is constrained to deny itself at the very outset: freedom is posited this side of any relation to being (the empty *cogito* as identical with the empty *volo*); *actuality is grounded sheerly and exclusively on potentiality!*

[24] We are here faced with what might be called the new "syllogism of identity" of reason: "In everything that we consider as given, there is already involved our own covert rational operation: and the sole basis of our own right to cognition of things is the fact that we initially create them for ourselves . . . The world we are experiencing is our own act; it is of our own making (*Die Welt, die wir erleben, ist unsre Tat*)" (W. Windelband, "Kulturphilosophie und transzendentaler Idealismus," in *Präludien,* Vol. II [Tübingen, 1921[7-8]], pp. 282f.).

3

Modern Principle of Immanentism or Conjunction and Thomist Principle of Transcendence or Causality

In that somber thriller, the evolution of modern thought, the hero (consciousness, the mind) has been made to assume an astounding number of disparate disguises; but one feature has never changed, nor indeed could it have been changed without the novel falling apart. That feature is the *cogito* or the principle of immanentism, expressed by Hegel in the formula that "the truth of consciousness is self-consciousness". This is recognizably the "principle of conjunction" often expressed in terms of the "identity syllogism" articulating the return of the mind upon itself in the recognition that the manifold and the heterogeneous are but the appearances or phenomena of the One and the homogeneous, the identical, and necessarily belong to or are "conjoined" with it. Thus, the principle of conjunction basically expresses the same contention as does the *cogito* in its consummation and self-realization, involving as it does the coincidence of the "result" with the principle and of the synthesis with the thesis, a terminal state of affairs which we have often designated as the "re-turn" (*Rückgang*) of the spirit into itself. The somber pilgrimage of the *cogito* is as pitiable as that of Ahasuereus: never does it find rest though it claims paradoxically never to wander abroad; always the solution is *given* and yet never; always it is present yet always deferred; everywhere it is and nowhere, *nusquam et ubique!*

Consider the paradoxical state of the God-problem in Descartes: God is excluded from the outset, in the most radical fashion, because of the doubt that has besieged the whole camp of being and meaning; yet God is posited, i.e., admitted forthwith as the *primum cognitum* and as the guarantee of subsequent knowing. God is admitted in virtue of the principle of the clear and distinct idea: the starting point is, to be sure, the

Idea of the most perfect Being; but what decides the promotion of God to the place of honor in the knowledge of the truth is the evidence of the "content" of the idea, its clarity and distinctness, the primordial and essential conjunction, in Descartes' position, of clarity-and-distinctness and the idea of God. The Cartesian proof is in no sense whatever introduced in order to substantiate a transcendence of any kind but rather precisely to reinforce and consolidate immanence to the point of immanentism and to weld the mind ever more firmly to itself at every stage of its appropriation to itself of the real. Thus, that which is ultimate, most difficult, most remote and for us most indeterminate and confused, i.e., God, is here taken as anterior terminal, for clearest and most distinct, for the most proximate and evident; not only this, but it is also taken (and this is the most important point for Descartes and likewise for our own investigation) as the principle of presence, of presentness, which is *substantiating* of all the subsequent awarenesses that the mind may be pleased to admit.

It is no accident, then, that Descartes came to be accused of making a double beginning, first with the *cogito* and then with the Idea of God, and so of falling into atheism not once but twice over, first with the *cogito* which effects a total confiscation of being and then with the Idea of God, as *prius cognitum fundans cognitionem,* calculated to restore the being lost to the mind, finite being which *in ratione essendi et cognoscendi* is antipodal to God. A truly weird method of procedure, but an immensely fascinating and beguiling one!

The development and evolution of the principle of immanentism shows the same enthralled fascination for the conjunction of truth and the mind and the effort to free the *cogito* from the dual "leap", first from the leap of the *cogito* to God and later from the *cogitare* of God to the *cogitare* of creatures.

Modern histories of thought have therefore been quite right in giving ever greater prominence to the radical transition effected by Spinoza with his notion of God as *causa sui,* a notion that makes short work of the ambiguity of the Cartesian beginnings and gives the first and fundamental formulation of the principle of conjunction. It explicitates, on the one hand, in most drastic fashion the ontological proof roughed out by Descartes; and it replaces, on the other hand, the principle of causality. It is no accident that Spinoza's *Ethics* opens with the definition of *causa sui* as the understanding point of the whole system: *"By causa sui (cause of itself), I understand that whose essence involves existence; or that whose nature cannot be conceived except as existing."* [1] This definition, which initiates modern metaphysics, is echoed, at the other end of the

[1] Spinoza, *Ethica,* P. I, def. 1; *Opera,* Vol. II, ed. Gebhardt, p. 45.

line of the definitive degradation of the divine into a merely human reality, by the Sartrian definition to the effect that "existence precedes essence". The opposition between the two is far more apparent than real; indeed the latter can be considered legitimately as the mandatory opposite pole of the anthropomorphizing magnet. Moreover the terminal doctrine of the Spinozan *Ethics* concerning *amor intellectualis* contains already in explicit form the principle of conjunction in a stage of transformation already drastically advanced by the resolution of the foundation of being into human reality: "The intellectual love of the mind for God is the Love of God itself, whereby God loves himself, not inasmuch as he is infinite, but rather inasmuch as he can be displayed by the essence of the human mind, considered under the aspect of eternity, i.e., the intellectual love of the mind for God is a part of the infinite love wherewith God loves himself." [2]

This point is of special importance in the discussion of the "ground" of modern atheism. The first definition conceals beneath the outward guise of a current Scholastic terminology the most radical overthrow and negation of that transcendence which had hitherto, for better or for worse, constituted the basis of Western thought. Even the little phrase *causa sui* itself is already an indication of the new road being taken: *causa* connotes dependence *in being* and is inapplicable to the Absolute which is in itself the fullness of all perfection. The Absolute can be called "cause" only with respect to the finite, to the manifold of beings dependent upon it, but not with respect to itself: within the Absolute there are, according to theology, the trinitarian emanations of the Word and the Holy Spirit, but they are "processions" in the identity of nature and therefore posit sheer derivation, not dependence. God is called "principle" not cause in this case: were the Father the "cause" of the Son, then the Son would be a creature and so too would the Holy Spirit, just as the Arians claimed. But the Spinozan definition aims at much more, namely, the identification in God of the finite with the Infinite, an identification pushed relentlessly forward with the successive definitions of *substance, attribute* and *mode,* expressive respectively of the two moments of concentration and expansion of the real, or again his inside and his outside in the co-existence which is a mutual grounding of the One and the many.

Causa sui is explained by the phrase *cuius essentia involvit existentiam.* This latter is the principle of conjunction in its crucial formulation, apparently harmless in its obviousness but laden with all the tempests that will lash modern thought ahead, *from within,* to its awful moment of truth, in terms of the logic of immanentism, which is the expulsion of

[2] Spinoza, *Ethica,* P. V, prop. 36, p. 302.

God. *Causa* is a term relative with respect to the effect and thus here God becomes to be the effect of himself, not like other things, each one of which derives from the other, but in an absolute manner proper to God, "inasmuch as the divine essence involves existence". Decadent Scholasticism had said that "in God there is an identity of essence and existence" and the formula was quite clumsy and inept because "existence" (*ex-sistentia*) is the fact of "standing outside of" one's own cause, and this can have no plausible meaning in God. It is to this imbecilic terminology that Spinoza appeals. Shrewdly he writes "whose essence involves existence" and not simply "whose essence is identical with his existence". This "involves" connotes a whole series of notions big with somber consequences: "implies", "demands", "comprehends"; there is a total coincidence of the logical and the metaphysical relation. This perfect coincidence is also present in St. Thomas' notion of God "whose essence is his very Being (Be-ing = *esse*); but Aquinas' *esse* is the exact opposite of the Scholastics' and Spinoza's *existentia.* Aquinas' notion of *esse* is that of pure subsistent Act, that supreme perfection which in God takes the place of essence.[3] Thus *esse* is expressive of God's absolute transcendence and the supereminence of his actuality over all creatures; it is then this very supereminence which, in St. Thomas' view of that total causality which is creation, becomes the ground of God's metaphysical immanence in creatures. Thus these two notions of God, the Thomist and the Spinozan, intermesh and diverge in an endless dialectic concerning which we may here limit our comments to the following most salient points.[4]

First, let us get meticulously clear the opposition between St. Thomas' *esse* and Spinoza's *existentia:* the former articulates God's absolute transcendence, the "separateness" of his fullness of perfection, God's conjunction with himself; the latter, on the contrary, articulates or at least requires the conjunction with God of the modes and attributes which come to constitute in a certain sense the "content" and the metaphysical "body" of God. This is an assertion of modern metaphysical immanentism which, as we have seen, activates and often decides the issue of its atheistic bias.

[3] On the absolute primordiality of *esse* in St. Thomas and on St. Thomas' uniqueness in maintaining this notion among Scholastics, cf. C. Fabro, *Participation et causalité,* (Paris-Louvain, 1960).

[4] Spinoza's relations with Scholasticism have constituted a fertile field for research and investigation (cf. J. Freudenthal, *Spinoza und die Scholastik* [Heidelberg, 1913]; *Idem, Die Lehre Spinozas,* auf Grund des Nachlasses [Heidelberg, 1927]. These investigations are notable for their total failure to make any distinction between the extrinsicist position of formalistic Scholasticism, against which Spinoza sets himself, and the genuine intrinsicist position of Aquinas' *esse* [*id quod est magis intimum*]. Such bemusing neglect of a crucial distinction makes all the more urgent a structural examination of modern thought).

Next there is Spinoza's *involves* over against St. Thomas' *is*. The *is* indicates a transcendence of any "content" like an essence of any sort in the interests of an assertion of *sheer Be-ing* (*esse purum*). Spinoza's *involvit*, on the contrary, indicates a process of constitution of Substance which is internal to its own being, by means of which it takes possession and assumes hegemony of the content and comes to be the "foundation" or "ground" of its own attributes and modes. Here the realm of existence belongs to God, the world and man, like extension and thought, are the actuations of God. This conjunctive trend, still only implicit in the Spinozan formula, will become explicit in the Hegelian principle to the effect that ". . . the external is the internal" [5] which amounts virtually to the transitional bridge to the Sartrian formula noted above.

Finally, and as a conclusion from the two points just treated, in St. Thomas the *esse's* transcendence connoted God's absolute sufficiency and subsistence within himself and guaranteed the full freedom of the creative act, which God could revoke at any moment, since in creation it is the creature that enters into relations with God and not *vice versa*. In the Spinozan conception, the Thomist mutual "creational" relation of cause-effect is replaced by the structural constitutive relation of substance-accidents. It is no longer a relation of dependence but of conjunction that can be exemplified precisely by the neo-Platonic analogy of the center and its radii or by Hegel's just mentioned analogy of external and internal, this latter a considerably more empirical picture!

In Spinoza, then, it is thinking that rules on being, and the relations internal to thought become the relations constitutive of being. Thus, does Spinoza transcend the Cartesian notion of *substantia finita,* to proclaim the indivisible unity of Being. This is existentialism pushed to its ultimate extreme, where if there were some essence (perfection) "outside of" God, God would not be God and the creature would be nothing. Admittedly Spinoza does not directly identify Substance with the attributes and modes, nor yet God with the world. Indeed, he distinguishes them, but in the unity that sustains and differentiates them, in the conjunction that links them. Thus, it is equally true that without God, the world is not world, and that without the world, God is not God. The logico-ontological priority belongs to God—*substantia prior est natura suis affectionibus* (substance is prior by nature to its attributes) [6]—but

[5] Cf. Hegel, *Wissenschaft der Logik,* Book II, Section II, Ch. 3C; *Enzyklopädie der philosophischen Wissenschaften,* §§ 138-141. Kierkegaard is quite right in attacking the Hegelian dialectical primarily from this angle and on this point: cf. *Enten-Eller,* Pref.; *C. W.*, Vol. I (Copenhagen, 1938²), p. III; *Afslutt. uvid. Efterskrift; C. W.*, Vol. VII, P. I, Ch. 2, pp. 45ff.; P. II, Ch. 1. The subjective problem, pp. 123ff. Cf. also *Papirer,* 1846-47, VII A 186; Italian translation by C. Fabro, Vol. I (Brescia, 1962²), p. 518 and translator's note on pp. 1027ff.

[6] Spinoza, *Ethica,* P. I, prop. 1; Vol. II, p. 45.

at the level of conjunction the nexus is necessary and inseparable on both sides. And the special theoretical element of the notion of God as *causa sui* lies in the significance of *causa immanens* as Spinoza himself specifies: God exists as *causa sui,* not as cause of anybody or anything, but *sui,* of himself, inasmuch as his reality lies in the self-expansion of the attributes and the self-realization of the modes.[7] On this point likewise, transcendental idealism travelled the road opened by Spinoza to the bitter end, culminating in the expression of the identity of the finite and the Infinite in the formula that violates all grammatical rules in Latin: *Deus est res cunctas,* where the *est* expresses the identity and the accusative expresses the causality which is preserved in identity or as "necessary progression", which is precisely what we mean by our use of the term "conjunction". [8] The above Latin sentence can only be rendered into English by breaking another rule and even here the English would be open to a benign interpretation: *God uses all things!*

Continuing the play on words, and granting that the Spinozan Substance wrests to itself the whole of reality and like Saturn devours its own children, the formula *Deus est res cunctas* can be said to parallel the perfectly grammatical German formula: "*(Gott) das Unendliche 'isst' das Endliche*" ([God] the Eternal 'eats' [same form as 'is' but with reduplicated 's'] or devours the finite). For such an immanentism,

[7] "The difficulty which most people find in conceiving the unity of the infinite with the finite or the fact that the former is immediately the latter originates in their misunderstanding of absolute identity and in their tendency to persist in imagining being as something different and really distinguishable from substance itself, whereas it is precisely substance as such. In the statement A is B, nothing else is really being said than: A is the *Esse* (the essence) [the original reads: *A ist das Esse* (*die Wesenheit*) and in this apposition we surprise the inverted essentialism of modern philosophy as a whole!] of B (which latter to this extent would therefore *not be* on its own, but now *is* in virtue of the nexus with A). Precisely such is the meaning of the statement: 'God is all things' which ought to be expressed in Latin not as *est res cunctae,* but rather, contrary to good accepted Latin usage, as *est res cunctas*" [Schelling's point is that the *est* must be converted into a transitive verb to do full justice to the ontological situation being articulated]. Thus this fundamental proposition: "the infinite is the finite" is the *analogatum primum* of all the other expressions of the unity of contraries, as e.g.: "the free is immediately and as such the enchained" (Schelling, *Aphorismen über die Naturphilosophie; C. W.,* Abt. I, Vol. VII (Stuttgart and Augsburg, 1861), p. 205 note. These aphorisms turn almost exclusively on the twinning of *natura naturans* and *natura naturata.*).

[8] "The accusative in this sentence is supposed to signal that, within the relationship between God and man, God is the sustainer and foundation of that which is as world: 'God is all things' = 'God sustains all things [in being]' " (W. Schulz, *Der Gott der neuzeitlichen Metaphysik* (Pfullingen, 1957), p. 67. The author remarks, rightly in our own opinion, that, whereas Descartes follows the analytic method in philosophy, Spinoza on the contrary introduces the synthetic method which is destined to be the characteristic method of modern thought: cf. pp. 59f., 64f.).

clearly, even though the finite can be said to be in the Infinite from the formal point of view, yet from the real point of view it is the Infinite that is and circulates and actualizes itself in the finite: the alleged interiority therefore actualizes itself (is actualized) only as exteriority and the One manifests itself only in and by way of the many. This is that genuine, simon-pure immanence-immanentism proper to modern thought, transforming itself at this crucial point in its evolution into the form that has catalyzed its more recent dissolutions.

The crucial advance of immanentism in Spinoza is clear, but just as certainly this immanentism is remaining in the current of thought opened up by Descartes and is still Cartesian entirely in its deepest depths: the appeal to forms of neo-Platonic pantheism, medieval and Renaissance, is nothing but extrinsic evocation (e.g., Hegel's evocation of Proclus and Böhme). Indeed, the *cogito* comes out more vehemently in Spinoza than in Descartes and the first definition of *causa sui* we have reported shows that Spinoza actually began where Descartes had said he was ending: [9] it is truly from the identity of being and thought, with the positing of the *causa sui,* or in other words from ontological immanentism that there is derived the assumption of the identity of the finite and the Infinite or metaphysical immanentism. It can easily be observed how artfully and consistently the three definitions of *causa sui,* Substance (III) and God (IV) coincide, in the series of Definitions opening the *Ethics.* But it is pertinent to note how there is a "transition" from the one to the other, a transition mediating (in an anticipation of the Hegelian method) the progress toward the identity that is the ultimate goal. Thus, between the *causa sui* and the *Substance* notion, there intervenes the notion of "finite" which is specified as being reserved to the attributes, with the limitation being specified in each attribute in terms of its own order: "A body is called finite because we always conceive another greater. So thinking is terminated by another thinking." Substance, on the contrary, is conceived as self-sufficiency: "By *substance,* I understand that which is in itself and is conceived through itself; i.e., that whose concept has no need of the concept of another thing from which is must be formed." Obviously "substance" is here primarily

[9] The definition of substance in the *Principia* is already virtually Spinozan: "By substance we can understand nothing else than a thing that exists in such a way that it has need of no other thing in order to exist. And certainly a substance needing no other thing can only be understood as being unique, to wit God" (*Principia Philosophiae,* § LI; *Ouevres,* Vol. VIII, ed. Adam-Tannery, pp. 21-25). But it should be specified that the concept of God as *causa sui,* in a positive and not simply negative sense, is already clearly spelled out in Descartes, in the *Responsiones ad primas objectiones* (*Oeuvres,* Vol. VII, ed. Adam-Tannery, pp. 99ff.) as I have shown elsewhere (cf. C. Fabro, *Dall'uomo a Dio* [Rome: Studium, 1966]).

discovered and designated not as *conceived* but as *conceiving,* active and therefore sufficient. We have here already the Leibnizian dynamism and even an adumbration of the Hegelian dialectic in the two definitions of attribute (IV) and mode (V). The definition of God (VI), the last of the series, links up with the first, that of *causa sui,* repeating it with the mediation of the "other" as Hegel would say, i.e., of the attributes: "By *God* I understand an absolute infinite being, i.e., a substance consisting of infinite attributes, each one of which expresses an eternal and infinite essence" [10]

The sufficiency of God's being is thus decided by thought, by the "mode" (or fashion) of conceiving that being as an identity of essence and existence which is made to coincide, as we have seen, with the identity of substance with its infinite attributes and modes. Thus, what was still in a tentative formulation in Descartes is here pushed forward in a few propositions to what Hegel will call the "beginning" of thought in itself as the Absolute.

Leibniz did indeed indignantly combat Spinozan monism and atheism, as we have seen, setting over against it his own monadic pluralism. But in point of fact he took a further crucial step toward metaphysical immanentism (the very immanentism proclaimed by Spinoza): for Leibniz identified substance (monad) with that "power" of energy which subsequently becomes self-consciousness itself as freedom. Leibniz's subsequent assertion of the "plurality" of the monads is nothing more than an extrinsic definition, as Hegel noted, because in fact the Monad is one, God, into whom all monads return and subsist. This Monad of monads is the real crux of thought, whereas that manifold constitutes the abstract or ideal and therefore untrue moment or element.[11] Kant, who was initially a Leibnizian, was shocked by his exposure to Hume into transferring or rather specifying the activity of the monad into the production of the *Ich denke überhaupt* and thus sacrificing the unity (in plurality) of the substance-monad. Active immanence-immanentism is actualized in the Kantian *a priori* as "productive" and not merely constitutive of itself, in a world of experience. In this sense, the Kantian critical philosophy is much more deeply submerged in immanentism than was Substance or the Monad, because here in Kant anthropology pure and simple takes the first step toward becoming itself

[10] Spinoza, *Ethica,* P. I, Definitiones, p. 45.

[11] Hegel, *Wissenschaft der Logik,* Book I, Section I, Ch. 3, p. 152. Despite the systematic differences between Leibniz and Spinoza, Heinze says they have these basic points in common: the stability of all the monads in the divine Monad; the coincidence of purposiveness with perfect rationality (optimism); and, finally and most crucially and significantly, intellectualistic determinism (cf. M. Heinze, "Leibniz in seinem Verhältnis zu Spinoza," *Neues Reich* II [1875], pp. 921ff., especially pp. 925ff.).

an "ontology", banishing metaphysics and equating truth, once and for all, to the potentiality of man (the transcendental Ego). Idealism, as we have seen, in an effort to salvage metaphysics, had recourse again to the active substance-monad as the structure of the absolute Ego which was supposed to be God but could in fact be nothing more than the spontaneity of human Reason henceforth possessed of sovereign freedom within itself: Immanentism here swells and ebbs in the strictest sense *ad infinitum,* in the irresistible flux of history and in the scattered manifold of nature. What here seems to be a contamination of metaphysics and empricism, of unity and plurality, of identity and diversity, actually amounts to the crucial step on the way to a reconciliation between the majestic world of the immutable Necessary and the empirical world of the mutable and contingent. For we have here a transcendence of the Leibnizian limit of the distinction between the principle of contradiction and that of sufficient reason, i.e., between the *truths of reason* and the *truths of fact.* Henceforth immanence is entirely in the hands of the human spirit and so has irrevocably become immanentism!

Hegel will be the one to effect a vigorous resolution of the immanentistic pressure of rationalism, by revealing the anthropological character of God which will be the premise for Hegel's own definitive expulsion of the mind. Hegel notes that Descartes, Malebranche, Spinoza and Leibniz have all posited God as that relation of soul and body, and precisely in the sense that the finitude of the soul, on the one hand, and matter, on the other, are merely determinations, and ideal determinations at that, each a function of the other and neither possessed of any veridical status whatever. Thus God, concludes Hegel, is for these philosophers not only, as is often the case, another word to indicate that incomprehensibility attaching to the dichotomy, but rather is conceived as the sole true *identity* of the two, soul and body. But either this identity is too abstract, objects Hegel, like that of Spinoza; or else it is downright *creative* like Leibniz's Monad of monads, in a purely *judging* (*urteilend*) capacity, with the result that Leibniz ends by establishing a difference between the soul and the corporeal, the material, leaving the identity resident solely in the *copula* of the judgment, and thus failing to proceed to any definitive absolute conclusion.[12]

And precisely in connection with this *resolutio omnium in Deo* effected by rationalism, Hegel has an observation that clearly brings to light the latent but already active atheism contained in the decision to conceive precisely as existing in God the unity of what initially presented itself in a reciprocal extrinsicality (*auseinander*): God is here simply accorded the privilege of having foisted upon him everything that

[12] Cf. Hegel, *Enzyklopädie der philosophischen Wissenschaften,* § 389; ed. Hoffmeister, pp. 334f.

man cannot succeed in comprehending. The word "God" is thus the makeshift stop-gap (*Aushülfe*) leading to a unity that is as such merely an object of opinion; it is not really shown how the manifold proceeds from this unity. Thus God has a much more important part to play in modern philosophy than he had in ancient philosophy, for now the main thrust is toward a comprehension of the absolute opposition of thought to being.[13] Descartes in fact was the man who saddled God with the burden of guaranteeing truth and safeguarding from error in knowledge of reality; Leibniz subsequently added the further burden of safeguarding from evil with the principle of sufficient reason that posits in God the necessary order and pre-established harmony of all the events of the world.

At this point in the decisive crisis of immanentism precipitated by rationalism, an investigation could pause over the various efforts undertaken to resolve the finite into the Infinite and rise to the level of God. It will here suffice for us to note that this whole project demanded from the very outset too high a price, namely, the denial that the finite was a genuine reality or truth; hence, the apparently so impressive development of rationalist speculation resolves itself, as we have noted, into a series of pretentious variations on the theme of the ontological proof. This argument comes, thanks to the principle of immanentism in its objective ontological aspect, to have in modern thought the meaning we have already seen: *only God really is.* And the same principle of immanentism in its subjective epistemological aspect insists that it is thought which enthrones the Absolute in consciousness, thus resolving the very presence of the Absolute into thought and act of thought so that it is thought itself which is ultimately enthroned in the place of the Absolute. Hegel and idealism begin with an "absolute" thought, later convert it into an absolute "thinking"; and because in this process *the founding and grounding principle is thought as actualized in man* (indeed, there is no clarity on the point of how it could be actualized elsewhere!), the very logic of the process itself demanded that a philosophy taking the *cogito* as its point of departure should not long delay in getting rid of the Absolute even as a predicate. And that, as we have seen, is exactly what happened, right on schedule! Thus, by a paradox that is in the final analysis consistency itself, metaphysical immanentism's sole valid argument for the existence of God resulted in the radical denial of God.

As always in these fundamental discussions, nothing is more instructive than to trace the Hegelian procedure through its essential steps.[14]

[13] Hegel, *Geschichte der Philosophie,* Vol. III; ed. Michelet, pp. 425f.

[14] Cf. Hegel, *Philosophie der Religion,* Part I, Ch. 2, Section 2, § III, "Die absolute Vermittlung"; ed. Lasson, pp. 206-225.

We have, says Hegel, God and his being. The mind has the assignment of showing us the connection between the two determinations or definitions, since they arc as such diverse, different. Note that point well: God and being are different. In the first instance, each has its own reflexive reference: God as God and being as being: i.e., God as the Absolute in itself and being as the unfolding of activity of human reality or "being-conscious" (*Bewusstsein*). Now, to "prove" (the existence of God), says Hegel, means to show the connection between the two; it implies that God and being-conscious as a totality do have a connection, a nexus despite their undeniable diversity, that they have an identity, and this identity must not be an abstract identity, for that would be sameness and consequently immediacy, and we should have naturalistic or intellectualistic pantheism. There is an exterior nexus that leaves the individual components (e.g., the building blocks in a building) each in their own being; and there is a sort of nexus that is found in the things themselves, such as the property of a right-angled triangle which makes the square on the hypoteneuse equal to the sum of the squares on the other two sides. But the proof to the existence of God is not of this sort because here in geometry the result is already contained within the premises, i.e., the very notion of a triangle.

In the ascent to God, those proofs that start from the finite present an interesting situation: the form in which they have been hitherto presented must indeed be rejected; but their content is valid and is the movement which leads from the finite to the Infinite. Initially we have two definitions mutually connected: God in general, the indeterminate image of God; and being (*Sein*). These two are to unite in a second moment. Hegel's starting point is sheer being, and his procedure is approximately this: because there is the finite, there is—there must be!—the Infinite as well. But this argumentation can be undertaken, notes Hegel, only inasmuch as the finite has not in itself any truth, is something contingent(*ein Zufälliges*), precisely a being which is in fact merely non-being. And this recognition of the non-being of the finite which comes out in positive form as an affirmation not of the finite but of the Infinite, this transition from the non-being of the finite to the existence of the non-finite or the Infinite—this is the proof of the existence of God! There are three elements or moments here, almost as in the Thomist approach of the five ways: the point of departure is the finite, immediate existence (*unmittelbares Dasein*); the next moment is that the finite in itself is nothing true, that it has no true being, is negative (*omnis determinatio est negatio*), or in other words that the being of the finite reveals itself as non-being. The third moment is that this negation of the finite is, for its part, an affirmation, arising out of that negation, and therefore infinite, absolute Being. Hegel's exact words are: "The third is that this negation of the finite is itself affirmation and therefore (*damit*) infinite Being";[15] he does not say "therefore a positing of infinite Being" or any thing of that sort; and this point is of capital importance for an understanding of the meaning of immanence-immanentism as "conjunction".

The situation is as if the veil of apparent being, of non-being, falls away at a certain moment from finite things and reveals them as in transparency Being itself which is the Absolute. And this is what Hegel accurately calls "absolute mediation" (*absolute Vermittlung*) which assumes, via total negation, the form of "transition from the first to the second immediacy". The first immediacy is the immediacy of the finite, the apparent which reveals itself as a "self-negation" (*sich-aufheben*), hence a non-being; the second is the essential immediacy, i.e., the emergence of the Absolute. The endless transition from finite to finite resolves nothing, for it is nothing but an infinite self-presentation or coming-to-presence of non-being (the *processus ad infinitum* which Hegel agrees with St. Thomas in calling *schlechte Unendlichkeit* [baneful infinity]). The true transition is from the finite to the Infinite; and this transition, be it carefully noted, is for Hegel not simple negation but true affirmation, being; it is the transition from the finite as negative to the Infinite as positive. Hegel calls it "interior mediation" (*innere Vermittlung*).

And the transition consists in a substantion-negation or negation-substantiation (a substantiating negation or a negative substantiation, or indeed perhaps even better a negational substantiation) of the finite which presented itself as being and is in reality non-being or mere appearance, whereas the Infinite is true Being. One does not therefore "pass over" from the finite to the Infinite, as in the Thomist proofs; rather the Infinite lies concealed in the finite and presents itself as its Reality; and this is what can be called *constitutive immanence*. Hegel warns against the formulation: "Because there *is* the finite, there is *also* the Infinite". For this says that the finite *is* and therefore there is the Infinite, so that the finite is here not only point of departure but foundation as well (*Grundlage*). The proper method of deduction is this: initially the finite presents itself, but then the Infinite which is the genuine, because the finite is not, because the finite is not true in itself, but is rather the self-negating contradiction, seeing that the truth of the finite is that affirmative which is called the Infinite. Thus, neither the finite nor the Infinite are left each in itself; that is the entirely abstract way of considering proper to the understanding. On the one side there is posited a world, on the other, God; and the knowing of the world is founded on

[15] *Ibid.*, p. 212.

the being of God. Thus, although we do indeed start from the finite to arrive at the Infinite, yet there is no mediation whatever between a finite and an Infinite, each of which is. Rather the point of departure negates itself: the finite reveals itself as negative and from the negation of this negation, i.e., from a mediation, there arises the Infinite; it is a self-abolishing mediation, mediation by means of the negation or abolition of mediation. And the result of the whole operation is what Hegel calls the "second immediacy".[16]

Hegel is insistent on the point that this whole procedure makes sense only if, and itself clearly indicates that, only the Infinite is and the finite has no true being. The finite from which the start is made negates itself, is negated (*wird aufgehoben*): Reason has the task of seeing that the finite has no truth at all, that it is only a limit(ation) and thus does not persist) there are no longer two because the finite disappears, fading away into a mere appearance, a shadow. This then is the development of the knowledge of God, that the point of departure (the finite) shall be denied, negated, refused subsistence by the spirit. The terminal of the transition, really attained by him who makes the transition, is not abstract, arid being, but rather the being that is the negation of negation, the positively true, so that finite being does not remain something other and there is no breach remaining between the finite and the Infinite. Finite being which reveals itself as accidental is that which negates itself and it is this negation, as we have said, which reveals itself as affirmation (of the Infinite) and this affirmation is the *absolutely necessary Being* (*das absolut notwendige Wesen*).[17]

Later in his exposition, Hegel appeals to the concept of "vitality"

[16] "The genuine transition consists not in change, in continuing alteration; rather is the truly other of the finite the infinite; and this latter is not mere negation of the finite; rather it is affirmative, Being . . . We have here not a relationship, not a mediation between two entities, each of which *is;* rather does the starting-point abolish itself; it is a self-abolishing mediation, mediation by means of the abolition of mediation" (*Philosophie der Religion,* p. 213). The end result is what Hegel calls "mediated immediacy" (*vermittelte Unmittelbarkeit*), and "essential immediacy" (*wesentliche Unmittelbarkeit*), which consequently emerges as the "self-abrogation of mediation" itself (cf. in this connection, C. Fabro, *Hegel, La dialettica,* pp. LXXIVff.). It is from this pseudo-theology centering round an essential immediacy conceived as a rediscovery or recovery by the Absolute of itself that the Hegelian Left will launch out on its demolition activities culminating in the dissolution and precipitation into atheism of the principle of immanentism.

[17] Hegel is being perfectly consistent with the principle of conjunction when he writes: "There are finite spirits. But the finite has no truth; the truth of the finite spirit is the Absolute Spirit. The finite is no true being; its very nature is to abolish, negate itself dialectically, and its negation is the affirmation as infinite, as in and of itself universal" (*Philosophie der Religion,* p. 218). It is in this section that Hegel seems to me to present the most pithy and forthright exposition of the scope and significance of the dialectic.

(*Lebendigkeit*) in general, the actual absolute vitality of the world in which "occurs" each particular life-phenomenon as a "realm of ends" in the conception of Kant and Aristotle. The final conception of the Absolute, after that of Being and Life, is that of Spirit (*Geist*). Here the argument is that the finite spirit has no truth; the truth of the finite spirit is (the) Absolute Spirit.

In the final analysis, therefore, Hegel's "real dialectic" seems to be binary rather than trifold: it consists in the incessant "negation" (*Aufhebung*) which is the transition from the finite to the Infinite. In this dialectic, the phenomenon or immediate being is just as indispensable in the human process of becoming as is the Absolute: the negation or transition is possible only on the basis of the incessant self-revelation of the negativity of the finite. For Hegel, in fact, it is this negativity of the finite which is the enormous motive power for the transition, so that on the one hand this world of the non-true which is the first immediacy is the subject-object of the dialectic directed to the comprehension of the Spirit and on the other hand this Spirit has no other "theater" of action and appearance than this world of phenomena.

We have already seen that Hegel's expressions on this point ("functional dualism") of God's immanence *without remainder* in the world have deep roots in the very structure of Hegelian thought. Baader too saw this[18] and noted Hegel's agreement with Böhme on the concept of *Geist* as arising as a "negation" that involves a "divesting" (*Entäusserung*); but Baader also hastened to point up the profound differences between Böhme and Hegel. Especially in the matter of the concept of Nature (*Natur*), Hegel knows only visible material and thus transitory nature, whereas Böhme posits primarily an "eternal nature" (*ewige Natur*) which is the Creator-God himself and thus God is absolute principle and first cause (*und ist also Gott der Urgrund und Grund*). Then, furthermore, Böhme always aims at distinguishing created reason from divine and absolute Reason, whereas Hegel always recognizes only absolute Reason so that finite reason plunges into rational universality and "goes down" as in Spinoza.

Finally, Baader feels that Hegel's devaluation of sensible knowledge as against philosophical knowledge must be corrected, so that the movement of knowledge shall not become detached from immediate knowledge but only free itself from that immediate knowledge to the extent that the limit itself guides and bears forward, determining as internal the

[18] F. von Baader, *Fermenta cognitionis,* Viertes Heft, §§ 17-18; *C. W.*, Vol. II, pp. 305ff. Later in the same work, Baader welcomes the Hegelian conception of Spirit (*Geist*), but with the insistent reservation that the finite shall maintain itself and continue to exist even in the *Aufhebung,* even though that finite be an evil spirit! (*ibid.*, Fünftes Heft, § 1, p. 326).

determinant (the positive, the empirical, etc.) which every movement of knowledge inhibits and determines from the outside. Actually a movement is free to the extent that is succeeds in dominating the exterior cause and opening within itself the interior principle of movement. And this holds for both elements of representation, its content (sensation) and its form (concept). This nexus of thought with the sensible sphere is for human knowledge as indispensible as is gravity for bodies on the earth: [19] thus the identity of form and content is untenable.

And Baader goes straight to the source of this pantheistic monism which eliminates the true productive interiority of the spirit: he attacks Spinoza as lacking the notion of secondary or dependent substantiality. Spinoza, says Baader, actually confounds the participation of secondary substances in absolute substance with the notion of these secondary substances forming and being a numerical part of that absolute substance. But if each and every individual thing is produced by God in such a way that it is insubstantial (*unselbstständig*), then it can easily be seen that the sum total of such insubstantiality will itself be insubstantial unable even to negate itself, and then nothing seems so ludicrous as the great panegyric on pantheism's concept of God and the world, the identity of God and the world or the consubstantiality of both, as being the result of the profoundest speculation! [20] If the finite is not being, it is incomprehensible how God can be Being; if the finite is not a cause in it own order, it is incomprehensible how God can be First Cause. And Baader insists the crucial point that must here be grasped is the "metaphysic of participation", since being like life cannot be actualized in solitude.

Against the Hegelian notion that ". . . the extrinsic reality of the Idea or the creature does not have its own being within itself but only in the Infinite", Baader objects: "The creature has its own being only in the participation (*Theilhaftseyn*) in the Being of God, but that does not mean, as in the Hegelian conception, that the creature does not have any being in itself and should want to have it like those ascetics who lament that the flame of love of God is destroying them." Hegel does indeed sometimes use the term "essence" or "being" as *Wesen* in opposition to "spirit" (*Geist*) understood as the "Self-less" (*ein Selbstloses*); but

[19] F. von Baader, *Fermenta cognitionis,* Fünftes Heft, §§ 1-2, pp. 326f. Baader has in mind the *Enzyklopädie der philosophischen Wissenschaften* in §§ 1-2. In § 3, Baader criticizes the minimist Hegelian conception of religion (§ 5), showing how the "mysteries" do not inhibit the "free motion" of knowledge; in the elevation to God, only the "baneful singularity" (*schlechte Einzelheit*) disappears, that singularity which has not only emancipated itself from unity, but has even gone so far as to exclude itself from that unity.

[20] F. von Baader, *Fermenta cognitionis,* Sechtes Heft, § 6, p. 400. There is an evident allusion not only to Schleiermacher but to Hegel as well.

even here it should be said that the creature just as much a being (essence) as a spirit and that the difference between God and the creature consists in the fact that God is the absolutely primordial unity of spirit and essence (being, whereas that unity as obtaining in the creature, is derived from God. Consequently it is just as mistaken to speak of a "flowing-back and dissolution" (*Refluenz-Auflösung*) of the created being (essence) into the being (essence) of God as to speak of the dissolution of the created spirit into the Creator-Spirit".[21] The being of beings lies not simply in affirmation or negation but also and primarily in "participation" from which we make the transition from the finite to the Infinite.

The basic nexus of finite and Infinite is therefore "participation" and this relationship, even though it be initially actualized for the finite spirit by God's free act, is nonetheless not consummated except by a decision that is a free act of man. And Baader expressly reproaches preceding philosophies, and especially that of Hegel, of a falsification of the concept of the finitude (*Endlichkeit*) of the creature.[22] This concept has two quite distinct degrees: the first birth or creation (as a participation of the Father) and the second birth or creation (which is the redemption) as a participation of the Word. In his first condition, the creature, as still incomplete, is not yet conformed to his own concept and is always pursued by a "beyond", by a duty, and so is unhappy (*unselig*) because he has not yet acquired the second birth, has not yet united himself with, i.e., been reborn of the Word (Son). But the reason for the creature's unhappiness, specifies Baader, is not the fact that he is not the infinite God himself; he is unhappy precisely because he is not yet grounded in God, not because (as the mystico-panthesitico-Spinozan conception would have it) he has not yet returned into God. Thus is modern philosophy intrinsically anti-Christian because it ignores or annihilates (reduces to nothing) the notion of creature, resolving the dependence of the creature on the creator into the conjunction of a phenomenon or appearance with the Essence or the All, the Whole,

[21] F. von Baader, *Revision der Philosopheme der Hegel'schen Schule,* pp. 33f. Here Baader attacks Carrière, protagonist of the Hegelian conception (cf. the defense of the sufficiency of nature and of the creature in its own order, inasmuch as it participates in God, a defense directed specifically against Hegel, in addendum [g] on p. 155. Also F. von Baader, *Bemerkungen über einige antireligiöse Philosopheme unserer Zeit,* §§ 18ff., especially § 27, pp. 489f.). Baader can therefore be said to have foreseen the theoretical fertility of Thomistic speculation on participation as a supersession of the formal immanence-transcendence tension, as this speculation is being developed in recent *Thomas-Forschung* (cf. in this connection, C. Fabro, *La nozione metafisica di partecipazione* [Turin, 1963 [3]]; *Idem, Participation et causalité.*

[22] The editor, F. Hoffmann cites *Hegels Werke* III, 137-73, i.e. *Wissenschaft der Logik,* Book I, Section I, "Die Endlichkeit"; pp. 116-146.

More technically speaking, modern philosophy fails to distinguish between being or becoming a part (*zum Teil werden*) and participating (*Theilhaftwerden*), and thus reduces the creature to the status of being a part of God.[23]

Baader's crucial call therefore is for a substitution of transcendent immanence as causality-and-participation for the monistic closed immanence that is immanentism, and of *Aufhebung* as *Erhebung* (a lifting oneself up and at the same time being lifted), i.e., actualization of the powers or perfections innate in the real with which every being is endowed from the outset, a substitution of this *Erhebung* interpretation of *Aufhebung* for the essentially negativistic notion of *Aufhebung* as "down-going" (going down like a ship) and loss of reality (*Untergang*). When Schopenhauer's capital work [24] appeared, Baader saw in it the same error of Hegelian immanentism, that of identifying finitude (*Endlichkeit*) with non-being and evil (*Schlechtigkeit*), so that the negative transcendence by annihilation of creatureliness as finitude constituted the only and radical means for the destruction of sinfulness. To Hegel's notion of religion, according to which ". . . the true content of the Christian faith must be justified by philosophy, not by history, since what the Spirit does must be effected only by what is in itself and by itself, not by a past (or future) but by what is absolutely present", Baader retorts that it is "just as un-biblical as it is unphilosophical to try to separate the *interior becoming* (what Hegel calls content) from the *exterior becoming* (what Hegel calls history, *Geschichte oder Historie*) as it is to mix them up together or to call the one the positive in abstraction from the other. Rather must philosophy's field of endeavor, the unity of this interior and exterior becoming, be kept intact against both excessively centrifugal and excessively centripetal tendencies. Thus will misunderstandings and equivocations be avoided and specifically there will disappear that opposition between philosophy and history which Hegel still wants to maintain." [25]

In the light of this proven Hegelian incomprehension of the finite, this

[23] *Ueber die Wahrheit* (Review); *C. W.*, Vol. I, p. 121, especially the note to pp. 23ff. In the *Fermenta cognitionis,* Baader repeatedly returns to this crucial and cardinal point, denouncing ". . . the Spinozan confounding of the creature with the creator" (Fünftes Heft, § 22, p. 352), and setting over against it the doctrine of Böhme which Baader interprets as asserting transcendence (*ibid.,* Sechstes Heft, § 1, p. 373). On Baader's critique of Spinozism and his realist theory of participation, cf. E. Susini, *F. von Baader et le romantisme mystique,* Vol. II (Paris, 1942), pp. 468ff.

[24] *Die Welt als Wille und Vorstellung* which Baader examines in the *Vorlesungen über Jakob Böhme's Theologoumena und Philosopheme* (1847); *C. W.*, Vol. III, pp. 359ff.; cf. especially p. 366 note).

[25] F. von Baader, *Vorlesungen über Jakob Böhmes Theologoumena und Philosopheme,* p. 430.

perversion of finitude into sheer objectivity and exteriority, we can understand how Hegel came so totally to misunderstand the *relation of faith and reason,* how he came to have such a wholly wrong notion of the redemption which, like every cure, is applied individually to individual subjects and not to the species *en masse!* This involves that claim for freedom of the individual, in the genuine notion of immanence, that Kierkegaard was already championing, with the aim of defending philosophy (principle of contradiction) rather than faith, in the first instance! It is the whole of modern philosophy which is here being arraigned in its most qualified representatives: Fichte, Schelling, Hegel, Schopenhauer. And Baader concludes that, even as another philosopher (in fact this was Schelling) asserted that the Son, hidden in the bosom of the Father, obtains personality, "selfhood" (*Selbstheit*) and hence reality, substantiality (*Wesenheit*) only with creation, so Hegel declares this Son to be just as "unreal, ungenuine" (*unwahrhaft*) as creatures themselves, since this Son is the other-being and exteriority of the Father. Nor is it then hard to see how Schopenhauer, starting from Hegel, went over into atheism: for Hegel in point of fact agrees (though only on the fundamental point) with those philosophers of nature who confuse God with the creature, with creation as a whole, since Hegel asserts that both (God and creature) commence and cohere only via becoming-other and self-emptying (*Anderssein und Entäusserung*). Consequently this God, says Schopenhauer, is always desirous of manifesting himself, of coming-to-presence in the phenomenon or appearance (*Erscheinung*); but this will is perpetually frustrated because God's appearance is wrecked each time in the void. Thus the fundamental error of the metaphysic of immanence which has become metaphysical immanentism turns on the concept of "finitude as creatureliness" (*Endlichkeit als Creaturlichkeit*). There has been a failure to see that the creature, the finite, can attain to its fullness without having to be transformed into the Infinite.[26] This is the crux of the entire question, so eminently diagnosed by Baader and Kierkegaard on the theistic side and by Feuerbach and Schopenhauer, together with Nietzsche, on the atheistic side: the former group to go back to the primordial ground of Being for the salvation of beings; the latter to push the *cogito* principle ruthlessly forward to its final disappearance into the void as it in turn causes being to vanish into nothingness!

The adventure of modern thought has come full circle with the philosophies of our own day. After three centuries of dramatic and enthralling

[26] *Ibid.*, p. 432. Baader therefore vigorously contests Hegel's pantheistic interpretation of Böhme (*ibid.*, p. 403 note and *passim* in all Baader's works. Cf. especially, in a context proximate to our own problematic: *Ueber den christlichen Begriff der Unsterblichkeit im Gegensatz zu den älteren und neueren nichtchristlichen Unsterblichkeitslehren*, 1835; *C. W.*, Vol. IV, pp. 281f.).

(in more ways than one!) escapades, that have kept time with the phases of the transformation of modern civilization, that modern thought has been brought home to its miserable hovel, the definitive void. Any attempt on the part of one of these present-day philosophies to acquire a content so as to justify some gesture at least of a firm stand is doomed from the outset: the new principle of freedom as sheer negativity is lying always in wait to dissolve every valiant plan and, like some grinning death's head, to remind them all that delay is pointless and that it is too late for regret or repentence. Philosophy as a discipline deriving from the *cogito* is utterly doomed and its doom is now manifest. But the adventure of man himself is not yet over and time has not run out entirely for *him!* Freedom awaits its restoration to its true foundation which is Being himself as act of all that presents itself to thought, as act of thought (but never *the* act of thought, of thinking!) and as guarantor of that thought which surges forward from the presentness of the world to the future, knowing that the Act that shall be its own fullness and consummation awaits it, the Act that shall give of his own fullness without destroying either the fullness or the substantiality of the questing fragile but doughty voyager.

4
Principle of Immanentism and Modern Science

Despite our repeated insistence throughout this volume on modern thought as the assertion of immanence and freedom against the metaphysical transcendence of ancient and especially medieval thought, we must caution that it would be a silly and impermissibly restrictive approach to reduce the *entire* phenomenon of modern philosophy, and with it the molding of the modern world, to any single principle or to any single simple idea. In every age, even in antiquity and indeed even in the Middle Ages themselves, man's questing spirit has never succeeded in quieting its restlessness which drives it unceasingly to the self-transcendent leap of a pursuit of its insatiable aspirations in an ever more complex dialectical evolution.

There is a tendency to conceive the modern era as the third age of mankind, the "Age of the Spirit", in the phrase of Lessing and the transcendental idealists, succeeding to the age of the hegemony of nature over man in antiquity and of the Absolute and the Church in Christian thought. But the real picture is considerably more complicated than any easy contrast between geocentrism and heliocentrism, between slavery and freedom.[1] Modern thought from its very outset returned to the mathematical approach to reality, seeing in the physico-mathematical sciences and in the manifold combinations of physical experience with mathematical reckoning the perfect and most valid paradigm of knowledge. Men like Telesio, Campanella and Giordano Bruno revived the ancient Stoic-hylozoistic conception of universal life and animation, in the wake of the resumption in Eckhart and Nicholas of Cusa of Pythagorico-Neo-Platonic

[1] The Marxists pretend to ignorance of the considerable debt owed by modern science to Greek thought and science, aside from the atomism of Democritus and Epicurus. Cf. in this connection, the remarks of the Protestant theologian A. Titius, *Natur und Gott,* Ein Versuch zur Verständigung zwischen Naturwissenschaft und Theologie (Göttingen, 1926), pp. 217ff. Also: P. Jordan, *Der Naturwissenschaftler vor der religiösen Frage* (Oldenburg-Hamburg, 1963), pp. 19ff.

speculations on the coexistence of the macrocosm-microcosm and of the finite-Infinite, i.e., of the coincidence of contraries and of opposites. And the survival of the metaphysical bent of mind was to make every effort, especially in Spinoza and subsequently in the transcendental idealists, to preserve in modern thought a meaning and a value for the Absolute. But this rationalist and idealist metaphysic has been definitively disposed of especially by post-Hegelian philosophy in its pushing of the principle of immanentism to its really logical conclusion, branding the rationalist and idealist metaphysics as simply a disguised theology, a pseudo-theology, a radical equivocation, a mystification and mystery-mongering on the subject of nature, a man and indeed God himself (Feuerbach).

Just as the panthetistic or panentheistic principle of modern immanentism can be linked directly to the hylozoistic monism of the classical world, so too the *new science* can be traced back, both in respect of its hypotheses and of its method, to Greek thought, without any unjust infringement of the creative originality of modern scientific endeavor. Historical research has contributed meticulous and salutary clarification on this point. There is not a single theory of modern science, from heliocentrism to evolution, that was not adumbrated and outlined by the Greek genius, even if the means and equipment were often subsequently lacking to develop and explicitate the theories. Indeed it is precisely the actual design and introduction of this equipment and of these methods that constitutes the merit of modern science and of the new conception of the world introduced by that science and leading to the establishment in the modern era, just as in Aristotle,[2] of a new and structural link between science and philosophy. The true and full significance of this nexus is far from having been exhaustively articulated for it is still in process of explicitation.

The break between the modern world and the medieval world must be admitted to be deep and mortal; it can be expressed paradigmatically in the radical opposition of immanentism and transcendence-orientation. The fact that Descartes, Spinoza, Leibniz and many other thinkers, right down to and including Heidegger himself, often continue to treat problems treated by Scholasticism and even to use Scholasticism's own terms, proves no continuity of thought but only points up the irreconcilable opposition. The persistence of these venerable terms henceforth sanctions an incontestable occupation right for a new kind of thought that proclaims once and for all the *regnum hominis*. This hegemony of

[2] But inversely, for whereas in Aristotle (or better, in degenerate Aristotelianism) it is philosophy which imposes conditions on science, in the modern age it is science which imposes conditions on philosophy. Not always, however, for in the wake of Kant, the idealists return to distorted Aristotelianism.

man was asserted in the new science before it was articulated or implemented in politics; and it was from the new science that the new philosophy took its chief inspiration. The new science had little trouble asserting itself against a Scholasticism that had ended up in a windy verbalistic philosophy of logic-chopping and an arrogant theology.[3] Humanism, rather vapid in the area of theory, turned confidently to the classical world; modern rationalism resolutely set out to take the straight road of science, based simultaneously on mathematics and experiment; and this was a sound step.

Philosophy likewise wished to avail itself of the happy insight of modern science into the study of phenomena; and exact science thus became the paradigm of knowing. The situation of a science influenced by philosophy (and sometimes by theology) was replaced by a situation of a philosophy stimulated and even guided by science: Descartes (and with him Malebranche, Spinoza, Pascal), Leibniz, Kant (and even Hegel!) were not only major philosophers but also more or less outstanding practicioners of science. And they determined to rescue philosophy from the miserable state into which it had fallen: philosophy, they contended, could survive only if it adapted itself to the criteria of science. This is the explanation of the origin of Descartes' "clear and distinct idea", of Leibniz's principle of sufficient reason, of Kant's synthetic a priori judgment. In scientific research into the laws of phenomena, man finds himself on the one hand in contact with experience and on the other hand he can operate directly in this world of phenomena with his own hypotheses, reckonings and experiments.

Rey may be extrapolating a little when he says that Kant's *Critique of Pure Reason* is "the justification of modern mathematics and of Newtonian physics . . . a demonstration of the legitimacy of modern science and an apology for its value".[4] But we feel that the statement is substantially accurate and provides the key to an understanding of the revolution or inversion of the axis of truth effected by the principle of immanentism. And science being a human endeavor and project, a human adventure and undertaking, man in science feels himself to be at the center of operations and even feels himself to be the pivot of truth: the supereminence of man, asserted in humanism in such florid and esoteric terms of rhetoric, found in the severity of scientific methodology its ample and total justification.

[3] Scholastic terminology finally disappears in Schelling and Hegel, to return in Heidegger. This witnesses primarily to the disintegration and speculative deficiency of that abstract philosophy which played at formalizing the empirical world. Hence, in reaction, the recourse to the *cogito* or the discovery (or hypothesis!) of the transcendental.

[4] Cf. A. Rey, *La philosophie moderne* (Paris, 1921), p. 23.

The second step was the application of science to technology: this produced the industrial revolution in the 19th century and is in process in our 20th century of effecting a social and political transformation throughout the world. What pure philosophy had not been able to effect over a period of tens of centuries and Christianity itself had not succeeded in doing in the course of two millennia, the notion of man as "pure practice", that claim which is the ultimate expression of the principle of immanentism and of the invasion by science into the "walled garden" of philosophy,[5] boasts that it is even now in process of accomplishing in our own day.

We do not mean to say that the whole of modern philosophy dissolves philosophy into science and *vice versa:* 19th-century positivism and 20th-century neopositivism express only a fraction of the logic of the principle of immanentism, and not the most pertinent portion at that, in our opinion. Positivism assumes the knowledge of phenomena as the first and last truth and considers the laws of phenomena as convertible with the real; neo-positivism rejects and repudiates any remnant of a thing-or-truth-in-itself and resolves truth into terms of a sheer analysis of language and of the verifiability of events. The transformation effected by the *cogito* principle in the course of its gradual evolution has become much more profound and complex. The crux of the matter is this, unless we are entirely mistaken: for Scholasticism (St. Thomas included), philosophy had no direct link with science, but aimed rather at instituting relations with theology and with revealed faith. And this for two reasons: for want of a science worthy of the name, in an age full of confused empirical guesswork, black magic, credulity and superstition; and in virtue of the haughtiness of a philosophy laying claim to a divine language instead of being content with human articulations.

St. Thomas stands out from this sorry scene for three excellent reasons: (a) he asserted vigorously the necessity of sensible experience in the natural sciences and the provisional and conditional character of physical hypotheses based on the observation of phenomena; (b) he posited quantity as the first accident of bodies, thereby recognizing the priority of extension over qualities and providing the basis for the necessity of a mathematical treatment of physical phenomena; (c) he expressly recognized the application of mathematics to physics, the possibility of an intimate collaboration of the two approaches to bodies, the

[5] Scientists themselves are today protesting this invasion: "My erstwhile faith in the superiority of the natural science approach over other approaches to knowledge and action now seems to me to be a self-deception, founded upon youthful enthusiasm for the clarity of physical theories as compared with the vagueness of metaphysical speculation" (Max Born, "Physik im Wandel meiner Zeit," (1958), in G. Noll, *Sein und Erkennen* [Munich, 1962], p. 9).

purely abstract approach that provides hints and guidelines and the experimental approach that verifies and consolidates.[6]

But St. Thomas was unable to realize and implement this magnificent program of the *mediate sciences* and his own disciples did not even grasp what he had in mind: they allowed themselves to become mired in verbal quibbles and perpetuated a hare-brained physics that died hard. The intimate tie-in instituted by decadent Scholasticism between philosophy and physics was continued in a no less loudly proclaimed tie-in between physics and theology, leading to an illicit solidarity of the two which was to occasion the modern crisis of science and faith, the reasons for which crisis lie in a situation that historiography is now in a position to clarify quite precisely. This does not alter the fact that the discord between the medieval and the modern world remains profound and the task of interpretation between the two is arduous indeed.[7]

It is the sense of values, at bottom, which has altered in modern man: authority has been transferred from a divine and sacral organism like the Church to science and culture, from dogma to reason; and for the obedient acceptance of dogmatic statements there has been substituted research and experiment in untrammelled freedom. The authority of science thus proclaimed must not be confused with the authority that used commonly to be attributed to the Church: although science does in many instances aim at supplanting metaphysics and theology, it still does not lay any claim to the right to make dogmatic pronouncements. The authority of science is proposed and accepted in purely rational terms: "No penalties fall upon those who reject it; no prudential arguments influence those who accept it. It prevails solely by its intrinsic appeal to reason. It is, moreover, a piecemeal and partial authority; it does not, like the body of Catholic dogma, lay down a complete system, covering human morality, human hopes and the past and future history

[6] The crucial text for a sane and sound methodology of knowledge is the (incomplete) Commentary on Boethius' *De Trinitate* (especially q. V, aa. 2-3. Cf. a. 3 ad 5, the brilliant references to the "sciences intermediate between mathematics and natural science"; ed. B. Decker [Leiden, 1955], p. 188, line 10); this is an anticipation of modern theoretical physics. But on the whole these comments remained without follow-up and without effect: recent investigations have shown that the positive contributions, so far as modern science is concerned, came primarily from nominalist Scholasticism.

[7] The abstract formalism of Baroque era Scholasticism seems to bear no mean responsibility for the estrangement of science from traditional philosophy: "Had the 17th century Scholastics had the boldness and discernment of the 13th century doctors, of a St. Thomas Aquinas or of a Gilles de Lessines, they would have been very careful not to tie their doctrines of the universe, of the soul and of God, to a science at best hypothetical and already outmoded; and they would not have presented medieval thought as a solid block, not one stone of which can be removed without toppling the whole edifice" (J. Chevalier, *Histoire de la pensée*, Vol. III [Paris, 1961], p. 28).

of the universe. It pronounces only on whatever, at the time, appears to have been scientifically ascertained, which is a small island in an ocean of nescience. There is yet another difference from ecclesiastical authority, which declares its pronouncements to be absolutely certain and eternally unalterable: the pronouncements of science are made tentatively, on a basis of probability, and are regarded as liable to modification. This produces a temper of mind very different from the medieval dogmatist." [8]

This whole frame of mind and approach to the question cannot be too often stressed, for it is vital to a comprehension of the animating spirit of the modern principle: indeed, even those extreme idealists and subjectivists, skeptics and deniers of science on principle, appeal to this approach whenever they want to go for classical metaphysics, of which modern thought has given no evidence of having even become acquainted with more than the pallid pupa represented by baroque Scholasticism.

This interpolation of science into the modern *cogito* has indeed proclaimed the victorious eruption of the new philosophy; but it has equally undeniably led that new philosophy into a dead-end conflict between objectivism and subjectivism. For there is nothing easily imaginable more objective than a science based on mathematical reckoning and subsequent experimental verification; and there is nothing easily imaginable more subjective than the *cogito* which assumes as substantiating principle the certainty of its own act of thought with respect to the object. There are indeed those who proclaim the conflict resolved by an appeal to "thought in general" or conceived in its universality and thus disencumbered of individual singularity, so that science itself, in its own self-constitution, tends to become the expression of this universality and thus to effect a reconciliation of the two clashing elements. But it is also true that the *cogito* principle aimed at asserting the primordiality of man's being (human be-ing) over against nature, at proclaiming man's *freedom* in the face of the professed necessity of physical laws; and such a freedom certainly cannot be said to have been satisfied with a mere realization of the scientific ideal, indeed this ideal would surely be freedom's Philippi!

Thus modern philosophy, like a fevered patient threshing about on his bed, has constantly swung back and forth between materialism and spiritualism, between empiricism and idealism, between subjectivism and objectivism, between naturalism and historicism. Science therefore

[8] B. Russell, *History of Western Philosophy* (London: George Allen and Unwin, Ltd., 1946), p. 512. This *theoretical* science, continues Russell, has been supplemented by a *practical* science representing an attempt to *change* the world and put it at the service of man. The most important discoveries have been steam and electricity (p. 513), and we might now add, nuclear energy.

has been very well-advised to shake off all philosophical allegiance and go its own way with its own methods, once those methods had been consolidated. This indeed is what it has certainly tried to do; yet ideologies seem still to be prejudicing its sense and capacity for good and truth.

It is time that philosophers grasp the fact that modern science remains entirely foreign and unrelated to the religious problem, both in its concepts and in its assignments, for the very simple reason that science deals with a field and area specified by material reality, whereas God is the Absolute Spirit and absolutely transcendent. Many scientists themselves are coming to this conviction on the limits of science's legitimate scope, the "strict observance" Soviet scientists always excepted, as we shall be explaining directly. If science as such and in virtue of its own specific object cannot and does not assert God, neither is it in any position to call him in question and still less to deny him: the proof of the existence of God stems from the demand of the integral human being. The founders of modern philosophy were almost all convinced theists: Descartes, Malebranche, Leibniz, in the rationalist tradition, whatever may be the case with Spinoza; and Bacon, Locke and Berkeley together with the whole Deist school, in the empiricist tradition. But, as we have said, in these cases the theist profession clashed with the demands of the principle of immanentism which resolves being into the finite limits of the potentiality of the human being. The greatest initiators of modern science, such as Copernicus, Kepler, Galileo, Huygens and Newton, were fervent theists and believers: and here the principle of immanentism had no part at all to play. They were impressed with the marvelous rationality of the cosmos, by its evidence of design, both in the world of the infinitesimally small studied by microphysics and in the world of the infinitely large studied by astrophysics. In contradistinction to modern philosophy which has made the *cogito* into the ground and foundation of the presence of being, modern science rejects and repudiates both positivism with its reduction of the reality of the world to perception and idealism with its conversion of the world into a creation of thought. If there is one discipline the science of our own decade can most easily do without, it is modern philosophy. Its own concepts and methods of rendering present physical reality (namely, experimentation) cannot and must not be those of philosophy.

The dogmatic Marxist "maximalists" assert as a positive demand of science itself the identity of science and materialism and hence of science and atheism. The Marxists of this kidney have a no less supremely superficial notion than do the positivists and the idealists about what ought to be understood by "reality" and what it connotes for man. For positivism, in the tradition of Bacon, Hobbes, Locke, Hume, *et al.*, down to Mach and his school (e.g., the physicist P. Jordan), reality consists in the *de facto* data of observation, both that of everyday life and that of experimental science. Little can be said against this approach as far as it goes, as even Born [9] the opponent of positivism freely admits. Marxism, especially in the wake of Lenin's critique of Mach,[10] rejects the phenomenist-positivist notion of science, considering it (and not without reason!) to be subjectivist and idealist. In 1848 the pro-Hegelian R. Haym had reproached Feuerbach with conceiving nature and spirit as having no nexus or correspondence whatever between them, of denying any link whatever between objective reality and the laws of science on the one hand and the mind's conception of the course of natural phenomena (order, purposiveness, etc.) on the other. Haym took exception to this passage especially: "Nature can generically *be understood only in terms of itself;* its necessity is not a human or logical, metaphysical or mathematical, i.e., abstract necessity, for nature is the only being to which no human measure can or ought to be applied, even though we do generally compare its phenomena to analogous human phenomena and apply such human expressions and notions as order, purpose, law, to it in order to render it intelligible . . . it is the requirement of our own language that compels us to use such terms." [11]

Feuerbach vigorously contested this criticism: "What is this supposed to mean? Am I supposed to be saying that there is no order in nature, so that, for instance summer could follow autumn, winter could follow spring or autumn winter? Or that there is no purpose in nature, as though, for instance there is no coordination between the longs and the aid, between the light and the eye, between sound and the ear? Or that there is no order in nature in the sense that I would be holding that, for instance, the earth sometimes revolves in an elliptical orbit and at others in a circular one, achieving its revolution round the sun sometimes in a year and sometimes in a quarter of an hour? What nonsense! What then did I want to say in that section? Simply to distinguish between what belongs to nature and what belongs to man; I did not say that there is

[9] M. Born, *Experiment and Theory in Physics* (Cambridge, 1943), Italian tr. (Turin, 1962), pp. 50ff. Cf. P. Jordan, *Der Naturwissenschaftler vor der religiösen Frage,* pp. 118ff.

[10] Cf. V. I. Lenin, *Materialism and Empiriocriticism* (Moscow: Foreign Languages Publishing House, n.d.). Actually the Marxists are again parading men and arguments from the crassest materialistic positivism, submissive to their class dogmatism, as can be seen e.g. in the anti-religious anthology of the chemist W. Ostwald, *Wissenschaft contra Gottesglauben* (Leipzig-Jena: Urania Verlag, 1960).

[11] The passage is a free rendition or paraphrased summary of Feuerbach (cf. *Das Wesen der Religion,* 1845, § 48; *C. W.,* Vol. V, ed. Bolin [Stuttgart, 1905], pp. 519f.).

nothing real in nature corresponding to our words and ideas on order, purpose and law; I only intended to deny the identity of thought and existence, to deny that the order, purpose, etc. are the same in nature as they are in man's head or feelings. Order, purpose, law are worlds man uses to translate the things of nature into his own language in order to comprehend them. These words are not devoid of meaning nor yet of object; but a distinction must be made between original and translation. Order, purpose, law are, in their human meaning, arbitrary inventions. Theism concludes *directly* from the fortuitous character of the order, purpose and laws of nature, to the assertion of their arbitrary origin and the existence of a being different from nature, who bears within himself the order, purpose and laws of a chaotic nature . . . The spirit of the theists . . . is in flat contradiction with nature, about the real character of which they understand nothing whatever. The theist understanding divides nature into two beings, one material and the other formal or spiritual; it then calls the former nature in the strict sense, and the latter it calls God." [12]

Lenin's comment is suggestive as an instance of adaptive exegesis. He holds Feuerbach to be admitting the objective regularity of nature and objective causality which is reflected only approximately in human ideas of order, law, etc.: "With Feuerbach the recognition of objective law in nature is inseparably connected with the recognition of the objective reality of the external world, of objects, bodies, things, reflected by our mind. Feuerbach's views are consistently materialistic. All other views, or rather, any other philosophical line on the question of causality, the denial of objective law, causality and necessity in nature, are justly regarded by Feuerbach as belonging to the fideist trend. For it is, indeed, clear that the subjectivist line on the question of causality, the deduction of the order and necessity of nature not from the external objective world, but from consciousness, reason, logic, and so forth, not only cuts human reason off from nature, not only opposes the former to the latter, but makes nature a *part* of reason, instead of regarding reason as a part of nature. The subjectivist line on the question of causality is philosophical idealism (varieties of which are the theories of causality of Hume and Kant), i.e., fideism, more or less weakened and diluted. The recognition of objective law in nature and the recognition that this law is reflected with approximate fidelity in the mind of man is materialism." [13]

No specialist knowledge is required to notice the obvious twisting of the Feuerbachian text: Feuerbach considers the human concepts to be an approximation at best and even downright "arbitrary" (*etwas Will-*

[12] L. Feuerbach, *Entgegnung an R. Haym; C. W.*, Vol. VII, pp. 519f.
[13] V. Lenin, *Materialism and Empiriocriticism,* p. 155.

kürliches); Lenin twists this to fit an immediate recourse to the simplist "reflection" (*Widerspiegelung*) theory of the direct and exact correspondence between the phenomena of nature and the human brain. In fact, Feuerbach can be said to have insisted on reducing the science problem like the God problem to the dimensions of human psychology; his approach is therefore diametrically opposed to the Marxist *Widerspiegelung* theory which conceives human cognition as a direct reflection of nature and therefore a byproduct of nature. Subsequently the Marxists embark, with an naivete approaching the ridiculous, on an explanation that science (and, to their mind, philosophy and art as well) can only be undertaken by the proletariat, i.e., be a product of the worker class, etc.[14]

The real conditions of science are far too complex to be able to be satisfied by this materialist theory of the material "reflection" of phenomena in the brain. Physics today (and indeed from the very introduction of the modern experimental method by Galileo) manipulates its instruments and its concepts simultaneously and convergently: ". . . fields, atoms, electrons, etc., which are partly possessed of the character of objects and partly not, but which do have one feature in common: that of not belonging to the ordinary world and having to be derived and deduced indirectly from experimental results. Often they are deduced initially via theoretical considerations, in some cases they become gradually more and more accessible to observation and thereby become "real": take, for instance, chemical molecules, which today can be photographed by the electronic microscope." [15]

We are left then with the Feuerbach notion of science as "approximation", but this approximation is achieved in a supremely objective form emancipated from any purely psychological profession of acceptance, achieved in fact solely via a complex and continuous labor of reflection, reckoning and experimentation.

In this work of comprehension of physical reality, modern science has been constrained to renounce the interpretation of all the aspects of a phenomenon via the observation of a *single type* and of a single system of concepts. There are at least two aspects to any fact and in each individual case a selection must be made of the one that is to be preferred. It is this partially subjective aspect of modern statistical physics —an aspect which Feuerbach, Marx, Engels or even Lenin could not

[14] Cf. e.g. the Russian philosopher G. Alexandrov's Introduction to the Russian translation of *Science versus Idealism,* by the English author M. Cornforth, reported in the German translation (Berlin, 1955), pp. 7ff. Cf. also the impudent defense of "atheistic science" on the part of M. Verret, in his *Les marxistes et la religion.*

[15] Cf. M. Born, *Experiment and Theory in Physics,* Italian tr., p. 58.

have known—that scandalizes many physicists brought up on the dogma of rigid determinism. The new physics is inclining toward what Nils Bohr has called the "principle of complementariety" [16] with its strange but suggestive evocation of the Aristotelian twin concepts of potency and act. It asserts that in the study of any problem, the researcher should work not with a single concept but with pairs of mutually opposed concepts, such as matter and life, body and soul, necessity and freedom. Even the simplest of sciences, physics, demands complementary and nuanced treatments of the various aspects of one and the same problem; it is quite impossible to refer everything to one *single* system or type or concepts as positivism, idealism, and to a far greater extent the dialectical materialism of Marxism, claim to be able to do. In biology, the animate substance is studied by physical and by chemical methods. But life itself is described and must be described in a completely different language containing such words as purpose, will, suffering, joy, habit, etc. The belief can of course be articulated, prior to any experimentation, that the cause of thought is to be sought in those chemico-physical phenomena transpiring in the brain, phenomena that have not yet been adequately studied. But Bohr cautions that when experimentation is undertaken on the brain of living beings, there occurs a disturbance of the very psychic phenomena the researcher wishes to study; the experiment is frustrated of its aim because the experimental subject has been modified by the research itself!

Innumerable quite profound books and treatises have been written on free will. Without it there is neither responsibility nor right and wrong, nor yet guilt and expiation. Our social theories are based on the hypothesis that every human being is free in his decisions. But how can this be reconciled with the laws of nature and with the notion of causality in general? According to these laws, what I am doing is simply the last link in a cause-and-effect chain for which I cannot be held responsible. When determinism began to totter, it was thought that an escape route had been found: if it is chance that rules in individual events, then it is up to the will, considered as an activity of the spiritual being, to make the ultimate choice. But this is completely untenable: the demon Will would then have to be continually paying attention to not violating *statistical* laws! Bohr thinks we have here a pseudo-problem: there are two aspects of the event, the physical one and the moral one, and they are comple-

[16] *Ibid.*, pp. 72f., where Born reports M. Bunge's refutation of the Marxist extrapolation from the new physics. P. Jordan has a more thorough analysis in his discussion of "complementarity" in *Der Naturwissenschaftler vor der religiösen Frage*, pp. 200ff., 208f., 341ff. (biology). Jordan holds that this notion of complementarity represents the culmination of the modern indeterministic conception of the world, prevalent in physics, biology and astronomy.

mentary and cannot be reduced the one to the other.[17] The conclusion must then be that precisely because of the fantastic developments and progress achieved in pure and applied science in the last fifty years, the simplism of the positivist, idealist, dialectical materialist and similar theories of science are completely untenable. We would certainly not say that science has again become a "theodicy" as once in the days of Newton, Nieuwentyt, Derham and their colleagues; but at least the barrage of atheistic conclusions being drawn by pseudo-scientific Marxist writings must be admitted to be sheer politically inspired extrapolations foreign to science as such. God is not to be found as a constitutive element of the physical world nor yet is he to be attained by the methods and procedures of the natural sciences; were that to be possible, he would no longer be God but rather a body or a physical state, a modification of bodies. If the idealists have not succeeded in getting matter to be forgotten, neither have the materialists succeeded in suppressing the spirit of God who is the crowning summit of the realm of spirit and who must therefore be sought by the methods proper to the spirit.

The same must be said of the other principle human problem in the understanding of life and history, namely, *free will,* which is radically compromised by any brand of materialism, especially dialectical materialism, with its reduction of human reality into the class struggle and its consequent proclamation of the most rigid historical economic determinism driving man necessarily from the primitive original state of nature, via feudalism, capitalism and socialism to the inescapable terminal state of communism. The genuine scientific approach on the contrary is quite sober on this point and repudiates as fantastic and dangerous the gratuitous speculations of determinists, whether they be materialist or idealist. In the study of the problem of freedom, science again can only put its trust in statistical laws which derive from the laws of large numbers (or individuals). How the single individual will behave is a problem that escapes science and on which the only competent authority would be the individual himself (if indeed even he!). This is the inescapable conclusion as soon as the human mind is admitted to be a special way-of-being, to have an ontological status proper to itself,

[17] M. Born, *Experiment and Theory in Physics,* p. 99. While Born acknowledges that "much of what physics thinks has been anticipated by philosophy", he rightly concludes that "our representation of the world does not adapt itself well to any known system: it is neither materialistic nor idealistic, neither positivist nor realist, neither phenomenological nor pragmatist, nor does it jibe with any other system" (p. 100). It is undeniable, in any case, that this conception at once recalls the deep significance of the Aristotelian-Thomist dualism, as soon as it has been disengaged from the factual limitations of ancient and medieval science and rethought (as we have pointed out just now) from the sheer point of view of methodological requirements.

namely, that of a thinking activity over against a nature that is an objective reality and the object of thinking, the inexhaustible challenge to knowing. The Marxists, following the lead of Marx and Engels, make a great point of the atheistic materialism of La Mettrie, d'Holbach, Meslier, Diderot and their like and consider themselves to be the legal heirs and successors of these men; but this in no sense redounds to their credit; rather, it simply points up the fact that their own stand has been transcended even by science itself, that science to which they are perpetually appealing. There can be no question of the impressive scientific results and breakthroughs that have been scored by Soviet scientists no less than (and no differently than!) Western scientists. But these successes have nothing to do with the profession of materialism or atheism. They come solely from the power of intuition and the proper use of the scientific method; and they have been facilitated by the fact that the Soviet Union, together with its competitor the United States of America, disposes of the proper equipment that is becoming ever more indispensible to successful experimentation. The problem of God simply does not enter into the picture here at all: the scientist who would presume to make the transition from his own theories or discoveries to a denial of God would simply no longer be operating as a scientist but only as a bad philosopher, repeating the same sort of error (in reverse!) as that perpetrated by those bad philosophers and less than brilliant theologians who presumed to dispute the value of Galileo's discoveries.

Let us now come to the heart of the matter, the Marxist notion of "matter" and let us take the exposition of that notion directly from the Great Soviet Encyclopedia which follows to the letter the classics of Marxism and especially the Lenin essay against Mach which we have already cited. This is an authoritative official Marxist text.[18] Let us begin with the definition of matter: "Matter (Lat. *materia*) is a philosophical category for the designation of objective reality given to man in his sensations; matter is copied, photographed, imaged by our sensations and exists independently of them. The only property of matter which philosophical materialism is bound to admit is its property of *being an objective reality,* of existing outside our consciousness." [19] And in order to avoid misunderstanding, the article hastens to point out that this matter is not to be confused with the notion modern physics has formed about nature and the properties of matter; and Engels is cited to the following effect: "matter (*Stoff, Materie*) is nothing but the totality of matter (*sic!*) from which this concept is abstracted, just as motion

[18] I am here following the official German translation of the Dietz Verlag (Berlin, 1950 [2]): "Die Materie," "Der Materialismus," "Materialismus und Empiriokritizismus".

[19] "Die Materie," p. 3.

(*Bewegung*) as such is nothing but the sum total of the forms of motion of sense-perception. Words like matter and motion are only abbrevations or shorthand (*Akbürzungen*) in which we synthesize many different things of sense-perception in terms of their common properties. Matter and motion can therefore be known only by investigation of the individual matters (*Stoffe*) and forms of motion and to the extent we know these, to the same extent do we know likewise matter and motion as such."[20] The two notions are therefore supposed to be mutually clarificatory; but anyone can see the insoluble muddle to which they lead.

The first definition (the official one) designates matter as a philosophical category and obviously in dialectical materialism it would be understood as being the fundamental and indeed only category of philosophy. Now this category is held to embrace and encompass the whole of objective reality given in our sensations, so that the sensations are sheer "copies", "photographs" "reproductions" and the mind a photographic plate having impressed upon it in a purely physical process of reception the sensory stimuli. Now this is a notion of matter which has no precise nexus with the philosophical tradition, unless it be held to be (in consideration of the studies of the young Marx) with the Democritan theory of "physical emanations" (ἀπορροαί). In any case it stands in the most shrieking contrast to the principle of immanentism of modern thought, to which, as we have seen, Marxism claims to adhere most strictly. But a patent contradiction and impossible situation emerges in this very notion with the attribution to this matter, as is one and only property, that ". . . *of being an objective reality,* of existing outside our consciousness".

We have only a few remarks to make on the meager content of such statements: in the first place, it is not clear how there can be any talk of outside and inside (and consequently of an opposition) in a conception in which knowing, cognition, is reduced to a simple physical "reflection" or "mirroring" (*Spiegelung*); secondly, the distinction made by Engels between the sum total of matter and the sum total of motion is far from clear; nor is it clear how there occurs the "coagulation" of the various

[20] And F. Engels is cited (*Dialektik der Natur* [Berlin: Dietz Verlag, 1955], p. 251). Marxist writers, both specialists and popularizing generalists, have followed Lenin's lead in unconditional adherence to Engels and have accepted the dogmas of evolution and absolute determinism, touting them as the definitive refutation of all religious conceptions of life and as an irrefutable proof of atheism. But the evolution of the physical and biological sciences in recent decades has seriously undermined these open-handed extrapolations, as we have been pointing out, and have gravely compromised both the Marxist method and the results it has produced. (For an extremely interesting overall treatment of this subject, cf. P. Jordan's recent work, *Der Naturwissenschaftler vor der religiösen Frage,* especially pp. 19ff., 97ff.: refutation of Haeckel.)

sensory qualities into the one and only matter and subsequently the disjunction into matter and motion; and finally, it is obscure just what might be the distinction between matter, which is the content received, and the mind which is the subject receiving and subsequently becoming reflective and operative in all fields of theoretical and practical activity. The psychology of antiquity, borne out by modern phenomenology, does not speak of sensations as an adequate primary content of sense experience; rather it speaks of "perceptions", which are apprehensions of a structured "whole" as such.[21] Sensations as such are considered as being "abstractions" which have neither meaning nor relevance if torn away from the whole (*thing* or *substance*) to which they belong. And in the most recent physics as well, as we have just seen, reality is conceived in terms of the "principle of complementariety", connoting the convergence and simultaneity of opposite features. But the official Soviet version is nothing daunted and proceeds to posit its own materialism as the only alternative to idealism, in a passage which would seem incredible were it not so clear (in its syntax and grammar!): "In opposition to idealism, which maintains that the material world, being, nature, are products of consciousness, of the mind, of the Idea, materialism, in full accord with natural science and socio-historical practice, considers consciousness to be a secondary phenomenon, derived from matter. The recognition of matter as an objective reality, existing independently of consciousness, is inseparably linked to atheism, whereas the denial of matter leads into the swamps of priestcraft." [22]

Now on the surface of syntax this seems clear enough, if perhaps a trifle involved. But in reality it is the most complicated muddle of verbiage I have ever encountered in my entire career; and I am convinced that a simple analysis of semantic logic applied to this text would show it to be absolutely meaningless. We shall pause simply to consider the concepts or notions involved, abstracting from their incredible and monstrous concatenation.

[21] The associationism of the old-style empiricism has been radically refuted by modern investigations into the field of perceptions and especially by the various *Ganzheits-* and *Gestalt* schools of psychology, beginning with the Aristotelian Brentano and his disciples von Ehrenfels, Meinong and Benussi in Austria; Wertheimer and his associates Köhler and Koffka in Berlin; Krüger, Sanders and disciples in Leipzig, etc., of all whom the Marxists feign ignorance (cf. C. Fabro, *Fenomenologia della percezione* [Brescia, 1961 [2]]).

In his *Experiment and Theory in Physics,* the Nobel Prize winner in physics, Max Born has also called attention to the importance of the Gestalt principle in the field of scientific discoveries and of their significance in forming a notion of the world. Born protests against the oversimplifications of dialectical materialism and the groundlessness of its scientific claims.

[22] *Grosse Sowjet-Enzyklopädie,* article "Materie", p. 4.

First of all, there is a re-statement of the old presupposition, the old Marxist alternative: materialism or idealism. The Marxists ought to know quite well (as in fact they do!) that the real traditional opponent of materialism is spiritualism, which has always opposed and continues to this day to oppose both materialism *and* idealism. Spiritualism distinguishes matter and spirit, soul and body, sensation and thought, instinct and freedom, against the deterministic physical necessity touted by both materialism and the equally necessitarian dialectic of idealism. Further the Marxists ought to know quite well (as in fact they do!) that they claim to be taking their inspiration, in their propounding of their own materialistic monism, from the materialism of antiquity and especially from 18th-century French Enlightenment materialism, whereas in reality they are propounding a new-style materialism, "dialectical materialism" which is nothing other than the latent anthropological notion of idealism (Feuerbach), developed moreover with a recourse to idealism (Hegelian dialectic). Finally, they know full well, or at least should be able without preternatural exertion to understand, that in their own conception there is a simultaneous assertion and negation of the *dualism* of matter and mind, of nature and man. One of two possibilities, then: either the human mind, which proceeds to the reflection of practical activity and science differs from matter; or else it is identical with matter. It would seem that it differs or must differ, at least in virtue of the evident fact that mind, consciousness (in man, at least!) proceeds to science and technology, a development that does not occur in the simple realm of matter outside of man. But on the other hand the monistic demand of the system requires the reality of human activity to resolve itself into matter and that is what the Marxists are aiming at securing with their assumption of the "dialectic", the principle of the conflict of opposites as the motive force in the progress of the processes of physical nature and of human history alike.

The Marxists make or profess to make explicit demands for reform and social renovation in terms of justice, but in their materialistic monism they are constrained to conceive this goal as the result of a "natural" evolution similar to that of the cosmic system or the solar system of that of the embryo, in the realm of biology, not to speak of the phylogenetic evolution of the amoeba (or of Haeckel's *Bathybius*), which the Marxists profess with enthusiastic candor. But in a system lacking in any real opposition between matter and spirit, necessity and freedom, the very demand of evolution, as indicating a development of progressive perfecting aimed at an ultimate goal, cannot be met by matter as it is presented and as it must necessarily be conceived by Marxism. Thus, *Marxism is operating simultaneously with various con-*

cepts of matter, diametrically opposed and mutually contradictory: matter as nature outside of mind and matter as totality of sensory qualities; matter as nature in itself and matter as endowed with movement; matter as opposed to (human) consciousness or mind and matter as principle of the development (evolution) of matter into mind and thus as substance of mind; natural evolution of the natural cosmos as distinct from the development of human institutions and again as fundamentally identical with a material and necessary dialectical process of social evolution. But if the sole forces in the field are material, and if all the demands, even those for social justice, originate and develop under the impulse of powers that can be reduced to material forces, then Marxism's claims and plans are vitiated from the outset, for the stronger will win and that will be the end of it!

Marxism thus shows itself to share fully the materialistic ideology of capitalism and thus can lay no claim to transcending it: on what higher principle can Marxism base its vaunted demand for justice? If the shape of the world to come which is most conformed to the dignity of man is supposed to be socialist and communal, then it must not and cannot be materialistic and dialectical but rather spiritualistic and personalistic. The simplest Marxist ought to know that Christian realism, especially in its Thomist form, vigorously asserts the reality of both matter and spirit: far from denying matters, as the just cited official Marxist text mendaciously maintains, it makes the greater part of the world derive from matter, excepting only thinking beings and the human soul, i.e., finite spirits and the Infinite Spirit who is precisely God.

Marxist ideology must face the insoluble dilemma of the very terms and fundamental concepts of its own system, or else accept the only possible solution. The first dilemma is created by the absolutely univocal and entirely static starting point of the theory of sensations as "reflections". As formulated by Lenin, this theory states: ". . . the whole of matter possesses a property essentially akin to sensation, namely, the property of reflection,"[23] i.e., the capacity to reflect itself or better and more accurately to be reflected in the mind, in consciousness. Then *simultaneously* this theory asserts: ". . . not the whole of matter possesses the property of reacting to stimuli. . . ." This is held to be "peculiar to relatively highly organized matter" of which the highest

[23] "As Lenin points out, it is logical to assume that the whole of matter possesses a property essentially akin to sensation, namely the property of reflection. But not the whole of matter possesses the property of reacting to stimuli and still less the faculty of sensing and thinking. These properties are peculiar to relatively highly organized matter; they are the result of a long and laborious evolution of this matter. The product of the highest stage of evolution of matter is human thought, consciousness, the mind" (*ibid.*, p. 7).

state or stage is thought.[24] We have explained why these solemn and gratuitous assertions of Marxist Scholasticism are meaningless, both separately and taken together. Therefore, it is not the proclamation of atheism that causes us to repudiate and reject materialism and idealism along with it (that idealism whose dialectic Marxism has abstracted); rather it is the manifold and insuperable meaninglessness of the two systems!

This brief treatment of the basic doctrines of Marxism suffices for our present purpose. We have now only to mention the high-handed fashion in which Marxists eliminate the opposition between matter and mind in this "official statement" which reiterates the notion of knowledge as a "reflection" and then goes on ingenuously to assert that "human practice" is the criterion of truth. This to an assertion, on the one hand, that knowledge is pure reception, receptivity and thus passivity; and on the other hand that its truth is the work of practice and therefore something distinct, even indeed something new added. The crux of knowledge is independent of man, for nature is asserted, in the realistic tradition, as being independent of and standing over against man; the crux of truth is dependent on man, for it lies in the dialectical and immanentistic dimension of practice, the bridge for the transition to the assertion of historical materialism.

But as Kierkegaard said of Hegel, it is easier to make the "dialectical transition" on paper than in fact: between these two elements of the Marxist position there intervenes not merely a distinction but an evident break and incurable opposition; and, indeed, the Marxists themselves quite candidly admit this opposition and then proceed with an incredible nonchalance to deny it! [25]

Hegel, too, began with opposites (being, non-being) which were subsequently to be transcended in becoming. But the Marxists begin with the opposition of two concepts, two notions, nature and matter and the mind as spirit; and they end by identifying mind and spirit with matter. They invoke and maintain in this strange methodology the conjunction of motion and matter (Toland's thesis); but whatever may be said of this thesis, on which the physics of our own day seems quite perplexed, the conjunction of motion and matter is a principle of Aristotelian phys-

[24] The Soviet Encyclopedia proceeds to bracket the Leninist theory of reflection (*Spiegelung*), also called the "copy theory" (*Abbildtheorie*), with Pavlov's theory of "conditioned reflexes" (p. 8), thus heavily underscoring the passive nature of the cognitive process.

[25] "Matter and consciousness, mind, are opposed, but only within the limits of the chief problem of philosophy, i.e. the problem of the relation of consciousness to being, for apart from matter and independent of it there is no mind, no consciousness and an existence of such a consciousness is impossible" (*ibid.*, p. 8).

ics which had as object the *physis* in the precise sense of *ens mobile.*[26] But it is a long and impossible step from this to an identification of thought with the processes of the brain; and the suspicion arises that for the Marxists any dualism between matter and spirit or any assertion of spiritualism or of man's freedom amounts to Papist Christianity,[27] a contention that Catholicism itself has never advanced.

Well, that is the best that Marxist ideology can do on the theoretical level. But this does not mean that theists can continue to dream their placid dreams. They must rather search for the real causes (in the absence of ideological ones) for the deep derangement of minds in the contemporary world.[28] It would seem that these causes lie rather in the sociological dimension, including such facts as the drive to industrialization which has created huge urban concentrations with the consequent unbridled pursuit of material well-being, the mirage of the easy buck, the weakening of moral and religious principles under the pressure of resentment that generates a spirit of revolt against the well-heeled!

It is on this level of human practice rather than on the ideological level, where Marxist thinkers cannot in the long run fail to take cognizance of the radical inconsistency of their own position, that Marxism must be met and answered. Yet the ideological element must always be kept in the foreground too, and it must be shown that Marxism claims to implement the impossible compromise between realist dualism and immanentist dialectic (Hegelian principle) in philosophy, and of mathematical mechanism and qualitative physics in science, and a whole host of other equally impossible compromises all along the line. The Marxists

[26] Cf. the definition in *Physics,* II, I, 192b 21 and the Aristotelian tradition, according to which the object of natural philosophy was *ens mobile* (being which is or can be in motion).

[27] "Thought is a product of the brain, and the brain is the highest product of matter; thought cannot, therefore, be separated from matter. The opposition of matter and mind, of being and thought, outside the limits of the chief problem of philosophy, stands in opposition to the results of science and leads to dualism and priestcraft" (*Grosse Sowjet-Enzyklopädie,* pp. 8f.).

[28] On the inadequacy of the mechanistic notion of science in Marxism and the general ambiguity of Marxist epistemology, cf. S. Docky, *Cienca y filosofia* (Universidad Nacional de Mexico, 1960), pp. 48ff. Docky reports that in Zurich the Marxist philosopher Rieger conversed with him ". . . as a realist—just like the Thomists—and not as an idealist" but only on the point of the objective reality of the external world. Docky distinguishes between Marxists as scientists and Marxists as philosophers: "Their stance as scientists is entirely correct. But their philosophy, in its denial of the existence of spiritual reality, is necessarily opposed to the reality of the free will in the human being, who forms part of the spiritual world. And so we consider that Marxism can only be defended within the limits of science, and not within the ambit of true and genuine philosophy" (*ibid.*). But the Cartesian conception of science founded on purely mathematical and mechanistic knowledge has been widely repudiated today, as we have seen in the case of Max Born and the protagonists of Nils Bohr's "complementarity principle".

give evidence of having realized the meaninglessness of the principle of immanentism in the scientific field; but they proceed to accept and welcome it in philosophy in order to explain the content of science and of human life. This is the crux of the whole drama of our culture: on the one hand, the revolt against a philosophy which, fallen into the hands of uninspired interpreters, is incapable of comprehending the development of science and society; on the other hand, the progressive disappearance of the spiritual Ego, Self, precisely in the context of that new philosophy which had initially enthroned the subject as against the object and freedom as against dogma and religion. But neither ideological diatribes alone without adequate social reforms, nor yet economic reforms without an inner righting of the axis of the spirit of man, will ever succeed in producing any appreciable results. The true struggle at the sheer level of the spirit is not between capitalism and socialism, but between religion and atheism: the basic difficulty is precisely that atheism is rampant throughout the whole of the modern world, and not only in the Marxist world; and the manifold channels of its penetration are the fragmented veins of the principle of immanentism.

In our structural analysis, we must limit our treatment to the essential element, pointing up the fundamental ambiguity of the atheism of dialectical materialism, a more serious ambiguity from this structural point of view than that of existentialist atheism. For the latter remains totally and radically faithful to the principle of immanentism in its most drastic meaning, that of the *cogito-volo* as constitutive and exclusive foundation and ground of the truth of being; this is the position of "constitutive nothingness" and though bleak is consistent! Marxism on the contrary claims to have overcome and transcended this sort of nothingness, this void, this zero-point, with its appeal to the reality of the world, both the "world" of immediate experience and the "world" of science. And Marxism is unaware or claims, at least, to be unaware of the incompatibility and impossibility of using simultaneously two opposing and mutually exclusive methods such as immanentistic monism and realistic dualism.[29] And it is not hair-splitting to maintain that Marxism is not only once but at least twice realist-dualist and monist-immanentist

[29] That the "malaise" is real and acute can be seen from the discussions in progress in the Communist countries on the nature and foundations of the dialectic, on the relations between logic and dialectic and between science and philosophy: e.g. those at the University of Moscow in December 1950 and those at the University of Jena on December 17 and 18, 1951, which have been collected in the two volumes of Proceedings: *Ueber die formale Logik und Dialektik* (Berlin: Verlag Kultur und Fortschritt, 1952); *Protokoll der philosophischen Konferenz über Fragen der Logik* (Berlin: Deutsche Verlag der Wissenschaften, 1953). Cf. the discussion in C. Fabro, *Materialismo dialettico e materialismo storico* (Brescia, 1966 [2]).

at once: it is realist-dualist first in the proclamation of the cognitive and epistemological immediacy of sensation; and again in its ontological distinction between outside nature and man; it is monist-immanentist first in its identification of sense impressions with knowledge (properly and adequately so styled) of nature in itself; and again in its recourse to the dialectic calculated to negate the distinction and fill the hiatus between matter and mind, between nature and spirit, so as to inaugurate the autocracy of material reality.

We must finally merely mention the curious fact that when the Marxists are attacked in the field of philosophy or ideology they appeal to science and tax their opponents with idealism, as we have seen; but when they are attacked in the field of science they race with Lenin to the ramparts of their own philosophy which is supposed to reconcile and consolidate absolute materialism with practice-oriented immanentism! [30]

[30] "The present-day theoreticians of Marxism initially present materialism as one philosophy *among others,* superior to the others in its ability to prove its validity *positively* by reference and appeal to the results of the scientific disciplines. Now, the crisis effected by the criticism which denies that such an appeal is a proof is compelling these theoreticians to a deeper review. Already there is coming into currency the idea that Marxist materialism is something other, in its theoretical aspect, than an ontology or epistemology, that, if it is *solidly grounded,* this is not to be understood in the sense in which a system such as that of Descartes or that of Husserl proclaimed themselves to be well-grounded. But an examination of the kind of justification being adduced in the current expositions of Marxism, in place of the traditional substantiation, reveals simultaneously that this sort of justification is not calculated to convince the philosopher and that it gives rise to serious conflicts and contradictions within materialism itself" (F. Chatelet, *Logos et Praxis,* Recherches sur le signification théorique du marxisme [Paris, 1962], p. 50. Cf. also on p. 104 the note on H. Lefebure's noteworthy work, in which ". . . it is too often admitted as self-evident that materialism is 'well-founded' in virtue of the fact that it possesses the instrument of truth." Chatelet quite rightly objects: "Objectivism [scientific objectivism, that is, to which Lefebure appeals], although it does indeed represent a deeper understanding of the theoretical assignment of Marxism, seems in this regard as little justified as 'class subjectivism' and the "Messianism of the proletariat'." Cf. also pp. 182-183). Chatelet himself feels he can obviate these deficiencies "by the rediscovery of the new way of thinking defined and applied by Marx" (Appendix, p. 197). But was not Marx himself the very man who posited that radical structural ambiguity from which stem these insoluble inconveniences?

Discussing the problem of what is called "physical indeterminism," the physicist P. Jordan asserts that Planck's discovery of energy quanta, from which this problem stems, has revealed nothing to us outside the mathematical laws of probability of the sources of the quanta. It is, writes Jordan, a spectacle of lofty beauty and mathematical harmony and it is *possible* to see in it, as Kepler did, an expression of the divine will; but it is *not necessary* to see this, not, at any rate, in the sense of any duty flowing from the necessity of laws of logic or thought. Similarly, there *can* be seen (but not with logical cogency) in the exuberant fullness of ever new decisions the divine action, a divine dominion and structure (*creatio continua*). Therefore both the notion of "pure chance" and the theological notion of purposiveness and teleology are foreign to science (P. Jordan,

We must therefore conclude that the "scientific diversionary maneuver" launched by Lenin and Marxist Scholasticism against theism and metaphysics peters out in a maze of positivistic and phenomenistic materialism which the Marxists are subsequently compelled to repudiate in the interests of their own social and political realism.

"Naturerkenntnis gibt den Glauben frei—Abbruch einer Mauer," *Zeitschrift für Religionsgeschichte,* XV [1963], pp. 161f.). For a deeper-probing and more thorough discussion of the principle of physical indeterminism (Heisenberg), cf. P. Jordan, *Der Naturwissenschaftler vor der religiösen Frage,* pp. 151ff.

Max Planck is known to have concluded from the discovery of the quanta to the notion of a theistic purposiveness and teleology in nature and in science; cf. the essays "Wissenschaft und Glaube," "Vom Wesen der Willensfreiheit," and "Religion und Naturwissenschaft" in *Vorträge und Erinnerungen* (Leipzig, 1949), p. 246ff., 301ff. The Marxist H. Vogel does not accept Planck's religious purposiveness or his theistic spiritualism (H. Vogel, *Zum philosophischen Wirken Max Plancks* [Leipzig: Akademie Verlag, 1961], pp. 155, 216ff.); indeed Vogel sets over against these Planckian conclusions the consistency of Lenin's atheistic materialism!

5

Conclusion: Immanentism and Atheism: Two Terms with but a Single Fate

Our conclusion must be that, unless our own investigation has completely misread the signs, then modern thought has encountered, in the philosophy of our own day, that "moment of truth" it has so richly deserved since the outset: the dissolution of the *cogito* principle into the structural atheism of consciousness as such, into an ontology whose content is man's being-in-the-world and whose foundation is consciousness itself as the meaning or condition of being-in-the-world. The atheistic bias of modern thought, that bias which distinguishes it from classical thought and which has opened up the new view of the world, is not an optional bias but a constitutive one, in the sense that any concession, direct or indirect, to transcendence is a distortion and a misunderstanding, indeed a total incomprehension of that very immanentism that characterizes the first step of modern thought, the immanentism chosen by modern thought as its starting point and trade mark. We must categorize as just such misunderstandings and incomprehensions all the efforts undertaken to salvage the Absolute within the confines of the principle of immanence, from the most imposing efforts of the age of rationalism to the feeblest and most muddled ventures of recent times. Anyone who, in the wake of the basic clarifications effected by Feuerbach, Kierkegaard and Nietzsche, takes the *cogito* as a starting point of the search for God, proves himself, by that very fact, to be singularly obtuse on the score of the modern world or at least (nay, above all!) on the score of the transcendence of God and the human spirit.

The principle of immanentism revealed its atheistic bias the very instant the Cartesian *cogito* appeared on the philosophical scene; and there has not been a single modern philosopher of any stature who has not been accused of atheism. Yet, this fact, significant as it is, does not constitute the deepest aspect of the problem nor yet the one most relevant to our own day and situation. The most important point to consider in order to avoid confusion and misunderstandings is the stark fact that modern philosophy, at the very outset, took a radically new starting point, the mind itself, and consequently inverted the whole outlook on being, embarking on the boldest and most enthralling (in both senses!) venture man has ever attempted, the effort to ground thought radically and totally *upon itself*! The *cogito* has plunged to an ontological "absolute zero" in the philosophical systems typical of our day; and it loudly professes this status, which represents at once its total degradation and its "essential verification", its final audit: a definitive acknowledgement of the non-being or nothingness of man, based precisely on the much-touted constitutive non-being of consciousness, of the mind. It is therefore no mere accident that the dynamic of this modern thought should have finally declared the non-being of God as solidary with the non-being of man. The mournful Odyssey of this "verification" or dissolution has been long and arduous; but the homing instinct of the *cogito* has from the outset precluded any uncertainty as to the final outcome and destination. And the precipitous plunge can by no means be accounted a total debit in the ledger of man's questing spirit.

We wish once more to underscore our contention that the plunge of the *cogito* to absolute zero is and always has been inevitable and constitutive of the very principle itself. The repeated efforts to arrest the atheistic pull of the *cogito* have become ever more infrequent and feebler as the centuries have progressed. They are sheer inhibitory phenomena, deriving either from a total failure to understand the *cogito* principle itself or from an intrusion of the personal attitude of the philosopher, superimposed on the internal consistency of the *cogito* to block it arbitrarily at the crucial moment. Thus we consider every species of theism which has appeared in modern thought to be counterfeit and an interloper: thought cannot transcend the human horizon imposed by the *cogito*.

And let it be clearly understood, in order to avoid all misunderstanding: the constant insistence on the intimate link between modern thought and the advent of modern science, an insistence that began with Descartes and has continued right down to the most recent claims and pretensions of Marxism and neo-positivism—this pet line is nothing but double-talk, which science itself has in our own day most resolutely squelched. Science has its own well-defined field of competency, its own methods, principles and concepts, and depends on philosophy only to the extent that any structured human activity may so depend. And, in any case, a philosophy like immanentism, which reduces the content of experience and consequently of science as well to a mentalistic manifestation, makes no sense to science and therefore is of no interest to it.

A quite different point, and once of much greater interest from the speculative point of view, is "polymorphism" displayed by the principle of immanentism in the three centuries of its evolution. Again and again it has fragmented into opposing segments: rationalism and empiricism, phenomenism and idealism, neo-idealism and neo-positivism, phenomenology and existentialism, etc. This fragmentation is a symptom of the skittishness and malaise of the *cogito,* which cannot be satisfied either with the sheerly immediate or with the entirely mediate. The radically absolute nature of the *cogito* principle and of consciousness which is its source, could not but make the choice of either of the opposing segments in the above-named pairs seem equally justified and well-founded, and any effort of either to rule out the other seem patently arbitrary. And yet each of the opposing positions *had* to exclude the other, in virtue of the demand of the *cogito* at "absolute zero". In this antithesis of ambivalence and indisputably patent equivocity, it becomes clear, moreover, that the *cogito* is not simply a reduction of reality to "representations" within the limits of some form of empiricism (e.g., Berkeley), nor yet the reduction of knowledge to representations (e.g., Descartes, Malebranche, Locke, Berkeley, Hume, Husserl and their like), even though this is the commonest way of presenting and interpreting modern immanentism.

The polymorphism of the *cogito* and the resultant conflicts between the opposing alternatives have been of signal value. In its frenzied efforts to vanquish doubt by securing the beachhead of the Absolute, the self-styled autonomous mind has, over the last three centuries, run through the whole motley gamut of its enthralling and fearsome potentials, clearly demonstrating that it can indeed fall back into nothingness but cannot manage to break through to being. Man grappled finitely with the Infinite on the right flank, and infinitely with the finite on the left; no matter if the challenger on the right flank was a pseudo-Infinite of content and the champion on the left was a pseudo-infinity of act; the battle has nonetheless revealed an extraordinary wealth of human resources and opened up new horizons in the great adventure of the exploration of human selfhood.

Until a few decades ago, virtually all theologians, Catholic and Protestant alike, drastically minimized the problem of atheism—and many still do. Their faces are set resolutely toward the past, or toward the atemporal abstractions too many of them had made the exclusvie scope of their science; the theologians had lost contact with the new event-complex and its radical inversion of the picture (and, in a very real though relative sense, of the reality) of the universe, by the replacement of the Creator-God by Atlas-Man as the sustainer of the whole, and by the subsequent discovery and proclamation that this Atlas is in fact an uprooted Antaeus, who is incapable, in his sorry plight, even of shrugging off the burden, since he evaporates on closer examination into an insubstantial cipher. The theologians have thus bowdlerized the atheism-problem and missed the mark even in their fulminations: the Protestants by excess with their alignment of atheism with the problematic of the Hidden-God who leaves man abandoned to sin; the Catholics, by defect, with their simplist and superficial tendency to refer all atheism back to the perennial whipping-boys (materialism, skepticism, relativism and the like). And finally, the intrusion of politics into the very camp of the theologians has engendered a regrettable shortsightedness, which causes even intelligent theologians to worry more about the practical consequences of a certain species of atheism—Communism—then about the root cause of the sickness unto death of the modern world, a sickness that feeds upon itself and spreads its contagion through every area of human life, theoretical and practical alike.

The positive strength and malice of modern atheism is firmly and univocally anchored in the *principle of immanentism,* the total inversion of the *foundation of freedom.* Our present investigation has clarified this nexus as it proceeded from stage to stage of the ragged but ruthless advance of the new philosophy. In this head-on assault by man on being, this assault destined to plunge men inescapably into the constricting confines of the finite, structural analysis reveals various distinct lines of force, apparently opposed but actually collaborating to tilt the principle of immanentism fatally down the slippery slope to its inevitable destination. And this destination—be it said clearly and uncompromisingly—is the weirdest and most paradoxical terminus ever to appear in the history of thinking beings. Descartes and rationalism had set out to substantiate cognition as a radically absolute principle, and the end result has been the establishment of such a radical primacy of volition as to blow cognition sky-high. Kant and idealism aimed at guaranteeing the primacy of mind and the hegemony of the interiority of the Self over against the alleged incursions of the exteriority of the world, and the end result has been a pulverization of the very term "mind" itself, leaving man in the perilous homelessness of a "Being-in-the-world", destined to vanish in the interests of the emergence of the world and history, fated to be recurrently scattered and absorbed by the unlovely labia of the osmotic situation.

In the wake of the effective repudiation of the Hegelian style of theologizing, the new Humanism was proclaimed, purporting to restore man to his true status as the primordial source of creative endeavor; and the end result has been the irretrievable loss of even minimal humanity in the abandonment of man to the individual frailties and the generic constitutive fragility of his existential status and situation. Man who laid bumptious claim to being the very foundation of the truth of being has emerged today as the only radically undefinable being, in the wake of his dissolution of his own being into a potency of potency or a radical void.

The semaphores on the mournful route of this mass migration to the void have been many and often have seemed to flag the migrant trains along radically divergent tracks. Many historians of philosophy have been hoodwinked by this apparent divergence, even the Marxists who had most interest in displaying their own humanism as the essence of a unitary and convergent interpretation of modern thought. Our present investigation has revealed the crucial stages or lines of force in the precipitation of the atheistic pith of the principle of immanentism: Descartes' introduction of a radical and deliberate doubt; Bayle's demonstration of the possibility of an atheistic ethic; Locke and Hume's stress on the priority of act over content; Enlightenment Deism's absolutizing of reason; the highlighting of the transcendental *I think* (*Ich denke überhaupt*) in the evolution from Kant to Hegel; Schopenhauer and Nietzsche's absolute voluntarism; radical humanism from Feuerbach to Sartre; absolute emergent evolutionism from Darwin to L. Morgan-Alexander-Whitehead. Each of these stages represents a drastic break with the preceding; each is a supersession of the previous immanentistic position; and each in its turn launches a still more radically immanentistic drive, calculated to sever all the toils in which its predecessor had been ensnared. The thrust has been toward a maturation of the principle of immanentism and the end result is a fatal plunge. The initial aim was to substantiate immanentism, the *cogito,* the *I think;* and the end result has been the total loss of the *I,* of the human self, squashed under the implacable roller of the "constitutive worldliness" of being itself, crumbled in the exteriority of the world. Today man is nothing but a being-for-science, a being-for-technology, a being-for-politics, a being-for-culture. Henceforth man is defined in terms of the world, or rather in terms of "chance", the parameter of the world. Therefore do we say that man is the only being left undefined and thus bereft of all knowledge of himself, in this inflated scientism.

But the phenomenon we have been analyzing is still deeper rooted and more drastic. Every effort or claim on the part of any one of these stands or stages to "supersede" or "transcend" another is futile: for the would-be innovator is simply conferring a new aspect of the position he would like to overcome, or more accurately he is simply providing it with a more appropriate terminology. Once the really constitutive aspect of Descartes' radical doubt (*cogito, ergo sum*) has been properly grasped, there can be no shying away from Sartre's contention that existence precedes essence, that the will conditions the truth. In this theoretical sense, neither Descartes nor Spinoza, nor Locke, nor Hume, nor Kant, nor Hegel, nor Marx, nor any of the other crucial thinkers have ever been or can be overcome or transcended; and so Sartre can be called more Cartesian than Descartes, and Marx more Hegelian than Hegel.

And there is a still deeper secret involved. All of the modern precipitates of the principle of immanentism can be said to be at once divergent and convergent, divergent in terminology and convergent in their bias toward the basic principle (immanentism). Cartesian voluntar ism agrees with Bayle in proclaiming ethics independent of religion; this same voluntarism leads Locke to assert the possibility of "thinking matter". These two principles suffice to explain the entire subsequent evolution of philosophy, culminating in the *Ich denke überhaupt* and the autonomous ethic of Kant on the one hand and in materialist, phenomenological, neopositivistic and historicist humanism on the other. We do not deny that modern thought set out with the aim of defending the Absolute, freedom, transcendence; [1] and this aim is a recurrent motif, amid all the fluctuations, stumbles and declines, down to the death of Schelling (1854), little more than a century ago.

The investigations I have undertaken in this work have made me personally keenly aware of this aim of modern thought, and I have expressed that awareness repeatedly in these pages. But the question remains for those interpreters who stop at the external tag affixed to a system: What is the explanation of the fact that precisely Spinoza and Hegel, the two philosophers with the strongest theological bias (on paper, at least) are the very thinkers most favored, most studied and most followed by the atheistic schools of present-day philosophy which make these two would-be champions of God the very basis of their own atheistic systems?

The chief points on which we insisted in our Introduction must therefore be reiterated uncompromisingly in our Conclusion: first, the absolute necessity of distinguishing sharply between the internal logic of a principle and the subjective intention of individual thinkers; and secondly, the demand for a God who is truly God in all the ramifications of his "metaphysical status".

[1] "For Descartes and Malebranche, for Spinoza and Leibniz, there is no solution for the *problem of truth,* except as mediated by the *God-problem:* the knowledge of the divine being constitutes the supreme principle of knowledge, from which flow all other derivative certainties" (E. Cassirer, *Die Philosophie der Aufklärung* [Tübingen, 1932], p. 211).

Concerning our first point, we would stress that the internal logic of a principle is the competency of reason which becomes ever more aware of the abrasive bias of the initial principle of immanentism, whereas the subjective intention of an individual thinker is dependent on the existential situation and is evanescent, as belonging to the empirical subject as such (the man Descartes, the man Kant, *et al.*) rather than to the principle itself.

Concerning our second point, we admit that it is exigent in the extreme: God must be recognized and acknowledged not only as Absolute but as Creator, not only as Creator but as Spirit, not only as Spirit but as free, not only as free but as Personal and Providential. But there is no other way to avoid toppling him either into the world or into man, to the fatal ruin of all three!

At the theoretical level, the level of internal logic, therefore, the consequences of radical atheism proclaimed by the various philosophical schools of our day hold good. They can be neither erased nor refuted by any merely marginal commentaries. Anyone desirous of undertaking a really penetrating critique of modern atheism must concentrate not on the problem of God but on the problem of being, that "starting-point problem" posed by Descartes and again at intervals by Locke, Hume, Kant, Schelling, Hegel, Heidegger *et al.:* the problem of the mind-being nexus, the question as to which is primary. Only the thinker who starts from the integral existent being and uses as his lever the radical integrity and transcendent power of Being (*esse*) discoverable in that integral existent, can hope to reach the Absolute Esse, the Infinite Act of Being who is God. Any thinker who takes the mind as his starting point is bound to be caught in the wash of the intrinsic finitude of the human dimension and sucked down into the ontological void. Finitude thus becomes the transcendental structure of the mind itself, so that by the very act of raising the mind out of the void, that finitude inevitably plunges it into that very same void. And essential or constitutive atheism consists in the positing of this finitude of man's horizon as the very foundation of the coming-to-presence, of the bestowal and constitution of being. To call such a stance humanism alters its intrinsic atheism not a whit; and this atheism no longer connotes an opposition to God or a polemic against God, in other words anti-theism; rather it connotes that radical absence and want engendered by "the "escape of God" from man and the "escape from God" on the part of man.

Protestant theologians today acknowledge the positive character of modern atheism; but they go on to talk of a continuous process of "secularization" whose initial fault they claim to have been the pretense to a "natural theology" and whose incentive they claim to have isolated in Scholastic speculation. Luther, they say, repudiated "reason, the whore" (*die Hure Vernunft*) with holy horror.[2] And they allege that the nihilism in which modern atheism is said to end is simply the consequence of this process of secularization of the world.[3] But we must insist that the realm of the Sacral cannot be detached from that of the Absolute: as the Sacral is the sign of value, so is the Absolute the foundation and key of interpretation. Protestant religious thought early perpetrated a radical compromise with the principle of immanentism, from the moment when pietism and subsequently the new theology which accepted, together with Hamann-Kant and Jacobi, the principle of autonomy and freedom, led to the abandonment of the Scholastic mold of 17th-century Protestant theology and to a rediscovery and renewed proclamation of the principle of interiority as "constitutive freedom", a principle which Hegel claims Luther to have asserted.[4] In this acceptance of freedom as the ultimate transcendental structure of the mind lies the germ of the entire disintegration effected by and epitomized in 20th-century atheism.

For the ancients, *fate,* the rationality or λόγος of the φύσις, which exacted submission even from the gods, modern thought has substituted man's lot (*Geschick*), a ceaseless struggle with the void, the nothingness now spewing forth in the wake of the advances of science and tech-

[2] Cf. M. Horkheimer, "Theismus-Atheismus," in *Zeugnisse,* Theodor W. Adorno zum 60. Geburtstag (Frankfurt a. M., 1965), p. 10.

[3] "The atheism that ends in nihilism is rather the consequence of the *secularization of the world,* a secularization of which the objectifying approach to nature is but a partial manifestation. Secularization can be simply characterized as that phenomenon wherein the world is imagined by man as an object and thereby becomes the object of technology. This secularization is effected in every area of life: in morality, in law, in politics" (R. Bultmann, *Der Gottesgedanke und der moderne Mensch* [1963], now appearing in *Glauben und Verstehen,* Vol. IV [Tübingen, 1965], pp. 115f.). In his analysis, Bultmann rightly stresses the Heideggerian concept of subject-ness (*Subjektität*) as expounded in Heidegger's essay on Nietzsche, in *Holzwege* (p. 236), a concept Bultmann identifies as ontic and distinguishes from the concept of subjectivity (*Subjektivität*), which is psychologico-epistemological. But this approach does not go to the root of the opposition between immanence and transcendence and remains, like Heidegger, a prisoner of immanetism, albeit an immanentism antipodal to the pre-Kantian sort.

[4] "What Luther began as faith, in the indistinct sentiment and witness of the spirit is the same thing that the still more mature Spirit is at pains to capture in *concept* and thus to free itself in the present and thereby to find itself in that present" (Hegel, *Grundlinien der Philosophie des Rechts,* Vorrede, ed. Hoffmeister [Hamburg, 1955], p. 17). There are more drastic but less well-known references to Luther, in this same context, in Hegel's other works, contemporary with this one, namely *Vorlesungen über die Philosophie der Weltgeschichte; C. W.,* ed. Lasson (Leipzig, 1925), p. 878; *Vorlesung über die Geschichte der Philosophie; C. W.,* ed. Michelet, Vol. III (Berlin, 1844), p. 230. We shall have scope to speak of the relation between Luther and Hegel in our forthcoming study, *Jesus Christ in Modern Thought.*

nology in their unremitting probing of beings without Being. And under this baneful constellation man is doomed to wander bemused amid the enormous silences of the endless spaces, no longer knowing himself in the wake of his denial of God.

This fateful confrontation was inevitable sooner or later for the human mind; this risk of loss in endless spaces in its own cosmic solitude could not be avoided. And the great variety of avenues followed by the *cogito* in its evolution has created whole new disciplines and fields of human endeavor, drastically more pithy and compelling than the detached analyses and classifications of the formalistic tradition and much closer (if only in contrast) to the deepest intuitions of metaphysics. Above all, the assertion of the primordiality of the mind and the absolute character of freedom (despite the obfuscation and radical deviation that becomes evident from the first moment when the *cogito* appears on the scene and has not culminated in the zero-point) has provided a *sui generis* expression of the constitutive primordiality and creative power of thought and of the consequent struggle waged by philosophy to save man from the sucking tentacles of the ontological void. As soon as the basic judgment has been passed, however, on the fundamental opposition involved, there is nothing to prevent the thinker from entering openheartedly into contact with the world, into the tension of technology and of that dialectic with his fellows which manifests itself in the conflicts of ethics and the vicissitudes of history, in the waste perpetrated by a "nature red in tooth and claw" and in the unending search for true and solid freedom.

The charge of radical and constitutive atheism that we have levelled against modern thought may seem on the one hand exaggerated and on the other irrelevant from the point of view of structural analysis. In fact, standard histories of philosophy do consider theistic bias to have been limited to a few episodes of sporadic deviationism, or else they use it as a proof that the *cogito* has therein achieved its goal. It may be readily admitted that the charge of atheism has often not been particularly felicitous in its historical actuality. For not only have such philosophers as Hobbes, Toland, Collins, Spinoza and their like been adjudged atheists from the word go; so have even such Catholics as Descartes, Malebranche and Herbert, the founder of Deism, who held religion to constitute man's essential distinguishing mark and the existence of God to be a truth innate in the human mind.[5]

From as early as the beginning of the 17th century, such terms as "naturalism", "Freethinking", "Freethinker" and *esprit fort* were virtu-

[5] Cf. G. V. Lechler, *Geschichte des englischen Deismus* (Stuttgart and Tübingen, 1841), pp. 450ff.

ally equivalent to atheism, when hurled against the Deists. In the heat of controversy, the term "atheist" and "atheism" ultimately came to have about the same meaning as "barbarian" and "barbarism" in the abusive rhetoric of classical antiquity: the charge of atheism and the epithet of atheist came to be hurled quite automatically at anyone presenting an idea of God or divine realities that did not square with the polemicist's own idea, which he considered both entirely adequate and absolutely inviolably sacred. There can be complete agreement, therefore, that for a few centuries—down to the point of Feuerbach and Kant's radical diagnoses—the contending parties, dazed by the smoke and dust of battle, did not always grasp with the desired precision the objective point at issue. The division of Christianity occasioned by the Reformation contributed decisively, by its elimination of objective authority in the area of faith, to the abandonment of Christianity as a historical religion of salvation in favor of that "eternal Christianity" or "reasonable and mystery-free Christianity" which proved to be the prologue and incubator of the positive and constructive atheism of 19th-and above all 20th-century philosophical schools.

The final word then must be a reiteration of the complexity of the atheism-problem, a complexity we stressed again and again in our lengthy Introduction. This problem is in very truth the Gordian knot of human life and thought, for its solution demands a supreme speculative effort and unflagging singlemindedness and courage; that solution must, moreover, engage the human person to the uttermost limit as the inner core of truth and the fulcrum of responsible action.

Bibliography

This bibliography is a listing of all the works referred to in the book. It is structured by the book's parts and, within each part's listings, is subdivided into 1) the principal works discussed in the part and 2) secondary studies and works which receive only passing treatment. Section 2) is a cumulative listing: secondary works are recorded only on their first appearance.

INTRODUCTION
Toward a Delimitation of the Notion of Atheism

Principal Works

Bayle, P. *Dictionnaire historique et critique*. 5th ed. Basle, 1738.
——— *Pensées diverses sur le comète*. Rotterdam, 1704.
Bouterwek, F. *Die Religion der Vernunft*. Göttingen, 1824.
Buddaeus, J. F. *Theses de Atheismo et Superstitione*. Jena, 1714. German edition, *Sätzen von Atheisterey und Aberglaube*. Jena, 1717. A French translation was published by L. Philon. Amsterdam: P. Mortier, 1740.
Descartes, R. *Correspondance. Oeuvres de Descartes,* Vol. V. Edited by C. Adam and P. Tannery. Paris, 1909.
——— *Meditationes de prima Philosophia. Oeuvres,* Vol. VII. Edited by Adam and Tannery. Paris, 1909.
Diderot, D. and d'Alembert. *Encyclopédie ou Dictionnaire raisonné des sciences, des arts et des métiers*. Paris, 1751; 2nd. ed. Lucca, 1758.
Feuerbach, L. *Grundsätze der Philosophie der Zukunft. Werke,* Vol. II. Stuttgart, 1904. Edited by M. G. Lange. Leipzig, 1950. English translation by Manfred H. Vogel, *Principles of the Philosophy of the Future.* Indianapolis-New York-Kansas City: The Library of Liberal Arts, Bobbs-Merrill, 1966.
Hegel, G. W. *Enzyklopädie der philosophischen Wissenschaften.* Edited by J. Hoffmeister. Leipzig, 1949.
——— *Philosophie der Weltgeschichte. Werke,* Vol. 1. Edited by Lasson. Leipzig, 1925.

Kraus, M. *Die Absolute Religionsphilosophie*. Dresden and Leipzig: Leonhardi, 1834.

Marx, K. *Kritik der Hegelschen Dialektik und Philosophie überhaupt. Oekonomisch-philosophische Manuskripte aus dem Jahre 1844,* M.E.G.A. (*Marx-Engels Gesamtausgabe*) Abt. I, Vol. 3. Edited by D. Ryazanov and V. Adoratsky. Moscow and Berlin, 1926ff.

——— *Zur Kritik der Nationalökonomie, Oekonomisch-philosophische Manuskripte aus dem Jahre 1844,* M.E.G.A. Abt. I, Vol. 3. Moscow and Berlin, 1926ff.

Rensi, G. *Apologia dell'ateismo*. Rome, 1925.

——— *Realismo*. Milan, 1952.

Schleiermacher, F. *Der christliche Glaube. Gesammelte Werke,* Vol. I. 7th. ed. by M. Redeker. Berlin, 1960.

——— *Ueber die Religion. Ausgewählte Werke,* Vol. IV. Leipzig, 1911.

——— *Zur Theologie. Gesammelte Werke,* Vol. I. 7th. ed. of M. Redeker. Berlin, 1960.

Spitzel, T. *Scrutinium Atheismi historico-aetiologicum*. Augsburg, 1633.

Valsecchi, A. *De fundamentis religionis et fontibus impietatis*. 2nd. ed. Venice, 1770. Italian edition, *Dei fondamenti della religione e dei fonti dell' empietà*. 7th. ed. Padua, 1805.

Wolff, C. *Theologia Naturalis*. Frankfurt and Leipzig, 1741.

Yvon, Abbé. article "Athée", *Encyclopédie* of Diderot and d'Alembert, Vol. I, fol. 798b ff. (1751 edition), fol. 692a ff. (1758 edition).

Secondary Works

Abbagnano, N. *Dizionario di filosofia*. Turin, 1961.

L'Athéisme contemporain. Geneva: Edition Labor et Fides, 1956.

Bacon, F. *De augmentatione scientiarum. The Works of Francis Bacon,* Vol. I, Edited by J. Spedding, R. L. Ellis and D. D. Heath. London, 1879.

Berkeley, G. *A Treatise concerning the Principles of Human Knowledge. Berkeley's Works,* Vol. I. Edited by A. C. Fraser. Oxford, 1901.

Brightman, E. S. *A Philosophy of Religion*. New York, 1946.

Brunschvicg, L. Héritage de mots, héritage d'idées. Paris, 1945.

——— "La querelle de l'athéisme," *De la vraie et de la fausse conversion*. Paris, 1950.

——— *La raison et la religion*. Paris, 1939.

——— *Bulletin de la société française de philosophie,* Vol. 28, no. 3.

Buonaiuti, E. *Giuseppe Rensi, Lo scettico credente*. Rome, 1944.

Dilthey, W. *Einleitung in die Geisteswissenschaften. Werke,* Vol. I. Leipzig, 1933.

Drews, A. *Die Spekulation seit Kant mit besonderer Rücksicht auf das Wesen des Absoluten und die Persönlichkeit Gottes.* Berlin, 1893.

Fabricius, C. *Der Atheismus der Gegenwart, Seine Ursachen und seine Ueberwindung.* Göttingen, 1922.

Fabro, C. *Dall'essere all'esistente.* Brescia, 1957, 1965.

——— *Dio, Introduzione al problema teologico.* Rome, 1953.

——— *Partecipazione e causalità secondo S. Tommaso d'Aquino.* Turin, 1961. French edition, *Participation et causalité selon S. Thomas d'Aquin.* Paris-Louvain, 1960.

——— "Il problema di Dio. Introduzione al problema teologico," *Orientamenti e problemi di teologia dogmatica,* Vol. II. Milan, 1957.

Flint, R. *Agnosticism.* Edinburgh and London, 1903.

Frank, E. *Philosophical Understanding and Religious Truth.* Oxford, 1945.

von Fürstenberg, E. *Der Selbstwiderspruch des philosophischen Atheismus.* Regensburg, 1960.

Guyau, M. *L'irréligion de l'avenir.* Paris, 1896.

Hazard, P. *La pensée européenne au XVIIIe siècle.* Paris, 1946. English translation, *European Thought in the Eighteenth Century.* Cleveland: World, 1964.

Heiler, F. *Die Religionen der Menschheit.* Stuttgart, 1959.

Herttenstein, M. J. F. *Quo jure antiqui quidam Philosophi Athei vocentur.* Ulm, 1709.

Jacoby, F. "Diagoras, d'Ἄθεος", *Abhandlungen der deutschen Akademie der Wissenschaften, Klasse für Sprachen, Literatur und Kunst,* Jahrgang 1959, Nr. 3.

Joel, K. "Antbarbarus," *Vorträge und Aufsätze.* Jena, 1914.

Joel, M. *Religionsphilosophische Zeitfragen.* Breslau, 1876.

Kant, I. *Kritik der reinen Vernunft. Kants gesammelte Schriften,* Abt. I, Vol. 3. Berlin: Reimer, 1911. English translation by F. Max Müller, *Critique of Pure Reason.* Garden City, New York: Dolphin Books, Doubleday & Company, Inc., 1961.

Kierkegaard, S. *Afsluttende uvidenskabelig Efterskrift. Samlede Vaerker,* Vol. VIII. Copenhagen, 1925. English translation by David Swenson, edited by Walter Lowrie, *Concluding Unscientific Postscript to the "Philosophical Fragments."* Oxford-Princeton, 1941.

——— *Begrebet Angst. Samlede Vaerker,* Vol. IV. Copenhagen, 1923. Italian translation by Cornelio Fabro, *Il concetto dell'angoscia.* Florence, 1953. English translation by Walter Lowrie, *The Concept of Dread.* Princeton, 1944.

——— *Papirer.* Copenhagen, 1910-1948. Italian translation by Cornelio Fabro, *Diario.* 2nd. ed. Brescia, 1962. English translation, *The*

Journals of Sören Kierkegaard: A Selection, edited and translated by Alexander Dru. Oxford, 1938.
Lacrois, J. "Sens et valeur de l'athéisme contemporain," *Monde moderne et sens de Dieu.* Paris, 1954.
Lagneau, J. *Célèbres leçons et fragments.* Paris: Alexandre, 1950.
Lange, F. A. *Geschichte des Materialismus.* Leipzig: Reclam, 1905.
Le Dantec, F. *L'ateismo.* Milan, 1925.
Leibniz, G. W. *Confessio naturae contra Atheistas. Gesammelte Werke,* Vol. IV. Edited by Gerhardt. Hildesheim, 1961.
——— *Opera philosophica.* Edited by Dutens. Geneva, 1768.
Marcel, G. *Le sens de l'athéisme moderne.* Paris-Tournai, 1958.
Maritain, J. *Court traité de l'existence et de l'existant.* Paris, 1947. English translation, *Existence and the Existent.* New York: Vintage Books, Alfred A. Knopf and Random House, Inc., 1966.
——— *La signification de l'athéisme contemporain.* Paris, 1949.
Mauthner, F. *Wörterbuch der Philosophie.* 2nd. ed. Leipzig, 1924.
Merleau-Ponty, M. *Eloge de la philosophie.* Paris: Gallimard, 1953. English translation by John Wild and James W. Edie, *In Praise of Philosophy.* Evanston, Ill.: Northwestern University Press, 1963.
Moreri, G. *Le Grand Dictionnaire Historique.* 2nd. ed. Basle, 1733.
del Noce, A. "Riflessioni sull'opzione ateistica," *Il problema dell'ateismo.* Brescia, 1962.
Philipps, J. T. *De Atheismo* or a History of Atheism in which many Writers, Ancient and More Modern, falsely accused of impiety are freed from the shameful stigma of Atheism; while others who seem to have thought less correctly of the Supreme Spirit are rightly refuted. London, 1735.
Reinmann, J. F. *Atheismi et Atheorum falso suspectorum apud judaeos, ethnicos, christianos, mahumedanos.* Hildesheim, 1725.
Riva, C. *Pensiero e coerenza cristiana.* Brescia, 1963.
Rosmini, A. *Logica.* 2nd. ed. Intra, 1867.
Scheler, M. *Vom Ewigen im Menschen. Gesammelte Werke,* Vol. I. 4th. ed. Berne: Francke Verlag, 1954.
Schlegel, D. B. *Shaftesbury and the French Deists.* Chapel Hill, N.C.: University of North Carolina Studies, 1956.
Schopenhauer, A. *Parerga und Paralipomena. Gesammelte Werke,* Vol. V. Edited by Frauenstädt. Leipzig, 1891.
——— *Ueber die vierfache Wurzel des Satzes vom zureichenden Grunde. Gesammelte Werke,* Vol. I. 2nd. ed. by Frauenstädt. Leipzig, 1916.
Stefanini, L. *Esistenzialismo ateo ed Esistenzialismo cristiano.* Padua, 1952.

Stephen, L. *History of English Thought in the Eighteenth Century*. London, 1881.
Trinius, J. *Freydenker Lexikon*. Leipzig and Bernburg, 1759; abridged edition, Turin, 1960.
Vatke, W. *Religionsphilosophie oder allgemeine philosophische Theologie*. Bonn: Preiss, 1888.
Voltaire, *Questions sur les miracles*. Geneva, 1765. *Oeuvres complètes de Voltaire*, Vol. XXV. Edited by Moland. Paris, 1883.

PART I

Controversies Surrounding the Atheism of Rationalism

Principal Works

Bayle, P. *Dictionnaire historique et critique*. 5th. ed. Basle, 1738.
——— *Pensées diverses sur le comète*. Rotterdam, 1704.
——— *Pensées philosophiques*. Edited by P. Vernière. Paris, 1961.
Descartes, R. *Epistola ad G. Voetium. Oeuvres de Descartes,* Vol. VIII. Edited by Adam and Tannery. Paris, 1909.
——— *Lettre apologétique aux Magistrats d'Utrecht. Oeuvres,* Vol. VIII. Edited by Adam and Tannery. Paris, 1909.
——— *The Philosophical Works of Descartes,* translated by E. S. Haldane and G. R. T. Ross. 2 volumes. New York, 1955.
Hardouin, G. *Athei detecti. Opera varia.* Amsterdam and The Hague, 1733.
d'Holbach, D. *Système de la nature*. 2nd. ed. London, 1774.
Kuyper, F. *Arcana Atheismi enervata. . . .* Rotterdam, 1676.
Montesquieu, C. *De l'Esprit des Lois*. Paris, An IV de la Republique; first edition, 1748.
More, H. *Opera Omnia*. London, 1679; reprinted Hildesheim, 1966.
Pufendorf, S. *Le Droit de la Nature et des Gens,* translated from the Latin by Baron J. Barbeyrac. Basle: E. Thourneisen, 1771.
Rousseau, J. J. *Emile. Oeuvres Complètes,* Vol. II. Paris: Hachette, 1856.
——— *La Nouvelle Eloise. Oeuvres Complètes,* Vol. III. Paris: Hachette, 1856.
Spedalieri, N. *Dei Diritti dell'uomo*. Milan: Silvestri, 1848.
Spinoza, B. *Cogitata Metaphysica. Opera,* Vol. I. Edited by C. Gebhardt. Heidelberg, 1924.
——— *Epistulae. Opera,* Vol. IV. Edited by C. Gebhardt. Heidelberg, 1924.

Spinoza, B. *Ethica. Opera,* Vol. II. Edited by C. Gebhardt, Heidelberg, 1924.

——— *Korte Verhandeling van God. . . . Opera,* Vol. I. Edited by C. Gebhardt. Heidelberg, 1924.

——— *Principia Philosophiae Cartesianae. Opera,* Vol. I. Edited by C. Gebhardt. Heidelberg, 1924.

——— *Tractatus Theologico-Politicus. Opera,* Vol. III. Edited by C. Gebhardt. Heidelberg, 1924.

Spitzel, T. *Scrutinium Atheismi historico-aetiologicum.* Augsburg, 1633.

Toland, J. *Adeisidaimon sive Titus Livius vindicatus.* The Hague: Thomas Johnson, 1709.

——— *Letters to Serena.* London, 1704.

Voetius, G. Preface to *Admiranda Methodus Novae Philosophiae Renati des Cartes.* Utrecht, 1643.

Voltaire, *Dictionnaire Philosophique.* Edited by J. Benda and R. Naves. Paris: Garnier, 1954.

——— *Lettres Philosophiques.* Edited by F. A. Taylor. Oxford, 1961.

——— *Philosophie.* Paris, n. d.

Secondary Works in addition to those already listed.

Abbadie, J. *Traité de la vérité de la religion chrétienne.* Rotterdam: R. Leers, 1688.

Bacon, F. *Essays.* Edited by F. Fiske Heard and R. Whateley. Boston and New York, 1871.

Blondel, M. *L'action.* Paris, 1936.

——— "Le Christianisme de Descartes," *Revue de métaphysique et morale,* 1896.

——— *L'être et les êtres.* Paris, 1935.

Bohrmann, G. "Spinoza in England," *Spinozas Stellung zur Religion.* Giessen, 1914.

Borkowski, S. D. *Der junge Spinoza.* Münster i. W., 1910.

——— "Der erste Anhang der Kurzen Abhandlung," *Chronicon Spinozanum,* III, 1925; previously published in *Der junge Spinoza.*

——— *Spinoza nach Dreihundert Jahren.* Berlin and Bonn, 1932.

Bouiller, F. *Histoire de la philosophie cartésienne.* Paris-Lyon, 1854.

Boyer, C. "Le 'Cogito' dans S. Augustin," *Descartes.* Series III Centenario del Discorso del Metodo. Milan, 1937.

Bredenbourg, J. *Enervatio Tractatus Theologico-politici una cum demonstratione, geometrico ordine disposita, NATURAM NON ESSE*

DEUM, cuius effati contrario praedictus Tractatus unice innititur. Rotterdam, 1675.

Brunschwicg, L. *Descartes et Pascal lecteurs de Montaigne.* 2nd. ed. New York-Paris, 1944.

Busson, H. *Le Rationalisme dans la littérature française de la Renaissance.* 2nd. ed. Paris, 1957.

Deborin, A. M. "Spinoza's World-View," Kline *et al., Spinoza in Soviet Philosophy.* London, 1952.

——— "Spinozismus und Marxismus," *Chronicon Spinozanum,* V, 1927.

Delbos, V. *Le Spinozisme.* 2nd. ed. Paris, 1926.

Desautels, A. R. *Les Mémoires de Trévoux et le mouvement des idées au XVIIe siècle.* Rome, 1956.

Erhardt, F. *Die Philosophie des Spinoza im Lichte der Kritik.* Leipzig, 1908.

Fabro, C. *La nozione metafisica di partecipazione secondo S. Tommaso d'Aquino.* 3rd. ed. Turin, 1963.

Feuerbach, L. *Pierre Bayle, Ein Beitrag zur Geschichte der Philosophie und Menschheit. Werke,* Vol. V. Stuttgart, 1905.

——— *Geschichte der neueren Philosophie von Bacon von Verulam bis Benedikt Spinoza. Werke,* Vol. III. Stuttgart, 1906.

——— *Vorläufige Thesen zur Reform der Philosophie. Werke,* Vol. II. Stuttgart, 1904.

——— *Das Wesen der Religion. Werke,* Vol. V. Stuttgart, 1905. English translation, *The Essence of Religion,* New York: Harper and Row, 1967.

Freudenthal, J. *Spinoza, Leben und Lehre.* Edited by C. Gebhardt. Heidelberg, 1927.

Gebhardt, C. *Spinoza.* Leipzig: Reclam, 1932.

Grünwald, M. *Spinoza in Deutschland.* Berlin, 1897.

Hallet, H. F. *"Aeternitas," A Spinozistic Study.* Oxford, 1930.

Hamelin, O. *Le Système de Descartes.* 2nd. ed. Paris, 1921.

Hazard, P. *La crise de conscience européenne.* Paris, 1935.

Hegel, G. W. *Geschichte der Philosophie.* Edited by Michelet. Berlin, 1844; reprinted as Vols. 17-18 of the Jubiläumsausgabe of Hegel's *Sämtliche Werke.* Stuttgart, 1959. Edited by J. Hoffmeister. Leipzig, 1944.

——— *Philosophie der Religion.* Edited by Marheinecke. Berlin, 1840; reprinted as Vols. 15-16 of the Jubiläumsausgabe of the *Sämtliche Werke.* Stuttgart, 1959. Edited by Lasson. Leipzig: Reclam, 1930.

——— *Wissenschaft der Logik.* Edited by Lasson. Leipzig, 1934.

Jaquelot, I. *Dissertations sur l'existence de Dieu, où l'on démontre cette vérité par l'histoire universelle, par la réfutation du système d'Epicure et de Spinoza, par les caractères de divinité qui se remarquent dans la religion des Juifs.* The Hague, 1697.

Jens, M. *Examen philosophicum sextae definitionis Partis I Eth. Benedicti de Spinoza sive Prodromus Animadversionum super unico veterum et recentiorum Atheorum Argumento nempe "una substantia."* Dort, 1698.

Jodl, F. *Geschichte der Ethik in der neueren Philosophie.* Stuttgart, 1882.

Jurieu, P. *Courte Revue des Maximes.* Amsterdam, 1591.

Kierkegaard, S. *Philosophiske Smuler. Samlede Vaerker,* Vol. IV. Copenhagen, 1923. Italian translation by C. Fabro, *Briciole di filosofia.* Bologna, 1960. English translation by David F. Swenson, *Philosophical Fragments.* Princeton: Princeton University Press, 1936.

Kline, G. *et al. Spinoza in Soviet Philosophy.* London, 1952.

Kortholt, C. *De Tribus Impostoribus.* Kiel, 1680. A bilingual edition has been published by G. Bartsch. Berlin: Akademie Verlag, 1960.

Labrousse, E. *Pierre Bayle.* The Hague, 1964.

Lachièze-Roy, P. *Les origines cartésiennes du Dieu de Spinoza.* Paris, 1932.

Lami. F. *Le nouvel Athéisme renversé ou Réfutation du Système de Spinoza.* Paris, 1696.

Law, E. *An Inquiry into the Ideas of Space, Time, Immensity, etc.* Cambridge, 1734.

LeClerc, J. *Bibliothèque Ancienne et Moderne,* Vol. XXIV. Amsterdam, 1724.

Lévêque, R. *Le problème de la vérité dans la Philosophie de Spinoza.* Strasbourg: Publications de la Faculté des Lettres de l'Université de Strasbourg, fasc. 17, 1923.

Lucchi, B. *Spinozismi syntagma.* Padua, 1738.

Malebranche, N. *Entretien d'un Philosophe Chrétien et d'un Philosophe Chinois sur l'Existence et la Nature de Dieu.* Amsterdam, 1704. Edited by A. Le Moine. Marseille, 1936.

Marx, K. and F. Engels. *Die Heilige Familie. K. Marx-F. Engels Werke,* Vol. II. Berlin, 1958. *Marx-Engels, Historisch-kritische Gesamtausgabe: Werke, Schriften, Briefe* (M.E.G.A.), Abt. I, Vol. 2. Edited by D. Rjazanov and V. Adoratsky. Moscow and Berlin, 1926ff.; edited by H. J. Fueter and P. Futh: Darmstadt, 1962. Bücherei des Marxismus-Leninismus, Vol. 41. Berlin: Dietz Verlag, 1953. English translation, *The Holy Family.* Moscow: Foreign Languages Publishing House, 1956.

Mason, H. T. *Pierre Bayle and Voltaire.* Oxford, 1965.

Masson, P. M. *Rousseau et la restauration religieuse*. 2nd. ed. Paris, 1916.

Mauthner, F. *Der Atheismus und seine Geschichte im Abendlande*. Stuttgart and Berlin, 1921.

Meinsma, K. O. *Spinoza und sein Kreis*. Berlin, 1909.

Nonnotte, Abbé. *Dictionnaire Anti-Philosophique*. Avignon, 1767.

Orcibal, J. "Descartes et sa philosophie jugés a l'Hôtel Liancourt," *Descartes et le Cartésianisme hollandais*. Paris, 1950.

Pascal, B. *Pensées*. Edited by Brunschwicg. Paris, 1917.

Pintard, R. *Le libertinage érudit dans la première moitié du XVIIe siècle*. Paris, 1943.

Plechanov, G. W. *Die Grundprobleme des Marxismus*. Berlin, 1958.

Poiret, J. *De Deo, Anima et Malo*. 2nd. ed. Amsterdam, 1685.

Pollock, F. *Spinoza, His Life and Philosophy*. London, 1899.

Powell, E. E. *Ueber Spinozas Gottesbegriff*. Halle a. S., 1899.

Presser, I. *Das Buch "De Tribus Impostoribus"*. Amsterdam, 1926.

Pünjer, G. C. B. *Geschichte der christlichen Religionsphilosophie seit der Reformation*. Braunschweig, 1880.

Randall, J. H. *The Career of Philosophy,* From the Middle Ages to the Enlightenment. New York: Columbia University Press, 1962.

Renner, K. *Das Selbstbewusstsein der Gottheit im Systeme Spinozas*. Godberg, 1906.

Rex, W. *Essays on Pierre Bayle*. The Hague: Nijhoff, 1965.

Sartre, J. P. *Descartes*. *Collection* Les classiques de la liberté. Paris, 1946.

——— *L'être et le néant*. Paris: Gallimard, 1943. English translation by Hazel Barnes, *Being and Nothingness*. London: Methuen & Co., 1957.

——— *L'existentialisme est un humanisme*. Paris, 1946. English translation by Philip Mairet, *Existentialism and Humanism*. London: Methuen & Co., 1948. English translation by Walter Kaufmann, in *Existentialism from Dostoievsky to Sartre*. Cleveland: Meridian Books, 1956.

Schlatter, A. *Die philosophische Arbeit seit Cartesius nach ihrem ethischen und religiösen Ertrag*. Gütersloh, 1932.

Schulz, W. *Der Got der neuzeitlichen Metaphysik*. Pfullingen, 1957.

Sortais, G. "Le cartésianisme chez les Jésuites français au XVIIe siècle," *Archives de Philosophie,* VI, 1929.

Souilhé, J. *La philosophie chrétienne de Descartes à nos jours*. Paris, 1934.

Soviet team of historians of philosophy. *Geschichte der Philosophie*. Berlin: VEB Deutscher Verlag der Wissenschaften, 1959.

Stephen, L. *An Agnostic's Apology and Other Essays*. London, 1904.

Stoupp, J. *La Religion des Hollandais*. Utrecht, 1693.

Strauss, L. *Die Religionskritik Spinozas als Grundlage seiner Bibelwissenschaft*. Berlin, 1930.
Thijssen-Schoute, C. L. "Le cartésianisme aux Pays-Bas," *Descartes et le cartésianisme hollandais*. Paris, 1950.
——— *Nederlands Cartesianisme*. Verhandelingen der Koninklijke Nederlandse Akademie van Wetenschappe, Afd. Letterkunde, Nieuwe Reeks, Deel LX. Amsterdam, 1954.
Thomassin, L. *Dogmata theologica*. Paris, 1680ff.
Thijssen-Schoute, C. L. *La Méthode d'étudier et d'enseigner Chrétiennement et solidement la Philosophie. . . .* Paris, 1685.
Trendelenburg, A. *Logische Untersuchungen*. Leipzig: S. Hirzel, 1870.
van del Linden, A. *Spinoza, seine Lehre und deren erste Nachwirkungen in Holland*. Göttingen, 1862.
de Velthuysen, I. O. L. *Tractatus de cultu naturali et origine moralitatis*. Rotterdam: R. Leers, 1680.
Vernière, P. *Spinoza et la pensée française avant la révolution*. Paris, 1954.
de Versé, A. *L'Impie convaincu, ou Dissertation contre Spinoza dans laquelle on réfute les fondements de son athéisme*. Amsterdam, 1685.
Wolfson, H. A. *The Philosophy of Spinoza*. New York, 1958.

PART II
Deism and Atheism in English Empiricism

Principal Works

Bentley, R. *Matter and Motion cannot think; or a Confutation of Atheism from the Faculties of the Soul*. London, 1692.
——— *Remarks upon a late Discourse of Free-Thinking*. London, 1713.
Berkeley, G. *Alcyphron, or the minute Philosopher. Berkeley's Works*, Vol. II. Edited by A. C. Fraser. Oxford, 1901.
——— *Commonplace Book. Berkeley's Works*, Vol. I. Oxford, 1901.
——— *Dialogues between Hylas and Philonous. Berkeley's Works*, Vol. I. Oxford, 1901.
——— *Syris. Berkeley's Works*, Vol. III. Oxford, 1901.
——— *The Theory of Vision or Visual Language shewing the immediate Presence and Providence of a Deity vindicated and explained. Berkeley's Works*, Vol. II. Oxford, 1901.
——— *A Treatise concerning the Principles of Human Knowledge. Berkeley's Works*, Vol. I. Oxford, 1901.
Brown, J. *Essays on the Characteristics of the Earl of Shaftesbury*. London, 1751.

Burnet, G., ed. *A Defence of Natural and Revealed Religion; being an Abridgment of the Sermons Preached at the Lecture founded by the Honble Robert Boyle, Esq., in Four Volumes, with a General Index.* London: printed for Arthur Bettesworth and Charles Hitch, at the Red Lion, in Pater-noster Row, 1731. French translation and expansion, *Defense de la Religion tant Naturelle que Revélée contre les Infideles et les Incredules:* Extraits des Ecrits publiés pour la Fondation de Mr. Boyle, par les plus habiles Gens d'Angleterre; et traduite de l'Anglois de Mr. Gilbert Burnet. The Hague: chez Pierre Paupie, 1738-1744.

Butler, J. *The Analogy of Religion natural and revealed to the Constitution and Course of Nature.* Originally published in 1736; reprinted Glasgow-London, 1827.

Herbert of Cherbury, *De Veritate.* Paris, 1633.

Clarke, S. *A Demonstration of the Being and Attributes of God more particularly in Answer to Mr. Hobbes, Spinoza and their Followers, Wherein the Notion of Liberty is Stated, and the Possibility and Certainty of it Proved, in Opposition to Necessity and Fate.* London, 1705.

——— *A Discourse concerning the Being and Attributes of God, the Obligation of Natural Religion, and the Truth and Certainty of the Christian Revelation.* London, 1716.

Collins, A. *A Discourse of Freethinking occasioned by the Rise and Growth of a sect called Freethinkers.* London, 1713.

——— *Essay concerning the Use of Reason.* London, 1707.

——— *Inquiry concerning Human Liberty.* London, 1715.

——— *Liberty and Necessity.* London, 1729.

Derham, W. *A Demonstration of the Being and Attributes of God from the Works of Creation.* The Boyle's Lectures of 1711-12; in Gilbert Burnet's *A Defence of Natural and Revealed Religion,* Vol. II. Italian translation, *Dimostrazione dell'Essenza ed Attributi di Dio dalle opere della sua Creazione.* Florence, 1719.

Gastrell, Bp. *Of the Certainty and Necessity of Religion in General.* The Boyle's Lectures of 1697; in Gilbert Burnet's *A Defence of Natural and Revealed Religion,* Vol. I.

Gurdon, B. *The Pretended Difficulties in Natural or Reveal'd Religion no Excuse for Infidelity.* The Boyle's Lectures of 1721-22. London, 1723. Burnet, Vol. III.

Hancock, J. *On Natural and Revealed Religion.* The Boyle's Lectures of 1706; in Gilbert Burnet's *A Defence of Natural and Revealed Religion,* Vol. II.

Harris, J. *Refutation of the Atheistical Objections against the Being and Attributes of a God.* The Boyle's Lectures of 1698; in Gilbert Burnet's *A Defence of Natural and Revealed Religion,* Vol. I.

Hobbes, T. *An Answer to a Book published by Dr. Bramhall, to the Reader. English Works,* Vol. IV. Edited by Molesworth. Aalen, 1962.
——— *Appendix ad Leviathan. Opera Latina,* Vol. III. Edited by Molesworth. Aalen, 1961.
——— *De Homine. Opera Latina,* Vol. III. Aalen, 1961.
——— *Liber de Cive. Opera Latina,* Vol. II. Aalen, 1961.
——— *Of Liberty and Necessity. English Works,* Vol. IV. Aalen, 1962.
——— *Philosophical Rudiments concerning Government and Society. English Works,* Vol. II. Aalen, 1962.
——— *The Question concerning Liberty, Necessity and Change. English Works,* Vol. V. Aalen, 1962.
Hume, D. *Dialogues concerning Natural Religion.* Edited by Norman K. Smith. 2nd. ed. Toronto-New York, 1947. German translation by Paulsen, *Dialoge über natürliche Religion.* Berlin, 1904.
——— *An Enquiry concerning the Human Understanding.* Edited by Selby-Bigge. Oxford, 1936.
——— *The History of Great Britain.* London, 1757.
——— *The Letters of David Hume.* Edited by J. Y. T. Grieg. Oxford, 1932.
——— *The Natural History of Religion. Essays and Treatises on several Subjects,* Vol. II. London, 1788.
——— *Treatise on Human Nature.* Edited by Selby-Bigge. Oxford, 1928.
Jacobi, F. H. *Idealismus und Realismus,* Ein Gespräch. *Werke,* Vol. II. Leipzig, 1816.
——— *Ueber die Lehre des Spinoza in Briefen an den Herrn Moses Mendelssohn.* Leipzig, 1785; 1789; *Werke,* Vol. IV. Leipzig, 1819.
——— *Von den göttlichen Dingen und ihrer Offenbarung.* Leipzig, 1798; *Werke,* Vol. III. Leipzig, 1816.
——— *Vorrede zugleich Einleitung in des Verfassers sämtliche philosophische Schriften. Werke,* Vol. II. Leipzig, 1816.
Leibniz, G. W. *Adnotationes subitaneae ad Tolandi "De Christianismo Mysteriis carente". Opera,* Vol. V. Edited by Dutens. Geneva, 1768.
——— *Lettres à La Croze. Opera,* Vol. V. Edited by Dutens. Geneva, 1768.
——— *Textes inédits.* Edited by G. Grua. Paris, 1948.
——— *Théodicée. Opera,* Vol. I. Edited by Dutens. Geneva, 1768. *Die philosophischen Shriften von G. W. Leibniz,* Vol. VI. Edited by C. J. Gerhardt. Hildesheim, 1961.
Leng, J. *Natural Obligations to Believe the Principles of Religion and Divine Revelation.* The Boyle's Lectures of 1717-18. London, 1719.

Lenin, V. I. *Materialism and Empiriocriticism.* Moscow: Foreign Languages Publishing House, no date. German translation, *Materialismus und Empiriokritizismus.* Berlin: Dietz Verlag, 1949.

Locke, J. *An Essay concerning Human Understanding. The Works of John Locke,* Vol. II. London, 1823; reprinted Aalen, 1963.

——— *The Reasonableness of Christianity.* London, 1695. *The Works of John Locke,* Vol. VII. London, 1823; Aalen, 1963. French translation by M. Coste, *Le Christianisme raisonnable,* tel qu'il nous est représenté dans l'Ecriture Sainte. 4th. ed. Amsterdam, 1740.

——— *A Second Vindication. The Works of John Locke,* Vol. VII. London, 1823; Aalen, 1963.

——— *Some Familiar Letters between Mr. Locke and Several of his Friends.* London, 1708.

Marx, K. and F. Engels. *Die Heilige Familie. K. Marx-F. Engels Werke,* Vol. II. Berlin, 1958. *Marx-Engels, Historisch-kritische Gesamtausgabe: Werke, Schriften, Briefe* (M.E.G.A.), Abt. I, Vol. 2. Edited by D. Rjazanov and V. Adoratsky. Moscow and Berlin, 1926ff.; edited by H.-J. Fueter and P. Futh: Darmstadt, 1962. Bücherei des Marxismus-Leninismus, Vol. 41. Berlin: Dietz Verlag, 1953. English translation, *The Holy Family.* Moscow: Foreign Languages Publishing House, 1956.

Antony Earl of Shaftesbury. *Characteristics of Men, Manners, Opinions, Times, etc.,* with a Collection of Letters by the Right Honourable Antony Earl of Shaftesbury. Three volumes. Basle, 1790. Edited in two volumes by John M. Robertson. London: Grant Richards, 1900; reprinted Gloucester, Mass.: Peter Smith, 1963.

——— *An Inquiry Concerning Virtue or Merit. Characteristics of Men, Manners, Opinions, Times, etc.,* Vol. II of the Basle edition; Vol. I of the Robertson edition.

——— *Letters to a Student at the University. Characteristics of Men, Manners, Opinions, Times, etc.,* Vol. I.

——— *Miscellaneous Reflections. Characteristics of Men, Manners, Opinions, Times, etc.,* Vol. II.

——— *The Moralists. Characteristics of Men, Manners, Opinions, Times, etc.,* Vol. II.

——— *A Prayer to God.* Shaftesbury Papers, G. D. 24; Bodl. XXVI, 7. In F. Heinemann, "The Philosophy of Enthusiasm, with materials hitherto unpublished," *Revue Internationale de Philosophie* VI, 1952.

Toland, J. *Adeisidaimon sive Titus Livius vindicatus.* The Hague: Thomas Johnson, 1709.

——— *Christianity not Mysterious.* London, 1696.

Toland, J. *Letters to Serena.* London, 1704. German translation, edited by E. Pracht, *John Toland, Briefe an Serena,* Ueber den Aberglauben, über Materie und Bewegung. Berlin: Akademie Verlag, 1959.

Valsecchi, A. *De fundamentis religionis et fontibus impietatis.* 2nd. ed. Venice, 1770. Italian edition, *Dei fondamenti della religione e dei fonti dell'empietà.* 7th. ed. Padua, 1805.

Woodward, J. *The Divine Original, and Incomparable Excellency of the Christian Religion, As founded on the Holy Scriptures, Asserted and Vindicated.* The Boyle's Lectures of 1709-10. London, 1712.

Secondary Works in addition to those already listed.

Bandini, L. *Shaftesbury,* Etica e religione, la morale del sentimento. Bari, 1930.

Benn, A. W. *The History of English Rationalism in the Nineteenth Century.* New York-London, 1906.

Blount, C. *Oracles of Reason.* London, 1693.

Bramhall, J. *The Catching of Leviathan. The works of the most Reverend Father in God, John Bramhall . . .* with a life of the author and a collection of his letters. Five volumes. Oxford, 1842-45.

von Brockdorff, C. *Die englische Aufklärungsphilosophie.* Munich, 1924.

Bruno, G. *Spaccio della Bestia trionfante. Le opere italiane di Giordano Bruno,* Vol. 2. Göttingen, 1888.

Bury, A. *The Account of the Growth of Deism in England.* London, 1696.

——— *The Naked Gospel.* London, 1690.

Cassirer, E. *Die Philosophie der Aufklärung.* Tübingen, 1932.

Catlin, G. *Thomas Hobbes, as Philosopher, Publicist and Man of Letters.* Oxford, 1922.

Chiappelli, B. *Il pensiero religioso di Shelley.* Rome, 1956.

Crous, E. *Die Religionsphilosophischen Lehren Lockes und ihre Stellung zu dem Deismus seiner Zeit.* Abhandlungen zur Philosophie und ihre Geschichte. Leipzig, 1910.

Cudworth, R. *Systema intellectuale.* Latin translation by Mosheim. Jena, 1733.

Diderot, D. *Pensées philosophiques. Oeuvres philosophiques.* Edited by P. Vernière. Paris, 1961. *Oeuvres de Diderot,* Vol. I. Edited by Assezat. Paris, 1875.

——— *Promenade du sceptique. L'allée des Maroniers. Oeuvres philosophiques.* Edited by P. Vernière. Paris, 1961.

——— *Réfutation suivie de l'ouvrage d'Helvétius intitulé l'Homme. Oeuvres philosophiques.* Edited by P. Vernère. Paris, 1961. *Oeuvres,* Vol. II. Edited by Assezat. Paris, 1875.

Diderot, D. Translation of *An Inquiry Concerning Virtue or Merit* by Shaftesbury. *Oeuvres,* Vol. I. Edited by Naigeon. Paris, 1821. *Oeuvres,* Vol. I. Edited by Assezat. Paris, 1875.

Dilthey, W. *Aus der Zeit der Spinozastudien Goethes. Gesammelte Schriften,* Vol. II. 4th. ed. Leipzig and Berlin, 1940.

Dodwell, H. *The Natural Mortality of the Human Soul clearly demonstrated.*

Fabro, C. *L'anima,* Introduzione al problema dell'uomo. Rome, 1955.

——— "Foi et raison dans l'oeuvre de Kierkegaard," *Revue de sciences philosophiques et théologiques,* 1948, pp. 169ff.

Fraser, A. C. *Locke.* Edinburgh-London, 1890.

Gibson, J. *Locke's Theory of Knowledge and its Historical Relations.* Cambridge, 1917.

Gizycky, G. *Die Philosophie Shaftesbury's.* Leipzig and Heidelberg, 1876.

Gueroult, M. *Berkeley,* Quatre études sur la perception et sur Dieu. Paris, 1956.

Hegel, G. W. *Enzyklopädie der philosophischen Wissenschaften.* Edited by L. von Henning. Berlin, 1840.

Heinemann, F. H. *David Hume,* The Man and his Science of Man, containing some unpublished Letters of Hume. Paris, 1940.

——— "Toland und Leibniz," *Beiträge zur Leibniz-Forschung,* edited by G. Schichkoff. Reutlingen, 1947.

Helfbower, S. G. *The Relation of John Locke to English Deism.* Chicago, 1918.

Hendel, C. *Studies in the Philosophy of D. Hume.* Princeton: Princeton University Press, 1925.

Hibben, Y. G. *The Philosophy of Enlightenment.* New York, 1910.

Hildebrandt, K. *Leibniz und das Reich der Gnade.* The Hague, 1953.

Holm, S. "L'attitude de Hobbes a l'égard de la religion," *Archives de la Philosophie* XII, 2, 1936.

Hutcheson, S. *An Inquiry concerning Moral Good and Evil. British Moralists,* Vol. I. London, 1738.

Jacques, A., ed. *Oeuvres philosophiques de Samuel Clarke,* nouvelle édition. Paris, 1845.

Kant, I. *Die Religion innerhalb der Grenzen der blossen Vernunft. Werke,* Abt. I, Vol. 6. Berlin, 1907.

Karpp, H. *Probleme altchristlicher Anthropologie.* Gütersloh, 1950.

Klemmt, A. *John Locke theoretische Philosophie.* Meisenheim-Glan-Wien, 1952.

Lechler, G. V. *Geschichte des Englischen Deismus.* Stuttgart and Tübingen, 1841.

Lempp, O. *Das Problem der Theodicee in der Philosophie und Literatur des 18. Jahrhunderts bis auf Kant und Schiller*. Leipzig, 1910.
Leroy, A. *La critique de la religion de David Hume*. Paris, 1930.
Leslie, C. *Short and Easy Method with the Deists. The theological works of the Reverend Mr. Charles Leslie,* Vol. I. London, 1721.
Limentani, G. *La morale della simpatia*. Genoa, 1914.
Lüers, A. *David Humes religionsphilosophische Anschauungen*. Dissertation. Berlin, 1909.
Lyon, G. *La philosophie de Hobbes*. Paris, 1893.
Magnino, B. *Il pensiero filosofico di D. Hume*. Naples, 1935.
Marx, K. and F. Engels. *Die Deutsche Ideologie. M.E.G.A.*, Abt. I, Vol. 3. Darmstadt, 1962.
K. Marx-F. Engels Werke, Vol. III. Berlin: Dietz Verlag, 1958.
Meinecke, F. *Die Entstehung des Historismus*. 2nd. ed. Munich, 1964.
Mintz, S. *The Hunting of Leviathan,* Seventeenth Century Reactions to the Materialism and Moral Philosophy of Th. Hobbes. Cambridge, 1962.
Moniglia, T. *La mente umana spirito immortale, non materia pensante*. Padua, 1766.
Mossner, E. C. *The Forgotten Hume, Le bon David*. New York: Columbia University University Press, 1943.
——— *The Life of David Hume*. Austin: The University of Texas Press, 1954.
Osske, I. *Ganzheit, Unendlichkeit und Form, Studien zu Shaftesburys Naturbegriff*. Berlin, 1930.
Parker, S. *Letter to a Deist*. London, 1677.
Platner, E. *Ueber den Atheismus,* Ein Gespräch. Leipzig, 1783.
Radicati, A. *Philosophical Dissertation upon Death*. Translated by John Morgan. London, 1733.
Rand, B., ed. *The Life, Unpublished Letters and Philosophical Regimen of Anthony Earl of Shaftesbury*. New York, 1900.
Robertson, G. *Hobbes*. Edinburgh and London, 1910.
Robertson, J. M. *A Short History of Freethought*. 3rd ed. London, 1915.
Rossi, M. *Alle fonti del deismo e del materialismo moderno*. Florence, 1942.
Scholz, H. *Die Religionsphilosophie des Herbert von Cherbury,* Auszüge aus *De veritate* und *De religione gentilium*. Giessen, 1914.
Serini, P. *Voltaire Scritti filosofici*. Bari, 1962.
Skelton, P. *Deism Revealed,* Or the Attack on Christianity Candidly Reviewed on Its Real Merits, as They Stand in the Celebrated Writings of Lord Herbert, Lord Shaftesbury, Hobbes, Toland, Tindal,

Collins, Mandeville, Doddwell, Woolston, Morgan, Chubb and Others. Two volumes. 2nd ed. London, 1751.
Smith, N. K. *The Philosophy of David Hume.* London, 1941.
Söderblom, N. *Natürliche Theologie und allgemeine Religionsgeschichte.* Stockholm and Leipzig, 1913.
Sorley, W. R. *A History of English Philosophy.* Cambridge, 1920.
——— *Moral Values and the Idea of God.* 3rd. ed. Cambridge, 1935.
Spanneut, M. *Le Stoïcisme des Pères de l'Eglise.* Paris, 1957.
Stäudlin, C. F. *Geschichte des Rationalismus und Supernaturalismus.* Göttingen, 1826.
Sullivan, R. J. *A View of Nature. Letters to a Traveller among the Alps with Reflections on Atheistical Philosophy, now exemplified in France,* Vol. I. London, 1794.
Tindal, M. *The Rights of the Christian Church.* London, 1709.
Tönnies, F. *Thomas Hobbes Leben und Lehre.* Stuttgart, 1925.
Troeltsch, E. "Deismus," *Realencyklopedie für protestantische Theologie und Kirche,* Vol. IV. Leipzig, 1898. Abridged version in *Aufsätze zur Geistesgeschichte und Religionssoziologie. Werke,* Vol. IV. Tübingen, 1925.
Viano, C. A. *John Locke, dal razionalismo all'illuminismo.* Turin, 1960.
Wild, J. *George Berkeley,* A Study of his Life and Philosophy. Cambridge, 1936.
Zabceh, F. *Hume, Precursor of Modern Empiricism.* The Hague, 1960.
von Zscharnack, L. *John Toland's Christianity not Mysterious (Christentum ohne Geheimnis) 1696.* Translated by W. Lunde. Studien zur Geschichte des neueren Protestantismus, 3. Giessen, 1908.

PART III
Enlightenment Atheism

Principal Works

Anonymous, *Examen des critiques du livre intitulé "De l'Esprit."* London, 1760.
Bergier, Abbé J. *Examen du matérialisme ou réfutation du Système de la Nature.* Tournai: J. Casterman, 1838.
Descartes, R. *Le Monde: Traité de la Lumière. Oeuvres de Descartes,* Vol. XI. Edited by C. Adam and P. Tannery. Paris, 1909.
——— *Des Passions de l'âme. Oeuvres,* Vol. XI. Edited by Adam and Tannery. Paris, 1909.

Diderot, D. *Apologie de l'Abbé de Prades. Oeuvres de Diderot,* Vol. I. Edited by J. Naigeon. Paris, 1821.
Edited by J. Assezat. Paris, 1875.

——— *De l'interprétation de la nature. Oeuvres philosophiques.* Edited by P. Vernière. Paris, 1961.
Oeuvres, Vol. II. Edited by Assezat. Paris, 1875.

——— *De la suffisance de la religion naturelle. Recueil philosophique,* Vol. I. London-Amsterdam, 1770.

——— *Entretien d'un philosophe avec la Maréchale de D***. Oeuvres philosophiques.* Edited by P. Vernière. Paris, 1961. *Oeuvres,* Vol. II. Edited by Assezat. Paris, 1875.

——— *Entretien entre d'Alembert et Diderot. Oeuvres philosophiques.* Edited by P. Vernière. Paris, 1961.
Oeuvres, Vol. II. Edited by Assezat. Paris, 1875.

——— *Lettre sur les aveugles. Oeuvres philosophiques.* Edited by P. Vernière. Paris, 1961.

——— *Pensées philosophiques. Oeuvres philosophiques.* Edited by P. Vernière. Paris, 1961.
Oeuvres, Vol. I. Edited by Assezat. Paris, 1875.

——— *Principes philosophiques sur la matière et le mouvement. Oeuvres philosophiques.* Edited by P. Vernière. Paris, 1961.

——— *Réfutation suivie de l'ouvrage d'Helvétius intitulé l'Homme. Oeuvres philosophiques.* Edited by P. Vernière. Paris, 1961. *Oeuvres,* Vol. II. Edited by Assezat. Paris, 1875.

——— *Le rêve d'Alembert. Oeuvres philosophiques.* Edited by P. Vernière. Paris, 1961. *Oeuvres,* Vol. II. Edited by Assezat. Paris, 1875.

Helvétius, C. *De l'Esprit.* Paris, Year II of the Republic.

——— *De l'Homme,* De ses Facultés intellectuelles et de son education. London, 1776; Paris, 1818.

——— *Le vrai sens du Système de la Nature.* London, 1774. German translation, *Neunundzwanzig Thesen des Materialismus.* Halle a. S., 1873.

d'Holbach, D. *Système de la nature.* 2nd ed. London, 1774.

Holland, M. *Les Réflexions philosophiques sur "Le Système de la Nature."* Paris, 1773.

Laharpe, J.-F. *Réfutation du Livre De l'Esprit.* Paris, 1797.

La Mettrie, J. O. de. *L'Homme machine.* Edited by M. Solovine. Paris: Boissard, 1921.

——— *L'Homme Plante.* Leyden, 1748. Edited by Francis Rougier. New York: Columbia University Press, 1936.

——— *Le Système d'Epicure. Oeuvres philosophiques de Monsieur de la Mettrie,* Vol. II. Amsterdam, 1764.

Lamourette, Abbé. *Pensées sur la philosophie de l'incredulité ou Réflexions sur l'esprit et le dessin des philosophes irréligieux de ce siècle.* Paris, 1786.

Liguori, A. *Breve Dissertazione contra gli errori de' moderni increduli x oggidí nominati Materialisti e Deisti.* Turin: Marietti, 1825.

——— *Riflessioni sulla verità della divina Rivelazione contra le principali opposizioni dei Deisti.* Turin: Marietti, 1825.

——— *Verità della Fede.* Turin: Marietti, 1825.

Marana, G. P. *L'Espion du Grand-Seigneur et ses Relations secretes envoyées à Constantinople, contenant les événements les plus considérables pendant la vie de Louis le Grand.* Amsterdam: chez Henry Weltstein, 1688.

——— *L'Espion dans les Cours des Princes Chrétiens, ou Lettres et Memoires d'un Envoyé secret de la Porte dans les Cours de l'Europe, où l'on voit les découvertes qu'il a faites dans toutes les Cours où il s'est trouvé, avec une Dissertation curieuse de leures Forces, Politique et Religion.* Cologne (Rouen): chez Erasme Kinkius, 1696. 15th. ed. London, 1742.

Meslier, J. *Le bon sens du curé Meslier suivi de son Testament.* Edited by d'Holbach and Voltaire. Collection *Scripta manent.* Dijon, 1930.

——— *Le Testament de Jean Meslier.* Edited by Charles, in three volumes. Amsterdam, 1864.

Nonnotte, Abbé. *Dictionnaire Anti-Philosophique.* Avignon, 1767.

Valsecchi, A. *De fundamentis religionis et fontibus impietatis.* 2nd ed. Venice, 1770. Italian edition, *Dei fondamenti della religione a dei fonti dell'empietà.* 7th ed. Padua, 1805.

——— *La Religione Vincitrice.* Genoa, 1776.

Vartanian, A. *La Mettrie's L'Homme Machine,* A Study in the Origin of an Idea, Critical Edition with an Introductory Monograph and Notes. Princeton: Princeton University Press, 1960.

Voltaire. *Dictionnaire Philosophique.* Edited by J. Benda and R. Naves. Paris: Garnier, 1954.

Secondary Works in addition to those already listed.

Anonymous. *La nouvelle Philosophei dévoilée,* et pleinement convaincue de Lèse-Majeste Divine et Humaine au premier chef. In France, 1770.

Belaval, Y. Preface to the 1966 reprint of the Paris 1821 edition of d'Holbach's *Système de la nature.* Hildesheim, 1966.

Belin, J.-P. *Le mouvement philosophique de 1748 à 1789.* Paris, 1913.

Bréhier, E. *Histoire de la Philosophie.* Paris, 1962.

Casini, P. *Diderot "philosophe"*. Bari, 1962.
Condillac, E. *Essai sur l'origine des connaissances humaines.* Edited by Raymond Lenoir. Paris, 1924.
Cotta, S. *Montesquieu e la scienza della società.* Turin, 1953.
Dieckmann, H. *Cinq leçons sur Diderot.* Geneva-Paris, 1959.
Du Marsais. "De la raison," *Recueil philosophique,* Vol. I. London-Amsterdam, 1770.
Engels, F. *Herrn Eugen Dührings Umwälzung der Wissenschaft.* 5th. ed. Stuttgart, 1904.
——— *Ludwig Feuerbach und der Ausgang der klassischen deutschen Philosophie.* Edited by Hajek. Philosophische Bibliothek, Vol. 230. Leipzig, 1947.
Hubert, R. *D'Holbach et ses amis.* Paris, 1928.
Kahn, L. *Metaphysics of the Supernatural as illustrated by Descartes.* New York, 1918.
Keim, A. *Helvétius,* sa vie et ses oeuvres. Paris, 1907.
Lenin, V. I. "Sur l'importance du matérialisme militant," *Marx-Engels Marxisme.* Moscow, 1947.
——— *Ueber die Religion.* Berlin: Dietz Verlag, 1956.
Ljublinski, S. *Voltaire-Studien.* Berlin: Akademie Verlag, 1961.
Luppol, I. K. *Diderot,* Ses idées philosophiques. French translation by V. and Y. Feldman. Paris, 1936.
Maritain, J. *The Dream of Descartes.* English translation by M. L. Andison. New York, 1944.
Momdshian, C. N. *Helvétius,* Ein streitbarer Atheist des 18. Jahrhunderts. Berlin, 1959.
Naigeon, J. A. *Le militaire philosophe.* London, 1768.
Plechanov, G. W. *Beiträge zur Geschichte des Materialismus.* Berlin, 1957.
Pluche, N.-A. *Histoire du Ciel, considéré selon les idées des poètes, des philosophes, et de Moïse.* Paris, 1739.
Robinet, J. B. *De la nature. Four volumes.* Amsterdam, 1763-66.
Rosenkranz, K. *Diderot's Leben und Werke.* Leipzig, 1866.
Soviet author team. *Grundlagen der marxistischen Philosophie.* Berlin: Dietz Verlag, 1959.
Szigeti, I. *Denis Diderot,* Une grande figure du matérialisme militant du XVIIIe siècle. Budapest, 1962.
Thielemann, L. "Diderot and Hobbes," *Diderot Studies,* Vol. II. Syracuse: Syracuse University Press, 1952.
Toldo, P. "Dell' 'Espion' di Gian Paolo Marana e delle sue attinenze con le 'Lettres Persanes' de Montesquieu," *Giornale storico della letteratura italiana,* XXIX (1897), pp. 45-79.

Torrey, N. L. Introduction to *Diderot Studies,* Vol. II. Syracuse: Syracuse University Press, 1952.

Vartanian, A. *Diderot and Descartes,* A Study of Scientific Naturalism in the Enlightenment. Princeton: Princeton University Press, 1953.

——— "From Deist to Atheist," *Diderot Studies,* Vol. I. Syracuse: Syracuse University Press, 1949.

Voltaire. *Précis de l'Ecclésiaste et du Cantique des Cantiques.* Geneva, 1759.

Wartofsky, M. W. "Diderot and the Development of Materialist Monism," *Diderot Studies,* Vol. II. Syracuse: Syracuse University Press, 1952.

Wollaston, W. *The Religion of Nature delineated.* London, 1724. French translation, *Ebauche de la Religion Naturelle.* The Hague, 1756.

Zebenko, M. D. *Der Atheismus der französischen Materialisten des 18. Jahrhunderts.* Berlin: Dietz Verlag, 1956.

PART IV

Disintegration of Idealism into Atheism

Principal Works

Fichte, I. H. *J. G. Fichte's Leben und literarischer Briefwechsel.* Sulzbach, 1830.

Fichte, J. G. *Angewandte Philosophie. Werke,* Vol. VI. Edited by F. Medicus. Leipzig, 1912.

——— *Die Anweisung zum seligen Leben oder auch die Religionslehre. Werke,* Vol. V. Edited by Medicus. Leipzig, 1912.

——— *Appellation an das Publikum. Werke,* Vol. III. Edited by Medicus. Leipzig, 1910.

——— *Auf einem Privatschreiben. Werke,* Vol. V. Edited by Medicus. Leipzig, 1912.

——— *Beitrag zur Berichtigung der Urteile des Publikums über die französische Revolution. J. G. Fichtes Werke, Erster Ergänzungsband.* Edited by R. Strecker. Leipzig, 1922.

——— *Briefe.* Edited by E. Bergmann. Leipzig, 1919.

——— *Darstellung der Wissenschaftslehre vom 1801. Werke,* Vol. IV. Edited by Medicus. Leipzig, 1911.

——— *Einige Aphorismen über Religion und Deismus. Nachgelassene Schriften,* Vol. I. Edited by R. Lauth and H. Jakob. Stuttgart, 1962.

Fichte, J. G. *Grundlage der Gesamten Wissenschaftslehre. Werke,* Vol. I. Edited by Medicus. Leipzig, 1908.

——— *Die Grundzüge des gegenwärtigen Zeitalters. Werke,* Vol. IV. Edited by Medicus. Leipzig, 1911.

——— *Der Herausgeber des philosophischen Journals gerichtliche Verantwortungsschriften gegen die Anklage des Atheismus.* In H. Lindau, *Die Schriften zu Fichte's Atheismus-Streit.* Munich, 1912.

——— *Ideen über Gott und Unsterblichkeit.* Edited by F. Büchsel. Leipzig, 1914.

——— *Logik und Metaphysik. Nachgelassene Schriften,* Vol. II. Edited by R. Lauth and H. Jakob. Stuttgart, 1962.

——— *Rückerinnerungen, Antworten, Fragen. Werke,* Vol. III. Edited by Medicus. Leipzig, 1910.

——— *System der Sittenlehre. Werke,* Vol. II. Edited by Medicus. Leipzig, 1909.

——— *Ueber den Begriff der Wissenschaftslehre. Werke,* Vol. I. Edited by Medicus. Leipzig, 1908.

——— *Ueber den Grund unseres Glaubens an eine göttliche Weltregierung. Werke,* Vol. III. Edited by Medicus. Leipzig, 1910.

——— *Wissenschaftslehre 'nova metodo'. Werke,* Vol. IV. Edited by Medicus. Leipzig, 1911.

——— *Zu "Jacobi an Fichte". Werke,* Vol. V. Edited by Medicus. Leipzig, 1912.

——— *Zweite Einleitung in die Wissenschaftslehre. Werke,* Vol. III. Edited by Medicus. Leipzig, 1910.

Forberg, F. C. *Entwicklung des Begriffs der Religion.* In H. Lindau, *Die Schriften zu Fichte's Atheismus-Streit.* Munich, 1912.

——— *Friedrich Carl Forbergs Apologie seines angeblichen Atheismus.* Gotha, 1799.

Hegel, G. W. *Berliner Schriften.* Edited by J. Hoffmeister. Hamburg, 1956.

——— *Enzyklopädie der philosophischen Wissenschaften.* Edited by Hoffmeister. Leipzig, 1949.

——— *Der Geist des Christentums und sein Schicksal.* In *Hegels Theologische Jugendschriften.* Edited by H. Nohl. Tübingen, 1907.

——— *Geschichte der Philosophie.* Edited by Michelet. Berlin, 1844. Reprinted as Vols. 17-18 of the Jubiläumsausgabe of the *Sämtliche Werke.* Stuttgart, 1959. Edited by J. Hoffmeister. Leipzig, 1944.

——— *Glaube und Wissen. Werke,* Vol. I. Edited by Lasson. Leipzig, 1930.

——— *Phänomenologie des Geistes.* Edited by Hoffmeister. Leipzig, 1937.

——— *Philosophie der Geschichte.* Edited by Gans. Stuttgart, 1961.

Hegel, G. W. *Philosophie der Religion.* Edited by Marheinecke. Berlin, 1840; reprinted as Vols. 15-16 of the Jubiläumsausgabe of the Sämtliche Werke. Stuttgart, 1959. Edited by Lasson. Leipzig, 1930.

——— *Philosophie der Weltgeschichte.* Edited by Lasson. Leipzig, 1925.

——— *Die Positivität der christlichen Religion.* In *Hegels Theologische Jugendschriften.* Edited by H. Nohl. Tübingen, 1907.

——— *Ueber die wissenschaftlichen Behandlungsarten des Naturrechts. Hegels Werke,* Vol. VII. Edited by Lasson. Leipzig, 1932.

——— *Wissenschaft der Logik.* Edited by Lasson. Leipzig, 1934.

Jacobi, F. H. *Brief an Fichte. Werke,* Vol. III. Leipzig, 1816.

——— *Sendschreiben an Erhard O. Werke,* Vol. I. Leipzig, 1816.

——— *Ueber das Unternehmen des Kriticismus, die Vernunft zu Verstande zu bringen. Werke,* Vol. III. Leipzig, 1816.

——— *Ueber die Lehre des Spinoza in Briefen an den Herrn Moses Mendelssohn. Werke,* Vol. IV. Leipzig, 1819.

——— *Von den göttlichen Dingen und ihrer Offenbarung. Werke,* Vol. III. Leipzig, 1816.

——— *Vorrede zugleich Einleitung in des Verfassers sämtliche philosophische Schriften. Werke,* Vol. II. Leipzig, 1816.

——— *Wider Mendelssohns Beschuldigungen in dessen Schreiben an die Freunde Lessings. Werke,* Vol. IV. Leipzig, 1819.

Kant, I. *Der einzig mögliche Beweisgrund zu einer Demonstration des Daseins Gottes. Werke,* Vol. II. Edited by E. Cassirer. Berlin, 1923.

——— *Kritik der reinen Vernunft. Kants gesammelte Schriften,* Abt. I, Vol. 3. Berlin: Reimer, 1911. English translation by Max Müller, *Critique of Pure Reason.* Garden City: Dolphin Books, Doubleday & Company, Inc., 1961.

——— *Die Religion innerhalb der Grenzen der blossen Vernunft. Kants gesammelte Schriften,* Abt. I, Vol. 6. Berlin, 1907.

——— *Was heisst sich im Denken orientieren? Werke,* Vol. IV. Edited by E. Cassirer. Berlin, 1926.

Lindau, H. *Die Schriften zu Fichte's Atheismus-Streit.* Munich, 1912.

Mauthner, F., ed. *Jacobis Spinoza Büchlein,* nebst Replik und Duplik. Munich, 1912.

Schelling, F. *Denkmal des Schrift von den göttlichen Dingen etc. des Herrn F. H. Jacobi und der ihm in derselben gemachten Beschuldigung eines absichtlichen täuschenden, Lüge redenden Atheismus. Werke,* Abt. I, Vol. 8. Stuttgart and Augsburg, 1861.

——— *Philosophische Unterschungen über das Wesen der menschlichen Freiheit und die damit zusammenhängende Gegenstände. Werke,* Abt. I, Vol. 7. Stuttgart and Augsburg, 1861.

Schelling, F. *Ueber das Wesen deutscher Philosophie. Werke,* Abt. I, Vol. 8. Stuttgart and Augsburg, 1861.

Schlegel, F. *Die Entwicklung der Philosophie. Werke,* Vol. XIII. Edited by J. J. Anstett. Munich, 1964.

——— *Neue Philosophische Schriften.* Edited by J. Körner. Frankfurt a. M., 1935.

——— *Ueber die Sprache und Weisheit der Indier. Werke,* Vol. VIII. Munich, 1964.

Schleiermacher, F. *Der christliche Glaube. Werke,* Vol. I. 7th. ed. by M. Redeker. Berlin, 1960.

——— *Dialektik.* Edited by R. Odebrecht. Leipzig, 1942.

——— *Grundriss der philsophischen Ethik.* Edited by D. Twesten. Berlin: Reimer, 1841.

——— *Reden über die Religion.* Edited by G. B. Pünjer. Braunschweig, 1879. English translation, *On Religion.* New York: Harper & Row, 1958.

Secondary Works in addition to those listed above.

Anonymous. *Epistulae nonnullorum Germaniae parochorum ad Germanos Kantianae philosophiae propagatores et asseclas.* Frankfurt, 1799.

Anonymous. *Absolutes Wissen und moderner Pantheismus.* Leipzig, 1829.

——— (by the same author) *Ueber die Wissenschaft der Idee.* Breslau, 1831.

von Baader, F. *Biographie und Briefwechsel. Werke,* Vol. XV. Edited by F. Hoffman. Aalen, 1963.

Bartsch, G., ed. *De Tribus Impostoribus,* Anno MDIIC. Berlin: Akademie Verlag, 1960.

Brunner, E. *Die Mystik und das Wort,* Der Gegensatz zwischen moderner Religionsauffassung und christlichem Glauben dargestellt an der Theologie Schleiermachers. Tübingen, 1924.

Chalybaeus, H. M. *Historische Entwicklung der spekulativen Philosophie von Kant bis Hegel.* Dresden, 1837.

——— *Philosophie und Christenthum.* Kiel, 1853.

Dieter, T. *Die Frage der Persönlichkeit Gottes in Hegels Philosophie.* Tübingen, 1917.

Drobisch, M. W. *Grundlehren der Religionsphilosophie.* Leipzig, 1840.

Erdmann, J. E. *Die Entwicklung der deutschen Spekulation seit Kant.* Stuttgart, 1931.

Erdmann, J. E. *Grundriss der Geschichte der Philosophie.* 3rd. ed. Berlin, 1878.

Erdmann, K. *Die Theologische und philosophische Aufklärung des sechzehnten und neunzehnten Jahrhunderts.* Leipzig, 1849.

Fabro, C. *Hegel, La dialettica.* Brescia, 1960; 2nd. ed., 1966.

Finger, O. "Johann Heinrich Schulz, ein Prediger der Atheismus," In G. Stiehler, *Beiträge zur Geschichte des vormarxistischen Atheismus.* Berlin: Dietz Verlag, 1961.

——— "Der Kampf Karl von Knoblauchs gegen den religiösen Aberglauben," In G. Stiehler, *Beiträge zur Geschichte des vormarxistischen Atheismus.* Berlin, 1961.

——— *Von der Materialität der Seele.* Berlin, 1961.

Fischer, K. *J. G. Fichte und seine Vorgänger.* 2nd. ed. Heidelberg, 1899.

Foucher de Careil, A. *Descartes et Spinoza.* Paris, 1863.

Friedmann, G. *Leibniz et Spinoza.* Paris, 1946.

Gogarten, F. *Fichte als religiöser Denker.* Jena, 1914.

Göschel, C. F. *Beiträge zur spekulativen Philosophie von Gott und von dem Gott-Menschen.* Berlin, 1838.

Grabmann, M. *I divieti ecclesiastici di Aristotele sotto Innocenzo III e Gregorio IX.* Rome, 1941.

Grassl, H., ed. Letter of Hegel to von Baader. *Hegelsche Studien* II, 1963.

Groos, H. *Der deutsche Idealismus und das Christentum.* Munich, 1927.

Gulyga, A. W. "Der 'Atheismusstreit' und der streitbare Atheismus in den letzten Jahrzehnten des 18. Jahrhunderts in Deutschland," in M. Buhr, ed., *Wissen und Gewissen,* Beiträge zum 200. Geburtstag Johann Gottlieb Fichte 1762-1814. Berlin, 1962.

Günther, A. *Die Justemilieus in der deutschen Philosophie gegenwärtiger Zeit.* 1838.

——— "Ueber Atheismus in metaphisichen Systemen," *Zeitschrift für Philosophie und spekulative Theologie,* III.

Hartmann, A. *Der Spätidealismus und die Hegelsche Dialektik.* Neue Deutsche Forschungen 163. Berlin, 1937.

Hauter, C. *Essai sur l'objet religieux.* Paris, 1928.

Hebeisen, A. *Friedrich Heinrich Jacobi,* Seine Auseinandersetzung mit Spinosa. Dissertation. Bern, 1960.

Heimsoeth, H. *Fichte.* Munich, 1923.

Heine, H. *Zur Geschichte der Religion und Philosophie in Deutschland. Ausgewählte Werke,* Vol. IV. Munich, 1957.

Heise, W. "Mathias Knutzen," in G. Stiehler, ed. *Beiträge zur Geschichte des vormarxistischen Materialismus.* Berlin, 1961.

Herweck, F. *Die Giessner Beteilung an dem Fichteschen Atheismusstreit.* Leipzig, 1913.

Hirsch, E. *Geschichte der neuern evangelischen Theologie*. Gütersloh, 1952.

——— *Die Religionsphilosophie Fichtes zur Zeit des Atheismusstreites in ihrem Zusammenhang mit der Wissenschaftslehre und Ethik*. Göttingen, 1914.

Hölters, H. *Der spinozistische Gottesbegriff bei M. Mendelssohn und F. H. Jacobi*. Universitas-Archiv 97. Emsdetten, 1938.

Horneffer, M. *Die Identitätslehre Fichtes in den Jahren 1801-1806*. Leipzig, 1925.

Jäsche, G. B. *Der Pantheismus*. Three volumes. Berlin, 1832.

von Knoblauch, K. *Anti-Hyperphysik zur Erbauung der Vernünftigen*. 1789.

——— *Nachtwachen des Einsiedlers zu Athos*. 1790.

——— *Spinoza der Zweite*. 1787.

——— *Spinoza der Dritte*. 1790.

Kojève, A. *Introduction à la lecture de Hegel*. Paris, 1947.

Krause, C. F. *Zur Geschichte der neueren philosophischen Systeme*. Leipzig, 1889.

Lange, J. *Prüfung der vernünftigen Gedanken des Herrn Wolf von Gott, der Welt*. . . . Halle, 1723, 1724.

Lau, T. L. *Meditationes, Theses, Dubia, etc*. Freistädt, 1719.

——— *Philosophische Untersuchungen über Gott, die Welt, den Menschen*. Freistädt, 1717.

Leese, K. *Die Religionskrisis des Abendlandes und die religiöse Lage der Gegenwart*. Hamburg, 1948.

Lévy-Bruhl, L. *La philosophie de Jacobi*. Paris, 1894.

Lindner, H. *Das Problem des Spinozismus in Schaffen Goethes und Herders*. Weimar: Arion Verlag, 1960.

Löwith, K. *Dio, uomo e mondo da Cartesio a Nietzsche*. Naples, 1966.

Lucacs, G. *Der junge Hegel*. Zurich-Vienna, 1848.

Lütgert, W. *Die Religion des deutschen Idealismus und ihr Ende*. Gütersloh, 1923.

Magnino, B. *Romanticismo e Cristianesimo*. Brescia, 1962.

Medicus, F. "Fichtes Leben," *Fichtes Werke,* Vol. I. Edited by F. Medicus. Leipzig, 1908.

Mendelssohn, M. *An die Freunde Lessing's. Werke*. Vienna, 1838.

——— *Jerusalem oder über religiösen Macht und Judenthum. Werke*. Vienna, 1838.

Mertel, F. *Das theologische Denken Schleiermachers*. Zurich, 1965.

Mesnard, P. "Comment Leibniz se trouva placé dans le sillage de Suarez," *Archives de Philosophie,* 1959.

Messer, A. *Fichtes religiöse Weltanschauung*. Stuttgart, 1923.

Meyer, F. *Eine Fichte-Sammlung*. Leipzig, 1921.

Nicolini, F. *La giovinezza di G. B. Vico (1668-1700)*. Bari, 1932.

——— *La religiosità di G. B. Vico*. Bari, 1949.

Pupi, A. *Alla soglia dell'età romantica*. Milan, 1962.

Rickert, H. "Fichtes Atheismusstreit und die kantische Philosophie," *Kant-Studien,* IV. Berlin, 1900.

Ritzel, W. *Fichtes Religionsphilosophie*. Stuttgart, 1956.

Rohmer, F. *Gott und seine Schöpfung*. Nördlichen, 1857.

——— *Kritik des Gottesbegriff in den gegenwärtigen Weltansichten*. 2nd. ed. Nördlichen, 1857.

Romang, J. P. *Der neueste Pantheismus oder die junghegelsche Weltanschauung nach ihrem theoretischen Grundlagen und praktischen Consequenzen*. Bern-Zurich, 1848.

Scherer, C. C. *Die Gotteslehre I. H. von Fichte*. Theologische Studien der Leo Gesellschaft 9. Vienna, 1902.

Schmid, F. A. *Friedrich Heinrich Jacobi*. Heidelberg, 1908.

——— *Die Philosophie Fichtes mit Rücksicht auf die Frage nach der "veränderten Lehre"*. Freiburg im Br., 1904.

Scholz, H. *Die Hauptschriften zum Pantheismusstreit zwischen Jacobi und Mendelssohn*. Berlin, 1916.

——— "Ein neues Dokument zu Fichtes religionsphilosophischer Evolution," *Kant-Studien* XXII, 1918.

Schulz, J. H. *Philosophische Betrachtungen über die jüdische Insonderheit*. 1786.

Spalding, J. J. *Bestimmung des Menschen*. Edited by H. Stephan. Giessen: A. Töpelmann, 1908.

Steinbeck, W. *Das Bild des Menschen in der Philosophie J. G. Fichtes*. Munich, 1938.

Stephan, H. *Spaldings Bestimmung des Menschen und Wert der Andacht*. Studien zur Geschichte des neuern Protestantismus, 1. Giessen, 1908.

Stiehler, G. *Beiträge zur Geschichte des vormarxistischen Materialismus*. Berlin: Dietz Verlag, 1961.

Stilling, P. M. *Den moderne Atheisme*. Copenhagen, 1844.

Thilo, C. A. *Die Religionsphilosophie des absoluten Idealismus*. Laugensalza, 1905.

Vaihinger, A. *Die Philosophie des "Als ob"*. 7th-8th. ed. Leipzig, 1913.

Valjavec, F. *Geschichte der abendländischen Aufklärung*. Vienna-Munich, 1961.

Verra, V. *F. H. Jacobi,* Dall'illuminismo all'idealismo. Turin, 1963.

Wagener, B. *Ueber die Beziehung Fichtes zu Spinosa und Leibniz*. Dissertation. Borna-Leipzig, 1914.

Wahl, J. "A propos de l'Introduction à la Phénoménologie de Hegel par A. Kojève," *Etudes Hégéliennes*. Deucalion 5. Neuchatel, 1955.

Wallner, N. *Fichte als politischer Denker*. Halle a. S., 1926.

Wirth, J. *Der religionsphilosophischer Gehalt der Atheismusstreitsschriften Fichtes*. Dissertation. Neustrelitz, 1926.

Wolff, C. "De peccato in philosophum," *Horae subsecivae Marburgenses*, a. 1731. Frankfurt and Leipzig, 1731.

Wolff, H. M. *Die Weltanschauung der deutschen Aufklärung*. Bern, 1949.

Wundt, M. *Fichte*. Stuttgart, 1927.

——— *Die deutsche Schulphilosophie im Zeitalter der Aufklärung*. Heidelberger Abhandlungen 32. Tübingen, 1945.

Zart, G. *Einfluss der englischen Philosophen seit Bacon auf die deutsche Philosophie des 18. Jahrhunderts*. Berlin, 1881.

Zeller, E. "Wolff's Vertreibung aus Halle; der Kampf des Pietismus mit der Philosophie," *Verträge und Abhandlungen*, Vol. I. Leipzig, 1865.

PART V

Explicit and Constructive Post-Hegelian Atheism

Principal Works

Bauer, B. *Das entdeckte Christentum*. Zurich, 1843. This edition was immediately confiscated by the Zurich censors; the first available edition is that of E. Barnikol, Jena, 1927.

——— and K. Marx. *Die Posaune des jüngsten Gerichts über Hegel den Atheisten und Antichristus*. In K. Löwith, ed., *Die Hegelsche Linke*. Stuttgart, 1962.

Engels, F. *Die Lage der arbeitenden Klasse in England*. Leipzig, 1845. *Marx-Engels Werke*, Vol. II. Berlin: Dietz Verlag, 1958.

——— *Werke und Schriften bis Anfang 1844*. *Marx-Engels, Historisch-kritische Gesamtausgabe: Werke, Schriften, Briefe* (M.E.G.A.), Abt. I, Vol. 2. Edited by D. Rjazanov and V. Adoratsky. Moscow and Berlin, 1926.

Feuerbach, L. *Aus dem Vorwort zur ersten Gesammtausgabe. Werke*, Vol. II. Edited by Bolin and Jodl. Leipzig, 1904.

——— *Ausgewählte Briefe. Werke*, Vol. I. Edited by Bolin and Jodl. Leipzig, 1904.

——— *Briefwechsel und Nachlass*. Edited by K. Grün. Leipzig-Heidelberg, 1874.

——— *Grundsätze der Philosophie der Zukunft. Werke*, Vol. II. Edited by Bolin and Jodl. Stuttgart, 1904. Edited by M. G. Lange. Leipzig,

1950. English translation by Manfred H. Vogel, *Principles of the Philosophy of the Future*. Indianapolis-New York-Kansas City: The Library of Liberal Arts, Bobbs-Merrill, 1966.

Feuerbach, L. *Grundsätze zur Reform der Philosophie. Werke,* Vol. II. Edited by Bolin and Jodl. Stuttgart, 1904.

——— *Kleine philosophische Schriften*. Edited by M. G. Lange. Leipzig, 1950.

——— *Pierre Bayle, Ein Beitrag zur Geschichte der Philosophie und Menschbeit. Werke,* Vol. V. Edited by Bolin and Jodl. Stuttgart, 1905.

——— *Ueber Philosophie und Christenthum. Werke,* Vol. VII. Edited by Bolin and Jodl. Stuttgart, 1906.

——— *Vorläufige Thesen zur Reform der Philosophie. Werke,* Vol. II. Edited by Bolin and Jodl. Stuttgart, 1904.

——— *Das Wesen des Christentoms. Werke,* Vol. VI. Edited by Bolin and Jodl. Stuttgart, 1906. English translation by George Eliot, *The Essence of Christianity*. New York, Evanston and London: Harper Torchbooks, Harper and Row, Publishers, 1957.

——— *Das Wesen des Glaubens im Sinne Luthers. Werke,* Vol. VII. Edited by Bolin and Jodl. Stuttgart, 1906. English translation, *The Essence of Faith According to Luther*. New York: Harper and Row, 1967.

Grassl, H., ed. Letter of Hegel to von Baader, *Hegel-Studien,* Vol. II. Bonn: Bouvier, 1963.

Hegel, G. W. *Geschichte der Philosophie*. Edited by Michelet. Berlin, 1844; reprinted as Vols. 17-18 of the Jubiläumsausgabe of the *Sämtliche Werke*. Stuttgart, 1959. Edited by Hoffmeister. Leipzig, 1944.

——— *Philosophie des Rechts*. Edited by J. Hoffmeister. Hamburg, 1955.

Lenin, V. I. *Aus dem philosophischen Nachlass*. Berlin, 1958.

——— *Religion*. New York: International Publishers, Little Lenin Library, 1933.

Löwith, K., ed. *Die Hegelsche Linke*. Stuttgart, 1962.

Marx, K. and F. Engels. *Basic Writings on Politics and Philosophy*. Edited by Lewis S. Feuer. New York: Doubleday and Co., Anchor Books, 1959.

——— *Briefwechsel zwischen Marx und Engels*. M.E.G.A., Abt. III, Vol. 1. Moscow and Berlin, 1928.

——— *Die Deutsche Ideologie*. M.E.G.A., Abt. I, Vol. 3. Moscow and Berlin, 1929. *K. Marx-F. Engels Werke,* Vol. III. Berlin: Dietz Verlag, 1958.

Marx, K. and F. Engels. *Die Frühe Schriften von K. Marx.* Edited by H.-J. Lieber and P. Furth. Darmstadt: Wissenschaftliche Buchgesellschaft, 1962.

——— *Die Heilige Familie. K. Marx-F. Engels Werke,* Vol. II. Berlin, 1958. M.E.G.A., Abt. I, Vol. 2. Edited by D. Rjazanov and V. Adoratsky. Moscow and Berlin, 1926. English translation, *The Holy Family.* Moscow: Foreign Languages Publishing House, 1956.

——— *Oekonomisch-philosophische Manuskripte aus dem Jahre 1844.* M.E.G.A., Abt. I, Vol. 3. Moscow and Berlin, 1929. English translation, *Economic and Philosophic Manuscripts of 1844.* New York: International Publishers, 1964.

——— *Ueber die Religion.* Berlin, 1958. English translation, Marx and Engels *On Religion.* Moscow: Foreign Languages Publishing House, 1957; New York: Schocken Books, 1964.

——— *Zur Judenfrage. K. Marx-F. Engels Werke,* Vol. I. Berlin: Dietz Verlag, 1958.

——— *Zur Kritik der Hegelschen Rechtsphilosophie. K. Marx-F. Engels Werke,* Vol. I. Berlin, 1958. The Introduction is translated in *On Religion.* New York, 1964.

Plechanov, G. W. *Die Grundprobleme des Marxismus.* Berlin, 1958.

Reding, M. *Der politische Atheismus.* Graz-Vienna-Cologne, 1957.

——— *Der Sinn des Marxschen Atheismus.* Munich-Salzburg-Cologne, 1957.

Strauss, D. F. *Der alte und der neue Glaube. Werke,* Vol. VI. Edited by E. Zeller. Bonn, 1877.

——— *Die christliche Glaubenslehre in ihrer geschichtlicher Erscheinung und im Kampfe mit der modernen Wissenschaft.* Two volumes. Tübingen-Stuttgart, 1840-41.

——— *Das Leben Jesu. Werke,* Vol. IV. Edited by E. Zeller. Bonn, 1877. English translation by George Eliot, *The Life of Jesus Critically Examined.* London, 1892.

Secondary Works in addition to those already listed.

Arvon, H. *Ludwig Feuerbach ou la transformation du sacré.* Paris: P.U.F., 1957.

Barth, K. *Die protestantische Theologie im 19. Jahrhundert.* Zurich, 1947. English translation, *Protestant Thought from Rousseau to Ritschl.* New York: Harper, 1959.

Blockmühl, K. E. *Leiblichkeit und Gesellschaft,* Studien zur Religionskritik und Anthropologie im Frühwerk von L. Feuerbach und K. Marx. Göttingen, 1961.

Cabanis, P. *Rapports du physique et du moral de l'homme.* 3rd. ed. Paris, 1815.

Calvez, J.-Y. *La pensée de Karl Marx.* Paris, 1956.

Carlyle, T. *Past and Present.* London: E. P. Dutton & Sons, Everyman's Library, no date.

Cornu, A. "L'idée d'aliénation chez Hegel, Feuerbach et K. Marx," *La Pensée* 17, 1928.

——— *Marx,* l'homme et l'oeuvre. Paris, 1934.

——— *Moses Hess et la gauche hégélienne.* Paris, 1934.

Cottier, M. M. *L'athéisme du jeune Marx,* ses origines hégéliennes. Paris, 1959.

Dicke, G. *Der Identitätsgedanke bei Feuerbach und Marx.* Cologne and Opladen, 1960.

Ehlen, P. *Der Atheismus im dialektischen Materialiamus.* Munich, 1961.

Fabro, C. *Feuerbach-Marx-Engels: materialismo dialettico e materialismo storico.* Brescia, 1962.

——— *Storia della filosofia.* 2nd. ed. Rome, 1959.

——— *Tra Kierkegaard e Marx.* Florence, 1952.

Fichte, I. H. *Ueber die christliche und antichristliche Spekulation der Gegenwart.* Bonn, 1842.

Fichte, J. G. *Briefwechsel.* Edited by Schulz. Leipzig, 1925.

von Frank, F. H. R. *Geschichte und Kritik der neueren Theologie* insbesondere der systematischen seit Schleiermacher. Erlangen and Leipzig, 1894.

Garaudy, R. *Dieu est mort,* Etude sur Hegel. Paris, 1962.

Gollwitzer, H. *Die marxistische Religionskritik und christlicher Glaube.* Tübingen, 1962.

Heusinger, I. H. G. *Ueber das idealistisch-atheistische System des Herrn Prof. Fichte.* Dresden and Gotha, 1799.

Hirsch, E. *Die idealistische Philosophie und das Christentum.* Gütersloh, 1926.

Hohof, W. *Die Bedeutung der Marxschen Kapitalkritik.* Paderborn, 1908.

——— *Warenwert und Kapitalprofit.* Paderborn, 1902.

Hyppolite, J. *Genèse et structure de la Phénoménologie de l'esprit de Hegel.* Paris, 1946.

Kierkegaard, S. *Breve og Aktstykker vedrorende S. Kierkegaard.* Edited by N. Thulstrup. Copenhagen, 1953.

Kortanek, A. M. *Schellings Seinslehre und Kierkegaard.* Munich, 1962.

Lacroix, J. *Le sens de l'athéisme moderne.* Tournai-Paris, 1958.

Landgrebe, L. "Das Problem der Dialektik," *Marxismus-Studien* III, 1960.

Löwith, K. "L'achèvement de la philosophie classique par Hegel et sa dissolution chez Marx et Kierkegaard," *Recherches philosophiques* IV, 1934-35.

——— "L. Feuerbach und der Ausgang der klassischen deutschen Philosophie," *Logos* XVII, 1928.

——— *Nietzsches Philosophie der ewigen Wiederkunft des Gleichen.* Berlin, 1935.

——— *Weltgeschichte und Heilsgeschichte.* Stuttgart, 1953.

Maier, H. *An der Grenze der Philosophie.* Tübingen, 1909.

——— "D. F. Strauss," *Verhandlungen des III. Internationalen Kongress der Philosophie.* Heidelberg, 1908.

Miotti, A. *Ueber die Falschheit und Gottlosigkeit des Kantischen Systems.* Vienna, 1801.

Nietzsche, F. *Gedanken. Werke,* Vol. VII. Munich: Musarion, 1920.

——— *Was den Deutschen abgeht. Werke,* Vol. XVII. Munich: Musarion, 1920.

——— *Wille zur Macht. Werke,* Vol. XIX. Munich: Musarion, 1920.

Nitzsch, K. I. *System der christlichen Lehre.* Bonn, 1829.

Nüdling, G. "Die Auflösung des Gott-Menschverhältnisses bei Ludwig Feuerbach," *Der Mensch vor Gott,* Festschrift Th. Steinbüchel. Düsseldorf, 1948.

——— *L. Feuerbachs Religionsphilosophie.* Die Auflösung der Theologie in Anthropologie. Paderborn, 1936; 2nd. ed., 1961.

Paulsen, F. *Philosophia militans,* Gegen Klerikalismus und Naturalismus. 2nd.-3rd. ed. Berlin, 1908.

Pfleiderer, O. *Die Entwicklung der protestantischen Theologie seit Kant und in Grossbritannien seit 1825.* Freiburg i. Br., 1891.

Popitz, H. *Der entfremdete Mensch, Zeitkritik und Geschichts-philosophie des jungen Marx.* Basel, 1953.

Rohr, H. *Pseudoreligiöse Motive in den Frühschriften von K. Marx.* Tübingen, 1962.

Runze, G. *Bruno Bauer, der Meister der theologischen Kritik.* Berlin, 1931.

Schelling, F. *Philosophische Briefe über Dogma und Kritik. Werke,* Abt. I, Vol. 1. Stuttgart and Augsburg, 1856.

Schilling, W. *Feuerbach und die Religion.* Munich, 1957.

Schweitzer, A. *Geschichte der Leben-Jesu-Forschung.* 4th. ed. Tübingen, 1926. English translation, *The Quest of the Historical Jesus.* London, 1910.

Staudenmaier, F. A. *Darstellung und Kritik des Hegelschen Systems.* Mainz, 1844.

——— *Die Grundfragen der Gegenwart.* Freiburg i. Br., 1851.

Steinbüchel, T. *Sozialismus*. Tübingen, 1959.
Stephan, H. *Geschichte der deutschen evangelischen Theologie seit dem deutschen Idealismus*. Edited by M. Schmidt. 2nd. ed. Berlin, 1960.
Thier, E. *Das Menschenbild des jungen Marx*. Göttingen, 1957.
Ullrich, H. *Der junge Engels*. Berlin: VEB Deutscher Verlag der Wissenschaften, 1961.
Vuillemin, J. "L'humanisme athée chez Feuerbach," *Deucalion* IV. Neuchayel and Paris, 1952.
Wetter, G. "Marxismo e ateismo," *Il problema dell'ateismo*. Brescia, 1962.
Willmann, O. *Geschichte des Idealismus*. Braunschweig, 1879.

PART VI

The Religious Atheism of Anglo-American Empiricism

Principal Works

Alexander, S. *Space, Time and Deity*. The Gifford Lectures at Glasgow 1916-1918. London, 1920; 2nd. ed., 1934.
Bradley, F. H. *Appearances and Reality*. London, 1893; 9th. ed., 1930.
——— *Essays on Truth and Reality*. Oxford, 1914.
Dewey, J. *A Common Faith*. New Haven: Yale University Press, 1934.
——— *Experience and Nature*. New York: W. W. Norton and Company, Inc., 1929.
——— *Problems of Men*. New York: Philosophical Library, 1946.
——— *Reconstruction in Philosophy*. New York: Henry Holt and Company, 1920.
——— "The Philosophy of Whitehead," *The Philosophy of Alfred North Whitehead,* edited by P. A. Schilpp. New York: Tudor, 1951.
Hartshorne, C. *Philosophers Speak of God*. Chicago: University of Chicago Press, 1953.
——— "Das metaphysische System Whiteheads," *Zeitschrift für philosophische Forschung* III, 1948.
——— "Panpsychism," *A History of Philosophical Systems,* edited by Vergilius Ferm. New York, 1950.
——— "Santayana's Doctrine of Essence," *The Philosophy of George Santayana,* edited by P. A. Schilpp. New York: Tudor, 1951.
——— "Whitehead's Idea of God," *The Philosophy of Alfred North Whitehead,* edited by P. A. Schilpp. New York: Tudor, 1951.
James, H., ed. *The Letters of William James*. Boston, 1920.
James, W. *Essays in Radical Empiricism*. New York: Longmans, Green and Co., 1938.

James, W. *A Pluralistic Universe*. New York: Longmans, Green and Co., 1909.

——— *Pragmatism,* A New Name for Some Old Ways of Thinking. New York: Longmans, Green and Co., 1907.

——— *The Varieties of Religious Experience*. New York: Longmans, Green and Co., 1902.

——— *The Will to Believe and Other Essays*. New York: Longmans, Green and Co., 1912; Dover Publications, 1956.

McTaggart, E. *The Nature of Existence*. Edited by C. D. Broad. Cambridge, 1927.

——— "The Personality of the Absolute," *Studies in Hegelian Cosmology*. Cambridge, 1901.

——— *Studies in the Hegelian Dialectic*. Cambridge, 1896.

Mill, J. S. *Nature, the Utility of Religion, Theism,* Being Three Essays on Religion. London, 1874.

——— *An Examination of Sir William Hamilton's Philosophy*. 4th. ed. London: Longmans, Green, Reader and Dyer, 1872.

Morgan, L. *Emergent Evolution*. New York: Henry Holt and Company, 1923.

Royce, J. *The Conception of Immortality*. Boston and New York, 1890.

——— *The Philosophy of Loyalty*. New York, 1920.

——— *William James and Other Essays*. New York: The Macmillan Co., 1900.

——— *The World and the Individual*. New York, 1899; Dover Publications, 1959.

Santayana, G. *The Realm of Essence; Book First of Realms of Being*. New York: Charles Scribner's Sons, 1927.

——— *The Realm of Matter; Book Second of Realms of Being*. New York: Charles Scribner's Sons, 1930.

——— "Dewey's Naturalistic Metaphysics," *The Philosophy of John Dewey,* edited by P. A. Schilpp. New York: Tudor, 1951.

Schilpp, P. A., ed. *The Philosophy of Alfred North Whitehead*. New York: Tudor Publication Company, 1951.

——— *The Philosophy of George Santayana*. New York: Tudor Publication Company, 1951.

——— *The Philosophy of John Dewey*. New York: Tudor Publication Company, 1951.

Whitehead, A. N. *Adventures of Ideas*. New York: The Macmillan Company, 1952.

——— *Essays in Science and Philosophy*. London: William Brendon and Son, 1948.

——— *The Function of Reason*. Princeton, 1929.

Whitehead, A. N. *Modes of Thought*. New York: The Macmillan Company, 1938.
——— *Process and Reality*. The Gifford Lectures, Edinburgh 1927-28. New York: Harper Torchbooks, Harper and Row, 1960.
——— *Science and the Modern World*. New York: The Macmillan Company, 1929.
——— *Science and Religion*. New York: Charles Scribner's Sons, 1931.

Secondary Works in addition to those listed above.

Baumgarten, E. *Der Pragmatismus,* R. W. Emerson, W. James, J. Dewey. Frankfurt a. M., 1938.
Bixler, J. S. *Religion in the Philosophy of William James*. Boston, 1926.
——— "Whitehead's Philosophy of Religion," *The Philosophy of Alfred North Whitehead,* edited by P. A. Schilpp. New York, 1951.
Brightman, E. S. *The Problem of God*. New York, 1930.
Christian, W. A. "The Concept of God as Derivative Notion," *The Hartshorne Festschrift, Process and Divinity,* edited by W. L. Reese and E. Freeman. Lasalle, Illinois, 1964.
——— *An Interpretation of Whitehead's Metaphysics*. New Haven: Yale University Press, 1959.
——— "Whitehead's Explanation of the Past," *A. N. Whitehead, Essays on his Philosophy*. Englewood Cliffs: Prentice-Hall, 1963.
Cohen, M. *A Preface to Logic*. London: George Routledge & Sons Ltd., 1946.
Collins, J. *God in Modern Philosophy*. London: Routledge and Kegan Paul, 1959.
Dakin, A. H. *Man the Measure,* Essay on Humanism as Religion. Princeton: Princeton University Press, 1939.
von Ehrenfels, C. "Ueber Gestaltqualitäten," *Vierteljahrschrift fuer wissenschaftliche Philosophie* XIV, 1890.
Fabro, C. *Fenomenologia della percezione*. 2nd. ed. Brescia, 1961.
Fagginger, J. A. *Humanism States its Case*. Boston, 1933.
Gates, J. F. *Adventures in the History of Philosophy*. Grand Rapids, 1961.
Hegel, G. W. *Erste Druckschriften. Werke, Vol. I.* Edited by Lasson. Leipzig, 1928.
Johnson, A. H. *Whitehead's Theory of Reality*. New York, 1962.
Knudson, A. C. *The Philosophy of Personalism*. Boston: Boston University Press, 1949.
Kuspit, D. B. "Whitehead on Divinity," *Archiv für Philosophie* XI.
Laird, J. "Memoir," in S. Alexander, *Philosophical and Literary Pieces*. London, 1939.
Lamont, C. *Humanism as a Philosophy*. New York, 1949.

Lamont, C. *The Illusion of Immortality*. 3rd. ed. New York, 1958.
Leclerc, J., ed. *The Relevance of Religion*. New York, 1961.
Lippmann, W. *A Preface to Morals*. New Edition. Boston: The Beacon Press, 1960.
Macintosh, D. C. "Contemporary Humanism," *Humanism, Another Battle Line,* edited by William P. King. Nashville, 1931.
Marcel, G. *La métaphysique de Royce*. Paris, 1945.
Mays, W. *The Philosophy of Whitehead*. New York, 1959.
Reck, A. J. "The Philosophy of Charles Hartshorne," *Studies in Whitehead's Philosophy*. The Hague, 1961.
Reese, W. L. and E. Freeman, eds. *The Hartshorne Festschrift, Process and Divinity*. Lasalle, Illinois, 1964.
Rosenfeld, L. C. *Portrait of a Philosopher:* Morris R. Cohen, in Life and Letters. New York, 1962.
Schüring, H.-J. *Studie zur Philosophie Francis Herbert Bradley*. Meisenheim an Glan, 1963.
Stokes, W. E. "Whitehead's Challenge to Theistic Realism," *The New Scholasticism* 38, 1964.
Williams, D. W. "How does God Act?: An Essay in Whitehead's Metaphysics," *The Hartshorne Festschrift, Process and Divinity,* edited by W. Reese and E. Freeman. Lasalle, 1964.

PART VII
FREEDOM AS AN ACTIVE DENIAL OF GOD IN EXISTENTIALISM

Principal Works

Bultmann, R. *Das Evangelium des Johannes*. 11th. ed. Göttingen, 1950.
——— *Jesus*. Tübingen, 1951. English translation, *Jesus and the Word*. New York: Charles Scribner's Sons, 1958.
Camus, A. *L'homme revolté*. Paris: Gallimard, 1951. English translation by Anthony Bower, *The Rebel*. New York: Vintage Books, Random House, 1956.
——— *Le mythe de Sisiphe*. Paris: Gallimard, 1942. English translation by Justin O'Brien, *The Myth of Sisyphus and Other Essays*. New York: Vintage Books, Random House, 1955.
Heidegger, M. *Einführung in die Metaphysik*. Tübingen, 1953. English translation by Ralph Manheim, *An Introduction to Metaphysics*. New Haven: Yale University Press, 1958.
——— *Erläuterung zu Hölderlins Dichtung*. 2nd. ed. Frankfurt a. M.; Klostermann, 1951.

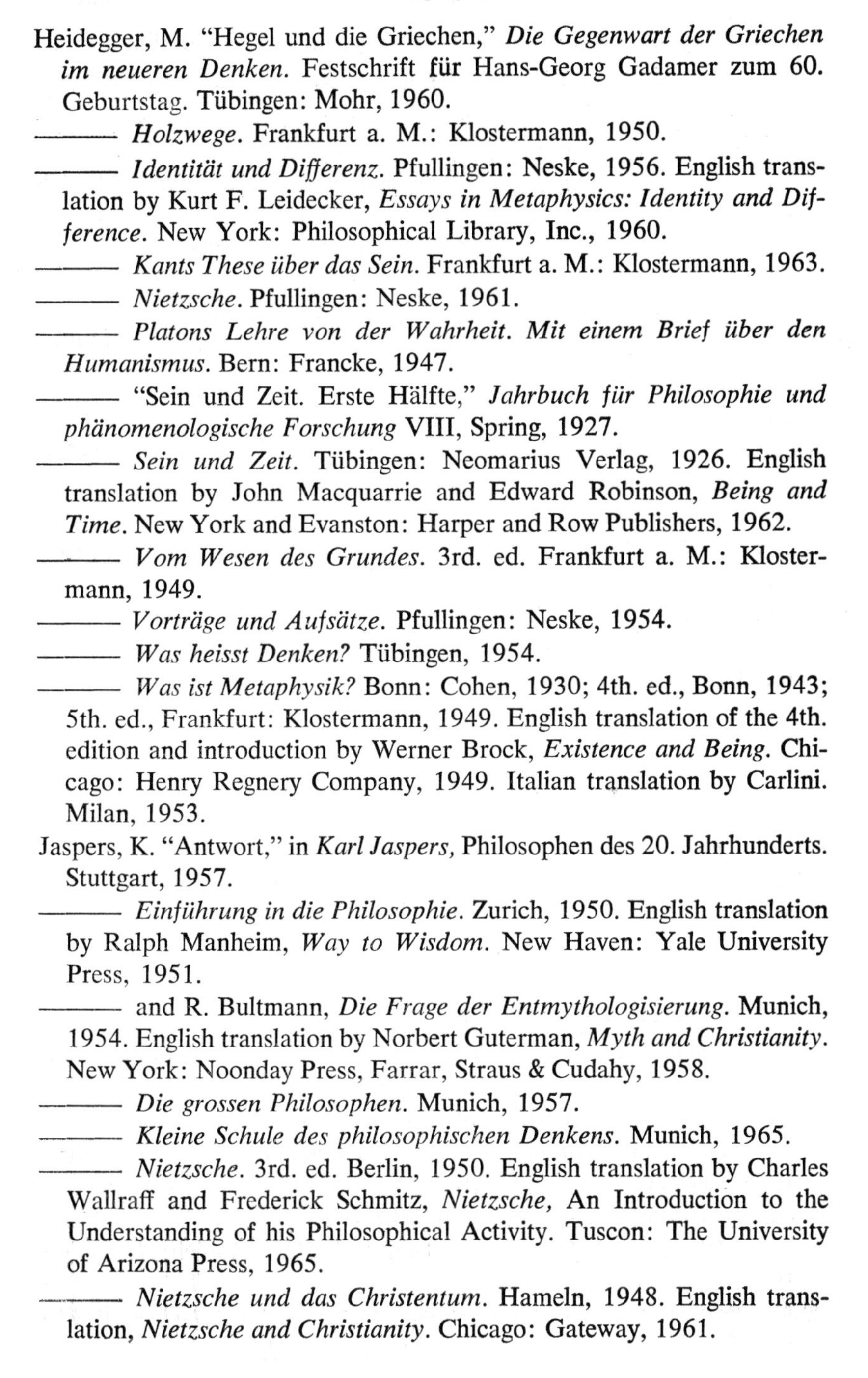

Heidegger, M. "Hegel und die Griechen," *Die Gegenwart der Griechen im neueren Denken*. Festschrift für Hans-Georg Gadamer zum 60. Geburtstag. Tübingen: Mohr, 1960.

——— *Holzwege*. Frankfurt a. M.: Klostermann, 1950.

——— *Identität und Differenz*. Pfullingen: Neske, 1956. English translation by Kurt F. Leidecker, *Essays in Metaphysics: Identity and Difference*. New York: Philosophical Library, Inc., 1960.

——— *Kants These über das Sein*. Frankfurt a. M.: Klostermann, 1963.

——— *Nietzsche*. Pfullingen: Neske, 1961.

——— *Platons Lehre von der Wahrheit. Mit einem Brief über den Humanismus*. Bern: Francke, 1947.

——— "Sein und Zeit. Erste Hälfte," *Jahrbuch für Philosophie und phänomenologische Forschung* VIII, Spring, 1927.

——— *Sein und Zeit*. Tübingen: Neomarius Verlag, 1926. English translation by John Macquarrie and Edward Robinson, *Being and Time*. New York and Evanston: Harper and Row Publishers, 1962.

——— *Vom Wesen des Grundes*. 3rd. ed. Frankfurt a. M.: Klostermann, 1949.

——— *Vorträge und Aufsätze*. Pfullingen: Neske, 1954.

——— *Was heisst Denken?* Tübingen, 1954.

——— *Was ist Metaphysik?* Bonn: Cohen, 1930; 4th. ed., Bonn, 1943; 5th. ed., Frankfurt: Klostermann, 1949. English translation of the 4th. edition and introduction by Werner Brock, *Existence and Being*. Chicago: Henry Regnery Company, 1949. Italian translation by Carlini. Milan, 1953.

Jaspers, K. "Antwort," in *Karl Jaspers,* Philosophen des 20. Jahrhunderts. Stuttgart, 1957.

——— *Einführung in die Philosophie*. Zurich, 1950. English translation by Ralph Manheim, *Way to Wisdom*. New Haven: Yale University Press, 1951.

——— and R. Bultmann, *Die Frage der Entmythologisierung*. Munich, 1954. English translation by Norbert Guterman, *Myth and Christianity*. New York: Noonday Press, Farrar, Straus & Cudahy, 1958.

——— *Die grossen Philosophen*. Munich, 1957.

——— *Kleine Schule des philosophischen Denkens*. Munich, 1965.

——— *Nietzsche*. 3rd. ed. Berlin, 1950. English translation by Charles Wallraff and Frederick Schmitz, *Nietzsche,* An Introduction to the Understanding of his Philosophical Activity. Tuscon: The University of Arizona Press, 1965.

——— *Nietzsche und das Christentum*. Hameln, 1948. English translation, *Nietzsche and Christianity*. Chicago: Gateway, 1961.

Jaspers, K. *Philosophie,* Vol. III: *Metaphysik*. 3rd. ed. Berlin, 1956.

——— and H. Zahrnt. *Philosophie und Offenbarungsglaube*. Hamburg, 1963.

——— *Der philosophische Glaube*. Munich, 1947.

——— *Der philosophische Glaube angesichts der Offenbarung*. Munich, 1962.

——— *Vernunft und Existenz*. Groningen: Batavia, 1935.

——— *Von der Wahrheit*. Munich, 1947. English translation of some sections by Jean T. Wilde, William Kluback and William Kimmel, *Truth and Symbol*. New York: Twayne Publishers, 1959.

——— "Wahrheit une Unheil der Bultmannschen Entmythologisierung," *Kerygma und Mythos,* Vol. III. Hamburg: Volkdorf, 1954.

Merleau-Ponty, M. *Eloge de la philosophie*. Paris: Gallimard, 1953. English translation by John Wild and James E. Edie, *In Praise of Philosophy*. Evanston: Northwestern University Press, 1963.

——— *Phénoménologie de la perception*. Paris: Gallimard, 1945. English translation by Colin Smith, *Phenomenology of Perception*. London: Routledge and Kegan Paul, 1962.

——— *Sens et non-sens*. Paris: Editions Nagel, 1948. English translation by L. Dreyfus and Patricia Allen Dreyfus, *Sense and Non-Sense*. Evanston, Northwestern University Press, 1964.

——— *Signes*. Paris: Gallimard, 1960. English translation by Richard McCleary, *Signs*. Evanston: Northwestern University Press, 1964.

——— *La structure du comportement*. Paris, 1949.

Nietzsche, F. *Also Sprach Zarathustra. Werke, Vol.* XIII. Munich: Musarion, 1924. English translation by R. J. Hollingdale, *Thus Spoke Zarathustra*. London, 1961.

——— *Aus dem Nachlass der Achtzigerjahre. Werke,* Vol. III. Edited by K. Schlechta. Munich, 1957.

——— *Die fröhliche Wissenschaft. Werke,* Vol. XII. Munich: Musarion, 1924. English translation by Kurt F. Reinhardt, *Joyful Wisdom*. New York: Frederick Ungar Publishing Co., 1964.

——— *Jenseits von Gut und Böse. Werke,* Vol. XV. Munich: Musarion, 1925. English translation by Marianne Cowan, *Beyond Good and Evil*. Chicago: Henry Regnery Company, 1955.

——— *Die neue Aufklärung. Werke,* Vol. XV. Munich: Musarion, 1925.

——— *Die Philosophie im tragischen Zeitalter der Griechen. Werke,* Vol. III. Edited by K. Schlechta. Munich, 1957.

Nietzsche, F. *Unzeitmässige Betrachtungen. Werke,* Vol. VI. Munich: Musarion, 1922.

——— *Wille zur Macht. Werke,* Vol. XIX. Munich: Musarion, 1929.

——— *Zur Genealogie der Moral. Werke,* Vol. XV. Munich: Musarion, 1925.

Sartre, J.-P. *Critique de la raison dialectique.* Paris, 1960.

——— *L'être et le néant.* Paris: Gallimard, 1943. English translation by Hazel Barnes, *Being and Nothingness.* London: Methuen & Co., 1957.

——— *L'Existentialisme est un humanisme.* Paris, 1946. English translation by Philip Mairet, *Existentialism and Humanism.* London: Methuen & Co., 1948. English translation in *Existentialism from Dostoievsky to Sartre.* Edited by Walter Kaufmann. Cleveland: Meridian Books, 1956.

——— "La liberté cartésienne," prefaced to *Descartes.* Geneva-Paris, 1946. Reprinted in *Situations,* Vol. I. Paris, Gallimard, 1947.

——— "M. François Mauriac et la liberté," *Situations,* Vol. I. Paris: Gallimard, 1947.

——— *Saint Genet, comédien et martyr.* Paris, 1952. English translation, *Saint Genet, actor and martyr.* New York: Mentor Books, 1963.

Secondary Works in addition to those listed above.

Birault, H. "De l'être, du divin, des dieux chez Heidegger," *L'existence de Dieu.* Tournai, 1961.

——— "La foi et la pensée d'après Heidegger," *Philosophies chrétiennes.* Recherches et Débats. Tournai, 1955.

Bonhoeffer, D. *Akt und Sein.* 3rd. ed. Munich, 1964.

Fink, E. *Nietzsches Philosophie.* Stuttgart, 1960.

Fraenkel, E. *Das Sein und seine Modalitäten.* Lexis II, 1949.

Hammelsbeck, O. "Theologische Bestreitung des philosophischen Glaubens," *Offener Horizont,* Festschrift für Karl Jaspers. Munich, 1957.

Hasse, H. *Schopenhauer.* Munich, 1926.

Holm, S. "Jaspers Religionsphilosophie," *Karl Jaspers,* Philosophen des 20. Jahrhunderts. Stuttgart, 1957.

Hommes, J. *Zwiespaltiges Dasein,* Die existenziale Ontologie von Hegel bis Heidegger. Freiburg i. Br., 1953.

Knudsen, R. D. *The Idea of Transcendence in the Philosophy of Karl Jaspers.* Kampen, 1958.

Krueger, G. "M. Heidegger und der Humanismus," *Studia Philosophica* IX, 1949.

Langan, T. *The Meaning of Heidegger.* A Critical Study of an Existentialist Phenomenology. New York: Columbia University Press, 1959.

Lohff, W. *Glaube und Freiheit,* Das theologische Problem der Religionskritik von K. Jaspers. Gütersloh, 1957.

Löwith, K. *Heidegger Denker in dürftiger Zeit.* Frankfurt a. M., 1953.

——— *Von Hegel zu Nietzsche.* 2nd. ed. Stuttgart, 1950.

Möller, J. *Existenzialphilosophie und katholische Theologie.* Baden-Baden, 1952.

Müller, M. *Existenzphilosophie im geistigen Leben der Gegenwart.* Heidelberg, 1949. French translation, *Crise de la métaphysique.* Paris, 1953.

Noack, N. *Die Philosophie Westeuropas.* Darmstadt, 1962.

Paumen, I. *Raison et existence chez Karl Jaspers.* Brussels, 1958.

Räber, T. *Das Dasein in der 'Philosophie' von Karl Jaspers.* Bern, 1955.

Reding, M. "Nietzsches Verhältnis zur Religion, Christentum und Katholizismus," *Festschrift K. Adam.* Düsseldorf, 1952.

Richardson, W. J. *Heidegger,* Through Phenomenology to Thought. The Hague: Martinus Nijhoff, 1963.

Ricoeur, P. *Phénoménologie existentielle* in "Philosophie-Religion," *Encyclopédie Française,* Vol. XIX. Paris, 1957.

——— "Philosophie und Religion bei Karl Jaspers," *Karl Jaspers,* Philosophen des 20. Jahrhunderts. Stuttgart, 1957.

——— and H. Dufrenne. *Karl Jaspers et la philosophie de l'existence.* Paris, 1947.

von Rintelen, F. J. *Philosophie der Endlichkeit als Spiegel der Gegenwart.* Meisenheim a. Glan, 1951.

Schelling, F. W. J. *Philosophische Schriften.* Landshut, 1809.

Schlechta, K. *Der Fall Nietzsche.* Munich, 1958.

Schöfer, E. *Die Sprache Heideggers.* Pfullingen, 1962.

Schopenhauer, A. *Ergänzungen zum ersten Buch. Werke,* Vol. III. Edited by Frauenstädt. Leipzig, 1916.

——— *Die Welt als Wille und Vorstellung. Werke,* Vol. II. Edited by Frauenstädt. Leipzig, 1916.

Schmaus, M. *Katholische Dogmatik.* 2nd ed. Munich, 1939.

Schrey, H.-H. *Existenz und Offenbarung,* Ein Beitrag zum christlichen Verständnis der Existenz. Tübingen, 1947.

——— "Die Bedeutung der Philosophie M. Heideggers für die Theologie," *M. Heideggers Einfluss auf Wissenschaften.* Bern, 1949.

Schuwer, L. "Intorno ai presupposti della demitizzazione: 'Wie kommt der Gott in die Philosophie,'' *Il problema della demitizzazione.* Rome, 1962.

Siegmund, G. *Der Kampf um Gott.* Berlin, 1957.

Ter-Georgian, W. *F. Nietzsches Stellung zur Religion.* Dissertation. Halle a. S., 1914.

Van Lier, H. *L'existentialisme de J.-P. Sartre* in "Philosophie-Religion," *Encyclopédie Française,* Vol. XIX. Paris, 1957.

Volkmann- Schluck, K. H. *Nietzsches Gedicht: "Die Wüste wächst, weh dem, der Wüsten birgt."* Frankfurt a. M., 1958.

——— "Zur Gottesfrage bei Nietzsche," *Anteile. M. Heidegger zum 60.* Geburtstag. Frankfurt a. M., 1950.

Walz, G. *La vie de Friedrich Nietzsche d'après sa correspondance.* Paris, 1932.

Welte, B. *Nietzsches Atheismus und das Christentum.* Darmstadt, 1958.

PART VIII

Theology of Atheism: Dialectical Theology and Death-of-God Theology

Principal Works

Altizer, T. J. J. *The Gospel of Christian Atheism.* Philadelphia: Westminster Press, 1966.

——— and W. Hamilton. *Radical Theology and the Death of God.* Indianapolis: The Bobbs-Merrill Company, 1966.

Barth, K. *Die christliche Dogmatik.* Zurich, 1927.

——— *Die kirchliche Dogmatik.* 5th ed. Zurich, 1947.

——— "Ludwig Feuerbach," *Die Theologie und die Kirche,* Vol. II. Zollikon-Zurich: Evangelischer Verlag, 1928. English translation, "Ludwig Feuerbach, An Introductory Essay," in George Eliot's translation of Feuerbach's *The Essence of Christianity.* New York: Harper Torchbooks, Harper and Row, Publishers, 1957.

——— *Die protestantische Theologie im 19. Jahrhundert.* Zurich, 1947. English translation, *Protestant Thought from Rousseau to Ritschl.* New York: Harper, 1959.

——— *Der Römerbrief.* Bern, 1919. English translation by E. C. Hoskyns, *The Epistle to the Romans.* Cambridge, 1933.

Bonhoeffer, D. *Akt und Sein.* Transzendentalphilosophie und Ontologie in der systematischen Theologie. Theologische Bücherei 5. 3rd ed. Munich, 1964. English translation by Bernard Noble, *Act and Being.* New York: Harper and Row, 1961.

——— "Concerning the Christian Idea of God," *The Journal of Religion,* 1932. *Gesammelte Schriften,* Vol. III. Edited by E. Bethge. Munich: C. Kaiser Verlag, 1966.

——— *Ethik.* Edited by E. Bethge. Munich, 1949. English translation, *Ethics.* Edited by E. Bethge. London: SCM Press Ltd., 1955.

——— "Die Frage nach dem Menschen in der gegenwärtigen Philosophie und Theologie." Antrittsvorlesung in der Aula der Berliner Universität am 31. Juli 1930. *Gesammelte Schriften,* Vol. III. Edited by E. Bethge. Munich, 1966.

Bonhoeffer, D. *Widerstand und Ergebung.* Edited by E. Bethge. Munich, 1951. English translation, *Letters and Papers from Prison.* New York: Macmillan, 1957.

Bultmann, R. *Glauben und Verstehen.* 2nd ed. Tübingen, 1954. English translation, *Essays, philosophical and theological.* London: SCM Press, 1955.

——— *Jesus Christus und die Mythologie.* Hamburg, 1965. English translation, *Jesus Christ and Mythology.* London: SCM Press, 1960.

——— *Kerygma und Mythos.* Theologische Forschung I. Hamburg: Herbert Reich, 1948. English translation, *Kerygma and Myth.* New York: Harper Torchbooks, Harper and Row, 1961.

——— *Theologie des neuen Testaments.* 2nd ed. Tübingen, 1954. English translation, *Theology of the New Testament.* New York: Charles Scribner's Sons, 1951.

——— "Zur Frage einer 'Philosophischen Theologie'," *Einsichten,* Vol. IV. Tübingen, 1965.

Ogden, S. M. "The Christian Proclamation of God to Men of the So-Called 'Atheistic Age'," *Concilium,* Vol. 16. New York: Paulist Press, 1966.

——— "The Temporality of God," *Zeit und Geschichte.* Dankesgabe an Rudolf Bultmann zum 80. Geburtstag. Tübingen, 1964.

Ogletree, T. W. *The 'Death of God' Controversy.* London: SCM Press Ltd., 1966.

Robinson, J. A. T. *Honest to God.* Philadelphia: The Westminster Press, 1963.

——— and David L. Edwards. *The Honest to God Debate.* London: SCM Press Ltd., 1963.

——— *The New Reformation?* London: SCM Press Ltd., 1965.

Tillich, P. *Biblical Religion and the Search for Ultimate Reality.* Chicago: University of Chicago Press, 1955.

——— *The Courage to Be.* New Haven: Yale University Press, 1953.

——— *Das Dämonische,* Ein Beitrag zur Sinndeutung der Geschichte. Sammlung Gemeinverständlicher Vorträge 119. Tübingen, 1926. English translation in *The Interpretation of History.* New York: Charles Scribner's Sons, 1936.

——— ed. *Kairos, Geisteslage und Geisteswendung.* Darmstadt, 1926.

——— *The Protestant Era.* Chicago: University of Chicago Press, 1948.

——— *Die religiöse Lage der Gegenwart.* Berlin, 1926. English translation, *The Religious Situation.* New York: Meridian Books, 1956.

——— *Religiöse Verwirklichung.* Berlin: Furche Verlag, 1929.

Tillich, P. *The Shaking of the Foundations.* New York: Charles Scribner's Sons, 1948.

——— *Systematic Theology.* Vol. I. Chicago: University of Chicago Press, 1951. Vol. II. Chicago: University of Chicago Press, 1957.

Vahanian, G. *The Death of God.* New York: George Braziller, 1961.

——— *No Other God.* New York: George Braziller, 1966.

——— "Theology and 'the End of the Age of Religion'," *Concilium,* Vol. 16. New York: Paulist Press, 1966.

——— *Wait Without Idols.* New York: George Braziller, 1964.

Van Buren, P. M. *The Secular Meaning of the Gospel.* New York: The Macmillan Company, 1966.

Secondary Works in addition to those listed above.

Adams, J. L. "Tillich's Concept of the Protestant Era," in P. Tillich, *The Protestant Era.* Chicago: University of Chicago Press, 1948.

von Balthasar, H. U. *Karl Barth. Darstellung und Deutung seiner Theologie.* Olten: Hegner, 1951.

Bandt, H. *Luthers Lehre vom verborgenen Gott.* Theologische Arbeiten VIII. Berlin, 1958.

Bouillard, H. *Karl Barth,* Genèse et évolution de la théologie dialectique. Paris, 1957.

Brunner, E. *Dogmatik.* Vol. I. Zurich, 1946. Vol. II. Zurich, 1950.

——— "Zum Problem der 'natürlichen Theologie' und der 'Anknüpfung'," *Der Mensch im Widerspruch.* 3rd ed. Zurich, 1941.

Bühler, P. *Die Anfechtung bei Martin Luther.* Zurich, 1942.

Dewart, L. *The Future of Belief,* Theism in a World Come of Age. New York: Herder and Herder, 1966.

Ebeling, G. "Luthers Reden von Gott," *Der Gottesgedanke im Abendland.* Stuttgart: Schaefer, 1964.

Fabro, C. "Review of H. Beck, *Der Akt-charakter des Seins",* in *Divus Thomas* 69, 1966.

Gadamer, H.-G. "Martin Heidegger und die Marburger Schule," *Zeit und Geschichte.* Dankesgabe an Rudolf Bultmann zum 80. Geburtstag. Tübingen, 1964.

Gherardini, B. *La parola di Dio nella teologia di Karl Barth.* Rome, 1955.

——— *La seconda Riforma,* Uomini e Scuole del Protestantesimo moderno. Brescia, 1966.

Gogarten, F. *Der Zerfall des Humanismus und die Gottesfrage. Stuttgart,* 1937.

Haible, E. *Schöpfung und Heil,* Ein Vergleich zwischen Bultmann, Barth und Thomas. Mainz, 1964.

Hamilton, K. *Revolt against Heaven.* Grand Rapids: Eerdmans, 1966.

Hamilton, W. *The New Essence of Christianity.* New York: Association Press, 1961.

Hartnack, J. *Wittgenstein und die moderne Philosophie.* Stuttgart, 1962.

Hasenhüttl, G. *Der Glaubensvollzug,* Eine Begegnung mit Rudolf Bultmann aus katholischem Glaubensverständnis. Essen, 1963.

Herrmann, W. *Die Wirklichkeit Gottes. Gesammelte Aufsätze.* Edited by F. W. Schmidt. Tübingen, 1923.

Hoffman, F. *Die erste Kritik des Ockhamismus durch den Oxforder Kanzler Johannes Lutterell.* Breslau, 1941.

Kamlah, W. *Der Mensch in der Profanität,* Versuch einer Kritik der profanen durch vernehmenden Vernunft. Stuttgart, 1949.

Kasch, W. F. "Die Lehre von der Inkarnation in der Theologie Paul Tillichs," *Zeitschrift für Theologie und Kirche* 58, 1, 1961.

Kattenbusch, F. "'Deus absconditus' bei Luther," *Festschrift für J. Kaftan.*

Kierkegaard, S. *Til Selvprövelse. Samlede Vaerker,* Vol. XII. Copenhagen, 1928.

Killen, R. A. *The Ontological Theology of Paul Tillich.* Kampen, 1956.

Knevels, W. *Die Wirklichkeit Gottes.* Stuttgart, 1964.

Köhler, W. "Der verborgene Gott," *Sitzungsbericht der Heidelbergischen Akademie der Wissenschaften, Philosophisch-historische Klasse,* 1942-43. Heidelberg, 1946.

Krause, G. "Dietrich Bonhoeffer und Rudolf Bultmann," *Zeit und Geschichte,* Dankesgabe an R. Bultmann zum 80. Geburtstag. Tübingen, 1964.

Krech, W. "Analogia fidei oder analogia entis?" *Antwort,* Festschrift zum 70. Geburtstag von K. Barth. Zollikon-Zurich: Evangelischer Verlag, 1956.

Löwith, K. "Die Sprache als Vermittler von Mensch und Welt," *Gesammelte Abhandlungen.* Stuttgart, 1960.

Luther, M. *Luthers Vorlesung über den Hebräerbrief 1517-18.* Edited by J. Ficker. Leipzig, 1929.

Matzak, S. A. *Karl Barth on God,* The Knowledge of the Divine Existence. New York, 1962.

Müller, J. T. *Die symbolischen Bücher der evangelisch-lutherischen Kirche.* 6th ed. Gütersloh, 1886.

Niesel, W. *Bekenntnisschriften und Kirchenordnungen der nach Gotteswort reformierten Kirche.* Zollikon-Zurich: Evangelischer Verlag, 1938.

Noll, G. *Sein und Existenz,* Die Ueberwindung des Subjekt-Objektsschemas in der Philosophie Heideggers und in der Theologie der Entmythologisierung. Munich, 1962.

Otto, R. *Das Heilige*. Breslau, 1917; revised edition, Munich, 1947. English translation, *The Holy*. New York: Oxford University Press, Galaxy Books, 1958.

Philipp. W. *Das Werden der Aufklärung in theologiegeschichtlicher Sicht*. Göttingen, 1957.

Pöggeler, O. *Dor Denkweg Martin Heideggers*. Pfullingen, 1963.

Ricca, P. *La "morte de Dio": una nuova teologia?* Turin, 1967.

Ries, J. *Die natürliche Gotteserkenntnis, im Zusammenhang mit dem Imago-Begriff bei Calvin*. Grenzfragen zwischen Theologie und Philosophie XIV. Bonn, 1939.

Rilliet, J. *Karl Barth théologien existentialiste?* Neuchatel, 1952.

Samuel, O. *Die religiösen und nichtreligiösen Offenbarungsbegriffe*. Theologische Forschung 16. Hamburg-Bergstedt, 1958.

Schlink, E. *Theologie der lutherischen Bekenntnisschriften. Einführung in die evangelischen Theologie,* Vol. VIII. 2nd ed. Munich: C. Kaiser Verlag, 1947.

Schmithals, W. *Die Theologie Rudolf Bultmanns*. Tübingen, 1966.

Schnübbe, O. *Der Existenzbegriff in der Theologie Rudolf Bultmanns*. Göttingen, 1959.

Stange, C. *Die Bedeutung des Gebetes für die Gotteserkenntnis*. Studien des apologetischen Seminars, Heft 37. Gütersloh, 1933.

Strauch, P. *Theologie der Krisis*.

Thomas, J. H. "Some Comments on Tillich's Doctrine of Creation," *Scottish Journal of Theology* 14, 2, 1961.

van Til, C. *The New Modernism,* An Appraisal of the Theology of Barth and Brunner. Philadelphia, 1946.

Wein, H. *Realdialektik,* Von hegelscher Dialektik zu dialektischer Anthropologic. Munich, 1957.

Wittgenstein, L. *Notebooks 1914-1916*. Oxford, 1961.

——— *Tradtatus Logico-Philosophicus,* With an Introduction by Bertrand Russell. London, 1922.

PART IX
THE INNER NUCLEUS OF MODERN ATHEISM

Principal Works

von Baader, F. *Bemerkungen über einige antirelegiöse Philosopheme unserer Zeit. Werke,* Vol. II. Edited by F. Hoffmann. Aalen, 1963.

——— *Erläuterungen zu Auszügen aus den Werken des hl. Thomas von Aquin. Werke,* Vol. XIV. Edited by F. Hoffman. Aalen, 1963.

von Baader, F. *Fermenta cognitionis. Werke,* Vol. II. Edited by F. Hoffmann, Aalen, 1963.

——— *Revision der Philosopheme der Hegel'schen Schule.* Stuttgart, 1839.

——— *Ueber den Begriff des Gut—oder positiv Nichtgut—oder negativ gewordenen endlichen Geistes.* Lucerne, 1829.

——— *Ueber den christlichen Begriff der Unsterblichkeit im Gegensatz zu den älteren und neueren nichtchristlichen Unsterblichkeitslehren. Werke,* Vol. IV. Edited by F. Hoffmann. Aalen, 1963.

——— *Ueber die Notwendigkeit einer Revision der Wissenschaft natürlicher, menschlicher und göttlicher Dinge.* Erlangen, 1842.

——— *Ueber die sich so nennende rationelle Theologie in Deutschland. Werke,* Vol. II. Edited by F. Hoffmann. Aalen, 1963.

——— *Ueber die Wahrheit* (Review). *Werke,* Vol. I. Edited by F. Hoffman. Aalen, 1963.

——— *Vorlesungen über Jakob Böhme's Theologoumena und Philosopheme. Werke,* Vol. III. Edited by F. Hoffmann. Aalen, 1963.

——— *Vorlesungen über religiöse Philosophie,* im Gegensatz der irreligiösen älterer und neuerer Zeit. *Werke,* Vol. I. Edited by F. Hoffmann. Aalen, 1963.

——— *Vorlesungen über spekulative Dogmatik.* Heft II. Münster, 1830. Heft IV. Münster, 1836.

Born, M. *Experiment and Theory in Physics.* Cambridge, 1943.

——— "Physik im Wandel meiner Zeit," in G. Noll, *Sein und Erkennen.* Munich, 1962.

Fichte, J. G. *Grundlage der Gesamten Wissenschaftslehre. Werke,* Vol. I. Edited by Medicus. Leipzig, 1908.

——— *Die Tatsachen des Bewusstseins. Nachgelassene Schriften,* Vol. I. Edited by R. Lauth and H. Jakob. Stuttgart, 1962.

Great Soviet Encyclopedia (*Bol'shaya Sovetskaya Entsiklopediya*). German translation, *Grosse Sowjet-Enzyklopedie.* Berlin: Dietz Verlag, 1950.

Hegel, G. W. *Die Beweise vom Dasein Gottes.* Edited by Lasson. Leipzig, 1930.

——— *Enzyklopädie der philosophischen Wissenschaften.* Edited by J. Hoffmeister. Leipzig, 1949.

——— *Geschichte der Philosophie.* Edited by Michelet. Berlin, 1844. Reprinted as Vols. 17-18 of the Jubiläumsausgabe of the *Sämtliche Werke,* Stuttgart, 1959.

——— *Grundlinien der Philosophie des Rechts.* Edited by J. Hoffmeister. Hamburg, 1955.

——— *Phänomenologie des Geistes.* Edited by J. Hoffmeister. Leipzig, 1937.

Hegel, G. W. *Philosophie der Religion.* Edited by Lasson. Leipzig, 1930.
——— *Philosophie der Weltgeschichte.* Edited by Lasson. Leipzig, 1925.
——— *Wissenschaft der Logik.* Edited by Lasson. Leipzig, 1934.
Planck, M. *Vorträge und Erinnerungen.* Leipzig, 1949.

Secondary Works in addition to those listed above.

Alexandrov, G. Introduction to the Russian and German translations of M. Cornforth, *Science versus Idealism.* Berlin, 1955.
Bultmann, R. "Der Gottesgedanke und der moderne Mensch," *Glauben und Verstehen,* Vol. IV. Tübingen, 1965.
Chatelet, F. *Logos et Praxis,* Recherches sur le signification théorique du marxisme. Paris, 1962.
Chevalier, J. *Histoire de la pensée.* Paris, 1961.
Descartes, R. *Principia Philosophiae. Oeuvres,* Vol. VIII. Edited by Adam and Tannery. Paris, 1909.
——— *Responsiones ad primas objectiones. Oeuvres,* Vol. VII. Edited by Adam and Tannery. Paris, 1909.
Dilthey, W. *Das Leben Schleiermachers.* 2nd ed. Berlin, 1922.
Docky, S. *Ciencia y filosofia.* Mexico City: Universidad Nacional de Mexico, 1960.
Engels, F. *Dialektik der Natur.* Berlin: Dietz Verlag, 1955.
Ettinger-Reichmann, R. *Die Immanenzphilosophic,* Darstellung und Kritik. Göttingen, 1916.
Fabro, C. *Dall'uomo a Dio.* Rome: Studium, 1966.
——— *Materialismo dialettico e materialismo storico.* 2nd ed. Brescia, 1966.
——— *Percezione e pensiero.* 2nd ed. Brescia, 1962.
Feuerbach, L. *Entgegnung an R. Haym. Werke,* Vol. VII. Edited by Bolin and Jodl. Stuttgart, 1907.
Fichte, I. H. *Psychologie,* Die Lehre vom bewussten Geiste des Menschen. Leipzig, 1864.
Freudenthal, J. *Die Lehre Spinozas,* auf Grund des Nachlasses. Heidelberg, 1927.
——— *Spinoza und die Scholastik.* Heidelberg, 1913.
Göschel, C. F. *Aphorismen über Nichtwissen und absolutes Wissen.* Berlin, 1829.
Heinze, M. "Leibniz in seinem Verhältnis zu Spinoza," *Neues Reich* II, 1875.
Horkheimer, M. "Theismus-Atheismus," *Zeugnisse,* Theodor W. Adorno zum 60. Geburtstag. Frankfurt a M., 1965.
Jordan, P. "Naturerkenntnis gibt den Glauben frei—Abbruch einer Mauer," *Zeitschrift für Religionsgeschichte* XV, 1963.

Jordan, P. *Der Naturwissenschaftler vor der religiösen Frage.* Oldenburg-Hamburg, 1963.

Kierkegaard, S. *Enten-Eller. Samlede Vaerker,* Vol. I. 2nd ed. Copenhagen, 1938. English translation by David F. Swenson and Lillian M. Swenson, *Either/Or.* Garden City: Doubleday, 1959.

Maier, H. *Philosophie der Wirklichkeit.* Tübingen, 1926.

Maimon, S. *Ueber die Progressen der Philosophie.*

Nelson, L. *Ueber das sogenannte Erkenntnisproblem.* Göttingen, 1908.

Ostwald, W. *Wissenschaft contra Gottesglauben.* Leipzig-Jena: Urania Verlag, 1960.

Pepin, J. "Histoire de la philosophie ancienne," *Histoire de la philosophie et de la métaphysique.* Paris, 1955.

Protokoll der philosophischen Konferenz über Fragen der Logik. Berlin: Deutsche Verlag der Wissenschaften, 1953.

Rey, A. *La philosophie moderne.* Paris, 1921.

Rickert, H. *Der Gegenstand der Erkenntnis.* 3rd ed. Tübingen, 1915; 4th-5th ed. Tübingen, 1921.

——— *Grundprobleme der Philosophie.* Tübingen, 1934.

——— "Die Heidelberger Tradition und Kants Kritizismus," *Deutsche systematische Philosophie nach ihren Gestalten.* Berlin, 1934.

——— *Die Logik des Prädikats und das Problem der Ontologie.* Heidelberg, 1930.

Russell, B. *History of Western Philosophy.* London: George Allen and Unwin, Ltd., 1946.

Schelling, F. *Aphorismen über die Naturphilosophie. Werke,* Abt. I, Vol. VII. Stuttgart and Augsburg, 1861.

Schuppe, W. "Bergmann's reine Logik und die Erkenntnistheoretische Logik mit ihrem angeblichen Idealismus," *Verteljahrsschrift für wissenschaftliche Philosophie* III, 1879.

——— *Grundriss der Erkenntnistheorie und Logik.* Berlin, 1894.

Susini, E. *F. von Baader et le romantisme mystique.* Paris, 1942.

Titius, A. *Natur und Gott,* Ein Versuch zur Verständigung zwischen Naturwissenschaft und Theologie. Göttingen, 1926.

Ueber die formale Logik und Dialektik. Berlin: Verlag Kultur und Fortschritt, 1952.

Vorret, M. *Les marxistes et la religion.* Paris, 1961.

Vogel, H. *Zum philosophischen Wirken Max Plancks.* Leipzig: Akademic Verlag, 1961.

Waitz, T. *Lehrbuch der Psychologie als Naturwissenschaft.* Brunswick, 1849.

Windelband, W. "Kulturphilosophie und transzendentaler Idealismus," *Präludien,* Vol. II. 7th-8th ed. Tübingen, 1921.

Index of Names

FIGURES IN ITALICS INDICATE THE PAGES WHEREIN THE NAME-ENTRY IS TREATED IN DEPTH

Index of Subjects

HIEBERT LIBRARY
3 6877 00077 9503